ISSN 0276-8178

Volume 78

Twentieth-Century Literary Criticism

Topics Volume

Excerpts from Criticism of Various Topics in Twentieth-Century Literature, including Literary and Critical Movements, Prominent Themes and Genres, Anniversary Celebrations, and Surveys of National Literatures

Jennifer Gariepy
Editor

Thomas Ligotti
Associate Editor

GALE

DETROIT · LONDON

STAFF

Jennifer Gariepy, *Editor*

Thomas Ligotti, *Associate Editor*

Susan Trosky, *Permissions Manager*
Kimberly F. Smilay, *Permissions Specialist*
Steve Cusack, Kelly A. Quin, *Permissions Associates*
Sandy Gore, *Permissions Assistant*

Victoria B. Cariappa, *Research Manager*
Michele P. LaMeau, Andrew Guy Malonis, Barbara McNeil, Gary J. Oudersluys, Maureen Richards, *Research Specialists*
Jeffrey Daniels, Tamara C. Nott, Tracie A. Richardson, Norma Sawaya,
Cheryl L. Warnock, *Research Associates*
Corrine Stocker, *Research Assistant*

Mary Beth Trimper, *Production Director*
Deborah L. Milliken, *Production Assistant*

Christine O'Bryan, *Desktop Publisher*
Randy Bassett, *Image Database Supervisor*
Robert Duncan, Michael Logusz, *Imaging Specialists*
Pamela Reed, *Imaging Coordinator*

Library of Congress Catalog Card Number 76-46132
ISBN 0-7876-2137-4
ISSN 0276-8178

Printed in the United States of America
10 9 8 7 6 5 4 3 2 1

Contents

Preface vii

Acknowledgments xi

Death in Literature 1
  Introduction 1
  Representative Works 1
  Fiction 2
  Poetry 115
  Drama 146
  Further Reading 181

Drugs and Literature 184
  Introduction 184
  Representative Works 184
  Overviews 185
  Pre-Twentieth-Century Literature 201
  Twentieth-Century Literature 242
  Further Reading 282

Television and Literature 283
  Introduction 283
  Representative Works 283
  Television and Literacy 283
  Reading vs. Watching 298
  Adaptations 341
  Literary Genres and Television 362
  Television Genres and Literature 390
  Children's Literature/Children's Television 410
  Further Reading 425

Literary Criticism Series Cumulative Author Index 429

Literary Criticism Series Topic Index 496

TCLC Cumulative Nationality Index 505

Preface

Since its inception more than fifteen years ago, *Twentieth-Century Literary Criticism* has been purchased and used by nearly 10,000 school, public, and college or university libraries. *TCLC* has covered more than 500 authors, representing 58 nationalities, and over 25,000 titles. No other reference source has surveyed the critical response to twentieth-century authors and literature as thoroughly as *TCLC*. In the words of one reviewer, "there is nothing comparable available." *TCLC* "is a gold mine of information—dates, pseudonyms, biographical information, and criticism from books and periodicals—which many libraries would have difficulty assembling on their own."

Scope of the Series

TCLC is designed to serve as an introduction to authors who died between 1900 and 1960 and to the most significant interpretations of these author's works. The great poets, novelists, short story writers, playwrights, and philosophers of this period are frequently studied in high school and college literature courses. In organizing and excerpting the vast amount of critical material written on these authors, *TCLC* helps students develop valuable insight into literary history, promotes a better understanding of the texts, and sparks ideas for papers and assignments. Each entry in *TCLC* presents a comprehensive survey of an author's career or an individual work of literature and provides the user with a multiplicity of interpretations and assessments. Such variety allows students to pursue their own interests; furthermore, it fosters an awareness that literature is dynamic and responsive to many different opinions.

Every fourth volume of *TCLC* is devoted to literary topics. These topic entries widen the focus of the series from individual authors to such broader subjects as literary movements, prominent themes in twentieth-century literature, literary reaction to political and historical events, significant eras in literary history, prominent literary anniversaries, and the literatures of cultures that are often overlooked by English-speaking readers.

TCLC is designed as a companion series to Gale's *Contemporary Literary Criticism,* which reprints commentary on authors now living or who have died since 1960. Because of the different periods under consideration, there is no duplication of material between *CLC* and *TCLC*. For additional information about *CLC* and Gale's other criticism titles, users should consult the Guide to Gale Literary Criticism Series preceding the title page in this volume.

Coverage

Each volume of *TCLC* is carefully compiled to present:

- criticism of authors, or literary topics, representing a variety of genres and nationalities

- both major and lesser-known writers and literary works of the period

- 6-12 authors or 3-6 topics per volume

- individual entries that survey critical response to each author's work or each topic in literary history, including early criticism to reflect initial reactions; later criticism to represent any rise or decline in reputation; and current retrospective analyses.

Organization of This Book

An author entry consists of the following elements: author heading, biographical and critical introduction, list of principal works, excerpts of criticism (each preceded by an annotation and a bibliographic citation), and a bibliography of further reading.

- The **Author Heading** consists of the name under which the author most commonly wrote, followed by birth and death dates. If an author wrote consistently under a pseudonym, the pseudonym will be listed in the author heading and the real name given in parentheses on the first line of the biographical and critical introduction. Also located at the beginning of the introduction to the author entry are any name variations under which an author wrote, including transliterated forms for authors whose languages use nonroman alphabets.

- The **Biographical and Critical Introduction** outlines the author's life and career, as well as the critical issues surrounding his or her work. References to past volumes of *TCLC* are provided at the beginning of the introduction. Additional sources of information in other biographical and critical reference series published by Gale, including *Short Story Criticism, Children's Literature Review, Contemporary Authors, Dictionary of Literary Biography,* and *Something about the Author,* are listed in a box at the end of the entry.

- Some *TCLC* entries include **Portraits** of the author. Entries also may contain reproductions of materials pertinent to an author's career, including manuscript pages, title pages, dust jackets, letters, and drawings, as well as photographs of important people, places, and events in an author's life.

- The **List of Principal Works** is chronological by date of first book publication and identifies the genre of each work. In the case of foreign authors with both foreign-language publications and English translations, the title and date of the first English-language edition are given in brackets. Unless otherwise indicated, dramas are dated by first performance, not first publication.

- Critical excerpts are prefaced by **Annotations** providing the reader with information about both the critic and the criticism that follows. Included are the critic's reputation, individual approach to literary criticism, and particular expertise in an author's works. Also noted are the relative importance of a work of criticism, the scope of the excerpt, and the growth of critical controversy or changes in critical trends regarding an author. In some cases, these annotations cross-reference excerpts by critics who discuss each other's commentary.

- A complete **Bibliographic Citation** designed to facilitate location of the original essay or book precedes each piece of criticism.

- Criticism is arranged chronologically in each author entry to provide a perspective on changes in critical evaluation over the years. All titles of works by the author featured in the entry are printed in boldface type to enable the user to easily locate discussion of particular works. Also for purposes of easier identification, the critic's name and the publication date of the essay are given at the beginning of each piece of criticism. Unsigned criticism is preceded by the title of the journal in which it appeared. Some of the excerpts in *TCLC* also contain translated material. Unless otherwise noted, translations in brackets are by the editors; translations in parentheses or continuous with the text are by the critic. Publication information (such as footnotes or page and line references to specific editions of works) have been deleted at the editor's discretion to provide smoother reading of the text.

- An annotated list of **Further Reading** appearing at the end of each author entry suggests secondary sources on the author. In some cases it includes essays for which the editors could not obtain reprint rights.

Cumulative Indexes

- Each volume of *TCLC* contains a cumulative **Author Index** listing all authors who have appeared in Gale's Literary Criticism Series, along with cross references to such biographical series as *Contemporary Authors* and *Dictionary of Literary Biography.* For readers' convenience, a complete list of Gale titles included appears on the first page of the author index. Useful for locating authors within the various series, this index is particularly valuable for those authors who are identified by a certain period but who, because of their death dates, are placed in another, or for those authors whose careers span two periods. For example, F. Scott Fitzgerald is found in *TCLC,* yet a writer often associated with him, Ernest Hemingway, is found in *CLC.*

- Each *TCLC* volume includes a cumulative **Nationality Index** which lists all authors who have appeared in *TCLC* volumes, arranged alphabetically under their respective nationalities, as well as Topics volume entries devoted to particular national literatures.

- Each new volume in Gale's Literary Criticism Series includes a cumulative **Topic Index,** which lists all literary topics treated in *NCLC, TCLC, LC 1400-1800,* and the *CLC* yearbook.

- Each new volume of *TCLC,* with the exception of the Topics volumes, includes a **Title Index** listing the titles of all literary works discussed in the volume. In response to numerous suggestions from librarians, Gale has also produced a **Special Paperbound Edition** of the *TCLC* title index. This annual cumulation lists all titles discussed in the series since its inception and is issued with the first volume of *TCLC* published each year. Additional copies of the index are available on request. Librarians and patrons will welcome this separate index; it saves shelf space, is easy to use, and is recyclable upon receipt of the following year's cumulation. Titles discussed in the Topics volume entries are not included *TCLC* cumulative index.

Citing Twentieth-Century Literary Criticism

When writing papers, students who quote directly from any volume in Gale's literary Criticism Series may use the following general forms to footnote reprinted criticism. The first example pertains to materials drawn from periodicals, the second to material reprinted from books.

[1]William H. Slavick, "Going to School to DuBose Heyward," *The Harlem Renaissance Re-examined,* (AMS Press, 1987); excerpted and reprinted in *Twentieth-Century Literary Criticism,* Vol. 59, ed. Jennifer Gariepy (Detroit: Gale Research, 1995), pp. 94-105.

[2]George Orwell, "Reflections on Gandhi," *Partisan Review,* 6 (Winter 1949), pp. 85-92; excerpted and reprinted in *Twentieth-Century Literary Criticism,* Vol. 59, ed. Jennifer Gariepy (Detroit: Gale Research, 1995), pp. 40-3.

Suggestions Are Welcome

In response to suggestions, several features have been added to *TCLC* since the series began, including annotations to excerpted criticism, a cumulative index to authors in all Gale literary criticism series, entries devoted to criticism on a single work by a major author, more extensive illustrations, and a title index listing all literary works discussed in the series since its inception.

Readers who wish to suggest authors or topics to appear in future volumes, or who have other suggestions, are cordially invited to write the editors.

Acknowledgments

The editors wish to thank the copyright holders of the excerpted criticism included in this volume and the permissions managers of many book and magazine publishing companies for assisting us in securing reproduction rights. We are also grateful to the staffs of the Detroit Public Library, the Library of Congress, the University of Detroit Mercy Library, Wayne State University Purdy/Kresge Library Complex, and the University of Michigan Libraries for making their resources available to us. Following is a list of the copyright holders who have granted us permission to reproduce material in this volume of *TCLC*. Every effort has been made to trace copyright, but if omissions have been made, please let us know.

COPYRIGHTED EXCERPTS IN *TCLC*, VOLUME 78, WERE REPRODUCED FROM THE FOLLOWING PERIODICALS:

American Literature, v. XLVIII, January, 1977; v. 57, October, 1985. Copyright © 1977, 1985 by Duke University Press, Durham, NC. Both reproduced by permission.—*American Studies,* v. 24, Spring, 1983 for "William James, Theodore Dreiser and the 'Anaesthetic Revelation'" by Lynn S. Boren. Copyright © Mid-American Studies Association, 1983. Reproduced by permission of the publisher and the author.—*The Antioch Review,* v. 34, Summer, 1976; v. 50, Summer, 1992. Copyright © 1976, 1992 by the Antioch Review Inc. Both reproduced by permission of the Editors.— *The Armchair Detective,* v. 18, Fall, 1985; v. 21, Summer, 1988. Copyright © 1985, 1988 by The Armchair Detective. Both reproduced by permission.—*The Boston Review,* v. IX, July/August 1984 for "The Art of Television Drama" by Martin Esslin. Copyright © 1984 by the Boston Critic, Inc. Reproduced by permission of the author.—*Canadian Literature,* No. 112, Spring, 1987 for "The Mystique of Mezcal" by Sue Vice. Reproduced by permission of the author.—*The Centennial Review,* v. XXXIV, Winter, 1990 for "Guiding Blight: The Soap Opera and the Eighteenth-Century Novel" by Deborah D. Rogers. Copyright © 1990 by The *Centennial Review..* Reproduced by permission of the publisher and the author.—*Children's Literature Association Quarterly*, v. 7, Fall, 1982; v. 12, Summer, 1987. Both reproduced by permission.—*CLA Journal,* v. XXXIV, December, 1990. Copyright © 1990 by The College Language Association. Used by permission of The College Language Association.—*Contemporary Literature,* v. 12, Summer, 1971. Reproduced by permission of The University of Wisconsin Press.—*The Critical Survey,* v. 3, 1991,. Reproduced by permission.—*Critique: Studies in Contemporary Fiction,* v. XXXIV, Winter, 1993. Copyright © 1983 Helen Dwight Reid Educational Foundation. Reproduced with permission of the Helen Dwight Reid Educational Foundation, published by Heldref Publications, 1319 18th Street NW, Washington, DC 20036-1802.—*Critique: Studies in Modern Fiction,* v. 17, 1975; v. XXIII, Winter 1981-82. Copyright © 1975, 1981 Helen Dwight Reid Educational Foundation. Both reproduced with permission of the Helen Dwight Reid Educational Foundation, published by Heldref Publications, 1319 18th Street NW, Washington, DC 20036-1802.—*Daedalus: Journal of the American Academy of Arts and Sciences,* v. III, Fall, 1982. Copyright © 1982 by the American Academy of Arts and Sciences. Reproduced by permission of Daedalus: *Journal of the American Academy of Arts and Sciences.—ELH,* v. 34, March, 1967. Copyright © 1967. Reproduced by permission of The Johns Hopkins University Press.—*Extrapolation,* v. 30, Summer, 1989. Reproduced by permission.—*The Georgia Review,* v. XXXVI, Winter, 1982. Copyright © 1982, by the University of Georgia. Reproduced by permission.—*Journal of Modern Literature,* v. 7, April, 1979. Reproduced by permission.—*Journal of Popular Culture,* v. VIII, Spring, 1975; v. 20, Summer, 1986; v. 23, Winter, 1989. All reproduced by permission.—*Journal of Popular Film and Television,* v. 15, Winter, 1988; v. 19, Fall, 1991. Copyright © 1988, 1991 Helen Dwight Reid Educational Foundation. Both reproduced with permission of the Helen Dwight Reid Educational Foundation, published by Heldref Publications, 1319 18th Street, NW, Washington, DC 20036-1802.—*The Kenyon Review,* v. 10, Fall, 1988 for "'The Body of This Death' in Robert Penn Warren's Later Poems" by Floyd C. Watkins. Copyright © 1988 by Kenyon College. All rights reserved. Reproduced by permission of the author.—*The Lion and the Unicorn: A Critical Journal of Children's Literature,* v. 11, October, 1987. Copyright © 1987. Reproduced by permission of The Johns Hopkins University Press.—*Literature and Psychology,* v. XXXI, 1981; v. XXXIX, 1993. Copyright © Editor 1981, 1993. Both reproduced by permission.—*Literature Film Quarterly*, v. 3, 1985; v. 21, 1993. © copyright 1985, 1993 Salisbury State College. Reproduced by permission.—*The Massachusetts Review*, v. VI, Winter-Spring, 1965; v. VII, Summer, 1966. Copyright © 1965, 1966. Both reprinted from *The Massachusetts Review,* The Massachusetts Review, Inc. by permission—*Michigan Quarterly Review*, v. XXXI, Winter, 1992 for "Perilous Parenting: The Deaths of Children and the Construction of Aging in Contemporary American Fiction" by Margaret Morganroth Gullette. Copyright © The University of Michigan, 1992. All rights reserved. Reproduced by permission of the author.—*The Midwest Quarterly,* v. VIII, January, 1967. Copyright © 1967 by *The Midwest Quarterly*, Pittsburg State University. Reproduced by permission.—*MLN,* v. 109, September, 1994. Copyright © 1994. Reproduced by permission of The Johns Hopkins University Press.—*Modern Drama,* v. XX, June, 1977. Copyright © 1977 University of Toronto, Graduate Centre for Study of Drama. Reproduced by permission.—*Modern Fiction Studies,* v. 22, Winter, 1976; v. 27, Winter, 1981-82. Copyright © 1976, 1981. Both reproduced by permission of The Johns Hopkins University Press.—*The Nathaniel Hawthorne Journal,* 1978 for "PBS Scarlet Letter: Showing Versus Telling" by Larry

COPYRIGHTED EXCERPTS IN *TCLC,* VOLUME 78, WERE REPRODUCED FROM THE FOLLOWING BOOKS:

Death in Literature

INTRODUCTION

Among the most frequently treated subjects in literature, death—present as a theme, symbol, or plot device—exists as one of the defining elements in the writing of modern poets, dramatists, and novelists. Intertwined with the origins of literature itself, human consciousness of mortality has for centuries provided the impetus for reflection on the causes, meaning, and nature of existence. And, while treatments of death are as varied as the authors who write them, scholars have perceived in modern texts—whether for the stage, in verse, or in prose fiction—certain clearly defined approaches to this topic of nearly universal interest.

Modern writers have frequently presented death as the ultimate existential dilemma, one which arouses terrible anxiety as it offers an avenue toward authentic self-discovery. Likewise, death is often perceived within a larger context, as part of the natural cycle of decay and renewal, or treated as a source of laughter, co-opted for humorous ends by writers of black comedy and absurdist drama, who nonetheless recognize the high seriousness of their subject. Death in literature also carries with it a range of symbolic implications, over the years having been aligned with ideas of retreat into solipsism, escape, alienation, and ultimately with the sources of meaning and the creation of literature itself.

In the modern novel and short story death has achieved a nearly ubiquitous presence. Critics observe in the works of Franz Kafka and D. H. Lawrence, for example, an almost obsessive concern with human mortality, which produces states of alienation, anxiety, and a potential retreat into the self in order to escape the omnipresent forces of death and decay. Death in the works of the Modernists is also frequently associated with solipsistic individuals, in relation to whom external and internal forces collude, symbolically cutting them away from humanity. Scholars acknowledge that the intense study of death undertaken by many Modernists also affords some writers the opportunity to more fully understand life and living. For writers like Gertrude Stein and Italo Svevo—in his *Confessions of Zeno* (1923)—the contemplation of human mortality leads to an understanding of personal identity and provides for an immanent meaning in life. Writers of the contemporary era have also often focused on the comic qualities of death under the umbrella of "black humor" fiction. Using the pretext of death as an inescapable part of the human comedy, such writers as J. P. Donleavy in *The Ginger Man* (1955), Thomas Pynchon in *Gravity's Rainbow* (1973), Kurt Vonnegut, Jr. in *Slaughter-house Five*, (1969) and Vladimir

Nabokov in *Pale Fire* (1962)—to name only a few—have used the subject of death as an ironic metaphor for life and art in the twentieth century. In the writings of these and other contemporary authors, death pervades the story and its protagonists' minds, and offers an absurd commentary on the brevity and meaninglessness of their lives and the finality of their deaths.

The symptoms of black humor fiction stretch beyond genre boundaries to the field of drama, in which the writers of modern tragicomedy and proponents of the theater of the absurd—represented by such writers as Samuel Beckett, Eugène Ionesco, and Harold Pinter—again study the humorous side of death. Critics have seen a wide diversity, nonetheless, in the writings of these dramatists. These range from Beckett, whose fatalism in the face of incomprehensibility demonstrates that laughter might be the only appropriate response to a violent and hopelessly absurd universe, to Ionesco, in whose tragicomic plays about death critics discern an affirmation of life. Other playwrights, including Eugene O'Neill and Tennessee Williams, have dealt with death as the defining feature of stage tragedy. Critic Philip M. Armato has characterized Williams's mid-career plays, among them *The Night of the Iguana* (1961), as "one poet's quest for a solution to the problems created by man's awareness of the inevitability of death." Elsewhere, Robert Feldman has seen in the characters of O'Neill's *Mourning Becomes Electra* (1931) a longing for death as an escape from the seemingly interminable pain of life.

Such tragic responses to death are more in line with the serious mood that tends to prevail in poetry on the subject. Critics find this attitude best exemplified in the musings of the twentieth century confessional poets, a group that includes such writers as Sylvia Plath, Anne Sexton, Robert Lowell, and John Berryman. For several of these writers, notably Plath and Sexton, death as a pretext for understanding life is of tantamount importance. In the poetry of these introspective writers, mortality exists as the defining sensibility, and is deeply rooted in a personal experience of the anguish of living and of death; an experience so intense for Plath and Sexton as to have culminated in their own suicides.

REPRESENTATIVE WORKS

Sherwood Anderson
 Winesburg, Ohio (short stories) 1919
John Barth
 The Floating Opera (novel) 1956

Samuel Beckett
Happy Days (drama) 1961
Saul Bellow
Mr. Sammler's Planet (novel) 1970
John Berryman
77 Dream Songs (poetry) 1964
Richard Brautigan
The Abortion (novel) 1971
Hermann Broch
Der Tod des Vergil [*The Death of Vergil*] (novel) 1945
Albert Camus
La peste [*The Plague*] (novel) 1947
Willa Cather
Death Comes for the Archbishop (novel) 1927
E. E. Cummings
Santa Claus—A Morality (drama) 1946
J. P. Donleavy
The Ginger Man (novel) 1955
Ernest Dowson
"The Dying of Francis Donne" (short story) 1896
Friedrich Dürrenmatt
Der Meteor [*The Meteor*] (drama) 1966
William Faulkner
As I Lay Dying (novel) 1930
John Hawkes
Second Skin (novel) 1964
Joseph Heller
Catch-22 (novel) 1961
Ernest Hemingway
A Farewell to Arms (novel) 1929
Henrik Ibsen
Når vi dýde vågner [*When We Dead Awaken*] (drama) 1906
Eugène Ionesco
Tueur sans gages [*The Killer*] (drama) 1959
Le roi se meurt [*Exit the King*] (drama) 1963
Henry James
"The Turn of the Screw" (novella) 1898
The Wings of the Dove (novel) 1902
James Joyce
Dubliners (short stories) 1914
Franz Kafka
Der Prozess [*The Trial*] (novel) 1925
D. H. Lawrence
The Man Who Died (novel) 1931
Robert Lowell
Life Studies (poetry) 1959
Thomas Mann
Der Tod in Venedig [*Death in Venice*] (novel) 1913
Der Zauberberg [*The Magic Mountain*] (novel) 1924
Vladimir Nabokov
Pale Fire (novel) 1962
Eugene O'Neill
Mourning Becomes Electra (drama) 1931
Walker Percy
The Last Gentleman (novel) 1966
Harold Pinter
No Man's Land (drama) 1975
Sylvia Plath
The Collected Poems (poetry) 1981

Thomas Pynchon
Gravity's Rainbow (novel) 1973
Rainer Maria Rilke
Duineser Elegien [*Duino Elegies*] (poetry) 1923
Anne Sexton
Live or Die (poetry) 1966
Wallace Stevens
The Auroras of Autumn (poetry) 1950
Italo Svevo
Confessions of Zeno (novel) 1923
Leo Tolstoy
Smert Ivana Ilyicha [*The Death of Ivan Ilych*] (novel) 1886
Mark Twain
The Adventures of Huckleberry Finn (novel) 1885
John Updike
The Centaur (novel) 1963
Kurt Vonnegut, Jr.
Slaughterhouse-Five (novel) 1969
Tennessee Williams
Suddenly Last Summer (drama) 1958
The Night of the Iguana (drama) 1961

FICTION

Charles Bernheimer

SOURCE: "On Death and Dying: Kafka's Allegory of Reading," in *Kafka and the Contemporary Critical Performance: Centenary Readings,* edited by Alan Udoff, Indiana University Press, 1987, pp. 87-96.

[*In the following essay, Bernheimer studies Franz Kafka's literary-existential exploration of the subject of death.*]

My title alludes to two very different books, Elizabeth Kübler-Ross's compassionate account of the feelings of terminally ill patients and Paul de Man's rigorous study of the self-destructiveness of literary texts.[1] This double allusion is intended to suggest the scope of Kafka's conception of death, which ranges from naturalistic reference to the writer's approaching end to near suspension of reference in the allegorical figuration of his writing destiny. A close analysis of two famous passages, frequently conflated by critics, will demonstrate how Kafka's different attitudes to death and dying are inscribed in his fiction as implied models for its reading.

The first passage is a diary entry written on December 13, 1914:

> Recently at Felix's. On the way home told Max that I shall lie very contentedly on my deathbed, provided the pain isn't too great. I forgot—and later purposely omitted—to add that the best things I have written have their basis in this capacity of

mine to meet death with contentment. All these fine and very convincing passages always deal with the fact that someone is dying, that it is hard for him to do, that it seems unjust to him, or at least harsh, and the reader is moved by this, or at least he should be. But for me, who believe that I shall be able to lie contentedly on my deathbed, such scenes are secretly a game; indeed, in the death enacted I rejoice in my own death, hence calculatingly exploit the attention that the reader concentrates on death, have a much clearer understanding of it than he, of whom I suppose that he will loudly lament on his deathbed, and for these reasons my lament is as perfect as can be, nor does it suddenly break off, as is likely to be the case with a real lament, but dies beautifully and purely away. It is the same thing as my perpetual lamenting to my mother over pains that were not nearly so great as my laments would lead one to believe. With my mother, of course, I did not need to make so great a display of art as with the reader. (D II, 102; T, 448-49)[2]

What strikes one immediately about this meditation is that Kafka, who usually experiences himself as weak, indecisive, and anxiety-ridden, here attributes mastery to himself, mastery indeed of that most extreme of human eventualities, his own death. And this remarkable assurance in the face of death he sees as the basis for a second kind of mastery, a control of the writing process so fine that he can create a text that is "möglichst vollkommen," as perfect, complete, entire as possible, "schön und rein," beautiful and pure.[3]

There is no doubt a certain cruelty in the game Kafka describes. Himself immune to the fear of death, he detaches himself from his reader in order to facilitate that reader's identification with the protagonist's feelings of loss, injustice, and confusion. Whereas the reader is convinced by the mimetic power of the literary work of the implacable finality of death, the writer rejoices in his ability to construct that finality as a textual effect. The death with which the writer identifies—"Ich freue mich ja in dem Sterbenden zu sterben"—is a fiction produced "with clear understanding" of its fictionality. The ground of that understanding, Kafka insists, is not literary; it is experiential. First the writer must be able to face his own death cheerfully, then he may write that death as part of a fictional game free of existential relevance.

The game of literature thus has a center that originates its freeplay while it stands outside that freeplay, to borrow terms from Derrida's critique of metaphysical structure. Kafka's concluding reference to his childhood lamentation to his mother suggests a psychoanalytic reading of this generative center. For the mother is the original source of contentment and frustration, the original ground in symbolic relation to which a game of mastery may be played—witness the famous *fort-da* game of Freud's grandson. The young Kafka's lamentation in deceitful excess of any felt pain prefigures his later artful deception of his reader. Both fictional elaborations are based on a fundamental confidence in existential reality, in life's biological origin in the first case, in its biological

end in the second. One might even speculate, given the associational logic of the passage, that the contentment Kafka believes he will feel on his deathbed is due in part to his fantasizing death as a return to the mother, a speculation that can be supported, as I have shown elsewhere, by an analysis of the letters to Felice and to Milena, in which Kafka expresses a regressive yearning to dissolve into these maternal presences.[4]

But if it is indeed this hidden fantasy scenario that sustains Kafka's confidence in the face of death, then matters are not quite as they seemed in our initial analysis. What appeared to be an experimental grounding for fictional freeplay may actually be a fantasy motivated by a wish to deny experience. This point of view would suggest that Kafka thinks himself able to die contentedly not because he has mastered the reality of his own death but because he has, in fantasy, never lived, never been born. "My life is a hesitation before birth" (D II, 210; T, 561), he noted in 1922. If his life has itself been a fiction, a duplicitous mirage, if he has been "dead . . . in his own lifetime" (D II, 196; T, 545), then the writing game in which he lives through his own death is not secondary to but rather a mirror image of the existential game in which he dies through his own life. The grounding in experience has been lost: fictional death mirrors fictional life. Kafka has not mastered his actual death: he has made the distinction between life and death into a literary game.

It now appears that Kafka may be deceiving himself in this passage and that his understanding may not really be much clearer than that of the reader he thinks he is tricking. He describes the freedom of writing as dependent on the writer's freedom from the terror of death. The literary work can achieve completion, he maintains, only if the artist can place himself imaginatively at the end of his life and not "suddenly break off" his writing as a result of this imagined placement *in extremis*. The beauty and purity of the work are thus qualities that reflect, and are grounded in, the wholeness of a biological life that will pass away without resistance. Not surprisingly, this view of a contented death corresponds to Kafka's most positive account of a happy birth—that of "The Judgment," written in one long night of inspired creativity. "The story came out of me," he observed, "like a real birth. . . . Only *in this way* can writing be done, only with such coherence, with such a complete opening out of the body and the soul" (D I, 278, 276; T, 296, 294). No breaking off here: the lament "verläuff schön und rein." Such a relation to writing, in which the text is born and dies as the biological extension of the author's being and achieves its coherence, its "Vollkommenheit," as what Kafka elsewhere calls "a blood relation" (D I, 134; T, 142) of its creator, this fantasized relation to writing that binds the freeplay of fiction to a maternal origin and makes it readable as what Barthes calls a "text of pleasure" was the focus of Kafka's literary ambition throughout the first period of his creative activity.

But in this same period Kafka was coming to realize with ever greater lucidity that to conceive himself as origin and ground of his writing, as existing outside its fiction-alizing game, was a wish-fulfilling delusion. I have suggested that a trace of the repression of this awareness is perceptible in the implied circularity of the associational logic in Kafka's reflection: he can imagine himself dying contentedly because this ending will be a return to his beginning. This circular fantasy cancels the temporal sequentiality of experience while it maintains the biological determinants of that sequence: maternal origin and physical death. The fantasy thus appears to have a primarily psychological genesis and to reflect a regressively narcissistic impulse. Kafka's sense of having mastered death is fostered by his repression of this regressive motivation. The attraction of this illusion of mastery may also account for his inability in this diary entry to move from an analysis founded in subjective psychology to one that perceives writing as the undoing of such a psychology and of its biological determinants.

Numerous passages in the diaries and letters to Felice, written in the period from 1912 to 1916, suggest that he was arriving at such a negative perception of his scriptive destiny even while he continued to assert writing's affirmative, mimetic potential. In these passages Kafka identifies his life entirely with writing. He comes into being, he declares, not at the point of his biological birth but at the moment of his body's being possessed by writing, as by a devil. "I have no literary interests," he tells Felice in 1913, "but am made of literature. I am nothing else, and cannot be anything else" (LF, 304; BF, 444). And what does this identification with writing entail? "It is not death, alas," says Kafka, "but the eternal torments of dying" (D II, 77; T, 420). Death in this sense belongs to life, whether it be approached with contentment or with lamentation. Dying, in contrast, suspends, or defers, the possibility of death—it is, in the phrase from Hegel that Maurice Blanchot makes the focus of his extraordinary article "Literature and the Right to Death," "that life which supports death and maintains itself in it," death in the process of becoming.[5]

The writer sustains death, maintains himself within it, by attempting to free language from any ground outside its own negativity. The writer never rejoices in his own death because he is always-already immersed in a process that removes him from life and offers him death as a "merciful surplus of strength" (D II, 184; T, 531). There can be no question of mastery here: the writer, made of literature, gives himself to an incessant activity of self-distancing, self-fictionalizing, to a game that suspends indefinitely the difference between life and death.

It is this state of suspended animation that Kafka describes with disturbing vividness in his letter to Max Brod of July 5, 1922. The context is an explanation of Kafka's fearful resistance to going on a trip to visit his friend Oskar Baum in the Georgental:

> Last night as I lay sleepless and let everything continually veer back and forth between my aching temples what I had almost forgotten during the last relatively quiet time became clear to me: namely, on what frail ground or rather altogether nonexistent ground I live, over a darkness from which the dark power emerges when it wills and, heedless of my stammering, destroys my life. Writing sustains me, but is it not more accurate to say that it sustains this kind of life? By this I don't mean, of course, that my life is better when I don't write. Rather it is much worse then and wholly unbearable and has to end in madness. But that, granted, only follows from the postulate that I am a writer, which is actually true even when I am not writing, and a nonwriting writer is a monster inviting madness. But what about being a writer itself? Writing is a sweet and wonderful reward, but for what? In the night it became clear to me, as clear as a child's lesson book, that it is the reward for serving the devil. This descent to the dark powers, this unshackling of spirits bound by nature, these dubious embraces and whatever else may take place in the nether parts which the higher parts no longer know, when one writes one's stories in the sunshine. Perhaps there are other forms of writing, but I know only this kind; at night, when fear keeps me from sleeping, I know only this kind. And the diabolic element in it seems very clear to me. It is vanity and sensuality which continually buzz about one's own or even another's form—and feast on him. The movement multiplies itself—it is a regular solar system of vanity. Sometimes a naive person will wish, "I would like to be dead and see how everyone mourns me." Such a writer is continually staging such a scene: He dies (or rather he does not live) and continually mourns himself. From this springs a terrible fear of death, which need not reveal itself as fear of death but may also appear as fear of change, as fear of Georgental. The reasons for this fear of death may be divided into two main categories. First he has a terrible fear of dying because he has not yet lived. By this I do not mean that wife and child, fields and cattle are essential to living. What is essential to life is only to forgo complacency, to move into the house instead of admiring it and hanging garlands around it. In reply to this, one might say that this is a matter of fate and is not given into anyone's hand. But then why this sense of repining, this repining that never ceases? To make onself finer and more savory? That is a part of it. But why do such nights leave one always with the refrain: I could live and I do not live. The second reason—perhaps it is all really one, the two do not want to stay apart for me now—is the belief: "What I have playacted is really going to happen. I have not bought myself off by my writing. I died my whole life long and now I will really die. My life was sweeter than other peoples' and my death will be more terrible by the same degree. Of course the writer in me will die right away, since such a figure has no base, no substance, is less than dust. He is only barely possible in the broil of earthly life, is only a construct of sensuality. That is your writer for you. But I myself cannot go on living because I have not lived, I have remained clay, I have not blown the spark into fire, but only used it to light up my corpse." It will be a strange burial: the writer, insubstantial

as he is, consigning the old corpse, the longtime corpse, to the grave. I am enough of a writer to appreciate the scene with all my senses, or—and it is the same thing—to want to describe it with total self-forgetfulness—not alertness, but self-forgetfulness is the writer's first prerequisite. (L, 333-34; Br, 384-85)

Here the writer's loss of any experiential ground, of any basis in duration, of any life outside his ongoing death, is seen as constitutive of his being-as-literature. Writing sustains his life, but that life involves a cannibalistic depletion of his biological existence. It is a diabolic reward for having denied life's sheltering happiness and its offer of a final and satisfying death. To write is to enter the darkness of unknowing, where language becomes a buzz of words that expresses no self but rather perpetuates its erosion, its continual, never-ending loss.

The contrast with the earlier passage we analyzed is striking. The writer who had pictured himself confronting death with contentment now has "a terrible fear of death." And this fear is related to precisely the same fictional staging of his own death that had previously given Kafka a reassuring sense of mastery. Now that mastery is considered vanity, the vanity of a self-enclosed linguistic system that can only metaphorically be considered a "Sonnensystem" (sunlight, Kafka declares earlier in the letter, would erase the writing he generates in the dark, nether regions). This is a solar system in which the sun is missing, outside itself, elsewhere. No longer is the activity of writing grounded in the experiential reality where Kafka had anchored it in his reflection of 1914. Then the writer was sustained in his fictionalizing activity by his memory of his non-fictional self's confidence that death need not be feared. Now that non-fictional self, "mein wirkliches Ich," is considered never to have lived, to have been a corpse all along. The writer's precarious existence is sustained by his ability to forget this dead self. But this forgetting can never be total. "Everything is allowed him, except self-oblivion," Kafka wrote in one of the aphorisms of the "He" series, "wherewith, however, everything in turn is denied him, except the one thing necessary at the moment for the whole" (GW, 158; B, 285). What remains of this denial is a trace that may be understood psychologically as a "sense of repining," the writer's regret for an ego that has never moved into its own house, or that may be understood reflexively as literature's mournful awareness that it can never "die beautifully and purely away" but must continue ceaselessly to feed sensually off of life.

Kafka's fear of death may be understood as a fear of this trace's being conclusively erased, causing a fusion of corpselike self and insubstantial writer. Such a fusion did at times appear desirable to Kafka as the achievement of self-oblivion and hence of wholeness. "After all," he wrote to Felice, "there can be no more beautiful spot to die in, no spot more worthy of total despair, than one's own novel" (LF, 142; BF, 231). Despair fosters the happy fantasy of an inscription that coincides with being by symbolizing its end. Kafka's novel here plays the role of his mother in the earlier passage. In fantasy, the novel

receives his despair as generously as his mother had received his laments. In contrast, the writer who fears his own death does not despair. He suffers, and suffering, Kafka wrote in a notebook, "is the only positive element in this world, indeed it is the only link between this world and the positive" (DF, 90; H, 108). Unreadable in itself, suffering stimulates the ongoing process of self-reading of which the Georgental letter is but one remarkable residue. Actually this residue, as Stanley Corngold has pointed out, is a kind of excess or surplus, produced in the midst of the self's suffering as an inexhaustible question about the mode of that production.[6] What is the difference, the text asks, between "I, myself" and "he, the writer?" Each is alive only insofar as the other is dead, and vice versa—"the two do not want to stay apart for me now," comments Kafka. It seems as if each could be read as a figure for the other, as if each were capable of functioning as either tenor or vehicle and "veer[ed] back and forth between [Kafka's] aching temples." Only the fundamental reference to physical suffering remains stable.

How can the analysis we have performed of these two passages linking writing and death help in the task of interpreting Kafka's fiction? First of all, it should alert us to the very different meanings that death can have for Kafka and to the contrasting conceptions of writing he associated with each. Thus if Kafka's prose is, as Roman Karst has observed, "a contemplation of dying—a poetic eschatology," the critic should beware of adding, as Karst does, "Everything in it is the desire for and expectation of the end—of that which the ultimate moment brings."[7] Such a desire for death translates in literary terms into a desire for wholeness, "Vollkommenheit," the finality of an ending that closes itself off from the incessant murmur of writing. It is a desire for death to be clearly definable as the absence of life and for writing to be free to elaborate its fictional inventions on the basis of their analogy to life's limited organic form and constricted temporal extension. Kafka no doubt felt this desire intensely, and it could be shown that it motivates not only many of his protagonists but also many of his critics. The critics who interpret Kafka in these terms implicitly allege not to be taken in by the secret game whereby he pretends, in the diary entry of 1914, to be duping his readers' understanding. But their claim to hermeneutic mastery is no more than a repetition of Kafka's own similar claim: they are grounding the literary game in lived experience and reassuring themselves thereby of death's reality outside linguistic freeplay. In this they resemble the family man in Kafka's story who finds nothing more worrisome about the mobile spool of tangled thread that calls itself Odradek and occasionally inhabits his house than the thought that Odradek may be unable to die and will most likely outlive him. Odradek, a word, the narrator tells us, of uncertain etymology, is also a being of uncertain ontology. A laughing figure ("Gebilde") for the enduring instability of the figural, he/it renders unreadable the distinction between life and death, creature and thing.

Walter Benjamin's observation that "What draws the reader to the novel is the hope of warming his shivering life with a death he reads about" applies to Kafka's protagonists.[8] They are most often readers of this kind, with the peculiar twist that the story with which they hope to warm their shivering lives is their own—the engagement story Georg Bendemann writes to his friend in Russia, the tale of dutiful work performance whereby Gregor Samsa attempts to justify himself to the chief clerk, the narrative of innocence Joseph K. futilely presents at his interrogation, the account of his being hired as Landsurveyor with which K. wishes to confront the Castle. In a sense, all these would-be stories are analogous to Kafka's claim that he is capable of meeting his death with contentment. Their goal is to narrativize a life in such a way that the present moment appears as its end and completion. Indeed, in "The Hunter Gracchus," the story that illustrates more explicitly than any other the issues I have been exploring, the hunter declares: "I had been glad to live and I was glad to die" (CS, 229; SE, 228).

But the hunter's death ship has taken a wrong turn and now, neither dead nor alive, the "fundamental error of [his] onetime death" ("der Grundfehler [seines] einstmaligen Sterbens") (CS, 229; SE, 287), mocks him forever. What has been lost, precisely, is the ground on which an individual's death can occur only once, the ground that justifies the narrative completion of his life. The hunter, like the other Kafka protagonists I mentioned, has lost himself in a space of fundamental error, of perpetual errancy. Like Odradek, who is "extraordinarily nimble and can never be laid hold of" (CS, 428; SE, 139), Gracchus is never more than provisionally and delusively present in any world. He has become an unreadable text, a floating signifier: "Nobody will read what I write here" (CS, 230; my translation; SE, 288), he declares in a surprisingly undisguised identification of his suspended existence with the writing process and a disturbing denial of what I as reader am presently engaged in doing.

A certain mode of psychoanalytic interpretation offers a way of reading this denial. Kafka, whose name is etymologically related to Gracchus, may be fantasizing a way out of the writer's predicament as illustrated by Gracchus's perpetual errancy: if his text is not read, if it is not put into motion through any reader's help, then Kafka can imagine it as a grave that will not be opened, as a death ship that will not be led astray. "Nobody knows of me" (CS, 230; SE, 288), says Gracchus, reminding us of Kafka's lifelong reluctance to publish and of his request, when faced with his own death, that Brod burn all his unpublished manuscripts, as if in a great funeral pyre. Thus we are brought back, via this biographical circuit, to the writer's narcissistic dream of a contented death and to his fantasy of dying inside his own texts. The denial of the reader now appears as a strategy to counter the diabolic activity of the writer, dramatized in the narrative as fundamental error. Error supports death and maintains itself in it. Thus conceived, error corresponds in psychoanalytic terms to the fundamental drive energizing all unconscious activity, the

death instinct. Gracchus seems to embody that instinct in its close relationship to the scriptive process. Constantly in motion, hovering between life and death while hoping for death's finality, Gracchus errs in much the same sense that the unconscious does. To refuse the effort to read the unreadable text of his errancy would thus be tantamount to denying the unconscious function of writing. And this, according to one psychoanalytic interpretation, may well have been Kafka's unconscious desire.

Psychoanalysis thus transforms the unreadable text into a readable one. It is essentially a hermeneutics, wherein meaning and understanding, however complex, qualified and mediated, are ultimately based in an extralinguistic truth.[9] If we can speak of the text as having an unconscious, we do so by analogy with the human psyche. "Psychology," Kafka wrote in one of his notebooks, "is the description of the reflection [Spiegelung] of the earthly world in the heavenly plane or, more correctly, the description of a reflection such as we, nurslings of the earth, imagine it, for no reflection actually occurs, we only see earth wherever we may turn" (H, 72; DF, 65-66). In these terms, Kafka's narratives become a kind of psychomachia: the protagonist wishes to tell a story of mastery, as if from the point of view of his death, of his reflection in the heavenly plane, and he battles against the erasure of this reflection, an erasure that represents the death drive within him. He wants to reach the imaginative space of his own death and thereby achieve the authority to narrate his life, but he is repulsed by the, to him, unimaginable activity of his own death impulse.

But there is perhaps a step beyond the circle of hermeneutic recuperation that Kafka's texts challenge their interpreters to take: this is what I call the step into allegory. Its epigraphs (or perhaps I should say epitaphs) could be Kafka's notebook observations, "The evolution of mankind—a growth of death-force" and "Our salvation is death, but not this one" (DF, 101; H, 123). The allegorical world is historical, it is in evolution, but, as Walter Benjamin observes in his brilliant discussion of allegory, "in this form history does not strike one as the process of eternal life so much as the advance of unending decay. . . . Allegories are in the realm of thoughts what ruins are in the realm of things."[10] In the allegorical world, death can never offer salvation because the very notion of salvation betrays the ongoing temporal erosion, the continual growth of death-force, that characterizes the ruinous allegorical landscape. This is a "Sonnensystem" from which the life-giving sun is absent; that sun is the center of a universe of truth of which the mournful allegorical world has no part.

The existence of the writer as Kafka describes it to Brod in the letter of 1922 is purely allegorical in Benjamin's sense. The corpse Kafka claims to have been his whole life long is the allegorical emblem *par excellence*. "The allegorization of the physis," comments Benjamin, "can only be carried through vigorously in respect to the corpse."[11] "I" has been a corpse his whole life long, Kafka tells us. One way of understanding this observation would be to say that "I" has spent his life attaining the neutrality of "it."[12] This depersonalizing process whereby "I" loses his humanity enables him, paradoxically, to recognize his identity, his selfhood, in the experience of suffering.[13] This empirical experience constitutes the referential, mimetic moment that always persists in any allegory but that remains outside that allegory's staging of its reading. Kafka, suffering sleeplessly in bed, only begins to read himself when he remembers that the ground of his life is "altogether nonexistent" ("gar nicht vorhanden"). At this point, when what is remembered is that memory itself has no coherent organic or referential basis, "I" and "he" become rhetorical fictions each of which signifies the death of the other.

The allegorical protagonist, here Kafka himself, attempts to capture this signification, that is, to coincide with his own death, by destroying the distance and difference that keep him alive as a figure. But this coincidence can never occur, for it would mean the literalization of the figure, its transformation into pure scriptive matter, the letter as corpse. Allegory tends toward this mute literalism. According to de Man, it "names the rhetorical process by which the literary text moves from a phenomenal, world-oriented to a grammatical, language-oriented direction."[14] "The cruelty of death," Kafka commented in his notebook, "lies in the fact that it brings the real sorrow of the end, but not the end" (DF, 101; H, 122). The hermeneutic impulse to read a life mimetically from the point of view of its end is frustrated by the allegorical impulse to figure that end rhetorically as the death of figuration. By staging the narrative of this frustration, Kafka's texts offer their readers a powerful dramatization of the life-and-death issues at stake in the act of reading.

NOTES

[1] Elizabeth Kübler-Ross, *On Death and Dying* (London: Tavistock Publications, 1970); Paul de Man, *Allegories of Reading: Figural Language in Rousseau, Nietzsche, Rilke, and Proust* (New Haven: Yale University Press, 1979).

[2] I have used the following abbreviations for Kafka's works, giving references first to the standard English translations (all published by Schocken Books in New York) then to the German originals (all published by Fischer Verlag in Frankfurt):

 B *Beschreibung eines Kampfes,* 1954
 Br *Briefe 1902-1924,* 1958
 BF *Briefe an Felice,* 1967
 CS *The Complete Stories,* 1971
 D I *Diaries 1910-1913,* 1948
 D II *Diaries 1914-1923,* 1947
 DF *Dearest Father,* 1954
 GW *The Great Wall of China,* 1970
 H *Hochzeitsvorbereitungen auf dem Lande,* 1953
 L *Letters to Friends, Family, and Editors,* 1977
 LF *Letters to Felice,* 1973
 SE *Sämtliche Erzählungen,* 1970
 T *Tagebücher,* 1954

[3] For a suggestive commentary on this passage, which has influenced my reading but from which it differs significantly, see Maurice Blanchot, "La mort contente," in *De Kafka à Kafka* (Paris: Gallimard, 1981).

[4] See Charles Bernheimer, *Flaubert and Kafka: Studies in Psychopoetic Structure* (New Haven: Yale University Press, 1982), pp. 139-67.

[5] Maurice Blanchot, "Literature and the Right to Death," in *The Gaze of Orpheus and Other Literary Essays,* edited by P. Adams Sitney (New York: Station Hill, 1981), p. 61.

[6] See Stanley Corngold's article in this book and his fuller discussion of what he calls the "surplus subject" in chapter five of his book *The Fate of the Self: German Writers and French Theory* (New York: Columbia University Press, 1986).

[7] Roman Karst, "Kafka or the Impossibility of Writing," *The Literary Review,* 26:4 (Summer 1983), p. 516.

[8] Walter Benjamin, "The Storyteller: Reflections on the Works of Nikolai Leskov," in *Illuminations,* edited by Hannah Arendt (New York: Harcourt, Brace & World, 1968), p. 101.

[9] In this sense, the final goal of the readable text is to abolish the activity of reading: "The ultimate goal of a hermeneutically successful reading is to do away with reading altogether," comments Paul de Man ("Introduction" to Hans Robert Jauss, *Toward an Aesthetic of Reception* [Minneapolis: University of Minnesota Press, 1982], p. ix). In contrast, "allegories are always allegories of metaphor and, as such, they are always allegories of the impossibility of reading—a sentence in which the genitive 'of' has itself to be 'read' as a metaphor" (*Allegories of Reading,* p. 205).

[10] Walter Benjamin, *Ursprung des deutschen Trauerspiels,* in *Gesammelte Schriften* I.1, edited by Rolf Tiedemann and Hermann Schweppenhauser (Frankfurt: Suhrkamp Verlag, 1974), pp. 353-54. My translation.

[11] *Ursprung,* p. 391.

[12] Michel Foucault mentions this process of authorial neutralization as one of the conceptual innovations most likely to make his readers uneasy: "Must I suppose that in my discourse I can have no survival? And that in speaking I am not banishing my death, but actually establishing it; or rather that I am abolishing all interiority in that exterior that is so indifferent to my life, and so *neutral,* that it makes no distinction between my life and my death?" *The Archeology of Knowledge* (New York: Harper & Row, 1976), p. 210.

[13] Kafka evokes a similar experience in one of the aphorisms of the *He* series: "He has the feeling that merely by being alive he is blocking his own way. From this sense

of hindrance, in turn, he deduces the proof that he is alive" (GW, 154; B, 280). The *He* series as a whole explores the problematic status of the third person Kafka both is and is not.

[14] "Introduction" to *Toward an Aesthetic of Reception,* p. xxiii.

David Cavitch

SOURCE: "Solipsism and Death in D. H. Lawrence's Late Works," in *The Massachusetts Review,* Vol. VII, No. 3, Summer, 1966, pp. 495-508.

[In the following essay, Cavitch explores Lawrence's representation of a retreat from the alienation and division of modern society into an "isolation of personal identity" and into death in his late fiction.]

Unlike D. H. Lawrence's earlier novels, *Lady Chatterley's Lover*[1] invites a gossipy sort of attention: the novel itself encourages readers to separate details of the characters' behavior from the fictional context which interprets them, and the result is that for nearly forty years the dissociated facts of the lovers' words and acts have given the novel notoriety that has caused widespread misrepresentation. But even now, five years after the courts in England and America have recognized that the fiction is not obscenely detailed in its sexual episodes, it is improbable that the general approach to *Lady Chatterley* will alter, because the work draws attention to circumstantial information that is deliberately garish and shocking. Connie Chatterley and Mellors are prominently interesting in the novel because of what they do and say from moment to moment, while the represented quality, or ambiance, of their lives is subordinated to a background that is too simple, too fanciful or too vague for most readers' interests. Lawrence reversed his usual treatment of his subject material when he brought personal and particularized data about the characters into the foreground of the fiction, and subordinated the generalized life-qualities which earlier characters embody.

Lawrence prizes Connie personally and he presents her with more evidence than she needs of his unequivocal sympathy. He excuses the weakness that initially led her into marriage with Clifford Chatterley by explaining it as the effect of immaturity and misguided modern feminism; she sought to retain "a pure and noble freedom in love." But Connie, as her father and older men approvingly notice, is basically "old-fashioned"—which assures us from the outset of her marriage that her error of judgment does not indicate a deep character fault. When Clifford returns from the war paralyzed and impotent, the sympathy in the novel's viewpoint attaches only to Connie, for Clifford's paralysis is symbolic of his incapacity for sympathy with others or any warm-hearted natural response. Connie's years of unfulfillment in marriage seem a cruelly wasteful penalty for her youthful mistake; she is completely deprived of intimacy and she has no place

with the cleverly talking, passionless men of her husband's society. As she comprehends the vacuity of her life, the vacuity of Clifford, the vacuity even of her liberty to have affairs or bear another man's child to rear in Wragby Hall, it is evident to the reader that anything Connie does to attempt sensual fulfillment will receive Lawrence's easy, unquestioning approval.

Oliver Mellors, whose love changes Connie's life, also suffers from a disastrous marriage. In his youth he knew women who gave him their spirit of love but they never really wanted the physical act of sex; Mellors reacted from them by marrying Bertha Coutts, whose aggressions during intercourse finally demonstrated her fierce sexual hatred. Embittered against women and against modern industrial civilization, Mellors withdrew from the world to a hermit's life as a gamekeeper on the Chatterley estate. But apparently, he would have been fully capable of tenderness and sympathy for a girl like Connie at any time before he met her. He, too, commands a single-minded sympathy in Lawrence's viewpoint.

The background of the lovers' separate misery and solitude reveals that civilization or "other people in the world" are mainly to blame for their troubles; the lovers themselves are free from the complexities or shortcomings of character that might defeat their chance for happiness together, and their romance is the story of their progress into a relationship uncorrupted by social evil. The narrative is the simplest of all Lawrence's major fictions and it introduces no complications that seriously interfere with the lovers' attention to themselves. Mellors' love-making brings Connie gently into full sensual responsiveness. She becomes pregnant, openly acknowledges her affair with Mellors, and at the end of the novel the lovers are anticipating divorces which will enable them to marry each other. The story centers on Connie's steady growth into a fulfilled woman; her uncomplicated nature flowers like the woods in springtime where she meets with Mellors:

> She was gone in her own soft rapture, like a forest soughing with the dim, glad moan of spring, moving into bud. She could feel in the same world with her the man, the nameless man, moving on beautiful feet, beautiful in the phallic mystery. And in herself, in all her veins, she felt him and his child. His child was in all her veins, like a twilight.
>
> . . . . .
>
> She was like a forest, like the dark interlacing of the oak-wood, humming inaudibly with myriad unfolding buds. Meanwhile the birds of desire were asleep in the vast interlaced intricacy of her body. (163)

For Connie and Mellors sexual relations are sweeter and simpler than for any earlier pair of Lawrence's protagonists. They are the first major characters who are absolutely free of self-revulsion or any fear of sex, and the novel concentrates attention on their sensuality. Lawrence describes their sexual intercourse in more explicit detail than in earlier fiction, as he tries to purify every word and act of any shameful associations. He introduces the diction of vulgarity to the lovers' dialogues, and even Mellors' occasional preference for the "Italian way" is alluded to in the novel as a necessary immersion in wholesome sensuality. The descriptions of their intercourse are not dominated by images of aggression, resistance, violation or loss of identity, nor do the lovers struggle to orgasms of horrific intensity.

The imagery of harmony and direct sensual fulfillment gives an astonishing new sweetness to Lawrence's style in *Lady Chatterley,* but the apparent rosiness of his vision only announces his retreat from a mimetic representation of life. To present characters who have perfect inner freedom for direct sensual fulfillment, Lawrence had to circumvent his own sense of reality. He created a conventionally artificial world where the lovers could act according to his ideal of love rather than according to his knowledge of experience. Connie and Mellors live in a world of pastoral idyll. Their love is dramatized only in the woods on the Chatterley estate, where rain falls softly through the darkness or the twilight and the fresh growth of spring scents the air. They dance nakedly in the glades and spread forest flowers on their bodies; they make love in a forest hut, or on the ground, and Connie returns in secrecy to her conventional place in the outer world. Anyone but the lovers enters the woods as an intruder. The arrival of a postman at Mellors' cottage and the return of Mellors' wife introduce the complications which threaten to defame their love. Only meanness thrives in the encircling world: the ugly works of the Chatterley coal mines line the rim of the forest, and in the manor-house the conversation of sophisticated guests displays the cynicism of modern society.

The contrast between the innocence of experience in the forest and the decadence of life in the world depends upon Lawrence's most facile judgment against modern industrial civilization. His evaluation of modern culture is made diagrammatically, and it is only effective to support the schematic structure of the novel.[2] As Connie matures into a sensual woman but forfeits her place in conventional society, Clifford climbs to success in the world. He forgoes his literary dilettantism and becomes a progressive business leader in the coal-mining industry, but inwardly he disintegrates and regresses to child-like dependency upon his housekeeper, Mrs. Bolton. Their perverse eroticism underlies Clifford's thriving in the outer world, while Connie and Mellors discover innocence in the privacy of the woods. A world peopled only by Clifford and his vitiated friends offers no defense against Lawrence's denunciations of its mechanization, its abuse of money and its hatred of life.

The attack against modern society is only superficially verified, because the atmosphere of romance dominates the novel. Lawrence wrote *Lady Chatterley* three times over in order to achieve the world of idyll in the final version, and in each text he reduced the lovers' connec-

tion with society and made the outer world less relevant in the fiction.[3] From the first version he rejected the gamekeeper's virulence towards other people, his lower class uncouthness and his social radicalism as a secretary of a Communist League. He rejected the distressing conclusion of the second version, in which Connie and her lover are beset by a coarse, prying gamekeeper as Connie weeps desperately over their unlikely prospects for future happiness. In the third version, Mellors takes a job on a farm and prepares to receive Connie and their child when they return from Italy. His letter to her displays confidence in their love, along with a stoical foreboding of a bad time of social violence ahead for the rest of the world as a result of the "mass-will of people, wanting money and hating life." But he assures her that the inevitable ruin of humanity that is fostered by industrial civilization can have no effect on their destiny: "All the bad times that ever have been, haven't been able to blow the crocus out: not even the love of women. So they won't be able to blow out my wanting you, nor the little glow there is between you and me." (363-64)

The conclusion of the novel repudiates any alternative to the evil imputed to society. Mellors believes that the world could be a better place if men would act more like men, which in his mind means wearing scarlet tights and white jerkins, but the fiction dismisses his hypothesis as a passing fancy; his brief remarks are absurdly irrelevant to Clifford's failure as a man or to Connie's triumph as a woman. He speaks from a child's notion of interchangeable personal identities; and even Mellors' Midlands dialect, which he uses almost exclusively with Connie, suddenly sounds like an infant's accents:

> Why, if men had red, fine legs, that alone would change them in a month. They'd begin to be men again, to be men! An' the women could dress as they liked. Because if once the men walked with legs close bright scarlet, and buttocks nice and showing scarlet under a little white jacket: then the women 'ud begin to be women. It's because th' men *aren't* men, that the women have to be. (263)

This frail proposal which is not even presented affirmatively is all that remains in *Lady Chatterley* of Lawrence's former passion for cultural reconstruction. He abandons the world to its madness—the result of humanity's incapacity for direct sensual fulfillment—and he precludes any possibility of the lovers' regenerative return to society. The novel marks the end of Lawrence's search for a new world of communal experience; in his art he no longer experiments with forms of social organization as a means of objectifying essential human character. The sensuality that flourishes in Connie and Mellors seeks no positive counterpart in the relationships of the larger world, and the novel rejects all likelihood that men's social experience will ever lead to anything but disaster.

Harmony among people can prevail only within the family relation implied at the end of the novel when Connie is pregnant and the lovers, though presently separated, anticipate marriage and being "together next year." But this family grouping even with its promise of new birth achieves no societal relevance in the fiction—Mellors and Connie plan to sever finally their connections with the world of social circumstances. The real meaning of Connie's pregnancy is reflected in Mellors' reinstatement to emotional security and his retrogressive freedom from the demands of sexual activity; and it is identified by the carefully discriminated parallel of sexual innocence in his relation with Connie, and Clifford's child-like happiness with Mrs. Bolton. Mellors' famous letter to Connie celebrates his re-achieved state of chastity in fact and in spirit, for he explains that his erotic nature is quieted by peaceful thoughts about her womb; and he enjoys his purity of consciousness in final detachment and immunity from the effects of present experience. The emblematic situation at the conclusion implies the stability of maternal rather than conjugal relations.

A similar disavowal of adult and circumstantial experience dominates all of Lawrence's last art, as other protagonists achieve their deepest desire in blissful quiescence. In "The Man Who Died," Lawrence's last completed work of fiction, the renunciation of purposive activity and direct personal relations becomes the meaning of Christ's resurrection. In his crucifixion the Man knew all the bitterness of human experience. Escaped from his tomb, he turns away from further entanglements with his disciples and he rejects his former mission as a mistaken effort to compel life unnaturally; he wanders aimlessly through a calm and sunlit Mediterranean world, slowly acquiring the full satisfactions of his "aloneness." A priestess of Isis gives him sexual fulfillment and she becomes pregnant by him. Not wishing, however, to be ensnared in "the little life of jealousy and property," he sails away again: the god-like man in the security of his little boat remains attached only to the womb of the mild-mannered woman. His fatherhood, like Mellors', points to his pre-natal identification and leads to his eternal freedom from the demands of making particular responses.

These disintegrations in Lawrence's fiction occurred partly because he lost interest in external experience during his long tubercular illness—and sexual experience particularly may have been only a memory in those last years—so that his strong regressive tendencies easily dominated his art. Even his descriptive writing indicates his withdrawal from realistic scenes to highly abstract settings, such as the idyllic Chatterley forest and the Mediterranean world of "The Man Who Died." The most prominent scene in the story seems properly Mediterranean in its painterly expanse of sea-space and bright light, but it offers no perspective or impression to suggest that the total view is directly seen. The details are generalized and conventional, and they are not brought to sharp definition by the sensibility of a perceiving intelligence; they reflect none of the complexity of "character," as Lawrence's descriptions previously did. Instead, the setting places the Man and priestess in a conceptualized world which aggravates the solipsism evident in the fiction:

The wind came cold and strong from inland, from the invisible snows of Lebanon. But the temple, facing south and west, towards Egypt, faced the splendid sun of winter as he curved down towards the sea, the warmth and radiance flooded in between the pillars of painted wood. But the sea was invisible, because of the trees, though its dashing sounded among the hum of pines. The air was turning golden to afternoon. The woman who served Isis stood in her yellow robe, and looked up at the steep slopes coming down to the sea, where the olive-trees silvered under the wind like water splashing. She was alone save for the goddess. And in the winter afternoon the light stood erect and magnificent off the invisible sea, filling the hills of the coast. She went towards the sun, through the grove of Mediterranean pine-trees and ever-green oaks, in the midst of which the temple stood, on a little, tree-covered tongue of land between two bays.

It was only a very little way, and then she stood among the dry trunks of the outermost pines, on the rocks under which the sea smote and sucked, facing the open where the bright sun gloried in winter. The sea was dark, almost indigo, running away from the land, and crested with white. The hand of the wind brushed it strangely with shadow, as it brushed the olives of the slope with silver.[4]

The fairly insubstantial materials of the composition—light, wind, the invisible sea—emphasize the purely tonal qualities of the setting, and the chief details are arranged by the syntax of logical organization: "*But* the temple. . . . *But* the sea . . . *though* its dashing . . . *save for* the goddess." This sort of description has the atmospheric effect of reducing vision to the sparest, unnaturally isolated details; it reveals little interest in actually examining the world.

In his life as in his fiction, Lawrence was no longer inclined to empirical observation; his travels around the earth were over and when he looked back upon his explorations he saw them as a completed adventure, one that led him to realize the greater expanse of inwardness he has to enjoy, as a late poem explains:

TRAVEL IS OVER

I have travelled, and looked at the world, and
  loved it.
Now I don't want to look at the world any more,
there seems nothing there.
In not-looking, and in not-seeing
comes a new strength
and undeniable new gods share their life with us,
  when we cease to see.[5]

The current of his imagination simply flowed away from the circumstances of external life to a passionate interest directly in himself. He was irritated by events which interrupted his attention or contradicted the harmonies of his subjective experience, and his attitude towards the common experience of other people became more petulant and satirical than ever. Most of the poems in *Pan-*

sies, Nettles, and *More Pansies* are prosy verses that expressed a moment's irritation with the vulgarity or evil of the world outside him. But he was impatient over objective reality, and he was more apt to dismiss it than to sustain even negative emotions about it, and so the poems are usually slight or inept.

His significant artistic achievements in these last years issue from his one remaining involvement with life: from about 1926 Lawrence knew that he was dying because of his recurrent tubercular attacks, and a group of death-poems from his posthumously collected *Last Poems* together with his piece of graveyard literature, *Etruscan Places,* comprise the best of his final art. He still drew upon immediate knowledge of experience in his preparations for dying, which represent death as a supreme satisfaction. In *Etruscan Places*[6] he describes his tour of the cities of the dead, tombs where corpses were provided with all the accoutrements necessary for a continuing life. Lawrence climbs in and out of the caverns dug under the hillsides or covered with mounds of earth, hurrying across the daylight from one dark descent to another: "And gradually," he writes, "the underworld of the Etruscans becomes more real than the above day of the afternoon. One begins to live with the painted dancers and feasters and mourners, and to look eagerly for them." (76)

The entire account is governed by his developing impression that in the awareness of death one sees more clearly just how life is individually, sensually experienced. He believed that the Etruscans felt no aversion for death and therefore they could represent life honestly by including it. Their art freely accepts the frailty and evanescence of all life-images; they knew no poignancy or horror over transience. For them, as Lawrence interpreted their tombs, death was the quickness, the subtlety of the life-experience. Even the irony of their ruined preparations for an after-life strikes him as soothing and true to the spirit in which they died:

> The tombs seem so easy and friendly, cut out of rock underground. One does not feel oppressed, descending into them. It must be partly owing to the peculiar charm of natural proportion which is in all Etruscan things of the unspoilt, unromanized centuries. There is a simplicity, combined with a most peculiar, free-breasted naturalness and spontaneity, in the shapes and movements of the underworld walls and spaces, that at once reassures the spirit. The Greeks sought to make an impression, and Gothic still more seeks to impress the mind. The Etruscans, no. The things they did, in their easy centuries, are as natural and as easy as breathing. They leave the breast breathing freely and pleasantly, with a certain fullness of life. Even the tombs. And that is the true Etruscan quality: ease, naturalness, and an abundance of life, no need to force the mind or the soul in any direction.

> And death, to the Etruscan, was a pleasant continuance of life, with jewels and wine and flutes playing for the dance. It was neither an ecstasy of bliss, a heaven, nor a purgatory of torment. It was just a natural continuance of the fullness of life. Everything was in terms of life, of living.

> Yet everything Etruscan, save the tombs, has been wiped out. It seems strange. One goes out again into the April sunshine, into the sunken road between the soft, grassy-mounded tombs, and as one passes one glances down the steps at the doorless doorways of tombs. It is so still and pleasant and cheerful. The place is so soothing. (28-29)

The descent to darkness and oblivion comforts Lawrence with the promise of peace and justification. The dying man journeys into an underworld, as in the pagan myths of death; there, his body is enveloped by unfathomable blackness and he is cleansed of his continuous awareness of separation, which is the distressing condition of life. In "Bavarian Gentians" Lawrence anticipates the loss of objective awareness in death by using intensive repetition of key words—*blue, dark* and *torch*—to surpass the descriptive and referential limitations of language. The effort of his style is to make speech so symbolic that his individual words directly express facts of consciousness, without first being metaphors or symbols that refer also to the external world:

> Not every man has gentians in his house
> in soft September, at slow, sad Michaelmas.
>
> Bavarian gentians, big and dark, only dark
> darkening the day-time, torch-like with the
>   smoking blueness of Pluto's gloom,
> ribbed and torch-like, with their blaze of darkness
>   spread blue
> down flattening into points, flattened under the
>   sweep of white day
> torch-flower of the blue-smoking darkness,
>   Pluto's dark-blue daze,
> black lamps from the halls of Dis, burning dark
>   blue
> giving off darkness, blue darkness, as Demeter's
>   pale lamps give off light,
> lead me then, lead the way.
>
> Reach me a gentian, give me a torch!
> let me guide myself with the blue, forked torch of
>   this flower
> down the darker and darker stairs, where blue is
>   darkened on blueness
> even where Persephone goes, just now, from the
>   frosted September
> to the sightless realm where darkness is awake
>   upon the dark
> and Persephone herself is but a voice
> or a darkness invisible enfolded in the deeper dark
> of the arms Plutonic, and pierced with the passion
>   of dense gloom,
> among the splendour of torches of darkness,
>   shedding darkness on the lost bride and her
>   groom.
>
>   (697)

The poem intentionally separates two planes of reality by using two kinds of language in opposition. The casual self-effacement of the opening lines ironically undervalues the poet's objective situation, and the more weighty emotional terms of the second line allow his mood to dominate the scene. Objective circumstances appear reflected in simple, logical statements in which they are only marginally, laterally developed. The room, the flowers, the time of year remain at the edges of the poem's field of awareness, where they frame the central, imagined world of oblivion. The actual situation is mildly reasserted in "frosted September," in the imperatives, and in the analytically simplified metaphor: "Reach me a gentian, give me a torch! / let me guide myself with the blue forked torch of this flower." The world from which the poet is ready to depart appears already subordinated to a lower level of reality, to a periphery of less intense consciousness.

For the central experience in the poem Lawrence uses language that is laden with compound adjectives and adjective clauses. The elaborate modifications tend to dissociate darkness as a substantial, complex quantity apart from the flower. It is darkness which suggests fire, smoke, light of the underworld and the myth of the soul's descent to oblivion and sensual experience in the deepest cavern of the earth. The qualifying constructions build on each other, as seemingly autonomous words crowd together in incremental, proliferating contact. *Dark* leads to "dark darkening," to "blaze of darkness," to "darker and darker" and other variations. Each sentence extends farther and farther away from the influence of the simple grammatical base that refers to the actual situation. The amount and density of modification break down the normal syntactical patterns that preserve the duality of objective circumstances and a perceiving intelligence. Modification in this poem replaces verbs, so that adjectives function as whole predicates and appear as acts of mind.

The poem gives artful form to the regressive feelings which undermine *Lady Chatterley* and "The Man Who Died" by properly identifying the pattern of action as an obliteration of consciousness and clearly associating death with the peace of maternal reunification in the embracing womb. Because of its linguistic complexity and its sustained discrimination between the poet's circumstances and his mood, "Bavarian Gentians" is probably an earlier poem than "The Ship of Death," in which Lawrence is more at ease with his desire for death and can generalize it and state it absolutely. He does not have to make the effort of a special language or maintain categories of reality to express his subjective experience precisely; his lines are shorter and more pliant, and his diction is simple and sometimes disarmingly casual. The emotional force of the poem is more conceptual and does not so noticeably arise from the words or structure of the poetic expression. Death is introduced as a heavy gravitation drawing all of nature downward; the elliptical compression of the opening lines avoids the qualification of any personal assertion:

> Now it is autumn and the falling fruit
> and the long journey towards oblivion.
> The apples falling like great drops of dew
> to bruise themselves an exit from themselves.

> And it is time to go, to bid farewell
> to one's own self, and find an exit
> from the fallen self.

(716)

The soul liberated from the body voyages over an unknown sea in a small boat, like the Man's boat and like the Etruscan's ship of death, drawn like Persephone into the density of darkness:

> There is no port, there is nowhere to go
> only the deepening blackness darkening still
> blacker upon the soundless, ungurgling flood
> darkness at one with darkness, up and down
> and sideways utterly dark, so there is no direction
>   any more.
> and the little ship is there; yet she is gone.
> She is not seen, for there is nothing to see her by.
> She is gone! gone! and yet
> somewhere she is there.
> Nowhere!

(719)

The journey ends at the first thread of dawn over eternity when the soul regains her lost body and enters it, "filling the heart with peace." Only death could finally promise Lawrence to remove the basic human sense of self-division and alienation from the life of the body, after he had lost serious hope for a new world of improved human relations in adult sex and social organization. He found that beyond the griefs of manhood or modernity, the isolation of personal identity was the final, rudimentary obstacle in the way of vivid, perfect experience.

NOTES

[1] *Lady Chatterley's Lover* was first published in Florence by G. Orioli in 1928. The Grove Press edition, New York, 1959, is used for citations within the text of this article.

[2] G. Armour Craig believes that "it is one of the ironies of modern social history that public censors should be so outraged by the thoroughness of the idyll yet so oblivious to the attack on modern technology." "D. H. Lawrence on Thinghood and Selfhood," *The Massachusetts Review,* I (Fall, 1959), 58. My own view is that the public has disregarded the novel's attack on technology because in *Lady Chatterley* Lawrence does not persuasively depict social evil.

[3] A general comparison of the three versions appears in E. W. Tedlock, Jr., *D. H. Lawrence Manuscripts, A Descriptive Bibliography* (Albuquerque, N. M., 1948), pp. 279-316.

[4] *The Tales of D. H. Lawrence* (London, 1934), p. 1116.

[5] *The Complete Poems of D. H. Lawrence,* edited by Pinto and Roberts (New York, 1964), p. 662. Additional references to poems will be cited in the text.

[6] *Etruscan Places* was first published in London by Martin Secker in 1932. The Heinemann edition, London, 1933, is used for citations within the text.

Keith Cushman

SOURCE: "The Quintessence of Dowsonism: 'The Dying of Francis Donne'," in *Studies in Short Fiction,* Vol. XI, No. 1, Winter, 1974, pp. 45-51.

[In the following essay, Cushman describes "The Dying of Francis Donne" as "a masterly delineation of the psychology of dying" in which its protagonist succeeds in escaping "the tyranny of time only by intellectual detachment and by death."]

The evidence suggests that Ernest Dowson thought more highly of his prose than his poetry,[1] but that has not been the verdict of the world. If Dowson has an audience at all these days, it is for his frail, languorous poetry, not for his stories, sketches, or translations, or for the two novels he collaborated on. For the most part the stories and sketches are interesting period pieces, pale, delicate variations on Dowson's characteristic themes of lost love and the tragic gap between the flux of life and the perfection of art. The end of "The Diary of a Successful Man" epitomizes the typical Dowson situation. The protagonist sits "in a cloud of incense" in the Church of the Dames Rouges, listening first to the "perfect litany" and then to the beautiful singing of a nun who had been his love years before. The "sweetness and power" of the singing mock the unhappiness of living, and the story closes with the "successful man" feeling "alone in utter darkness."[2] Estrangement is usually the keynote. Most of Dowson's stories bring to mind the composition played by the young Russian pianist in "An Orchestral Violin": a "mad *valse*" which "thrilled the nerves painfully, ringing the changes between voluptuous sorrow and the merriment of devils, and burdened always with the weariness of 'all the Russias,' the proper *Welt-schmerz* of a young, disconsolate people" (p. 50). Too often Dowson's own *Weltschmerz* feels like little more than adolescent yearning; his suffering did not enjoy the authority of a wide range of experience. Almost all the stories seem the work of a writer who has not reached maturity.

Only in "The Dying of Francis Donne" did Dowson break through to significant work in short fiction. Published in *The Savoy* in August 1896, the piece has been unduly neglected partly because of questions of definition: is it a story or a sketch? It seems obviously a short story to me,[3] but whatever it is—short story, sketch, or study—"The Dying of Francis Donne" is both artistically austere and rich in felt experience. More than any other Dowson story, it is capable of leaving a more than historical impact on a reader. Certainly it is, in Derek Stanford's phrase, a "grim authentic *tour-de-force*"[4]—and *authentic* is a crucial word in a canon marred by artificiality and self-indulgence. "The Dying of Francis Donne" is a masterly delineation of the psychology of dying; the pattern of Donne's death agony is scientifically verifiable. The story is also excellent in its own right, and deserves to endure as a fascinating expression of—and comment on—*fin-de-siecle* aestheticism.

Francis Donne is a successful physician who has risen to public eminence because of his writing and lectures. This dual profession is important, for Donne is an artist as well as a doctor; he is "great not only in the scientific world, but also in the world of letters" (p. 104). His popularity arises from his ability to clothe the "dry bones" of science in "so elegantly literary a pattern." He is also a characteristic *fin-de-siecle* writer in being misunderstood: the lectures have become a "social function" and have "almost succeeded in making science fashionable" (p. 105).

But Donne is primarily a physician, not an artist, and in this profession he is even more a child of the end of the century. "The Dying of Francis Donne" is a very brief story, but it confronts no less a theme than the tragedy of being trapped in our mortality. Francis Donne's entire life has been devoted to coming to terms with his dilemma. His strategy is unmistakably that of the aesthete, and his "tired spirit" (*ibid.*) and "morbid self-consciousness" (p. 106) also place him in the 90's. Donne is above all detached: one of the technical accomplishments of the story is the brilliant manner in which the near-solipsism is rendered. The point, however, is that Donne's detachment is a defense. The only way he can confront the problem of decay and death is to remove himself from life itself. He copes with the "absurdity" (p. 103) of the human situation by trying to keep that situation at a distance.

Donne is essentially a sort of decadent version of Roger Chillingsworth. He has lived exclusively with his mind, because the mind can order and control: "He had lived so long in the meditation of death, visited it so often in others, studied it with such persistency, with a sentiment in which horror and fascination mingled; but it had always been, as it were, an objective, alien fact, remote from himself and his own life." In the objectification of death, there seems a way to control and order life, and so Donne lives secure with his "analytical habit," with a mind that is "so exquisite a mechanism of syllogism and deduction" (*ibid.*) Death is kept at arm's length and studied for its own sake, as if it has no bearing on Donne's life.

Of course this distancing is illusory, and the story begins with the protagonist's moment of truth: Donne knows he is to die. He tries to deny this knowledge, but faced with reality, reason must yield to "casuistry." The detached observer is forcibly jerked back into life and started on the relentless process toward decay and dissolution. The image of mind as exquisite mechanism gives way to the image of "a hunted animal at bay" (*ibid.*). Donne had known he was living in an illusion—one of his lectures is entitled "Limitations of Medicine"—but the fact remains that once the illusion is shattered, his entire world caves in. The "dull, immutable pain commences" (p. 104) and doesn't let up, and the august, austere, eminent public figure is reduced to "puerile tears" (p. 106). The rest of the story follows Donne's path from London to Brittany to the moment of extinction.

In its modest way the story is as much a depiction of the aesthete's yearning to get beyond flux and sensation as Pater's *Marius the Epicurean.* Marius refuses to give up the search for the "Ideal, among so-called actual things."[5] He wants to enjoy the fruits of his sensations, but he also longs for a principle of permanence beyond the constant flux, a principle he discovers in the primitive Christianity practiced in the church in Cecilia's house. Like Marius, Donne delights in the "pleasant sensuousness of life, the joy of the visible world" (p. 105); "his absorbing interest in physical phenomena had made him somewhat a materialist" (p. 108). But once the pain begins and he himself is reduced to nothing more than a physical phenomenon, his philosophical control breaks down. He decides to discontinue the escape offered by morphia, for he realizes that he should reserve use of the drug for the time when the pain will be unbearable. Work offers no escape, for the pain has already gotten the upper hand. Donne withdraws to the bleak coast of Brittany, preferring the "kind indifference of strangers" to the "intolerable pity of friends" (p. 107). It is there that he will end his days— and attempt to discover some final ordering.

All of Dowson's writings are colored by his world-weariness and ennui and by his nostalgia for a harmony that never existed. His life offered more than ample occasion for melancholy: one thinks immediately of the suicides of his parents, the tuberculosis, the hopeless longing for the nymphet with the unlikely name Adelaide Foltinowicz. The other side of dissipation and being faithful to Cynara in his fashion was a kind of stoicism. In Thomas Hardy's works there is a real element of affirmation in the self-conscious stance of facing a cruel universe without flinching. In contrast, Dowson's stoicism is much closer to pathos. He endures because he has no choice, but there is a wistful, almost adolescent quality about his yearning for a better world. "The Dying of Francis Donne" is a success partly because for once Dowson has found a form that allows him to distance his own self-pity and world-weariness. The story is intensely personal of course, but it is also a self-contained artistic construct that needs no autobiographical interpretation. At he same time Dowson's characteristic nostalgia and ennui are unmistakably present, especially in the third section, which describes Donne's life in the fishing village "on the bleak and wave-tormented coast of Finisterre" (*ibid.*).

The description of sea and village, a carefully wrought impressionist tableau, is one of the most skillful passages in the story:

> Bleak and grey it had been, when he had visited it of old, in the late autumn; but now the character, the whole colour of the country was changed. It was brilliant with the promise of summer, and the blue Atlantic, which in winter churned with its long crested waves so boisterously below the little white lighthouse, which warned mariners (alas! so vainly), against the shark-like cruelty of the rocks, now danced and glittered in the sunshine, rippled with feline caresses round the hulls of the fishing-boats whose brown sails floated so idly in the faint air.
>
> Above the village, on a grassy slope, whose green was almost lurid, Francis Donne lay, for many

silent hours, looking out at the placid sea, which could yet be so ferocious, at the low violet line of the Island of Groix, which alone interrupted the monotony of sky and ocean (*ibid.*).

This descriptive set-piece is included to define the cruel indifference of the universe to man and his labors. Man's "little white lighthouse" cannot help much in the face of the "shark-like cruelty of the rocks" and the "feline caresses" of the waves. Donne's state of mind is "almost peace" as his thought subsides into "lethargy and blank," but he envies the fishermen and their wives the "grim and resigned fatalism" that comes so easy because death is such an everyday affair to them. A "poor little grey church" (*ibid.*) is at the center of the scattered houses that make up the village, suggesting another sort of order unattainable by Donne. The story contains a nostalgia for the simple lives of the fishermen. Their fatalism and their Christianity allow them a consistent stance toward the universe and toward their mortality. Donne can only go to the cemetery and tell himself, "'And in a little time I shall lie here'" (p. 108).

As he descends toward death, Donne's efforts to transcend sensation and find a principle of permanence become even more intense: ". . . . His purely physical knowledge seemed but a vain possession, and he turned with a passionate interest to what had been said and believed from time immemorial by those who had concentrated their intelligence on that strange essence, . . . the Soul. . . . " (pp. 108-109). In search of his soul and "an harmony of life," he reads, like des Esseintes and Dorian Gray, Greek philosophy and early Christian theology. However, Plato's *Phaedo,* the Emperor Hadrian's address to his soul, and the "triumphant declarations of the Church"—*"Ubi est, mors, victoria tu? Ubi est, mors, stimulus tuus?"*—can be of no help. The dying Donne is a man in the middle, denied the simple faith of the fishermen, denied the complex systems of faith of earlier eras. Denied "certitude" (p. 109), he sinks into "a drugged, unrestful sleep" (p. 110). The only certitude he is granted is that of death.

And yet Dowson does allow his protagonist a happy ending of sorts. Perhaps there is a bit of wish-fulfillment in the conclusion. Mark Longaker commends the story to "anyone who wishes to know the essential voice of Dowson when his dread malady was tightening its grip."[6] No doubt this is true, and it is interesting that Dowson lets Francis Donne go out happily: "The corporal capacity of smiling had passed from him, but he fain would have smiled" (*ibid.*).

Even more interesting, however, is the way Dowson describes the death. The "immense and ineffable tiredness" becomes "this utter luxury of physical exhaustion, this calm, this release" (*ibid.*). Donne's life had been devoted to escaping from life, but his long dying had wrenched him back to the everyday world of change and decay. Much to his delight, he discovers that the transition into death is a release back into a sort of formal perfection, into a kind of changeless nirvana. The lifetime dedicated to living outside time had ended rudely and abruptly when the dying set in, but at the moment of death Donne is transported back to a world of timelessness, into the bliss of blankness and nirvana.

Donne is even granted a moment of ecstasy as he expires, an epiphanic point in time of complete clarity and perception. During these "few minutes of singular mental lucidity, all his life flashed before him in a new relief. . . . All that was distorted in life was adjusted and justified in the light of his sudden knowledge" (*ibid.*). This extended moment of clarity and insight is of course a surrogate for religious experience. Dowson can find no way to construct an order out of the chaos, and so he must settle for the heightened *moment* of order. Because the yearning for order is so intense, Dowson has a particularly high emotional stake in the moment when it comes. Thus there is an unmistakable ecstasy in the "singular mental lucidity" with which Donne passes from life. This moment of insight allows him to understand, order, and aesthetically arrange his entire life just as he leaves time for the timelessness he has always yearned for. The generation of the 90's were descendants of Arnold the poet, wandering between two worlds, one lost, and the other powerless to be born. This type of ecstasy is a commonplace in the poetry and fiction they wrote.[7]

And so at long last Francis Donne completes his dying. He is an aesthete to the very end: as he passes from consciousness "he could yet just dimly hear, as in a dream, the sound of Latin prayers, and feel the application of the oils upon all the issues and approaches of his wearied sense." Then unconsciousness, "and that was all" (*ibid.*). O death, where is thy sting?

"The Dying of Francis Donne" is richly cadenced and harmonious, and its sharp sense of experience is all the more effective because of its understatedness. The story is something of a miniature, but its economy and compression are such that it is able to confront the largest questions of all. At the same time "The Dying of Francis Donne" contains an important commentary on Dowson's own life and on *fin-de-siecle* aestheticism in general. It is a mistake to interpret aestheticism exclusively in terms of developments in the arts. The phenomenon is more directly a response to breakdown in the culture at large. Writers retreated to the formal perfection of art and to the doctrine of art for art's sake as a defense against chaos: "These fragments I have shored against my ruins." This link between the aesthetic stance of these writers and man's metaphysical dilemma is made clear by the life and dying of Francis Donne.

Dowson seems to be saying that the harmonies of art offer no real escape from the despair of living. Donne is able to escape the tyranny of time only by intellectual detachment and by death. These two forms of escape are directly related, and surely the effect is to question the detachment implicit in aestheticism, in attempting to convert one's life into a work of art.

Donne's "burning sense of helplessness" (p. 106) is emphasized in his dying, but his loneliness throughout is even more terrible. The "eminent surgeon" who dies early in the story is an "acquaintance" (p. 105), not a friend. He goes to Brittany to escape the "intolerable pity of friends," but no friends are in evidence and it is hard to believe Donne *has* close friends. The simple inhabitants of the fishing village are "kindly" (p. 107), but they necessarily allow him to maintain his shell of isolation. The companions by his deathbed are a nurse, a faithful servant, and a priest. One thinks back to the work Donne tries to do early in the story to take his mind off the recent discovery that he is dying: "He had selected the work of a distinguished German savant upon the cardiac functions, and a short treatise of his own, which was covered with recent annotations, in his crabbed handwriting, upon 'Aneurism of the Heart'" (p. 106). This detail is in the story to tell us that Donne is suffering above all from heartlessness. Instead of coming to terms with man's fate, he has tried to escape it, and as a result his life has been a living death, cold and sterile, without community, without love, without even emotion.

Donne learns that he cannot escape his mortality: no one can. But his decision to seek detachment is also a decision to deny life itself. The deepest and most profound meaning of this story is that the life of aethetic detachment is nothing more than a long dying. "Dust thou art and to dust thou will return," Dowson's epigraph tells us; this is the main fact the story presents. Nevertheless, another message resonates through the carefully measured prose: the aesthete's headling flight from life is a horrible mistake. "The Dying of Francis Donne" is something of a personal testament. Apparently Ernest Dowson had learned to measure the cost of the life he had chosen.

NOTES

[1] Ernest Dowson, *The Stories of Ernest Dowson,* ed. Mark Longaker, (Philadelphia, 1947), p. 1.

[2] *The Stories of Ernest Dowson,* pp. 35-37. Subsequent references to this volume will be incorporated in the text.

[3] Dowson himself is responsible for some of the confusion. He called it a "story" when it was just "under weigh" in early April 1896, but three weeks later he referred to it as "my story or study rather" (*The Letters of Ernest Dowson,* ed. Desmond Flower and Henry Maas, Rutherford, N. J., 1967, pp. 352, 358). In its printed form it is subtitled "A Study." Thomas Burnett Swann classifies it as a sketch because "it lacks both conflict and detailed characterization" (*Ernest Dowson,* New York, 1964, p. 82). This comment seems to me, however, to misrepresent the piece, for there is ample *inner* conflict and the author's control of point of view (that of a near-solipsist) explains the absence of detailed characterization.

Mark Longaker, who should know best, also seems to consider it a sketch in associating it with the five brief prose-poems of *Decorations.* He vaguely declares that "The Dying of Francis Donne," "Absinthia Taetra," and "The Visit" are "unmistakably poetic" (*The Stories of Ernest Dowson,* p. 9).

It seems true enough that Dowson wrote his best prose "in the pieces in which he was not burdened by the necessity of telling a sustained story" (*Stories,* p. 9), but this does not necessarily make "The Dying of Francis Donne" a sketch. Certainly it is confusing to categorize it with the wraith-like pieces in *Decorations,* all of which are about half-a-page in length, especially since it manages to compress quite an extensive action into eight pages. It may also be germane to observe that "The Dying of Francis Donne" is unlike the other short prose pieces in being devoid of self-conscious literary posturing.

[4] Derek Stanford, *Short Stories of the 'Nineties: A Biographical Anthology,* New York, 1968, p. 204.

[5] *Marius the Epicurean: His Situation and Ideas,* London: Dent, 1885, p. 83.

[6] *The Stories of Ernest Dowson,* p. 121.

[7] Cf. Chapter 7, "Ecstasy," pp. 154-176 of John A. Lester, Jr., *Journey Through Despair, 1880-1914: Transformations in British Literary Culture* (Princeton: Princeton University Press, 1968). Dowson is mentioned regularly in this work.

Barbara A. Davis

SOURCE: "Zeno's Ontological Confessions," in *Twentieth Century Literature,* Vol. 18, No. 1, January, 1972, pp. 45-56.

[*In the following essay, Davis examines Zeno Cosini's struggle to comprehend the meaning of his existence in Italo Svevo's* Confessions of Zeno *as a process that can only be understood in relation to his own death.*]

Zeno Cosini, the fictional (and somewhat autobiographical) author of Italo Svevo's *Confessions of Zeno,* writes the following fable:

> THE CRAB (impaled on a hook, reflectively):
>   Life is
> sweet, but one must watch where one sits down.
>
> THE JOHN DORY (just off to the dentist): Life is
>   sweet,
> but one must rid it of those treacherous monsters
>   who
> hide steel fangs in tasty flesh.[1]

Both the crab and the John Dory fish of the fable are able to accept life in a way that Zeno himself is unable to do despite his efforts throughout most of the writing of his confessions. What Zeno does not realize when he writes

the fable for the amusement of his fellow office workers is that the reason his crab and fish are able to accept life is that they are facing death.

Although Zeno in his confessions refers repeatedly to death—the death of others (his father, Copler and Guido) as well as death in the abstract—he does not really confront it or allow it to be incorporated into his vague notions about life until his own habit of daily existence is interrupted by the war. Zeno mentions his experiences and thoughts about death only in order to aid in the process of his psychoanalysis. He feels that he is searching out the basis of a psychological problem; his analyst, Dr. S., has suggested that Zeno write about his life, hoping that "in the effort of recalling his past he would bring it to life again, and that the writing of his autobiography would be a good preparation for the treatment" (preface).

What the psychoanalyst does not realize, and what Zeno does not realize until more than a year after writing the major portion of his confessions, is that Zeno's underlying problem is not one of psychology (although he may indeed have serious psychological problems) but of metaphysics. His concern, even fascination, with death, as revealed in the confessions, indicates the ontological problem which pervades the whole of his expression and explanation of his life. Zeno is actually attempting to identify his being, to grasp the continuity of his essential self as he exists in time. In writing his confessions Zeno reveals his efforts to find pattern and structure in his existence from childhood up to the present. He seems, however, not to be conscious of this intent; he believes himself to be reporting the facts of his existence for analysis by Dr. S.

The very structure of the confessions indicates Zeno's search for order as he writes about his life. By dividing his autobiography into sections, he can classify life as a series of major events: the last cigarette, the death of his father, the story of his marriage, wife and mistress, a business partnership, and finally, psychoanalysis. Svevo has not allowed his character the comfort of fitting into a job category, a category which serves as identification for most men (one *is* a doctor, a professor, or a business man, for example). He is a man of leisure who is desperate to know what his existence means. He deals with this problem on a subconscious level by attempting to identify himself in relation to the external world of fixed objects and objective knowledge. When this fails, he searches internally for the meaning and explanation of his being—also without success.

Zeno reports his sense of the loss of an external and objective reality with the death of his father. The extremely self-conscious Zeno, who is bewildered by the sense of continual change in life, sees his father as something quite stable in the midst of an otherwise uncertain world: "My pursuit of health had led me to study the human body. He, on the other hand, had succeeded in banishing from his memory all thoughts of that terrible machine. As far as he was concerned the heart did not beat, and he had no need to remind himself of valves and veins and metabolism to explain why he was alive. . . . For him the earth was motionless and solid, poised between its poles" (p. 30).

The death of his father is significant for Zeno psychologically (as Dr. S. later points out), but it is clear from his expression of the experience that it is also significant ontologically. Zeno feels that it is necessary to "go into my father's story in so far as it helps me to recollect my own." He further justifies his recollection saying: "Probably no one will believe me, but this brief note records the most important event in my life" (p. 27). Zeno becomes rather explicit about the ontological effect that his father's death has on him: "My father's death . . . was an unmitigated catastrophe. Paradise had ceased to exist for me, and at thirty I was played out. . . . I cannot help believing I should not have lost that happy and inspiring faith [in my possibilities] if my father had not died. His death destroyed the future that alone gave point to my resolutions" (p. 28). Lee Jacobs, in her article, "Zeno's Sickness Unto Death," explains that "Zeno's father served as a stationary pole around whom the son could freely orbit until the death of his father fragmented Zeno's certainty about ever finding a coherence of identity. The death of his father represents the death of God in Zeno's life."[2] His father had been an objective point for Zeno to stand in relation to, a source for his own identity from his earliest memory up to the present. The father provided his son with some sense of continuity through thirty years of existence, and during this time Zeno had remained childishly dependent on his father, as he is later dependent on others, to make decisions for him. Therefore, with the death of his father imminent, Zeno can only ask himself: "What is there for me to do in the world now?" (p. 40).

At the end of the chapter concerning "the death of my father" Zeno asserts that after his father's death "I returned to the religion of my childhood and held to it a long time" and that "I daily with my whole heart commended my father's soul to the care of some unknown being" (p. 54). But a belief in an external and objective "higher being" outside himself is a fabrication, a rationalization for Zeno. He had previously told his father that he looked upon religion "simply as a phenomenon to be studied like any other" (p. 35). Later, after his marriage, Zeno compares his own intellectual study of religion (reading Renan and Strauss and "a critical edition of the Gospels") to his wife's easy-going, non-introspective practice of the conventions of religion: "Religion for me was a very different thing. If I had only believed, nothing else in the world would have mattered to me" (p. 152). Because religion cannot provide the objective knowledge of reality that he is searching for, Zeno substitutes superstition for it, at times, as a guide to behavior. At a dinner party with his in-laws, Zeno listens to his ill father-in-law jealously curse another guest who reaches for a glass of wine: "That is the third! May it turn to gall in his stomach!" Zeno reacts with superstition: "This pious hope would not have troubled me if I myself had not been

eating and drinking at the same table, and had not realized that every mouthful of wine I drank would have a like blessing bestowed on it. So I began eating and drinking secretly" (p. 202). During the same meal he reacts similarly to a malicious comment made by his father-in-law by crossing his fingers "under the table to avert his wish, which I know boded me no good" (p. 205). At another point in the confessions Zeno listens to Guido's statement that it is a bad omen to pay one's debts too quickly, and again he reveals his superstitious nature: "It is indeed a widespread superstition at all gaming-tables that other people's money brings one good fortune. I don't really believe this, but when I play I omit no precaution" (p. 324).

Because he is unable to really believe in a higher being and because he has lost his father as a stable point of reference, Zeno looks to other people in his environment, hoping to identify his place in existence by defining himself in relation to society. One of these people is a kind of father-substitute, in fact his future father-in-law, Giovanni Malfenti. In a search for identity Zeno attempts to imitate what appears to be an enviable reality, the personality of a man he admires. After admitting that Giovanni Malfenti "was so entirely different from me and from anyone whose friendship I had enjoyed up to that time" (p. 56). Zeno continues to explain his own actions: "When I admire anyone I at once try to be like him. So I began to imitate Malfenti" (p. 57). What Zeno admires in Malfenti is not great intelligence, insight or purpose, but rather his ignorance: "He . . . was an important business man, ignorant and pushing. But his ignorance gave one an impression of quiet strength which fascinated me. I loved to watch him and envied him for what he was" (p. 56). Zeno is fascinated with Malfenti for the very reason that the man is "ignorant" in the sense that he does not seem to be constantly questioning the "realities" of everyday life by which he lives. Malfenti, for example, has a list of business commandments, which he copies into Zeno's notebook in order to help him. His world runs quite smoothly by a set of established rules.

Even more fascinating to Zeno—although also somewhat confusing—is the world of women. In his autobiography, his relationship to various women apparently provides him with an illusion of continuity. He is always generalizing about women even when talking about an individual woman such as his wife or his mistress. Because his attitudes towards women (as a category, not as individuals) can provide Zeno with this illusion of continuity in existence, he emphasizes the role of women as he relates the story of his life. Henri Bergson in his essay on art and reality in *Laughter* explains this kind of emphasis: "My senses and my consciousness . . . give me no more than a practical simplification of reality. In the vision they furnish me of myself and of things, the differences that are useless to man are obliterated, the resemblances that are useful to him are emphasized; ways are traced out long in advance along which my activity is to travel. . . . The *individuality* of things or of beings escapes us unless it is materially to our advantage to perceive it."[3]

Admittedly, there is psychological significance in Zeno's comments about women, as demonstrated in his assertion that "it is a great sign of inferiority in a man not to understand women" (p. 74). But Zeno's statements also indicate that his generalizations concerning women are motivated by an attempt to establish the opposite sex as a stable and objective point in his small world. There are both psychological and ontological implications in his vision of a wife: "All the qualities lacking in myself, and which I longed to possess, I gave to her; she was to become not only my wife but a second mother to me, who would equip me for a full virile life, encourage me to fight and help me, to be victorious" (p. 73).

Throughout the *Confessions* Zeno attempts to define "women" by various characteristics in order to establish them as a fixed point of reference for himself. But even Zeno is unable to do this. He says at one point: "Women always know what they want" (p. 172), but at another time he says: "It is difficult for men to know exactly what it is that women do want, for they often do not know themselves" (p. 331). He also observes: "Women always insist on the fiction that they have been raped" (p. 190), but at another point in his narrative he seems to put at least one woman in the role of seductress: "When I go over the story of my first infidelity I have distinctly the sense of having been seduced" (p. 167). At the very beginning of the confessions Zeno recalls telling the psychoanalyst of "my troubles with women. I was not satisfied with one or even with many; I desired them all!" (p. 12). Later, however, in speaking of his friend, Copler, Zeno says, "I don't know why the poor man had such a mania for talking about women" (p. 155). It is his own emphasis on women that Zeno perceives, and he makes various other generalizations about women: "Women are made like that. . . . Their life can never be at all monotonous" (p. 208); . . . no woman can consent to be slighted in public, whatever treatment she may put up with in private" (p. 226); Women are always like that, and Augusta was unusually excited, even for a woman, at the thought of my personal losses" (p. 294); and . . ."for a woman to remain passive is a form of giving consent" (p. 321).

From the viewpoint of psychology, Zeno might be viewed as the male ego that must assert his superiority over the female species in order to conceal his own feelings of inadequacy or inferiority. From an ontological viewpoint, however, he may be viewed quite differently. By generalizing about women Zeno is able to classify and objectify them. He tries to present them as creatures that exist according to certain predictable and set standards— "women always" . . . or "women never" . . . or "all women" . . . or "no woman . . ." To Zeno, who feels himself to be without any such stable standards of behavior, a lost being in the flux of time, the position of "women" (as he sees it) is somewhat enviable. Women do not seem to have to think about what they are doing, as he does. His comments about his wife, Augusta, illustrate this envy as well as the desire to find such untroubled certitude in existence for himself. He says at one point: "I became so fond of her that I formed the great

hope that I might in the end grow like Augusta, who was the personification of health" (p. 140). The insecurity of his own existence and his envy of his wife's existence is evident when he talks about her: "Augusta walked boldly along the path so many of her sisters have trodden before her on this earth: those who are content to find all their happiness in law and order, or else to renounce it all together. . . . I felt obliged to treat it [her security] with the same respect I had previously shown to spiritualism. It might be true, and so might faith in human life" (p. 141).

Poor Zeno who is so bewildered by time and change in life is startled to find in observing his wife that "every act of hers showed that she believed in eternal life" (p. 141). He envies what he sees as Augusta's state of health, that is, her ability to exist in the present moment and to be able to find meaning in objective, stationary forces in a well-ordered sense of time. Zeno explains:

> I understood at last the meaning of perfect health in a human being, when I realized that for her the present was a tangible reality in which we could take shelter and be near together. I tried to be admitted to this sanctuary. (p. 141) . . . [For Augusta] the world goes round but everything else stays in its place. And these stationary things are of immense importance; a wedding-ring, jewels and clothes . . . also her evening dress, which must on no account be worn in the daytime, and only in the evening if I put on dress clothes. Then there were hours of meals . . . and also bedtime. All these hours had a genuine existence and were always in their right place. (pp. 141-142)

Zeno finds too, that Sunday Mass, the Austrian and Italian officials ("who made the streets and houses safe for people") and the doctors ("who had gone through all their medical training in order to cure us if by some unhappy chance we fell ill") were all sources of external authority and security for his wife, Augusta.

But Zeno finds comfort in none of these things. He even attempts to attribute an objective reality to time itself. He finds "significance," for example, in certain dates: "First day of the first month in the year 1901. Even today I feel that if only that date could repeat itself I should be able to begin a new life" (p. 11). Zeno himself states his attempt to make the abstract idea of time a reality: "And then Time, for me, is not that unimaginable thing that never stops. For me, but only for me, it comes again" (p. 11). But as much as Zeno would like to find concrete reality in the concept of time, to be like his wife, or at least "be admitted to this sanctuary," he is a man who finds only that "time is really very ill-ordered" (p. 381) and that there is no reality he can grasp that is external to himself which might help him to affirm his place in existence.

For Zeno then, there is no objective reality by which he can discover the meaning or the value or even the certainty of existence. The concepts of religion, of other individual personalities, of society, and of time do not provide Zeno with the organizing and identifying force for which he is searching. Gian-Paolo Biasin, in his article "Literary Disease: From Pathology to Ontology," explains that through the character of Zeno, Svevo is able to express "the breaking down of a whole 'vision du monde' which is to be replaced by another: the world of objects is no longer a 'datum' of certainty; the world of others is no longer meaningful in itself or its institutions. What comes to the fore is awareness of the self, with all the ambiguities and the anguish inherent in the discovery of how unstable, contradictory and absurd the relationship of the self to the world of others and of objects can be.[4]

By the time Zeno begins his confessions he has turned to the "self," trying to find identity and continuity of existence within himself rather than through the external world and its concepts of objective reality—which indeed present him only with contradiction and confusion. When Zeno does attempt to look within himself, however, it is not consciously for the meaning of existence but for the basis of his so-called psychological problems. Indeed, he begins his autobiography with his account of "the last cigarette:"—"When I spoke to the doctor about my weakness for smoking he told me to begin my analysis by tracing the growth of that habit from the beginning" (p. 5). Zeno explains how enduring his habit has been: "My days became filled with cigarettes and resolutions to give up smoking, and, to make a clean sweep of it, that is more or less what they are still. The dance of the last cigarette which began when I was twenty has not reached its last figure yet" (p. 9). But the "last cigarette" problem is deeply based in Zeno's ontological dilemma. The fact that he chooses to emphasize this habit in his confessions indicates the meaning of the last cigarette as a symbol of continuity in existence. Zeno the boy smoked cigarettes and tried to stop just as Zeno the man over fifty smokes cigarettes and tries to stop. Although he has physically altered and his world has been constantly changing, Zeno can feel that there is still something that is essentially his own being, that is, the organism that smokes cigarettes and tries to break his habit. That the problem is metaphysically based can be demonstrated in the fact that Zeno couples his "last cigarette" with attempts to discover the meaning of life: "'2 February, 1886. Today I finish my law studies and take up chemistry. Last cigarette!!' That was a very important last cigarette. . . . I was irritated by canon law, which seemed to me so remote from life, and I fled to science in the hope of finding life itself. . . . That last cigarette was the emblem of my desire for activity (even manual) and for calm, clear, sober thought" (p. 9).

More evident than the last cigarette throughout the autobiography is the development of various diseases, aches, and pains in the physical organism, Zeno Cosini. Again, it is the psychological aspect, the problems of the "malade imaginaire" that Zeno thinks he is revealing for Dr. S.'s benefit. But again, he actually indicates that his psychological need is stimulated by an ontological concern. Zeno's condition of ill-health is caused by his constant efforts to observe his own actions and thoughts, to conduct his self-analysis. Disease in any form is for Zeno a manifestation of this extreme consciousness of self. Perhaps the best example of this problem, as noted by several critics, is Zeno's limp.[5] His friend, Tullio, has told him that "when one is walking rapidly each step takes no more than half a second, and in that half second no fewer than fifty-four muscles are set in motion." Zeno reacts characteristically: "I listened in bewilderment. I at once directed my attention to my legs and tried to discover the infernal machine. I thought I had succeeded in finding it. I could not of course distinguish all its fifty-four parts, but I discovered something terrifically complicated which seemed to get out of order directly I began thinking about it. I limped as I left the cafe." (pp. 94-5).

Because Zeno wishes to observe life at every point he is unable to deal with the constant flux of time. He describes his problem of ill-health in connection with his violin playing and metaphorically demonstrates his inability to give himself up to the flow of time and the rhythm of life:

> I could play well if I were not ill, but I am always pursuing health even when I am practicing balance on the four strings of a violin . . . after I have been playing one of those rythmic figures it clings to me and I can't escape from it, but get it mixed up with the following figure so that I play it out of time. . . . The music that is produced by a well-balanced physique is identical with the rhythm it creates and exploits; it is rhythm itself. When I can play like that I shall be cured. (pp. 103-104)

Zeno's problems in writing his confessions are much the same as his problems in playing the violin—trying to be conscious of each act and thought, and trying to arrange all of these individual moments of action and thought into a coherent pattern that will define "Zeno." The very act of writing is a conscious attempt to organize the events of his life and to impress the account with a sense of continuity in order to assert the reality of his existence in time. From the beginning, however, Zeno realizes the difficulty (if not the actual impossibility) of bringing the whole of his life to conscious expression. Bergson has explained this problem in saying that "between nature and ourselves, nay, between ourselves and our own consciousness a veil is interposed; a veil that is dense and opaque for the common herd,—thin, almost transparent, for the artist and the poet" (Bergson, p. 151). Zeno begins with this problem in his introduction: "See my childhood? Now that I am separated from it by over fifty years, my presbyopic eyes might perhaps reach to it if the light were not obscured by so many obstacles. The years like impassable mountains rise between me and it, my past years and a few brief hours in my life. . . . The present surges up and dominates me, the past is blotted out" (p. 3). And in the final chapter of the confessions, Zeno shows himself well aware of what he has attempted to do in writing his autobiography. He asserts that "a written confession is always mendacious. We lie with every word we speak" (p. 368). He realizes that he has not presented "reality" at all: "And by dint of pursuing these memory-pictures, I at last really overtook them. I know now that I invented them. But invention is a creative act, not merely a lie . . . I thought my dream-pictures really were an actual reproduction of the past. . . . I remembered them as one remembers an event one has been told by somebody who was not present at it" (pp. 368-69).

Zeno's last chapter, "Psychoanalysis," is written in May of 1915 and finally March of 1961. There is a space of time of one year between this last section and the earlier confessions, which were interrupted by the war. Within this time, Zeno has confronted the paradox of life and has discovered why all his attempts to find the meaning of existence, whether in external objects and objective knowledge or in the depths of his own personality, have failed. He has determined that life cannot be defined except in death. His attempts to classify specific behavior, particular thoughts, and certain moments have not been successful because each succeeding act or thought or moment in time has modified, in some way, the preceding actions, thoughts and moments. Only at the end point of all these fragments can the totality be asserted or defined. John Freccero in his article, "Zeno's Last Cigarette" explains that "in Zeno's purely spatial imagination, the present moment is conditioned by the one that went before, that one in turn conditioned by its predecessor, and so on, back into the past, toward the origin of the individual and of the species. In a sense, then, the past exists in the present, and moves with it into the future."[6] It is through this concept that Zeno Cosini is analogous to the ancient Zeno of Elea. Freccero explains the "puzzle of Zeno of Elea:"

> If we imagine the trajectory of an arrow flying through space, it must be said that at any given moment it occupies a given space and is therefore momentarily motionless, requiring another moment before it can occupy the next successive position. Hence the trajectory is made up of an infinity of successive moments for the gradual transition from place to place. But these infinite moments cannot be said ever to reach the continuity that we perceive. Motion itself cannot be deduced. At each separate moment the arrow is motionless, all the time it is moving. Just as one can never place enough mathematical points side by side in order to make up a straight line, it is impossible to deduce the trajectory of the arrow from the logical states, the transversal cuts, that go to make it up. It will never reach its target. (Freccero, p. 52)

The "arrow" is analogous to the present moment of consciousness in Zeno Cosini's imagination. This present consciousness follows a path from the past into the future. The path, the pattern of all those present moments, can only be viewed at the end point—death. Actually, Zeno has unconsciously hinted at this concept throughout his confessions showing himself concerned but also frightened by the final "present moment." It may even be said that he has a certain preoccupation with death—but little real understanding of its possible significance for him. On the night before Zeno's father takes to his death bed, the father tells his son: "I feel as if I knew almost

everything. It must be the result of my great experience" (pp. 36-7). He wants to pass on this great knowledge to Zeno but is unable to express himself: "What I am after is not at all complicated. It is only a matter of finding a single word, and I know I shall find it" (p. 37). But if he did actually grasp a kind of totality of experience, it went with him to his death. Zeno later realizes that "the word he had been searching for, which he so much wanted to confide to me had escaped him forever" (p. 51). The arrow must complete its trajectory; the present moments are completed at the moment of death.

At one point, Zeno even expresses the idea that life must be viewed in terms of death, not because he believes it, however, but because he is trying to impress Ada in the days of courtship: "I stuck to my idea, and asserted that death was really the great organizing force of life. I was always thinking about death and so I had only one sorrow: the certainty that I must die. Everything else became so unimportant that I could welcome it with a smile, even laugh at it. I think my reason for talking in this way was that I wanted to show them I had a sense of humor, which had often before made me popular with women" (p. 71). It is only after the shock and violence of war that Zeno realizes the truth of such a statement. In his last entry (in March of 1916), Zeno relates his realization that his past attempts at analysis (both self-analysis and psychoanalysis) have been useless. To be classified in the context of the Oedipal Complex does not allow for life's totality, for the completed path of the ancient Zeno's arrow. Categorization is false, as Zeno sees it, because it does not admit to the flux of time and life. Zeno Cosini says of his written confession: "I should be able to write it all over again with absolute certainty now; how was it possible for me to understand my life when I did not know what this last part was going to be? Perhaps I only lived all those years in order to prepare for it!" (p. 397).

In his final vision, Zeno places himself in the context of all mankind. Life for all men is finally defined only in the face of death: "Life is a little like disease, with its crises and periods of quiescence, its daily improvements and setbacks. But unlike other diseases life is always mortal. It admits of no cure" (p. 397). And it is man who has made life a disease, according to Zeno. "Health," he says, "can only belong to the beasts, whose sole idea of progress lies in their own bodies"—not in the machine which "creates disease because it denies what has been the law of creation throughout the ages" (pp. 397-398). His vision for the world, as for himself as an individual, can only be death. As an individual, only at the last moments of all the moments in a life can the whole, the totality, be grasped—without the diseased and distorted interpretations of analysis. Similarly, the world of man can only be restored to wholeness, to health, by death: "Perhaps some incredible disaster produced by machines will lead us back to health" (p. 398).

Zeno's is a dark view of man—"parasites and disease." It is not his Oedipal Complex or any other psychological problem that leads Zeno to his viewpoint, however. It is his attempt and subsequent failure to grasp reality within life—before death—that has led him to his pessismistic onotology. There is no hope here for the "death and resurrection" conversion that might be expected at the end of one's "confessions." And Zeno's truest words are expressed in his final vision:

> We need something more than psychoanalysis to help us. (p. 398)

NOTES

[1] Italo Svevo, *Confession of Zeno*, trans. Beryl DeZoete (1923; rpt New York: Vintag-Knopf, 1958), p. 279.

[2] *Italian Quarterly*, 11, No. 44 (Spring 1968), 59.

[3] Henri Bergson, *Laughter*, trans. Cloudesley Brereton and Fred Rothwell (New York: MacMillan Co., 1911), pp. 151-152.

[4] *Modern Language Notes*, 82 (Jan. 1967), 80.

[5] See especially P. N. Furbank, *Italo Svevo: The Man and the Writer* (London: Secker and Warburg, and Berkeley and Los Angeles: University of California Press, 1966) and Gian-Paolo Biasin "Literary Disease: From Pathology to Ontology" (note 4 above).

[6] *Modern Language Notes*, 77, No. 1 (1962), rpt. in Sergio Pacifici, ed., *From Verismo to Experimentalism: Essays on the Modern Italian Novel* (Bloomington: Indiana University Press, 1969), pp. 36-37.

Larry R. Dennis

SOURCE: "Mark Twain and the Dark Angel," in *The Midwest Quarterly*, Vol. VIII, No. 2, January, 1967, pp. 181-97.

[*In the following essay, Dennis discusses Mark Twain's handling of death in* The Adventures of Huckleberry Finn *and in his unfinished "The Great Dark."*]

The confrontation with death, the Dark Angel, is a recurring thematic element in Mark Twain's writtings, from the rhetorical refrain of "Is he dead?" which punctures the narratives of the native guides in *The Innocents Abroad* to the specter of the spider-squid which lurks in the waters of "The Great Dark," the incomplete manuscript Bernard DeVoto includes in *Letters From the Earth*. Sometimes the confrontations are frankly autobiographical, sometimes they are elaborations of incidents Twain has merely read or heard about, and sometimes they are purely imaginative, but regardless of their genesis, each represents an earnest attempt to place the fact of death in a tenable perspective. Necessarily, this perspective implies an attitude toward the whole of life. It is the intent of this essay to explore some of the perspectives which Twain's creative imagination allowed him to take.

In *Life Against Death*, Norman O. Brown writes that "the construction of a human consciousness strong enough to accept death is a task in which philosophy and psychoanalysis can join hands—and also art." If I understand him correctly, what Brown means by a consciousness strong enough to accept death is a consciousness where life and death are reconciled, where they form an organic unity. The conditions of "civilization," however, negate this possibility, and life and death are seen as antithetical.

From boyhood on, neither death nor violence were alien to Mark Twain, as DeLancey Ferguson points out in *Mark Twain: Man and Legend*:

> Young Sam in the course of his boyhood saw a Negro killed when his master flung a lump of slag at his head. He saw old man Smarr shot down in a drunken brawl, and watched the wounded man cough out his life under the weight of a Bible some pious fool had laid upon his chest. He saw the rowdy young Hyde brothers try to kill their uncle—one kneeling on his chest while the other repeatedly snapped an Allen revolver that would not go off . . . He saw a drunken tramp burn to death in the jail, because some of the boys had kindly given him matches and tobacco. One night he saw a drunken ruffian set off with the avowed purpose of raping a widow and her daughter at "the Welshman's," and saw the sequel when the elder woman, after warning the scoundrel to be gone before the count of ten, riddled him with slugs from a steadily aimed shotgun.

The Dark Angel was an intrinsic part of the Hannibal, Missouri, community of Twain's boyhood. He is also an acknowledged element in St. Petersburg, the village where Huck lives in the opening chapters of *Huckleberry Finn*. But Huck is given a perspective toward death which is denied to all the other characters in the novel and which is impossible for Twain himself to assume.

Richard P. Adams, in his introduction to Twain in *American Literary Masters*, rightly sees the pattern of death and rebirth as the most significant structural element in *Huckleberry Finn*, but he fails to consider the psychological and philosophical import of the pattern. Nowhere else in Twain's output is the theme of life and death treated more fully, and nowhere else is what Norman Brown calls "the possibility of redemption . . . in the reunification of instinctual opposites" offered as it is in Huck himself.

The theme of death is introduced in the first chapter of *The Adventures of Huckleberry Finn*:

> After supper she got out her book and learned me about Moses and the Bulrushers; and I was in a sweat to find out all about him; but by-and-by she let it out that Moses had been dead a considerable long time, so then I didn't care no more about him, because I don't take no stock in dead people.

Huck does not attach any meanings or values to life that are beyond life. For Huck, death is the act of dying, but even to be dying is an act of living. To be dead is to be external to both living and dying. The antithesis does not exist in Huck's particular perspective.

It would be incorrect to categorize Huck as Adamic in his attitude. As Twain points out in "Reflections on Religion" (published in the *Hudson Review,* Autumn '63):

> To Adam is forbidden the fruit of a certain tree—and he is gravely informed that if he disobeys he shall die. How could that be expected to impress Adam? Adam was merely a child in stature; in knowledge and experience he was in no way the superior of a baby of two years of age; he could have no idea what the word death meant. He had never seen a dead thing, he had never heard of a dead thing before. The word meant nothing to him. If the Adam child had been warned that if he ate of the apples he would be transformed into a meridian of longitude, that threat would have been the equivalent of the other, since neither of them could mean anything to him.

Huck's is not Adam's innocence; Huck has seen death. In a very real sense his response is nonhuman altogether, that is, his awareness is instinctive at almost animal level. Huck's journey brings him into contact with the multiple guises that civilization grants death, and although Huck remains uncorrupted by these encounters and maintains his essential vision, it is only because Twain himself wills it so.

The conclusion of the first chapter juxtaposes life and death in the nonhuman way that Huck acknowledges them. It is after his lesson about Moses and everyone else has gone to sleep for the night except Huck. Listening, Huck hears the wind, an owl, a dog, and a whippoorwill, and each is associated with death. But within nature life and death are not contradictive, that is, the possible outcome of dying plays no role in living. This is essentially Huck's perspective. The world outside the Widow Douglas' house is alive, teeming with noise and pulsing with life, but as Huck himself notes, " . . . the house was all as still as death now." There is a vital distinction. Death, in this case, is "still," and there is no life associated with it. In fact, it is death as antipodal to life.

Houses continually form a viable threat to Huck's very existence. Living within houses means imprisonment to Huck, physically and psychically, for they deny him that perspective which permits a wholeness to the life-death unit and fragments the unit into polarities. Growth under Miss Watson's tutelage is a series of negative imperatives: "Don't put your feet up there, Huckleberry," "Don't scrunch up like that, Huckleberry—set up straight," "Don't gap and stretch like that, Huckleberry—why don't you try to behave?" Each of Miss Watson's attempts to civilize Huck, to regiment his behavior into society's accepted etiquette, even involves physical restriction.

Pap, Huck's father, is essentially a victim of society, yet at the same time he is a representative of that society. In one sense he frees Huck from the restraints of civilization by taking him from the Widow Douglas, but this new freedom becomes imprisonment in the literal sense of the word. Pap takes Huck off to a cabin across the river, but each time he goes into St. Petersburg he leaves Huck locked in the shack. During one of Pap's alcoholic fits, the cabin almost becomes a real house of death for Huck as his father chases him with a knife. When Pap collapses in alcoholic stupor, Huck says, "Then he laid stiller, and didn't make a sound. I could hear the owls and the wolves, away off in the woods, and it seemed terrible still." This reflection echoes the feelings Huck had voiced at the Widow Douglas'.

The associations between houses and death are undeniably established in the episode which has come to be called by critics and commentators "the house of the dead." The house which comes floating down the Mississippi even contains its own corpse, as Huck and Jim discover when they climb into it to see if there is anything they can salvage for their own use.

The stillness of the corpse again illustrates the dual way in which death is regarded: Death as still, the way in which "civilization" regards it, and death as dynamic, the vision of nature. Death as stillness exists where there is no longer life potential. Huck also states, in response to Jim's warning that the corpse is "too gashly" to look upon, that he doesn't want to look at it. Huck's declaration places him on the side of nature.

Huck does manage to effect an escape from the cabin where Pap has imprisoned him. In order to guarantee his freedom Huck is compelled to devise a plan which will liberate him from all future restrictions. The experiences with Pap have been a bitter lesson, and Huck does not wish to jeopardize his liberty again. The means of a complete escape is by a ritual slaying of the self. It is Huck's simulated death that is the agent of his freedom, and this is consistent with his attitude toward death and life, because in his framework, unarticulated, life and death are not antipodal. Dying is living; living, dying. Life is growth, change, potentiality, while death, when opposed to life, is fixed, static, and negative. The pig is slaughtered and evidence is placed to indicate the murder of Huck Finn. For Huck the slaying of the self results in the effacement and freeing of the self. In all subsequent social intercourse, each time he leaves the river for the shore, he assumes a new identity. At one time he is Sarah Williams, and in order to convince the watchman to go out to the *Walter Scott* and "save" the murderers, he invents a history for himself; he tells Buck Grangerford his name is George Jackson; at the Phelps' farm he even becomes Tom Sawyer.

Immediately after his ritual self-slaying Huck gets into the canoe he has cached in a brake nearby. The slaying becomes even more emphatically a form of rebirth when the river is recognized as a symbol of life in the Freudian tradition. The river itself provides Huck with the means of his escape: The canoe that comes floating downstream. For Huck the rebirth even involves a new awareness of his sense faculties, as if he were discovering them for the first time:

> I got out amongst the driftwood and then laid down in the bottom of the canoe and let her float. I laid there and had a good rest and a smoke out of my pipe, looking away into the sky, not a cloud in it. The sky looks ever so deep when you lay down on your back in the moonshine; I never knowed it before. And how far a body can hear on the water such nights!

The river is really a double symbol. At the same time that it is a symbol of life, it is also a symbol of death. The swift waters which carry the canoe downstream are part of a flood farther upstream. ("The House of the Dead" is also carried downstream by the destructive power of the river.) But the death aspects of the river are integral to its life-giving force. That is, these two qualities, life-giving and death-bringing, are *not* antithetical. They are in fact part of *one* force. Huck's perspective toward death and life is identical with the river's reconciliation of these two forces. For Huck, death can free one *from* life and free one *for* life at the very same time. Death forms an integral element of the whole.

Huck's attitute toward death is quite different from that manifested by his father, who in his fit of delirium tremens cries out: "Tramp—tramp—tramp; that's the dead; tramp—tramp—tramp; they're coming after me; but I won't go—Oh, they're here! don't touch me—don't! hands off—they're cold; let go—Oh, let a poor devil alone!" The associations Pap makes with death are traditional. For Pap death is a physical thing: It is sensory; it is cold. He has accepted the objective personification of death common among the primitive, the unsophisticated. Pap's vision of death is an emotive response, nonrational, and as if to emphasize this very aspect Twain has Pap deliver his version of death in an alcoholic fit.

The threat of death is very real to Pap, and he believes that the only way he can come to terms with it is to kill the Dark Angel. Pap chases Huck around the cabin, calling him the Angel of Death, and attempts to slay death with a clasp knife, believing that then he will be free of mortality. Because Pap has objectified death, he mistakenly believes that Huck is the Dark Angel. His blurred, blind vision seizes on Huck as the only other being in the room, the incarnation of his fears.

In one sense Pap's mistaken identification of Huck as the Angel of Death is not altogether inaccurate. After his own ritual self-slaying Huck is free of the actual threat of death. (The episode with Pap comes prior to his simulated death, and the one other time he is threatened, the threat is instantly dispersed.) A number of deaths occur throughout the remainder of the book where Huck is a witness.

The first time Jim sees him after the ritual self-slaying, he mistakes Huck for a ghost: "Doan' hurt me—don't! I hain't ever done no harm to a ghos'. I awluz liked dead people, en done all I could for 'em. You go and git in de river agin, whah you b'longs, en doan' do nuffn to ole Jim, 'at 'uz awluz yo' fren'." Later when Huck and Jim have been separated by the fog on the river, Jim's first words on seeing Huck again are: "Goodness gracious, is dat you Huck? En you ain' dead—you ain' drownded—you's back again?" Jim's incredulity is not unwarranted from the traditional perspective, but then Huck offers a vision which is more encompassing. (It should be remarked that the dynamics of this vision occur between Huck and the reader, not between Huck and those he encounters in the progress of the narrative. Huck is not a proselytizer.)

Pap's fear of death is one guise that society has granted the fact of death, but the attitude of the Grangerfords and the Sheperdsons places death in an entirely different perspective. The Grangerfords and Sheperdsons have made death acceptable by cloaking it in romanticism and sentimentality. Emmeline Grangerford is the high priestess of the cult of romantic death and, appropriately enough, she herself is dead. Her room has been turned into a shrine, and her paintings have a place on the living room walls. In the series of paintings Twain is burlesquing the stylized response to death: "Shall I Never See Thee More Alas," "I Shall Never Hear Thy Sweet Chirrup More Alas," "And Art Thou Gone Yes Thou Art Gone Alas." These tableaulike drawings represent the stock responses of a sentimental heart. Huck's reaction reflects his philosophy: "These was all nice pictures, I reckon, but I didn't somehow seem to take to them . . ." Emmeline's drawings are static, stylized. They are theatrical postures without validity experientially. A flair for the dramatic characterizes the entire Grangeford family—from the elaborate morning greetings to the arrangement of the furniture in the house.

Death has become a way of life for the Grangerfords in their feud with the Sheperdsons. It is a way of life unfamiliar to Huck, as Buck Grangerford discovers to his surprise when Huck asks what a feud is. Huck is surprised in his own turn to learn that Buck does not even know the origins of the feud. He merely subscribes to it without questioning its validity. Huck cannot comprehend this way of life which is committed to death. As Huck sees it, and as Twain sees it, these terms deny any value to life. The values, as Colonel Grangerford points out, are either in killing honorably or dying bravely. This emphasis on death negates the intrinsic wholeness of the life-death unit.

Huck happens to be present when his friend Buck Grangerford falls victim to the terms of death as the way of living. (Huck is in a tree watching the scene below, which hints of Pap's allegation of Huck as the Angel of Death.)

> All of a sudden, bang! bang! bang! goes three or four guns—the men had slipped around through the woods and come in from behind without their horses! The boys jumped for the river—both of

them hurt—and as they swum down the current the men run along the bank shooting at them and singing out, "Kill them! kill them!" It made me so sick I most fell out of the tree. I ain't going to tell all that happened—it would make me sick again if I was to do that. I wished I hadn't ever come ashore that night, to see such things. I ain't ever going to get shut of them—lots of time I dream about them.

Huck's moral revulsion at the futility and waste of the feud-life is shared by Twain. Huck's dreams echo Twain's. The romantic, sentimental attitude toward death becomes an anaesthetic, numbing one to the potentialities and possibilities of life. The episode concludes with Huck's reunion with Jim and the renewal of their life on the raft. Huck tells us that he "never felt easy till the raft was two mile below there and out in the middle of the Mississippi."

Huck's encounters with death as a corruption of the life-death unit generate a rhythm. Ashore, death becomes antipodal to life, that is, it is not felt as integral, but is something suspected of being external, separate. It is conceived as something imposed from without, and this is reinforced in the novel by the fact that death generally means being shot. Experience of the river acknowledges the life-death organic unit. One generates the other.

On shore Huck sees the methods by which death, and consequently life, have been corrupted by society, and he is repelled by this vision back to the unpolluted river. Each attempt to reconcile himself with life ashore only makes Huck aware of how impossible the task is.

The Boggs-Sherburn episode emphasizes this pattern. Death is again the central issue. Some commentators have read it as a treatise on mob psychology, but it seems to me that Henry Nash Smith's reading is closer, although he cannot relate Huck's visit to the circus which follows Sherburn's contemptuous speech to the lynch mob. In *Mark Twain, The Development of a Writer*, Smith sees Sherburn as ultimately a precursor of "the mysterious stranger," and compares his cold-blooded killing of Boggs to Satan's indifferent murders of the small people he has made. He writes that "Sherburn belong to the series of characters in Mark Twain's later work that have been called 'transcendent figures' . . ." However, Satan in "The Mysterious Stranger" is in the literal sense a transcendent figure, whereas Sherburn, after all, is only a man. Sherburn's "transcendent" powers are not manifestations of his supernaturalism but only parts of a pose, similar to that of the Grangerfords and Sheperdsons. The pose is another way of coming to terms with death. Sherburn shoots Boggs without hesitancy, without regret. In his scheme, death is negligible because life is equally so, as he clearly indicates in his speech to the lynch mob. Again Huck is witness.

Huck first encounters Boggs "a-tearing along on his horse, whooping and yelling like an Injun, and saying out—'Cler the track, thar. I'm on the waw-path, and the price of coffins is a gwyne to rise.'" He addresses Huck, asking him if he is prepared to die, but he rides on before Huck can answer. Huck does admit he was scared, but the threat was never really a potent one. Boggs, whooping and hollering "and weaving about in the saddle," is a travesty of the Dark Angel. As one of the townsmen points out, "I wisht old Boggs 'd threaten me, 'cuz then I'd know I warn't gwyne to die for a thousan' year."

Smith points out that the Boggs-Sherburn episode is linked with Twain's own experience, and that the shooting resembles the slaying of "Uncle Sam" Smarr in Hannibal when Twain was only nine. Sherburn shoots Boggs cold-bloodedly, without remorse, for threatening him with death and then contemptuously dismisses the lynch mob which has congregated to avenge Boggs' killing. In this instance neither Huck nor Twain evaluates the episode editorially, as Huck does the Grangerford-Sheperdson feud. But the circus scene which immediately follows the dispersal of the lynch mob offers an imaginative evaluation.

The parallels that can be drawn between this scene and the Boggs-Sherburn episode are too obvious to neglect. What the circus scene does is to reverse the previous situation. The ringmaster can be equated with Sherburn, in that he seems to control life in the ring as Sherburn controlled the mob; Boggs is again drunk, but this time it is the feigned intoxication of a clown-athlete. The audience represents the townspeople, who are merely spectators at both events, as Huck is. The "drunk" pesters to be allowed to ride one of the circus horses, and the ringmaster finally, arrogantly, concedes. The "drunk" frantically attempts to remain astride the galloping horse as the audience howls with glee, and as the townspeople laughed at Boggs. But Huck does not share the crowd's feelings: "It warn't funny to me, though; I was all of a tremble to see his danger." The "drunk," shedding layers of clothes, metamorphosizes into a handsome young acrobat to the chagrin of the ringmaster and the pleasure of Huck. The circus scene represents an attempt to check the arrogance of Sherburn, his indifference to both life and death, by checking the arrogance of his prototype, the ringmaster. This reversal of the earlier action is qualified by being set in a circus, a fantasy world. In reality on shore the possibility of metamorphosis does not exist, only the alternatives of Sherburn and Boggs, both equally unacceptable to Huck.

The next major episode in *The Adventures of Huckleberry Finn* deals with the Duke and the Dauphin's attempt to steal Peter Wilks' estate from the lawful heirs. It is clear from this episode that Twain thinks death within the framework of civilization has been corrupted and that instead of giving meaning to life, it gives only opportunity for degradation and depravity. It blinds people to the truth, as it blinds Peter Wilks' family and friends to the true identities of the Duke and the Dauphin. For Huck the obsequities to the forms and rituals of death are as much pretense and sham as the Duke and the Dauphin's titles. He even describes the funeral piety in terms of acting: "It worked the crowd," "give the next woman a show." Huck's description of the funeral as an orgy is apt. "I never seen anything so disgusting," Huck concludes, as the Duke and the Dauphin act out their remorse above Peter Wilks' coffin. Huck's remark applies to his other encounters on shore with the phenomenon of death as well.

In *Huckleberry Finn* Twain seems to be saying that the vision, Huck's perspective, which can give life its full value is that vision which can give death its full value. Huck's encounters ashore with the Dark Angel illustrate the negation of these value possibilities when life and death are seen as opposite poles. Life ashore sees death cutting off life, while Huck is just as aware of death's life-giving possibilities, and as if to firmly underline this thesis Twain ends the novel with the Dark Angel giving life to Huck and Jim again. Jim is freed from his slave status by the Widow Douglas' deathbed gesture, while Huck is finally told that the corpse in the house of the dead was his father, freeing him from authority and reprisal. The pathos of *Huckleberry Finn* is that Huck's perspective is no longer possible for Mark Twain. It is an imaginative position at best. As Twain himself discovered in *Life on the Mississippi,* the river herself had been civilized.

In *Roughing It,* Twain describes what it felt like to be dying:

> We were all sincere, and all deeply moved and earnest, for we were in the presence of death and without hope. I threw away my pipe, and in doing it felt that at last I was free of a hated vice and one that had ridden me like a tyrant all my days. While I yet talked, the thought of the good I might have done in the world, and the still greater good I might now do, with these new incentives and higher and better aims to guide me if I could only be spared a few years longer, overcame me and the tears came again. We put our arms about each other's necks and awaited the warning drowsiness that precedes death by freezing.

Of course this passage is suspect, placed as it is at the end of a chapter for the greatest possible comic effect—something like the tall-tale teller who ends his narrative by being consumed by the bear. But at least this passage does represent another perspective. The foreboding of the Dark Angel's presence is expressed in terms of regret. He does not fear death, and in the world of *Roughing It* death was too frequent to be feared, but it still remains in opposition to life. The perspective is only a stance, and one which Twain shares with the Southwestern humorists. Hennig Cohen and William B. Dillingham, in their introduction to *Humor of the Old Southwest,* state that these men "sought through humor to reduce this fearful spectre (death) to less awful proportions . . . The reader is taken into a real-unreal place where suffering and ugliness and death do not clash with horseplay so much as they become part of it." It would be impossible to imagine Huck saying what the hero of *Roughing It* says. Huck would stay alive as long as he possibly could, not because he feared death, but because being alive he had no alternative except to live. He would not be deeply moved by the presence of death. For Huck, death has no presence, only life has presence.

Twain's later writings shift from the perspectives held by Huck and the personna-hero of *Roughing It.* In "Reflections on Religion" he believes that "the dead are the only human beings who are really well off . . ." and he says in his autobiography that his daughter Jean "has been enriched with the most precious of all gifts—that gift which makes all other gifts mean and poor—death." The Twain who could write this way was a man who could no longer see the value of life. But his attitude toward death is not the romantic and sentimental vision of Emmaline Grangerford. There is no alternative to the disenchantment of the shore. Only Huck could "light out" for the better world because he hadn't been there. Twain had, and it was all the same.

Death becomes release from a life which is essentially dead—that is, dead to the possibilities of self-fulfillment, self-expression. "The Mysterious Stranger" attempts to reconcile the facts of life and death in dream. There is an awakening to a supraconsciousness that includes both life and death, but is beyond them. Huck's consciousness reconciles life and death in life.

Freudian psychology asserts that in dreams going away on a journey can be a symbolic form of dying. The journey motif is central to both *The Adventures of Huckleberry Finn* and the incomplete manuscript, "The Great Dark." In "The Great Dark" the journey, which is literally to death, occurs within a dream framework.

The central figure in the manuscript, Mr. Edwards, "was thirty-five years old, and seemed ten years younger, for he was one of those fortunate people who by nature are overcharged with breezy spirits and vigorous health, and from whom cares and troubles slide off without making an impression." Mr. Edwards can be seen as Huck reborn at the conclusion of *Huckleberry Finn;* his wife's motherly solicitude makes him as young as his children. He is the innocent again, the naif, who must make a journey of discovery. Edwards' life suddenly begins anew on board ship in a way similar to Huck's rebirth on the river.

In the world of "The Great Dark," however, there are no shores. The ship sails in pitch darkness—the stars which Huck saw lying on his back in the bottom of the canoe have been extinguished. The Mississippi which Huck came to know has become a black and unfathomable expanse where all the laws of nature have been suspended. The garrulous mate, Turner, tells Edwards that the gulf stream has gone to the devil, and informs him surreptitiously, "Well, you spoke of tonight. It ain't tonight at all; it's just noon now."

The mate's astonishing revelations do not really frighten Edwards. He has the Superintendent of Dreams who he believes is controlling the world. His presence is a justification in Edwards' mind for the terrors of the great dark and for the suspension of nature's laws. Besides, Edwards cannot feel real terror in the nightmare which surrounds him because he does not think it is real. When the Superintendent asks Edwards, "Are you quite sure it [the nightmare voyage] is a dream?" Edwards' self-assurance is suddenly shaken: "It was as if he had hit me, it stunned me so. Still looking at me his lip curled into a mocking smile, and he wasted away like a mist and disappeared." And the Superintendent never reappears. The terrible phenomena of the great dark have to be accepted as reality and not as fantasy. This is an extension beyond the view offered in "The Mysterious Stranger" where the possibility of life as dream still existed.

The first book of "The Great Dark" establishes life at sea as the only life; the second book defines that life in images of death, the most nightmarish of which is the spider-squid. The image of death as a spider also appears in *Huckleberry Finn* in one of Emmeline Grangerford's unfinished paintings in which a young woman is represented with three sets of arms. But Emmeline has died before deciding which set of arms is best. Huck says that although the woman in the picture has a sweet face "there were so many arms it made her look too spidery, seemed to me." The inhabitants aboard ship in the great dark cannot romanticize death in the way Emmeline Grangerford was capable of doing. Here, too, as in the world of the feud, death is a way of life, but for Edwards, his wife, and his friends, no other possibility exists.

The ship becomes the house of the dead which comes floating down the Mississippi. Edwards, his wife, and family have their own apartment—"chairs and carpets and rugs and tables and lamps and books and everything lovely, and so warm and comfortable and homey; and the roomiest parlor . . . ever struck in a ship too."

All the possible perspectives toward death explored in *Huckleberry Finn* are denied to Edwards. He cannot romanticize it as Emmeline Grangerford could—the spider-squid must be accepted on its own terms; and when the Superintendent of Dreams wisps away, the advantage of Sherburn-like assurance is denied Edwards. Even the captain, who must face the threats of the mutineers in a fashion similar to Sherburn's facing the lynch mob, no longer is able to command arrogance and superiority in the face of death. In "The Great Dark" life is seen as horror and death is seen as horror, and there is no possibility of viewing them as a unit with the magic potentialities of fulfillment as Huck does. For Edwards there is no reality beyond the nightmare.

The only human consciousness Twain had discovered that was strong enough to come to terms with death was Huck's. But Huck's perspective could only exist in a special world. Once the river dried up, as even the pitch-like waters of "The Great Dark" do, life is symbolically and literally denied. And when life cannot be understood, neither can the Dark Angel, death.

Wendy B. Faris

SOURCE: "1000 Words: Fiction Against Death," in *The Georgia Review*, Vol. XXXVI, No. 4, Winter, 1982, pp. 811-30.

[*In the following essay, Faris investigates the modern use of narration as the postponement of death—culled from the tradition of* The Thousand and One Nights—*in the work of such writers as Marcel Proust, Jorge Luis Borges, John Barth, Vladimir Nabokov, and others.*]

When Scheherazade staves off her death for 1001 nights by telling a continuously enthralling chain of stories to her captor, the king, she dramatizes an intriguing aspect of all literary discourse: its capacity to simulate the postponement of human death through the prolongation of fictional life. For narrators and readers alike, the end of a text represents a small death of sorts; its postponement, continued life.[1] Scheherazade's story has endured and continues to fascinate modern writers and theorists because it pictures the basic human desire to live on and on, but also because it is susceptible to varied and—as we shall see—often contrasting interpretations. After investigating some theoretical implications of Scheherazade's stance and her strategy, I will turn briefly to modern texts by Proust, Borges, Barth, Nabokov, and several others which illustrate in varying degrees and forms a resurgent interest in her story.

That Scheherazade's stance symbolizes fiction which postpones its own closure at first appears to contrast with, perhaps even to contradict, the idea that we crave "the sense of an ending" in life and in literature.[2] According to Frank Kermode, one of the imagination's mercies is closure. I am tempted to counter that another of the imagination's mercies is the postponement of closure—especially when it is imagined as death—but the problem is more complicated than this, as Kermode recognizes. Man's desire for endings can be seen as a particular instance of his desire for form. The imposition of form on chaos may represent the affirmative power of life over the dissolving power of death. One might argue, with Kermode, that novels that postpone their endings must have a strong sense of closure to fight against in order to play this game. And Scheherazade's stories, which constitute the *The Thousand and One Nights*, would never have been told without her deathly sense of her ending, and that of her family. Nevertheless, I believe the paradigm of *Arabian Nights* (as it is most commonly known) does represent a narrative impulse that complements the one Kermode describes. Perhaps Scheherazade and her literary descendants provide a protest from inside fiction against necessary but nonetheless frightening endings. Scheherazadian narrators fight bravely, if uselessly, against the end which figures their own deaths.

This oscillation between ending and continuing, between apocalypse and renewal, appears in the very number 1001. In the context of Scheherazade's achievement, it stresses man's power to begin over and over again, to keep on narrating—or living—forever. Visually, too, the sign constitutes a symmetrical, self-reflecting, regenerative pattern. If one imagines a conceptual mirror between the two zeros in 1001, the number consists of a perpetual reflection of its two parts. Bruno Bettelheim maintains that "'thousand' in Arabic means 'innumerable,' so 1001 signifies an infinite number," and he notes that translators and compilers who worked on the tales often took the figure 1001 literally, adding tales to make up the count.[3] Nevertheless, for western readers, the number 1001 perhaps represents not so much the indefinite notion of infinity as the moment of endless beginnings, the idea that there is always "one more," even when a millennial point has been reached. Scheherazade's own tale does end, but, as we shall see in a moment, it funnels into the new beginning of children.

Bettelheim interprets the frame tale of *Arabian Nights* as a parable for the integration of a personality. Because he wishes to study the "uses of enchantment," he emphasizes the therapeutic value of Scheherazade's tale. For Bettelheim, King Shahriyar and Scheherazade "meet in the great crises of their lives: the king disgusted with life and full of hatred of women; Scheherazade fearing for her life, but determined to achieve his and her deliverance" (p. 87). It seems to me that Bettelheim exaggerates a bit here. Scheherazade's crisis is not really her own; it is brought on by the king's disgust. His problem is psychological, while hers may be political. Nevertheless, a crisis it is. Scheherazade manages to restrain the king, the "uncontrolled id," from vengefully laying waste the kingdom only through telling a wide variety of fairy tales. (Man's psychological problems are too complex to be cured by single stories, according to Bettelheim; the necessary catharsis takes many.) Scheherazade symbolizes the ego, but an ego so dominated by superego and separated from the selfish id that it risks its own life to obey a moral obligation: she wishes to save the king's future victims from death. But as Bettelheim argues, Scheherazade's present strategy can only postpone her execution, not abolish it. She needs more than her single moral motivation to be fully successful: only when "superego (the wish to deliver 'the daughters of the Muslims from slaughter') and id (her love for the king, whom she now wishes to deliver from his hatred and depression) both endow the ego—has she become a fully integrated person. . . . As she declares her love for the king, he declares his for her" (p. 89).

Bettelheim's idea of Scheherazade's initial selflessness is strengthened by Emmanuel Cosquin's early historical study of the frame tale of *Arabian Nights*.[4] Cosquin claims that the primary motive for Scheherazade's actions is saving her father, the Vizir, from the king's anger when the supply of virgins runs out: Scheherazade's narration thus holds off not only death but unjust vengeance; it overcomes absolute power. The narrative voice that wishes never to stop speaks not only against its own death but against the deaths of its father, sisters, future husband—and readers. It stresses the communal nature of the narrative act.

Tzvetan Todorov would presumably disapprove of these psychological interpretations of Scheherazade's story: for him *The Thousand and One Nights* "can be considered as a limit-case of literary a-psychologism," a refutation of the idea that character and action are inevitably linked in fiction and that action serves the primary function of revealing personality.[5] In a narrative like *Arabian Nights,* according to Todorov, all character traits are immediately causal. In Sinbad's story, for example, we learn no more of his character than is necessary to provoke his actions: "Sinbad likes to travel (character trait)   Sinbad takes a trip (action): the distance between the two tends toward a total reduction" (p. 68). Todorov illustrates his own theory by proceeding immediately to Scheherazade's stories—her verbal action—without discussing her character or situation. In *The Thousand and One Nights* itself, just after we learn that Scheherazade is clever, she begins to tell the tales, and for the rest of the book, they, not she, hold our interest. Her artistic vocation—her "speech-act," as Todorov terms it—stems less from her character than from her situation, which is in turn caused by the actions of others: "The speech-act receives, in the *Arabian Nights,* an interpretation which leaves no further doubt as to its importance. If all the characters incessantly tell stories, it is because this action has received a supreme consecration: narrating equals living . . ." (p. 74). Scheherazade must narrate to avoid death, not to "express herself."

In discussing both *Arabian Nights* and the works it has inspired, it will be useful for us to keep in mind both Bettelheim's psychological interpretation and Todorov's "a-psychologism." Indeed, as I've suggested earlier, this interaction of contrasting interpretations may help explain the continuing popularity of the tales. Todorov's attention to formal causal action and his consequent elucidation of fictional structure points toward a consideration of the particular narrative strategies used by Scheherazade and her successors. But Bettelheim's focus reminds us that it is also essential to consider the emotional force that underlies these strategies in *Arabian Nights* and in its modern descendants. Scheherazade's tales insistently impel the reader forward, away from the teller, to another tale; yet sometimes it is rewarding—and moving—to reflect the whole tale backwards onto the teller, as a measure of his—or, in this case, her—need.

Roland Barthes provides a slightly different view of *The Thousand and One Nights* when he locates narrative, and particularly Scheherazade's stories, in the realm of "exchange." According to Barthes, "narrative (as an anthropological activity) is founded on some kind of exchange: a narrative is given, is received, is structured *for* (or *against*) something, of which it is in some sense the counterweight. . . . In *The Thousand and One Nights* each new story buys a day of survival for Scheherazade. . . . The narrative recounts the contract of which it is the stake."[6] Barthes compares Scheherazade's bargain with that of the storyteller in Sade's *The 120 Days of Sodom.* The latter makes an agreement with a group of libertines that if she will entertain them with stories, they will never harm her, no matter what they do to other women. It is true, as Barthes claims, that Scheherazade is in a similar situation. But unlike Sade's storyteller, she never has an explicit bargain. She must rely on the force of her narrative to stay alive; her implicit "contract" must be renegotiated each night.

Besides presenting Scheherazade as the archetypal narrator, narrating for her life, *Arabian Nights* contains various textual strategies for the prolongation of fictional life, strategies which reiterate stylistically the situation of Scheherazade and prefigure numerous modern literary conventions. Of course, any narrative employs numerous techniques to keep itself going, and the incentive to keep on narrating can be applied to storytelling of *all* kinds; this explains in part Scheherazade's continuing position at the center of literary tradition. Some form of embedding, some "Chinese box" structure, is probably the most striking Scheherazadian technique. The end of narration is postponed by stories within stories within stories that may lead forever onward, changing their narrators. This structure may contain an example of mise-en-abyme (a miniature portrait of a narrative within itself) noted by André Gide, though Gide's original idea does not necessarily imply repetition ad infinitum.[7] Narration may also, of course, be puffed up, drawn out, by extensive repetition of words or scenes, or by the inclusion of unusually large quantities of intertextual allusions. Or the finality of a fictional ending may be postponed by a circular structure of one kind or another. The presence of theories of cyclical time achieves conceptually a similar effect. This circular form characterizes *The Thousand and One Nights* as a whole, for it begins and ends with Scheherazade, but it does not describe the story of Scheherazade herself. Her story ends with an exit to the world that includes death. Though she has provided the model for (an albeit feverish) immortality of sorts, Scheherazade accepts her own mortal status gladly in the end and lives happily with her husband until they are visited by "the Destroyer of delights and the Severer of societies."[8] On the other hand, the cycles of the natural world affirm her continuity, holding the promise of ongoing life through her children at the end of the story.

Because Scheherazade has become a powerful sign of the storyteller—of either sex—discussion of her specifically feminine qualities is rare.[9] It is an essential point, however, that within the story of *Arabian Nights,* Scheherazade redeems the honor of her sex. The reason that King Shahriyar sleeps each night with a virgin and has her beheaded in the morning is that he and his brother have discovered that many women—including their own wives—are unfaithful. During her three years of storytelling, Scheherazade is presumably faithful to the king. But more than just faithful, Scheherazade is clever; her victory over the king not only redeems women, it also achieves a kind of revenge on men like him who wish to punish women for insubordination. Outside her own story, Scheherazade serves a similar corrective function by standing in contrast to Belladonna, or the fatal lover. If sex is a death game which the king plays, then fabulation in this case counteracts it; and when combined with sex, it is a source of renewal rather than revenge, for Scheherazade's children by Shahriyar have grown up parallel with her narrative. They are not a substitute for literary creativity; rather, they confirm the life-sustaining powers demonstrated by Scheherazade's narration. They also, of course, link her substantively, indissolubly, with

her "reader"—or listener—King Shahriyar. Viewed in this context, the structure of her tale is like a genealogical chart: from one unit is born another. And it is just such a chart, a royal one, to which she contributes with her children. The old metaphor of the male poet coupling with the female muse to produce the word-child undergoes a reversal of sorts. Here the inspirational force, the muse, is death; Scheherazade confronts death, couples with the king who represents this threat, and produces her stories and her children.

Robert Alter maintains that self-conscious novels often prove to be long meditations on death. The writer's mortality receives more explicit scrutiny in texts where he or a surrogate appears. Alter suggests that a consideration of death in the novel might therefore be instructive. Such a study could investigate "how the novel manages to put us in touch with the impossible implications of human mortality through the very celebration of life implicit in the building of vivid and various fictions."[10] The narrative impulse behind *The Thousand and One Nights* fits Alter's idea of mortality's presence as seen through the building of fiction: Scheherazade's continuing presence in texts by Proust, Borges, Barth, and Nabokov records the urge to fight against death, or at least to postpone it, with narrative itself.

Proust's Marcel is possibly the most eminent modern admirer—and imitator—of Scheherazade. His fondness for *Arabian Nights* is well known; he mentions it over and over again throughout *Remembrance of Things Past*. Most significantly, of course, near the end of *Time Regained* he directly compares his own work to *The Nights*. In doing so, he first points up only the most superficial similarity between the two texts—their great lengths. He finally acknowledges, however, a kind of subconscious current of continuity:

> . . . And I should live in the anxiety of not knowing whether the master of my destiny might not prove less indulgent than the Sultan Shahriyar, whether in the morning, when I broke off my story, he would consent to a further reprieve and permit me to resume my narrative the following evening. Not that I had the slightest pretension to be writing a new version, in any way, of the *Thousand and One Nights*. . . . But . . . you can make a new version of what you love only by first renouncing it. So my book, though it might be as long as the *Thousand and One Nights,* would be entirely different. . . . And only if you faithfully follow this truth will you sometimes find that you have stumbled again upon what you renounced, find that, by forgetting these works themselves, you have written the *Thousand and One Nights* or the *Memoirs* of Saint-Simon of another age. But for me was there still time? Was it not too late?[11]

This passage is embedded in thoughts of death. It is as if the pages Marcel writes must force their way through the idea of death, putting off its takeover of his system. He invokes the powerful precedent of *The Nights* and Scheherazade's earlier success in postponing death as an antidote to the mortal weakness he feels creeping through him and also, perhaps, to stave off with words the deaths of his grandmother, his mother, Albertine. (Has not Scheherazade saved an entire female population with her fictions?[12]) The allusions might also indicate a desire for narrative life to continue on and on like Scheherazade's stories.[13] That this reference appears near the end of the novel heightens Marcel's sense of urgency, his fear of not finishing; but it also suggests his fear of finishing—and reinforces our sense that he keeps himself alive by continuing to write.

Throughout the novel, Marcel's narrative means of drawing out instants of involuntary memory prolongs their time-killing effect.[14] Georges Poulet argues that Marcel's use of memory to structure his work serves principally to bolster a fragile self, to affirm continuity in the face of dissolution and death.[15] By establishing the continuity of his past and present selves, Marcel can also believe in his future. This is Why the tales in *Arabian Nights* make such appropriate bedtime stories; in fact, it is one of the favorite bedside books in *Remembrance of Things Past.* A child always wishes bedtime stories to continue forever, to postpone endlessly the approach of darkness and sleep—clear, if unconscious, analogues for death. Marcel's fear of death, like Scheherazade's, is associated with the nighttime embrace, and his fear, like hers, motivates an ingenious narrative strategy: a story within a story. Marcel feels as if he will die unless his mother comes upstairs to him. Before he "buries himself" in his bed, however, he decides to write her a note summoning her upstairs for something too important to put into writing. But the chain of invention goes beyond this initial tale. In order to get his grand aunt's servant, Françoise, to take the note to his mother, Marcel must invent a story: he says that his mother has requested that he ler her know about a missing object, and he claims that she will be angry if she's not informed via the note.

Just after this episode in *Swann's Way,* the "petite madeleine" scene provides a seminal revelation that will eventually culminate in Marcel's assumption of his role as narrator: like the bedtime scene it is also preceded by the presence of death. Marcel explains that so far he had only evoked Combray through his voluntary memory:

. . . To me it was in reality all dead.

Permanently dead? Very possibly.

There is a large element of chance in these matters, and a second chance occurrence, that of our own death, often prevents us from awaiting for any length of time the favours of the first. (1, 47)

The repetition of the word *dead* in an incomplete sentence, unusual in Proust, makes it seem almost as if death has cut the narrative impulse temporarily short in those two minimal phrases comprising a scant paragraph. He goes on to explain that he thinks there is much to be said for the Celtic belief that "the souls of those whom we have lost" are captive in trees or animals until we chance to pass by and release them. Marcel is, of course, not literally threatened by death here. The idea appears indirectly. He speaks of "our own death" as a second hazard that further endangers the incomplete resurrection of the past. But in a sense the impersonal expression "the souls of those whom we have lost" makes it possible to include Marcel in their ranks: the same verb *tressaillir* ("tremble") describes both their reawakening from death and Marcel's shuddering sensation when the crumbs of tea-soaked madeleine reawaken his past and point towards the future narration that seems to prolong his life.

At the very end of *Swann's Way,* a remembered scene in the Bois de Boulogne progressively loses life until Marcel cries, " . . . and houses, roads, avenues, are as fugitive, alas, as the years." In a sense, the past dies, and with it the self, as the narration comes to an end, though in this particular case it is only a temporary end. One of the attractions of a many-volume work like Proust's is perhaps the sense of survival that each new volume permits.

The most striking similarity between the work of Jorge Luis Borges and *The Thousand and One Nights,* which he, like Proust in his time, has long admired, is the technique of *récits enchassés,* or Chinese box stories.[16] Borges' stories, unlike Scheherazade's (and Proust's), are generally very short, so that the technique postpones endings in a metaphorical rather than a structural sense. "Tlön, Uqbar, Orbis Tertius," for example, contains several layers or boxes: the "I" of the narrator finds in a particular set of encyclopedias an article on the land of Uqbar, whose literature of fantasy in turn mentions the imaginary region of Tlön. Two years later he comes upon a volume of the first encyclopedia of Tlön, which, interestingly enough, has 1001 pages, and from which we learn about Tlön's philosophical and linguistic systems. These two boxes are finally encased in a third, for Borges adds a postscript which recounts another "intrusion" of Tlön into our world and further delays the end of the story. Postscripts are perhaps the most frequent of Borges' frames, but other stories are framed in other ways. The text of "The Garden of Forking Paths" is introduced by a reference in a history of the First World War and constitutes the statement of Dr. Yu Tsun as reported by another narrator. "The Immortal" is introduced as a manuscript inserted in a volume of Pope's translation of the *Iliad* and succeeded by a postscript describing various reactions to it. The short story of "The Two Kings and Their Two Labyrinths" is embedded in the longer story of "Abenjacán el Bojarí," which precedes it.

Another common element in Borges' stories is the final death of the narrator; this is, of course, one reason for the postscripts. In "The Secret Miracle," Jaromir Hladik is miraculously granted a year's time to finish his play in the moments before he is killed by a firing squad. The story seems to dramatize the uncanny sense we often have that a narrator's death at the end of a text has been postponed by the very force of his desire to keep on narrating. A different kind of postponement occurs in pieces where a Borges figure speaks of himself. This I/

Borges practices an infinite regression into the self. The famous ending of "Borges and I" describes this retreat from the deathlike immobility of definition: "Years ago I tried to free myself from him [Borges] and went from the mythologies of the suburbs to the games with time and infinity, but those games belong to Borges now and I shall have to imagine other things. Thus my life is a flight and I lose everything and everything belongs to oblivion, or to him."[17]

Besides these implicit similarities to *Arabian Nights* and Borges' numerous references to it throughout his works, Borges renders explicit homage to *The Nights* in two recent poetic works. "Metaphors of the Thousand and One Nights," is filled with such elements as Sinbad, the genie, and the queen—to which Borges adds images to describe Scheherazade's tale (including a map of time and his "own" symbol, a labyrinth) that serve to expand *The Nights* into a metaphor of temporal and spatial infinity. His one-word sentence—"Todo." ("Everything.")—signals this comprehensiveness. Borges' poem is a tribute to the richness of *Arabian Nights* as a storehouse of images for later literature, and like its subject it has a progressive structure in which one unit springs from the last. Moreover, as in his essay "Partial Magic in the *Quixote*,"[18] Borges proposes that Scheherazade, on the six hundred and second night, tells her own story, which necessitates the infinite retelling of all of the tales she has told the king.

> "The Book is in the book. Without knowing it,
> The queen tells the king the already forgotten
> Story of them both."

The poem ends:

> The arabs say that no one can
> Read to the end of the Book of Nights,
> The Nights are Time, which never sleeps.
> Keep reading as the day dies
> And Scheherazade will tell you your story.[19]

The text, in contrast to the day that dies, continues into the reader's life and proves the Arabs correct: the poem might be considered an imaginary prologue to *The Nights* in which the reader, like the king, will find one of the series of stories to be his own.

Borges' one-page parable "Someone" evokes a distinguished literary ancestor by describing the imaginary composition of *The Thousand and One Nights* in a nostalgically elegiac tone. In a dusty plaza, at the center of a circle of listeners, "The man talks and gesticulates. He doesn't know (others will) that he belongs to the lineage of the *confabulatores nocturni,* to the nighttime rhapsodizers, which Doublehorned Alexander assembled as consolation in his sleeplessness. He thinks he's speaking to a few people for a few coins and in a lost yesterday he weaves the Book of the Thousand and One Nights."[20] One thinks immediately of Funes the Memorious (whose endless interwoven memories resemble *Arabian Nights* and whom we meet at night) and also of Borges, now blind, himself a perpetual *confabulator nocturni.*

Over twenty years before these two works, Borges devoted an uncharacteristically long essay to "The Translators of the *1001 Nights.*" Consideration of its translation fits one more box around the story composed of many boxes. Borges goes even further in this direction, for he inserts the first translators he discusses into a serial structure that resembles *Arabian Nights* itself: "Lane translated against Galland, Burton against Lane; in order to understand Burton one must understand that hostile dynasty."[21] Here it is not Scheherazade who keeps herself alive by storytelling, but her translators, who wish to obliterate their predecessors so that they can live on through their own translations.

At the end of the essay, after discussing the relative merits of the various translations, Borges suggests additional reasons for his fascination with the tales which tie his own tales to Scheherazade's. First, history and fantasy are inextricably mixed: "When the magical events ran out, the scribes had to fall back on historical or pious bits of information, whose inclusion seemed to sanction the good faith of the rest. In the same volume the ruby that ascended to heaven coexists with the first description of Sumatra" (p. 132). Then Borges points to the six hundred and second night when Shahriyar hears his own story from the queen: like the frame tale, one story contains others. Finally, Borges describes the encased tales in *The Nights* as seeming more concrete than the ones they grow out of, antechambers confused with mirrors, masks behind faces, until "no one knows which is the real man and which his idols" (p. 133). Now we sense that we have passed from an account of *Arabian Nights* to a description of the Borgesian works it has engendered. Borges' tales prolong Scheherazade's series.

John Barth provides the most explicit rewriting of *The Thousand and One Nights* in his novella *Dunyazadiad.* Here he suggests that the relationship between writer and reader assures that every narrator's life hangs figuratively on his powers of narrative invention as surely as Scheherazade's hangs literally on hers. In his essay "Muse, Spare Me," Barth comments on the affinity that he feels for Scheherazade, her narrative position and procedures: "The whole frame of those thousand nights and a night speaks to my heart, directly and intimately—and in many ways at once, personal and technical."[22] Barth continues in the tradition of *The Nights* by creating multiple frames for his fictional text.[23] His principal innovation is to dwell on comparisons between erotic and narrative activities—perhaps his individual strategy for avoiding death in the commercial literary world.

In the *Dunyazadiad,* the story of Scheherazade is told by her younger sister Dunyazade, after which an omniscient narrator tells the story of Dunyazade herself. Dunyazade's account of her sister's activities includes a figure she calls the genie, an obvious analogue for Barth himself, who appears to Scheherazade in her hour of need. His presence adds to the original frame tale yet another frame—from the inside, so to speak—that turns out to suggest an infinite regression of frames. This genie as an archetypal department-of-English narrator (bespectacled, balding, continually struggling to produce a worthy addition to the world's store of literature), temporarily usurps the function of Scheherazade: he tells her the tales she will tell the king. But the genie, in turn, remembers these tales from his copy of *Arabian Nights,* whose existence *this* Scheherazade in *this* story apparently ignores. So we ask ourselves, who "really" came first, the genie or Scheherazade? And since the chicken-and-egg question reverberates infinitely, the origin of the narrative oscillates dizzily between the two figures, between ancient and modern stories, implicitly questioning the origin of narration per se. (As Todorov has pointed out, *The Thousand and One Nights* itself posits no true beginning for its storytelling, since it starts with the words "it is told" [p. 78].) As if to suggest the continuing nature of all narrative experience, the *Dunyazadiad* begins *in medias res.*

The generalized narrator figure of the genie wishes to participate in the ancient and seminal literary scene of *Arabian Nights,* to adopt Scheherazade's powerful narrative stance and return reinforced to his own worktable. He inserts himself in the origins he admires, couples intellectually, imaginatively, with Scheherazade as his muse, saying that "he desired her only as the old Greek poets their Muse, as a source of inspiration."[24] The Scheherazadian need to oppose death with fiction also appears in the story of Dunyazade and Shahzaman, King Shahriyar's brother, which follows the tale of Scheherazade. The machinations that lead up to this scene are too complicated to summarize here (they are delightfully ingenious, in true "Arabian" fashion); but finally, to gain the trust—and the love—of Dunyazade, Shahzaman lets her hold a razor blade ready to castrate him, and says: "All I ask is leave to tell you a story, in exchange for the one you've told me; when I'm finished you may do as you please" (p. 49). He lends force to his narrative by duplicating the scene where fear of death motivates the narrator—and perhaps softens the listener.

Shahzaman's strategy works, partly because he persuades Dunyazade to believe in the "philosophy of *as if,*" central to both the art of storytelling and the art of love. *As if*— the sign of the storyteller—is the genie and Scheherazade's favorite expression, too; they even apply it to the equation between narrative and sexual art:

> . . . they seemed to mean that writing and reading, or telling and listening, were literally ways of making love. Whether this was in fact the case, neither [the genie] nor Sherry cared at all; yet they liked to speak *as if it were* (their favorite words), and accounted thereby for the similarity between conventional dramatic structure—its exposition, rising action, climax, and dénouement—and the rhythm of sexual intercourse from foreplay through coitus to orgasm and release. Therefore also, they believed, the popularity of love . . . as a theme for narrative. (pp. 32-33)

Here, as always in a discussion of *Arabian Nights* and its descendants, thematic and structural concerns merge:

loving and storytelling are interdependent. Discussion of two famous examples, the *Odyssey* and the *Decameron*— the first largely told in bed, the second "a kind of *substitute* for making love"—confirms the idea; repeated comparisons between love- and story-making invest the narrative process with sexual energy, and vice versa. Both are then, of course, increasingly powerful weapons against death. Cleverly polivalent phrases like "passionate virtuosity" and "narrative inexhaustibility or profligacy" cement the connection between narrating and loving. "Narrative, in short," the genie and Scheherazade agree, "was a love-relation, not a rape: its success depended upon the reader's consent and cooperation, which she could withhold or at any moment withdraw; also upon her own combination of experience and talent for enterprise, and the author's ability to arouse, sustain, and satisfy her interest . . ." (p. 34). In the original tale, the reciprocal nature of narrative is indicated by the king's insomnia: he has something to gain from Scheherazade's storytelling.

The *Dunyazadiad* illustrates a central point in Barth's well-known essay on "The Literature of Exhaustion."[25] Just as Shahriyar and his brother Shahzaman are disenchanted with the repetitiously unfaithful conduct of women, so Barth and his double, the genie in the *Dunyazadiad,* claim to be disenchanted with the repetitive and exhausted nature of narrative. If there's nothing new to say, nor any new ways of saying it, why not be quiet. But for a writer to fall silent is almost to die, so that narration—of any sort—means continued life. Barth suggests in his essay that the solution to the problem of "exhausted" literature is to write about the problem. The magic sentence in the *Dunyazadiad* with which Scheherazade inadvertently summons the genie dramatizes this idea. Scheherazade has been trying to imagine *which* story will change the king's mind and save everyone, just as exhausted writers have been trying to imagine a new subject, style, or point of view. When "Sherry" says, "It's as if—as if the key to the treasure *is* the treasure," the genie appears (p. 16). We realize that it is not the content of a particular story that will save her, but storytelling itself, the structure of the narrative, especially the kind of endless narrative that glorifies invention and is nourished by love—the mutual trust of teller and listener.

Just as the relationship between teller and listener, or writer and reader, is reciprocal, so too the resolution of Scheherazade and the genie's modern narrative problems requires a similar cooperation. No narrative can exist alone. Literary discourse is a communal enterprise and asks that we recognize the interdependence of ancient and modern texts. Scheherazade suggests her implicit awareness of this literary communality early on, when she claims that the only stories she knows are the ones she tells Dunyazade at bedtime—"the ones that everybody tells" (p. 20). Similarly, the genie says that he has "gone forward by going back, to the very roots and springs of story. Like Scheherazade herself, he has used materials received from narrative antiquity and methods older than the alphabet for entirely present ends; in the time since Sherry's defloration he had set down two-thirds of a projected series of three *novellas*" (p. 36). These are, of course, the ones we are reading. Like the king and Scheherazade, we see ourselves in the tale. The *Dunyazadiad* ends with Scheherazade) and the genie's magic sentence, as if to conjure up another storyteller and deny once again the deathlike ending of narrative.

The first chapter of Barth's novel *The Floating Opera* ("Tuning My Piano") forms an interesting postscript to this discussion. Here the narrator, Todd Andrews, claims that he will have a hard time getting started in his role as narrator. So he seems not to fit my paradigm of narrators desperate to save themselves from extinction by telling endless stories. But Todd also says that "I know enough about myself to realize that once the ice is broken and the ink is flowing, the pages will follow all too easily, for I'm not naturally a reticent fellow, and the problem will be to stick to the story, and finally to shut myself up."[26] Already we can see Todd oscillating-between two opposing tendencies—one, never to start narrating, and the other, never to stop: between fictional death and fictional life. This opposition is suggested by Todd's very name, as he himself points out: "*Tod* is death, and this book hasn't much to do with death; *Todd* is almost *Tod*—that is, almost death—and this book, if it gets written, has very much to do with almost-death" (p. 9). Todd has the subject matter of his novel in mind here, but I would argue that, in a larger context, his discussion suggests the life and death aspects of all narration. This book, precisely because it may not even get started, has to do with "almost death" for its narrator.

Just before this last passage, Todd reveals his Scheherazade-like tendencies: "Every new sentence I set down is full of figures and implications that I'd love nothing better than to chase to their dens with you, but such chasing would involve new figures and new chases, so that I'm sure we'd never get the story started, much less ended, if I let my inclinations run unleashed" (pp. 8-9). Todd makes several comments about trying to get on with less digressions, but is not really successful in doing it. Digressions are healthy signs of life in Scheherazadian narrators. From their point of view, "Everything, I'm afraid, is significant, and nothing is finally important" (p. 12). He decides to "stick to the facts," and not comment. That way, he may digress, but at least he will have some hope of reaching the end: "and when I lapse from grace, I shall at any rate be able to congratulate myself on my excellent intentions" (p. 13). And so it goes: back and forth, back and forth. He must reach the end without digressions but he won't be able to resist digressions. "Now watch," he says, "how I can move when I really care to." He doesn't really care to, however, since in his capacity as narrator this sort of movement only draws him nearer to the end, and to death. Significantly, Todd combines the constant presence of death in his life with a reference to his writing. His chronic heart trouble means that "someday, any day, I may fall quickly dead, without any warning—perhaps before I complete this

sentence . . ." (p. 11). We venture to hope that, somehow, the flow of his sentence will assure the continued beating of his heart. We learn in Barth's most recent work, *Letters* (1979), that Todd has, in fact, continued to write, continued to live. Barth postpones the end of his character's narration and so postpones the end of his own as well.

I have saved Nabokov until last because *Ada* contrasts so markedly with the *Dunyazadiad*. Whereas Barth explicitly retells the story of *The Thousand and One Nights* and suggests that Scheherazade is the very model of the modern narrator, Nabokov mentions *The Nights* only obliquely. In *Ada* the implications for narrative theory are indirect, yet the text insistently adopts Scheherazade's stance, for it constitutes a masterful artifice of postponement. It can thus serve as a bridge between Proust, Borges, and Barth, who invoke Scheherazade overtly, and a number of other texts that illustrate the paradigm of *Arabian Nights* though they do not allude to it specifically.

Ada is a story of gaps, of continually displaced desire—hence part of its erotic charm. Van and Ada meet first as children and conduct hurried trysts in gardens and palatial country houses throughout their youth, but Ada marries someone else, and so the full satisfaction of their mutual desire is endlessly delayed.[27] The love story consists of moments snatched here and there. Near the end of the novel, after the death of Ada's husband, when she and Van are finally about to meet for a good long rendezvous at a Swiss hotel, the strategy of delayed satisfaction reaches a peak of marvelously comic exaggeration. After an intimate dinner for two, when Van tells Ada fondly that they have their old rooms back, plus, significantly, an extra bedroom, Ada announces that she has bad news for him: she must return to Geneva "to retrieve my things and maids" from customs.[28] Van is left that night to cool his "ardor" alone, by writing (of course). Ada comes back to the hotel in the middle of the night, and they reunite joyfully the next morning. The delay (besides keeping the reader waiting) has permitted Van to finish his work on "The Texture of Time." Indeed, it is almost as if satisfied desire signals a kind of death (deflection of the energy to write?), for "a little later" that morning (presumably after their lovemaking), "Van . . . was kissing her dear cold hands, gratefully, gratefully, in full defiance of death" (p. 427).

Before this encounter, when Van is waiting for Ada, we overhear parts of "The Texture of Time" as Van composes it. At first, Van's purpose appears to be to describe (yet again—there are references to Bergson and Proust) the nature of time. He does touch on various theoretical concerns—time and space, relativity, the past, present, and future. But, more significantly, Van has couched his study of time in amorous terms. It forms an integral part of his love for Ada. He begins by saying that "I wish to caress Time." He wants to measure "the Tender Interval," to extract time "from its soft hollow." In writing about time with sensual words, he conquers time by having his love assimilate it.[29] Van's description of his literary project also describes *Ada* itself. Very near the end, he applies to himself the kind of countdown that readers experience as they finger the few pages left in a book, pages that announce the imminent fictional end of the characters and of reading. Van tries to sleep "on one side only, so as not to hear his heart: he had made the mistake one night in 1920 of calculating the maximal number of its remaining beats (allowing for another half-century), and now the preposterous hurry of the countdown irritated him and increased the rate at which he could hear himself dying" (p. 430). Like Proust, then, to counteract this sense of personal death, Van uses time against itself in his work. At the end of Part Four, which contains passages from "The Texture of Time," time remains undefined, except in amorous terms. Ada wonders whether it is worthwhile attempting such a definition, and the part ends with her words: "We can never know Time. Our senses are simply not meant to perceive it. It is like—" (p. 427). Van and Ada's love prevails—its end, like that of the open-ended novel that contains it, repeatedly postponed.

A final postponement/perpetuation of "Vaniada" is foretold just before it occurs: "One can even surmise that if our time-racked, flat-lying couple ever intended to die they would die, as it were, *into* the finished book, into Eden or Hades, into the prose of the book or the poetry of its blurb" (p. 443). This is just what does happen: Van and Ada die into the finished book, into fictional life; the remaining pages of *Ada* do contain just this "blurb." After cliché-ridden summaries, the puff ends with a promise that the book also contains "much, much more." The final change of voice constitutes the narrator's metamorphosis into a generalized literary voice—the book reviewer, a comically reduced and reductive yet still eternal reader.

A specific reference to *Arabian Nights* is woven into a love scene between Van and Ada: "on a willow islet amidst the quietest branch of the blue Ladore," Van says:

> "Now I'm Scheher, . . . and you are his Ada, and that's your green prayer carpet."
>
> Their visits to that islet remained engraved in the memory of that summer with entwinements that no longer could be untangled. (p. 167)

Their "entwinements" of memory recall the complications of Scheherazade's narrative and its descendants, and they too are strengthened by embraces. In the phrase Van utters on the islet, we witness the merging of Van and Ada into "Scheher-his-Ada," into "Vaniada," a cooperative narrating voice similar to Barth's combination of the genie and Scheherazade. In *Ada*, Van narrates, but Ada reads and annotates, as we do. Together they constitute a replica of Scheherazade, delaying the end of their desire, their book, and their lives. At the end of this chapter, the aging Van makes an addition to his earlier text concerning Ada's identity. As he thus lengthens his narrative, he admits that "I am weak. I write badly. I may die tonight. My magic carpet no longer skims over crown

canopies and gaping nestlings, and her rarest orchids. Insert" (p. 170). As with Marcel, Jaromir Hladik, Todd Andrews, and Scheherazade, the reader senses that his storytelling is keeping him alive.

The list of strategies for postponing fictional death in modern literature and of texts that incorporate them seems, appropriately enough, to be almost endless. Several of Faulkner's narrators—Addie Bundren, Quentin Compson, Rosa Coldfield—project the sense that they are somehow staving off death and dissolution by telling their stories. Their descendants in *The Death of Artemio Cruz, One Hundred Years of Solitude,* and *The Obscene Bird of Night* do the same. The frantic narrator of *Death on the Installment Plan* fights with words against the sure approach of death in the title. He emits them so fast they are punctuated primarily by ellipses, as if his world would cave in on him were he ever to stop talking. Likewise, as Barbara Hardy points out, many of Beckett's characters seem to "narrate for dear life."[30] Earlier in the century, the dialogues between Naphta and Settembrini in Thomas Mann's *The Magic Mountain* take on a similar urgency, though in an entirely different mode. The narrative on the mountain owes part of its magic to the presence of death it fights against. More recently, the narrator of Robbe-Grillet's *In the Labyrinth* postpones the end of his text with numerous repetitions of scenes and details before his final, disillusioned exit from the stage. There, particularly, the reader confronts what seems like a pure desire to narrate, and perhaps all that keeps him going is his pure desire to read.

Carlos Fuentes has recently called *Finnegans Wake* a "scheheracharade"; the term can extend to the self-generative tendency of much modern fiction that, like *Finnegans Wake*, prolongs itself through extensive wordplay: "Through puns, Joyce destroys one word so that another or several more are born from the ruins of the mangled term. So in its very definition *Finnegans Wake* is a Scheheracharade, a vicoclometer, a collidoscope or kaleidoscope of collisions, a multiformograph and a meanderthal, a story of meanders, a valley of labyrinths."[31] In *Finnegans Wake* narration can perhaps be imagined to have gone beyond death and emerged on the other side; even death has not stopped the force of words.

In Gide's *The Counterfeiters*, when we look over Bernard's shoulder as he reads Edouard's diary (which includes among other things Laura's letter and the plans for Edouard's novel), we re-create the embedded structure of Scheherazade's tale, though here the pattern lacks some of the urgency of her story and plays on the idea of bad faith—counterfeiting—involved in narrative invention. It is almost a voyeuristic rather than a lifesaving endeavor. Here, as in *The Thousand and One Nights*, it is clear what is the frame and what the tale, though the reader may forget a given tale's frame when he is in the midst of it. This clarity often disappears in the Chinese box technique of Scheherazade's more recent descendants. As we have seen in Barth's retelling of *The Nights*, the end of a series of boxes may be indefinitely postponed by the oscillation between "pictures" and "frame." This is the case in Nabokov's *Pale Fire* also: has Shade invented Kinbote—or Kinbote, Shade?

Perhaps Julio Cortázar achieves the ultimate postponent of narrative death in his novel *Hopscotch*. There the fearful sentence of individual and narrative death ("bang, it's over") is commuted indefinitely by directions to go on to another set of chapters, the last two of which contain directions that lead to one another and back again ad infinitum. A cheap trick, perhaps, but one that Scheherazade might not scorn to use, for wouldn't she agree that all's fair in fiction's war with death?

NOTES

[1] Steven Cohan deals with some of these same issues in an excellent article, "Narrative Form and Death: *The Mill on the Floss* and *Mrs. Dalloway,*" *Genre,* 11 (Spring 1978), 109-29.

[2] See Frank Kermode, *The Sense of an Ending: Studies in the Theory of Fiction* (New York: Oxford Univ. Press, 1966).

[3] Bruno Bettelheim, "The Frame Story of *Thousand and One Nights,*" in *The Uses of Enchantment: The Meaning and Importance of Fairy Tales* (New York: Knopf, 1976), p. 87.

[4] Emmanuel Cosquin, "Le Prologue-cadre des *Mille et une nuits,*" in *Etudes Folkloriques* (Paris: Champion, 1922), pp. 264-347.

[5] Tzvetan Todorov, *The Poetics of Prose,* trans. Richard Howard (Ithaca, N.Y.: Cornell Univ. Press, 1977), p. 67.

[6] Roland Barthes, *Sade, Fourier, Loyola* (Paris: Seuil, 1971), p. 165.

[7] André Gide, *Journal: 1889-1939* (Paris: Gallimard, 1948), p. 41.

[8] *The Book of the Thousand Nights and a Night,* trans. Richard F. Burton (New York: Heritage Press, 1934), p. 3641.

[9] An exception to this critical lack is Judith Grossman, "Infidelity and Fiction: The Discovery of Women's Subjectivity in *Arabian Nights,*" *The Georgia Review,* 34 (Spring 1980), 113-26.

[10] Robert Alter, *Partial Magic: The Novel as Self-Conscious Genre* (Berkeley: Univ. of California Press, 1975), pp. 243-44.

[11] Marcel Proust, *Time Regained,* trans. Andreas Mayor, in *Remembrance of Things Past,* trans. C. K. Scott Moncrieff and Terence Kilmartin, 3 vols. (New York: Random House, 1981), III, 1101-2. All subsequent Proust citations are to this edition.

[12] See Michel Butor, *Les Sept Femmes de Gilbert le Mauvais* (Montpellier: Fata Morgana, 1972), p. 45, in which Butor imagines Marcel in terms of both Shahriyar, compelled to kill off the women he loves, and Scheherazade, attempting to save by narration the female population of his world.

[13] Leo Bersani discusses Marcel's strategies for maintaining an open-ended personality in "Proust and the Art of Incompletion," in *Aspects of Narrative: Selected Papers from the English Institute,* ed. J. Hillis Miller (New York: Columbia Univ. Press, 1971), pp. 119-42.

[14] Leo Spitzer discusses many ways in which Proust retards the ending points of his sentences, as he does the end point of the novel, in "Le Style de Marcel Proust," in his *Etudes de style* (Paris: Gallimard, 1970). See also Susan Suleiman, "The Parenthetical Function in *A la recherche du temps perdu,*" *PMLA,* 92 (1977), 458-70.

[15] Georges Poulet, "Proust and Human Time," in *Proust: A Collection of Critical Essays,* ed. René Girard (Englewood Cliffs: Prentice Hall, 1962), pp. 154-56.

[16] Both Borges and Nabokov refer in formal autobiographical pieces to old family editions of *Arabian Nights.* For both of them, the encounter with the tales was a seminal experience and stands near the origin of their literary careers. See Jorge Luis Borges, "An Autobiographical Essay," in *The Aleph and Other Stories, 1933-69* (New York: Dutton, 1970), p. 209; Vladimir Nabokov, *Speak, Memory* (1951; rev. ed. New York: G. P. Putnam's Sons, 1966), p. 244.

[17] Borges, *Labyrinths,* trans. Donald A. Yates and James E. Irby (New York: New Directions, 1962). In "The Zahir," the Borges persona resists in similar fashion a final self-definition.

[18] Borges, *Labyrinths,* pp. 193-96. Todorov cites this as a supreme example of literary embedding: "Nothing will ever again escape the narrative world, spreading over the whole of experience." *The Poetics of Prose,* p. 72.

[19] Borges, "Metáforas de las mil y una noches" in *Historia de la noche* (Buenos Aires: Emecé, 1977), pp. 21-23, my translation.

[20] Borges, "Alguien," in *Historia de la noche,* p. 27, my translation.

[21] Borges, "Los traductores de las *1001 noches,*" in *Historia de la eternidad* (Buenos Aires: Emecé, 1953), p. 99, my translation.

[22] "Muse, Spare Me," *Book Week* (26 September 1965; reprinted in *The Sense of the Sixties,* eds. Edward Quinn and Paul J. Dolan (New York: Free Press, 1968), pp. 440-44.

[23] The Chinese box structure is common to many of Barth's tales. At one point in "Menelaiad," for example,

dialogue is carried on from inside nests of up to seven sets of quotation marks. Punctuation like this constitutes a kind of shorthand, a sign, that refers to Scheherazade's stance. And as John O. Stark argues, "The reader, after he peels off all the layers of the onion, finds in the last layer only the impetus of storytelling," the vital impulse of fiction fighting death. See *The Literature of Exhaustion* (Durham: Duke Univ. Press, 1974), p. 121.

24 Barth, "Dunyazadiad," in *Chimera* (New York: Fawcett, 1973), p. 24.

25 *Atlantic Monthly* (August 1967), pp. 28-35.

26 Barth, *The Floating Opera* (New York: Avon, 1967), p. 7.

27 Ellen Pifer stresses the inhuman, unearthly nature of Van and Ada's passion; in this, Nabokov continues the fairy-tale atmosphere of the original *1001 Nights: Nabokov and the Novel* (Cambridge: Harvard Univ. Press, 1980), pp. 132-57.

28 Vladimir Nabokov, *Ada* (New York: Fawcett, 1969), p. 423.

29 Nabokov has suggested that "both memory and imagination are a negation of time," and perhaps also of death; "An Interview with Vladimir Nabokov," by Alfred Appel, in *Nabokov: The Man and His Work,* ed. L. S. Dembo (Madison: Univ. of Wisconsin Press, 1967), p. 32.

30 *Tellers and Listeners: The Narrative Imagination* (London: Athlone Press, 1975), p. 167.

31 Carlos Fuentes, *Cervantes o la crítica de la lectura* (Mexico: Joaquín Mortiz, 1976), p. 107, my translation.

David Galef

SOURCE: "The Self-Annihilating Artists of 'Pale Fire'," in *Twentieth Century Literature,* Vol. 31, No. 4, Winter, 1985, pp. 421-37.

[*In the following essay, Galef equates Kinbote's retreat from reality and ultimate suicide in Vladimir Nabokov's* Pale Fire *with the creation of his distorted and self-reflexive work of art.*]

The self-reflexive quality of Nabokov's *Pale Fire,* a fictional creation governed by its fictional creator, applies not only to the structure but also to the characters. As a group, they are self-referential, appearing as shadows, twins, and inverted images of one another. Though one may assign a central position to Kinbote as the author or manipulator, the source of his art remains in question. Critical suggestions for tracing the real Kinbote are numerous: Kinbote as a merging of Shade's artistic vision

and Gradus' urge toward destruction; Kinbote as Shade's aggrandizer, with Gradus as foreshadowed doom.[1] In the scholarly scuffle, not enough attention has been paid to a humbler figure, the character of Hazel Shade, the poet's daughter who commits suicide. Hazel functions as an interpretive key, revealing much about Kinbote and his grand extrapolation. In her cameo role, she represents the book's confabulation in miniature, the mixed success of art and annihilation.

As a character, Hazel appears only as a shadow across the work, an evoked memory. Though Shade never mentions his daughter's name in the cantos, her name is significant and provides a literary reference, a line from Scott's *The Lady of the Lake;* a stag who "deep his midnight lair had made / in lone Glenartney's hazel shade."[2] The romance of the Western Highlands serves as an ironic commentary on the real Hazel Shade, who is utterly devoid of dark beauty. Shade's descriptions, from the anxious parents' point of view, are both sorrowful and telling:

> Nature chose me so as to wrench and rend
> Your heart and mine. At first we'd smile and say:
> "All little girls are plump" or "Jim McVey
> (The family oculist) will cure that slight
> Squint in no time." And later: "She'll be quite
> Pretty, you know"; and, trying to assuage
> The swelling torment: "That's the awkward age."[3]

The picture is clear enough: Hazel is obese and unattractive, saddled moreover with a disfiguring squint. The little parental lies soon give way to Shade's confession, "It was no use, no use" (p. 44). Left out of most social activities, Hazel becomes moody and introspective, a bookish type by default. In one particularly wrenching passage, Shade relates:

> while children of her age
> Where cast as elves and fairies on the stage
> That *she'd* helped paint for the school pantomime,
> My gentle girl appeared as Mother Time,
> A bent charwoman with slop pail and broom. . . .
> (p. 44)

The image directly invokes Hardy's Father Time, another child wise and soured beyond his years, also doomed to die. In Hazel's situation, the ugly appearance of life extends unforgivably to herself.

Escape into books affords a temporary solace. Academia even offers a chance to excel, albeit to the exclusion of social life:

> The prizes won
> In French and history, no doubt, were fun;
> At Christmas parties games were rough, no doubt,
> And one shy little guest might be left out.
> (p. 44)

Inevitably, the scholastic seclusion becomes its own prison. She reads alone in her bedroom and the words themselves become emblematic of isolation: she pronounces *grimpen* as "Grim Pen" (p. 46), the four walls of her world.

The brief summation of Hazel's adolescence affords the same dismal view: "Alas, the dingy cygnet never turned / Into a wood duck" (p. 44). Teen-age romance is forever denied her, and the telephone remains silent. Since Hazel has become her own plaguesome reality, a change of scenery does her no good, and a trip to France only occasions more unhappiness:

> And she returned in tears, with new defeats,
> New miseries. On days when all the streets
> Of College Town led to the game, she'd sit
> On the library steps, and read or knit. . . .
>
> (p. 45)

She has gradually withdrawn from society but can take no comfort from her isolation. Since the world remains alienating and unchangeable, she tries to create a world of her own.

As Shade points out in his description, Hazel "might have been you, me, or some quaint blend" (p. 43), but she becomes perverse: "She had strange fears, strange fantasies, strange force / Of character . . ." (p. 45). Her father represents an edifying contrast. By his own admission, in his childhood he was "lame, asthmatic, fat" (p. 37), but was able to turn outward reality into art. Nabokov presents no clear source for the creation of good art. Hazel grows stunted from nurturing parents, while John Shade, orphaned early in life and brought up by "dear bizarre Aunt Maud" (p. 36), produces viable (there is no other word) art. If Nabokov does put forth a statement regarding art, it is concerned with the importance of connections. Aunt Maud, for instance, may have a taste for "realistic objects interlaced / With grotesque growths and images of doom," but she also lives "to hear the next babe cry" (p. 36). Morbid associations are fine, provided they are connected to life at one end.

Hazel's vision eventually turns inward, the imploded art of fantasy. The first indications are harmless enough, reversals of normal vision through palindromes: "She twisted words: pot, top, / Spider, redips. And 'powder' was 'red wop'" (p. 45). In her games with the lexicon of everyday life, she resembles her father, who enjoys the permutations of Word Golf. When words fail to transform reality to her satisfaction, however, she reaches beyond reality.

One of the words associated with Hazel is chtonic [sic] (p. 46),[4] a key to her developing interest. Forsaking the world which has forsaken her, she finds some romance in the creation of a private spirit world. As with Eliot in *Four Quartets,* from which the words *chthonic, grimpen,* and *sempiternal* are borrowed, she wants to go beyond mortal experience. Unlike Eliot or her father, however, she cannot write verse but can engage only in eidolism. Taking her cue from the recent death of her great-aunt Maud, she makes havoc in the name of the returned

spirit; she tries to bend natural law. A dog basket flies through the air; a scrapbook perambulates itself. Throwing things about is insufficiently arousing, however, and she succumbs to artistic elaboration. Kinbote narrates:

> But soon the poltergeist ran out of ideas in connection with Aunt Maud and became, as it were, more eclectic. All the banal motions that objects are limited to in such cases were gone through in this one. Saucepans crashed in the kitchen; a snowball was found (perhaps, prematurely) in the icebox; once or twice Sybil saw a plate sail by like a discus and land safely on the sofa; lamps kept lighting up in various parts of the house; chairs waddled away to assemble in the impassable pantry; mysterious bits of string were found on the floor; invisible revelers staggered down the staircase in the middle of the night; and one winter morning Shade, upon rising and taking a look at the weather, saw that the little table from his study upon which he kept a Bible-like Webster open at M was standing in a state of shock outdoors, on the snow. . . .
>
> (pp. 165-66)

As the parents quickly realize, Hazel is the instigator rather than the observer of these phenomena, the author of a private world of signs and images. What one may term an artistic universe, however, Shade's former typist Jane Dean labels "'an outward extension or expulsion of insanity'" (p. 166). The appraisal is not far from the truth. Where creation ceases to have any relevance to outward reality, it borders on madness. When art loses the vital connection to a world outside the artist, it becomes bound up with death. Art and obsession can become dangerously, fatally mixed.

True artistic obsession does not consume itself at once; it first expands its scope. Hazel's exploration of the spirit world resurfaces in a night vigil in an old barn, as she listens for personal messages. The barn episode is briefly mentioned in lines 345-47 of the poem and enlarged upon in Kinbote's commentary. Kinbote even goes so far as to create a mock scenario entitled "THE HAUNTED BARN" (p. 190), in which Hazel cannot bear the homey, deflating common sense of her parents. Her contact with the spirit world is moot; her hope of abstracting a pattern from what she envisions remains just a wish:

> The jumble of broken words and meaningless syllables which she managed at last to collect came out in her dutiful notes as a short line of simple letter-groups. I transcribe:
>
> pada ata lane pad not ogo old wart alan
> ther take feur far rant lant tal told
>
> (p. 188)

In "'The Viewer and the View,'" David Walker tries to piece together the bits to form a vague prophecy of Shade's death, but the analysis seems more wishful thinking than solid scholarship.[5] The meaning of Hazel's recopied farrago lies rather in the process itself, as Shade notes in Canto Two: *Life is a message scribbled in the dark* (p. 41). The allusion is nonetheless sympathetic. If

Hazel looks for meaning in a patternless existence or attempts to impose her own meaning, at least she cannot be blamed. As Nabokov has Kinbote relate at the close of "THE HAUNTED BARN," *Life is hopeless, afterlife heartless* (p. 192). Nabokov's tone, filtered through Kinbote, is that of a practicing artist: Hazel's necrotic vision is a perversion of art; hence, her art is a jumble. The sympathy is not for the artistic failure, but for the suffering of another human being. Significantly, John Shade later makes a poem from the incident, showing that art can be derived from any materials, provided it does not lose its attention to life. Mad art deals too much with death.

By the time of her sad blind date, Hazel has come near to madness. Reality is once more impinging upon her, forcing her half out of this world:

> She hardly ever smiled, and when she did
> It was a sign of pain. She'd criticize
> Ferociously our projects, and with eyes
> Expressionless sit on her tumbled bed
> Spreading her swollen feet, scratching her head
> With psoriatic fingernails, and moan,
> Murmuring dreadful words in monotone.
>
> (p. 45)

The urge for creation and the will to hate have reached a terrifying balance. The same madness which reduces her days to misery, however, also keeps her alive. She continues to believe, in the face of all opposing evidence, that somehow circumstances may change. As Shade notes, "I think she always nursed a small mad hope" (p. 46).[6] The failure of the date with Pete Dean kills that last hope, turning hate into self-destruction and creative evasion into the ultimate escape.

Hazel's last evening is actually her attempt to rub out her old identity. Images of blurriness and blankness pervade the scene, particularly during the fateful bus ride:

> *More headlights in the fog. There was no sense*
> *In window-rubbing: only some white fence*
> *And the reflector poles passed by unmasked.*
>
>   . . . . .
>
> *"I think," she said,*
> *"I'll get off here." "It's only Lochanhead."*
> *"Yes, that's okay." Gripping the stang, she*
> *   peered*
> *At ghostly trees. Bus stopped. Bus disappeared.*
>
> (p. 49)

The ghostly landscape of Lochanhead is evocative of Scott's Glenartney, but in a dreary, spiritually effacing enclosure. In this white, nonreflecting scene, Father Time patrols the lake, an adumbration of death. Hazel meets no one, however; in her last act of retreat, she is in perfect isolation: "The lake lay in the mist, its ice half drowned. / A blurry shape stepped off the reedy bank / Into a crackling, gulping swamp, and sank" (p. 51). The lake, elsewhere in the work a great reflective body, has become an opaque surface. If mirrors are reflecting surfaces

elsewhere in *Pale Fire,* they are even there no substitute for life. Mirrors, rather, represent art, and both, when blurred, are an attenuation of life. Hazel herself, a "blurry shape" halfway to evisceration, has lost the contours of her appearance. In an odd sense, by submerging herself, she has become Scott's "lady of the lake." Her final remove from reality is permanent. In a last irony that Hazel might have appreciated, she remains in her parents' memory as "a domestic ghost" (p. 41), a spirit at last.

In comparison to Hazel Shade, Charles Kinbote is a far grander artist, and a work of art in his own right. In his need to transform base reality, he creates the entire kingdom of Zembla through his bizarre annotation. Moreover, the true conundrum of *Pale Fire* revolves around Kinbote, since his warped commentary creates not only new facts and characters, but also "the monstrous semblance of a novel" (p. 86), the text itself. Nonetheless, Kinbote—be he Charles II or demented Botkin—suffers the same fate as Hazel. Based on a labyrinthine structure of false mirrors and props, his fantasy world eventually encloses him, leaving him in darkness.

Through Kinbote's magniloquent self-revelations, one learns a good deal more about him than about Hazel, but without the same objectivity. One may speculate about the change in Hazel's story if she had related it herself; the fact remains that Kinbote cannot hide his madness, since it is inexorably linked with his Zemblan creation. Delusions of grandeur and attendant paranoia shine through the most glittering passages describing his royal past:

> A group of especially devout Extremists calling
> themselves the Shadows had got together and swore
> to hunt down the King and kill him wherever he
> might be. They were, in a sense, the shadowy twins
> of the Karlists and indeed several had cousins or
> even brothers among the followers of the King.
>
> (p. 150)

Kinbote's use of the third person, rather than serving as modesty's cloak, only allows the conceits of Zembla and King Charles II full exposure. Where Hazel's art is solipsistic, Kinbote's creation is megalomaniac. Hazel, for example, shuns real mirrors, whereas Kinbote glories in them, from using "a fop's hand mirror" (p. 121) to gazing at his multiple reflection in "a triptych of bottomless light, a really fantastic mirror, signed with a diamond . . ." (p. 111). As in Nabokov's art, Kinbote's images collect and reflect endlessly.

If the magnitude of Kinbote's creation dwarfs Hazel's, the etiology is the same: an aesthetic retreat from reality. On the most pedestrian level, Kinbote is a boringly tenacious pedant with homosexual urgencies, a lonely expatriate in America whose one claim to fame is a book on surnames. Though one cannot judge how far back Kinbote began to construct his imaginary kingdom, the conditions for its creation are well established by the time he settles in New Wye:

> Often, almost nightly, throughout the spring of
> 1959, I had feared for my life. Solitude is the

playfield of Satan. I cannot describe the depths of my loneliness and distress. There was naturally my famous neighbor just across the lane, and at one time I took in a dissipated young roomer (who generally came home long after midnight). Yet I wish to stress that cold hard core of loneliness which is not good for a displaced soul.

(p. 95)

The same embittered isolation that encompassed Hazel surrounds Kinbote. As an expatriate, he is far from home; as a homosexual in staid New Wye, he leads an inverted life; as a social misfit, he alienates everyone. As he relates in his foreword, a clubwoman "said to me in the middle of a grocery store, 'You are a remarkably disagreeable person. I fail to see how John and Sybil can stand you,' and, exasperated by my polite smile, she added: 'What's more, you are insane'" (p. 25).

Apparently, Kinbote gets along with almost no one, and his endless sexual trysts are probably more than half-imaginary. If one adds up all the people in his claimed liaisons, the figure might total half of New Wye. More revealing is the betrayal by a roomer named Bob, who brings in "a fiery-haired whore from Exton who had left her combings and reek in all three bathrooms" (pp. 26-27). Most of Kinbote's sexual escapades seem to stem from bribes on his part, and one is even led to question the handsome physiognomy with which he credits himself. A fellow faculty member, Gerald Emerald, refers to him as "the Great Beaver" (p. 24). The discrepancy between Kinbote's imagined life and his real circumstances may be greater than many critics assume. David Walker has suggested that Kinbote's motel room is actually the padded room of an asylum.[7] One cannot rule out this possibility; in any event, Kinbote's alienation is incontrovertible.

All the factors which circumscribe Kinbote in his own little hell do not, of course, make him an artist; they merely provide the impetus for escape. Kinbote's resemblances, or Zemblances, to Hazel do not apply only to mental anguish, though. The transformations they ring on reality are also of the same mind. Discussing Hazel's fascination with palindromes, Kinbote mentions his own predilection for turning things backward: "But then it is also true that Hazel Shade resembled me in certain respects" (p. 193). Playing with words leads inevitably to playing with worlds in a Joycean mode.[8] As always, Kinbote's efforts eclipse Hazel's. Where she is content with "red wop" from "powder," Kinbote changes Jacob Gradus into d'Argus, Jacques de Grey, Jack Grey, all reflections in "a really fantastic mirror, signed with a diamond by its maker, Sudarg of Bokay" (p. 111). The obnoxious faculty member Gerald Emerald becomes, through a Russian twist, Izumrudov, "of the emerald." Nodo and Odon, two of the Shadows, are half-brothers and reversals of one another. The shades and reflections become ubiquitous. What turns up in Shade's poem may be enfolded into Kinbote's gossip anent New Wye, or triply folded into his chronicle of Zembla. The pair of Soviet spies who appear in one incarnation as Andronikov and Niagara and in another as Andron and

Niagarushka (pp. 244, 255) may just be a transformation that gets out of control. The point is that while Hazel synthesizes a mirror level of meaning through words, Kinbote develops an entire world around such principles, an exegetical edifice of words. The kingdom of Zembla and Kinbote's role in it grow to include a deposed king, secret passages, crown jewels, and its own Shadows. Kinbote, though mad to think that Shade would write a poem about such an unbelievable landscape, is right in one respect: his Zembla is a work of art. Nabokov has stated, in a typically Nabokovian manner, "art, at its greatest, is fantastically deceitful and complex."[9] In this respect, at least, he accords Kinbote an accolade.

Kinbote's dealings with reality are another matter altogether. The result of Kinbote's exegesis on Shade's poem, for instance, is deranged poetry. He consistently warps everything around him into reflections of himself, his own type of art. Fortunately for the text, Nabokov has endowed Kinbote with a brilliant imagination, in many ways more inventive and lexically interesting than Shade's. In describing a process as mundane as the ventilation of a house, he can be absolutely coruscating: "The heating system was a farce, depending as it did on registers on the floor where from the tepid exhalations of a throbbing and groaning basement furnace were transmitted to the rooms with the faintness of a moribund's last breath" (p. 19).

He is a verbal prestidigitator, not unsurprisingly in the Nabokovian vein, capable of turning dross into flowers like the conjurer mentioned in the foreword. Shade, too, is capable of artistic transformation—Kinbote uses the conjurer analogy to apply to the poet, not himself—but his art remains grounded in the mundanities of everyday life. He does deal with life, art, and death, but his approach is the opposite of Kinbote's reading public events out of his private fantasy. As Lucy Maddox points out, "Shade attempts to translate public fate into private significance. . . . "[10] Kinbote, on the other hand, moves toward structures as vaporous as Hazel's spirits.

Kinbote's commentary on his word-creations is elucidating if somewhat skewed. He sees himself as an appropriator of patterns, a thief with artistic tendencies, but his language belies the statement:

> Although I am capable, through long dabbling in blue magic, of imitating any prose in the world (but singularly enough not verse—I am a miserable rhymester), I do not consider myself a true artist, save in one matter: I can do what only a true artist can do—pounce upon the forgotten butterfly of revelation, wean myself abruptly from the habit of things, see the web of the world, and the warp and the weft of that web. Solemnly I weighed in my hand what I was carrying under my left armpit, and for a moment I found myself enriched with an indescribable amazement as if informed that fireflies were making decodable signals on behalf of stranded spirits, or that a bat was writing a legible tale of torture in the bruised and branded sky.
>
> (p. 289)

Kinbote's art is as beautiful as it is otherworldly, but by now one must be wary of his pronunciamentos. His evaluation of the package he carries—"I was holding all Zembla pressed to my heart" (p. 289)—is a fantastic importation to the scene, having no basis in reality. Rather, all of Zembla resides in his head. The references to charmed fireflies or a *Myotis sublatus* writing messages hearken back to Hazel and her private world of signs. Shade's art is solid in its reassuring weight of index cards. Kinbote's and Hazel's arts, while not inferior conceptions, represent ethereal, escapist visions.

One may view the emerging parallels between Kinbote and Hazel as just that: not exact equivalencies but correspondences between the characters. Nabokov puts it more strongly: "There are no 'real' doubles in my novels."[11] In the absence of outright doppelgängers, then, the suicide-daughter is a hazel shade of Kinbote. The affiliation between the two even helps explain certain phenomena outside their mad art. Shade's infinite patience with Kinbote, for example, makes perfect sense when one realizes that Shade sees his deranged daughter again in his next-door neighbor. If Shade is overly tolerant to Kinbote through an Oedipal link, the relationship also works in reverse. As Phyllis Roth notes in her analysis: "The evidence of the Oedipal situation in the novel is extensive. To begin, Kinbote sees himself as the child of Sybil and John. The most apparent manifestation of this is his rivalry with their deceased daughter Hazel Shade."[12] In fact, Kinbote's constant desire to see Shade represents more than collaring the nearest available neighbor; it is a childish bid for attention. Similarly, Hazel's attempts to subvert her parents' reality with her own fantasy are monstrously realized in Kinbote's perversion of Shade's poem. The danger lies in the fantasy taking over the artist, as well as reality.

Kinbote and Hazel suffer ultimately from a lack of relevance to their surroundings. If, as June Perry Levine suggests for a reading of the novel, "Significance is achieved by interconnection,"[13] betrayal arises through a loss of connection. The relation between the made-up image and the self is blanked out, as if one looked into a mirror and saw no reflection. Rejected by Pete Dean, Hazel becomes hazier, as others simply ignore her presence. Wrapped in her spiritual fancies, she has become a wraith even before her death. Kinbote encounters a similar betrayal when reality excludes him. Attaching his entire identity to Shade's presumed exposition of Zembla, he becomes mentally disjointed when he finds nothing of himself there:

> I started to read the poem. I read faster and faster. I sped through it, snarling, as a furious young heir through an old deceiver's testament. Where were the battlements of my sunset castle? Where was Zembla the Fair? Where her spine of mountains? Where her long thrill through the mist? And my lovely flower boys, and the spectrum of the stained windows, and the Black Rose Paladins, and the whole marvelous tale? Nothing of it was there! The complex contribution I had been pressing upon him with a

hypnotist's patience and a lover's urge was simply not there. Oh, but I cannot express the agony!
>
> (p. 296)

Apart from his personal myth, he is less than real; he is nonexistent. Accordingly, he attempts to re-create the entire structure of Zembla in a lonely motel room in Cedarn, Utana. Here, Kinbote shows greater imaginative force than Hazel, trying once more to resurrect himself through art. The burden of maintaining such a fantasy is too heavy, though. Not only does it exhaust the creator, but it also drags him down, further and further away from any connection with the real world. In his lucid moments, he dreams of the end of the farce he has created, the extinction of himself.

In a self-reflexive fiction, even the end is internally generated. If Hazel engineers her own finish, Kinbote creates a character for that purpose, a destructive anti-force named Gradus lurking in the Zemblan terrain. Though in some senses a mere construct, Gradus has a motivation, the act of regicide, and a personality which stands for all that Kinbote detests:

> Mere springs and coils produced the inward movements of our clockwork man. He might be termed a Puritan. One essential dislike, formidable in its simplicity, pervaded his dull soul: he disliked injustice and deception. He disliked their union—they were always together—with a wooden passion that neither had, nor needed, words to express itself.
>
> (p. 152)

Gradus is against deception, Kinbote's delight; he cannot use words, Kinbote's stock-in-trade. Nonetheless, Kinbote works upon him as with all his other creations, granting him a half-dozen aliases and a woefully inept record of assassinations. As the idea of creation blooms in Kinbote's brain, so does the idea of annihilation.

Once Kinbote has created Gradus, the henchman assumes a seemingly independent existence. He leaves Zembla and follows the path of the exiled king through Europe. He even appears in Shade's poem—as noted by Kinbote—through the sinister permutations of "gradual," "gray," and the unused variant "Tanagra dust" (pp. 77, 231). Since Kinbote associates the gunman who kills Shade with Gradus, the death Gradus represents becomes paired with Shade:

> His departure for Western Europe, with a sordid purpose in his heart and a loaded gun in his pocket, took place on the very day that an innocent poet was beginning Canto Two of *Pale Fire*. We shall accompany Gradus in constant thought, as he makes his way from distant dim Zembla to green Appalachia, through the entire length of the poem, following the road of its rhythm, riding past in a rhyme, skidding around the corner of a run-on, breathing with the caesura, swinging down to the foot of the page from line to line as from branch to branch, hiding between two words (see note to line 596), reappearing on the horizon of a new

canto, steadily marching nearer in iambic motion, crossing streets, moving up with his valise on the escalator of the pentameter, stepping off, boarding a new train of thought, entering the hall of a hotel, putting out the bedlight, while Shade blots out a word, and falling asleep as the poet lays down his pen for the night.

(p. 78)

The link between Shade's poetry and Gradus' journey toward America is based on Shade as the creator, yet Kinbote's own fiction is based on the poem. David Packman comments on the relation: "The novel measures its unfolding in relation to Gradus's trajectory. The road he covers is the text's narrative line. In his journey Gradus covers real roads that, in the representation, become lines of words upon the page."[14] Words create the situation and its undoing, and therein lies the double nature of Kinbote's logorrhea. As with Hazel, his art is fatally tinged. Reading Gradus into Shade's poem, he sees beyond art into death: "we cannot help reading into these lines something more than mirrorplay and mirage shimmer. We feel doom . . ." (p. 135). The artistry which produced Gradus is flawed. It embraces and encompasses death as an alternative to reality.

Though Gradus begins as something of a nullity, he begins to achieve a larger-than-life quality, overshadowing the other Zemblan figures as the notes progress:

> Gradus is now much nearer to us in space and time than he was in the preceding cantos. He has short upright black hair. We can fill in the bleak oblong of his face with most of its elements such as thick eyebrows and a wart on the chin. He has a ruddy but unhealthy complexion. We see, fairly in focus, the structure of his somewhat mesmeric organs of vision. We see his melancholy nose with its crooked ridge and grooved tip. We see the mineral blue of his jaw and the gravelly pointillé of his suppressed mustache.
>
> (p. 277)

The physical closeness is startling, as if one were looking through a microscope. The personification to end the fiction has become of interest in himself as Kinbote focuses in. Nabokov, too, believes in the microscopic approach:

> There is, it would seem, in the dimensional scale of the world, a kind of delicate meeting place between imagination and knowledge, a point, arrived at by diminishing large things and enlarging small things, that is intrinsically artistic.[15]

Nabokov, however, is capable of maintaining the proper proportion and distance. When Kinbote employs the same technique, he has fallen in love with his creation again, in this instance collaborating with his demise. He has assumed the role of a royal fugitive tracked by a gray assassin, all part of his intricate pattern. As always, the attempt is to dislocate reality, not that his friend Shade was killed by a criminal madman from the local asylum, but that the killing was the result of a continental web of intrigue and a tragicomically inept aim. In transforming Jack Gray into

Jacob Gradus, though, Kinbote internalizes the figure as part of his creation. Kinbote's future promises "a bigger, more respectable, more competent Gradus" (p. 301), but since this new Gradus really sprang into being after Shade's death, he is present from the start of Kinbote's foreword. He has become part of Kinbote's art, a destructive force in the artist's mind.

Evidence of Kinbote's concomitant desire to murder and create occurs throughout his notes, usually adjacent to a particularly unpleasant reality. Describing his betrayal at the hands of his former roomer Bob, he posits a way to halt the memory:

> At times I thought that only by self-destruction could I hope to cheat the relentlessly advancing assassins who were in me, in my eardrums, in my pulse, in my skull, rather than on that constant highway looping up over me and around my heart as I dozed off only to have my sleep shattered by that drunken, impossible, unforgettable Bob's return to Candida's or Dee's former bed.
>
> (p. 97)

Self-destruction and self-aggrandizement meet in Kinbote's mind as twin evasions of circumstance. As his creation progresses, however, its poetry is insufficient to mask his drab hideaway, and the secondary solution poses an escape. The retreat into the dark, the vitiation of his creation, begins to have physical effects: "Whatever energy I possessed has quite ebbed away lately, and these excruciating headaches now make impossible the mnemonic effort and eye strain that the drawing of another such plan would demand" (p. 107). The plan referred to is the drawing of Onhava Palace, once an invention that Kinbote could have elaborated on endlessly. Now, elaboration in the face of dumb reality is draining him. When his creation draws to an end, his created existence may also flow away. In a not-to-be-missed parentheses, he hints "(see eventually my ultimate note)" (p. 101).[16] In fact, as Hazel's failure at living is discernible from the start, Kinbote's end, too, begins with his introduction of himself. It is a portrait of a mind tearing itself to pieces, spewing out polychrome fragments for an imagined audience.

Kinbote heralds his mental decline from the start of his extravagant foreword. Unable to marshal his thoughts on the page, he complains of a competing reality: "There is a very loud amusement park right in front of my present lodgings" (p. 13). Lunacy has bloomed in the third paragraph. Even before that non sequitur of non sequiturs, though, he talks of "Canto Two, your favorite" (p. 13), as if he were conversing with an invisible confidant. Actually, the work is as much a confession as it is an arrogation of the text. In the conclusion to his foreword, he claims, "without my notes Shade's text simply has no human reality at all" (p. 28), but even at this early juncture one is aware of inversions. Kinbote's own commentary is precisely the self-referential creation he claims Shade's poem is. He does have some realization of the truth, and his greatest moments of expatiation contain, as Nabokov would have considered anagramatically apt, some expiation.

As a master creator, Kinbote bows to an even greater creator, though in typically Kinbotian fashion he promulgates "our Zemblan brand of protestantism" (p. 224). Just as Hazel hung on a spirit world, Kinbote depends on an afterlife, which he views more and more as a welcome relief from "these dark evenings that are destroying my brain" (p. 123). As he develops the idea of religion in his notes, God provides the divine afflatus, the opposite of nihilistic despair. More important, God provides a comforting afterlife which Kinbote uses as a rationale for suicide:

> With this divine mist of utter dependence permeating one's being, no wonder one is tempted, no wonder one weighs on one's palm with a dreamy smile the compact firearm in its case of suede leather hardly bigger than a castlegate key or a boy's seamed purse, no wonder one peers over the parapet into an inviting abyss.
>
> (p. 220)

Kinbote's interest in suicide corresponds to his tendency to fantasize. Ever the artist, he imbues the final act with a poetry of its own. Of the various means of divorcing soul from body, he prefers falling:

> The ideal drop is from an aircraft, your muscles relaxed, your pilot puzzled, your packed parachute shuffled off, cast off, shrugged off—farewell, *shootka* (little chute)! Down you go, but all the while you feel suspended and buoyed as you somersault in slow motion like a somnolent tumbler pigeon, and sprawl supine on the eiderdown of the air, or lazily turn to embrace your pillow, enjoying every last minute of soft, deep, death-padded life, with the earth's green seesaw now above, now below, and the voluptuous crucifixion, as you stretch yourself in the growing rush, in the nearing swish, and then your loved body's obliteration in the Lap of the Lord.
>
> (p. 221)

Seen in this light, self-murder becomes more a change of scenery than the onset of darkness. Life is a *shootka* ("little joke" in Russian). The phrase "death-padded life" shows an artistic merging of two extremes—but death precedes. As for the scenery around him, it has become repulsive: "We who burrow in filth every day may be forgiven perhaps the one sin that ends all sins" (p. 222). Kinbote's original fantasy was to occlude base reality, and the dream of death which supersedes it is another such attempt. What he cannot abide is a void, and once he has assured himself of a hereafter, he moves ineluctably toward it.

By the time of his last note, he has arrived at the same spiritual nadir as the suicidal Hazel. The final paragraphs have an uncanny valedictory note: "Yes, better stop. My notes and self are petering out. Gentlemen, I have suffered very much, and more than any of you can imagine" (p. 300). As to his future plans, he is hazy: other disguises, other semblances. The stage play he thinks of writing, however, shows his realization that he has in-

vented himself: "a lunatic who intends to kill an imaginary king, another lunatic who imagines himself to be that king, and a distinguished old poet who stumbles by chance into the line of fire, and perishes in the clash between the two figments" (p. 301).

With the recognition that his existence has been a figment, he has little to do but end the game. His projections for continued existence are merely a last misdirection, an unwillingness to go out without the possibility of an encore. If, in this day and age, one can still trust the author's judgment of his work, one has only to go to Nabokov for the eschatology. In an interview, he refers to "the day on which Kinbote committed suicide (and he certainly did after putting the last touches to his edition of the poem). . . . "[17] A consummate artist, with an emphasis on "consummate," Kinbote finishes first his commentary and then himself. As Hazel's headnote, so to speak, was *"Life is a message scribbled in the dark"* (p. 41), Shade's poem also provides an italicized tribute to Kinbote: *"Man's life as commentary to abstruse / Unfinished poem"* (p. 67). The twin epitaphs represent two existences almost irrelevant to reality, lived out rather through transmutation and fantasy. Final judgment, if not suspended, is at least moot. Nabokov obviously applauds consummate artistry, but when the vision consumes the artist, one can only laud the art and lament the means.

Though one may resent Kinbote's falsification of reality as opposed to Shade's poetic extension of life, the sympathy of the work seems to rest in the end with Kinbote. Against the arrogance of the artist, one detects a maundering vulnerability, Kinbote's recognition of himself as an aberration. "Imagine a soft, clumsy giant" (p. 17), he puts forth as a self-description in his foreword, and the evocation is apt. Here, the parallel with Hazel lends a useful perspective: both figures are freaks, in Nabokov's artistic conception and in their own artistic dreams. The author extends appreciation for their art, sympathy for their lives. This compassionate bond goes a long way toward refuting those critics who insist that Nabokov's vision is brilliant but cold. His sense of affection, though belittling at times, might almost amount to love. As Mary McCarthy wrote:

> Love is the burden of *Pale Fire*, love and loss. Love is felt as a kind of homesickness, that yearning for union described by Plato, the pining for the other half of a once-whole body, the straining of the soul's black horse to unite with the white. The sense of loss in love, of separation . . . binds mortal men in a common pattern—the elderly couple watching TV in a lighted room, and the "queer" neighbor watching *them* from his window. But it is most poignant in the outsider: the homely daughter stood up by her date, the refugee. . . . [18]

The fatal vision of a flawed artist is always of interest to the depicter, and not just as a cautionary tale, or for the setting up of a reflexive frame. One feels tenderness for one's creations, particularly those who seem too frail for life. As for the art produced by such figures, a distorting mirror has its own special reflection.

NOTES

[1] Andrew Field, in *Nabokov: His Life in Art* (Boston: Little, Brown, 1967), goes so far as to suggest that Kinbote is a creation of Shade's.

[2] Sir Walter Scott, *The Complete Poetical Works of Sir Walter Scott,* Cambridge ed. (Boston: Houghton Mifflin, 1900), p. 156. I am indebted to Mary McCarthy's article "A Bolt from the Blue" (*New Republic,* 4 June 1962, pp. 21-27) for this reference.

[3] Vladimir Nabokov, *Pale Fire* (New York: Putnam's, 1962), pp. 43-44. All subsequent references refer to this edition, and are cited parenthetically in the text.

[4] Though this misspelling of *chthonic* may be only a typographical error, it appears that way in all editions of *Pale Fire.*

[5] David Walker, "'The Viewer and the View': Chance and Choice in *Pale Fire,*" *Studies in American Fiction,* 4: 213.

[6] See William K. Wimsatt, ed., *Alexander Pope: Selected Poetry and Prose,* 2nd ed. (New York: Holt, 1972). "A small mad hope" is the modern, reduced equivalent of Pope's "Hope springs eternal in the human breast: / Man never Is, but always To be blest" (*An Essay on Man,* Epistle I, lines 95-96). Shade was a scholar of Pope and wrote his poem in Popeian couplets. The original reference to Zembla, "At Greenland, Zembla, or the Lord knows where," also stems from *An Essay on Man:* Epistle II, line 224.

[7] Walker, "'The Viewer and the View,'" p. 219.

[8] The comparison with Joyce is particularly salient with respect to a passage from *Ulysses,* where Martha writes a letter to Henry Flower, a.k.a. Bloom: "I called you naughty boy because I do not like that other world" (James Joyce, *Ulysses* [New York: Random House, 1961], p. 77). The overflow from words to worlds crops up continually in ensuing passages.

[9] Vladimir Nabokov, *Strong Opinions* (New York: McGraw-Hill, 1973), p. 33.

[10] Lucy Maddox, *Nabokov's Novels in English* (Athens: Univ. of Georgia Press, 1983), p. 19.

[11] Alfred Appel, Jr., "An Interview with Vladimir Nabokov," in L. S. Dembo, ed., *Nabokov: The Man and His Work* (Madison: Univ. of Wisconsin Press, 1967), p. 37.

[12] Phyllis A. Roth, "The Psychology of the Double in Nabokov's *Pale Fire,*" *Essays in Literature* (Western Illinois University), 2:222-23.

[13] June Perry Levine, "Vladimir Nabokov's *Pale Fire:* 'The Method of Composition' as Hero," in *International Fiction Review,* 5:108.

[14] David Packman, *"Pale Fire:* The Vertigo of Interpretation," in his *Vladimir Nabokov: The Structure of Literary Desire* (Columbia: Univ. of Missouri Press, 1982), p. 83.

[15] Vladimir Nabokov, *Speak, Memory* (New York: Putnam's, 1966), pp. 166-67.

[16] Nabokov's use of parentheses would make a small study in itself. He is the only author I am aware of who regularly locates the most significant part of a sentence within real or tonal brackets.

[17] Appel, "An Interview with Vladimir Nabokov," p. 29.

[18] McCarthy, "A Bolt from the Blue," p. 26.

Bruce A. Goebel

SOURCE: "'If Nobody Had to Die': The Problem of Mortality in Gertrude Stein's 'The Geographical History of America'," in *Philological Quarterly,* Vol. 70, No. 2, Spring, 1991, pp. 237-52.

[*In the following essay, Goebel probes the interwined crises of personal identity and mortality in Gertrude Stein's fiction.*]

While still quite young, Gertrude Stein overheard that her parents had planned for only five children. As the seventh child, it made her "feel funny" to think that her birth had depended upon the deaths of two earlier Stein children. This sudden awareness of mortality, or as she put it, this loss of the "everlasting feeling," haunted her the rest of her life. In *Everybody's Autobiography,* written at the age of sixty, she acknowledges:

> Then there was the fear of dying, anything living knows about that, and when that happens anybody can think if I had died before there was anything but there is no thinking that one was never born until you hear accidentally that there were to be five children and if two little ones had not died there would be no Gertrude Stein, of course not.[1]

Feeling the tenuousness of mere animal existence, she struggled to counter such a limited definition of herself. As a child she was adventurous and thought of ways of becoming immortalized in the "folklore of California."[2] Thus, even in her youth she was aware of the transcendent quality of language and stories. Later in life, she would increasingly turn to her writing as a means of countering the self-doubt brought on by her awareness of death.

Her concern with mortality is one of the unifying elements underlying her oeuvre, so much so that one could claim this fear as the driving force behind her innovative aesthetic project. As Catherine N. Parke suggests:

> Stein's invention of an alternative to scepticism, an alternative for which she invented a new kind of narrative to embody her radical, non-sceptical theory of knowledge, arose paradoxically from her own radical self-doubt—a doubt quite literally about her existence. . . . [3]

Stein's work is, in this sense, persistently ironic, simultaneously striving to create an immortal testament to the human mind that can erase and transcend the flawed, mortal nature of human existence. In the tradition of utopian visionaries, she uses the drawbacks of human nature as a motivational muse for the creation of a more perfect world in art. As a result of this paradox, my own discussion of Stein may appear paradoxical as well. While her ultimate goal may have been to create a transcendent text, thoroughly understanding her work requires taking into account the very human human nature from which she desired to escape. By connecting the living Stein with her aesthetic, almost mythic persona, my critical project necessarily includes what she hoped to deny.

For her, the very process of writing was a means of continually defining and redefining her self, taking command of her own existence. As a result, she spent a great deal of time thinking about the formation and function of identity, what effect external influences had upon it, and how she might best replicate its essence in language. In the early part of her writing career, she saw relationships as a primary source of an identity which existed beyond a person's physical being. By bonding her own identity with that of an other, or a group of others, she could transcend the mortal limitations of the isolated individual. A number of critics, especially Richard Bridgman in his discussion of *QED* and Jayne Walker in her explanation of *The Making of Americans* have noticed Stein's concern with identity and mortality in her early work.[4] Perhaps Stein anticipated the immanent self of Virginia Woolf's Mrs. Dalloway in the way she relied upon the connections between people to safeguard identity. But her version of a communally constructed self was, at this stage, particularly naturalist. In one of her Radcliffe themes she wrote: "You must submit yourself sooner or later to be ground in the same mill with your fellows . . . Be still, it is inevitable."[5] She embraced this deterministic attitude about the formation of identity as the foundation of her early writing. *QED,* her first novel, explores the possibilities of human connection. The story loosely follows one of her first lesbian relationships and represents an early attempt to define herself and understand her sexuality. Much of her approach to the love triangle in the novel can be found in the implications of the title, *Quod Erat Demonstrandum,* or freely translated as *What Had She Proved.* This classic signature to a geometric problem suggests that she saw the relationships of the characters in a mathematically determined way. By placing herself, in the role of Adele, within a sort of human equation, she hoped to determine a definitive self. But this attempt ends up in stalemate and exclusion when the characters transcend such limiting intentions and can no longer communicate, leaving the idea of transcendence through human connection rather questionable. The conflict between the content—lesbian relations which in themselves constitute a denial of biological and cultural determinism—and the form of the novel—a sort of determined Victorian romance with hints of naturalism—left no possibility for resolution. The resulting sense of frustration and isolation could only have served to intensify her fear.

She experienced a similar dilemma within her next major work, *Melanctha.* This naturalist novella, based upon much the same relationship with variations in gender, reveals Stein's perception of her characters as essentially static, and she portrays this through the rhythmic repetition of their "thinking, loving, and resisting." Her style of characterization blends a less radical form of what she would later call the "continuous present" with her early belief that that an individual's essence, the ingrained patterns of repetition that hide beneath seemingly varied but largely irrelevant behaviors, could be captured at any single moment in her life. The overriding definition of identity is fixed. Melanctha spontaneously experiences the moment, Jeff analyzes experience from a distance, and neither can ever break from their respective modes. With Melanctha's death, the sense of inevitable fate abounds. Despite her innovations with dialogue and her first tentative movements toward a "continuous present," Stein again found herself trapped in a literary genre which denied any possibility of transcending death.

It wasn't until the writing of *The Making of Americans* that she discovered a satisfying literary means of escaping mortality. She begins the novel as a sort of family chronicle in yet another attempt to define herself within a historical and biological context. Indeed, after reading Otto Weininger's *Sex and Character,* an anti-feminist tract that categorized people along a continuum that stretched from "total male" to "total female," she embraced the idea of creating an all-encompassing typology of humanity and set out to define everyone in order that "the enigma of the universe could in this way be solved."[6] By discovering the right types and constructing a system of classification which might permanently identify her, she could negate history, condense all humanity into a structural definition, and discover her own part in it. However, she quickly became aware of the reductiveness of such an approach and still couldn't avoid the fact that each of her characters eventually died. Death always seemed to be the last word. Significantly, upon the recognition of her failure, she writes of her own mortality:

> I tell you I cannot bear it this thing that I cannot be realizing experiencing in each one being living I say again and again I cannot let myself be really resting in believing this thing, it is in me now as when I am realizing being a dead one, a one being dying and I can do this thing and I do this thing and I am filled with complete desolation.[7]

This situation was all the more painful because she had projected much of her own identity into David Hersland, the final character in *The Making of Americans.* With his death, Stein faced the necessity of creating a new source for that "everlasting feeling."

Leon Katz suggests that she found such a source in another of Weininger's tenets. He quotes Weininger:

> Memory only vanquishes time when it appears in a universal form as in universal men. The genius is thus the only man—at least, this and nothing else is his idea of himself; he is, as is proved by his passionate and urgent desire for immortality, just the man with his strongest demand for timelessness, with the greatest desire for value . . . His universal comprehension and memory forbid the annihilation of his experiences with the passing of the moment in which each occurred; his birth is independent to his age, and his work never dies.[8]

While her fear of death and the corresponding desire for immortality may have come early in her life, Katz claims that upon reading Weininger, she accepted the idea of this "highest 'type' of human being—the only true individuality—in terms of achieving the promise of immortality by escaping from the contingency of time." Katz says that "Stein follows Weininger's system of values to its end by insisting that victory over time is achieved only by means of those qualities and capabilities of mind and spirit that belong to the genius or the saint alone" (16). While such a claim gives more credit to Weininger than he probably deserves, it does help to explain the experimental nature of her works that follow *The Making of Americans.* By recognizing herself as a genius, she might claim a sense of timelessness and do away with, at least in her art, the need for genealogical relationships.

Stein quickly developed the literary means by which to demonstrate her genius. Recognizing that historical connections necessarily tied one's identity to time and thus mortality, she began more actively experimenting with a "continuous present." By writing in the present and ignoring the past and the future, she found a comfortable means by which to avoid thoughts of death. As Janet Hobhouse notes in her biography of Stein:

> By constant returns to a point of beginning, the "continuous present suspends the inevitability of arriving at this end. To someone who, since adolescence had a fear of "death, not so much of death as of dissolution," the discovery would obviously have deep psychological appeal . . . It became a form of meditation that enabled her to remove herself from the real world, with its real and cruel passage of time.[9]

In effect, Stein found a temporary resolution by shifting her focus from character to language itself. Significantly, at this same time she also separated from her brother, Leo, a severing of connection to her genealogical past, and began her relationship with Alice, one which denied biology, genealogy, and patriarchy. Having discovered a means to deal with, or avoid, the threat of death, she finished *The Making of Americans,* a project that had

been in a frustrating state of inertia for years, and she went on to write some of her most famous experimental works—*Tender Buttons,* her portraits, and her plays.

For the most part, the problem of mortality thematically disappeared from her work for the next twenty years, surfacing only by implication in the stylistic means by which she avoided it. Not until the writing of *The Autobiography of Alice B. Toklas* did she once again experience a major crisis of identity and mortality. The writing of *AABT* may have triggered old fears in a number of ways. Much has been made of the possibility that Alice co-authored the book. The need for such a collaboration may have led Stein to question the permanence of her artistic gift by which she had successfully countered death. Also the necessity of writing to please an audience bothered her a great deal. With the great success of *AABT,* her relationship to her audience increasingly disturbed her, in part no doubt because of a fear of the power of the public to shape her later work and force a social identity upon her. Catherine N. Parke suggests that Stein was particularly concerned by the presence of an audience because of "the political, social, and personal dangers of immature dependence on others to prove one's identity" and believed "such immaturity to be one of the motives of the kinds of institutionalized violence (betrayal, lying, war) which we perform against ourselves and one another" (562). Perhaps more immediately important, however, was Stein's sense that an audience threatened her control of time and mortality. In *Stanzas in Meditation,* written concurrently with *AABT,* she acknowledges the presence of this new audience, "I have tried earnestly to express / Just what I guess will not distress . . . ," but it leaves her disturbed: "I feel very carefully they can be there / Or in no pretence that they change the time / Time which they change. / It troubles me often which can or can it not be / Not only in and because their share."[10] She believed the audience to be usurping her artistic power over time. She knew the public demanded the kind of autobiography that conforms to the traditional narrative time of history.

Significantly, she infused many of her works immediately subsequent to the publication of the autobiography with images of death. In *Blood on the Dining Room Floor,* she ostensibly wrote a murder mystery about a woman who falls to her death. The detective novel fascinated her because it so closely paralleled what Brooks Landon refers to as the "discovery process of perception."[11] She apparently attempted to create a detective novel that violated generic expectations by not offering a solution or even an ending, but rather continuously circling and recircling the narrator's perceptions. By her own admission, however, she failed. The circumstances about the woman's death are sufficiently unclear, and Stein creates suspicion through innuendo suggesting the character Alexander as potential murderer. However, this misdirection fails to hide the novel's deeper concerns with suicide and death.

It was during this intense struggle with mortality and identity that Stein began to write *The Geographical His-*

tory of America and for the first time openly confront her fears. Thus *GHA* assumes a significant place in both her psychological and literary development. She begins simply enough, "In the month of February were born Washington Lincoln and I,"[12] returning to her fortunate birth and her subsequent desire for fame and immortality. But in case we might miss the seriousness of her intent she immediately follows with "Let us not talk about disease but about death. If nobody had to die how would there be room enough for any of us who now live to have lived. We could never have been if all the others had not died. There would have been no room" (53). While this simplistic justification for the necessity of death belies the importance that the problem of death poses, it did provide Stein with a focal point upon which she could deliberate the question:

> Now the relation of human nature to the human
>   mind is this.
> Human nature does not know this.
> Human nature cannot know this. . . .
> But the human mind can. . . .
> This is the way human nature can sleep, it can
>   sleep by not knowing this.
> The human mind can sleep by knowing this.
>
> (53-54)

Thus, Stein directly confronted the problem that had haunted her throughout her career, and she set out to discover the ways in which the knowledge of death was beneficial or detrimental to humans *being* and the corresponding literary work of a transcendent genius.

In order to more clearly understand the kind of reasoning which the rest of *GHA* demonstrates, one must first come to grips with Stein's conception of human nature and human mind, a task made difficult by a lack of linear argument. *GHA* digresses and regresses, but nevertheless moves toward resolution. Rarely focusing on any subject for long, Stein rethinks, contradicts, circles, and returns to original pronouncements or suddenly changes her mind. Because of this, any distinction of what she meant by human nature and human mind must be tentatively pieced together. It helps to approach *GHA* as she approached a painting by Cezanne—not looking for a linear progression, but rather taking it all in and resolving it as a whole. In this way certain patterns do appear.

As Allegra Stewart notes in her discussion of *GHA,* Stein structured her response to mortality around the duality of being and existence.[13] For Stein, human nature was most closely tied to daily life, the actions and impulses of an individual. It consisted of memory, emotions, desires, and a connection to history. She closely associated human nature with animals, especially dogs. In so doing she suggested that it partly consisted of a primal, instinctual quality which was not interesting in comparison to other things human. One of the central paradoxes of human nature was that while within it there was no awareness of death, its historical nature rooted itself in death. Writing of wild animals she notes:

> wild ones are as if they were there with nothing to
> happen to them as if they lived there which they

do so that nobody thinks they die there which they do.

> That is what peace is but always there is some one who has not felt that this could be done that any wild animal living where it it is living could naturally go on being living until it became dead. Dead is not uninteresting and yet it is not any more uninteresting than that to any animal or human nature.

So that is peace. (84)

Thus while animals die, they are not disturbed by death, and so it is with human nature. While we act, we are not conscious of death. It is only in a reflective state, when we observe from outside the repetitious cycle of birth-dying-death, that fear is generated, or so Stein seemed to think. For this reason, the pleasure she found in her daily life with Alice, with Paris and rural France, with food and sex, did not contradict her claim that daily life was not a fit subject for reflection or art.

One of the peculiar problems that human nature presented to Stein was its relationship to identity. She writes, "human nature acts as it acts when it is identified when there is an identity" (143), and exemplifies this concept by referring to a bicycle race: "They are they because all who are there know they are they and on no account cannot they not be no not as long as they are in the race" (142). This imposing of identity from the outside, defining one's self by association the other members of the race, parallels Stein's early attempts at classifying people in *The Making of Americans* and runs counter to her belief that a genius is self-created and thus only has the identity that she herself chooses. Memory, too, in its role of creating and sustaining historical identity, was suspect. Stein felt, as Allegra Stewart says, "that memory (with its freight of the past) interferes with creation" and identity, as a part of human nature, is uncomfortably "part of cosmic existence and the temporal order" (37). Because these other-created selves were inherently temporary, she found them to be at best unimportant and at worst a threat to her sense of transcendence. Precisely "because everyday human nature tells what it was" Stein associated it with history and traditional literary narrative.

The human mind, on the other hand, generated a creative process which allowed her to transcend animal reality in favor of the symbolic. Stein closely associated it with the act of writing. It had no connection with memory, reflection, or truth; it simply "knows what it knows." It "plays," creates, "says yes" to new experience and "does not cry." To her the human mind was not concerned so much with right, wrong, or true as with what worked in her attempt to create an acceptable illusion of order in the world, to create a new self unbounded by space and time. Allegra Stewart believes that Stein achieved her goal through a meditative state in which:

> another self seems to have momentarily emerged,
> as a result of one's detachment from the net of

ordinary care, worry, or self interest. During such moments of focus, time, place, memory, and identity sink into nothingness . . . time cease[s] to flow. (36)

Her association of the human mind with writing points to the importance of art as a means of transcending the problem of existence. In essence Stein tried to create both an alternative world and an alternative entity, rather than identity, which would grant her immortality.

In effect *GHA* represents the history of Stein's personal search for transcendent identity. Sensing a threat to her artistic vision, she began gradually to reexamine and refine her definitions of human nature and the human mind and explore their connection to art. As a result *GHA* concurrently functioned as her example of the human mind at work—writing, experimenting with and challenging a variety of literary techniques and genres. She first attacks chronological narrative, both argumentatively and stylistically. She proceeds from Chapter 1 to Chapter one, to Chapter 3, followed by 3, 4, 5, 6, 7, 2, 3, 1 and so on. She refused to acknowledge a progression and flatly states "There is no reason why chapters should succeed each other since nothing succeeds another" (90). Such succession is part of human nature not human mind. By disrupting narrative progression Stein hoped to deny both time and the daily sequential events of human existence. Such disturbing coincidences of daily life motivated her to write *Blood on the Dining Room Floor,* and she returns to the central crime of that novel in *GHA* in order to exemplify the inevitable outcome of traditional narrative:

> So Madame Reverdy was the wife of a hotel keeper . . . She had four children that is they did three boys and a girl and the girl had a curl but she got very stout. She still is but not as stout as she was.
>
> The three boys were very good looking when they were younger.
>
> Now it is just the same as the older is married and the younger is a one lunger and the third is a cook. But all this had not happened when the mother was no longer their mother as she had become dead that is she had killed herself just as much to be dead as not . . . No one can care to know what happens to anyone although everybody listens to any one who tells about what happened to any one.
>
> I feel that it is a failure not to live longer. (71)

This kind of story, not unlike *Three Lives,* follows traditional narrative progression which inevitably leads to death, thus threatening Stein's sense of transcendence. Understandably she saw this as a failure. As a result she made every effort to subvert chronological order and negate the necessity of decay.

For much the same reason she laments "what is the use of being a little boy if you are growing up to be a man" (58), an exclamation made in *GHA* and many other

works. Within the understanding of the human mind, a person exists only in the present moment. In this sense one's childhood is irrelevant. At best it is merely time wasted getting to the present. In *What Are Masterpieces,* however, she reveals its more ominous implications by prefacing this same claim with, "It has been said of geniuses that they are eternally young,"[14] and going on to explain that "no one is content with being a man and boy but he must also be a son and a father and the fact that they all die has something to do with time but has nothing to do with a masterpiece" (93). Because of her need to transcend death in her writing and remain eternally young, Stein had no choice but to ignore such socio-historical referents as family and childhood. She even went so far as to claim that she thought "nothing about men and women because that has nothing to do with anything." Since the very definitions of men and women (the subject of *The Making of Americans*) are based upon difference and social relationship, to explore them would immerse her in a time bound, mortal context.

Stein located the source of her denial of social relationships in the fact of her Americanness. She perceived the United States to be a vast flat-land, an image reinforced by the aerial view she saw when flying across country during her 1933 lecture tour. This image was crucial for her in a number of ways. First of all, the presence of so much empty space in the United States relieved the fear of overpopulation that she expressed in the first page of *GHA*. In addition, such space offered the advantage of further separation from others and the necessity of movement across distances. In Stein's view the vast spaces which divided Americans negated any formation of a national "daily life."[15] Unlike England, which because of its enclosed geographical space had developed a "daily island life" and subsequently remained rooted in the dying habits of the nineteenth century, the United States was characterized by its diversity and its overwhelming individualism. Thus, it was natural for her to believe that it was the first country to enter the twentieth century. Such a country was the ideal place for the birth of a self-created genius who had no connections to past or future. In *Lectures in America* she notes that:

> the disembodied way of disconnecting something from anything and anything from something was the American one. The way it had of often all never having any daily living was an American one.
>
> Some say that is repression but it is not repression it is lack of connection, of there being no connection with living and daily living because there is none . . . (53-54)

She implies that this American disconnection arose from a denial of the body and that such a denial was necessary if one was to be "living" as opposed to "daily living" which she associated with death. It is important to remember that she was referring to life within art as much as outside it. While she made claims about the actual (as opposed to artistic) consequences of daily living for individuals and nations, she was not beyond enjoying daily life herself. Nevertheless, the social separation which she felt as the geographical essence of the United States was an integral part of her artistic conception of life of the human mind.

The disconnection inherent in the vastness of American geography also served to reinforce Stein's preference of continual present over traditional narrative time. In *GHA* she writes:

> I do not know where I am going but I am on my way and then suddenly well not perhaps suddenly but perhaps yes I do know where I am going and I do not like it like that.
>
> Because of this there is no such thing as one and one.
>
> That has a great deal to do with the relation of human nature to the human mind it also has a great deal to do with the geographical history of America. (92)

Whether in terms of writing or traveling, she felt most comfortable not knowing where she was going. When she did know where she was going, the concept of living in the present moment—"such a thing as one and one"—was disrupted, she was placed in a chronological context, and felt the subsequent anxiety of mortality. Surrounded by open space, however, Stein was not defined by where she had come from or where she was going. Such linear concepts didn't exist in a land where there were no points of departure or destinations but only the space in between. In the America of her imagination, Stein lived in a continual present of pure movement. For her it was "something strictly American to conceive a space that is filled with moving, a space of time that is filled always filled with moving. . . . " Indeed, "the straight lines on the map of the United States of America make wandering a mission . . . it has a great deal to do with the relationship between human nature and the human mind and not remembering and not forgetting and not as much as much having tears in one's eyes" (93). She directly connected movement with spontaneous discovery and perception as well as with the vanquishing of memory and the tear causing anxiety of death. In her vision, movement becomes one of the primary means of transcendence.

A genre which she most severely criticizes in *GHA* is autobiography. Considering her conception of human mind, her dislike of identity, and her insistence upon historical and social disconnection, one can easily appreciate why she considered autobiography a suspect genre. She believed that when anyone was doing anything, especially writing, "you do not have time and identity inside you," and if you are writing correctly, "you are seeing what you are seeing" (181) or, in other words, your writing is simultaneous with your observation. Clearly the kind of self-reflection normally required by autobiography could not exist in the world of her writing. In addition, by writing about herself, she faced the danger of

being identified from the outside. Such a connection between her and an audience would fix her in a social context, thus bringing on the anxiety of death. Paradoxically, in order to reinforce her self-conception of transcendent genius, she needed an audience's recognition and confirmation.

One of the primary obstacles that Stein confronted when writing autobiography was its insistence upon a beginning, middle, and end. Such historical progression, based upon daily life, arose out of human nature and not the human mind. Convinced that a masterpiece, because of its timeless quality, could only be written in the human mind, she felt autobiography was not only an anxiety producing genre but simply an inferior one as well. In *GHA*, she explains that she had already grown beyond the possibilities of such writing:

> But autobiography which has no be in it demands of me that I say that the day that I knew that there was time enough to say all that was so of human nature then I did not do so any more . . . The human mind is not so because being within it has nothing to do with identity or time or enough. (193)

She alludes to her writing of *The Making of Americans* which came to a conclusion only after she realized that anyone could go on listing the actions of everyone. Artistically, such a listing no longer presented an interesting challenge, not to mention that such a listing always led to death. She also notes the special problem that memories of childhood presented:

> I had a family. They can be a nuisance in identity but there is no shadow of doubt that that identity the family identity we can do without.
>
> It has nothing to do with anything if there is no time and identity . . . The human mind lives alone. (196)

A genius, created of herself, is not bound by biological genealogy but is free to select her own artistic heritage and define herself as she chooses.

She accomplished this in *AABT*, creating for herself an almost mythic persona, serving, as Paul Alkon suggests, "as the perfect embodiment of Gertrude" transforming her "unsatisfactory life into eminently satisfactory art."[16] Such an approach approximated a metaphysical philosophy which seemed to be the ultimate destination of her creative journey. Early in *GHA* she offhandedly mentions that a European could never invent a religion. This remark implies, however, that an American, especially a genius, could. She wanted her audience to approach her work with the same reverence with which they read the Bible. But Stein was not interested in a traditional conception of religion; her understanding of Judaism left no room for heaven or any transcendence of that kind. There was, however, something about religion which did appeal to her, "because religion does know that there is no time and no identity and no enough and no human nature in the human mind" (195), but she felt that:

religion is timid and so it does not say why or how
but it does say where and saying where it must
look over there.

So little by little which is not enough I found that
enough is not enough and not enough should be
treated roughly. So finally I became so attached to
one word at a time. . . . (195)

Stein intended no less by her writing than the creation of
a personal religion and demanded that religion be purely
of the mind, founded, as Allegra Stewart suggests, on the
"mystery of creativity" (29).

Thinking beyond this world, she again found reason to
bridle at the problem of identity. Such a limited concept
had little place in the expansiveness of the human mind,
"The more likely a universe is to be connected with identity the less likely is a universe to be a universe" (157).
For her the human mind was the sole determiner of the
universe, and through it "anything is very near" (162).
This need to move artistically toward the abstract and the
impersonal led directly to such works as *Tender Buttons,* the
portraits, and the plays. In *GHA* she identifies the essence of
these works as a kind of literary romance by stating that
there was "some relation between romance and the human
mind" (160). Like the human mind, the literary romance was
abstract, highly symbolic, and had few direct equivalents in
the physical world. Significantly, she felt that "there is no
romance if anybody is to die by and by" (165). One can see
more clearly why the determined naturalism of *QED* failed
to fulfill her aesthetic project. Having associated the romance with the human mind, she encountered problems in
attempting to reason out the source of romance. Because
romance "is what makes landscapes but not flat land" (163),
it was not within the human mind; however, since "I am I
because my little dog knows me . . . has nothing to do with
romance," (168) it also was not of human nature. Why this
discrepancy in her reasoning suddenly became clear to her
one can only guess. But once it had, the only possible conclusion for her was that "romance is in between human
nature and the human mind but has nothing to do with either" (173). This was no easy compromise for one so desirous of a complete split between human nature and the human mind, and her first reaction was to state, "I wonder if
you could be cured of not knowing that" (173). It is problematic to say her recognition of the discomforting paradox
underlying her art represents a turning point in the text. She
began writing *GHA* because she suspected just such a conflict and the frequent plea to "leave well enough alone"
suggests that she knew what might result. Nevertheless, this
is one of the first overt signs within *GHA* of her psychological acceptance of the necessity of human nature and mortality as part of an artistic continuum.

Despite frequent repetitive regressions to earlier arguments, the rest of *GHA* moves quickly, if reluctantly,
toward a tentative reconciliation of human nature with
the human mind. Stein notes at this point that:

everything else is as well finished as begun
  everything except to find out what is or is not

interesting.
Leave well enough alone means nothing now
  because nothing is alone.
That is it.
Not even the human mind.

(176)

She recognized that the challenge was "to accustom oneself to the problem the problem of why if human nature
is not interesting are masterpieces supposed to be interesting because of the subject of human nature in them"
(201). She came to the conclusion that while one must
tell of human nature, it was the style of the telling, not
the human nature, which made a masterpiece a masterpiece. "What is seen may be the subject but it cannot be
the object of a masterpiece" (210), or, in other words, the
portrayal of human nature may, unfortunately, be necessary in writing, but it should never be the purpose.

Taken out of the context of her life, these changes in
perspective appear painless enough, but the anxiety that
accompanied the writing of *GHA* can scarcely be over-
emphasized. Throughout the book Stein refers to crying
and tears. This was no idle experiment but rather an examination into very foundation of her perception of the
world with the distinct possibility of proving that perception false. If it is true that Stein's artistic gift arose out of
her idiosyncratic vision as a kind of defense mechanism
against the threat of mortality, the writing of *GHA* and,
more specifically, the forced recognition of human nature
and death could very easily have disrupted the psychological basis from which her writing sprang. Thus when
she states toward the end of *GHA*, "I would kindly not
like to know what a masterpiece is" (213), and pleads to
herself as well as her readers to "Leave masterpieces
alone" (232), she essentially expresses a wish not to have
begun the project. One feels almost certain that it was an
agonizing moment, and if she had stopped it would have
been understandable.

Fortunately, she had the strength and courage to push
forward. She candidly asks herself "Do I do this so that
I can go on or just to please any one. As I say it makes
no difference because although I am always right is being
right anything" (237). Within that statement can be found
the means of compromise; The correctness of her artistic
vision was not as important as an appreciation for the
creative process itself. After all, "what difference does a
masterpiece make if there is no dog to be" (242). A genius needs an audience, as threatening as they may be
when they impose an identity upon her. And so Stein
came to a reluctant reconciliation with human nature:

it is so evident that identity is not there at all but
it is oh yes it is and nobody likes what they have
not got and nobody has identity. Do they put up
with it. Yes they put up with it. They put up with
it. . . . (243)

Clearly she was aware of the tenuous paradox upon
which she based her argument for transcendence. However, even if she had to accept the existence of identity,

it was uninteresting to her artistically. While she had to admit its presence in her life, she could still avoid it in her work. She continued her literary experiments, especially with a continuous present. There is an easing of tension in the works following *GHA*. In *Everybody's Autobiography* she no longer feels the need to hide behind Alice's persona, and the result is a less mythic more human portrayal of herself. While she may never have lost her fear of death, she confronted and came to an understanding of that fear. And, as she says in the last line of *GHA*, "I am not sure that is not the end."

NOTES

[1] Gertrude Stein, *Everybody's Autobiography* (1937; rpt. New York: Cooper Square, 1971), p. 115.

[2] John Malcolm Brinnin, *The Third Rose: Gertrude Stein and Her World* (Boston: Little, Brown and Co., 1959), p. 15.

[3] Catherine N. Parke, "'Simple Through Complication': Gertrude Stein Thinking," *American Literature* 60 (Dec. 1988): 570.

[4] Richard Bridgman, *Gertrude Stein in Pieces* (New York: Oxford U. Press, 1970 and Jayne Walker, *The Making of a Modernist* (U. of Massachusetts Press, 1984).

[5] Bridgman, p. 41.

[6] Gertrude Stein, *Lectures in America* (1935; rpt. Boston: Beacon Press, 1985), p. 142.

[7] Stein, *The Making of Americans* (1925; rpt. New York: Something Else Press, 1966), p. 729.

[8] Leon Katz, "Weininger and *The Making of Americans*," *Twentieth Century Literature,* 24 (1978): 24.

[9] Janet Hobhouse, *Everybody Who Was Anybody: A Biography of Gertrude Stein* (New York: Doubleday, 1975), p. 55.

[10] Stein, *The Yale Gertrude Stein* (Yale U. Press, 1980), p. 433.

[11] Brooks Landon, "'Not Solve It But Be In It'": Gertrude Stein's Detective Stories and the Mystery of Creativity," *American Literature* 53 (1981): 489.

[12] Stein, *The Geographical History of America: or the Relation of Human Nature to the Human Mind* (1936; rpt. New York: Vintage, 1973), p. 113.

[13] Allegra Stewart, *Gertrude Stein and the Present,* (Harvard U. Press, 1967).

[14] Stein, *What Are Masterpieces* (1940; rpt. New York: Pitman, 1970), p. 90.

[15] Stein, *Lectures in America,* p. 161.

[16] Paul Alkon, Visual Rhetoric in *The Autobiography of Alice B: Toklas,*" *Critical Inquiry* 1 (1975): 881.

Margaret Morganroth Gullette

SOURCE: "Perilous Parenting: The Deaths of Children and the Construction of Aging in Contemporary American Fiction," in *Michigan Quarterly Review,* Vol. XXXI, No. 1, Winter, 1992, pp. 56-72.

[*In the following essay, Gullette discusses the implications of children's deaths in contemporary midlife "decline" or "recovery" fiction, seeing these deaths as indicative of a fear of aging and of anxiety about parenting.*]

1

Children do still die, alas, in life—but the risk of their doing so may now be greater in American fiction than in American reality.[1] I want first to emphasize the fictionality of this event when it is taken up to motivate a plot. In fact, infant mortality has dropped in the so-called First World (although it has gone up shockingly in what some are now calling the Fourth World, our inner cities), and many children's diseases are preventable or treatable. In fiction, however, even about the middle class, children are still dying. Indeed, there seems to have been a spurt of child-deaths since 1960, when the publication of John Updike's *Rabbit, Run* seemed to give writers renewed permission to use the plot. [See appendix for "Selected Bibliography".] The writer who chooses this plot knows it has the potential to shock and disturb the reader.

All the fictional children who die are under the age of majority; mostly, well under; and several are infants. At such ages, they don't die by their own hand nor in cars they are driving themselves. Most die by accident; only one of illness. In other words, the issue producing these deaths cannot be suicide, or any actual social or medical problem of childhood. One fictional child dies for what might be called political reasons: as a result of the experience and dread of slavery, in Toni Morrison's *Beloved*. But aside from *Beloved*, the deaths in these novels cannot be blamed on the outside world's coercions; and in all of them the main narrative interest is conceived as being domestic and psychological.

In the most sensational cases, all written by men until Morrison wrote *Beloved*, a parent kills his own child (usually it is a male parent) accidentally, or is somehow complicitous in the child's death. Many children's deaths have to be contrived, but plots that contrive parental complicity are often more unlikely than usual. In Heller's *Something Happened*, the son has been slightly wounded in an auto accident, but the father, overreacting and hug-ging him, smothers him to death. In *Ironweed,* Frances Phelan drops his thirteen-day-old son while changing his diaper, and the infant dies. In *Rabbit, Run,* it's the mother, who is drunk, who drowns the infant while giving it a bath, but the father, her husband, has run off and left her, so he too is guilty. In *The World According to Garp,* one son dies and another loses an eye in a bizarre accident for which both mother and father can be said to be at fault, but the reader is asked, I believe, to blame the mother more. I think that hostility toward women, who produce children, is involved in these stories where male authors construct plots so that it is *women* who kill the children (many readers will recall the archetypal one, *Medea*). *Beloved* goes back to the days of slavery to find the circumstances in which a *mother* might plausibly kill her own child. And there is one plot written by a woman in which the grandmother is at fault for the death: Rosellen Brown's *The Autobiography of My Mother.* On a scale from innocence to guilt, there's a complete range in these novels, from cases where the parents are clearly innocent and doubt it only in the first moment of grief, to cases where they are clearly guilty and know it, with cases of moral ambiguity or fudged responsibility in between. But in a sense that will need to be expanded later, by making the children so young and so vulnerable, all these novels take it that, even in the most innocent, accidental cases, parents are somehow *responsible.*

No novelist in this list has in fact killed his or her child; nor, as far as I know, has any of the writers lost a child. But we always want to pay extra attention to plots that strain the mimetic: great psychological pressures (and beyond them, great cultural pressures) must be at work producing them. I suspect there are many more novels containing or concerning the deaths of children than I have listed, but even if there were no others, we would want to pay attention to these.

After their fictionality, the next thing to say about this group of novels is that they are not about the children themselves. One proof is that the children often have only walk-on parts, with very few lines. In many nineteenth-century novels, the treatment was quite different. Dickens and Louisa May Alcott and other writers did give the children who would die full personalities; and the reader was asked to sit by the deathbed, and was taught how to behave in a last illness, and led to shed tears for that particular child. We now label such scenes sentimental, perhaps because of our aversion to death and dying, and they have vanished from contemporary fiction, depriving us of an emotional outlet and a form of life. But the main point here is that focusing on the death as belonging to the child has become (for now, for fiction) culturally impossible.

2

If these novels are not about the children, whom are they about? As my reference to parental responsibility implied, they're about *us*—the fictional midlife character (I or she or he) who stands in for us. Then why do authors writing about *us* kill our children? I'm going to try to answer this question, understanding that analyzing cultural phenomena as they occur is an intellectual operation fraught with complications and undecidables.

My theory begins with the idea that these plots are fundamentally about *aging.* Probably all plots are. Aging is what characters *do* in narrative, whatever else they do. Or, put another way, what we all-too-vaguely call "temporality" in narrative is the sum of the author's ways of representing a character's life-in-time. How characters react to the passing of time—most of all, whether they fear it or not—contributes largely to a novel's attitudes toward aging. Even if a main character doesn't finally learn to fear it, a plot may teach us that *we* should. Usually without our knowing it, then, we are receiving from fiction constant signals about time: its passing, its effects, and "individual" reactions to it—in short, aging.

Some midlife fictions, but fortunately not all, convey little but the fear of aging, while others conquer fears associated with aging and demonstrate that aging can be in some ways a cure.

The novelists I'm talking about ranged in age from 36 to 56 when they were writing these books—not old, now. So, this is the moment to notice that worrying about aging in our culture can begin at puberty; that death anxiety can overwhelm adolescents; and that the subjective clock can begin audibly ticking even before a character has stepped over the threshold of marriage and the first child is born.[2]

The novel itself has grown up through the life course during the past two centuries. From *Tom Jones,* through Austen, much of Dickens and Eliot, and up through Harlequin Romances, the novel's main characters have been adolescents, and the crucial event that has served as the marker of adulthood has been their wedding. By the "marker" I mean the event that spelled forward movement in the life course if you achieved it, and failure for life if you didn't. Eventually, however, there began to be novels about what goes on *after* the wedding. At first these were novels about adultery or the mere threat of adultery. It's notable that as soon as there are novels about even the threat of adultery (or cuckoldry), children are at risk. In Rousseau's *Julie* (1763), Julie dies after rescuing a child of hers who fell into the water, and on her deathbed confesses her repressed love for her erstwhile lover, whom she was not allowed to marry; and in Goethe's *Elective Affinities* (1809), one of the punitive outcomes of another repressed adultery is that a baby dies (in water). Franco Ferrucci, one of the few literary critics who has dealt with this theme, thinks that earlier writers from Goethe to Mann (all his examples are male) identified their creativity with child-figures, and that when a child is killed off it expresses a (man's) fear that he is losing precious qualities such as creativity and energy.[3] If true, this too represents a fear of aging—which a Romantic view might describe as the movement that gradually draws us further away from childhood. At the same time (as if that were not bad enough) aging past childhood inexorably leads us, female and male alike, into sexuality.

Just as in the nineteenth century, many contemporary novels about young-adulthood still express guilt or a warning about sexuality. We can read into them either the awareness that sexuality is hedged with social restrictions, especially for women, or the writer's internalized belief that punishment *should* follow sexual wrongdoing. Nowadays, in a sexually freer age, the same dreads require a plot in which real adultery *precedes* the child's death. *Rabbit, Run* has such a plot, and so does *The World According to Garp.* In the first case it is the man's sexuality that is dangerous and needs to be controlled, and in the second, although the man has had affairs (treated as mere harmless flings), it is the woman's adultery that causes all the trouble and is so dreadfully punished. Many people in our culture have thrown away the links between sex and sin, and sin and punishment, and sin and death. But some people—women and men—who have internalized these associations will continue to kill fictional children because of them.

In general, however, as sexuality and adultery have become less fraught, children are less likely to figure as the instruments through whom guilty parents are punished. Instead, they have become signs of the burdensome responsibility of adulthood—a fate common to all (parents). Novels concerning the death of children construct and reinforce the notion that the long process of child-tending begins at the birth of the vulnerable infant, and that it goes on until some time after sixteen (when, presumably, the child becomes responsible for herself or himself). These novels are thus part of the way our culture envisions the middle of the life-course—as a period whose central passage is a perilous parenting. Once this is generally established in the culture, of course, a writer need not (theoretically) even be a parent to use the material. It could be said that the theme of the death of the child is part of the price we pay (some may decide that it's part of the gain we get) for the fact that fiction has now finally written itself into this arena of the life course.

In case we are so embedded in our own cultural constructions that we think the focus on *this* risk perfectly "natural," let me point out that fiction could conceive of adulthood quite otherwise. There's no end of real and imaginable risks. Novels could conceive of the span of the middle as primarily spousal (or fraternal or filial) rather than parental—and some do. But for the moment in the fiction of adulthood, the death of a child is more critical than the death of a spouse, parent, or sibling. Perhaps divorce and remarriage have made spouses seem more replaceable, and commitment to spouses less obligatory. When women write about the death of the men in their lives, for example, it turns out to be because they have lived the facts, not imagined them. (If a Lael Tucker Wertenbaker or an Oriana Fallaci wants to write about the death of a man, she does it in a documentary form.) Children are now the irreplaceable: caring for them is

obligatory, and loving them is obligatory. Therefore, the loss of a child can presumably be read by all novel readers, even those without children, as an "unmitigated loss." The list of alternative risks in midlife fiction could be considerably extended. The major risk could be job loss, as in *Death of a Salesman;* it could be nuclear holocaust, as in Carolyn See's *Golden Days;* it could be the survival of a child who needs chronic care; it could be the cancer of an adult character, as in Larry McMurtry's *Terms of Endearment.* Yet despite all other possibilities, for this important and well-known subset of novels written between 1960 and now, the chosen "unscheduled event," the worst risk, has its source in the generation we produce and are responsible for. Why?

3

Novels about the death of children reflect or utilize great anxiety about parenting—more than normal anxiety. *Normal* anxiety about responsibility and caretaking and unreadiness produces a different plot, less intense and dramatic—plots like those Margaret Drabble and Anne Tyler produced in their young-adulthood, in the Sixties and Seventies: Drabble's *The Garrick Year* (1964) and *Thank You All Very Much* (also known as *The Millstone,* 1965); Tyler's *Celestial Navigation* (1974) and *Earthly Possessions* (1977). These are about women who cope. Maybe the babies *almost* die: in *The Garrick Year* they are almost asphyxiated, and little Flora falls into the river, but both times they are saved—by their mother. She gives up a tasty adultery so she can fix her full attention on her children. Tyler seems to have taught herself how durable babies are—after her second novel, *The Tin Can Tree,* they are not at risk—but she certainly gives a complete picture of the unremitting attention they require: the paraphernalia of childhood lead to all the thickenings of life, high chairs first, and then "income tax and license renewals . . . bank statements and dental appointments and erroneous bills . . ." as the heroine says in the aptly titled *Earthly Possessions.* But these are novels about being a young (female) adult who finds she is able to bear the burdens and responsibilities of adulthood. The protagonists learn through practice that they are capable mums, that women survive parenting handily. Fathers scarcely have a role, but mothers can manage even alone. This is young-adult fiction in which aging shows that women become independent, competent and successful at a central life-course task. Later on, when the risk became having children leave the nest, they each wrote life-after-mothering stories: Tyler in *Searching for Caleb* (in 1975, when her children were in fact not yet in their teens) and Drabble in *The Middle Ground* (1980).

Plots in which children die, on the other hand, emphasize the vulnerability of children in order to heighten the sense of risk for their parents that comes from proceeding this far in the life course. They assert that dreadful things can happen to us—that we create and then must endure terrible risk. They are fictional expansions of Francis Bacon's saying (so mysterious to young people) that children offer "hostages to fortune." That's why they assert that we adults are to some degree responsible even for events out of our control. *Our* danger begins with the baby. "I was responsible for the survival of this creature," Lynne Sharon Schwartz's heroine says (ominously) when her first baby is born. When Tyler's Macon Leary starts fathering again, even though the child is not biologically his own, he feels

> a pleasant kind of sorrow sweeping through him. Oh, his life had regained all its old perils. He was forced to worry once again about nuclear war and the future of the planet. He often had the same secret, guilty thought that had come to him after Ethan was born: From this time on I can never be completely happy.
>
> Not that he ever was before, of course.[4]

In *Beloved,* Sethe decides not to have another baby. "She was frightened by the thought of having a baby once more. Needing to be good enough, alert enough, strong enough, *that* caring—again. Having to stay alive just that much longer. O Lord, she thought, deliver me. Unless carefree, motherlove was a killer." We don't realize at this point how ambiguous her wording is.

In these fictions, the most anxious parents are the very ones who kill their children; anxiety itself kills. In *Beloved,* Sethe, only twenty-eight days escaped from slavery, fears the future for her children so much that she hastily tries to kill all of them when the slavers arrive to drag them back into humiliation and suffering. Hers is the most rational anxiety: how was she to know in 1855 that if she let Beloved live, the Emancipation Proclamation would eventually free her? But other novels show that the peril for parent and child is created by the parents' own exaggerated fear. In John Irving's *Garp,* this becomes quite explicit in one of Garp's own stories: "*The World According to Bensenhaver* is about a man who is so fearful of bad things happening to his loved ones that he creates an atmosphere of such tension that bad things are almost certain to occur." This explanation—male fear about coping with the responsibilities of adulthood—accounts directly for another father-caused death in *Something Happened* and indirectly for those in *Rabbit, Run* and that other runaway's story, *Ironweed.*

If we revise classic psychoanalysis, we arrive at a related, more disturbing explanation for why parentlove can be a "killer." Some parents repress a fear that a new child means a kind of death for themselves: to avoid this, the child has to be killed first—a preemptive strike. This is what Laius tried to do when he heard from the oracle that his son Oedipus would grow up to kill him: he had Oedipus put out on the mountain to die. The oracle voices a new father's anxiety for himself, a fear that something awful and uncontrollable will happen in the future; in this dire case, caused by his own progeny. The Oedipus story needs to be rewritten to locate Father Laius's complex as the source of the tragedy.

The level of anxiety in these novels, I want to suggest, varies with the writer's fear of time. More precisely, of aging. Aging can be defined in our culture today as that very feeling that something awful and uncontrollable will happen in the future. Particularly in a society terrified of aging, the birth of a baby, the existence of a child and the development of an adolescent—or even the apprehension of these events—can and do trigger a whole set of related fears: about sexual decline, economic powerlessness, surviving our own parents, being survived, losing self while caring for another, losing the parenting role. A mélange of guilts and fears, hard to disaggregate. In turn, these can trigger ambivalence about children, the ostensible cause.

In most of our own life stories, I imagine, ambivalence turns out to be a passing moment, related to our own inexperience and our projection of a baby's fragility. It need not get associated negatively with aging. As I said with regard to Tyler and Drabble, the experience of mothering can be used in fiction to show that aging brings competence and relief from fear. But if aging, for whatever private and/or cultural reasons, becomes or remains dreadful, some writers will reach for a young-adult or midlife disaster-plot—and kill children.

Ambivalence about children is not a characteristic of men alone, who until recently in our culture have been distanced from children, and have also deprived themselves of the remarkable life-course benefits that come from hourly, daily, detailed, parenting. Psychoanalysis of women's dreams shows that pregnant mothers often have severe ambivalence about becoming mothers. Now we also have evidence from novels set in young-adulthood and the midlife that *being* a mother creates ambivalence too (small wonder). The gender-based difference is that women, in most cases, cannot escape the unremitting attentiveness that helps to overcome irrational anxiety. And this explains why young-adult fiction about surviving parenting without death has been written mainly by women and why the *Rabbit, Runs* and *Something Happeneds* and *Garps* have male authors. But it's not difficult to explain Rosellen Brown's novel and Maureen Howard's and others. Women, of course, can also feel that their aging is negatively charged—that they have even more to fear from time than men do. We can't be surprised that women too have produced novels about the death of children, and even a few novels in which the surviving mothers are not allowed to recover.

4

In answer to the first problem this essay proposed, then: when authors kill children they construct the question, "Can I survive the *worst* that life can shove at me?" Implicitly, this question means, "Can I survive my own worst fear of aging?" When a plot acutely poses the question as "Is time on my side or against me?" the reader answers the question, "Should I damn aging or value it?"

Some readers like a universal answer, an answer good for every case. If we look to these novels, though, they can be divided roughly into two camps on the basis of what happens *after* the death of the child: recovery novels and decline novels. The existence of a few borderline narratives should not obscure a rather binary division on the question of "survival": that is, whether the bereaved parent can recover and begin life again and perhaps even know that she or he has recovered.

The ones I prefer are the cure stories. In the last section of this essay I hope to justify this preference—not on the grounds that meliorism is per se for each of us a better belief and attitude than pessimism (although I do believe it is, as do—according to therapists—most therapists). Instead, I'd like to make a case that the cure stories can teach us more because they have thought through the complete condition of loss with more imaginative completeness. They give us a fuller account of the entire experience. It's true that with the exception of *Disturbances in the Field,* they omit the parents' reception of the news of the death of the child, and thus deemphasize the first moment of loss. Nevertheless, they tell us what mourning is like and how to deal with it, as the decline stories do not.

Recovery plots do not hustle us into consolation, as some people think the culture at large does: they say instead what Frank Bascombe says at the end of *The Sportswriter,* looking back at the four years since his son died. "Grief, real grief, is relatively short, though mourning can be long." No recovery novel recommends oblivion—on the contrary, they all value memory. But they trust the process of healing that occurs over time. They count on time to bring relief from what they identify as the most hurtful parts of loss: the self-blame and the ingenious self-punishments, the irrational anger at the other spouse, if present; the sense that *nothing* of one's self is left (that one's identity is constituted solely by being a parent), the shock of the rediscovery of loss over and over. Novels that describe recovery comment on the spirit—they say that it has some strength in the face of the vicissitudes of adult life. Novels with older characters who have aged and suffered and yet demonstrate survival probably carry more conviction. Even in our culture, for some things, it helps to have aged a little. At thirty-four, Updike described as a discovery an observation he had made, via aging, about aging. "We do survive every minute, after all, except the last."[5]

The other kind of novel—which I call the decline narrative—doesn't say right out that we succumb. It isn't heavy on expository comment. But it implies this by various narrative strategies. One of these strategies is to end right after the death of the child. Still in the nightmare, before any healing has begun. In *The Autobiography of My Mother,* Rosellen Brown has the protagonist's only child vanish into an abyss three pages before the end. The grandmother should have been holding the four-year-old's hand; just before she vanished, the child's mother tried to shout to her to hold onto the child's hand, but she wasn't heard above the circumambient noise. The three pages left don't provide even for the beginning of

grief. They don't even try to: they're holding us in the shock of the first moment. They provide only enough time for the protagonist to get an awful kind of revenge on her seventy-two-year-old mother. The daughter has always been a "mess"; the mother is an elderly respected lawyer, well-organized but chilly; more detached from her daughter than critical of her, but her criticisms are implicit. The revenge, in the last page, is to see her mother, no longer omnipotent, but guilty at last, collapse and cry. This view of young-adult parenting forces us up against the daughter's self-pity, her inability to take over adult responsibility. The gist of the ending is "my life fails forever because you failed me and you continued to fail me, and now it's your fault I don't have my daughter: there wasn't much before and now there's nothing at all. How can I possibly survive adulthood?"

Something Happened also ends shortly after the doctors tell Bob Slocum that his boy would have lived if Bob had not smothered him in his frenzy of anxiety at seeing him lying on the ground suffering. The child's death illustrates, and ends, the adult's neurotic identification with him. Slocum has told us that the "the boy" (whom he never calls by name) is the only person he truly loves. He too has put all his eggs in this one basket. "I have this constant fear something is going to happen to him . . . I think about death. I think about it all the time. I dwell on it. I dread it. I don't really like it." Even the boy's tonsillectomy was a narcissistic horror for Bob: he had to leave the boy alone at night in order to try to escape from the child's pain. "I identify with him too closely, I think." What he identifies with is the child's vulnerability—not his sweetness or docility, but, Slocum tells us, his failures at school, his fear of the dark, the way he expects the worst from time and longs to have it come—"just to get it over with." The identity between them on their negative sides almost makes one think that Slocum needs his son to die to kill his own vulnerability by proxy. Heller shows us that for Slocum, the Child signifies not creativity, but weakness. Before the boy's death, Slocum already feels guilty. "I think I'm in terrible trouble. I think I've committed a crime. The victims have always been children." Rabbit Redux, three years earlier, thought almost the same thing about his guilt: "He knows he is criminal, yet is never caught." And Heller could have been talking about the two first Rabbit novels when he noticed that "The victims have always been children." If one weak small victim dies, will the grownup be free of weakness and smallness? And in fact in the few pages after the boy's death, Slocum succeeds in all his financial and status ambitions, but of course none of them can matter any more.

I think there should be a moratorium on killing a child in the last quarter of a novel; a fortiori, on the last page. Such a structure not only refuses to conceptualize recovery, it can barely show grief. Its mode after the death is the fictional equivalent of shocked silence: the end of a chapter, the blank page. Or the intentionally inadequate response: "I miss him" (Heller). The implication is that this state of loss will go on forever. Worse, such a fictional structure can be filled with fearful anticipation all the way along, up to the death. Even if the death occurs relatively early in the novel, room is made to construct fearful anticipation of the future. In *Rabbit, Run* as soon as Janice gets drunk and decides to give the baby a bath, every reader knows what will happen. There are some excruciating pages to get through, as we approach the inevitable with horror and aversion. (A friend of mine when young, with a first baby, closed the book at this point and picked it up again twenty years later.) Even in *Disturbances in the Field,* a recovery novel, the first half is full of dread, foreshadowing some awful event. "Everything had the chance to be so beautiful, and look what has happened," the narrator says, when nothing has yet happened, and Schwartz won't let her tell us what happened for another 150 pages. Decline novels force us through the fictional experience that *fears* come true. By midlife we usually have learned that fears don't *all* come true, and we learn to control anxiety, and even discard some anxieties. Novels like these construct anxiety again.

Some do this also by forcing us through the correlative experience, that *hopes* of a certain kind don't come true. At one point, at a pot party, Schwartz's Lydia imagines her midlife-to-come as a relatively "safe" space of life. "Perhaps my greatest problem would be boredom. . . . the relief of growing up and believing that . . . things will happen, but you will be so ripe with experience as to be unable to feel wonder or terror, knowing that anything is possible and everything finally subsides. That was what I thought, high and ignorant." We're being warned in such novels to level down our hope and bring up our anxiety level; as another character says, "You can't afford to get overconfident when you're hot. The gods don't like that." As if our attitude could call down reward and punishment on our kids. One page after she has dared to say that she will be unable to feel "wonder or terror," two of Lydia's four children die. That's as quick as punishment comes in fiction. Not sexual sin but *hope* can be the adult crime in contemporary decline stories.

Pessimism, on the other hand, is "safe." If you want to be safe, anticipate the worst. Decline narratives are in effect warnings about how to regard the future—it's not merely part of what they mean, but their main meaning. Treating the death of a child this way recalls and emphasizes what is sacred and secret and scary about the event in life. The effect of this treatment is to lower the reader's suspicion of the fictionality of the fiction, and wash over the resultingly less resistant reader with this flood of forebodings.

And yet Lydia recovers: so that while the first two-thirds of the plot punishes her crudely and obviously for overconfidence—for foolishly anticipating a braver kind of "safety"—the overall plot shows how she can recover (not from hope disappointed, a minor casualty at the cognitive level, but) from actual loss.

The recovery section of *Disturbances in the Field* seems weak and clichéd to me. Yet many readers love and admire the book. I think this is precisely because it opens up a small space in which to make conscious the superstition inherent in pessimism, and because it suggests that over the life course we recover not just from loss but from our false belief in the magic powers of our mind to control life and death. Underlying many fictional deaths is the writer's more or less conscious fear that our ambivalence about our children will kill them. The recovery novel says that our children may die, but not because we *wanted* them to.

5

Time is a friend in recovery novels, but friendship can work slowly. In all but *Disturbances in the Field,* the death has occurred years before the novel opens, sometimes ten or twenty years before, giving the protagonists a long retrospect. These slow-recovery narratives are constructed so that the accident or the crime occurred in passionate, dangerous young-adulthood, while the healing takes place in a more contemplative midlife. These are safe-at-last stories. Francis Phelan in *Ironweed* dropped his baby and left his home twenty-two years before. It takes that long before he can bear to remember Gerald and think about his other crimes; then in two days at the age of fifty-eight he expiates and stops trying to run or die. Sethe in *Beloved* killed her baby when she was nineteen; having punished herself for eighteen years by solitude, celibacy and forgetfulness, at thirty-seven she finds courage to take up with a man, remember, overexpiate, forgive herself, and begin to recover. Hannah Burke, the sixtyish therapist in *Other Women,* whose children died several decades before, finds that she has been punishing herself unknowingly. She has deprived herself of the risk of new relationships because of an unconscious fear of "the inevitable aftermath": withdrawal. Her cure at sixty takes the risky form of making a friend who is the age her lost daughter would have been. As a therapist, she argues most wryly and explicitly for the value of time. "What about her own despair? It didn't seem to be around much anymore. . . . The older she got, the less anything could upset her for very long. Maybe the only real cure for her clients was the aging process. But that could take years."

Even where recovery does not take so long, midlife protagonists can be grateful to time. As Lydia Rowe's marriage to Victor begins to disintegrate because they mourn so differently, she prophesies, "This land of ours, coarsened by blight, cannot endure. It's only a matter of time" (*Disturbances in the Field*). And they do separate. But other things too are a matter of time: Lydia buys a coloring book, one of the ways she already knows of making herself feel that she can get things back in her own control. She starts playing music again; she calls friends; eventually she plans to ride on buses and work on snow. (And eventually she wants her husband back, and he returns.) When you start using your strengths in your favor, employing your multiple identities in your favor, braving your superstitions, the healing process is underway. Where decline narratives threaten parents (and non-parents too), recovery novels are written as if to sufferers of any loss, to offer help.

One way recovery novels themselves differ is in showing how active a character can be in reducing grief, regaining control, restoring self-esteem. Updike shows recovery as a rather passive process. Ten year after Janice Angstrom drowned her baby, "that was terrible, the most terrible thing ever, but even that had faded, flattened, until it seemed it hadn't been her in that room but an image of her, and she had not been alone, there had been some man in the room with her . . ." (*Rabbit Redux*). Ten years after the other death for which he is partly responsible, Harry Angstrom in *Rabbit Is Rich* feels that "The years have piled on, the surviving have patched things up, and so many more have joined the dead, undone by diseases for which only God is to blame, that it no longer seems so bad, it seems more as if Jill just moved to another town, where the population is growing." The recoveries happen *between* the novels (which Updike in fact wrote ten years apart), so that we don't see the stages of the cure: it looks as if "time" alone had done the trick.

The Sportswriter makes Frank Bascombe an active, self-conscious optimist: a man who goes into his familiar mental gymnastics whenever anything bad happens to him—it is open to us to believe that he has learned these routines from having survived his little boy's death. "All we really want is to get to the point where the past can explain nothing about us and we can get on with our life." The past "should be just uninteresting enough to release you the instant you're ready (though it's true that when we get to that moment we are often scared to death.)" Frank has a positive belief in the future. "There is mystery everywhere. You have only to let yourself in for it. You can never know what's coming next. Always there is the chance it will be—miraculous to say—something you want."

Mental manipulations that are somewhat less self-conscious get built into the recovery narratives that other writers invent. When Hannah Burke's surviving children have grown up and left, she could use this to create a catalogue of postmaternal, postmenopausal losses for herself, but instead she converts it into a good feeling: "Occasionally she felt lonely, but it was easy to convert that into a sense of delicious solitude" (*Other Women*). No progress novelist treats such conversions for the sake of recovery ironically; many admit a category of what we might call *valuable* illusions. To help console himself for his son's death, Macon Leary in *The Accidental Tourist* creates an image of Ethan aging in heaven.

> And if dead people aged, wouldn't it be a comfort?
> To think of Ethan growing up in heaven—fourteen
> years old now instead of twelve—eased the grief a
> little. . . . The real adventure, he thought, is the
> flow of time; it's as much adventure as anyone
> could wish. And if he pictured Ethan still part of
> that flow—in some other place, however
> unreachable—he believed he might be able to bear
> it after all.

By giving his son an independent, parallel life, Macon gives himself permission to have such a life: it marks one end within his continuum of mourning.

The decline novel maximizes shock, helplessness, guilt, and loss as the content of adulthood, and makes them appear timeless and irreversible; whether we have lost a child or not, its effect (unless we resist its message) is to make adults dread the next blow from the future. The midlife recovery novel, on the other hand, uses its painful subject to invent ways of imagining a life we might still want after loss. By showing recovery coming in time, it puts time on our side. Once we know that, we put ourselves on the side of time. We may thus find ourselves, to our fine surprise, also praising aging.

NOTES

[1] This essay was originally a talk given at the Wellesley Center for Research on Women, and one of the Center's Working Papers. It expands a short section of Chapter VII of the author's *Safe at Last in the Middle Years: The Invention of the Midlife Progress Novel* (Berkeley: University of California Press, 1988). The emphasis in that chapter, "In Defense of Midlife Progress Novels," is on how Western pessimism (as embedded in decline theories about the life course) has affected the production and reception of midlife narratives. As one part of the defense I briefly discuss the way suffering is represented in such novels. In this essay, I concentrate on one form of midlife suffering: the loss of a child, viewed as a fictional construction of midlife risk.

[2] Psychologist Joann Montepare asks undergraduates "What appeals to you about getting older?" "What do you fear about it?" They fear many of the future life events I list on p. 63. The measure Montepare uses is called a "fear-of-aging scale." (*Nota bene:* not a "hope-of-aging scale.") At large in the culture, the idea that very young people fear aging may seem peculiar. But our refusal to conceive of aging as an issue of consciousness—our persistence in thinking it can be nothing but bodily decay, a problem for "old" people—is part of the decline ideology. In Donald Hall's poem, "My Son My Executioner," for example, the parents who "start to die together" when their baby is born are twenty-five and twenty-two. Hall wants us to treat this situation as an irony, but once we recognize that fear of aging commonly begins in adolescence, sometimes as early as puberty, we may not feel that such poems deconstruct anything; they actually reinforce the early-aging phenonemon.

[3] Franco Ferrucci, "The Dead Child: A Romantic Myth," *Modern Language Notes,* June 1989, pp. 117-134. I owe an earlier debt to Shaun O'Connell, whose talk on the dead child in contemporary fiction, delivered at Harvard about twelve years ago, kindled my interest in the topic. See also Garrett Stewart, *Death Sentences* (Harvard University Press, 1984) and Reinhard Kuhn, *Corruption in Paradise: The Child in Western Literature* (University Press of New England, 1982).

[4] Lynne Sharon Schwartz, *Disturbances in the Field* (NY: Harper and Row, 1983), p. 133; Anne Tyler, *The Accidental Tourist* (NY: Knopf, 1985), p. 258.

[5] John Updike, "One Big Interview," *Picked-Up Pieces* (NY: Knopf, 1975), p. 519. This interview took place in 1966.

A SELECTED BIBLIOGRAPHY

1960. John Updike, *Rabbit, Run.* Infant (second child), drowned by drunken mother.

1971. John Updike, *Rabbit Redux.* "Child" (Jill), frail underage woman, dies in her sleep when "protector's" house is burned.

1974. Joseph Heller, *Something Happened.* Nine-year-old (favorite child) knocked down in auto accident; dies asphyxiated by father's hug.

1976. Rosellen Brown, *Autobiography of My Mother.* Four-year-old girl (only child) falls off cliff: neither mother nor grandmother is holding her hand.

1978. John Irving, *The World According to Garp.* One son blinded and the other dies in auto accident: father and mother both at fault.

1981. John Updike, *Rabbit is Rich.* Father has recovered from deaths in earlier volumes of the trilogy. One adult child in family.

1983. Lynne Sharon Schwartz, *Disturbances in the Field.* Two children (one boy, one girl, youngest of four) die in bus accident on ski trip in snowstorm in 1981.

1983. William Kennedy, *Ironweed.* Thirteen-day-old infant dies from a fall when drunken father drops him. Two other children in family.

1984. Lisa Alther, *Other Women.* Two children, girl and boy, asphyxiated in freak home accident in which mother too nearly dies. Two other children in family.

1985. Anne Tyler, *The Accidental Tourist.* Only son, twelve, shot by holdup man at camp (first time away from home).

1986. Maureen Howard, *Expensive Habits.* Only son, sixteen ("Baby") stabbed by holdup man.

1986. Richard Ford, *The Sportswriter.* First child, son, nine, dies of Reyes' syndrome. Two other children in family.

1987. Toni Morrison, *Beloved.* Infant (one of four) killed by mother when slavers come. Present time 1873; flashback to 1855.

Mildred Hartsock

SOURCE: "The Most Valuable Thing: James on Death," in *Modern Fiction Studies,* Vol. 22, No. 4, Winter, 1976, pp. 507-24.

[*In the following essay, Hartsock focuses on Henry James's intellectually pragmatic perception of death as a "termination" and his emotional faith in the supreme value of life.*]

Everyone has recognized that for Henry James the living of the fully conscious life is a supreme value. Critics speak of his "ordeal of consciousness," his "religion of consciousness," his "idea of consciousness."[1] James himself had asked, " . . . what is morality but high intelligence?"[2] and he had shown characters, like Lambert Strether or Maggie Verver, achieving creative awareness and others, like John Marcher or Merton Densher, achieving it too late. But, despite the general recognition of this theme in the fiction, there is still a profound disagreement about what it means in terms of a philosophic stance. No one expects a novelist to be a philosopher; and in the Preface to *The Portrait of a Lady,* James had disposed of the claims of the moralist and the propagandist when he said that the only moral requirement of the work of fiction is that it should manifest "the amount of felt life concerned in producing it."[3] But in no sense does his statement nullify the fact that a novelist's presuppositions about life and death will affect his way of conveying that "felt life."

There are those who claim that Henry James had no particular philosophic bent. Martha Banta dubs him a supreme eclectic and says that he would use any idea which would work for him.[4] Ralph Barton Perry, biographer of William James, concludes that Henry was philosophically naïve.[5] Other critics still follow the interpretation of Quentin Anderson, who sees James as the heir to his father's thought: as a kind of Swedenborgian idealist or modified transcendentalist in whom "the impulse of Emerson's generation to practice a Carthusian individualism came to artistic fulfillment."[6] Generally echoing Anderson's views, John Goode has recently said that James affirms "a level of reality beyond the phenomenal."[7]

Robert Reilly, though he directs attention to the novelist's ethical kinship to William James, describes the "typical Jamesian protagonist" as "an Emersonian individual who exists in an unintellectualized faith-state that will lead him to unique moral action." This protagonist, Reilly continues, "is not in touch with law but with the divine."[8] For Yvor Winters, James is in the thought-tradition of the "long discipline of the Roman, Anglo-Catholic, and Calvinist churches"; but his moral sense, Winters concludes, was "finally destroyed by Emerson's 'antimoral' philosophy."[9] For Philip Rahv, James "approaches the world with certain presumptions of piety that clearly derive from the semireligious idealism of his family background . . . and from the early traditions and faith of the American community." This faith, Rahv believes, was converted to secular ends, but "one might venture the speculation that his wordly-aesthetic idea of an élite is in some way associated . . . with the ancestral and puritan idea of the elect. . . . "[10] Ross Labrie agrees.[11]

For Edward Rich Levy, Henry James was a Pragmatist: "The pragmatic theory of inquiry . . . was to become the keynote for his approach to characterization; tychism as the principle of consciousness was to form the theme of his novels, in their assertion of the possibility of growth in conscious awareness and of the supreme value of that consciousness of life as a possibility."[12]

Clearly Henry James cannot have embraced all of these philosophic positions simultaneously, and no one has adduced any evidence of a progression or change from one to another. If, then, there are ways of adjudicating among them, they must be further explored. At the heart of every philosophy is the philosopher's solution to the most stubborn of the ineluctable human problems—death. To understand how James looked at death and how it is used in his fiction may, therefore, invalidate some of the above views and may provide evidence for a tenable, if partial, interpretation of his *Weltanschauung*.

The statements and comments of James on death are generally known from his letters, his notebooks, and his prose essays; but they need to be examined for pattern and consistency.

The letters reveal persistent shock at human "terminations" and a firm refusal to engage in what Wallace Stevens called "sleek ensolacings."[13] Even absolutists, of course, feel and express grief—and idealists and those supported by theological conviction as well. But the language of James suggests more than personal sorrow. "Extinction" is the word most often used to describe the fate of the loved dead. After the death of William in 1910, Henry wrote to Edith Wharton that he sat "stricken in darkness" over his "beloved brother's irredeemable absence." He adds that his relation to William and his affection for him "and the different aspect his *extinction* has given for me to my life are unutterable matters. . . . "[14] In a letter to Edward Marsh, he spoke of the death of Rupert Brooke: "This is too horrible and heart-breaking. If there was a stupid and hideous disfigurement of life and outrage to beauty left for our awful conditions [the War] to perpetuate, those things have been now supremely achieved, and no other brutal blow in the private sphere can better them for making one stare through one's tears." He saw Brooke's death as a "stupid *extinction* of so exquisite an instrument and so exquisite a being" (II, 472). To Mrs. Wilfred Sheridan, whose husband was killed in World War I, James wrote that he could offer her *no consolation* except the happiness of her having been associated with him in marriage (II, 499). In another troubled letter about the death of Brooke, he insists that death must be confronted without evasion. He advises: " . . . all my impulse is to tell you [Edward Marsh] to entertain the pang and taste the bitter-

ness for all they are 'worth—to know to the fullest extent what has happened to you and not miss one of the hard ways in which it will come home" (II, 469).

The death of James's mother in 1882 was a profoundly disturbing experience for him. It elicited one of the rare statements he ever made that might suggest some hope of an afterlife:

> her death has given me a passionate belief in certain transcendent things—the immanence of being as nobly created as hers—the immortality of such virtue as that—the reunion of spirits in better conditions than these. She is no more an angel today than she had always been; but I can't believe that by the accident of her death all her unspeakable tenderness is lost to the beings she so dearly loved. She is with us, she is of us—the eternal stillness is but a form of her love.[15]

Even here, however, the "transcendence" seems chiefly a perpetuation of her memory in the living. And in the same letter he uses the term *extinction*. After the father's death, Henry told William: "As I stood there and looked at this last expression of so many years of mortal union, it was difficult to believe that they [the parents] were not united again in some consciousness of my belief."[16] The negative phrasing, though, more than hints that Henry shared William's uncertainty on the point. Late in life, when Henry visited the family graves in Mt. Auburn cemetery, there is no word of ultimate union in a "beyond" with those loved and lost: only a determination to know and to savor once again what these dead have meant to him. He feels "how not to have come would have been miserably, horribly to miss it. . . . Everything was there, everything *came;* the recognition, stillness, the strangeness, the pity and the sanctity and the terror, the breath-catching passion and the divine relief of tears." He stood there facing "the pity and tragedy" of all the past.[17]

If no evidence existed beyond the passages already cited, a wide gap between Henry James and Emerson or Whitman or other romantics is clearly visible. One cannot imagine James concluding a threnody on the death of a small son with the comforting thought that he is "Lost in God, in Godhead found."[18] Nor can one imagine his finding anything but nonsense in Whitman's certainty:

> Has anyone supposed it lucky to be born? I hasten to inform him or her it is just as lucky to die, and I know it.[19]

James did not know it. For him death was the Beast in the Jungle, and he is closer to our own day than he is to the romantic idealist tradition.

More direct evidence is available from other letters and from the late essay on immortality contributed to Howells' volume *In After Days, Thoughts on the Future Life*. In a letter to William following the latter's publication of the literary remains of Henry James, Sr., Henry separates himself from any kind of transcendental absolutism:

It comes over me as I read them [his father's writings] how intensely original and personal his whole system was, and how indispensable it is that those who go in for religion should take some heed of it. I can't enter into it (much) myself. I can't be so theological nor grant his extraordinary premises, nor throw myself into conceptions of heavens and hells, nor be sure that the keynote of nature is humanity. . . . (I, 111-112)

To be taken with equal seriousness is his letter to Mrs. William James to thank his brother for a copy of "his 'Immortality' lecture . . . which I have read with great appreciation of the art and interest in it. I am afraid I don't very consciously come in to either of the classes it is designed to pacify—either that of the yearners, I mean, or that of the objectors. It isn't the difficulties that keep me from the yearning—it is somehow the lack of the principle of the same" (I, 305).

The essay for Howells, "Is There a Life After Death?," gives the fullest explicit statement on death and its aftermath.[20] The major thrust is an affirmation of life and an impatience with all who are "dead" before they die. To be indifferent to the question of immortality, James says, is "below the human privilege"; and of those who do not consider it, it may be asked "whether they are distinguishable as 'living' either before or after" (p. 602). Ross Labrie says that James means that "each man must earn an afterlife through raising his level of awareness in this life." An "immortal élite" thus inheriting life-after-death would be, he continues, "analogous to the religious ideas of American Puritans like Jonathan Edwards."[21] One can only insist that James implies nothing of the kind. He simply seizes the occasion to rebuke those who, in their worry over survival, fail to live the life they have. After this rebuke, James develops, through the central part of the essay, the evidence that death is indeed a termination:

> he sees "nothing so much written over the personalities of the world as that they are finite and precarious and insusceptible. All the ugliness, the grossness, the stupidity, the cruelty, the vast extent to which the score in question is a record of brutality and vulgarity, the so-easy non-existence of consciousness . . . these things fairly rub it into us that to *have* a personality need create no presumption beyond what this remarkably mixed world is by itself amply sufficient to meet." (p. 605)

Wholly repudiating the claims of the spiritualism flourishing at the time as "absolutely not established," James laments:

> . . . we begin by pitying the remembered dead, even for the danger of our indifference to them, and we end by pitying ourselves for the final demonstration of their indifference to us. "They must be dead, indeed," we say; "they must be dead as 'science' affirms. . . . " (p. 607)

To this point, there is no hint of faith, either in a Christian deity or in any concept of spiritual oneness in the universe which might make death something other than a brutal ending. A "tough-minded" man is simply brooding over the nothingness that may yawn at life's end. But James continues:

> Living or feeling one's exquisite curiosity about the universe fed and fed, rewarded and rewarded—though I don't say definitely answered and answered—becomes the highest good I can conceive of, a million times better than not living. . . . (p. 610)

Recognizing a growth and change in consciousness, he must then concede that there may be realizations "I am condemned as yet but to dream of." On the continuation of consciousness after death he will at least keep an open mind. His concluding statement could have been written by his brother William—it is so essentially the pragmatist's position:

> I "like" to think . . . that this, that and the other appearances are favorable to the idea of the independence . . . of my individual soul; I "like" to think even at the risk of lumping myself with those shallow minds who are happily and foolishly able to believe what they would prefer. It isn't really a question of belief . . . it is on the other hand a question of desire, but of desire so confirmed, so thoroughly established and nourished, as to leave belief a comparatively irrelevant affair. . . . If one acts from desire quite as one would from belief, it signifies little what name one gives to one's motive. (p. 614)

The prevailing tone of the essay is tentative. It reflects a pained admission that rational evidence indicates that death is an end, but it refuses to close the door on the possibility that future explorations of consciousness *might* alter the weight of the evidence. The essay is a rejection of absolutism and a hesitant commitment to openness and futurity. It is pragmatic in the sense of William James's *Will to Believe.*

Henry's comments on his brother's thought are, of course, well known. In 1907 he wrote to William: " . . . I was lost in the wonder of the extent to which all my life I have . . . unconsciously pragmatised." And later he wrote of *The Pluralistic Universe:* "As an artist and a 'creator' I can catch on, hold on, to pragmatism and can work in the light of it and apply it. . . . "[22] Ralph Barton Perry has called these statements mere fraternal compliments from a novelist wholly naïve in philosophy. But the evidence of the immortality essay, not to speak of the very substantial arguments of Edward Rich Levy based upon consideration of certain novels, prefaces, and reviews, forces a skeptical view of Perry's conclusion.[23] Quite evidently Henry James *had* thought about his brother's views, particularly his views of religious experience, and perhaps had reached similar positions independently.

Nevertheless, the letters and the fiction suggest that, though Henry James chose, on the level of intellect, an open-ended pragmatism regarding death, he more often, on the deeper levels of feeling, holds to the dominant tone of the essay on immortality: "What it comes to is that our faith or our hope may to some degree resist the fact . . . of watched and deplored death, but that they may well break down before the avidity and consistency with which everything insufferably continues to die" (p. 608). It is hard to see what Quentin Anderson could have meant when he said that the taste of Henry James, Sr., for "the unconditioned, which led to an explicit denial of the reality of sexuality and death, is present in the novelist."[24] To the contrary, death is a grim fact in many of the stories and some of the novels, and an examination of how the death-theme is used in the fiction confirms the most persistent value in the work of James: the value of life itself. He states it explicitly in his often-quoted letter to Grace Norton: "I don't know *why* we live—the gift of life comes to us from I don't know what source or for what purpose; but I believe we can go on living for the reason that . . . life is the most valuable thing we know anything about, and it is therefore presumptively a great mistake to surrender it while there is any yet left in the cup." He advises her: "Don't melt too much into the universe, but be as solid and dense and fixed as you can, and those of us who love and know, live so most" (I, 101).

Generally in the stories and novels, death is used in one of three interrelated ways: 1) to show that life must be lived in a present not unduly burdened by the weight of the past; 2) to awaken those living-dead whose consciousness is hardly more active than if they were already in the grave; 3) to rebuke, with artistic obliquity, those whose conventionality or fear of life would fatally repress fulfillment of the individual.

James was always sensitive to the claims of the dead upon the living; he had profound feeling for the "visitable past." George Stransom, in "The Altar of the Dead," defends his ritual observances for the dead: "This was no dim theological rescue, no boon of a contingent world; they [the dead] were saved better than faith or works could save them, saved for the warm world they had shrunk from dying to; for actuality, for continuity, for the certainty of human remembrance."[25] But the point of the story, finally, is that, while our bonds with the past and with the dead are ineradicable and enrich our lives, death cannot be allowed to keep men from loving and living. Stransom's hurt that a friend has dishonored a dead wife by remarrying is the obverse of his later discovery that his own love for his altar-companion actually honors the dead more by honoring life more. The same theme is at the heart of *The Aspern Papers*: a story which lovingly and appreciatively creates the ambience of the past but focuses upon old Juliana's willingness to surrender her cherished mementoes of the dead poet to ensure the happiness of the living Tina. Though James did, indeed, hate invasions of privacy, the story is not primarily about that hatred. The papers are Juliana's only counter with which to bargain for poor Tina's one chance at life; and they are a small price to pay. Tragedy, here, lies in the fate of Tina and the thoughtless manipulations of her "suitor."

Juliana knows that death-in-life from lack of love is a far greater cause for concern than the preservation of tokens from the dead past.

Any discussion of James's views on death must take account of his stories of the occult—the so-called "ghost" stories. In a preface to a collection of eighteen such tales, called *Henry James: Stories of the Supernatural*, Leon Edel describes these stories as concerned with "the mysterious world of daylight ghosts"; James, he says, "knew uncannily—how to make us walk in his company, in the broad daylight of our own lives—with our own ghosts."[26] Martha Banta, too, in *Henry James and the Occult* rightly agrees that the "ghosts" are the vocabulary, the metaphor for something strictly human: they are the "catalysts to self-knowledge." They never, she observes, speak in a literal sense "of belief in other beings, other worlds, or other lives than those discernible by the human eye and the human heart in this world and this time."[27] These stories, however, are interestingly apposite to James's several ways of using death in his fiction.

Two early stories, "DeGrey: A Romance" (1868) and "The Last of the Valerii" (1874), deal with the curse of the past when it impinges unduly upon the present. In the first, all of the DeGrey brides, over a number of generations, have died unexpected deaths. Margaret, fully aware of the family curse, marries Paul DeGrey with the passionate conviction that she can and will live life fully in the face of it: "Then raising her head, with her deep-blue eyes shining with the cold light of an immense resolve—a prodigious act of volition—'Father Herbert,' she said, in low, solemn accents, 'I revoke the curse. I undo it. I curse it!'"[28] Thereafter, she is blooming and happy and fulfilled while Paul weakens and sickens and finally dies. Both Edel and Banta believe that this is an instance, not uncommon in James, of psychic vampirism—of a wife's draining the vigor from a husband. Professor Banta extends the theme far beyond this story: "Is not vampirism," she asks, "the blood-brand that ought to be stamped upon what is most unhealthy in James' fiction? Are not Alice Staverton, May Bartram, Milly Theale, Maggie Verver, Miriam Booth [sic], Isabel Archer, and others soul-suckers of the men whose wills come under their spell?"[29] Though disproof does not fall within the context of this paper, I should say that the answer is a resounding "No!" And the story of DeGrey would appear to have a quite other theme. Margaret lives because she sturdily repudiates the Hawthorne-like "curse"; Paul dies because he permits himself to be a psychic victim of the dead past. Another near-victim is the Count Valerio in "The Last of the Valerii." When the archeological interests of his wife lead to excavations of relics from the ancient past of his family, the Count falls in love with that past. His withdrawal from the present and from his wife culminates in an actual return to the worship of Juno and to other ancient rites. Edel says that the story makes the reader "aware that the past harbors within it unspeakable evil—haunting evil." Though I agree with him that the theme is the danger of living in the dead past, I think that the charm of the story is in the seductive evocation of that past through its descriptive details. Good *or* evil, the past is not viable: it leads to a death-in-life. The story's ending is amateurishly incredible, but the theme is sufficiently established.

Perhaps the most poignant of the tales dealing with the past and the dead is "Maud-Evelyn," written in 1899. A middle-aged couple, unable to accept the death of their young daughter, forge the future for her that she never had. A young man who meets them by chance is chosen as the suitor and husband of the long-dead Maud-Evelyn. With motives perhaps mixed at the outset, the young man gradually comes to believe in the fiction in which he and the parents and the dead child, now a fictive woman, are living. The living girl whom he was to have married sums up the strange obsession: "It's the gradual effect of brooding over the past; the past that way grows and grows. They make it and make it. They've persuaded each other—the parents—of so many things that they've at last also persuaded *him.* It has been contagious."[30] This is a cult of the dead more extravagant than the ritual observances of George Stransom. The living woman, however, brings Stransom back to life and acceptance; the living girl in "Maud-Evelyn" can only share blighted final hours with a man utterly committed to the dead and to death. The story displays a psychological realism familiar enough—and a pathos that comes from the goodness and sensitivity of the people really destroyed by their own fantasies. Ghosts and fantasy-figures are natural symbols of those unreal, real haunting presences which signify unhealthy relationship to the past.

Another death attributable to the destructiveness of a senseless tradition is that of young Valentin de Bellegarde in *The American.* Dying of a pointless duel fought for the "honor" of Noemie, Valentin is attended by Christopher Newman. Newman feels anger at the meaningless dying: "You might have done something better than this. It's about the meanest winding up of a man's affairs that I can imagine!" Valentin answers: "It is mean—decidedly mean. For you see at the bottom—down at the bottom, in a little place as small as the end of a wine-funnel—I agree with you."[31] The youth dies apologizing—apologizing for the hollow values of the ancient house of Bellegarde. But neither he nor his sister has been able to summon the courage to defy the horrendous pressures of enslavement to the accumulated traditions that kill the possibilities of life in the present. Whether such pressures be a commitment to the dead or to the dead past, whether they be commitment to conventional values in the present—James knew that they were the stuff of a tragic denial of life, and they provide the theme of much of his fiction. The pride of French aristocracy and the Puritan ethos of Woollett, Massachusetts, can come to the same deprivation.

The several deaths by suicide in the fiction of James throw further light upon the novelist's passion for that "most valuable thing"—life. The fatal fall of Roderick Hudson may or may not have been suicide. Rowland, lashing himself for having driven Roderick into despair,

convinces himself that the tormented young man had made a false step in the mountain-top storm. But the matter is left in doubt. The fact of importance is that, in effect, Roderick was dead before he died. There was nothing left in the cup for him. Caught up in a hopeless passion for Christina Light, Roderick had abandoned his art, the people who loved him, and his own Self. Rowland had forced him to contemplate his tragedy: to see himself as a man self-destroyed, because he could not make the saving choices. And, however he may have died on the cliff, his life was already expended. In a much better novel, *The Princess Casamassima,* Hyacinth Robinson, too, lacks the courage and vigor to make the hard choice. Committed to the anarchists who champion the poor, Hyacinth feels increasingly drawn to the arts and way of life to which the Princess has introduced him. He decides that violent revolution is incompatible with the preservation of high culture—and he most choose between them: "To desert one of these presences [the social need and the cultured values] for the other—that idea was the source of shame, as an act of treachery would have been. . . . "[32] But, as I have said elsewhere: " . . . the supreme act of treachery is to desert both with a bullet through the heart." James means for us to see " . . . that Hyacinth sees too little and loves life too little, for all his awakening awarenesses."[33] Both Roderick and Hyacinth are artists *manqué,* one a selfish man, the other a sensitively good man—but both unable to see, as James did, that it is a mistake to surrender life "while there is any yet left in the cup" (Letters, I, 101).

A hero who *may* belong to the same category is the young pacifist Owen Wingrave. Included in *Henry James: Stories of the Supernatural,* "Owen Wingrave" cannot really be called a "ghost story." Leon Edel rightly points out that the only ghost is the pressure of the past and of family. But the question remains: how shall we interpret the death of Owen? He is found dead on the floor of the "haunted" room where his ancestor had mysteriously died: "He was all the young soldiers on the gained field."[34] Edel cites Bernard Shaw's objection to the story on the ground that Owen, in his pacifism, had viable choices other than death. To this cavil, James replied: "You simplify too much."[35] And, though the story is troubling, perhaps Shaw did. James would appear to be saying that, given Owen's strong sense of family (like Valentin's), he could not repudiate family—hence chose to die himself rather than to inflict death upon others. If this is indeed the meaning, then Owen's death would have a more positive significance than that of Hyacinth or Roderick.

Two of the best tales, "The Author of Beltraffio" and "The Turn of the Screw," seem closely related in a common theme: the death which is always implied in a denial of life. According to the admiring disciple who recounts the story of the author of Beltraffio, Mark Ambient is a very great novelist whose wife fears and despises his art and desperately tries to shield their child from the influence of his father. To the younger writer, the troubled father confesses the deep chasm between his own and his wife's view of the world:

It's the difference between making the most of life and making the least, so that you'll get a better one in some other time and place. Will it be a sin to make the most of that one too, I wonder; and shall we have to be bribed off in the future state as well as in the present? Perhaps I care too much for beauty—I don't know, I doubt if a poor devil *can;* I delight in it, I adore it, I think of it continually, I try to produce it, to reproduce it. My wife holds that we shouldn't cultivate or enjoy it without extraordinary precautions and reasons. She's always afraid of it, always on her guard.

Ambient worriedly concludes:

I don't know what the end will be. Moreover, I care for seeing things as they are; that's the way I try to show them in any professed picture. But you mustn't talk to Mrs. Ambient about things as they are. She has a mortal dread of things as they are.[36]

The end is that the mother, in effect, chooses to let the child die sooner than expose him to the dangerous, open world of a father who prefers to see things as they are. She withholds medicine from Dolcino, desperately ill with diphtheria, and turns the doctor away. The story clearly expresses, through Ambient, many of James's own feelings and convictions about his art. Mrs. Ambient, indeed, seems almost a fictionalized, feminized version of the critic [Besant] to whom James had addressed *The Art of Fiction.* But beyond his view of the novelist's art, Ambient expresses a view of life: it should be totally exposed, honestly encountered, and fully lived. His wife's Puritan view logically culminates in a death-choice. As an ironical twist at the end, Mrs. Ambient for the first time reads her husband's "black" novels.

Everyone, now, who writes about "The Turn of the Screw" feels tempted to apologize for adding to the bulky bibliography. The debate, of course, has centered about the question of the ghosts: are they real or are they the sick creations of an hysteric spinster-governess? The question should be phrased differently: what is the meaning of these very real "ghosts"? For all of Henry James's ghosts are "real" in the sense that they have psychological meaning; *never,* in the sense that they are emanations from a world beyond death. All of the James ghost stories can be read on more than one level: first, simply as old-fashioned tales of terror but finally as portrayals of an inner reality. What, then, could the ghosts of Peter Quint and Miss Jessel *mean.* Edmund Wilson, who advanced the so-called Freudian view of the governess, and Robert Heilman, who argued for the story as religious allegory, have set, perhaps, the dominant patterns of interpretation.[37] Certainly, the artistry of the tale lies, as James said in his Preface that it did, in the carefully preserved ambiguity which allows many possible meanings. Nevertheless, the Wilson and Heilman views strain credulity—Heilman's because it is utterly unlike James to frame a religious allegory and Wilson's because it takes no account of the narrator's introduction and because it denies the *felt* realness of the "ghosts," a feeling that Quint and Jessel *are* a force that has some meaning beyond the question of the governess' interpretation of them.

On balance, the essay of Joseph J. Firebaugh seems to me to come closer to intelligent explication and to some sensible accounting for the death of Miles. He recognizes, as one has to, the hint of "boyish homosexuality" in Miles: "If that is the nameless crime, it is still knowledge. . . . He gives this knowledge to his schoolmates, those he 'liked' moreover, in love rather than malice." Firebaugh assumes, without much evidence, that Quint had had a "corrupt purpose"; but, more convincingly, he says that the governess "destroys the children by imposing on them images of evil formed in her conviction of the essential sinfulness of mankind."[38] It is more than possible to see the governess as the "good" woman the narrator feels her to be and at the same time to argue that she belongs in that large company of the good who go into panic when they confront forms of experience unknown and, therefore, frightening to them. Homosexuality as a carefully covert theme is suggested, not only by the reasons for Miles's expulsion, but also by the pairing of Miles and Quint and of Flora and Miss Jessel. James's interest in that theme is present, of course, elsewhere and is a matter for discussion in the last two volumes of Edel's biography. I would hazard a guess that "The Turn of the Screw" could be the story Edel says James never wrote because he had for many years lived it. Edel notes that three years after the death of his sister Alice (1892), James "thought of a story he might write about 'the existence of a peculiar intense and interesting affection between a brother and sister.' As he recorded this in his notebook, he spoke of 'two lives, two beings, and one experience.'"[39] There can be no question about the nature of the relationship of Alice with Katherine Loring, as that is made clear both by Edel and by certain letters of James.[40] And from both the Edel biography and from the literary expressions of the theme of homosexuality, it may be inferred that James had good reasons for his deep understanding of his sister's problems. If, indeed, "The Turn of the Screw," written in 1897-98, may covertly reflect that "one experience" of brother and sister, then the fate of Miles and the illness of Flora would symbolize, as usual in James, the belief that whatever interferes with the fullness of life for the individual is veritable death.

Two other short stories have particular relevance to the theme of death in the work of James, "The Middle Years" and "The Beast in the Jungle." What death means to the artist is the concern of "The Middle Years." Martin Dencombe, his latest novel in his hands, his illness and his years upon him, senses "the completion of a sinister process; feels the chill of this dark void." His last chance is ebbing away: "He had done all he should ever do, and yet hadn't done what he wanted." There is no speculation about some expansion of his artist's consciousness after death: "A second chance—that's the delusion. There never was to be but one."[41] For James, death is the Beast in the Jungle, for it terminates the chance to know and to feel and to create. The beast that leaps out at John

Marcher is death—his tragic perception at the grave of May Bartram not only that life has a term but also that life itself can be a death-in-life when consciousness fails: "Since it was in Time that he was to have met his fate, so it was in Time that his fate was to have acted."[42] Death is not felt as a tragedy for May Bartram: she has "had her man," has known love in full consciousness. It is Marcher, "powerless to penetrate the darkness of death," who throws himself upon her tomb in an agony of recognition too late. Death is as shocking to James as it was to the existentialist writers of recent time. For him, the brutality of death can give a sharper poignancy to the living of life and can be the spur that awakens the unawakened.

When Isabel Archer, at the death-bed of Ralph Touchett, cries out that she would sooner die than lose him, Ralph assures her: "you won't lose me—you'll keep me. Keep me in your heart; I shall be nearer to you than I've ever been. Dear Isabel, life is better; for in life there's love. Death is good—but there's no love."[43] And Isabel turns back to life and to responsibility.

Milly Theale, too, believes that life is better. *The Wings of the Dove,* the most tragic of James's novels, is, in one sense, focused upon the death of its heroine. The emphasis upon Minnie Temple as model for Milly has perhaps influenced some readers to suppose that the tragedy is Milly's. But no matter how filled with pathos her situation is and no matter how cruel the deception practiced, Milly's death cannot be called tragedy. Hers is death from a natural cause and is the *donnée* of the novel: nothing could have forestalled her fate—no choice of hers, no choice of Densher's or Kate's. F. W. Dupee, mis-reading the role of Sir Luke Strett, says that Milly's "physician hopes that she may recover if she falls in love."[44] But this is not at all what the physician means. Strett is, in effect, the voice of Henry James. After questioning Milly and learning of her circumstances and after sensing her courage and capacity for life, Sir Luke expresses to her the characteristic philosophy of James: live as fully as you can in *whatever* time you have. "You've the right to be happy," he tells her. "You must make up your mind to it. You must accept any form in which happiness may come. . . . It's a great, rare chance."[45] Milly grasps his meaning perfectly. At the end of the second visit, she asks: "Shall I . . . suffer?" (XIX, 246). Strett replies that she will not. "And yet then live?" she persists. "My dear young lady," he answers, " . . . isn't to 'live' exactly what I'm trying to persuade you to take the trouble to do?" (XIX, 246). In the chapter following that conversation, Milly understands what Sir Luke has done for her. He has not lied to her; he has not offered her pity; he refuses to conjure up visions of sick-rooms and medicines and suffering. She knows she will die, but she feels how wonderful it is, the "strange mixture that tasted at one and the same time of what she had lost and what had been given her" (XIX, 248). The bloom was gone "from the small old sense of safety. . . . But the . . . idea of a great adventure, a big dim experiment or struggle in which she might, more responsibly than ever before, take a hand, had been offered her instead" (XIX, 248). She must

pluck the nettle danger from the flower safety; she must take up "some queer defensive weapon, a musket, a spear, a battle-axe" and assume a military posture (XIX, 248). She reflects: "It was wonderful to her . . . she had been treated—hadn't she?—as if it were in her power to live, and yet one wasn't so . . . unless it came up quite as much, that one might die" (XIX, 248). She knows; Sir Luke knows; Susan Stringham soon finds out; Kate Croy is sure—that Milly, in fact, will soon die. But Sir Luke commands Milly to lay claim to those kingdoms of the earth which she had earlier viewed from her mountain-top: he frees her to live with a valiant intensity while she can.

Sir Luke reenters the situation at a crucial later time in Venice after Lord Mark's revelation to Milly of the Densher-Croy plot and after she has "turned her face to the wall." Oscar Cargill says that Kate and Densher commit psychological murder of Milly.[46] This view is a sentimentalizing of a doom that was inevitable anyway. But more than that, it overlooks the final role of Sir Luke Strett. After he spends a day with Densher, never mentioning Milly at all, he evidently concludes that there is in Densher a genuine concern and caring for Milly. Later, he gives Densher the word that Milly will receive him. In effect, his good offices turn Milly's face *away* from the wall and back toward life. The greatness of Milly Theale is not that she "forgives": it is that she is capable of opting for life when she is in the very embrace of death. Those who speak of Milly's getting some sort of "revenge" surely miss the point. But those go equally astray who see Milly as somehow transcendent in death—a sort of abstract symbol of the holy spirit. John P. O'Neill feels that, as Milly looks at the Bronzino portrait, she "arrives at a kind of joy, partly aesthetic, partly mystical, over a fact of experience [death] which . . . is most feared. She sees the fusion of life and death poetically. . . . "[47] The details do not support O'Neill. Milly sees death with an absolute horror and is in protest against it to the end. She is a loving woman, however, who decides that, though she cannot live, she can give the gift of life to Merton Densher. We never see the letter which she writes to Densher. Its importance lies in how the receipt of it affects him. The tragedy of the novel is the tragedy of Densher and Kate Croy. His obsessive guilt turns him away from the gift of life offered by Milly and toward a cruel testing of Kate. It is the goodness in him which creates his shame, but he is not, finally, good enough. He cannot summon the strength to read the letter; he can only put the burden upon Kate in an accusatory way. The beauty of Milly's nature has so moved him that we feel in him, at the end, the devotion of the "mari" in "Maud-Evelyn": he will live henceforth with a ghost. Kate, understanding how Milly has changed them both, nevertheless still loves Densher. For him she had propagated a cruel deception and ventured a stupendous risk for herself in her willingness that Densher should marry the dying Milly. She does care for Milly, and her motives had been not wholly evil—more imprescient than designedly evil. She had been wrong. But she is still capable of life and of facing guilt. The tragedy, then, is a tragedy of waste and a surrender to guilt, an outcome that Milly could not have willed. Like

James her creator, Milly speaks for life. She fears and hates death and draws all her weapons against it. It is a bitter irony that her last defiance of death—an act of life—should destroy where she had hoped it would save. But, as always in James, memory of the dead *is* destructive when it turns the living away from pursuit of their lives.

Letters, essays, novels, stories show Henry James to be consistent in his view of death. Death is a termination. If, like his brother William, he was intellectually open to the idea that the future might bring new insights to bear upon the problem, emotionally he is sure that death is the enemy, the Beast in the Jungle. To confront it honestly may catapult the living into a fuller consciousness; to make a cult of it—whether of the loved dead or the dead past or a dead set of values—is to impede the embrace of life.

Leon Edel, in his last volume of the biography, describes the pathetic clutching at consciousness and the reaching, still, for his craft as James neared his end.[48] That life for him was indeed the "most valuable thing" is manifest in a letter written, just two years before he died, to the despairing Henry Adams:

> Of course we are lone survivors, of course the past that was our lives is at the bottom of an abyss— if the abyss *has* any bottom . . . I still find my consciousness interesting—under *cultivation* of that interest. Cultivate it *with* me, dear Henry. . . . (II, 361)

The views James had of death and of life place him very far from the position of any of the familiar varieties of philosophic idealism. Without metaphysical supports, he was closer to the questioning and often doubting twentieth century. But his faith in the interest of life did not wane.

NOTES

1 Dorothea Krook, *The Ordeal of Consciousness in Henry James* (Cambridge at the University Press, 1962); Martha Banta, *Henry James and the Occult* (Bloomington: Indiana University Press, 1972); Ross Labrie, "Henry James's Idea of Consciousness," *American Literature,* 39 (January, 1968), 516-529. Many others, of course, have explored the role of consciousness in James.

2 *The Golden Bowl* (New York: Charles Scribner's Sons, 1905), I, 90.

3 Leon Edel, ed., *Henry James, The Future of the Novel* (New York: Vintage Books, 1956), p. 49.

4 Banta, p. 53.

5 Ralph Barton Perry, *The Thought and Character of William James* (Boston, MA: Little, Brown and Co., 1935), I, 429.

6 Quentin Anderson, *The American Henry James* (New Brunswick, NJ: Rutgers University Press, 1957), pp. 352-353.

7 John Goode, "The Pervasive Mystery of Style: *The Wings of the Dove,*" in John Goode, ed., *The Air of Reality: New Essays on Henry James* (London: Methuen & Co., 1972), p. 245.

8 Robert J. Reilly, "Henry James and the Morality of Fiction," *American Literature,* 39 (March, 1967), 25.

9 Yvor Winters, *In Defense of Reason* (Denver, CO: University of Denver Press, 1947), p. 306.

10 Philip Rahv, *Literature and the Sixth Sense* (New York: Houghton Mifflin Co., 1969), p. 123.

11 Labrie.

12 Edward Rich Levy, *Henry James and the Pragmatic Assumption* (Ann Arbor, MI: University Microfilms, 1964), p. 87.

13 Wallace Stevens, "Esthetique du Mal," *Collected Poems* (New York: Alfred A. Knopf, 1954), p. 322.

14 Percy Lubbock, ed., *The Letters of Henry James* (New York: Charles Scribner's Sons, 1920), II, 168, All references will be to this edition.

15 F. O. Matthiessen and Kenneth Murdock, eds., *The Notebooks of Henry James* (New York: Oxford University Press, A Galaxy Book, 1961), p. 41.

16 A letter to William cited by Leon Edel, *Henry James, The Middle Years* (Philadelphia, PA: J. B. Lippincott Co., 1962), p. 62.

17 *The Notebooks of Henry James,* pp. 320-321.

18 Brooks Atkinson, ed., *The Writings of Ralph Waldo Emerson* (New York: The Modern Library, 1950), pp. 775-783.

19 Gay Wilson Allen and Charles T. Davis, eds., *Walt Whitman's Poems* (New York: New York University Press, 1955), p. 75.

20 F. O. Matthiessen, ed., "Is There a Life After Death?" *The James Family* (New York: Alfred A. Knopf, 1961). The essay first appeared in a collection edited by Howells, entitled *In After Days, Thoughts on the Future Life* (New York: Harper & Brothers, 1910). References will be to this edition.

21 Labrie, pp. 528-529. F. O. Matthiessen says that James argues for survival in a "loosely neo-Platonic way," *Henry James, The Major Phase* (New York: Oxford University Press, 1944), p. 147. Neo-Platonism, however, is based upon belief in the upward journey of the soul toward God or the One. This ultimate goal finds no expression in James. Frederic Harold Young, in an analysis of the thought of Henry James, Sr., points out that the elder James never developed any specific doctrine of

immortality. In Chapter IX of Part Two, Young explains the role of consciousness in the father's philosophy but makes clear that it did stem from theological assumptions never made by the younger Henry. *The Philosophy of Henry James, Sr.* (New Haven, CT: College and University Press, 1951), pp. 164-225.

[22] Perry, I. 428. See Richard A. Hocks, *Henry James and Pragmatistic Thought* (Chapel Hill: University of North Carolina Press, 1974) for a recent analysis of James's pragmatism.

[23] Levy's unpublished doctoral dissertation, previously cited, makes a convincing demonstration of elements of pragmatism in the work of Henry James. He deals with *Roderick Hudson, The Sacred Fount, The Ambassadors,* and certain reviews and essays.

[24] Anderson, pp. 352-353.

[25] Clifton Fadiman, ed., *The Short Stories of Henry James* (New York: The Modern Library, 1945), p. 353. William Troy has pointed out the contemporary relevance of this story and shown it to be wholly without theological implications. "The Altar of Henry James" in F. W. Dupee, ed., *The Question of Henry James* (New York: Henry Holt, 1945).

[26] Leon Edel, ed., *Henry James: Stories of the Supernatural* (New York: Taplinger, 1970), p. xiv.

[27] Banta, p. 3.

[28] *Henry James: Stories of the Supernatural,* p. 56.

[29] Banta, p. 85.

[30] *Henry James: Stories of the Supernatural,* p. 617.

[31] *The American, The Novels and Tales of Henry James* (New York: Charles Scribner's Sons, 1907), II, 394.

[32] *The Princess Casamassima, The Novels and Tales of Henry James* (New York: Charles Scribner's Sons, 1908), VI, 264.

[33] Mildred E. Hartsock, "The Princess Casamassima: The Politics of Power," *Studies in the Novel,* I (Fall 1969), p. 305.

[34] *Henry James: Stories of the Supernatural,* p. 352.

[35] Edel, Preface to "Owen Wingrave," *Henry James: Stories of the Supernatural,* p. 314.

[36] "The Author of Beltraffio," *The Novels and Tales of Henry James* (New York: Charles Scribner's Sons, 1909), XVI, 45-46.

[37] Edmund Wilson, "The Ambiguity of Henry James," *The Triple Thinkers* (New York: Oxford University Press, 1948). Robert Heilman, "The Turn of the Screw as Poem," *The University of Kansas City Review,* 14 (Summer 1948), 277-289.

[38] Joseph J. Firebaugh, "Inadequacy in Eden: Knowledge and *The Turn of the Screw,*" *Modern Fiction Studies,* 3 (Spring 1957), 57-63.

[39] Leon Edel, *Henry James, The Middle Years,* p. 306.

[40] See Edel, *Henry James, The Middle Years,* pp. 67-68; 126-129; 134-136; 299-304.

[41] Fadiman, p. 315.

[42] Fadiman, p. 575.

[43] *The Portrait of a Lady, The Novels and Tales of Henry James* (New York: Charles Scribner's Sons, 1908), IV, 413-414.

[44] F. W. Dupee, *Henry James* (New York: Dell Publishing Co., 1965), p. 217.

[45] *The Wings of the Dove, The Novels and Tales of Henry James* (New York: Charles Scribner's Sons, 1909), XIX, 245. Other references will be to this edition.

[46] Oscar Cargill, *The Novels of Henry James* (New York: The Macmillan Co., 1961), p. 340.

[47] John P. O'Neill, *Workable Design* (Port Washington, NY.: Kennikat Press, 1973), p. 111.

[48] Leon Edel, *Henry James, The Master* (Philadelphia, PA: J. B. Lippincott Company, 1972), pp. 542-554.

Brooke Horvath

SOURCE: "Richard Brautigan's Search for Control Over Death," in *American Literature,* Vol. 57, No. 3, October, 1985, pp. 434-55.

[*In the following essay, Horvath describes the efforts of the countercultural heroes in Brautigan's fiction as they attempt to resist the dominant culture of American society, associated in Brautigan's novels with "dealing and desiring death."*]

Ludwig Wittgenstein once noted that "Death is not an event in life. Death is not lived through."[1] However, as Kierkegaard and others have forcefully argued, the prospect of death is life's central fact and the repression of this fact life's primary task. For Ernest Becker, moreover, man's heroism lies in his impossible efforts to transcend creatureliness, to deny death by means of "life-enhancing illusion."[2] Among such illusions might be placed statements such as Wittgenstein's and the fiction of Richard Brautigan.

As Becker writes early in *The Denial of Death,* "The irony of man's condition is that the deepest need is to be free of the anxiety of death and annihilation; but it is life itself which awakens it, and so we must shrink from being fully alive" (p. 66). For Becker, this dilemma is inherent to consciousness, a consequence of human nature more than nurture. His views thus oppose those of Marcuse or Norman O. Brown, whose works speak to the desire for unrepressed living while pointing an accusing finger at society as the cause of repression. Yet throughout the Sixties, Brautigan created characters seeking not greater freedom but greater control over their lives: over their creatureliness, their thoughts and emotions. But, further, although shrinking from life should not be seen exclusively as a result of social antagonism toward freedom and self-expansiveness, society can exacerbate this existential timidity. And in *Trout Fishing in America* (completed 1961, published 1967), *A Confederate General from Big Sur* (completed 1963, published 1964), *In Watermelon Sugar* (completed 1964, published 1968), and *The Abortion: An Historical Romance 1966* (1971) the global village falls to ataractic communes and isolated dreamers seeking escapes from history, time, and change.

I

The American 1960s was often violent and deadly. The decade brought the country Vietnam and nightly body counts, the Cuban missile crisis and renewed atmospheric nuclear testing, Birmingham Sunday and the Days of Rage, Watts and Newark, Charles Whitman and Richard Speck, assassinations and alarms of overpopulation and eco-death. Strange, unnatural death and explicitly detailed acts of irrational, unexpected violence clearly obsessed the decade's fiction. Brautigan suggested the inseparability of death from his vision of the Sixties in the title of his fourth novel, *The Abortion: An Historical Romance 1966,* thereby underscoring the death-obsession which his critics have frequently noticed percolating through his work.[3] This obsession underlies the now-famous vignettes of blighted landscapes and polluted streams, perverted myths, frustrated hopes, corrupted values, corporeal and spiritual death in *Trout Fishing in America.* Brautigan's disappointment with our times underlies as well the sense of degeneration informing *A Confederate General,* evoked through the novel's contrast of present-day America with the Civil War years and of the heroic images that war typically conjures up with both the imagined behavior of Lee Mellon's ancestor Augustus and the observed behavior of that border psychopath Lee. *In Watermelon Sugar* reveals its author's critique of society in its images of an alternative community and of the Forgotten Works: those remains of a self-destructive civilization so far fallen into ruin that its survivors, 171 years later, can no longer identify many of its simplest artifacts.

Additionally, Brautigan's *idée fixe* habitually works itself out in stories of dropouts or of those living along the mainstream's more ragged tributaries, for his characters customarily sound retreats: to Big Sur, to what remains of the wilderness, to the emotionless science-fiction com-

mune of iDEATH, to the cloistered utopia Vida and the narrator share in *The Abortion.*[4] Such a conjunction of death, destruction, and disaffiliation suggests that Lee, Vida, and the rest share a countercultural view of the dominant culture as dealing and desiring death; in which case, disengagement from society might understandably follow. But further, to the extent that fear of death may be considered the primary motivational factor in men's lives, disengagement may result not only because death is ubiquitous within the confines of the establishment but because, even when most admirable, most heroic, the dominant culture offers promises of transcending death that no longer convince. When such promises fail to inspire belief, the individual is forced back upon himself to create his own illusions of control, his own means of defusing death fears. In short, our world makes closet neurotics of us all when we must forego, in some measure, giving allegiance to the dominant culture as savior and attempt instead to erect private stays against dissolution.[5]

To free themselves from the anxiety of death, Brautigan's heroes seek to control the life that awakens it, seek the know-how of dominating life through self-imposed restraints upon life and self. Lee Mellon, for instance, may possess a certain amount of barely serviceable survival know-how, but, as importantly, he also has the know-how to shape his life into a denial of death. In this connection, Hugh Kenner has recently observed how-to literature's venerable tradition in America. Infiltrating the work of our best writers (Kenner points to *Walden, Moby-Dick, Life on the Mississippi,* and *Death in the Afternoon*), how-to literature has over the years metamorphosed into "a genre sui generis, the indigenous American literature of escape."[6] Similarly, Brautigan's Sixties seekers put a premium on self-reliance, on know-how, as a way of creating the illusion that one is master of one's life, hence of one's destiny. In this respect, *The Abortion* is in a sense only a terribly *au courant* how-to manual (how to resolve a problematic pregnancy easily, safely, and relatively emotionlessly); *In Watermelon Sugar,* a mock blueprint for structuring utopia; and Lee Mellon, that "Confederate general in ruins,"[7] a half-assed, latter-day Thoreau.

Brautigan's is, however, a curious brand of how-to self-reliance. Two comments reprinted on the back cover of the Dell edition of *Trout Fishing* clarify the nature of these novels as how-to literature. A reader at the Viking Press noted that "Mr. Brautigan submitted a book to us in 1962 called *Trout Fishing in America.* I gather from reports that it was not about trout fishing." *Fly Fisherman* magazine, on the other hand, told its readers that "reading *Trout Fishing in America* won't help you catch more fish, but it does have something to do with trout fishing."[8] The point is that Brautigan, foregoing even a facade of practical instruction, foregrounds instead the escapism underlying America's indigenous genre no less than it underlies the musings of armchair and weekend anglers. He focuses on the how-to of escape: not only from a particularly deadly society but from too much life generally, and from the fear of being overwhelmed by this life, the life awakening fears of death.

Such concerns may be described as religious insofar as they manifest a preoccupation with death and its transcendence and insofar as the desire to transcend death lies at the heart of religious belief. Brautigan's fiction as how-to, then, involves creating a private religion that promises a triumph over death. This combination of self-reliance and spiritual necessity—requiring the reshaping of a received but no longer viable tradition or, more drastically, the constructing of a private alternative to fit personal needs—characterizes as well a large part of religious thought in America. America's history of do-it-yourself religion might be seen to begin with the Puritans' covenant theology and their vision of the New World as the New Israel. This tradition informs the Enlightenment appropriation of Puritanism, the Transcendentalist and Romantic revisions of Puritanism and Unitarianism, the merger of civil and millennial expectations that became so centrally a part of nineteenth-century thought, the Campbellites and Millerites (indeed, America's history of utopian communities in general), the work of Joseph Smith and Mary Baker Eddy, Emerson's plea for religious self-reliance and James's *Varieties of Religious Experience*, Henry Adams and the Beats. In short, whenever spiritual dissatisfaction has flowered, Americans have been quick to "make it new," to clear some imaginative ground upon which to raise their personal solutions.

II

As man's capacity for killing increased in scale, as incomprehensible death seemed increasingly omnipresent, as conventional religious belief as a means of resolving death fears continued to collapse, literary theorists began speaking more and more of literature's function in terms of its ability to give endings meaning.[9] It is art's ability to control its ends, its power to resee and to reorder reality, that Brautigan foregrounds in his first completed novel, *Trout Fishing in America.* "Rembrandt Creek," one of the novel's two "lost chapters" (published in *Esquire* three years after the book's appearance), seems to offer a heuristic for interpreting *Trout Fishing*'s intention: "Often I think about Rembrandt Creek and how much it looked like a painting hanging in the world's largest museum with a roof that went to the stars and galleries that knew the whisk of comets."[10] Like the name arbitrarily assigned to the creek, this passage reminds the reader of the possibility of transforming life into art. More explicitly still, Brautigan emphasizes fiction's ability to legislate endings by the conclusion he here offers. The penultimate chapter of the novel ends with the narrator expressing his desire to "write a book that ended with the word Mayonnaise" (p. 181). Then, on the next and final page, postfixed to the letter concluding *Trout Fishing* but having nothing to do with this letter, the following appears: "Sorry I forgot to give you the mayonaise" (p. 182). (Not to strain, but the fact that "mayonnaise" is here misspelled—in all editions of the novel, as far as I can tell—may suggest that the narrator's wish to control his story's ending has been at best imperfectly realized.) Finally, the book's overall style and structure highlight art as symbolic transcendence: through its collage construction and lack of narrative line,

the novel seems intent on converting time into space and thereby halting America's progressive decay, while this tactic of atemporality likewise creates a sense of timeless presence that erases mortality as a function of time-boundedness.[11]

On the other hand, like the Biblical prophet, who assumes a countercultural stance to speak against his culture's numbness to death, Brautigan as controlling author has constructed a witty, dispassionate jeremiad to criticize his country's passionless capitulation to death, America's degeneration and forgetfulness concerning its hopes and dreams: which he does by ironically mirroring in his book's construction the sense of that eternal now that Walter Brueggemann labels "the lewd promise of immortality" and argues is always an illusion the establishment finds necessary to maintain to deny the possibility of newness, of alternative beginnings. By voicing through its series of koan-like sketches the despair over death and dissolution America has provoked, is blind to, and cannot countermand, *Trout Fishing* expresses the grief that must precede dismantling and energizing toward a new beginning. That is, through its language of grief, through its dark humor, through its awareness of death fears suppressed so long they have been forgotten in numbness, Brautigan's first novel opens the possibility of controlling death insofar as the novel now allows the future to be imagined alternatively.[12]

However, Brautigan's fiction attempts to solve the problem of death not only by finding an energizing language of grief and hope, not only by imposing "coherent patterns" providing ends consonant with beginnings and middles,[13] but also by intercalating within these patterns accounts of characters who themselves seek controls over death, controls they would like to think proffer freedom, dignity, and hope—characteristics of the "best" illusions, according to Becker (p. 202). Toward this end, the characters of *A Confederate General, In Watermelon Sugar,* and *The Abortion* resort, variously, to fantasy, simplification of perception and response, ritualized and routinized behavior, and an effort at shutting down the self by maintaining a cool aloofness from emotion, from too much introspection, and from anything else that might cause a loss of self-control. Self-reliance for these characters is achieved not by expanding the sphere of their competence but by reducing life's scope and possibility (the less-is-more approach) or by wrapping themselves in private myths that imaginatively render life harmless. The problem with such ploys lies in the fact that rather than penetrating a numbness to death and so engaging in that "embrace of deathliness [that] permits newness to come,"[14] these characters typically spin illusions enhancing numbness by camouflaging its underlying anxiety: those fears of death with which they refuse to wrestle.

III

A Confederate General, with its hard-drinking, dope-smoking, gun-toting, womanizing dropouts Lee and Jesse, might seem to illustrate not the characterization of

Brautigan's heroes just drawn but that craziness that may easily result from the need to contrive private rituals. Yet neurosis and psychosis are ways of seeking to control life and to neutralize the terror of eventual annihilation— though such strategies cost too much, which is part of the reason why Lee and Jesse seem finally to be leading unenviable lives.

In an early discussion of *A Confederate General* Terence Malley objected that Jesse's replacement of Lee as the novel's center of attention works to the book's detriment. Malley found Jesse's slide into psychological instability too radical a change from his earlier role as humorous sidekick, and the melancholic temperament he comes to exhibit, too perplexing.[15] Yet from first to last the book is Jesse's, not only because he is its narrator and central consciousness but because what *A Confederate General* in fact chronicles is Lee's effect on Jesse: the gradual undermining of this shy loner's precarious psychological balance through his acquaintance with Lee, that "end product of American spirit, pride and the old knowhow" (p. 93).

The reader learns little about Jesse's life prior to his meeting Lee, but one suspects it was quietly desperate. Well read, given to paying visits on the elderly woman living below him, conscientious (he leaves a newfound lover's bed, for example, to recover a drunken Lee before the police find him), Jesse finds his days nonetheless clouded by depression. The most unlikely experiences emerge from his mind in metaphoric shrouds: "a rush of wind came by the cabin. The wind made me think about the Battle of Agincourt for it moved like arrows about us . . ." (p. 111). Against this habitual disposition, Jesse favors small life-enhancing illusions, such as humor— which attempts to distance despair and to deflate its seriousness—or the book about the soul he reads shortly after joining Lee at Big Sur: "The book said everything was all right if you didn't die while you were reading the book, if your fingers maintained life while turning the pages" (p. 66). Similarly, after obsessively reading and rereading Ecclesiastes, Jesse finds a way of bringing its gloomy world view under control by reducing the text to its punctuation marks, which he then carefully tabulates night by night, Qoheleth's vision mastered by being reduced to a "kind of study in engineering" (p. 74).

Yet at the time Jesse is practicing such pathetic rituals, he has already fallen into the manic world of Lee Mellon. Lee's exuberance doubtless attracts the withdrawn Jesse, who finds fascinating material for his death-suffused outlook in Lee's martial fantasy and violent behavior. Throughout the novel, Jesse has occasion to relate instances of Lee's sadism, as when Lee threatens to shoot two teenagers caught trying to siphon gas from his truck (pp. 76-80). If heroism is, at root, the courage to face death, and sadism, like mental illness generally, "a way of talking about people who have lost courage" (Becker, p. 209),[16] Lee's sadistic behavior is a logical consequence of his lifestyle, as is the fantasy role he assigns himself: the outlaw descendent of the fictitious Confederate general Augustus Mellon.

Lee leads a life of petty violence, squalor, and penury; as a self-reliant outlaw, he is inept: his hold-ups net him petty cash; he cannot shoot straight because he is "excitable" (p. 65); and although while holed up in an abandoned house in Oakland he successfully taps a gas main, he cannot control the resulting flame and is consequently seen for a time minus eyebrows. To give such a life meaning and the heroic dimension that would justify it, Lee must resort to sadism and fantasy: as the Confederate General of Big Sur, he gains self-worth by proxy and a precedent for abandoning the conventions by which lesser men must live.

The martial imagery draping Lee and the book is, however, primarily Jesse's doing, for he has masochistically bought into Lee's fantasy life to add vicarious grandeur to his own failed heroics. As Jesse observes while the two teenagers grovel at gunpoint and he stands by, ax in hand, "Do you see how perfect our names were, how the names lent themselves to this kind of business? Our names were made for us in another century" (p. 78). But eventually, these fantasies become themselves too overwhelming, no longer a means of controlling life but now a threat to self-control. Johnston Wade may be the final straw here, for, unlike the fantasies of the others (even Lee, threatening the teenagers, knows his gun is not loaded), Wade's are so out of control and dangerous that Lee finally resorts to chaining Wade to a log to keep everyone safe. Further, Wade, as a deranged insurance magnate on the lam because convinced his family is out to get him, offers an unsettling reminder not only of society's power to destroy but also of both the trapped individual's recourse to fantasy-control and the destructive potential of fantasy itself.

After a few hours of Wade, Jesse confesses, "I wanted reality to be there. What we had wasn't worth it. Reality would be better" (p. 126). But life at Big Sur will continue to tip Jesse's delicate balance: "I was really gone. My mind was beginning to take a vacation from my senses. I felt it continuing to go while Lee Mellon got the dope" (p. 152). By the final chapter, Jesse has fallen into sexual impotence and, looking back, concludes, "The last week's activities had been a little too much for me, I think. A little too much of life had been thrown at me . . ." (p. 154).

Jesse fails to find the illusions he needs, leaning instead on the crutch of others' fantasies, which offer him small hope, smaller dignity, and at best a loser's kind of freedom. Unable to discover a way of ordering his life into a meaningful, heroic whole, Jesse, not surprisingly, finds no satisfying end for his story but rather five alternative conclusions followed by "more and more endings: the sixth, the 53rd, the 131st, the 9,435th ending, endings going faster and faster, more and more endings, faster and faster until this book is having 186,000 endings per second" (p. 159).

IV

According to Nietzsche, most men employ either "guilty" or "innocent" means in their struggles against life's "deadening dull, paralyzing, protracted pain," which only the courageous have the capacity to experience without a soporific. Guilty means always involve "some kind of an *orgy of feeling*," whereas innocent means include a "general muting of the feeling of life, mechanical activity, the petty pleasure, above all 'love of one's neighbor' . . . the communal feeling of power through which the individual's discontent with himself is drowned in his pleasure in the prosperity of the community."[17] In *A Confederate General* Lee and Wade represent the employment of guilty expedients, which submerge Jesse and his more innocent stratagems. Well aware of the dangers of excess, and more fortunate than Jesse in avoiding these dangers, the characters of *In Watermelon Sugar* and *The Abortion* likewise favor innocent maneuvers. In both books, characters find asylums wherein carefully regulated and ritualized fantasies—do-it-yourself religions—achieve a drastic shutting down of self that masks a failure of heroism and voids death anxiety more successfully than anachronistic secession and more predictably than dope.

In the world of Watermelon Sugar, simple, quietly routine days pass without disturbing emotions, thoughts, or desires. Whatever happens is seen to have happened for the best and as it must, and whatever displeases tends to disappear from view, like Margaret's note: "I read the note and it did not please me and I threw it away, so not even time could find it."[18] Personality has been so repressed that most of the community's art, to choose one telling example, stands as the work of anonymous artists who typically favor harmless subjects, electing to produce statues of vegetables and books on innocuous topics like pine needles and owls. In iDEATH, the community's spiritual center, as in Watermelon Sugar generally, "a delicate balance" obtains, as the narrator acknowledges (p. 1). To safeguard this life's emotional and intellectual deep sleep, virtues conducive to placidity must be cultivated; consideration and politeness are fetishized, and small, unsophisticated pleasures prevail. To experience such innocent joys, emotion must be carefully monitored, and even sexual desire must be satisfied with passion well under control (p. 34).

Further, all actual or potential threats to the community's well-being must be neutralized. Books, for example, are unvalued. Written by those who can find no satisfaction in more communally useful employment, books are seen as odd, solitary pursuits. If they do not, as in *Farenheit 451,* represent such subversive dangers as curiosity and originality of thought, this is because no one pays them any mind. Although only twenty-three books have appeared in 171 years, even these go largely unread (pp. 11, 135), the possibility of life's growing too large averted by simple disregard, which also serves to defuse the nearby evil of the Forgotten Works:

> Nobody has been very far into the Forgotten Works, except that guy Charley said who wrote a book about them, and I wonder what his trouble was, to spend weeks in there.
>
> The Forgotten Works just go on and on and on and on and on and on and on and on and on. You

get the picture. It's a big place, much bigger than we are. (p. 82)

Other sources of unrest fade from view as readily. The tigers, the once-great threat to Watermelon Sugar, required the most active opposition. Exterminated and subsequently mythologized, the tigers, symbols of human aggressiveness and instinctual need, have taken the theological problem of Blake's tyger with them, leaving only their remembered virtues—their math prowess and beautiful singing voices—for souvenirs. On the other hand, inBOIL and his gang, like Margaret, obligingly remove themselves through suicide, the end of their restless dissatisfaction with iDEATH. However, their deaths, although violent, trouble utopia only momentarily because Watermelon Sugar is a world with the know-how to repress death anxiety by masking death's reality behind numbing familiarity, spurious immortality, and soporific funereal wisdom. InBOIL may kill himself to reveal iDEATH's true meaning, what the death of the self really entails: that it means more than the death of the ego (Ideath), of the id (IDeath), of thought (IDEAth); that Charley and the rest have made a mockery of iDEATH, have, in fact, failed to confront it. Yet nestled firmly in their numbed, death-in-life existence, iDEATH's inhabitants cannot be flushed by literal death so easily. In the midst of the mass suicide of inBOIL and his gang, the narrator's girlfriend responds only by fetching a pail and mop to clean up the "mess" their bleeding to death has made. And although other deaths may elicit more sympathetic responses, they do not provoke much more emotion. Watching in the Statue of Mirrors (in which "everything is reflected") as his former girlfriend Margaret hangs herself, the narrator remarks, "I stopped looking into the Statue of Mirrors. I'd seen enough for that day. I sat down on a couch by the river and stared into the water of the deep pool that's there. Margaret was dead" (p. 136; see the similar reaction of Margaret's brother, p. 142).

Naming its center iDEATH, a place as changeable as death is various (pp. 18, 144-45), the community can pretend to be living with and in "death," which is further familiarized through elaborate burial rituals that leave the dead "in glass coffins at the bottoms of rivers" with "foxfire in the tombs, so they glow at night and we can appreciate what comes next" (p. 60). However, the community must pay a great price for this anxiety-free life. The shutting down of self practiced in Watermelon Sugar has reduced tremendously the scope of human responseability. Moreover, the elaborate defensive armor forged here is not without chinks: unpacified dissidents like inBOIL; unhappy, ostracized souls like Margaret; and the restless, nameless narrator as well. Not only does the narrator see behind the shared illusions of iDEATH ("We call everything a river here. We're that kind of people," p. 2); he has written a book ("I wonder what his trouble was"): a book very different from the others written in Watermelon Sugar; a book that builds toward the suicide of iDEATH's latest dropout and ends on the day of the black sun; a book that implicitly gives the lie to the utopian triumph over death this world seems to represent by showing Watermelon Sugar as the restricted, dehumanizing, hopeless, and deadly place it finally is.

V

The Abortion continues Brautigan's interest in characters attempting to retreat from life. The narrator, again nameless, appears in the novel's first two books as a recluse operating a library to which San Francisco's lonely, frustrated residents can bring manuscripts to be recorded in the Library Contents Ledger, shelved (but never borrowed or read), and eventually moved to caves for permanent storage (where "cave seepage" will insure their destruction). Life, the narrator confesses, "was all pretty complicated before I started working here,"[19] but now, safe within the library—tellingly described as a prison, a church, a funeral parlor, an asylum, a time machine, a monastery (pp. 71, 77, 84, 85, 105, 178)—the ritualized, isolated life he leads in this building he has not left once in three years insulates him from history, time, and change. As he remarks upon finally emerging, "Gee, it had been a long time. I hadn't realized that being in that library for so many years was almost like being in some kind of timeless thing. Maybe an eternity" (p. 70).

The cause behind the narrator's re-entry into life is Vida, a relentlessly beautiful girl who arrives one evening with a book for the stacks. She also is in retreat from life; as she tells the narrator, "I can see at a glance . . . that you are something like me. You're not at home in the world" (p. 51). Vida's unease centers upon her body, not despite but because of its beauty: "My book is about my body, about how horrible it is to have people creeping, crawling, sucking at something I am not," she explains (p. 45).

If the library represents a refuge from life, Vida (Spanish for life) enters as a threat to the narrator's innocent defenses: mechanical activity, petty pleasures, muted feeling. "Yes,' I said, feeling the door close behind me, knowing that somehow this at first-appearing shy unhappy girl was turning, turning into something strong that I did not know how to deal with" (p. 49). The narrator rightly feels such qualms, for Vida's beauty—the terrible beauty of life—is a perilous thing capable of wrecking havoc wherever it reveals itself. A middle-aged man, for instance, spotting Vida in the airport, "stood there staring on like a fool, not taking his eyes off Vida, even though her beauty had caused him to lose control of the world" (p. 117). And Vida's beauty can conjure death anxieties even more directly: "The driver continued staring at Vida. He paid very little attention to his driving. . . . I made a mental note of it for the future, not to have Vida's beauty risk our lives" (p. 177).

Yet Vida's beauty does risk their lives. The narrator finds himself far from the library riding in a taxi because Vida's appearance has caused life to enter his world in one particularly troublesome fashion: she has become pregnant, and the two must seek a Tijuana abortion, endangering Vida in obvious ways (and through the very source of her existential dis-ease), endangering the narra-

tor insofar as this fall into physicality constitutes the immediate cause for his forced return to the world. "It looks like our bodies got us," Vida concludes, to which the narrator replies, "It happens sometimes" (p. 67), seeking comfort, like Jesse, in the assumption of a light-hearted attitude.

Indeed, although the narrator's good-natured stoicism falters momentarily as he waits in the doctor's office for the abortion to begin, for the most part he and Vida respond splendidly to life's sudden eruption in their midst. Just as Vida drags the narrator from his womblike existence to "live like a normal human being" (p. 189), so he more than reconciles her to her body. By novel's end, Vida is in fact supporting him by working in a North Beach topless bar (p. 191).[20] Similarly, the narrator's outlook changes during the course of his adventure. Flying to San Diego en route to Tijuana had left him green with nausea and desirous of a return to timelessness (p. 120). However, by the time of his return flight, mere hours later, he can remark cavalierly, "From time to time the airplane was bucked by an invisible horse in the sky but it didn't bother me because I was falling in love with the 727 jet, my sky home, my air love" (p. 183). And even earlier, only minutes after leaving the abortionist's, he finds it hard to keep a straight face when the hotel desk clerk reveals his belief that "People should never change. . . . They are happier that way" (p. 173). Returning to find he has lost his library position, the narrator adjusts quickly, moving into an apartment with Vida, Foster (his only other friend and a former library employee), and Foster's girlfriend and raising money for the library at a table across from Sproul Hall at Berkeley, where he becomes the hero Vida had assured him he would be (pp. 113, 192).

But in what sense is the narrator a hero? And how have he and Vida made their rapid transition from passive withdrawal to active participation in the world? The answer to the first question usually involves the narrator's personality. Beatle-like in appearance, gentle, caring, tranquilized, the narrator embodies, ostensibly, the virtues of heroism as redefined by the counterculture. Thus Malley describes him as a "strange, passive, low-keyed hero of our time" desiring an escape from the American experience, and Charles Hackenberry, plugging into the story's allegorical possibilities, sees in Brautigan's romance a "portrait of the peace movement's heroism and efficacy, its solution to the unwanted pregnancy of American intervention in Asia."[21] But I would suggest that the narrator considers himself heroic because he has triumphed over death. This feat accounts as well for his and Vida's altered attitudes toward the world, attitudes that in fact begin to change when they decide to seek an abortion, for this decision seems to place control over death (choosing its time and means) and so over life in their hands.

Although Hackenberry illustrates that *The Abortion* enacts the archetypal heroic quest, he carefully notes that the book is as much a parody of the romance as it is a romance-proper. It is parodic for the same reasons the narrator's control over death fails as a liberating, dignifying, and hopeful life-enhancing illusion. Like Lee and inBOIL, *The Abortion*'s narrator has attempted to control life and death by becoming the agent of death (in this case, the indirect agent). But his triumph is ephemeral. He has not seized control of his life; he has not even severed his connection with the library. But more to the point, his triumph lacks heroism, involving as it does a Foster-financed, antagonist-free trip to Tijuana for a relatively guiltless, untroubling termination of his girlfriend's pregnancy. The hotel clerk's wish may cause the narrator to smile, but the object of his quest is the fulfillment of this wish: to remain the same, to deny life and change: "Vida's stomach was flat and perfect and it was going to remain that way" (p. 133). The abortion was inexpensive and painless, and one gets what one pays for: in this case, a cheap, temporary illusion that will be obsolete in a few years.

VI

A Confederate General, In Watermelon Sugar, and *The Abortion* present searches for illusions capable of allaying death anxiety and of controlling the life that awakens this anxiety by overwhelming us self-conscious animals with the knowledge of our inherent finitude and biological enslavement. These searches end no more successfully than the search in *Trout Fishing* for pristine trout streams or for the continuance of traditional American myths and ideals, and one might conclude that Brautigan holds no hope of discovering a saving illusion that does not necessitate shutting down the self, smothering emotion, limiting human possibility. Yet stepping back, so to speak, beyond these stories and their narrators to the level on which both become components of Brautigan's imaginative acts, one returns to the sphere of art as life-enhancing illusion. In "Tire Chain Bridge," a brief, three-page stop along the route of *The Tokyo-Montana Express* (1980), Brautigan presents in small compass a paradigmatic exploration of the possibilities and limits of art as death-defying illusion.

"Tire Chain Bridge" takes the form of a parable about the Sixties. It begins:

> The 1960s:
>
> A lot of people remember hating President Lyndon Baines Johnson and loving Janis Joplin and Jim Morrison, depending on the point of view. God rest their souls.
>
> I remember an old Indian woman looking for a tire chain in the snow.[22]

The story, set in 1969, is quickly told. Its narrator and his girlfriend are driving across New Mexico after a snowfall, looking for "some old Indian ruins." They find them, after a fashion, in the persons of an old Indian man and his sister. The man is encountered first, "standing patiently beside a blue Age-of-Aquarius pickup truck parked on the side of the road." He is not in any trouble;

in fact, "Everything's just fine": he only waits for his sister, who is a mile or so down the road looking for a lost tire chain valued at three dollars. The narrator is pleased to learn that road conditions improve ahead but has trouble believing someone is really "out there," searching in such wintry weather beneath the indifferent mesas for a used tire chain. But driving on, he soon finds her and asks foolishly if she has found the chain yet. Glancing "at the nearby 121,000 square miles, which is the area of New Mexico," she answers simply, "It's here someplace."

> "Good luck," I said, ten years ago in the Sixties that have become legend now like the days of King Arthur sitting at the Round Table with the Beatles, and John singing "Lucy in the Sky with Diamonds."
>
> We drove down the road toward the Seventies, leaving her slowly behind, looking for a tire chain in the snow with her brother waiting patiently beside a blue pickup truck with its Age-of-Aquarius paint job starting to flake.

So the story ends. Although brief, seemingly artless, and lightly told in a style matching the content's superficial slightness, "Tire Chain Bridge" means more than meets the casual eye, but what? Surely one must push beyond Edward Halsey Foster's opinion that the story illustrates an ability to laugh good-naturedly at the world's leftover hippies.[23] True, the narrator's retrospective glance back does appear to offer a biting (though hardly acerb) assessment of the decade's foibles and delusions. Its heroes and villains, once as large and seemingly eternal as the New Mexican mesas, barely survived the decade, and—like the narrator's road, which disappeared into "a premature horizon"—they have already vanished into legend. Yet what sort of legends have they left us? Is the Age of Aquarius a fit substitute for Camelot? Are the Beatles the best the period could serve up in the way of heroes worthy to sit beside Arthur and his knights? Is "Lucy in the Sky with Diamonds" what we have in lieu of *Morte d' Arthur?*

If a parable, the lesson of "Tire Chain Bridge" would seem to be that the Sixties was a time of hopeless searching and of passive complacency: both inadequate responses to a cold world in which life exists, like this story, between death and dissolution. Further, these quests, however solemn and sincere, were worse than hopeless: they were so absurd as to be unbelievable ("'What?' I said, not quite hearing or maybe just not believing . . ."). The boon sought was trivial, the seekers caricatures of knights errant capable of mistaking a used tire chain for the Holy Grail. But if the searches were ludicrous, the alternative response was an exercise in misguided smugness: to wait beatifically in the assurance that "everything's just fine" while another conducts one's search, seeks one's solutions. Hoping to salvage a three-dollar investment but oblivious to his truck's slow corruption, the brother would seem to be the man who knows the price of everything and the value of nothing. Similarly, the Age of Aquarius itself—self-satisfied, commercialized, soon bogged down in trivialities and (like the Beatles) in internal feuding—was already beginning to chip and fade even as it was being proclaimed a *fait accompli.*

Such a reading follows Brautigan's recent critics in their efforts to free his work from a too-narrow and perhaps spurious identification with the counterculture.[24] But I think the reading just offered does not tell the entire story. In the first place, metamorphosis into legend is not necessarily a shameful fate; to seat the Beatles beside Arthur may be a means not of undercutting their stature but of enhancing it. And with its acid-induced celebration of wonder, of emancipation from an overly repressive and joyless sense of reality, "Lucy in the Sky," the lay of Woodstock Nation, may be in its way a fitting successor to the songs of the troubadours, an appropriate anthem for the Children's Crusade of the Sixties.

But in terms of a close reading of Brautigan's story, it is perhaps more important to note that the Indian couple is heading not out of but into bad weather, and so the tire chain is well worth looking for: it could save their lives. To see the chain only in terms of its meager monetary worth discloses not only a faulty but a dangerous value system, just as it is wrong to fault the brother for worrying more about the chain than about his pickup: for want of the chain, the truck may be lost. Moreover, direction of motion is problematic here. Although the Indians seem to be dawdling "in the middle of nowhere" and the narrator ostensibly heading toward better weather, the road he travels is, like the year in which the story is set, a bridge into the Seventies, a decade equated in the opening and closing paragraphs with death—Joplin in 1970, Morrison in '71, Johnson in '73—and with disintegration: the flaking paint, the Beatles' death as a group in 1970, the evaporating sensibility of the Sixties. This dissolution hits closer to home for the narrator in that he and his "long since gone girlfriend" broke up after their travels together; and it is emphasized structurally by the girlfriend's disappearance into an infrequent "we" after paragraph six, the only paragraph in which she is spoken of.

Yet looking back to tell his tale, the narrator recalls as his talismanic figure not his girlfriend, not the mesas, not the Indian ruins he was looking for and presumably found, not the decade's dead or disbanded culture heroes, but a woman "looking for a tire chain in the snow." It is she who orients his perspective on the past. The narrator, apparently, cannot recall this woman without the accompanying thoughts of death and deterioration framing her story, yet in recollection her eyes "[echo] timelessness," placing her symbolically among those mesas that "had been witnesses to the beginning of time." Just as she stands alone in the snowy landscape—her patient searching akin to neither her brother's inertia nor the narrator's heedless forward progress into the Seventies and the end of the road—so she stands apart from the decade's famous dead and their failed heroics.

Tire chains are, of course, a means of controlling one's movement along dangerous routes. The woman's search becomes, then, a defiance of death, a search for control in a deadly environment. There is no reason to suppose she enjoys her cold, lonely task, undertaken possibly only to please her brother, who lingers metaphorically closer to the Seventies, content to let whatever will be, be. Yet unlike him, she acts, purposefully if hopelessly, her actions sounding a small triumph of life over death, her conviction that the chain is "here someplace" becoming, however unconvincingly or absurdly, a denial of death: a denial echoed by the story's surface tone, which implies that nothing terribly fearful or serious is here at issue.

However, a sorrow underlies the story's placid surface. This sadness derives not so much from the narrator's necrology or wistful recounting of things past as from his recognition of the futility of the woman's paltry stay against destruction (and, by extension, of the limits of his own death-defying art). Her seeking may bridge the loss surrounding her, but the narrator has located these structurally peripheral memento mori at the story's thematic center. He has anchored his story-proper—of the salvific bridge the woman's action erects—in death at both ends: in the physical deaths with which "Tire Chain Bridge" begins and in the symbolic, spiritual death with which it ends. This latter anchorage involves the extinction of a way of seeing, of imagining the world: possibilities flatten out and dead-end, like the mesa-topped horizon behind the narrator's forward-fleeing Jeep. Structurally, then, "Tire Chain Bridge" gives in to death. And so it is no wonder that the narrator's style has been affected by his acknowledgment of death's centrality, of the limits of control, of the losing battle recollection as an artistic method wages against entropy. And consequently, it is no wonder that the story should sound so flat and artless, that beneath its surface calm should be heard a "melancholy, long, withdrawing roar."

The story, in fact, would seem to deflate its own implicit pretensions as a stay against decay, just as and because it undermines the promise of the woman's seeking. Yet if seeming to succumb to the death it argues is inescapable, "Tire Chain Bridge" acts upon us as it does only by virtue of its remaining an accomplished fact even while proclaiming itself a fading, futile, gesture. The story's telling establishes a small, coherent world of order, and, through its direct engagement of death, "Tire Chain Bridge" permits the "fruitful yearning" that alone allows newness and hope to come.[25] Perhaps Becker is correct when he writes that, in the face of death's inevitability, "The most that any one of us can seem to do is to fashion something—an object or ourselves—and drop it into the confusion, make an offering of it, so to speak, to the life force" (p. 285). The woman has fashioned herself; the narrator, his story. It would seem that, like his creator, he cannot do otherwise.

VII

Several years ago John Clayton complained that Brautigan's "politics of imagination," with its implied hope of "salvation through perception," was not only insufficient but dangerous because its vision might seduce readers into abandoning the struggle to make this world a better place.[26] One can understand Clayton's objection, yet he is wrong to dismiss Brautigan's work as unrebelliously or merely escapist, as lacking a social consciousness. Clayton's error lay in missing the centrality in Brautigan's fiction of death and the anxiety an awareness of death engenders. This awareness is ineradicable; as the narrator of one short story observes, "you cannot camouflage death with words. Always at the end of the words somebody is dead."[27] Death-obsessed, Brautigan's characters find they must dissociate themselves from a culture that both throws death constantly in their paths and fails to give it meaning. These characters typically retreat into private life-enhancing religions, but habitually this ploy does not, as in *Trout Fishing* or "Tire Chain Bridge," engage life-and-death fears head-on and fruitfully; rather, it intensifies that hopelessness and numbness that make death so fearsome within the establishment. A year ago, Richard Brautigan committed suicide; why, I would not presume to say. His work, however, continues to forward an especially severe critique of American society, one that moves beyond politics into prophecy, implicitly sounding a call for repentance, for a turning from death toward life.

NOTES

[1] *Notebooks 1914-1916,* 2nd ed., trans. G. E. M. Anscombe, ed. G. H. von Wright and G. E. M. Anscombe (Chicago: Univ. of Chicago Press, 1979), p. 75e.

[2] *The Denial of Death* (New York: Free Press, 1973). Further references are to the paperback edition (New York: Free Press, 1975) and are included parenthetically within the text.

[3] See, for example, Tony Tanner, *City of Words: American Fiction 1950-1970* (New York: Harper & Row, 1971); Ihab Hassan, *Contemporary American Literature: 1945-1972* (New York: Ungar, 1973); and Jack Hicks, *In the Singer's Temple: Prose Fictions of Barthelme, Gaines, Brautigan, Piercy, Kesey, and Kosinski* (Chapel Hill: Univ. of North Carolina Press, 1981).

[4] Brautigan's characters as dropouts have been the subject of much commentary. See, for example, John Clayton, "Richard Brautigan: The Politics of Woodstock," *New American Review,* 11 (1971), 56-68; Terence Malley, *Richard Brautigan,* Writers for the Seventies (New York: Warner, 1972); W. T. Lhamon, Jr., "Break and Enter to Breakaway: Scotching Modernism in the Social Novel of the American Sixties," *boundary* 2, 3 (1975), 289-306; and Manfred Pütz, *The Story of Identity: American Fiction of the Sixties* (Stuttgart: J. B. Metzlersche Verlagsbuchhandlung, 1979).

[5] My discussion here is much indebted to Becker; see pp. 198-99 particularly.

[6] "The Wherefores of How-To: Pascal, BASIC, Call Up a Literary Tradition," *Harper's,* March 1984, p. 92.

[7] *A Confederate General from Big Sur* (1964; rpt. New York: Delta / Seymour Lawrence, 1979), p. 18. Further references are included parenthetically within the text.

[8] *Trout Fishing in America* (New York: Dell, 1967). Further references are included parenthetically within the text.

[9] See, for example, Frank Kermode, *The Sense of an Ending: Studies in the Theory of Fiction* (New York: Oxford Univ. Press, 1967) and Peter Brooks, *Reading for the Plot: Design and Intention in Narrative* (New York: Knopf, 1984).

[10] "Rembrandt Creek," in *Revenge of the Lawn: Stories 1962-1970* (New York: Pocket Books, 1972), p. 42.

[11] According to Frederick Hoffman, fictions positing no hopes for an afterlife often, in attempting to articulate their "mortal no," work to convert time into space. See *The Mortal No: Death and the Modern Imagination* (Princeton: Princeton Univ. Press, 1964).

[12] Brueggemann develops the notion of prophecy sketched here in his book *The Prophetic Imagination* (Philadelphia: Fortress Press, 1978).

[13] See Kermode, p. 17.

[14] Brueggemann, p. 113.

[15] Malley, pp. 104-09.

[16] In this quotation, Becker is summarizing Alfred Adler. See Adler's *The Practice and Theory of Individual Psychology* (London: Kegan Paul, 1942), chap. 21.

[17] Friedrich Nietzsche, *On the Genealogy of Morals,* trans. Walter Kaufmann and R. J. Hollingdale, ed. Walter Kaufmann (New York: Vintage, 1969), p. 136.

[18] *In Watermelon Sugar* (1968; rpt. New York: Dell, 1973), p. 65. Further references are included parenthetically within the text.

[19] *The Abortion: An Historical Romance 1966* (1971; rpt. New York: Pocket Books, 1972), p. 53. Further references are included parenthetically within the text.

[20] Even earlier, Vida had mellowed to the point where Foster (keeper of the caves and arranger of the abortion) could make her laugh by swearing, "My God, ma'am, you're so pretty I'd walk ten miles barefooted on a freezing morning to stand in your shit" (p. 78). That Vida can laugh at such a remark is particularly revealing, for as Becker explains, "excreting is the curse that threatens madness because it shows man his abject finitude, his physicalness, the likely unreality of his hopes and dreams" (p. 33).

[21] Malley, p. 75, and Charles Hackenberry, "Romance and Parody in Brautigan's *The Abortion*," *Critique,* 23, ii (1981-1982), 34.

22 In *The Tokyo-Montana Express* (New York: Delacorte / Seymour Lawrence, 1980), p. 94. Because the story is so short (running from p. 94 to p. 97), I will not include page references in the text.

23 *Richard Brautigan* (Boston: Twayne, 1983), pp. 120-21.

24 The two most recent book-length studies of Brautigan, for example, assert among their principal intentions the desire to free the novelist from the critical error of reading him primarily in terms of Sixties concerns. Foster in his Preface claims that "Brautigan's best works were in fact never quite what they were alleged to be. Although they certainly do reflect a special time in American history, the time they reflect has little to do with America in the late 1960s and early 1970s." Mare Chénetier, *Richard Brautigan* (New York: Methuen, 1983), offers the thesis that Brautigan "has always been much more akin to the metafictionists of the seventies than to the naive flower-children of what I should like to call the pre-Nixapsarian sixties" (p. 16).

25 The phrase is Brueggemann's, p. 113.

26 Clayton, pp. 56, 59.

27 "The World War I Los Angeles Airplane," in *Revenge of the Lawn*, p. 169.

Mary Joseph

SOURCE: "Suicide in Henry James's Fiction: A Sociological Analysis," in *CLA Journal*, Vol. XXXIV, No. 2, December, 1990, pp. 188-211.

[In the following essay, Joseph interprets the many characters in Henry James's fiction who take their own lives in terms of the classifications of suicidal behavior adduced by Émile Durkheim in his Suicide: A Study in Sociology.*]*

Suicide among major fictional characters of the nineteenth century—Hardy's Eustacia and Little Father Time, Tolstoy's Anna Karenina, and Flaubert's Madame Bovary, to name a few—impresses one with its pervasiveness in the imaginative world of eminent authors of the time. Writing in the period following the glorification of the suicidal deaths of Werther and Chatterton, and emphasizing the workings of the minds of his characters by working "an acre of embroidery on an inch of canvas," Henry James calls attention to the portrayal of self-willed deaths in his fiction. Having grown up in a highly individualistic family that emphasized the exercise of free will, and being one who reveled in the probing of his character's consciousnesses, James considered important the role of will in matters of life and death. Because characters who willfully courted death at their own hands through violent means and those who died because of the more passive loss of will to live are equally self-destructive, the term suicide is used in the sense of Émile Durkheim's late nineteenth-century definition as applying to "all cases of death resulting directly or indirectly from a positive or negative act of the victim himself, which he knows will produce this result."[1] Thus, Daisy Miller's willful contracting of fatal malaria and the fatally ill Milly Theale's turning her face to the wall are as much suicidal acts as Hyacinth Robinson's putting a bullet through his heart and Agatha Grice's consumption of poison.

Ten instances of physical suicide and eight instances of symbolic suicide (death as a result of the loss of the will to live) in a total of sixteen novels and tales are closely analyzed here. Analyses of these eighteen suicides in the light of penetrating sociological studies of the phenomenon by such notables as Émile Durkheim, Louis Dublin, Edwin Shneidman, A. Alvarez, and Philippe Aries show James's fictional suicides to be reflections of the real-life phenomenon. The temporal and geographical universality, the irrationality, and the inexplicability of self-destruction make the scholarly studies and observations, irrespective of their time and place, enlightening. The comprehensiveness and timing (last decade of the nineteenth century) of Durkheim's study make his observations especially relevant to the analysis of James's suicide fiction. While reflecting the universality, the irrationality, and the inexplicability of the phenomenon, James's fictional suicides also show conformity to characteristics of the real-life phenomenon during his time. Thus, in the delineation of his suicidal characters, James shows himself to be very much a man of his times and of his milieu.

I

In a total of nine novels and tales, there are ten instances of obvious or suspected suicides where the concerned individuals resort to violent means to end their lives. In "Osborne's Revenge," Robert Graham, a deluded young man of literary bent, "had shot himself through the head in his room at the hotel."[2] Before doing it, however, he had sent to his best friend, Philip Osborne, a letter describing his mental state and his reasons for taking this drastic step. Three years later, in *Watch and Ward,* a widower, distraught over his financial situation, kills himself in the presence of his young daughter. When others arrive on the scene, his hand still holds the pistol from which "he had just sent a bullet through his brain."[3] An 1874 story, "Madame de Mauves," is singular in having two suicides. The impoverished Baron de Mauves, husband of the innocent and wealthy American Euphemia, shoots himself in the head[4] because his virtuous wife refuses to forgive his transgressions after he has reformed himself. The other suicide in the story, his sister's husband, having lost his fortune and fearing his wife, had earlier shot himself in the head (13:249). *Roderick Hudson* (1874-75), the first work which raises the question of intention, provides ample textual evidence and foreshadowing to justify labeling Roderick a suicide.

More than a decade after *Roderick Hudson* (1875), in *The Princess Casamassima* (1885-86), Hyacinth Robinson's dead body is discovered within a room locked from the inside, leaving no question as to how he came to his end: "Mr. Robinson has shot himself through the heart" (6:431). "The Modern Warning" (1888), containing one of two suicides by poisoning in James's fiction, depicts the only married woman to take her own life. Another tale published the same year, "The Patagonia," contains the other female suicide. Grace Mavis disappears one night from the Patagonia. Though her body is not recovered, she may safely be considered a suicide since no indication is given of a possible accidental fall and since we have no reason to suspect that anyone on board would deliberately push her into the ocean. "Sir Edmund Orme" (1891), the only Jamesian ghost story with a suicide, has the only male suicide who resorts to poisoning. After keeping suicide out of his fiction for almost two decades, James returns to it in "A Round of Visits" (1910). Newton Winch, depressed over his unethical financial transactions, shoots himself through his temple just as the police arrive at the door for him and as his friend Mark Monteith goes to open the door for them.

Certain interesting facts emerge from a surface observation of these suicides. Except for the two tales published in 1888, "The Modern Warning" and "The Patagonia," all of the physical suicides are men. For those who seek violent deaths at their own hands, the most often used means is the gun. Five of these choose to send bullets through their brains, while one sends it through his heart. Two choose to end their lives by poisoning, one falls from a mountaintop, and another drowns herself. The two women choose comparatively less violent forms of self-destruction: Agatha in "The Modern Warning" takes poison, while Grace Mavis aboard *The Patagonia* chooses drowning. All except Robert Graham in "Osborne's Revenge," Lambert in *Watch and Ward,* and M. Clairin in "Madame de Mauves" are protagonists or major characters. The suicides of the Baron in "Madame de Mauves," Roderick Hudson in the novel of that name, Hyacinth Robinson in *The Princess Casamassima,* Agatha in "The Modern Warning," Grace in "The Patagonia" and Newton Winch in "A Round of Visits" are all culminating activities in the respective works. Robert Graham's suicide, which takes place early in "Osborne's Revenge," provides the background for Philip Osborne's revenge. Sir Edmund Orme's suicide, which had taken place several years before the current action, accounts for his ghostly presence in the story named after him. The suicide in *Watch and Ward* is unique in not having much bearing on the main action of the plot. Lambert's suicide remains in the background as the event that orphaned Nora, making Roger Lawrence's entry into her life possible. The mental stability of Robert Graham, Lambert, and Roderick Hudson appears to be questionable. All of the other physical suicides seem to be in command of their mental faculties.

II

In addition to the ten instances of physical suicide, there are several examples where James's characters lose their will to live and subsequently lose their lives or give up the trappings of living in the physical world. Three tales and four novels containing eight such voluntary deaths, most of them results of a combination of illness and loss of will, offer a compelling study in the psychology of self-destruction. Durkheim's definition of suicide permits us to view these deaths as suicides.

Two Civil War stories present protagonists who lose their will to live when they face rejection in love. In "The Story of a Year" (1865), a wounded young soldier has made a remarkable recovery. However, when he realizes that his "intended," Lizzie, is romantically interested in someone else, he dies after releasing Lizzie from her commitment to him. Ironically, at the same time, he utters part of the wedding vows, asking Lizzie to be his for a little while, "holding my hands—so—until death parts us" (*CT,* 1:97). "A Most Extraordinary Case" (1868) has another Civil War hero, Colonel Ferdinand Mason, who recovers from a grievous ailment when love nourishes him, but who suddenly makes himself a martyr at the altar of love when he realizes that the girl he adores will soon marry someone else. The narrator makes it perfectly clear that Mason dies because he loses his will to live. He bequeaths most of his wealth to Horace Knight, Caroline Hofmann's would-be-husband: "From this moment his strength began rapidly to ebb, and the shattered fragments of his long-resisting will floated down its shallow current into dissolution" (*CT,* 2:365). To the young doctor, Horace Knight, Mason's death is quite inexplicable; it was "the most extraordinary case" he had ever heard of. Clearly, both deaths, altruistically motivated, result from disappointment in love and consequent loss of the will to live.

"Longstaff's Marriage" depicts contradictory ways in which a man and a woman respond to rejection and acceptance of love. Reginald Longstaff, who proposes to Diana Belfield while supposedly on his deathbed, has the fortune or misfortune of being refused. The rejection, instead of worsening his condition, makes him recover. Later on, the tables are turned when Diana becomes gravely ill and proposes to Reginald. Instead of holding a grudge and refusing her, Longstaff gladly marries her. However, quite oddly and deliberately, in a paradoxical demonstration of love, Diana dies. Rejection of the deathbed marriage proposal boosts Reginald into vigor and life, while acceptance under similar circumstances kills Diana. Longstaff and Belfield exercise their wills in opposing ways. Acceptance of her love prompts Diana Belfield to will herself to die as an act of altruism.

The American (1876-77), first of the two full-length novels in this group, contains two instances of voluntary giving up of life. Stephen Spender considers the entire Bellegarde family of *The American* suicidal: "It repels the inflow of new American life, and it even suicidally refuses the money which might revive its splendour.[5] The aristocratic Claire de Cintre, when caught between family loyalty and love of her American suitor, chooses to enter a convent. Insofar as it means being dead to the world, the action may be considered a symbolic suicide. In this, she may be compared to John Donne, who, according to Alvarez, "finally negotiated his middle-life crisis by taking holy orders instead of his life."[6] That Claire views her entering a convent as a suicidal act is evidenced in her choice of words to Newman. She calls her going away "death" and adds, "Let me bury myself" (2:365). When pressed about where she is going, she says, "I am going out of the world. . . . I am going into a convent" (2:418). Her words clearly do not express the enthusiasm of a person who joins a convent prompted by admirable, noble, and selfless motives. The idea of her being dead to the world is underscored by Newman's own experience of Claire's self-denial. He tells Mrs. Tristram: "I feel like a widower . . . as if my wife had been murdered and her assassins were still at large" (2:512). He further views her as entombing herself in a cell (2:419) and he refers to the convent as "the stony sepulchre that held her" (2:531). Earlier, her brother, Valentin de Bellegarde, had courted physical death in a duel over an obviously disreputable young woman.

Daisy Miller and Milly Theale stand at two ends of the spectrum of characters who die when they lose their will to live. Daisy, the earliest of James's female innocents abroad, shows that even young Americans of sturdy stock (quite healthy and planning to remain so) can suddenly lose their will to live and therefore die, while Milly Theale demonstrates how a strong will to live can sustain even a fatally ill person and how that person can die as soon as she loses her will to live. Twice Daisy declares her intention to remain healthy. First, when her mother and Mrs. Walker try to dissuade her from going to the Pincio with Giovanelli because she might catch the fever, she asserts: "I don't want to do anything that's going to affect my health—or my character either!" (18:54). Later, at the Colosseum, when Winterbourne criticizes Daisy's Italian escort for his indiscretion in taking her there, Daisy, still very much sure of herself, responds, "I never was sick, and I don't mean to be! . . . I don't look like much, but I'm healthy!" (18:88), thus arrogantly expressing her will to live.

However, repeated acts of rejection by Daisy's compatriots in Rome gradually kill her zest for life. The innocent Daisy—who, early in the tale equates the other Americans' not speaking to her and her mother with their (her family's) not speaking to the others and thus being "exclusive" (18:28)—gives up when she suspects that Winterbourne does not believe in her innocence. Despite all her innocence and bravado, the insult in Mrs. Walker's deliberately turning her back to Daisy, who was trying to take leave of the hostess before leaving the party, is not lost upon Daisy. She "turned very pale and looked at her mother" (18:73) and soon turns away, "looking with a small white prettiness, a blighted grace, at the circle near the door" (18:73). Such a reaction belies Winterbourne's suspicion that she simply does not feel and does not know about all the cold shoulders that were turned upon her (18:80).

The scene at the Colosseum demonstrates the ultimate dispiriting of Daisy. When she realizes that Winterbourne has been observing her and Giovanelli and has turned away without speaking to her, she tells her escort, "Why it was Mr. Winterbourne! . . . He saw me and he cuts me dead!" (18:86). An irate Winterbourne, having heard this, confronts her and Giovanelli about the stupidity of their being in "a nest of malaria." Giovanelli quickly exculpates himself and assures Daisy's concerned friend, "I assured Mademoiselle it was a grave indiscretion but when was Mademoiselle ever prudent?" (18:87), underscoring the defiant nature of Daisy's actions. Still anxious for Winterbourne's approval, Daisy asks him if he believed that she was engaged. Winterbourne's response, apparently expressing indifference in the matter, is the final stroke, making her declare, "I don't care whether I have Roman fever or not" (18:89).

The willful nature of Daisy Miller's death makes it conform to Durkheim's definition of suicide. Her actions as well as the observations of those who know her well testify to the active role of her will in her contracting malaria and her subsequent passivity and loss of the will to live. When she is taken seriously ill, even her brother Randolph affirms, "It's going round at night that way, you bet—that's what has made her so sick" (18:90). After Daisy's funeral, when an indignant Winterbourne confronts Giovanelli with his responsibility in taking her to the Colosseum, he again expresses the willful nature of her act by saying, "She did what she liked!" (18:92)—she caught malaria! Her death, therefore, results from a positive *and* a negative act which she knows will result in death. She dies as much from her Roman fever as from losing her will to live. Her surrender, while she is still very young, in the face of adverse criticism is also in the Romantic tradition.

If an otherwise robust Daisy Miller, in the face of unfair criticism, loses her vibrant interest in life to the point of losing her will to live, a fatally ill Milly Theale, in *The Wings of the Dove* (1902), hangs on to life by the sheer power of her will until betrayal in love provokes her to release her precarious hold on it. Much of the beauty and aesthetic value of the novel lies in James's careful and persistent delineation of the power of Milly's will in her life as well as in her death.

Milly's strong will to live is clearly evident throughout the novel in her attempt to live life to the fullest, even after she becomes aware of the fatal nature of her illness. F. O. Matthiessen points to the end of the chapter that introduces Milly as proof that James intended her to be far from suicidal.[7] During their brief sojourn in the Alps, Milly's friend and confidante, Susan Stringham, comes upon Milly one afternoon seated on the "dizzy edge" of a precipice, on "a slab of rock at the end of a short promontory." In the passage detailing Mrs. Stringham's thought processes, James inserts one sentence that removes beyond the shadow of a doubt the fear that Milly entertained any suicidal thoughts: "If the girl was deeply and recklessly meditating there she wasn't meditating a jump" (19:23-24). Soon after this Milly reappears at the inn where Susan Stringham is still meditating on what she saw and its implications, only to conclude, "She wouldn't have committed suicide; she knew herself unmistakeably reserved for some more complicated passage" (19:125). In addition to the narrator's assurance that the "thousand thoughts, for the minute, [that] roared in the poor lady's ears" did not reach Milly's ear, we now have Susan Stringham's categorical conclusion that Milly "wouldn't have committed suicide." In view of what happens later when Milly gives up on life, Mrs. Stringham's assurance that Milly "knew herself unmistakeably reserved for some more complicated passage" is full of ironic import. Later on, Milly describes herself to Sir Luke as "a survivor—a survivor of a general wreck" (19:241). Even when she returns from the doctor's office she cannot help entertaining hopeful thoughts: "It was of course as one of the weak that she had gone to him—but oh with how sneaking a hope that he might pronounce her, as to all indispensables, a veritable young lioness!" (19:251) As Matthiessen points out, "One aspect of her situation that he [James] penetrates with psychological depth is the relation between her delicate vitality and the will to live. Sir Luke knows that she needs love to sustain her, to relax the tension of her loneliness, and . . . he urges her to 'take the trouble' to live."[8] James devotes a scene to Milly's meditations as she returns from the doctor's office through Regent's Park. At the end of her meditations, she stands up and looks "at her scattered melancholy comrades—some of them so melancholy as to be down on their stomachs in the grass, burrowing; she saw once more, with them, those two faces of the question between which there was so little to choose for inspiration. It was perhaps superficially more striking that one could live if one would; but it was more appealing, insinuating, irresistible in short, that one would live if one could" (19:254).

After painstakingly demonstrating her intense will to live through the probing of her consciousness and that of Susan Stringham in lengthy passages, James reports her fatal resolve indirectly through the simple sentence, "[S]he had turned her face to the wall" (20:323), thus underscoring the active nature of her will in her death. Only through a symbolic act, and not through any violence, would Milly reveal the loss of her will to live. Mrs. Stringham reports to Densher, on Milly's death: "She has turned her face to the wall" (20:270). Densher repeats the phrase when he in turn reports it to Kate, emphasizing the heavy blow that Mark has given: "The way it affected her was that it made her give up. She has given up beyond all power to care again, and that's why she is dying. . . . One can see now that she was living by will. . . . [H]er will, at a given moment, broke down, and the collapse was determined by that fellow's dastardly stroke" (20:320-21). As in the case of Daisy Miller, the perception of evil in the world surrounding her puts a sudden end to Milly's life. Cargill, Bowden, and Fowler, among others, observe the element of will in Milly Theale's life and death. According to Cargill, "the whole story of Milly Theale is the story of her will to live, strengthened by love, but finally destroyed by the revelation of the plot against her."[9] According to Bowden, "it is her will to

live, her firm determination to enjoy as much of life as possible, that makes her courage attractive and her death tragic."[10] Virginia Fowler sees Milly as continuing to exert an influence on the world through her bequest to Merton Densher. Fowler adds: "[B]ut she can do so only by dying. And death is, though perhaps unconsciously, to some extent self-willed."[11]

The Pupil (1891) contains the touching story of an ailing young man who loses his will to live when he experiences what he considers the ultimate rejection by his family and, perhaps, by his tutor as well. Unlike Daisy Miller and Milly Theale in his poverty, Morgan Moreen resembles Daisy in his tender age and Milly in his serious illness. Though he dies of a heart attack, it is clear that James intended the element of will to color his death as strongly as it colors the deaths of Daisy and Milly. In his preface to the New York edition, James compares Morgan Moreen to Hyacinth Robinson of *The Princess Casamassima* and says, "[I]t is much in this manner [the manner of Hyacinth Robinson] . . . that Morgan Moreen breaks down—his burden indeed not so heavy, but his strength so much less formed."[12] In pointing up the similarity between Morgan Moreen's death and the death of Hyacinth Robinson, a clear suicide, James attributes a self-willed element to young Moreen's death. The Romantic notions of youth, waste, and self-willed early death come together in Morgan's premature death. In contrast to the physical suicides, women dominate the group of symbolic suicides. In this cluster of tales and novels, a combination of illness and loss of will results in the deaths of the protagonists. Claire de Cintre and her brother Valentin in *The American* are exceptional in being in perfect health when they will their deaths, whether physical or symbolic.

III

The various definitions of suicide offered by philosophers, psychologists, and sociologists underscore the multiplicity of attitudes toward killing oneself. A. Alvarez, Avery D. Weisman, and Charles W. Wahl emphasize the attention-getting, immortality-guaranteeing, and guilt-provoking aspects of suicide. According to Alvarez, "suicide is simply the most extreme and brutal way of making sure that you will not readily be forgotten. It is a question of a kind of posthumous rebirth in the memory of others."[13] According to Avery D. Weisman, "wanting to die, crying for help, or seeking oblivion are only a few of the many motives for suicide. Just as a religious person ponders the promise of immortality, so is a suicidal person lured by the prospect of a special kind of death which only an act of self-destruction will achieve."[14] Weisman sees suicide also as "only an extreme form of self-destructive behavior in which the wish to obliterate oneself happens to coincide with the wish to discover oneself through death. Suicide is a product of a mood, a time, and a season, but self-destructive acts assume many guises and may often endure throughout an entire lifetime."[15] The tendency for self-destruction manifested in Roderick Hudson all through his life illustrates this. Wahl also emphasizes this aspect of suicide when he refers to the "magical" aspects of suicide and says that suicide "is not preeminently a rational act pursued to achieve rational ends, even when it is effected by persons who appear to be eminently rational. Rather, it is a magical act, actuated to achieve irrational, delusional, illusory ends."[16] The completely unexpected suicides of Grace Mavis in "The Patagonia" and of Agatha Grice in "The Modern Warning," two outwardly rational women, may be explained in these terms. It is also possible, as Wahl explains to those to whom suicide appears to be against man's normal self-preservative instinct, that death by one's own hand expiates self-guilt and inflicts it on others. Voluntary death, he goes on to say, may be regarded "not only as a surcease from pain in this world . . . but also as an act whereby one acquires powers, qualities and advantages not possessed in the living state."[17] Since such attention-getting suicides are also guilt-provoking, and since such a heavy burden of guilt would be destructive, an element of murder characterizes the effects of such suicides on survivors. The suicide may unconsciously believe, "like Sampson in the temple, that by an act of self-destruction he is encompassing the destruction of myriads of others. The suicide, when he dies, kills not one person, but many. He commits not only suicide but vicarious matricide, patricide, sororicide, fratricide, and even genocide."[18]

Love-related suicides best illustrate this murderous aspect of self-destruction. In "Osborne's Revenge," Robert Graham, though he fails to make the desired impression on his lady-love, clearly intends for her to feel responsible for his death. The desperate Baron de Mauves, through his suicide, must have sought his cruel wife's sympathy and immortality in her thoughts. Daisy Miller, in rather willfully contracting Roman fever and then losing her will to live, points her accusing finger at her harsh critics. Milly Theale, despite her noble and unselfish intentions, makes Merton Densher feel guilty enough to make him modify his marriage proposal to Kate Croy, in effect cancelling his engagement to her. In the sheer number of survivors who would feel guilty over a suicide, Roderick Hudson remains unsurpassed in James's fiction. His mother, his patron/brother, his faithful fiancée, and perhaps even his femme fatale must have felt the destructive impact of his suicide. Thus, as Weisman points out, "suicide offers both masochistic gratification and atonement for homicidal wishes. Although suicide may relieve guilt and hatred, the victim is also free to destroy others by his act."[19]

To Camus, "killing yourself amounts to confessing. It is confessing that life is too much for you or that you do not understand it."[20] Alvarez also points to the confessional aspect of suicide when he says, "Like divorce, suicide is a confession of failure. And like divorce, it is shrouded in excuses and rationalizations spun endlessly to disguise the simple fact that all one's energy, passion, appetite and ambition have been aborted."[21] As such, suicide may be considered the ultimate purgation. All of the physical suicides in Henry James's works proclaim failure of one

kind or another, while all the symbolic suicides in his fiction proclaim failure in love. Robert Graham, in attributing his suicide to unrequited love, proclaims his failure in that department. Lambert's suicide in *Watch and Ward* proclaims his financial failure. The Baron de Mauves kills himself because he fails to regain his wife's love and respect. His brother-in-law's suicide, which preceded the Baron's own, testifies to his financial failure. Roderick Hudson and Hyacinth Robinson both experience failure in love, with Roderick's failure extending into his artistic career. Agatha, in "The Modern Warning," fails to reconcile her love for her brother and country with her love for her husband and his country. Grace Mavis aboard *The Patagonia* jumps overboard when she fails to maintain her reputation. Failure of self-esteem provokes Newton Winch's suicide in "A Round of Visits."

IV

During the last decade of the nineteenth century, Émile Durkheim conducted the investigation of suicide that resulted in the publication of his well-known book *Suicide: A Study in Sociology.* In the early chapters Durkheim tries to negate doctrines that ascribe suicide to extra-social factors such as mental alienation, racial characteristics, heredity, climate, temperature, and finally the then-popular doctrine of "imitation." Through his study, Durkheim comes up with categories of suicide. The first one, which he calls egoistic suicide, results from lack of integration of the individual into society. He supports this by pointing out that the suicide rate is lowest among Catholics and Jews, followers of religions that closely integrate the individual into the collective life. In contrast, among Protestants, because of the high state of individualism, the rate is high. However, of all great Protestant countries, England has fewest suicides, because religious society there is much more strongly constituted (*D,* pp. 160-61). Egoistic suicide happens also when the individual is not well integrated into the family. In times of crisis, since society naturally gets to be strongly integrated, the suicide rate falls.

Interestingly, a high rate of integration leads to the second type of suicide, the one Durkheim labels "altruistic": "If excessive individuation leads to suicide, insufficient individuation has the same effects. When man has become detached from society, he encounters less resistance to suicide in himself, and he does so likewise when social integration is too strong" (*D,* p. 217). Here the individual takes his own life because of higher commandments. The unquestioning obedience to authority expected of and generally given by members of armed forces, even in modern society, would be a case in point. According to William James, mankind's common instinct for reality, which makes man admire heroism, also makes sacred that supreme gesture of heroism, a person's willingness to risk death and suffer it heroically in the service he has chosen.[22]

Among the self-willed deaths in James's fiction, those of Hyacinth Robinson and the protagonists of the two Civil

War stories come close to being altruistic ones. The symbolic murder which the revolutionaries of *The Princess Casamassima* plan would require an act of obedience from a committed revolutionary. In the beginning, Hyacinth Robinson is eager to prove his commitment. However, his revolutionary allies recognize the change in him after his European travel. When Poupin accuses him of having changed and declares that that changes everything, an indignant Hyacinth retorts: "Does it alter my sacred vow? There are some things in which one can't change. I didn't promise to believe; I promised to obey" (6:371). If Hyacinth had carried out the order contained in his letter, that alone would have been suicidal because the murder would have gotten him the death penalty. His decision to murder himself rather than commit the symbolic murder planned by the revolutionaries gives his suicide an altruistic dimension because of its sacrificial nature. At the same time, in going against the command of the revolutionaries, he falls short of being altruistic in the revolutionary cause. The protagonists of the two Civil War stories lose their will to live when they realize that the girls they love would be happier with other mates. Since they are motivated by unselfish motives, their deaths approach altruistic suicide.

A lack of integration into family and society is generally considered the major cause of suicide. Several of the physical suicides in James's fiction appear to have family members and/or friends who care deeply for them. Alienation in these cases originates from inside the characters. Hyacinth Robinson, though without his natural parents, has several surrogate parents. His problem lies in his inability to reconcile within himself the pulls of opposing social strata. "[A] little bookbinder who had so much more of the gentleman about him than one would expect" (5:198), Hyacinth is "the illegitimate child of a French impropriety who murdered one of her numerous lovers" (5:36), an English aristocrat. He grows up with a loving foster mother in a lower-class tenement. As a young man, he enters upper-class society, mainly through the whim of the Princess Casamassima. The narrator tells us, "His present position wasn't of his seeking—it had been forced upon him" (6:28-29). That is not to say that he was not charmed by its glitter. At about the same time, he is also initiated by a brother-figure, Paul Muniment, into a revolutionary group in London. The revolutionary zeal burns in him for a while. After the death of his foster mother, Pinnie, he has the opportunity to tour Europe. A change in attitude toward the various classes, which had already been at work in him, surfaces strongly during his travels. He writes to the Princess about how happy he is, how guilty he feels about that happiness and about the contrast between himself and Hoffendahl, the revolutionary leader (6:143-36). Upon his return home, Hyacinth even entertains thoughts of moving upward into an elite class through writing (6:155-56). Torn between the conflicting loyalties to upper-class society and the anarchists, feeling equally rejected by the Princess and Millicent Henning, and betrayed by Paul Muniment and the Cause, Hyacinth feels all alone; and instead of murdering the enemy of the Cause, he kills himself.

Hyacinth's suicide, then, in addition to being the result of a sense of alienation, may also be viewed as an example of a classic psychological type of suicide—the desire to kill someone else turned toward the self.

Among the other suicides in James's fiction, Robert Graham in "Osborne's Revenge" has a friend who cares deeply for him and would spare no expense in his service. The sense of alienation at being rejected by his wife forces the reformed but rejected Baron de Mauves to take his own life. Roderick Hudson has a mother and a fiancée who adore him, a brother-figure who patronizes him in the best possible way, and many who admire his sculpture. An obsession with the charming Christina Light makes him alienate himself from his family, his friends, and his work. Inexplicably, like Melville's Bartleby, he chooses not to belong. The transplanted Agatha, in "A Modern Warning," in spite of having a loving husband and a loving brother, had been made to feel like a traitor by the latter. Newton Winch, in "A Round of Visits," through manipulation of large sums of money entrusted to his management, naturally feels alienated. However, strangely enough, he shoots himself immediately after having found a sympathetic ear in an old friend. James's pupil, in the midst of a family he is ashamed of, feels completely alone when he feels that his tutor, the only person to whom he feels close, rejects him. Milly Theale, an heiress, has no family. Fatally ill, she chooses to travel in Europe. Betrayal in love by a young man and a young woman she trusts makes her feel even more alone in a foreign country.

A third kind of suicide, the one that Durkheim calls "anomic," comes about from lack of regulation of the individual by society. Changes in status quo, like sudden wealth or divorce, can bring about suicide. Anomic suicide is essentially passionate in nature, though the passion is ignoble, characterized by anger and all the emotions customarily associated with disappointment (*D*, pp. 284-85). The suicide of the man misunderstood, very common in days when no recognized social classification is left, belongs to this group. The supreme example would be Goethe's Werther, "the turbulent heart as he calls himself, enamoured of infinity, killing himself from disappointed love, and the case of all artists who, after having drunk deeply of success, commit suicide because of a chance hiss, a somewhat severe criticism, or because their popularity has begun to wane" (*D*, p. 286). James's Roderick Hudson clearly falls into this category.

Individual forms of suicide could be mixtures of the different categories like ego-anomic, altruistic-anomic, and ego-altruistic. With available statistics Durkheim finds a correlation between suicide and social phenomena like family, political and economic society, and religious groups. According to Durkheim, the correlation indicates decisively that each society has a collective inclination towards suicide, a rate of self-homicide which is fairly constant for each society so long as the basic conditions of existence remain the same. The American translator/editor of Durkheim's book sums up the sociological aspect of self-destruction in this way: "The individual inclination to suicide is explicable scientifically only by relation to the collective inclination, and this collective inclination is itself a determined reflection of the structure of the society in which the individual lives" (*D*, p. 16). He continues: "From the point of view of psychoanalytic psychiatry, it may be said that every individual has what we may call a suicide-potential, a tendency to self-murder which varies in degree of intensity from individual to individual." The degree of intensity of this potential is established in infancy and early childhood by fears, anxiety, frustrations, loves, and hatreds engendered in the individual by the family environment in terms of eliminatory processes, weaning, sex education, sibling rivalry, rejection, or over-acceptance by the parents and degree of dependence. Where through excessive mother-love, father-rejection, or inferiority induced by siblings the individual is not readied for responsible adulthood according to the customs and mores of the society in which he is to participate, the suicide potential of an individual may be very high (*D*, p. 23). To sum up, "[a]ll of the emotions manifested in suicides are, then, explicable in terms of the life-history of the individual, particularly the channeling of the basic psychic configurations through the family" (*D*, p. 24). Even in other cases, the trials and tribulations of adulthood may provoke suicide.

After dividing suicide in general into three categories, Durkheim classifies the suicides of the insane into four kinds. When a person kills himself to escape from an imaginary danger or disgrace, or to obey a mysterious order from on high, he calls it maniacal. Lambert's suicide in *Watch and Ward* approaches this category. A man who demands one hundred dollars from a complete stranger in a hotel lobby obviously must be mentally deranged. Lambert projects an aspect of "grim and hopeless misery" (p. 21) and an "image of fallen prosperity, of degradation and despair" (p. 22). With a face "as white as ashes" and eyes "as lurid as coals" (p. 22), to Roger Lawrence he appears "simply crazy" (p. 22). That the man considers himself thus is obvious from the words he uses to preface his abrupt demand for the money: "You'll think me crazy, I suppose. Well, I shall be soon. Will you lend me a hundred dollars?" (p. 22). His almost violent reaction to the offer of a tenth of the amount he asked for, his threat to cut his own throat (p. 24), and his eventual suicide, all testify to the deranged state of his mind. Lambert's bizarre suicide, then, might be labelled what Durkheim calls "maniacal."

Durkheim connects melancholy suicide with a general state of extreme depression and exaggerated sadness, causing the patient no longer to realize sanely the bonds which connect him with people and things about him (*D*, p. 63). Robert Graham's suicide in "Osborne's Revenge" may be placed in this category. Though Philip Osborne and Robert Graham have been best friends, Osborne is puzzled by Graham's behavior preceding his suicide. Spending the summer at certain medicinal springs, Graham fails to stay in touch with his best friend. When correspondence is demanded, the reply reveals an unsettled mind. Graham claims that the "infernal waters," instead of doing him good, have poisoned him. In somewhat incoherent terms he refers to a young lady's charms that hold him there, while he declares his intention to return and claims that he is not "cracked" (*CT*, 2:13). When he appears, Osborne finds him physically improved but "morally . . . a sad invalid. He was listless, abstracted, and utterly inactive in mind" (p. 15). He dispatches another incoherent letter from Minnesota, where his best friend has sent him for diversion. The coherent conclusion to this letter proclaims his suicidal bent: "Life has lost, I don't say its charm . . . but its meaning. I shall live in your memory and your love, which is a vast deal better than living in my own self-contempt. Farewell" (p. 17). The narrator's posthumous appraisal of Graham, who is three years Osborne's senior, as "slight, undersized, feeble in health, sensitive, indolent, whimsical, generous, and in reality of a far finer clay than his friend" (p. 18), and the description of Graham by "disinterested parties" as "an insignificant, lounging invalid, who, in general company, talked in monosyllables, in a weak voice, and gave himself the airs of one whom nature had endowed with the right to be fastidious, without ever having done a stroke of work," help us make an objective evaluation of Robert Graham. His mental state before his suicide clearly blinds him to the strong bond of friendship with Osborne; therefore, he becomes obviously melancholic and attracted by the idea of death. Osborne's investigations after his suicide reveal that his best friend was laboring under delusions of betrayed love, when there actually was no love felt by the object of his affections. A third type of suicide of the insane, what Durkheim labels "obsessive suicide" or "anxiety suicide," has no relevance to James's fiction. It is caused by no motive, real or imaginary, but solely by the fixed idea of death, which, without clear reason, has taken possession of the person's mind (*D*, p. 64).

Roderick Hudson's suicide may be considered a combination of melancholy suicide and Durkheim's fourth category—impulsive or automatic suicide. As unmotivated as the obsessive suicide, impulsive suicide has no cause in reality nor in the patient's imagination. Instead of being produced by a fixed idea obsessing the mind for a shorter or longer period and only gradually affecting the will, it results from an abrupt and immediately irresistible impulse. "The sight of a knife, a walk by the edge of a precipice, etc., engenders the suicidal idea instantaneously and its execution follows so swiftly that patients often have no idea of what has taken place" (*D*, p. 65). Durkheim's description of a certain kind of suicide existing from antiquity in his chapter on "Individual Forms of the Different Types of Suicide" seems to fit Roderick Hudson's suicide. A condition of melancholic langor and general indifference characterized by heightened inner life and producing alienation typifies this type of suicide (*D*, pp. 278-79).

V

What emerges from this survey of sociological dimensions of suicide is the conviction that James portrays his fictional suicides, both physical and symbolic, quite realistically. That his suicidal characters can be used to illustrate conclusions on self-destruction reached by sociologists, psychologists, and philosophers is the ultimate testimony to his realism. Even in the matter of statistics, James's suicides parallel the trends in society. More men than women and more single people than married people will their own deaths. Durkheim points out that the suicides of women form only a small fraction of that of males (*D*, p. 99). Only two out of James's ten physical suicides are women. This also confirms Durkheim's observation in relation to egoistic suicides: that suicides among married persons are much fewer, though not due to the influence of conjugal society, but of the family society (*D*, p. 189). With the breakup of the marriage, more divorced men than women commit suicide, because men enjoy more benefits in marriage. In the total of eighteen suicides (ten physical and eight symbolic) in this study, only six have ever been married. Three of those are men who shoot themselves—the deranged widower Lambert in *Watch and Ward* and the desperate Baron de Mauves and his brother-in-law in "Madame de Mauves." The widowed Claire de Cintre of *The American* takes the veil, while Agatha of "The Modern Warning" poisons herself in spite of a happy marriage, and Diana of "Longstaff's Marriage" wills her death. There is something of Richard Cory in the unexpectedness of many of these suicides; Charles W. Wahl's view of suicide as a magical act that enables a victim to fulfill many of his unfulfilled wishes in real life offers a rational explanation for this irrational act:

> [B]y equating the world with the self, [the suicide] affirms the same fallacy as the medieval mystics who said, . . ."Nothing outside my own mind is real; the world and all persons in it are, in reality, me." Therefore, to kill oneself is to kill everything that there is, the world and all other persons.[23]

In conclusion, as Edel points out in the general introduction to *The Complete Tales of Henry James,* James wanted "to leave a multitude of pictures of [his] time, projecting [his] small circular frame upon as many different spots as possible" (p. 7). Without doubt, in the depiction of self-willed death, as in other aspects of his milieu—artistic, upper-class, leisured—he did succeed in what he wanted to accomplish.

NOTES

[1] Émile Durkheim, *Suicide: A Study in Sociology,* trans. John A. Spaulding and George Simpson (Glencoe, Ill.: Free Press, 1951), p. 44. Hereafter cited parenthetically in the text as *D,* followed by the page number(s).

[2] Henry James, *The Complete Tales of Henry James,* ed. Leon Edel, 12 vols. (Philadelphia: Lippincott, 1961), II, 17. Hereafter cited parenthetically in the text as *CT,* followed by the volume and page number(s).

[3] Henry James, *Watch and Ward* (New York: Grover, 1959), p. 29. Hereafter cited parenthetically in the text.

[4] Henry James, *The Novels and Tales of Henry James,* 26 vols. (New York: Scribner's, 1909), XIII, 331. Hereafter cited parenthetically in the text by vol. and page number(s).

[5] Stephen Spender, *The Destructive Element* (London: Jonathan Cape, 1935), p. 40.

[6] A. Alvarez, *The Savage God: A Study of Suicide* (New York: Random, 1972), p. 165.

[7] F. O. Matthiessen, *Henry James: The Major Phase* (New York: Oxford Univ. Press, 1944), pp. 63-64.

[8] Ibid., p. 67.

[9] Oscar Cargill, *The Novels of Henry James* (New York: Hafner, 1971), p. 339.

[10] Edwin T. Bowden, *The Themes of Henry James: A System of Observation Through the Visual Arts* (New Haven: Yale Univ. Press, 1956), p. 93.

[11] Virginia C. Fowler, *Henry James's American Girl: The Embroidery on the Canvas* (Madison: Univ. of Wisconsin Press, 1984), pp. 88-89.

[12] Henry James, "Prefaces to the New York Edition," *European Writers and the Prefaces,* ed. Leon Edel (New York: The Library of America, 1984), p. 1170.

[13] Alvarez, p. 108.

[14] Avery D. Weisman, "Self-Destruction and Sexual Perversion," in *Essays in Self-Destruction,* ed. Edwin S. Shneidman (New York: Jason Aronson, 1967), p. 265.

[15] Ibid.

[16] Charles William Wahl, "Suicide as a Magical Act," in *Clues to Suicide,* ed. Edwin S. Shneidman and Norman L. Farberow (New York: McGraw, 1957), p. 23.

[17] Ibid., p. 27.

[18] Ibid., p. 30.

[19] Weisman, p. 266.

[20] Albert Camus, *The Myth of Sisyphus and Other Essays,* trans. Justin O'Brien (New York: Vintage, 1955), p. 5.

[21] Alvarez, p. 100.

[22] William James, *The Varieties of Religious Experience* (New Hyde Park, N.Y.: University Books, 1963), p. 364.

[23] Wahl, pp. 29-30.

Thomas LeClair

SOURCE: "A Case of Death: The Fiction of J. P. Donleavy," in *Contemporary Literature,* Vol. 12, No. 3, Summer, 1971, pp. 329-44.

[*In the following essay, LeClair observes developments in Donleavy's sustained treatment of the theme of death in his novels.*]

"I'll die with a case of death," says Sebastian Dangerfield, hero of J. P. Donleavy's *The Ginger Man,* when his wife threatens to have him evicted from their flat.[1] Sebastian manages to charm his way through this and the other "indignities" the world subjects him to, but his "case of death" is not so easily dispensed with. It hangs on, showing its symptoms in daydream and nightmare, during intercourse and argument. Although Donleavy does not allow this condition to reach literal consummation in *The Ginger Man,* the "case of death" and the psychic effects it works on his characters are the controlling elements in *The Ginger Man* and his other novels—*A Singular Man, The Saddest Summer of Samuel S,* and *The Beastly Beatitudes of Balthazar B.* Donleavy's fictions are not, of course, simply case histories of the terminal self. They are about the classical rogue as well as the modern victim, twentieth-century Tom Joneses as well as funny Joseph K.'s, man inside yet outside of society in Dublin, New York, and Vienna. The novels range from variations of the humorous—slapstick, scatological, sardonic—to the sentimental in an idiosyncratic style that conveys the pressure of time on language. But such features of Donleavy's work are finally extensions of and returns to death, the test of man's mettle in landscapes made pale by death's presence.

It is in *The Ginger Man,* the first of his four novels, that Donleavy best displays his virtual obsession.[2] The novel is marked by what Martin Heidegger called "thrownness," man's initial reaction to finding himself in the world of time. Sebastian is the absurd man whose expectations far exceed the possibilities of reality: "But the world was made for me. Here long before I arrived and they spent years getting it ready. Something got mixed up about my assets" (109). When the novel opens, Sebastian's assets are indeed in disarray, and their condition worsens as he attempts to live off the capital of the past and future. But the situation is not completely his own doing, for he has been thrown into poverty by his father-in-law's refusal to pay the dowry promised for Marion and his own father's unexpected parsimony and longevity. The sense of "thrownness"—"In debt in death" (266), says Sebastian—caused by the Dangerfields' economic privation is magnified by the alien quality Dublin presents to the American Sebastian and the British Marion. They feel dropped into an environment militantly at odds with their own aristocratic pretensions, for the Ireland of *The Ginger Man* is the world of darkness the Protestant ascendancy has cursed since the beginning of English control. The setting the Dangerfields inhabit is the damp backstreet land of Simon Daedalus, a place of crying children, fecal stink, and never warm enough fires. Their flats tell the dismal story. The first, tottering on the edge of an abyss, has a screeching one-eyed cat in the attic and a "history of death" (19). The second overlooks a laundry and a main thoroughfare to Dublin's cemeteries and is itself overlooked by commuters in passing trains.

The third, bordered by dog manure in front and a tangled garden in back, is the last apartment in a dead-end street. The poverty of Ireland is not, however, a simple economic problem; it is bound up with the spiritual malaise hinging on a sexual repression Sebastian finds appalling. Unable to buy contraceptives, the Irish live in constant fear of having children, "brought down upon them by the wrath of God for screwing" (243), says Sebastian. "Dublin," writes Donleavy in a travel article, "is a city where the fundamental juice of life is evaporated away by the brooding restrictions."[3] Unable to become a part of the womb-like atmosphere of Trinity College, Sebastian finds that life flourishes only in the moments made meaningful through his own independent resources or, finally, in emigration.

These economic and social manifestations of "thrownness" experienced by Sebastian are, however, best considered as externalizations of the elemental homelessness of man in time, where, Heidegger insists, man has his most basic existence. The world may, as Sebastian believes, have "eyes and mouths" (220) which threaten to martyr him, but the real danger, he also realizes, is within, where time is eating itself outward at an unknown rate to Nothing. His comment about intercourse sums up his attitude toward life in general: "Matter, all of it, of time" (55). Early in the novel Sebastian tries to reassure himself: "No time to be nervous now. With youth on my side" (30); but his is a youth with what Frank Kermode calls the "sense of an ending" which affects the style of the middle as well as recollections of the beginnings.[4] Sebastian's visions of the end, as the following example illustrates, are not idly morbid daydreams but dynamic centers of consciousness which direct psychic and physical action:

> If they get you in the medical school they hang you up by the ears. Never leave me unclaimed, I beg of you. Don't hang me all swollen, knees pressing the red nates of others where they come in to see if I'm fat or lean and all of us stabbed to death on the Bowery. Kill you in the tenement streets and cover you in flowers and put in the juice. By God, you hulking idiots, keep the juice away from me. Because I'm a mortician and too busy to die. (55)

Under the pressure of his imagination, Sebastian speeds up his activities toward the state of continual motion. Busyness is thus both a result of his awareness of the end and a way of escaping it. He immerses himself in the destructive element so that he may not think of destruction, or as he puts it: "In it all to get away from it all" (162). The aim of this variation of the *carpe diem* approach to life is not to expand the present moment to fruition but to fill the present to overflowing with acts which circumvent thought and diminish the experience of duration. Inactivity is no less important than activity: loss of tension, exhaustion, and sleep are the valuable byproducts of Sebastian's hyperindustry, itself caused by the threat of consciousness. It is not surprising, then, that the past and the future furnish solace for Sebastian, whose terror is concentrated on the present as it verges on an uncertain near future. A quilt of idyllic innocence and loneliness, Sebastian's memories combine the pure pleasures of youth with Holden Caulfield's tormented adolescence, yet Sebastian's past in America offers him a constant refuge from his experience of duration. After evoking the Americana of an amusement park, Sebastian says simply: "I want to go back" (126).

Despite his attachment to the simpler time of the past, it is the future that most mitigates his present, for Sebastian expects to be made gloriously rich by his inheritance. But given his helplessness in time, he can neither comfortably wait for the future nor work toward it. Patience seems the gift of the godly—those who believe time will be destroyed rather than do the destroying—and continued effort to attain future wealth, such as studying for a law degree, requires the faith of the investor in his capital, impossible when that capital is time. Time, as physical succession, must be denied, through the strategies of consciousness or action, until the "golden udder" (61) of the future magically descends to him.

For Heidegger anxiety about time and "Nothingness" was a challenge, the acceptance of which conferred authenticity on man's life. The Heideggerian hero is a major man of will, flesh, and blood; but Donleavy's hero is a marginal man of flesh and blood whose will has been usurped by visions, both daylight and nocturnal, of "that last and final chill, the one to be avoided at all costs" (191). Sebastian doesn't choose between authentic and inauthentic existence; from the very beginning of the novel he is in desperate flight from anxiety, time, and death. Although he is best remembered by friends and readers for his sexuality, his Don Juanism is but an aspect, important to be sure, of a more basic psychological defense against destruction: the closed self. Sebastian's is a static selfhood which protects itself by offering the world multiple variations in identity: the masks of solicitous husband, ironic raconteur, young aristocrat, or helpful friend are but a few. This tactic precludes, of course, the possibility of love, a mediation unconsidered in *The Ginger Man.* Without love, the circle of anxiety viciously turns in ever lessening revolutions of man against himself and toward the still point of solipsism. Arland Ussher, who contributed an introduction to the first American edition of *The Ginger Man,* has said that without death we would be "mere solipsists,"[5] but in Donleavy's novel death has both a centrifugal and centripetal effect. It pushes man outward into the physical world while simultaneously pulling him toward a destructive isolation of the self within that world. The nearest Sebastian can come to love is the vague goodwill he manages to feel toward his friends and several women, especially Mary, his last partner.

Although he enjoys a sensual aesthetic and the challenge of conquest, Sebastian makes sex a device of both memory and forgetfulness. In the scenes describing coitus with Marion and Chris, he crosshatches the pleasure of the present with recollections of the past, both of

which offer him liberation from anxiety. It is the "silent minute" Sebastian mentions in the following passage, however, that best diverts him: "Her hair lay athwart in clean strands on his body and for the next silent minute he was the sanest man on earth, bled of his seed, rid of his mind" (96). But sexual activity, which the existential psychoanalyst Rollo May calls "the most ready way to silence the inner dread of death,"[6] can as well call up death. Sexuality and death are mingled in the long passage quoted earlier, the ending of an interior monologue which begins while Sebastian and Marion sport themselves and which contains Sebastian's identification of the beginning (semen) and end (embalming fluid) of life: "Starts and ends in antiseptic smell" (55). Punned on by the Elizabethans, the climax of sex and life is no laughing matter for Sebastian. When the lusty Mary avers during intercourse: "I don't care if we die," Sebastian is quick to scotch any such notions. "Don't say that. Give God ideas. We must discourage that attitude" (186).

As persons, the women in Sebastian's life have no value. He was originally attracted to Marion because of her breasts and fashionably bucked teeth (which later turn out to be dentures). His first mistress, Chris, who shows some complexity of personality, is nothing more than a change of scenery and a refuge from Marion's onslaughts. Miss Lilly Frost, the older maiden whose conquest is a victory over the funereal flower as well as the chill of death, is simply on tap as a boarder at the Dangerfields', and Mary, though matching and sometimes overmatching Sebastian's ardor, is primarily identified by her bovine breasts and ready money. The men in the novel are likewise flattened out by Sebastian's defensive relation with the world. Clocklan, Malarkey, and MacDoon are fellow sufferers useful to share conversation and the odd pint with, but are kept at a distance. It is only O'Keefe, a fellow American, whom Sebastian can allow intimacy, perhaps because O'Keefe is obviously harmless. For Donleavy, O'Keefe, in his absurd virginity, is a convenient foil for Sebastian's athletic sexuality. Both are down and out, but Sebastian keeps his erotic grip. O'Keefe, rebuffed by man, woman, and beast, plunges into despair and voices a wish for death—an unforgivable sin in Sebastian's eyes.

Sex, if procreation is avoided, is an inexpensive way to forget time, but partners are not always available. More expensive is Sebastian's other passion: alcohol, preferably accompanied by a good feed to quiet the gnawing of hunger which can grow into dread. The methods Sebastian uses to satisfy his lust for drink, wily charm and craftiness, humorously parallel the techniques he employs in his seductions. When nothing is left to pawn, Sebastian wheedles credit and charity in the same manner that he purchases Marion's favors with a compliment or persuades Lilly to sleep with him out of pity for his loneliness. Though an early drink or two is welcome fortification for the day, Sebastian's greatest need is for the extended nightcap to avert dreams of death that leave him a trembling shambles.

These evasive strategies are but stopgaps between the present and the future. Sebastian aims to glut himself with everydayness that he might forget the end. The way he sees it, "death [is] an obstacle to overcome till the good ripe years of lust, gluttony and sloth" (209-210) come rolling in with his inheritance. Seeing him as a forerunner of the alienated rebels of American fiction in the sixties, one critic states that Sebastian "cares little for material goods or for the security that a bourgeois life offers."[7] But Sebastian is clearly no social rebel; he is rather a temporarily displaced person whose assets, once cleared up, will allow him a life of unthinking bourgeois bliss. In an idyllic flashback, he recalls his notion that he and Ginny Cupper, his first sexual partner, were "so rich we could never die" (58). But Ginny is killed in an auto accident. The richness of youth disappears, yet Sebastian holds on to his belief in material richness, which he hopes will numb his mind, as his ultimate measure against awareness. The law degree he wants but cannot "sit still" long enough to obtain; the business magazines, "the bible of happiness" (25) he pores over; his fantasies of cozy home scenes before the fire; his fervent pleas for money ("I want to see dollars. Thousands of them"); and his defense of conformity ("Too many damn people trying to be different. Coining phrases when a good platitude would do and save anxiety"; 31)—all demonstrate the quality of life dear to Sebastian. He and his friend O'Keefe are, like the expatriates of an earlier time and the hipsters of the fifties, living on the margin of the world, but not by choice. Impoverished and stigmatized, Donleavy's Americans want to return home to the streets of gold, "the deep carpeted womb of the idle rich" (46). The aim is peace, the life of the body with the death of the mind summed up in one of Sebastian's moments of desperation: "I need a long trolley ride in the womb, to take me out of this" (61).

The image Heidegger uses to describe the kinds of evasions Sebastian employs is flight, an image that Donleavy builds into the structural principle and dominant metaphor of *The Ginger Man*. Developed by the escapades of the hero, the plot of the novel plunges forward like those of the episodic novels of initiation so common in contemporary fiction. Sebastian is, however, no questing knight or unheeded saint, but is rather a harried pseudo-aristocrat who cares nothing for the knowledge that experience brings. In fact, he wants to avoid it. Unlike Bellow's all too human Henderson, Barth's innocent Giles, or Ellison's naive Jack the Bear, Sebastian is in possession of his secret, if not of the resources to put it into effect. But since the world refuses to recognize the truth of his master principle—that the world was made for him— Sebastian is forced to flee what he feels is a vengeful society. Victimized by his "inferiors" and his awareness of death, he lives by fits and starts, by acts of immediate creation and flight. He flees his wife, his mistresses, his friends, landlords, the police, and the public to whom he feels unfairly exposed (once literally) in scenes sometimes comic to the reader but always serious to him. Donleavy gives these chases symbolic resonance with his title, which presumably alludes to the fable of the gingerbread man who leads his pursuers a merry chase until he is outwitted by the fox. Sebastian, who emphatically declares: "I don't want to be caught by anybody" (253), is somewhat less and somewhat more than human in his flight from extinction. And this is the paradox of the death theme in the novel. Because of his uncontrollable awareness of death, Sebastian sacrifices human attachment and responsibility but gains, like the gingerbread man, a desperately joyous excitement in his avoidance of death, a manic existence impossible without the threat of an imminent ending. Sebastian is not the Heideggerian hero who manages to make terms with his death and thus live authentically; he is simply man fleeing who fails to achieve his goal of forgetting death and who paradoxically lives life, in both its joy and sadness, more intensely because of his failure.

Related to the strategies of evasion and flight are the funereal and religious themes which fill out Donleavy's analysis of death. Sebastian's cultivation of the funereal—demonstrated by his reading of the In Memoriams, his watching the funerals pass his flat, his reading of a religious pamphlet on death, and his fantasizing about burial in Woodlawn or Austria—is a way to make death an impersonal event. The religious theme further documents Sebastian's flight before death. The Irish people are comically flayed for their piety, an example of which is Miss Frost's conclusion that anal intercourse is less a sin than vaginal; and the clergy, in their repressive and destructive prying, are beyond humor. For Sebastian, though, religion is a comic crutch. The Blessed Oliver Plunkett is a minor if efficacious figure in a theology which has God as the patron saint of luck. Sebastian's fondness for the Pope, who keeps "dignity" in the world; his claims to be a forgiver of sins; his venerable saint's name; and his assurances that Jesus would look with favor upon one who had lain with the ginger man are simultaneous denials of the religious view and acceptances— at very long odds—of Pascal's wager. To a man whose heart is "Twisted/With dying" (285), these paradoxes— attraction to and repulsion from the funereal, ironic denial of religion and covert affirmation of it—are not bothersome, for the extremity of Sebastian's psychic situation produces not only the quick footwork of literal flight but also dazzling leaps of logic.

Several major strands of imagery further define Sebastian's situation and, more generally, the view of life in the novel. The ending of one of Sebastian's ditties— "In this dark gloom/We live like beasts" (19)—sets the key for the bestial references that pervade *The Ginger Man*. The Irish populace have the "eyes of cows and the brains of snakes" (80), Skully the landlord is a "black beast" (146), Malarkey a bull, and O'Keefe "half man, half beast" (211). Sebastian too is both man—"a little frightened man looking out and seeing all the prowling animals" (254)—and beast—"a mad stallion" (289)—but he is "shrewdest of the beasts" (269), the need for shrewdness being clearly explained by Sebastian's biology lecture to O'Keefe. Sebastian says there are books about the animals that didn't fight: "They put a little word at the bottom of the page to tell you something. Extinct. To be avoided" (247). These and the other beast references do more than reinforce what is clear—that these lives verge toward the subhuman; they also help to account, at least in Sebastian's mind, for the cause of this condition, the threat of extinction which forces man toward the animal in his struggle for survival. Sebastian's "spider walk" (215), an improvement in mobility, makes this bond between animality and survival clear.

The other major concentration of imagery, centering on the sea and ships, also focuses on destruction and preservation. Through most of the novel the sea is an image of "death and disaster" (192), and Sebastian is the captain of an imaginary ship that threatens to go under: "Close the watertight compartments. Latch the hatches. Seal up, we're going down you mad bastards" (188). The sea is also a good index of Sebastian's view of space, a concept largely defined by his experience of time. Although Sebastian most fears being trapped, wide open spaces give him a sense of dissolution and sadness. Small, warm rooms, where he feels in control, shut out time and are thus his ideal forms of space.

But the sea can also be kind. At the end of the novel, Percy Clocklan, having undergone a marvelous sea change, is a combination Lazarus and Santa Claus in Rolls Royce who showers wealth and comfort on the severely discouraged Sebastian, just one of the multiple ironies of the London section in which Donleavy recapitulates and reverses some of the themes developed in the rest of the novel. The irony of death as creator and destroyer of life is given several final twists with Clocklan's resurrection from the Irish Sea and with Dangerfield Senior's death, which creates the riotous celebration of life led by MacDoon but which ends in disappointment when the terms of the will are disclosed. The death and religious themes unite in Donleavy's conjoining of Easter and Christmas: Sebastian sails from Ireland on a "crucifixion Friday" (285) to be born again on Christmas eve. The good news is "Dangerfield Lives" (297). Even the beast and sea imagery are turned to joyous use. Sebastian is now "king beast" (342), the jovial kangaroo and performer of the moo dance, for, in an ironic parallel of Stephen Daedalus' flight, Sebastian has crossed the sea to "travel East. To the more established civilizations" (284). This last section of the novel thus moves toward what can only be called a happy ending. Sebastian has been thrown into wealth, time is at his disposal, he suffers no demands, and he has full opportunity for sex and drink—in short, the happiness he has projected from the beginning. Then the final terrifying vision that denies the flimsy defenses so long abuilding:

> On a winter night I heard horses on a country road, beating sparks out of the stones. I knew they were running away and would be crossing the fields where the pounding would come up into my ears. And I said they are running out to death which is with some soul and their eyes are mad and teeth out.
>
> God's mercy
> On the wild
> Ginger Man.
>
> (347)

In symbolic terms, here is the gingerbread man at the time of his greatest triumph—he has crossed the river on the nose of the fox only to find himself in the power of that force from which he has fled.

By treating as irrelevant in *The Ginger Man* those values not directly related to personal survival, Donleavy set for himself a problem in fictional development. He could either continue to push the counters of chaos into different positions or could move toward some mediation of this chaos. In *A Singular Man* (1963) he chooses to tread again some of the ground of *The Ginger Man*, but he also takes a half step toward a compromise with traditional values by reappraising and redefining his theme of death. This movement is no leap into an easy world of surety before death. In fact, *A Singular Man* suggests that man's dreadful relation with death must be extended to extremity before it can be mediated. Only then will value and existence interpenetrate. Thus *A Singular Man* begins where *The Ginger Man* ends, with the knowledge that wealth and comfort do not cleanse the mind of death. O'Keefe has proven a man of wisdom:

> "But Jesus, when you don't have any money, the problem is food. When you have money, it's sex. When you have both it's health, you worry about getting rupture or something. If everything is simply jake then you're frightened of death." (*GM*, 45)

Sebastian ignores O'Keefe's ladder of anxiety, but George Smith, hero of *A Singular Man*, cannot. He lives it.

The concrete links with which Donleavy connects the two novels lead to the more significant thematic similarities and revisions. Both Sebastian Dangerfield and George Smith have a black maid, Matilda, a habit of "beep-beeping" (replying to questions with some variety of "beep") unwanted acquaintances, a desire for a strong metal door for their homes, a fear of becoming a cadaver, and a penis larger than normal, but the relationship between the two heroes is essentially one of transmutation. George Smith is Sebastian Dangerfield with his hopes fulfilled, a wealthy American who need not worry about money, food, or drink. An executive of some reputation, mostly bad, Smith has an apartment well stocked with the necessities for survival, including the person of Matilda, a caricature of the lusty, full-bodied Mary of *The Ginger Man*. But health and death, though the former is cultivated at a gymnasium, are beyond Smith's control. An avatar of the contingency-conscious Dangerfield, Smith too has visions of the end which send him scurrying from his own consciousness: "I might be popped into a plain pine coffin. Unclaimed. Lifted on a barge. With hundreds of others. A number and body photographed on a slab. Don't want to go down that way dead. Like an amputated arm or leg."[8] The defenses of his prototype are, however, soon proved inadequate. A retrenchment, a shuffling of priorities, is necessary for Smith to exist in the peace both he and Sebastian so frantically demand.

The major shift in strategy is Smith's increased reliance on the "closed self." Sebastian wanted to be protected, but he would make the forays into the world that were necessary for him to avoid awareness. Smith avoids exposure whenever possible. He has a special steel door built into his apartment, a limousine with bulletproof glass, and a hermit's distrust of others: "don't let them get in close, keep everyone at arm's length, stop smiling kindly" (6). Sebastian too denied others respect, but allowed himself physical contact. Smith, in a later stage of withdrawal, is afraid of even distant contact though it may offer a respite from anxiety. He would like nothing more than to bed down Sally Tomson but spends most of the novel working up enough courage to make a move toward this end. He does manage to talk Miss Martin into staying with him at his remote cottage, but their happy sexual experience is the result of a spider in her bedroom rather than action initiated by George. But Smith is not always innocently ineffectual. The other extreme of this same defense—domination—also contributes to his isolation. He is sometimes ruthless with women and violent with strangers, and he is at best a mockingly distant listener to the woes of his old friend Bonniface.

Undone in the midst of wealth and luxury, unable to attain Sebastian's satisfaction in sexuality, George boards up the self in smaller and smaller spaces. His auto, cottage, tiny office, the rented hearse, all symbolize his attempt to reduce the pressure of time by reducing space, but it is his mausoleum that best illustrates his retreat from the spacious world as well as his absorption in the funereal, one of Sebastian's defenses here magnified into primary importance. Sebastian's interest in the funereal most often turned toward the death of others, but he was also much concerned with the state of his body after death. He directed the morticians at large to leave the cover of his coffin loose, and fantasized about "a rich tomb of Vermont marble in Woodlawn Cemetery, with automatic sprinkler and evergreens" (*GM*, 55). George's mausoleum is more than a fantasy, it is a project which both illustrates his fear of the world and his desire to be a part of it. "They said why did I do it. Build a monstrous monument," George thinks to himself; the answer: "Because I had no friends. No respect" (131). Early in the novel his wife Shirl tells him that traffic will stop for him only when he is dead. George's mausoleum assures this attention, for it is, as he says, a "monstrous" structure, the largest in Renown Memorial Cemetery. Several years under construction, built of imported marble, with foundations reaching thirty feet beneath the ground, the mausoleum is not only for the world's view; rather, it is a physical and psychological retreat, complete with fireplace, air-conditioning, and other conveniences: "Go to the mausoleum while still alive and live in it. Withstanding the regulations that say you must be dead. A pity. Be quiet there, on the marble, satin pillow under head" (94).

Both the contingency plan of George Smith and the fictional strategy of Donleavy in *A Singular Man* are summed up in the laconic statement of a taxi driver in the novel: "I got to go somewhere. Too much responsibility going nowhere" (200). Sebastian's defenses, essentially the busyness of nowhere, are inadequate. George, bearing the same consciousness of death, goes to the physical somewhere of his mausoleum and, near the end of the novel, the psychological somewhere of a variety of love. He finally breaks out of his self-imposed isolation—"I walked away alone from Dynamo House. Nothing to protect me from the outside world" (297)—but finds that death still gets the last laugh: he hears on his car radio that Sally has been killed in an auto accident.

Although George's attempt to break down the barriers of radical subjectivity fails, the ending of the novel, Sally's funeral, does not have the terror of Sebastian's final vision. There is, at the end of *A Singular Man,* a somewhere to go even if the hero can't get there. That love might be a way to cope with death, an idea beyond the ken of Sebastian, is a possibility throughout *A Singular Man,* although Smith fails to realize that love is a mutual relationship until the end, and even then we doubt that he is capable of a new life. Thus, it is only when his hero is forced to psychological extremity that Donleavy allows love to surface as the antidote, or at least anodyne, to the "case of death" that has forced the hero to the boundary.

Man pushed toward madness is the subject of *The Saddest Summer of Samuel S* (1966), in which Donleavy further mediates contingency by questioning the sanity of a world that works against the hero's attempt to get a grip on his life before death.[9] Samuel S, ten years older than George Smith, is a paunchy, down-and-out American intellectual-playboy "tightrope walking above the abyss" (43) in Vienna where he has been seeing a psychiatrist each week for five years. In an attempt to cure himself (neither he nor the doctor knows what cure means), Samuel refuses to have sexual relations without meaning. A duchess offers to maintain him in return for physical favors, his landlady offers to let him play a symphony upon her body, and a young American college girl offers him a gratuitous lay, but he refuses each one to protect himself. He tells the co-ed: "For you this is just a tourist itinerary. For me it's a steam shovel full of sod flipped on my coffin" (71). From Sebastian Dangerfield's point of view, Samuel S is indeed insane, but Samuel's attempt to impose value on his personal chaos is the effort implicit in Smith's actions at the end of *A Singular Man.* Samuel, in his innocent hope for a significant sexual relation, is not mad at all. It is the doctor, an investor in oral contraceptives and munitions, who is "nuts" (89), and Abigail, the American co-ed who has had sexual relations with her dog and writes letters to her father while she is nude, is none too fit.

Like other Donleavy heroes, Samuel S has visions of the grave dancing in his head:

> Sprinkle me
> With anther dust
> Sprinkle me
> With lime.
> Sow me
> Beneath the buttercups
> After all
> The pantomime.
>
> (42)

Withdrawn into a room of pulled shades, Samuel S also defends himself against his sense of the end by retreating before the mobilized weapons of the world—other persons. But Samuel, more than George Smith, recognizes the need for contact and acts upon this recognition:

> Pull in the outposts of life, the dreams, ambitions, the distant deals. So that some passing grabber swishing his scimiter doesn't lop them off. End up just being alive, the only thing that matters at all. Feel the way carefully while there are still teeth left in one's head. Beware reaching for that little flower, its stem earthed to a buried electric cable to send you flying clear across the grassy field. I reach out. (51)

The co-ed to whom Samuel reaches out and to whom he finally proposes is, like Miss Tomson of *A Singular Man*, unready to enter into the relationship he needs. At the end of the novel she leaves him, like George Smith at the end of his novel, immobile, depleted, contemplating death. Samuel's ethic, "do not try to look big, making others feel small" (35), and his gesture toward accommodation with traditional values (he wants a marriage and children) are, then, ultimately unsuccessful; but not because of Samuel S. He is the singular man who has earned the right to love and accommodation but who finds the world has called in its out-posts. The possibility of love is real, but the probability remote: a further stage in Donleavy's own movement toward a fiction that assumes but does not capitulate to chaos.

In Donleavy's most recent novel, *The Beastly Beatitudes of Balthazar B* (1968), possibility becomes actuality, the relationship Samuel S wants is reached—if only for a short time—by Balthazar B, the novel's hero, who falls in love with Elizabeth Fitzdare, a minor character in *The Ginger Man*. When she and the promise of marriage and a family die in a riding accident, Balthazar resigns himself to loneliness: "Hurry up to die. So little reason left to live. Take a ship across the Atlantic, jump down into the cold waves."[10] The tone of sadness here and throughout much of the novel stems primarily from Balthazar's role as beatific victim. His inherent weakness turns his awareness of death into pathos and low comedy. When Balthazar and his beastly double Beefy are expelled from Trinity, Donleavy mixes death with comic pathos:

> A roll of drums beating. Cannons firing salvos. In a coffin two blank parchments. Of ungranted degrees. Drawn on a gun carriage. Hooves echoing their clatter up and down Dublin streets. . . . Go down to death bravely. When you go. Neither to weep nor smile. (212)

The reader laughs here and elsewhere, but Balthazar, from whose point of view this is told, is unable to counter disappointment with Sebastian's mirthless laugh.

Balthazar's quest for a family and his attainment of a brief moment of love minimize the role of death in *Beastly Beatitudes*. In contrast to the end-burdened consciousness of *The Ginger Man* and *A Singular Man*,

Beastly Beatitudes presents death as an event that moves characters in predictable ways, the most basic being the hero's establishment of a defensive gap between himself, the innocent victim of death's event, and those around him. The absence of an intensely time-conscious hero slows down the movement of the novel. Though *Beastly Beatitudes* is organized chronologically, time is no longer Heraclitus' river which man tries to capture with a sieve. Balthazar is drawn to the past because of the unknown son he has fathered upon his governess, but the present would be acceptable to Balthazar if only it contained love, a word superficially defined by the context of the novel when compared with Sebastian's elucidation of death in *The Ginger Man*. In *Beastly Beatitudes* Donleavy disperses the desperate energy of man in time into a preoccupation with space and setting, the evocation of which takes up large portions of the novel. The panoramic replaces the dramatic, large developed blocks of experience replace the fragmented actions of the earlier novels. Retreating from the sometimes unfunny comedy of the boundary situation, Donleavy transforms the metaphysical farce of his earlier work into weak-kneed satire directed variously against the French gourmet-whoremonger, the English public school, and Irish woman-hood, and into a musty sentiment illustrated by Balthazar's accounting for Beefy's acts. At the end of the novel, Balthazar quotes a diary entry written in verse which reveals that Beefy performs his physical and mental contortions because he is an orphan: "I want/A mommie/And a daddy" (391). As character turns into sentimental caricature and plot becomes an excuse for setting, language slides off into cliché, the result of the narrator's and author's banality without the pressure of time.

Beastly Beatitudes is thus the culmination of a development that began with *A Singular Man*. By retreating from extremity forced by his characters' intense awareness of death to a position illustrated by "Something born *nudges* you *gently* to do and die" (*BB*, 180; my emphasis), Donleavy widens the fictional realms he can explore (the first eight chapters of *Beastly Beatitudes* were published in *The Saturday Evening Post*), but sacrifices the intensity that would make the exploration interesting. This is not to imply that death's presence in extreme form is a requisite of good fiction, but simply that the slackness of technique in *Beastly Beatitudes* seems to stem from Donleavy's new approach to death, the element that gave *The Ginger Man* its vigor and tension. In *A Singular Man* and *The Saddest Summer of Samuel S*, Donleavy was in the process of discovering a value—heterosexual love—that would stand against death, but he realizes this value in *Beastly Beatitudes* only by sentimentalizing the relationship of man to time and death. He dilutes death, only to water down love into a kind of barely post-adolescent lyricism. Incapable of a mature understanding of death, Donleavy's hero fails to persuade us that his love is mature or, more important, convincing. Donleavy attempts to retain the balance between value and death as denier of value by shifting his presentation of death from consciousness to external event, but Balthazar's reactions are all too usual. The effect is one of bathetic deflation leaving the collapsed skin of sentiment to cover the bones of an ordinary *Bildungsroman* plot. The reader of Donleavy's other novels searches for the irony that won't turn against this sentiment and restore the vision of basic man—ginger man—but finds only a gentle humor that nibbles at the edges of sentiment.

NOTES

[1] New York, 1966, p. 139. Page references of quotations from this text are given in parentheses in the discussion.

[2] Martin Heidegger's analysis of death in *Being and Time* sheds considerable light on Donleavy's treatment of death. I have therefore adopted, rather generally, some of Heidegger's terminology in my discussion.

[3] J. P. Donleavy and Richard Joseph, "Traveler, Consider My Dublin," *Esquire*, LXVII (1967), 122; Donleavy ends this piece with the assurance that should the traveler die in Dublin, the Irish "will always mourn a stranger" (208).

[4] *The Sense of an Ending* (New York, 1967).

[5] *Journey Through Dread* (New York, 1955), p. 55.

[6] See Rollo May, *Love and Will* (New York, 1969), pp. 99-121.

[7] William David Sherman, "J. P. Donleavy: Anarchic Man and Dying Dionysian," *Twentieth Century Literature*, XIII (1968), 220.

[8] *A Singular Man* (New York, 1967), p. 226.

[9] *The Saddest Summer of Samuel S* (New York, 1967), p. 78.

[10] *The Beastly Beatitudes of Balthazar B* (New York, 1968), p. 363.

Thomas LeClair

SOURCE: "Death and Black Humor," in *Critique: Studies in Modern Fiction*, Vol. 17, No. 1, 1975, pp. 5-40.

[*In the following essay, LeClair discovers continuities in the presentation of death in the works of such black humor writers as J. P. Donleavy, Joseph Heller, John Barth, John Hawkes, Walker Percy, Kurt Vonnegut, Jr., and Thomas Pynchon; he additionally studies the sociological implications of these author's comical representations of death.*]

That Black Humor has become a fit subject for the literary historian as well as the literary anatomist is demonstrated by the recent publication of three books—Charles B. Harris's *Contemporary American Novelists of the Absurd*, Raymond M. Olderman's *Beyond the Waste Land*, and Max F. Schulz's *Black Humor Fiction of the Sixties*—which advance theories about the cultural causes of Black Humor.[1] Harris, Olderman, and Schulz rightly emphasize social dissonances and intellectual uncertainties as stimuli for the novelists they discuss, but a new sense of the finality of human existence causes much of the social disjunction and intellectual futility that Black Humor presents.[2] Although this proposition has about it the reductionism of Pynchon's Herbert Stencil, both the centrality of death in Black Humor and the importance of recognizing its centrality without discounting the Black Humorists' other concerns can be demonstrated. The theses of this essay are that the "blackness" of Black Humor is primarily funereal, that the fact and awareness of death are the basic sources of the pessimism or nihilism in such fiction, that the presence of death in such fiction does much to explain the kinds of heroes presented, the strategies of selfhood they adopt, and the kinds of endings and forms the writers employ, and that the Black Humorists' concern with death gives their fiction both a philosophical ultimacy and an artistic rationale. The argument begins with comments on John Updike's *The Centaur* and Saul Bellow's *Mr. Sammler's Planet,* which are controls for and, in Bellow's case, an introduction to the discussion of the Black Humorists. Although the death theme in all of the novels by the following authors will be discussed, it is seen as best presented in a representative novel by each: J. P. Donleavy, *The Ginger Man;* Joseph Heller, *Catch-22;* John Barth, *The Floating Opera;* John Hawkes, *Second Skin;* Walker Percy, *The Last Gentleman;* Kurt Vonnegut, Jr., *Slaughterhouse-Five;* and Thomas Pynchon, *Gravity's Rainbow.* These are central and representative works of Black Humor; works by Terry Southern, Bruce Jay Friedman, James Purdy, and Donald Barthelme have not been included since they do not seem to take death as a central subject.

Modern writers other than the Black Humorists have dealt with death as a basic subject for fictional investigation, but the degree to which death pervades Black Humor and the way in which Black Humorists present death set them off from other novelists. Frederick J. Hoffman has analyzed modern Continental, English, and American authors' treatment of death, but his main interest was in the effects of modern mass violence rather than in the effects of an individual's conception of his own natural end or his responses to the natural deaths of those close to him.[3] Murder, whether individual and for personal gain or mass and for political gain, is sometimes present in the Black Humorists' fiction, but they primarily concern themselves with the effects of an individual's *consciousness* of death rather than with the event itself. Consciousness may be stimulated by some violent event (suicide is prevalent), but usually an unfocused thought of death as a possibility or death from disease or accident sets the characters to thinking about mortality and devising strategies for coping with their consciousness. The emphasis on the consciousness of death influences the form of experience in the novels. Instead of using death as an event to round off action (as in *The Great Gatsby, A*

Farewell to Arms, or *Light in August*), the Black Humorists most often place the event of death in the past before the action of the novel begins, near the beginning of the novel, or present it as a continuing process or perpetual possibility throughout the novel. Because death is a radical given, the flow of experience is from, instead of toward, the end. In concentrating on the characters' internal responses rather than on objective situations of violence, the Black Humorists also avoid the pornography of violence which saturates our pulps and popular films. Presented as it affects consciousness, death is apprehended by most Black Humor characters as a contractive end, as a final and ultimate denial of the future rather than a way to some futurity or immortality. By closing rather than opening possibilities, death becomes an element of existence, a process that is simultaneous with living. For the Black Humorists, man alive is in the midst of death; in their fiction, death is more than a convenient resolution for plot and more than a distant necessity for their characters—it is a cause of action rather than an effect, an end which dictates beginnings and middles. In their emphasis on the consciousness of death as a source of motivation, the Black Humorists have some antecedents in American fiction. Hemingway's whole career, it now seems, was a response to death of the self. Faulkner's *Sartoris* and *As I Lay Dying* both have the death of others as ground subjects. A basic theme in Wolfe's *Look Homeward, Angel* is Eugene Gant's growing awareness of time and death. More recent novelists have also given us characters who muse on their own or others' extinction. Carson McCullers, Norman Mailer, John Updike, and Saul Bellow have, in one or more novels, turned their attention to the meaning of personal extinction as a basic theme. Although Updike and Bellow have most consistently created characters who are tested by their awareness of death, they both handle the idea of death traditionally. *The Centaur* and *Mr. Sammler's Planet* have in common with Black Humor the centrality of death and characters who reveal themselves through their attitudes toward mortality, but the responses of the heroes, the resolutions and modes of the novels, and the authors' implied views are quite different from those in Black Humor.

The Centaur (1963) records the confrontations of two persons—George Caldwell and his son, Peter—with their consciousness of mortality. During the four days of the novel's action, George Caldwell, a middle-aged schoolteacher, entertains the possibility of and then accepts the certainty of his death. As he progresses from ambivalence—fear of death and longing for death—to the acceptance of death as part of a natural and spiritual economy, his son is initiated into a mortal world by becoming aware of his father's struggle. Death is presented as an internal process (rather than external event) which George and Peter Caldwell continually contemplate:

> Since, five days ago, Caldwell grasped the possibility that he might die, took it into himself as you might swallow a butterfly, a curiously variable gravity has entered the fabric of things, that now makes all surfaces leadenly thick with

heedless permanence and the next instant makes them dance with inconsequence, giddy as scarves. Nevertheless, among disintegrating surfaces he tries to hold his steadfast course.[4]

Caldwell's life is filled with economic privation, social isolation, professional frustration, mechanical failures, and the imagery of wasted junk, yet "he tries to hold his steadfast course." His fear of death could send him off on the kinds of adventures a hitchhiker recounts; his failure could send him winging toward the peace of resignation, but Caldwell continues his responsibilities as father, husband, and teacher. In very nearly the last words of the novel, "Chiron accepted death" (222)—and the life of cooperation and sacrifice the school-lesson volvox had introduced along with death. Caldwell-Chiron also accepts, without defining it, a religious faith which had been undermined by his sense of mortality. At the end of the novel, he is left on the boundary of earth and heaven with the promise of an eternal reward: immortality.

Peter Caldwell recalls the novel's four days as an adult in New York City, where he is "an authentic second-rate abstract expressionist living in an East Twenty-third Street loft with a Negro mistress" (81). In its proud elegiac tone, the novel implicitly honors Caldwell senior's religious acceptance of mortality and devalues Peter's responses to death, love and art (the first a way to make present time sacral, the second a way to stop time). For both men, death, as a time-release poison within, is the central fact of their existence which requires a definite response; their awareness is without desperation, if with sorrow. Updike's own view of the Caldwells filters through the Centaur myth which confers dignity upon George Caldwell for his sacrifice for others and his courage to continue as a hero of the ordinary. As the epigraph from Karl Barth—"Heaven is the creation inconceivable to man, earth the creation conceivable to him. He himself is the creature on the boundary between heaven and earth"—suggests, Updike's view is ultimately religious. The boundary between heaven and earth is most specifically man's mortality which must be considered a natural end *and* beginning rather than a wall or an easy avenue to transcendence. In his Epilogue, Updike gives Caldwell-Chiron the immortality of the Centauri constellation, an ending of undeniable, if indirectly stated, hopefulness.

A very similar resolution, devoid of Christian elements, is achieved at the end of *Mr. Sammler's Planet* (1970). Like George Caldwell, Artur Sammler instructs the disrespectful young, senses a general degeneration and personal ending, suspects nature and sexuality, lives in insane confusion, and yearns for the order of the past or the promise of a transcendent future. Also like Caldwell, Sammler is separated from his contemporaries by a consciousness of death which pervades the novel. Sammler and his wife were "killed" by a Nazi death squad, but somehow Sammler survived. Now he lives in New York City with his special and, despite his disclaimer, prideful knowledge of death. In the three days of the novel's present, Sammler changes his conception of death and accepts a life of moral responsibility even though he is an aged man. The stimulus for the change is Elya Gruner, who is dying of an aneurism. Gruner accepts his death, maintains his generous nature, and continues to perform his daily responsibilities. Sammler, abstracted and detached by his survival, learns from Gruner that the awareness of death does not confer a magical potency nor does it excuse selfishness. Under the pressure of such recognition and of events which demand his practical response, Sammler disavows his attempt at a pure spiritual transcendence. The novel ends with his prayer for Gruner which affirms Sammler's new knowledge, paralleling Caldwell's, that a moral contract in which the self sacrifices for others is the connection between heaven and earth. Many of the dualities of *The Centaur*—heaven/earth, intellection/natural appetites, futurism/nostalgia, parental responsibility/adult freedom—are present in *Mr. Sammler's Planet* and are resolved in much the same way. Death, the lateness of time, and the wideness of space tempt Sammler to escape from quotidian responsibilities, but Sammler changes and thus becomes, because of his advanced age, a special hero of the ordinary. Bellow does not, as Updike, hold out the promise of immortality, but Gruner's courage, Sammler's new knowledge and new beginning, and the prayer which concludes the novel suggest that death need not force men to abandon the "ordinary forms of common life" for terrified action or selfish disengagement.[5]

Sammler's continuing analysis of his culture is not invalidated by his change from abstraction to responsibility; in fact, his reflections are used to prefigure his shift, for Sammler does not follow out his own prescriptions until he learns that anyone can know the truth about death. Such commentary, a synthesis of sociological, psychological, and philosophical theories, makes *Mr. Sammler's Planet* a good, if negative, introduction to the world presented by Black Humor. Sammler, presumably, believes that modern historical processes have awarded men increased freedom from economic, political, social, and religious restrictions, but that the freedom has resulted in the new suffering of individual selfhood. Subject to a flooding of information and alternative forms of life by the media, the individual in our time loses the ability to give design to cultural phenomena. He retreats into subjectivity, makes impossible demands on complex realities, refuses "(death being sure and final) to go away from this earth unsatisfied" (34). Since "humankind could not endure futurelessness" and since "death was the sole visible future" (71), the individual selects out of the universally disseminated grab-bag of information the notion of Romantic transcendence, now debased to terms of immanence, to satisfy his longing for happiness. This "debased Romanticism" or "dark Romanticism" includes the following ways of coping with the thought of finality: primitivism, irrationality, mystery cults, sexuality, criminality, madness, and cultivation of freedom, spontaneity, innocence, and wholeness. The individual sacrifices religious or ethical criteria for aesthetic standards, thus making life a spectacle in which one acts or watches. If the actors are to elicit interest in their aesthetic life, they

must mythologize themselves, must "expand by imagination and try to rise above the limitations of the ordinary forms of common life . . . hoping perhaps to get away (in some peculiar sense) from the death of their species" (135-6). Imaginative distinction and originality rather than imitation become rules for personality. This "passion for the infinite caused by the terror, by *timor mortis,* needed material appeasement" (167), but man's imagination is overtaxed by the need to produce a figure of stature, a form of selfhood which would satisfy the promise of history and mitigate the fear of finality. Frustrated by his failed quest for transcendent singularity and ecstatic authenticity, the individual has a "peculiar longing for nonbeing" (214) and apocalypse. Bellow thus brings the circle of death to a full close: from fear of death to a longing for annihilation. Sammler renounces his own wish for death and his compulsive attraction to the actions of "dark Romanticism," but the heroes in Black Humor novels cannot accommodate themselves with Sammler's religious humanism. They live in the world he describes, a world of terror, debased Romantic gestures, aesthetic standards of behavior, and apocalypse, but they create it because other mediations between them and their deaths—religious faith, social faith, love, "the ordinary forms of common life"—have wasted away or have disintegrated under the pressure of finality. Taken together, the seven novels discussed below present the circular pattern of death analyzed in *Mr. Sammler's Planet:* self-assertion to imaginative construction to confusion and longing for annihilation.

Many of the themes of the debased Romanticism that Bellow describes are personified by Sebastian Dangerfield, the hero of J. P. Donleavy's *The Ginger Man* (1955).[6] A poor American law student in Ireland, Dangerfield fears "that last and final chill, the one to be avoided at all costs" (191). Because his waking moments and nightmares are filled with elaborately imaged anxieties about his imminent and total annihilation, Dangerfield's primary daily project is avoiding the fact and thought of death. Although Donleavy uses the fable of the gingerbread boy—a figure running from parental authority, rather foolish bystanders, and extinction—to structure his picaresque novel and give symbolic resonance to its numerous chase scenes, the police, the landlords, and women who pursue Dangerfield are actually externalizations of his anxiety about internal time eating itself outward at an unknown rate to Nothing. His comment about intercourse sums up his attitude toward life in general: "matter, all of it, of time" (55). Terrified of time's irreversible progress toward putrefaction, Dangerfield flees his own consciousness through spontaneous, often criminal busyness and the resulting exhaustion, by drinking and whoring, by fantasizing about his rich past and future, by reveling in the funerals of others, and by pretending to himself and the Blessed Oliver Plunkett a religious faith. He becomes a closed self who protects his precious subjectivity by denying the value of others, by adopting masks and disguises, and by irrationally asserting the primacy of his own desires. Dangerfield's life is a combination of major defeats and minor victories, but near the end of the novel his hopes for wealth, sexual satiety, and peace seem answered, ironically enough, by his father's death. However, all his strategies for evading his consciousness of the end are exploded by his final reverie of death's horses running out to sea with him. The novel ends with a sad and despairing prayer: "God's mercy/On the wild/Ginger man" (347). Dangerfield's assertion of self (in the ways Bellow identifies as Romantic) brings only temporary relief from the fear of extinction which drives him to desperate denials of conventional codes.

Although *The Ginger Man* presents a man whose heart is "twisted with dying" (285), the mode of the novel is comic. Much of the action is slapstick, and the limited humanity of the characters makes them satiric objects or grotesque jokes, but most of the comedy in the novel is verbal. Dangerfield continually outwits and outtalks his "enemies" and uses his irony to pretend to himself that death is escapable and that he has "dignity." The reader is invited to laugh at some of Dangerfield's more innocent foibles and scrapes, but most often Donleavy sets up an alliance between his hero-narrator and the reader to laugh at respectability, morality, and weakness. It is a Dionysian laugh, but when death erupts into Dangerfield's consciousness, laughter often falters as a protective device. We are left with the same horror Dangerfield feels, a horror unmediated by religious belief, personal relationships, or the now mirthless laugh. We are like the gingerbread boy whose manic, taunting laugh has ended in the wolf's throat. Donleavy's achievement is thus primarily rhetorical. Through his shifting first- to third-person stream of consciousness, time-shattered syntax, and epitaphic rimes, he reverses our ordinary criteria of judgment and has us rejoice at Sebastian Dangerfield's continual reversal of others' expectations. Moral issues are reduced by the more basic question of life and death, and only an affirmation of vitality at any cost saves the novel from complete nihilism.

Donleavy's other novels also begin with the hero's awareness of death and the gap between self and the world such awareness causes; a clear progress is made, however, from the manic and comic desperation of *The Ginger Man* to the pathetic and sentimental resignation of *The Onion Eaters*.[7] *A Singular Man* takes a protagonist very like Dangerfield into a paranoid separation from life and death symbolized both by his fixation on his mausoleum and the novel's title. The heroes of *The Saddest Summer of Samuel S, The Beastly Beatitudes of Balthazar B,* and *The Onion Eaters* all attempt to overcome their fear of their own death or their sadness about the death of others through love, but Donleavy too often sentimentalizes their relations by giving them an adolescent quality. The vitalistic technique of *The Ginger Man* slides in later novels toward more unified action, descriptions of setting, static consciousness, cliche, and even silence. The relative failure of Donleavy's later novels is instructive. With *The Ginger Man* he had explored a variety of ways to cope with death and found them ultimately wanting. Forced into seeking some resolution to

his characters' victimization by their own consciousness, Donleavy turned away from the tension comedy creates to heterosexual love but (modifying Leslie Fiedler's thesis) found difficulty writing persuasively about love because of the effects of death. Only by diminishing death's effect and reducing his heroes' stature, as he does in *The Beastly Beatitudes,* does Donleavy make the man-woman relation more meaningful than the male alliance he treats in most of his fiction. Death, then, causes the bleakness of the characters' lives in Donleavy's fiction and also, after *A Singular Man,* reduces the author's ability to produce a fiction which avoids sentimentality—an illustration that death forces men, as characters in and creators of fiction, into pitiful weaknesses and sad resignation.

Sebastian Dangerfield has a severe "case of death" (139), but Yossarian in Joseph Heller's *Catch-22* (1961) is the Black Humor hero whose "deep-seated survival anxieties" most obviously and completely control his life.[8] Although *Catch-22* is a war novel, the death in it is not just a result of war; the logic of death that Heller establishes early in the novel makes his ending false. Yossarian's anxieties about death are evident before he reaches the war zone—he tells Mrs. Scheisskopf to "be *furious* you're going to die" (184)—and are extreme: he will not resign "himself submissively to the idea that he must die someday" (51) and thinks about war that he "could have lived without it—lived forever, perhaps" (69). As the missions mount, Heller has Yossarian become aware of death's reality and move from anxiety to paranoid evasive strategies which evidence a demonic and desperate imagination at work. The major raids trace Yossarian's progress toward an ever more probable death and the resultant paranoia: over Ferrara he loses courage, over Bologna he is reduced to a quivering hulk of terror, over Avignon he finds out Snowden's secret, and over Parma he is wounded himself. As the probability of death for Yossarian increases, the deaths of others become increasingly mysterious and absurd, as though death's power increased an increment in its repetition. Kraft's exploding in thin air and Clevinger's disappearing in a cloud begin a progress toward absurdity that ends with Dobbs and Nately colliding in mid-air and Dunbar and Major Major simply disappearing. Given the shortening odds, death's voracious consumption, and the almost ubiquitous Nately's whore, Yossarian decides to desert, but the condition of his now desperate, even murderous consciousness and the charnel state of the world make his renunciation of Cathcart's deal illogical and the ending of the novel sentimental. Yossarian has accepted the deal when he is wounded by Nately's whore, an act which precipitates his full consideration of Snowden's secret. But only if one interprets the spirit in "the spirit gone, man is garbage" (450) as principle, an interpretation at odds with Yossarian's original interpretation (177) and with the physical situation, can one accept Yossarian's change from a thanatophobic victim to a charitable idealist. Yossarian has said he would like to live in a hospital so doctors would operate at the first sign of an emergency and has said that, if worst comes to worst, death is made to behave in the hospital, yet he leaves the hospital to find Nately's whore's kid sister in Rome and *then* go to Sweden, a mission contradictory to his long-standing and persistent "mission against mortality" (180). Although Yossarian does not believe that his moral action will earn him a reward outside of time, Heller insists on his running *to* responsibilities, as if the author—against all the evidence he has adduced—wanted to demonstrate that the fear of death need not reduce man to amorality.

In order to multiply the evidence of death's power and to increase the relevance of his war-time situations to life in an America at peace, Heller gives the reader, in the term he uses to describe Snowden's intestines, "God's plenty" of death independent of the war. Nature, as Yossarian finds in his walk through the mushroom-filled woods, is hostile, and the sun is dying. Dunbar sees decades zipping through his hands; time finally catches the old man in Rome. Disease threatens Doc Daneeka and finishes Chief White Halfoat and the old colonel in the hospital. One could also be murdered by an Aarfy or Flume, be killed by a prank (Kid Sampson), or could accidentally drown. Suicide is McWatt's end, and Hungry Joe, the man nearest Yossarian in paranoia, just plain dies. To reinforce such multiple mortality, Heller introduces several long lists of ways to die, including a list of terminal diseases. The point is that if Scheisskopf, Wintergreen, Milo, and Cathcart were deposed, if the war were ended, if the planes were grounded, these men would still have natural or accidental death to cope with, and Yossarian would still have survival anxieties. War gives men a chance to do their worst to others and makes manifest those anxieties that make the act of living a fearful business; ultimately Heller suggests that the absurdity of dying in war is only in degree greater than the absurdity of dying anytime, anywhere. For a war novel, *Catch-22* does not linger on the details of the events of death. Only in the Snowden episodes does Heller force us (and Yossarian) to bear the ironic, grisly details of death, and even in the Snowden sequences Yossarian's reactions are the primary subject of attention. Heller shares with the other Black Humorists, then, an interest in death as an element of existence, both as it affects the living and is a result of stupid policy decisions by a self-serving bureaucracy. For Heller, as for Donleavy and others, death is an absolute end (the chaplain, the man presumably most capable of accepting death, has terrifying, death-filled night-mares) which forces men into closed survival systems or desperate flight. That Heller felt the need to lessen the burden of survival in the ending of *Catch-22* illustrates, like Donleavy's recent novels, that affirmation for the writer who knows and presents death's potency is desired but difficult to achieve.

In his more recent *Something Happened,* Heller treats paranoia and survival anxieties within a peacetime context. His hero, Bob Slocum, fears closed doors, fellow workers in his corporation, his family, and madmen in the street, but most of all he fears death: "I think about death. I think about it all the time. I dwell on it. I dread it. I don't really like it. Death runs in my family, it seems. People die from it, and I dream about death and weave ornate fantasies about death endlessly and ironically."[9] Although he treats it ironically here, his own death, the deaths of mother, father, brother, the random deaths he witnesses, the feared deaths of his wife and children, all force him to live his diminished life from a survival kit, force him to protect himself with Yossarian-like verbal and physical deceptions. Like Yossarian, too, Slocum wants to "outlive everyone, even my children, my wife, and the Rocky Mountains" (327). Slocum would like to love and help his family, but his ego's desperate need for preservation prevents all but helpless good will: "all of them but my dead father petitioning me for some kind of relief that I cannot give them because I am in such helpless need myself" (401). Ultimately, something does happen in the novel, and Bob Slocum destroys the person he loves most—his son, a double for himself—because of his morbid anxieties and vulnerability. A profound study of domestic life and the ramifications of death anxiety in our time, *Something Happened* extends the primal (and social) insights of *Catch-22.*

The terror of death's possibility and the manic activity and desperate physicality that it produces in *The Ginger Man* and *Catch-22* give way in John Barth's *The Floating Opera* (1956) and John Hawkes's *Second Skin* (1964) to less obvious anxieties and more subtle methods of self-protection. When threatened by that "last and final chill" or Snowden's secret, Dangerfield and Yossarian momentarily deceive themselves and others, but the hero-narrators of *The Floating Opera* and *Second Skin* expand and refine the strategy of deception to, *literally,* an art. They make their narrations life "stories," elaborate fictions which conceal or deny the degree to which death has dictated their lives. Barth's Todd Andrews—the name means "almost death"—has as his stated purpose explaining why he did not commit suicide.[10] As Todd rambles through his account, he reveals a death-filled past (his cold-blooded murder of a German soldier and the suicide of his father) and a highly contingent present (Todd has a heart disease that could kill him at any moment). He says that his faulty heart is "the condition of my existence, the great fact of my life" (48) and that the "masks" of rake, saint, and cynic have protected him from thinking about his imminent demise. In June of 1954, these masks are no longer efficacious, so Todd plans to kill himself, along with seven hundred others, and thus rid himself of his anxiety about time and extinction. As Todd explains why he did not commit suicide, contradictions and inconsistencies prove him an unreliable and, probably, an intentionally deceiving narrator. Indirectly revealed through boat imagery and the floating opera metaphor is Todd's rationale for "autobiography" and life: ultimate irresponsibility to fact, irrelevance of contradiction, formal integrity, and life as a fiction to be given an aesthetic order. Because the facts of time and death cannot be physically avoided, mediated by relations, placed in some satisfactory rational order, or transcended through religious faith, Todd invents fictional selves and roles to substitute for himself. The ultimate role is the fiction, *Todd's* fiction, called *The Floating Opera.* Ebenezer Cooke in *The Sot-Weed Factor* sums up Todd's visceral truth:

"That lives are stories, he assumed: that stories end, he allowed—how else could one begin another? But that the story-teller himself must live a particular tale and die—Unthinkable! Unthinkable!"[11] At the end of *The Floating Opera,* Todd projects a more ambitious, and presumably false, account of his life which the reader sees as further fictionalization of a life made miserable by its contact with the event and thought of death. Closed off from others by his inability to accept the "unthinkable" fact of mortality as end, Todd is left to the fate of Beckett's heroes—spinning webs of words against an impossible silence.

The Floating Opera is an excellent introduction to Barth's whole career, for although Andrews is sometimes ludicrous in his generalizations, he is the first of a line of protean fictionalizers with whom Barth identifies himself, and the novel itself has beneath its false realistic surface many of the qualities of Barth's later, more elaborately artificial fictions. In an interview, Barth commented that, like Todd Andrews, he was made nervous by "fact": "a certain kind of sensibility can be made very uncomfortable by the realization of the *arbitrariness* of physical facts and the inability to accept their *finality* . . . this impulse to imagine alternatives to the world can become a driving impulse for writers. I confess that it is for me."[12] Barth's response to arbitrariness and finality, also like Todd's, is to create alternative fictional universes with the same qualities—exploited conventions, outrageous artifices, virtuosity and idiosyncrasy, confuted expectations—Todd admired in his legal cases and employed in his "autobiography." In *The End of the Road* the arbitrariness and finality of fact, especially Rennie Morgan's death, are again responsible for radically unreliable narration. The narrator, Jake Horner, under the tutelage of a protean psychotherapist, denies any responsibility to fact in his "mytho-plastic" approach to life, a strategy which allows the imagination to distort reality to protect the self from others and from its consciousness of itself. Although personal death and duration do not as obviously press upon characters in Barth's later works (*The Sot-Weed Factor, Giles Goat-Boy, Chimera*), all have protean fictionalizers (Henry Burlingame, Harold Bray, Polyeidus) who defend themselves against the finality of reality by denying identity, honesty, sincerity, and responsibility, and by assuming disguises or illusions. The fictional qualities of these novels—baroque artificiality, parody, overelaboration—are reflections of their covert heroes' survival strategies, for the novels themselves offer historical, allegorical, or mythological alternatives to the mundane reality in which the author's body has its existence. The comedy of such protean fiction stems from Barth's continual confuting of what seem to be the most valid expectations—physical, moral, and aesthetic. Barth finds man a pretentious fool, a being whose finest power—the mind—can do little to mediate the fact that it will be extinguished. Only the solipsistic imagination can both protect and make interesting a life whose temporality and physicality are a burden.

The hero of John Hawkes's *Second Skin,* a retired seaman called Skipper, shares with Todd Andrews a history of death, including a father's suicide, but in the novel the threat of time has been put away by Skipper's escape to an island of notime. Like Todd, Skipper proposes an autobiography, but in attempting to make a romance of his life he reveals a tragedy of innocence—innocence perverting and innocence perverted. Skipper's father, mother, wife, and only daughter have committed suicide; his son-in-law was murdered. Their deaths have caused Skipper some concern for his own longevity—he always thinks of his own safety before others'—and have made him consider his role in their deaths. Skipper rejects his possible guilt because his present life on a paradisiacal "wandering island" proves, *he says,* his innocence.[13] Skipper claims to be a man of "courage and love," but Hawkes allows the reader to see that Skipper has failed at marriage, has arranged the futile marriage of his daughter to a homosexual, and perversely kept his daughter in his power. These failures, Hawkes also suggests through imagery and Skipper's associations, are the result of Skipper's refusal to consider how the deaths of his father and mother retarded his psychological growth. Skipper's affections were focused on his mother; when she died, he was frozen into a pre-adolescent sexuality which he refuses to admit.[14] The childhood deaths have also caused Skipper to cultivate a sentimental avoidance of facts and an "innocence" that allows him to evade his responsibilities to others. Because Skipper does not try to understand what Hawkes calls "the sack of the past slung around our necks," he becomes the selfish agent of suffering and death in his adult life, the Papa Cue Ball that knocks others into their graves.[15] In *Second Skin* death is both the cause and the effect of man's fictionalizing reality. The desperation or pessimism that death caused the characters in the previous novels belongs, in *Second Skin,* only to the reader who sees through Skipper's self-congratulation to a death-avoiding, dangerous, guilty "innocence." For Skipper, his narrative frees him from his unfortunate past, allows him a second, or new, skin. Hawkes's mode of narration, however, directs the reader to another meaning of the title: the self-protective garment of words that hides the "naked history" (15) of Skipper's life with death, death that extends no promise of a future.

Hawkes's work before *Second Skin* also treated the relationship of death and innocence, but in *Second Skin* and *The Blood Oranges* he best employs the comic mode. "Charivari" describes two middle-aged "innocent" adolescents destroying themselves and another. Naive attempts to controvert or preserve history produce the violence and death in *The Cannibal.* Both *The Beetle Leg* and *The Lime Twig* have characters who victimize themselves when they become fixed to their seemingly innocent fantasies of violence and death. In *Second Skin* Hawkes found a method of narration—first-person unreliability—which allowed him to treat "disability and inadequacy and hypocrisy with brutal humor" and the necessary detachment.[16] Skipper entertains us with his clownish actions, but the "brutal" comedy Hawkes mentions is produced by the incongruity of Skipper's conception of himself and the reality he allows to be revealed.

The novel has classical elements of comedy—hero's life integrated on a higher plane, love triumphing over death, lush pastoral setting, release from the past, new youthful innocence—but Hawkes uses them as parody to exploit the discrepancy between his false comic hero and the heroes of Shakespeare's comedies. In *The Blood Oranges,* Hawkes combines parallels with *Twelfth Night* and a fantasy setting with an "innocent" narrator who helps destroy two marriages and drives a friend to suicide to again question the value of good intentions and self-deception. In the more recent *Death, Sleep & the Traveler,* the hero is almost a parody of Hawkes's dangerous innocent. Allert Vanderveenan, attached to his fantasies of physical failure and sexual experiment, kills a young girl but maintains, in the last words of the novel, "I am not guilty."

In Walker Percy's *The Last Gentleman* (1966), the self-congratulatory innocence of Hawkes's Skipper modulates into Bill Barrett's insistent obtuseness and contrived indifference as responses to death. Bill's father, like Skipper's, killed himself and thus left his son in confusion, but the gradual dying of young Jamie Vaught from leukemia in the present time of the novel is the mainspring of Percy's episodic plot and the test of his characters. As Jamie's traveling companion, Bill might be expected to consider the meaning of contingent time, Jamie's death as a process of life, and his own mortality, but even at Jamie's deathbed Bill considers death as a public event, plays games to normalize the little time left, and refuses to let the thought of his own mortality penetrate his sluggish synapses. By choosing to remain ingenuously obtuse to death while searching for someone to direct his life, Bill shuts out others almost as surely as the more desperately active Dangerfield or rationally passive Andrews. Percy's other characters, including Jamie himself, are also measured by their reactions to death. Jamie's response is a restless but total avoidance until, minutes before his death, he accepts baptism. His parents resolutely deny the doctor's prognosis; his sister, Kitty, thinks only of her career as a Southern belle; and his sister-in-law, Rita, tries to save him through the latest technology and considers his death, in Heidegger's words, a matter of "public occurrence." Opposing these avoiders are Percy's *raissoneur,* Jamie's brother, Sutter, who believes "the certain availability of death is the very condition of recovering oneself" and who has put alienated men into terminal wards in order that they might recover themselves, and Jamie's sister, Val, a Roman Catholic postulant and the agent of Jamie's baptism.[17] After reading Sutter's notebooks and witnessing Jamie's baptism and death, Bill, at the very end of the novel, intimates that he may be a Parsival come twice to the Fisher King, that he may, just may, be willing to consider the authentic questions mortality raises. Because he lives in an environment where "death is as outlawed now as sin used to be" (291), Bill's interest in Sutter's philosophizing about death may well lapse into the obtuseness with which he has covered death and his life.

Percy has commented that "what it means to be a man living in the world who must die" is his major concern and that the dying youths in his novels are a "litmus test: to see which sphere of existence each protagonist lived in."[18] In *The Moviegoer,* when protagonist Binx Bolling accepts his half-brother Lonnie's death, he moves one step in his search for an answer to the death-in-life he lives and perceives around him. In *Love in the Ruins,* Tom More despairs over his daughter's death, recovers himself through a suicide attempt, overcomes his pride, exorcizes his devil, marries, and finally accepts grace in a resolution similar to the one in *Mr. Sammler's Planet.* Percy's fiction has been moving to just such spiritual comic resolution, for both *The Moviegoer* and *The Last Gentleman* poise their heroes on the edge of marriage, reintegration of life, and a hopeful future. Percy's comedy is, then, more traditional than that of other Black Humorists, more assuredly satiric, less pessimistically ironic and desperate. However, his placing man's avoidance or grudging acceptance of mortality at the center of his novels, his sense of a comically inverted world, and his malice toward conventional religious, social, and scientific pieties are consonant with the practices and attitudes of other Black Humorists.

The protagonists of *The Ginger Man, Catch-22, The Floating Opera, Second Skin,* and *The Last Gentleman* are all survivors of others' deaths as well as escapees from their consciousness of their own mortality, but those of Kurt Vonnegut most intently concentrate on the experience of survival. In his seven novels Vonnegut presents the by-products of twentieth-century violence, men deprived of normal responses and traditional purposes, men pitifully befuddled or insanely inspired by their survival of mass or individual death. *Slaughterhouse-Five* (1969) is the late paradigm of a virtual obsession, perhaps because it treats Vonnegut's own survival of the Dresden bombing. In the introductory chapter, Vonnegut presents himself as a "pillar of salt," a man whose responses to personal death have been scrambled by his knowledge of the filled "corpse mines" of smoldering Dresden.[19] How does an accidental man, a sport of nature whose law seems premature death, write a novel about an experience that inspires only silence?—that is the question Vonnegut solves by using a tone of sepulchral bemusement and the artifice of Tralfamadore, a planet where death is just another experience. In his comments about himself and Dresden experience, Vonnegut parallels the responses Robert Lifton found in the survivors of atomic attack. In the spell of a grotesque, unanticipated, and profoundly unnatural mass death, the survivor, says Lifton, is both attracted to and repelled by the experience he has illogically escaped. His guilt (for not dying) and his revulsion activate both a psychic numbing (Vonnegut's irony) and a search for a world-order (Tralfamadore) which will account for his suffering and the deaths of others. Lifton also states that such a death-focused imagination becomes painfully sensitized to the extremities of sadness and humor, a comment that applies directly to Vonnegut.[20] Vonnegut uses irony and artifice as ways into the silence that follows massacre, but his hero, Billy Pilgrim, finds only in the delusion of Tralfamadore, with its denial of time and offering of sex, a way to cope with *his* survival of Dresden and the many deaths before and after. Confronted with an overwhelming quantitative and qualitative reality of death which fits no rational category, Billy progressively distorts time and space and seizes upon the impossible category of Tralfamadore. His knowledge and space travels set him apart from his contemporaries, but his isolation makes little difference. His delusions hurt no one, and, besides, this world with all its comforts could do little to mediate Billy's memory. Diminished by his knowledge and magnified by his delusions, Billy finally accedes to his murder by another survivor of Dresden as the ultimate affirmation of his Tralfamadorian faith in the irrelevance of death's finality.

The comedy in *Slaughterhouse-Five* issues from the futility and mechanical repetition of phrase and action. The torment of time and the cruelty of the scenes we and Billy are forced to see mount a picture of life so horrible and determined that laughter is our only response. Billy cannot laugh and so goes mad; the reader, encouraged by Vonnegut, finds the irrelevance of man's gestures and the stupidity of his errors so pervasive that crying or rage would be reactions affirming a dignity absent in Vonnegut's death-defiled creatures. To produce the head-shaking, mirthless laugh, Vonnegut says death is necessary: "you have to have death quite near, or terror, or you don't laugh out loud . . . you just sort of snicker to yourself."[21] Or, as he quotes Celine in *Slaughterhouse-Five*, "no art is possible without a dance with death" (18). *Slaughterhouse-Five* is the "Duty-Dance with Death" that Vonnegut had been working toward in his previous novels. Both *Player Piano* and *The Sirens of Titan* have dehumanized survivors of wars as heroes. In *Mother Night* Vonnegut presents the first of his artist-heroes, Howard Campbell, Jr., who cannot cope with a memory of death, which is also a collaboration with Nazism. *Cat's Cradle* has as its narrator a man who survives (underground, as Vonnegut survived Dresden) the end of the world, only to be attracted to a comically futile suicide. Eliot Rosewater, hero of *God Bless You, Mr. Rosewater,* works out a crazy plan of charity and benevolence to expiate his guilt for killing innocent German firemen. In *Breakfast of Champions,* one of the two protagonists, Dwayne Hoover, goes mad not long after his wife commits suicide by drinking Drano. Vonnegut's survivors do not explicitly worry much about their own deaths; they are too busy trying to cope with their awareness of others' unnatural and grotesque extinction. Unable "to reinvent themselves and their universe" (87), they stumble along in a dance with a partner they did not choose until their consciousness of death brings them to madness or suicide.

With Vonnegut's heroes' madness and surrender to the death that has traumatized them, we approach the "peculiar longing for non-being" that Bellow identified as the result of death anxieties. In the fiction of Thomas Pynchon, the urge toward abandonment of anxieties and self is given detailed and complicated expression. Although Pynchon's most recent novel, *Gravity's Rainbow* (1973), would be impossible to describe here, it should

be seen as fulfilling the death-caused apocalyptic strain in his imagination. In *V.,* Pynchon's first novel, the three main plot lines converge in a Dance of Death and end in what he calls "a dream of annihilation."[22] The protean V. takes into herself ever greater amounts of the inanimate or dead world and ends on Malta preaching the gospel of sterility. Benny Profane originally fears falling apart into fragments of inanimateness but eventually becomes a member of the Whole Sick Crew—representatives of the varieties of Romantic decadence—and ends running through a darkened Malta to the sea. Although Benny is capable of human kindness, he "yo-yos" toward an end of randomness. Herbert Stencil fears his degeneration to stillness, so follows the murderous V. and, perhaps, a twentieth-century disease or apocalyptic Plot With No Name. Stencil's purposeful but anxious quest also takes him toward the possibility of a personal ending if he should find the Circe-like V. As Frank Kermode has said, any ending, but especially an apocalypse, gives an order to the anarchy of experience in process, gives a meaning simply by ending what may have had no meaning without the closure.[23] Pynchon's attitude toward Stencil's and other characters' need for some hierophantic ending or encompassing principle of dissolution seems that of the old sailor, Mehemet: "Why say a disease? Only to bring it down to a size you can look at and feel comfortable?" (433). In *The Crying of Lot 49,* Pynchon returns to the quest for certainty with Oedipa Maas's search for what she hopes is a pattern of history and contemporary event which will give her presence in that pattern some meaning. However, the acronyms of the organization she hopes to find—D.E.A.T.H. and W.A.S.T.E.—and the violence surrounding the supposed Tristero empire give it a threatening, even slightly apocalyptic quality. For Oedipa, though, either paranoia or the secret empire are preferable to her present life in a kitsch America. If Oedipa is not forced into her quest by fear of death, she does share Stencil's tendency toward a fused revelation-destruction.

Gravity's Rainbow begins near the end of World War II in London, where the novel's main protagonist, Tyrone Slothrop, and other characters wait in terror for the sudden and mindless death brought by the German V-rockets. When dispatched to the continent as a secret agent, Slothrop, like other Pynchon questers, fails to find the special rocket (00000) and plastic device (*Schwarzgeraet*) he seeks, but through his crisscrossing of Europe the rocket has become more than a death-dealing weapon: it has become the holy object in an apocalyptic religion, a symbolic vehicle for escaping from, overcoming, and then surrendering to death. Major Weissmann, who appeared in *V.* and is now "Blicero," the personification of death, summarizes the appeal of the rocket for the German scientists and military men who know it: "I want to break out—to leave this cycle of infection and death. I want to be taken in love: so taken that you and I, and death, and life, will be gathered, inseparable, into the radiance of what we would become."[24] Another character reinforces the sexual and suicidal meanings of the rocket when she describes its "great airless are as a clear allusion to certain secret lusts that drive the planet and herself, and Those who use her—over its peak and down, plunging, burning, toward a terminal orgasm" (223). In *V.* Pynchon had entertained the possibility that "the act of love and the act of death are one" (385). At the end of *Gravity's Rainbow,* Blicero dramatizes the notion and his idea that Europe means death and perversion when he sends rocket 00000 aloft with Gottfried, his homosexual companion, inside a plastic shroud—an ultimate act of murderous pederasty. Although Blicero's act develops naturally from the etiology of the rocket, the original appeal of the rocket was not its terminal and self-destructive orgasm. Franz Poekler, one of the early scientists working on the rocket and a major character in the novel, first sees the rocket as a way to escape his "fear of extinction" (406) and to transcend the earth through science. The rocket, however, comes to have a life of its own, an arc that mirrors the once rising and now falling fortunes of Nazi Germany; it begins with the promise of victorious escape, peaks at a moment of stilled time, surrenders to gravity and death, and plunges to the earth and a glorious annihilation. The Germans in the late stages of the war identify with this last phase and give it majestic connotations of sexual climax: the ordained and glorious failure of the physical.

Although those who pursue Blicero and rocket 00000—Slothrop, the Herero Enzian, the Russian Tchitcherine—fail, their quests uncover a possible plot that pales the Rilke-influenced German *Goetterdaemmerung.* Coincidences and connections suggest the existence of an international rocket cartel—a "They" who conspire to make the self-destructive arc of the rocket the symbol for their actions—suicidally exhausting the world's energy resources for "Their" power and economic gain. For the collective "They," "the Serpent that announces, 'The World is a closed thing, cyclical, resonant, eternally-returning,' is to be delivered into a system whose only aim is to *violate* the Cycle" (412). A key figure in violating the world's contractive cycle is a psychologist turned chemist, Laszlo Jamf, who has responded to his own hatred of extinction and the deadly determinism of nature's pattern by discovering molecular displacement and plastics, a discovery that accelerates progress toward what Pynchon calls "Absolute Zero" or entropy. The rocket system, including its mysterious plastic component, represents all "Their" technology and industrialization, is "an entire system *won,* away from the feminine darkness" (324) of the earth's innards, but in its rainbow arc the rocket also symbolizes only half a circle, does not replenish the land, and thus represents the slogan of the supposed "They": "Once, only once" (413). As with the other Black Humorists, death for Pynchon is the driving force, the efficient cause of behavior, but in *Gravity's Rainbow* Pynchon removes its effects from the personal realm to a destructive conspiracy in the tissues of history itself. That some lead the world to suicide and that most applaud or, at least, foolishly concur with the "progress" toward Zero prove that the old mediations of our mortality, personal and cultural, have surrendered to the apocalyptic "dream of annihilation." "Their" irreversible pursuits are summarized by Jamf: "the absolute. Life *and*

death. Win *and* lose. Not truces or arrangements, but the joy of the leap, the roar, the blood" (577, my italics). Pynchon's comment on the Faustian impulse of science comes when Jamf replaces the chemical formula $C—H$ of pre-plastic time with a formula for deathless inanimateness: "in enormous letters, $Si—N$" (580).

Norman Brown, following Freud, has stated that "man aggressively builds immortal cultures and makes history in order to fight death."[25] In *Gravity's Rainbow,* Pynchon uses World War II Germany and the rocketry it spawned as perfect symbols for the culture of the West which builds its own final destruction because of its fear of mortality. These symbols of "control" and entropy, however, inhabit the same frame occupied by the comic collection of mystics, spiritualists, Skinnerites, Dale Carnegie zealots, and other maniacs housed at the "White Visitation," as if Pynchon were trying to cancel out his profundity with his comic banality. *Gravity's Rainbow* is filled with comic artifices—weird names, grotesque minor characters, mistaken identities, pratfalls, silly disguises, comic-book dialogue, fantasies, tall tales, linguistic jokes, games, musical-comedy impersonations, songs, and asides to the reader—which develop an alienation effect and suggest that, after all, the ultimacy of *Gravity's Rainbow* is not without its attendant foolishness. Perhaps no other method could reflect the foolish and sometimes life-supporting banalities that go on while "Their Control" and the rape of Gravity are proceeding with the certainty of a countdown. We *do* get and spend our private energies in our private ways underneath skies already plotted with the rockets' parabolic routes to our annihilation—perhaps the ultimate comic incongruity registered by the novel's beginning and ending. The novel opens with "A screaming comes across the sky" (3) and ends with the Mitch Miller invitation to "Follow the bouncing ball" (760) along one of Pynchon's songs: "Now everybody—"

If the books discussed above are representative, death, in its elemental and pervasive presence, is the primary source of the pessimism in Black Humor, is, in Henry James's words, "the real distinguished thing."[26] When Bruce Jay Friedman made his collection of Black Humorists in 1965, he found in the *Zeitgeist* "a fading line between fantasy and reality" and "a nervousness, a tempo, a near-hysterical new beat in the air, a punishing isolation and loneliness of a strange, frenzied new kind" which he offered as motivation for his group of writers.[27] Recent books on Black Humor have extended and refined Friedman's visceral analysis. In a study of Heller, Barth, Pynchon, and Vonnegut, Charles Harris finds their fiction a response to a "meaningless universe," a world made absurd by the "new logic" of modern science, technological control of life, social and political madness, and a general loss of the self.[28] Paralleling Harris, Max Schulz concentrates on "pluralism, conformity, and an irresolute value system" in his comments on the background of Barth, Vonnegut, Pynchon, Berger, Friedman, and others.[29] As described by Friedman, Harris, Schulz, and others, the manifest absurdities of life in America and the impossibility of rationally encompassing them are, indeed, stimuli for the Black Humorists' imaginations, yet the textual evidence offered by Black Humor suggests that death, apprehended as finality, is what makes rational explanations and social forms meaningless, absurd, useless. In terms that are not meant to be reductive, death is the uncaused cause, the prior physical and metaphysical fact that disturbs man's powers, undermines his structures, and questions his works. Tracing the intellectual history of the sense of finality (and futility) would be impossible here; most Black Humor, however, reflects Vonnegut's sentiment in *Mother Night:* "When you're dead you're dead."[30] Such futurelessness causes some Black Humor characters to jettison inhibitions and conventional codes and forces others into desperate strategies of evasion or physical transcendence, but the result is the same: a radical skepticism about or denial of traditional modes of behavior as logical responses to a now contracted existence. By radically foreshortening moral imperatives and reducing life to a matter of personal survival, the new nihilistic logic tramples on the beliefs and principles of many readers, yet as Yossarian found in *Catch-22* there remains about it that "spinning reasonableness." If death is total extinction, perhaps all is permitted. In any event, if the world were better organized, if science broke through the Uncertainty Principle, if political leaders were not retired movie actors, that is, if all minor absurdities were cleared away, men would still be left to the primal encounter with their death and the desperation it causes when a sense of futurity is absent. To see Black Humor in any less absolute terms is to miss the philosophical and psychological ultimacy of these writers and to misunderstand their pessimism about conventional ways of making do, for the basic problem in Black Humor is not social and intellectual but personal and metaphysical, the problem of death.

In the two novels—*The Centaur* and *Mr. Sammler's Planet*—used as contrasts, the protagonists share the Black Humor heroes' hypersensitivity to death and are undermined by their awareness, yet by accepting themselves and the forms of ordinary life, they continue to or learn to carry out their daily moral responsibilities. Caldwell and Sammler are tempted by manic despair, self-delusion, denunciation of God, and abandonment to mortality, but at the ends of their novels they accept time and death, accept their place in a physical world, take their place in a spiritual universe, and turn toward future responsibilities. Because death is not a final and ultimate event for them, they retain a sense of the future and hope. The social worlds of the Black Humor novels are no more absurd or threatening than Updike's or Bellow's, but an absence of personal futurity, or a presence of finality, in Black Humor instigates the quite different responses of its protagonists to death. The heroes of these novels adopt survival strategies best described as evasive, singular, aesthetic, and protean. Unable to entertain the possibility of death and live a life of contented normalcy, these heroes construct elusive and illusive selves through elaborate acts of deception of both themselves and others. Trying to protect their precious subjectivity,

Black Humor heroes become singular men for whom the outside world and others are the agents of annihilation. These strategies of avoiding or denying death and asserting the self are aesthetic, for they ignore humanistic, social, and religious conventions or responsibilities in favor of their creators' subjective and frequently amoral purposes. Forced by their consciousness into desperate acts of physicality, parody, and delusion, these absurd protagonists often seem shifting dramatizations of themselves, what Lifton has called "protean man."[31]

The Black Humor heroes' conceptions of themselves and their relationship to death define the nature of time in their fiction. If threatening time cannot be wrung of its fullness through vitalistic action, it can be slowed down, spatialized, or humanized by becoming fictional, and so allow escape to a delusion of no-time or some momentary transcendence. No matter what the strategy for disturbing the irreversible and mechanical order of Zeno's time, futurity, whether immanent or transcendent, remains highly contingent, sometimes possible but unlikely or parodied. These novels do not end with the repose and hope found in *The Centaur* and *Mr. Sammler's Planet,* but with depair, futile affirmation, bogus happiness, confusion, madness, or suicidal dreams. Either the heroes are too strong in their self-assertion or too weak from their conflict with death to love and carry out the moral responsibilities that Caldwell and Sammler accept. Most of these heroes are positive that the examined life is not worth living, and some of their creators share their distrust of a reality fraught with finality. Caldwell and Sammler are men devoted to the development of consciousness, but many of the Black Humor heroes and some of the Black Humorists themselves find consciousness, in its openness to all the messages mortality sends, the enemy. Only in Hawkes's *Second Skin* and Percy's *The Last Gentleman* of the seven novels discussed in detail does one find implicit condemnation of their death-evading heroes. In none of the novels does one find the faith in man's humanity and his relation with God that is expressed in *The Centaur* and *Mr. Sammler's Planet.* These comparisons and generalizations should not suggest that death causes all the anxieties nor controls all the facets of Black Humor, but they do suggest that basic to such fiction is a consciousness of death as final end which challenges traditional responses to mortality and undermines all value systems. Although an individual's terror of death may be produced by breakdowns in society and a general malaise, in Black Humor the fear of death is the given, is presented as the cause rather than the effect of the gap between the hero and himself, between the hero and his world. These writers are probably at the end of the historical process Bellow describes in *Mr. Sammler's Planet,* but in their fiction death is a beginning and not a part of some larger analysis.

The comic mode in which Donleavy, Heller, Barth, Hawkes, Percy, Vonnegut, and Pynchon work is also closely related to the centrality of death in their novels. The humor or comedy in their fiction has multiple sources, is of various kinds, employs many different devices and methods, and proceeds toward different ends. The focus of laughter demonstrates the variety: Donleavy and Heller have the reader laugh with their heroes at other characters; Hawkes, Percy, and Vonnegut focus laughter on their heroes; Barth sometimes laughs at the reader; and Pynchon and Vonnegut direct the reader's laughter at themselves. Death as final end, however, creates a basic incongruity. With the contraction of time and the sense of finality in Black Humor comes an attendant reduction of inherited human stature. His spiritual or social immortality cancelled by doubt and love diminished by fear, man in Black Humor begins to look very much like the "sick animal"—the animal that sees ahead of itself to death—that Norman Brown has called him. When a limited being assumes certain dignities although the conditions or beliefs supporting those dignities have eroded, when he insists against contrary internal and external evidence upon his own importance, when he thrashes violently about in his closed space and revolts against his necessary end, a basic and ultimate incongruity between self-assertion (life) and self-recognition (life ending) results and gives rise to the comedy in Black Humor.[32] Most of the heroes in these novels are not essentially defined as social outcasts, stupid vulgarians, or grotesque caricatures, that is, as butts of social comedy. Rather, they are reduced to their often desperate and foolish actions, their single-minded manias, clownish self-deprecation or exaggerated self-assertion, by the consciousness of their own death or the death of others. They are victims of their imaginations, for they can imagine unending life yet daily know mortality. The incongruity is, again, not primarily social but personal and metaphysical: these are men psychologically worse than we are.

The comedy which comes out of this painful existential incongruity would probably be called ironic by Northrop Frye, a "comedy that brings us to the figure of the scapegoat ritual and the nightmare dream, the human symbol that concentrates our fears and hates."[33] Black Humor protagonists do suffer and live our deepest fears, but the energy, freedom, and imaginative resourcefulness of these characters and the formal playfulness of the novelists themselves make the fiction less bitterly ironic than pessimistically comic. An older, traditional comedy was, in Wylie Sypher's words, "a Carrying Away of Death, a triumph over mortality by some absurd faith in rebirth, restoration, and salvation."[34] Black Humor heroes have no such transcendent faith but do have character traits of an older comedy—craft, wit, imagination, vitality, resiliency, protean changeability, amorality, persistence, life itself—which enable them to match for a time the implacable power of their adversary. These characters are frauds, imposters, cheats, tricksters, and fools who manage in a clownish dance with death to spin death and themselves dizzy for a moment. They display a gallows humor that crazily works, for although madness and desperation are pervasive, they hold out against death, a temporary comic draw. None of the heroes, despite their anxieties, dies within the present time of their novels; they do survive, even if minimally and without the promise of a future. Although these heroes have comic character traits, Black Humor departs from traditional comic form by leaving its protagonists in the middle of their struggle and by tending toward death rather than life. Because the two terms of Black Humor's fundamental incongruity—self and death—are held in a relative balance, the fiction does not characteristically end in tragedy or pathos, although verging toward them.

Laughter is the novelists' primary rhetorical method of preserving such balance. Through a variety of artifices and control of tone, the Black Humorists alternate moments of painful awareness with moments of laughter, either the characters' or the reader's. Laughter does not "carry away" death, but it does create for the reader a literary environment in which death can be presented. Without the various kinds of laughter the novelists elicit, the reader might not tolerate that subject—death—which gives rise to the comedy and, in Vonnegut's view, intensifies it. As Norman Brown says, humor "openly confronts ideas that are in themselves painful or are connected with painful images, and thus it is instrumental in overcoming the automatic machinery of defense."[35] Once death is confronted, laughter can and often does function as a defense, a way of intellectually conquering the experience presented or evading it. Because laughter establishes distance between a person and his experience, it "makes possible an affirmation of life without the necessity of Meaning."[36] In *The Centaur* and *Mr. Sammler's Planet* comic futility turns into spiritual comedy, laughter becomes prayer, and a transcendent "meaning" is achieved. The Black Humor novels discussed here maintain a tension between comic persistence and deathly finality, between humor and blackness.

If one grants that the finality of death largely accounts for the Black Humorists' pessimism and their characters' actions and also contributes to the basic comic incongruity exploited in their fiction, critical judgments are affected. Black Humor has been criticized for its distortion, reduction, and simplification of human life and for the resultant literary dandyism, extravagance, and frivolity. A philosophical case can be made that death's finality need not reduce man's stature or cause despair; however, most of the Black Humorists begin with such an assumption—which critics have not so much refused to grant as simply ignored. If considered in social terms, less ultimate than the Black Humorists suggest, Black Humor could perhaps be called sentimental: exaggerated responses to the conditions of institutions and individual identity. But if their assumption—death's finality causes desperation—is accepted, then the outrageous acts of the heroes and the novelists' attempts to register the outrageousness and desperation with extravagant fictional techniques should be judged in relation to that *donnee*. Do the novelists, then, find the proper fictional terms and forms to execute their assumptions about life? Black Humor seems to flow in good Forsterian fashion from the existential conceptions of character and situation inherent in the novels. Some of the novels thrash the literary decorum dictated by the realistic novel, but the disorder, artifice, seeming artlessness, foiling of expectations, irrelevance, parody, and other techniques are valid methods for creating an atmosphere in which death can be considered and for reflecting the often bizarre and outlandish gestures of the fiction's characters. If, as Barth says, "the artist's mode or form" is to be "a metaphor for his concerns," then conventions must be pressed, perhaps parodied, to register the unconventional man, ridden with the new finality, that the fiction creates.[37]

Barth and Vonnegut exemplify the different technical extremities to which writers can be forced by the ultimacy of death. Because Vonnegut wishes to reduce the world in his fiction to those basic matters on which men act, he gives us minimal prose and childlike illustrations in *Breakfast of Champions* as correlatives of simplified moral and psychological questions. Barth pushes literary decorum toward the other extreme. The arbitrariness and finality of the world encourage him to create a huge, monstrous, parodistic, artificial alternative to reality in *Giles Goat-Boy*. Their extremities are a logical outgrowth of basic assumptions that their authors have about the nature of mortality and man. The critical passwords for these and the other Black Humor fictions are "blurring of fact and fiction," epistemological uncertainty, and multiplicity, but the Black Humorists make certain that one fact remains unblurred by artifice, one single and absolute: taxes may be repealed but not death. Borges summarizes just such certainty:

> Denying temporal succession, denying the self, denying the astronomical universe, are apparent desperations and secret consolations. Our destiny (as contrasted with the hell of Swedenborg and the hell of Tibetan mythology) is not frightful by being unreal; it is frightful because it is irreversible and iron-clad. Time is the substance I am made of. Time is a river which sweeps me along, but I am the river; it is a tiger which destroys me, but I am the tiger; it is a fire which consumes me, but I am the fire. The world, unfortunately, is real; I, unfortunately, am Borges.[38]

Because the Black Humorists consider death in just these contractive terms, it becomes the absolute, like God or society in earlier fiction, which demands extraordinary fictional strategies. William May says that in contemporary America "only death—not life—has sufficient energy, vitality, and lure to command the morning headlines and to reduce men to attentiveness before it, like a priest at his daily devotions."[39] He further explains Americans' simultaneous avoidance of and preoccupation with death by using the category of the sacred, which demands a special response, a fearful attraction. In literary terms, the ultimacy of the subject of death drives the novelists to work out, implicitly or explicitly, an aesthetic rationale of freedom and possibility which recognizes that only by twisting conventions and confuting expectations can the novelist communicate the desperation of man in endtime. The new aesthetic also expresses the authors' rebellion against the value system inherent in the very form of the realistic novel. If one does not share the Black Humorists' philosophical assumptions, one can still understand their engagement with ultimacy as a result of excessive awareness and, perhaps more significantly, an introduction to a common future.

The effect Black Humor has upon Americans' consciousness of death is a subject even more speculative than the influence of American life on Black Humor, yet the parallel growth of Black Humor and the new discipline of thanatology has interesting implications. In 1956 the American Psychological Association held a symposium on death; some of the papers given decried the lack of research into all aspects of death.[40] Between 1956 and 1972, the bibliography on death has greatly increased, but much of the research remains inconclusive.[41] The thanatologists generally agree that death has replaced sex as *the* taboo in America. As old people are shunted into retirement centers, as functionaries replace the family in caring for the dying, as Americans gain increasing control over natural processes and view themselves in the mechanistic terms of responsible producer and unfailing consumer, death becomes a crime, an unforgivable denial of the American myths of potency and expansiveness. Worshipping the suspended time of youth, the American adult engages in both verbal deception—the abounding euphemisms which veil reality—and material deception—the funeral and burial practices which mightily attempt to hide the fact of death. Whether or not these deceptions are "therapeutic" is not so easily answered. The existentially rooted psychologists, following Heidegger and Binswanger and best represented by Rollo May in this country, are positive that the acceptance of death "makes the individual existence real, absolute, and concrete."[42] Norman Brown, in his reinterpretation of Freud, agrees that repressing mortality, a constituent of existence, has destructive results. Others, including Reich and Horney, are not so sure. Ernest Becker's view is also instructive; following Otto Rank and agreeing largely with the existential therapists and Norman Brown, Becker says that death is a more primal psychological problem than the Oedipal complex and that the repression of death is evidenced in and controls much of our action. However, he says that the problem of mortality is of such magnitude that man cannot exist without some repression and concludes that "the question for the science of mental health must become an absolutely new and revolutionary one, yet one that reflects the essence of the human condition: On what level of illusion does one live? . . . What is the 'best' illusion under which to live? Or, what is the most legitimate foolishness?"[43] If one accepts Becker's theses, Eliot Rosewater's comment to his psychiatrist in *Slaughterhouse-Five*—"I think you guys are going to have to come up with a lot of wonderful *new* lies, or people just aren't going to want to go on living" (87-8)—is not as ridiculous as it seems, and the defensive strategies of some Black Humor heroes are not as crazy as they might have first appeared. Perhaps these writers are intoducing the new, post-existential man: death-haunted, illusion-creating, and slippery—but hardly ever, in Rollo May's terms, "real, absolute, and concrete."

The Black Humorists register both the American tendency toward the evasion or denial of death and the psychologists' uncertainty about the value of confronting death, yet by concentrating on the consciousness of death as a cause of action, Black Humorists bring death out of the concealment favored by most Americans and allow the reader to consider at a distance the problem of mortality. The novelists' comic mode breaches the defenses that the thanatologists find in Americans, but the comedy in Black Humor may also diminish the seriousness of mortality and the need to confront it. Thus considered, Black Humor is a simultaneous advance upon and retreat from death; it both endangers and protects its readers' consciousness in its fusion of death and comedy. Whether or not Black Humor is useful as imaginative thanatology, the novelists have again anticipated the psychologists and have charged ahead with case studies before the subject was frozen into ideologies. Part of the Black Humorists' achievement is to have picked up the signals of the race and converted them into fictions which do not shy away from ultimacy, fictions which render ultimacy in forms both new and effective.

NOTES

[1] Charles B. Harris, *Contemporary American Novelists of the Absurd* (New Haven: College and University Press, 1971); Raymond M. Olderman, *Beyond the Waste Land* (New Haven: Yale Univ. Press, 1972); Max F. Schulz, *Black Humor Fiction of the Sixties* (Athens: Ohio Univ. Press, 1973); books with valuable essays on Black Humor are Harry Levin, ed., *Veins of Humor,* Harvard English Studies, No. 3 (Cambridge: Harvard Univ. Press, 1972) and Louis D. Rubin, Jr., ed., *The Comic Imagination in American Literature* (New Brunswick: Rutgers Univ. Press, 1973).

[2] To demonstrate here the existence of such a sense of finality in the culture at large or the newness of it in anything but degree is not possible, but convincing arguments are made by Robert Jay Lifton and Eric Olson, *Living and Dying* (New York: Praeger, 1974) and Philippe Aries, *Western Attitudes toward Death: From the Middle Ages to the Present,* trans. Patricia M. Ranum (Baltimore: Johns Hopkins Univ. Press, 1974).

[3] Frederick J. Hoffman, *The Mortal No* (Princeton: Princeton Univ. Press, 1964); see also Robert Detweiler, "The Moment of Death in Modern Fiction," *Contemporary Literature,* 13 (1972), 269-94.

[4] John Updike, *The Centaur* (Greenwich: Fawcett, 1963), p. 149. Subsequent page references to the novels discussed are to the editions cited.

[5] Saul Bellow, *Mr. Sammler's Planet* (Greenwich: Fawcett, 1970), p. 135.

[6] J. P. Donleavy, *The Ginger Man* (New York: Dell-Delta, 1966); published earlier than any of the other novels considered here, *The Ginger Man* should be recognized as an important seminal work in Black Humor.

[7] Donleavy's latest novel, *A Fairy Tale of New York,* has a fighting hero and a *Ginger Man* atmosphere; it was written, Donleavy says, quite early in his career.

[8] Joseph Heller, *Catch-22* (New York: Dell, 1962), p. 312.

[9] Joseph Heller, *Something Happened* (New York: Knopf, 1974), p. 343.

[10] John Barth, *The Floating Opera,* Rev. ed. (New York: Bantam, 1972), p. 3.

[11] John Barth, *The Sot-Weed Factor* (New York: Grosset and Dunlap, 1966), p. 288.

[12] John Enck, "John Barth: An Interview," *Wisconsin Studies in Contemporary Literature,* 6 (1965), 8.

[13] John Hawkes, *Second Skin* (New York: New American Library, 1965), p. 44.

[14] See Norman O. Brown's chapter "Death and Childhood" in *Life Against Death* (New York: Vintage, 1959) for a psychological commentary that fits all too well Hawkes's hero.

[15] John Hawkes, "Notes on *The Wild Goose Chase*" in "Symposium: Fiction Today," *Massachusetts Review,* 3 (1962), 787.

[16] Enck, p. 146.

[17] Walker Percy, *The Last Gentleman* (New York: New American Library, 1968), p. 291.

[18] Walker Percy, "From Facts to Fiction," *Washington Post Book Week,* 25 December 1966, p. 6; letter to Thomas LeClair, 1 November 1971.

[19] Kurt Vonnegut, Jr., *Slaughterhouse-Five* (New York: Dell-Delta, 1969), p. 19.

[20] Robert Jay Lifton, *Death in Life: Survivors of Hiroshima* (New York: Random House, 1967).

[21] "We Talk To . . . Kurt Vonnegut," *Mandemoiselle,* August 1970, p. 296.

[22] Thomas Pynchon, *V.* (New York: Bantam, 1964), p. 191; Dance of Death references are found on pp. 185, 243, 276, and 282.

[23] Frank Kermode, *The Sense of an Ending* (New York: Oxford Univ. Press, 1967).

[24] Thomas Pynchon, *Gravity's Rainbow* (New York: Viking-Compass, 1973), p. 724; compare Dr. Lal's attraction to the rocket in *Mr. Sammler's Planet.*

[25] Brown, p. 101.

[26] Quoted in Kermode, p. 164.

[27] Bruce Jay Friedman, "Foreward," *Black Humor* (New York: Bantam, 1965), p. viii.

[28] Harris, pp. 17-32.

[29] Schulz, pp. 3-15; see also Olderman's introductory chapter.

[30] Kurt Vonnegut, Jr., *Mother Night* (New York: Avon, 1967), p. vii.

[31] Robert Jay Lifton, "Protean Man," *Partisan Review,* 35 (1968), 13-27; the consciousness of death drives "protean man" to his disguises and fluidity.

[32] Lifton, in his preface to *Living and Dying,* says he believes death is "the ultimate source of mockery per se."

[33] Northrop Frye, *Antomy of Criticism* (New York: Atheneum, 1966), p. 45.

[34] Wylie Sypher, "The Meanings of Comedy," in *Comedy: Meaning and Form,* ed. Robert W. Corrigan (San Francisco: Chandler, 1965), p. 37.

[35] Brown, p. 65; discussing death in literature, Anthony Alvarez, *The Savage God: A Study of Suicide* (New York: Random House, 1972), p. 262, says "the real resistance now is to an art which forces its audience to recognize and accept imaginatively, in their nerve ends, not the facts of life but the facts of death and violence."

[36] Olderman, p. 28.

[37] John Barth, "The Literature of Exhaustion," *Atlantic,* August 1967, p. 32.

[38] Jorge Luis Borges, "A New Refutation of Time," trans. James E. Irby, in *Labyrinths* (New York: New Directions, 1964), pp. 227-8.

[39] William F. May, "The Sacral Power of Death in Contemporary Experience," in *Death in American Experience,* ed. Arien Mack (New York: Schocken, 1973), p. 104.

[40] Herman Feifel, ed., *The Meaning of Death* (New York: McGraw-Hill, 1959).

[41] Robert Kastenbaum and Ruth Aisenberg, *The Psychology of Death* (New York: Springer, 1972); see also Edith Wyschogrod, ed., *The Phenomenon of Death* (New York: Harper and Row, 1973) for a good selective bibliography.

[42] Rollo May, Ernest Angel, and Henri F. Ellenberger, eds. *Existence: A New Dimension in Psychiatry and Psychology* (New York: Basic Books, 1958), p. 49; see also Rollo May, *Love and Will* (New York: Norton, 1969).

[43] Ernest Becker, *The Denial of Death* (New York: Free Press, 1973), pp. 189, 202.

William W. Rowe

SOURCE: "'Confession' and Death," in *Leo Tolstoy,* Twayne Publishers, 1986, pp. 87-105.

[In the following excerpt, Rowe comments on Leo Tolstoy's varied approaches to the theme of death in his fiction.]

The treatment of death in Tolstoy's works can be viewed as a gradual clarification of some of his primary concerns. His two greatest novels are similarly Tolstoyan in many ways, but they are also revealingly different. Despite its emphasis upon death, *War and Peace* celebrates life; despite its moments of hope and joy, *Anna Karenina* darkly anticipates death. Prince Andrew's death, seen as a quite positive "awakening," contrasts sharply with Anna's ugly demise. Still more revealingly, only one of the five major characters in *War and Peace* (Natasha) attempts suicide, and she regrets the impulse in time to set her own recovery in motion. In addition to Anna Karenina's long-anticipated suicide, Vronsky tries to kill himself, and his going off to war at the end has been interpreted as a form of suicide; Levin is so close to suicide that he desperately avoids potential instruments of self-destruction; and both Kitty and Karenin experience despair little less intense than the sufferings of the other three. In short, the transition from *War and Peace* to *Anna Karenina* is a rather ominous one. The nature of the change can be suggested by asking whether the title *All's Well That Ends Well* could seriously have been considered for the latter novel, as it was for the former. Levin's agonized search for the meaning of life and his narrow escape from suicide lead directly to Tolstoy's *Confession.* Tolstoy had long focused upon the fear of death, especially upon the significance of how we face death and how this reflects back upon our lives, but now these concerns were to become a major moral theme of his literary work.

CONFESSION

Though the censor banned Tolstoy's *Ispoved'* (*Confession*) in April of 1882, the work circulated in manuscript copies, one of which was read by Ivan Turgenev. In October of that year Turgenev wrote to author Dmitry Grigorovich that the *Confession* was "remarkable for its sincerity, truthfulness, and strength of conviction," but added that it "ultimately leads to the most sombre denials of all human life."[1]

Tolstoy added a two-page postscriptlike conclusion to his *Confession* in 1882, but the work was written essentially from his perspective of 1879. Having lived half a century, he divided his maturity into three segments: the years prior to his literary success, the period before marriage, and fifteen years of married life. His *Confession* opens with the frank admission that by the age of sixteen he had genuine faith only in self-perfection. He had ruefully noticed, moreover, that his attempts to achieve moral goodness were ridiculed. Perhaps still worse, his elders encouraged him to be ambitious, greedy, lascivious, and vengeful. Now at fifty, he recalled this early decade of his life with horror: "I killed people in war, challenged others to duels in order to kill them . . ." (16:110). Despite his "lying, robbery, lechery, drunkenness, violence, and murder," others praised him as a comparatively moral man.

Literary fame encouraged Tolstoy to adopt the values of his fellow authors, which, he eventually realized, were no better than his previous standards. He proudly assumed that he could promote "progress" by teaching men without knowing *what* to teach them. Six years passed in this way, save for two indelibly disturbing experiences: an execution he witnessed in Paris and the death of his brother Nicholas. "When I saw how the head parted from the body—both the one and the other thumping separately into the box—I understood, not with my mind but with my entire being, that no theories about the reasonableness of our existing progress could justify this deed" (16:113). His brother's death, Tolstoy adds, similarly exposed the inadequacy of a belief in progress as a guide to life. "A wise, good and serious person," Tolstoy wrote, "he fell ill while still young, suffered for more than a year, and died in agony, not understanding why he had lived and still less why he had to die."

After his marriage, Tolstoy declared, his efforts at self-improvement were focused upon securing the best possible life for himself and his family. However, he still did not know "how to live;" he was plagued by doubts about the meaning of life. His condition resembled that of a sick man who realizes that what he took for an indisposition is actually more important than anything else in the world—"death." His meaningless life had led him to an abyss of destruction: "All my strength drew me away from life. The thought of suicide came to me just as naturally as thoughts of how to improve my life had come before" (16:117). Tolstoy then recalled how he, like Levin in *Anna Karenina,* had avoided ropes and guns as seductive, almost irresistible temptations. Only the faint hope of finding some other answer, plus the fact that there would always be time for suicide, kept him alive. Yet he increasingly saw life as an evil and stupid joke, inevitably followed by stench, worms, and obscurity.

At this point, Tolstoy wrote, he resembled the traveler in an Eastern fable who was overtaken on a plain by an enraged beast. Climbing into a dry well, he clings to a branch growing from a crack on its side, while at the bottom a dragon waits to devour him. Two mice, one black and one white, gnaw at the branch, while the traveler licks a few drops of honey from its leaves. "So I too clung to the branch of life," Tolstoy explained, "knowing that the dragon of death was unavoidably awaiting me." The white and black mice of day and night kept gnawing at the branch, and the joys of life now failed to assuage his fear of the dragon: "Those two drops of honey which diverted my eyes from the cruel truth longer than the rest, my love of family and of writing—art as I called it—were no longer sweet to me." Both his family and his writing,

Tolstoy sadly concluded, would necessarily end in death. He was then attracted even more strongly to suicide, because he could not answer the question, "Is there any meaning in my life that my inescapably imminent death would not destroy?" (16:122).

Tolstoy's desperate quest brought him to some discouraging insights. Socrates taught him that "the destruction of the life of the body is a blessing" (16:132). Schopenhauer contributed the notion that life is "that which should not be—an evil," and Solomon proclaimed that everything in the world is "vanity and triviality." Finally, Tolstoy formulated a view patterned on the words of Buddha: "one must free oneself from life."

The search for an answer among his peers also left Tolstoy bitterly frustrated. Though convinced that life is "an evil and an absurdity," he refused to seek escape in epicureanism. Yet he still declined to "end this stupid joke," hoping that his pessimism was somehow invalid. At last, again like Levin, he realized that a faith which "made it possible to live" was perhaps necessarily outside of reason. A turning to "unlettered folk" (pilgrims, monks, sectarians, peasants) seemed to confirm this. Finally, "a voice within" Tolstoy exclaimed that God is life: "Live seeking God, and then you will not have a life without God" (16:152). He was thus "saved from suicide," although he nevertheless concluded that the institution we call the Church has handed down to us both truth and falsehood.

Tolstoy completed his *Confession* in 1882 by describing a recent dream in which he seemed to find faith (16:163-65). The dream may be interpreted as a solution to the dilemma of the traveler hanging by a branch in the Eastern fable he had related three years earlier. Lying on his back in a bed suspended above a bottomless abyss, Tolstoy feared that he would tumble into the abyss. He then discovered that by "looking only upwards" (even though the space above was also "bottomless") he could overcome his fear: there was then "no question of falling." Even though it would make "no sense" if he were awake, he realized that at the head of his bed stood a slender pillar whose firmness "was undoubted despite the fact that there was nothing for that slender pillar to stand on." And just before Tolstoy awoke, a voice seemed to counsel him that if he continued to look up, his fear of death would not return.

DEATH AS INTIMIDATION

The perception of death as an inevitable, threatening presence goes back to young Nicholas Irtenyev's reaction to his grandmother's death in *Boyhood.* That reaction—"an oppressive fear of death"—is carefully distinguished from "grief" and seen as a vividly unpleasant reminder that "I too must die some day" (1:176). In *War and Peace,* this terrifying reminder evidently causes the coolly self-composed Prince Vasily Kuragin to break down and cry when old Count Bezukhov dies: "Everything will end in death, everything," he tells Pierre.

"Death is terrible" (4:109). And in *Anna Karenina,* as Levin attends his brother, "death, the inescapable end of everything, confronted him for the first time with irresistible force" (8:383). "Levin now saw only death and the approach of death in everything," Tolstoy tells us. And later, when his brother does actually die, the Tolstoy-like Levin is haunted by a "still stronger" feeling of terror at the inexplicable inevitability of death (9:81).

This feeling of excruciating intimidation rose to a crescendo in the story "Zapiski sumasshedshego" ("Memoirs of a Madman"), written in 1884 and reworked several times during the next twenty years but published only in 1912. The tale reflects a nocturnal ordeal of Tolstoy's in the town of Arzamas, where, as he wrote to his wife in September of 1869, "suddenly I was overcome by despair, fear and terror, the like of which I have never experienced before. . . . May God preserve anyone else from experiencing it."[2]

As the story opens, the narrator tells us that he has been officially declared sane, although he has concealed his true feelings because an insane asylum would hamper his "mad work" (12:43). He is, however, convinced of his own insanity, whose roots he discovers in three childhood experiences. First, when he was happily falling asleep at the age of five or six, confident of the harmony all around him, he had overheard a domestic squabble that filled him with "cold terror." The child hid his head beneath his blanket, to no avail. Second, he recalls seeing a serf boy beaten by a man who kept strictly declaring "You won't." Though the boy said "I won't," the beating (and the refrain of "You won't") continued, causing the young spectator to undergo a second fit of near madness. Finally, the narrator's aunt told him about the persecution of Christ. Unable to understand how His torturers could beat Him even as He forgave them, the lad sobbed and hit his head against the wall.

These three rather stylized episodes are linked by a common thread of anguish induced by man's inhumanity to man. Taken together, they suggest the beginning of a stark, moralistic parable. As John Bayley has observed of Tolstoy's fiction after his *Confession:* "His many methods—his tentative plotting, his discursive variety—all give place to a single dedicated and selfconscious method."[3]

The narrator's symptoms of "madness" were temporarily suppressed, he suggests, by the sexual corruption of his youth. In his tenth year of married life, however, he experienced the first of three additional "attacks." On the way to purchase from a "fool" an estate "with large forests" he planned to sell enough wood from the rich forests on the estate to regain the purchase price—he stopped over at Arzamas. During the night he was overcome with such uncanny horror that he desperately wondered what its cause could possibly be.

> "I am here," inaudibly answered the voice of death. A chill seized my flesh. Yes, death. It would come—here it was—but it ought not to be. . . .

And this inner laceration was terrible. . . . In life there was nothing; there was only death, but it ought not to be. (12:47)

He began to pray, which helped only as a diversion, and then returned home without buying the estate.

The next attack of "Arzamas terror" occurred, appropriately enough, after he attended a performance of "Faust," when again he felt lacerated by the ominous presence of "death, the destroyer of everything." Again he vainly prayed for a solution to his agony, and his health deteriorated.

The final attack occurred while the narrator was out hunting in winter. "I had been a hunter all my life," he declares (12:51). The hunt is unsuccessful: the wolves break through the ring of beaters. On the trace of a hare, the narrator is again thwarted: "It jumped out so that I did not see." He turns back, but suddenly feels lost. Afraid of freezing, he turns back twice more, to be overcome by the same Arzamas terror, "but a hundred times worse." Shaking with fear, he wonders: "Is death here? I don't want it. Why death?" He prays again, though this time not to reproach God, but in the realization that he himself is guilty. He prays for God's forgiveness, and the terror soon subsides. At the same time he finds his way out of the forest: "I had not been far from the edge." Emerging, he returns home in a new "joyous" state and prays for forgiveness for his sins.

This third and last episode seems intended to be read metaphorically: the narrator, who has been "a hunter (or seeker) all his life," finally realizes (as he repents his sins) that he is close to the edge of the woods after all. Tolstoy's use of the forest to suggest that the narrator is (morally) lost is a nice touch, for it was by purchasing an estate "with large forests" from a "fool" that he had planned to take advantage of his fellow man. Moreover, the narrator's fear of freezing to death in the forest recalls the "chill" that had seized his flesh as he was on the way to buy the estate. It is even possible to interpret the uncontainable wolves as the narrator's former passions; the elusive hare that he "did not see" as the faith he had been vainly seeking; and the three times he "turns back" when lost in the forest as the three times he turns to God in prayer.

At the end of the story, the narrator refuses to buy another estate, "joyously" realizing that it is a sin to live on "the poverty and misery" of the peasants, "our brothers." This joyous feeling, we are told, marked the beginning of his true madness. Leaving church one day, he sees beggars at the exit:

> And it suddenly became clear to me that all this ought not to be. Not only should it not have been, but it was not, nor was there death and fear, nor was my former laceration still within me, and I now feared nothing. Then the light fully illuminated me, and I became the way I now am. (12:53)

Giving away all the money he has with him, the narrator walks home on foot, talking with the people. Thus ends the parable: the narrator's "madness" is actually his enlightened understanding of the truth that we are all brothers, and the "mad work" to which he refers at the beginning consists of helping his fellow man. And as we also finally realize, the repeated phrase "ought not to be" precisely echoes the narrator's earlier reaction to the ominous presence of death, suggesting that just as he was lost when close to the edge of the forest, so was he also near to discovering the enlightened truth of brotherhood that destroys the fear of death and perhaps even death itself.

DEATH AS PUNISHMENT

In Tolstoy's largely moralistic world, a life wrongly lived often ends in a tortured death. "I firmly believe that people are punished," Tolstoy wrote in 1907, *"not for their sins but by their sins."*[4] He wrote this to Mikhail Artsimovich, with whose wife his married son Andrey was having an affair. Tolstoy deplored his son's conduct, speaking of "its disastrous consequences whatever happens." A sinful course, he evidently believed, determines its own further path of suffering. Much of what befalls Anna Karenina illustrates this belief: her suicide can be viewed, quite simply, as the end of the inexorable earthly suffering that begins with her adultery. In his *Confession*, Tolstoy later declared that among the Russian upper classes, who spend their entire lives in idleness, amusement, and dissatisfaction, "a death without terror and despair is the rarest exception" (16:145-46).

In *Kreitserova sonata* (*The Kreutzer Sonata*, written 1887-89), Tolstoy presents contemporary upper-class attitudes towards sex and marriage as containing the seeds of death. Though somewhat deranged, the protagonist Pozdnyshev evidently expresses the author's own views, however extremely formulated. (In his afterword to the work, Tolstoy provided evidence that this was so.) After his wife courageously persuaded Alexander III to allow its publication in 1891, however, Tolstoy had strong misgivings about the story. There was "something nasty" in it, he wrote to Chertkov, "something bad about the motives which guided me in writing it, such bitterness has it caused."[5] Though *The Kreutzer Sonata* was justly criticized as one-sided and distorted, it has an infectious intensity (as Chekhov was quick to observe) that challenges the reader to deal with Pozdnyshev's arguments.

Essentially, the tale consists of Pozdnyshev's extensive, controversial explanation of why he killed his wife. He begins by declaring that what we call "love" is merely lust. "Spiritual affinity!" he scornfully exclaims. "In that case, why sleep together?" (12:130). Contemporary marriage, he contends, leads either to violence or deception; it often engenders "that terrible hell which causes people to become drunkards, shoot themselves, or kill and poison themselves and each other."

Pozdnyshev then relates the story of his life, portions of which resemble Tolstoy's other writings and reported descriptions of his own past. For example, Pozdnyshev's

declaration that when taken to a brothel at age fifteen, he afterwards wanted to weep while still in the prostitute's room (12:135), parallels a similar one made by Tolstoy. And the insistence that the equation "beauty is goodness" is false (12:137) parallels a contention advanced early in *What Is Art?* When Pozdnyshev, just prior to marriage, shows his future wife the diary accounts of his former debauchery (12:138), one thinks of Levin in *Anna Karenina* and of the author himself as well.

Pozdnyshev likens the linkage between women and sex to that between the Jews and money: both have retaliated for their oppression by seeking sexual or financial control over others (12:144). He compares his own honeymoon, with its vulgar disenchantments, to the deceptions of a cheap side show. Sex, he concludes, is "not natural," and we should abstain from it, even though this would mean "the end of the human race." Can anyone, he asks, who looks upon the world doubt this? "It is just as doubtless as death" (12:147).

After the honeymoon, Pozdnyshev's marriage deteriorates still further, as increasingly frequent arguments lead to cold hostility. Their mutual hatred, he declares, was that of "accomplices in a crime:"

> How is it not a crime that she, poor thing, got pregnant the very first month, and yet our swinish intercourse continued? Do you think I am digressing from my story? Not at all! I am only relating to you how I killed my wife. The fools! They think that I killed her then, with the knife, on the fifth of October. I killed her not then, but much earlier. The very same way that everyone now kills, everyone. . . . (12:151)

Pozdnyshev next deplores what he considers contemporary hypocrisy with regard to "women's rights." The failure of his marriage, he now admits, was not his wife's fault, for women's education will always depend on men's view of them. The only solution, he contends, is to alter the way men regard women and women regard themselves. Doctors also come in for harsh criticism, and Pozdynshev's attack on the "cynical undressing and feeling her everywhere" (of Pozdnyshev's wife by a doctor) recalls Kitty's plight as described early in Part II of *Anna Karenina*. Moreover, these "priests of science" show Pozdynshev's wife how to avoid having any more children. At this point she turns to music and becomes involved with Trukhachevsky, a violinist who accompanies her piano playing. Tolstoy himself had been stung, while courting Valerya Arseneva in 1856, by rumors that she had become amorously involved with her music teacher, and his wife Sonya in 1896-98 would develop a strange passion for the composer and pianist Sergey Tanaev. As Tolstoy did Tanaev, Pozdnyshev treated Trukhachevsky with exaggerated politeness; Pozdnyshev's wife may well have been as innocent of actual adultery as Sonya, though circumstances in *The Kreutzer Sonata* are suggestively compromising. The first epigraph to the story comes from Matt. 5:28, which says that any man who looks upon a woman with lust has already sinned with her in his own heart. The reader may be tempted to apply these words to Pozdnyshev's wife, though we see her suspicious responses to Trukhachevsky only through the eyes of her increasingly jealous husband. Pozdnyshev emphasizes that early in life he himself became depraved in his imagination, and that after sex with a prostitute he was "ruined forever." Edward Wasiolek even goes so far as to argue that "Pozdnyshev kills his wife not because she may have had an affair with Trukhachevski . . . but because he himself [Pozdnyshev] has slept with his wife."[6]

Pozdynshev tells us that the court eventually acquitted him as a deceived husband who had killed to defend his outraged honor. He insists, however, that "all husbands who live as I lived must either live dissolutely, separate, or kill themselves or their wives, as I did" (12:167). Both he and his wife, Pozdnyshev adds, had been on the verge of suicide. This may again remind us of *Anna Karenina* (even though Vronsky and Anna do not marry), especially since Pozdnyshev tells his story on the train and recalls that in his jealous despair he was strongly tempted to commit suicide by throwing himself under a moving railway car (12:185). One critic has called *The Kreutzer Sonata* "a gargoyle on the cathedral of *Anna Karenina*."[7]

Pozdnyshev's jealousy reaches an extreme pitch as his wife and Trukhachevsky perform Beethoven's Kreutzer Sonata together, and his insistence that music mysteriously agitates the listener without any resolution (12:179) closely resembles a section of *What Is Art?* (15:181-82). The structure of Tolstoy's novel has been imaginatively related to Beethoven's sonata,[8] and readers of the story in English translation will probably not realize that just before Pozdnyshev kills his wife, the word "crescendo" is inserted in the Russian text to describe his feverish mood.

Pozdnyshev's murder of his wife, when he unexpectedly returns home late at night to find her at the piano with Trukhachevsky, is well prepared, and its description is vivified by Tolstoy's technique of "making strange." For example, Pozdnyshev recalls that as he wildly pursued his rival, "a weight" hung on his arm (12:191); the next sentence reveals that "the weight" was his wife. And though we have twice read of Pozdnyshev's intention to stab his wife in her side, the deed itself is graphically blurred: "I heard and remember the momentary resistance of her corset and of something else, followed by the sinking of the knife into something soft." As she dies, Pozdnyshev's wife tells him that she hates him, then cries out, "evidently frightened by something in her delirium." She tells someone or something to go ahead and "kill, kill" her, adding: "Only everyone, everyone, and him too" (12:196). These words echo Pozdnyshev's earlier assertion that he had killed her "the very same way that everyone now kills, everyone" and therefore reinforce his contention that contemporary upper-class attitudes toward sex and marriage contain the seeds of death.

In Tolstoy's story "Mnogo li cheloveku zemli nuzhno" ("How Much Land Does a Man Need?" 1886), the greed of a peasant is directly punished by death. The hero Pakhom purchases as much land as he can encompass on foot in a single day. His greed takes him too far, and though he races back to the starting point just before the sun has set, he drops dead from exhaustion. The answer to the title question thus becomes "enough to contain his body," enough for a grave.

The tale may be read as a Tolstoyan condemnation of land ownership, but it is also more carefully crafted than the critics have realized. After a public reading of the story at Moscow University, Tolstoy's wife wrote him: "the impression was that *the style* is remarkably austere, terse, not a single extra word; everything is true and precise, like a musical chord; there is much content, few words, and it is satisfying to the end."[9]

As the twelve-page story begins, Pakhom's wife is arguing with her sister, who is visiting from the city. Country life is difficult, she admits, "but we don't know anxiety." In the city, she claims, people either make too much or lose everything; moreover, city people are often tempted by the Evil One. Pakhom, who has been listening, emphatically agrees, adding that their only problem is a lack of land. With enough land, he exclaims, he "wouldn't be afraid of the devil himself!" (10:358). The devil, who has been eavesdropping from "behind the stove," takes this boast as a challenge.

Already the main events of the story have been efficiently prefigured. Not only will Pakhom "know anxiety" as the Evil One tempts him, but the notion of making too much or losing everything accurately applies to his quest for land throughout the rest of the story.

As Pakhom obtains more and more land, it satisfies him less and less. Numerous references to his feeling "cramped" or "confined" (*tesno*) reinforce the irony (10:360-63) and perhaps also suggest the devil's influence: Pakhom's heart burns with desire as he feels cramped by lack of land. Tolstoy even puns upon the word when Pakhom quarrels with his neighbors: "Pakhom began to live on more spacious lands but in a more confined world." The ultimate irony of Pakhom's "confinement by land," however, is realized by his grave at the end, as he obtains "all the land he needs."

Learning that the Bashkirs will sell rich land for a low price, Pakhom visits them and strikes a deal with their Chief: "a thousand roubles for a day." As he encompasses the land, Pakhom will mark the corners by digging distinctive holes with a spade. However, if he fails to return to the starting point before sunset, he loses his money. That night in a dream Pakhom sees the Chief laughing loudly and holding his belly; thereafter he is transformed, in retrogressive succession, into two other men who figure in Pakhom's quest for more land and then finally into the devil, who laughs loudly over the prostrate body of a barefoot man wearing only trousers and a shirt. Looking more closely, Pakhom realizes that he is that man, and wakes up in terror (10:365).

The Bashkirs gather at daybreak on a small hill. Pakhom puts his money in the Chief's hat, set on the ground to mark the starting and finishing point. Armed with a spade, he sets off in the direction of the rising sun. After encompassing a great deal of fertile land and digging holes at the first two turns, Pakhom removes his boots to walk more easily. A second echo of his dream occurs after the next turn when he becomes fatigued and thinks: "If I lie down, I might fall asleep." As he walks on, it becomes "very hot"; "sleep" begins "to influence" him. The Russian word for "sleep" also means "dream," and it is used of the dream that Pakhom now seems to be reenacting. The extreme heat may further suggest the faint but increasing influence of the devil, who appropriately accepted Pakhom's "challenge" behind the stove and appeared in his dream.

Pakhom fights off the desire to sleep but walks on dangerously far to encircle some particularly rich-looking land before making the final turn. Seeing that the sun is now quite low, he digs a last hole and heads back towards the hill on which the Bashkirs await him. Realizing in horror that "the sun will not wait," Pakhom discards his extra clothes in further reenactment of his dream, keeping only the spade for support. As he dashes along, his "heart pounding like a hammer," he has an eerie feeling that death may be near. The setting sun now becomes "large, red, and bloody."

Pakhom rushes madly on, and the sun disappears. But he hears the Bashkirs shouting on the hill and realizes that there it is still light. With a last desperate effort he reaches the finish, where the Chief is laughing loudly and holding his belly. Recalling his dream, Pakhom collapses with blood flowing from his mouth. His grave is dug with the same spade he had used to make the holes marking the turns in his journey.

These holes, we see, were miniature suggestions that Pakhom in his feverish quest was digging his own grave, much as the "cramped" feeling that his increasingly spacious lands had ironically engendered in him is now realized in the confines of the grave itself. The image of the sun (which "will not wait") is particularly successful, as it races in its arching journey across the sky against the wide curve of Pakhom's greed upon the ground. He had decided, we recall, to set off in the direction of the rising sun. Later in the day, the sun's intense heat, recalling the devil's own element, appropriately "influences" Pakhom to lie down and sleep in a premature realization of his devil-induced dream. The fact that Pakhom's heart pounds like a hammer while the sun turns blood-red is a grimly apt anticipation of the blood that issues from his mouth as he dies. At the end, both Pakhom and the sun disappear beneath the ground after tracing their curving courses above the earth—a focus that appropriately reinforces the deadly playfulness of the story's title.

DEATH AS INSPIRATION

Tolstoy's preference for the simple life of the peasants is reflected in his descriptions of their deaths. Thus in *Childhood,* the peasant woman Natalya Savishna "accomplished the best and greatest deed in this life: she died without regret or fear" (1:107). In his *Confession,* Tolstoy would write that unlike the nobility, the simple folk "approach death with tranquility, and most often with joy." This death, he concludes, is "the greatest happiness" (16:146). The Tolstoyan inference is that an unselfish, hard-working, natural life is rewarded by an inspiring, almost triumphant transition to the next world.

Even with this in mind, it is difficult to understand Tolstoy's story "Tri smerti" ("Three Deaths"), published in 1859. He worked especially hard on the story's ending (which features the death of a tree), but it puzzled many readers nonetheless. Ivan Turgenev wrote Tolstoy that "Three Deaths" was generally popular among St. Petersburg readers, "but they find the ending strange and don't even completely understand its connection with the two preceding deaths; those who do understand—are dissatisfied."[10] Some critics suspected that Tolstoy was losing his powers as an artist.[11] In a letter to Countess Alexandra, he attempted to explain the idea behind the story:

> three creatures died—a lady, a peasant and a tree. The lady is pitiful and loathsome because she has lied all her life, and lies when on the point of death. Christianity, as she understands it, doesn't solve the problem of life and death for her. . . . The peasant dies peacefully just because he is not a Christian. His religion is different, even though by force of habit he has observed the Christian ritual: his religion is nature, which he has lived with. . . . The tree dies peacefully, honestly and beautifully. Beautifully—because it doesn't lie, doesn't put on airs, isn't afraid, and has no regrets.[12]

The three deaths seem valued in proportion to their closeness to nature. The "beautiful" death of the tree, as a part of nature itself, is better even than that of the "natural" peasant. Still, Tolstoy's explanation may not seem entirely satisfactory.

The story invites diverse interpretations. One of Tolstoy's best critics has observed: "The dying peasant who gives his new boots away, instinctively acts for the good of others."[13] But as another well-known critic has noted, this is "just not true," much as we would like it to be: the peasant grudgingly agrees only after he has been asked repeatedly, scolded for being wasteful, and promised a gravestone in return.[14] The second critic goes on to explain that the themes of class difference between peasant and noblewoman and of true and false Christianity are, like the excoriation of the hypocrisy attendant on the noblewoman's dying, invitations to misinterpret the story. This critic finds in it an "implication" (which he terms an outrageous violation of both Christian and humane feeling) "that compassion, grief, and pity are false." In support of this, however, he renders Tolstoy's opinion (in the above letter) that the dying tree "has no regrets" (*ne zhaleet*)[15] as "doesn't pity" (which the Russian could indeed mean, but which seems misleading in this context since it is the other trees which do not pity the dying one). He also appears to agree implicitly with Tolstoy that the death of the tree is beautiful because it "has no fear"—even though, as the first critic has noted, the author himself "appears to have forgotten" that in the story "he had described the tree as 'tottering on its roots in fear.'"

In view of such problems, "Three Deaths" should be interpreted cautiously, but it can also be seen, ultimately, as a suggestive exploration of the development of human life in its broadest natural context. The story is constructed upon contrasts within similarities. As it begins, we see the lady, who is pale, thin, and sickly, riding in a carriage with her maid, who is pink, plump, and healthy. The lady's hat, hanging inside the carriage, sways "before the nose" (3:59) of the maid. Yet when the edge of the maid's coat "barely touches" the lady's leg, she irritably pushes it away with the single word "Again," whereupon the maid moves further away, blushing furiously. They soon pass a church and the maid crosses herself. The lady is slow both to understand why and to follow her example.

These two initial themes—the clothing and the cross—recur in the story of the old peasant. As he nears death, a young peasant asks him for his new boots, which he will presumably no longer need. The old man agrees, provided that the young peasant buy him a gravestone. The young man later fails to do this, but does place a cross on the grave, for which purpose he cuts down the tree at the end.

The tree, then, is put to a useful purpose, like the new boots of the old peasant. Earlier, when the old man had been slow to part with them, the cook had reproached him by declaring that he had no "need" for them: he "will hardly be buried in new boots" (3:64). This point was important to Tolstoy. At the end of his story "Kholstomer" ("Strider"), a man is indeed buried in a new uniform and new boots (12:42). The man was "of no use to anyone," we learn, and yet his burial was "an extra difficulty for people." In sharp contrast, the body of the dead horse Strider is variously useful: people use his skin and his bones, and a wolf feeds his flesh to her cubs, who howl "joyously."

When the tree is cut down to make a cross at the end of "Three Deaths," the surrounding trees fill out the new space with their branches "still more joyously." And in the story's last sentence, these trees' branches and leaves rustle "joyously and peacefully" and "majestically." When the lady dies, her face is described as "stern, peaceful and majestic" (3:70). The carefully established contrast between "stern" and "joyous" reflects the contrast, as in "Strider," between a burdensome death and a useful one.

The tree's death, which Tolstoy called "peaceful, honest and beautiful," has a still greater, though also elusive, importance in the story. The cook, who had reproached the old peasant for being slow to give away his boots, has a dream which, she believes, foreshadows his death. In the dream he gets up from his sickbed and chops wood, saying that he wants to do something useful, whereupon the cook awakens to realize that he has just died. Though she does not know it then, her dream still more specifically predicts the death of the tree: the old man, she dreams, "seizes an axe" and "the chips fly all over." At the end of the story the young peasant "took his axe," and when he kills the tree "the chips were flying."

The peasant cook is thus attuned, through her dream, to the two deaths that Tolstoy viewed with approval. Another link is that the peasant's religion, in Tolstoy's words, is nature, and the tree, a part of nature, is carefully personified as it dies. First, we read that its leaves "whispered something," and a robin sitting on one of its branches moved to another tree. "The tree," we are told, "shuddered with its whole body . . . tottering on its roots in fear." Finally, "lowering its limbs," the tree falls to the earth, and "the robin whistled and fluttered higher." After this, the birds gather to "chirp something happy," while the other trees whisper joyously, peacefully, and majestically.

Whether or not one sees the hint of a departing soul in the robin that flies upward from the body of the dying tree, clearly nature itself is elaborately and even triumphantly personified by this "majestic" ending. Despite Tolstoy's apparent failure to remember the fear of the dying tree, the three deaths are admired to the extent they approach a harmony with the natural world around them. The death of the tree, as the surrounding trees "still more joyfully" fill out the new space with their branches, promotes this natural harmony. Attempting to answer the question "What is the aim of human life?" Tolstoy at nineteen had written in his diary: "If I begin with a view toward nature, I see that all within her is constantly developing and that each component part unconsciously facilitates the development of the other parts. Man himself is such a part of nature, but endowed with consciousness; he ought then to strive, just as the other parts, consciously employing his spiritual faculties, for the development of everything in existence."[16] The fact that the tree in "Three Deaths" is used to make a cross, enabling one man to atone for his broken promise to another, makes the harmony of the tree's "beautiful" death particularly inspiring.

In "Alesha Gorshok" ("Alyosha The Pot," 1905), the death of a simple-minded, overworked peasant proves unexpectedly beautiful. The story's main theme is ironic offensiveness: Alyosha's nickname is a life-long reminder that as a child he had once broken a pot while running an errand. Continually mistreated, he worries most about offending others. The cook Ustinya is the only person who "pities" him, but their hopes of marriage are crushed as an offense to his employer and his father. When Alyosha injures himself fatally at work, he fears that "the master will take offense" (14:200). Before dying, he prays "only with his hands and his heart," feeling in his heart that just as this world is good if you obey and do not offend, so will all be good in the next one. As he dies, Alyosha is repeatedly "astonished at something." The subtle, touching implication is that his meek obedience and fear of offending others have finally been rewarded by an enlightened insight into the sacred value of his own goodness.

DEATH AS ENLIGHTENMENT

In Tolstoy's most famous short story "Smert' Ivana Il'icha" ("The Death of Ivan Ilych," 1886), the hero discovers a shattering truth just before he dies: his entire life has in a real sense been a protracted "death." Ivan Ilych is a sort of Russian Everyman whose disease is also deliberately generalized. As his surname Golovin suggests (*golova* means "head"), Ivan Ilych has functioned "from the head" rather than "from the heart." He has lived exclusively for his own pleasure, never questioning the value of such an existence. His striving toward the "pleasant" and the "proper" is relentlessly exposed as frivolous and false.

The repetitive pattern of Ivan Ilych's self-centered life is reflected in the circular nature of the story. For example, his daughter's fiancé is a court examiner, the same post Ivan Ilych himself held when he became engaged to his wife. Moreover, he "receives the same treatment from his doctor, when on trial for his life, as he himself had been accustomed to mete out to others in court."[17] In still another subtle circle, the odd taste produced by his medicine recalls one of the symptoms of the disease itself. Finally, after a painful, three-day struggle in a symbolic black sack (which has been likened to Jonah's three days of learning humility in the belly of the whale),[18] Ivan Ilych quite literally "sees the light." Comprehending the folly of his former existence, he thinks: "Death is over"—and dies.

The transformation of Ivan Ilych, who finally realizes that his life has been a sort of death, follows a simple formula: the concepts "pleasant" and "proper" are replaced by "pity" and "understanding." As his affliction worsens, he realizes that only his peasant servant Gerasim and his son Vasya "understand and pity" him (12:98). Just before his death it is revealed to him that his life was not what it should have been, but that this can still be remedied (12:106). He then begins to "pity" both his wife and son, as we learn from two short, separate sentences. Finally he attempts to express this "pity," but then breaks off, "knowing that the one to whom it mattered would understand." As Ralph Matlaw has put it: "The understanding Ivan Ilych reaches and the pity that he feels are contrasted with his inability to communicate and his indifference whether he does, and the discovery that his salvation no longer depends on external expression but on inner conviction."[19]

Deciding, in his new compassion for his wife and son, to relieve both them and himself of suffering, Ivan Ilych abruptly discovers that pain, and even death itself, seem to be vanishing.

> There was no fear whatsoever because death, too, was no longer.
> In place of death there was light.
> "So that's what it is!" he announced aloud.
> "What joy!"
>
> (12:107)

All of this strongly recalls the narrator's "joyous" experience at the end of "Memoirs of a Madman," when his fear of death disappears as he sees the "light" of the brotherhood of man. Ivan Ilych's enlightenment, however, is merely a hopeful component of his inexorable death.

In "Khoziain i rabotnik" ("Master and Man," 1895), Tolstoy's tale of two men lost in a snowstorm, the hero who "sees the light" acts nobly before he dies. Having tried to abandon his servant Nikita in an attempt to save himself, the merchant Brekhunov then dies while using his own body warmth to save Nikita's life. The story has been demonstrated to contain symbolic echoes of Christ's passion, including the crowing of a cock, a Peter who turns away, and even Brekhunov's crucifixlike posture during his self-sacrificing death.[20] Most contemporary readers were deeply moved by the hero's change of heart, though one critic complained that if Brekhunov indeed forgot about himself and thought only of Nikita (as Tolstoy tells us), the exploit was too unexpected and unmotivated.[21]

On the other hand, John Bayley argues that Tolstoy renders the merchant Brekhunov's noble impulse "both moving and convincing" by using business-related images to describe his thoughts and actions.[22] For example, Brekhunov warms Nikita in order to save his own life as well: he acts "with the same decisiveness with which he used to clinch a good business deal" (12:337). Nevertheless, one could disagree with Bayley's opinion that the merchant remains true to his "nature and personality" throughout the story. After Brekhunov has sheltered Nikita's body with his own, he is "amazed" by "a joy he had never before experienced." Tears fill his eyes, and he soon thinks "neither about his own legs nor about his own arms, but only about how to warm the peasant lying beneath him." The goodness of Brekhunov's deed thus seems to acquire an unexpected momentum capable of transcending selfish calculation. Though he now thinks "boastfully," as in concluding a business deal, that he is saving Nikita, Brekhunov soon has a dream in which his new feeling of joy is said to be "completed" (12:339): he is summoned by the one who bade him lie down upon Nikita. "I'm coming!" he cries "joyously"—and "awakens, but awakens not at all as the same person he was when he fell asleep." Indeed, Brekhunov now exhibits an attitude toward his servant that he could presumably never have felt before: "and it seemed to him that he was Nikita, and Nikita was he, and that his life was not in his own self, but in Nikita." Tolstoy obviously intended to demonstrate that Brekhunov dies a transformed person, fully aware of a sacred bond with his fellow man.

Brekhunov's dream, in which his new joy is "completed" by the realization that he has been motivated to save

Nikita by the one who is now summoning him, exemplifies Prince Andrew's idea (in *War and Peace*) that "God is love" and that, as a particle of love, man returns to the eternal source at death. As he dies, Prince Andrew realizes that "death is an awakening." In a letter of 1892, Tolstoy expressed his own belief that "death is an awakening." Our life, he explained, is like a dream compared to "the more real, actual, true life from which we come when we enter this life, and to which we return when we die. . . . But even that truer life is only one of the dreams of another, still truer life and so on to infinity, to the one last true life, the life of God." Tolstoy knew this "for certain," he declared: "when I die I shall rejoice that I am waking up to that more real world of love."[23]

NOTES

[1] Knowles, *Tolstoy: The Critical Heritage*, 32.

[2] Christian, ed., *Tolstoy's Letters*, 1:222.

[3] Bayley, *Tolstoy and the Novel*, 192.

[4] Christian, ed., *Tolstoy's Letters*, 2:667.

[5] Ibid., 2:478.

[6] Wasiolek, *Tolstoy's Major Fiction*, 163.

[7] Albert Cook, "The Moral Vision: Tolstoy," in Matlaw, ed., *Tolstoy: A Collection of Critical Essays*, 126.

[8] See Dorothy Green, "*The Kreutzer Sonata:* Tolstoy and Beethoven," *Melbourne Slavonic Studies* 1 (1967); Green's argument is summarized by R. F. Christian, *Tolstoy*, 232-33.

[9] Tolstoy, 10:533.

[10] Ibid., 3:468.

[11] Simmons, *Leo Tolstoy*, 197.

[12] Christian, ed., *Tolstoy's Letters*, 1:122.

[13] Christian, *Tolstoy*, 89.

[14] Wasiolek, *Tolstoy's Major Fiction*, 33.

[15] L. N. Tolstoi, *Polnoe sobranie sochinenii v 90-kh tomakh* [Complete works in 90 volumes] (Moscow, 1928-58), 5:301.

[16] Eikhenbaum, *Young Tolstoi*, 10.

[17] Christian, *Tolstoy*, 237.

[18] See Boris Sorokin, "Ivan Il'ich as Jonah: A Cruel Joke," *Canadian Slavic Studies* 5, no. 4 (Winter 1971):503.

[19] Matlaw, ed., *Tolstoy: A Collection of Critical Essays*, 6.

[20] See E. W. Trahan, "Tolstoy's 'Master and Man'—A Symbolic Narrative," *Slavic and East European Journal* 7, no. 3 (Fall 1963):258-68.

[21] L. N. Tolstoi, *Sobranie sochinenii v dvadsati dvukh tomakh,* 12:474.

[22] Bayley, *Tolstoy and the Novel*, 95.

[23] Christian, ed., *Tolstoy's Letters*, 2:490-91.

David Stouck

SOURCE: "'Winesburg Ohio' as a Dance of Death," in *American Literature*, Vol. XLVIII, No. 4, January, 1997, pp. 525-42.

[*In the following essay, Stouck illuminates the tragic world view offered in Sherwood Anderson's* Winesburg, Ohio *by highlighting its affinities with the "medieval concept of life as a Dance of Death."*]

Sherwood Anderson's implied purpose in *Winesburg, Ohio* is "to express something" for his characters, to release them from their frustration and loneliness through his art. This motive is revealed in the prayer of Elizabeth Willard (mother of the nascent artist George Willard), who, sensing the approach of her death, says: "I will take any blow that may befall if but this my boy be allowed to express something for us both" (p. 40).[1] The view of art, however, in this book does not suggest the fulfillment of that prayer. Artists, like the old man in the introductory sketch and like Enoch Robinson in "Loneliness," are among those least capable of expressing themselves to others, either in their life gestures or in their art. The old man in "The Book of the Grotesque" is a pathetic figure preoccupied with fantasies about his failing health. He has a vision of people in a procession and a theory about the "truths" that make them grotesques; but he does not publish the book he is writing about these people, for he realizes it would represent only *his* truth about them, that it is not possible to express the truth for someone else. Enoch Robinson, the pathologically shy painter, tries to reach out to others through his work, but his paintings fail to make even his fellow artists experience what he has thought and felt.

The central insight in the book concerning human relationships is that each man lives according to his own "truth" and that no one can understand and express fully that truth for someone else. Or, put another way, every human being in this world is ultimately alone. In desperate reaction to this vision Elizabeth Willard, near the end of her life, seeks out death as her companion:

> The sick woman spent the last few months of her life hungering for death. Along the road of death she went, seeking, hungering. She personified the figure of death and made him now a strong black-

haired youth running over hills, now a stern quiet man marked and scarred by the business of living. In the darkness of her room she put out her hand, thrusting it from under the covers of her bed, and she thought that death like a living thing put out his hand to her. "Be patient, lover," she whispered. "Keep yourself young and beautiful and be patient." (p. 228)

In this one vivid paragraph are telescoped many of the book's central concerns: the suffering mother, frustration and loneliness, life as unending movement, the search for love, and the power of death. Describing death as Elizabeth Willard's lover, Anderson suggests not only a central theme but perhaps a principle of structure in his book—namely, the medieval concept of life as a Dance of Death.

I

Anyone familiar with Anderson's writing is aware of the frequency of the word death in his titles. In *Winesburg, Ohio* "Death" is the title of a key sequence concerning Elizabeth Willard. "Death in the Woods" is the title of one of Anderson's most accomplished short stories and was made the title of a collection of stories published in 1933. One of the best stories in that collection is titled "Brother Death," a story of a boy who must die young but who, unlike his older brother, never has to part with his imagination. "Death" and "A Dying Poet" are two of the titles in *A New Testament* and "Death on a Winter Day" is a chapter title from *No Swank.* In the *Sherwood Anderson Reader* we find a magazine piece titled "A Dead Dog" and a sequence from the unedited memoirs published as "The Death of Bill Graves." The suggestion in these titles that Anderson was more than casually preoccupied with the theme of death is quickly borne out by an examination of his novels, stories, and memoirs.

In almost every book Anderson published the death of a beloved character is of crucial significance and casts the protagonist's life in a wholly different perspective. And on a more philosophical level Anderson saw modern man, alienated from creativity by mechanized factory work and by a repressive Puritan ethic, caught up in a form of living death. These two forms of death—the death of an individual and the death of a society—correspond to the distinction in late medieval art between a dance of Death and the dance of the dead. Holbein's *Dance of Death,* artistically the most sophisticated expression of this theme, depicts Death claiming various individuals and leading them away singly from this life. The more popular representations, such as the relief on the cemetery at Basel, depicted the dead either in a procession or dancing with the living. One of the popular beliefs associated with the Dance of Death was that the dead appeared to warn the living of their fate.[2] Such images and themes, as will be shown, were a part of Anderson's imagination throughout his career as a writer.

The death of Sherwood Anderson's mother when the author was eighteen likely determined, more than any other experience, the persistent preoccupation with death in his fiction. The mother's death is recorded several times in Anderson's writings, in both semi-autobiographical and fictional form. For some of Anderson's protagonists the death of the mother changes radically the course of their lives and initiates an unending quest to find a home and a place in the world. In *Windy McPherson's Son* Sam's mother dies when the hero is still a youth and he seeks in the motherly Mary Underwood someone to fill that role. His later attachments to women follow the same pattern. When he marries Sue Rainey he envisions a whole family of children, for he wants himself to be part of a family with Sue mother to them all. Because Sue cannot give birth to living children, the marriage fails for a long time, and Sam becomes an alcoholic, guilt-ridden over the deaths of motherly women he has known. Only after he has found three children to adopt does he go back and resume his life with Sue. In the more ideological novel *Marching Men,* the death of Beaut McGregor's mother has a similar profound effect on the course of the protagonist's life. The death of Beaut's mother is imaged as a Dance of Death in the manner of Holbein. Death personified comes unexpectedly one night up the stairs to the old woman's room, sits grim and expectant at the foot of the bed and carries the old woman away before morning. Grief stricken over the death of this humble and obscure figure, McGregor dedicates himself to a vision of mankind's purposeful march toward perfection, a march that will give the anonymous lives of people like his mother order and meaning.

In more directly autobiographical writings the mother's death initiates the youth into the world of experience and awakens him to his own mortality. In A *Story-Teller's Story* it is an experience of profound alienation for the boy; Anderson writes "for us there could be no home now that mother was not there."[3] Similarly in *Winesburg, Ohio* it occasions George Willard's departure from the town in which he has grown up. In *Tar: A Midwest Childhood* the mother's death spells the end of childhood and innocence. The day after his mother's funeral, Tar crawls inside a box car on a railroad siding and for the first time in his life thinks about his own death—what it would be like to be buried under a load of grain. When later he hurries up the street, forcing himself to take up his paper route again, we are told in the book's closing lines that although he did not know it he was "racing away out of his childhood."[4] In each instance the mother's death awakens the hero to the mortal view of existence and raises the difficult question of life's meaning and purpose.

Adult life in Anderson's fiction is repeatedly imaged as processional movement along a road. In *Marching Men* mankind is represented as shuffling in disorderly fashion toward death. Beaut McGregor's vision is that the procession will become orderly and dignified when men cease to serve the ambitions of individual leaders and march for the betterment of human kind. All of Anderson's writing is remarkable for its sensitivity to movement as a characteristic mark of American life. In *Poor White* it is the rapid change of America from a rural to an industrial nation; swarms of men, like the sky full of moving, agitated clouds, are seen moving from the prairies into the cities. The young, optimistic spirit of the country, we are told, made it "take hold of the hand of the giant, industrialism, and lead him laughing into the land."[5] But in *Many Marriages* those people working in factories, living side by side without communicating to each other, are represented collectively as a city of the living dead. When John Webster decides to leave his business and his timid, repressed wife, he feels he has come back from the dead. By contrast other people in the novel are imaged as moving steadily toward the throne of Death, who is also described as the god of denial. Death is personified as a general with an army made up not of the physical dead but of the living dead.

> Death had many strange tricks to play on people too. Sometimes he let their bodies live for a long time while he satisfied himself with merely clamping the lid down on the well within. It was as though he had said, "Well, there is no great hurry about physical death. That will come as an inevitable thing in its time. There is a much more ironic and subtle game to be played against my opponent Life. I will fill the cities with the damp fetid smell of death while the very dead think they are still alive . . . I am like a great general, having always at his command, ready to spring to arms at the least sign from himself, a vast army of men.[6]

Anderson sees America made up of lonely, frustrated individuals who cannot communicate with each other and who form a procession of the living dead. The same image occurs in *The Triumph of the Egg* in the long story "Out of Nowhere into Nothing." The heroine, Rosalind Wescott, returns from Chicago to her home town to find that her people "in spirit were dead, had accepted death, believed only in death" (p. 266).[7] The whole town, she feels, lies in the shadow of death: her mother, whose face appears death-like, sits like "a dead thing in the chair" (p. 248); and Rosalind feels she must herself run away "if she doesn't want death to overtake her and live within her while her body is still alive" (p. 185).

In *Dark Laughter,* Anderson's most Lawrentian novel, life is imaged as a dance. For the central character, Bruce Dudley, the image functions initially to suggest life's energy and potential rhythms ("Dance life . . . Pretty soon you'll be dead and then maybe there'll be no laughs"[8]), but the image acquires a darker dimension when Dudley thinks of his dead mother as having been "part of the movement of the grotesque dance of life" (p. 90).

As far as I know Anderson never referred to *Winesburg, Ohio* as incorporating the Dance of Death idea. The different images, however, fall together suggestively—life as a procession, life as a dance, life as a living form of death. He did frequently personify death in his writings, including in *A Story-Teller's Story* a traditional image of Death, the Grim Reaper, coming for the author (p. 404),

and in the *Notebooks* an image of himself old and dying and listening to "the sound of the tramping of many feet."[9] Moreover, we do know that he conceived of the frustrated and defeated characters in his early stories as among the living dead. In a letter to M.D. Finley, December 2, 1916 (the period in which he was composing the Winesburg stories), he says:

> Men's fears are stories with which they build the wall of death. They die behind the wall and we do not know they are dead. With terrible labour I arouse myself and climb over my own wall. As far as I can see are the little walls and the men and women fallen on the ground, deformed and ill. Many are dying. The air is heavy with the stench of those who have already died.[10]

The same idea appears in *A New Testament* in "The Story Teller" where Anderson describes his tales as people dying from cold and hunger, while in his memoirs he says that dead people, such as his mother, would return to him in dreams and he concluded they wanted their stories told.[11]

Winesburg, Ohio may not have taken shape directly around the Dance of Death idea, but it was most certainly influenced by a book, Edgar Lee Masters's *Spoon River Anthology,* of which the central theme is death. Masters's poems were published in book form in the spring of 1915 (the year Anderson probably started writing the Winesburg stories), and we know that Anderson read the book shortly after its publication.[12] He professed a distaste for Masters's poems which critics have explained in the light of Masters's relationship with Anderson's second wife, but it may also reflect a literary debt that Anderson was reluctant to acknowledge.[13] However that may be, there is no denying some fundamental similarities between the two books. Both *Winesburg* and *Spoon River* depict in episodic fashion a cross-section of life in a small midwestern town. In both books at the deepest level there is an intransigent sense of despair. The Spoon River poems are vignettes of lives lived at cross-purposes, with recognitions after death that life has been wasted and is now forever irrecoverable. Masters's poems incorporate the medieval idea of the dead appearing to warn the living of their inevitable end. The voices of the dead, each one telling a story from the tomb, was a formal design which must surely have influenced Anderson considerably, for we have seen him speak of his Winesburg characters as each walled in by fears and already dead or dying. Anderson's characters are not presented as spirits returned from the dead, and yet in a very important sense that is what they are, for the characters in *Winesburg, Ohio* are people from the narrator's memory of his home town, and many of them, most significantly the mother, are in fact long dead.[14]

But what is particularly suggestive, given the fact that Anderson had seen Masters's book, is that several of Oliver Herford's illustrations for the first edition of *Spoon River Anthology* depicted the Dance of Death in various forms. Death swinging a lariat appears twice and, placed above the first of the poems, serves as a controlling visual motif throughout the collection. Death is also shown in the manner of Holbein leading away a child in one sketch and beckoning to a drunk in another. But two of the illustrations suggest actual situations in the Winesburg stories. One shows Death in bed as a lover and we are reminded of Elizabeth Willard's erotic personification of death in her last days. The other presents Death approaching an older man who has just taken a young wife, and we think of Doctor Reefy, whose young bride is snatched away from him by Death only a few months after the couple are married. Anderson may not have consciously conceived of his stories being arranged like a medieval Dance of Death, but it is hard to believe that the Masters's book with its death theme and design did not influence his imagination at some fundamental level.

II

In *Winesburg, Ohio* the idea of death does not signify only the grave, but more tragically it denotes the loneliness and frustration of the unlived life. As in *Poor White* we are aware in *Winesburg, Ohio* of movement as characteristic of American life, but here it is the restlessness of the individual who grows increasingly oppressed by his loneliness and his inability to express himself to others. In each story when the character reaches an ultimate point of insupportable frustration or recognizes that he can never escape his isolation, he reacts by waving his hands and arms about, talking excitedly, and finally running away. In a very stylized pattern almost every story brings its character to such a moment of frenzy where he breaks into something like a dance.

The introductory sketch, "The Book of the Grotesque," is either ignored by critics or dismissed as a murky and confusing allegory. That Anderson intended it to carry significant weight in relation to the rest of the book is clear when we remember that "The Book of the Grotesque" was the publication title Anderson first gave to the whole collection of stories. In its oblique and terse fashion the sketch defines the relationship of the artist to his characters. The subject is an old man who is writing a book about all the people he has known. The first thing we notice is that the writer is preoccupied with fantasies about his failing health. When he goes to bed each night he thinks about his possible death, yet paradoxically that makes him feel more alive than at other times; thoughts of death heighten his awareness to things. In this state the old writer has a waking dream in which all the people he has known are being driven in a long procession before his eyes. They appear to the writer as "grotesques," for each of these characters has lived according to a personal truth which has cut him off from the others. These are the characters of Anderson's book. The procession they form is like a dance of the dead, for as mentioned above most of these people from Anderson's childhood are now dead. The youth in the coat of mail leading the people is the writer's imagination and also his death consciousness—his memory of the past and his awareness that

loneliness and death are the essential "truths" of the human condition. We are told in this sketch that the old carpenter, who comes to adjust the height of the writer's bed and who instead weeps over a brother who dies of starvation in the Civil War, is one of the most lovable of all the grotesques in the writer's book. Just such a character apparently befriended Anderson's lonely mother in Clyde, Ohio;[15] this detail indicates both the personal and the elegiac nature of the book.

The first story, "Hands," tells about Wing Biddlebaum whose unfulfilled life typifies the other life stories recounted in the book. From his little house on the edge of town Wing can watch life pass by: " . . . he could see the public highway along which went a wagon filled with berry pickers returning from the fields. The berry pickers, youths and maidens, laughed and shouted boisterously. A boy clad in a blue shirt leaped from the wagon and attempted to drag after him one of the maidens, who screamed and protested shrilly. The feet of the boy in the road kicked up a cloud of dust that floated across the face of the departing sun" (p. 27). With its archetypal images of the public highway, youths and maidens, the berry harvest, and the cosmic image of the sun, the scene Anderson has created is a tableau depicting the dance of life. By contrast Wing Biddlebaum ventures only as far as the edge of the road, then hurries back again to his little house. He lives in the shadows of the town. Yet, like the berry pickers, his figure is always in motion, walking nervously up and down his half decayed verandah. His hands especially are always moving and are compared to the beating wings of an imprisoned bird. In *Tar* Anderson tells us that likely "the memory of his mother's hands made him think so much about other people's hands" (p. 276), again creating a link between his fictional characters and dead mother. Wing's story of being accused of perverted love for the boys he teaches ends in his flight from a small Ohio town. The newspaper reporter George Willard, persona for the young Anderson, listens sympathetically to Wing as he tries to describe his pastoral dream of living like the classical teacher Socrates; but his hands, caressing George Willard, betray him and he runs away to resume his endless pacing in the shadows of his old house.

Several of the stories follow the basic pattern of "Hands": a misfit in the town is telling George something of his story but cannot express himself completely; he begins to wave his hands about helplessly and breaks into a run. In "Drink" Tom Foster, a gentle, passive boy, is described as living "in the shadow of the wall of life." Like Wing Biddlebaum he watches the parade of life pass him by. But he conceives an affection for the banker's daughter Helen White, and one spring night he goes for a long walk and gets drunk on a bottle of whiskey. He becomes a grotesque figure moving along the road: "his head seemed to be flying about like a pinwheel and then projecting itself off into space and his arms and legs flopped helplessly about" (p. 218). He tries to tell George Willard that he has made love to Helen White, but the reporter won't listen because he too loves the banker's daughter. They take a long walk in the dark. Tom raises his voice to an excited pitch to explain that he wants to suffer because "everyone suffers," but George does not understand him.

In the story "'Queer'" George does not get an opportunity to understand. Elmer Cowley, oppressed by his sense of being different from everyone else, resolves that he will be like other people. He goes on a long walk in the country where he encounters the half-wit named Mook. Walking up and down and waving his arms about, he tells Mook that he won't be queer any longer, and then goes on to tell of his resolution to George Willard, whom he sees as typifying the town and representing public opinion. They go on a walk together but Elmer cannot explain himself to the reporter: "He tried to talk and his arms began to pump up and down. His face worked spasmodically. He seemed about to shout" (p. 198). Having failed to communicate to anyone, he decides to run away from the town, but as he is leaving on the train he calls George Willard down to the station to try once again to explain. Still speechless he breaks into a grotesque dance: "Elmer Cowley danced with fury beside the groaning train. . . . With a snarl of rage he turned and his long arms began to flay the air. Like one struggling for release from hands that held him he struck out, hitting George Willard blow after blow on the breast, the neck, the mouth (pp. 200-201).

George is similarly struck at by the school teacher, Kate Swift. Like so many of the characters in the book Kate takes long walks alone at night; one night she walks for six hours. In the eyes of the town she is a conventional old maid, but inside, her passionate nature yearns for companionship and for significant achievements. She half loves George Willard, her former pupil, and in her desire to see his genius flower, she goes to the office of the newspaper to talk to him. Like George's mother she wants him to be a serious writer and to express something for the people of the town. But confused by her love for the boy, she cannot express herself adequately and winds up beating him on the face with her fists, and then running out into the darkness. That same night the Reverend Curtis Hartman, who for weeks has paced the streets at night imploring God to keep him from his sinful habit of peeping into Kate Swift's bedroom window, bursts into the office of the Winesburg *Eagle* "shaking a bleeding fist into the air" as an emblem of his triumph. He has broken the church study window through which he had "peeped," so that now it will be repaired and he will no longer be able to indulge in his sin. Over and over inarticulate characters in a moment of passion wave their hands in the air and burst into a run.

Two of the stories present a macabre vision of life's "truth." In "The Philosopher" Doctor Parcival tells George Willard about his childhood, but when he reaches the point of telling about his father's death in an insane asylum, he breaks off and paces distractedly about the newspaper office. Doctor Parcival is another of the book's failed artists; he is writing a book and his sole vision is that life is a form of crucifixion, a long torture and dying as it was for Christ on the cross. "Respectability," the story of the cuckold Wash Williams, also involves a vision of living death. In reaction to his wife's faithlessness Williams holds the idea that all women are corrupt and dead.

Wash Williams is perhaps most remarkable for his hideous physical appearance. He is compared to "a huge, grotesque kind of monkey, a creature with ugly, sagging, hairless skin below his eyes and a bright purple underbody" (p. 121). Everything about Wash, including the whites of his eyes, looks unclean, everything except his hands which in striking contrast are well cared for. There is a medieval grotesqueness in the description of several of the characters; as in medieval art, the twisted inner nature of the people is manifested in imperfections and distortions of the physical body. Doctor Reefy in "Paper Pills" has a huge nose and hands; the knuckles of his hands are "like clusters of unpainted wooden balls as large as walnuts fastened together by steel rods" (p. 35). This stylized image of the doctor's physical body anticipates the description of his character as being like the sweetness of the gnarled apples left on the trees in autumn, and the image of the little balls of paper on which he has written a number of truths. Some of the characters are almost like gargoyles on medieval buildings. Doctor Parcival, who believes all men are crucified, has a yellowed mustache, black irregular teeth, and a left eye that twitches, snapping up and down like a window shade. Elmer Cowley's father has a large wen on his scrawny neck; he still wears his wedding coat which is brown with age and covered with grease spots. Elmer too is grotesque in appearance: extraordinarily tall, he has pale blond almost white hair, eyebrows, and beard, teeth that protrude, and eyes that are the colorless blue of marbles. Characteristically many of the physical portraits focus on hands. The hands of Tom Willy, the saloon keeper, are streaked with a flaming red birthmark, as if the hands had been dipped in blood that dried and faded. Tom Foster's grandmother has hands all twisted out of shape from hard work. When she holds a mop or broom handle they look like "the dried stems of an old creeping vine clinging to a tree" (p. 211). There are two half-wits in Winesburg as well: Turk Smollet, the old wood-chopper, who talks and laughs to himself as he passes regularly through the village, and Mook, the farm hand, who holds long involved conversations with the animals. Perhaps it is not accidental that George Willard thinks of the Middle Ages one night when he is walking through the town, and that the first word that comes to his lips when he looks up at the sky is "Death" (p. 184).

In some of the stories George Willard does not appear except of course as implied narrator; the characters nevertheless are pictured as breaking into a run or dance at peak moments of frustration or loneliness. Jesse Bentley in "Godliness," who has a vision of being a Biblical patriarch, runs through the night imploring God to send him a son; years later when he takes his grandson to sacrifice a lamb, hoping God will send him a visible sign of His blessing, the scene ends with the flight of the grandson from Winesburg. In "Adventure" Alice Hindman, who has been waiting for years for the return of her lover, one night runs out naked onto the lawn in the rain. In the story of the two farm hands, entitled "The Untold Lie," the moment of truth brings Ray Pearson to run across the field to save his friend, Hal Winters, from marriage.[16] Repeatedly the most vivid images in the book are those of characters in grotesque or violent motion: Louise Bentley, the estranged daughter of the Biblical patriarch, driving her horse and carriage at breakneck speed through the streets of Winesburg; Jesse Bentley's drunken brothers driving along the road and shouting at the stars; Enoch Robinson described as "an obscure, jerky little figure bobbing up and down the streets when the sun was going down" (p. 173); Hal Winters' father, Windpeter Winters, drunk and driving his team along the railroad tracks directly into the path of an onrushing locomotive. Such images seem to have coalesced to form a grotesque procession in the writer's memory.

The procession becomes a Dance of Death when the writer comes to recognize his own mortality. The death of his mother awakens George Willard to both the brevity and the loneliness of human exisence. Elizabeth Willard, perhaps more than any of the other characters, seeks some kind of release from her perpetual loneliness. As a young woman she had been "stage-struck" and, wearing loud clothes, paraded the streets with traveling men from her father's hotel. Like the other grotesques her desire to escape loneliness is expressed in movement. Once she startled the townspeople by wearing men's clothes and riding a bicycle down the main street. After she married and still found no communion with another human being, she drove her horse and buggy at a terrible speed through the country until she met with an accident. (The image of a woman hurt in an accident or disfigured in some way recurs several times to the eyes of the artist figures in the book: one of Enoch Robinson's paintings depicts a woman who has been thrown from a horse and has been hurt [p. 170], while the old writer in the introduction is crying over "a woman all drawn out of shape" [p. 23].) Eventually when her long illness comes we are told that Elizabeth went along the road seeking for death: "She personified the figure of death and made him now a strong black-haired youth running over hills, now a stern quiet man marked and scarred by the business of living" (p. 228). As a young woman she had taken several lovers before she married; now her lover is Death.

"Sophistication," the penultimate chapter, is shaped around George's growing awareness of life as a procession or dance toward death. In the background is the Winesburg County Fair: people are moving up and down the streets and fiddlers sweat "to keep the feet of youth flying over a dance floor." But in spite of the crowds George Willard feels lonely; he wants someone to understand the feeling that has possessed him since his mother's death. Significantly we are told that "memories awoke in him" and that he is becoming conscious of life's limitations. The narrator, reflecting on youth, generalizes: "There is a time in the life of every boy when he for the first time takes the backward view of life. . . . If he be an imaginative boy a door is torn open and for the first time he looks out upon the world, seeing, as though they marched in procession before him, the countless figures of men who before his time have come out of nothingness into the world, lived their lives and again disappeared into nothingness" (p. 234). At this point George sees his own place "in the long march of humanity. Already he hears death calling" (pp. 234-235). And in the last chapter he joins the procession when he leaves on the train, and Winesburg becomes a "background on which to paint the dreams of his manhood."

III

Twenty years after the Winesburg stories were written, Sherwood Anderson created a drama out of his famous collection of stories. *Winesburg, Ohio: A Play*[17] focuses more squarely on the figure of George Willard and the events, particularly the death of his mother, that precipitate his growth into manhood and nurture his desire to become a writer. The death theme running through the stories also stands out more boldly in the play. Nine scenes comprise the play and the first scene is set, like a Spoon River poem, in the Winesburg cemetery on the day of Windpeter Winters's funeral. The Winesburg people are seen formed in a procession and their conversation inevitably turns to the macabre. The young people, by contrast, create a dance of life; despite the sobriety of the occasion, they tease and jostle one another as the irrespressible life instinct demands expression. One of the sub-plots in the play involves Belle Carpenter, who has become pregnant and who goes to Doctor Reefy in Scene two to ask for an abortion. Reefy counsels against this request and says to Belle "there are always two roads—the road of life and the road of death" (p. 30). This image describes the two main narrative threads in the play: in the foreground is George's involvement with three different women in Winesburg and his sexual awakening, while in the background Elizabeth Willard makes elaborate preparations to die. Her death, as in the stories, precipitates George's departure from Winesburg, but the road of life he sets out on is also the road of death, for Elizabeth Willard, in prayer, has made her promise to come back from the dead if she sees her son becoming "a meaningless, drab figure." The fulfillment of that prayer eventually places George on the road back to Winesburg.

In his later books as well Sherwood Anderson continued to use the Dance of Death motif as a measure of life's brevity and misdirection. When Red Oliver, the principal character in the novel *Beyond Desire,* is about to be killed for his peripheral involvement in a strike, a dancing death figure appears in the form of a limping stationer who exhorts the soldiers to shoot the communist leaders of the strike.

> The little stationer of Birchfield, the man with the
> bad feet had followed the soldiers to the bridge.
> He had come limping along the road. Red Oliver
> saw him. He was dancing in the road beyond the

soldiers. He was excited, filled with hatred. He danced in the road, throwing his arms above his head. He clenched his fists. "Shoot. Shoot. Shoot. Shoot the son-of-a-bitch." The road sloped down sharply to the bridge. Red Oliver could see the little figure above the heads of the soldiers. It seemed dancing in the air over their heads.[18]

Just before the fatal shot is fired we are told that Red "saw the absurd little stationer dancing in the road beyond the soldier" and that he asked himself whether the little man "represented something" (p. 355). Anderson seems to be asking the reader at this point to give the figure thoughtful consideration. The image is reminiscent of such Winesburg figures as Elmer Cowley and Wing Biddlebaum who claw at the air with their hands and dance about in a hopeless effort to communicate with other people. The stationer in *Beyond Desire* is an emblem of countless repressed twentieth-century men who find an outlet for their frustrations in violent mob action.

Anderson himself used the term "dance of death" when he was writing his *Memoirs*. In that posthumous volume he registered his horror at the spectacle of World War II in an entry entitled "The Dance Is On."[19] He begins, "It's a crazy dance of death now" referring to the war, but he quickly extends the image to include all the mechanical, dehumanizing forces of the modern industrial world. Anderson did not believe that modern industry was in itself negative. In *Beyond Desire* and his last novel, *Kit Brandon*, he describes the cotton mills as dancing with life, and in this entry from the *Memoirs* he points to a cloth mill and says "here is a gay dance, a purposeful dance. See the many colored cloth rolling out of the flying machines in the cloth mills." But he also saw a "monster" latent in the industrial process, an uncontrollable appetite for production and profit without reference to the needs of the human community. The monster's consuming, destructive power is imaged by Anderson in a sequence titled "Loom Dance" in *Perhaps Women* where a group of factory girls working at the loom are stricken with choreomania; they become mindless robots of production unable to stop their movements. The question Anderson puts in his *Memoirs* is "Can the dance be made, not a dance of death, but of joy and new life?" He equates the dance of life with man's ability to reach out and communicate with his fellow man: "Can men come out of their selves to others?" Although Anderson despairs at the world around him, he believes that "men never intended it to be the dance of death," rather "dreamed of making it a great new dance of life." Similarly Anderson in his epitaph insisted that "Life not Death is the great adventure."

But the question still to be asked is what is gained by viewing *Winesburg, Ohio* in the light of the recurrent death imagery in Anderson's writing. Most obviously it directs us to something dark and pessimistic in the book that recent critics, unlike the early reviewers, have either ignored or explained away.[20] In a period of rapid economic growth and expansion, Anderson was drawing attention to the tragedy of those people, like his own par-

ents, who did not succeed, and who were alienated from each other by economic failure and by the repressive American Puritan ethic. Seeing the lives of such people as a form of living death underscores the social tragedy that the book presents, and also suggests a continuity between Anderson's early writing and those later books and stories such as *Many Marriages* and "Out of Nowhere into Nothing" where he envisions America as a land of the dead. As a Dance of Death *Winesburg, Ohio* functions as social satire to warn the living of what is happening to their lives.

The Dance of Death idea is most closely associated with the mother figure and directs us to a personal tragedy implicit in the book—the narrator's sense of filial guilt. While she lived, Elizabeth Willard and her son seldom spoke to each other; before her death Elizabeth prayed that her son would some day "express something" for them both. But the artist's central insight in the book is that all truth is relative to the individual, so that he cannot really express anything for his characters—he can only hint at their secret, repressed lives. Ironically, in attempting to give dignity to the lives of his people, the narrator has made them grotesques, and like the old writer in the introduction must be left to whimper like a small dog at the "woman drawn all out of shape" (p. 23). At best the narrator, like the author of the *Spoon River Anthology*, has erected out of love a series of tombstones for the people he once knew. The Dance of Death perspective functions then as a framework around the book reminding us that these characters are now gone, and that they were never released from the agony of their loneliness while they lived. This tragic personal emotion is described by the narrator in "Sophistication" when he says: "One shudders at the thought of the meaninglessness of life while at the same instance, and if the people of his town are his people, one loves life so intensely that tears come into the eyes" (p. 241).

The narrator's sympathy and love for his people makes more poignant the failure of art to expiate his filial guilt. Anderson had dedicated the book as an expression of love to his mother; we cannot help feeling that it has come too late. But this of course does not mean that *Winesburg, Ohio* fails as a work of art. On the contrary, seeing the book as a Dance of Death further testifies to its richness of pattern and form. The medieval Dance of Death was a highly ritualized art and it is that quality of stylized repetition which is most striking formally in Anderson's book. To see *Winesburg, Ohio* as a Dance of Death is not only to underscore rightly its essentially tragic nature, but also to recognize its considerable artistry.

NOTES

[1] This and subsequent page references to *Winesburg, Ohio* are to the "Compass Book" edition (New York, 1960).

[2] For a comprehensive treatment of the historical origins of the Dance of Death see James M. Clark, *The Dance of*

Death in the Middle Ages and the Renaissance (Glasgow, 1950).

[3] *A Story-Teller's Story* (New York, 1924), p. 127.

[4] *Tar: A Midwest Childhood* (New York, 1930) p. 346. All references are to the same text.

[5] *Poor White in The Portable Sherwood Anderson,* ed. Horace Gregory (New York, 1949), p. 162.

[6] *Many Marriages* (New York, 1923), p. 217.

[7] *The Triumph of the Egg* (New York, 1921). All references are to this text.

[8] *Dark Laughter* (New York, 1925), p. 68. All references are to this text.

[9] *Sherwood Anderson's Notebooks* (New York, 1926), p. 22.

[10] See William A. Sutton, *The Road to Winesburg* (Metuchen, N.J., 1972), pp. 446-447.

[11] See *Sherwood Anderson's Memoirs: A Critical Edition,* edited by Ray Lewis White (Chapel Hill, 1969), pp. 524-526.

[12] See William L. Phillip's article "How Sherwood Anderson Wrote *Winesburg, Ohio*" in *The Achievement of Sherwood Anderson: Essays in Criticism,* ed. Ray Lewis White (Chapel Hill, 1966), pp. 71-72.

[13] See Sutton, pp. 299-300. Anderson's second wife, Tennessee Mitchell, had been the poet's mistress and this may have prompted Anderson's dislike of the book. But Anderson seems to have encouraged the myth that his stories were appearing in print before Masters's poems. This is demonstrably untrue and suggests Anderson was concerned about the question of originality.

[14] Typically Anderson gave two different accounts about the source of his Winesburg characters. At one point in his memoirs he says that the tales came "out of some memory or impression got from boyhood in a small town," but only a couple of pages further he claims that the characters were portraits done of his fellow boarders in a cheap Chicago rooming house on Cass Street. See *Sherwood Anderson's Memoirs: A Critical Edition,* pp. 346-348. Probably both accounts are true, but certainly figures like the mother, Doctor Reefy and the old carpenter are from Clyde, Ohio. See also William L. Phillips, "How Sherwood Anderson Wrote *Winesburg, Ohio,*" pp. 69-74.

[15] See *Tar: A Midwest Childhood,* pp. 71, 85.

[16] Anderson told his son in a letter that "The Untold Lie" was inspired by the memory of sitting on a train once and seeing a man run across a field. *Letters of Sherwood Anderson,* selected and edited with an introduction and notes by Howard Mumford Jones and Walter B. Rideout (Boston, 1953), p. 357.

[17] *Plays: Winesburg and Others* (New York, 1937). All references are to this text.

[18] *Beyond Desire* (New York, 1961), p. 354. All references are to this text.

[19] "The Dance Is On," *Sherwood Anderson's Memoirs: A Critical Edition,* pp. 552-553.

[20] For example, in his introduction to the 1960 "Compass Book" edition Malcolm Cowley concludes that "*Winesburg, Ohio* is far from the pessimistic or destructive or morbidly sexual work it was once attacked for being. Instead it is a work of love, an attempt to break down the walls that divide one person from another, and also in its own fashion, a celebration of small-town life in the lost days of good will and innocence." And in his article "*Winesburg, Ohio:* Art and Isolation," *Modern Fiction Studies,* VI (Summer, 1960), 106-114, Edwin Fussell sees the loneliness and frustration of the characters being dissolved by the future art of George Willard, who will give these people a voice.

POETRY

Harold Bloom

SOURCE: "Death and the Native Strain in American Poetry," in *Social Research,* Vol. 39, No. 3, Autumn, 1972, pp. 449-62.

[*In the following essay, Bloom selects a representative poem from both Wallace Stevens and W. B. Yeats in order to contrast American and British poetic conceptions of death, and observes that the former is generally more solipsistic than the latter.*]

> Shall we be found hanging in the trees next
>   spring?
> Of what disaster is this the imminence:
> Bare limbs, bare trees and a wind as sharp as salt?
>
> The stars are putting on their glittering belts,
> They throw around their shoulders cloaks that
>   flash
> Like a great shadow's last embellishment.
>
> It may come tomorrow in the simplest word,
> Almost as part of innocence, almost,
> Almost as the tenderest and the truest part.

This is Wallace Stevens in expectation of an imminent death. The context is the American Sublime; the poem is his masterpiece, *The Auroras of Autumn.* When the poem attains its resolution, the auroras cease to be a spell of light or false sign of heavenly malice, and are seen as an innocence of the earth. Death, which may come tomorrow, is not called part of that innocence, but *almost* part of it—even almost what it is in Whitman, the tenderest and truest part of innocence. Whitman and Stevens, both central to American poetic tradition, are wholly at the American imaginative center in their visions of death. Mortality, when confronted by the native strain in our poetry, is neither religiously denied nor transformed into something strangely rich. Death is part of the family, and its enigma is assimilated to the mystery of origins, where it is granted the true priority.

I want to contrast the visions of death in British and American poetry, and though I will take my instances of both free-style, I will keep coming back to a central poet of each tradition and a central text of death in each poet. Yeats and Stevens are inevitable contraries, being the largest heirs, respectively, of British and American Romanticism. I want two mysterious, hieratic poems, pre-elegies for the poet's own death, and out of a number of possibilities I choose Yeats' *Cuchulain Comforted* and Stevens' *The Owl in the Sarcophagus.* Yet to apprehend these poems we need to know other poems by Yeats and Stevens, and the inescapable poems of their precursors: Blake, Shelley, Keats and Browning for Yeats; these same poets, but also the American line of Emerson, Whitman, and Dickinson for Stevens. This discussion, then, attempts to illuminate Yeats by his ancestors and by his contrary, Stevens, and also to see through Stevens and his American ancestry a peculiarly national vision of death. Yeats, though esoteric, moves towards a broader European account (and acceptance) of death, but the American poetic story of death is less universal, and probably more of an evasion of death our death, an evasion that is the ultimate triumph of imaginative solipsism.

Blake and Emerson, two very different Romantic founding fathers, had a common disinterest in death, unlike their major disciples. Blake said he could not think that death was more than a going-out from one room into another, which is a dismissal we might expect from a consciousness strong enough to believe that "The ruins of Time build mansions in Eternity." Emerson, in his best essay, *Experience,* has resort to death as a final antidote to the illusoriness of all phenomena: "Nothing is left us now but death. We look to that with a grim satisfaction, saying, There at least is reality that will not dodge us." Yet this is Emerson in a fine exasperation with his (and our) own skepticism. More often, he is subtly dialectical in his devaluation of death. Aged thirty-nine, he writes in his journal, "The only poetic fact in the life of thousands and thousands is their death. No wonder they specify all the circumstances of the death of another person." At forty, he protests, "Now, if a man dies, it is like a grave dug in the snow, it is a ghastly fact abhorrent to Nature, and we never mention it. Death is as natural as life, and should be sweet and graceful." At the age of fifty-one, he

sums up the strength of his wisdom, but with the resignation of the seer who doubts the communicability of his vision:

> A man of thought is willing to die, willing to live; I suppose because he has seen the thread on which the beads are strung, and perceived that it reaches up and down, existing quite independently of the present illusions. A man of affairs is afraid to die, is pestered with terrors, because he has not this vision. Yet the first cannot explain it to the second.

Emerson and Blake, who disagree on most things, including the relative goodness of the natural man, are nearly at one in their realization that death is not *materia poetica.* Wordsworth, the other prime founder of Romanticism in the poetry of our language, is much closer to all later Romantics in his poetic anxieties about death. Yeats, though consciously repelled by Wordsworth, followed after Wordsworth's imaginative patterns quite as much as Stevens did, and Stevens is an overt Wordsworthian. In this, Yeats and Stevens repeat the contrast between Shelley and Keats, both of whom developed Wordsworth's central arguments—but Shelley by opposing their naturalism and Keats by making such naturalism even more heroic.

Wordsworth fought the *consciousness* of death because he had begun by identifying the poetic spirit with the intimation of immortality. His means for fighting a self-consciousness so destructive was to beget again the glory of his youth by the pursuit and recapture of after-images, defined by Geoffrey Hartman as re-cognitions leading to recognitions. By entering again into the gleam of immortality, through recollected images, Wordsworth almost persuaded himself that he could renovate his consciousness so as to attain again the child's freedom from any sense of mortality.

Shelley, a skeptic yet a visionary, apprehended the Wordsworthian gleam as a constant inconstant, a flickering sense of what he called the Intellectual Beauty. Primarily an erotic poet, Shelley centered his concern on the shadow of ruin that haunted every manifestation of the Intellectual Beauty, particularly in heterosexual love, in all its glory and in its cyclic decay. Death, for Shelley, is essentially the absence or ruin of Eros. For Keats, with his faith in the senses, death is part of the body, and part therefore of Eros. Even as Keats is incapable of unperplexing joy from pain, so he discovers we cannot unperplex bodily love from death. It is—Keats sings—in the very temple of delight that veiled Melancholy has her solitary shrine. After the quester, Keats adds, proves capable of viewing this, he is capable only of a distinguished death: "to be among her cloudy trophies hung." As Hart Crane says of his idioms in one of his elegies, so we might say of Keats's questers: "They are no trophies of the sun." Like Stevens after him, Keats yields graciously to what Freud would call the Reality Principle. Yeats outrageously and splendidly would not so yield, and in this he had both English Romantic and Victorian precursors (Browning most powerfully), even as Stevens was schooled in yielding by the two best American Poets, Whitman and Dickinson.

Browning's triumph over the Reality Principle does not come through his vehement temperament, much impressed as we may be when he growls at us that he would no more fear death than he would any other battle. We are more moved when Childe Roland dauntless touches the slug-horn to his lips even as a horrible and nameless death closes upon him. But a kind of vehemence is involved in Childe Roland too, and I will return to Browning's magnificent invention when *Cuchulain Comforted* becomes the main text, for *Cuchulain Comforted* is Yeats' version of *Childe Roland to the Dark Tower Came.* Though Santayana attacked Browning and Whitman together as "poets of Barbarism," there is nothing in common between the two, including their clashing visions of death. This rapid induction to a contrast between British and American poetries of death can move to Yeats and Stevens by way of Whitman's contrast to Browning, with a side glance at Dickinson's severe originalities in this, her great subject.

Whitman, in the concluding sections of *Song of Myself,* meets death our death as being indistinguishable from an Orphic Eros, a release that is fulfillment:

> And as to you Death, and you bitter hug of
>   mortality,
>   it is idle to try to alarm me.
>
> To his work without flinching the accoucheur
>   comes,
> I see the elder-hand pressing receiving supporting,
> I recline by the sills of the exquisite flexible
>   doors,
> And mark the outlet, and mark the relief and
>   escape.

Here, as at the end of *The Sleepers,* neither we nor Whitman know precisely whether we are talking about a womb or a tomb, birth or death. Yet Whitman, unlike Browning or Yeats, is not concerned about personal immortality in the sense of an individual survival. "I shall clasp thee again," Browning insists, and in his last *Epilogue* reminds us he always "Held we fall to rise, are baffled to fight better,/Sleep to wake." Browning's is a highly individual, truly a private Protestantism, yet it is still Protestant, but Whitman's religion is American Orphism, which is a very different faith. Dickinson, who had in common with Whitman only Emerson as prime precursor, shares in this Orphism but with a very different emphasis, and an accent entirely her own creation.

Emerson was Orphic about everything except death, which may suggest he was more an Orphic speculator than an Orphic believer. He had fostered a faith that Whitman, Thoreau, and Dickinson all possessed, yet he entertained it more speculatively than they did. American Orphism, which seems to me still the religion of the ongoing native strain in our poetry, emphasizes not the potential divinity of man but the actual divinity already present in the creative spirit. Divination, in every sense of that term, is the enterprise of the native strain in American poetry. What Wordsworth hesitantly affirmed becomes literal doctrine in American Romanticism. The American Orphic not only worships the gods Bacchus, Eros, and Ananke or Necessity, as the ancient followers of Orpheus did, but he seeks to become those gods. Zeus, Apollo, Jehovah and Christ count for less in American poetry than Bacchus, Eros and Ananke do, for the American Orpheus begins in the Evening-land, and so starts out in the belief that he is already a quasi-god, who perhaps can evade true death through divination, by joining gods like Dionysus, Eros, and Ananke, all of whom include death, and so surmount it.

Dickinson is too strong and too subtle to divinate without every kind of shading reservation. What matters in her is consciousness, and this is rarely so much consciousness of death as it is the consciousness of consciousness, even when it is death that is being apprehended:

> This Consciousness that is aware
> Of Neighbors and the Sun
> Will be the one aware of Death
> And that itself alone
>
> Is traversing the interval
> Experience between
> And most profound experiment
> Appointed unto Men—
>
> How adequate unto itself
> Its properties shall be
> Itself unto itself and none
> Shall make discovery.
>
> Adventure most unto itself
> The Soul condemned to be—
> Attended by a single Hound
> Its own identity.

A consciousness that she tells us is not solipsistic, since it is aware of other selves and of the external world, will some day be aware of dying, and will be altogether solitary, autonomous, and unable to communicate its final knowing to others. This final adventure will be a quest indistinguishable from the quester, and yet the quester will know herself as a shaman might, surviving so long as her totemic hound survives. This division between soul or character, and self or personality or identity is a distinction made in different ways in Browning, Whitman and Yeats, yet never as starkly as Dickinson conveys it. What matters in her is a heroism that says only consciousness matters. Death interests her as a challenge to consciousness, but not as a challenge to any other capacity for heroism.

Heroism meant nearly everything to Yeats; he overvalued violence because he was so desperate in his search for the heroic character. His central hero is the legendary Cuchulain, who inspired his finest verse-dramas, *At the Hawk's Well* and *The Only Jealousy of Emer.* Yeats's last play, left unrevised, is *The Death of Cuchulain;* his last poem-but-one is the majestic *Cuchulain Comforted,* as good a poem as ever he wrote. Yeats dated it 13 January 1939; on January 28 he died. Dorothy Wellesley, who heard Yeats read aloud a prose version of the poem, gives this as part of her memory of it: One of the shades speaks to Cuchulain, the just-slain hero:

> . . . you will like to know who we are. We are the people who run away from the battles. Some of us have been put to death as cowards, but others have hidden, and some even died without people knowing they were cowards . . .

In the poem, *Cuchulain Comforted,* the Shrouds tell Cuchulain their character: "Convicted cowards all, by kindred slain/Or driven from home and left to die in fear." They omit those who die, their cowardice still unknown by others. Cuchulain, "violent and famous," is the antithesis of a coward, and so is Browning's obsessive quester, Childe Roland, who nevertheless enters the after-life ringed by cowards and traitors, failed fellow-questers, just as Cuchulain does. Is Yeats, like Browning, struggling with an obscure sense of self-betrayal, of a moral cowardice he believes himself not to have expiated?

As Helen Vendler has noted, the beautiful close of *Cuchulain Comforted,* "They had changed their throats and had the throats of birds," echoes Dante's great vision of Brunetto Latini, who is in Hell, yet seems one of the victorious and not among the defeated. This is the accent of celebration and not of bitterness, and we can say therefore that Yeats, though equivocal, is not turning against the theme of heroism in this death-poem. The cowards are transfigured, even as Roland's failed companions are transfigured when they stand ranged about him as a living flame, as he sounds his last trumpet of a prophecy. The hero has joined the failures, blent into one final state where the antithesis between heroism and cowardice, success and failure, has broken down far more thoroughly, somehow, than the unbreakable antithesis between life and death.

Yeats compels us, in *Cuchulain Comforted* as in a surprising number of other poems, to a close knowledge of his system in *A Vision.* The weight of Yeats-criticism is against me here, but the critics are wrong. *Cuchulain Comforted* does not make full sense unless we understand the precise difference between the supernatural states inhabited in the poem respectively by the Shrouds and by Cuchulain. In terms of Yeats's system, the Shrouds are moving through the last moments of the state called the Shiftings, until in the poem's last line they pass into the state Yeats calls the Beatitude. Cuchulain, less advanced than the Shrouds, moves in the poem from the Phantasmagoria or third phase of the state of Meditation into the Shiftings. To translate this, we need to turn to *A Vision.*

After you die, Yeats tells us there, you find yourself in a state he calls The Vision of the Blood Kindred, a kind of farewell to the sensuous world, to things as they were, to images and impulses. The following state is the Meditation, which is in three phases, called in sequence the Dreaming Back, the Return, and the Phantasmagoria. In the whole of the Meditation your labor is to see your past life as a coherent whole, an achieved form, like a work of art. Yet the Meditation is not a creative state; it is confused, imperfect, unhappy, and begins with the painful Dreaming Back, in which all the events of your past life recur. In the Return phase, which is a kind of antithesis of artistic creation, you deconstruct all the events of your life until they are turned into pure knowledge, divested of all accident, all passion. You are ready then for the Phantasmagoria, which is where we meet Cuchulain in the poem, leaning upon a tree, suffering again the wounds and blood of his destruction, and so at work exhausting, as Yeats says, "not nature, not pain and pleasure, but emotion." When emotion is exhausted, in this nightmare parody of poetic vision, Cuchulain will be ready to join the Shrouds in the Shiftings, where moral good and moral evil, and particularly courage and cowardice, are cast off by the Spirit. In this shifting of your whole morality as a man, you are emptied out, and are made ready for the Shrouds' tranfiguration into complete equilibrium or wholeness, at once a condition of unconsciousness and an epiphany or privileged moment of consciousness: "They had changed their throats and had the throats of birds."

Though *Cuchulain Comforted* takes you only so far (for dramatic reasons), Yeats's system in *A Vision* takes you all the way back to rebirth again. The Shrouds, and Cuchulain when he is ready, will pass next to the Purification, which means mostly that you become very simple, free of all complexity, in an occult state. You may linger in the Purification for centuries, while your thin Spirit seeks out a living person to somehow help you into the Foreknowledge, a kind of launching pad towards Rebirth.

If we return to *Cuchulain Comforted* with these arbitrary but peculiarly fascinating Yeatsian distinctions firmly in mind, we can begin to understand the poem's design upon us. The cowards, until the last line of the poem, remain cowards, "Mainly because of what we only know/The rattle of those arms makes us afraid." What is it that they know? In the terms of Yeats's system, they know what Cuchulain has not yet realized, that all of us must live again, and since they are not yet in the Beatitude, they retain enough of their nature to fear the hero's weapons. But in deeper terms, belonging to European literary tradition at least since Homer, they know something that humanly impresses us more. They are comforted by their momentary communal experience ("And all we do/All must together do") but they know what Yeats the poet so greatly knows, which is what Homer knew, that in dying as in living any sense of community is rapidly evanescent. Cuchulain may be degraded (if indeed that is Yeats's entire intention, which I doubt), yet he remains the hero. In encountering Cuchulain, who can bear the solitude of dying as he can bear the solitude of being reborn, they encounter their own foreboding that in rebirth they must experience again the condition of being alone, which as cowards they cannot tolerate.

What then is Yeats most crucially saying about death, or rather about dying, in this fascinating but veiled

Dantesque poem, with its muted *terza rima?* Very much, I think, what his master Shelley said about death in *Adonais* and *The Triumph of Life* and what his fellow-student of Shelley, Browning, was saying in *Childe Roland to the Dark Tower Came.* The consciousness of death's necessity calls into question the purposiveness of all human action that is not somehow communal, and yet the dignity of dying, for a poet, demands a questing mode of action that is either wholly solitary or that admits the possibility of the community only of a band of brothers, the precursors of poet and hero, or as we now should say, the poet-as-hero. Yeats, as perhaps the last of the High Romantics of European tradition, confirms his tradition's view of death even as he seems to qualify or even degrade it. Death matters because it can be *materia poetica,* but only when it becomes an opportunity for the poet to pass a Last Judgment upon himself. Was he enough of a hero? Did he surmount his precursors, or if he joined them in failure, was he at least worthy of such a joining? Death is, therefore, even for a poet or hero, a social phenomenon essentially, and the standards it must meet (or evade) involve some sort of vision of the communal, however specialized that vision may be.

How un-American this is, and how far even from Emerson, let alone Whitman and Dickinson and their descendants all through American poetry, including Hart Crane and Wallace Stevens. Because our poets are such gorgeous solipsists, from Emerson on, their vision of dying has no relation to this European dialectic of the communal and the solitary. Browning, a passionate egomaniac, is all but selfless compared to Whitman and Dickinson, whose spirits make contact only with divisions in their own selves. Yeats, compared with Wallace Stevens, is drowned in the dramas of other selves; there are *people* in his poems, but Stevens magnificently knows only himself, attaining his greatest peace when he can intone most persuasively:

> And if there is an hour there is a day,
>
> There is a month, a year, there is a time
> In which majesty is a mirror of the self:
> I have not but I am and as I am, I am.

What can so great an "I am" meditate when it comes into the region where we all must die? Browning is not a better poet than Dickinson, or Yeats than Stevens; the problem here is not one of aesthetic loss and gain, but of an imaginative difference that I am rather dismayed to find may be at its root a social difference. Our native strain goes down deeper still, and must be related to the differences between British and American Puritanism, since both poetries for the last two hundred years are, in a clear sense, displaced Protestantisms. But rather than lose myself in a labyrinth I am not competent to explore, I want to return us to a text, with a brief overview of Stevens' *The Owl in the Sarcophagus,* after which I will conclude with a contrast between Yeats and Stevens as representative British and American poets of death.

The Owl in the Sarcophagus is an elegy for Stevens' friend, Henry Church, to whom *Notes toward a Supreme Fiction* had been dedicated. Written in 1947, when Stevens was sixty-eight, it is also a kind of pre-elegy for Stevens' own death, some eight years later. In Stevens' work, it stands chronologically and thematically between *Credences of Summer,* essentially a celebratory, naturalistic, Keatsian poem, and *The Auroras of Autumn,* a Wordsworthian poem of natural loss, and of the compensatory imagination rising up, not to redress loss, but to intimate what Stevens beautifully calls "an innocence of the earth." *The Owl in the Sarcophagus* yields up the world celebrated, however qualifiedly, in *Credences of Summer* and reaches towards the divination of *The Auroras of Autumn,* where the only consolation offered is the wisdom of acceptance, of completion, a wisdom testifying to the mind's power over our consciousness of death. *The Owl in the Sarcophagus* does not go so far; it does not leave us with Stevens' "The vital, the never-failing genius,/Fulfilling his meditations, great and small." But it does give us a lasting sense of "the beings of the mind/In the light-bound space of the mind, the floreate flare . . ." or more starkly of what Stevens also calls "the mythology of modern death."

The Owl in the Sarcophagus is a vision of two forms that move among the dead, "high sleep" and "high peace," two brothers, and a third form, "the mother of us all,/The earthly mother and the mother of/The dead." This is an American Orphic Trinity, ultimately derived from Emerson, though Stevens was evidently not wholly aware of his full relation to this particular precursor. Stevens' "high sleep" is a version of Dionysus, however strange or even oxymoronic the image of a Dionysiac sleep must seem. But then, Stevens' "high peace" is a transformed Eros, and an erotic peace is rather far from the experience of most of us. The Orphic Great Mother, probably derived by Stevens from Whitman's *The Sleepers,* is a transfigured Ananke, Necessity divested of her dread and made into a figure of ultimate consolation (as she is also in certain passages of Emerson's *The Conduct of Life*). In Stevens' elegy, the consolation is attained by a magical metamorphosis of the mind's consciousness of death into the opposite of such consciousness, a child asleep in its own life:

> These are death's own supremest images,
> The pure perfections of parental space,
>
> The children of a desire that is the will,
> Even of death, the beings of the mind
> In the light-bound space of the mind, the floreate flare
> It is a child that sings itself to sleep,
> The mind, among the creatures that it makes,
> The people, those by which it lives and dies.

When we contrast Stevens and Yeats on death, we might begin by remembering Stevens' insistence that poetry must satisfy the human desire for resemblances. Against *A Vision*'s multi-phased life-after-death or rather death-between-lives, we can set a sardonic prose statement by Stevens:

> What a ghastly situation it would be if the world
> of the dead was actually different from the world

of the living and, if as life ends, instead of passing to a former Victorian sphere, we passed into a land in which none of our problems had been solved, after all, and nothing resembled anything else in shape, in color, in sound, in look or otherwise.

The world of the dead in *The Owl in the Sarcophagus* is only what, "Generations of the imagination piled/In the manner of its stitchings," and Stevens speaks of his mother of the dead as "losing in self/The sense of self," very much in Dickinson's manner. His elegy is profoundly American in making dying an ultimate solipsistic adventure, at once Bacchic, erotic and necessitarian, and as much an act of solitary fulfillment as the writing of a poem is. Dying has priority in divination, even as becoming a poet establishes priority in divination. Major American poets see dying as only another assertion in the self's expansiveness, another huge effort to subsume the universe. Dying, whatever else it is for our native strain, for the genius of America, is not a social act. Even Yeats knows what European poets always knew, that dying makes a gesture towards community, but the American imagination has another goal always.

The greatness of *Cuchulain Comforted* is that, like *The Man and the Echo* and certain other late poems of Yeats, it shows its poet both powerfully employing and yet standing clear of his own mythologies. This is his advantage over Stevens, and the general advantage of the less solipsistic British over our own poets. Still, the whole movement of modern poetry is towards a progressive internalization of every sort of quest, and Yeats is most Romantic and most like American poets when he defies everything that is external and societal. Against *Cuchulain Comforted,* with all its magnificence of Yeats-against-Yeats, its seeming degradation of heroism, we can set Yeats himself, in a late prose manifesto, celebrating the unique power of the poets: "The world knows nothing because it has made nothing, we know everything because we have made everything."

Mikhail Ann Long

SOURCE: "As If Day Had Rearranged Into Night: Suicidal Tendencies in the Poetry of Anne Sexton," in *Literature and Psychology,* Vol. XXXIX, No. 1&2, 1993, pp. 26-41.

[*In the following essay, Long explores the suicidal urge in Anne Sexton's poetry.*]

> as if day had rearranged
> into night and bats flew in the sun.

Was Anne Sexton's poetry primarily about the nature of the closed world of suicide? Most critics agree on the fact that Sexton definitely wrote about wanting to die, and the nature of suicide, from a very personal point of view. Many critics believe that at least some of Sexton's poetry reflects this suicidal "lust." According to Diane

Hume George, there are "at least twenty poems primarily dedicated to explaining what it feels like to want, or need, to die" (*Oedipus Anne* 126). Kathleen Spivack, in her article "Poet and Friend" notes that "Anne was obsessed with death—one has only to read *Live or Die* to see to what extent" (35). Spivack goes on to tell us that:

> Ultimately, death took precedence in her imagination. Anne had . . . almost a what-the-hell attitude toward death: Her wish to destroy herself was a deep compulsion. (30)

So Sexton's deep-seated desire to die is apparent to most, if not all of her critics, and readers. But is it omnipresent, woven into the fabric of all, or nearly all, of her poetry, or is it only in a few pieces?

Sexton resumed writing poetry (she had written as a child and young woman), according to Maxine Kumin's introductory essay in Sexton's *Collected Works,* after her first breakdown and suicide attempt. Her psychiatrist Dr. Martin Orne encouraged her writing as a kind of therapy, an emotional outlet, to enable her to return to, or develop, a stable inner life. Therefore all of her published poetry was written after she had entered Allen Alvarez's "closed world of the suicide." This explains the unremitting background of despair and pain that is clearly visible in even the most pleasant of her poems. But the obvious connection between Sexton's urgency towards death and suicide and her poetic expression is blurred in most critics' minds. They fail to analyze Sexton's work based on the fact that since she was suicidal during her entire writing career, her poetry could well be judged by assuming this suicidal nature as foundational to any real understanding.

Was Sexton consciously aware of her desire to die? According to Ari Kiev in his 1971 article about "Suicide Prevention,"

> The suicidal act in most of our patients was characterized by impulsivity and the absence of premeditation. . . . patients were often so emotionally disturbed at the time of the attempt that they not only did not consider but could not use the telephone to call for help. . . . Another factor which cuts across age, sex and diagnostic groups, was non-recognition of an underlying psychiatric illness or emotional disturbance which the patient was experiencing prior to the attempt. (40)

Although this impulsive behavior may have characterized several of Sexton's suicide attempts, the overall thrust of her writing indicates premeditated action on her part. Her poems clearly reflect her understanding of, and attempt to come to terms with, her mental illness and suicidal behavior. She tried to work these conflicts out on paper as well as with numerous therapists and psychiatrists. Another suicidologist, Joseph Richman, discusses the fact that

> Suicide itself is a communication. It is a cry for help, an appeal to others, a method of retaliation or revenge, an expression of atonement and a confession . . . What has been largely overlooked

. . . is the reciprocal, two-way nature of communication. . . . There also seems to be an imperviousness or non-reception to verbal messages from the suicidal person by the relatives. (49)

This "reciprocal nature" of suicide as communication comes into play not only with the family and friends of Sexton but with her readers since she expressed her despair and her darker nature in her poetry. This communication was used by Sexton to attempt to reach other souls that were as tormented as she herself was.

Sexton, writing as a "confessional poet," undoubtedly used her own persona in much of her poetry. Kumin refers to "Sexton's deeply rooted conviction that poems not only could, but had to be, made out of the detritus of her life" (xxx). Therefore her poetry can be assumed to be a reflection of her underlying view of life and her deepest feelings about suicide. I will provide an alternative reading for several of Sexton's apparently non-suicidal poems, by isolating Sexton's suicidal tendencies as a major thematic element that runs through not only the "suicide/death" poems, but many of the others, and by analyzing her poetry using data from a study of *Suicidal Women: Their Thinking and Feeling Patterns* done by Charles Neuringer and Dan J. Lettieri in 1982.

In their study Neuringer and Lettieri postulated that "the key to suicide does not lie in the area of personality and motivational forces but is the product of the cognitive and intellectual organization of the suicidal individual. . . . there is a particular style of thinking. . . . that leads some people to organize their experience in such a way that suicide is the only possible choice for them" (vi). Originally Neuringer had also hoped to compare this potential using gender but was unable to as no comparable study had yet been conducted using male potential suicides.

The Neuringer study consisted of forty women, thirty of whom had evidenced definite suicidal tendencies, and a control group of ten who were in crisis but not suicidal. All thirty of the suicidal women had contacted a suicide "hotline" in Los Angeles, and had been analyzed concerning their suitability for this particular study. The potential suicides were divided into groups of ten and ranked from low to high suicide potential. The subjects were then followed for three weeks, on a daily basis, using a combination of questionnaires and personal interviews to monitor their mental and emotional status. The findings isolated data on four "ingredients" and attempted to find the pattern for identifying potential suicides. I will be dealing with the findings for the highly suicidal woman since Sexton clearly fell in this category throughout her writing career.

The first "ingredient" is the subject's attitude toward life, death, and suicide. According to Neuringer the highly suicidal woman does not find life attractive. Her evaluations of life are in the negative zone. Death seems to be perceived as non-frightening, neutral, or even attractive. A desire to escape from her life seems to predominate (84-85).

The second "ingredient" in the suicidal personality is the particular manner the subject chooses to organize her way of viewing the world. Neuringer maintains that this consists of dichotomous thinking carried to one or more extremes. Stark alternatives and extreme polarities of life and death characterize the highly suicidal woman's thinking patterns. "No-Win" situations and severely limited problem-solving mechanisms seem to be part of the pattern. "The massive dichotomous thinking [of the highly suicidal woman] curtails the use of conceptual and intellectual tools that could provide a wide variety of alternative solutions to their difficulties. . . . For these women life and death are perceived as clear and opposing alternatives; intermediate ways of living are not possible" (86). Howard M. Bogard also describes this dichotomous thinking in his article, the "Collected Thoughts of a Suicidologist" when he describes how differently a situation can appear to a suicidal person. He states that

The loss of jobs, love objects and status must be viewed within the eye and the psychology of the individual involved. The loss of a a job will mean something far more devastating to a man who has rigorously overinvested his work . . . Should a man's career be part of a compensatory struggle to deny feelings of minimal self worth, loss of his position will set off feelings of failure, humiliation, impotence, uselessness, depression and perhaps of suicide. Thus, if I lose my job, I am nothing . . . if I am nothing I am [or should be] dead. (30)

This is a clear illustration of the fact that alternate ways of living do not appear possible to the suicidal person.

The third "ingredient" of the suicidal personality seems to be the suicidal urge that is more or less present at all times. The desire or urgency fluctuates from day to day but only within a narrow range: "The person never feels free enough from suicidal feelings to develop adequate problem-solving behavior. . . . The horror continues and will continue, reinforced by the very presence of negative life attitudes and dichotomous thinking. These lethal ingredients to not permit the adoption of life-saving orientations" (87). Allen Alvarez explains this urge very clearly in his book *The Savage God:*

For them [the suicidal ones], the act is neither rash nor operatic nor, in any obvious way, unbalanced. Instead it is, insidiously, a vocation. . . . there never seems to have been a time when one was not suicidal . . . so the suicide feels he has always been preparing in secret for this last act. (108)

So death is always in the back of their minds, a viable choice if nothing else works out.

The final "ingredient" is the affective state, the level of feelings and emotions. The highly suicidal woman reports greater suffering, and "seems to be living in a world devoid of interest and [apparently] joyless. They cannot be aroused by stimuli; they are angry and dissatisfied by what they are and what they do; they feel inadequate, they dislike themselves and are profoundly depressed" (89). Otto Rank isolated this tendency in his 1945 book *Will Therapy and Truth and Reality* when he states that the suicide

> perceives himself as unreal and reality as unbearable, because with him the mechanisms of illusion are known and destroyed by self-consciousness. He can no longer deceive himself about himself and disillusions [sic] even his own ideal of personality. He perceives himself as bad, guilt laden, inferior, as a small, weak, helpless creature, which is the truth about mankind, as Oedipus also discovered in the crash of his heroic fate. All other is illusion, deception, but necessary deception in order to be able to bear one's self and thereby life. (qtd. in Becker 188)

Neuringer attempts to find a relationship between these ingredients for the seriously suicidal woman and finds that, in addition to this already "lethal brew" there is one final factor not found in the other women in the study. The "seriously suicidal woman is not oriented toward others. . . . [therefore] possible social restraints in the environment have no inhibiting power for her . . . [this] allows her to act in socially non-sanctioned ways and. . . . makes the decision to escape from life easy" (91/92). These findings concur on a scientific level with Allen Alvarez's more colloquial description of the "closed world" of the suicide in his book.

A close examination of Sexton's poems, one about death and suicide, and several others that do not appear to be about death, will reveal Neuringer's five "ingredients."

"Sylvia's Death" (126), written in 1963 is probably the best of Sexton's explorations of wanting to die. Diane Hume George dislikes this poem intensely, making her reasons clear in her discussion of Sexton's so-called "suicide series" in her book *Oedipus Anne*. George sees the poem as "self-serving, self-pity[ing] and self-aggrandizing" and she feels that she is "overhearing a pathetic competition between suicides, one accomplished and one potential, full of petty jealousy and envy masquerading as eulogy" (136). This view of the poem is echoed by Kathleen Spivack when she discusses Sexton's "jealousy that Sylvia had actually managed to kill herself" (35), but if this poem is viewed as an expression of Sexton's actual feelings about Plath's death, and about her own suicide attempts, then perhaps the apparent pettiness and jealousy could be construed as simply symptoms of the suicidal mind set rather than self-pity.

Neuringer's first "ingredient" can be seen in this poem with Sexton's expressed view of life as "a dead box of stones and spoons," and death as "an old belonging," and finally her view of suicide as "the ride home with our boy." These attitudes reflect a necessary view of death, one which makes suicide a plausible alternative to Sexton rather than simply expressing pettiness and envy.

The second "ingredient" is the dichotomous or polarized view of life and death. This must be assumed in this

poem because death is the only subject. Death is not only affirmed as precious, "the death we drank to," but is seen as the only thing of value throughout the poem. Sexton does not remind Plath of the beauties of life, indeed she never refers to any values of life at all. She merely reiterates their previous obsession with death as "the one we talked of so often."

The third "ingredient" is the suicidal urge which appears near the end of the poem: "And I see now that we store him up/year after year, old suicides/and I know at the news of your death,/a terrible taste for it, like salt," Alvarez refers to this endless desire when he quotes an English novelist as saying "For me suicide's a constant temptation. It never slackens . . . it's been a pattern ever since I can remember" (108).

The fourth "ingredient" is the emotional or affective state of mind of Sexton and she is clearly feeling abandoned by Plath, left behind in this terrifying life where "the moon's bad/and the king's gone,/and the queen's at her wit's end/." Death is obviously preferable, and Sexton seems to feel only that Plath has gone ahead, without warning Sexton of her departure for the promised land. Sexton herself had a pact with Maxine Kumin that seems similar. She was to ask Kumin for the "Death Baby" if she ever decided to kill herself again. Possibly Sexton felt that Plath had owed her a similar warning in their suicidal "closed world."

The final factor, according to Neuringer, was the feeling of isolation from the surrounding culture's social mores. This lack of interest in what is important to "other people" seems obvious when Sexton does not remind Sylvia of her obligation to stay alive for her children's sakes. It is also apparent from the fact that Sexton herself, a potential suicide, was completely unaware that Plath was on the verge again. Allen Alvarez (also a member of the "closed society" of which he wrote) refers to his own lack of perception when he admits that he as a fairly good friend of Plath, completely missed the message, and finally he rationalizes this oversight by trying to prove that Plath really didn't mean to kill herself. So Sexton's loss of contact with the world outside could also be assumed by her feeling that she did not have a responsibility to stay closely enough in touch with her friend's pain or terrors to attempt to alleviate or deflect them. So all five ingredients can be found in this "suicide" poem. But can they be found in Sexton's other, less stridently death-oriented, poetry?

Unlike "Sylvia's Death," "The Nude Swim" is a poem that has probably never been classified as a suicide/death poem. It appeared in *Love Poems* in 1969. William H. Shurr sees the poem as part of a record of a love affair, and although he feels that the poem "derives its setting and quite likely [its] personae from Anne's European trips with her husband" (254), still he perceives the poem on a very superficial "travel documentary" level. The poem does appear to be a momentary break in Sexton's on-going depressive state, and yet when analyzed according to Neuringer's criteria, it has all of the "ingredients" for a suicidal interpretation. A brief plot summary isolates some of its key elements. Two people swim into an "unknown grotto," where they can "lose all their loneliness," and the "real fish" ignore them. The water is clear and buoyant, and the speaker poses on its surface mimicking a painting of a seductive woman. Her companion tells the speaker that her eyes are "seacolor/ skycolor" which then seems to destroy her mood.

Sexton's view of life, death and suicide in this poem appears to be that life is only pleasant when one escapes to an exotic place like Capri, and even there reality looms so large that a further escape to an "unknown grotto" is required to allow the speaker to "release [her] loneliness." Entering the "unknown grotto" can be seen as mysterious or even ominous. Water is a symbol of the subconscious, of oblivion, and can be death-dealing as well as life-giving. Therefore the "clear [and] buoyant" water becomes significant as a symbol when the speaker floats on top of it, plays with it, and finally views it as "a couch as deep as a tomb." Sexton's dichotomous thinking is apparent in the juxtaposition of "real" with unreal fish. The real fish are able to survive in the water, and they ignore these unreal fish as they "trail" over the surface. The speaker and her companion seem only to be pretending to be alive and will never be "real."

The suicidal urge can be traced in the speaker's perceptions of the swim as a momentary release from her loneliness, and yet she knows that she is only posing, only pretending to be a vivid and sensuous woman, while she is floating on the unreal and tomb-like water. Her affective state appears dreamy as she describes this fantasy scene. But her companion destroys the mood by telling her that she is "sky" and "sea colored," a positive view of the speaker basically, and this is a reminder of the living world of which she is a part. This compliment forces her to close her eyes, in an attempt to remain hidden, and then to revert to an ashamed and self-hating state. This is a reenactment of her usual feelings of inadequacy, and worthlessness which are typical of a suicidal person.

The isolation of the cave and the swimmers from the "real world" of Capri indicates that the speaker is oriented away from the world. She has lost touch with others and feels suffocated and constrained by the real world. This freedom of the cave, in reality, is freedom for the speaker to toy with oblivion and death.

In another poem from *Love Poems* (1969), "For my Lover, Returning to his Wife," Sexton again exhibits the "particular style of thinking" that Neuringer contends leads to suicide. Paul Lacey describes the entire volume of poems as "affirm[ing] the body in a way not to be found in her earlier poetry. . . . the whole body and its separate parts are celebrated and delighted in" (13). Karl Malkoff describes the *Love Poems* as "further[ing] the reintegration of the self" (285). But within the actual poem itself Sexton's view of life, death, and suicide is again clearly weighted against the speaker's own right to existence. She compares herself to the "Wife" and finds

that the wife is "solid" while the speaker is "a water-color./I wash off." This also provides a concise view of the dichotomy between the real world of "the wife," and the unreal world of "the mistress" and as usual the speaker loses. She "wash[es] off." She is "momentary," and an "experiment." Therefore, she perceives the wife as the ideal that she, the speaker, cannot attain, and realizes that her only alternative is to disappear. This disappearance is part of the on-going urge toward total oblivion. To die is to lose her awareness that she is not "solid" like the wife, and will enable her to forget that she has been "wash[ed] off" and dissolved.

And in the speaker's muffled anger and rage at being abandoned, there are curious echoes of what she feels she is not. Sexton's own affective state shows in her description of the wife. If the wife is "exquisite," "fireworks," "real," "harmony," and his "have to have," in addition to the "bitch in her," then what is the speaker? The opposite descriptive adjectives are ugly, boring, unreal, and inharmonious, and his unnecessary object. That the wife has a "bitch in her" does not mitigate the speaker's sense of being second-best. And the speaker clearly agrees with the lover that she is less valuable than his wife when she "give[s] him permission. . . . [to] answer the call . . . [to] climb her like a monument . . . [because] she is so solid."

Sexton does not consider herself a part of the real world within the context of the poem because she describes herself as "momentary," "a luxury," with her hair "rising like smoke," and her very existence is "out of season." And while she does not discuss suicidal feelings in direct terms, the absence of any rationale that would enable her to live, coupled with her complete invisibility, and lack of worth in her relationship to the lover and his wife, would lead most seriously disturbed people to feel like death was a serious alternative to such despair. Instead of rationalizing her situation, or rejecting and devaluing her lover, she has turned the knife of worthlessness against her own life. Or in the words of Neuringer, the speaker has organized her thinking patterns "in such a way that suicide is the only possible choice" for her (86).

In "The Double Image" the suicidal undertones are even more markedly present. Published in her first book, *To Bedlam and Part Way Back* in 1960, it is ostensibly a long explanation, addressed to her three-year-old daughter, of Sexton's suicide attempts, and therefore her past inability to be a good mother for the child. Written as though Sexton now felt "together" and stable, the poem's speaker is in reality precariously balanced on the verge of oblivion. Greg Johnson describes the poem as "tender [with a] carefully modulated voice . . . firmly aligned on the side of health" (176). And although Johnson describes Sexton as aware of her "continued vulnerability" he focuses on her "desire for an affectionate, healthy relationship with the child." In truth Sexton is already isolated from life and unable to relate to her child at all.

Beginning with the first section, and running throughout the poem, her view of life can be seen as strongly negative: nature "goes queer," and autumn leaves do not believe in themselves or else they fall. Life "was an old debt," that is filled with "blame" and "doom," and can be understood only by "witches" and "ugly angels" who tell Sexton what her life means, and what she must do. Sexton warns her daughter that if she doesn't believe in herself she will fall as the leaves are falling. By the second section of the poem life is filled with lies and hypocrisy where one is locked up in the cupboards of a church. Death, on the other hand, is "simpler than [she'd] thought," and will, with the witches' help, "take away [her] guilty soul."

The suicidal view of life as having only one solution or alternative to death is seen in her repeated failures to find a place to be, not only for her daughter, but for herself. Sexton tries to die, she ends up in a mental hospital, she then tries to go home again to her mother's house, again she tries to die, she tries to go back to her husband in Boston, and so on and so on. She seems to be searching for the perfect place in the world for her weary spirit to rest, and exist, and never seems to succeed. The end of the poem remains inconclusive since, although she has her daughter back with her full time, she does not tell the reader where they finally are, or even give the feeling that they really are settled at all.

Sexton's desire to die, and also her separation from the immediacies of the world, are seen in her use of language and imagery that distances, not only the audience, but the speaker, from the story being unfolded. A formal, unemotional retelling of all of these desperate failures of the spirit on Sexton's part creates a sense of disinterest in, or at best, clinical curiosity about, the details of her life. She is not committed to this life, or even to this child. She calls her daughter an "image," a "small piglet," a "butterfly girl," a "splendid stranger," and "a small milky mouse." All terms of endearment to be sure, but also basically non-human terms, and such terms could also serve to remove the child from the immediate world where her mother would feel responsibility for her. So the child could conceivably end up being part of the world that Neuringer feels the suicidal person can ignore. However adorable, who needs to feel responsible for an image or a mouse?

Sexton's affective state is the most easily isolated. It consists of total despair, a complete and over-riding sense of guilt and failure, and a self-image that is disastrous. Sexton sees herself through her mother's eyes, or at least as she imagines her mother sees her, and what she finds is the "stony head of death," "the double woman who stares/at herself, as if she were petrified/in time," and most dreadfully, she sees herself as "rot[ting] on the wall, [her] own/Dorian Gray." Sexton has no hope for her own future or for the future of the relationship with her child. She begins the poem in futility, "all the medical hypothesis/that explained my brain will never be as true as these/struck leaves letting go," and ends it in guilt and confusion: "I, who was never quite sure/about being a girl, needed another/life, another image to remind me./And this was my worst guilt; you could not cure/nor

soothe it. I made you to find me." The final terrifying fact that the reader notices is that the entire poem, with the exception of the opening line, is written in the past tense. The poems ends in the past, not in the present or the future.

Sexton's *Live or Die* (1966) ends with the poem "Live." Paul Lacey finds that this poem "express[es] a new equilibrium" (13), and Robert Boyers calls it "a triumph of determination and insight, a final resolution of irreconcilabilities that had threatened to remain perpetually suspended and apart. . . . a rebirth of astounding proportions" (69). Most other critics also agree that the poem affirms life and announces Sexton's determination to live. But in this poem Neuringer's five "ingredients" appear clearly, and they do so with even more violence simply because the tone is so strong and positive. This poem does not offer a counter to Sexton's suicidal nature but rather represents her state of mind when she is feeling stronger and more capable of dealing with her problems. Clearly however, her on-going obsession with death, her inability to achieve equilibrium in her life, her vision of the world as joyless and cruel, and her lack of connection with the people around her remain as marked and symptomatic as in her other works.

Beginning with Sexton's view of life, death, and suicide, we see immediately that she remains obsessed with death although she describes it in less seductive terms. Death, relegated to the background like "mud, day after day," is still far from being safely removed from her. The assumption that Sexton is merely setting the stage for her reader in the first two stanzas by explaining her emotional state does not ameliorate her terrifying view of life. She calls herself mutilated, dismembered, "somebody's doll" and says that she has a "dwarf's heart." The only human is the "death-baby," which has been cooked and sewn with "little maggots" by "somebody's mother." And in the subsequent supposedly affirmative stanzas, life remains "a dream," and even less positive, a magic ritual as she "turn[s her] shadow [and not her substance] three times round." Sexton maintains that life has given her "the answer" and she sees it as "moving feverishly." Her tone becomes increasingly angry and even sarcastic as she progresses through the poem and describes her "new" outlook. Sexton's depiction of the sun or life as an egg with a tumbling center is as deadly as her other more obviously negative life images. She ends "Live, Live because of the sun,/the dream, the excitable gift." Such images are not necessarily positive since none of the three is susceptible to man's control, and the effects of these images are equally uncontrollable and unknown. The sun can kill and so can a dream. And what exactly is an "excitable gift?" It is something offered by another person, at their convenience, and for their own reasons. To "excite" means to set in motion, awaken, call forth, or stir-up, according to the Oxford English Dictionary, and all these terms are capable of being extremely positive or extremely negative. That Sexton chooses such strong words capable of divergent and polarized meanings is indicative of her true inner mood.

Sexton's view of herself becomes increasingly impenetrable; she decides that she needs a "purifier," and sleeps in a "corruptible bed." While she feels that she is not a "killer," she remains hidden behind an "apron" and carries her kisses inside her "hood." Her role appears to be to "love more if they come," to nurture, to feed, and to provide roses (beauty) from "the hackles" (her inner anger) of her throat. She is not creative in herself she says; her typewriter is the one that writes and does not break. In fact, she herself has frequently broken and been yelled at and told to shut-up by the people in her world. Ironically, the hammer or the power to kill herself has not been discarded because she has come to love life, but because she now understands that "people don't like to be told/that you're sick."

Sexton's mood remains strongly dichotomous as she portrays her world as a heartless place where her pain is used sadistically, or trivialized, by those around her. When she burns, they roast marshmallows over her flames, and when she freezes emotionally, they skate on her in cute little costumes. When she becomes a witch, they paint her pink, disguising her real nature for a moment. Even more indicative of their insensitivity is her comment that rather than help her change or get well, those around her simply oversimplify her complexity, and say that she is as "nice as a chocolate bar" when she is crazy.

But the primary key to Sexton's mood is that the people around her remain inhuman, or at best non-human, throughout the poem. Her lovers are "celery stalks," her husband is a "redwood," and her two daughters are "sea urchins." Even the puppies are not compared to living creatures but are called "cordwood [and] birch trees." So Sexton remains oriented away from those around her, and while she is not going to wear her hospital shift or quote her Black Masses at this time, she does not unequivocally state that they are no longer in her repertoire of life. Suicide and death remain in the recesses of her mind because life continues to be something that she "all the time want[s] to get rid of."

So Neuringer's five "lethal ingredients" can be found in many other Sexton poems, certainly many more than the twenty or so ostensibly "suicidal" poems that the critics cite. And these ingredients may well be present in them all, either wholly or in part. Sexton's view of the world seems always a little askew, and her sense of futility is always very strong. The awareness of all her incapacities, failures, and secret sins, seems to underlie many, if not all, of her poems. And Sexton constantly reiterates her view that death is easy, plausible, welcoming, and so attractive that "I am in love with it" (in the poem "Leaves That Talk"). Perhaps Diane Hume George's theory of the existence of a special language of the suicide is true, and this special language has muffled Sexton's deathly view of life in the minds of critics. Perhaps only someone who has also heard the "green girls" can understand Sexton's language, and agree with her that "They call, they call their green death call. They want me. They need me./I

belong lying down under them,/letting the green coffin fold and unfold/above me as I go out" (541).

Other elements, of course, go into the making of Sexton's, or any poet's work. Gary Blankenburg, among other critics, notes that Sexton's poetry is written primarily from the stance of "mental, physical, and spiritual illness" (103). Sexton suffered severe bouts with mental illness during her entire writing career, and indeed much of her poetry can be viewed from the therapeutic angle. There are numerous critical articles written about Sexton's therapy sessions, her hospitalizations, and her frequent descent into mental distress. But she was also a consummate poet. Anyone capable of writing such lines as "Johnny, your dream moves summers/inside my mind" (23), or " . . . what/I remember best is that/the door to your room was/the door to mine" (55), was a gifted craftsman of the language. That she also had a strong sense of humor about life and death can be seen by lines such as "the dead turn over casually,/thinking . . . /Good! No visitors today" (89). These and hundreds of other perfectly crafted lines prove that Sexton's poetry is readable on any number of levels.

But her suicidal tendencies drove her, and ultimately claimed her, and stopped her mouth with death. Ernest Becker seems to be describing Sexton, and all creative geniuses, when he discusses the root of the suicidal wish:

> What we call the well-adjusted man has just this capacity to partialize the world for comfortable action . . . men aren't built to be gods, to take in the whole world; they are built like other creatures, to take in the piece of ground in front of their noses . . . as soon as a man lifts his nose from the ground and starts sniffing at eternal problems like life and death, the meaning of a rose or a star cluster-then he is in trouble. (178)

And Sexton definitely began sniffing at eternal problems, eternal paradoxes, and so lost her way forever. But her poetry remains to tell us about ourselves, the darker parts, the parts of ourselves that we try to ignore. And she tells us, whether we understand her or not, how it feels to live in the endless night of a suicidal nature.

WORKS CITED

Alvarez, A. *The Savage God: A Study of Suicide.* London: Weidenfeld and Nicolson, 1972.

Anderson, Dorothy B., and Lenora J. McClean, eds. *Identifying Suicide Potential.* Proc. of a Conference at Columbia University's Teachers College. New York: Behavioral Publications, 1971.

Becker, Ernest. *The Denial of Death.* New York: The Free Press, 1973.

Blankenburg, Gary. "Anne Sexton: The Voice of Illness." *Anne Sexton: Telling The Tale.* Ann Arbur, MI: U. of Michigan P., 1988.

Bogard, Howard M. "Collected Thoughts of a Suicidologist." *Identifying Suicide Potential.* Eds. Dorothy B. Anderson and Lenora J. McClean. New York: Behavioral Publications, 1971.

Boyers, Robert. "Live or Die: The Achievement of Anne Sexton." *Salamagundi.* Vol. 2. 1967: 61-71.

Durkheim, Emile. *Suicide: A Study in Sociology.* Trans., John A. Spaulding and George Simpson. Glencoe, Ill.: The Free Press, 1951.

George, Diana Hume. *Oedipus Anne: The Poetry of Anne Sexton.* Chicago: U. of Illinois P., 1987.

Kiev, Ari. "Suicide Prevention." *Identifying Suicide Potential.* Eds. Dorothy B. Anderson and Lenora J. McClean. New York: Behavioral Publications, 1971.

Lacey, Paul A. *The Inner War: Forms and Themes in Recent American Poetry.* Philadelphia: Fortress Press, 1972.

Malkoff, Karl. "Anne Sexton." *Crowell's Handbook of Contemporary American Poetry.* New York: Crowell, 1973.

Neuringer, Charles, and Dan J. Lettieri. *Suicidal Women: Their Thinking and Feeling Patterns.* New York: Gardner Press, 1982.

Richman, Joseph. "Family Determinants of Suicide Potential." *Identifying Potential Suicide.* Eds. Dorothy B. Anderson and Lenora J. McClean. New York: Behavioral Publications, 1971.

Sexton, Anne. *The Complete Poems.* Boston: Houghton Mifflin, 1981.

Shurr, William H. "Anne Sexton's *Love Poems:* the Genre and the Differences." *Anne Sexton: Telling the Tale.* Ed. Steven E. Colburn. Ann Arbor: U. of Michigan P., 1988.

Spivack, Kathleen. "Poets and Friends." *Boston Globe Magazine.* 9 Aug. 1981: 10+.

Marjorie Perloff

SOURCE: "Death By Water," in *ELH*, Vol. 34, No. 1, March, 1967, pp. 116-40.

[*In the following essay, Perloff surveys the development of Lowell's elegies from bitter reflections on the death of the New England Puritan tradition to meditative pieces on the subject of human mortality.*]

> . . . the earthbound event which meant most to the Puritan was death. His life was harder than that of most men of his time; as a pioneer, he was overbearingly aware of the dangers to body and soul of his enterprise. . . . His most important poems are called forth by the ever-threatening imminence of death. These poems are elegies— lengthy, discursive and elevated—most often on the death of good men and powerful. . . . For the occasion of a death, the point just before the final proof of election or damnation, gave the Puritan poet his greatest opportunity. Now a man newly dead would really *know*. And the poet would bear witness to that knowledge, if only he could work out the way of getting it.[1]

One of the poems that Roy Harvey Pearce cites in support of the above generalization is a late seventeenth-century elegy on William Bradford by Josiah Winslow.[2] In 1944, nearly 300 years later, Josiah Winslow's descendant, Robert Lowell, wrote an elegy on his grandfather Arthur Winslow, in which the Puritan tradition of the New England Winslows is totally rejected by a poet who is himself paradoxically the "ideal follower of Barth and Calvin."[3] Surely no other modern American poet has been as obsessed with death and last things as has Lowell: from *Land of Unlikeness* (1944) to *For the Union Dead* (1964), his most characteristic and celebrated poems have been elegies, particularly elegies on his maternal or Winslow relatives.[4]

Although the subject matter of these elegies has remained remarkably constant during the twenty years of Lowell's career to date, structure and tone have undergone a radical revision, a change that can be summed up in Yeats's famous statement, "We make out of the quarrel with others, rhetoric, but of the quarrel with ourselves, poetry." "In Memory of Arthur Winslow" and "The Quaker Graveyard in Nantucket" (1946) display a bitterly disdainful preacher-poet who regards the lives of the dead relatives he has presumably come to mourn as so many exempla of the ultimate failure of the New England Puritan vision. In such recent Winslow elegies as "My Last Afternoon with Uncle Devereux Winslow" (1959) and "Soft Wood" (1964), however, the poet no longer quarrels with his relations and ancestors; the "I" of these poems is the quietly meditative, delicately humorous and humble self who would rather *see* than *judge*. For this speaker, the death of loved ones becomes a way of understanding, not God's predestination of the Elect and the Damned, but simply what Wallace Stevens has called in one of his cryptic titles, "How to Live. What to Do."

I. "IN MEMORY OF ARTHUR WINSLOW"

Both Hugh Staples and Jerome Mazzaro, in the only two book-length studies of Lowell to date, consider "In Memory of Arthur Winslow" one of the finest poems in *Land of Unlikeness*.[5] According to Mazzaro, the poem reveals "the successful interplay . . . of personal and traditional levels"; "theology, liturgy, mythology, history and personal observation are fused" (pp. 7, 17). Similarly, Staples comments, " . . . in the fine elegy to his grandfather. . . . Lowell displays, in a sustained effort, his astonishing ability to move with ease from the moral geography of Boston . . . to the cosmic scene, in which symbolism from both Christian and pagan traditions are harmoniously fused" (p. 29).

The metrical form of "In Memory of Arthur Winslow" has also been praised. As Allen Tate pointed out in his introduction to *Land of Unlikeness,* every poem in the book has a strict formal pattern either invented by Lowell or borrowed from other poets.[6] In this case, the stanza form is derived from Matthew Arnold's "The Scholar Gypsy": each iambic pentameter stanza has ten lines rhyming *abcbcadeed;* in each case, the sixth line is shortened to three stresses. This strict metrical form is, according to Staples, an excellent means of controlling the violence of the imagery.[7]

"Fusion" and "control" are, however, strange terms to apply to an elegy that fails to fulfill the most basic requirements of the form: it contains no lament and a very dubious consolation.[8] Despite the mythological and liturgical allusions and the carefully wrought stanza form, this elegy presents a poet at war with himself: he comes to mourn and to memorialize his grandfather but ends by attacking him, dwelling on his sins, and implying that, as a representative of his social class and religious sect, Arthur Winslow is one of the damned.

The poem is divided into four parts.[9] In the first, "Death from Cancer," the speaker addresses his grandfather directly. Cruelly honest, he morbidly tells the dying man that it is useless to wrestle with the "crab":

> The claws drop flesh upon your yachting blouse
> Until longshoreman Charon come and stab
> Through your adjusted bed
> And crush the crab.

The reference to Charon, the terrible ferryman who rows the souls of the dead across Acheron, the River of Woe, into the underworld, implies that Winslow's death is a prelude to greater suffering, an implication borne out by lines 9-10: "You ponder why the coxes' squeakings dwarf / The *resurrexit dominus* of all the bells." Because he has no true Christian faith, Arthur cannot hear the *resurrexit dominus;* as Staples points out, "the language of the Vulgate remains for him literally an unknown tongue" (p. 30). The first stanza, then, suggests that Winslow's death is equivalent to his damnation.

In the second stanza, the image of Christ walking the waves is introduced, ostensibly as a contrast to the frightening image of Charon. The muddy waters of Boston Basin and the Charles River suddenly become the miraculous waves on which Christ will "run / Arthur upon a trumpeting black swan / Beyond Charles River to the Acheron / Where the wide waters and their voyager are one." Mazzaro observes, "With 'trumpeting black swan' Lowell reinserts the classical idea that a swan utters a cry before death, and here, with 'trumpeting' rather than 'honking,' he further suggests that Winslow would be welcomed in heaven. . . . In conjunction with death, the

swan also invites a favorable comparison of the qualities of King Arthur with those of Arthur Winslow, whose journey to afterlife resembles that of the monarch's epic swan journey to Avalon" (p. 8).

This interpretation may well reflect Lowell's intentions, but how is the swan symbolism related to the other images in the poem? Mazzaro explains, "The faithful called over the Acheron succeed in crossing the water to heaven only while they, like Peter in the water-walking episode in the Bible, have faith in Christ" (p. 9). But, as the first stanza has implied and as the rest of the poem will make clear, Arthur Winslow did not have faith in Christ. How then can he cross the "wide waters" of the Acheron to heaven? And how does the speaker *know* with such assurance what Arthur's fate will be?

The poem never comes to terms with these questions; the salvation theme is abruptly dropped, and in Part II, "Dunbarton," Arthur Winslow's burial is rendered with cruel and disenchanted precision. The cold "granite plot" of the "half-forgotten Starks and Winslows" at Dunbarton symbolizes the spiritual aridity of the New England Puritan tradition. The speaker is revolted by what he sees: at his grandfather's funeral, thoughts of the dead man are obscured by his agonized perception of his living relatives, arriving in limousines with their crutches, both physical and mental, in order to perform their hollow rites in this landscape with its "gray" grass, "yellow" stones, and "rotten" lake. Even the "dwarf pines" (everything looks "dwarfed" to the jaundiced eye of the speaker) are envious ("green") of their more robust ancestors as they wait pointlessly for the "landed Promise" of the Mayflower Compact, a promise that has never been fulfilled.

In the second stanza of "Dunbarton" the speaker addresses his ancestors directly: "Oh fearful witnesses, your day is done. . . . " The faith of the Pilgrim Fathers, the religious zeal that once made them "point their wooden steeples lest the Word be dumb," is dead; in modern Boston, the Protestant creed is reduced to empty posturing: "The preacher's mouthings still / Deafen my poor relations on the hill. . . . " The relations are "poor" because they have no faith; only a "cold sun" "melts" on his grandfather's casket and the graves of the unbelieving, materialistic Winslows are viewed as "sunken landmarks."

It is usual to read "Dunbarton" as the devout Catholic's critique of the shortcomings of Protestant theology.[10] But such a reading ignores the poem's tone: the angry and oracular voice that delivers the denunciation is one familiar to readers of Lowell's famous dramatic monologue "Mr. Edwards and the Spider," a poem in which Jonathan Edwards, the great Puritan divine, tells his relative Josiah Hawley that, struggle though he may, he is predestined to eternal damnation:

> It was in vain you set up thorn and briar
> In battle array against the fire
> And treason crackling in your blood;

> For the wild thorns grow tame
> And will do nothing to oppose the flame;
> Your lacerations tell the losing game
> You play against a sickness past your cure.
> How will the hands be strong? How will the heart
> endure?[11]

"Mr. Edwards and the Spider" and its companion piece, "After the Surprising Conversions," succeed because Lowell uses the persona of Edwards to dramatize the peculiarly Puritan dilemma in which the sinner must confront the truth of the angry God directly, with no mediator, "no middle term, no gentle order, no Christ."[12] In using the mask of Edwards, Lowell lets the situation speak for itself; we *see* what it means for the isolated self to cower before a cruel God. But when Lowell uses the voice of the Calvinist preacher to castigate Calvinist preachers and to berate his Calvinist ancestors, the prevailing impression is one of confusion rather than of fusion. The elegy traditionally contains attacks on certain groups hostile to the dead man commemorated—the clergy in "Lycidas," the reviewers in "Adonais"—but in "In Memory of Arthur Winslow" it is the subject of the elegy, Winslow himself and the tradition he stands for, that is under attack.

The same indignant moral tone continues to prevail in Part III, "Five Years Later." Paraphrasing Mark Antony, the speaker says, "This Easter, Arthur Winslow, five years gone / I came to mourn, not to praise the craft / That netted you a million dollars . . . ," but we look in vain for the promised lament. Instead, this section of the elegy specifies the sin that removed Arthur from Christianity—his materialistic greed which brought him to Colorado in search of gold. Arthur's name is linked to that of Cotton Mather as well as to those of earlier Winslows: Edward (1595-1655), the sometime governor of Plymouth, who came over on the Mayflower and built the "blockhouse" mentioned in line 12; his grandson Edward (1669-1753), a well-known sheriff and silversmith; and General John Stark (1728-1822), the Revolutionary War general who founded the township of Dumbarton.[13] All these men shared Arthur Winslow's materialism and ambition, but at least they made substantial contributions to the government and cultural life of America, whereas the poet's grandfather achieved no fame outside the family circle and is remembered by the speaker as one whose thirst for wealth was his ruling passion. The harshness of the speaker's judgment is intensified by the fact that again he addresses Grandfather Winslow, now "five years dead," directly. Even standing beside the grave on Easter Sunday, he can neither forget nor forgive.

In Part IV, "A Prayer for my Grandfather to Our Lady," however, the poet seems to remember the requirements of the elegy form and provides what looks like a conventional consolation motif. Images of salvation are now introduced: Hugh Staples points out, for example, that "the poet, in his role of mediator, puts the words from the *Miserere* (slightly altered from *me* to an inclusive *nos*) into Latin: *Lavabis nos et super nivem dealbabor,* in his

effort to effect a kind of posthumous conversion" (p. 30). Again, however, the overall emphasis of this section is less on conversion than on sin and destruction, Jonathan Edwards' ruling themes. The speaker begins by telling Our Lady that "Neither my father nor his father" with their "clippers" and "slavers"—symbols of materialistic exploitation—have reached "The haven of your peace." This categorical statement again comes dangerously close to asserting Grandfather Winslow's damnation. The prayer that follows is less a prayer for Arthur Winslow that it is a prayer for the poet himself:

> Beached
> On these dry flats of fishy real estate,
> O Mother, I implore
> Your scorched, blue thunderbreasts of love to
> pour
> Buckets of blessings on my burning head
> Until I rise like Lazarus from the dead. . . .

Marius Bewley writes of this passage, "This is a network of conflicting connotations that operates at cross-purposes. 'Thunderbreasts' . . . is meant to suggest the mythical Thunderbird of various Indian tribes which was supposed to bring rain, and so the word may imply the life-giving qualities of Our Lady's love. But Our Lady and the Thunderbird . . . belong to traditions too remote to coalesce imaginatively." As for the phrase "Buckets of blessings on my burning head," it "suggests that Our Lady is dousing a halo."[14]

This verbal confusion (what Bewley calls the Gilbert-and-Sullivan quality of the passage) reflects the larger structural irresolution of the poem. The ostensible "Prayer for my Grandfather" begins as a diatribe against him and then turns inward upon the speaker, the *lavabis nos* nothwithstanding. The Puritan habit of "tortuous introspection to test the validity of grace in the soul" (Bewley, p. 159) seems to collide with the professed Catholic prayer. In the second stanza, moreover, Lowell suggests that the stained glass windows of the Protestant Trinity Church in Boston represent the limits of Winslow's religious faith; the "painted Paradise of harps and lutes," reminiscent of the painted city of Babylon, must sink like Atlantis, the symbol of materialism, into the Devil's jaw.[15] Grandfather Winslow's weak Protestantism, a ceremony without faith, is thus doomed.

Mazzaro argues that line 15, "And knock the Devil's teeth out by the roots," is the crucial line: " . . . this sinking will defeat the Devil for teeth are regenerative organs" (p. 18). Salvation is, in other words, reaped out of destruction. But whose salvation is in question? The "I" now comes into the foreground as the agonized speaker "strikes for shore."[16] For him, religion is not just a matter of "painted idols"; he begs the Blessed Mother to "run to the chalice and bring back / Blood on your fingertips for Lazarus who was poor." Lowell here employs a double Biblical allusion both to the Lazarus of Luke xvi, 19-31 as well as to the more famous Lazarus of John xi. It can be argued, as Mazzaro does (p. 98), that Lowell ironically reverses the positions of the rich and the poor man in Luke, so that the "poor Lazarus" for whom Christ must intercede is none other than the rich man, Arthur Winslow. But if the meaning of Stanza II is thus that Winslow will be saved by Christ after all, it is hardly stated very forcefully; on the contrary, the syntax of the passage suggests that it is the speaker himself rather than his grandfather who is the "Lazarus who was poor"; the movement of the elegy is, consequently, a sudden leap from a condemnation of Arthur Winslow to a final prayer for the speaker's salvation.

"In Memory of Arthur Winslow" is ultimately a failure because one is never sure whether the poem is social satire or elegy; tone and theme clash throughout. The larger structure does not cohere for there is no relationship between the final prayer to Our Lady and the blistering attack on Winslow piety in Part II and on Winslow materialism in Part III. Nor is there a meaningful development of the central water imagery. The poem contrasts two very different meanings of water: to the unbeliever Arthur Winslow, water is an indifferent natural element; it is Boston Basin, where the "clippers" and "slavers" of his ancestors satisfied their greed, it is the "sun-struck shallows" where the "midday Irish" fish for chub, it is the "rotten lake" at Dunbarton. To the Christian speaker, on the other hand, water is the symbol of salvation: the waves where "the ghost of risen Jesus walks," the "wide waters" to which the "trumpeting black swan" brings the soul of Arthur Winslow, the "buckets of blessing on my burning head," and the *lavabis nos* from the liturgy. But these two contradictory aspects of water are never reconciled or even related within the elegy. R. P. Blackmur, reviewing *Land of Unlikeness* in 1945, made a comment that illuminates the problem: " . . . in dealing with men his [Lowell's] faith compels him to be fractiously vindictive, and in dealing with faith his experience of men compels him to be nearly blasphemous. . . . What is thought of as Boston in him fights with what is thought of as Catholic; and the fight produces not a tension but a gritting."[17] Marius Bewley similarly speaks of the "collision between the Catholic tradition and the Apocalyptic Protestant sensibility" in Lowell's early poems (*Complex Fate,* p. 160). The poet has yet to learn to fuse the personal and the universal.

II. "THE QUAKER GRAVEYARD IN NANTUCKET"

In his second major elegy, Lowell consciously tried to move from the personal to the impersonal or mythic mode that one associates with Eliot: "The Quaker Graveyard in Nantucket" is to "In Memory of Arthur Winslow" what "The Waste Land" is to "Portrait of a Lady." Not only is Warren Winslow, Lowell's young cousin killed in World War II who is the nominal subject of the elegy, hardly felt as a presence in the poem, but the narrator now recedes as well. What remains is an impersonal vision of the terrible effects of spiritual alienation at any moment in history: Ahab's whale hunt in *Moby Dick* is used in the elegy as the central symbol of man's attempt to abuse his dominion over nature.

Of all Lowell's poems, this is the one most frequently and fully explicated,[18] and it would be superfluous to attempt another full-scale analysis here. What is important for our purpose is that, although Lowell here avoids the embarrassingly self-righteous tone of his earlier elegy and does not attack Warren Winslow personally, he still has great difficulty in articulating the total structure of the elegy. Like "In Memory of Arthur Winslow," "The Quaker Graveyard" contains no lament, and again the consolation, this time explicitly placed in Section VI, "Our Lady of Walsingham," is not integrated into the poem, which deals with the rapacity and greed of the New England Protestants of the nineteenth century, who are linked in Lowell's mind to the modern patriotic capitalists, here represented by Warren Winslow, who fought for a meaningless cause in World War II.

"The Quaker Graveyard" has been compared to "Lycidas" by a number of critics.[19] Hugh Staples lists the following parallels between the elegies of Milton and Lowell: the death of a young man to whom the poet has a more than casual yet less than intimate relationship, death by drowning, the unrecovered body, the movement beyond the lament to a larger consideration of contemporary and universal issues, and the "answer to the apparent futility of a young man's death, but in terms of Catholic mysticism rather than through the more or les orthodox Protestant solution of Milton" (p. 45). Both Lowell and Milton, moreover, draw upon classical and Biblical sources for their patterns of imagery; both pay indirect homage to great figures in their native tradition— Thoreau and Melville in Lowell's case, Theocritus, Bion and Virgil in Milton's. Both use place names to evoke the *genius loci:* for the Hebrides, Namancos and Bayona, Lowell substitutes Nantucket, Martha's Vineyard and Walsingham (pp. 45-46). Even the verse form of "The Quaker Graveyard" resembles that of "Lycidas": its 194 lines are "divided like the 193 lines of 'Lycidas' into a loose structure of pentameter lines, varied by an occasional trimeter. Each stanza has its own highly intricate rhyme scheme, repeated in only two cases (stanzas II and VII . . .), yet differing from each other only slightly. Like Milton, then, Lowell adapts the *canzone* form to his own uses . . . (p. 45).

Yet surely the differences between the two elegies outweigh these superficial similarities. Whether we think of "Lycidas" as a symphony, as does Marjorie Nicolson,[20] or as a rondo, as does Northrop Frye,[21] its structure is "musical" in that the motif of lament and consolation, introduced in the opening lines of the poem with the symbolism of myrtle and laurel, "echo antiphonally"[22] throughout the elegy so that the final climactic affirmation, "Weep no more, woeful shepherds, weep no more, / For Lycidas, your sorrow, is not dead . . . ," has been prepared for all along.

There is no such contrapuntal development in "The Quaker Graveyard." Lowell's elegy begins on a note of horror: the epigraph from Genesis, "Let man have dominion over the fishes of the sea and the fowls of the air and the beasts, and the whole earth, and every creeping creature that moveth upon the earth," is an ironic commentary on the awful abuse of this privilege by the Quaker whalers and their Godless modern descendants. What follows is a powerfully concrete description of death at sea.[23] The "bloodless" corpse of the drowned sailor, "a botch of reds and whites," is retrieved only to be cast back into the sea, the source of all creation. The theme of Part I is the horror and finality of death when viewed by those who have no belief in immortality. There is no hope for Warren Winslow and his fellow sailors in this nightmare vision: when the corpse is pitched out to sea, "dreadnaughts shall confess / Its hell-bent deity. . . . " As materialists, these sailors must reckon with the pagan deity Poseidon, the "earth-shaker," the cruel sea god. For them, death is final and irrevocable: "ask for no Orphean lute / To pluck life back."

The imagery of violence and destruction that pervades Part I is not modulated or significantly altered in subsequent sections, and the structural problem of the elegy is that Lowell does not quite seem to know where to go next. There is very little development in the first five sections: what happens, briefly stated, is that the poet shifts from the opening vision of contemporary wartime destruction to its historical counterpart, the meaningless voyage of Ahab's *Pequod*. The World War II battleship and the *Pequod* are explicitly linked in Part II, and the sinful pride of the Quakers of Nantucket is related in Part III to the same sin as it manifests itself in modern warfare. These sins are further specified in II and III as being sins against Christ (the "hurt beast," "IS, the whited monster"), and Part IV is, as Mazzaro observes, a kind of dirge for Christianity, which has been "killed" by the godlessness of Ahab's sailors and their modern counterparts (p. 39). Part V graphically describes the disposal of the whale's rotting viscera, an act evidently symbolic of the overwhelming evil that can be overcome only through the intercession of Jonas Messias—Christ. The complicated symbolism and rhetoric of these five sections mask a basic confusion: if the *Pequod* was, in fact, sent "packing off to hell" (IV), and if the figure of Warren Winslow merges with Ahab's mariners, why will Christ intercede for him? What, in other words, is the progress from sin to salvation?

Part VI, which is an adaptation of the description of Our Lady of Walsingham in E. I. Watkin's *Catholic Art and Culture*,[24] does not answer these questions and its function in the poem is puzzling. In an idyllic rural English setting, barefoot penitents are seen, walking along "the munching English lane," beside a gently flowing stream, and the speaker tells Warren Winslow, "Sailor, you were glad / and whistled Sion by that stream." But the image of the Virgin herself does not fulfill the sailor's expectations:

> There's no comeliness
> At all or charm in that expressionless
> Face with its heavy eyelids. As before,
> This face, for centuries a memory
> *Non est species, neque decor,*
> Expressionless, expresses God. . . .

Irvin Ehrenpreis observes that in Part VI Lowell is trying to juxtapose two attitudes toward the afterlife: he "puts the snug, familiar salvation that his cousin might aspire to

beside the Catholic vision of the universal but quite unknowable God reflected in the image of Our Lady of Walsingham" ("The Age of Lowell," p. 78). Hugh Staples agrees that the conventional conception of heaven outlined in Stanza I, a conception which is, incidentally, reminiscent of Grandfather Winslow's "Painted Paradise of harps and lutes," is rejected for "a loftier interpretation of the Godhead. . . . a state in which all human aspirations and concerns must be left behind," the state of mystical union (p. 51).

Most commentators have praised the "affirmation" of this section. Richard Fein writes, "Mary is there for the sailor to see, even if he fails to understand the nature of her restraint."[25] Ehrenpreis, however, voices a minority opinion; he finds Part VI "bathetic": it has "a posed air, a willed simplicity. This forced tone seems the more regrettable because Lowell's passage is meant to deliver the positive alternative to the errors he denounces with such thoroughness" (p. 79).

The placing of Part VI is, in fact, the central weakness of the elegy. It is curious that those critics who praise Lowell's perceptive handling of the American scene in the poem have failed to ask why the locale of Part VI should be Walsingham. What does the English shrine in its pastoral setting have to do with the precarious existence of the Quakers in Nantucket? How shall the "world" "come to Walsingham" when Lowell's world of S-boats and whalers has rejected Christianity? Secondly, and more specifically, if the "Sailor" (Warren Winslow) is made "glad" by the conventional description of heaven presented in the first stanza of VI, he is evidently incapable of understanding the significance of the face that "goes / Past castled Sion," just as Grandfather Winslow was incapable of hearing the *resurrexit dominus*. In this case, the consolation can lie only in the speaker's superior vision of God; the sailor who is memorialized in the elegy is beyond redemption. The result is a certain smugness; it is as if the speaker were saying, "*I* know that 'She knows what God knows,' whereas my poor cousin is satisfied with his limited vision of paradise."

Within the larger context of the whole elegy, the shrine of Our Lady of Walsingham stands in sharp opposition to the Quaker Graveyard in Nantucket, and it is hard to see how these two symbolic locales can be fused. Again, to use Blackmur's phrase, there is "not a tension but a gritting." Part VII is therefore a rather lame conclusion. Richard Fein insists that VII is a "reaffirmation of God's covenant with man that despite man's dying in the sea . . . God's will remains above destruction" (p. 268), and Mazzaro writes, "The poet having achieved the harmony of mystical union and its vision, Part VII reexamines the world without the sinister effects of the earlier sections" (p. 42). Granted the speaker says, "It's well" that the Atlantic is "fouled with blue sailors / Sea-monsters, upward angel, downward fish,"[26] but the "empty winds" are still "creaking," the "greased wash" is still "exploding on a shoal-bell," and the act that the poet finally associates with the "time / When the Lord God formed man from the sea's slime" is the destructive movement of "blue-lung'd combers" that have "lumbered to the kill." The final affirmation, "The Lord survives the rainbow of His will," impressive as it is in itself, thus seems rather forced. It has not been implicit all along as has Milton's consolation; even in the concluding section of the elegy, Lowell seems preoccupied with violence and destruction. It is as if the poet took one section of "Lycidas," the so-called "digression" in which Milton attacks the clergy (lines 109-31), and made this angry attack, which is only one motif in "Lycidas," the substance of his vision. One remembers "The Quaker Graveyard" for its merciless invective against man-made violence and horror, a horror never really transcended within the limits of the elegy. For Warren Winslow, "dead at sea," the Virgin's "expressionless / Face with its heavy eyelids" seems to be beyond reach. As for the speaker, he never really comes to terms with the meaning of death as does the "I" of "Lycidas"; he may understand that the "expressionless" face "expresses God," but he cannot *relate* that expression to anything or anyone in his environment. He knows only that the dead who inhabit the Quaker Graveyard in Nantucket are eternally damned. Again the tone of the elegy belies its intended theme.

III. "MY LAST AFTERNOON WITH UNCLE DEVEREUX WINSLOW"

On a first reading, "My Last Afternoon with Uncle Devereux Winslow," the first of the fifteen autobiographical poems in Part IV of *Life Studies* (1959),[27] seems less impressive than "The Quaker Graveyard." No one would compare this new elegy to "Lycidas": gone are the classical, historical and Biblical allusions, the complex liturgical symbolism, the oracular tone, the tight canzone form.[28] The resulting "prosaic" or "flat" quality has disturbed certain readers: Mazzaro, for example, writes, "The reader feels 'he has been here before,' and most of his interest as a result in clinical. The structure of the poem follows the timeshift technique and concentrates on the tension and on the incidental observations of Lowell playing, his hands first on a pile of earth and then on a pile of lime. There is no single illumination to be drawn from the observations" (p. 111).

Like "In Memory of Arthur Winslow," "My Last Afternoon" is divided into four parts, but the resemblance ends there. In the new elegy, we do not move logically from sickness, to burial scene, to "lament" for the dead man, to a prayer for his salvation. Part I characterizes Grandfather Winslow's summer home as it appeared to the narrator as a small boy, and the central character is Arthur Winslow himself, no longer the ruthless, godless capitalist of the earlier elegy, but a kindly if misguided man who has tried to place his individual stamp on his environment. Part II is a brief vignette in which Lowell depicts the boy's image of himself. Part III abruptly shifts to Grandmother Winslow's sister, Great Aunt Sarah, a lonely and aimless spinster who spends her days practicing for the concert she is never to give. Only in Part IV does Uncle Devereux, the boy's romantic hero, appear and his premature death is related. The elegy ends on a note of death and there is no explicit consolation, no stated hope that the soul of Uncle Devereux will be saved.

Nevertheless, "My Last Afternoon with Uncle Devereux Winslow" is a much more unified, if less ambitious work than Lowell's earlier elegies. Hugh Staples has shown that the seemingly random observations of the narrator "are integrated by a carefully planned and executed pattern of imagery based on the elements of earth, water and air. . . . in Part I, the basic image is that of earth and the minerals that compose it. . . . the mineral images . . . though they suggest the wished-for permanence, are themselves mutable. Lifeless, they stand opposed to the world of human experience" (p. 79).

This is a very just observation and one that deserves further development. The elegy's epitaph, "1922: the stone porch of my Grandfather's summer house," provides us with a key to the whole poem. The connotations of "stone porch"—lifelessness, the grave, death—immediately reverse those of "summer house"—youth, warmth, vitality, life. The whole poem moves between these two poles, and yet, as the syntax of the epigraph makes clear, these opposites are found in conjunction; it is the "summer house" that has the "stone porch." Thus, unlike "In Memory of Arthur Winslow," this elegy does not set up a simple contrast between good and evil, salvation and sin; here it is difficult to extricate one from the other. Lowell manages to avoid the "gritting" or clash of opposites found in the earlier poem by a careful manipulation of tone. The mature narrator may well understand the futility of the lives of the Winslows, but for the young boy, his former self, "Nowhere was anywhere after a summer / at my Grandfather's farm." Moreover, "stone porch" and "summer house" are introduced at the very outset of the poem so that Lowell here avoids the jarring effect of Part VI of "The Quaker Graveyard," in which the religious consolation, totally unprepared for, is suddenly introduced.

The seemingly random opening sets up the structural pattern:

> "I won't go with you. I want to stay with
>   Grandpa!"
> That's how I threw cold water
> on my Mother and Father's
> watery martini pipe dreams at Sunday dinner.

The "cold water" of line 2 becomes the poem's central life symbol: it is the water of salvation, although here salvation has only a human, not a supernatural dimension.[29] For the narrator's parents, "cold water" is an alien element; they have only "watery martini pipe dreams." The whole farm is characterized by a lack of water; even the poplar trees are "Diamond-pointed, athirst," and they "parade" unhappily "From Grandmother's rose garden" to "a scarey stand of virgin pine, / scrub, and paths forever pioneering." Throughout Part I images of earth and water are carefully juxtaposed: Grandfather Winslow's "disproportioned" world is one of "Alpine Edwardian" cuckoo clocks, "slung with strangled, wooden game," of "fool's-gold nuggets," of "octagonal red tiles, / sweaty with a secret dank, crummy with ant-stale." But when the maids, Sadie and Nellie, appear at sunset, "bearing pitchers of ice-tea, / oranges, lemons, mint and peppermints," they remind the boy who watches them from the stone porch of "sunflowers" and "Pumpkins floating shoulder-high." For the child, such moments are enough to prove that "Nowhere was anywhere after a summer / at my Grandfather's farm," but the narrator sees the inherent futility of the Edwardian elegance:

> The farm, entitled *Char-de-sa*
> in the Social Register,
> was named for my Grandfather's children:
> Charlotte, Devereux, and Sarah.

Not only does the silly, pretentious name *Char-de-sa* seem comically inappropriate for a farm, but the off-rhyme "Char-de-*sa*" / "Social Regis*ter*" intensifies the hollowness of Winslow *moeurs contemporains*. (The same effect is created in Part III, where the meaningless round of Aunt Sarah's activities is summed up by off-rhyme in the lines, "Aunt Sarah, risen like a phoe*nix* / from her bed of troublesome sna*cks* and Tauch*nitz* clas-si*cs*.") Part I ends on a note of death as the narrator recalls the demise of "Cinder, our Scottie puppy" ("Cinder" is again a mineral image) and sits "mixing black earth and lime," the two substances that will "blend to the one color" as an emblem of Uncle Devereux's death at the end of the elegy.

Part II presents the death-life paradox in terms of the boy's vision of himself in the mirror. The perfection of his "formal pearl gray shorts" (again a mineral image) gives the boy an illusion of permanence: he feels that he has "the Olympian / poise of my models in the imperishable autumn / display windows / of Rogers Peet's boys / store. . . . " A he studies his reflection in the mirror, however, "Distorting drops of water / pinpricked my face. . . . " Life is not the false stasis of the shop window mannequin; it is flux, change, movement. The reality must be faced even if it is unpleasant: "I was a stuffed toucan / with a bibulous multicolored beak."

The seemingly random shift to Aunt Sarah in Part III presents a new variation on the same theme. Aunt Sarah's station is indoors, this side of the "lake-view window in the billiards-room"; she places a wall between herself and the water. The only event that can make her "rise like a phoenix" from her neurotic invalid's bed is the command of her sister, who, needing "a fourth for 'Auction'," casts "a thirsty eye / On Aunt Sarah." The stone motif recurs in the image of the "naked Greek statues" that adorn Symphony Hall, "deathlike in the off-season summer," where Aunt Sarah formerly practiced on her soundless piano for her mythical recital.

The account of the actual physical death of Uncle Devereux, which is the subject of Part IV, jolts the reader with a sudden shock of recognition: it is only now that one realizes that all along the poem has been talking about death, the life-in-death of all the Winslows, whose carefully accumulated possessions are as ephemeral as the proper clothes, clever student posters, and "double-barrelled shotguns" of Uncle Devereux, who is "dying of the incurable Hodgkin's disease." Again, Part IV opens with a water image:

> I picked with a clean finger nail at the blue anchor
> on my sailor blouse *washed white* as a spinnaker.
> What in the world was I wishing?
> . . . A sail-colored horse browsing in the
>   *bullrushes* . . .
> A fluff of the west wind puffing
> my blouse, kiting me over our seven chimneys,
> troubling the *waters*. . . .
>   [italics mine]

It is a lovely daydream, an escape to a world of water, whiteness and wind, but the reality rapidly intrudes with the ironic lines, "As small as sapphires were the ponds: *Quittacus, Snippituit* / and *Assawompset*. . . . " Not only are the long Indian names of the little ponds amusingly pretentious; more significant is the fact that in Uncle Devereux's world it is difficult to distinguish life from death: water and mineral images merge—ponds become sapphires. Uncle Devereux is, in more than one sense, "closing camp for the winter":

> At the cabin between the waters,
> the nearest windows were already boarded.

The "cabin between the waters" is a key phrase in the elegy; the Winslow world is itself a "cabin between the waters," a lifeless entity surrounded by, but not participating in, the waters of life.

The description of the "disproportioned" world of Grandfather Winslow's stone porch in Part I has prepared us for the "helter-skelter" of Uncle Devereux's cabin where everything is incongruous, beginning with his attire, inappropriate for a sportsman, in "his severe / war-uniform of a volunteer Canadian officer." The only person whose thirst is quenched here is "Mr. Punch," grotesquely depicted as "a water melon in hockey tights," "tossing off a decanter of Scotch." The other posters similarly reflect the lack of direction in Uncle Devereux's life: "*La Belle France* in a red, white and blue toga / was accepting the arm of her 'protector,' / the ingenu and procine Edward VII," and the narrator sardonically concludes:

> The finest poster was two or three young men in
>   khaki kilts
> being bushwhacked on the veldt—
> They were almost life-size. . . .

This terrible death of young men who are "almost life-size" prefigures Uncle Devereux's own death, explicitly referred to in the next line. The poignancy of the closing verse paragraph resides in the ironic contrast between the Winslows' illusion that one can live forever and the reality of death. Lovingly, year in and year out, Grandfather Winslow has "pencilled" "the white measuring-door" with Uncle Devereux's heights until his son reached the eminence of six feet in 1911. To the very end, Devereux maintains the illusion of "Olympian perfection" (II); he is, in the eyes of the young boy, a figure of superhuman strength and splendor: "His blue coat and white trousers / grew sharper and straighter. / His coat was a blue jay's tail, / his trousers were solid cream from the top of the bottle. / He was animated, hierarchical. . . . " It is a splendid image but ultimately as "death-like" as the "naked Greek statues" in Symphony Hall: Uncle Devereux is no more than a "ginger snap man in a clothes-press"—one wrong movement and he will break in two. The black pile of earth and the white pile of lime will "blend to the one color."

The final verse paragraph of the poem contains the only passage in the elegy reminiscent of Lowell's earlier allusive technique: in recording his reaction to the pointless arguments between Grandfather Winslow and the dying Devereux, the speaker remembers:

> I cowered in terror.
> I wasn't a child at all—
> unseen and all-seeing, I was Agrippina
> in the Golden House of Nero. . . .

The classical reference is not particularly obscure; what Lowell evidently means is that, just as Agrippina "cowered in terror" after her son Brittanicus was poisoned and, fearing for her safety, spied on her treacherous son Nero behind palace doors, so the child, "unseen and all-seeing," makes an unconscious connection between the death of others—in this case Devereux—and his own annihilation. Again, like Agrippina, the speaker in Lowell's elegy has to maintain the aristocratic tradition in the face of a decadent world. The fall of his house symbolizes the fall of a larger social order.[30]

But such explication does not take us very far. If one considers the function rather than the source of the passage, it becomes readily apparent that the lines are out of key with the rest of the elegy. The tone throughout has been one of quiet understatement, of ironic implication; the narrator has kept his eye squarely on the objects that surround him and has read their lesson obliquely. In the structure created by the contrasting earth and water imagery, the sudden reference to Agrippina seems strained and overly explicit. We do not need to be told that the speaker "wasn't a child at all," for the poem has already dramatized the intensity of the child's vision, and the insistence on his "all-seeing" power seems laboured and sentimental. It is the only time that tone falters in this otherwise superbly articulated poem.

As an elegy, "My Last Afternon with Uncle Devereux Winslow" stands at the opposite pole from "In Memory of Arthur Winslow" and "The Quaker Graveyard." In the early elegies, the death of the relative was used as a mere starting point for a satiric attack on the evils of contemporary civilization. "Uncle Devereux Winslow," outwardly so unlike a classical elegy like "Lycidas," is actually closer to it than is "The Quaker Graveyard," for Lowell's new elegy does contain the lament for the pre-

mature death of the young man which is a basic requirement of the elegy form. Because we see Devereux both from the angle of vision of the child and from that of the mature narrator recalling his childhood, we can sympathize with the dying man, who is the boy's hero, even as we judge him. "Uncle Devereux Winslow" also contains the consolation motif essential to elegy, even if only implicitly: the poet-speaker, in the act of recalling his childhood, has learned that only by accepting the lives of others can one go beyond them. The central theme of the poem—the need to accept the flux of life, to "throw cold water" on one's "watery martini pipe dreams," to leave "the cabin between the waters"—is surely one that transcends the local concerns of the Lowell-Winslow family. Despite what seems an undue autobiographical emphasis, "Uncle Devereux Winslow" is paradoxically, a more impersonal poem than the two earlier elegies which strain unsuccessfully to make the death of one man symbolic of the death of the whole New England tradition.

IV. "SOFT WOOD"

The very title of Lowell's most recent volume of poetry, *For the Union Dead* (1964), reveals the poet's continuing concern with the problem of mortality. But after what amounted almost to an obsession with his family in *Life Studies* (the volume might more accurately be called *Death Studies*), Lowell now turns to more public subjects, and the title poem of the new volume is a brilliant generalized lament in the tradition of Gray's "Elegy in a Country Churchyard." The new collection does, however, contain one Winslow elegy, the poem "Soft Wood" which is written in memory of Harriet Winslow, the poet's aunt. Compared to, say, "The Quaker Graveyard," this is a slight, unimposing lyric, but its offhand casualness turns out to be a carefully calculated effect.

"Soft Wood" is curiously reminiscent of Yeats's "The Wild Swans at Coole": in both poems, the central thematic antithesis is between the eternal renewal or "immortality" of nature and the mortality of man. Just as Yeats's speaker asks about the swans, "Among what rushes will they build, / By what lake's edge or pool / Delight men's eyes when I awake some day / To find they have flown away?", Lowell's lament for mortality in Stanza VI is followed by the statement, "Yet the seal pack will bark past my window / summer after summer." Even the 6-line stanza of "Soft Wood" resembles that of "That Wild Swans at Coole," although the stress pattern is different, and Lowell uses no regular rhyme scheme as does Yeats.[32]

Matthew Arnold's "The Scholar-Gypsy," which provided Lowell with the stanza form for "In Memory of Arthur Winslow," here furnishes him his witty opening metaphor: the seals, happily swimming "in their barred pond at the zoo," oddly remind the speaker of the mysterious Oxford boy who disappeared from the university in the remote past, became a gypsy, and returned to haunt students of subsequent generations. In Arnold's poem, the scholar-gypsy becomes the symbol for the free, instinctive, natural life, unencumbered by the normal man's "sick fatigue," "Languid doubt," "heads o'ertax'd," and "palsied hearts"; similarly, Lowell's seals, which pop up suddenly on the surface of the water and then unexpectedly disappear again, symbolize the instinctive and irrational element in life.

The seals are "happy" because they are at home in nature, just as Yeats's swans find the cold streams "Companionable." The lines "and no sunflower turns / more delicately to the sun / without a wincing of the will," recall Yeats's lines, "Passion or conquest, wander where they will / Attend upon them still." The natural world is the seals' habitat and so there is no need for a "wincing of the will."

Stanza II opens with the line "Here too in Maine things bend to the wind forever." "Too" is a puzzling word; it implies that it is a good thing for "things" to "bend to the wind forever," that this action resembles the turning of sunflower to sun. The rest of the stanza bears out this implication: along the Maine coast, one has the illusion of being able to live forever—the "painted soft wood" of the oceanfront houses stays "bright and clean" indefinitely as the air blasts "an all-white wall whiter," and the wind, tinged with the aroma of salt and evergreen, is a welcome force. But it is already clear that the difference between seal pond and Maine seaport is that in the latter eternal life is only an illusion: "To bend to the wind" is ultimately to die.

The illusion persists in the next stanza in which wind imagery is replaced by that of water: "The green juniper berry spills crystal-clear gin, / and even the hot water in the bathtub / is more than water, / and rich with the scouring effervescence / of something healing, / the illimitable salt." This magically healing water recalls the water imagery of "Uncle Devereux Winslow": it is the water of life, health, salvation. But the positive emphasis is undercut by the contrast between this water and the pond the seals swim in: water is not man's natural habitat—he must crush the juniper berry in order to extract the flavoring for "the crystal-clear gin," and the "hot water in the bathtub" is, after all, a man-made product.

It is therefore not surprising that in the fourth stanza a note of doubt enters. "Things last," the narrator says cryptically, but the wind that formerly blew "Through curtain and screen / touched with salt and evergreen," now becomes, in a transformation that recalls the poems of Wallace Stevens, "the wind smashing without direction." The ceaseless monotony of the air blast reduces the mind to nothingness so that man forgets his responsibilities: "only children seem fit to handle children." And even the "fresh paint on the captains' houses" cannot hide the fact that the wood is becoming "softer."

The whitening action of the wind upon "soft wood" recalls another image to the narrator's mind in Stanza VII: the dazzling display of power in the days when the captains' "square-riggers used to whiten / the four corners of the globe." But their command of the ocean was, again, short-lived and illusory: the captains hardly "outlast their possessions, / once warped and mothered by their touch." Not only is the acquisition of "things" that supposedly "last" useless, but in the stanza's final line, the human body itself is seen as a thing, as one more useless possession: "Shed skin will never fit another wearer." This ominously quiet line with its feminine endings ("nev*er*," "anoth*er*," "wear*er*") suddenly forces the reader into an awareness that all along it has been death, not life, that has been the subject of the poet's meditation. It is the same effect that Lowell created in Part IV of "Uncle Devereux Winslow" (see above), but in "Soft Wood" it is achieved with greater economy.

The phrase "shed skin" reminds one of the seals (sealskin) to whom the poet now returns. "Shed skin" is no problem in the seal world, for new seals "will bark past" the poet's window "summer after summer." But for human beings, especially for the aged, it is different. "This is the season / when our friends may and will die daily. / Surely the lives of the old / are briefer than the young." Just as the wood seems to be eternally white, so the young seem immortal; if "the lives of the old / are briefer," it is because the young are daily made aware of the termination of these lives.

Only now, in the last stanza, does Lowell attack the subject of the elegy directly: "Harriet Winslow, who owned this house, / was more to me than my mother. . . . " This is the first and only instance of pure praise of the dead relative in Lowell's Winslow elegies. The speaking voice has come a long way from the strident prophecy of the preacher, castigating Grandfather Winslow for his sins in "In Memory of Arthur Winslow." One can accept the flat statement of these lines because Lowell has already dramatized Harriet Winslow's world in which "the juniper berry spills crystal-clear gin," and "even the hot water in the bathtub" has "a scouring effervescence." As the personification of that world, Harriet Winslow seemed immortal to her young nephew; the truth that she has "bent to the wind" is almost impossible to grasp. The distance between the speaker and the lamented dead is measured in the last three lines of the elegy by the symbolic distance between Washington, city of heat waves and air-conditioning, and Maine with its whiteness, water, wind, and evergreen. "Breathing in the heat wave" is the opposite of breathing the fresh air that "blows through curtain and screen" of Harriet Winslow's house; the heat waves of Washington also stand opposed to the ocean waves of Maine. The air-conditioning is thus "a drug that numbs"—one forgets the heat, but simultaneously its "air blast" alerts the poet to the painful recollection of an air blast that was natural and ennervating.

In "Soft Wood," lament and consolation come together in the climatic line "Shed skin will never fit another wearer." The speaker laments the mortality of his beloved relative, but he knows that there is another level of awareness at which "shed skin" is no tragedy. The elegy's water symbolism is functional here: the seals are at home in the water but, because they are mindless, they accept it blindly "without a wincing of the will." Harriet Winslow, on the other hand, lives near the water but not in it; she is not at home in nature as are the seals, and the wind can become a terrifying sound in her mind; however, she and the poet who mourns for her can do what the seals cannot—they can see, assess, understand. "Knowing" is thus the crucial verb in the last stanza.

In the well-known *Paris Review* interview, Lowell insisted that his recent "Agnostic" poems are not thematically different from his earlier Catholic ones: " . . . I don't feel my experience changed very much. . . . it's very much the same sort of thing that went into the religious poems—the same sort of struggle, light and darkness, the flux of experience. The morality seems much the same."[33] This comment is extremely misleading; it can only remind us how right D. H. Lawrence was when he said, "Never trust the artist. Trust the tale." For the "morality" of "Soft Wood" is not at all that of the early elegies. In "In Memory of Arthur Winslow" the sharp contrast between the waters of Boston Basin and the "waves" on which the "ghost of risen Jesus walks" is never resolved; Geoffrey Hartman has recently described such irresolution in Lowell's early poetry as "an unfortunate grinding together of natural experience and supernatural emblem."[34] The same "grinding together" occurs in "The Quaker Graveyard," in which the image of the destructive waters of the Atlantic and that of the gurgling stream near the shrine of Our Lady of Walsingham seem to be created on different poetic planes. The poet's vision fails to reconcile the horror and the glory. But in "My Last Afternoon with Uncle Devereux Winslow," and even more in "Soft Wood," there is a new and delicate balance between sympathy and judgment, between lament and consolation. There is no "quarrel with others" in "Soft Wood"; the poem succeeds because it resolves the tensions between natural experience: the poet's awareness of Harriet Winslow's death, and supernatural emblem: the life-giving water of Maine. The poet's tears are salt, but the salt water of the ocean is "illimitable."

NOTES

[1] Roy Harvey Pearce, *The Continuity of American Poetry* (Princeton, 1961), pp. 24-25.

[2] Pearce, p. 29.

[3] Randall Jarrell, *Poetry and the Age* (New York, 1953), p. 212.

[4] Lowell's emphasis on death has been pointed out by a number of critics. See, for example, Josephine Jacobsen, "Poet of the Particular," *Commonweal*, LXXXI (1964-65), 345-50; Christopher Ricks, "The Three Lives of Robert Lowell," *New Statesman*, LXIX (26 March, 1965), 496. It is curious to note that, although "91 Reverse Street," the autobiographical sketch of Lowell's early life in *Life Studies,* deals almost exclusively with Lowell's paternal relatives, the poetry in the same volume concerns itself with the Winslows rather than the Lowells.

[5] Staples, *Robert Lowell: The First Twenty Years* (New York, 1962), and Mazzaro, *The Poetic Themes of Robert Lowell* (Ann Arbor, 1965). "In Memory of Arthur Winslow" is also singled out for praise by Irvin Ehrenpreis, "The Age of Lowell," in *American Poetry,* Stratford-upon-Avon Studies 7 (New York, 1965), pp. 75-76.

[6] (Cummington, Mass., 1944). Pages of introduction are unnumbered.

[7] Staples writes, "In deliberately accepting the artistic demands imposed by traditional forms, Lowell has found a means of controlling the volcanic flow of his imagination" (p. 19). See also Ralph J. Mills Jr., "Robert Lowell," *Contemporary American Poetry* (New York, 1965), p. 140.

[8] By definition, the elegy is a poetic genre which contains both lament and consolation: thus Stephen F. Fogle writes in the *Encyclopedia of Poetry and Poetics* that an *elegy* is "A lyric, usually formal in tone and diction, suggested either by the death of an actual person or by the poet's contemplation of the tragic aspects of life. In either case, the emotion originally expressed as a lament, finds consolation in the contemplation of some personal principle" (Princeton, 1965), p. 215.

[9] Since *Land of Unlikeness* appeared in a limited edition of 250 copies and is not readily available, I use as my text the version of "In Memory of Arthur Winslow" in *Lord Weary's Castle;* the edition used is *Lord Weary's Castle and the Mills of the Kavanaughs* (Cleveland: Meridian Books, 1965). There is a detailed comparison of the two versions, which are not essentially different, in Mazzaro's book, pp. 4-19.

[10] See Mazzaro, pp. 12-13; Staples, pp. 28-29; Mills, pp. 125-36.

[11] *Lord Weary's Castle,* p. 58.

[12] The phrase is Denis Donoghue's: see Chapter V of *Connoisseurs of Chaos: Ideas of Order in Modern American Poetry* (New York, 1965), p. 154.

[13] See Mazzaro, p. 15.

[14] "Some Aspects of Modern American Poetry," *The Complex Fate* (London, 1952), p. 161.

[15] See Apocalypse 18: 22. Mazzaro gives a detailed explication of this passage (pp. 16-18), and Staples locates the source of "The painted paradise of harps and lutes" in François Villon's "Ballade—Que Villon Feist à la Requeste de sa Mère, Pour Prier Nostre Dame" (p. 98).

[16] In the *Lord Weary's Castle* version, quotation marks surround the second stanza; Staples therefore concludes

that the speaker of the second stanza is Grandfather Winslow himself. The text does not, however, support such a reading: the "I" says that he finds "no painted idols to adore," whereas Arthur Winslow clearly does admire the "painted paradise." Moreover, the prayer to the Blessed Virgin ("Mother, run to the chalice. . . . ") is perfectly consistent with the speaker's prayer in the first stanza. Staples' argument that the "lavabis *nos*" indicates a modulation to the voice of Arthur Winslow (p. 9) is not convincing. The quotation marks are not the only sign of confusion in the second stanza; even Mazzaro, whose praise for the elegy is almost unqualified, notes that it makes no sense for the speaker to "strike for shore" when he has just said that he is "beached / On these dry flats of fishy real estate" (p. 19).

[17] *Kenyon Review,* VII (1945), 348.

[18] See Staples, Chapter IV *passim;* Mazzaro, pp. 37-44; Richard Fein, "Mary and Bellona: The War Poetry of Robert Lowell," *Southern Review,* I (1965), 826-31; Mills, pp. 141-44. For the text, see *Lord Weary's Castle,* pp. 8-14.

[19] John Thompson, in a review of *Life Studies* in *Kenyon Review,* XXI (1959), 485, writes, "'The Quaker Graveyard,' for instance, is an elegy which may be compared at length and in detail with 'Lycidas' without suffering much at any point." See also Staples, pp. 45-52.

[20] *John Milton: A Reader's Guide to his Poetry* (New York, 1963), pp. 105-11. Marjorie Nicolson describes the structure as that of a sonata-symphony with an overture and three movements.

[21] Literature as Context: Milton's 'Lycidas'," *Fables of Identity* (New York, 1963), p. 121. Frye writes, "The body of the poem is arranged in the form ABACA, a main theme repeated twice with two intervening episodes as in the musical rondo. The main theme is the drowning of Lycidas in the prime of his life; the two episodes, presided over by the figures of Orpheus and Peter, deal with the theme of premature death as it relates to poetry and the priesthood respectively. . . . The most difficult part of the construction is the managing of the transitions from these episodes back to the main theme."

[22] See Nicolson, p. 106.

[23] The imagery of this passage is taken from the opening chapter of Thoreau's *Cape Cod;* see Staples, p. 101.

[24] Lowell himself points out his source in the Preface to *Lord Weary's Castle;* for the full source, see Staples, pp. 103-04.

[25] Fein, "Mary and Bellona," 828.

[26] Even this supposedly affirmative image is ambiguous. The allusion is to *Paradise Lost,* I, 462-63; here Milton describes the fallen angels who arrive in Hell, having

died for Mammon, as "Sea-monsters, upward angel, downward fish." The fallen angels, in other words, maintain some semblance of their former radiance even as they enter Hell. By analogy, it would seem that the "blue sailors" also enter Hell. Why, then, does Lowell write "It's well"?

[27] This text used is *Life Studies* (New York: Vintage Books, 1959), pp. *55-59.*

[28] "Uncle Devereux Winslow" is written in free verse paragraphs of varying length: the lines range from two stresses ("one winter") to six ("What were those sunflowers? Pumpkins floating shoulder-high?"), and there is occasional rhyme as in "my Great Aunt S*arah*" / was learning Samson and Del*ilah*").

[29] A remark made by Lowell about "Skunk Hour" is relevant here: "I hope my readers would remember John of the Cross's poem. My night is not gracious, but secular, puritan, agnostical. An Existentialist night," *The Contemporary Poet as Artist and Critic,* ed. Anthony Ostroff (Boston, 1964), p. 107.

[30] See Richard Calhoun, *Explicator,* XXIII (1965), Item 38.

[31] *For the Union Dead* (New York, 1964), pp. 63-64.

[32] Yeats's stanza is a4b3c4b3d5d3—a ballad stanza plus an unequal couplet. Lowell's stanza has no regular pattern; the lines range from 2 to 6 stresses and there is occasional rhyme as in "screen" / "evergreen" and "Gypsy" / "happy." The most striking sound effects in the poem are those created by assonance and alliteration, as in the opening line, "Sometime*s* I have *s*upposed *s*eals. . . ."

[33] *Writers at Work, The Paris Review Interviews, Second Series* (New York, 1963), p. 352.

[34] "The Eye of the Storm," *Partisan Review,* XXXII (1965), 279.

Constance Scheerer

SOURCE: "The Deathly Paradise of Sylvia Plath," in *The Antioch Review,* Vol. 34, No. 4, Summer, 1976, pp. 469-80.

[*In the following essay, Scheerer traces Plath's rejection of mythic paradise—which she evokes using imagery of death—in her poetry.*]

> Green alleys where we reveled have become
> The infernal haunt of demon dangers;
>
> . . . . .
>
> Backward we traveled to reclaim the day
> Before we fell . . .

All we find are altars in decay. . . .
Sylvia Plath, "Doom of Exiles," 1954

In Ted Hughes's "Notes on the Chronological Order of Sylvia Plath's Poems," included in *The Art of Sylvia Plath,* he refers to several written in 1956-57, calling their vision of "the deathly paradise" a "chilling" one. The comment is haunting, also puzzling: how can "paradise" be "deathly"? Sylvia Plath was, Hughes adds, evolving her own pantheon of deities at the time, her special cosmic vision. Although she was inspired by the works of "primitive painters" from Henri Rousseau to Leonard Baskin, he explains, the vision was an internally felt experience and very much her own.

Paradise is, by definition, not deathly. A concept common to many myths and religions, it is invariably defined as the starting point for humanity, also as the time when human beings possessed the ideal life, including intimate contact with God or gods. In pagan or pre-Christian faiths or stories, the original state of innocence and bliss can be recaptured only by a return: this was often meant literally and forms the cyclical pattern of Oriental religions or pagan philosophies. With the coming of the Judaeo-Christian tradition, paradise, our first home, takes on an eschatological meaning as well. Its idyllic condition waits in some uncertain future time, a going-forward to a place or state won through God's redemptive power and grace. The word "paradise," of Persian origin, means simply "walled garden," and this aspect is retained with its traditional imagery and lavish beauty in many Plath poems as it is in paintings by Rousseau.

A deathly paradise is, however, of darkling, sinister import, presided over by presences divine but daemonic—mythic figures or power, impersonalized archetypes without concern for what they create. Within the walls of such death-gardens ravaging figures sometimes prowl and destroy, like the tigers of Rousseau's mysterious canvases, or the archetypal sow who swills down the very cosmos itself as she wallows in the "walled garden" of her legendary sty in the Plath poem, "Sow." Although they contain by implication humanity's beginnings and endings, death, not life, is the ruling principle of these anti-Edens. Moreover, their inhabitants have no freedom of choice in the old Miltonic sense of having been made "Sufficient to have stood though free to fall." They are human but hapless, at the mercy of deity or deities. The deathly paradise, then, is deathly not only because it affirms death instead of life but also because it swallows up purpose and individuality. Its ultimate affirmation is a negation: the search for an identity means the search for non-identity. The discovery of purpose discloses that there is no purpose.

On this paradox Sylvia Plath's vision is based. Having told us in "The Death of Myth-Making" (1959, uncollected) what our world would be like—dull and mechanized—ruled only by the ugly, limiting vision of Reason and Common Sense, she demonstrates in her poetry how the mythic, in its immemorial pre-Christian, even pre-

Graeco-Roman dress of birth and death, seasonal and vegetative changes, moon and sea phases, and archaic concept of beginnings and endings, is the only way to express the cosmos, is, in fact, the only way the cosmos can express itself.

Early uncollected poems, scattered through Aurelia Plath's edition of her daughter's *Letters Home,* help us trace the poet's developing vision. A fragment about an archaic garden-figure of a boy, significantly described as "eyeless," tells us that his function is to make us forget our own mortality because his frozen, impersonal youth is eternal. "Doom of Exiles" is a "Paradise Lost" in miniscule, an apprehension of "fallen man" in a world without hope of salvation. In "the ramshackle meadow" of "Temper of Time," the snake lurks as a shadow while "apples go/Bad to the core." In the south of France, sketching the walled garden of a nunnery from the outside, Sylvia bursts into tears. "I knew it was so lovely *inside,*" she writes her mother (italics mine). A Rousseau-painting poem, "Pursuit," is animated by "the terrible beauty of death." The panther who symbolizes male sexuality as well as the death-lust has an easy time of it, ravaging the land "Condemned by our ancestral fault"— the lost paradise again. But this poem goes farther. No wall, it says, can keep death out of a paradise already spoiled, penetrated by a power at once fatal and erotically attractive.

These early poems prefigure the twenty-eight or thirty "garden" poems in *The Colossus.* Among them "Snakecharmer" deserves attention, partly because it is one of the poems Ted Hughes found especially "chilling," and partly because it is a more complete realization of the anti-Edenic vision than is found in earlier works. Inspired by Rousseau's "La Charmeuse de Serpents," "Snakecharmer" reaches back into an archaic world. Turning the painting's female snakecharmer into a male demigod, perhaps a principle of ageless, archetypal function, the poet creates a cultic figure possessing the secrets of life and death, creation and destruction. What this snakecharmer pipes, has forever piped, and will eternally pipe, is a *private* Eden, expressive of his personal, whimsical vision. He is uninterested in plan or purpose, in gods or men. he pipes a lush, green, watery world into existence, then, as the mood takes him, out of existence again. By his piping he not only creates this world but peoples it—with snakes. It seems at first as if his garden and its occupants exist only so long as he wills them to be.

When the snakecharmer tires, however, his creatures become part of "the simple fabric,/ Of snake-warp, snake-weft"—in other words, there is an *idea* of snakes, almost in a Platonic sense, a "cloth" without whose prior existence no particular snakes could be given form. Soon, as the piper pipes, his snakes undergo change: they become "Leaf, become eyelid; snake-bodies, bough, breast/ Of tree and human." The piper as creater-destroyer is actually piping the human race. This is a pre-Genesis as well as an anti-Genesis concept of paradise and human origins: humanity is not driven forth into the human condition by a stern yet just and compassionate God who is also prepared to redeem His children. Humanity, in this "paradise," is a ripple on a green, watery surface, a flick of a serpent-tongue, an inhalation of a piper's breath. "Eden" is a painted backdrop, cool, silky, witty, amoral, perhaps a cosmic joke. Yet because of that "simple fabric," that pre-existent "idea" of snake-humanity, the vision is no literal "pipe-dream," and its "reality" is what gives the piece its "chilling" quality.

Like "Snakecharmer," the other garden poems of *The Colossus* present a garden that is off-center, strange, anti-Edenic. It may be a death-garden ("The Manor Garden"), or a garden combining death and the erotic ("The Beekeeper's Daughter"), or a garden without any potential for redemption ("The Burnt-out Spa"), or a garden in which the snake still burns like a jewel and has the last laugh, even though he has been slain by the yardman—a further symbolizing of humankind as incapable of overcoming the "snake," of keeping death out of paradise ("Medallion"). Perhaps it is a garden closed into a super-egg, attainable only through peering in—the great Alice-in-Wonderland daughter on her knees at the tiny window behind which lives and looks sadly back at her the eye of the dead father ("The Beekeeper's Daughter"). It may be made along the lines of a mechanical model ("The Stones"), or created by or for an "Absolutely alien/ Order" ("Mussel Hunter at Rock Harbor"). But in each case it is a frightening garden, one which traps without sheltering, rejects even when it entices.

Moreover, whoever controls the garden, however it is described, holds the secrets of origins and ends, of life and death. The presence, the persona, god or demi-god, human or partly human, differs markedly from one poem to the next, but the control is always absolute, and the meaning (or meaninglessness) of each garden is at this power's descretion. As divorced from control of their own destiny as the snake-descended humanity of "Snakecharmer," the "controlled" are set apart in every poem. Sometimes they are voiceless appendages, sometimes helpless pleaders, occasionally welcomers crying out in greeting. But they are always placed in irreconcilable polar opposition to the "controller," or power.

"The Surgeon at 2 A.M." (CW) [For the reader's convenience, and where the source is not otherwise clear from the context, editions of Sylvia Plath's works will be designated in parentheses in the text by symbols as follows: (A) *Ariel;* (C), *The Colossus* (American edition); (CW) *Crossing the Water;* (WT) *Winter Trees.*] is a rather different poem in this tradition. Again the central metaphor is the garden and its creator-lord. This time the garden is biological, within the body of a particular patient undergoing emergency surgery late at night, afterwards in a ward where many patients lie recovering. The surgeon, the poem's power and persona, first presents a garden in his patient on the table: it is internal, beneath the skin, containing the "bell-bloom" that is the heart, the "tubers and fruits/ Oozing their jammy substances," the "lung-tree." Snake-imagery is present, too, but is equated by the

surgeon with "orchids" and beauty. "I am so small," says the surgeon, "In comparison with these organs!" But the surgeon is not small in relation to his job: he is playing God. He does not pretend to create human beings: he does *re*-create them. His skill at rearranging internal parts brings life out of death and saves the bodies in which the souls, invisible, are anchored. Next, orderlies are "wheeling off" the patient and putting him to bed in the ward. The surgeon, tagging along yet remote and detached, continues to muse, admiring the results of his craft and seeing himself as divinely inspired "gardener." In a world where all is blue—light, linen, angelic atmosphere—he contemplates, not without considerable satisfaction, the drugged faces that "follow [him] like flowers." The garden-concept has expanded from a particular patient to a ward filled with patients, saved, reborn, turning in concert to the doctor-as-God.

The poem, however, is more complex. Death imagery is introduced at the end. The sleepers are described as lying in "gauze sarcophagi." Blue, hue of heaven, gives way to red, symbol of anguish, wounds, death, vividness, power. "I am the sun," the self-admiring surgeon comments. It is an Eden, this hospital, but an Eden man-made. The very purity (i.e., innocence) is artificial ("The white light . . . hygienic as heaven"). The presiding deity is a physician who saves bodies, not souls. Rebirth is physical, into a world of new teeth, a gall bladder extracted, a limb of flesh replaced by "clean, pink plastic." The soul, that reality which the surgeon posits while admitting he had never "seen" it, is not medicine's province. (Tonight, from the patient who has just undergone surgery, it has temporarily receded, like a ship's light, and stands watch.)

If it was the poet's intention to portray a compassionate figure in her surgeon, she did not succeed. He is detached, cool, admiring the body as "a Roman thing," a superb piece of engineering, and himself as its perfecter. A telling aspect of the poem is that neither on the operating table nor in the ward do patients have "faces" for the surgeon; on the ward, "Grey faces, shuttered by drugs," make an expressionless expanse of uniformity. In its own way, the garden-vision of this poem is fully as chilling as that of "Snakecharmer," its Eden as eerie and as limited. In this garden of the faceless, no seeds of redemption have been planted. The surgeon is pleased to accept responsibility for the total "garden," but not for the individual blooms. He is also attracted, actually, by human suffering, something he can control and manipulate at will without himself becoming a part of it—an attitude found in several Plath poems. The "Adams" and "Eves" of his "Eden" are described in such terms as "A lump of Chinese white/ With seven holes thumbed in" (a head), or "a pathological salami" (tissues awaiting analysis). There is a hint of medical-school student humor here: there is depersonalization, too. And there is an implied irony: why go through surgery only to wake to a world of tubes and plastic, or artificial replacements? Is this our destiny—even our *physical* destiny? Moreover, the surgeon who equates the "snakes" in his patients with "orchids" and splendor ignores the "snake" in his own soul. A surgeon is not meant to be a father-confessor, but this surgeon's pride is the real serpent in his hospital-garden. His is not the Eden of the caring God, but the Eden of a man who plays at being God, not humble before his powers but floating in exalted detachment ("I am the sun").

There is purpose and order in the surgeon's garden of life and death, but his control over it is startlingly akin to that of the snake-charmer. The surgeon is happy as he "worms" and "hacks"—he revels in lovely red blood. Perhaps he is the moral evocation of the snakecharmer; but for a mere hair which the centuries have drawn he might turn and "hack" his "flowers" to purposeless shreds. He does not, of course (although the theme still appears in "mad doctor" movies): the amorphous shimmer of the snakecharmer's world has been replaced by a clean, decent, ordered vision. But it is a paradise no less deathly in a nonphysical sense, because it is both man-made and man-redeemed. In a way, snakecharmer and surgeon inhabit the same mythic world. The snakecharmer belongs to the primal life before individual consciousness came into being—or became important: the surgeon is part of the Romantic or post-Renaissance world in which human individuality receives an emphasis little known in antiquity (although born with the birth of Christianity). But both personas are controlling figures alienated from their worlds—creators parted from their creatures. Both "garden poems" romanticize the alienated superfigure at the expense of faceless sufferers.

If we take the sequential publication of Sylvia Plath's poetry as a roughly accurate guide to the development of her thought and vision—we know, for instance, that the poems of *The Colossus* were completed by 1959, that the poems of *Crossing the Water* follow along in sequence more or less, and that the poems in *Winter Trees* are contemporaneous with those in *Ariel* and probably written during the last nine months or so of the poet's life— we note that garden imagery and metaphor grow less frequent. As "the garden" drops away, "the journey" takes its place—anything to get on board that train (ultimately the death-train), to find the "terminus" for which the "suitcases" are packed, to ride that horse, churn with those churning pistons. Such garden poems as do appear are more decadent. For instance, in "Leaving Early" (CW) the garden has moved indoors into a cold, artificial atmosphere charged with crackling hatred. A mysterious "lady" appears, "creator" of a cluttered, degenerate, messy apartment, and later is seen (an aspect quite possibly never intended by the poet) as pathetic victim of the poem's persona in a cosmos of lacerating tensions whose "Eden" is not only deathly but "lousy." The poem, first printed in August 1961, belongs to the same period as "I Am Vertical" (CW), an attempt to cancel the alienating barriers between self and nature, creature and creator. This poem's speaker longs for the death which will make her one with the garden, in this case the totality of Nature: it is restful, pleasant, but impersonal, and purity has no part in it. In "Among the Narcissi" (WT) we sense at once that the recuperating old man has not long to live as he hobbles among his "children," the white-paper flowers. But the garden's true response is not to the man but to an overpowering sense of cosmos or godhead—neutral, alien, fearsome. To it the flowers do obeisance; of it, frail old Percy remains innocently unaware.

It is not until the poem "Tulips" (A) that the metaphors of garden/Eden and purity/innocence cross one another for the first (and almost the last) time. This garden is an "excitable" mass of huge, intense, scarlet flowers, brought to the suffering speaker's hospital room where they oppress and disturb her. She does not simply *want* to die—that would be easy enough. She now feels that she is ready, *worthy,* by a process of preparation—"I am a nun now, I have never been so pure." But someone has brought her a red garden, forcing vivid life upon the peaceful death-whiteness of purified readiness. "Tulips" does not only set up a confrontation between life and death but between the faceless and the face-endowed as well, i.e., between the impersonal, nonindividuated, primal, and mythic, and the personal, individual, cared-for and caring, here-and-now. The speaker wishes to be effaced: the tulips will not let her. They not only force existence on the speaker but pain and self-awareness as well.

From this point on, the poems of *Ariel* pick up speed, merging into the imagery of the gallop, the piston, the mad journey, the agony. One last garden of death ("The Moon and the Yew Tree") presents a quiet graveyard of rest after despair, but is left behind like a way-station receding into distance while the themes of purity and redemption move harder and faster with the striking hooves, the turning wheels, the churn of pistons. "Ariel," "Getting There," "Fever 103°," "Totem," "Years," "Words"—all tell of cosmic trips without destination or even a clear point of origin, divorced from the human and the individualized. All the while the lusted-for goal (for which the self has been packed into its cosmic suitcase) is death—death in the form of sweeping-away of identity, melding into the primal/impersonal.

There are no more gardens (perhaps a touch or two of garden imagery). There are no creator-figures, either, only machines on the move, and one pitiable old queen-bee with "wings like torn shawls" who ascends, red and terrible, into the cosmos, taking the poet's self along with her, a lost and defeated identity in a world found more and more alien and alienating. In "Strings," there is a final hint, in the tradition of "Snakecharmer" or "The Surgeon," of a presiding, commanding, alien power who skips in from the mythic and skips out again, leaving a few tangible clues in the form of shed garments, symbolizing the concrete dropping away from the abstract and the continuing possibility of an eternal forming power in the cosmos. In "Edge," almost the last poem Sylvia Plath ever wrote, the themes of purity and the garden cross once again with a power and effect not found in "Tulips" as, in a series of marbleized images, "the woman," now "perfected" by death, folds her children back into herself and makes of her act a self-created garden, the "deathly paradise" come true.

Two things seem clear as we trace through the poetry of Sylvia Plath: she rejects both the primal and the eschatological paradise and seeks redemption elsewhere and in a different form; Edenic imagery and metaphor for the search for purity find different voices. The quest for the garden and the quest for the lost innocence are almost never the same quest. Sometimes her simpler nature poems hold out a kind of hope, resolution, promise, for example, "Black Rook in Rainy Weather" (CW). Certain mother-child poems hint at a similar transforming power: in "Child" (WT) the speaker comes closer to God in the clear beauty of her baby's eye than in any "paradise" (the glimpse is almost at once negated as she also sees in that same pure eye the reflection of the cosmos as "dark/ Ceiling without a star"). A deeply mythic distrust of gardens as sources of purity is voiced in "Three Women" (WT): the wife, safely delivered of a healthy son and concerned with how to shield him from the world's pain, asks "How long can I be a wall around my green property?" "Not very long," is the implied reply, and it brings us face to face with the metaphysical basis of Sylvia Plath's distrust of Eden, of the paradise of life.

Her trouble lies, not necessarily in the garden per se, but in the *wall* around it. Mythic or real, stylized like Pope's or roving into nature like Wordsworth's, gardens are designed to protect, to keep certain things in and other things out. Even though her poetry depicts a world of alienations—man from man, man from nature, man from God (perhaps mother and child form the one abiding exception)—alienation is what Sylvia Plath cries out against most in her poetry. If we live in a garden, or seek one as a perfect spot, we are always closed in *with* something or *from* something. If evil has got in, like the tiger in Rousseau's paintings, we are trapped with it: if we are barred from the garden, on the outside, there is no way back in, no way to find the lost innocence. Paradise, ultimately, is deathly for Sylvia Plath, not because it is a source of death but because it promises or threatens to prevent death. Like that mysterious "birthday present" always "waiting," it will not "let down the veil," it keeps its wall up. As under the "bell jar" where one breathes only one's own self-poisoning air, one is trapped in and by a garden, or barred from it, unable to cope with one's sins. This is why many Plath poems express a world without help, refuge, salvation, redemption. For many, paradise is bliss with its confining order: for Sylvia Plath it was not. In one sense a daughter of Eve, the poet in a deeper sense is closer to Persephone who, as Milton wrote in effect, while gathering flowers became herself the flower gathered. Ravishment by Dis was the price Persephone paid for her aimless, primal flowerpicking in which, as John Armstrong writes in *The Paradise Myth*, the girl surrenders to "the imperative need to counteract the oppressiveness of the idyllic confine. . . ."

A price has to be paid for the refusal of the garden's walls. In Sylvia Plath's poems we see the same price

being paid over and over as her poetic voices seek yearned-for purity outside the "idyllic confine." Her personas continually express the cosmology of aliens in the world who are at the same time muffled and inaccessible behind the garden wall. Her poems perpetually ask Alan Watts's questions: How far out can I get? How lost without being utterly lost? No sure answer is given, but there is a rejection of all experiences which may be likened to what the poet called a "shut box." The garden as first-and-final home is shunned. So is the body, another form of trap. In "Getting There" (A), the poet writes, "And I, stepping from this skin/ Of old bandages . . . old faces. . . ." In "Apprehensions" (WT) it is the mind that is the prison, and in "Event" (WT) marriage is seen as a crippling confinement, turning into torment the bed once experienced as "paradise." "Last Words" (CW) envisions a "box" as a happy world, pretty sarcophagus with "a face on it," and one is tempted to see this as a clinging to the individual personality, to walls that protect selfhood—until one remembers that in the archaic, non-individuated world, a magical use was made of objects but not of the body or the personality.

It is an unendurable paradox: Sylvia Plath, who could not tolerate the wall, the constriction, the garden, also felt lost and alien in the expansion of the unconfined universe. Does this mean that death was to her the ultimate expansion, therefore the ultimate restriction—the last, walled, confining garden? One begins to suspect that, despite the frantic need for freedom, motion, and wildness, this was so. The poet always sought purification, redemption in the dynamic, the active; and yet the purifying act, in her poems as in her life, took place in enclosures: the love of the dead father in the sugar-egg; the fruition of motherhood in the dark, closed, blooming womb; death in the cellar-ledge of her mother's basement; death, finally, in the "shut box" of the gas oven, as if her myths of origins and ends were finally translated into realities.

The origin of humanity's sense of being lost and alienated has been well defined by Alan Watts in his *Beyond Theology: The Art of Godsmanship:*

> [Man] is kicked out of Paradise, because Paradise is having a connection—roots in the garden, stem from the branch, current to the light. To be unaware of the connection is to have one's heart in the wrong place—far out in the fruit instead of within, in the tree. It is to feel that one's basic self is isolated within the body's envelope of skin, forgetting that the self is the whole circulating current from which embodiments come and go . . . endless variations upon one theme.

But Sylvia Plath's poems tell us that life in alienation, in perpetual polar tension with "other," is not worth it, and that wall-less life cosmically, mythically blended with the universe is simply not possible. The poet longs to creep back, not into the conventional womb, but into the archaic world of feeling, governed not by morality or stern justice and duty but by an indifferent, amorphous, mysteriously attractive, destructive/life-giving, goddesslike power which reveals no secrets as to our origins and makes no promises as to our ends. But surrender to this deathly paradise even as an act of the imagination gives small comfort. The death-garden may not judge, neither does it save. It may promise rebirth, but not of the individual consciousness. And it appears to be totally without love.

When the garden poems with their controlling figures have faded from her work, one realizes that, because of the sheer number and variety of their personas—sacred or secular, human or daemonic, male or female—no one accepted figure, power, or control exists. Even the moon, possibly the greatest single deity-figure, only occasionally fulfills the controlling function, and her presence, too, is always charged with ambiguity since, like those dark mother-goddesses of primal times, she presents a fearsome combination of the destructive and the maternal. It begins to appear as if setting in motion a world and its inhabitants and ordering its meaning and their end is a game at which any number may play. It comes as no surprise when Sylvia Plath, no longer speaking through some persona but in a voice all too patently and painfully her own, decides to undertake the task herself.

Therefore in "Edge," written a day or so before her death, she creates her own, new myth. In the only other poem except "Tulips" in which images of purity cross those of the garden, the persona folds in upon herself and into herself (taking her children with her) and completes rites of purification which paradoxically convert self and children into a sealed garden, where neither hope, life, nor redress bloom and flourish, yet where a strange "perfection" waits. "Edge" states that the only real "journey" is a moveless, static in-folding; the only garden the last, not the lost one. The marbleized Greek necessity of the poem's vision refuses to affirm the infinite value of human life or the existence of the divine and the transforming in the universe. "Edge" does away with the alien power of "other," but at a terrible cost. The primal and/or eschatological meaning of "garden" is denied, and the poetic persona *becomes* the garden, self-created. Self is the wall, the idol and monument, the creator, end, and aim of this garden. In its concept of the ultimate "home," "Edge" offers us the most "chilling" definition of "the deathly paradise," with the self as controlling deity, not from *hubris* but from the pathos of utter despair, in a world which can offer no place "to get to."

Floyd C. Watkins

SOURCE: "'The Body of This Death' in Robert Penn Warren's Later Poems," in *The Kenyon Review,* Vol. 10, No. 4, Fall, 1988, pp. 31-41.

[*In the following essay, Watkins evaluates Warren's vacillation between skepticism and a religious view of mortality in his last two collections of poetry,* Rumor Verified *and* New and Selected Poems.]

Many varieties of religious experience are everywhere present in the characters, the meditations, and the fiction and poetry of Robert Penn Warren. No novel is more permeated by the subject, perhaps, than *All the King's Men.* Jack Burden alone ranges from an unalleviated determinism which views God Himself as the Great Twitch (derived from the image of a hitchhiker's uncontrollable tic in his face) to some kind of belief which accepts in its own way the Scholarly Attorney's statement about the glory of God. It would be impossible to determine for long whether Warren's meditations search more for a belief in the self or for a belief in God. Once I put the question as bluntly as I could to Warren and asked, "Red, what is your belief about God?" He replied directly that he cannot believe but that he has a great yearning. It is almost as if he wears a collar tugged at with as much power as that in George Herbert's poem but with no definable source of the pull and no destination toward which Warren and the personae may be pulled.

In a paragraph in a letter to me nearly ten years ago Warren wrote of his mighty struggles with a variety of literary efforts—so much to be done and so little time to do it, each day or over the long haul. With an abrupt change of subject, apparently, in the last sentence he asked me to pray for his soul. At first I took the request as strictly and literally religious, and I did try to carry out his request in my own also uncertain way.

Years later I see that there were unknown quantities of various elements mixed up in that request: something of a mere exclamation, no doubt; some religious element also, no doubt; some unstated allusion to the artistic as well as the spiritual soul; a goodly degree of ambivalence which I had at first failed to note. The remark can range in its seriousness from a mere aside to the overwhelming subject of meditation, especially in Warren's later years. The poems between that old time of my simple question and Warren's brief answer have been like calderas of molten rock shot through by pressured jets of other rocks and opinions. The lines of force or belief have changed with almost every poem, so to speak, but it may be that in *Rumor Verified* (the last single volume of new poems)[1] and in *New and Selected Poems*[2] Warren has achieved some of his spiritual desires, with or without modifying the intensity of his yearnings.

The Italian epigraph of Warren's last separate volume of poems, *Rumor Verified,* derives from the *Inferno* of Dante's *Divine Comedy.* A translation records how Dante and his companion, Virgil,

> saw some of
> The beautiful things that Heaven bears; and
> Thence we issued forth to see again the stars.[3]

Stars or *stelle* in Italian—a "sweet and hopeful word" according to the translator—appears in the final sentence of each of the three divisions of the *Comedy.* For Warren the epigraph is accordingly at least partly happy. By 1980 Warren, the central persona of his lyrical poems, is coming out of hell to see the stars and "some of the beautiful things that Heaven bears. . . . " The late poems seem to progress toward acceptance and possible belief in a divine being after skepticism and yearning for faith in earlier poems. The title poem of the volume asks "what can you do?" and answers:

> Perhaps pray to God for strength to face the
>   verification
> That you are simply a man, with a man's dead
>   reckoning, nothing more.
> (Rumor Verified, p. 30)

Used by a ship in a fog, dead reckoning steers for a goal without the benefit of astronomical observations, and here it implies that the poet may hope or yearn without the assistance of heavenly guidelines which may exist even though they are obscured in this part of the voyage.

In contrast, three short epigraphs to the previous volume, *Being Here*, show a desire for "Absolute Time," a thirst for rather than knowledge of "the power . . . of time" and God striving "to define His own Being." Not one of the ten collections of poems published before *Rumor Verified* focuses on the fundamental questions of death, time, and eternity. The epigraph of *Altitudes and Extensions* in Warren's *New and Selected Poems,* is also taken from a Christian writer. In the *Confessions* (Book IV, Chapter XII) Saint Augustine asks, "Will ye not now after that life is descended down to you, will not you ascend up to it and live?" The descent of life is a reference to Christ's Incarnation, and the ascent is that of the soul up to the spirituality of Christ. The proportions of metaphor and of faith vary considerably from one poem to another. If Warren's views have not changed, the quotation is either strictly ethical or psychological—that is, not religious at all. Yet the poems, the epigraph, and Warren's yearnings struggle for or even attain a belief in divinity. The epigraph pleads without qualification. Always before this Warren's characters and personae in his fiction and poetry (except for the saints and the fanatics) vacillated between belief and doubt. "Lord, I believe," says the father of a son healed by Christ: "help thou mine unbelief" (Mark 9:24, the Bible, King James Version).

Given mortality, no human being ever attains absolute belief without some wavering. Two of Warren's poetic predecessors (Robert Frost and Emily Dickinson) shifted back and forth between nearly absolute faith and deep skepticism. A similar vacillation appears in nearly all of Warren's late lyrics. From his early days as a Fugitive until *Promises* (1957), his poems were less religious, more worldly. Like the falling leaves in Allen Tate's "Ode to the Confederate Dead," Warren's earlier poems "sought the rumour of mortality"; his latest poems, however, offer rumors and intimations of immortality. If the hope of the epigraphs in the last two published volumes is fulfilled, Warren's great yearning for a belief in God is at least partially attained. The poems may be meditations on the strong possibilities of immortality and God.

The very titles of the poems before World War II indicate preoccupations with worldly conditions and emotions, psychology, and the troubles of a young poet who believes in no theologies and no beliefs, who has miles to go before he begins to ponder the problems of death and immortality. Titles like "Terror," "Pursuit," "Crime," "History," and "Bearded Oaks" suggest flight from horror rather than seeking for belief. Some titles of late poems present a contrast: "Mortal Light," "Immortality over the Dakotas," "Hope," "Doubleness in Time." Other titles suggest the old fears of mortality and of oblivion. The remarkable thing is not only the changes and development of subject, but also the high quality of poetry regardless of age and life or death.

From *Night Rider* (1939) to *A Place to Come To* (1977), from the first to the last, Warren's fiction deals with violent episodes and inner struggles, sometimes with the emphasis mainly on one, as in the violence of *Wilderness;* sometimes on another, as in the issues of *At Heaven's Gate* and *The Cave;* always to some degree on both, as in *All the King's Men.* Excluding the long narrative and historical poems, the development of the poetry is more consistent and definable. He began with metaphysical lyrics, changed to a mingling of narrative and lyric from the early 1950s until the late 1970s, and then became much more consistently meditative in the later years.

Clear-minded as his older poetry is, its content has obviously grown old and thoughtful along with the poet. Many details of early life have been forgotten; the images of childhood have vanished (*Rumor Verified* 53); life in the past seems to be something like the image of a shed snakeskin (*Rumor* 53); the poet does not see some images face to face but, like the figure of Christ on the Journey to Emmaus in *The Waste Land,* "just beyond the corner of the eye" (*Rumor* 63); time and space have changed (*Rumor* 21); and he wonders whether "all wisdom [is] learned too late" (*Rumor* 21). Perhaps no two poems by Warren illustrate more effectively the change in the workings of the poet's mind as it deals with the unknown than "Dragon Country: To Jacob Boehme" (*Promises: Poems,* 1957)[4] and "The Corner of the Eye" (*Rumor Verified,* 1981). In the early poem the dragon comes to the state of Kentucky and leaves a great turd steaming in a misty field on a frosty morning. He tears up Jack Simms's hog pen and reduces it to a "bloody mire," rips mules from the trace chains of a wagon and kills the teamster, leaves a "track of disrepair," and then vanishes. Men disappear, and only Jebb Johnson's boot with some part of the leg inside is left of him. Physical and supernatural as well, the dragon is a mighty presence to strike fear and prayer into the hearts of men. The poem in images and spirit is particularly Southern, and it may suggest that in the country, the region, the South, it may be more possible to believe in evil and the possibility of good.

In later poems like "The Corner of the Eye," spirits, good or evil, are not nearly so corporeal and carnal as the dragon. This poem occurs in a state of mind, whether in a blacksmith shop or New York City, rather than in the state of Kentucky. More vague than the dragon, the subject and spirit of the poem exist truly only in the peripheral vision

> while the full moon,
>
> Phthisic and wan, above the East River, presides
> Over the last fragment of history which is
>
> Our lives.
>
> *(Rumor Verified,* p. 63)

This is one kind of verification of rumor. Death is verified more than immortality, but in the volume there is some of both. The tall tale and the folklore of "Dragon Country" do not appear in the later poem, and the unseen and unknown thing at the "corner of the eye," psychological, poetic, or even religious, "has stalked you all day, or years, breath rarely heard, fangs dripping" ("The Corner of the Eye"). And now, any moment, great hindquarters may hunch, ready to vanish or spring on the victim. Is it a dragon, or God, or "*merely* [emphasis mine] a poem, after all?"

Some poems rumor the finality of death with no hint even of immortality—almost in defiance of the hopeful epigraph. Some are ambivalent. Stanzas on the death of the father and on a friend drowning under "time's windless wash" culminate in the cast-off skin of an old garter snake. Possibly

> this bright emptiness
>
> Is all your own life may be—or will be—when,
>
> After the fable of summer,
>
> (that is, the fiction of a full life—)
>
> a lithe sinuosity
>
> Slips down to curl in some dark, wintry hole, with
>   no dream.
>   ("Questions You Must Learn to Live Past,"
>   *Rumor Verified,* p. 54)

That dark wintry hole without even a dream of life seems at first to be the completely black oblivion of the grave after the living being has cast away forever the "bright emptiness" of the snakeskin, or mortality. But the darkness of the hole may suggest merely the unknown, hibernation before awakening, sleep with no dream instead of nothingness of death, because it is life—"a lithe sinuosity"—which of its own volition moves ("slips down") into the hole to await in darkness perhaps even the resurrection of the body. Read a poem one way, look again out of the corner of the eye, read it again, and then read it the opposite way. Both ways are there.

That same ambivalence is at the center of one of Warren's best poems in *Rumor Verified.* The ambiguity of the title of the volume appears again forcefully in the title of the poem *"Blessèd Accident." Blessèd* is a word

of God used by one with a trust in God; *accident* is a word utterly without God or without any scheme or plan of any kind in the universe; and it is a word used by a person who cannot believe in anything systematic, not even the determinism of the naturalists. No spirit, that is to say, exists to make a determination, even with malignity. The poem begins when the persona is "relatively young"—in the quoted words of the beginning of Dante's Inferno, *"Nel mezzo del camin"*—in the middle of the poem, in the middle of the journey or middle of life. Looking back on the first part of the journey, you see storm, wreckage, sunlight, heavy burdens, the injuries of a hard journey, and other uncertainties and adversities. Turning away from a vista on a hilltop, the speaker asks whether you have found yourself in bed, and

> have you
> Grasped out and found the hand, clasped it, and
>   lain . . . ,
>
> felt
>
> Slow tears swell, like bursting buds of April, in
> Your eyes, your heart, and felt breath stop before
>
> That possibility, doomful, of joy, and the awful
>   illogic of
> The tremor, the tremble of God's palsied hand
>   shaking
>
> The dice-cup? Ah, blessèd accident!
>   *(Rumor Verified,* p. 12)

In this poem there is human love in the clasped hand, the tears, the buds of spring, joy. For once, it looks as if the mood is altogether of joy without the terror of disbelief or the doubt of yearning. It is, indeed, "blessèd." Then the accident lies in the phenomenon of God, as supernatural as that old folkish but powerful dragon in *Promises* long before. But God has the tremors, trembles, the shakes from palsy. His is the hand, nevertheless, which is shaking the dice-cup—not the limb or claw of some malevolent creature or of an omnipotent and benevolent divinity. The "blessèd accident" with which the poem ends may be that the cup is in God's hand. That may be the luck from the time of creation when the eternal crap game began, or, in another time, it may be the ultimate end, the roll and turn of the dice. The dice, certainly loaded (they are in the hand of God, though he is weak), are nevertheless controlled, or fixed, favorably. The roll is a good one, I think, a winner, a seven rather than a crap out or a failure to make the point in gambling. It is a rough world, what with the palsy and all the weakness, but there is a decision, there is more than a yearning, and because God's hand holds the dice the accident is "blessèd." Is this a weak faith at last, or must we wait for another poem to find a different answer and the old yearning? Some rumor is verified, but the nature of the verification is still somewhat uncertain.

The tremendous increase of Warren's interest in the questions of life and death which are beyond answering and almost beyond pondering is in a strange—if not inexplicable—way an indication that there has been a change in his yearning for religious belief, an increase, perhaps, in his faith—an increase which may find expression only in poetry, and which even in poetry he may not certainly know or be altogether aware of. The great number of poems about belief, doubt, yearning, possibility, uncertainty, hope, and so forth show a new spiritual status and more belief of some kind. Warren's later poems suggest what a layperson, an amateur appreciator of his poetry, once remarked: "A man who writes poems like that believes in God somehow whether he knows it or not." The speculations about mortality and other possibilities deal with birth, life, death, immortality, and the Bible. In "The Whole Question" Warren meditates on the change from whatever occurs before life to what life is itself,

> If it can be said that you dreamed anything
> Before what's called a hand slapped blazing
>   breath
> Into you, snatched your dream's lulling nothing-
> ness into what Paul called the body of this death.

(New and Selected Poems, 1923-1985, p. 54)

In the biblical passage which Warren quotes here (Romans 7:24) there is the hope of some kind of deliverance from the life that comes after birth and from death itself. Paul hopes, and Warren's omission of the hope may indicate a less optimistic view but possibility nevertheless. Paul's entire question of which Warren quoted only a fragment is "Who shall deliver me from the body of this death?" (Romans 7:24)

The ultimate in doubt and hope comes when Warren discusses in "The Place" a time of "unbounded loneliness":

>   This
> Is the hour of the self's uncertainty
> Of self. This is the hour when
> Prayer might be a possibility, if
> It were.

(New and Selected Poems, 1923-1985, p. 60)

Well, is it? The thought has at least crossed the mind and stayed there until he put it in the line of the poem. And that may be a beginning, as uncertain as these things of faith are.

In much of his poetry Warren writes in abstractions, as he does here, but on other occasions his images are hard enough to dull the finest steel for swords or fleshy enough to bleed with a small scratch. "The Place" ends with a stanza almost this concrete—certainly as sensuous as a shadow or light—about this life, the wait for death, eternity—at least as everlasting as the stars—and the *knowledge* (note the certainty of the word in the quotation)—of whatever is beyond all knowing:

> You think of the possibility of lying on stone,
> Among fern fronds, and waiting
> For the shadow to find you.

> The stars would not be astonished
> To catch a glimpse of the form through interstices
> Of leaves now black as enameled tin. Nothing
>   astounds the stars.
> They have long lived. And you are not the first
> To come to such a place seeking the most difficult
>   knowledge.

(New and Selected Poems, 1923-1985, p. 61)

The end of man is to know, and beyond all the questions, "difficult" as they are, there may be knowledge.

Whether Warren is writing about a historical person or an event or a crime, meaning is almost always associated with a particular place, and great numbers of his characters in fiction and in poetry make journeys back to the places of their childhood or of wondrous or monstrous events in their lives in search of meaning. For this reason Billie Potts comes home ("The Ballad of Billie Potts"), Jeremiah Beaumont tries to return to face the consequences of his crime *(World Enough and Time),* and the persona (Warren) and his father go to the plantation of Lilburn and Isham Lewis where these nephews of Thomas Jefferson chopped to pieces a living slave on a meat block *(Brother to Dragons).* The journeys in Warren's last two volumes of poetry are usually to lonely places of natural settings by streams or field or forest. They are returns to the places of the most profound meditations of the beginnings and endings of Warren's poetic and spiritual life. "Why Boy Came to Lonely Place" may or may not be a return to the same spot as that in "The Place." He asks himself whether he had clambered "these miles of distance / Only to quiver now in identity." Spiritually, in this poem the search is much more significant than the discovery of meaning which results. He is not himself by virtue of creation and God, but "by luck, disaster, or chance. . . . " First he went to the place at age thirteen, "ignorant, lost in the world" *(New and Selected Poems, 1923-1985,* p. 56). At the time of the meditations involved in the writing of the poem he speaks "the name they gave you" in a passage reminiscent of Billie Potts's changing his name, loss of his identity, and search for a new and then the old identity in Warren's first long poem.

"Why Boy Came to Lonely Place," like so many other late lyrics by Warren, turns on the subject of the life remaining before death. To know who and what he is, personally and spiritually, he says his name—almost like an American Indian with a secret name which reveals an identity known only to the person and his parents: "You say the name they gave you. That's all you are." Then he attempts to know himself mortally and physically by moving his fingers down his face. What he is, he will be only during his mortality on this earth. So the person wonders how many more years he will live, "how many years you'll be what you are." But he asks what that is and answers, "To find out you came to this lonely place." It is a place of his childhood. In time, it is the last short interval before death, and the main implication, the unstated question or conclusion of the poem, is that he will be something different after the years of life and death. But this poem—one of the most skeptical of all the late poems—finds no better answer about what the persona will be after death than is known about what he is before.

Poem after poem and image after image in Warren's last poems seem to represent efforts either to reach the ultimate in doubt or to go to the edge of immortality for a glimpse over the edge into whatever is next—death, nothingness, speculation, faith, or even an unknowable afterlife itself. The title of the second poem in Warren's last volume describes just that line between earthly being and the vanishing into nothingness or the seam that stitches together mortality and the existing unknown, "Mortal Limit." A hawk rides in the "updraft in the sunset over Wyoming" and becomes a "black speck" hanging beyond an indeterminable height. Perhaps its gold eyes will see "New ranges rise to mark a last scrawl of light" (*New and Selected Poems, 1923-1985*, p. 6). And then, at the moment of finality or definition, the poem suggests lines from the ending of "The Ballad of Billie Potts," Warren's first long poem:

> For the beginning is death and the end may be
> 　　life,
> For the beginning was definition and the end may
> 　　be definition,
> And our innocence needs, perhaps new
> 　　definition. . . .

> *(Selected Poems: 1923,* p. 17)

After crime and flight Billie Potts sought to return home; death and whatever may come afterward, whatever definition, is the ultimate home for both the hawk and for Billie:

> Beyond what range will gold eyes see
> New ranges rise to mark a last source of light?
>
> Or having tasted that atmosphere's thinness, does
> 　　it
> Hang motionless in dying vision before
> It knows it will accept the mortal limit,
> And swing into the great circular downwardness
> 　　that will restore
> The breath of earth? Of rock? Of rot? Of other
> 　　such
> Items, and the darkness of whatever dream we
> 　　clutch?

> *(New and Selected Poems, 1923-1985,* p. 6)

All we may clutch here is the dream and the dream is darkness, but darkness is the unknown; whether or not it is oblivion and nothingness, it is not given to us to know in this "mortal limit." Thus doubt is a necessity, and faith is a hope if not a possibility. That is the terrible limit of mortality.

The very next poem in the volume repeats the theme in an altogether different figure. The persona, in a plane over the Dakotas, presses his brow "at the two-inch-thick plane-window glass" to look at darkness he

can't get in.
It's as though you were at last immortal.

Then the poet has a vision of a man far below

> 　　down there, with collar up on the dirty
> 　　　　sheepskin,
> Snow on red hunter's cap, earflaps down.
> Chores done. But he just can't bring himself to go
> 　　in.
> The doctor's just said he won't last till another
> 　　winter.

Seeing his wife sitting before a dying fire inside,

> 　　he can't go in.
> He knows that if he did he might let something
> 　　slip.
> He couldn't stand that. So stares at the blackness
> 　　of sky.
> Stares at lights, green and red, that dread the dark
> 　　of your immortality.

> ("Immortality over the Dakotas," *New and
> Selected Poems, 1923-1985,* p. 7)

The blackness, the lights, the dark, immortality—all gather into a plural and complex, enigmatic oxymoron of contradictions that can be only the puzzle at the center of the existence of the soul—the simultaneous faith and doubt at which Warren has arrived in these last poems. The yearning has simultaneously intensified and arrived at more certainty. The haunting question (the basis of whatever faith may be possible) is what the hunter, the persona-poet in the airplane, and the other personae of these poems, including that stonelike figure of Pharaoh arrives at with

> Unblinking gaze across
> Sands endless.
>
> If we can think of timelessness, does it exist?

> ("Old Dog Dead," *New and Selected Poems,
> 1923-1985,* p. 20)

Old as it is, the statue of Pharaoh is still in time. Remotely, perhaps, Warren is echoing the philosophical proof of mortal existence which ended, at least for a moment, in Descartes's "Cogito, ergo sum," or "I think, therefore I exist." If that principle did work about mortal matters, Warren would seem to ask, will it also work for immortality? This time it is a question rather than a conclusion. Finitely, "I think; therefore I am." In infinity, if I think of immortality, does it exist? Who is to say yes, Warren has pondered all these years, but now he seems to have come at least to the point where he can say, "Who is to say not?" The next stanza, intentionally or not, echoes the Christian hymn in which the worshiper comes to the garden alone to be with God.

> 　　Tell me,
> Is there a garden where
> The petal, dew-kissed, withereth not?

> ("In the Garden")

One of Warren's last poems, "First Moment of Autumn Recognized," is a description of the next world, immortality, paradise, in images as knowable to the five senses as the Garden of Eden is to the most unwavering fundamentalist or creationist. It has all the perfection and beauty of the Garden before the Fall of man, presumably a spirituality not possible for man after the Fall itself, therefore presumably a poem on a subject matter as undiscernible to a mere fallen mortal as the Garden in Genesis, the first-created Adam and Eve in Genesis, and Paradise in the *Divine Comedy:*

> Hills haven the last cloud. However white. From
>   brightest blue
> Spills glitter of afternoon, more champagne than
>   ever
> Summer. Bubble and sparkle burst in
> Tang, taste, tangle, tingle, delicious
> On tongue of spirit, joyful in eye-beam. We know
> This to be no mere moment, however brief,
> However blessed, for
> Moment means time, and this is no time,
> Only the dream, untimed, between
> Season and season. Let the leaf, gold, of birch,
> Of beech, forever hang, not vegetable matter
>   mortal, but
> In no whatsoever breath of
> Air. No-embedded in
> Perfection of crystal, purer
> Than air. You, embedded too in
> Crystal, stand, your being perfected
> At last, in the instant itself which is unbreathing.
>   (*New and Selected Poems, 1923-1985,* p. 62)

To believe this passage and to accept it both as a figure and a statement of the certainty of knowledge might be even the sin of hubris, of belief in a knowledge that is not only unlimited but even forbidden, the sin of equality with the angels or with God himself. Doubter that he has been, Warren could never accept that. So he ends the poem with a shift to the old doubt and vacillation:

> Can you feel breath brush your damp
> Lips? How can you know?

Well, to return to life, you don't. But for a moment Warren seems to have looked on Paradise itself. Another poem ends with the promise of an unknown beyond sufferings of an angry life. "If Snakes Were Blue" speculates on life and death and whatever else there may be, and it ends with some kind of vision:

> In the distance lift peaks
> Of glittering white above the wrath-torn land.
>   (*New and Selected Poems, 1923-1985,* p. 65)

Warren confronts this subject meaningfully in his introduction to Ernest Hemingway's *A Farewell to Arms,* a work filled with religious characters and questions and problems even when the hero and some others do not attain a meaningful faith. The milieu of the lost generation, World War I, the moral and religious issues of the time and the book excruciatingly reflect twentieth-century and modern variations of the troubles of mankind in any age since the Fall. In defining the spiritual conditions of the characters of *A Farewell to Arms,* Warren suggests the world of his own fiction and poetry:

> *A Farewell to Arms* is a love story. It is a compelling story at the merely personal level, but it is much more compelling and significant when we see the figures of the lovers silhouetted against the flame-streaked blackness of war, of a collapsing world, of nada. For there is a story behind the love story. That story is the quest for meaning and certitude in a world that seems to offer nothing of the sort. It is, in a sense, a religious book; if it does not offer a religious solution it is nevertheless conditioned by the religious problem.[5]

Similarly, Warren's own works and his poems are "conditioned by the religious problem," but even more extensively and extravagantly, I think, than Hemingway's. More also than Faulkner's. More than the works of any unbelieving writer of importance that I know in the twentieth century. There are great varieties of change, figures, and beliefs and disbeliefs in all the corpus of Warren's works. In the last two volumes of poetry there is more concern with religion than ever before. The poems are religious poetry even more than *A Farewell to Arms* is a religious book. At times they become poems of faith, in which Warren is more than a mere yearner for belief. I am not at all sure but what that spontaneous reaction from the little old lady in Sunday School contained a great deal of truth: Warren (at times) believes in God whether he knows it or not.

NOTES

[1] Robert Penn Warren, *Rumor Verified* (New York: Random House, 1981).

[2] Robert Penn Warren, *New and Selected Poems, 1923-1985* (New York: Random House, 1985).

[3] Dante Alighieri, "Inferno," *The Divine Comedy,* trans. Charles S. Singleton (Princeton: Bollingen Series, LXXX, 1970), p. 369.

[4] Robert Penn Warren, *Promises: Poems 1954-1956* (New York: Random House, 1957).

[5] Robert Penn Warren, Introduction to *A Farewell to Arms,* by Ernest Hemingway (New York: Scribner's, 1953), pp. xxvii-xxviii.

DRAMA

Philip M. Armato

SOURCE: "Tennessee William's Meditations on Life and Death in 'Suddenly Last Summer', 'The Night of the Iguana' , and 'The Milk Train Doesn't Stop Here Anymore," in *Tennessee Williams: A Tribute,* edited by Jac Tharpe, University Press of Mississippi, 1977, pp. 558-570.

[*In the following essay, Armato studies Williams's portrayal of human perceptions of death in his dramas, concluding that "underneath the guise of southern decadence, Tennessee Williams practices the art of a decidedly Christian playwright.*]

In Tennessee Williams' autobiography, the chapter dealing with his life in the sixties might well be entitled "The Inferno." His recent description of these years is chilling. Before publication of *Memoirs* he had told Rex Reed that they culminated in a "protracted death wish that lasted roughly from 1963 until my release from the psychiatric hospital [1969] where I came within a hairbreadth of death." Even before these most difficult years of spiritual and physical suffering, *death,* Williams admits in the same interview, had been an "excessively recurring theme" in his plays. His preoccupation with mortality is certainly understandable to those who are familiar with his biography. He has suffered from childhood diphtheria, numerous nervous breakdowns, two heart attacks, a tumor, prolonged bouts with alcohol/drugs and the untimely death of his personal secretary Frank Merlo from lung cancer in 1963.

Williams is the only American playwright who has regularly grappled with the problem of death. The three plays under consideration here, written during Williams' "Inferno" period, are peopled with the dying and with memories of the already dead: *Suddenly Last Summer,* 1958 (Sebastian Venable), *The Night of the Iguana,* 1961 (Frank Faulk and Jonathan Coffin called "Nonno"), *The Milk Train Doesn't Stop Here Anymore,* 1963 (Alex, Harlon Goforth, Sally Ferguson, Madelyn's mother, an unnamed suicide and, of course, Sissy Goforth). These plays can be seen as the spiritual documents of one poet's quest for a solution to the problems created by man's awareness of the inevitability of death. It is to Williams' credit that he has not merely "survived" his years of pronounced physical and spiritual crises. During this time of most difficult circumstances, he has created plays which attempt to see death steadily and see it whole.

In *Suddenly Last Summer,* Williams presents two diametrically opposed ways of looking at death, the Christian and the existential. Sebastian Venable embodies the existential vision of death while the rival Christian view is expressed by the life of Venable's namesake, Saint Sebastian. Here, Williams uses juxtaposition to develop his first meditation on death. The life of the modern, profane man Sebastian Venable is contrasted with that of the ancient, saintly man St. Sebastian.

Sebastian Venable is despairing modern man. Mrs. Venable's description of her son's two visits to the Encantada islands reveals his grimly existential view of life. Sebastian's fascination stemmed from Melville's description of these islands as cinder heaps "looking much as the world at large might look—after a last conflagration." Sebastian, like his fellow poet Melville, sees the islands as symbols of a greater reality. For him, they come to represent the existential void, the sterility of

existence. Instead of turning away from the void Sebastian, like Camus' young poet-emperor Caligula, decides to confront it. He persuades his mother to tour the Encantadas with him.

During his first tour, Sebastian discovered signs of life in the midst of the island's desertlike terrain. He saw sea turtles depositing their eggs on the beach. Surely the turtles are a hopeful sign; life can thrive in the midst of sterility. He plans to return when the eggs are ready to be hatched. On his return, Venable witnesses a savage spectacle. The newly hatched sea turtles are slaughtered by carnivorous birds as they desperately attempt to escape into the sea. Mrs. Venable says her son was fascinated by this brutal display. He spent the whole day in the ship's rigging, under the blazing tropical sun, gripped by the spectacle on the beach.

However, when Sebastian climbs down from the rigging and announces to his startled mother that he has seen God on the beach, it becomes apparent that he is interested in the brutality only insofar as it symbolizes a larger truth. This "truth" is inextricably bound to his sarcastic reference to divinity. God, Sebastian implies, presides over a sterile, decimated world in which helpless creatures (the baby sea turtles, man) are brutalized by death (the carnivorous sea birds). That other young poet, Camus' Caligula, puts it succinctly: "Men die, and they are not happy." Venable's confrontation with the starkest facts of existence has a harrowing effect upon him. The "sickness unto death" which is caused by despair over the human condition finds its literal representation in the tropical fever-delirium that Sebastian contracts while watching the slaughter. Although he is nursed back to physical health by his mother, his continuing spiritual malaise is emphasized by his wish to enter a Buddhist monastery where meditation might cure him of despair.

"If there is no God, everything is permitted," argues Ivan Karamazov. Sebastian Venable might very well add the corollary: "If God exists but he is cruel, cruelty is the principle of order in the universe and, therefore, should not necessarily be shunned by man." Sebastian's conduct after the Encantada episode is that of a man so overwhelmed by evil/death that life and humanistic values no longer hold any ultimate meaning for him. The last days of Sebastian Venable, as sketched by his cousin and traveling companion Catharine Holly, are marked by frustration, confusion, and cruelty. Catharine reports that Sebastian was restless and moved fitfully from place to place, he could no longer concentrate on his poetry, he used Catharine to procure young boys for him, he took advantage of their poverty by paying them for performing indecencies and in moments of anger scornfully called them "beggars."

Sebastian's understanding of the Encantada episode's meaning is the force that motivates his corrupt behavior. The Encantadas taught him that existence is a cruel absurdity which cannot be improved upon, because its cruelty is a part of God's plan: *"He!—accepted!—all!—*

as—how!—things!—are! . . . even though he knew that what was awful was awful, that what was wrong was wrong."

Surely Sebastian's polluted life finds its source in the brackish waters of his own nihilism. Also, however, Venable's brutal death results from his despairing posture. Sebastian convinced himself that man's central business on earth was to suffer and die. Because he sees himself as merely a victim in the scheme of things, he begins to act like one. As Catharine explains, Sebastian's actions are an attempt to complete "a sort of!—*image!*—he had of himself as a sort of!—*sacrifice* to a!—*terrible* sort of a— . . . God? . . . Yes, a—*cruel* one" (p. 397). The meaning of Venable's death is clear. Convinced that man can play only the role of victim on earth, he despairingly orchestrates his own murder by antagonizing the desperate and brutal beggar boys of Cabeza de Lobo. In a perverse and masochistic manner, the wish is father to the deed here. By acting upon his definition of himself as a victim, he creates the conditions of his own victimization. Because Sebastian believes death and suffering make la condition humaine absurd and cruel, his life degenerates into a cruel absurdity.

The act of meditation invites the questioning that is caused by an examination of opposing ideas. If Williams' play confined itself to only an investigation of Venable's existential despair, it could be called a *statement* but certainly not a meditation. This, however, is not the case. An alternative vision of life and death is presented, albeit cryptically, by the play's allusions to Sebastian Venable's namesake, St. Sebastian.

Using a method reminiscent of Eliot's "The Waste Land," Williams builds his complex allusion to St. Sebastian by setting up parallels between the saint's life and that of his modern counterpart, Sebastian Venable. For instance, both fall seriously ill while exercising their vocations, both are nursed back to health by women, both have many followers. And, finally, the mutilated bodies of both men are found lying in a gutter after they have been beaten to death.

The network of allusions to the life of St. Sebastian in *Suddenly Last Summer* creates a level of meaning in the play best classified by "mock-heroic." As Joyce's Leopold Bloom is mocked by the correspondence that exists between his banal, modern life and the heroic adventures of Ulysses, as Eliot's licentious secretaries suffer a diminution by comparison with their ancient counterparts, the rhine maidens, Sebastian Venable seems all the more venal when he is compared to the heroic saint. Clearly, the exemplary life of St. Sebastian demonstrates an alternative to the corruption that characterizes the life of despairing modern man.

The saint, an early martyr, is most renowned for his courage and constancy in the face of death. His legend holds numerous examples of saintly fortitude; for instance, Butler's *Lives of the Saints* tells of Sebastian's undaunted

bearing in the "face of the clouds of arrows shot at him" and his practice of always taking the most dangerous posts. Sebastian's constancy, his refusal to despair in the face of death, is an expression of the early Christian belief in a benevolent deity. Because God was good, human existence was charged with an ultimately positive meaning—resurrection through Christ. Armed with his faith in a loving God and therefore in a meaningful universe, Sebastian prepared both himself and his fellow martyrs for death. His death at the hands of the antichristian emperor Diocletian symbolized his total devotion to Christ, his fellow Christians, and principle.

The function of the mock-heroic analogy that Williams sets up between St. Sebastian and Sebastian Venable is twofold. First, the exemplary conduct of St. Sebastian throws into relief the shameful behavior of Sebastian Venable. For instance, Venable, unlike the saint, quarrels with God's plan; he becomes totally demoralized over the fact of death. His demoralization leads to a nihilistic inability to love. Unlike St. Sebastian, Venable does not care a whit for his followers (the boys of Cabeza de Lobo), his mother, his cousin or, for that matter, himself. His death is an expression of a masochistic self-contempt. Truly, Williams' ironic pun on Sebastian's last name reveals his character. Venable is not venerable; unlike St. Sebastian, he deserves pity, not veneration. Second, the decimation of *meaning* that characterizes Venable's modern world is emphasized by the contrasting *meaningful* world of the ancient saint. The ancient view that death was a meaningful part of God's total plan facilitated a positive outlook that found its expression in lives of fortitude, charity and saintliness. The modern notion of death as the "everlasting nay" robs life of its meaning and leads, naturally enough, to acts of despair, cowardice, and corruption.

Suddenly Last Summer is clearly the most static of Williams' mature dramas. Of all his plays, it is the one that approaches closest to the condition of poetry. For instance, not only does Williams fail to develop an explicitly dramatic conflict between Venable and a foil, but he also does not present the audience with a living, breathing Venable. Moreover, although the memories of Venable's mother and his cousin give the audience a rather complete portrait of him, his counterpart, Saint Sebastian, is merely alluded to. The challenge must have been clear to Williams. If he wished effectively to dramatize an antinomy central to his time, the opposition between the absurd and the Christian views of existence, he would have to embody these opposing views in luminous dramatis personae. This is precisely Williams' greatest achievement in *The Night of the Iguana*. For here, he masterfully creates a modern, believable saintly couple (Hannah Jelkes and her grandfather Jonathan Coffin). And also he presents his audience with a most compelling portrait of "absurd man," the Reverend T. Lawrence Shannon, defrocked. Through a marvelous series of confrontations between these three characters, Williams further investigates the effect the two world views have on their adherents' spiritual health and life conduct.

Many similarities exist between Lawrence Shannon and his prototype Sebastian Venable. Their most important shared experience is witnessing an event which causes both to question the value of life and the benevolence of God. The Encantada episode propelled Venable into a period of spiritual turmoil, and a grim scene on an unnamed tropical island adds impetus to Shannon's growing despair. There he saw two old natives picking carefully through a pile of excrement in an attempt to find sustenance. The island of excrement becomes Shannon's Encantadas for it also symbolizes the harshness of human existence. Man, like the two old natives, picks his way through life in an attempt to find something of value, but he is always frustrated because life is a dungheap. This experience also convinces Shannon that God is cruel. For as Venable saw God presiding over the Encantadas' slaughtering sea birds, so Shannon sees God in the fierceness of a tropical thunderstorm, a storm described by images which recall the savage birds of the earlier play: "The storm, with its white convulsions of light, is like a giant white bird attacking the hilltop of the Costa Verde."

Shannon is not, however, a mere carbon copy of Venable. Although both characters see life as an absurdity, Shannon emphasizes a different aspect of the problem. Venable was most dismayed by death's contribution to the absurdity of the human condition. Shannon, however, compulsively focuses on the harsher aspects of life and actually sees death as a benevolent liberator. Shannon's identification with the bound iguana lizard objectifies and amplifies his view of the human state. Like the iguana, tied to a post, helplessly waiting to be slaughtered by the native boys, man, helplessly tied to earth by his life, cannot evade the inevitable suffering of existence. Only death can free one from the slings and arrows of outrageous fortune. If, like Shannon, one does not have the courage to commit suicide, one's position is much like that of the tied iguana. Man's greatest hope, Shannon explains, is to get beyond the end of his rope (to death) quickly so that his inevitable suffering will be minimized: "I'll get my flashlight, I'll show you. . . . See? The iguana? At the end of its rope? Trying to go on past the end of its goddam rope? Like *you! like me!*" Insofar as Shannon is typical of despairing modern man, we may see the nature of our spiritual turmoil in his iguana symbol. However, just as Venable's anguish was answered, albeit cryptically, by the example of St. Sebastian, so Shannon's view of life does not go unchallenged. An alternative to despair is posited by Hannah Jelkes and Jonathan Coffin. Hannah's life philosophy and Jonathan's death philosophy function as powerful rejoinders to those, like Shannon, who are hateful of life and in love with the idea of death. Williams achievement in creating an answer to Shannon that is embodied by flesh and blood characters earmarks the "special" brilliance of *The Night of the Iguana.*

Hannah Jelkes stands as an example of courage and understanding in the face of tribulation. Like Shannon and Venable, she also has experienced harrowing moments, but, unlike the two men, she has never allowed herself the luxury of despair. Her experience with the lonely, Austrian salesman effectively demonstrates the saintly response to life's trials. Certainly, Hannah's conduct during this episode serves as an example of what is finest in human nature.

While traveling in Singapore with her grandfather, Hannah accepted the salesman's invitation to join him on a boat ride. During the excursion, he asked for a piece of Hannah's underwear and performed a fetishistic act with it. Appalled by the story, Shannon immediately characterizes the event as a "sad, dirty little episode." It is Hannah's spirited rejoinder to this pessimistic characterization that distinguishes her exemplary approach to life. She does not become disgusted with life after this episode, nor did she envision, during the perverse act, a rancorous, cruel God enjoying her humiliation while egging the Austrian on. Instead, she calls the event a "love experience" and values it as such. Moreover, she does not rebel against the fact that life will often present moments of trial; instead, she wisely submits to the truism that one must "Accept whatever situation you cannot improve." Hannah's two-fold response of affection and endurance clearly shows the saintly virtues of charity, understanding, and courage. Surely, Williams argues through Hannah that love and courage, not hate and cowardice, are the virtues needed if one wishes to remain spiritually afloat in life's troubled waters.

Hannah's exemplary attitude toward life is supplemented by grandfather Nonno's response to the problem of death. Nonno strikes a balance between Venable's terror of death and Shannon's active death wish. The nature of Nonno's admirable thanatopsis is revealed in the lovely poem he completes just before he dies. The poem takes the form of a prayer for courage in the face of extinction. Its speaker observes that an orange tree branch remains calm and unruffled even though a violent tropical storm is approaching. The branch animistically realizes that the storm will soon destroy it, but it refuses to despair: "And still the ripe fruit and the branch/Observe the sky begin to blanch/Without a cry, without a prayer,/With no betrayal of despair." The speaker concludes the poem by praying for that virtue which allows the branch to face death with such equanimity: "O Courage, could you not as well/Select a second place to dwell,/Not only in that golden tree/But in the frightened heart of me?" The poem's lesson is clear. Life is to be valued, for it is as precious and beautiful as the orange branch; therefore, actively desiring death, as Shannon does, is perverse and wrongheaded. But also, to turn craven in the face of the inevitable, as Venable does, is to sin against one of life's most important beautifiers, the virtue of courage. In short, man, like the orange branch, should glory in earthly existence but courageously accept death's dominion. Insofar as Nonno dies at the end of the play without any trepidation of spirit, he stands as Williams' most effective example of modern man's potential to accept death as gracefully as Socrates or St. Sebastian.

The Milk Train Doesn't Stop Here Anymore is the last of Williams' plays which presents death as a central concern. Here, Williams accepts his greatest challenge, the creation of a protagonist who is in the process of slowly dying from cancer. He portrays the special turmoil of a person in the prime of life, Sissy Goforth, who remains in love with living while slowly dying. The list of playwrights who have not grappled with this exceedingly common problem is immense. Williams' insights into the psychology of the disease-sufferer are new, fresh, and, at times, startling. This most recent dramatic statement about death distinctly follows in a logical progression from earlier positions developed in *Suddenly Last Summer* and *The Night of the Iguana*. In short, the similarities that exist between Sissy Goforth and Venable/Shannon clearly show that all three are members of the same family, despairing modern man.

Just as Shannon puzzled over the nature of existence during his sabbatical on a hilltop overlooking the Mexican coast, as Venable sought answers to overwhelming questions from his crow's nest above the ocean, Sissy Goforth ponders life's mysteries in her mountain villa perched above the Mediterranean Sea. Venable and Shannon experienced harrowing events which caused them to doubt the benevolence of God or His universe. Likewise, Sissy is spectator to a death scene which has contributed to the development of her present "fear and trembling." This scene was the panic-stricken death of her first husband, Harlon Goforth, who suffered a massive stroke while performing the act of love with Sissy. It is clear that the look of terror in Harlon's dying eyes has profoundly affected Sissy's heart and mind, for her present description of this long past event is marked by panic and trepidation of spirit: Harlon had "death in his eyes, and something worse in them, terror. . . . I move away from death, terror! . . . I go straight to the door . . . onto the terrace! . . . It's closed, I tear it open, I leave him alone with his death." Sissy literally ran away from Harlon's death. Like Venable's Encantadas and Shannon's isle of excrement, this grim variant of coitus interruptus aptly symbolizes man's ultimate frustration and victimization by death. Because she is afraid of death and cognizant of its dominion, Sissy lies to herself about the seriousness of her physical condition. Sissy's self-deception is a product of the despair created by the fear of death. Escape from this form of despair is possible only if Sissy learns, as Nonno learned, to accept death, to *face it* with courage.

Sissy, then, must courageously confront the reality of her own situation if she wishes to defeat Self-Deception and Despair, two of man's ogres. Like Shannon, she is lost in the wilderness, but, luckily, she also is not without a guide. Here, as in *The Night of the Iguana*, Williams creates an artist-teacher who offers wise counsel about the nature of reality to a despairing protagonist. Through this typically Williamsian figure, Christopher Flanders, the playwright makes his last (so far) major statement about the problem of death. The statement is a harsh one, for Williams was undoubtedly influenced by the slow decay of his friend Frank Merlo; it is not, however, a despairing one. For clearly, Chris as Williams teaches Sissy and us to face the grimmer aspects of existence "With no betrayal of despair."

Christopher Flanders utilizes two of his artistic creations, a mobile and a parable about suicide, as mediums through which his lesson is conveyed. Just before his final confrontation with Sissy, he hangs the mobile entitled "The Earth Is a Wheel in a Great Big Gambling Casino" from her bedroom ceiling. The mobile functions as a preamble to all that Chris will say about life and death. Its title suggests that the earth is merely a minor cogwheel in the limitless gambling casino of the universe; clearly, the title alludes to the Copernican astronomy which ushered in modern man's recognition of his unimportance in the "scheme of things." Visually, the mobile makes a second statement which logically proceeds from the first. Just as it randomly tilts and sways while being buffeted by the uncontrollable force of the wind, so helpless, diminished man is assaulted by the uncontrollable pushes and pulls of chance and fate in the gambling casino of the universe. The implications of this lesson are clear: (1) To live is to operate in a universe ruled by gambling odds. (2) Therefore, wisdom is the realization that our destinies are not controlled by ourselves, but by two lords of life, Chance and Fate. (3) Therefore, the fault, dear Brutus, does lie in our stars!

If Chris's total statement is the lesson taught by the mobile, he could certainly be accused of negativism. Luckily, for Sissy, this is not the case. Chris's second creation, the suicide parable, suggests how one might ultimately defeat the grim reality so aptly symbolized by the trepidating mobile. While walking past an ocean inlet, Chris saw an old gentleman on the beach calling for help as if he were drowning in the sand. On closer inspection, he sees the signs of a horrible disease in the old man's ravaged countenance. The old man confesses to Chris that he is no longer able to stand the extreme pain of his condition. He asks Chris to help him end it all. Obligingly, Chris carries him out into the water where the tide wafts him out "as light as a leaf." The moral of this story is clear. The diseased old man screams for help on the sandshore of life, because he finds the burden of existence unacceptable. Concomitantly, death, then, becomes his friend and liberator. The wisdom of the old man's exemplary thanatos encompasses the lesson that Chris is attempting to teach Sissy: When one's luck runs out, as the old man's has, in the casino of life, death is to be revered, not feared. By courageously embracing death we, like the old gentleman—St. Sebastian—Socrates, revolt against a tyrannical existence made up of hours of lead.

After hearing his parable, Sissy asks Chris to help her into the bedroom, just as the old man had asked Chris to carry him out to sea. Now, Sissy also desires death. She describes her new feelings about life and death in a final symbolic statement. An investigation of the statement's implications suggests that Sissy will not face death with the fear and trembling of a Harlon Goforth. Indeed, she has learned Chris's lesson well.

The preamble to Sissy's new perception of life and death is expressed in the symbolic statement which gives the play its title: The "milk train doesn't stop here anymore."

This assertion clearly shows Sissy's realization that those aspects of life which are nutritive to the human spirit, precious, and of value, will no longer visit her, for the milk train which refuses to stop symbolizes these positive aspects of existence. Here, Sissy faces the essential absurdity of the human condition. In short, she is aware that: (1) At any given moment, the precious things in life may cease to stop at our door. (2) There seems to be no logical reason for this to happen. (3) The situation must be accepted as a fait accompli, for nothing can be done about it.

Sissy's new perception of death is a logical progression from the vision of life described above. Now she wisely realizes that when life becomes a horrible burden—when the positive aspects of existence symbolized by the milk train are no longer forthcoming, death is to be actively submitted to, not feared: "It's my turn, now, to go forth [to die]. . . . I'll do it alone. I don't want to be escorted. I want to go forth alone." These final lines show that Sissy, like the old gentleman, faces the harshness of reality in an absurd universe and courageously accepts death, the only antidote to a poisonous existence. By facing her situation, she casts off self-deception. By gracefully accepting death, she conquers despair. Clearly, Sissy is spiritually a victor over life's vicissitudes. For as soon as she dies, a gust of wind triumphantly whips out her flag, and a bugle in the background plays reveille in honor of her awakening, not taps.

Milk Train's most important departure from *Night of the Iguana* is in the severe asceticism of its statement. Although chaste, self-disciplined Hannah Jelkes practiced a life of denial, she and Nonno clearly reveled in the physical beauties of life. A much colder eye is cast upon earthly existence in *Milk Train,* for its message is contemptum mundi. Yet, *Milk Train* is not a retraction of the warmer regard for human life posited in *Iguana.* Both plays present important views of life. In short, *Iguana* is a play for those who still have hope; *Milk Train* is surely a play to comfort the hopeless.

In one area, however, the plays coincide in a manner that sets their protagonists apart from Sebastian Venable in *Suddenly Last Summer.* Hannah, Nonno, Shannon, Chris and Sissy see human charity as life's most precious treasure. They know that life is often like a penal colony, a hostile environment that makes creating, loving, and clear perceiving difficult. But this knowledge does not propel them into the viciousness of a Sebastian Venable. They still love, after their own manner. Even Larry Shannon warmly regards Hannah/Nonno and embraces Maxine Faulk at the end of *Iguana.* It is the later plays' preponderance of love that sets them apart from the coldness of *Suddenly Last Summer.* Although the later plays are certainly somber, they cannot be construed as defeatist, for part of their lesson is "Love thy neighbor as thyself." They show that even in a harsh universe love, charity, compassion are still possible. The despair that destroyed Sebastian Venable's humanity can be exorcised from the human spirit. Underneath the guise of southern decadence, Tennessee Williams practices the art of a decidedly Christian playwright.

Edith A. Everson

SOURCE: "E. E. Cummings' Concept of Death," in *Journal of Modern Literature,* Vol. 7, No. 2, April, 1979, pp. 243-54.

[*In the following essay, Everson analyzes E. E. Cummings's multifaceted view of death in his poetic drama* Santa Claus, *which emphasizes death's destructive and rejuvenating qualities.*]

At the heart of E. E. Cummings' most characteristic work is a keen sense of the mystery and miracle of life. But this American poet has a great deal to say about death as well, not only in the lyrics, but also in a morality play in which Death is one of the leading characters. By analyzing particular passages in these writings, one may arrive at an understanding of Cummings' concept of death and of its place in his world of values. A study of this kind both presupposes and affirms a basic integrity among the values the poet upholds. And such an inquiry also recognizes the complexity of his vision, for this concept of death is many-sided, manifesting itself in widely varying contexts and under differing lights. For example, death may be shown to have positive value as an experience that is natural to and inseparable from the ongoing process of life. Considered in this vital sense the concept is, in this paper, designated by the verbal form, "dying." On the other hand, death may be revealed as a negative, life-denying condition, one that is associated with the conventions of society which, Cummings believes, oppress the individual and inhibit his intuitive and spontaneous impulses. In this negative aspect the concept is here named by a more static word, the noun, "death." I propose to examine not only these major aspects, but also their subdivisions, and thus to round out the concept of death that emerges in E. E. Cummings' work.

To search for this concept is to become involved in a paradox, however, for concepts are among the things of which Cummings disapproves. In a letter to his sister written in May 1922, the poet discusses the notion of the "best possible world." He asks, "What does 'the best' mean! Can you eat it, like a beefsteak? Can you smoke it, like tobacco? Or is it a mere concept?" He goes on to ask if there is any reason why another "mere concept, e.g. 'the worst,' should be less acceptable than its fellows." Cummings points out that both notions are useless, for to him "concepts do not exist."[1] This nominalist attitude is borne out in his poetry, where he often ridicules generalizations and abstractions and celebrates all that is individual and concrete. A partial answer to the contradiction might point out that the concept sought here will derive its shape from particular poetic instances. But a complete resolution of the problem is impossible, for the fact is that Cummings' expressions are not always concrete. Indeed, the poet does, frequently and deliberately, use general concepts and abstract ideas, particularly in his later works. Paradoxically, however, Cummings enlists abstractions in the service of proclaiming his unchanging gospel of the concrete and the unique.

One of the most obvious examples of Cummings' use of general ideas is discovered in his morality play, *Santa Claus*.[2] In this poetic drama Cummings follows the traditional method of allegory, that of presenting characters that are abstractions, in order to point to a moral. As Charles Norman has noted, this play "reveals Cummings in a didactic vein."[3] Since the character Death is a kind of walking definition, this drama is a reasonable beginning point for an inquiry into Cummings' concept of death. First of all, then, a summary of *Santa Claus* should provide a basis for relevant commentary, and Cummings' shorter poems may supply corroboration for the ideas that emerge. It is noteworthy that the characters' names, including that of Death, are capitalized in this play. Since Cummings rarely capitalizes proper names, perhaps his doing so here suggests that he assigns particular weight to the play's characters as indexes to his views on the concepts of which these actors are incarnations.

As the play opens, Death is strolling on the stage. He wears a skeleton suit and mask, which crudely imitate the way in which death is usually represented. Santa Claus, in a red, traditional but moth-eaten suit, enters slowly, appearing despondent. To Santa's complaint that no one will take what he has to give, Death replies that neither will anyone give what he, Death, would like to take. He explains further that people cannot take because they do not live in an actual world. Rather, says Death, they live in a negative world, characterized by blurred sameness, repression of natural impulses, greed, laziness, blindness, artificiality, and triviality. Death says to Santa:

> Imagine, if you can, a world so blurred
> that its inhabitants are one another
> —an idiotic monster of negation:
> so timid, it would rather starve itself
> eternally than run the risk of choking
> so greedy, nothing satisfies its hunger
> but always huger quantities of nothing—
> a world so lazy that it cannot dream;
> so blind, it worships its own ugliness:
> a world so false, so trivial, so unso,
> phantoms are solid by comparison.
>
> (*Santa Claus*, 11)

Santa is unable to imagine such a world, but Death explains that this is an age of salesmanship, not of gifts, and he persuades Santa to sell the thing that people will buy most readily: knowledge without understanding. Death explains that because people do not really exist they will eagerly buy something which does not exist. Therefore Santa becomes a scientist (salesman of knowledge without understanding) after exchanging masks with Death, and he sells stock in "wheelmines" to a credulous, greedy mob. Science, Santa tells the crowd, has turned them all into supermen, equal beings. Hitherto they had been mere individuals, but now they have been freed from their

humanity. The "supermen" cry "gimme," "Long live Science," and "Hooray for wheelmines!" (*Santa Claus*, 11-14).

But all is not well. Because of an accident in a wheelmine, the angered crowd soon turns on Santa, to whom they refer as "Mr. Science." Death has watched developments with some satisfaction because he really desires to ruin Santa. He now advises the perturbed Santa that the nonexistent wheelmines have been able to turn people into monsters only because the people themselves, like the wheelmines, do not exist. After all, he points out pedantically, "two negatives . . . make an affirmative." When Santa is surprised to learn that people do not exist, Death says that he wishes they did exist, in which case he, Death, would not be such a skeleton. Next, Death advises Santa that he can be saved from the mob's fury only if he convinces his public that he does not exist. A little child appears and tells the crowd that the man before them is not Science, but Santa Claus. Since the mob is very sure that Santa Claus does not exist, they must consider their intended victim nonexistent and therefore innocent, and so they withdraw (*Santa Claus*, 14-16).

Santa and Death meet again, and this time Death asks for Santa's "fat" in exchange for his own skeleton. Because Death's advice has proved "efficacious," Santa readily agrees, and they exchange suits of clothes. Death, it seems, wishes to keep a date with a "swell jane" who prefers plump men, although he points out that he has never loved a woman. When Santa claims to have done so at one time, Death replies, "Well, everybody makes mistakes," and he leaves for his date (*Santa Claus*, 17).

The child approaches again, and she knows Santa for himself, even though he is now completely attired in the clothes of Death. She tells Santa that she has lost someone, a woman who is very beautiful. Moreover, both she and the woman have lost someone else. When Santa asks who that "someone" is, the child looks directly at him and replies, "You." Next, a woman enters, weeping because the world is joyless since knowledge has taken love away. She asks death (the word is uncapitalized) to take her, mistaking Santa for physical death because of the costume he is wearing. The woman then believes herself to be dying, but suddenly she hears the voice of her lost lover, for it is Santa who is under the attire of Death. She asks her lover to protect her from "deathless lifelessness," or unending nonexistence in a world that values only nonexistent things (*Santa Claus*, 17-19).

Soon the mob returns, and they are carrying a pole from which dangles the corpse of Death disguised as Santa. This time the child has told them that their victim is not Santa Claus, a claim which is perfectly true, since it is Death in Santa's disguise whom they have taken. Believing him, therefore, to be "Mr. Science," they have killed him. The crowd is unaware, however, that by means of another strange double negative, they have mistakenly laid hands on the real villain. At this point the play concludes, as the child and her mother, Joy and Love, are reunited with each other and with Santa, whose face, when his mask is removed, is revealed to be that of a young man (*Santa Claus,* 19).

It seems at first that the play presents chiefly the negative aspect of Cummings' concept of death. But it soon becomes apparent that there is considerable complexity in the character of Death; he is not a simple morality figure. Norman Friedman notes that Death, although he is cast as the villain who created the "unworld," is nevertheless capable of great insight, speaking sometimes in the voice of Cummings. This is certainly true in his statement, cited above, where Death speaks of a "blurred world," with inhabitants that form an "idiotic monster of negation." And Santa is also complex, for he is said to have understanding, but he is also extremely naive. Friedman justly points to the exchange of masks and costumes as symbolic acts suggesting the complex natures of the play's leading characters.[4]

Although interpretation of the play is not the primary concern here, a clear view of the character of Death is necessary if Cummings' concept is to be completely understood. It seems to me that most critical commentary on the play neglects to note that not only Santa, but Death as well, has been greatly affected by the disappearance of love from the world. Both Death and Santa are in disguise at the play's beginning, a fact which suggests that they have both assumed identities other than their natural ones. Much criticism assumes that Death is only a deceiver, while Santa is a "good" character. Both, however, exist on more than one level, and in their costumes they have become something like institutionalized versions of their true selves. The importance of this view lies in the fact that it shows each character to have at least two natures. Death's underlying character allows him to speak, at times, with friendliness and even with wisdom, perplexing the reader who expects Death to be only a villain. Death in his true character is indeed wiser than Santa, who is only a young man under his disguise. Death's costume is a crude imitation of the appearance of natural death, or "dying." He has become a caricature of himself, and he has become evil. His two identities, then, the assumed one and the true one, correspond with the death-dying dichotomy already suggested. This duality of character is also expressed in a poem in Cummings' collection *Xaipe*

> . . . dying
> 's miraculous
> why?be
>
> cause dying is
>
> perfectly natural;perfectly
> putting
> it mildly lively(but
>
> Death
>
> is strictly
> scientific
> & artificial &
> evil & legal)[5]

What, then, is included in the notion of "dying," the aspect of death that is "natural" in Cummings' work? First of all, this term suggests the experience that is commonly called physical death. In *Santa Claus,* Death is speaking, at least in part, of the physical death of the individual when he tells Santa that, if people really existed, then he, Death, would not be such a skeleton. He seems to be suggesting that those who live fully will not find dying so formidable, so skeleton-like, as do those who live in an "unworld." The Woman of the play illustrates this idea, for she is one that had been truly alive until she became separated from her lover. She does not fear dying, but actually seeks it in preference to the "deathless lifelessness" of the unworld. Similar commentary on physical death appears in Cummings' poem "anyone lived in a pretty how town" (*Poems,* 370). Here the lovers, "anyone" and "noone," are the only ones in the community who are living in the proper sense. As Barry Marks writes of this pair, when they die they "merge their love with the love at the heart of things."[6] Lovers, more than anyone else in Cummings' world, "have the great advantage of being alive"; they need not fret because they are not "undying" (*Poems,* 464).

But although "dying" is natural, Cummings does not look upon it as the doorway to another conscious existence, for he writes, "death, as men call him, ends what they call men" (*Poems,* 421). Man, he believes, must live with uncertainty until "the final curtain strikes the world away," leaving the stage to "shadowy silence" (*Poems,* 60). Cummings would agree with Wallace Stevens, who writes that the individual should gladly acknowledge his place in "the heavenly fellowship/Of men that perish."[7] In a letter written to Dr. Richard Hoffman in 1953, Cummings comments further on this idea, explaining that he is against the socialist "compulsory heaven-on-earth," because for him such a world is too much like the "escapist unworld of a so-called future life, immemoriably postulated by conventional religions. . . . " "Eternity, Cummings believes, has its only real significance in the present; eternity means "not time-adinfinitum, but timelessness." The poet values not a future life, but what he calls an "illimitable now," an unbounded possibility for growth in the present life (*Letters,* 225).

This emphasis upon growth leads to another view of "dying," one which considers it to be inseparable from "living." In *Santa Claus* the interchanging of masks and costumes suggests that the true natures of the characters representing "living" (Santa) and "dying" (Death) are very closely identified. But in closely associating "dying" and "living," the poet is not thinking of "dying" chiefly as an aging process, as the steady growth toward maturity which is simultaneously a move toward death. Cummings places his emphasis upon renewal rather than upon a process whereby energy is "consumed with that which it was nourished by." The rejuvenating power of death is foremost in this view. On one level, of course, this process is manifested in the cyclical rebirth of all natural things. Cummings, for example, refers to death as earth's "rhythmic lover," whose embrace is followed by the birth of spring (*Poems*, 40). This renewal, as already suggested, takes place at the expense of the individual life. But Cummings writes of another form of dying-living, one in which human beings may participate during their lifetimes. This form of dying involves a kind of self-giving, a rejection of self-consciousness in favor of all that is "natural which is infinite which is yes" (*Poems*, 464). In the beginning of *Santa Claus,* Death desires to take, but people are unable to give. Sometimes this statement is read as a condemnation of Death, as evidence of his evil, grasping character. This assumption is misleading, however, for people in the unworld are in need of learning the kind of giving which is a form of dying, just as they must learn to take. Giving and taking (paralleling dying and living) belong together in Cummings' world. Dying requires self-giving, and such an act leads to growth and to spiritual renewal.

Cummings' most frequent use of this idea is in association with the notion of the self-abnegation of lovers in the act of physical love, where giving is followed by taking, dying is followed by renewal. Such references are in the tradition of the Elizabethan lyricists, who often used "dying" as a metaphor for sexual climax. In Cummings' poem, "that which we who are alive in spite of mirrors," Cummings refers to the "dying" of lovers in the act of love and to the new life which follows (*Poems*, 279). And in another poem he suggests that those who give themselves freely and spontaneously turn the "corner of Nothing and Something" and find new life (*Poems*, 129). In the play, as the Woman gives herself to "dying" (physical death), she pictures symbolically the act of love, with Cummings' emphasis upon the renewal which follows self-giving. For in "dying" the woman is greeted by the voice of her lover, Santa Claus, the character who, in his true nature, represents life. Rejuvenation follows giving, as further suggested when Santa takes off his mask, revealing himself to be a young man. And parallel to this notion of the self-abnegation of lovers is a kind of dying which is prerequisite to artistic creation. Cummings' love poems may often be read as symbolic commentary upon the act of artistic creation, where the artist's giving of himself brings into being something completely new. More often, however, when dealing with the subject of art, Cummings emphasizes the need to destroy before creation may take place. I shall discuss this more violent concept later, but first it is necessary to look at Death's other major aspect.

Thus far the forms of death described are those of which Cummings would approve. They are associated with the character called Death in Cummings' play, but they belong to him in his natural identity, that which is covered up by the costume symbolizing his corruption. But his masquerade creates a character who is the spirit of death in a different sense. He is the prefix "un" that precedes the words "world" and "life" in Cummings' custom-made vocabulary. A thoroughgoing deceiver, he is the one who ruins the world of *Santa Claus.* He represents everything that is opposed to spontaneity, to joy, to life, and to love. He is a crude imitation of the living, becoming what

Henri Bergson has called "something mechanical encrusted upon the living," a kind of rigidity "applied to the mobility of life. . . . " Bergson associates this concept with comedy, with situations and individuals that are in need of corrective laughter.[8] Cummings, however, takes a more solemn view of this artificiality, conceiving of it as a form of death for the individual, even while biological life is present. In *The Enormous Room,* imprisonment becomes a metaphor for this "unlife." Writing of his departure from La Ferté-Macé, the dismal, filthy French prison in which he was unjustly confined for several months during World War I, Cummings says that he left "non-existence" and moved back into "reality."[9]

In analyzing the static, rigid side of Cummings' concept of death, one may recall Death's description of the "unworld" of Cummings' play. There death has a blurring effect upon the people, so that they "are one another." They are so completely governed by social conventions that individuals are no longer to be found among them. Holding all of the general, popular views, they all have the same values. Ideas and opinions have become completely standardized. The inhabitants of this world are nothing but mirrors of each other, and they worship "same." Cummings writes that such a monotonous existence makes birth into a kind of death, for there is nothing ahead but lifelessness for one born into such a world.

> worshipping Same
> they squirm and they spawn
> and a world is for them,them;whose
> death's to be born
>
> (*Poems,* 314)

The people in such a world cannot call their souls their own. In another poem Cummings writes of the Cambridge ladies who live in "furnished souls" and who sleep smugly under the sameness of conventionality. They hold all the widely accepted views and attitudes, but they are completely indifferent to the mystery and imaginative excitement that might be theirs if they would only look at the unconventional moon, which is high above them. Their rigidity shows in their "permanent" faces, as they rehearse the current gossip and fail to look upward, for

> . . . the Cambridge ladies do not care, above
> Cambridge if sometimes in its box of
> sky lavender and cornerless, the
> moon rattles like a fragment of angry candy
>
> (*Poems,* 58)

Dogmatic systems are forms of death in Cummings' world. Conventional religions, as I have already noted, belong to the unworld. But Cummings is particularly disapproving of systems that are upheld by authoritarian means. He attacks communism, for example, in his poem, "kumrads die." The "kumrads" of the poem die, both physically and spiritually, "because they're told," because they allow themselves to be governed by an impersonal body of dogma. They "won't believe in life" sufficiently to assert their individuality and humanity. Thus, like the followers of any kind of rigid system, they lack spontaneity. And they commit the sin of lovelessness; they are afraid to love (*Poems*, 296).

Any form of knowledge that seems to be pursued separately from feeling is, for Cummings, a form of death. Perhaps this is why, as Richard S. Kennedy has shown, the poet valued the independence and friendships afforded him during his Harvard years far more highly than the university's "academic side." Kennedy notes, of course, that Cummings was a superior student in literature and languages, indeed becoming "one of the best-educated young men in the country." But he was scornful of philosophy, and in later years he continued to dislike purely intellectual pursuits.[10] In his writings it becomes evident that modern science and technology belong to his kingdom of death. For it is knowledge (science) that provides the non-existent commodity that the crowds in *Santa Claus* buy so eagerly. It is Death who is responsible for the suggestion that Santa become a "knowledge salesman" and that the knowledge sold must be free of understanding. For Cummings, thinking without feeling is "dying thinking / huddled behind dir / ty glass mind" (*Poems*, 255). In the play it is Santa Claus who articulates Cummings' epistemology, which recognizes intuition rather than reason as authoritative. When Santa proclaims to the mob that they have been under the influence of a deceiver, he challenges them to discover the truth in their ability to "feel it" in their hearts. "Your hearts will tell you as my heart has told me," he assures them. Complete understanding, then, comes from the heart, but knowledge alone is, in Cummings' words,

> . . . the foetal grave called
> progress, and negation's dead undoom
>
> (*Poems*, 345)

For Cummings "all ignorance toboggans into know/and trudges up to ignorance again" (*Poems*, 412).

Another form of death is commercialism, in which buying and selling replace giving and taking. At the play's beginning people are unable to give or to take. Yet, as a result of Death's suggestion, they are invited by Santa to buy stock in "wheelmines." In this commerical situation they seem to be more than willing to take as they cry "gimme." They wish to make millions on a small investment, a desire which is a form of corruption, of death, in Cummings' world. In "my specialty is living" Cummings presents a young man who is unable to earn his bread because he is not willing to "sell his head" (*Poems*, 339). He wishes to create freely, not in accordance with specifications dictated by someone else. Nor does he wish to set a price on the results of his work. Nature does not bargain and exact a price for what it has to offer, and it does not ask permission to express its own character. When "serpents bargain for the right to squirm," to do what is natural to them, when the sun "strikes to gain a living wage," when "rainbows are insured," then, says Cummings, he will "believe in that incredible/unanimal mankind (and not until)" (*Poems*, 441).

Buying and selling love is a form of death to which Cummings devotes considerable poetic commentary. In "little ladies more/than dead" he describes prostitutes who, years after he has known of them, come back to his memory. He writes that such women "dangle the old men and the hot men" and that they are "carefully dead" (*Poems*, 97-98). They take care with their practice of death, and their employers take care that the women practice death profitably. In another reference to death, Cummings writes of a young prostitute whom he calls "kitty," referring to her body as "Death's littlest pal" (*Poems*, 59).

All of the manifestations of the static, evil side of Death's character have this in common: they are all forms of denying and suppressing life. Even more fundamentally, perhaps, they directly oppose love, which Cummings calls "the every only god/who spoke this earth so glad and big" (*Poems*, 378). Death comprises the evil in a universe in which love is foundational. Norman Friedman points out that love has always been Cummings' chief subject, one to which he devoted well over one-fifth of his poems.[11] In view of this, what is then to be done with the evil manifestations of death so that love and life may triumph? The answer is that, paradoxically, death must die. This is the meaning of the execution of Death at the conclusion of *Santa Claus*. It is innocence in the person of the Child that causes the mob unwittingly to put to death the real villain. This ending shows symbolically that vitality and love (allied with innocence rather than with knowledge) are capable of defeating the death which threatens to suppress all that is natural. Cummings writes:

> but the proud power of himself death immense
> is not so as a little innocence
>
> (*Poems*, 456)

Death must be destroyed in the practice of art and also in ordinary living. In *The Enormous Room* Cummings writes that "for an educated gent or lady to create is first of all to destroy" (307). Here the form of death to be destroyed first is obviously some of the dead material of education. Cummings is, however, referring also to his poetics, by which he destroys not only ideas of the past, but also traditional syntax, spelling, meter, rhyme, punctuation, and verse forms. The result of his violent attack upon language, ideas, and forms is a body of work which offers much superb poetry abounding in fresh ideas and exciting new techniques. And Cummings also advises destruction of traditions in the broader context of creative living. In a letter to his sister written in 1922, he writes that "to destroy is always the first step in any creation," and he suggests further that his sister challenge all those ideas she has been taught and that she rather experience and evaluate life on her own (*Letters*, 84-85). Whether in relation to living or to creating art, death must be destroyed.

In the conclusion of *Santa Claus* Death's execution clears the way for the triumph of both love and creativity. If "dying" has also died, this is not at all inappropriate, since it is, after all, the function of "dying" to die. Love is asserted in the final moments of the play, and living follows dying, for the young man's face is revealed when the mask is removed, and he is reunited with the Woman and with their child, Joy. In another poem Cummings gives us lines which seem to apply directly to the triumph of Love in the play's ending:

> so (unlove disappearing) only your
> less than guessed more than beauty begins the
> most not imagined life adventuring
> who would feel if spring's least breathing should
>   cause
> a colour
>   and i do not know him
>   (and
> while behind death's death whenless voices sing
> everywhere your selves himself recognize)
>   (*Poems*, 323)

Love has won, and Death, in his unsympathetic character, has lost. But this enemy's destruction is never final. Another poem comments on Death's casual manner in accepting defeat and on his ability to revive and to begin his evil work again:

> death(having lost) put on his universe
> and yawned:it looks like rain
> (they've played for timelessness
> with chips of when)
> that's yours; i guess
> you'll have to loan me pain
> to take the hearse,
> see you again.
>
>   (*Poems*, 324)

NOTES

[1] E. E. Cummings, *Selected Letters of E. E. Cummings*, eds. F. W. Dupee and George Stade (Harcourt Brace and World, 1969), p. 85. Hereafter cited in text as *Letters*.

[2] E. E. Cummings, *Santa Claus (A Morality), Harvard Wake*, V (Spring 1946), 10-19. Hereafter cited in text as *Santa Claus*.

[3] Charles Norman, *E. E. Cummings: The Magic-Maker* (Duell, Sloan, and Pearce, 1964), p. 171.

[4] Norman Friedman, *E. E. Cummings: The Growth of a Writer* (Southern Illinois University Press, 1964), pp. 148-149.

[5] E. E. Cummings, *Poems: 1923-1954* (Harcourt Brace, 1968), p. 432. Hereafter cited in text as *Poems*.

[6] Barry A. Marks, *E. E. Cummings* (Twayne, 1964), p. 39.

[7] Wallace Stevens, "Sunday Morning," in *The Collected Poems* (Knopf, 1969), p. 66.

[8] Henri Bergson, "Laughter," in *Comedy*, Introduction by Wylie Sypher (Doubleday, 1956), pp. 74, 84-85.

[9] E. E. Cummings, *The Enormous Room* (The Modern Library, 1934), p. 314. Hereafter cited in text as *Room*.

[10] Richard S. Kennedy, "E. E. Cummings at Harvard: Studies," *Harvard Library Bulletin*, XXIV (July 1976), 267-270, 296.

[11] Norman Friedman, *E. E. Cummings: The Art of His Poetry* (Johns Hopkins University Press, 1960), p. 28.

Robert Feldman

SOURCE: "The Longing For Death in O'Neill's 'Strange Interlude' and 'Mourning Becomes Electra'," in *Literature and Psychology*, Vol. XXXI, No. 1, 1981, pp. 39-48.

[*In the following essay, Feldman illuminates the influence of Sigmund Freud's concept of the death instinct on Eugene O'Neill's plays* Strange Interlude *and* Mourning Becomes Electra, *but acknowledges that O'Neill's characters seek death as an escape from the pain of living, rather than as an instinctual urge.*]

The longing for death is a theme which appears in many of the plays of Eugene O'Neill.[1] *Strange Interlude* and *Mourning Becomes Electra*, which represent the middle period of O'Neill's career wherein the playwright was preoccupied with ideas, are two lengthy plays that repeatedly give expression to this theme. Generally speaking, the literary critics have regarded these two plays as heavily influenced by the psychology of Sigmund Freud. However, their analyses primarily have focused upon the subject of the Oedipus complex rather than the Freudian concept of the death instinct.[2] Therefore, part of my study will refer to Freud's theories on death, which I find parallel to this theme, to support my own argument and to illustrate that the two plays are accessible to a Freudian interpretation from another angle. But in addition to observing the similarity of the ideas of the psychoanalyst and the playwright, I will attempt to demonstrate some of the distinctions between their visions of life and death and between psychoanalysis and playwriting.

Arthur H. Nethercot's detailed articles on "The Psychoanalyzing of Eugene O'Neill" reveal that the extent of Freud's influence on O'Neill is a debatable issue. O'Neill himself objected to the critics' charges that his plays were patterned too closely along Freudian lines. In 1929, in response to a request by Martha Carolyn Sparrow, a graduate student, for personal information concerning this influence, the playwright put forth his defense:

> There is no conscious use of psychoanalytical material in any of my plays. All of them could easily be written by a dramatist who had never heard of the Freudian theory and was simply guided by an intuitive psychological insight into human beings and their life-impulses that is as old as Greek drama. It is true that I am enough of a student

of modern psychology to be fairly familiar with the Freudian implications inherent in the actions of some of my characters while I was portraying them; but this was always an afterthought and never consciously was I for a moment influenced to shape my material along the lines of any psychological theory. It was my dramatic instinct and my personal experience with human life that alone guided me.

I most certainly *did not* get my ideas of Nina's compulsion [in *Strange Interlude*] from a dream mentioned by Freud in "A General Introduction to Psychoanalysis." I have only read two books of Freud's, "Totem and Taboo" and "Beyond the Pleasure Principle." . . . But the "unconscious" influence stuff strikes me as always extremely suspicious! It is so darned easy to prove! I would say that what has influenced my plays the most is my knowledge of the drama of all time—particularly Greek tragedy—and not any books on psychology.[3]

We can appreciate O'Neill's fervent reply, for the phenomenon of the death wish already was present in his plays preceding the appearance of the English translation of Freud's book, *Beyond the Pleasure Principle,* in which the psychoanalyst introduced his concept of the death instinct. The death wish can be detected in characters like Smitty of *The Moon of the Caribbees* and Robert Mayo of *Beyond the Horizon* (two of the playwright's early achievements). But it is necessary to note that O'Neill admitted he read *Beyond the Pleasure Principle,* for it is in this work that Freud defines his theory of the death instinct. Essentially, this is the innate tendency on the part of the organism to return to its original inorganic state. Freud postulated that the death instinct arose when inorganic matter came to life as a result of a disturbance by external forces. However, in opposition to the death instinct is the life instinct, whose aim is to preserve organic substance. Since both instincts are said to be conservative by nature, life is pictured as a perpetual battleground of conflicting forces. This dualistic view of nature is analogous to the backdrop of *Strange Interlude* and *Mourning Becomes Electra.* Gregory Zilboorg, a Freudian analyst, "praised the insight of *Strange Interlude* and its effective dramatization of the stratification which makes us all ' . . . in our "normal" daily life go on unsuspecting that we are but a sort of endless dynamic battlefield rather than a compact whole.'"[4]

If we were to obtain no evidence of O'Neill's reading of *Beyond the Pleasure Principle* other than the letter he wrote to Miss Sparrow, which was dated 1929, it would be conceivable that O'Neill read the book before or during his writing of *Strange Interlude* (1926-1927) since *Beyond the Pleasure Principle* was first translated into English in 1922; and certain that he read it during, if not before his work on *Mourning Becomes Electra* (1929-1931). However, the critic Egil Törnqvist has pointed out that "By 1925 O'Neill possessed not only Freud's *Beyond the Pleasure Principle* but also *Group Psychology and the Analysis of the Ego.*"[5] Törnqvist notes that "Both copies, which are now in Yale University Library, are

signed 'Eugene O'Neill, Bermuda '25.'"[6] Thus it is probable that O'Neill read Freud's book before he wrote these two plays.

Another factor which could have contributed to the strong Freudian overtones in these two plays is O'Neill's own brief encounter with psychoanalysis in 1926. According to Arthur Nethercot and W. David Sievers, the playwright consulted with Dr. Gilbert V. Hamilton, a Freudian psychiatrist, who cured him of his drinking problems.[7] Dr. Hamilton had been given a grant to investigate through psychoanalysis the marital problems of a number of individuals and published his findings in *A Research in Marriage,* which later became the popular version *What Is Wrong with Marriage?* by Hamilton and Kenneth Macgowan. Nethercot claims that while working with O'Neill, "Hamilton, however, in his abbreviated six weeks' treatment, went considerably beyond his [O'Neill's] primary problem, and afterward O'Neill told Macgowan, who was also questioned about his marital habits, that now 'he had no trouble understanding that he hated and loved his father, and that he was suffering from an Oedipus complex.' Hamilton also told Macgowan later, '*There's a death wish in O'Neill*'" [italics mine].[8]

In *Strange Interlude* and *Mourning Becomes Electra,* the longing for death, or the death wish, is a recurring phenomenon. In both plays, much of the dramatic action stems from war—a metaphor for the conflicts of life.[9] Early in the first act of *Strange Interlude,* it is established that Nina Leeds, the heroine, lost her lover, Gordon Shaw, when his plane crashed during World War I. From that traumatic moment on, Nina longs to recapture the past and to lose herself through love relationships with the following male figures: Sam Evans (her husband), Doctor Edmund Darrell (her new lover), Charles Marsden (a father substitute), and Gordon Evans (her son, a substitute for her original lover or object choice). At the end of the final act of the play, we have come full circle as Nina watches her son fly away with his lover and comments: "Gone. My eyes are growing dim. Where is Ned [Darrell]? Gone, too. And Sam is gone. They're all dead. Where are Father and Charlie? *(With a shiver of fear she hurries over and sits on the bench beside Marsden, huddling against him)* Gordon is dead, Father. I've just had a cable. What I mean is, he flew away to another life—my son, Gordon, Charlie. So we're alone again—just as we used to be."[10]

Nina literally and predictably decides to settle down with Charles Marsden, for each finds shelter from the problems of living in the other's embrace which represents a marriage of death. In a mournful mood, Nina reflects upon her situation now that her husband is dead: "I am sad but there's comfort in the thought that now I am free at last to rot away in peace . . . I'll go and live in Father's old home . . . Sam bought that back . . . I suppose he left it to me . . . Charlie will come in every day to visit . . . he'll comfort and amuse me . . . we can talk together of the old days . . . when I was a girl . . . when I was happy . . . before I fell in love with Gordon Shaw and all this tangled mess of love and hate and pain and birth began!" (p. 214).

And herein lies an important distinction between Freud's conception of the death instinct and O'Neill's view of the longing for death as expressed through Nina and Charlie: these characters strive to return to the state of nonexistence not because of a built-in instinct, but because they cannot bear the pain of being alive; and therefore, they choose psychological death as a means of escape from the tortures of living. Charlie reckons that "Age's terms of peace, *after the long interlude of war with life* [italics mine], have still to be concluded" (p. 212). The boundaries of the play—between which lies the strange interlude of life—are marked by death. Life, then, is the strange interlude, or more accurately, the *terrifying* interlude beyond which the characters yearn to pass. Near the closing lines of the play, Charlie turns to Nina and says: "So let's you and me forget the whole distressing episode, regard it as an interlude, of trial and preparation, say, in which our souls have been scraped clean of impure flesh and made worthy to bleach in peace" (p. 221), to which Nina replies: "It will be a comfort to get home—to be old and to be home again at last—to be in love with peace together—to love each other's peace—to sleep with peace together!—*(She kisses him—then shuts her eyes with a deep sigh of requited weariness)*—to die in peace! I'm so contentedly weary with life!" (P. 222).

Thus Freud's world-view, which is represented in the biological battle between life and death instincts, can be differentiated from what we may call the O'Neillian spiritual struggle which manifests itself in the reaction of the individual will to choose to live or die when it is confronted by a world of continuous conflict.[11] I think that this partly explains O'Neill's resistance to the critics' strict Freudian comparisons between his plays and the psychoanalyst's studies. After analyzing his complete works, one can infer that the playwright is not content with a mechanistic-rationalistic view of life.[12] He may share with Freud an antipathy toward conventional religious attitudes, but he is not willing to dismiss or reduce the question of religion to an illusion, much less renounce it in favor of modern science which, as his plays indicate, cannot alone solve the mysteries and complexities of the human dilemma. Moreover, O'Neill convincingly demonstrates that even illusions (see the plays *Gold* and *The Iceman Cometh*) are necessary for man's survival.

Recalling O'Neill's remark in the 1929 letter that "the 'unconscious' influence stuff strikes me as always extremely suspicious! It is so darned easy to prove!", we can believe that the playwright had no intention of subordinating art to science. This skeptical attitude toward the science of psychoanalysis is expressed in *Strange Interlude* through the private thoughts of Charlie in reference to Doctor Darrell: "Giving me the fishy diagnosing eye they practice at medical school . . . like freshmen from Ioway cultivating broad A's at Harvard! . . . what is his specialty? . . . neurologist, I think . . . I hope not psychoanalyst . . . a lot to account for, Herr Freud! . . .

punishment to fit his crimes, be forced to listen eternally during breakfast while innumerable plain ones tell him dreams about snakes . . . *pah, what an easy cure-all!* [italics mine] . . . sex the philosopher's stone . . . 'Oh Oedipus, O my king! The world is adopting you!'" (p. 86).[13]

However, the language of *Strange Interlude* appears to be a curious contradiction to these sentiments of Charlie Marsden, who may be O'Neill's mouthpiece in this instance. On the one hand, the playwright brought before the public an innovative dramatic technique to express the subconscious thoughts and hidden motives of his characters. Kenneth Macgowan observes that "This device was more than soliloquy and it did more than expose the thoughts of people. It was a living and exciting dialog of a new kind. To the dramatic contrasts and conflicts of ordinary spoken dialogue O'Neill added the contrasts and conflicts of thought. There was the speech of Nina against the speech of Charlie, the thought of Nina against the speech of Nina; the thought of Nina against the thought of Charlie and sometimes the speech of one against the thought of the other."[14]

But O'Neill's utilization of this technique to penetrate through the exterior of his characters in order to reveal their inner complexities is extremely mechanical. Oedipal wishes and death wishes are too neatly mapped out and occupy the attention of the characters to such an exclusive degree that the complexes become living abstractions.

In addition to this, there seems to be some confusion between subconscious and self-conscious thoughts. For example, concerning death wishes, Professor Leeds, Nina's father, in an aside in Act One is gratified to learn of the death of Gordon Shaw because Leeds desires to possess his daughter: "*(thinking angrily)* Her eyes . . . I know that look . . . tender, loving . . . not for me . . . damn Gordon! . . . I'm glad he's dead!" (p. 72). Even at best, sometimes, people have only a dim perception of their neurotic conflicts. But, as in many passages in the play like this one, O'Neill's characters give us the impression that they are aware of their psychological conflicts and simply are withholding their thoughts from others. A few minutes later, Leeds himself divulges his death wish to his daughter in ordinary dialogue:

> PROFESSOR LEEDS: . . . You are young. You think one can live with the truth. Very well. It is also true I was jealous of Gordon. I was alone and I wanted to keep your love. I hated him as one hates a thief one may not accuse nor punish. I did my best to prevent your marriage. I was glad when he died. There. Is that what you wish me to say?
>
> NINA: Yes. Now I begin to forget I've hated you. You were braver than I, at least. (p. 75.)

It was a great achievement of Freud to have discovered in human beings the existence of unconscious mental processes. The task of the psychoanalyst is to bring to the awareness of the patient the repressed or unconscious conflicts of his or her experience for the purpose of restoring the patient to a state of mental health. But the task of the playwright is to dramatize conflicts without resorting to explanation; that is, the characters should be acting out, not speaking about, their problems. The playwright must carefully avoid having his characters explain their own conflicts independent of the process of the struggle for self-knowledge, for if he fails to do so the reaction of the reader or the audience will be one of disbelief.

Nevertheless, one has to admire O'Neill for his energy and ability to transport his characters through the nine acts of *Strange Interlude* to a destination echoing the one at which Freud arrived in *Beyond the Pleasure Principle:*

> Moreover it is possible to specify this final goal of all organic striving. It would be in contradiction to the conservative nature of the instincts if the goal of life were a state of things which had never yet been attained. On the contrary, it must be an *old* state of things, an initial state from which the living entity has at one time or other departed and to which it is striving to return by the circuitous paths along which its development leads. If we are to take it as a truth that knows no exception that everything living dies for *internal* reasons—becomes inorganic once again—then we shall be compelled to say that *'the aim of life is death'* and, looking backwards, that *'inanimate things existed before living ones'.*[15]

O'Neill continued to pursue the theme of longing for death in *Mourning Becomes Electra,* a play of epic proportions. In his notes for the play, O'Neill raised this question: "Is it possible to get modern psychological approximation of Greek sense of fate into such a play, which an intelligent audience of today, possessed of no belief in gods or supernatural retribution, could accept and be moved by?"[16] Eventually he found the answer to his question: yes. For all its faults, *Mourning Becomes Electra* is O'Neill's contribution to our need for new myths in its fresh, even though limited, interpretation of the world as we know it today.

The external forces of classical fate have been transformed into internalized forces—namely, Oedipus complexes and death wishes that torment the Mannon family throughout the history of their existence. O'Neill "urged himself to 'try for prose with simple forceful repeating accent and rhythm which will express driving insistent compulsion of passions engendered in family past, which constitute family fate.'"[17] He achieved his goal but not by avoiding the kind of self-conscious language that proved to be detrimental to *Strange Interlude.* The youngest generation of Mannons, Orin (Orestes) and Lavinia (Electra), has inherited the sins of its ancestors, as Orin points out to his sister: "(*with a quiet mad insistence*): Can't you see I'm now in Father's place and you're Mother? That's the evil destiny out of the past I haven't dared predict! I'm the Mannon you're chained to!" (p. 356). Indeed the problem is that the characters *literally* resemble their predecessors in appearance and behavior

to the point of absurdity. It seems to me that O'Neill has exaggerated the idea, which reappears in many of his other plays and in the works of Freud, that the past determines the present and the future.

In *Beyond the Pleasure Principle,* Freud relates the death instinct to part of this idea which he terms "the repetition compulsion: " . . . we cannot escape a suspicion that we may have come upon the track of a universal attribute of instincts and perhaps of organic life in general which has not hitherto been clearly recognized or at least not explicitly stressed. *It seems, then, that an instinct is an urge inherent in organic life to restore an earlier state of things* which the living entity has been obliged to abandon under the pressure of external disturbing forces."[18] He adds that "the most impressive proofs of there being an organic compulsion to repeat lie in the phenomena of heredity and the facts of embryology."[19]

O'Neill, on the other hand, signifies that when the individual is under the pressure of external disturbing forces of life, he or she reacts by harboring death wishes in the form of longing to return to the past or dreaming of a nonexistent paradise free of conflict. In *Mourning Becomes Electra,* as in *Strange Interlude,* war (in this case the Civil War) is symbolic of the constant battle of life. "Haunted by death" (p. 323), Christine Mannon (Clytemnestra), who used to "believe in heaven," but "now knows there is only hell" (p. 323) bemoans her lost youth: *"(Then with bitter longing)* If I could only have stayed as I was then! Why can't all of us remain innocent and loving and trusting? But God won't leave us alone. He twists and wrings and tortures our lives with others' lives until—we poison each other to death!" (p. 286). Unable to endure life after her lover, Adam Brant (Aegisthus), is killed by her son when the latter discovers their secret affair, Christine "turns and rushes into the house" (p. 328) to commit suicide.

Ezra Mannon (Agamemnon), the husband of Christine and victim or her malice, before being murdered by her, confesses to his wife that her hatred of him was the reason why he entered the Mexican War: "I was hoping I might get killed" (p. 270). Now after his return from the Civil War and desiring to mend their marriage, Ezra, to no avail, utters his longing to escape from the perils of the present: "I've been thinking of what we could do to get back to each other. I've a notion if we'd leave the children and go off on a voyage together—to the other side of the world—find some island where we could be alone a while. You'll find I have changed, Christine. I'm sick of death! I want life!" (p. 270). The irony is that Ezra is longing for some otherworldly existence because life itself is a form of death: "That's always been the Mannons' way of thinking. They went to the white meeting-house on Sabbaths and meditated on death. Life was a dying. Being born was starting to die. Death was being born" (p. 269).

In the exact same vein, Christine's son, Orin, describes how, during the Civil War, he "wanted to desert and run home—or else get killed" (p. 300) because he longed for his mother's love. And after he was wounded in action, he, too, dreamed of going to the Islands on the other side of the world—the South Sea Islands which "came to mean everything that wasn't war, everything that was peace and warmth and security" (p. 300). These "Blessed Isles" represent the womb to which the Mannon men, including Adam Brant, long to regress, for it is only within the womb that all one's needs are satisfied and no conflicts can emerge. In his notes for the play, O'Neill "wrote that the islands should represent among other things the 'mother symbol—yearning for prenatal non-competitive freedom from fear.'"[20] He also "talked about ' "Island" death fear and death wish' . . . and after the play was completed, he spoke about 'the life and death impulses that drive the characters on to their fates.'"[21] And in *Beyond the Pleasure Principle,* Freud similarly states that "The dominating tendency of mental life, and perhaps of nervous life in general, is the effort to reduce, to keep constant or to remove internal tension due to stimuli (the 'Nirvana principle', to borrow a term from Barbara Low)—a tendency which finds expression in the pleasure principle; and our recognition of that fact is one of our strongest reasons for believing in the existence of death instincts."[22]

When Orin actually goes to the Islands, it is no surprise that "They only [make] [him] sick" (p. 346), for what he really longs for is to reenter his mother's womb; consequently, "the Blessed Isles" (p. 243) exist only inside his imagination, not in external reality. Having lost his mother and continually hounded by guilt (the furies), Orin can find no peace in life and seizes on his sister's taunting remark that "[He'd] kill [himself] if [he] weren't a coward" (p. 365) as an avenue of escape:

> ORIN: . . . *(He stops abruptly and stares before him, as if this idea were suddenly taking hold of his tortured imagination and speaks fascinatedly to himself)* Yes! That would be justice—now you are Mother! She is speaking now through you! *(More and more hypnotized by this train of thought)* Yes! It's the way to peace—to find her again—my lost island—Death is an island of peace, too—Mother will be waiting for me there—*(With excited eagerness now, speaking to the dead)* Mother? . . . You're here in the house now! You're calling me! You're waiting to take me home! . . . (pp. 365-366.)

Orin then *"turns and strides toward the door"* (p. 366) and commits suicide.

After a Freudian slip, Lavinia, the last Mannon, realizes that she, like other Mannon figures, was goaded to revenge not out of a sense of justice but because of selfish desire. Finally, she decides to take upon herself all of the Mannons' sins:

> LAVINIA: . . ."I'm the last Mannon. I've got to punish myself! Living alone here with the dead is a worse act of justice than death or prison! I'll never go out or see anyone! I'll have the shutters

nailed closed so no sunlight can ever get in. I'll live alone with the dead, and keep their secrets, and let them hound me, until the curse is paid out and the last Mannon is let die! *(With a strange cruel smile of gloating over the years of self-torture)* I know they will see to it I live for a long time! It takes the Mannons to punish themselves for being born! (p. 376.)

Following her speech to Seth Beckwith, the Mannons' gardener, Lavinia *"ascends to the portico—and then turns and stands for a while, stiff and square-shouldered, staring into the sunlight with frozen eyes. Seth leans out of the window at the right of the door and pulls the shutters closed with a decisive bang. As if this were a word of command, Lavinia pivots sharply on her heel and marches woodenly into the house, closing the door behind her"* (p. 376).

One is struck by the way in which Nina and Charlie of *Strange Interlude* and the members of the Mannon family come home to rest. In both plays, the house is a symbol of death. According to Freud, "the dwelling-house was a substitute for the mother's womb, the first lodging, for which in all likelihood man still longs, and in which he was safe and felt at ease."[23] For all her talk of living, Lavinia has returned to the Mannon house only to die. To be more precise, she, like Nina and Charlie of *Strange Interlude,* has become a living-death figure. Her Christ-like decision to suffer for the sins of "everymannon" by remaining *"bound here* [italics mine]*—to the Mannon dead"* (p. 375) is merely a mask to conceal her terror of living in the world of reality. Sealing herself off from society by literally *shutting her self in the house.* Lavinia does not experience the joy of courageously confronting her conflicts in a constructive manner, but only indulges herself in masochistic delight in having found a neurotic pseudosolution to the problem of guilt.

The image of being bound plays an important part in the theme of the longing for death in these two plays. It represents the characters' self-imposed confinement which reflects their inability to exist between the limits of life or spiritually to transcend them; that is to say, within the dualistic framework depicting the battle between the forces of life and death, the characters cling to the pole of death in order to escape the tragic tension of life.[24] The image is paradoxical because the characters long to go "beyond the horizon"[25]—beyond the boundaries of their existence in search of peace and security, but they discover that this can only be accomplished through regression. Hence, the characters *bind* themselves to death—to the womb-tomb shelter of the past.

The theme of the longing for death in *Strange Interlude* and *Mourning Becomes Electra* bears a striking resemblance to Freud's concept of the death instinct as it is described in *Beyond the Pleasure Principle.* This is understandable, for O'Neill most likely read *Beyond the Pleasure Principle* prior to writing the two plays whose language suggests a knowledge of this book. But I contend that O'Neill's reading of *Beyond the Pleasure Prin-*

ciple reinforced his *own* concept of the death wish, which is expressed through his characters as a longing to be delivered from the pain of living. We must credit the playwright for his unique, personal vision and distinguish it from that of the psychoanalyst since in O'Neill's writings the death wish is not instinctual but a choice on the part of the individual to eliminate life's tragic tension through self-destruction.

NOTES

¹ Critics who similarly have dealt with the subject of death in these two plays, but not specifically from this point of view, or only tangentially to it, are: Inger Aarseth, "A Drama of Life and Death Impulses: A Thematic Analysis of 'Mourning Becomes Electra,'" *Americana Norwegica,* 4 (1973), 291-304; Leonard Chabrowe, *Ritual and Pathos: The Theater of O'Neill* (New Jersey: Associated University Presses, 1961): Edwin A. Engel, *The Haunted Heroes of Eugene O'Neill* (Cambridge: Harvard University Press, 1953); Bryllion Fagin, "Eugene O'Neill Contemplates Mortality," in *O'Neill and His Plays: Four Decades of Criticism,* ed. Oscar Cargill et al. (New York: New York University Press, 1961), pp. 424-430; Doris V. Falk, *Eugene O'Neill and the Tragic Tension* (1958; rpt. New Jersey: Rutgers University Press, 1969); and John Henry Raleigh, *The Plays of Eugene O'Neill* (Carbondale: Southern Illinois University Press, 1965).

² Tom F. Driver, in his article "On the Late Plays of Eugene O'Neill," *The Tulane Drama Review,* 3, No. 2 (Dec. 1958), 8-20, notes that not much critical attention has been paid to Freud's notion of the death wish and then briefly discusses this idea in relation to O'Neill's *The Iceman Cometh.*

³ Arthur H. Nethercot, "The Psychoanalyzing of Eugene O'Neill," *Modern Drama,* 3, No. 3 (Dec. 1960), 248.

⁴ W. David Sievers, *Freud on Broadway: A History of Psychoanalysis and the American Drama* (New York: Hermitage House, 1955), p. 116.

⁵ Egil Törnqvist, *A Drama of Souls: Studies in O'Neill's Supernaturalistic Technique.* (New Haven: Yale University Press, 1969), p. 36.

⁶ Törnqvist, p. 36n.

⁷ See Arthur H. Nethercot, "The Psychoanalyzing of Eugene O'Neill," *Modern Drama,* 8, No. 2 (Sept. 1965), 154; and Sievers, p. 116.

⁸ In 1912, O'Neill tried to commit suicide by taking an overdose of the drug Veronal. Croswell Bowen, in his book *The Curse of the Misbegotten: A Tale of the House of O'Neill* (New York: McGraw-Hill Book Co., 1959), p. 26, remarks that "In this suicide attempt O'Neill was giving positive expression to an inner drive that was to be noted by others at many stages in his life—a drive which

Freudian analysts have called the 'death instinct' and which Brooks Atkinson, a few years after O'Neill's death, so nicely described as an 'infatuation with oblivion.'"

⁹ Cf. Raleigh, p. 57.

¹⁰ Eugene O'Neill, *Strange Interlude* (1928), rpt. in *Three Plays of Eugene O'Neill* (New York: Vintage Books, 1959), p. 221. All further references to *Strange Interlude,* and all references to *Mourning Becomes Electra* (1931), will be included in the text.

¹¹ Cf. Chabrowe's comment, p. 106.

¹² Cf. Chabrowe, p. 106.

¹³ Edwin A. Engel, p. 214, notes that "Insofar as psychoanalysis may be considered a science (its method, at least, is claimed to be empirical) it shares with biology O'Neill's contempt."

¹⁴ Kenneth Macgowan, "The O'Neill Soliloquy," in *O'Neill and His Plays: Four Decades of Criticism,* ed. Oscar Cargill et al. (New York: New York University Press, 1961), p. 451.

¹⁵ Sigmund Freud, *The Standard Edition of the Complete Psychological Works of Sigmund Freud,* trans. James Strachey, XVIII (1955; rpt. London: The Hogarth Press, 1975), 38.

¹⁶ Doris M. Alexander, "Psychological Fate in Mourning Becomes Electra," *PMLA,* 68, No. 5 (Dec. 1953), 923.

¹⁷ Travis Bogard, *Contour in Time: The Plays of Eugene O'Neill* (New York: Oxford University Press, 1972), p. 338.

¹⁸ Freud, p. 36.

¹⁹ Freud, p. 37.

²⁰ John Stafford, "Mourning Becomes America," *Texas Studies in Literature and Language,* 3, No. 4 (Winter 1962), 551n.

²¹ Törnqvist, p. 38.

²² Freud, pp. 55-56.

²³ Sigmund Freud, *Civilization and Its Discontents,* trans. James Strachey (1930; rpt. New York: W. W. Norton & Co., 1962), p. 38.

²⁴ See Doris Falk's book for an excellent Neo-Freudian interpretation of O'Neill's plays.

²⁵ With reference to the theme of longing for death, O'Neill's *Beyond the Horizon* can be considered a prototypical play in which its protagonist, Robert Mayo, finds

freedom from pain in actual death, while his wife, Ruth, grows content with figurative or living death.

Jan Kott

SOURCE: "Ionesco, or a Pregnant Death," in *The Dream and the Play: Ionesco's Theatrical Quest,* edited by Moshe Lazar, Undena Publications, 1982, pp. 121-32.

[*In the following essay, Kott observes the tragic-farcical impression of death in Eugène Ionesco's plays.*]

We all know that we shall die. But Ionesco knows it even as he eagerly reaches for a menu in a restaurant. Even while he eats, he knows he is dying. Each of Ionesco's doubles, the Bérengers in his comedies, knows it too. Not only is death constantly present in everything Ionesco writes, but it is present as *dying*—one's own and other people's, universal and incessant.

"When the bells toll for a funeral I am overcome with a mysterious anguish, a sort of fascination. We know all the people who die."[1] This is one of the earliest entries in "Scattered Images of Childhood" from Ionesco's *Fragments of a Journal.* A few pages later, he writes " . . . when I was four or five years old I realized that I should grow older and older and that I should die. At about seven or eight, I said to myself that my mother would die some day and the thought terrified me."[2] And once again: " . . . the only thing one can know is that death is there waiting for my mother, my family, myself."[3]

Many years later, in his reminiscences of the Vaugirard Square, close to where he spent his Parisian childhood, Ionesco wrote: "When memory brings back a picture of that street, when I think that almost all those people are now dead, everything does indeed seem to me to be a shadow and evanescence. My head spins with anguish. Really, that *is* the world: a desert of fading shadows."[4] And the following two lines, which could have concluded Bérenger's long monologue at his last meeting with the Killer: "It's to Death, above all, that I say 'Why?' with such terror. Death alone can, and will, close my mouth."[5]

Ionesco's double in *The Killer* says: "We shall all die, this is the only serious alienation." In *Fragments of a Journal* we read: "The human condition is beyond bearing."[6] And further: "I cannot understand how it should be that for hundreds and hundreds and hundreds of years men have accepted life and death in these intolerable conditions: have accepted an existence haunted by the fear of death, amid war and pain, without showing any real, open decisive reaction against it. . . . We are caught in a sort of collective trap and we don't even rebel seriously against it."[7]

One could go on and on citing such quotations, but they are tiresome in their monotony: death is the process of dying, there is no cure for it and no reconciliation. It is

as if there were nothing else to say. Ionesco had intended to write his dissertation at the Sorbonne on "Sin and Death in Poetry After Baudelaire." He never completed his thesis. Smitten by death, he became an author of comedies.

According to my simple definition of this theatrical genre, comedy is a spectacle which evokes laughter. "Nothing is more difficult," wrote Molière, "than to amuse *les honnêtes gens.*" Ionesco is one of the finest, if not the finest of modern playwrights who make us laugh. His plays amuse me and amuse us all. The comic power of *The Bald Soprano, The Lesson* and *Amédée* compares only with that of Chaplin's early films. They arouse and continue to arouse loud laughter.

What kind of laughter is it, and what is its object? "When I say: is life worth dying for? I am still using words. But at least they are comic."[8] In other words, dying can be amusing when it is talked about or performed. "For my part," Ionesco explains, "I have never understood the difference people make between the comic and the tragic. As the 'comic' is an intuitive perception of the absurd, it seems to me more hopeless than the 'tragic.' The 'comic' offers no escape. I say 'hopeless' but in reality it lies outside the boundaries of hope and despair. . . . For it seems to me that the comic is tragic, and that the tragedy of man is pure derision."[9]

The tragic is a source of metaphysical consolation. The tragic without metaphysics—ordinary dying which nothing will justify, the absurd without hope—is ridiculous. "Pure derision," writes Ionesco. And where does it occur? On stage. The *ridiculous-tragic* is a theatrical genre. In 1960 he wrote: "But when these older writers use the comic and mix it with the tragic, in the end their characters are no longer funny: it is the tragic that prevails. In my plays it is just the opposite: they start by being comic, are tragic for a moment and end up in comedy or tragi-comedy."[10]

The term as well as the theatrical genre of tragi-comedy, or tragico-comedy, was invented by Mercury, the god of transformation. "What's that? Are you disappointed/To find it's a tragedy?" he chides Plautus' Amphitryo; "Well, I can easily change it./I am a god, after all./I can easily make a comedy,/And never alter a line."[11] Ionesco called *The Bald Soprano* an anti-play, *The Lesson* a comic drama, *The Chairs* a tragic farce. In *Victims of Duty,* Nicolas explains to the Detective: "No more drama nor tragedy, the tragic's turning comic, the comic is tragic and life's getting more cheerful . . . more cheerful."[12]

"Tragi-comedy" would in this case be a misleading term. The "cheerful life" Nicolas envisions for the Detective is a "tragic farce." Using Aristotelian terms, we would say that terror is to be accompanied by laughter rather than by pity and compassion.[12a] The tragic hero must first perform his role clownishly. As a result of this clownish mockery, the terror of his tragic situation is revealed for a moment, only to be overcome by laughter so that life can become "more cheerful" again.

Ionesco has been transforming the *ridiculous-tragic* into the *tragic-ridiculous,* both in his reflections, and in his plays from *The Chairs, Jack, or the Submission* and *Amédée,* to *The Killer* and *Exit the King.* This dual exchange of theatrical signs, the inverted sequence of the tragic and the ridiculous, seems to give the formula for tragic buffoonery. The best and perhaps the oldest description of this theatrical genre, was given by Peter Quince in *A Midsummer Night's Dream* after he assembles his actors for the first rehearsal. "Marry, our play is 'The most lamentable comedy and most cruel death of Pyramus and Thisby.'" (I,ii, 11-12)

The "most cruel death of Pyramus and Thisby," as the long title indicates, is a "comedy," but it is a "most lamentable" one. This little play, performed by Athenian craftsmen is a burlesque of *Romeo and Juliet,* which one of the Quartos called "The most excellent and lamentable tragedie." The most cruel death of Romeo and Juliet as well as the most cruel death of Bérenger in *The Killer* and in *Exit the King* have been made comic. Nevertheless these comedies are "most lamentable." "Take a tragedy;" Ionesco wrote in his *Notes and Counter Notes;* "accelerate the movement and you will have a comic play . . . ," and more emphatically: "A burlesque text, play it dramatic. A dramatic text, play it burlesque."[13]

The first performances of Ionesco's plays in the 50's aroused simultaneous delight and resistance, admiration and horror at their astounding novelty. And yet, most astounding in Ionesco's tragic farces was their reversion to the most ancient and the most persistent tradition of comic theatre and carnival pageantry: the world is set on its head, the beggar is proclaimed king, the ship of fools represents the human condition, clowns conduct laical and religious rites, death struts in a procession of masks through city streets, dying is equated with breeding, and life becomes "more cheerful."

> The darkness has scarcely descended into the narrow, highwalled street before lights are seen moving in the windows and on the stands; in next to no time the fire has circulated far and wide, and the whole street is lit up by burning candles. . . . It becomes everyone's duty to carry a lighted candle in his hand, and the favorite imprecation of the Romans, "Sia ammazzato," is heard repeatedly on all sides.

> "Sia ammazzato chi non porta moccolo:" "Death to anyone who is not carrying a candle." This is what you say to others, while at the same time you try to blow out their candles.

In this way, Goethe begins his description in *Italian Journey* of the 1788 Carnival in Rome.

> The louder the cries of *Sia ammazzato,* the more these words lose their sinister meaning and you forget that you are in Rome, where, at any other

time but Carnival, and for a trifling reason, the wish expressed by these words might be literally fulfilled.

> Just as in other languages curses and obscene words are often used as expressions of joy or admiration, so, on this evening, the true meaning of *Sia amazzato* is completely forgotten, and it becomes a password, a cry of joy, a refrain added to all jokes and compliments. . . .

> All ages and all classes contend furiously with each other. Carriage steps are climbed; no chandelier and scarcely a paper lantern is safe. A boy blows out his father's candle, shouting "Sia amazzato il Signore Padre!" In vain the old man scolds him for this outrageous behaviour; the boy claims the freedom of the evening and curses his father all the more vehemently.[14]

Ionesco wrote in his *Notes,* " . . . laughter alone respects no taboo . . . the comic alone is able to give us the strength to beat the tragedy of existence."[15] His earlier "intuition of the absurd," like his "tragedy of existence," is a debt paid to the philosophy fashionable in the 50's. Ionesco's true "intuition," however, was the return to carnival celebration where, like in the ancient Saturnalias, our modern *Angst* was present, but where masks of Death were accompanied by masks adorned with phalluses, and with this inversion of signs, funeral rites were turned into rites of wedding.

"There is nothing unfamiliar," continues Goethe, "about seeing figures in fancy dress or masks out in the streets under the clear sky. They can be seen every day of the year. No corpse is brought out to the grave without being accompanied by hooded religious fraternities. The monks in their many kinds of costumes accustom the eye to peculiar figures. There seems to be the Carnival all the year round. . . . "[16] I once watched in New Orleans an amateur theatre troupe which chose a funeral as the subject for a ballet. The rhythmic wailing to blues melodies gradually became more and more ecstatic. Voices rose to an ever higher pitch as a coffin was lifted higher and higher. From beneath long black skirts legs squiggled out as if they had a life of their own. A moment later the coffin swayed in the air, like the dancing hips and bellies.

New Orleans is one of the few places where old carnival traditions, which link together images of sex and death, still retain their compelling symbolism. As Goethe continues in his description of the Roman Carnival, "On the side streets are young fellows dressed up as women, one of whom seems to be far advanced in pregnancy. . . . As if from shock, the pregnant woman is taken ill, a chair is brought and the other women give her aid. She moans like a woman in labour, and the next thing you know, she has brought some misshapen thing into the world, to the great amusement of the onlookers."[17]

According to the oldest traditions of Saturnalia, the woman who gives birth is Death. "In the famous Kerch terracotta collection," writes Bakhtin in *Rabelais and His*

World, "we find figurines of senile pregnant hags. Moreover, the old hags are laughing. It is pregnant death, a death that gives birth. There is nothing completed, nothing calm and stable in the bodies of these old hags. They combine a senile, decaying and deformed flesh with the flesh of new life, conceived but as yet unformed."[18]

The body, Bakhtin writes, is shown in its two-fold contradictory process of decay and growth: a pregnant death. The Saturnalian and carnival signs epitomize the perpetuity and continuity of life and thereby negate completely Samuel Beckett's cruel vision of continuous dying: " . . . one day we were born, one day we shall die, the same day, the same second . . . they give birth astride of the grave. . . ."[19]

The death that gives birth in a carnival farce is not a young woman, pregnant with a new death, but an old hag pregnant with a new foetus. The body, which is decaying, conceives. Awe occasions laughter: in the symbolism of carnival it is one and the same body.

> One of the fundamental tendencies of the grotesque image of the body is to show two bodies in one: the one giving birth and dying, the other conceived, generated, and born. This is the pregnant and begetting body, or at least a body ready for conception and fertilization. . . .
>
> In contrast to modern canons, the age of the body is most frequently represented in immediate proximity to birth or death, to infancy or old age, to the womb or the grave, to the bosom that gives life or swallows it up. But at their extreme limit the two bodies unite to form one. The individual is shown at the state when it is recast into a new mold. It is dying and yet unfinished; the body stands on the threshold of the grave and the crib.
>
> The unfinished and open body (dying, bringing forth and being born) is not separated from the world by clearly defined boundaries; it is blended with the world, with animals, with objects. It is cosmic, it represents the entire material bodily world in all its elements. It is an incarnation of this world at the absolute lower stratum, as the swallowing up and generating principle, as the bodily grave and bosom, as a field which has been sown and in which new shoots are preparing to sprout.[20]

Remarkably, this description of carnival imagination and wisdom which served Bakhin to introduce the world of Rabelais, is also a surprisingly apt introduction to the world of Ionesco's *Jack, or the Submission* and *The Future Is In Eggs.* In both plays, Ionesco appears to be reusing the old formula for a comedy of manners about two families, a shy young man, an ugly miss, a matchmaker, an engagement, a wedding, and a long wait for progeny. But the "naturalistic comedy" becomes a carnival farce, almost an animal farm. The characters are all "Jacks" or "Robertas" with identical face-masks. Their bodies are unfinished, at once decaying and growing. Herded together, they begin to lose even their human shape. Body parts multiply as with the three noses of Roberta II or the nine fingers on her hand.

Jack: . . . You're rich, I'll marry you. . . .

[They put their arms around each other very awkwardly. Jack kisses the noses of Roberta II, one after the other, while Father Jack, Mother Jack, Jacqueline, the Grandparents, Father Robert, and Mother Robert enter without saying a word, one after the other, waddling along, in a sort of ridiculous dance, embarrassing, in a vague circle, around Jack and Roberta II who remain at stage center, awkwardly enlaced. Father Robert silently and slowly strikes his hands together. Mother Robert, her hands clasped behind her neck, makes pirouettes, smiling stupidly. Mother Jack, with an expressionless face, shakes her shoulders in a grotesque fashion. Father Jack pulls up his pants and walks on his heels. Jacqueline nods her head, then they continue to dance, squatting down, while Jack and Roberta II squat down too, and remain motionless. . . . The darkness increases. On stage, the actors utter vague miaows while turning around, bizarre moans, croakings. The darkness increases. We can still see the Jacks and the Roberts crawling on the stage. We can hear their animal noises, then we don't see them any more. We hear only their moans, their sighs, then all fades away, all is extinguished. Again, a gray light comes on. All the characters have disappeared, except Roberta, who is lying down, or rather squatting down, buried beneath her gown. We see only her pale face, with its three noses quivering, and her nine fingers moving like snakes.][21]

In *The Future Is In Eggs,* the barnyard changes into a chicken coop. Roberta II lays eggs, one after the other. She is oviparous. There is no limit to multiplying by way of eggs and the eggs are all the same. The future is in the eggs. Indistinguishable Jacko-Robertas will hatch from them. But even in this carnival chicken coop of boundless fertility, where individuality has been eradicated and life is reduced to the egg, death is present. Even before the young wife begins to lay eggs in a basket, grandfather Jack dies. To "die" means to enter an empty frame. As a matter of fact, he will shock the whole family when he steps out of his frame for a moment to hum to himself.

For Freud laughter is the bribe accepted by the censor of morals for permitting a joke that exposes prurient desires and forbidden wishes. However, more strictly prohibited and suppressed to the depths of the subconscious, is the dread of death, the fear that we will die. All of us. The bribe for revealing this dread and this fear is also laughter. The archaic pregnant Death laughs. Amidst piles of carnival litter, the begetting of a misshapen monster by a man dressed as a woman, evokes riotous laughter. Dread of the end spawns a jolly spectacle. "Death and death throes, labor, and childbirth are intimately interwoven. On the other hand, these images are closely linked to laughter. When death and birth are shown in their comic aspect, scatological images in various forms nearly always accompany the gay monsters created by laughter in order to replace the terror that has been defeated."[22]

With characteristic insight, Goethe perceived the same interwoven images of death, sex and birth in the carnival pantomimes performed on the streets of Rome: "In the course of all these follies our attention is drawn to the most important stages of human life: a vulgar Pulcinella recalls to us the pleasures of love to which we owe our existence; a Baubo profanes in a public place the mysteries of birth and motherhood, and the many lighted candles remind us of the ultimate ceremony."[23]

Pulcinella, as he left the *commedia dell' arte* for the streets, always wore a black leather mask with an enormous hooked nose over his eyes and brow. Harlequin had a similar mask, but his costume was different. Pulcinella wore a large white cylindrical hat, white breeches and jacket, a hump on his back and padding in his belly.

Entertainment for Children,[24] Domenico Tiepolo's ironic title for his series of a hundred wash drawings, is a great "tragic farce." This sad and cheerful, bitter and derisive story covers in a hundred scenes the life of Pulcinella—from his birth out of a turkey's egg to his banishment from eighteenth century Venice.

The title drawing of Tiepolo's *Divertimento per li Regazzi* shows old Pulcinella pensively gazing at a monument inscribed with the title of this series. Perched on his shoulder is a puppet of a beautiful Venetian woman who is smiling flirtatiously. Her head is inclined away from the tomb, in her hand is a fan. She is blithely swinging her legs, having drawn them out from beneath her dress. Possibly, the drawing symbolizes the death of Carnival and the approach of Lent. Or perhaps it is a burlesque parody of a passion play in which Christ arises from his grave.

Pulcinella dies, but not forever. In a Pier Leone Ghezzi drawing from the early eighteenth century, Pulcinella suddenly arises from his bier, terrifying a family of peasants. In one of the drawings from Tiepolo's *Divertimento,* Pulcinella's skeleton, wearing the same large white, cylindrical hat, leaps out of a Rococco grave. Death itself wears the clown hat of Pulcinella.

In Domenico Tiepolo's drawings, the streets of Venice are peopled with Pulcinellas. They paw young women under the ledges of terraced vineyards; dance at village celebrations, hunt for partridges, ride elephants in the circus, collect rent from peasants, and stare inquisitively at camels, which like Pulcinellas themselves, have humps on their backs. Not all of the Pulcinellas are male; women also wear the hooked-nosed masks. Pulcinellas have Pulcinella wives and Pulcinella children, who enter the world with potbellies, humps, and black noses. But the Pulcinella in Tiepolo drawings, and perhaps also in some lost story, is not merely the actor and hero in a Venetian comedy of manners or a carnival pantomime. Here he is incarcerated; other Pulcinellas visit him in prison. As in the paintings of Callot and Goya where the atrocities of the Napoleonic Wars are depicted, so in Tiepolo's *Entertainment for Children* we find scenes of hangings and executions. A blind-folded Pulcinella, still wearing a black-nosed mask, awaits execution bound to a stake. Another Pulcinella lies on the ground, already shot. The execution squad itself, rifles poised for firing, consists of Pulcinellas in white hats. In another drawing, Pulcinella, bereft of his hat, but still in his black-nosed mask, dangles from a scaffold where a crowd of Pulcinellas has gathered. The hangman is on a horse and wears the white Pulcinella hat; he, too, is Pulcinella. Pulcinella is the hangman and the hanged man; he is the executioner and the executed. Wars and revolutions are also a tragic farce: the actors and victims are Pulcinellas. Pulcinella is a new Everyman.

All Bérengers in Ionesco's plays are his doubles and at the same time, Everyman. In two small rooms in a basement of the Frick Collection in New York, where in the winter of 1980 *Entertainment for Children* was exhibited for the first time, I suddenly saw Ionesco's great theatre. Perhaps the Professor in *The Lesson* who rapes and murders his fourteenth pupil in a row, ought to wear the Pulcinella black mask with a hooked nose and the white hat. Perhaps the Pupil, who is able to multiply multi-digit numbers in her head but cannot subtract, and who suffers a sudden toothache, should wear not only the blouse and the short skirt of a school-girl, but also a little mask with a black hooked nose.

Perhaps the Old Man and the Old Woman in *Chairs* should also wear Pulcinella masks. Surely, the Orator who after the suicide of the Elders proclaims his final message to empty chairs, should be masked like Pulcinella and could display a hump as well as a pot-belly. Wearing the white blouse of Punch and Pierrot and a huge Pulcinella hat, he would draw letters on the black-board and gesture with his hands like a deaf man. In *Amédée or How to Get Rid of It,* gigantic legs of a corpse gradually slide into Amédée's and Magdalena's dining room. This corpse may be a murdered lover or the Past. In any case, it is also Death. But here, Death is present only as the legs of a giant dummy. As in carnival imagery, this Death is "a gay monster created by laughter in order to replace the terror that has been defeated."

We "do die," writes Ionesco, "It is horrible and cannot be taken seriously. How can I trust in a world that has no stability, that flits away? One moment I can see Camus, I can see Atlan and suddenly they are gone. It's ridiculous. It almost makes me laugh. Anyway, King Solomon has already exhausted the subject."[25] Or, "King Solomon is my master," and yet again, "Yes, the leader I follow is King Solomon; and Job, that contemporary of Beckett."[26] Job and Beckett—the comparison is obvious, but what is Solomon's place in this company? "I am the most foolish of men,"[27] says Solomon in *Ecclesiastes*. Precisely this sentence is the one Folly cites with delight in Erasmus' *The Praise of Folly*.

King Solomon frequently appears in Medieval ribaldries as well as in Medieval and early Renaissance morality plays. His wisdom is always foolish. Ionesco could have written a tragic farce, "Solomon and Job Discourse on Death." In this "Dialogue of the Dead" we would hear again Lucian's derisive laughter.

The Death which comes to Bérenger in the epilogue to *The Killer,* does not utter a word. This is no longer the archaic pregnant Death, nor the gay carnival Death which gives birth to a new creature in order to overcome the terror. It is the Medieval Death which calls with a sickle on Everyman. Unbridable, irrevocable and ruthless, this Death has no respect for human honor or dignity. When the fifteenth century Everyman proposes a tribe, Death responds with indignation:

> Everyman, it may not be, by no way.
> I see not by gold, silver, nor riches,
> Ne by pope, emperor, king, duke, ne princes;
> For, and I would receive gifts great,
> All the world I might get;
> But my custom is clean contrary.
> I give thee no respite. Come hence, and not tarry.[28]

In *The Killer,* Death is silent. Bérenger, all alone, must carry on a Medieval dialogue with Death:

> You're poor now, aren't you? Do you want some money? I can find you work, a decent job. . . . No. You're not poor? Rich then?. . . . Aaah, I see, neither rich nor poor! (Chuckle from the KILLER)[29]

According to Ionesco's stage directions Killer-Death is supposed to be " . . . very small and puny, ill-shaven with a torn hat on his head, and a shabby old gabardine; he has only one eye, which shines with a steely glitter . . ."[30] All Medieval texts talk about the hideousness of Death. Yet in folk drama, in the Sicilian Opera dei Puppi, and in the Polish folk theatre, Skeleton-Death is also quite funny. In the Italian theatre of marionettes, Death diligently saws off heads of sinners which then roll off stage to the merriment of the spectators. In Polish folk theatre, King Herod's head is a cabbage which Death reaps, like a peasant his crops. Death in Ionesco merely chuckles as it drowns its victims, in a basin in the Radiant City, where Death gathers its harvest to the perpetual accompaniment of *cris de Paris:* the banter of concierges, the mumbling of vagabonds, and the shouts of street vendors. Ionesco's chuckling Death could wear the mask of Harlequin with a hooked nose and have Pierrot's powdered white face. *The Killer* is a tragic farce performed on city streets.

We "do die," Ionesco repeats. "It is horrible and cannot be taken seriously." *Exit the King* is a comedy about dying. It is the only modern comedy about dying and the only *comedy* with a hero and the main actor who begins *dying* in the very first scene before he dies in the last one. If Bérenger were dying in a real bed, if he were mourned by a *real* wife and a *real* mistress, if he were treated and operated on by *real* doctors, if a *real* nurse rearranged *real* pillows for him, this *play* would be insufferable. But Bérenger, who is dying in Ionesco's comedy, is a King.

"The King," wrote Stanislaw Jerry Lec, "is naked . . . but under such splendid robes."[31] Bérenger is dying in splendid robes of royalty. He is King, a fairy tale King, a King in a palace assembled by children out of cards; he is King of a carnival masquerade.

Bérenger does not die. The King dies in the company of Queen Marguerite, who was his first wife, Queen Marie, his second wife, and the Doctor, who does not take care of him and who is at once, "a surgeon, a hangman, a bacteriologist, and an astrologer." Bérenger is dressed up as King so that he can die only as King.

Among the most enduring of carnival amusements is the crowning and uncrowning of the beggar enacted so that he can later be abused, scourged and chased. The beggar's coronation in the marketplace shows traces, according to Frazer, of an ancient ritual in which the king's substitute was killed annually in order to "resurrect" the real king. In the carnival travesty, death cannot be taken seriously. The inhabitants of the Isle of Winds in Rabelais' utopia emit gases when they die and their souls, like this unbecoming gas, leave their bodies *via rectum.* In Seneca's satire *Ludus Morte Claudii,* Caesar dies in the act of defecation.

In *Le roi se meurt, ou la cérémonie,* the ceremonies of dying are carnivalesque. " . . . we do die. It is horrible and cannot be taken seriously." Bérenger is Ionesco's double. King Bérenger dies to enable Ionesco not to die.

I saw *The Bald Soprano* and *The Lesson* for the first time when they opened in Warsaw. I think it was 1956. Subsequently, whenever I was in Paris I would go to the little theatre in the Rue de la Huchette, where *The Lesson* and *The Bald Soprano* were continually running. When I was there last in 1965, I was not sure whether the same actress was still playing the Pupil. She seemed less childish. After the performance I visited the Ionescos. I recorded my recollections from this evening in my diary, which was later published in *Theatre Notebook:*

> "Of course, it's the same actress," said Eugène. "*The Lesson* will go on being performed for another fifty or seventy years. One day the Pupil will die. I mean really die, not just on the stage. She will go to heaven, and St. Peter will sternly ask her: 'What did you do in life, my child?' And she will reply, 'What did I do? I was eighteen when I began to act the Pupil in M. Ionesco's play at the theatre in the rue de la Huchette. Then I got engaged, to be married, and I went on acting the Pupil. Then I got married. I went on acting the Pupil. Then I got pregnant for three months. I stopped acting the Pupil. Then my daughter was born. I went on acting the Pupil. Then I got a divorce. I went on acting the Pupil. Then I got married again. I went on acting the Pupil. Then my son was born. I went on acting the Pupil. Then I got divorced again. I went on acting the Pupil. Then my daughter had twins. I had to leave Paris for two weeks. Then I went on acting the Pupil.' And St. Peter will say, 'M. Ionesco can hardly wait for you; he is attending a rehearsal of *The Lesson.*'"
>
> Ionesco looked at me, became very sad all of a sudden and said in a choked whisper, "It's not true; I shall not die."[32]

NOTES

* This essay was translated from the Polish by Michael Kott.

[1] Eugène Ionesco, *Fragments of a Journal,* trans. Jean Stewart (New York: Grove Press, 1968), p. 8.

[2] Ionesco, *Fragments,* p. 10.

[3] Ionesco, *Fragments,* p. 20.

[4] Eugène Ionesco, *Notes and Counter Notes: Writings on the Theatre,* trans. Donald Watson (New York: Grove Press, 1964), p. 154.

[5] Ionesco, *Fragments,* p. 27.

[6] Ionesco, *Fragments,* p. 21.

[7] Ionesco, *Fragments,* p. 31.

[8] Ionesco, *Fragments,* p. 73.

[9] Ionesco, *Notes,* p. 27.

[10] Ionesco, *Notes,* p. 119.

[11] Plautus, "Amphitryo" in *The Rope And Other Plays,* trans. E. F. Watling (London: Penguin Books, 1965), p. 230.

[12] Eugène Ionesco, "Victims of Duty," in *Plays II,* trans. Donald Watson (London: John Calder, 1958), p. 309.

[12a] J. S. Doubrovsky, "Ionesco and the Comic of Absurdity," *Yale French Studies* (23, 1959), p. 9. "This non-Aristotelian theater presents us with a problem which Aristotle had not foreseen: that of pity and fear for which *laughter* is a chatharsis."

[13] Ionesco, *Notes,* p. 228; p. 182.

[14] J. W. Goethe, *Italian Journey,* trans. W. H. Auden and E. Mayer (New York: Pantheon Books, 1962), pp. 467-68.

[15] Ionesco, *Notes,* p. 144.

[16] Goethe, *Italian Journey,* p. 448.

[17] Goethe, *Italian Journey,* pp. 460-61.

[18] Mikhail Bakhtin, *Rabelais and His World,* trans. Helen Iswolsky (Cambridge, Massachusetts: The M.I.T. Press, 1968), pp. 25-26.

[19] Samuel Beckett, *Waiting for Godot* (New York: Grove Press, 1954), p. 57.

[20] Bakhtin, *Rabelais,* pp. 26-27.

[21] Eugène Ionesco, "Jack or the Submission," in *Four Plays,* trans. Donald M. Allen (New York: Grove Press, 1958), p. 109.

[22] Bakhtin, *Rabelais,* p. 151.

[23] Goethe, *Italian Journey,,* p. 16.

[24] Marcia E. Vetrocq, ed., *Domenico Tiepolo's Punchinello Drawings* (Indiana University Art Museum, 1979).

[25] Ionesco, *Notes,* p. 110.

[26] Ionesco, *Notes,* p. 156.

[27] Erasmus, "The Praise of Folly," in *The Essential Erasmus* (New York: New American Library, 1964), p. 164.

[28] "Everyman," in *Everyman and Medieval Miracle Plays,* ed. A. C. Cawley (New York: Dutton, 1959), p. 210.

[29] Eugène Ionesco, *The Killer and Other Plays,* trans. Donald Watson (New York: Grove Press, 1960), p. 105.

[30] Ionesco, *The Killer,* p. 97.

[31] S. J. Lec, *Unkempt Thoughts,* trans. Jack Galazka (New York: St. Martins Press, 1962), n.p.

[32] Jan Kott, *Theatre Notebook 1947-1967,* trans. Boleslaw Taborski (New York: Doubleday, 1968), p. 220.

Rosette Lamont

SOURCE: "Death and Tragi-Comedy," in *The Massachusetts Review,* Vol. VI, No. 2, Winter-Spring, 1965, pp. 381-402.

[*In the following essay, Lamont considers representative plays by Samuel Beckett, Eugène Ionesco, and Jack Richardson in order to examine the modern dramatist's comic interpretation of human suffering and death.*]

There is no solution to the unbearable, and the new theatre attempts to offer no solutions. It is concerned with scrutinizing man exposed to what George Steiner calls "the murderousness and caprice of the inhuman."[1] The most unavoidable truth of all is that of man's mortality. Death, one's own and that of those we love, is the central preoccupation of our contemporary dramatists.

Pierre Aimé Touchard, a former Administrateur of the Comédie Française, and a close friend of Ionesco, defines the tragic climate as one in which "men recognize themselves . . . recognize themselves in others . . . recognize one another . . . come to full consciousness in the beautiful."[2] And he affirms: "What constitutes the tragic atmosphere is not the play but the spectator," because "I call Dionysian tension the state in which the spectator feels himself tied so intimately to the destiny of the characters that he loses the awareness that this destiny is not his own."[3] Thus, Dionysian tension is achieved when we identify with the hero to the extent that his fate becomes our fate, his death our own. Speaking of Shakespeare's Richard II, Ionesco says: "it is *I* who die with Richard II."[4]

What is true of the death of Richard is even more so of Hamlet's death. A character in a play acquires greater reality than a member of the audience: his struggles and suffering take precedence over those of the people watching him. The audience loses sight of the fact that it is watching an actor, and experiences the emotions of pity and terror for a human being whose life unfolds upon the stage. To dramatize the situation of audience vis-à-vis *dramatis persona,* Shakespeare shows his Hamlet as a so-called "real" person as compared to the players who perform the piece he has written. Yet, Hamlet himself was struck with wonder at the actor's emotion over Hecuba. It seemed to him that the player could feel more grief over the fictional Hecuba than he experienced over his father's death. It is then that Hamlet, whose tragic duties are "real," decides to use the device of a play as a "mouse-trap" to capture the truth of his situation, and confirm the veracity of the ghost's revelations. But the audience of *Hamlet* cannot help retaining in part of its mind the knowledge that Hamlet is just a character within Shakespeare's imitation of an action, that he himself is made of "the stuff of dreams," as evanescent as the substance of which the characters of the play within the play are composed. By making one of the central episodes of his tragedy a play within the play, Shakespeare achieves two effects: he affirms the reality of his hero, allowing the spectator to identify completely with the protagonist; and he demonstrates that a narrow, almost invisible line divides reality from fiction—the stage of a theatre from the stage of life.

Hamlet the person plays many parts: a clown, a fool, a madman. He is his own *dramatis persona* within an ironic tragi-comedy mocking the vitiated ritual celebrations of the corrupt court of Denmark. The melancholy Prince of Denmark "plays himself" unto death, retaining to the end a sharp self-consciousness. His ironic detachment allows him to see himself reflected in the mirror of his lucidity, the crystallized myth of the character he is and chooses to become. He watches himself grieve, brew a dreadful vengeance; he spies on his own fascination with death, his longing "not to be." But above all he wants to retain consciousness to the end, and like his great contemporary, the poet Donne, he could say: "I would not that death should take me asleep. I would not have him meerly seise me, and onely declare me to be dead, but win me, and overcome me. When I must shipwrack, I would do it in a Sea, when mine impotencie might have some excuse; not in a sullen weedy lake, where I could not have so much as exercise for my swimming. Therefore I would fain do something; but that I cannot tell what is no wonder. *For to chuse, is to du:* but to be no part of any body, is to be nothing" (my own italics).[5]

Like Donne, Hamlet sees all the possibilities of action and finds it difficult *to choose,* and *do.* Having been

"shipwrecked" and rescued by pirates, Hamlet learns that Claudius plotted his death, and that his university friends, Rosencrantz and Guildenstern, were to deliver him in England to his executioners. Yet he still fails to kill the king, and agrees to participate in the ritual joust against Laertes, with whom he had already grappled in the fresh grave of Ophelia. Hamlet, the ironic actor of himself, the mocker of Claudius's court of appearances, is brought to death in the last ritual feast of the play, a fencing match, with the rules of the game subtly altered by the treacherous king.

As he learns from the lips of the dying Laertes of the poisoned sword, Hamlet speaks with a mixture of amazement, resignation and a kind of secret joy: "I am dead, Horatio!" At this moment he knows, as does the audience in the theatre, that he has reached the end of his tragic destiny, *le dénouement.* Once again he sees himself objectively, almost as though he were sitting among the people in the theatre; he shares their wonder at the thought that a man who moves, breathes, and addresses a friend, can know that he has "not half an hour of life." How else can we explain Hamlet's peculiar use of the present tense with a future meaning? He does not say: "I am dying!" or "Soon, I'll be dead," but chooses to speak of an unavoidable future in the present to suggest that the creature on the stage is pregnant with mortality.

In *Death and Elizabethan Tragedy,* Theodore Spencer has drawn a number of parallels between Hamlet's state of mind and Donne's. He also shows that the Metaphysical poet and Shakespeare's protagonist are spiritual heirs of St. Bernard de Clairvaux. "Indeed if we consider the development of the European mind from this point of view," he writes, "all its various changes from the time of St. Bernard of Clairvaux (1095-1155) to the time of Shakespeare may be seen as parts of one unbroken movement, and the creation of Hamlet may be regarded as a remote consequence of St. Bernard's contemplation of the sufferings of Christ."[6] St. Bernard's "emphasis . . . on the human pains of Jesus" created a new sensibility, and thus "the continued contemplation of Christ's death made the individual contemplate, with increasing fervor, his own."[7] Indeed, one could draw a line from the Sermons of St. Bernard through Villon's Testaments, Donne's Anniversaries and Sermons, Hamlet's soliloquies, Baudelaire's Spleen poems and his "Une Charogne," Mallarmé's *I gitur,* right to Beckett's *Malone Dies.* The common denominator in all these works is what one writer calls "a self-conscious death which would be the fulfillment of being."[8]

In his *Notebooks of Malte,* Rilke states that each one of us carries his death as a fruit does its seed. When Hamlet says, "I am dead," and indeed repeats these words once more, we realize that we have been watching all along one of the living dead, a man who absented himself from "felicity" in order to carry out his duty as son and Prince of Denmark. But like Donne, Hamlet is fascinated by death to the extent that it heightens his apprehension of the process of living. Death would confer on him a finality he cannot experience while alive. He would no longer have to enact the madman, or choose his vengeance. He could leave his story to Horatio. But the awareness of the void, of nothingness, sweetens the very pain of the present moment. Pain and suffering are still awareness, the state of being alive. "We die every day, and we die all the day long," says Donne in a sermon,[9] and in "The Second Anniversary" he lingers lovingly over the throes of a dying body:

> Thinke thy selfe labouring now with broken
>   breath,
> And thinke those broken and softe Notes to bee
> Division, and thy happyest Harmonie.
> Thinke thee laid on thy death-bed, loose and
>   slacke / . . .
> Thinke thy selfe parch'd with fevers violence, /
>   . . .
> Thinke thy friends weeping round, and thinke that
>   they
> Weepe but because they goe not yet thy way. / . . .
> Thinke that they shroud thee up / . . .
> Thinke that thy body rots, / . . .
> Thinke thee a Prince, who of themselves create
> Wormes which insensibly devoure their state. /
>   . . .
> Thinke that they bury thee . . .

It is this very contemplation of the process of living which is also the process of dying which constitutes the philosophical basis of much of our contemporary art. The Tragi-Comic mode is the dramatic expression of this particular sensibility.

In a world turned upside down, a world deprived of heroes, tragedy is no longer possible. Tragedy presupposes, according to Friedrich Duerrenmatt, "guilt, despair, lucidity, vision, a sense of responsibility,"[10] and above all it depends on a hierarchical order. In a society ruled by mass production, a civilization which equates people and things as products to be consumed, the state loses its physical reality. The mighty who were formerly our standard for measuring virtue have themselves turned into replaceable expressions of blind cruelty; they are the puppets of Evil. Old newsreels reveal the extraordinary resemblance between Hitler and Jarry's Ubu. "Objective humor," the term André Breton uses to describe the spirit of Jarry's work,[11] is the weapon the artist wields against the tyranny of mediocrity, and the "banality of evil." According to Duerrenmatt, "the comical exists in forming what is formless, in creating order out of chaos." Thus "comedy is the mousetrap in which the public is easily caught." Duerrenmatt believes, however, that "the tragic is still possible if pure tragedy is not" for "we can achieve tragedy out of comedy."

Tragi-comedy, whether it is called *comic drama, tragic farce, pseudo drama,* or turned on its head to be termed "comi-tragedy," is the dominant mode of our ironic age. It mirrors the passionate anarchy our artists oppose to an absurd world, a meaningless society, devitalized speech. It embodies our puzzlement with the world, and suggests the groping for a question rather than an answer. As

Ionesco writes in "Brief Notes for Radio": "I look and I see pictures, creatures that move in a kind of timeless time and spaceless space, emitting sounds that are a kind of language I no longer understand or ever register. 'What is all this?' I wonder. 'What does it all mean?' And out of this state of mind, which seems to spring from the most fundamental part of my nature, is strangely born at times a feeling of despair that the world should be so utterly ephemeral and precarious, as if it all existed and did not exist at the same time, as if it lay somewhere between being and non-being: and that is the origin of my tragic farces."[12]

Samuel Beckett's *Happy Days*[13] is the soliloquy of a silly, optimistic, middle-aged woman, Winnie, who is clearly shown interred alive in a steadily growing mound of earth. In Act I Winnie is buried to her waist, and can still move her arms, shoulders, and head. In Act II her head alone is visible, and she is reduced to moving her eyeballs.

Despite this horrifying situation, Winnie keeps on chattering pleasantly about the past and present, those "happy days." She is speaking mainly to herself, although ostensibly her questions and remarks are addressed to her husband, Willie, who inhabits a hole at the foot of the mound, to the back, and out of range of Winnie's limited view. Willie interrupts his wife's monologue with occasional readings from the obituary page, or the clarification of points of syntax. His most illuminating comment is an explanation of what the word *hog* means as an answer to Winnie's query concerning the inscription on her hair brush, "genuine pure hog's setae."

> WINNIE: What is a hog, Willie, please!
>   *(Pause)*
> WILLIE: Castrated male swine *(Happy expression*
>   *appears on Winnie's face)* Reared for
>   slaughter.
>   *(Happy expression increases.)*

Clearly Winnie thinks the definition suits the speaker, her husband. Nor would she be averse to seeing him slaughtered. For that matter he probably feels the same way about her, for he crawls in at the end "dressed to kill." A devastating comment on married life.

Winnie's incessant chatter is punctuated by an equally incessant activity. She goes through the routines of life, brushing her teeth, combing her hair, applying lipstick, performing in fact the many trivial chores women go through in the course of their daily existence. A social worker or psychiatrist might call her well-adjusted, but Beckett leaves us no doubt as to his ironic view as he has her quoting from *Romeo and Juliet* while applying make-up to her doomed face. "Ensign crimson. Pale flag." The words uttered by Romeo as he looked down upon a Juliet he imagined dead:

> beauty's ensign yet
> Is crimson in thy lips and in thy cheeks
> And death's pale flag is not advanced there

have an ironic ring in the mouth of this narcissistic middlebrow, paralyzed not by a soporific drug which makes the living Juliet seem dead, but by the ever tightening girdle of the earthly grave which will swallow all. The disconnected quotations which crowd her brain, the disconnected gestures which testify to the fact that this woman is still alive cannot disguise the fact that, in the words of Hamlet fingering the skull of Yorick, "to this favor she must come."

As Winnie extracts the various articles necessary to her toilet from a handbag, she is delighted and amused by what she finds. ("The depths in particular, who knows what treasures.") It is important at this point to recall that the image of the bag recurs throughout Beckett's work. The narrator of *How It Is* is a crawling creature like Willie with a fifty-kilo coalsack of wet jute tied round his neck. The contents of the sack are a can opener, a bit of rope, and some cans of food. These objects are not only vital necessities; they offer points of reference without which man would be lost. The dying Malone, for example, finds it important to make an inventory of his possessions: "When I have completed my inventory, if my death is not ready for me then, I shall write my memoirs. . . . Dish and pot, dish and pot, these are the poles."[14] The sack and its contents become symbols for our material possessions, pitiful reductions of the baroque grandeur of a San Simeon, or the painting collection of a Getty, ultimately futile in the face of destruction.

The narrator of *How It Is* uses his sack for spiritual comfort as much as for convenience: "the sack again other connections I take it in my arms talk to it put my head in it rub my cheek on it lay my lips on it turn my back to it again clasp it to me again say to it thou thou."[15] The sack takes the place of the soft breast of the mother or that of a woman one loves. It is also a kind of womb into which Beckett's men try to crawl. It represents and replaces the secret recesses of woman, the comfort of love.[16]

Among the commonplace objects within Winnie's bag one seems to float up from the bottom despite the fact that "the weight of this thing would bring it down." The revolver defies the laws of gravity, just as Winnie herself at times feels that she "would simply float up into the blue" did not the girdle of the earth clasp her loins so tightly.

> WINNIE: Don't you ever have that feeling,
>   Willie, of being sucked up? *(Pause)* Don't you
>   have to cling sometimes, Willie?

> WILLIE: *Sucked* up?

The word rouses Willie out of his habitual silence. Clearly for him it has only erotic implications. Winnie, however, feels that sometimes she can escape "natural laws."

Winnie's revolver used to belong to Willie, but she has taken it away from him at his own request. Clearly he prefers "to be" despite much posturing ("Remember how you used to keep at me to take it away from you? Take it away, Winnie, take it away, before I put myself out of my misery. . . . Your misery!") Though Winnie's misery may be greater than Willie's, she much prefers a life of "lasting woe" to not being. The word Paradise is significantly forgotten or lost, "Oh fleeting joys—oh something lasting woe," but there can be many happy days still. Winnie, with a kiss, sets the revolver within reach, but since by the second half of the play she has lost the use of her arms the weapon stays where she has placed it, a useless object among many others. Winnie prefers to "absent" herself "from felicity awhile."

Winnie's situation, which recalls that of the Damned of Dante's *Inferno,* is actually that of any person past his or her prime. Beckett shows how futile it is for a woman of fifty to pretend that she will live forever. We say that a person has one foot in the grave; Beckett's Winnie has both feet in, as well as the whole lower portion of her anatomy. In that she reminds us of Nell, the inhabitant of one of the twin garbage cans of *Endgame.* Almost all of Beckett's characters are either immobilized or half-paralyzed. When they are not confined to a wheel chair (Hamm in *Endgame*), a jar *(The Unnamble),* an urn (the lovers' triangle of *Play*), they must content themselves with crawling through the slime as does "the worm-like hero of *Comment c'est*" who sustains his failing strength on tins of fish, nibbling "at morsels of the body of Christ, taken from a vacuum-packed tabernacle, until he loses his appetite and discards his canned sustenance into the ubiquitous mud." The French have a wonderful expression for loss of vitality: "Il est diminué." Alice in Wonderland, for example, is constantly shrinking or growing. At one time she almost snuffs herself out of existence by using the white rabbit's fan. She stops just in time when she sees that she has been able to slip her hand into his tiny glove. The Unnamable is also shrinking within his jar.

> I have dwindled. I dwindle. Not so long ago, with a kind of shrink of my head and shoulders, as when one is scolded, I could disappear. Soon, at my present rate of decrease, I may spare myself the trouble of closing my eyes, so as not to see the day, for they are blinded by the jar a few inches away. . . . Wrong again, wrong again, this effort and this trouble will not be spared me. For the woman, displeased at seeing me sink lower and lower, has raised me up by filling the bottom of my jar with sawdust which she changes every week, when she makes my toilet. It is softer than the stone, but less hygienic. And I had got used to the stone. Now I'm getting used to the sawdust. It's an occupation. . . . And today, if I can still open and close my eyes, as in the past, I can no longer, because of my roguish character, move my head in and out, as in the good old days.[17]

The situation of the Unnamable, of Winnie, and even to some extent of Lewis Carroll's youthful heroine is a perfect objective correlative for the sapping action of time. Eugène Ionesco says again and again in his critical writings that we are killed by time. Beckett allows us to witness the murderous action of time.

Though most of Beckett's characters are resigned to their awful situation, and accept it as "normal," in the way Kafka's Gregor Samsa adjusts to his metamorphosis, Winnie does more than accept. Though she is visibly half out of this life, she remains as cheerful as though she were immortal. She remembers a couple stopping in front of her mound, and the husband telling his wife that if he were Willie, he "would dig her out" with his "bare hands," but she does not resent the fact that these strangers passed judgment on her husband without offering any concrete help. She thinks of them as of characters in a dream, content with having memories. "Strange thing, time like this, drift up into the mind (Pause.) Strange? (Pause.) No, here all is strange. (Pause.) Thankful for it in any case. (Voice breaks) Most thankful." Though she has a moment of weakness, Winnie has real courage. Her constant chatter is both foolish and endearing; at the same time it is quite typically feminine. Beckett has succeeded in creating one of his most successful female characters.

Winnie the chatterbox and Willie the silent partner are on one level: the typical British couple of grade B movies. If we did not see Winnie imbedded in earth, we could imagine the same conversation at the breakfast table, the wife talking a blue streak, the husband hiding behind his paper (as Willie does at the bottom of the mound). He regales his wife with tidbits such as: "Opening for smart youth. Wanted bright boy," which set her off on long, sentimental reminiscences of the bright boys she used to want. There was a gentleman with a tawny moustache, Johnson, Johnston, or Johnstone, who by any other name would still have kissed her in the toolshed. As to Willie, he seems to listen but he does not talk. Winnie reminds him: "You were never one to talk, I worship you Winnie be mine and then nothing from that day forth only tidbits from Reynolds news." Once in a while, however, husband and wife seem to share a joke as when they laugh for a long time over the word "formication," but even then Winnie cannot be sure that they are not "diverted by two quite different things." She forgives Willie for picking his nose and eating his pickings, all "natural, human" things as she says. Even the fact that he is no longer "the crawler" she gave her heart to can be endured so long as he pretends to listen to her. Marriage as Beckett portrays it is a "solitude à deux."

> Ah yes, if only I could bear to be alone, I mean prattle away with not a soul to hear. Not that I flatter myself you hear much, no Willie, God forbid. (Pause.) Days perhaps when you hear nothing. (Pause.) But days too when you answer. (Pause.) So that I may say at all times, even when you do not answer and perhaps hear nothing, something of this is being heard, I am not merely talking to myself, that is in the wilderness, a thing I could not bear to do—for any length of time.

Willie's silent listening allows Winnie to retain her identity, and gives her an aim in life. The statement recalls a scene in *Endgame*. Hamm orders Clov to wake up the old Nagg, Hamm's father, and make him listen to the novel Hamm is writing. Nagg refuses to listen and is bribed by the promise of a piece of candy. However, once the story has been told, he is informed that there is no longer any candy in the house. He at once retorts triumphantly by declaring that he had not been listening all along. Winnie is also writing a novel which Willie must listen to. It is the story of Mildred, a five year old girl who has been given a "waxen dolly" whose "China blue eyes . . . open and shut," like Winnie's eyes, the only part of her body she can still move. Clearly Winnie is writing *A la recherche du temps perdu*.

For Beckett, conversation and literature are forms of what Pascal calls "le divertissement," possibly the "supreme game" of Mallarmé, but a game nevertheless, one of man's inventions to divert himself from the thought of death—a way of killing time while it is killing you.

Happy Days is a comedy about the tragedy of the marriage relationship, and the inescapable catastrophe of final dissolution. Conversation, optimism, love are illusions. In some ways things have greater reality than people. ("Ah yes, things have their life, that is what I always say, things have a life. (Pause.) Take my looking glass, it doesn't need me.") The looking glass may not need Winnie, but she needs it to be sure that she is. Her other looking glass is her husband who, at the end of the play, appears in striped trousers and morning coat, crawling up the mound, a wild expression on his face: re-awakened desire mingled with despair. He utters only one word: "Win," which can be taken for the nickname of Winnie, or the proclamation of his victory. Winnie then sings a ditty, a flat, sentimental tune. Thus Beckett buries with the singer the whole notion of romantic love.

Winnie's chatter and her singing are like the whistling of a frightened man. They culminate in the dreadful silence at the end of the play when the two old people face one another for the last time. The stage directions are more telling than many parts of the dialogue, which must be taken ironically: "Smile off. They look at each other. Long pause."

"What must come to an end is already ended," says Ionesco's Bérenger Ier in *Exit the King*.[18] King Bérenger, like Hamlet, is informed that he must die at the end of the play. ("MARGUERITE. You are going to die in an hour and a half, you are going to die at the end of the show.") Thus Ionesco reminds his audience that they are in a theatre, and that a tragi-comic marionette must disappear at the end of the spectacle which is its span of life. But is there a marked difference between ourselves and these dramatis personae? Are we not merely players upon the stage of the world, puppets which must bow out once we have played our part?

Hamlet and Bérenger Ier remind us, their "frères humains" who must live after them, that our moments are counted. All of us share the condition of being what Beckett calls "co-detenus";[19] that is, inhabitants of that cell to which Pascal compared the world. The difference between us and Hamlet or the King is therefore of a relative nature. By revealing his consciousness of the inevitable end and speaking of the future in the present tense, Shakespeare's protagonist voices our own preoccupation with our approaching dissolution. For Ionesco's King the future is already an irretrievable past.

"I have always been obsessed by death," confesses Ionesco. "Since the age of four, when I first knew I was going to die, this anguish never left me. . . . I write in order to cry out my fear of death and my humiliation at the thought of dying."[20] In *Dionysos* Touchard says, "Everyone knows that death can also be a subject of farce." (p. 31) Ionesco has written a farce which makes us laugh at our own mortality.

When Molière was fatally ill, he wrote a comedy on the subject of his malady. The audience does not empathize with Argan's pains, real or imaginary, for he is the object of ridicule—a miserly hypochondriac who arranges a marriage between his daughter and a foolish doctor in order to receive free treatment at home. Yet, Molière himself was no imaginary invalid. Like Hamlet, he could have exclaimed: "I am dead!" the evening he collapsed in the chair in which he was enacting the grotesque hypochondriac. If his play appears to be pure comedy on the surface, a perfect example of the illiberal juest, the last performance of this comedy revealed it to have been all along a metaphysical farce, for the author of the metaphysical farce wishes above all to communicate within a humorous form his deepest anguish, his nightmares, fears, his private world.

King Bérenger is a Hamlet turned clown. In his case the "antic disposition" assumed by the Prince of Denmark in order to disguise his purpose is no longer a mask but his face. Yet, though we laugh at this cowardly "bourgeois" king, we realize that we are laughing at Everyman—in fact, at our own fear of death.

Nascentes morimur, says the poet. King Bérenger, the sovereign of a mythical kingdom, is told at the beginning of the play that he will die at the end of it. At first he finds it impossible to believe, and he is outraged at the notion that the sacred person of the king should be subject to the indignities suffered by his subjects. Death is guilty of *lèse-majesté*. He tells his doctor, who is also the surgeon, hangman, bacteriologist and astrologer of the realm, "I will die, yes, I will die. In forty years, in fifty years, in three hundred years. Later. When I'll be willing, when I'll have time, when I decide." Yet, little by little, as his strength begins to fail, King Bérenger realizes that he must die like everyone else. The rest of the play is a desperate and comic outcry of despair, a refusal of the unavoidable. Bérenger Ier may be a coward, spiritual brother to the great cowards of literature—Sancho Panza, Falstaff, Ubu Roi—but he is also human fear stripped bare.

In his pensée on "le divertissement," Pascal suggests that people consider it a privilege to be a king because a sovereign is surrounded with courtiers whose sole func-

tion it is to occupy every moment of his time and divert him from the thought of death. This thought is so unbearable, says Pascal, that a simple man who does not entertain it is happier than a mighty king with sufficient leisure to contemplate his end. Pascal equates hunting with war and spectacle with affairs of state as means of escape from contemplation of man's perishable nature.

Bérenger Ier will not be allowed any *divertissements*. In fact his first wife (he has two simultaneously, the shrewish, realistic Marguerite and the beautiful, tender, loving Marie) insists that he be told the truth. Marguerite resents the fact that he did not spend years of his life preparing for the ultimate moment, and preaches a caricature of Montaigne's philosophy when she says: "You were condemned, you ought to have thought of it since the very first day, and then every day, five minutes a day. It wasn't much. Five minutes a day. Then ten minutes, a quarter of an hour, half an hour. That's how one keeps in training. You ought to have kept it as a permanent thought, a background to all your other thoughts." Marguerite's *Ars Moriendi* is solidly grounded in St. Augustine's "First dialogue" ("We must picture to ourselves the effect of death on each several part of our bodily frame, the cold extremities, the breast in the sweat of fever, the side throbbing with pain, the vital spirits running slower and slower as death draws near, the eyes sunken and weeping, every look filled with tears, the forehead pale and drawn, the cheeks hanging and hollow, the teeth staring and discolored, the nostrils shrunk and sharpened, the lips foaming, the tongue foul and motionless. . . . This, then, is what I meant by sinking down deeply into the soul.") as well as in Montaigne's pagan wish to be found by Death "planting" his "cabbages, indifferent to him and still more to the state of [his] garden."[21]

The young queen has been much at fault as Marguerite lets her know: "It's your fault if he isn't ready, it's your fault if he'll be taken off guard. You let him go on his merry way, you even helped him get off the straight and narrow. Ah! the sweetness of life. Your balls, your merrymaking, your feasts and parades, your official dinner parties, your fiery words and your fire works, your weddings and wedding trips!" Strangely enough, Marie's love proves ineffectual as the end approaches, for Ionesco seems to imply that love has meaning when you are well, when you like yourself enough to enjoy another human being. Sartre explains this feeling most convincingly in "The Wall." His prisoner, who expects to be shot at dawn, no longer knows what love means for "death had disenchanted everything." He no longer wishes to see the woman he loves. "I would not even have wanted to hold her in my arms. My body filled me with horror because it was grey and sweating—and I wasn't sure that her body didn't fill me with horror. Concha would cry when she found out I was dead, she would have no taste for life for months afterwards. But I was still the one who was going to die. . . . I was alone."[22]

At the edge of death man can only love and pity himself. The King shrieks: "Enter into me you outsiders, be me, get under my skin." But as Camus and Malraux say over and over again, we have no "semblables" (fellow beings). No one will sleep for us on the floor out of friendship when we are in jail (Camus, *The Stranger*) and when we die, we are alone. "They are all strangers. I thought they were my family. I'm afraid . . ." moans Bérenger, and when Marie questions him: "Do you still love me? . . . Do you love me at this moment? I'm here . . . here . . . look . . . Try to see me . . . try to see me a little?" Bérenger answers: "I love myself still, despite everything I love myself, I still feel myself. I see myself. I look at myself." He is saying in fact that Becoming is still far from Non-Being, even though he is in the process of becoming a void. If King Bérenger were a poet he might have addressed Marie in the words of Donne:

> Study me then, you who shall lovers bee
> At the next world, that is, at the next Spring:
> For I am every dead thing,
> In whom love wrought new Alchimie.
> For his art did expresse
> A quintessence even from nothingnesse:
> He ruin'd mee, and I am re-begot
> Of absence, darknesse, death: things which are
> not.

In this play Bérenger may be a king but he is above all a man. His name is revealing, for it is that of the anti-hero of *The Killer,* and of the last human being left among rhinoceroses. It is also the name Ionesco has chosen for the protagonist of the *féerie Pascalienne (Le Piéto de l'Air)* he wrote in the same year as *Exit the King,* in which a writer, the very portrait of his creator, finds that his gift of levitation allows him to explore *les deux abîmes* and many others which surround our planet. For Ionesco, Bérenger is the average man of good will who is often forced to be a hero in spite of himself. Though he would prefer to survive in peace, he is ready to fight when his principles are violated. For those who know Ionesco's private mythology, Bérenger Ier sounds as ludicrous and funny as Jourdain Ier.

This is the first level of tragi-comedy. We have a sovereign, the traditional noble hero of tragedy, yet this character is not what he appears to be at first; he is simply the average man and shares the common fear of mortality. But does this make him any less tragic? Kings must also die. As Touchard points out, "Fear, so dear to Aristotle, can bring about a comic explosion as readily as tragic anguish."[23]

Because Bérenger Ier is a king, his death has a significance beyond the disappearance of an individual. His death is symbolic of the disintegration (or plague) of his kingdom, the decline and fall of his whole universe. The King's doctor, who is also the greatest scientist at court, observes: "Spring which was with us last night left us at two-thirty. November has come." All notion of time is lost in a plague-ridden world ("Lightning is transfixed in the sky, frogs rain from clouds, the thunder threatens.") Marguerite interprets these happenings as "signs." The King's world is sliding towards entropy.

THE DOCTOR: Your Majesty, scores of years ago, or three days ago, your empire was flourishing. Within three days you lost the wars you had won. The ones you had lost, you lost all over again. . . . Since your harvests have rotted and that our continent [sic] has been invaded by the desert, vegetation began to flourish in the neighboring countries which were deserts last Thursday.

Echoing the words of a famous predecessor of Bérenger Ier, the doctor exclaims: "Après lui, le déluge!"

It is clear that Ionesco is presenting not only a dying man, but also a dying world. The history of scientific progress is brilliantly derided by Ionesco. The King, we are told, has actually been living for hundreds of years. It was he who invented steel, balloons, airplanes. He built Rome, New York, Moscow, Geneva and Paris. He was responsible for revolutions and counter-revolutions, for religion, for the Reformation and the Counter-Reformation. He created literature by writing *The Iliad* and *The Odyssey.* It was he, in fact, and not Bacon, who composed tragedies and comedies under the pseudonym of Shakespeare. Not too long ago he was able to split the atom. Now he is a dying man too weak to switch on the light.

This brief resumé of human progress is drawn by the Guard who serves the role of Chorus in the play. Ionesco believes that man's pride in his scientific achievements is one of the most dangerous illusions. In his private journals (a section of which appears in *Notes and Counternotes*) he writes: "History is an uninterrupted sequence of enormous aberrations. . . . Ideology is only an alibi for bad faith. . . . The wind of idiocy is blowing, and night, the dark night of foolishness engulfs us." What will remain of the King and his recorded achievements? "He will be a page in a book of ten thousand pages which will be placed in a library among a million libraries." Then one day the paper of all these books will have turned to dust, or the library will have burnt to the ground. What then? Wherein does man's greatness lie?

Ionesco's answer is that it is life itself which is beautiful. *Exit the King,* a tragi-comedy about the fear of dying, is above all a paean to life. There is an extraordinarily moving scene at the core of the play which deals with the simple joy of being alive. It is a scene between the King and his humble servant, Juliette. Although she has great pity for the dying king, she considers her own life a hard one. The King questions her about her existence. As she makes up a list of complaints we become suddenly aware that this harsh fate is paradise to the dying monarch, that indeed he would exchange all the trappings of his state for one more day of humble living. Thus, when Juliette complains of the cold she feels when she gets up at dawn to start her working day the King, thinking of the cold touch of death, cries out: "It isn't the same cold!" and then, astonished, questions her: "You don't like feeling cold?" To feel cold when you are alive is to be aware that you are living. Suffering itself can be pleasure, for you are made cognizant of your body, and you know that pain will be followed by relief.

JULIETTE: I wash the laundry of the whole
    house . . .
    My hands hurt, my skin is chapped.
THE KING: It hurts. One feels one's skin.
JULIETTE: I scrub floors . . . My whole back
    aches.
THE KING: That's right. She's got a back. We've
    got a back.

How wonderful to have a back that can hurt, hands that
can chap, a skin that feels. How marvelous to be alive. "It
is endless," moans Juliette. "Endless!" delights the King.
He is not echoing her words, for they do not speak on the
same level. Juliette is complaining of endless toil, a
world without rest, and the King, picking up the word
"endless," thinks of a world without end, without the end
of death.

Bérenger Ier is sorry that so much has escaped his notice.
"I haven't been everywhere," he sighs. Now that it is too
late he realizes that he should have found joy in the simplest moments of living, in the most insignificant gestures.

JULIETTE: My room has no windows.
THE KING: (in the same raptured voice). No
    windows! One goes out. One looks for light,
    and finds it. In order to go out you must turn
    the key in the lock, you open the door, you
    turn the key again, you close the door.

The man who speaks in this way, the lover of life, is the
man who knows that "he *is* dead." A painter celebrates
life in its evanescent beauty, gives eternity to an arrangement of flowers, to a ray of light upon the table cloth, to
a piece of bread and a knife upon the bread board. The
ill-named *nature morte* is a *nature éternellement vivante*.
All art is in a sense a celebration of life. Boris
Pasternak's poet-hero, Yuri Zhivago, thinks at the most
tragic moment of his life: "Art, including tragedy, expresses the joy of existence." In the same way Ionesco
writing about death bids in this play a kind of tender
farewell to life.

In his private journals Ionesco writes: "The longer I live, the
more tied I feel to life. I sink ever deeper into it. . . . How
hard it will be to tear myself away! I have grown used to
it; grown used to living. I am less and less prepared to
die." There is a danger which is almost as great as that of
death. It is the dulling of the senses through habit, the
inability to have fresh, spontaneous reactions, what
Ionesco called in conversation "l'usure du temps" (the
sapping action of time). People become trapped in routine; they grow thick with well-being. Those are the living dead. The image Ionesco uses for this way of feeling
is that of slime. In *Victims of Duty*, his anti-hero,
Choubert, is caught in a marsh of memory and life in
which he must drown. In a little-known short story,
"Slime," Ionesco describes a man's gradual disintegration. This travelling salesman finds that he is slowing
down. His digestion is sluggish, his mouth thick with a
coated tongue. He can no longer walk as he used to, and

takes to staying in his room and dieting in the hope of
recapturing the lightness of youth. One day he decides to
set out once again for one of his usual trips. He embarks
on a painful walk through the country; suddenly slipping
on the wet earth, he falls into the mud. There he stays,
very much like Beckett's crawlers, and waits. Gradually
his limbs begin to detach themselves from his body. With
fascination, the man watches his hand sink into the marsh.
He experiences a strange detachment, as though the hand
did not belong to him at all, a kind of horror with matter
which reminds us of Sartre's hero in *Nausea*. Finally, there
is nothing left except the grey surface of the primeval ooze.

Marguerite accuses the King of being caught "in the
warm slime of the living." She, *"la reine-à-tout-faire"* (a
word made up of queen and *bonne-à-tout-faire,* which
means "maid-of-all-work") calls her husband "un petit
bourgeois." He has, according to her, all the failings of
the bourgeois, a love of comfort and well-being, of food
and fun, a sentimental attitude. Now he must leave all
those things he loved, and since every man creates the
universe anew, his world will die with him. Like God "he
had organized his universe. He had invented trees, flowers, smells, colors. . . . He had imagined oceans and
mountains." Every man's agony is the agony of Christ;
Bérenger, caught in the slime of life, and "in a hedge of
thorns," finds it hard to loosen his hold on the sweet
earth. Marguerite urges him to do so: "Let go, open your
fingers, I order you to loosen your fingers, release the
plains, the mountains. . . . It was nothing but dust."

Exit the King is a triumphant example of the tragi-comic
mode. It is a play about death which is an affirmation of
life, a farce which manages to blend humor and anguish.
It echoes the fear and trembling of a Pascal, the wisdom
in regard to physical suffering of the Montaigne of *De
l'Expérience*. It is in fact a philosophical cartoon, ironic
yet immensely tender. Ionesco has been able to communicate beyond his anguish his profound respect for this
vulnerable creature, Man.

In his preface to *Gallows Humor*,[24] Jack Richardson
quotes James Thurber in support of his notion that tragi-
comedy ought to be written as one word. He explains that
there is no fundamental difference between the two
genres when they are practiced with high seriousness.
Comedy "is not something categorically separated from
life's lamentations," he writes, and on its highest level it
is not free of the tragic flaw, that basic concept of tragedy. "The idealistic myopia of Don Quixote, the pathetic
pretensions of Monsieur Jourdain, the chaotic hedonism
of Falstaff, all these are qualities which, had the eye
viewing them been a sly one, might have served tragic
purposes." Richardson's declared aim is "to move" the
audience to laughter. Like Shaw he does not wish merely
to tickle or bustle them into laughter. The comic emotion
is also a way of purging, of liberating an audience. To
make them laugh at their weaknesses, at their own mortality, such is the aim of Jack Richardson in this play
which is kindred in so many ways to the theatre of
Beckett and Ionesco.

Richardson is the American apostle of what the French call *humour noir*. "Gallows humor," or *Galgenhumor*, has been analyzed by Sigmund Freud in a chapter of his *Wit and the Various Forms of the Comic*. Freud gives two examples of grim wit: The rogue who on the morning of his execution (the day happens to be a Monday) remarks: "This week is beginning well." And the pathetic story of the man who requests a scarf for his neck in order not to catch cold on the way to the gallows. Ionesco also indulges in a bit of *Galgenhumor* in *Exit the King* when Marguerite, who is a strict disciplinarian, scolds the king for walking around the palace barefoot. "What a nasty habit to walk around barefoot." The young wife Marie is worried for his health, and orders: "Put on his slippers. He's going to catch cold." She unconsciously indulges in gallows humor, for she knows that the king is dying and will not have time to catch cold. The logical Marguerite tries to call her attention to this fact: "Whether he catches cold or not is of no importance. It's simply a bad habit," but in so doing she carries *Galgenhumor* a step farther—for what is the importance of good or bad habits, of what is fitting or not fitting, for a monarch in the face of death? Marguerite's strict sense of dignity, of *comme il faut*, is more ludicrous in the face of death than Marie's loving concern.

Gallows Humor is a play in two parts, independent but connected by their theme, which is that it is difficult these days to tell the living from the dead, the hangman from the hanged. Richardson feels that it is easy to make "the hapless mistake of the average who are sure that they are alive solely because they eat, excrete and sleep."

The play opens with a Medieval Prologue in which Death appears in full dress and assures the audience that it will not be seen for the rest of the performance. Death states the theme and serves as Chorus to the plays. "That one-time basic distinction between the quick and the dead has become far too abstract today for one with my earthbound mind, and this fundamental confusion was showing up in my performance."

The two plays are about "an upper-middle-class type" who has killed his wife in a fit of metaphysical doubt and who is now to be hanged by a hangman and a warden who are obviously less alive than the man they are dispatching from this world. Richardson's theme is *ennui*, the wasteland of our lives, the deadening effect of habit, lack of courage, lack of imagination.

In the first play, eroticism, the world of the senses, and the poetry of love, are mocked, reduced as they are to the ministrations of the Welfare State prostitute who is sent to the prisoner in order to provide him with some last kicks before the kick-off. A Mary Magdalene of the sociological paradise, she comes to administer the Last Rites and wheels in the Last Supper on a tea tray decked with silver Queen Anne dish covers and sauceboats. Her victim is one of the living dead.

This man's neat world collapsed one day in court when, as a lawyer for Mrs. Gogarty versus the Municipal Bus Company, he lost that simple suit for damages on account of his client's fit of the hiccups. The jury, reduced to the state of a group of undisciplined, giggling children, returned with the irrational verdict of "guilty." Defeated by a humorous failing of the body, a grotesque, involuntary physiological phenomenon, Walter, the lawyer, experienced a veritable fall from Grace reminiscent of that suffered by Jean Baptiste Clamence, the lawyer-anti-hero of Camus' *The Fall*. Both men had to come to the realization that they could not trust the ordered universe in which they saw themselves as respected citizens. "What was left that couldn't be hiccuped out of existence?" is the question Walter cannot answer. What he fails to realize is that this chaos is the stuff of life itself, whereas his orderly universe was a living petrification.

This model husband, this worthy citizen, experiences, however, the fascination of chaos, of the void. Like Thomas Mann's Aschenbach he submits to the "lure for the unorganized, the immeasurable, the eternal," and surrendering to *Natur* finds himself "on the wrong trains, in the wrong beds, with the wrong people." He no longer recognizes his Steppenwolf face when he encounters it in the mirror. In a moment of utter lawlessness, he kills his innocent, faithful wife by striking her head with a golf club. He can only recall that when her skull was hit, it sounded "like a good shot."

Now a reformed character, Walter has gone back in his cell to a routine existence. He spends his last hours sewing on his number patch, 43556, and his only regret is that the numbers in it are not all even. He is also tidying up his cell, and does not welcome the intrusion of Lucy, for how can one expect "a number to make love?" Lucy cannot stand defeat, however—her professional honor is at stake. "Make love to me, Walter, and you won't mind the hangover of the gallows," she cries out, littering the neat cell with ashes and chicken bones. After she has managed to tear off the number patch, chaos is definitely re-established and Walter, full of the hopes of life, sinks into her professional arms: "Maybe the rope will break or the hangman come down with a bad cold," he whispers musingly. Freud's story has been subtly altered so that it is the hangman and not the hanged who is in danger of catching a cold, and indeed as we meet him in Part II, we realize that he is less alive than his victim.

The same actor who plays Walter plays the Hangman in Part II. He is a timid man who would like to hide his face under a hangman's hood. This notion does not fit the Welfare State, in which hangmen proceed to their business in Madison Avenue suits. The Warden will not allow this childish masquerade. While the Hangman goes up to his room to fetch his hood in the hope of swaying him, the Warden makes a play for Martha, the Hangman's wife. In her sloppy breakfast dressing gown, she reminds us a little of Lucy for the good reason that the same actress plays both parts.

Apparently the Warden has had his eye on this woman for twenty years but had to repress his extravagant desires for the sake of his children, "the twins." Now that the twins are "almost chemical engineers," and the warden's wife spends her time riding streetcars, there is a chance to seize the day. Martha agrees: "All right, tomorrow, three o'clock in front of the supermarket steps." But the Warden is busy with an inspection team. He could see her Saturday afternoon, but she has her card game. Monday seems safe enough to her, but the Warden assures her that if he were to leave his desk for one moment on the first day of the week he could not catch up on his work for the rest of it. Appointment books in hand, Martha and her would-be lover have to come to the conclusion that their weeks don't match. The Warden then begs for one mad kiss. It is of course at this very moment that the Hangman appears, properly hooded. His universe is shattered at this sight, and for a moment he experiences the same dreadful freedom which landed his victim in the death cell. He decides to walk out on the execution and his wife in order to become more like the fellows he has been hanging, those men whose pulses beat faster than his own.

Martha does not appear to be taken aback by this announcement. She simply suggests that he help her with the dishes. He does, day-dreaming all the while quite audibly about tropical climes. Martha punctuates his Baudelairian *voyage imaginaire* with brief comments: "That still looks wet to me. You're getting water on your trousers, Walter." Finally she hands him an apron, the symbol of his enslavement. Indeed when the Hangman heads for the door, his wife reminds him to untie the apron strings and return the apron. Then she proceeds to remind him that he has an appointment with the dentist, and that he must also accompany her to her sister's house for Friday dinner. He really ought to schedule his desertion for the following week. The wayward Hangman is considerably deflated at this point, and the *coup de grâce* is his wife's statement that she needs him, for she depends on all his little functions in the way she has come to depend on the telephone, the electricity and the plumbing. At this sublime moment she is like the wife in Anouilh's *Waltz of the Toreadors* who taunts her old roué of a husband, calling him one of her possessions, "her garbage can."

Beside himself with rage, the Hangman tries to strangle his wife. He would be ready for the gallows himself had he the necessary strength and skill to carry out his purpose. Richardson's Hangman, though, has no talent for killing. However hard he squeezes his wife's neck, she continues talking in an irritatingly calm tone. In fact she is obviously enjoying the performance for "this is the closest" they have come to sex in many years. Since he cannot kill his wife, the Hangman realizes that he might as well go on to his execution. Martha buttons him up so he won't catch a cold.

The modern dramatist is concerned primarily with the irrevocability of human suffering, the No-Exit situation of Man. The protagonists of the anti-plays, perhaps because they are suffering the action rather than initiating

it, seem to have lived their lives, retaining, like Dante's Dwellers in Hell, only the memory of their earthly sojourn. The tragic sense of life which informs the Metaphysical Farce lends a muted universality to a world in which the distinction between living and having lived disappears in a constant oscillation of the mind tuned to the only inevitable catastrophe, that of the final dissolution of consciousness. The tragi-comic mode allows us, in this Age of Anxiety, to defeat our ghosts with paroxysms of laughter.

NOTES

[1] *The Death of Tragedy* (London: Faber and Faber, 1961), p. 5.

[2] *Dionysos* (Paris: Editions Montaigne, 1937), p. 39.

[3] *Ibid.,* p. 31.

[4] "Experience of the Theatre," *Notes and Counternotes* (New York: Grove Press, 1964), p. 136.

[5] John Donne, "Letter to Sir H. Goodere, September 1608," *Complete Poetry and Selected Prose.* Edited by John Hayward (New York: Random House, 1929), p. 455.

[6] New York: Pageant Books, 1960 (Originally published by Harvard University Press), pp. 15-16.

[7] *Ibid.,* pp. 16, 21.

[8] Robert Ellrodt, *L'Inspiration Personnelle et l'Esprit du Temps chez les Poétes Metaphysiques Anglais* (Paris: Jose Corti, 1960), vol. 1, p. 151.

[9] Sermon XV, 1st Friday in Lent at Whitehall, March 8, 1621/2, *op. cit.,* p. 602.

[10] "Problems of the Theatre," *Tulane Drama Review,* Oct., 1958, p. 20.

[11] "Situation Surréalistes de l'objet (1935)," *Manifestes du Surréalisme,* Paris, 1962, p. 319.

[12] *Notes and Counternotes,* p. 136.

[13] Samuel Beckett, *Happy Days* (New York: Grove Press, 1961), Act 1, p. 47.

[14] Samuel Beckett, *Malone Dies* (New York: Grove Press, 1956), pp. 6-7.

[15] Samuel Beckett, *How It Is* (New York: Grove Press, 1964), p. 17.

[16] Ruby Cohn reminds us that *"Vider son sac"* in French means "to have one's say," and that "the phrase is entirely fitting for the way the Beckett hero spews forth his monologue." (*Samuel Beckett: the Comic Gamut,* Rutgers,

1962, p. 194.) Certainly this applies to Winnie, who empties her bag in full view of the audience while soliloquizing to her heart's content.

[17] *The Unnamable* (New York: Grove Press, 1958), pp. 60-61.

[18] *Le Roi se Meurt* (Paris: Gallimard, 1963), p. 82.

[19] *Molloy* (Paris: Les Editions de Minuit, 1951), p. 15.

[20] *Notes and Counternotes,* p. 227.

[21] Spencer, *Death and Elizabethan Tragedy,* pp. 38, 60.

[22] *Intimacy and Other Stories* (New York: New Directions, 1948), pp. 26-27.

[23] *Dionysos,* p. 25. A similar view is held by Elder Olson in *Tragedy and The Theory of Drama* (Detroit: Wayne U. Press, 1961), p. 152.

[24] New York: E. P. Dutton, 1961.

Sister Corona Sharp

SOURCE: "The Dance of Death in Modern Drama," in *Modern Drama,* Vol. XX, No. 2, June, 1977, pp. 107-16.

[In the following essay, Sharp evaluates modern stage adaptations of the medieval Dance of Death, especially in the grotesque comedies of Dürrenmatt and Ionesco.]

The Dance of Death and the Triumph of Death are themes that appeared across late medieval and Renaissance Europe in the visual arts, poetry and drama.[1] Death snatching people away became a favourite subject of didacticism. In Germany, France and Switzerland, particularly, the lasting impressions made by extant murals, verses and plays have continued into our time. Quantity of scholarship alone shows the growing interest in the subject. In modern drama, there are two distinct manifestations of the influence of the Dance of Death: first, the imitative Dance of Death plays, like Emil Wächter's, produced at the Berne Festival, 1962-64; and second, the more original adaptations of the theme such as Auden's *The Dance of Death,* Dürrenmatt's *The Meteor* and Ionesco's *Massacre Games.*[2] Auden's familiarity with Germany perhaps included the Dances of Death on view before World War II. Dürrenmatt grew up near Berne and Basel, locations of *Totentänze,* and Ionesco learned his first lessons in staging death from puppet shows in the Luxembourg Gardens.

Historical evidence of dramatic performances of the Dance of Death goes back to 1393 in France. That dramatic presentations existed from the beginning—soon after the outbreak of the Black Death, 1347—is clear from the pictures, where conflict was suggested from the first. The Renaissance artists Niklaus Manuel Deutsch (c. 1484-1530), Bernese playwright and painter, and Hans Holbein the Younger (1497-1543), who spent some time in Basel, added realism and violence to their creations of the Dance. Holbein's *Images of Death* are complete scenes, crowded with characters, detailed scenery and intense dramatic conflict. Both Manuel and Holbein specialized in the grotesque comedy and social satire that replaced the dignified allegory and metaphysical meaning of the older Dances. Although drama gradually displaced the processional dance, the Renaissance artists retained the motif of music. Death as musician is prominent in the German tradition, whereas the French tradition generally prefers Death as gravedigger, carrying coffins or coffin lids, mattocks and shovels, though these objects may be combined with the pipe, and the dead figures—messenger of Death, or Death himself, depending on the text—are usually executing dance steps.

In the three plays under discussion, these aspects of the Dance of Death are present. Dance and music appear most prominently in Auden's play, with social satire as well. Dürrenmatt, imbued with the spirit of Manuel and Holbein, has transferred Renaissance realism to his play, together with a disconcerting touch of otherworldliness. His satire, too, prevails along with grotesque comedy. In Ionesco, we find the most stunning use of the medieval Dance of Death. In his play, the ominousness of Death, his dignity and irresistible power are vested in the allegorical Black Monk, who stalks his victims. Anonymous type characters come and go. Above all, the metaphysical aura, so strong in this author's later work, obtrudes in the midst of universal dying. Though devoid of theological meaning, this aura signifies man's helplessness before transcendence. Although the appearance of Death is sombre, Ionesco has injected the Grand Guignol farce in which he is now an expert, and in this context, it reflects the comic cavorting of the corpses in numerous Dances.[3] Ionesco rejects realism categorically, of course, and by doing so he locates his work in fantasy. Rapid changes of scenes, simultaneous staging and use of lighting reinforce the vagueness of location. Common to Dürrenmatt and Ionesco is the medieval levelling of death, which carries off the rich and poor, the great and weak. The medieval hierarchy has its counterpart in a cross-section of modern society. Of the three playwrights, Auden alone parodies medieval didacticism in a half-serious exaltation of Marxism. Structurally, *The Meteor* and *Massacre Games* resemble the episodic scenes of Holbein, though Dürrenmatt's play is more tightly knit with a semblance of plot. Auden's play is in a single unit.

Auden's *The Dance of Death* (1933), performed by Rupert Doone in their Group Theatre, is only a lesser achievement in the Auden canon. More a cabaret act than a play, it presents Death the Dancer allegorically, first as Sun God, creator and destroyer, then as middle-class Fascism, trying to mislead the Chorus of confused Englishmen. Opposition comes from the working-class audience. The Dancer's tricks to deceive the Chorus are interpreted by an Announcer and consist of callisthenics, war, racism, organized pleasure and feats of daring. Death dances and makes the Chorus dance to mime these activities. The small jazz orchestra emphasizes the comic atmosphere that prevails through the light satiric tone of the lyrics and the low comedy of the cockney speeches. The play is a medley of commentary, song, dialogue, audience participation and other theatrical devices used in a Brechtian manner. Before his death, which signifies the end of the middle class, the Dancer bequeaths the sources of wealth to the audience, then the Chorus introduces the saviour figure by singing to Mendelssohn's Wedding March:

> O Mr. Marx, you've gathered
> All the material facts
> You know the economic
> Reasons for our acts.
>
> (*Enter* Karl Marx *with two young communists*)
> K.M. The instruments of production have been too much for him. He is liquidated.[4]

Writing just prior to the mass dying inaugurated by Hitler, Auden did not treat his subject with the grimness and horror of later dramatists. His interest in the theme, however, is also evident in his serious war poem "Danse Macabre." The evocative power of his *Dance of Death* remains only guesswork until it is once again produced. Its significance for us is the combination of the dance motif with allegory in a modern cabaret act, thus bringing an ancient tradition to public awareness, as the medieval murals were intended to have popular appeal. This free use of the theme resembles the originality of Dürrenmatt and Ionesco.

In Dürrenmatt we find a playwright wholly obsessed with death. It is a peculiar aspect of his dramatic art that he places death in a grotesquely comic universe. Having had its première in 1966, *The Meteor* represents "grotesque theatre," a type of play based on the philosophical proposition that man's fate is grotesque but logical and therefore not absurd, when his careful planning is thwarted and reversed through chance, and he is thus reduced to the worst possible end. In *The Meteor,* Dürrenmatt has transposed the elements of the Dance of Death into an unexpected pattern: death prevails through the paradoxical and comic agency of Schwitter, the man who desperately desires death, dies several times, but keeps on resurrecting. He is the meteor that destroys the representatives of modern society. Extravagant comedy was captured in the Zürich première, when the renowned actor Leonard Stekel hurtled through the play, increasingly berserk and terrifying, tossing wet diapers and funeral wreaths in his frantic dance and then succumbing to comic despair.

Dürrenmatt has inherited the earthy humour and violence of Germanic artists and writers before him. He sees modern man as the victim not only of society, but even more of a demythologized transcendent force that reduces him to total frustration. This force is paradoxical chance. Dürrenmatt stands apart from Absurd Theatre on

account of his view of existence and the moral purpose of his writing. He seeks to put a model of the real world on the stage to dramatize its grotesqueness. This formula works well for *The Visit,* where reality is parodied on various levels of unreality and where the moralist's accusing finger is pointed squarely into the auditorium. But when Dürrenmatt tackles theological mysteries such as life, death and immortality, as he does in *The Meteor,* the artistic purpose becomes confused. The blend of surface realism with myth and eschatology renders the play exceedingly difficult to stage. Schwitter, the Nobel Prize author who in revulsion against existence burns his manuscripts and millions and tries desperately to die—strangely enough without thinking of suicide—is from the start a grotesque and improbable figure. Unwittingly he exerts a lethal influence on the clergyman, the artist, the contractor, the surgeon, his call-girl wife and finally, his mother-in-law, the toilet attendant. Here we have a burlesque of the Dance of Death procession of classes: instead of the pompous Pope of the Middle Ages, Dürrenmatt presents a timid and holy little minister; and instead of the peasant or cripple, the lowliest person is the toilet attendant, a semi-mythical figure who rises from her blue-tiled underworld, where she ekes out a living from the pennies dropped into her plate, and turns out to be a successful capitalist after all. In the meantime, Schwitter, the would-be corpse, makes love with the artist's wife in the same bed where he tries to die. Some of his victims are overwhelmed by his resurrections: the religious-minded die of joy, the agnostics of despair. Others are destroyed simply by chance for having strayed into the path of this meteor, which symbolizes the death force.

In an interview, Dürrenmatt indicated that Schwitter is a symbolic figure. He represents the self-destructive side of man, desiring his own death to excuse his brutal and nihilistic egoism.[5] As the most grotesque character, he receives—paradoxically—the grace of a miracle. But he rejects it. That is the dialectic of the play.[6] It is Schwitter who gives the play its metaphysical turn. He declares: "Death rushes toward one like a locomotive. Eternity is whistling about your ears, new creations roar into being, crash apart—the whole thing a gigantic accident."[7]

The human problem posed in the play is the agony of man as unwilling instrument of the death force. Here the medieval agent of Death has been re-created in a startling fashion and made to serve another metaphysical problem, the mystery of the afterlife. Dürrenmatt uses inversion much as Manuel does, for Schwitter, the death-figure, leaps and cavorts with more energy than the living. The violence of *The Meteor* is reminiscent of the shock effects in Manuel and Holbein.

As a Lazarus-figure Schwitter is an innovation in modern drama.[8] From death he brings back an uncontrollable rage, an uncomprehending frustration and a growing horror of his predicament. One wonders from which existence he has rescued his abiding sense of irony. But it pervades the play, which consists of a series of comic reversals juxtaposing the glory of this world (success and money) with Schwitter's loathing of it. Renaissance wealth is parodied in the character of the tycoon contractor, modelled on the moneylender in Basel and the rich man in Holbein, but Dürrenmatt's original contribution is the toilet attendant and wealthy madam. Mixing his Swiss scatology with social satire, Dürrenmatt makes the Nobel Prize winner acknowledge the superiority of this woman's achievement. Compared to it literature and art are nothing, he says, addressing the already dead woman. "Death alone is the only reality," he adds, "the only imperishable thing."[9] This is the final stage in the demythologizing of death begun in the sixteenth-century German Dances. Death no longer symbolizes transition into eternity—it represents only the end of man's mortal life and the scattering of his goods. This horrible joke is evident in Holbein's picture of the rich man: Death is scooping up his pile of gold while he leaps up in horror. Hence I interpret *The Meteor* as a twentieth-century version of the secular spirit of the Renaissance combined with a burlesque of the social types and of the corpse dancing vigorously out of the charnel-house.

That the end finds Schwitter more alive than ever remains Dürrenmatt's joke on the audience, who may indeed reject it as happened in Zürich. To Schwitter's final cry, "When will I finally croak?," a spectator shouted, "Soon, I hope!" In the secularized scheme of things it is of course no joke, since the death force will swallow up life. Dürrenmatt also parodies the medieval preacher and theme of redemption by introducing the Salvation Army, who sing in jubilation over Schwitter's "miraculous" resurrection. But their faith and joy are wasted on the man who has consistently rejected any suggestion of divine intervention. Although hampered by surface realism and the confusion of paradox, Dürrenmatt tries to convey the theological statement of real resurrection. Traces of the Dance of Death are also evident in *The Visit,* part of which Peter Brook choreographed (1958), and in *Portrait of a Planet* (1970), which the author linked expressly with the Dance of Death.

While Dürrenmatt shows the influence of the Swiss Dances, Ionesco's *Massacre Games* reveals an affinity with the French tradition of the *danse macabré* (accented until the seventeenth century) as exemplified in the pictures of Guyot Marchant (1485) that are copies of the Paris Dance and show Death as gravedigger. For its graphic details the play is based on Defoe's *Journal of the Plague Year* (1722). The Dance element was emphasized in the Paris production (1970) when the market scene was choreographed. Allegory is prominent in the figure of the Black Monk. The dramatic quality inheres in the separate scenes.

Ionesco believes that one must laugh at death. In 1969 he asserted that a dead person is derisible because he is no longer master of himself.[10] Death is the deliberate joke in *Massacre Games.* The title alone stresses the play element in Ionesco's approach. A *jeu de massacre* is the game "Aunt Sally," played at fairs, in which the players throw sticks at the pipe in the mouth of a wooden woman's head. In this play, Death plays his grisly game with human beings. The basic irony in this game resembles that of the merry dance to which Death invites his reluctant guests. Ionesco also makes death itself ridiculous by dehumanizing all the characters, creating the effect of a gigantic puppet show. The surrealism of the Black Monk is emphasized by the marionette-like appearance and movements of the other characters, and the possible use of actual puppets and dummies on stage. In the Paris production, Death himself collapsed at the end like a giant puppet.

Briefly, the play consists of seventeen disconnected scenes showing the ravages of the plague in an unidentified town. Each scene presents another segment of society: shoppers at market, the rich man in his mansion, prisoners in jail, young people making love, a traveler at an inn, the city father giving a speech. The last scene shows the cessation of the plague and the beginning of the great fire. The resemblance of the play to the Dance of Death is in the use of allegory, social types and the theme of mass dying. The choice of the plague as the means of death is an even more significant resemblance. Hellmut Rosenfeld states that "all medieval pictures of the Dance of Death were painted or renovated immediately before or after catastrophes of plague."[11] Originally intended as spiritual warnings, they eventually were invested with a magical power to avert epidemics or cure victims of the disease.

Since the writings of Artaud and Camus, the plague has taken on new symbolic meaning for the modern mind. The universal dying witnessed in our century also invites artistic parody and requires the distancing of comedy to check emotion and control the gruesomeness of the subject. In its effects, it is a control different from yet similar to that of the medieval paintings with their austere detachment. It is different from the comedy of the Renaissance artists and of Rowlandson, who direct their attention to the social evils of their day and lure the viewer to immerse himself in the spectacle. Although Ionesco's career started in the Theatre of the Absurd, I do not think he writes exclusively in this vein any more. He has moved on to a theatre of myth, archetype and dream, shot through with a mystical vision and perception of the transcendental that take him back to medieval forms and symbols.

Ionesco found a vivid account of the 1665 London plague in Defoe's story. It is a description of shocking events cushioned by pious moral reflections arising from the pragmatism of a business man, Defoe's narrator, H. F. The *Journal* contains many dramatic scenes. Over half of Ionesco's scenes are borrowed directly from or based partly on the *Journal.* Even dialogue and some props are transferred from the source, the most outstanding being the wonderful profusion of stolen hats. When we come to this scene we realize why Ionesco chose 1880-1900 for the setting. What other reason but the comic exploitation of that heyday of millinery art? H. F.'s solemn interruption of the looting in the hat shop is transformed into Ionesco's riot of screeching women who "dress up with absurd ostentation, feathers flying to the four corners of the stage. They fight over the things. They have hats of all colours, the stage is covered with an improbable number of gaudy clothes."[12] Another farcical scene based directly on Defoe is the fumigating scene in the rich man's house. Defoe also tells of watchmen posted to shut up and guard houses of stricken families. Essentially they are decent fellows doing an impossible job. But Ionesco changes them into armed policemen who aid the plague in decimating the population. Uniformed in black, they appear to be Death's own henchmen. Another detail is the cruelty of the nurses. H. F. narrates these tales and piously questions their authenticity; but Ionesco rejects the moralizing and dramatizes the situation starkly: the nurse murders her patient and takes her money. Persons committing suicide, running naked through the streets or throwing themselves out of windows in distraction, are found in both works. In every instance the sober realism of Defoe is transmuted by Ionesco into eerie fantasy or grotesque farce.

In adapting Defoe and the Dance of Death, Ionesco modifies his satire. The impersonal element derived from more primitive theatre neutralizes it. Both puppets and stilts, and the mechanical repetition of acts, the depersonalized mass dying and the brevity of scenes disallowing audience identification, render the play as uncommitted as possible. The satire itself is pushed to the limits of improbability. For example, in discussing the pollution problem, the Fifth Housewife says: "I remember we used to have to wash carrots, or else they gave you leprosy." Presently she comments: "O, eggplants are cancerplants." (p. 9) Political satire fares the same way. The revolutionary politician declares: "This dying is political! We're playing into the hands of our oppressors by dying." (p. 73) The moderate politician says: "Our leaders are obsessed with death, they are neurotic about it. They make up a morbid and decadent government." (p. 79)

By his ingenious combination of history with surrealism and symbolism, Ionesco has created a unique Dance of Death play that reflects the allegorical quality of the medieval Dances. Of primary importance is the Black Monk mounted on stilts. The symbolic function of black is evident in the *Würzburger Totentanz* (c. 1360), where the Dead Man says he leads "the dance of black brothers" and is himself called the "black man."[13] The frequent, silent appearances of the Monk create the uncanny feeling that the Dance of Death plays and *Everyman* must have raised in their original audiences.[14] Like the medieval Dances, too, Ionesco's play evokes no pity, and so his omission of Defoe's pathetic and sentimental scenes is deliberate. All suggestions of charity and religious reverence for God's punishment, however, are suppressed or distorted. Ionesco also omits three scenes he could have exploited for comic effect: Defoe's tales of the living piper accidentally carried out in the dead cart, of the man stricken with plague who swam the Thames and thereby was cured, and of the reconciliation of the

religious sects. It seems that these were passed over because they end happily. In Ionesco, too, government and authority are presented in a foolish or sinister light, whereas Defoe defends them. By these means Ionesco's Dance of Death has stripped away every trace of secular glory depicted in the Dances from the beginning. For the medieval and Renaissance mind this world was intensely attractive; for Ionesco it is so only in snatches and then for immaterial reasons.

Without a theological centre, Ionesco's mystical bent, discussed at length in his *Conversations* with Claude Bonnefoy and evident especially in *The Killer,* leads him to experience moments of brightness and euphoria followed by terrible obscurity and heaviness. Amid all the puppetry of this play, suddenly an old couple hobble onto the stage and begin to recount these contradictory experiences of life. To the Old Woman, "Everything is a miracle" (p. 88), the world is "sweet and mysterious" and everything makes her happy (p. 93). The Old Man, however, has never felt this. To him, "every instant is burdensome and empty" (p. 89), and "The universe is a great steel ball, impenetrable" (p. 93). Her sadness is in his resistance to her love; his sadness is in his failure to have challenged existence (p. 93). Then the plague strikes her down. That this scene is to be played straight, without farce or grotesqueness, indicates the artistic purpose: the old couple have an intense experience of existence; its incommunicability stresses the essentially private nature of mystical insight; it may come as ecstasy or as abandonment. This is a dramatization, not of the absurdity of life, but of an experience beyond the limits of reason that is substantiated in much mystical writing. This transcendence possesses something of the medieval otherworldly quality; we realize here the presence of the intangible, the visionary, the mysterious. The scene ends and we see the looting, the gravediggers, the dead cart and the final farce of the "man of middle age, middle height and . . . middle class" being crammed into a coffin while the audience starts applauding (p. 106). Why did Ionesco insert this surprising scene into his puppet show if not to offer a glimpse of the mystery of life and death? Beyond social satire, beyond grotesque comedy, mystery envelops humanity, but only a few perceive it. What Dürrenmatt fails to achieve because of his surface realism, Ionesco succeeds in through his peculiar concept and use of theatre: "I want only to render my own strange and improbable universe."[15]

Initially an art form inspired by religious conviction and otherworldly orientation, the Dance of Death play has moved in our century in two opposite directions. First, there are those plays and musical compositions with dialogue that adhere closely to the originals and are best performed, like the modern *Everyman* in Salzburg, in or close to the church edifice. The other course, followed by such dramatists as Auden, Dürrenmatt and Ionesco, takes the basic Dance or drama of Death into wider and unexpected areas of adaptation best suited to the theatre with its technical equipment. For Dürrenmatt and Ionesco, at least, the theatre is still suitable for a projection of metaphysical realities such as the mysteriousness of life and the horror of death. Realism is inadequate to dramatize these experiences, whereas the styles of surrealism and symbolism can create the required distance. Strindberg's *The Dance of Death* stands behind Dürrenmatt, who wrote his own adaptation, turning it into a marital boxing match. The naturalism in this Strindberg work is a deceptive cloak disguising elements more commonly found in expressionistic and absurd drama. Jarry's *King Ubu* is the acknowledged forerunner of Ionesco's dramatic art, and much might be said of Father Ubu as a dancing figure of Death drawn from the puppet theatre. The grotesque comedy central to Jarry's work has remained the strongest theatrical means of defying death and distancing its horror. A comic intension, I believe, was operating under cover in the medieval Dances of Death alongside of the overt didactic purpose, for the irony of being invited to a merry dance against one's will is a comic predicament and the joke played on man in his unpreparedness. From their interviews and their entire dramatic work, we may conclude that Dürrenmatt and Ionesco write grotesque comedies about death in order to distance its horror from themselves.

NOTES

[1] Hellmut Rosenfeld's *Der mittelalterliche Totentanz* (Köln, 1954, 1968) is a reliable history of the Dance of Death, with annotated bibliography. The identity and date of the oldest Dance of Death text, however, are disputed. Stephan Cosacchi, *Makabertanz* (Meisenheim, 1965), believes the Spanish *Danza general de la Muerte,* which he dates after 1350, to be the oldest. Rosenfeld refutes this hypothesis, claiming the honour for the Latin Dance of Death, which he ascribes to a German Dominican, c. 1350.

[2] Emil Wächter, *Der Berner Totentanz nach Niklaus Manuel,* Musik von Heinrich Sutermeister (Bern, 1964). Hugo Distler, *Dance of Death,* ed. Malcolm Johns, trans. Brigitte Rauer, Opus 12, No. 2, Motet for All Saints' Sunday. Dialogue based on the *Lübecker Totentanz* by Johannes Klöcking (Marquette, 1970). Another interesting play with music is Hans Henny Jahn's *Neuer Lübecker Totentanz,* Musik, Yngve Jan Trede (Hamburg, 1954), wherein two figures of Death appear, a fat one and an emaciated one. Several minor German authors have written imitative Dance of Death plays. W. H. Auden, *The Dance of Death* (London, 1933); Friedrich Dürrenmatt, *Der Meteor* (Zürich, 1966); and Eugène Ionesco, *Jeux de massacre* (Paris, 1970).

[3] Théâtre de Grand Guignol was a Parisian theatre of horrors that flourished from 1896 to the early 1960's. Farces alternated with plays of horror almost from the start.

[4] Auden, *The Dance of Death,* p. 38.

[5] "Lazarus, der Fürchterliche. Urs Jenny im Gespräch mit Friedrich Dürrenmatt," *Theater heute,* 7 (Feb. 1966), 12.

[6] Violet Ketels, "Friedrich Dürrenmatt at Temple University," *Journal of Modern Literature,* 1 (1970), 100. [Interview].

[7] *Der Meteor,* p. 47. Trans. mine.

[8] The case of Edgar in Strindberg's *The Dance of Death* is not entirely similar, for although he claims to have died and returned, the author's chief concern is not with the mystery of resurrection.

[9] *Der Meteor,* p. 68.

[10] Nelly K. Murstein, "Une Entrevue avec Eugène Ionesco," *The French Review,* 45 (Feb. 1972), 618.

[11] Rosenfeld, "Der mittelalterliche Bilderbogen," *Zeitschrift für deutsches Altertum,* 85 (1954), 75, and *Der mittelalterliche Totentanz,* pp. 59, 299.

[12] *Jeux de massacre,* p. 98. Trans. mine. Further references to this play are indicated in the text.

[13] Quoted in *Der mittelalterliche Totentanz,* pp. 311, 317. Death clad in monkish garb occurs in late medieval art. Such a statue is in the Badisches Landesmuseum, Karlsruhe. Hans H. Hofstätter, *Art of the Late Middle Ages* (New York, 1968), p. 202, supposes it to have been part of a Dance of Death group.

[14] In *La Soif et la faim* (1964), Ionesco presents sinister figures in monkish costume. Their silent Brother Superior also walks on stilts.

[15] *Notes and Counter Notes* (New York, 1964), p. 159.

FURTHER READING

Anthologies

Enright, D. J., ed. *The Oxford Book of Death.* Oxford: Oxford University Press, 1983, 351 p.
    Offers literary selections from throughout history on the subject of death.

Criticism

Ackerman, R. D. "Death and Fiction: Stevens' Mother of Beauty." *ELH* 50, No. 2 (Summer 1983): 410-14.
    Studies the figure of the Mother of Beauty in Wallace Stevens's writing as a symbolic construct that encompasses the ideas of "natural decay and procreative renewal."

Barreca, Regina, ed. *Sex and Death in Victorian Literature.* London: Macmillan, 1990, 264 p.

Includes several essays on the Victorian eroticism of death.

Boym, Svetlana. *Death in Quotation Marks: Cultural Myths of the Modern Poet.* Cambridge, Mass.: Harvard University Press, 1991, 291 p.

Examines the relationship between literature and biography, regarding the concept of the death of a poet in "both figurative and literal terms."

Burkman, Katherine H. "Death and the Double in Three Plays by Harold Pinter." In *Harold Pinter: You Never Heard Such Silence*, edited by Alan Bold, pp. 131-45. London: Vision Press Limited, 1984.

Probes Pinter's use of doppelgangers, or doubles, in his dramas *A Slight Ache* (1961), *Old Times* (1971), and *No Man's Land* (1975) as figures that "threaten death or stand for death itself," but offer his protagonists the opportunity to discover a "meaningful kind of existence."

Damiani, Bruno and Mujica, Barbara, eds. *Et in Arcadia ego: Essays on Death in the Pastoral Novel.* New York: Lanham, 1990, 178 p.

Investigates the omnipresent figure of death in the Renaissance pastoral novels of Miguel Cervantes, Sir Philip Sidney, and others.

Doebler, Bettie Anne. *"Rooted Sorrow": Dying in Early Modern England*, Rutherford, N. J.: Fairleigh Dickinson University Press, 1994, 296 p.

Study that "focuses upon themes of death, despair, and comfort in seventeenth-century literature" by probing the cultural implications of works by such writers as Spenser, Milton, Shakespeare, and Donne.

Fausset, Hugh I'Anson. "The Death Theme in Rilke's Life and Poetry." In *Poets and Pundits: Essays and Addresses*, pp. 155-69. London: Jonathan Cape, 1947.

Explores the "conflict of life and death" Rainer Maria Rilke determined to resolve in his *Duino Elegies* and *Sonnets to Orpheus.*

George, Diana Hume. "Anne Sexton's Suicide Poems." *Journal of Popular Culture* 18, No. 2 (Fall 1984): 17-31.

Discusses poems Sexton wrote in the seventeen-year period between "her first suicide attempt and her final and successful one."

González, Eduardo. *The Monstered Self: Narratives of Death and Performance in Latin American Fiction.* Durham, N. C.: Duke University Press, 1992, 275 p.

Examines the relationship between death, mutability, and monstrosity in the works of Jorge Luis Borges, Mario Vargas Llosa, Augusto Roa Bostos, and other Latin American writers.

Goodwin, Sarah Webster and Bronfen, Elisabeth, eds. *Death and Representation.* Baltimore, Md.: The Johns Hopkins University Press, 1993, 336 p.

Probes textual, psychological, semantic, historical, ideological, and gendered representations of death in literature and art.

Guenther, Beatrice Martina. *The Poetics of Death: The Short Prose of Kleist and Balzac.* Albany: State University of New York Press, 1996, 216 p.

Discusses Kleist's and Balzac's "subversive" representations of death.

Hoffman, Frederick J. "No Beginning and No End: Hemingway and Death." In *Interpretations of American Literature*, edited by Charles Feidelson, Jr., and Paul Brodtkorb, Jr., pp. 320-31. New York: Oxford University Press, 1959.

Argues that Hemingway's fiction describes "a form of death to which the twentieth century is peculiarly heir," an unreasonable "death that comes as a violent disruption of life."

Kay, Dennis. *Melodious Tears: The English Funeral Elegy from Spenser to Milton.* Oxford: Clarendon Press, 1990, 296 p.

Analyzes the English tradition of elegy in the sixteenth and seventeenth centuries.

Langer, Lawrence L. *The Age of Atrocity: Death in Modern Literature.* Boston: Beacon Press, 1978, 256 p.

Focuses on the legacy of death reflected in twentieth-century literature by such authors as Thomas Mann, Albert Camus, Aleksandr Solzhenitsyn, and Charlotte Delbo.

Nesbet, Anne. "Suicide as Literary Fact in the 1920s." *Slavic Review* 50, No. 4 (Winter 1991): 827-35.

Concentrates on the incorporation of authentic suicide stories into the fiction of German and Russian writers of the 1920s as "modernist experiments in the literary cohabitation of life and text."

Roudané, Matthew C. "On Death, Dying, and the Manner of Living: Waste as Theme in Edward Albee's *The Lady from Dubuque*." In *Edward Albee: An Interview and Essays*, edited by Julian N. Wasserman, pp. 65-81. Houston, Tex.: The University of St. Thomas, 1983.

Evaluates the theme of wasted lives in Albee's drama *The Lady from Dubuque.*

Schleifer, Ronald. *Rhetoric and Death: The Language of Modernism and Postmodern Discourse Theory.* Urbana: University of Illinois Press, 1990, 252 p.

Considers "the relationship of power and meaning with a 'sense' of death that developed in the modernist era."

Shapiro, Michael J. "Terminations: Elkin's *Magic Kingdom* and the Politics of Death." In *Reading the Postmodern Polity: Political Theory as Textual Practice*, pp. 140-57. Minneapolis: University of Minnesota Press, 1992.

Regards Stanley Elkin's ironic rendering of a postmodernist discourse of death in his novel *Magic Kingdom.*

Spinrad, Phoebe S. *The Summons of Death on the Medieval Renaissance English Stage*. Columbus: Ohio State University Press, 1987.

> Investigates the dramatic representation of death as it developed on the English stage in the Middle Ages and the Renaissance.

Stamelman, Richard. *Lost Beyond Telling: Representations of Death and Absence in Modern French Poetry*. Ithaca, N. Y.: Cornell University Press, 1990, 291 p.

> Concentrates on the poetics of loss in the work of eight French poets, from Charles Baudelaire to writers of the contemporary era, and one French critic, Roland Barthes.

Steward, Garrett. *Death Sentences: Styles of Dying in British Fiction*. Cambridge, Mass.: Harvard University Press, 1984, 403 p.

> Considers representations of mortality and closure in the writings of Charles Dickens, George Eliot, Thomas Hardy, D. H. Lawrence, Virginia Woolf and other British authors.

Wheeler, Michael. *Death and the Future Life in Victorian Literature and Theology*. Cambridge: Cambridge University Press, 1990, 456 p.

> Discusses death, judgment, heaven, and hell in relation to Tennyson's *In Memoriam*, Dickens's *Our Mutual Friend*, Newman's *The Dream of Gerontius*, and Hopkins's *The Wreck of the Deutschland*.

Drugs and Literature

INTRODUCTION

For thousands of years artists and writers have turned to intoxicants in the belief that these substances enhance their artistic abilities and output. Illicit drugs, including laudanum, opium, heroin, marijuana, mescaline, and LSD have held special appeal for certain writers wishing to expand the boundaries of their perception and of their work. Widely used as pain killers throughout Asia, Egypt, and South America, drugs such as opium and hashish were staples of early medical practice, and continued to play an important part in medicine around the world through the early twentieth century. Drugs were also commonly used in religious ceremonies because of their alleged ability to intensify the visionary experiences sought by the devout. Portrayals of drug use in literature can be traced back to the earliest examples of written stories; the classical Greek poet Homer depicts Helen of Troy using the opium derivative *nepenthe* as an antidote to her overwhelming grief. Opium and hashish became known to western Europe when medieval Christian Crusaders brought poppies and hemp plants back from the Middle East, Greece and Turkey. Western writers including Geoffrey Chaucer and William Shakespeare mention drugs in their works. In the Romantic period of the early nineteenth century, a virtual explosion of drug use erupted among writers, a phenomenon perhaps most famously recorded by Thomas De Quincey in his autobiographical *Confessions of an English Opium-Eater*. Romantic poets Samuel Taylor Coleridge, Percy Bysshe Shelley, William Wordsworth, Lord Byron, and John Keats all produced what many critics consider their best works while under the influence of opium and laudanum (a liquid form of opium commonly prescribed as a pain killer in the nineteenth and early twentieth centuries). Nineteenth-century French writers such as Théophile Gautier, Arthur Rimbaud, and Charles Baudelaire became known collectively as the Hashish Club because of their drug experiments, and the American poet and horror writer Edgar Allan Poe wrote of drug-induced hallucinations in some of his short stories. Although laudanum and morphine were frequently prescribed to women during this period for a variety of physical and perceived emotional ailments, and many women are known to have become addicts as a result of their medical treatment, women writers—with the notable exceptions of Mary Shelley, Charlotte Brontë, and Elizabeth Barrett Browning, all of whom were familiar with drugs and wrote of them—rarely wrote about drug use except in nonfiction criticizing the so-called cures then used to treat women's "illnesses." Such treatments were usually designed to keep the patient in a constant stupor. In the twentieth century, as debates raged in the United States and Europe over possible causes of and treatments for widespread drug addiction, writers sought new means of exploring what they considered different planes of reality, mostly through hallucinogenic drugs. Aldous Huxley maintained that religious ecstasy could be reached using hallucinogens, and he recorded his attempts to prove it in his book *The Doors of Perception*, which became an important inspiration for other writers trying to attain euphoria or conversion. Writers of the Beat Generation in the 1950s, influenced by Huxley and wishing to explore what they believed were untapped areas of the human mind, wrote of their own drug experimentation in Beat outposts in San Francisco and Mexico. Among the best-known writers of this era were William S. Burroughs, Jack Kerouac, Neal Cassady, Allen Ginsberg, Tom Wolfe, and Ken Kesey, all of whom employed their drug use as a starting point for some of their best works. Timothy Leary, perhaps the most famous proponent of the use of LSD, also published accounts of some of his experiments with psychedelic substances. The hope that drug use can stimulate creativity and open new vistas for the imagination continues among many writers and artists; however, late twentieth-century literature also includes a number of cautionary tales about the dangers of addiction, which often end in destitution and death.

REPRESENTATIVE WORKS

Charles Baudelaire
  Les Fleurs du mal (poetry) 1857
  Les Paradis artificiels [contains "Le Poème du haschisch" and "Un Mangeur d'opium"] (poetry) 1860
André Breton
  Entretiens, 1913-1952, avec André Parinaud (interviews) 1952
Samuel Taylor Coleridge "Christabel" (poetry) 1816
  "Kubla Khan" (poetry) 1816
  "The Pains of Sleep" (poetry) 1816
Thomas de Quincey
  Confessions of an English Opium-Eater (autobiography) 1822
Theodore Dreiser
  Laughing Gas (drama) 1915
  Plays of the Natural and the Supernatural (drama) 1916
Théophile Gautier
  "Club des Haschischins" (essay) 1846
Aldous Huxley
  Antic Hay (novel) 1923

The Doors of Perception (nonfiction) 1954
William James
　　The Will to Believe (essays) 1897
Malcolm Lowry
　　Under the Volcano (novel) 1947
Alexander Trocchi
　　Cain's Book (novel) 1960
Tom Wolfe
　　The Electric Kool-Aid Acid Test (nonfiction) 1968
Stephen Wright
　　Meditations in Green (novel) 1983

OVERVIEWS

Ernst Jünger

SOURCE: "Drugs and Ecstacy," in *Myth and Symbols: Studies in Honor of Mircea Eliade,* edited by Joseph M. Kitagawa and Charles H. Long, The University of Chicago Press, 1969, pp. 327-42.

[*In the following essay, Jünger examines the influence of drugs on personality and the portrayal of this influence in literature over several centuries.*]

> Qu'elle soit ramassée pour "le bien" ou pour "le mal," la mandragore est crainte et respectée comme une plante miraculeuse—En elle sont renfermées des forces extraordinaires, qui peuvent multiplier la vie ou donner la mort. En une certaine mesure donc, la mandragore est "l'herbe de la vie et de la mort."
>
> 　　　　Mircea Eliade, "Le culte de la mandragore en
> 　　　　　　　　Roumanie," *Xalmoxis,* 1938

The influence of drugs is ambivalent; they affect both action and contemplation, will and intuition. These two forces, which seemingly exclude each other, are often produced by the same means, as everyone knows who has ever observed a drinking party.

It is, however, questionable whether wine can be considered a drug in the strict sense of the word. Perhaps its original power has become domesticated in the course of millennia of use. We hear of its greater power, but also of its greater mystery, from myths in which Dionysus appears as the lord and host of feasts with his entourage of Satyrs, Sileni, Maenads, and beasts of prey.

The triumphant conquest of Dionysus took place in a reverse order from Alexander's—from India across the Near East to Europe—and his conquests were of a more lasting nature. Dionysus is considered, like Adonis, to be the founder of orgiastic festivals, whose periodic recurrences are deeply interwoven with historical event. An exuberant phallic worship was connected with these festivals. Phallacism was not the content of the Dionysia but

one of the revelations which confirmed the mystery and its binding power. In contrast to the Dionysia, according to an ancient author, "the festivals of Aphrodite in Cythera might be called the pious games of children."

This original power of wine has vanished; we see it return, in a milder form, in the autumn and spring festivals of the wine countries. In rare instances only the intensification of the lust for life, colors, melodies, and grotesque pictures reveals a trace of the ancient mystic world with its uncanny, contagious power. Archaic features then appear in the faces, leaps, and dances. More than anything else, the mask is essential in this as a symbol of the "reversed world."

If we compare the triumphs of Alexander and Dionysus, we touch upon the difference between historical and elemental power. Success in history, as the conquest of Babylon, for example, shows, is fleeting and tied to names. The moment does not return in the same form; it becomes a link in the chain of historical time. But if we consider changes in the elemental world, neither names nor dates are important and yet changes take place time and again, not only below historical time but also within it. They burst forth like magma from its crust.

But let us stay with wine. Alexander was forced to retreat from India, while Dionysus even today reigns as a nameless host. Wine has changed Europe more forcefully than has the sword: even today it is considered to be a medium of cultic transformation. The exchange of new poisons and ecstasies, and also of new vices, fevers, and diseases, lacks the kind of definite dating by which coronations or decisive battles are remembered. Such exchanges remain in the dark, in the entanglement of the roots. We can surmise the events, but we can neither know their extent nor penetrate their depth.

For Europeans, Cortez' landing in Mexico in 1519 belonged to the historical order; for the Aztecs, this event belonged to the magical order of the world. In the latter world order dream is more powerful than consciousness; the presentiment has greater binding force than the word. In those contacts there is an oscillating element which is understood sometimes as booty and sometimes as a gift, then again as guilt or expiation—for example, in the sacrifice: on the one hand Montezuma, on the other Maximilian, both emperors of Mexico. Below the surface seeds, images, and dreams are given and received in an alternation which destroys some tribes and strengthens others. Yet its effect cannot be exactly described or dated.

Statistics, even if they are precise, can only extract figures from a problem. The problem in its depth is not touched by them; it remains in the strict sense of the word "a matter in disguise." This applies especially to domains that border on the psyche, as well as to any "behavior," including animal behavior, and no less to our subject of drugs and induced ecstasy.

To mention in this connection one of America's great gifts to Europe, tobacco, we have rather precise figures concerning the relation between nicotine and a number of diseases. These findings belong to the field of statistics. If we are to acknowledge them, however, we must first accept the idea of "utility" under which they were established.

Usefulness, in this case, is of a hygienic nature. Yet, from a different point of view, smoking could also imply something beneficial—the word "enjoyment" itself indicates this possibility. One might think of the easing of conversation, of the shortening of a tedious hour or the rapid passage of a gloomy one, of some association that may be prompted in this way, or simply of any moment of happiness. Any concentration, but any relaxation, too, must be paid for. Is the enjoyment worth the price? Here lies the problem for which statistics can only supply data. It arises for the smoker every time he thinks of lighting a cigarette.

Statistics merely confirm a fact which has always been known: drugs are dangerous. He who becomes involved with them takes a risk which becomes greater the less he calculates. In this respect, however, in comparing loss and gain, statistics are of value.

We include wine and tobacco in our consideration because it is advisable to start from rather well-known factors. Both are only marginals of our subject proper. They will be touched less the more exactly we define the word "drug." For Baudelaire wine opens, along with hashish and opium, the gate to artificial paradises. Justifiably, the friend of wine is disinclined to consider wine as a drug. He prefers wine growers and coopers rather than chemists and manufacturers to be occupied with wine. Still, from the growing of the wine to the resurrection of the grapes from the cellar, the care and skill of wine growers and craftsmen are devoted to wine; it is still regarded as a divine gift of miraculous, transforming power. It is blood of the earth and blood of gods.

To consider wine as a drug would mean no more than one comment among others—for instance, that wine contains alcohol. Tobacco seems to fit better in this category. Nicotine gives us an idea of what is possible in the sphere of alkaloids. In the smoke offerings which are made daily on our planet, there is an indication of the lightness, the spiritual liberation of the great dreams of flight. But compared with the magic power of opium, nicotine gives only a slight uplift, a mild euphoria.

Like many other etymological explanations, the one for the word "drug" is unsatisfactory. Its origin is obscure. As in the case of the word "alcohol" there are derivations from the Spanish-Arabic and also from medieval Latin. The origin from the Dutch *drog,* dry, is more likely. Drugs were materials obtained from many countries; they were traded through herb lofts and pharmacies and used by physicians, cooks, and perfumery and grocery dealers. From the beginning the word had a tinge of mystery, of magical manipulation, especially if the materials were of oriental origin.

In our definition a drug is a substance which produces a state of ecstacy. It is true, however, that something specific must be added to distinguish these substances from others used as medicine or simply for enjoyment. This specific factor should not be sought in the substance itself, but rather in the purpose of its use, because medicine too, as well as other stuffs taken for the sake of pleasure, may be used, in this restricted sense, as intoxicating drugs.

In a passage of his *Midsummer Night's Dream* Shakespeare speaks of the "common" sleep, which he distinguishes from stronger, magical states. The former brings dreams, the latter visions and prophecies. In a similar way the ecstasy produced by a drug shows particular effects which are difficult to describe. He who seeks this type of intoxication does so with specific intentions. And he who uses the word "drug" in this sense presupposes an understanding on the part of his listener or reader which cannot be defined more exactly. He sets fact on a border line.

Infusions and concentrations, decoctions and elixirs, powders and pills, ointments, pastes and resinous substances, all these can be used as drugs in this specific sense. The substance may be solid, liquid, gaseous, or smoke-like; it may be eaten, drunk, inhaled, smoked, sniffed, or injected. To attain a state of ecstasy not only a certain kind of substance is required, but also a certain quantity and concentration thereof. The dosage may be too low or too high; in the former case it will not lead beyond soberness, and in the latter it will cause unconsciousness. It is well known that in the case of drug addiction it becomes more and more difficult to adhere to the golden mean—on the one hand lies depression, and on the other the dosage becomes ever more threatening. The price that must be paid for pleasure rises ever higher. Then, the only choice is to reform or to perish.

As the effect of the drug diminishes, either quantity or concentration can be increased. That is the case with the smoker or drinker who first increases his usual consumption and then reaches for stronger kinds. This indicates at the same time that mere pleasure no longer suffices. A third possibility lies in a change in periodicity—in the transition from daily habit to rare, festive excess. In the third case, not the dosage but the receptivity is increased. The smoker who can muster up the discipline to be content with one cigarette in the morning will none the less be satisfied, because he achieves an intensity of pleasure hitherto unknown to him despite his greater former consumption. However, this again adds to temptation.

The sensitivity may become very great and, correspondingly, the dosage very slight, even minimal. We have known ever since Hahnemann that even the slightest traces of substances may become effective, and modern chemistry confirms this fact. In every case, however, the prescription must be supported by a special receptivity. For this reason homeopathic medicines do not help everyone. They presuppose homeopathic behavior. For the sensitive person a hint is enough. That is a universal law, not only in the field of hygiene but also in the general conduct of life. In the opposite case, there is an applicable proverb: "a rough log needs a rough wedge."

Thus the dosage may become minimal. Under certain circumstances, some substances which are commonly believed to be neutral may even become intoxicating, such as the air we breathe. Jules Verne's "Idea of Doctor Ox" is based on this principle. Under the false pretense of planning to build a gasworks, Doctor Ox induces an intoxicated state in the inhabitants of a small town by adding pure oxygen to the air. Thus, through concentration, a substance which we inhale with every breath of air we take becomes "poisonous." Paracelsus: "Sola dosis facit venenum."

Doctor Ox distilled the air. From this it can be assumed that for sensitive people it may become intoxicating in itself. And so it is indeed. There are probably few people for whom Goethe's words "youth is intoxication without wine" have not become reality, at least for some moments. Certainly this requires untouched receptivity, one of the signs of youth. In any case, however, external factors will also contribute to that effect, either through "higher potencies" of known or unknown substances or atmospheric influences. In novels we find flowerly phrases such as "the air was like wine"; the inexplicable gaiety arises from almost immaterial sources.

Yet the "happy hour" may bring melancholy as well. It may have an exhorting, warning power, and this quality makes it no less beneficial, because threatening dangers often announce themselves in this manner. Apart from perceptions, which are equally difficult to explain or deny, there are many experiences for which refined receptivity suffices as an explanation. Alexander von Humbold, in his "Reise in die Äquinoktialgegenden" ("Journey to the Equinoctial Areas"), deals extensively with the phenomena which preceded volcanic eruptions and earthquakes. In this connection he discusses the agitation of men and animals that may justly be called premonition as well as perception.

Up to the present day man has tried time and again to extract substances or psychogenic forces out of the atmosphere, so to speak. Mesmer, for example, taking magnetism as his starting point, believed he recognized a "fluid" which emanated from the human body and could be conserved in certain objects, such as storage batteries. In medicine, Mesmerism became hardly more than a fashion; its influence, however, survived in literature. E. Th. A. Hoffmann was especially fascinated by it. Mesmer's dissertation had already caused a sensation: "De planetarum influxu" could as easily have been the title of a piece of writing by Novalis or a contribution to the *Athenäum*.

More significant, although less well-known than Mesmer, is Carl Ludwig von Reichenbach; he excelled not only as a natural philosopher but also as a geologist, chemist, and industrialist. Reichenbach claimed he had found in "Od"

a substance whose force or emanation may be compared to Mesmer's fluid. This Od, though present everywhere in nature, is more easily perceived by delicately organized beings, whom Reichenbach called "sensitive," or, in case of special sensitivity, "highly sensitive" creatures. Reichenbach, in whom a gift for natural philosophy was united with the exactness of the natural scientist, attempted to prove the existence of Od experimentally. For this purpose he employed sensitive persons in the same way as a nearsighted person uses spectacles. He developed methods which we would call "tests" today. Although he used no instruments, he nevertheless made very fine differentiations. A person who could not detect a difference in temperature between the small and large ends of a chicken egg held in two fingers did not qualify as a sensitive person. Reichenbach ventures to penetrate into regions which, though neither remote nor closed, are inaccessible to dull senses.

Physicists, however, were just as unwilling to take notice of Od as psychiatrists and neurologists were to give consideration to sensitive persons. As a natural scientist Reichenbach grieved about this; as a philosopher he could disregard it. He came up with his idea at a most unfavorable time. This is even more true of Fechner, who considered the mathematical-physical view of the world as the "night side" of the universe, and drew from Reichenbach's writings the greatest benefit for his "psychophysics."

Fechner's thoughts about the animation of celestial bodies and of plants faded away without an echo in an era in which mechanistic theories forced their way with unprecedented force. In medicine, a massive positivism was in preparation, and out of its hybris a surgeon boasted that he had never seen a soul in his work.

Such opposing views give rise to the impression that the mind of the age was busy in two wings of a building without any doors between the two. One might also think of a double mirror whose two sides are separated by an opaque layer. Nonetheless, there have been and will be periods which approximate a oneness of view. It can never be fully attained because both the mathematical-physical view of the world and the natural-philosophical view of Reichenbach and Fechner are only aspects of the "inner self of nature" (*Inneren der Natur*).

Thus, the dosage which leads to intoxication can be minimal if the receptivity is great enough. In this respect, too, some sensitive persons are especially susceptible. The norms which the legislator feels must be established—in traffic laws, for instance—can only give an approximate standard. It will become ever stricter because the empirical world daily proves anew that intoxication and technology are clashing powers which exclude each other. Truly, this does not apply to drugs as such. On the contrary, their number and the extent of their use increase steadily. There are a growing number of achievements in which the proper use of drugs is not only indicated but indispensable. This becomes a science in itself.

The receptivity which leads to ecstasy can become so strong that mere ways of behavior suffice and drugs become superfluous. This is a prerogative of ascetics; their close relationship to ecstasy has always been known. Added to temperance, staying awake, and fasting is solitude, which the artist and the scholar also need, temporarily at least. The flow of images in the Thebais were "tele-visions" which were not dependent on drugs, let alone on equipment.

The thinker, the artist who is in good form, knows phases in which new light flows toward him. The world begins to speak and responds to the mind with swelling force. Objects seem to charge themselves; their beauty, their meaningful order come out in a new way. This being-in-good-form is independent of physical well-being; it is often in contrast to the latter, almost as if images had easier access in a condition of weakness than at other times. It is true, however, that Reichenbach has already warned against confusing sensitivity and illness—after all, it is not easy to avoid error here. The difficulty becomes especially obvious in disputes in which conclusions are drawn about the psyche of the artist on the basis of his work. It is no coincidence that our own time is so rich in controversies of this kind. Probably states of heightened sensitivity precede not only the productive phases in the life of the individual but also changes of style within a culture. These developments are connected with an almost Babylonian confusion, not only of forms of artistic expression but of language in general.

Jung-Stilling calls this receptivity a "faculty of clairvoyance" and means by this a heightened susceptibility which can be gained by a certain way of life: "finally, however, a pure, devout man may also achieve ecstacies and a state of magnetic sleep through prolonged exercises and a godly way of living." According to him "the soul works in the natural state through the brain and the nerves, in the magnetic state without either." Only after death does man gain the full power of clairvoyant sleep, because he has been completely separated from the body; this capacity is far more perfect after death than it can be in life.

Jung-Stilling's clairvoyants correspond roughly to Reichenbach's highly sensitive men; in the language of the present day they might be understood as extremely rare but recurring mutants. Clairvoyance can be developed, yet it must be inborn. Thereby Jung-Stilling explains, among other things, those cases in which warning dreams or apparitions are perceived not by the person in danger but by a third person who plays the role of the receiver. This faculty need not be coupled with ethical or intellectual endowment; it may appear in a dull existence as well as in a person full of genius. In the figure of Prince Myshkin Dostoevsky describes someone with a highly developed faculty of clairvoyance who seems to be an idiot in the eyes of the people around him. In old and new biographies one comes again and again upon the figure of the highly sensitive person who, before a fire, a stroke of lightning, or some other accident, is seized by indomitable unrest or oppression in breathing and leaves the room where he had been with others who remained unconcerned.

States of excitation or meditation, similar to those of intoxication, may also occur without the use of toxic drugs. This points to the possibility that drugs awaken faculties which are more comprehensive than those produced by a specific intoxication. They are a key—though not the only one—to realms that are closed to normal perception. For that with which one strives to achieve the idea of intoxication is hardly adequate unless it is broadened to comprise manifold and even contradictory phenomena. We started from the observation that drugs influence the will as well as contemplation. Within this ambivalence there is a large scale of variability which leads on either side to unconsciousness and finally to death. Drugs may be wanted as excitants and stimulants, as somnifacients, narcotics, and hallucinogens; they serve both narcotization and stimulation. Hassen Sabah, the old man from the mountain, was familiar with this scale to its full extent. He led the Fedavis, the votaries who were later also called the Assassins, from the peace of artificial paradises to the frenzy of running amok against princes and satraps. Not the same thing but something closely related can be found within the entanglement of our technological world. Its tendencies include both the flight into insensitivity and the intensification of the mechanism of motion through the use of stimulants.

The legislator must simplify this abundance. He considers intoxication "to be the state brought about by the use of drugs, especially the state of acute alcoholic poisoning." It is up to him to decide in every individual case whether or not intoxication had to do with a particular act, which might also be an act of omission. To judge in what state of consciousness the punishable deviation begins is especially difficult because there are drugs which, at least temporarily, further technical achievement. Champion fighters have always known such drugs, but the borderline which separates doping from permitted stimulation is fluid.

Every year there appear in the market new drugs whose dangerous effects are often not recognized until the damage has been done. With others the damage is minimal but accumulates in decades of use to an often disastrous degree. This applies both to stimulating drugs such as tobacco and to narcotics such as mild sleeping pills. Added to this is the fact that stimulants and narcotics are often used in addition to one another, or rather against one another. The saw moves to and fro. One might also think of weights on a scale: for every weight a counterweight is put on the scale. Thus an artificial equilibrium is maintained until one day the scale beam breaks.

The outsider, the sober person, notices above all in the spectrum of inebriation the side on which motion takes place. There the state of being different cannot be ignored; it announces itself far and wide to eyes and ears. The words for this condition refer, at least in the beer and wine consuming countries, to excessive drinking or heightened activity. They are mostly derived from the Latin *bibo* and *ebrius,* or the old high German *trinkan* and the Gothic *drigkan.* On the other hand, *Rauschen* denotes a lively movement, like that of wings, which becomes, also acoustically, noticeable as *Geräusch.* The movement may become violent—the Anglo-Saxon *rush* implying *stürzen* (onrush) should be mentioned here. One should further think of heightened, vibrant vitality. *Rauschzeit* is mating time. It is said of the wild boar that he becomes *rauschig.* Some animals gather in swarms; immediately following the mating flight termites drop their wings.

Rauschzeit is swarming time; men and animals congregate. For this very reason the active, will-determined side of inebriation is best known. The inebriated person does not shy away from society. He feels happy in the festive excitement and does not seek solitude; he often behaves conspicuously, but he enjoys greater license in his behavior than the sober person. One prefers seeing a laughing person to seeing a sad one; the slightly tipsy person is regarded with benevolence, frequently as the one who drives away boredom and cheers up everyone. A messenger of Dionysus enters and opens the gate to a mad world. This is contagious even for the sober individual.

This heightened activity that cannot be overlooked has given the word *Rausch* an important connotation. Generally speaking, in language also the visible side of things claims a greater share than the hidden side. An example of this is the word "day." When we pronounce it we also include the night in it. So the bright side also comprises the shadow. Generally we hardly think about that. Similarly, the word *Rausch,* though it stresses the apparent heightening of the vital, includes also its lessening: the lethargic and motionless states which closely resemble sleep and dream.

Inebriation manifests itself in various, often contrary phenomena; drugs produce the same varying effects. Nevertheless, they both complement each other to create a complex of wide range. It is said of Hassan Sabah that he led his Assassins into a world of blissful dreams or into that of murder through the use of the same drug, hashish.

He who seeks a state of insensibility behaves differently from the person who, in the manner of enthusiasts, intends to attain ecstasy. The former does not seek society but solitude. He is closer to addiction; for this reason he generally seeks to conceal his actions, which are also devoid of any festive element. The "secret drinker" is considered to be a questionable type.

He who takes drugs heavily and habitually must do this secretly for the simple reason that drugs, in most cases, come from dubious sources. Their use leads into a zone of illegality. Therefore it is one of the signs of anarchy if such heavily intoxicated individuals no longer shy away from the public. After World War I, for example, one could watch drugged persons in coffee houses "staring holes into the air."

However, the drugged person avoids society not only because he has to fear it for various reasons. By his very nature he is dependent on solitude; his disposition is not communicative, but receptive, passive. He sits as if he were facing a magic mirror, motionless, absorbed in himself, and it is always his own self that he enjoys, be it as pure euphoria or as a world of visions created by his innermost being and flowing back to him. There are lamps whose fluorescent light can change a gray stone into a piece of gold ore. Baudelaire, who calls hashish "a weapon for suicide," mentions, among other effects, the extraordinary chill following the use of the drug, which he includes in the "category of the lonely joys." This feeling of chill, also produced by other narcotics, is not only of a physical nature. It is also a sign of loneliness.

Narcissus was the son of a river god and the nymph Liriope. His mother was just as much enchanted with his beauty as she was frightened by his coldness. Worried about his fate, she asked the seer Tiresias for advice and heard from him the oracle: her son would be endowed with longevity unless he should recognize himself. The enigmatic prophecy was fulfilled when Narcissus, returning one day from the hunt, thirstily bent over a spring and saw his reflected image. The youth fell in love with the phantom and consumed himself in unrequited longing for his own image until he perished. The gods changed him into a flower of intoxicating scent, the narcissus, which has carried his name to the present day and whose blooms like to bend over quiet waters.

Probably the Narcissus myth, like many others, has only been preserved in its rudiments; its great theme seems to have been his longing. The nymph Echo also became a victim of this feeling; she longed in vain for the embrace of Narcissus and consumed herself in her sorrow until nothing remained of her but her voice.

Narcissus "became acquainted with himself," but he did not know himself. "Know yourself!" was written above the temple of Apollo in Delphi; Narcissus failed in this most difficult task like so many before and after him. The word "to know" has a double meaning; Narcissus entered into an erotic venture, while Faust chose an intellectual one. Faust wanted, according to Mephistopheles, "Helen in all women"; Narcissus, turned inward, vainly sought his self in his reflected image.

Exactly this consuming longing is also a mark of drugs and their use; the desire again and again remains behind the fulfillment. The images are enticing, like a Fata Morgana; the thirst becomes more burning. We might also think of entering a grotto which branches out into a labyrinth of increasingly narrow and impracticable passages. There threatens the fate of Elias Fröböm, the hero of Hoffmann's "The Mines of Falun" ("Die Bergwerke zu Falun"). He does not return, he is lost to the world; a similar thing happened to the monk of Heisterbach who lost his way in the forest and did not come back to his monastery until three hundred years later. This forest is time.

We believe that the substances which produce narcotic intoxication are finer, more ethereal than those which exert the will. Faust, after the great conjuration in his nocturnal study, is first led to the coarse drinkers in Auerbach's cellar and only then into the witch's kitchen.

We speak of "narcotic scent." The word is derived from the Greek ναϰόω, "to dull the senses." In southern Europe there are some kinds of narcissi whose scent is considered to be dangerous. Euphoria and painlessness follow the inhalation of volatile substances such as laughing gas or ether. At the turn of the century, the latter was in fashion as a drug, and Maupassant devoted a special study to it. In classical magic, smoke is frequently mentioned, not only as a narcotic but also as an excellent medium for the visions that follow narcotization. We find such scenes in "A Thousand and One Nights" and also in the works of authors like Cazotte, Hoffmann, Poe, Kubin, and others.

The conjecture suggests itself that the aspect of intoxication that is turned toward visions is also more significant with regard to quality. If we want to form an opinion on this, we must go back to the common root from which forms of imagination of such variety arise. The risk that we take in using drugs consists in our shaking a fundamental pillar of existence, namely time. This of course is done in different ways: depending on whether we narcotize or stimulate ourselves, we stretch or compress time. In turn, the traversing of space is connected with this factor: on the one hand, the endeavor to increase the motion, on the other the rigidity, of the magic world.

If we compare time to a stream, as has always been done, to the stimulated person the stream seems to narrow, to flow more rapidly downward in whirlpools and cascades. Thoughts, miming, and gestures adjust to this pace; the stimulated person thinks and acts faster and more impulsively than the sober one, and his actions become less calculable. Under the influence of narcotic drugs, however, time slows down. The stream flows more quietly; the banks recede. As narcotization begins, consciousness floats as in a boat on a lake whose shores it no longer sees. Time appears boundless; it becomes an ocean.

This leads to the endless opium dreams as described by de Quincey. He fancies "to be buried for millennia in the bowels of eternal pyramids." In *Suspiria de Profundis*, a collection of essays that appeared a quarter of a century after the *Confessions of an English Opium-Eater*, he looks back on this tremendous expansion of time and says that to describe it astronomical standards would not be sufficient. "Indeed, it would be ridiculous to measure the span of time one lives through in a dream by generations—or even by thousands of years."

The feeling of being distant altogether from the human consciousness of time is confirmed by others, for in-

stance, Cocteau: "Tout ce qu'on fait dans la vie, même l'amour, on le fait dans le train express qui roule vers la mort. Fumer l'opium, c'est quitter le train en marche; c'est s'occuper d'autre chose que de la vie, de la mort."

Time runs faster at the animal pole, more slowly at the vegetative pole. This fact sheds also some light on the relation between narcotics and pain. Most people become acquainted with narcotics because of their anesthetic properties. The feeling of bliss, of euphoria, connected with their use leads to addiction. The fact that it is especially the depressed who so easily fall victim to morphine is explained by their existence as such being already painful to them. Many narcotics are at the same time hallucinogens. In isolating morphine in 1803, Sertürner separated the pain-stilling potency of opium from the eidetic power. Thereby he helped countless suffering people, but at the same time he robbed of its colors the poppy juice praised by Novalis.

He who strives for visions wishes neither to escape pain nor to enjoy euphoria by means of a narcoticum; he seeks a phantasticum. He is not motivated by the fear of suffering but by curiosity, perhaps also by presumption. In the magic and witchery of the Middle Ages, the world of the alkaloids came in again and again: conjuration with the aid of potions, ointments, and fumes of mandrake, thorn apple, and henbane.

Conjuration was counted among the capital crimes in those days. The phenomena were more credible at the time than today. For Faust the realm of ghosts, though it has largely become a spiritual world, is still "not closed," yet he is only concerned with the success of his conjuration. Religious or moral scruples no longer worry him. Likewise, in our time, the intellectual devoted to the Muses is confronted with the question of what the drug can impart. His final aim cannot be the kinetic intensification of powers, happiness, or even freedom from pain. He is not even interested in the sharpening or refinement of insight but, as in Faust's cabinet, in "that which enters."

This "entering" does not mean that new facts become known. The enrichment of the empirical world is *not* meant. Faust strives to get out of his study, while a man like Wagner will remain there and feel happy the rest of his life. "It is true, I know much, but I want to know all"—there is no end to that, and in this sense the discovery of America also belongs to facts; no spaceship can lead out of that world. No acceleration, even if it carried us to the stars, can annul the primary dictum, "From yourself you cannot flee." This also applies to the intensification of the vital force. Multiplication, even involution, does not change the cardinal number. More is expected from that which enters than intensification of a dynamic or vital kind. At all times it was hoped that it would bring an increase, a complement, an apposition. That does not imply involution but addition.

In conjuration, be it with the aid of asceticism or by other means, formerly no one doubted that something strange would join in. Since then the intellect has gained such superior power that this conviction is only defended by a rearguard. Ultimately, however, it is of mere topographical significance whether an addition comes from outside or from within, whether its origin is the universe or the depth of one's self. Not the point at which the probe is started, but the one that it reaches is decisive. Here the vision is so strongly convincing that there is neither room nor need to question its reality, much less its origin. Where reasons, authorities, or even means of force are necessary to ensure its reality, the vision has already lost its power; it lives on, but henceforth its effect is merely that of a shadow or an echo. Yet, "the readiness is all."

R. A. Durr

SOURCE: "Imagination, the Unifying Power," in *Poetic Vision and the Psychedelic Experience,* Syracuse University Press, 1970, pp. 3-30.

[*In the following essay, Durr discusses the way psychedelic drugs affect one's focus of attention and the way writers and artists have used this phenomenon to unleash their imaginative abilities.*]

One of the most emphasized fundamentals in the total complex of the psychedelic or imaginative experience is its quality of absolute absorption: attention. To whatever the subject turns, his whole being is given. "Under the influence of the mushroom, one's power of concentration is far more pronounced than normally. You become deeply absorbed in whatever you may be thinking. There is no external distraction."[1] Huxley cites a passage from *The Tibetan Book of the Dead:* "'O nobly born, let not thy mind be distracted.' That was the problem—to remain 'undistracted.' Undistracted by the memory of past sins, by imagined pleasures, by the bitter aftertaste of old wrongs and humiliations, by all the fears and hates and cravings that ordinarily eclipse the Light."[2] The mind thoroughly awakened but undistracted, free of its habitual fixations, is able—being empty—wholly to receive, or what amounts to the same thing, being unbiased, balanced, is able wholly to act. One recalls a Zen anecdote of how, when the master was asked what is the Way, the Tao, he replied, Attention. The question came then, To what? And the answer: Attention! and again, Attention!—not to any what, not to any thing, but to the great Nothing, the inconceivable, a "sesame bun," maybe.

Gerald Heard believes that "it is the unique quality of *attention* which LSD can bestow that will or will not be of benefit. Intensity of attention is what all talented people must obtain or command if they are to exercise their talent. Absolute attention—as we know from, for example, Isaac Newton's and Johann Sebastian Bach's descriptions of the state of mind in which they worked—is the most evident mark of genius functioning."[3] Not only creative thought but creative living attends upon the power of attention. Alan Watts comments that "the psychedelics expand attention," and he employs an interesting metaphor: "They make the spotlight of consciousness a floodlight which not only exposes ignored relationships and unities but also brings to light unsuspected details—details normally ignored because of their lack of significance, or their irrelevance to some prejudice of what ought to be. . . . Time after time, this unprogrammed mode of attention, looking *at* things without looking *for* things, reveals the unbelievable beauty of the everyday world."[4] Sidney Cohen makes a similar point: "This total awareness Meister Eckhart calls 'the now moment.' A few people can experience such total attention spontaneously. With LSD this timeless, selfless relationship with the percept is achievable by many. When it happens, the object is invested with a profound significance. The separation between the one who sees and the seen vanishes."[5]

Years ago, Coventry Patmore, in a little essay on "Attention," expressed these ideas in his own fine prose. He saw that "realities, far lovelier than any 'ideal,' stand about us, willing to be wooed and longing to be won" but that "through inattention to their own true desires and capacities, men walk, as in a dream, among the trees of the Hesperides, hung with fruit the least savour of which includes the summed sweetness of all the fleshpots of Egypt, yet so far surpasses it as, once tasted, to supersede for ever the lust of the eyes, the lust of the flesh, and the pride of life; but they do not dream of plucking them." They are starving at a plenteous board, as Traherne put it. What is requisite, Patmore saw, is "the hardly acquired habit of suspending *active thought,* which is the greatest of all enemies to *attention*"; for "good thoughts are the free children of God, and do not come by thinking."[6] "Yet how vast are the rewards of a habit of attention, and how joyful an answer can the few who still practise it give to Wordsworth's question":

> Paradise and groves
> Elysian, Fortunate Fields—like those of old
> Sought in the Atlantic main—why should they be
> A history only of departed things,
> Or a mere fiction of what never was?
> For the discerning intellect of man,
> When wedded to this goodly universe
> In love and holy passion, shall find these
> A simple produce of the common day.[7]

To which might be added another passage from Wordsworth:

> Nature for all conditions wants not power
> To consecrate, if we have eyes to see,
> The outside of her creatures, and to breathe
> Grandeur upon the very humblest face
> Of human life.
> (*The Prelude,* XIII, 283-87)

Now it is precisely such absorbed attention to the life and work at hand that, East and West, has been recognized to keynote the creation and reception of art. Coomaraswamy explains that Eastern esthetics assumes "that knowledge arises only in the act of knowing, by an immediate assimilation (*tadakarata*) to its object, neither knower nor known existing apart from the act of knowledge."[8] Thus, in the tradition of Chinese art, the student is admonished: "Draw bamboos for ten years, become a bamboo, then forget all about bamboos when you are drawing."[9] The metaphysical ground of the creation of art is simply assumed; except from that mode of being and knowing which is the identity of subject and object there could be no organic, original art, but only the spurious manufactures, the re-combinations of the clever fancy. In the West the epistemology of the Platonic tradition consistently taught that "in perfect knowing, subject and object are identical"[10] and that "whatever intellect intellectually perceives, it perceives from itself. And whatever it possesses, it possesses from itself. But if it perceives intellectually by and from itself, it is itself that which it perceives."[11] (*Intellect* here is not used to mean reason or rationality, as it does today, but rather imagination or intuition. In his famous letter to Flaccus, Plotinus explains: "To the last [intuition] I subordinate reason. It is absolute knowledge founded on the identity of the mind knowing with the object known."[12]) This was also the epistemology of the great Scholastics, Aquinas declaring that "knowledge comes about insofar as the object is within the knower" (*Summa Theologica,* I, Q. 59, A. 2). Eckhart puts it in his cryptic way: "What absorbs me, that I am, rather than mine own self."[13] Dante translates this tradition into the principle of art when he asserts, "Who paints a figure, if he cannot be it, cannot draw it."[14] Schelling, in *Transcendental Idealism,* envisioned the faculty of imagination in accordance with these theories, for he saw the imagination as the organ of truth, the reconciler of the apparent opposites of subject and object, active and passive, determiner and determined. In the imaginative act ideological dualities vanish; there is only the one act of self-consciousness, though we regard it *in terms of* subject and object, active and passive, determiner and determined. This is the original act of imagination wherein the infinite *Urselbst* manifests and knows itself in the finite, the primary act of imagination repeated in every mind conscious of an external world, and raised in seers and poets to the power of Self-realization.

In the following verses Thomas Traherne is using words with a strictness in accord with the precision of scholastic thinking: "Sure Man was born to Meditat on Things, / And to Contemplat the Eternal Springs / Of God and Nature . . . /" ("Dumnesse"). Meditation, a discursive process, is by definition involved with *things,* with the data of experience conceptualized, since every "thing" is a "think," an abstraction from the indivisible flow of life. To meditate is natural for man, a highly useful tool and means. But contemplation is its own end. It is that order of knowing and being which is non-discursive, non-dual, im-mediate, in which knower and known are not to be regarded as entities but as the two terms of a single act: thus contemplation is of the "Eternal Springs" of both God and Nature. In mystical language contemplation is of the *Ein-soph,* the No-thing, and hence the ineffable since "beyond" all language, all conception, all dualities, all terms, in-fin-ite. In Eastern terminology this act is called

dhyana, cha'n, zen. And in the language of Romantic philosophy and esthetics, this is the Imaginative Act.

The magnificent idea of the imagination as finally formalized by the Romantics and their immediate predecessors constitutes an exact compendium of the various facets of the psychedelic and esthetic experiences with which we are mainly concerned. In summarizing the idea, I will use the language of Blake, Wordsworth, and Coleridge for the most part, since they perhaps more than any of their contemporaries fully realized the psychological and philosophical implications and metaphysical profundities of the doctrine.

Of course, the idea of the imagination is not unique to the early nineteenth century, and there are many analogous conceptions in earlier thought. In his *Vanity of the Arts and Sciences,* Cornelius Agrippa, for example, maintained that the Word of God is the only religious authority and that the Word is to be interpreted by the imagination and not by rationality—an argument later expounded by the Anabaptist and Quaker movements, where the "inner light" is roughly equivalent to imaginative vision. The influence of Boehme is apparent here, and that great mystic had much to say about the imagination, as is reflected in Schelling's thesis on it. The humanist doctrine of the microcosm, regarding man as a "little world," is congruent, since it is through imagination, as Paracelsus said, that man discerns his relation to the macrocosm, the "great world." One also recognizes close resemblances in the speculations of the "spiritual alchemists" of the earlier seventeenth century, or in the conception of "right reason" of Milton and the Cambridge Platonists.[15] Traherne's "right apprehension" is exactly imaginative vision. Peter Sterry anticipated the Romantic formulation very closely in designating the imagination the faculty wherein the spiritual and corporeal worlds are united, and he anticipated Blake in proclaiming God Himself the supreme poet, the exemplar of imaginative being. The traditional belief in the poet as inspired, prophetic,[16] as in the Bible and classical culture, was assumed throughout the Renaissance and is a corollary of the idea of imagination: it is the Muse or the Holy Ghost who works through the poet, and thus his mode is suprarational, intuitive, imaginative.[17] Shakespeare conveys the general understanding of the term as regarded from the standpoint of "cool reason" in this famous passage from *A Midsummer-Night's Dream:*

> The lunatic, the lover and the poet
> Are of imagination all compact:
> One sees more devils than vast hell can hold,
> That is, the madman: the lover, all as frantic,
> Sees Helen's beauty in a brow of Egypt:
> The poet's eye, in a fine frenzy rolling,
> Doth glance from heaven to earth, from earth to
>   heaven;
> And as imagination bodies forth
> The forms of things unknown, the poet's pen
> Turns them to shapes and gives to airy nothing
> A local habitation and a name.
>
> (V. i. 7-17)

This is intended as a sort of gentle satire by the bemused Duke, prototype of the rational man, but the true idea is still recognizable: the inspired vision, the cosmological eye, liberated from the despotism of the passive eye, encompassing heaven and earth, creatively embodying the invisible in form.[18] Poetic genius has always been seen as near akin to madness, especially by the discriminating eye of such as the "realistic" Theseus; and the beautiful and beauty-making power of love is but a *modus operandi* of the genial spirit of imagination.

But it will be enough for our purposes to recall briefly the idea's more immediate evolution in eighteenth-century thought toward the definitive statement made by the major Romantics. At least as early as the third Earl of Shaftesbury, the doctrine of "sympathy" had become disengaged from its former alchemical associations to play an increasingly important role in counteracting the prevailing Lockean-Hobbesian mechanistic views of man and nature. For while Locke was thought to have conceived of man's mind as merely passive and generalizing, and Hobbes portrayed man as the complete egoist, Shaftesbury argued that we have a moral "sense," an intuitive, spontaneous power of apprehension and response, a "sympathetic imagination." The idea found coherent expression in Adam Smith's *Theory of the Moral Sentiments,* and was general amongst the rest of the "Scottish School of Common Sense." Although Smith did not seek to controvert the empirical basis of Locke's system, he nevertheless contended that man is capable of empathizing with another by a mysterious act of imagination, and that, moreover, this act does more than merely associate superficies; it effects entrance into the very essence of the object thus apprehended. The mind is not to be regarded as a simply passive recipient of stimuli, for it is a power, and by its act of sympathetic imagination it becomes that which it knows. By some, Abraham Tucker (*The Light of Nature Pursued,* 1768, 1778), for example, imagination was considered to afford knowledge of the All, of divinity. What had begun in the early eighteenth century as moral philosophy tended by the nineteenth toward metaphysics and religion.

With Hazlitt, the various and often nebulous connotations surrounding the idea of a sympathetic imagination became crystallized in a theory of imagination worthy of those propounded by his great Romantic peers. Hazlitt believed that by virtue of its imaginative power art attains to revelations of Truth, of Reality transcendent of time and space. But this Truth, or Reality, is in no sense an abstraction: it is the imaginative realization of the essence, or "quiddity," of the "concrete particular." Art, by its energy of apprehension, its gusto, realizes the incomparable, ineffable "isness" of objects; and if our reaction is adequate we are released from our "habitual mind" and afforded at least momentary entry into the realm of essence.

For Coleridge, imagination denotes that act of total mind effecting, or revealing, the identity of subject and object, man and nature, in the *Sum,* or I Am, thus enabling man to transcend his "fixed and dead" conceptual world of *natura naturata* with its limited notions of self and to realize his true being as part and parcel of the "One Life of God."[19] The spiritual principle in man and the essence or *Natur-geist* of the natural world are of one ground, God. In nature imaginatively apprehended the spiritual principle in man, the "intuition and the immediate spiritual consciousness of God" (*BL,* I, lxxiii), called Reason by Coleridge, knows itself symbolically; for nature is itself a spontaneous symbolic manifestation of that same infinite mind—symbolic in the Coleridgean sense "that it always partakes of the reality which it renders intelligible: and while it enunciates the whole, abides itself as a living part in that unity of which it is representative" (*BL,* I, lxxiii). The imagination is thus the "unifying power," the "esemplastic power," as he called it, enabling the poetic genius—the True Man in every man, as Blake taught—to recognize that "each thing has a life of its own, and yet they have all our life" (*BL,* I, xxxiv), to "make the external internal, the internal external, to make nature thought, and thought nature . . ." (*BL,* II, 258).

> The artist must imitate that which is within the thing, that which is active through form and figure, and discourses to us by symbols—the *Natur-geist,* or spirit of nature. (*BL,* II, 259)

> If the artist copies the mere nature, the *natura naturata,* what idle rivalry! . . . Believe me, you must master the essence, the *natura naturans,* which presupposes a bond between nature in the higher sense and the soul of man. (*BL,* II, 257)

The true work of art is a spontaneous symbolical emanation of infinite mind as "natural" as nature herself; it is the peer of nature, not its copy: it manifests the power of imagination, "the reconciling and mediatory power, which incorporates the reason in images of the sense, and organizes, as it were, the fluxes of the sense by the permanent and self-circling energies of the reason" (*BL,* I, lxxiii).

Thus Coleridge assigned to the imagination, this "living Power and prime Agent of all human Perception," a deific character, for it is "a repetition in the finite mind of the eternal act of creation in the infinite I AM" (*BL,* I, 202). Imaginative man is a creator; through him God creates and knows and loves. Therefore Blake asserts, "Where man is not, nature is barren" (*The Marriage of Heaven and Hell*). Traherne, that great lover of the world, of nature, concurs. Without man's joyous, loving "Thought," or "Right Apprehension"—Imagination—creation is as nothing, in vain:

> The World within you is an offering returned. Which is infinitly more Acceptable to GOD Almighty, since it came from him, that it might return unto Him. Wherein the Mysterie is Great. For GOD hath made you able to Creat Worlds in your own mind, which are more Precious unto Him then those which He Created: And to Give and offer up the World unto Him, which is very Delightfull in flowing from Him, but much more

in Returning to Him. Besides all which in its own Nature also a Thought of the World, or the World in a Thought is more Excellent then the World, becaus it is Spiritual and Nearer unto God. The Material World is Dead and feeleth Nothing. But this Spiritual World tho it be Invisible hath all dimensions, and is a Divine and Living Being, the Voluntary Act of an Obedient Soul. (*Centuries*, II, 90)

Emerson, another lover of nature, is of their party in explaining the age-old idealism of the transcendentalist of 1842 in New England:

> The idealist, in speaking of events, sees them as spirits, He does not deny the sensuous fact: by no means; but he will not see that alone. He does not deny the presence of this table, this chair, and the walls of this room, but he looks at these things as the reverse side of the tapestry, as the *other end,* each being a sequel or completion of a spiritual fact which nearly concerns him. This manner of looking at things transfers every object in nature from an independent and anomalous position without there, into the consciousness.... Mind is the only reality, of which men and all other natures are better or worse reflectors.... His thought—that is the Universe. ("The Transcendentalist")

In the words of Zen: "The triple world is but one Mind. Outside the Mind there is no other reality; Mind, Buddha, all Sentient Creatures—these are not different things" (*Kegonkyô*).

It is by virtue of the mysterious power of imagination, in heightened mode (Coleridge's secondary, or poetic, imagination), that the poet creates; for it is only in the imaginative act that the poet's "heart and intellect" become "intimately combined and unified with the great appearances of nature" (*BL,* I, xxxiv), and that, as Wordsworth put it, he attains the visionary power to "see into the life of things" and so is inspired and capable of rendering the intelligible world in terms of the natural world. The imagination, in sum, to adopt some verses from Traherne's marvelous "My Spirit,"

> Acts not from a Centre to
>   Its Object as remote,
> But present is, when it doth view,
>   Being with the Being it doth note.
>   Whatever it doth do,
> It doth not by another Engine work,
> But by it self; which in the Act doth lurk.
>   Its Essence is Transformed into a true
>   And perfect Act.
>   And so Exact
> Hath God appeared in this Mysterious Fact,
>   That tis all Ey, all Act, all Sight,
>   And what it pleas can be,
>   Not only see,
> Or do; for tis more Voluble then Light:
>   Which can put on ten thousand Forms,
>   Being clothd with what it self adorns.

While it is not always explicit in Coleridge's writings, it is everywhere implicit that the act of imagination, being

an act of total mind, can be the functioning of man's true being only, his very Self, and never of the mere ego, "the unsubstantial, insulated Self," "the false and guilt-making centre of Self,"[20] just as, in Blake, Imagination *is* the real man in every man. It was fundamental to Coleridge throughout his life that in joy (and for the Romantic poets *Joy* is synonymous with blessedness, the spiritual mode of his veritable life of the imagination), "in joy individuality is lost."[21] Man's object in life is "to lose and find all self in God," "to leave behind, and lose his dividual phantom self, in order to find his true Self in that Distinctness where no division can be—in the eternal I AM, the Ever-living Word."[22]

The foundation of Blake's theory of the imagination[23] is the Berkeleyan *esse est percipi* and also *esse est percipere* (since we *are* even when we are not being perceived): One's being consists in his being imagined, perceived, by another, thus becoming a part of another's particular pattern of reality, and it consists in his own imaginative acts, as perceiver, relating another vitally to his own reality. Reality in Blake is always individual—"Every man's wisdom is peculiar to his own individuality" (*Milton,* 4)—since the idea of a "general nature" is just that, an *idea,* or abstraction:

> What is General Nature? is there such a thing?
> What is General Knowledge? is there such a
>   thing?
> Strictly Speaking All Knowledge is Particular.[24]

And by the same token, reality is mental:

> Mental Things are alone Real; what is call'd
> Corporeal, Nobody Knows of its Dwelling Place:
> It is in Fallacy, & its Existence an Imposture.
> Where is the Existence Out of Mind or Thought?
> Where is it but in the Mind of a Fool.[25]

It is not that nature is not "there" for all men to see—"... All of us on earth are united in thought, for it is impossible to think without images of somewhat on earth"[26]—but that there is no general or abstract "thing-in-itself" nature apart from the kind and degree of perception, the imaginative pattern, in a man's mind: "Every Eye sees differently. As the Eye, Such the Object."[27] Thus, "a fool sees not the same tree that a wise man sees" (*The Marriage of Heaven and Hell*) because the fool is less imaginative, more ratiocinative, and so forms only a diminished, spectral transaction with the tree; he knows only the Lockean "reflection" of the tree, the mass "ratio," or preconception, an abstraction out of general nature, *natura naturata.* But the wise man lives in gusto, exuberance, and pays attention, the price of clear vision. Because he is more imaginative, he is more alive, and his tree is proportionately more real, more distinctly individual than the generalized tree of the fool: "the clearer the organ the more distinct the object" (*The Marriage of Heaven and Hell*). The greater the imagination, the more nearly Man. It is in this sense that Emerson deems the poet representative. "He stands among partial men for the complete man, and apprises us not of his wealth, but of the common wealth. The young man reveres men of genius, because, to speak truly, they are more himself than he is" ("The Poet").

The ultimate Self, the Poetic Genius in man, is God. Thus for Blake imaginative vision is in the strictest sense divine vision. It is not that by it we see God, for God cannot become an object of perception. ("No man hath seen God at any time," John 1:18: can the seeing eye see itself? or is God some thing?)[28] It is rather that God is the one and only Percipient (in the terms of our present discussion): in the act of imaginative perception we see *as* God sees. "The Eternal Body of Man is The Imagination, that is, God himself. . . . It manifests itself in his Works of Art (In Eternity All is Vision)" (*The Laocoön*).

The idealistic cast of Blake's or Coleridge's poetry and thought is recognized, but even good readers of Wordsworth often miss the metaphysical sophistication of his vision, which never assumed subservience of the mind to nature (*natura naturata*), mere passivity (*The Prelude*, VI, 736). Recollecting a period in his life when he *had* been guilty of such subservience, such thralldom, he repudiates it as anomalous:

> I speak in recollection of a time
> When the bodily eye, in any stage of life
> The most despotic of our senses, gained
> Such strength in *me* as often held my mind
> In absolute dominion.
> > (*The Prelude*, XII, 127-31)

But this defection proved no more than transient, in that stage of his life:

> I had known
> Too forcibly, too early in my life,
> Visitings of imaginative power
> For this to last: I shook the habit off
> Entirely and for ever, and again
> In Nature's presence stood, as now I stand,
> A sensitive being, a *creative* soul.
> > (*The Prelude*, XII, 201-207)

(That he had not shaken the habit off for ever but after seeing for a while in glimpses saw finally not at all is the mystery and tragedy associated with the name of Wordsworth.)

Unlike Blake or Coleridge, Wordsworth is a poor theorizer and not to be trusted when he sets out to write or talk about his own poetry. Blake's comment is to the point: "I do not know who wrote these Prefaces: they are very mischievous & direct contrary to Wordsworth's own Practise."[29] It is the poetry itself, the poetry of the "Great Decade" especially, which bears witness to the genuineness of Wordsworth's imagination. It may be worthwhile to cite some passages from that poetry which tend to intimate his theory more accurately at least than his various prose comments of a theoretical nature.

The following verses from "Tintern Abbey" are among the most famous in the English language, but their idealistic cast is not commonly remarked:

> And I have felt
> A presence that disturbs me with the joy
> Of elevated thoughts; a sense sublime
> Of something far more deeply interfused,
> Whose dwelling is the light of setting suns,
> And the round ocean and the living air,
> And the blue sky, and in the mind of man;
> A motion and a spirit, that impels
> All thinking things, all objects of all thought,
> And rolls through all things.
> > (93-102)

This "presence" is neither an effluence from within nor an influence from without, neither subjective nor objective, but the confluence and identity of subject and object—the "field" of the act of knowing. It is not "here" nor "there," but *present*, the "blended might" of mind and nature (Preface to *The Excursion*), an "ennobling interchange of action from within and from without" (*The Prelude*, XIII, 375). He goes on then to affirm his love of nature or, appositively, "of all the mighty world/ Of eye, and ear," and adds, clumsily perhaps, "both what they half create,/ And what perceive." Mind and nature are one creative process, the working of "one great Mind" (*The Prelude*, II, 254).

The Prelude, which traces "the growth of a poet's mind," is full of relevant passages. In Book I, for example, he addresses the "Wisdom and Spirit of the universe" as "Thou Soul that art the eternity of thought/ That givest to forms and images a breath/ And everlasting motion . . . / (II, 401-404). What kind of division can the analytic intelligence discover here between the mind of man and the Mind of the universe? The very "forms and images" in man's thought owe their animation, their *life*, to "the eternity of thought," the "Wisdom and Spirit of the universe."

> Hard task, vain hope, to analyse the mind,
> If each most obvious and particular thought,
> Not in a mystical and idle sense,
> But in the words of Reason deeply weighed,
> Hath no beginning.
> > (*The Prelude*, II, 228-32)

Compare Traherne:

> The Thoughts of Men appear
> Freely to mov within a Sphere
> Of endless Reach; and run,
> Tho in the Soul, beyond the Sun.
> The Ground on which they acted be
> Is unobserv'd Infinity.
> > ("Consummation")

Another passage from *The Prelude:*

> How shall I seek the origin? where find
> Faith in the marvellous things which then I felt?
> Oft in these moments such a holy calm
> Would overspread my soul, that bodily eyes
> Were utterly forgotten, and what I saw
> Appeared like something in myself, a dream,
> A prospect in the mind.
> > (II, 346-52)

The heart of Wordsworth's poetry, it might be said, lies in his "spots of time," his moments of intensely realized experience; and in the famous passage in Book XII of *The Prelude* he tells us that their "renovating virtue"

> chiefly lurks
> Among those passages of life that give
> Profoundest knowledge to what point, and how,
> The mind is lord and master—outward sense
> The obedient servant of her will.
>
>   (219-23)

Texts could be multiplied, but let it suffice to say that for Wordsworth, when he was most worthy of himself, the various worlds of man and nature

> Were all like workings of one mind, the features
> Of the same face, blossoms upon one tree;
> Character of the great Apocalypse,
> The types and symbols of Eternity,
> Of first, and last, and midst, and without end.
>   (*The Prelude,* VII, 635-40)

In his moments of imaginative vision, Wordsworth is one of the great knowers of Suchness. In the passages cited, and in many others like them, he is sometimes trying to render such moments in poetry, and sometimes trying to explain their significance. Perhaps it is true, as Blyth suggests,[30] that the latter tendency eventually opened a rift between him and nature that finally cut him off from the sources of imaginative power.

Shelley also moved toward the thought that finite mind was part of the workings of one great Mind and that in imaginatively apprehending nature man is knowing himself, his Self. "Mont Blanc" provides an instance closely comparable to the drift of Wordsworth's intuitions:

> The everlasting universe of things
> Flows through the mind, and rolls its rapid waves,
> Now dark—now glittering—now reflecting gloom—
> Now lending splendour, where from secret springs
> The source of human thought its tribute brings
> Of waters,—with a sound but half its own, . . .
>
> Dizzy Ravine! and when I gaze on thee
> I seem as in a trance sublime and strange
> To muse on my own separate phantasy,
> My own, my human mind, which passively
> Now renders and receives fast influencings,
> Holding an unremitting interchange
> With the clear universe of things around . . .
>   (1-6, 34-40)

And like the other Romantics, Shelley saw that most men were ignorant of this primal "Power": "The secret Strength of things/ Which governs thought, and to the infinite dome/ Of heaven is as a law . . ." (139-41). For men are like sleepwalkers embroiled in their own phantasies:

> who lost in stormy visions, keep
> With phantoms an unprofitable strife,
> And in mad trance strike with our spirit's knife
> Invulnerable nothings—
>   ("Adonais," 39)

It should be clear now that the statement that all things are of one Suchness, the workings of one Mind, does not mean that "everything is the same," an indistinguishable mass, "matter." Quite the contrary: the suchness shared by all things is manifest as unique individual existence, or "isness," as clearly perceived, as divinely imagined— not a *separate* existence, but a *distinguished* existence. As Huxley understood it in his mescaline experience:

> "Within sameness there is difference. But that difference should be different from sameness is in no wise the intention of all the Buddhas. Their intention is both totality and differentiation." This bank of red and white geraniums, for example—it was entirely different from the stucco wall a hundred yards up the road. But the "is-ness" of both was the same, the eternal quality of their transience was the same.[31]

Compare Emerson, in "Art":

> A squirrel leaping from bough to bough and making the wood but one wide tree for his pleasure, fills the eye not less than a lion—is beautiful, self-sufficing, and stands then and there for nature. A good ballad draws my ear and heart whilst I listen, as much as an epic has done before. A dog, drawn by a master, or a litter of pigs, satisfies and is a reality not less than the frescoes of Angelo. From this succession of excellent objects we learn at last the immensity of the world, the opulence of human nature, which can run out to infinitude in any direction. But I also learn that what astonished and fascinated me in the first work, astonished me in the second work also; that excellence of all things is one.

Leary, Alpert, and Metzner put it this way: "In the state of radiant unity, one senses that there is only one network of energy in the universe and that all things and all sentient beings are momentary manifestations of the single pattern."[32] Francis Huxley also attempts to explain the paradox:

> One of the most fascinating experiences to be gained under LSD is that during which the subject-object distinction is done away with. It is replaced, not by that state imputed to infants unable to distinguish things in the outside world from themselves, but by a recognition that nothing that exists and is experienced can be properly classified as "an object" since the very act of experiencing it makes it part of yourself and therefore of your subjectivity. Strangely enough, however, this recognition does not necessarily destroy the thing's individuality: it remains itself however much it also becomes a vehicle for the awareness of yourself.[33]

Blake's note on a text of Swedenborg's is relevant here: "Essence is not Identity, but from Essence proceeds Identity & from one Essence may proceed many Identities. . . . If the Essence was the same as the Identity, there could be but one Identity, which is false."[34]

Words like *suchness* or *isness,* a wrenching of conventional diction, are apropos because they refuse the assignment of some kind of generalized quality, or name, to a perception, an assignment which is always ex post facto, Lockean reflection—the attempt of memory to stop and classify the relational flux of life. But the event, reality, is precisely ineffable, utterly outside the realm of language, ratios, classifications, and thus incomprehensible or at least paradoxical to rational, dualistic thought. All actual experience is incomparable, which is why all comparisons are odious, an assault upon true being, as D. H. Lawrence said:

> The moment you come to compare them, men are unequal, and their inequalities are infinite. But supposing you *don't* compare them. Supposing, when you meet a man, you have the pure decency not to compare him either with yourself or with anything else. Supposing you can meet a man with this same singleness of heart. What then? Is the man your equal, your inferior, your superior? He can't be, if there is no comparison. He is the incomparable. He is single. He is himself.[35]

All generalizations, all comparisons, regarded as real rather than as merely useful, support

> The tendency, too potent in itself,
> Of use and custom to bow down the soul
> Under a growing weight of vulgar sense,
> And substitute a universe of death
> For that which moves with light and life informed,
> Actual, divine, and true.
>
> *(The Prelude, XIV, 157-62)*

Only the imaginative act, "Right Apprehension," the realization of the Suchness of things, can shake off this "weight of vulgar sense." In imaginative vision everything exists as in itself it is, just so, incomparable and wonderful, because imagination is not "I" but God seeing through me. Poetry, imaginative art, is "the reconciler of man and Nature" and brings "the whole soul of man into being" precisely because its perspective is non-egotistical, non-partisan; it sees with the cosmological eye totally absorbed yet dispassionate, indiscriminate. In this view, even Achilles dragging Hector's outraged body around the walls of Troy, the carnage of the *Nibelungenlied*, Chaucer's Summoner and Pardoner, Macbeth or Iago, are Good: are incomparable acts in the cosmic play of life immense in power, pulse, and passion. In the world of art, the world of imagination, we become ourselves, Spectator of the spectacle.

Keats is another great poet who, with very slight philosophical bent initially and with very little tutelage (Hazlitt's writings and lectures, principally), intuited the central insights represented by the term Imagination. He clearly distinguished "the poetical character," that kind of which he was a member, from "those who have a proper self, Men of Power" (to Benjamin Bailey, November 22, 1817), or the "egotistical sublime; which is a thing per se, and stands alone." For he perceived that the origin of poetry is *non ego*, that "as to the poetical Character itself . . .

> it is not itself—it has no self—it is every thing and nothing—It has no character—it enjoys light

and shade; it lives in gusto, be it fair or foul, high or low, rich or poor, mean or elevated.—It has as much delight in conceiving an Iago as an Imogen. What shocks the virtuous philosopher delights the chameleon Poet. It does no harm from its relish of the dark side of things any more than from its taste for the bright one, because they both end in speculation [that is, for Keats, the Spectator absorbed by the spectacle].

(To Richard Woodhouse, October 27, 1818)

Because the poet—as Poet, as inspired, in the imaginative act, not necessarily as member of society, father, lover, friend, and so forth—is not a self-contained, discriminating ego, "he is continually in for and filling some other Body." He has the *"Negative Capability"* of remaining open, inconclusive, attentive in "the midst of uncertainties, Mysteries, doubts, without any irritable reaching after fact & reason" (to George and Thomas Keats, December 21, 27 [?], 1817)—the wisdom of insecurity.

> Go not too near a house of rose,
> The depredation of a breeze
> Or inundation of a dew
> Alarm its walls away;
> Nor try to tie the butterfly;
> Nor climb the bars of ecstasy.
> In insecurity to lie
> Is joy's insuring quality.
>
> (Emily Dickinson)

And because the poet will let things be, because he is empty, unconsolidated, mindless, he is capable of making what Keats called "the empathic entrance into essence." "Wherein lies happiness?" he asks in the early *Endymion*,

> Wherein lies happiness? In that which becks
> Our ready minds to fellowship divine,
> A fellowship with essence; till we shine,
> Full alchemized, and free of space. . . .
>
> (I, 777-80)

He imagined a kind of "Pleasure Thermometer"—unfortunate phrase—"a regular stepping of the Imagination towards a Truth" (to John Taylor, January 30, 1818), an increasing intensification of imaginative apprehension ("The excellence of every Art is its intensity, capable of making all disagreeables evaporate, from their being in close relationship with Beauty & Truth," to George and Thomas Keats, December 21, 27 [?], 1817) progressing from the tactile, the miracle of touch, through the supersensuosity of music, to the "chief intensity" of love. Each degree, truly experienced (our minds must be "ready," passively attentive), is capable of bringing us "into a sort of oneness," so that "our state/ Is like a floating spirit." But the two highest degrees, of friendship and love, are "Richer entanglements, enthralments far/ More self-destroying . . ." (*Endymion*, I, 798-99).

It is this kind of ego-dissolving love, empathy, intense relaxed awareness of the present moment, that is the poet's joy and gives him power to see into the life of things. "I scarcely remember counting upon any Happiness—I look not for it if it be not in the present hour—nothing startles me beyond the Moment. The setting sun will always set me to rights—or if a Sparrow come before my Window I take part in its existence and pick about the Gravel" (to Benjamin Bailey, November 22, 1817). Thus to the poet's sight, as Emerson wrote,

> The hush of natural objects opens quite
>   To the core: and every secret essence there
>   Reveals the elements of good and fair;
> Making him see, where Learning hath no light.
>
> > ("The Poet")

> 'Tis the man who with a bird,
> Wren or Eagle, finds his way to
>   All its instincts; he hath heard
> The Lion's roaring, and can tell
>   What his horny throat expresseth,
> And to him the Tiger's yell
>   Comes articulate and presseth
> On his ear like mother-tongue.
>
> > ("Where's the Poet?")

"This insight," said Emerson, "which expresses itself by what is called Imagination, is a very high sort of seeing, which does not come by study, but by the intellect being where and what it sees . . ." ("The Poet"). It is clear that, despite the variance among their symbols and terms, this "very high sort of seeing" is the heart of all romantic, mystical, or visionary literature, and the veritable core of the psychedelic experience.

As Wordsworth insisted, the subject matter of this kind of imaginative experience and poetry is most often "nothing special," "incidents and situations from common life," man's "primal passions" ("Preface" to the 1800 edition of *Lyrical Ballads*), his archetypal being, shared by every man, however uncommon may be the poet's symbolic rendition. "Miraculous power and marvelous activity—/ Drawing water and hewing wood" (Ch'uan Teng Lu). But recognizing these incidents and situations from common life as miraculous and marvelous, the stuff of poetry, is a question, as we have seen, of imaginative being, of "Right Apprehension," as with Traherne:

> Giv but to things their tru Esteem,
> And those which now so vile and worthless seem
>   Will so much fill and pleas the Mind,
> That we shall there the only Riches find,
>   How wise was I
>   In Infancy!
>   I then saw in the clearest Light;
> But corrupt Custom is a second Night.

To Dr. Johnson a blade of grass was *nichts als* a blade of grass, but to Whitman "a leaf of grass is no less than the journeywork of the stars,"

> And the pismire is equally perfect, and a grain
>   of sand, and the egg of the wren,
> And the tree-toad is a chef-d'oeuvre for the highest,
> And the running blackberry would adorn the parlors

> of heaven,
> And the narrowest hinge in my hand puts to scorn
>   all machinery,
> And the cow crunching with depressed head
>   surpasses
>   any statue,
> And a mouse is miracle enough to stagger sextillions
>   of infidels
> And I guess I could come every afternoon of my life
>   to look at the farmer's girl boiling her iron
>   tea-kettle and baking shortcake.
>
> > ("Song of Myself")

The effect of imaginative vision, in Coleridge's words, is "to find no contradiction in the union of old and new; to contemplate the ANCIENT of days and all his works with feelings as fresh, as if all had then sprang forth at the first creative fiat. . . . To carry on the feelings of childhood into the powers of manhood; to combine the child's sense of wonder and novelty with the appearances, which every day for perhaps forty years had rendered familiar; 'With sun and moon and stars throughout the year, / And man and woman . . . '" (*BL*, I, 59).

Sidney Cohen remarks in this connection that "Only a very few are able to retain the novelty of the first sensory experience after repeated exposures. One of the unique qualities of LSD is its capacity to temporarily bring back the vividness of newness."[36] Thus, a statement frequently found in the psychedelic reports is to the effect of having rediscovered the "divine ordinariness"[37] of life. Jane Dunlap, for example, reports that an enduring consequence of her sessions with LSD was "a markedly noticeable increase in the appreciation of beauty. . . . Not only did almost any lovely object take on still more graceful lines, often becoming luminous and sparkling with jewels, but I could see beauty in hundreds of commonplace things I had not thought of as being even attractive before."[38] "The invariable mark of wisdom," Emerson wrote, "is to see the miraculous in the common" ("Nature").

This visionary world, fresh with a childlike wonder and joy, is not to be sought for as remote in space or time; it is as near as here and as present as now. Thomas Traherne was one who wished to remind us where our true felicity was to be found. Like the birds in Huxley's *Island*, "Here and now, boys, here and now" is the song Traherne never tires of singing.

> By the very Right of your Sences you Enjoy the World. Is not the Beauty of the Hemisphere present to your Ey? Doth not the Glory of the Sun pay Tribut to your Sight? Is not the Vision of the WORLD an Amiable Thing? Do not the Stars shed Influences to Perfect the Air? Is not that a marvellous Body to Breath in? . . . Prize these first: and you shall Enjoy the Residue. . . . *Be faithfull in a little, and you shall be Master over much.* . . . If you be Negligent in Prizing these, you will be Negligent in Prizing all. There is a Diseas in Him who Despiseth present mercies, which till it be cured, he can never be Happy. He esteemeth nothing that he hath, but is ever Gaping after more: which when he hath He despiseth in

like manner. . . . Being therefore all Satisfactions are near at hand, by going further we do but leav them: and Wearying our selvs in a long way round about, like a Blind man, forsake them. They are immediately near to the very Gates of our Sences. It becometh the Bounty of God to prepare them freely: to make them Glorious, and their Enjoyment Easy. For becaus His Lov is free so are his Treasures. (*Centuries*, I, 21, 23)

Not knowing how near the truth is,
People seek it far away,—what a pity!
They are like him who, in the midst of water,
Cries in thirst so imploringly,
They are like the son of a rich man
Who wandered away among the poor.

(Hakuin)

No one better understood than Traherne "that it did not so much concern us what Objects were before us, as with what Eys we beheld them . . ." (*Centuries*, III, 68). For he remembers how, in the dark days of his apostasy, when he had caught the disease of ignorance, he too had "pin'd for hunger at a plenteous Board" ("Solitude").

> Thoughts are the most Present things to Thoughts, and of the most Powerfull Influence. My soul [when I was a young child] was only Apt and Disposed to Great Things; but Souls to Souls are like Apples to Apples, one being rotten rots another. When I began to speak and goe. Nothing began to be present to me, but what was present in their Thoughts, Nor was any thing present to me in any other way, then it was so to them. . . . All Things were Absent which they talkt not of. (*Centuries*, III, 10)

And as they, the adults, "the old grey realists," talked only of getting and spending, success and failure, right and wrong, the sun and moon and stars went out, and he, "being Swallowed up therfore in the Miserable Gulph of idle talk and worthless vanities, thenceforth . . . lived among Shadows, like a Prodigal Son feeding upon Husks with Swine" (*Centuries*, III, 14).

These poets are associated in the popular mind with Nature, justly enough; but it is not sufficiently recognized that their Nature is metaphysically subtle, inseparable from "The mind of man/ My haunt; and the main region of my song" (Wordsworth, *The Recluse*, 793). The visionary, it is worth repeating, is typically not philosophically naive. It is axiomatic with him that "The Sun's Light when he unfolds it/ Depends on the Organ that beholds it" (Blake, "The Gates of Paradise").

> I feel that a Man may be happy in This World. And I know that This World is a World of imagination & Vision. I see Every thing I paint in This World, but Every body does not see alike. To the Eyes of a Miser a Guinea is more beautiful than the Sun, & a bag worn with the use of Money has more beautiful proportions than a Vine filled with Grapes. The tree which moves some to tears of joy is in the Eyes of other only a Green thing that stands in the way. Some See Nature all Ridicule

& Deformity, & by these I shall not regulate my proportions; & Some Scarce see Nature at all. But to the Eyes of the Man of Imagination, Nature is Imagination itself. As a man is, So he Sees. As the Eye is formed, such are its Powers.[39]

> "What," it will be Question'd, "When the Sun rises, do you not see a round disk of fire somewhat like a Guinea?" O no, no, I see an Innumerable company of the Heavenly host crying, "Holy, Holy, Holy is the Lord God Almighty."[40]

"'The Nature of my Work is Visionary or Imaginative,' said Blake: 'it is an Endeavor to Restore what the Ancients call'd the Golden Age.' *By vision*," Northrop Frye precisely interprets, "*he meant the view of the world, not as it might be, still less as it ordinarily appears, but as it really is when seen by human consciousness at its greatest height and intensity*. It is the artist's business to attain this heightened or transfigured view of things, and show us what kind of world is actually in front of us, with all its glowing splendours and horrifying evils."[41]

Thus these men know very well what must be done in order to reveal the world again as freshly sprung forth "as at the first creative fiat." The work is to be accomplished, in Coleridge's words, "*by awakening the mind's attention from the lethargy of custom*, and directing it to the loveliness and the wonders of the world before us; an inexhaustible treasure, but for which, in consequence of the film of familiarity and selfish solicitude we have eyes, yet see not, ears that hear not, and hearts that neither feel nor understand" (*BL*, II, 6; my italics).

> For love, and beauty, and delight,
> There is no death nor change; their might
> Exceeds our organs, which endure
> No light, being themselves obscure.
> (Shelley, "The Sensitive Plant")

According to this epistemology and ontology, then, subject and object, mind and thing, man and nature are, in reality, inseparable, the two terminals of a single imaginative act. But in practice, due to "the lethargy of custom" and "in consequence of the film of familiarity and selfish solicitude," one of the terminals—man—has become insulated so that the spark, the flash that reveals reality, remains inert, *in potentia*. The poet is that man on whose mind and heart the egotistical film has not formed, or at least not hardened, so that now and again—in "spots of time"—in him the circuit is completed, and the currents of universal Being flow through him. His is then no longer an insular ego-consciousness, but a cosmic consciousness. In traditional language, he is inspired, breathed into by a divine power, sacred Muse, or Holy Ghost, so that he sees all things *sub specie aeternitatis* and finds that all which we behold is full of blessings. This is that "glad day" when Imagination, the Real Man, awakens in eternity's sunrise.

That the psychedelic experience is very frequently imaginative in the sense of the word that I have been outlining is the root of its kinship with literature, with the world of art; their various contiguities stem from this source.

NOTES

[1] "Four Psilocybin Experiences," *Psychedelic Review* (*PR* hereafter), I (1963), 226.

[2] Aldous Huxley, *The Doors of Perception* and *Heaven and Hell* (New York: Harpers, 1963), p. 58.

[3] "Can This Drug Enlarge Man's Mind?" *PR*, I (1963), 17.

[4] "A Psychedelic Experience: Fact or Fantasy?" in *LSD: The Consciousness-Expanding Drug,* ed. David Solomon (New York: Putnam, 1964), p. 125.

[5] *The Beyond Within: The L.S.D. Story* (New York: Atheneum, 1964), p. 50.

[6] *In Religio Poetae, etc.* (London, 1907), pp. 33, 36.

[7] *Ibid.,* pp. 34-35.

[8] A. K. Coomaraswamy, *The Transformation of Nature in Art* (New York: Dover, 1956), p. 12.

[9] In D. T. Suzuki, *Zen and Japanese Culture* (London: Princeton, 1959), p. 31.

[10] Plotinus, *Enneads,* V, 1. 4, ed. B. S. Page; trans. Stephen Mackenna (London: Pantheon, 1957), p. 372.

[11] *Select Works of Plotinus,* trans. Thomas Taylor (London, 1817), p. 292.

[12] R. M. Bucke, *Cosmic Consciousness* (New York: Dutton, 1923), p. 122.

[13] C. de B. Evans, *Meister Eckhart by Franz Pfeiffer* (London: Allenson, 1931), I, 380.

[14] Coomaraswamy, *Transformation,* p. 176.

[15] It is understood that by the word *imagination* the Cambridge Platonists, like most thinkers of their time, meant what Coleridge later clearly defined as *fancy,* and thus *imagination* is a pejorative term in their vocabulary. In finding in their thought an analogy to the Romantics' idea of imagination, I mean only that, unlike Hobbes and the mechanistic philosophers whom they opposed, they had experienced and affirmed the ascendancy in man of suprarational, intuitive powers of mind that are correlative to the power of imagination as defined by the Romantics. More specifically, in Cudworth's epistemology, which insisted upon the active, creative function of the mind in relation with "outer reality," and which attributed reality to the mind's images (and not only to the mathematically "clear and distinct ideas" of the New Philosophers), there is the firm basis for a theory of the imagination. See, e.g., his *True Intellectual System,* III, 432.

[16] *Prophetic* in the proper sense of the word, as defined by Whitman, e.g., in *Specimen Days* (1882): "The word prophecy is much misused; it seems narrow'd to prediction merely. That is not the main sense of the Hebrew word translated 'prophet'; it means one whose mind bubbles up and pours forth as a fountain, from inner, divine spontaneities revealing God. Prediction is a very minor part of prophecy. The great matter is to reveal and outpour the Godlike suggestions pressing for birth in the soul."

[17] For an excellent study of "The Poet and His Muse," see Sir Herbert Read, *The Origins of Form in Art* (New York: Horizon, 1965), Chapter VI. He concludes that "the Muse is clearly an archetypal figure conceived at the dawn of civilization to represent [Coleridge's "shaping power of the imagination"], and such an archetype is still serviceable for a modern theory of poetry, for an adequate philosophy of art."

[18] See the commentary of Paul A. Olson on this passage, in "A Midsummer Night's Dream and the Meaning of Court Marriage," *ELH,* XXIV (1957), 97-98. He cites Pico della Mirandola and Peter de la Primaredaye as representatives of the Renaissance idea of imagination as the power of realizing and embodying universal form. See also Northrop Frye's essay on "The Imaginative and the Imaginary" in *Fables of Identity* (New York: Harcourt, 1963), pp. 151-67.

[19] See especially Chapter XII of the *Biographia Literaria,* ed. J. Shawcross, 2 vols. (London: Oxford University Press, 1954). References to this edition will appear as *BL.* Shawcross' Introduction is still one of the most comprehensive general surveys of Coleridge's thought, and for the convenience of the nonspecialist reader I have cited several of Coleridge's statements from Shawcross' discussion, where they appear in a context more coherent perhaps than in Coleridge's work at large.

[20] S. T. Coleridge, *Confessions of an Inquiring Spirit,* ed. H. St. J. Hart (London: Stanford, 1957), pp. 80, 52.

[21] *The Philosophical Lectures of Samuel Taylor Coleridge,* ed. Kathleen Coburn (London: Princeton, 1949), p. 179.

[22] *BL,* I, 186; *Confessions,* ed. Hart, p. 70. Cf. Essay xi of Coleridge's *The Friend,* where he affirms that "the groundwork . . . of all pure speculation is the full apprehension of the difference between the contemplation of reason, namely, that intuition of things which arises when we possess ourselves, as one with the whole, which is substantial knowledge, and that which presents itself when transferring reality to the negations of reality, . . . we think of ourselves as separated beings." The latter, "the abstract knowledge which belongs to us as finite beings, . . . leads to a science of delusion."

[23] I am indebted to Northrop Frye's brilliant account of Blake's theory, *Fearful Symmetry: A Study of William Blake* (Boston: Beacon, 1962).

[24] *Ibid.,* p. 15.

[25] *Ibid.,* pp. 14-15.

[26] *Ibid.,* p. 20.

[27] *Ibid.,* p. 19.

[28] Cf. The *Kena Upanishad:* "That which is not seen by the eye, but by which the eyes see; *that,* understand truly, is Brahman and not what the world worships." I once put a similar idea into verse as "The Case of Me, Myself, and I":

> mind subdued to Word,
> word subdued to Mind,
> who seeks shall find
> eye has not seen, ear heard,
> the Seer of every mind,
> the Hearer of every word.

[29] Annotations to Wordsworth's Poems, in Geoffrey Keynes, ed., *The Complete Writings of William Blake* (London: Random House, 1957), p. 783. R. H. Blyth is another who mistrusts Wordsworth's Prefaces, especially the later ones. He offers "a definition of imagination as the faculty was exercised not theorized by Wordsworth himself," a definition with which the present book is in agreement: *"It is the power by which we become so united—or better, by which we realize our original unity with persons, things, situations so completely—that we perceive them by simple self-consciousness"* (*Zen in English Literature and Oriental Classics* [New York: Dutton, 1960], pp. 420-21).

[30] *Zen in English Literature,* Chapter 27.

[31] *The Doors of Perception,* p. 62.

[32] Timothy Leary, *The Psychedelic Experience* (New York: University Books, 1964), p. 65.

[33] *Hallucinogenic Drugs and Their Psychotherapeutic Use,* ed. R. Crocket, R. A. Sandison, and A. Walk (Springfield, Ill.: Charles C Thomas, 1963), p. 176.

[34] Keynes, *Complete Writings of Blake,* p. 91.

[35] D. H. Lawrence, "Education of the People," in *Phoenix: The Posthumous Papers of D. H. Lawrence,* ed. E. D. McDonald (London: Viking, 1961), p. 602.

[36] *The Beyond Within,* p. 48.

[37] *Ibid.,* p. 168.

[38] *Exploring Inner Space: Personal Experiences Under LSD-25* (New York: Harcourt, 1961), p. 199.

[39] Blake, letter to Dr. Trusler, Aug. 23, 1799.

[40] Blake, quoted in Frye, *Fearful Symmetry,* p. 21.

[41] *Fables of Identity,* p. 143, my italics.

PRE-TWENTIETH-CENTURY LITERATURE

Anuradha Dingwaney and Lawrence Needham

SOURCE: "A Sort of Previous Lubrication: DeQuincey's Preface to 'Confessions of An English Opium-Eater'," in *Quarterly Journal of Speech,* Vol. 71, No. 4, November, 1985, pp. 457-69.

[*In the following essay, Dingwaney and Needham examine the "rhetorical strategies" of Thomas de Quincey's preface to his* Confessions of an English Opium-Eater.]

> We shall endeavour to bring up our reader to the fence, and persuade him, if possible, to take a leap which still remains to be taken in this field of style. But, as we have reason to fear that he will "refuse" it, we shall wheel him round and bring him up to it from another quarter. A gentle touch of the spur may then perhaps carry him over. Let not the reader take it to heart that we here represent him under the figure of a horse, and ourselves in a nobler character as riding him, and that we even take the liberty of proposing to spur him. Anything may be borne in metaphor. . . . But no matter who takes the leap, or how; a leap there is which must be taken in the course of these speculations on style before the ground will be open for absolute advance.
>
> De Quincey, "Style."

As a master prose stylist, Thomas De Quincey is most celebrated for the dream sequences of his *Confessions of an English Opium-Eater* and *Suspiria de Profundis* which provide instances of what he called "impassioned prose," or that "record of human passions."[1] As a theorist of style, De Quincey is best remembered for popularizing, if not introducing, the idea of organic style. For Travis Merritt and others, De Quincey's creative prose and critical commentary signal the advent of "organicist and expressivist principles" of composition which influenced the direction of English prose style during the nineteenth century.[2] These ideas hold that the language of prose or poetry embodies and expresses the original ideas, insights, sentiments, and passions of an author, or, in the words of De Quincey, manner is confluent with the author's matter, or, again, echoing his mentor William Wordsworth, style is "the incarnation of the thoughts."[3]

For the Romantic author exploring subjective experience, then, style was the outward phase of some inner process, the *material expression* of some mental phenomenon. In its extreme formulation, this expressive theory of discourse held that language records the flux and reflux of the mind at the moment of perception. Style is neither premeditated nor mechanically applied to subject matter out there, but is the spontaneous expression of some inner condition. As the writer's perceptions, thoughts, and feelings move to the center of his preoccupations, fidelity to subjective experience, not an audience's response, becomes the end of style which ultimately is judged as to how authentically, genuinely, or sincerely it reflects the author's state of mind. M. H. Abrams, whose *The Mirror and the Lamp* perhaps best documents the shift from pragmatic to expressive theories of art, sums up this important change in the following fashion: "The purpose of producing effects upon other men, which for centuries had been the defining character of the art of poetry, now serves precisely the opposite function: it disqualifies a poem by proving it to be rhetoric instead."[4] At best, the writer soliloquizes, and "the poet's audience is reduced to a single member."[5]

While De Quincey undeniably espoused organic and expressivist principles of style, we must not forget that he also maintained that style is sometimes "ministerial" to thought. In its "ministerial" capacity, style is not the embodiment of thought or the spontaneous expression of an author's perceptions, thoughts, or feelings; rather, style is the disposition of an author's materials to produce intended effects in an audience. Thus, in his essay, "Language," De Quincey devoted considerable attention to the characteristics of "ministerial" style, or that style which is "contemplated as a thing separable from the thoughts" ("Language," p. 262). The "ministerial" style has two functions: first, "to brighten the *intelligibility* of a subject which is obscure to the understanding" either through "previous mistreatment" or by nature of its complexity; second, "to regenerate the normal *power* and impressiveness of a subject which has become dormant to the sensibilities" ("Language," p. 260). Although De Quincey admitted initially that this view of style constitutes a "narrow valuation of style" compared to style considered as the "incarnation of the thoughts," he quickly recanted arguing that "these offices of style are not essentially below the level of those other offices attached to the original discovery of truth" ("Language," pp. 260-61). Style, "in its ministeriality," provides "light to *see* the road" and "power to *advance along* it" and is a "great organ of the advancing intellect—an organ which is equally important considered as a tool for the culture and *popularization* of truth" ("Language," p. 261).

For De Quincey, then, style had two important offices: first, to express an original thought; second, to popularize or illuminate an original truth for an ignorant or misinformed audience. Recalling De Quincey's status as a professional writer for the important periodicals of his day, one might expect that he gave some thought to the second of these offices, the popularization of truth, and several observations in his essay, "Style," confirm this expectation. "A man," said De Quincey,

> who should content himself with a single condensed enunciation of a perplexed doctrine would be a madman and a *felo-de-se* as respected his reliance upon that doctrine. Like boys who are throwing the sun's rays into the eyes of *a mob* by means of a mirror, you must shift your lights and vibrate your reflections at every possible angle, *if you would agitate the popular mind extensively.*[6]

Displaying a subject from every station at every possible angle would certainly illuminate any subject "previously mistreated" through ignorance or narrow valuation and render that subject in its full complexity, thus fulfilling the first function of the "ministerial" style, "to brighten the *intelligibility* of a subject." It would lend a subject power and impressiveness as well. As an example, in his essay, "Rhetoric," De Quincey described how Jeremy Taylor transformed "unaffecting and trite" subject matter by surveying it "from novel stations and under various angles." Taylor's treatment provided "new infusions of thought and feeling," and a "field absolutely exhausted throws up eternally fresh verdure."[7]

Given De Quincey's extensive statements on the subject, it is surprising that critics have not addressed themselves to the "ministerial" style[8]—surprising especially because De Quincey's observations on the "ministerial" style explain and justify a characteristic style of his which has been variously judged to be "prodigal," "digressive," or "discontinuous."[9] Of course, these judgments reflect an expressivist/organicist perspective which views style as a verbal reflex of thought and feeling. Thus, in De Quincey's case, a "digressive" or "discontinuous" style is symptomatic of his disorientation; according to one critic, he is "unwittingly beguiled into wandering."[10] We think, however, that the "excrescences" of De Quincey's style, those "adjuncts," "digressions," and "discontinuities" that so often show up in his work, are, in fact, instances where De Quincey eddied about a complex topic and viewed it from every possible angle to orient and familiarize the popular mind with a difficult, perplexed doctrine. Admittedly, eddying about a complex topic may suggest intellectual profligacy and an unrestrained style, but De Quincey argued that such movement "ought no longer to be viewed as a licentious mode of style, but as the just style in respect to those licentious circumstances," that is, those circumstances related to writing about a novelty for a popular audience. This style, he contended, constitutes "the true art of popular display" ("Style," p. 140).

In the analysis which follows, we show how De Quincey practiced what he theorized about the "ministerial" style in his essays. We have chosen the preface to De Quincey's most famous work, *Confessions of an English Opium-Eater,* to demonstrate how he employed the "ministerial" style to familiarize the mind with a complex and novel subject. In selecting the preface, we are, of course, taking heed of De Quincey's own remarks on the necessity to "minister" to a reader's needs when the subject is particularly complex or novel: "There is," observed De Quincey, "a sort of previous lubrication, such as a boa-constrictor applies to any subject of digestion, which is requisite to familiarize a mind with a startling or complex novelty. And this is obtained for the intellect by varying the modes of presenting it,—now putting it directly before the eye, now obliquely, now in abstract shape, now in the concrete . . ." ("Style," p. 140). If any work demanded "previous lubrication," De Quincey's *Confessions of an English Opium-Eater* certainly was it. First published in two installments in *London Magazine* (1821), then in book form (1822), and finally in a revised edition (1856), the *Confessions* consternated some contemporary reviewers who expressed concern over the author's startling treatment and disconcerting presentation of what they considered to be a dangerous subject, opium. First, they charged De Quincey with "general moral laxity,"[11] and, more importantly, took him to task for exploiting a subject like opium-eating without taking, as one review put it, "sufficient care to render his communications salutary, or even harmless. While treating of a vice *never before depicted in such glowing colours,* he has neither been earnest enough in denouncing its moral turpitude, nor sufficiently positive in warning men against its dangers."[12]

Couched within the moral objection was a formalist objection against the work's ostensible discontinuities and inconsistencies. While highlighting the dangers of opium-eating, for example, the *British Review* made an explicit causal connection between excessive opium-eating and an unconnected or discontinuous text: "A brain morbidly affected by long excess of indulgence in opium cannot be reasonably expected to display a very consistent or connected series of thoughts and impressions. The work before us is accordingly a performance without any intelligible drift or design."[13]

We believe that De Quincey was aware that his reader would misapprehend his work and so designed the preface to serve as the "sort of previous lubrication" he thought so necessary "to familiarize the mind with a startling or a complex novelty." We argue that the self-intricating prose of the preface constitutes a fine example of style in its "ministerial" capacity, and that De Quincey achieved the ends of "ministerial" style, in *Confessions,* in two ways: First, he adopted a strategy of accommodation and challenge—whereby he accepted the reader's viewpoint only to undermine and replace it with another—to move his reader from a narrow, prejudicial valuation of opium to an enlarged view of its paradoxical power. Second, the preface's "licentious" style rehearsed the reader in the activity requisite to understanding the difficult, involved text which followed. In this case, style is "ministerial" in another sense: in addition to illuminating the intelligibility and power of the subject, style serves to guide the reader through the experience of reading, thus providing not only "light to *see* the road" but also "power to *advance along* it."

Accommodation and Challenge

De Quincey's aim in the *Confessions,* stated in the concluding sentence of its preface and reiterated in his "Introductory Notice" to *Suspiria,*[14] was to "emblazon the power of opium": "What I contemplated in these Confessions was to emblazon the power of opium . . . over the grander and more shadowy world of dreams" (p. 93).[15] Yet, in the "Pains of Opium," he observed that given the "ignorant horror which everywhere invested opium, I saw too clearly that any avowed use of it would expose me to

rabid persecution" (p. 304). If an admission of opium use was likely to produce such disastrous consequences, then writing about it for the express purpose of "emblazoning" its power was an enterprise fraught with considerable difficulty. How was De Quincey to overcome his readers' hostility and prejudice? We argue that he devised a complex rhetorical strategy of accommodation and challenge through which he sought to make the reader view opium in a different light. Once this was achieved the reader would approach the work with more comprehension, and, perhaps, with more sympathy. Specifically, De Quincey elicited his audience's approval by first inhabiting their preconceptions, occupying what M. H. Abrams has, in another context, designated "the terrain selected by the opposition," before overturning their expectations and enlarging their sympathies.[16]

Our recognition of this strategy of accommodation and challenge in the preface makes sense of what would otherwise be seen simply as a confusion of purposes in *Confessions.* Initially, for example, De Quincey identified "instruction" as the end of *Confessions* in his preface: "I trust," he said, that [*Confessions*] will prove, not merely an interesting record, but, in a considerable degree, instructive" (p. 93). The instructiveness of his record, at first resided in "the benefit resulting to others, from an experience [of opium addiction] purchased at so high a price" (p. 93). The record would, De Quincey implied, warn its readers against the dangers of opium-eating. Later, a more specific benefit was suggested. By demonstrating how he "untwisted, almost to its final links, the chain which fettered" him (p. 94), De Quincey suggested that an account of his struggle and progress provided a model for and encouraged other opium-eaters' efforts in the same direction, and, moreover, proved that the "chain" could, in fact, be broken. But the reader who took these implied claims seriously was likely to be disappointed. For *Confessions* was ultimately not intent on warning persons against opium's dangers (although these dangers were, indeed, an important part of the record), nor was it intent on providing a model others might emulate. Both these misconceptions, encouraged by the preface's opening argument, De Quincey "corrected" elsewhere (and, we will argue, in the preface as well). For example, in his retrospective account of *Confessions* in the "Introductory Notice" to *Suspiria,* he remarked: "I have elsewhere explained that it was no particular purpose of mine, and *why* it was no particular purpose, to warn other opium-eaters" (p. 451).

As for providing a model other opium-eaters might emulate, De Quincey did not really provide one. First, his record testified to extreme suffering which would deter, not encourage, others to launch on a similar effort at withdrawing from opium. "I triumphed," he concluded his "annal of suffering," "But infer not, reader, from this word 'triumphed,' a condition of joy and exultation. Think of me as one, even when four months had passed, still agitated, writhing, throbbing, palpitating, shattered" (p. 326). Next, as De Quincey pointed out, each individual case is different: "I would not presume to measure the efforts of other men by my own. Heartily I wish him more resolution; heartily I wish him equal success. Nevertheless, I had motives external to myself which he may unfortunately want" (p. 326). Finally, he undercut his assertion of triumph over opium addiction altogether. In the "Appendix" to *Confessions* when it first appeared as a book in 1822, De Quincey remarked: "Those who have read the Confessions will have closed them with the impression that I had wholly renounced the use of Opium. This impression I meant to convey . . . because I, who had descended from so large a quantity as 8,000 drops to so small a one (comparatively speaking) as a quantity ranging between 300 and 106 drops, might well suppose that victory was in effect achieved" (p. 435). However, "the fact is," his "Introductory Notice" to *Suspiria* made clear, "I overlooked, in those days, the *sine qua non* for making the triumph permanent. Twice I sank, twice I rose again. A third time I sank . . ." (p. 449).

If the aim of *Confessions* was not to "instruct" by warning against the dangers of opium or indeed, by providing a model for others to emulate, why did De Quincey mislead his readers about his work in the preface's opening argument? A passage in the "Introductory Narration" of *Confessions* indirectly provides the answer. Here, De Quincey pointed approvingly at G__'s insight into Grotius's method of argument. Grotius, G__ suggested, initially accommodated hostile views, even though it entailed abstaining from "certain advantages of his argument," because his audience which "would have been repelled on the very threshold from such testimonies as being in a spirit of hostility to themselves, will listen thoughtfully to suggestions offered in a spirit of conciliation, much more so if offered by people occupying the same ground at starting as themselves" (pp. 143-144). We can see the opening argument of the preface as De Quincey's Grotian gambit. Confronted with a hostile and uncomprehending audience, De Quincey did exactly what Grotius did: he inhabited the "same ground at starting" as his audience to deflect their immediate hostility and secure their thoughtful attention before overturning their preconceptions about opium and testifying to its powers.

Certainly De Quincey seemed to conciliate his readers and seemed to inhabit their stance admirably. The preface's opening exemplified this strategy of audience accommodation. His tag, "courteous Reader," and his "apology" for "breaking through those restraints of delicate reserve, which for the most part, intercept the public exposure of our errors and infirmities" (p. 93) were the more obvious attempts at accommodation. Less obvious, though no less effective, was De Quincey's attempt to place the *Confessions* within the framework of his readers' expectations. He trotted out the palliative most literature traditionally employs: *Confessions* is "instructive,"[17] and suggested a subject bound to elicit his readers' instant approval: *Confessions* will warn against the dangers of opium. But the reader who expected, therefore, the argument to proceed along the lines of a "moral denunciation" was mistaken. "Guilt [read moral culpability]," asserted De Quincey next, "I do not acknowledge"

(p. 94). Guilt, moreover, was for De Quincey relative to the "probable motives and prospects of the offender, and the palliations, known or secret, of the offense" (p. 93). Immediately thereafter, De Quincey implied that "intellectual . . . pursuits and pleasures" were his palliations for eating opium: "My life has been, on the whole, the life of a philosopher: from my birth I was made an intellectual creature; and intellectual in the highest sense my pursuits and pleasures have been, even from my schoolboy days" (p. 94). Realizing, however, that he may have gone too far, and have startled the reader who viewed opium-eating as a gross indulgence, De Quincey conceded that opium-eating may be a "sensual pleasure." But, we should note that "may be" is the operative term, for De Quincey prefaced his statement with the hypothetical construction: "*If* opium-eating *be* a sensual pleasure . . ." (p. 94).[18] Furthermore, he argued that his offense, if any, would be mitigated by circumstances peculiar to his own case.

By this point, then, "Instruction" in the narrow sense (of warning against opium) was no longer at issue. Contemporary readers who expected a "moral denunciation" were now placed in the position of having to weigh De Quincey's justification for opium-eating, and this was halfway to acknowledging the legitimate uses of opium. But, typically, what De Quincey gives with one hand he takes away with the other. In keeping with his characteristic procedure, then, De Quincey somewhat undermined his own justification for opium-eating by suggesting that it may be "open to doubts of casuistry" (p. 94). Again, however, the recalcitrant reader who was all too willing to agree with De Quincey's hesitant proposition was in for a surprise. Immediately, De Quincey confronted the reader with a long list of opium-eaters. While the reader might dismiss De Quincey's justification for opium-eating as special pleading, he or she could not as easily dismiss the list De Quincey provided. An argument by numbers, the list included, first, "the class of men distinguished for their talents" and well-known figures of that time (p. 94). Talent and eminence, linked here with opium-eating, were brought into the service of making opium-eating almost respectable. More specifically, opium's ability to relieve excruciating pain was the palliation offered in this segment of the argument: "a later undersecretary of state (viz., Mr. Addington, brother of the first Lord Sidmouth, who described to me the sensation which first drove him to opium in the very same words as the Dean of Carlisle—viz., that he felt as though rats were gnawing at the coats of his stomach)" (p. 95).

If the reader did not accept this argument, De Quincey had another to offer: working class people also eat opium. Why? Because "The lowness of wages, which, at that time, would not allow them to indulge in ale or spirits" (p. 96). Lest the moralist complain that this was no justification (why, after all, must they "indulge in" anything at all?), De Quincey had yet another argument. Moving from what readers might see as a trivial justification to what he conceived of as the genuine justification for eating opium, De Quincey remarked:

Wages rising, it may be thought that this practice would cease: but, as I do not readily believe that any man, having once tasted the divine luxuries of opium, will afterwards descend to the gross and mortal enjoyments of alcohol, I take it for granted [and here opium is made a universal pleasure] that

Those who eat now who never ate before,
And those who always ate, now eat more

(p. 96).

The shift from working people to a universal class of opium-eaters is a little facile and would be disturbing if De Quincey had not stacked up considerable evidence as he proceeded from the individual case to the universal, gathering more and more opium-eaters along the way: first himself, then talented and eminent men, then the common man, and, finally, everyman, since De Quincey asserted that opium-eating would be even more prevalent if it were not for the "medical writers, who are [opium's] greatest enemies," and, thus, induce "fear and caution" to prevent people from "experiencing the extensive power of this drug" (p. 97).

The shift accomplished, De Quincey could now muster and present all the evidence in support of his more accurate statement of intent: that he will "emblazon the power of opium." A catholic anodyne, opium encompasses medicinal, physiological, and psychological benefits. It could, for instance, intercept "the great English scourge of pulmonary consumption," relieve unbearable physical pain, and counter "the formidable curse of *taedium vitae*" (p. 97), which is certainly a universal malady, cutting across class and income.

De Quincey neatly turned the tables on the moralists who denounced opium by denouncing them himself in the penultimate paragraph of the preface. The doctors of the soul (the moralists), like the doctors of the body (the "medical writers" De Quincey rebuked earlier) were "ignorant, where they are not hypocritical, childish where not dishonest" when they targeted opium for their "moral denunciations," because "opium, or any agent of equal power, is entitled to assume that it was revealed to man for some higher purpose than that it should serve as a target for moral denunciations" (p. 97). The reader, too, stood rebuked. Schooled by the moralists, the reader who expected (encouraged, certainly by the preface's opening) the preface (and the work it precedes) to proceed along the lines of a "moral denunciation" was jolted out of his preconceptions and forced to re-examine and, perhaps, revise them. Finally, most of the preface's opening argument was rendered suspect by the concluding three-fourths of the preface. Suggesting primarily that *Confessions* will warn against the dangers of opium, it was contradicted by the concluding sections which justify opium-eating and assert opium's powers.

The preface, then, disoriented the reader, initially inhabiting assumptions that it subsequently overturned to dispose the reader to assume an open-minded attitude toward opium. Yet it is worth noting that, while warning against the moral dangers of opium was not the preface's (or the text's) concern, the preface still wished to record (as did the text) the "infirmity and misery" which result from opium addiction. Thus, De Quincey's reiteration of the word "misery" in the opening argument qualified his insistent claims about opium's pleasures and benefits. Though De Quincey was intent on celebrating the powers of opium, opium was for him a paradoxical power, "a kind of oxymoron," says Roger Porter, "'a dread agent of unimaginable pleasure and pain,' while its very name awakens 'vibrations of sad and happy remembrances,' . . . opium brings 'revulsion' and 'resurrection,' the lowest depths of hell and an 'apocalypse' of divine enjoyment."[19] (It is no accident, therefore, that in the segment in the preface where he justified opium-eating, De Quincey also pointed to the polarities of fascination and enthrallment, "divine luxuries" and "sensual pleasure" that opium engendered). Having corrected a narrow prejudicial valuation, he did not want to err in the opposite direction.

To accurately reflect this paradox, De Quincey attempted a difficult balancing act that some might argue failed. If opium does contain self-contradictory powers, why did De Quincey dwell more on the justification for opium-eating and on its pleasures in the preface? The response to such readers is simple: because the reader was already convinced about the dangers of opium, they needed to be merely suggested; whereas, because the reader needed to be convinced about opium's pleasures, they were stated explicitly and at great length. In this, the preface clearly anticipated the text, where the section on "Pleasures of Opium" is virtually unqualified, but the "Pains of Opium" are prefaced by a protracted argument about opium's beneficent agency. De Quincey was insistent that the pleasures of opium are as real as the pains. He accurately reflected this paradox in the preface which anticipates in both structure and emphasis De Quincey's subtle and more substantial delineation of opium's paradoxical agency in his text.[20]

REHEARSING THE READER

The preface compelled the reader to re-examine his or her prior conceptions of opium and encouraged a rich and comprehensive understanding of its powers. But this is not all the preface tried to accomplish. The preface sought also to reform the reader's reading habits by rehearsing him or her in the art of careful reading. "Most contemporary readers," De Quincey complained in his essay on "Style," "are repelled from the habit of careful reading." Brought up primarily on newspapers, and, therefore, "shrinking from the plethoric form of cumulation and 'periodic' writing in which the journalist supports or explains his views," these readers had learned the "trick of short-hand reading" whereby they knew the "art of catching at leading words and the cardinal and hinge joints of succession which proclaim the general course of a writer's speculation" ("Style," p. 162). Contemporary readers must have been consternated and perplexed when confronted with *Confessions*. To capture the "self-contradictory powers" of opium in words, De Quincey often yoked together contraries and made acute qualifications and discriminations which undermined his assertions. Oftentimes, too, De Quincey illuminated his point by rambling away from it to another point which seemed to have little apparent connection with what was at issue. To follow the back-and-forth movement of De Quincey's *Confessions,* where he mentioned or conceded a point only to overturn it or qualify it subsequently, moreover, to see the contradictions as an index of his complex treatment of his subject and not as uncertainty about it, the reader had to read attentively and carefully.[21]

As an exemplary instance of De Quincey's characteristic procedure, we can consider what Malcolm Elwin has characterized as the "circumlocution of [*Confessions'*] hesitant opening" (p. xviii). De Quincey opened his work with the question: "I have often been asked—how it was, and through what series of steps, that I became an opium-eater" (p. 104), to which he provided a brief answer; "simply an anodyne it was, under the mere coercion of pain the severest, that I first resorted to opium" (p. 104). But the reader who expected next a record of the steps which led to De Quincey's opium-eating had a long wait. Instead, the reader was treated to "a long disquisition on the differences between [De Quincey] and Coleridge as opium-eaters," which Elwin finds "interesting and relevant but disconcerting to the reader who has learned nothing of De Quincey's case" (p. xviii). This "disquisition" is more than "interesting and relevant"; it was crucial to De Quincey's effort to "emblazon the power of opium," an effort not fully accomplished by his explanation of his reason for launching on his own opium career. At the heart of this "disquisition" lay De Quincey's defense of opium as more than an anodyne: "Any attentive reader, after a few moment's reflection, will perceive that whatever may have been the casual *occasion* of mine or Coleridge's opium-eating, this could not have been the permanent *ground* of opium-eating; because neither rheumatism nor toothache is any abiding affection of the system . . . And once the pain ceased, then the opium should have ceased. Why did it not? Because [we] had come to taste the genial pleasure of opium" (pp. 109-110). If we grant, moreover, De Quincey's insistent claim about *Confessions* in its 1822 version—"Not the opium-eater, but the opium is the true hero of the tale" (p. 431)—then the defense of opium's power this "disquisition" contained becomes more significant than the narrative it interrupts.

De Quincey's wish for an "attentive reader" was no empty signal. For De Quincey, here as elsewhere, followed what Vincent de Luca calls "the elusive path of revelation."[22] The reader was, for instance, not confronted with the chief insight of the "disquisition" immediately: De Quincey's overt defense of opium extended beyond its properties as an anodyne. Instead, the reader arrived at it by way of De Quincey's condemnation of Coleridge's "gross misstatements of fact in regard to [their] several opium experiences" (p. 108). These misstatements De Quincey proceeded to locate in Coleridge's "flighty . . . partial and incoherent reading"

(p. 108). De Quincey's aim here was to undermine Coleridge's credibility. With good reason too. Coleridge was more famous and, like De Quincey, known for his opium-eating. To some readers, he may even have appeared the authority on opium-eating. Thus, De Quincey who wished to invest himself with this authority, especially since then his defense of opium would be more credible, annihilated Coleridge's authority by showing his position on opium to be mistaken, and, ultimately, indefensible.

The significance of this "disquisition" was not yet exhausted. Like Coleridge, there were contemporary readers who were aware of and even comfortable granting opium's use as an anodyne. As an anodyne, however, the "disquisition" and the text made clear, the power of opium was not sufficiently accounted for, and, certainly not adequately celebrated. Thus, when De Quincey took Coleridge to task, he was also taking his readers to task for having, at best, a reductive and inadequate understanding of opium's powers.

Elwin is right when he states that this "disquisition" disconcerted the reader. Not only did it disrupt the discussion with which *Confessions* opens, it also took a long time to come to its point. There were, of course, other such disruptive (because discontinuous with what precedes or follows) passages in the text. The opening of "Pains of Opium" was a prime example. The "Pleasures of Opium" closed with: "Here opens upon me an Iliad of woes"; then we get the title "Pains of Opium," followed by an epigraph from Shelley's *Revolt of Islam:*

> As when some great painter dips
> His pencil in the gloom of earthquake and eclipse
> (p. 291).

Naturally, the reader expected to read about De Quincey's "Iliad of woes," with "pictures" of opium's "pains" that approximated "the gloom of earthquakes and eclipse." Did the reader get these? No. What the reader got, instead, were a "few explanatory notes" on the beneficent agency of opium before De Quincey "[fell] back into the current of [his] regular narrative" (p. 308). ("Few," incidentally, is a misleading word because the "notes" comprise seventeen pages of an elaborate and dense argument.) Like the "disquisition," these "explanatory notes" were important because they constituted the crucial corrective to the misery and suffering of opium addition this section documents. Furthermore, these "notes" contained a defense of opium's power and a denial of opium's dangers. De Quincey insisted that the fault lay not with opium, but with him for his inertia and awful nightmares. And he exploded two common misconceptions about opium's destructive agency: "either you must renounce opium, or else infinitely augment the daily ration; and secondly . . . you must content yourself, under any scale of doses, with an effect continually decaying . . . At this point I make a resolute stand, in blank denial of the whole doctrine" (p. 294). Finally, like the "disquisition," these "explanatory notes" contained an assertion of his own authority on the subject of opium, which strengthened his claims on behalf of opium's benefits: "reflective experience so extensive as my own . . ."; "I had reached [this] position [of authority] . . . as a result of long, anxious, vigilant experience" (pp. 306, 298).

Both the "disquisition" and the "explanatory notes," although they contained explicit appeals for the reader's attention ("Any attentive reader, after a few moments of reflection . . ."; "Reader, who have thus far accompanied me, I must request your attention, before we go further, to a few explanatory notes"; pp. 109, 291), might have merited scant attention from the reader intent on pursuing the discussion/narrative they interrupted. (In fact, one reader, Elwin, unequivocally asserted that "De Quincey's popularity—if not his reputation—suffered from the tedium of the long preamble" of which the "long disquisition" is a substantial part; p. xviii). Yet because these passages, and others like them, were crucial to De Quincey's complex delineation of opium's power, they deserved careful attentive reading—a skill the preface taught the reader to develop.

If we recall that "leading words and the cardinal and hinge joints of transition" in popular, journalistic discourse allowed the contemporary reader to be inattentive, then De Quincey's leap without any overt transition from one statement of intent (*Confessions* was moral instruction on the dangers of opium-eating) to another statement of intent (not moral instruction, *Confessions* was, rather, an attempt to "emblazon" opium's power) could be legitimately seen as De Quincey's effort to counteract his reader's "habit of care[less] reading." Within the larger argument of the preface, moreover, the argument justifying opium-eating itself broke up into an array of discrete arguments which were bound together not by "the cardinal and hinge joints of transition," but rather by the incremental support they provided for De Quincey's assertion of opium's power in the preface's conclusion. Comprehending these discrete arguments and making out the relationship among them required the reader to be alert to each new move. The reader had to be even more attentive because De Quincey moved so swiftly from one argument to another in this segment justifying opium-eating. Indeed, the mental gymnastics evident in this segment of the preface's argument absolutely required close and steady attention from the reader because the reader must create its coherence and meaning. The preface thus warned its readers and taught them to be attentive.

CONCLUSION

"The last word," said Hoyt Hudson in his article on De Quincey's prose, "the last word is, read De Quincey."[23] Hudson's own appreciative reading of De Quincey reveals a sensibility attentive to general rhetorical strategies which "attract and influence a more or less defined audience."[24] In this regard we have come full circle in our efforts to demonstrate that De Quincey was a skilled tactician who guided the responses of his readers; only we have read De Quincey as selected passages from his essays on rhetoric, style, and particularly, language suggest

that he might best be read whenever he is inducting an audience into a complex subject.

De Quincey's stature as a skilled tactician or conscious prose artist cannot be emphasized enough. Critics attracted to his sometimes original comments on the nature of rhetoric and style understandably have deflected attention from his practice to his theory of discourse, often overlooking, however, the mutually illuminating relationship between practice and theory we hope to have demonstrated in our analysis.[25] Critics who have analyzed his prose craft almost exclusively have embraced expressivist assumptions about style, often with disastrous consequences for any estimation of De Quincey as a conscious prose stylist. Thus, De Quincey is often portrayed as being at the mercy of his materials; his writing is either a reflex response to his perceptions, thoughts, and feelings, or is symptomatic of problems below the level of consciousness.[26] Of course, the best critics have argued that the "plasticity" of his prose is well suited to follow "the subtlest contours of experience," and their argument is sanctioned by De Quincey's dictum that style incarnates thought or that manner is confluent with matter.[27] Yet we have tried to suggest in our reading of the preface to the *Confessions* that style is sometimes something else as well: style is "ministerial."

In its ministerial capacity, style in *Confessions* either serves "the absolute interest of the things expounded" or guides the reader through the activity of reading. We have argued that the two functions of the "ministerial" style are often interrelated. On the one hand, amplifying a subject or viewing it from various, novel stations challenges a reader's narrow, sometimes prejudicial estimation of the matter at hand and directs the reader to view it under more complex relations. On the other hand, rehearsing the reader in the activity of reading about a complex subject instills a method which prepares the reader to further investigate a complex truth. In De Quincey's words, style not only provides "light to *see* the road," but also "power to *advance along* it."

In this connection, we would suggest finally that the "ministerial" style ultimately provides the reader a way of apprehending a complex truth on the way to original thought. This observation squares with De Quincey's comments on the "path" or method of philosophical inquiry. The purpose of philosophical investigation, he noted, was "not so much to accumulate positive truths in the first place as to rectify the position of the human mind and to correct its mode of seeing." By "raising the station of the spectator," it brings "a region of new inquiry within his view."[28]

The figures of the road, the viewing station, and the prospect are not casually chosen by De Quincey, but are meant to suggest the encompassing figure of the excursion to which he often compared reading his prose. Reading his *Confessions,* he explained in *Suspiria de Profundis,* was like embarking on an excursion to the Lake District. What should the true sojourner desire, he asked, the shortest or the most beautiful route (p. 454)? Having travelled the route himself, De Quincey casts himself as a guide who displays the beauties of the place and indicates the way to achieve yet more beautiful prospects. Samuel Taylor Coleridge, whose prose, like De Quincey's, has been characterized as rambling or vagrant, also employed the figure of the excursion to apologize for yet ultimately to justify his prose style. Noting his "imperfection of form," Coleridge nonetheless concluded that he would not "regret this defect if it should induce some future traveller engaged in a like journey to take the same station and to look through the same medium at the one main object. . . . "[29]

What De Quincey and Coleridge seemed to be trying to express through their metaphorical vehicles is a view of style that falls outside traditional categories. At times, style is neither simply expressive, a tag usually describing the function of style for the nineteenth century, nor is it managerial, a broad tag describing a variety of functions of style for the eighteenth century. On the one hand, as we have argued, style need not simply express mental phenomena without regard for the audience. On the other hand, style need not simply dispose or manage material to best present a preconceived thought, nor need it manage the responses of an audience conceived as passive spectators before compelling phenomenal evidence. Style, to use De Quincey's tag, is sometimes "ministerial." If De Quincey is credited with popularizing, if not introducing, the notion of organic/expressive style, perhaps he should be credited as well for introducing a style which serves a ministerial function. We have attempted to define some of the characteristics and functions of that style. Of course, the compass of our analysis is limited and hardly does justice to the full range of rhetorical strategies that De Quincey employs in his prose. We can only say with Hoyt Hudson, read De Quincey, hoping that in some small measure we have given light to see the road and power to advance along it.

NOTES

[1] The *Collected Works of Thomas De Quincey,* I, ed., David Masson (London: A. & C. Black, 1896), p. 14.

[2] Travis Merritt, "Taste, Opinion, and Theory in the Rise of Victorian Stylism," in *The Art of Victorian Prose,* ed., George Levine and William Madden (New York: Oxford University Press, 1968), pp. 4-5; Laurence Stapleton, *The Elected Circle: Studies in the Art of Prose* (New Jersey: Princeton University Press, 1973), p. 127.

[3] From "Language" in *Selected Essays on Rhetoric by Thomas De Quincey,* ed., Frederick Burwick (Carbondale: Southern Illinois University Press, 1967), p. 262. Hereafter, all citations, including page numbers from "Language" will appear parenthetically within the text.

[4] M. H. Abrams, *The Mirror and the Lamp: Romantic Theory and the Critical Tradition* (New York: Oxford University Press, 1953), p. 25.

[5] Abrams, p. 25.

[6] From "Style," in *Selected Essays in Rhetoric,* p. 139. Emphasis added. Hereafter all citations, including page numbers, from "Style" will appear parenthentically within the text.

[7] From "Rhetoric" in *Selected Essays in Rhetoric,* pp. 124-25.

[8] Most critics mention De Quincey's essay, "Language," which explicitly refers to the "ministerial" functions of style; few actually apply the essay to their criticism. Sigmund K. Proctor is the only writer we are aware of who has considered style in its "ministerial" capacities. Suggestively, he terms "ministerial" style a mode of "ingratiation." See *Thomas De Quincey's Theory of Literature* (New York: Octagon Books, Inc., 1966), pp. 194-201. See also Hoyt Hudson's "De Quincey on Rhetoric and Public Speaking," in *Historical Studies of Rhetoric and Rhetoricians,* ed., Raymond F. Howes (Ithaca: Cornell University Press, 1961), pp. 198-214. Although Hudson does not refer to De Quincey's essay, "Language," he identifies some of the "rhetorical" aspects of his style.

[9] J. Hillis Miller, *The Disappearance of God: Five Nineteenth-Century Writers* (Cambridge, MA: Belknap Press, 1963), p. 28; V. A. De Luca, *Thomas De Quincey: The Prose of Vision* (Toronto: University of Toronto Press, 1980), pp. 9-10, 13; Judson Lyon, *Thomas De Quincey* (New York: Twayne, 1969), p. 92.

[10] Miller, p. 28.

[11] John O. Hayden, "*Confessions* and the Reviewers," *Wordsworth Circle,* 6 (1975), 276.

[12] Cited by Hayden, 277.

[13] Cited by Hayden, 278.

[14] "The object of [*Confessions*] was to reveal something of the grandeur which belongs *potentially* to human dreams . . . it is certain that some merely physical agencies can and do assist the faculty of dreaming almost preternaturally . . . beyond all [other agencies] is opium, which seems to possess a specific power in that direction." *Confessions of an English Opium-Eater in Both the Revised and the Original Texts With its Sequels, Suspiria De Profundis and the English Mail Coach,* ed., Malcolm Elwin (London: MacDonald, 1956), pp. 447-48. Unless otherwise indicated, all citations from De Quincey's *Confessions* and *Suspiria* are from this edition; hereafter, we will provide page numbers parenthetically within the text.

[15] We have used the "Original Preface to The Confessions (As revised in 1856)" and the 1856 revised version of the text. Although the contemporary reviews we cite in our introduction were responding to the 1822 version,

John O. Hayden correctly points out that "much of this contemporary criticism, moreover, applies to the later edition as well" (278). We base our argument on the assumption that the two texts and their prefaces are alike in design and function. Though we can see with most critics that the 1856 version is longer and more discursive, we agree with De Quincey who observed, in a letter to his youngest daughter, "nothing has been added which did not originally belong to the outline of the work, having been left out chiefly through hurry at the period of the first [publication]."

[16] Cited by Margaret W. Ferguson, *Trials of Desire: Renaissance Defenses of Poetry* (New Haven: Yale University Press, 1983), p. 1. Ferguson's book is the best one we know of about defensive strategies writers exploit to justify their projects. Though she discusses only defenses proper, much of what she says illuminated De Quincey's curious preface to us.

[17] Emphasis added.

[18] Emphasis added.

[19] Roger J. Porter, "The Demon Past: De Quincey and the Autobiographer's Dilemma," *Studies in English Literature,* 20 (1980), 592.

[20] Roger Ramsay correctly notes that the structure of *Confessions* embodies "the fundamental rhetorical gambit of paradox." He lists, too, the juxtaposition of opposites in the argument—"pain/pleasure, dreaming/waking, guilt/innocence, self-conquest/self-indulgent"—and in the imagery—"heaven/hell, stomach/mind, summer/winter, imprisonment/freedom." See "The Structure of De Quincey's *Confessions of an English Opium-Eater,*" *Prose Studies,* 5 (1978), 23, 27-8.

[21] Ian Jack thinks De Quincey was uncertain about his purpose. See "De Quincey Revises his *Confessions,*" *PMLA,* 72 (1959), 122-23.

[22] Vincent De Luca, p. 14.

[23] Hudson, p. 214.

[24] Hudson, p. 199.

[25] See Weldon B. Durham, "The Elements of Thomas De Quincey's Rhetoric," *Speech Monographs,* 37 (1970), 240-48; Paul M. Talley, "De Quincey on Persuasion, Invention, and Style," *Central States Speech Journal,* 16 (1965), 243-54; and Wilbur S. Howell, "De Quincey on Science, Rhetoric, and Poetry," *Speech Monographs,* 13 (1946), 1-13.

[26] Miller, pp. 27-8; Lyon. p. 57; De Luca, p. 8.

[27] D. D. Devlin, *De Quincey, Wordsworth, and the Art of Prose* (London: The Macmillan Press, Ltd., 1983), p. 110.

[28] In *Collected Writings of Thomas De Quincey,* X, ed., David Masson (London: A. & C. Black, 1897), pp. 78-9.

[29] Cited by Wayne C. Anderson, "The Dramatization of Thought in Coleridge's Prose," *Prose Studies,* 6 (1983), 268.

Molly Lefebure

SOURCE: "Consolations in Opium: The Expanding Universe of Coleridge, Humphrey Davy and 'The Recluse'," in *The Wordsworth Circle,* Vol. XVII, No. 2, Spring, 1986, pp. 51-59.

[*In the following essay, Lefebure explores the experimentations of the English Romantics with opium.*]

The Romantics experimented with many drugs, within the respective contexts of pharmacy and picturesque experience. Opium was the best known and most used because it was the most accessible and the most effective. Throughout history it has been the most valuable medicinal drug known to man; also throughout history opium has been resorted to for purposes other than the purely medicinal: "It is in the faculty of mental vision, it is in the increased power of dealing with the shadowy and the dark, that the characteristic virtue of opium lies," De Quincey assures us in his essay, *Coleridge and Opium.* While Coleridge himself says that opium has the power, "To bring forth Thoughts—hidden before . . . and to call forth the deepest feelings" (NB 3320 21½.14).

Opium: the Milk of Paradise: the miraculous drug that, in its divine, first or honeymoon phase, can be physician, philosopher, companion; fund of inexhaustible invigoration, or source of dreams, profound and delicious consolations! So-called opium dreams occur not in true sleep, but under conditions of pleasurable morphine narcosis; De Quincey describes them as spectra rather than dreams and Coleridge too defines the experience of opium dreaming as a condition in which voluntary ideas pass before the eyes more or less transformed into vivid spectra.

These day dreams or visions (as the Romantics loved, euphemistically to call them) are founded on real events and situations, or at least ideas arising from real events and situations, around which (to quote Coleridge) are constructed a series of desirable, pleasure fulfilling variations which, to use his highly descriptive term, "stream" along, "yet with reason at the rudder" (NB 1718 16.105). He tells us what it was like, "When in a state of pleasurable & balmy Quietness I feel my Cheek and Temple on the nicely made up pillow . . . the fire gleam on my dear Books, that fill up one whole side from ceiling to floor of my Tall Study—& winds, perhaps are driving the rain, or whistling in frost, at my blessed Window, whence I see Borrodale, the Lake, Newlands—wood, water, mountains, omniform Beauty—O then as I . . . sink on the pillow . . . what visions have I had, what dreams—the

Bark, the Sea; all the shapes & sounds & adventures made up of the Stuff of Sleep and Dreams, & yet my Reason at the Rudder / O what Visions . . . & I sink down the waters, thro' Seas & Seas—yet warm, yet a Spirit" (*Ibid*).

And all the time everything is expanding; the opium universe is literally an expanding one. "Space swelled," says De Quincey in *Confessions,* "and was amplified to an extent of unutterable and self-repeating infinity." Endless, bottomless oceans; fathoms measureless to man; vast deserts; giant cities. Time, likewise, holds no terrors; the opium eater feels in possession of eternity. The capacities too of the heart, the mind, appear to be miraculously limitless; again to quote De Quincey, "The moral affections are in a state of cloudless serenity, and high over all the great light of the majestic intellect." And he exults, "Thou has the keys to Paradise, O just, subtle, and mighty opium!"

A yearning to escape, a longing for distant unknown shores, not necessarily physical, permeated Romanticism. The dream, the dream world, afforded the very essence of escape. Opium produced dreams of particular beauty, nightmares of peculiarly gothic horror. Thus inevitably the dream-possessed Romantic imagination was also an opium impregnated imagination. Coleridge knew what he was doing when, in 1816, desperately short of money, he sold Murray *Kubla Khan, The Pains of Sleep* and *Christabel,* to be released to the world as a trio of opium dreams, or visions. To what extent these poems were influenced by opium is not our concern here; the point is that Romantic popular taste was overwhelmingly for so-called opium poems. Similarly, when De Quincey's *Confessions of an Opium Eater* appeared it was an instant stupendous success and remained the most successful work that he ever wrote.

What might be described as an elitist drug circle, based upon Clifton, Bristol, had sprung into flourishing existence by the close of 1798, centered upon the newly founded Pneumatic Institute which, financed by the Wedgwoods, was the brainchild of Dr. Thomas Beddoes, the founder and principal. Dr. Beddoes, a radical in politics as well as in his medicine, was dedicated to experimental modes of medical treatment: he was an ardent practitioner of what today we call "alternative medicine." Yet, fundamentally, his medical knowledge was sound and he was a brilliant diagnostician; nor was his experimentation in vain; we should not treat lightly the man who discovered digitalis and who, moreover, discovered and promoted the young Humphrey Davy.

The Pneumatic Institute (or Institution, we find it called both) consisted of a small hospital for patients, a laboratory for experimental chemical research and a lecture theatre. Of the entire enterprise Humphrey Davy was made superintendent, taking up the appointment in 1798. He was nineteen years of age and a newly fledged apothecary and surgeon, having just completed the two years of study, apprenticeship and assistantship, which in those

days comprised the training of a medical man. He had also fallen in love with chemistry, which he had virtually been teaching himself over the past three years. Indeed the youth had come to Beddoes's notice because of his researches on heat and light and a new hypothesis on their nature, to which Beddoes became a convert. Davy was initially engaged as superintendent of the laboratory only, it being Beddoes's intention to treat his patients with a variety of drugs, acids, herbal remedies and, particularly, gases—these last referred to by Beddoes as "factitious airs." Cases of a wide variety of complaints were accepted in his hospital, but pulmonary disease cases above all.

Davy speedily made his impact upon the Pneumatic Institute; quickly being promoted, as aforesaid, to become superintendent of not only the laboratory but the entire complex. In April, 1799, he made his famous discovery of nitrous oxide, described by the Institute as "a pleasure producing air" but popularly known as "laughing gas." Davy officially used it to produce relaxation in his patients, especially those suffering from rheumatism and paralysis, and also for depression. His notebooks for the period abound with accounts of his experiments with nitrous oxide; there is an account of how he experimented with it upon himself and burst out laughing and stamped about the floor in glee. There are also accounts of the reactions of his patients; one paralytic, when asked how he felt after breathing the gas, said that "he felt like the sound of a hass" while another, rendered practically speechless by the novel treatment, could only gasp that "he felt he did not know how" (Royal Institution Lib., Box 20 20b). A rheumatic patient responded to the gas with wonderful "thrilling" in his lame leg (*Ibid* 20a).

But Davy's most dramatic successes with the gas were scored when he demonstrated its effects upon members of the enthusiastic audiences who flocked to hear him lecture on the subject of the new discovery. Many (Thomas Wedgwood was one such) responded to the gas by shouting and rocking with laughter and dancing wildly; others responded with sensations of thrill and sublimity. Others found that it left them unmoved. The Robert Southeys were among those who tried it; he laughed immoderately, but she, by nature apathetic, was "very little affected, only rendered giddy" (R.I., Box 20, 20b). As always with drugs, personal psychology played a large element in individual experience. Modern medicine recognises that some temperaments succumb to drug addiction more readily than others, though the reason for this is not yet fully understood. De Quincey, too, remarks upon this phenomenon. No one was a more interesting example than Davy himself.

In true Romantic vein Davy hurled himself at every new experience and sensation which presented itself. When he discovered a gas he unhesitatingly inhaled it (in 1799, he nearly killed himself inhaling carburetted hydrogen). When he produced a new acid, he swallowed it; some odd things happened to him. When he was experimenting with galvanic electricity he gave himself shocks. When he attempted to advance an hypothesis that the fixed alkalines and earths are metallic bases united to oxygen, and in their uncombined state are possessed of such powerful affinity for oxygen as to be capable of decomposing water, he visited Vesuvius when it was in eruption and took appalling risks with his life on the edge of the crater experimenting with fresh lava. When he was asked by the government to advise upon improving sanitation in Newgate prison he spent so much time in the prison applying himself firsthand to the problem that he contracted typhus, in the form of so-called gaol fever, and lay at death's door (and, he firmly believed, suffered as a result from ruined health in his later years).

Every drug that came within his reach he sampled; opium, marijuana (in those days known as "bhang"), hyoscyamine were all tried enthusiastically by him; he exchanged notes upon them with Coleridge. It is significant that when Tom Wedgwood wished Coleridge to procure some bhang for him the first person to whom Coleridge applied for the drug was Davy.

When Davy sampled a gas, acid, or drug he did so in style, with *panache:* here he is exploring the consolations to be found in nitrous oxide (the episode is described by him in a notebook entry for 1800—like Coleridge, he was a lifelong keeper of notebooks): "After eating a supper, drinking two glasses of brandy and water, and sitting for some time on the top of a wall by moonlight reading Condorcet's *Life of Voltaire,* I requested Mr Dewyer (his laboratory assistant) to give me a dose of air." The results, says Davy, were "thrilling." "I lost all connection with external things: trains of visible images passed rapidly through my mind, and were connected with words, in such a manner as to produce perceptions perfectly novel. I existed in a world of newly connected and newly modified ideas." He derived special pleasure from inhaling gas alone, in darkness and silence, occupied only by ideal existence, as he put it; the delight that he felt on these occasions was often "intense and sublime." One May night, in the moonlight, he respired six quarts of freshly prepared nitrous oxide and had pleasurable sensations "so intense and pure as to absorb existence" (*Ibid*).

For all his experimentation with drugs Davy never became addicted to any of them. He himself attributed his, so to speak, objectivity in this respect to the fact that his approach was that of "an experimental and inductive philosopher." "Philosophy, chemistry, and medicine are my professions," he wrote to his mother in 1800 (Davy, John, *Coll. Works of Humphrey Davy: Vol. I., Memoirs of his Life*). It was natural that he should speak of himself as a philosopher, and that everyone who knew him, or knew of him, should refer to him as such: at that time "philosophy" was a broad term covering the methodical pursuit of almost any branch of knowledge; for instance, we find Thomas Poole speaking of a laboratory as "an extensive philosophical apparatus" (*Works* i 465). More exact names for specific fields of enquiry were "metaphysical philosophy" and "natural philosophy"; most of what we now call science came under this last heading. Davy, however, had too broad a spectrum of inter-

ests and too wide a vision to be confined within the single category of "natural philosopher"; that is to say, as a scientist pure and simple. He spilled over into the sphere of metaphysical philosophy. For that reason Southey, in a lighthearted but perceptive moment, coined for Davy the name "metapothecary," which delighted Davy who throughout his life was fired with immense enthusiasm for what he described as the "sublime" in chemistry, adding, "The most sublime and important part of chemistry is as yet unknown" (*Works* i 55).

Davy and Coleridge first met in Bristol in October, 1799. Coleridge's sojourn in Bristol on that occasion was but fleeting; he and Cottle departed on their famous visit to Wordsworth in the north and on his return Coleridge went straight to London to work in Fleet Street for Stuart. Davy was in London, visiting, late that autumn and during this time he and Coleridge cemented the foundation of what was to be a lifelong friendship based on mutual deep affection and intense intellectual stimulation. The young Davy had a breadth of interest and vision, a flexibility of mind and gift of imagination that delighted Coleridge, who declared, "Every subject in Davy's mind has the principle of vitality. Living thought springs up like turf under his feet" (CL 355). Twenty years later Coleridge still held Davy in highest esteem as "the father and Founder of philosophic Alchemy, the Man who *born* a Poet first converted Poetry into Science and *realized* what few men possessed Genius enough to *fancy*" (CL 1358).

Davy all his life wrote poetry, for which he had a passion. He was a Cornishman, and of markedly Celtic temperament; by the age of five he was composing and reciting verses. He was visionary by nature; his paternal grandmother had a reputation for the second sight. She lived in a haunted house and took ghosts absolutely for granted. These things she often discussed with her small grandson, and it was from her that Davy inherited his lifelong feeling of neighbouring the invisible. From her, too, he received many wild tales and anecdotes derived from ancient Cornish oral-tradition mythology. As a schoolboy he enjoyed a great reputation as a teller of tales; that is, as a story teller in the bardic tradition. In the evenings after school he would install himself in an announced place (for instance an empty cart outside the Star Inn at Penzance, the town where he was born in 1778, and where he grew up) and, before an "enraptured audience" of young contemporaries, would embark upon long stories of wonder and terror, many of them handed down over generations and passed on to Davy by his grandmother (*Works* i 5). His early poems, surviving in his adolescent notebooks, are bardic chaunts rather than verse and possess a naturally wild note. We find "The Death of Merlin" (R.I. notebook 13h), "The Spinosist," and an untitled chaunt "My eye is wet with tears" (*Ibid* 13c); all unfinished. The last is by far the most remarkable and is based on a theme to which Davy was to return repeatedly:

> My eye is wet with tears
> For I see the white stones
> That are covered with names
> The stones of my forefathers' graves

The grass grows upon them
For deep in the earth
In darkness and silence the organs of life
To their primitive atoms return

Through ages the air
Has been moist with their blood
Through ages the seeds of
   the thistle has fed
On what was once motion and form

The white land that floats
Through the heavens
Is pregnant with
   that which was life
And the moonbeams
   that whiten it came
From the breath and spirit of man

Thoughts roll not beneath the dust
No feeling is in the cold grave
Neither thought nor feeling can die
They have leaped to other worlds
They are far above the skies

They kindle in the stars
They dance in the light of suns
Or they live in the comet's white haze

These poor remains of frame
Were the source of the organs of flesh
That feed the control of my will
That are active and mighty in me . . .

The poem then loses its way, stutters a few more fragmented lines and breaks off.

In his adult years Davy, in addition to writing conventional rhymed verse, also wrote a considerable amount of what might be called "poetic prose." This sounds untempting, but in fact he was a much finer writer of prose than of verse. Many of the poetic prose passages in his notebooks relate to what he himself described as dreams or visions; as a true Romantic he instinctively loved visions and daydreams and used them as vehicles for his poetic prose. Moreover in a man of his background, with his strong inherent strain of Celtic mysticism and gifts of imagination, a propensity to dream vivid dreams (without the aid of drugs) and a disposition to attach importance to them is scarcely surprising. However we know from the Coleridge-Davy correspondence that Davy experimented with opium and had experience of opium dreams; indeed the fact that Davy knew the pleasures of opium meant that he was able to share Coleridge's enthusiasm for pleasurable visionary drug experience and that Coleridge did not have to dissemble when speaking to Davy of opium. Some of the Davy notebook entries are obviously written while under the influence of some drug or gas; the handwriting sprawls, staggers and lopsidedly climbs up the page, to expire in scribble, or a blot. All in the cause of science!

His brother and biographer, John Davy, observes how interesting it is to compare Davy's early poems and reflections with those of a later period, particularly in notebooks and *Consolations in Travel.* "We may trace in the former the germs of many of the latter; and, indeed, the resemblance is often so marked, that the trains of thought have very much the character of recollections" (*Works* i 19). Opium, when working harmoniously, produces reticulative trains of thought which, like interminable skeins of seaweed, may float submerged, out of view, then surface to glisten in the light, then submerge again; always steadily carried forward by currents and tides and so never static, yet on reappearance fundamentally the same skein. Study of Coleridge's letters and notebooks (especially the letters) reveals this trait most markedly; reticulative skeins of ideas surfacing repeatedly, often phrased in almost the same words as were used years previously; indeed "trains of thought [which] have very much the character of recollections." It is an important factor to bear in mind when considering the plagiarisms and doubtless accounts for many—though by no means *all*—of them.

Fascinatingly we find the same reticulative skeins of ideas running through Davy's lifelong notebook entries relating to dreams or visions of spirits and celestial beings, and his exploration of boundless skies. In notebook 20a (probably dating to 1799-1800) there occurs a poetic prose passage which John Davy calls "a sketch of a reverie" allegedly experienced within view of the moonlit ruins of Tintern Abbey and embodying a development of the train of thought first met with in "My eye is wet with tears." Whether or not the prose passage is describing a dream resulting from actual opium, there is no gainsaying that it is tinctured with the essence of opium dreaming, particularly the theme of exploring vast distances: not, as in Coleridge's case, through fathomless seas, but above the stars, following "immeasurable paths of ether." To quote,

> I awoke at midnight; the recollection of indistinct but painful visions passed across my mind; the spectre of horrible images still trembled in my eyes . . . Restless, and filled with vivid imagination, I was unable to sleep; I arose and stole to the window. The moon had just sunk beneath the ruins of the abbey, and her broken and trembling light shone through the west window upon the burying-ground . . . For a few minutes I was lost, and swallowed up in impression. No longer connected with the earth, I seemed to mingle with Nature; I pursued the dazzling of the moonbeams; I raised myself above the stars, and gave imaginary beings to the immeasurable paths of ether. But when I cast my eyes on the remains of mortality—when I considered, that in that deserted spot, where the song of the nightingale and the wings of the bat were the only signs of life, thousands of thoughts . . . had rolled through the minds of a hundred intelligent beings,—I was lost in a deep and intense social feeling. I began to think, to reason, What is existence? . . . Nothing remains of them but mouldering bones; their thoughts and their names have perished. Shall we, too, sink in the dust? shall we, too, like those beings, in the course of time be no more? shall that ever-modified consciousness be lost in the immensity of being? No, my friend, individuality can never cease to

exist; that ideal self which exists in dreams and reveries, that ideal self which never slumbers, is the child of immortality, and those deep intense feelings, which man sometimes perceives in the bosom of Nature and Deity, are presentiments of a more sublime and energic state of existence.

Twenty-nine years later we find Davy jotting in his journal, "It is revealed to me that moons, which roll round the planets, are the places of expiation for offending spirits; and that the consummation of all things will be, when the moons rush to the planets, the planets to their suns, the suns to one great centre—when all will be light and joy, and all matter animated by one pure and undivided breath of Omnipotence" (*Works* i 440). This is yet a further variation on the original theme of "My eye is wet with tears." We should remind ourselves of De Quincey's observation, "It is in the faculty of mental vision, it is in the increased power of dealing with the shadowy and the dark, that the characteristic virtue of opium lies" and his further remark that opium calls "into sunny light the faces of long buried beauties" (*Confessions*). Opium aids, and indeed promotes, associative and reticulative memory.

In adulthood Davy wrote a considerable amount of verse, not without feeling and sincerity, but (considering his adolescent chaunts and the poetic prose visions which he continued to write throughout his life) disappointingly conventional both in style and content. Nonetheless he clearly prided himself on his accomplishments as a poet and gained quite a reputation as such. Though remaining largely unpublished during his lifetime (there was some posthumous publication), his poems were privately circulated and enthusiastically read and recited. In his early period at Bristol, Davy became friendly with Robert Southey and at Christmas, 1799, had two poems, *The Tempest* and *The Sons of Genius,* in the *Annual Anthology* which Southey at that time edited. Coleridge (we cannot but feel somewhat surprisingly) had no hesitation in sharing Southey's approbation of Davy's verse, particularly *Lines Written after Recovery from a Dangerous Illness;* the earlier draft was written in 1799; a later draft, (*Works* i 114-116) was written in 1807, following his attack of typhus. Coleridge assured Davy, "I will venture to affirm that there were never so many lines which so uninterruptedly combined natural and beautiful words with strict philosophical Truths, i.e. *scientifically* philosophic" (CL 356).

Coleridge, when he penned these lines, was in that dizzily enthusiastic state of adulation which always occurred in the opening phase of any friendship important to him. Instead of perplexing ourselves as to why Coleridge waxed so enthusiastic over Davy's verse, we should read the latter's scientific essays, lectures and notebooks. From these we receive an understanding of the quality which his contemporaries found so remarkable in his demonstrations and addresses—namely his "peculiar style of poetical illustration and his comprehensiveness of mind" (*Works* i 91-93). The actual notebooks, overflowing with scientific experiments described as they were performed (in several instances the notebook's pages are splashed and burned with acid), poems, essays,

metaphysical observations, details of visions, poetic prose passages, notes of reading and reflecting, mathematical calculations, chemical data, and innumerable little fleeting sketches, give us a wonderful insight into the comprehensively varied creative processes of this extraordinary genius. And we fully understand Coleridge's maturely considered pronouncement that Davy was "the Man who *born* a Poet first converted Poetry into Science and *realized* what few men possessed Genius enough to *Fancy.*"

Coleridge, all his life, revealed an extraordinary habit of travelling in and out of spheres of influence; not only did he himself magnetize, but he appeared to be cognizant of and to respond to powers of magnetism in certain others. Principally, during the years 1797 to 1810, Coleridge swung between Poole and Wordsworth; and in the spring and early summer of 1800, a battle of remarkable intensity went on between the conflicting magnetic pull of Nether Stowey on the one hand and Grasmere on the other. Coleridge's letters reveal how deeply he was torn between west and north, Poole and Wordsworth, and how close he came to abandoning a move to the Lakes and settling, instead, near Poole—and Davy, a new counter attraction to Wordsworth.

During this same period of autumn and spring, Coleridge was revealing an almost obsessive concern upon the subject of Wordsworth's progress with *The Recluse,* that immense philosophical poem, the brain child of Coleridge, which was to be the greatest and most comprehensive philosophical poem of all time, and dealing (we here need scarcely remind ourselves) with Nature, Man and Society.

With all opium addicts, as De Quincey observes and experience confirms, intellectual or creative ambition infinitely outruns capacity for achievement—hence the passion for projecting vast works which defy completion: it is part of the expanded universe of opium. In the case of De Quincey, he planned an (unrealised) *magnum opus* to which he gave the title of an unfinished work of Spinoza's, *De Emandatione Humani Intellectus:* in the case of Coleridge gigantic schemes flowed from him as from God in the beginning, creating a world of vast continents. Like God, too, Coleridge was confident that seven days, or at the most a fortnight, might see each project completed. Within the space of twelve months we find him outlining a *magnum opus* provisionally entitled *Organum verè Organum, or an Instrument of practical Reasoning in the business of real Life:* next a gargantuan study of Shakespeare; and hot on the heels of that a further enormous work, *Consolations and Comforts from the exercise and right application of the Reason, the Imagination and the Moral Feelings.* Whatever the consolations Coleridge was planning to derive from Reason and the Rest, we detect here, without a shadow of doubt, consolations from opium.

And Coleridge, of course, knew all this himself. In an opium impregnated notebook entry, written in Malta at the close of 1804, addressing himself, he jots, "One might make a very amusing Allegory of an embryo Soul up to birth!—Try! it is promising!—You have not above 300 volumes to write before you come to it—and as you write perhaps a volume once in ten years, you have ample Time, my dear Fellow!—Never be ashamed of schemeing— you can't think of living less than four thousand years, and that would nearly suffice for your present schemes—To be sure, if they go on in the same Ratio to the Performance, there is a small difficulty arises—but never mind! look at the bright side always—and die in a Dream! OH!" (NB 2373 21.553). The last is a groan of despair.

In a certain sense it may be said that Wordsworth, through Coleridge, also became a victim of opium impregnated ambition and its resultant conceptual *folie de grandeur*. As we all know, Coleridge persuaded Wordsworth that he was capable of unique achievement as a philosopher-poet who would write a Miltonic work, "the first and finest philosophical Poem"; the project originally having been discussed by the two poets at Alfoxden in the winter of 1797-98, and the scheme extending in scope and bulk as Coleridge advanced further into opium's grotesquely expanded landscape and loaded Wordsworth with concepts of an increasingly Piranesi-like structure: in 1804, Wordsworth was estimating that *The Recluse* would come to ten or twelve thousand lines, but in 1814 he was outlining an even vaster work which, if completed, might have comprised some 33,000 lines, 22,500 more than *Paradise Lost*. Wordsworth was seduced by Esteesian eloquence into believing that he had the powers to produce this immense work, a classic example of an opium eater's fantasy—with the difference that Wordsworth had embarked upon this impossible mammoth project at the urging of an opium eater, not as an opium eater himself.

Of course, we ourselves should be grateful, because as a result the world was given *The Prelude;* but for Wordsworth, without doubt, the burden which this vast project placed upon him proved of intolerable weight.

But, to repeat, in the autumn of 1799 and the spring of 1800, we find Coleridge revealing an almost obsessive interest in Wordsworth's progress with *The Recluse*. Indeed, it would be no exaggeration to say that Coleridge pestered Wordsworth with enquiries as to how the work was going and revealed impatience at the thought of William wasting his time on short poems. "Of nothing but the *Recluse* can I hear patiently" is a typical growl from Coleridge, and "I grieve that the *Recluse* sleeps," he was sighing heavily in February, 1800.

During this period Coleridge was back in the west country and consolidating his friendship with Davy, the two men meeting daily, as Coleridge informed Southey, each stimulating the other with talk and ideas; chemistry and science, metaphysics and poetry. According to John Davy at some point round about this time Humphrey Davy received from "a distinguished poet . . . a close friend of Davy . . . a proposal that he and Davy should write a

joint work, a philosophic epic" (*Works* i 71). It is difficult to think this distinguished poet could have been anyone else but Coleridge. It certainly wasn't Wordsworth, and Southey, though nursing a plan for a full length poem on Mahomet, was promised to write this with Coleridge; nor does any surviving evidence in correspondence concerning this projected joint work on Mahomet suggest that it was to be a philosophical poem dealing with the themes put forward by Coleridge to Wordsworth. To be sure, in one of Davy's notebooks (13c) there are some sketchy notes on "Mehomet" but there is no development of these, either in prose or poem form. But in this same notebook there does occur an outline plan of a lengthy epic poem in six books in blank verse, the subject of which was the deliverance of the Israelites from Egypt, and to be entitled "Moses." The theme revealed by the outline plan is recognisably that of Coleridge's Nature, Man and Society, treating man as man in contact with external nature, man in the pastoral and other early stages of society, and man in a state of highly organized civilization (in this instance of ancient Egypt of the pyramids), with a picture of degeneracy and vice, terminating with the departure of the Israelites, and the march across the desert, "a redemptive process in operation" with "promised future glory and restoration," to quote from Coleridge's outline originally proposed to Wordsworth.

Davy's actual outline headings give Book One commencing with the meeting of Moses and Zipporah and the daughters of Jethro, and entailing a description of pastoral scenery and patriarchal manners. Book Two headings read, "The Great Festival of the God of Nature—Customs of the Midionites—Moonlight Scene, and the Reflections of Jethro on the System of the universe—History of Moses—His earliest impressions connected with Pharoah's daughter—The knowledge of his family etc. . . . " Book Three details the growing love of Moses for Zipporah and their happy pastoral life. Gradually Moses comes to believe himself under the immediate inspiration of the Deity. Headings continue, "His dreams—Theory of Jethro—Moses resolves to return to Egypt."

With Book Four the tranquil pastoral passage is over; we are now with civilization and decadence. Moses meets Aaron and is reunited with Pharoah, the companion of his youth. Continue the headings (rather unexpectedly), "Jacobinical sentiments" (presumably voiced by Moses— one cannot imagine them coming from Pharoah). As a result, "Pharoah calls the Magicians." Book Four concludes with the Plagues and Lamentation for the Death of the First Born.

Headings for Book V read: "March through the Desert— Miraculous appearance of the Son of God—Destruction of Pharoah and the Army—Moses' Song—Amalek overcome." Book Six: "Meeting of Jethro—his Counsels— Institution of Laws—Communion with God on Mount Sinai—Mosaic Account of Creation. End."

Then come some jotted notes on the leading characters: "Moses a great but enthusiastic Man . . . Zipporah his

Superior in reasoning powers and sensibility—Pharoah a Despot—Jethro a Wonder, a philosophic Priest—Joshua a Hero, i.e. a Murderer—Miriam the Prophetess, the sister of Moses, a wonderful woman."

Accompanying this outline were several fragments of blank verse revealing that actual composition of this work had been commenced by Davy. The style is strongly reminiscent of Coleridge's *Destiny of Nations* (written in 1797 and intended as part of his own projected great philosophical poem—hence the reason why Coleridge referred to it as his "epic slice," a cutlet, so to speak, from the main body of the intended leviathan). Undoubtedly Davy had read *The Destiny of Nations,* attentively. It was not the best of Coleridge's blank verse—and Davy was not Coleridge. Yet Davy's exuberance, ebullience of attack, is wholly Coleridgean. We are, for instance, given a spirited Miriam:

> 'And loud she struck the harp, and raised the
>   song,
> Her ebon tresses waving in the wind;
> Her dark eyes sparkling, and her bosom
> Throbbing with transport high—'Thou, thou art
>   he,
> The chosen one of God—the man foretold,
> The saviour of thy people!'

In another passage we see the infant Moses in his cradle among the bullrushes, symbolizing man in his natural beginning, in closest contact with Nature,

> 'Gently flowed on the waters, as the sun
> Shone on them in full brightness; the tall plants,
> Shadowing around the little cradle, grew
> In full luxuriance. Fishes sported in the wave,
> Myriads of lovely insects fill'd the air . . . '

Nonetheless, then Pharoah's daughter discovers the infant Moses, she knows at once that she must save him, not simply because he appeals to her as a helpless baby, but because she sees him as Man, the ultimate masterpiece of Creation,

> 'Shall all things live, and Thou, the masterpiece
> Of all things living, perish?'

Other passages relate to communion with God on Mount Sinai, on the natural instincts of motherhood, Jethro's reflections upon the presence of mystery in Nature:

> 'But often in the heavens my wandering eye
> Has seen the white cloud vanish into forms
> Of strange unearthly lineaments.
> And often in the midnight's peaceful calm
> Have I been wakened by strange unearthly tones,
> And often in the hour of sacrifice
> Felt strange ideal pleasures.'

Further passages deal with the impact of Nature upon Man:

> 'In vain the aspiring spirit strives to pierce
> The veil of Nature, dark in mystery;

> In vain it strives, proud in the moving force
> Of hopes and fears, to gain almighty power,
> To form created intellectual worlds.'

Within the context of collaboration of Coleridge and Davy in the writing of a philosophic epic poem entitled "Moses," it may or may not be significant that, at the close of 1799, we find Coleridge writing to Southey from London, and mentioning Moses (passingly): "Spinosism (if Spinosism it be and i'faith 'tis very like it) disposed me to consider this big City as that part of the Supreme *One,* which the prophet Moses was allowed to see" (CL 316). Coleridge's mind as aforesaid, was nothing if not reticulative and this introduction of Moses into the London scene is suggestive, if nothing more, that Coleridge at that time had Moses on his intellectual map.

Yet despite Davy's initial enthusiasm for Moses, Zipporah and Jethro, within the framework of a philosophic poem treating with Nature, Man and Society, the epic failed to find completion. As his biographer puts it, Davy's "genius was destinied for other efforts." In 1801, he became professor of chemistry at the Royal Institution and accordingly left Bristol for London. He went on to become one of the most famous men internationally of his day. His greatest achievement was undoubtedly the invention of the miners' safety lamp, which has been seen, at least by the mining industry, as of greater benefit to mankind than any philosophical epic in blank verse.

The Davy-Coleridge friendship survived twenty-five years, until seriously failing health forced Davy to spend the greater part of his remaining years of life abroad. He died at Geneva, at the age of fifty-one. During the final months before his death, a seriously sick man, he diverted himself by writing a small book entitled *Consolations in Travel, or the Last Days of a Philosopher,* dedicating it to Thomas Poole. It consisted of a series of dialogues, which he committed to paper quickly, in consecutive order; the final dialogues, virtually composed on his deathbed, were dictated. The characters were Ambrosio, a classical scholar and historian, a liberal Roman Catholic, based on Davy's friend and chief companion while in Rome, Monsignor Spada (Davy was not a Catholic, but admired the discipline and doctrines of Rome); next, Philalethes, based on Davy himself; next, The Unknown, Davy's notion of the ideal chemical philosopher; and finally Eubathes, who it is said bore a striking resemblance to a fellow scientist and secretary of the Royal Society, Dr Wollaston.

The first dialogue is entitled "The Vision," the basic theme of which is, in sum, that in the progress of society no useful discovery is ever lost, all great and real improvements are perpetuated and that, in consequence, the welfare of mankind is in continuous progression (this of course being the great nineteenth century creed). The setting is the Colosseum in Rome and, according to Davy, he based this episode on a vision experienced by him in the Colosseum and recorded by him in a notebook entry dated November 9, 1819: "One moonlight night, when the summer seemed to pass into the autumn . . . I was walking in the Colosseum full of sublime thoughts . . . when of a sudden I saw a bright mist in one of the arcades, so luminous that I thought a person must be advancing with a light. I approached towards it, when suddenly it enveloped me; an aromatic smell, like that of fresh orange flowers, seemed to penetrate . . . my respiratory organs, accompanied with sweet sounds, so low that they seemed almost ideal; and a sort of halo, of intense brilliancy, and of all the hues of the rainbow, above which appeared a female form of exquisite beauty . . . a voice, distinct, but like that of a flute, said, 'I am one of the Roman deities! You disbelieve all the ancient opinions, as dreams and fables; nevertheless they are founded in truth. Before the existence of man, and some time after, a race of beings who are independent of respiration and air occasionally dwelt on the globe . . . In the early stage of society we condescended to instruct man . . . The last time I was here—'"

Here the notebook entry breaks off and is immediately followed by the account of another dream:

> I had on the 7th April, 1821, a very curious dream, which, because it has some analogy to the preceding *day dream* [Davy's italics, which, in conjunction with the words 'day dream' strongly suggests that the above was an opium dream], I shall detail:—I imagined myself in a place partially illuminated with a reddish hazy light; within, it was dark and obscure; but without, and opening upon the sky, very bright. I experienced a new kind of sensation, which it is impossible to describe. It seemed as if I became diffused in the atmosphere, and had a general sense of balmy warmth. [Compare with Coleridge's phrase (above), 'Yet warm, yet a Spirit']. Floating a little while in the atmosphere, I found that I had wings . . . I rose in the air; and . . . found myself in the sky, amidst bright clouds and galaxies of light. It seemed as if I was altogether entering a new state of existence . . . I seemed in communication with some intelligent being, to whom I stated . . . that I now knew what it was to have a purer and better existence, but that I hoped for something still more perfect . . . that I hoped to be, ultimately, in a world of intellectual light . . . After this my dream became confused; my fields of light changed to a sort of luminous wood filled with paths, and the bright vision degenerated into a common dream. (*Works* i 434-436)

In the first dialogue of *Consolations*, Philalethes-Davy is left alone in the Colosseum to ruminate among the moon-lit ruins, and before long there appears a spirit, the genius of the place. This tutelary genius takes him soaring aloft above the earth, in an infinity of space, but first Philalethes-Davy is treated to a species of lengthy monologue upon the development of mankind, presented as a series of visions, or spectra, obviously inspired by Coleridgean concepts of Nature, Man and Society. We are, in fact, being regaled, through the soaring Philalethes-Davy, with an opium-type dream based, albeit loosely at times, on the original project for *The*

Recluse, or, alternatively, *Moses;* yet in extraordinary, psychedelic terms, transposing *The Recluse* into something astounding indeed. Having traced suffering mankind through his various stages of progression, he is left behind entirely, and Philalethes-Davy is escorted by the genius higher and higher through the ether on a stage by stage exploration of the successive higher states of existence, approaching steadily nearer to the infinite and divine Mind. Incredible shapes and monsters are seen, miraculously and amazingly hued; they float and stream around the travellers, with weightless motion. Says the genius, "The universe is everywhere full of life, but the modes of this life are infinitely diversified, and yet every form of it must be enjoyed and known by every spiritual nature before the consummation of all things." Philalethes-Davy is then taken even higher, to the cometary world; much closer, indeed unpleasantly close, to the sun. All becomes hazy, crimson scarlet, and searing hot. Finally the genius can escort Philalethes-Davy no higher, because the genius herself, himself, itself, is not yet sufficiently highly developed to be capable of progressing nearer to the infinite and divine Mind. Finally Philalethes-Davy awakens from the dream, to find himself seated in the Colosseum, with his servant shaking his shoulder to rouse him. (In this vision-sequence we are reminded of Coleridge's prefix to the *Ancient Mariner,* which, translated from the Latin, reads: "I readily believe that in the sum of existing things there are more invisible beings than visible. But who will explain the great family to us—their ranks, their relationships, their differences, and their respective duties? What do they do, and where do they live? The human mind has always sought knowledge of these things, but has never attained it").

The second dialogue is entitled, "Discussions Connected with the Vision in the Colosseum," and is set on the summit of Vesuvius. This discussion treats upon dreams; there is discussion of man as an animal, man as a reasoning, developing intellectual being, and man as a religious being. There is concentration upon Christian religion: Ambrosio defends the Mosaic account of the creation of Man, maintaining "that man was created with a religious feeling, or instinct, or innate knowledge, as represented by Moses, which declining with the passage of time and the advance of man's progress, was supplanted by Revelation and the derivation of Christianity from Judaism"—a Coleridgean argument presented in highly Coleridgean vein.

In Dialogue Three, the Unknown joins the discussion and deals with the geological structure of the globe and surmised structural changes that it has undergone, including the latest scientific explanations of how living organisms came into being. The Unknown in this dialogue does most of the talking. He goes on to describe how he changed from a youth sceptic into a believer. And then something quite remarkable happens; the Unknown launches into the account of a dream he once had when in Palestine:

> I was walking along that deserted shore which contains the ruins of Ptolemais, it was evening; the sun was sinking in the sea; I seated myself on

a rock, lost in melancholy contemplations . . . The janissary, who was my guide, and my servant, were preparing some food for me . . . and whilst I was waiting for their summons to the repast, I continued my reveries . . . I fell asleep. I saw a man approaching me, whom at first I took for my janissary, but as he came nearer I found a very different figure; he was a very old man with a head as white as snow; his countenance was dark, but paler than that of an Arab, and his features stern, wild, and with a peculiar, savage expression; his form was gigantic, but his arms were withered, and there was a large scar on the left side of his face which seemed to have deprived him of an eye. He wore a black turban and black flowing robes, and there was a large chain round his waist which clanked as he moved . . . He called out, 'Fly not, stranger, fear me not, I will not harm you, you shall hear my story, it may be useful to you . . . You see before you a man who was educated a Christian, but who renounced the worship of the one supreme God for the superstitions of the pagans . . . I became an apostate in the reign of the emperor Julian, and I was employed by that sovereign to superintend the re-erection of the temple of Jerusalem, by which it was intended to belie the prophecies and give the death-blow to the holy religion. History has informed you of the result; my assistants were most of them destroyed in a tremendous storm, I was blasted by lightening from heaven' (he raised his withered hand to his face and eye) 'but suffered to life, and expiate my crime in the flesh. My life has been spent in constant and severe penance, and in that suffering of the spirit produced by guilt, and is to be continued as long as any part of the temple of Jupiter in which I renounced my faith, remains in this place. I have lived through fifteen tedious centuries . . . but I hope my atonement is completed . . . You have just thrown the last fragment of the temple over a rock. My time is arrived, I come!' As he spoke these last words, he rushed towards the sea, threw himself over the rock, and disappeared. I heard no struggling, and saw nothing but a gleam of light from the wave that closed above him.

Surely we have here a variation upon the Arab of Book Five of *The Prelude,* and the dream based on a dream dreamt by Descartes, as recorded in Baillet's *Life:* the Arab with the stone and the shell. We have "the glittering light" that is "The waters of the deep gathering upon us" as the Arab in *The Prelude* informs the enquiring stranger—the dreamer: in *Consolations* the gleam of light comes from the wave that closes over the Arab's head when he leaps into the sea. This dream sequence, if we accept the *Prelude* 1805 version, was Coleridge's dream; and though he may have taken it direct (with slight alteration) from Descartes, it is equally possible that it was an opium dream of Coleridge's, based on the reality of what he had read in the *Life.* Certainly Davy's Unknown, the dream of this dream in *Consolations,* makes it clear enough, in the euphemistic currency of the day, that his is an opium dream. And yet the Arab in *Consolations,* like the Ancient Mariner, has spent his extended life, fifteen centuries of it, in "constant and severe penance, and in that suffering of the spirit produced by guilt": which was not the case with the Arab in *The Prelude.*

Dialogue Four of the *Consolations,* called "The Proteus, or Immortality," deals with the pleasures of travel, a fishing adventure when Philalethes is nearly drowned, considers respiration and animal body heat and moves, discursively, into discussion of the soul: its immateriality and consequent immortality, founded on the postulate that sensibility and intelligence cannot result from any possible combination of any insensate unintelligent atoms. Dialogue Five, entitled "The Chemical Philosopher," attempts a definition of civilization and the attributes of the best type of chemical philosopher, who finally emerges as the apogee of all that civilized man stands for. Dialogue Six, entitled "Pola, or Time," discusses the destruction of civilizations and the operation of time, philosophically considered, and the certain and immutable laws of destruction, concluding with speculations on the infinite universe and the eternal mind by which the universe was created and is governed. And so Philalethes returns to his original theme of intelligences of a higher order than man, under the ultimate influence of a divine will. The dialogue ends with reference to the natural progression of successive rise and fall.

And with the conclusion of Dialogue Six, Davy succumbed to a fatal cerebral haemorrhage, and presumably soared upward on his own progression towards the ultimate influence of divine will. Dialogues seven and eight were cobbled together by his biographer and brother, John Davy, in the role of literary executor, and they need not be considered here.

The reader of *Consolations* emerges from the experience feeling bemused, confused, amazed. Indeed stunned, in the manner of the Wedding Guest when the Ancient Mariner had finished with him. No attempt is made to conceal the fact that much of the material in *Consolations* is drawn from opium dream sequences. Some of it sounds distinctly Coleridgean; some of it takes us back to hints we have been given in the outline for "Moses"; some of it stems, regressively through the series of visions described by Davy in his noteboks, from "My eye is wet with tears," the chaunt composed by Davy over a quarter of a century earlier.

Haunting visions flash before us as we read. *The Ancient Mariner* and *The Recluse* seem to have become inextricably mixed; the reticulative process of the opium dream! These *Consolations* are not all opium; but there is much, very much of opium in them, and we can never be certain when we are dreaming and when we are awake. And how much of it is Davy, and how much Coleridge, we shall never know. Perhaps Davy did not know either. He had had many many long and marvellous conversations with Coleridge over the years. In 1804, before Coleridge had left for Malta, Davy had told him, "Thoughts which you have nursed have been to me an eternal source of consolation . . . You will live with me as a recollection possessed of creative energy—as an imagination ringed with fire, inspiring and rejoicing" (*Works* i 449).

I pass, like night, from land to land,

I have strange power of speech;
The moment that his face I see,
I know the man that must hear me;
To him my tale I teach . . .

Coleridge had known Davy's face. And Davy never forgot the tale.

Claire Lyu

SOURCE: "'High' Poetics: Baudelaire's Le Poeme du hachisch," in *MLN,* Vol. 109, No. 4, September, 1994, pp. 698-740.

[*In the following essay, Lyu discusses the tension in Baudelaire's* Le Poème du haschisch *between the poet's desire to pronounce a distinct separation of poetry and hashish and his ultimate inability to keep them apart.*]

From the very beginning of *Le Poème du hachisch*[1] in *Les Paradis artificiels,* Baudelaire is quite insistent in distinguishing his voice from the intoxicated voice, and his writing about intoxication from the lived experiences of intoxication themselves. It is indeed clearly stated at the end of the first section that his writing will be based on secondhand and not firsthand experiences and that it accounts for intoxicated moments lived by others but not by the poet himself. The poet speaks, or at least starts out by speaking, with a sober voice that is not and has not been intoxicated:

> Aujourd'hui, je ne parlerai que du hachisch, et j'en parlerai suivant des renseignements nombreux et minutieux, extraits des notes ou des confidences d'hommes intelligents qui s'y étaient adonnés longtemps. Seulement, je fondrai ces documents variés en une sorte de monographie, choisissant une âme, facile d'ailleurs à expliquer et à définir, comme type propre aux expériences de cette nature. (404)

The term "expériences" ("comme type propre aux expériences de cette nature") needs to be understood in its double meaning, as experience and experiment. As opposed to other people's personal experiences of hashish, Baudelaire sets up his writing on hashish as an experimentation. These two "expériences," therefore, are to be carefully kept apart since the poetic writing is more of an experimentation on hashish rather than a personal experience of it. The experiment, here, is to be carried out by using other people's experiences: Baudelaire experiments with experiences.[2] Thus, the "renseignements" nombreux et minutieux, extraits des notes ou des confidences" supplied by other intoxicated people will guide his voice in his speaking ("j'en parlerai *suivant*"), and these "documents variés" will be incorporated into his writing of the monograph ("je *fondrai* ces documents variés en une sorte de monographie") Keeping in mind the desire of the poet to differentiate his voice and his writing from the intoxicated voice and writing, it is, however, to the way in which the poet's sober voice speaks following ("suivant") the intoxicated voice, and to the way in which the poet writes his monograph by melting ("je fondrai") various documents that I wish to be attentive.

The verb "fondre" means to melt, to amalgamate as well as to smelt and to cast. The gesture of "fondre" which constitutes the mode of writing of the poetic monograph therefore contains within itself three distinct movements: melting of "fondre" leads not only to mixing by fusion, but also to purifying by separation as well as to giving form by casting. The underlying image of metal work is worth taking note of here. In *Littré,* some of the recurrently cited examples when reading through the ensemble of entries related to "fondre" such as "la fonderie," "le fondeur," "fondu(e)," and "la fonte" are "la fonte des métaux, du minerai" for separating impurities from pure metal and refining it, "fondre une cloche, une statue" for casting objects and "fondeur en caractères d'imprimerie" for making printing fonts. "Fondre" is therefore the act, the process of working the metal, which, through melting—thus making disappear whatever initial form there might have been—either mixes or separates, and in so doing refines and finally arrives at giving a new form through casting. It is interesting to notice the frequent references to statues and printing fonts in these common expressions that are quoted, as it will precisely be a problem, in our text, of form, both visual and written, a problem of the graph and the graphic of the monograph. What follows will be a reading of Baudelaire's text that will try to elaborate to what degree these various movements of "fondre" are at work in the monograph. The dynamics of the gesture of "fondre," founding and shaping Baudelaire's monograph, then, will be our point of departure.

The text constantly oscillates between the desire and the attempt to keep poetry and hashish separate, on the one hand, and the difficulties and the failure in marking and maintaining the difference between these two, on the other. The desire of poetry to set itself apart from hashish, to establish the poetic experience as other than the hashish experience, and to purify itself of all possible contamination by hashish, be it in the past, present or future, makes the poet/Apollo figure pronounce an ultimate severe sentence against hashish at the end of the text.[3] This desire of separation has to be given full consideration in order to understand the other side of the story, that is, the fusion of the two leading to a quasi-impossibility in separating them, their close resemblance as that which exists between the molded form and its mold.

It should not be forgotten that, despite its gesture of cutting hashish away from poetry, the first text of *Les Paradis artificiels* is entitled *Le Poème du hachisch.* The monograph which condemns hashish so harshly in the name of poetry thus places the very two terms that it is trying to keep at a distance in an intimate proximity. The writing about hashish, the assertion that it is not poetry, becomes a poem in and of itself. Distance and proximity between poetry and hashish, then, form and generate *Le Poème du hachisch.*

POETRY AND HASHISH

Le Poème du hachisch is composed of five sections: I. Le Goût de l'infini; II. Qu'est-ce que le hachisch?; III. Le Théâtre de Seraphin; IV. L'Homme-Dieu; V. Morale. Of central concern to us at the moment is the third section "Le Théâtre de Séraphin," the longest of all five, set up explicitly as a stage at the center of the text. Various experiences of hashish intoxication, "un tableau de voluptés artificielles" (399) as they are called in the dedication, are presented to us exclusively on the stage of this theater. From the very start, a difference is introduced between the two voices: the intoxicated voices are staged whereas the poetic voice stages. The staging of the intoxicated voices consists in presenting them as anecdotal voices telling four stories that function at a different textual level from the main development of the text recounted by the poetic voice. The stage of the third section is the only space in the entire text in which the intoxicated voices are allowed to speak. No other section of the text lets them speak so directly, and the only other place where they are heard is in the beginning of the fourth section, "L'Homme-Dieu." There, however, Baudelaire is quoting some "merveilleux passages" of Poe, "ce poète incomparable, ce philosophe non réfuté, qu'il faut toujours citer à propos des maladies mystérieuses de l'esprit" (427). The intoxicated voices of the fourth section therefore stand less as noxious intoxicated voices themselves than as the poetic voice of Poe.

Intoxicated voices are thus exclusively presented on the stage of the "Théâtre de Séraphin." Baudelaire seems very cautious in framing this third section, and in presenting the episodes of intoxication. The third section begins as follows:

> Qu'éprouve-t-on? que voit-on? des choses merveilleuses, n'est-ce pas? des spectacles extraordinaires? Est-ce bien beau? et bien terribles? et bien dangereux?—Telles sont les questions ordinaires qu'adressent, avec une curiosité mêlee de crainte, les ignorants aux adeptes. On dirait une enfantine impatience de savoir, comme celle des gens qui n'ont jamais quitté le coin de leur feu, quand ils se trouvent en face d'un homme qui revient de pays lointains et inconnus. Ils se figurent l'ivresse du hachisch comme un pays prodigieux, un vaste théâtre de prestidigitation et d'escamotage, où tout est miraculeux et imprévu. C'est là un préjugé, une méprise complète. (408)

Subsequently, Baudelaire goes on to undo what he qualifies as "un préjugé" and "une méprise complète" that one usually has with respect to hashish, by saying that it does not give any extraordinary or miraculous vision. Hashish is, in a way, a bad spectacle that does not offer what it seems initially to promise. This initial framing gesture which opens the hashish spectacle by designating it as bad spectacle repeats itself again at the closing of the scene. The very beginning of the fourth section operates the transition from the theatrical stage of hashish back to the sober and serious main discussion of the text conducted by the poetic voice:

> Il est temps de laisser de côté toute cette jonglerie et ces grandes marionnettes, nées de la fumée des cerveaux enfantins. N'avons-nous pas à parler de choses plus graves: des modifications des sentiments humains et, en un mot, de la *morale* du hachisch? (426; original emphasis)

The show is over, and we are to leave the theater. The hashish spectacle and the main text discussing the moral of hashish do not share the same space, since the former has to be left aside ("laisser de côté") in order to resume the latter. The changing of the voice—from the intoxicated one to the poetic one and vice versa—requires a change of space, or at least a change of sides or "côté." Between the two, there exists a passage to be crossed and a space to be exited.

This overall framing of the third section which separates and isolates the part of the text where the intoxicated voices speak is reiterated even within the third section, at the beginning and the end of each story, or anecdote, of intoxication. Anecdotes are set up so as to occupy a different space from the main text. They are held and confined strictly to their own place on stage, kept inside quotation marks, as if the curtains have to be opened and closed for each one of them. They are not to invade or contaminate the space of the poetic voice. They are quarantined, a particularly pertinent terminology for the case in hand, since it is precisely a question of a fear of contamination, and, as we shall see later, of vessels, of transport(ation) and traveling through passages, between here and there. For each contact and passage between the two voices, then, there is a quarantining gesture at work, as if there were a necessity to find an antidote to each anecdote.

The most interesting and telling moments of this occur between the second and the third anecdote. They are the moments of passages out of the second anecdote into the main development and again from the main development into the third anecdote. In the first case, the poetic voice takes over the intoxicated voice by interrupting it, and it interrupts it by leaving the space of the anecdote. In order to continue its main narration, the poetic voice has to come back to its own space: it announces "[j]e reviens au développement régulier de l'ivresse" (416). The place of the anecdote appears as that from which one has to come back ("revenir") in order to go on. It is a space which is to be left: a parenthetical one that needs to be closed, sealed, and "laissé de côté" as we already saw. It appears as a place, an isolated place that leads to nowhere except to go back out the way one came in. There is no going further in or from the anecdote, as it only brings one back to where one was before entering its space. Its space is not where a "développpment régulier" takes place. If the space of the poetic voice is that of regularity, the anecdotal voice, then, would seem to occupy a space of irregularity. The relationship between the two voices appears more complicated than what was announced before, since the poetic voice, in its position following ("suivant") the intoxicated voice, may very well find itself in an impasse. The anecdotal path, therefore, leads to nowhere, as far as the poetic regular development is concerned, if one adopts the position of a "suivant." It is only by leaving, departing and coming back from it that one could possibly hope to be led by an anecdotal path. It is a path, but a curious path that does not lead if one is inside it and follows it, but leads only if one leaves it and is outside of it.

In the second case, the poetic voice introduces the third anecdote as: "Avant d'aller plus loin, je veux, à propos de cette sensation de fraicheur dont je parlais plus haut, reconter encore une anecdote qui servira à montrer jusqu'à quel point les effets, même purement physiques, peuvent varier suivant les individus" (416). Anecdotes have to be dealt with before any going further: "Avant d'aller plus loin." They seem to stop, or at least to delay momentarily the movement of the main text. They block the road, or are off the road. Anecdotes help, however, to show or to prove ("une anecdote qui servira à montrer") what the main text says. What and how it may help to show or to prove remains an open question at this point. Nonetheless, the auxiliary position of helping ("*servira* à montrer") again shows its place aside, "à (de) côté." Meanwhile, to discern which one is the "suivant" of which becomes a delicate issue, since, if the poetic voice announced itself to be a "suivant" of the intoxicated voice, the latter, in its position of helping, or of a "servant" is also a "suivant" of the former.

Since anecdotes precede any going further, and since one can only come back from an anecdote, this means that coming back precedes going further. There is a seemingly unusual temporality involved in this anecdotal passage which is that returning precedes departing. Anecdotes thus seem constantly to impose on the text a movement of coming back to which I will return later. For now, I would like to turn to individual anecdotes, and discern the various movements of the "fondre" between the poetic voice of the main text and the intoxicated voices of the anecdotes.

Each anecdote is told by a different person: the first one is told by Baudelaire, who claims to have witnessed the scene that he is reporting. The second one is told by a man, the third one by "un littérateur," and the fourth and the last one, which is also the longest of all four, by a woman. Except for the first one then, all of them consist in lengthy quotations in which the intoxicated voices speak directly. We have already seen that the central poetic motivation of the text consists in a constant effort to distinguish and to cut away hashish from poetry, and to purify the latter from the former. Hashish is often described as possessing an invasive and expansive—poisonously contaminating—force ("l'humeur conquérante et envahissante du poison" [411]) against which the poet tries to find an antidote.

The story of the second anecdote, then, seems to presage the difficulties Baudelaire will soon encounter in putting into effect his desire of separation and purification. Baudelaire seems to be in a situation similar to the per-

son in this story: an intoxicated man, suddenly remembering that he is invited to dinner in a "soirée d'hommes sérieux," proceeds to find a "réactif" that will annul the effect of hashish and enable him to go to dinner and to behave normally during the meal. And yet, in his attempt to obtain "un moyen d'adoucissement ou de réaction," he only confuses and scares the pharmacist. Not only is he not capable of getting the "réactif" that he wishes, but also, he precisely gets one which is wrong: in his benevolent desire to reassure the pharmacist "qu'il n'y avait pas de danger, qu'il n'y avait pas, *pour lui,* de raison de s'alarmer" [original emphasis], he only creates a terrible mistrust. He is then simply asked to leave the store without any means to purify his system of hashish.

Similarly, Baudelaire, in his very gesture of trying to purify poetry of hashish, entangles the two all the more intricately. The story ends with a last comment: "'Mais, je n'oublierai jamais les tortures d'une ivresse ultra-poétique, gênée par le décorum et contrariée par un devoir!'" (415). The hashish voice describes itself as "une ivresse ultra-poétique." Thus, it speaks of itself in terms of poetry, claiming itself to be poetic, and even, too poetic or more poetic than poetry itself. It is beyond poetry which it almost exceeds ("ultra"): it is on the other side of poetry. Here, we encounter again the structure of the "à [de] côté." If, however, the poetic voice constantly tries to establish a distance between itself and the intoxicated voice, and to introduce an insurmountable difference between the two sides they occupy, the intoxicated voice tries, on the contrary, to move in a closer proximity, almost to be on the side of the poetic voice.

It is not surprising, then, that with the third anecdote, the hashish voice begins a gradual mixing of the sides, reversing the spatial structure of the "à (de) côté" which we have seen operating between the two voices, between the staged hashish and the staging poetry. In a way, we have already seen the unstability of the structure of the "à (de) côté" in the problematic position of the "suivant," as it was difficult to pin down which one was on which side. Now, things start to shift sides in a quite obvious manner, because in this story, it is no longer a scene of intoxication that a sober poetic eye beholds, but an intoxicated man that is a spectator of an artistic stage representation. Hashish has left the stage to which it was confined and now occupies poetry's off-stage area, the loge: the intoxicated man is in the "salle," the "boîte" (417) or the "loge" (418) of a theater. This taking over of the side, going over to the other side, coincides with the intoxicated man's putting himself in the position of a poet through an explicit comparison: "Rien ne m'en choquait, et *je ressemblais un peu à ce poète* qui, voyant jouer *Esther* pour la première fois, trouvait tout naturel qu'Aman fît une déclaration d'amour à la reine" (418; my emphasis, except for *Esther*).

The tendency of hashish to gravitate around and towards poetry in an endless attempt to come close to and merge with it can be best seen in a passage between the third and the fourth anecdotes, where Baudelaire says the following concerning the hallucinatory state caused by the ingestion of hashish:

> C'est alors que commencent les hallucinations. Les objects extérieurs prennent lentement, successivement, des apparences singulières; ils se déforment et se transforment. Puis, arrivent les équivoques, les méprises et les transpositions d'idées. Les sons se revêtent de couleurs, et les couleurs contiennent une musique. Cela, dira-t-on, n'a rien que de fort naturel, et tout cerveau poétique, dans son état sain et normal, conçoit facilement ces analogies. Mais j'ai déjà averti le lecteur qu'il n'y avait rien de positivement surnaturel dans l'ivresse du hachisch; seulement, ces analogies revêtent alors une vivacité inaccoutumée; elles pénètrent, elles envahissent, elles accablent l'esprit de leur caractère despotique. (419)

One notices again the invasive force of hashish as the analogies that it occasions "pénètrent," "envahissent," and "accablent l'esprit de leur caractère despotique." More important, however, is the way in which hashish hallucination operates: "les équivoques," "les méprises," and "les transpositions d'idées." With "transposition" being the shifting of sides and of respective positions, the movement of hashish moving into the loge of poetry appears, indeed, as the proper movement of hashish hallucination. Moreover, the movement of the intoxicated voice that constantly aims at mingling and conflating itself with the sober poetic voice seems to be the movement, precisely, of the "equivoque." It proceeds to operate a literal equivocation, to have the same voice as the poetic voice.

Similar terms are used again in the following paragraph, to explain further the process of hallucination: "Par une équivoque singulière, par une espèce de transposition ou de quiproquo intellectuel, vous vous sentirez vous évaporant, et vous attribuerez à votre pipe (dans laquelle vous vous sentez accroupi et ramassé comme du tabac) l'étrange faculté de *vous fumer*" (420; original emphasis). This time, there is an acting out of the transposition, as the intoxicated person (thinks he) is sitting in his pipe in lieu of his chair. The transposition has taken place. The "équivoque," "méprise," "transposition" of the previous paragraph become "équivoque," "transposition," and "quiproquo" in this passage. There is a variation in the enumeration, but a very slight one, because only "méprise" is replaced by "quiproquo." The replacing of the word "méprise" by "quiproquo" which, in turn, is a certain "méprise," enacts the very notion of taking one thing for another in a gesture of transposition. Here, then, seems to start the operating of the poetic voice in the mode of the "équivoque," "méprise," "transposition" and "quiproquo" of the hashish voice. This goes hand in hand with the already familiar movement of the hashish voice which tries to become the poetic voice. The sober voice of the poet, in the very passages where it tries to expose the mechanisms of hashish hallucination, where its sobriety should all the more form a contrast to the intoxicated state of hallucination, begins to be "équivoque," to have the same voice as hashish, and to speak equivocally.

Would the poetic equivocation be the same as the hashish equivocation? The passage on hallucination quoted above seems to say no, since there still exists an effort to maintain a difference in what appears more and more as ambiguously similar. Baudelaire carefully formulates a possible objection ("Cela [the state of hashish hallucination], dira-t-on, n'a rien que de fort naturel, et tout cerveau poétique, dans son état sain et normal, conçoit facilement ces analogies") which already contains in itself an answer. Here, through the objection, a subtle difference is being introduced between the poetic state and the intoxicated one by positing the former as "sain et normal." This seems to qualify the hashish state as sickly and abnormal, and indeed, there are times in the text when the term "malade" is used to refer to the intoxicated state: "réplique en égoïste un des malades," "[v]ouloir guérir un homme malade de trop de vie, malade de joie!" (413), "la vie morale du malade" (434), etc. The oppositional motif between sickness, death and health is very much present all throughout the text, together with that of the pharmaceutics of "réactif" and poison,[4] the story of a medical surgery (439) and the comparison of hashish to suicide (439).[5]

Short of being able to establish a more solid difference, Baudelaire tries to maintain the separation between the two voices by having recourse to the opposition between health and sickness. One senses, however, that this new category of differentiation is a highly problematic one if one remembers that Baudelaire has called the poems of *Les Fleurs du Mal*, "ces fleurs maladives" in the dedication to Théophile Gautier. *Le Poème du hachisch* could almost be a "fleur maladive." Thus the formulation of Baudelaire, that there is the healthy equivoque of poetry which is different from the sickly equivoque of hashish shows less the existing marked difference than the desire to mark the difference.

Returning, now, to the problem of the equivoque and transposition between poetry and hashish, only two paragraphs after the previously mentioned passages, it is Baudelaire, the poetic voice, which produces this time a very serious "méprise." It is a passage where he is again talking about hallucination:

> Quand je parle d'hallucinations, il ne faut pas prendre le mot dans son sens le plus strict. Une nuance très importante distingue l'hallucination pure, telle que les médecins ont souvent occasion de l'étudier, de l'hallucination ou plutôt de la méprise des sens dans l'état mental occasionné par le hachisch. Dans le premier cas, l'hallucination est soudaine, parfaite et fatale; de plus, elle ne trouve pas de prétexte ni d'excuse dans le monde des objets extérieurs. Le malade voit une forme, entend des sons où il n'y en a pas. Dans le second cas, l'hallucination est progressive, presque volontaire, et elle ne devient parfaite, elle ne se mûrit que par l'action de l'imagination. Enfin, elle a un prétexte. Le son parlera, dira des choses distinctes, mais il y avait un son. L'œil ivre de l'homme pris de hachisch verra des formes étranges;

mais, avant d'être étranges ou monstrueuses, ces formes étaient simples et naturelles. L'énergie, la vivacité vraiment parlante de l'hallucination dans l'ivresse n'infirme en rien cette différence originelle. Celle-là a une racine dans le milieu ambiant et dans le temps présent, celle-ci n'en a pas. (420-21)

Baudelaire has taken up the very delicate issue of trying to distinguish what he calls pure hallucination in the clinical sense from hashish hallucination. With the intoxicated state already having been compared to the sickly state, the desire to differentiate the "malade" of the pure medical hallucination ("Le *malade* voit une forme, entend des sons où il n'y en a pas") from "l'homme ivre pris de hachisch" will encounter some difficulties, since the latter was previously called also a "malade." What would be the difference between the pure medical hallucination and the hashish hallucination if both of the subjects are "malade"? Would there be an impure "malade" of hashish as opposed to a pure "malade" of the clinical case? From opposing health to sickness, Baudelaire moves to oppose sickness to sickness, and the terms of differentiation are becoming harder to maintain or even to establish.

By the end of the passage, Baudelaire himself comes to perform a major "méprise," being unable to keep the two on their respective and distinct sides. The final sentence of the paragraph, "[c]elle-là a une racine dans le milieu ambiant et le temps présent, celle-ci n'en a pas," takes the pure medical hallucination for the hashish hallucination and vice versa. "Celle-là," which, according to this final sentence, should refer to the hashish hallucination, in fact, according to the structure of the paragraph, refers precisely to the pure medical hallucination. The poetic voice unknowingly takes one for the other, although it started out by saying that "[u]ne nuance très importante distingue l'hallucination pure, . . . de l'hallucination ou plutôt de la méprise des sens dans l'état mental occasionné par le hachisch." It is unable to keep the distinction it has set out to show itself, and takes "celle-là" for "celle-ci," "là-bas" for "ici" and "there" for "here." The poetic voice performs a literal, or a textual transposition by switching the two sides, and putting here what should be there, and there what should be here. The two "côtés" are reversed.

If the poet's project initially consisted in undoing the "préjugé" and the "méprise complète" (408) concerning hashish, and if here more than anywhere else, hashish appears as the culprit of "méprise des sens" (420), it is clear that by now, the poet himself "se méprend" by taking the wrong side. *Le Poème du hachisch* performs a continual "méprise," and the mutual gesture of "se méprendre" between the poetic voice and the hashish voice stands out as its central movement. Considering this final poetic "méprise," the first sentence of the paragraph above becomes interesting. Baudelaire started out by saying: "Quand je parle d'hallucinations, il ne faut pas prendre le mot dans son sens le plus strict. Une nuance très importante distingue l'hallucination pure, telle que

les médicins ont souvent occasion de l'étudier, de l'hallucination ou plutôt de la méprise des sens dans l'état mental occasionné par le hachisch." The gesture of "ne pas prendre le mot dans son sens le plus strict" is immediately followed by a gesture that distinguishes: "[u]ne nuance très importante distingue," and ends with a peculiar and inevitable "méprise." Would the "ne pas prendre le mot dans son sens le plus strict" be to "méprendre" then? If "distinguer" becomes "méprendre," would this mean that the gesture which differentiates inevitably leads to confusion?[6]

In fact, this unavoidable coupling of opposing movements, of that which distinguishes and that which confuses, enacts the very meaning of the word "nuance." For if Baudelaire claims that "[u]ne nuance très importante distingue," but proceeds immediately afterward to confuse this distinction, it is mainly because nuance stands for both variation and sameness, variation within the same, the imperceptible difference within the identical. *Littré* gives, for example, and I only quote two out of five possible meanings here, "[d]egré d'augmentation ou de diminution que présente une même couleur; différence ou changement de couleurs, surtout dans leur passage d'un ton à un autre," and "[d]ifférence délicate et presque insensible qui se trouve entre deux choses du même genre." Nuance, we can therefore say, given our context, is another instance of the movement of "fondre," which separates while it amalgamates. It stands for the play, the oscillation between these two movements of separation and mixture, for the passage from one to the other, to the other that is still the same: "surtout dans leur passage d'un ton à un autre [of the same color]." This passage, at the same time that it indicates a differential relation, indicates also a relation of similitude or even of identity. It is a passage that separates and links simultaneously, a passage that may be crossed, but only to arrive at the same.

Therefore, Baudelaire's final poetic "méprise" is perhaps more than justifiable, since he only faithfully obeys the logic of this differential passage of nuance. He manages, by crossing the passage from "here" to "there" which is in fact "here," to render perceptible the nuance between the two kinds of hallucination, as was his plan. Baudelaire may thus even be almost voluntary ("presque volontaire") in performing this "méprise," a quality attributed to hashish hallucination in our passage, and which appears more and more as a poetic one as it is said to ripen by the action of imagination ("mûri[r] . . . par l'action de l'imagination"). One may read then, the "sens" of the "ne pas prendre le mot dans son sens le plus strict" as the direction of this crossing, the ambiguous directionality of the passage leading both to here and there. The strictest "sens" or direction of a word would be that which goes against this free-floating, unpredictable bi-directionality of the nuanced passage that crosses over while it crosses back at the same time. A poetic reading of a word would take an altogether different direction from that of the "sens le plus strict," by liberating it from its strict uni-directionality. Hence, both in writing and in reading, it becomes always a question of taking, or not taking, or taking wrongly a direction, a side, or a path, as we have seen it happen with the "à (de) côté" of the anecdotal path. "Prendre" would always, in a sense, be a "méprendre."

Immediately following this "méprise," the fourth anecdote, which is also the last one, is introduced as follows:

> Pour mieux faire comprendre ce bouillonnement d'imagination, cette maturation du rêve et cet enfantement poétique auquel est condamné un cerveau intoxiqué par le hachisch, je raconterai encore une anecdote. Cette fois, ce n'est pas un jeune homme oisif qui parle, ce n'est pas non plus un homme de lettres; c'est une femme un peu mûre, curieuse, d'un esprit excitable, et qui, ayant cédé à l'envie de faire connaissance avec le poison, décrit ainsi, pour une autre dame, la principale de ses visions. Je transcris littéralement. (421)

The role of the anecdote goes from "servir à montrer" (416) to "mieux faire comprendre." It is now engaged in the process of understanding. What it makes more clear is the proximity between the "cerveau intoxiqué par le hachisch" and the "cerveau poétique" (419). What appear as the characteristics of the latter are to be found in the former: "bouillonnement d'imagination," "maturation du rêve" and "enfantement poétique." With the last term in the series, "enfantement poétique," the intoxicated voice becomes poetic and feminine. In this fourth anecdote, it is a woman who speaks. Unlike any of the previous male anecdotal voices, the female voice seems to necessitate, in its rendering, a certain adjustment in the poetic voice. The mode of speaking of the poetic voice goes from "je raconterai encore une anecdote" to "[j]e transcris littéralement." Between this change from "raconter" to "transcrire," there occurs another parallel change that seems to motivate it. It is no longer "un jeune homme oisif qui parle," but "une femme un peu mûre . . . qui . . . décrit." The change here, then, is three-fold: "jeune" becomes "un peu mûre," "un homme" becomes "une femme" and "parler" becomes "décrire." This last one triggers, in turn, the most important change: the movement of the poetic voice from "raconter" to "transcrire," as I have pointed out. The woman who describes makes the poet transcribe. The problem of writing appears at this point in the text in a subtle way by means of the word "écrire" in "décrire" and "transcrire." It is apparently a woman who initiates the poet into writing, who puts him in the mode of writing. What is it about the woman's story that causes Baudelaire to transcribe and not tell? Why is it a woman and not a man who initiates writing, or at least, makes the question of writing emerge?

In order to understand the place and the importance of the female voice as it relates to the poetic and the intoxicated writings as well as the significance of its full emergence at this point of the text, a slight detour back is necessary. The fourth anecdote is not the first passage in which a female figure appears. There are, in fact, two previous and important places: the third anecdote, and the dedication.

Going back to the third anecdote, I have already mentioned that in this story, the structure of the beheld/beholding, staged/staging which exists between poetry and hashish is reversed, since it is an intoxicated man who is viewing, from the loge, a scene of an artistic representation. Here is how the scene and the experience of being the spectator is described by the intoxicated man:

> Quant à la scène (c'était une scène consacrée au genre comique), elle seule était lumineuse, infiniment petite et située loin, très loin, comme au bout d'un immense stéréoscope. Je ne vous dirai pas que j'écoutais les comédiens, vous savez que cela est impossible; de temps en temps ma pensée accrochait au passage un lambeau de phrase, et, semblable à une danseuse habile, elle s'en servait comme d'un tremplin pour bondir dans des rêveries très lointaines. On pourrait supposer qu'un drame, entendu de cette façon, manque de logique et d'enchaînement; détrompez-vous; je découvrais un sens très subtil dans le drame créé par ma di traction. Rien ne m'en choquait, et je ressemblais un peu à ce poète qui, voyant jouer *Esther* pour la première fois, trouvait tout naturel qu'Aman fit une déclaration d'amour à la reine. (418; original emphasis)

Here, the intoxicated voice generates "un sens très subtil" out of the "lambeau de phrase." The way in which this subtle meaning is created, and the way in which the "drame" is "entendu" deserve attention. First, it is distraction which creates new meaning: "je découvrais un sens très subtil dans le drame créé par ma distraction." Distraction comes from Latin *distrahere* which means to break up, to pull apart in different directions. Hence, distraction is a force that separates by drawing away, by breaking and dividing an ensemble. This force of fragmentation appears as the unique force capable of delineating a limit of separation, of tracing and drawing a contour that is definite. It makes something definite emerge from something indefinite: "*le* drame" ("le drame créé par ma distraction") is created out of "*un* drame" ("un drame, entendu de cette façon"). Second, following directly from the first, is that here, "entendement" seems to be based on fragmentation, taking into account only a "lambeau de phrase," and operating in a temporally discontinuous fashion of "de temps en temps." Third, the "entendement" of the dramatic scene does not stem from hearing: "Je ne vous dirai pas que j'écoutais les comédiens, vous savez que cela est impossible." There is a divorce between understanding and hearing in this "entendement" as the former no longer depends on the latter. In this reversed or intoxicated beholding then, "entendement" is separated, diverted or distracted from itself, and emerges from a certain "non-entendement."

What is interesting is that the figure that is given metaphorically to stand for that which generates this "entendement" is "une danseuse," a female figure. This brings us back to the question raised above concerning the woman. If the woman of the fourth anecdote introduces and mediates the question of writing between poetry and hashish, the female dancer of the third anecdote introduces and mediates the issue of understanding (/ hearing) or "entendement." The "pensée" of the intoxicated man is "semblable à une danseuse habile," in that it assembles fragments of sentences into a new understanding: it uses these fragments "comme d'un tremplin pour bondir" as a female dancer would do.

This process of generating a new "entendement" through fragmentation which is mediated by a metaphorical female figure appears as a mirror-image of Baudelaire's subsequent writing process. In the fourth section "L'Homme-Dieu," Baudelaire will proceed in a manner similar to that of this intoxicated man/female dancer, and adopt the method of the spring-board. He will incorporate various fragments of the previous four anecdotes, especially the fourth one by the woman (the way in which the immediate visual surroundings transform themselves, the presence of the divinities of Antiquity and the motif of water (430), all were already told by the woman and only by her [421-24]), into his own poetic monograph: "mais nous ne nous servirons de son [the woman's] récit que pour en tirer quelques notes utiles qui compléteront cette description très sommaire des principales sensations engendrées par le hachisch" (424). The terms which Baudelaire uses to refer to his monograph in this sentence: "cette *description* très sommaire des *principales sensations,*" are very similar to the ones he used for the woman's story: "c'est une femme . . . qui . . . *décrit* . . . la *principale de ses visions*" (421; my emphasis), which shows again the approximation of the poetic and the intoxicated writings through the woman. He fashions his writing according to her writing, writes his over hers, transposes hers into his: he trans-scribes her writing.[7]

In the passage quoted above of the third anecdote, there are precisely two instances of similarity: "ma pensée . . . semblable à une danseuse habile," and "je ressemblais un peu à ce poète." Through comparing himself with a female dancer, the intoxicated man is led to compare himself with a poet. The figure of the female dancer therefore appears as that which allows, helps and even induces the movement of a mutual approach between hashish and poetry. With this prelude, it is no coincidence then, that the woman of the fourth anecdote takes on a similar function of making the intoxicated and the poetic voices merge.

The most important fact stemming from these observations is that the moments in the text when the crucial question of writing and understanding is raised are moments when the hashish voice and the poetic voice are the most intricately equivocated. At these moments of equivocation, genders seem to merge as well. The female voice, or the movement of the female body ("danseuse") becomes the privileged medium through which the amalgamating, transposing (the jumping from the spring-board in order to reach the other side) and the separating (force of distraction) activity of "fondre" takes place. Writing and understanding occur, or at least their possibilities are suggested, in moments and states of indecisiveness between hashish intoxication and poetic sober-

ness, between the female and the male. Here, then, the status of the speaking/writing/understanding subject is put into question as it is no longer the case that these three activities are performed by a perfectly definable integral subject with a clear and distinct voice. If, on the one hand, the "entendement" is based on a certain "non-entendement" in that the subject to be understood is necessarily fragmented, then, on the other hand, it is also the case that the subject doing the understanding itself undergoes an inevitable fragmentation in the very moment of this "entendement." The subject of understanding, in both senses of the word, is fragmented and multiple. Therefore, speaking/writing/understanding only take place in (or out of or "à [de] côté de") a discontinuous, fragmented, undecidable and unstable temporal and spatial domain. It is a domain which wavers between oppositions, occupying simultaneously or successively the two ends of the pole. No speaking/writing/understanding subject is one or whole, as several (or at least two) speak/write/understand at the same time within it.

It is to the dedication of *Les Paradis artificiels* that one has to turn in order to understand the undecidability of the speaking/writing/understanding subject, and its relation to the moments of eruption and presence of the woman in the text. In the dedication, Baudelaire, in discussing the "raison de cette dédicace," raises the question of the woman as it relates to the writing of *Les Paradis:*

A

J. G. F.

Ma chère amie,

Le bon sens nous dit que les choses de la terre n'existent que bien peu, et que la vraie réalité n'est que dans les rêves. Pour digérer le bonheur naturel, comme l'artificiel, il faut d'abord avoir le courage de l'avaler, et ceux qui mériteraient peut-être le bonheur sont justement ceux-là à qui la félicité, telle que la conçoivent les mortels, a toujours fait l'effet d'un vomitif.

A des esprits niais il paraîtra singulier, et même impertinent, qu'un tableau de voluptés artificielles soit dédié à une femme, source la plus ordinaire des voluptés les plus naturelles. Toutefois il est évident que comme le monde naturel pénètre dans le spirituel, lui sert de pâture, et concourt ainsi à opérer cet amalgame indéfinissable que nous nommons notre individualité, la femme est l'être qui projette la plus grande ombre ou la plus grande lumière dans nos rêves. La femme est fatalement suggestive; elle vit d'une autre vie que la sienne propre; elle vit spirituellement dans les imaginations qu'elle hante et qu'elle féconde.

Il importe d'ailleurs fort peu que la raison de cette dédicace soit comprise. Est-il même bien nécessaire, pour le contentement de l'auteur, qu'un livre quelconque soit compris, excepté de celui ou de celle pour qui il a été composé? Pour tout dire enfin, indispensable qu'il ait été écrit pour *quelqu'un*

J'ai, quant à moi, si peu de goût pour le monde vivant que, pareil à ces femmes sensibles et désœuvrées qui envoient, dit-on, par la poste leurs confidences à des amis imaginaires, volontiers je n'écrirais que pour les morts.

Mais ce n'est pas à une morte que je dédie ce petit livre; c'est à une qui, quoique malade, est toujours active et vivante en moi, et qui tourne maintenant tous ses regards vers le Ciel, ce lieu de toutes les transfigurations. Car, tout aussi bien que d'une drogue redoutable, l'être humain jouit de ce privilège de pouvoir tirer des jouissances nouvelles et subtiles même de la douleur, de la catastrophe et de la fatalité.

(. . .)

(399-400; original emphasis)

Scholars have long been debating over the identity of the mysterious acronym J. G. F.—the only other place where this same acronym appears is in the poem *L'Héautontimorouménos* (78)—placed at the head of the dedication, standing for the person to whom *Les Paradis* is dedicated.[8] Within the context of what has just been said above, what is important in our case, however, is less to identify the individual person behind these three letters than to try to think about the significance of the female figure in *Les Paradis,* whoever it may be.

This dedication sets in relief the question of the woman—especially her ambiguous position—with respect to poetry and hashish. The woman is, in the second paragraph, presented as possibly occupying the very opposite pole of drugs, as she is considered "[la] source la plus ordinaire des voluptés les plus naturelles," and drugs, "voluptés artificielles." The opposition woman/drug is reinforced by the opposition natural/artificial that is parallel to it. This initial oppositional structure is, however, immediately thrown into question, since the natural world is said to penetrate the spiritual world ("le monde naturel pénètre dans le spirituel"), and the woman to haunt and to fecundate the imaginations of others ("elle vit d'une autre vie que la sienne propre; elle vit spirituellement dans les imaginations qu'elle hante et qu'elle féconde"). In fact, the precariousness of the oppositions between artificial and natural, drug and woman is present even in the first paragraph as Baudelaire writes: "Pour digérer le bonheur naturel, comme l'artificiel, il faut d'abord avoir le courage de l'avaler." The term "comme" in "le bonheur naturel, *comme* l'artificiel" bridges the natural and the artificial, and functions in a very slippery manner, as it can mean both "or" or "as." In the first case (the natural *or* the artificial), the relationship between the two is that which keeps them apart and distinguishes them, since they are posited as mutually exclusive. In the second case (the natural *as* the artificial), there precisely occurs the opposite movement of superposing the two and blurring the limit set by the first case. This indeterminacy of the mediating term "comme" makes the natural and the artificial as inclusive of each other as they are exclusive. The logic of the "comme" is similar to that of the nuance which we saw as constituting a passage that both separates and links at the same time.

Although apparently being the opposite of drugs, the woman, nonetheless, exists in the invasive mode of the contaminating drugs. Moreover, she is said to penetrate and to fecundate, two activities traditionally attributed essentially to men. In the dedication then, the natural and the artificial, the male and the female merge. The woman appears as that which defies all apparent and traditional opposition, existing and operating in a mode which makes all attempts to define and confine her in a definite or definitive way difficult: she cannot be taken, we could say, "dans son sens le plus strict." She is a force which contains within itself all oppositional movements as she projects "la plus grande ombre ou la plus grande lumière" in an indifferent and an undifferentiated manner, and in so doing annuls precisely all oppositions. She is the figure of amalgamation as she is natural, artificial, female and male alternatively and all at once.

If, in the dedication, the woman takes on the male role of penetration and fecundation, in the text itself, the male poet, or the "cerveau poétique"[9] proceeds to take on the female role and to conceive and give birth: "tout cerveau poétique, dans son état sain et normal, conçoit facilement ces analogies" (419), "cet enfantement poétique auquel est condamné un cerveau intoxiqué par le hachisch" (421). This interpenetration between the male poet and the woman becomes complete as Baudelaire says that the mysterious woman of the dedication is "quoique malade, toujours active et vivante *en moi*" [my emphasis]. The woman has come inside the poet. The taking in of the woman, the conceiving the woman by the poet is doubly conceptive / conceiving: it is to conceive the principle of conception itself. This conception is double also in that with the woman, sickness has come inside the poet as well. Rather than perfect health, sickness is what persists in a manner that never ends ("toujours"), and precisely because of this, becomes the active and living force within the poet. Sickness is therefore related to the power to conceive and to perpetuate the poetic life. It overcomes death and turns death into the continuum of life that lives on forever. It is as if the poet draws his active and lively energy from sickness, from the woman, from the sick woman. The woman who lives on inside the poet constitutes the forever continuing locus of action, life and conception for him. The woman, therefore, contaminates the health and the gender of the poet, and this she does in an essentially vital way. It follows as an inevitable consequence then, that the poetic voice which is "sain" and "normal" is also the voice of the "malade," of the woman and of the sickly intoxication, and that poetic writing is the writing of the woman and also of hashish.

Given this internalization and conceiving of the woman and intoxication by the poet, Baudelaire is right to point out that only to the "esprits niais" will the "raison de cette dédicace" appear strange. For, dedicating *Les Paradis* to a woman should seem as natural as a woman talking to another woman, which is the case in the fourth anecdote, because it is the poet who is a sick woman (in) himself who writes to a sick woman. It may be this logic of the dedication which determines the logic of the fourth anecdote, which is told by a woman to another woman. For we are not informed as to how Baudelaire came to know of it. In the three previous cases, all of them with men, Baudelaire stated in a clear manner how he had gained knowledge of them: he has witnessed the first one, and for the other two, the very persons involved in the experiences of intoxication had recounted the stories to him ("une personne m'a raconté" [413] for the second and "me dit celui-ci" [416] for the third). Here, neither did he see what went on, nor did he hear the story from the woman. Would this leave the poet to remain outside the circle of communication, to be excluded from it? Not quite so, for here, the dialogue which seems to shut off the poet, and to be external to him is, in fact, the most engaging one for him, the most intimate one within him, he, who has in himself a woman, and who, in the dedication, writes to that same woman.

The dedication and the fourth anecdote are similar in that they both happen between women. They are both directed toward a woman—the dedication to "ma chère amie," and the fourth anecdote to "une autre dame"—and they both are spoken by a female voice because the poet has a woman inside him, and because the fourth story is said to have been told by a woman. It is interesting to notice the proximity, if not the identity, between the person who writes and the person toward whom writing is directed. If, in the fourth anecdote, a woman describes to another woman that is not herself ("une femme . . . qui . . . décrit ainsi, pour une autre femme"), in the dedication, there is a sense in which these two women collapse together onto and into the poet. Baudelaire, in a way, is dedicating *Les Paradis* to himself, to himself as woman, but to himself nonetheless. Therefore the dialogue between the two women, at the same time that it excludes the poet, is, in turn, included in the poet. Writing, if it is to be true poetic writing, shares the same "raison" as the "raison de cette dédicace": one writes toward oneself, the identical and the other within oneself. Hence writing is a relation one has with oneself, which can only emerge out of a relation of identity with respect to oneself, but identity as constituting a difference. The woman who "quoique malade, est toujours active et vivante en moi" is inside the poet at the same time that she is outside of him. The woman thus makes the poet be both inside and outside of himself, be himself and other than himself. She generates the undecidability within the poet. From this distance between oneself to oneself, through this passage that has been opened within oneself by the undecidability—as nuanced gradations—there occurs writing. Writing, then, moves along the distance and passage within the one who is writing from one side to the other. And in so doing, it also makes the one who is writing travel through oneself from one side to the other. It makes the writer transpose or transport him or herself. Writing, therefore, never occurs in the restricted and narrow space of the "sens le plus strict." The reason why a woman and not a man becomes the force motivating writing for the poet is be-cause she constitutes the principle of identity and difference for him, the imperceptible nuance within him, and lets there be a distance through and across which writing can be written. It is because woman exists in and out of the poet, making him both inclusive and exclusive of himself, that she is linked, in a fundamental way, to writing which exists in the same modalities.

The woman therefore is the force of "fondre" at work in the poet, as she divides and splits while amalgamating: "Toutefois il est évident que comme le monde naturel pénètre dans le spirituel, lui sert de pâture, et concourt ainsi à opérer cet amalgame indéfinissable que nous nommons notre individualité, la femme est l'être qui projette la plus grande ombre ou la plus grande lumière dans nos rêves." Paradoxically, what constitutes the indivisibility of individuality is an "amalgame indéfinissable." It is a mixture, something of a composite nature which never-theless cannot be sorted out, like various nuances which nonetheless compose one single color. Therefore what we saw previously as the fragmented and multiple subject of writing/speaking/understanding is at the same time an indivisible unity, indivisible by virtue of its fragmented multiplicity.

We have already seen that with the fourth anecdote, the poet's voice and writing merged with those of the woman. There, the woman describing made the poet tran-scribe. This modeling, by the poet, of his writing in the mode of writing of the woman seems, at first sight, to take place again here in the dedication. Baudelaire writes in the third paragraph: "pareil à ces femmes sensibles et désœuvrées qui envoient, dit-on, par la poste leurs confi-dences à des amis imaginaires, volontiers je n'écrirais que pour les morts." This statement is, however, immedi-ately contradicted by the following sentence introduced by a "mais": "Mais ce n'est pas à une morte que je dédie ce petit livre; c'est à une qui, quoique malade, est toujours active et vivante en moi." Baudelaire proceeds to do the opposite of what he just said above about how he could easily and quite willingly write to dead people, and without any further explanation other than a swift move through a "mais" (which is not an explanation in itself), simply states that he is not going to do what he just said he might do. *Les Paradis* will not be dedicated to imaginary or dead people, but to a living person or at least to a person who lives on and survives within the poet. Hence the writing of *Les Paradis* is not directed toward death, but moves away from death. It is not for a dead person but for a person beyond death who is "toujours active et vivante en moi." Writing is thus di-rected to the part in oneself that survives and continues beyond death, to that part that has resisted and keeps resisting death. It addresses itself to the "toujours" within oneself, and maintains it. The temporality of "toujours" is that of the convalescent sickness which makes death con-tinue through life. The part of oneself to which writing is directed is therefore that minimal part of oneself that goes on to exceed oneself. Given this relationship be-tween writing, death and oneself, hashish, which Baudelaire compares explicitly to suicide ("[q]ue je le [hashish] compare au suicide, à un suicide lent, à une arme toujours sanglante et toujours aiguisée, aucun esprit raisonnable n'y trouvera à redire" [439]), appears as that from which writing diverts itself, as that which writing precisely is not. Suicide is a gesture that puts an end to oneself, terminating the relation one has with oneself. Far from maintaining the "toujours" within oneself, it negates and suppresses all possibilities of a continuum in the mode of "toujours." The gesture of writing therefore is not the suicidal gesture of hashish. Here, poetry goes against hashish, and this time, the negation and differentiation do not break down. Poetry simply is not hashish.

Thus the gesture of dedicating which is the poetic gesture *par excellence* marks a radical difference between poetry and hashish, in that it reveals a drastic divergence between the two *vis-à-vis* the question of death. If hashish is slow suicide, thus moving unidirectionally toward death as its only and final possibility, poetry is more akin to the state of convalescence ("quoique malade, toujours active et vivante"). Convalescence is an undecided and, therefore, privileged state that contains both life and death, sickness and health in its perspective.[10] To reformulate this along the lines of our previous development, one could say that hashish takes death "dans son sens le plus strict," in that it takes the narrow, limited, and ultimately no-way-out direction, whereas poetry takes it in a different direction, or "sens." If hashish, in its path with the direction of the "sens le plus strict" only arrives at the dead-end street of suicide, poetry takes death as continuing beyond itself, continuing even and all the more through life, as the principle of continuation ("*toujours active et vivante*") of the poetic life itself. At the moment when the question of the direction, life and survival of poetry emerges, poetry detaches itself from hashish, with which it was so closely equivocated, and takes on its own direction, orientation, meaning, or its own "sens." What is this "sens" of poetry that is different from that of hashish then?

THE *SENS* OF POETRY

As might be expected, the term "sens" is perhaps one of the most crucial words in the text of *Le Poème du hachisch.* The expression "le bon sens" opens the dedication, and it could be said that the entire task of bringing to light the "sens" of poetry rests upon a precise understanding of this "bon sens."

Littré defines "le bon sens" as "la saine et droite raison." The "raison" which is contained in the "bon sens" must be thought, then, in conjunction with various occasions in which the word "raison" itself appears in the text. Among numerous such occasions, there are three that are of importance here. First, there is "la raison de cette dédicace" (399). The second case is when Baudelaire writes, after he has transcribed the woman's anecdote, "[v]oilà une femme évidemment raisonnable" (424). Finally, in the third case, the term "raisonnable" reappears toward the end of the text:

> Que je le [hashish] compare au suicide, à un suicide lent, à une arme toujours sanglante et toujours aiguisée, aucun esprit *raisonnable* n'y trouvera à redire. Que je l'assimile à la sorcellerie, à la magie, qui veulent, en opérant sur la matière, et par des arcanes dont rien ne prouve la fausseté non plus que l'efficacité, conquérir une domination interdite à l'homme ou permise seulement à celui qui en est jugé digne, aucune âme philosophique ne blâmera cette comparaison. (439; my emphasis)

In this last instance, the "esprit raisonnable" is the one that agrees with the comparison Baudelaire establishes between hashish and suicide. The "esprit raisonnable" is "raisonnable" in that by accepting this comparison, it also acknowledges the fundamental difference between poetry and hashish. It is an "esprit" which knows that poetry directs itself toward the part "toujours active et vivante," and that it directs itself neither toward death nor toward suicide. It is thus an "esprit" capable of seeing the different "sens" of poetry that diverges from hashish. Hence, reason here, in this "raisonnable," is the faculty of distinguishing hashish from poetry. It is interesting to notice that in the passage above, the "esprit raisonnable" is put in parallel with the "âme philosophique." Neither the former nor the latter questions the comparison made between hashish, on the one hand, and suicide or black magic, on the other, the comparison which marks an undeniable difference between poetry and hashish. Therefore, philosophy, in the context of *Le Poème du hachisch,* is the faculty of reason capable of separating and distinguishing intoxication from true and pure poetic experience. In this light, we may be able to understand why Baudelaire considers *Le Poème du hachisch* a philosophical study: "Dans les études philosophiques, l'esprit humain, imitant la marche des astres, doit suivre une courbe qui le ramène à son point de départ. Conclure, c'est fermer un cercle. Au commencement j'ai parlé de cet état merveilleux, où l'esprit de l'homme se trouvait quelquefois jeté comme par une grâce spéciale" (440-41). Baudelaire follows the circular curve that, according to him, all philosophical studies trace, by referring back to the "commencement" of his writing. *Le Poème du hachisch* is a philosophical study in that it establishes the reason—both the faculty of reasoning as well as the cause and justification—which has the power to cut away hashish from poetry. It is no accident then that the figure which appears at the end to deliver the final sentence condemning hashish is a poet/philosopher ("Je me figure un homme [dirai-je un brahmane, un poète, ou un philosophe chrétien?] placé sur l'Olympe ardu de la spiritualité"), and that this poet/philosopher speaks with the voice of "nous," the "nous" of poets and philosophers against intoxication ("tandis que nous, poètes et philosophes, nous avons régénéré notre âme . . . nous avons créé à notre usage . . . nous avons accompli le seul miracle . . ." [441]).

If one keeps in mind the specific meaning of reason and philosophy stemming from this third example, the "raison" in the first two cases can readily be understood. The apparently gratuitous comment made after the woman's story ("[v]oilà une femme évidemment raisonnable") becomes fully justified as the woman of the fourth anecdote together with the woman of the dedication contain within themselves the reason of poetry. And they indeed contain the reason of poetry, because, as we have seen, they allow poetic writing to be written in a "sens" that is different from that of hashish, and direct poetry to take a path other than the path of suicide. It is the woman "toujours active et vivante" toward whom poetry is oriented, not toward the deadly suicide of hashish. Therefore, since the woman separates hashish from poetry, and gives to poetry its own direction, she becomes, herself, the reason of poetry. The "femme évidemment raisonnable" of the fourth anecdote and the "raison de cette dédicace" all share the same reason, which is that poetry and hashish need to be differentiated, and that they are indeed essentially and vitally different.

The "bon sens" then, shares this same reason as well. It stands, most of all, for the ability to distinguish poetry from hashish. It posits the "sens" of poetry as necessarily other than the "sens" of hashish, and subtly slips in a form of judgment by qualifying the "sens" of poetry as the "bon sens," which consequently condemns the "sens" of hashish as the "mauvais sens." If, however, the "bon sens" is essentially linked to reason according to the definition of *Littré* ("la saine et droite raison"), and justly so in our context, it is not so sure that it necessarily is "sain" or "droit" in our case. The woman who is the "raison" of the dedication is sick, as are the poems of *Les Fleurs du Mal* that are sick flowers. Whether or not this reason is indeed "droite" remains uncertain as well, since the directionality of the "sens" of poetry seems—and I shall come back to this later—not so straight.

To go back to the "bon sens" of the dedication, the second sentence suggests that this "bon sens," which stands, in fact, for the faculty of judgment separating poetry from hashish, might first of all be the sense of taste. The "bon sens" is, before anything else, a "bon goût": "Pour digérer le bonheur naturel, comme l'artificiel, il faut d'abord avoir le courage de l'avaler, et ceux qui mériteraient peut-être le bonheur sont justement ceux-là à qui la félicité, telle que la conçoivent les mortels, a toujours fait l'effet d'un vomitif." The "bon sens" therefore comes from nowhere else than the throat. It is a question of passages across the throat, for this "bon sens" or taste originates from a double crossing of the throat: there is not only swallowing ("avaler") but also vomiting ("l'effet d'un vomitif"). Digestion appears then as an activity resulting from the coupling of these two opposite movements. For there to be digestion, throat has to be opened up to allow passages in both directions. Hence, this "bon sens" is double. There are at least two "sens" within it.

Swallowing is necessary for digestion since "[p]our digérer . . . il faut d'abord . . . avaler." This seemingly ordinary and usual fact, however, is immediately upset because vomiting precedes swallowing: those who deserve to swallow happiness are those who experienced the "effet d'un vomitif." Only those who have vomited deserve to swallow. Swallowing leads to vomiting as the "vomitif" needs to be swallowed in order to induce throwing up, but the reverse equally holds true: vomiting leads to swallowing. In this circuitous and nauseous movement between vomiting and swallowing, there always exists an aftertaste of the vomitive in the throat that swallows. Swallowing tastes like vomiting. What one swallows is always a "vomitif": it is to swallow the act of vomiting itself. Moreover, "concevoir" tastes like vomiting as well: "ceux-là à qui la félicité, telle que la conçoivent les mortels, a toujours fait l'effet d'un vomitif." Therefore the two movements that receive and take into the body: "concevoir" and "avaler," are intimately linked to the oppositional movement that takes out and throws up out of the body: "vomir." There is externalization, expulsion and refusal in the midst of internalization, ingestion and acceptance. It is furthermore this radical rejection and absolute negation through the act of vomiting that paradoxically allows digestion to take place, since only those who experienced the vomitive effect are said to deserve happiness, happiness which is to be swallowed and digested. A passage through an absolute negation, the vomitive mobilizes and readies the throat to take in and to accept, or to accept again. The "bon sens" of poetry thus consists of introducing a radically different "sens" into the already existing one, to introduce the outward directionality into the inward directionalities of conceiving and swallowing. Constituting the crucial direction within the "bon sens," this outward directionality of the "vomitif" becomes a movement of radical negation through which hashish is negated in an absolute manner by being thrown up and out.[11] Poetry's "bon sens" separating out and condemning hashish has a taste of a "vomitif." Poetry's "bon goût" throws up. Oddly enough then, throwing up tastes good, and it is in good taste to throw up. Here, poetry's "bon sens" opposes itself in a quite literal sense to the "sens commun."

That it is a question indeed of the throat, a passage across the throat, and taste, is confirmed subsequently by the title of the first part of *Le Poème du hachisch*, "Le Goût de l'infini." The taste of the infinite is described precisely in terms of swallowing and vomiting, of filling the throat and emptying out the throat that is overly filled. Here, passion is what goes in and out of the throat: "L'esprit humain regorge de passions" (403). The word "regorger," which indicates a filling of the throat to the limit, and over the limit, so as to overflow, contains in it the word "gorger," which means to fill with food, to stuff to excess, to the level of the throat. There is almost then, an "avant-goût" of "regorger" in "gorger," or an "après-goût" of "gorger" in "regorger." The word "regorger" therefore indicates the moment when "avaler" turns into "vomir," when the directionality of going-in reverses itself to that of going-out. This bi-directional passage across the throat, in a temporality of before and after, seems to be what generates "le goût de l'infini." It may very well be the taste, an "avant-goût" or an "après-goût" of the infinite. Passion which goes over the limit of the throat ("le trop-plein de cette passion débordante") makes "le goût de l'infini" go overboard. And perhaps this is why the taste constantly crossing the throat in both directions is qualified as "un goût qui se trompe souvent de route" (402).

This notion of "se tromper de route," however, needs to be given more thought, as it occurs within the context of taking, not taking, or taking wrongly a path which is a problem that has preoccupied us previously. The passage goes as follows:

> Hélas! les vices de l'homme, si pleins d'horreur qu'on les suppose, contiennent la preuve (quand ce ne serait que leur infinie expansion!) de son goût de l'infini; seulement, c'est un goût qui se trompe souvent de route. On pourrait prendre dans un sens métaphorique le vulgaire proverbe: *Tout chemin mène à Rome,* et l'appliquer au monde moral; tout mène à la récompense ou au châtiment, deux formes de l'éternité. (402-03; original emphasis)

The status and the use of the proverb "Tout chemin mène à Rome" in this passage is very curious. The proverb, describing a situation where multiple paths all lead to one place, indicates a case where there can be no mistake, and no difference in taking one road as opposed to another. It is a situation where various ways will all end up at a same location. It makes Rome into a center, the only center there is, at the same time that it renders all roads infallible, equivalent and identical to each other. Therefore the proverb stands for a situation that is precisely the opposite of that which it is called to exemplify, of the situation of "un goût qui se trompe souvent de chemin." For how can there be mistakes in taking certain roads if all of them will eventually lead to Rome? The proverb seems strangely out of phase and out of context with the rest of the passage, and all the more so as Baudelaire, in his reading of it, denies the centrality of Rome and the infallibility of the roads. In his version of the proverb: "tout mène à la récompense ou au châtiment, deux formes de l'éternité," Baudelaire splits the unique center, Rome, "the eternal city," into two extreme end points ("récompense" or "châtiment"), and concomitantly introduces an ineffaceable difference among the roads, as some will lead to one end and others to the other end which is, in no case, near the first end.

This gesture of splitting the one and the unique and introducing a difference into that which is undifferentiated is the gesture that takes "dans un sens métaphorique le vulgaire proverbe." Therefore, among the innumerable undifferentiated roads or directions, it is the metaphorical direction ("sens") that is the only one capable of making and marking a difference. The centripetal and therefore the unique directionality toward Rome, which constitutes the vulgar and common "sens"—one could say the "sens unique" or the "sens le plus strict"—of the proverb, becomes double as the road of the metaphor is taken: one can arrive either at "la récompense" or at "le châtiment." This metaphorical "sens" gives an altogether different and new "sens" (as direction, orientation, meaning) to the most common, vulgar and used everyday expression.[12] It liberates the expression from the "sens unique" and the "sens le plus strict," that is, from the narrow stricture of uni-directionality, and confers instead a freer bi-directionality. Here, one can say that the bi-directionality of the "bon sens" is introduced into the uni-directionality of Rome. It opens up the restriction of the center to allow passages in two directions. Here, in this bi-directionality then, are echoed all other bi-directionalities we have encountered: the double crossing of the throat in the "avaler"/"vomir," the state of sickness in convalescence having both life and death in its perspective (as opposed to the one-way dead-end street of suicidal hashish), writing as stemming from this double perspective of sickness, and the double position of the poet who is both inclusive and exclusive of himself through the figure of woman. This last instance of bi-directionality is all the more pertinent to the case of the proverb, as both—the double position of Rome and that of the poet—express a relation within the same, a relation with oneself. The poet being outside and inside of himself, thus being himself and other than himself, operates under the same logic as Rome split in two, as Rome that has become so remote to itself. In this spatial structure of the metaphor, Rome is as far away as it is close to itself. Within Rome and eternity, Baudelaire has thus introduced a metaphorical distance which allows passages to be crossed in new directions and which lets new meaning (or direction, orientation) emerge. Making Rome the farthest place from itself and therefore not identical to Rome is similar to the dynamics of the nuance which we saw as being one of the most important poetic movements. If nuance marks the imperceptible difference within similarity and the passage from one side to the other that is nonetheless the same, metaphor functions with the same dynamics, creating a relation within the self that marks a difference within identity. This imperceptible difference, however, is at the same time an enormous and an insurmountable one. It is the difference between "la récompense" and "le châtiment."[13]

With Rome having become the most distant place from itself, the distance which now exists between Rome and Rome is the metaphorical distance. Both *Furetière* and *Littré* establish a relation between metaphor and "transport," and define metaphor as "*transport* d'un mot propre à un sens figuré" ("transport" in *Furetière*), "la métaphore est une figure par laquelle on transporte, pour ainsi dire, la signification propre d'un nom à une autre signification . . ." ("transport" in *Littré*). Metaphor, therefore, is about places, about changing places, and about going from one place to another. The question of metaphor will necessarily entail, then, the question of space and of displacement. Metaphore is about taking a trip, and with the proverb of Rome taken metaphorically, we are indeed in the middle of a journey, and doubly so, since the proverb itself is about going to Rome, and as given by the two dictionaries, metaphor is itself a trip, a trip of the "sens."

In fact, more than double, it is rather on a multiple journey that *Le Poème du hachisch* embarks. One is constantly taking trips or being told stories of trips. "Le goût de l'infini" is described as the desire to get away from the miserable dwelling place ("fuir, ne fût-ce que pour quelques heures, son habitacle de fange" [402]), and the second section "Qu'est-ce que le hachisch?" begins by referring to "[l]es récits de Marco Polo," and "de quelques voyageurs anciens" (404). Hashish itself is said to have taken a long trip from the East to the West: "Le hachisch, en effet, nous vient de l'Orient" (405), and the intoxication triggered by the ingestion of hashish becomes, in turn, a trip in itself: "Vous êtes maintenant suffisamment lestés pour un long voyage. La vapeur a sifflé, la voilure est orientée, et vous avez sur les voyageurs ordinaires ce curieux privilège d'ignorer où vous allez" (410). The verb "lester" operates here an interesting amalgamation between ship and stomach, taking a trip and eating, as it means both to ballast a ship as well as to stuff oneself with food, which describes perfectly the trip effectuated by swallowing hashish, a spoonful of green jam. There is also a brief mention of the trip of Orpheus to the underworld (428) and the trip of the text itself as tracing a curve going back to the point of departure (440), both of which I will discuss later.[14]

The importance of the proverb of Rome in the context of these numerous trips is that the entire writing of *Le Poème du hachisch* can be said to reduplicate the gesture of taking the proverb metaphorically, since Baudelaire is trying to show how, while people may think they are going to Rome (or paradise), they actually are ending up either in the "paradis d'occasion" or "enfer" (441). The movement of "bon sens" or reason of the text which separates the directionality of poetry from that of hashish is identical to the movement which takes the proverb metaphorically and separates those paths leading to "récompense" from those leading to "châtiment." Therefore, the metaphorical reading of the Rome proverb that splits Rome bears direct relation to the fundamental differentiating gesture of *Le Poème du hachisch.*

Where does this multiple journey lead then? Going back to the Rome proverb, are we still taking a trip to Rome and going to Rome? Is Rome still the unique direction of all the roads? Not quite so, since metaphor transports the "sens," the "sens" of the proverb, which is Rome, is itself transported, displaced and taken somewhere else as well. Rome is no longer (at or in) Rome in the topographical space governed by metaphor: it is no longer the center of attraction, it is no longer where all the routes are going, and thus it is no longer the "sens" of the journey. As Rome loses its position as the center and direction of trip, it is no longer the meaning of the proverb either. It is no longer the "sens" of the proverb in all senses of this word. A new direction is taken. With the splitting open of the initial unique center, Rome becomes unattainable and paths diverge out, deviating further and further away from it. Poetry displaces Rome out of Rome, out of its place and context. It de-centers Rome. This means that Rome can never be in its own place and context in a poetical text, and the proverb of Rome, as I have already pointed out, is indeed out of phase and off center here in Baudelaire's text.

From this disappearing of Rome as the central "sens" giving way to new "sens," forms emerge, for "la récompense" and "le châtiment" are "deux *formes* de l'éternité." Therefore, it is at the moment—and only then—of an irreversible splitting, dividing and differentiating, that forms are created. Form is itself division and distinction, as only the dividing or the differentiating gesture is capable of tracing a limit, setting a boundary and thus drawing or carving out the contours of a form. This is an instance similar to the one we have already encountered in the third anecdote, where distraction, which is a force that pulls apart and splits an ensemble, was seen as the power generating a new "sens subtil," and the definite "*le* drame" out of an indefinite" "*un* drame." It is also the moment in the movement of "fondre" where new forms are created through casting. Melting and amalgamating lead, only when they are coupled with separation and purification, to giving forms by casting. It is no coincidence then that Apollo—the god of sun, light, and most of all, of purification, and whose exemplary sculptural representations stand for perfection of corporeal form[15]—is the figure delivering the final sentence that condemns hashish, and thus separates hashish from poetry in a manner that is irrevocable. When the dynamics of "fondre" is at work, that is, at the moment when initial amalgamating gives, through separating and purifying, a final form through pouring and casting, this final form that emerges, operates in turn, the separating and purifying activity from which it has emerged. Form thus constantly renews and redefines its own contour and traces over and over again its own delimitation.

Forms that emerge from the splitting of the Rome proverb, splitting occasioned by the metaphorical movement, are the new "sens" of the proverb. If there is a "transport" of the "sens propre" to "sens figuré" in metaphor, Rome, in our case, has been taken to its "sens formé," to its "deux formes de l'éternité."

That the poetic "sens" diverges drastically from and goes against the hashish "sens" is shown further by the only other proverb in the text. Baudelaire refers to this proverb when describing the self-induced apotheosis of an intoxicated person:

> Suivrai-je plus loin l'analyse de cette victorieuse monomanie? Expliqueraije comment, sous l'empire du poison, mon homme se fait bientôt centre de l'univers? comment il devient l'expression vivante et outrée du proverbe qui dit que la passion rapporte tout à elle? (436)

The proverb "la passion rapporte tout à elle" expresses a similar topographical structure as "tout chemin mène à Rome," in that it posits a center which establishes its own unfailing centrality by drawing everything to itself. If poetry, through its metaphorical gesture, consists in transporting and transposing the center to the most remote outskirts, and therefore in denying the very notion of center through this displacement or decentralization, hashish affirms the center, and more than that, it places the intoxicated person in this centrality, and turns him or her into the center ("mon homme se fait bientôt centre de l'univers"). If poetry changes altogether the direction and the meaning of the proverb by diverging out from it and from the center and taking its own course, hashish does not and cannot proceed in this manner. Hashish only faithfully follows the path laid out by the expression without being capable of detaching itself from it. It is unable to take a different road and incapable of differentiating itself. Hence, it stays at the level of common, vulgar and conventional everyday meaning. It does not go against the restricted "sens unique" of the proverb, never goes out of the way, and therefore never gets out of Rome.

In fact, the inability of hashish to go out and exceed boundaries is repeatedly insisted upon. Hashish never seems capable of crossing the limit, and never seems to go overboard: "Dans l'ivresse de hachisch, rien de semblable. Nous ne sortirons pas du rêve naturel," "[l]e cerveau et l'organisme sur lequel opère le hachisch ne donneront que leurs phénomènes ordinaires, individuels, augmentés, il est vrai, quant au nombre et à l'énergie, mais toujours fidèles à son origine" (409). Later, toward the end, we have: "le hachisch ne révèle à l'individu rien que l'individu lui-même," "[e]lles [thoughts one had during moments of intoxication] tiennent de la terre plutôt que du ciel" (440). Hashish does not go or get out of the natural, the individual, the origin and the everyday life of this world. The "velléités de nausée" (410) of hashish that only flirt with the faint desire to vomit without ever crossing the limits of the throat can therefore justly be contrasted to the good taste of poetry that does indeed throw up.

The tendency which hashish has to be constantly drawn to the center makes hashish incapable of staying away from and not collapsing onto it. Hashish cannot keep itself at a distance from the center, or from anything at all, for that matter. It simply abolishes all distances:

> Il arrive quelquefois que la personnalité disparaît et que l'objectivité, qui est le propre des poètes panthéistes, se développe en vous si anormalement, que la contemplation des objets extérieurs vous fait oublier votre propre existence, et que vous vous confondez bientôt avec eux. Votre œil se fixe sur un arbre harmonieux courbé par le vent; dans quelques secondes, ce qui ne serait dans le cerveau d'un poète qu'une comparaison fort naturelle deviendra dans le vôtre une réalité. Vous prêtez d'abord à l'arbre votre passion, votre désir ou votre mélancolie; ses gémissements et ses oscillations deviennent les vôtres, et bientôt vous êtes l'arbre. De même, l'oiseau qui plane au fond de l'azur *représente* d'abord l'immortelle envie de planer au-dessus des choses humaines; mais déjà vous êtes l'oiseau lui-même. (419-20; original emphasis)

Here, the "cerveau intoxiqué" is presented as operating in an opposite manner from the "cerveau poétique." What the latter holds only for "une comparaison (fort naturelle)," the former holds for "une réalité." This means that whereas the poet is capable of distinguishing

himself from the tree and the bird, keeping himself at a distance from them, the intoxicated person collapses this distance and becomes the tree and the bird. Hence, hashish turns the similarity of comparison into an identity and in so doing abolishes the necessary distance which needs to be respected and maintained. This distance which is maintained in the act of comparison is, again, the metaphorical distance. Thus here, again, hashish goes precisely against the metaphorical direction and distance of poetry.

Furthermore, by collapsing personal existence with external objects, hashish makes one live with a certain objectivity which contradicts what the "bon sens nous dit" in the dedication. The very first sentence of the dedication, we will remember, goes as: "Le bon sens nous dit que les choses de la terre n'existent que bien peu, et que la vraie réalité n'est que dans les rêves." The objectivity of the intoxicated state consists in conferring abnormally exaggerated importance, weight and existence to external objects that one should know, if one had the "bon sens," "n'existent que bien peu." If the "bon sens" teaches us to suspect "les choses de la terre," and thus to suspect objects or objectivity, hashish encourages the development of this objectivity and leads to the error of collapsing the terms which should be kept at a distance. Hashish makes one take representation for reality, as is the case in the passage above. The intoxicated person takes him or herself for the bird which he/she should know only represents his/her immortal desire to soar. It confuses art, writing and representation with life. When describing the hallucinatory state of hashish just one paragraph later, Baudelaire writes: "N'êtes-vous pas alors semblable à un roman fantastique qui serait vivant au lieu d'être écrit?" (420). Hashish confuses writing with living as it generates a novel which lives. The experience of writing and that of living, however, have mutually exclusive "lieux," as living occurs "au lieu de" writing, taking its place in a movement of substitution. Therefore, to confuse writing and living, or to make a novel live, apart from being an impossible task according to the "bon sens" of poetry, simply makes writing vanish. There is no longer writing or art, writing/art ceases to be writing/art when it becomes reality. It is by and through the distance it maintains with respect to reality that writing exists, and hashish, being incompatible with all notions of distance, is fundamentally incompatible with writing.

The fault of hashish in the passion proverb is therefore double. It is faulty not only for going to the center and believing in the center which no longer exists according to the metaphorical "bon sens" of poetry, but also for living the center by being the "expression *vivante*" of the proverb. By becoming the living proverb and the living center, hashish negates twice the poetic "sens" of metaphor.

As the poetic "sens" goes against the "sens unique" of Rome, of hashish and of their centrality, it consequently also goes against the infallibility of all roads. Poetry makes the infallibility of Rome fail, and in so doing, makes hashish fail. Thus the gesture which takes the Rome proverb metaphorically is the most powerful gesture of attack poetry launches against hashish. Poetry makes the infallibility of Rome fail precisely because this infallibility of Rome stands for the very immorality of hashish:

> Il est vraiment superflu, après toutes ces considérations, d'insister sur le caractère immoral du hachisch. . . . Si l'Eglise condamne la magie et la sorcellerie, c'est qu'elles militent contre les intentions de Dieu, qu'elles suppriment le travail du temps et veulent rendre superflues les conditions de pureté et de moralité; et qu'elle, l'Eglise, ne considère comme légitimes, comme vrais, que les trésors gagnés par la bonne intention assidue. Nous appelons escroc le joueur qui a trouvé le moyen de jouer à coup sûr; comment nommerons-nous l'homme qui veut acheter, avec un peu de monnaie, le bonheur et le génie? C'est l'infaillibilité même du moyen qui en constitue l'immoralité, comme l'infaillibilité supposée de la magie lui impose son stigmate infernal. (439-40)

The "moyen de jouer à coup sûr" of the "joueur escroc" is equivalent to the infallibility of roads all leading to Rome. If this infallibility is where the immorality of hashish lies ("[c]'est l'infaillibilité même du moyen qui en constitue l'immoralité"), then the gesture of morality would be the introduction of the possibility of failure.

In the Rome proverb, both Rome and eternity are split into "la récompense" and "le châtiment." Therefore, poetry attacks and destabilizes the infallibility both in space and in time, by splitting not only the spatiality of Rome, but also the temporality of eternity. This happens because division in space cannot occur without division in time. With the roads being split as they are, one will be led to "la récompense" half of the time, and the other half of the time, to "le châtiment." It is to restore the "travail du temps" into the dubious "coup" of the "à coup sûr." The instantaneousness in the temporality of the "coup" seems to be what goes the most against the constant effort which poetry must make in order to produce poetic writing. On two other occasions, the expression "d'un seul coup" is used to describe the way in which hashish operates: "d'emporter le paradis d'un seul coup" (402), "les moyens de s'élever d'un seul coup, à l'existence surnaturelle" (441). If hashish operates "à coup sûr," in other words, if it belongs to the temporality of the easy and instantaneous "d'un seul coup" that is always guaranteed to work, poetry happens precisely under the opposite temporality of a perpetually renewed effort which is not guaranteed to work. There is not necessarily work, or "œuvre" at the end of a long and persevering effort at work. There is only uncertainty and possible failure after endless sessions of the daily work of writing. Works of poetry and writing can only possibly be, if there are to be any, through "l'exercice journalier de notre volonté" (402), "la bonne intention assidue" (439), "le travail successif" and "l'exercice assidu de la volonté et la noblesse permanente de l'intention" (441). The "travail du temps" which is inscribed in the temporality of "journalier," "assidu," "successif" and "permanent" of poetic work, and which nonetheless has no guarantee and

certainty of working, is therefore in direct opposition to the temporality of hashish, of that of "d'un seul coup," which works "à coup sûr."

Thus the "sens" of poetry takes on a different temporal direction as well. It is not the path of the instantaneous and effortless "d'un seul coup" leading to infallibility that poetry takes, but that of the persevering renewal in the repetition of daily effort, whose outcome, if it is not a failure, is, at the most, uncertain. It is the inscription of poetry and "œuvre" in the temporal and spatial domain marked by uncertainty and failure that is the act of morality, the moral of poetry which *Le Poème du hachisch* is about. With the notion of uncertainty and failure that is at the heart of poetry and writing, it is to Orpheus that we are led, Orpheus that Baudelaire mentions only once and in a very fleeting manner, but in whom, nonetheless, the final "sens" of poetry lies.

THE RETURN OF ORPHEUS

It is Orpheus returning from the underworld that we have in the fourth section, "L'Homme-Dieu" of *Le Poème du hachisch*:

> Je veux, dans cette dernière partie, définir et analyser le ravage moral causé par cette dangereuse et délicieuse gymnastique, ravage si grand, danger si profond, que ceux qui ne reviennent du combat que légèrement avariés, m'apparaissent comme des braves échappés de la caverne d'un Protée multiforme, des Orphées vainqueurs de l'Enfer. (428)

It is in the context of detoxification of intoxication, of returning from the battle against hashish that Orpheus appears: "ceux qui ne reviennent du combat que légèrement avariés, m'apparaissent comme . . . des Orphées vainqueurs de l'Enfer." It is the movement of coming back, of severing oneself from hashish, of cutting and detaching oneself from it which makes one comparable to Orpheus. Here, by directing itself away from hashish, and therefore differentiating its "sens" from hashish, poetry emerges as poetry. The direction of Orpheus, the poet, is finally to move away from hashish in a movement of a return. It is only in this return that poetry and poet may exist.

Before the return, however, there was the descent to hell, to the underworld of the dead. In this descent toward the dead, then, would Orpheus be going against the "sens" of poetry which consists in turning away from death? The song of Orpheus echos through the underworld:

> O positi sub terra numina mundi
> In quem reccidimus, quicquid mortale creamur;
> Si licet et falsi positis ambagibus oris
> Vera loqui sinitis, non huc, ut opaca uiderem
> Tartara, descendi, nec uti uillosa colubris
> Terna Medusaei uincirem guttura monstri;
> Causa uiae coniunx, in quam calcata uenenum
> Vipera diffudit crescentesque abstulit annos.[16]

Orpheus goes down to hell not in order to court death in itself but in order to bring back Eurydice, his wife, to life. It is to make Eurydice live, continue beyond and survive her death. Orpheus, therefore, may be going down toward death, but this movement toward death takes place only in order to move away from it, to make Eurydice part from her own sad death. Thus, the move toward death is more a move toward life, toward death but only for its continuation through life. Orpheus goes down toward his wife, the most intimate woman "toujours active et vivante" in himself, in order to make her "toujours active et vivante" through and beyond death. Hence, his going down toward death does not go against the "sens" of poetry. On the contrary, it is the movement of poetry in its fullest "sens," because in this descent, the voice and the song of Orpheus undo the death of Eurydice by annulling the effect of the deadly poison ("uenenum [v]ipera diffudit") that killed her. And let us not forget that hashish is called poison in *Le Poème du hachisch.* Therefore, Orpheus' song is the ultimate antidote. Poetry is the antidote *par excellence.*

Orpheus' descent to hell, therefore, can most appropriately be inscribed within the "sens" of poetry, sharing the same "sens" as the "raison de [la] dédicace" of *Le Poème du hachisch,* in that it is a movement toward the woman "toujours active et vivante." This, however, is only half of the trip. For even after the descent, and the approval Orpheus obtains from the gods of the underworld to take back Eurydice with him, the returning path remains yet to be taken. And it is this returning portion of the trip which surfaces in our text as Baudelaire places it parallel to the return from the battle against hashish.

Something happens during this return from the battle. Something happens to that which is returning. Some slight damage seems to occur. Baudelaire writes: "ceux qui ne reviennent du combat que légèrement avariés." The term "avarie" stands for damages that occur during transport(ation). Something goes wrong, but only slightly, during the "transport." What is it that is being transported and only lightly damaged during the trip Orpheus makes? Orpheus has gone down to the underworld in order to find and bring back Eurydice, and yet, the going down to the underworld and the power of his song to move the gods of hell who grant him the privilege of taking back Eurydice with him, all this amounts to losing her during the return trip. How, then, can the trip of Orpheus be qualified as only "légèrement avarié?" Is losing Eurydice, who is the very reason why Orpheus goes down to hell, and who is the very reason why he sings, the woman "toujours active et vivante" in him, only a minor loss? How can the term "lightly damaged" be applied to the loss of Eurydice? How can Orpheus, who has lost Eurydice on his return be a "vainqueur de l'Enfer"? Would it not be, on the contrary, the failure of Orpheus, and the failure of the work of poetry that the failure to bring back Eurydice represents? Why is this "avarie" only "légère"? Why would such a serious loss be so light? What does "légèrement" mean?

It may be possible to understand the "légèreté" of this immense failure and uncertainty of the poetic movement

through the "regard insouciant, léger, d'Orphée" of Blanchot's "Le Regard d'Orphée."[17] Lightness, here, does not mean that the loss of Eurydice is a small, negligible or an unimportant one. It is lightness rising from the seriousness and the immensity of the weight of loss. In the story of Orpheus and Eurydice, and as Blanchot writes, the loss and forgetting of the "œuvre" appears as the most profound exigence and the fundamental movement of the "œuvre" itself. It is, then, in this liberation of the "œuvre" from the unilateral stricture of the "sens unique," in the moment of its opening to the uncertainty of its being and the possibility of its failure that lightness is felt, the lightness of the "œuvre," of the gaze of Orpheus, and of the return which nonetheless bears within itself the most profound gravity.

When Baudelaire compares himself to "ces femmes sensibles et désœuvrées" in the dedication, he makes the "sens" ("*sens*ibles") of poetry lie in the experience of its own "désœuvrement" ("désœuvrées"). Blanchot sees a similar movement in the experience of Orpheus as he writes: "mais ce désir et Eurydice perdue et Orphée dispersé sont nécessaires au chant, comme est nécessaire à l'œuvre l'épreuve du désœuvrement éternel."[18] The moment of "désœuvrement" is the moment when poetry liberates itself from and into "tous les sens," and experiences its limits breaking in a movement of distraction and dispersion which is true poetic experience. Lightness then, is the weight of the "œuvre" and of the "désœuvrement," the weight of the "œuvre" through the "désœuvrement." It is the weight of poetry finally gaining and liberating all its senses. Lightness, then, is the sheer weight of poetry.

The gesture of morality of *Le Poème du hachisch* which introduces failure and uncertainty into the infallibility of Rome and hashish is therefore not a gesture that bears the heaviness and the rigidity of a judgmental sentence. It is rather a light touch imparting lightness. It is to introduce the failure, the failure so immense but so light and carefree of the gaze of Orpheus.

The return of Orpheus is a story of a gaze turning, a gaze ever so light and free from care that it turns. This turning or the tour of the gaze, however, is only a detour since he cannot look at Eurydice and cannot "regarder le centre de la nuit dans la nuit."[19] Therefore, the return of Orpheus is a story of a gaze, which, in its (in)ability to look at the center, makes a (de)tour. It is a story of a gaze turning toward and/or away from the center. *Le Poème du hachisch* also is a story of a center and of a tour around the center. Or rather, it is a story of a non-center, since, with Rome split in two, the trajectory of *Le Poème du hachisch* which started out by moving toward the center, proceeds to move away from the center.

At the end, however, an altogether different direction seems to be taken:

> Dans les études philosophiques, l'esprit humain,
> imitant la marche des astres, doit suivre une courbe

qui le ramène à son point de départ. Conclure, c'est fermer un cercle. Au commencement j'ai parlé de cet état merveilleux, où l'esprit de l'homme se trouvait quelquefois jeté comme par une grâce spéciale. (440-41)

Neither centripetal nor centrifugal, the final trajectory of *Le Poème de hachisch* is that of a circle: a circular trajectory that neither affirms the center as would be the case with a centripetal movement, nor denies the center as would be the case with a centrifugal motion. Here, we are traveling through a trajectory that bears an entirely different relationship to the center: a center that is never attained but which exists nonetheless. In this circular trajectory, the center is both far and close: far in that the circumference of the circle will never cross or reach it and close in that the center is always present in the middle of the circle and is that which determines the circle. The topographical logic of the circle in which the center lies both at the greatest distance and in the closest proximity, all the while that it is being maintained at a constant distance, may be the ideal logic of metaphor of *Le Poème du hachisch.* Perhaps this is why, Baudelaire gives the shape of a circle to his monograph: "Pour idéaliser mon sujet, je dois en concentrer tous les rayons dans un cercle unique, je dois les polariser; et le cercle tragique où je les vais rassembler sera, comme je l'ai dit, une âme de mon choix" (429). The writing of the monograph is presented as an idealization ("[p]our idéaliser mon sujet") into a unique and tragic circle.

What about the gaze then? Where does it turn to? With the writing of *Le Poème du hachisch* going back to its beginning, and the pen of the poet tracing and closing a circle, a perfect metaphorical shape finally is drawn. The gesture of splitting Rome in a metaphorical move achieves its ideal end or beginning in the motion of a circle. And this ideal metaphorical circle is traced by "imitant la marche des astres." The poetic monograph and the entire writing of *Le Poème du hachisch* take on the shape of a circle, the shape of a perfect metaphor, by joining the stars in the sky. It is therefore to the sky, to the stars in the sky at night that the poetic gaze turns. Blanchot's Orpheus tries to look into the night, to "le centre de la nuit dans la nuit," and this, in order to look at Eurydice. The gaze in *Le Poème du hachisch* also seems to turn to the night and to the woman. For the woman in the dedication "qui, quoique malade, est toujours active et vivante en moi . . . tourne maintenant tous ses regards vers le Ciel, ce lieu de toutes les transfigurations" (400). By closing the circle and by going back to the beginning of the writing, Baudelaire goes back to the dedication, and the poet's gaze follows the woman's gaze to the sky. Writing returns and the gaze turns, and turns to the woman, to the night, to the stars and to the sky. To the sky which is uniquely and only naturally so, and this from the very beginning, contained within the artificial paradise, the "Ciel" of and in *Les Paradis artificiels.* It may then be only in the sky of the artificial paradise that possibly and ultimately the gaze of the poet with that of the woman, and the gaze of Orpheus with that of Eurydice meet. It is only through writing, and

at the end of writing which brings one to the beginning, that one attains the stars in the sky. There, where the lightly floating and carefree gaze has risen, the gaze of Orpheus, the poet, may not only be able to turn but also be returned, and it may even be possible to "regarder le centre de la nuit dans la nuit." And, perhaps, the rising of the poet's gaze from hell to the sky of *Les Paradis,* may be what makes the poet the ultimate "vainqueur de l'Enfer."[20]

NOTES

[1] *Le Poème du hachisch,* in *Œuvres complètes,* ed. Claude Pichois (Paris: Gallimard, 1975), I: 399-441. Paginations will be given in the text.

[2] *Le Poème du hachisch* experiments a lot: the second section, "Qu'est-ce que le hachisch?," is all about various chemical experimentations and preparations of hashish.

[3] *Le Poème du hachisch* ends as follows:

Mais l'homme n'est pas si abandonné, si privé de moyens honnêtes pour ganger le ciel, qu'il soit obligé d'invoquer la pharmacie et la sorcellerie; il n'a pas besoin de vendre son âme pour payer les caresses enivrantes et l'amitié des houris. Qu'est-ce qu'un paradis qu'on achète au prix de son salut éternel? Je me figure un homme (dirai-je un brahmane, un poète, un philosophe chrétien?) placé sur l'Olympe ardu de la spiritualité; autour de lui, les Muses de Raphaël ou de Mantegna, pour le consoler de ses longs jeûnes et de ses prières assidues, combinent les danses les plus nobles, le regardant avec leurs plus doux sourires les plus éclatants; le divin Apollon, ce maître en tout savoir (celui de Francavilla, d'Albert Dürer, de Goltzius ou de tout autre, qu'importe? N'y a-t-il pas un Apollon, pour tout homme qui le mérite?), caresse de son archet ses cordes les plus vibrantes. Au-dessous de lui, au pied de la montagne, dans les ronces et dans la boue, la troupe des humains, la bande des ilotes, simule les grimaces de la jouissance et pousse des hurlements que lui arrache la morsure du poison; et le poète attristé se dit: «Ces infortunés qui n'ont ni jeûné, ni prié, et qui ont refusé la rédemption par le travail, demandent à la noire magie les moyens de s'élever, d'un seul coup, à l'existence surnaturelle. La magie les dupe et elle allume pour eux un faux bonheur et une fausse lumiere; tandis que nous, poètes et philosophes, nous avons régénéré notre âme par le travail successif et la contemplation; par l'exercice assidu de la volonté et la noblesse permanente de l'intention, nous avons créé à notre usage un jardin de vraie beauté. Confiants dans la parole qui dit que la foi transporte les montagnes, nous avons accompli le seul miracle dont Dieu nous ait octroyé la licence!» (441)

[4] Hashish is called poison several times in the text: "pour livrer au poison toute liberté d'action" (410), "ces esprits que le poison a aiguisés" (412), "l'action du poison sur la partie spirituelle de l'homme" (426), etc. In *Un Mangeur d'opium,* opium is called "la panacée, le *pharmakon népenthès* pour toutes les douleurs humaines" (465; original emphasis).

[5] Within this context of health, medicine and pharmacology (*Le Poème du hachisch* is indeed a study of the preparation, uses and effects of hashish on men, a true pharmacology of hashish), it is interesting to note that both "équivoque" and "quiproquo" have meanings related to medicine. *Littré* gives for "équivoque": "Terme de médecine. Signe équivoque, signe qui peut convenir à plusieurs maladies," and for "quiproquo": "Un quiproquo d'apothicaire, médicament donné l'un pour l'autre."

[6] The movement of differentiation and purification inevitably involving the reverse movement of mixing and contamination can clearly be seen in the second section "Qu'est-ce que le hachisch?" There, the chemical process through which hashish is purified to the form of "l'extrait gras" appears as a process which constantly contaminates hashish with other chemical substances:

> L'*extrait gras* du hachisch, tel que le préparent les Arabes, s'obtient en faisant bouillir les sommités de la plante fraîche dans du beurre avec un peu d'eau. (406; original emphasis)

> Les expériences faites par MM. Smith, Gastinel et Decourtive ont eu pour but d'arriver à la découverte du principe actif du hachisch. Malgré leurs efforts, sa combinaison chimique est encore peu connue; mais on attribue généralement ses propriétés à une matière résineuse qui s'y trouve en assez bonne dose, dans la proportion de 10 pour 100 environ. Pour obtenir cette résine, on réduit la plante sèche en poudre grossière, et on la lave plusieurs fois avec de l'alcool que l'on distille ensuite pour le retirer en partie; on fait évaporei jusqu'à consistance d'extrait; on traite cet extrait par l'eau, qui dissout les matières gommeuses étrangères, et la résine reste alors à l'état de pureté. (406-07)

Purification of hashish consists of mixing the plant of hashish with butter and water in the first case, and with alcohol and water in the second case. The extraction or the pulling out of the "principe actif du hachisch" requires a constant adding and mixing in of foreign substances. It is interesting to notice that hashish in its pure form is inedible due to its repugnant odor. The "extrait gras" has to be mixed with sugar and various spices such as vanilla and cinnamon, and the "résine" with chocolate or ginger, if they are to be edible (406-07). Pure substance, therefore, is not ingestible. Purity smells bad, and gives nauseous feelings. One can say that ingesting and eating necessitate a certain preliminary contamination, a rendering impure of a pure substance. Eating then is essentially an impure act.

Furthermore, the subtext of alchemy and poetry to this passage on the chemistry of hashish cannot be overlooked. The poetic enterprise which extracts the essence of things has been compared to chemistry and alchemy by Baudelaire in one of his "projets d'un épilogue pour l'édition de 1861":

> Anges revêtus d'or, de pourpre et d'hyacinthe,
> O vous! soyez témoins que j'ai fait mon devoir

> Comme un parfait chimiste et comme une âme sainte.
> Car j'ai de chaque chose extrait la quintessence,
> Tu m'as donné ta boue et j'en ai fait de l'or.
>   (192)

Poetry, chemistry and alchemy bear affinities in that they are arts of extraction that use in a skillful manner the technique of mixing and separating. They are activities that rest upon a constant *va-et-vient* between these two opposite movements.

[7] With the fragments of anecdotes being incorporated into the poetic monograph in the mode of the dancer's springboard, anecdotes no longer simply occupy a place that has to be closed up and left. They have become, not only a point of departure, but also a point of return. If previously, the "développement régulier de l'ivresse" needed to leave the anecdotal path aside or behind, now, the monograph requires a constant going back to anecdotes.

[8] A list of possibilities are given in Pichois' notes to *L'Héautontimorouménos* (986). In the notes to *Les Paradis*, Pichois writes that Baudelaire's wish ("Il importe d'ailleurs fort peu que la raison de cette dédicace soit comprise") has been granted since no one has yet been capable of determining the identity of this woman. More recently, in *Le Secret de Baudelaire*, (Paris: Jean-Michel Place, 1991), Henri Lecay has come up with a suggestion that it stands for Félicité Ducessois, the sister-in-law of Baudelaire, the wife of his half-brother, Alphonse.

[9] Baudelaire consistently uses the term "cerveau" for the male poet, and for the woman, "cervelle" is used. The woman of the fourth anecdote says: "le poison se mit de nouveau à jouer avec ma pauvre cervelle" (422).

[10] For the figure of the convalescent as a prototype for artistic genius, see the third section of *Le Peintre de la vie moderne* (II, 687-940), in which the painter of modern life, M.G., is compared to an eternal convalescent.

[11] Hashish, presented as a spoonful of green jam, is an edible but nauseous happiness:

> Voici la drogue sous vos yeux: un peu de confiture verte, gros comme une noix, singulièrement odorante, à ce point qu'elle soulève une certaine répulsion et des velléités de nausée, comme le ferait, du reste, toute odeur fine et même agréable, portée à son maximum de force et pour ainsi dire de densité. (. . .) Voilà donc le bonheur! il remplit la capacité d'une petite cuiller! le bonheur avec toutes ses ivresses, toutes ses folies, tous ses enfantillages! Vous pouvez avaler sans crainte; on n'en meurt pas. (. . .) Ainsi, c'est dit: vous avez même, pour lui donner plus de force et d'expansion, délayé votre dose d'extrait gras dans une tasse de café noir; vous avez pris soin d'avoir l'estomac libre, reculant vers neuf ou dix heures du soir le repas substantiel, pour livrer au poison toute liberté d'action; tout au plus dans une heure prendrezvous une légère soupe. (409-10)

[12] In *Le Poème du hachisch,* the poetic voice always goes against the common everyday language, and this is achieved through a gesture of separation. There are three clear instances of this. The first one is the case of the Rome proverb in which the gesture separating Rome from Rome makes the poetic meaning diverge from the conventional and "vulgar" meaning of the proverb. The second one, and we have already seen this as well, is when the desire to "ne pas prendre le mot dans son sens le plus strict" was immediately followed by the nuance which distinguished. The third instance is Baudelaire's attempt to undo the "préjugé" and the "méprise complète" that common readers have concerning the word hashish. The poet's first gesture is again to mark a difference: "Et, puisque pour le commun des lecteurs et des questionneurs le mot hachisch comporte l'idée d'un monde étrange et bouleversé, l'attente de rêves prodigieux . . . *je ferai tout de suite remarquer l'importante différence qui sépare* les effets du hachisch des phénomènes du sommeil" (408; my emphasis)

[13] Thus the distance and proximity of the metaphorical space shares the same logic as that of the nuanced passage that separates and links at the same time. The "ou" of the "à la récompense *ou* au châtiment" of the Rome proverb operates such a passage, as well as the "comme" of "le bonheur naturel, *comme* l'artificiel" of the dedication. There is another instance of this in the "et" of "Opium *et* hachisch" which is the subtitle of *Les Paradis artificiels.* Opium and hashish are similar in that they both are drugs that are opposed to poetry. Nevertheless, an enormous difference is introduced between them, first, at the sheer level of the structure of *Les Paradis* which is that of a diptych (it is composed of *Le Poème du hachisch* and *Un Mangeur d'opium*). Together, hashish and opium form the writing of *Les Paradis,* but they are distinct from each other. Therefore, not only Rome but paradise is split in two as well. Second, in the passage where hashish is compared to opium in our text, hashish is similar to opium in that "[c]es deux caractéristiques de l'opium sont parfaitement applicables au hachisch." Subsequently, however, they become clearly distinguished from each other as "dix années d'*intoxication* par le hachisch" is contrasted to "dix années de *régime* d'opium" (428; my emphasis).

Here, in the text of *Le Poème du hachisch* then, metaphor seems to function as the dynamics of the nuanced passage operated by "ou," "comme" and "et."

[14] Derrida in "Le Retrait de la métaphore" (1978), published in *Psyché: Invention de l'autre* (Paris: Galilée, 1987) 63-93, discusses the issue of the metaphor in terms of transportation, orientation, proximity and distance among others.

[15] "Apollon" in *Dictionnaire des mythologies,* ed. Yves Bonnefois, Flammarion, 1981.

[16] *Metamorphoses,* X: 17-24.

[17] In *L'Espace littéraire* (Paris: Gallimard, 1955), 225-32.

[18] Blanchot, 228.

[19] Blanchot, 225.

[20] I would like to thank the American Association of University Women Educational Foundation for their American Fellowship, which supported the writing of this essay.

Alexandra K. Wettlaufer

SOURCE: "Paradise Regained: The Flaneur, the Badaud, and the Aesthetics of Artistic Reception i Le Poeme du haschisch," in *Nineteenth-Century French Studies,* Vol. 24, No. 3 & 4, Spring-Summer, 1996, pp. 388-97.

[*In the following essay, Wettlaufer contends that* Le Poème du haschisch *serves as an outline of Baudelaire's aesthetic philosophy as well as his statement about the tenuous benefits of drug experimentation.*]

Les Paradis artificiels is generally acknowledged to be the only published work that Baudelaire himself considered complete and definitive; in a letter to editor Julien Lemer he maintained, "je trouve le livre bon comme il est, je n'y ajouterai rien, je n'en retrancherai rien" (*Correspondance* 2: 442).[1] Yet the two essays that constitute *Les Paradis artificiels* are too often dismissed as a peculiar hybrid of self-referential moralizing (*Le Poème du haschisch*) and idiosyncratic translation (*Un Mangeur d'opium*). While the volume shares some thematic similarities and possibly even a structural affinity with Baudelaire's poems, *Les Paradis artificiels* also provides significant insights into the author's formal and aesthetic concerns vis-à-vis the relationship between author, reader and text.[2] On the most obvious level, *Les Paradis artificiels* sets forth the poet's condemnation of the facile and fleeting paradise of drug consumption. However this pair of essays that appeared in 1860, during the juncture between the first and second editions of *Les Fleurs du mal,* is as much about art as it is about drugs, and represents an important embodiment of Baudelaire's aesthetic theories of the production and the reception of meaning in a work of art. This second, but still fundamental level of meaning will be manifested in the thematic and formal tensions between the explicit and the implicit, between the "dit" and the "non-dit," and between the "lisible" and the "scriptible" within the text.

In many ways *Les Paradis artificiels* appears to be a text in conflict with itself. While ostensibly preaching the evils of opium and hashish, the author presents and even reproduces these states of intoxication in vivid and evocative detail, and while adamantly denying any points of intersection between the supernatural experiences of drugs and of art, his text creates a striking set of parallels between the two states. Nor is this implied similitude limited to the drug-related essays, for in *Exposition universelle de 1855,* in *Edgar Poe, sa vie et ses œuvres* and in *Richard Wagner et Tannhäuser à Paris,* to name only a few examples, Baudelaire also compares the experience of viewing a painting, reading a work of literature, and hearing an opera to "les vertigineuses conceptions de l'opium."[3] Nevertheless, the two essays of the *Paradis artificiels* will explicitly deny this resemblance, enunciating instead a stark contrast between the *toxicomane* and the artist. Baudelaire opposes the temporary transcendence engendered by the consumption of drugs to the more legitimate paradise of art: where the artificial, narcotic nirvana is achieved through the repression of self and the reality principle, the true, artistic paradise is achieved conversely through suffering and the active expression of self. Implicit, however, within the text, is the contrast and *intersection* between the experience of drugs and the experience of art: between the *effect* of narcotics and the *effect* of art on the perceiving consciousness. For if the *haschischin* or opium eater as *producer* of hallucinations is compared (unfavorably) to the poet, as *perceiver* of these hallucinations he is tacitly compared to the reader. In other words, the "creation" of the hallucination is in fact separable from the perception of the hallucination and the two processes function as separate metaphors for artist and audience.

In both *Le Poème du haschisch* and *Un Mangeur d'opium* Baudelaire presents an implicit theory of reader response based on a visual paradigm that shares much with the narcotic experience. Hallucination *and* reading are equally described in terms of *viewing:* the drug-induced reverie, as well as the text at hand, are consistently referred to as "tableaux," while the hallucinator and the reader are "spectateurs," observers of a series of mental scenes synthesized in the mind and unfolding before the mind's eye. Baudelaire's use of the tableau metaphor at the beginning of the *Poème du haschisch* is especially telling, for here he sets up a parallel not only between hallucinating, reading and viewing, but between his own critical text and a work of visual art as well. In the brief introduction to the volume, a "dédicace" in letter form offered "A. J. G. F." (also the recipient of "L'Héautontimorouménos"), he explains that what will follow will be "un tableau de voluptés artificielles"—visual, dramatic, evocative, and as implied by both "tableau" and "volupté," undeniably artistic (1: 399).[4] He repeats the painterly metaphor a page later, asserting, "tu verras dans ce tableau un promeneur sombre et solitaire, plongé dans le flot mouvant des multitudes" (1:400), implicitly positing a modern aesthetic of *flânerie.* The reader is led to believe that in the pages to follow she will *see* a contemporary Jean-Jacques, documenting in these updated reveries the state of the artist's soul in the modern city. However, in the first of many paradoxes that will characterize these essays, although Baudelaire claims that he will paint the portrait of a solitary stroller plunged into the surging stream of the Parisian populace, neither the street nor the multitudes are evident in either essay, and the *flânerie* will be entirely psychological in nature.

Indeed the *flâneur*—the Parisian idler, first cousin of the dandy and denizen of the teeming boulevards and arcades of the modern metropolis—would seem at first to have little in common with the solitary and self-contained hashish smoker and opium eater of Baudelaire's *Paradis artificiels.* Where the *flâneur*'s activity takes place outdoors and in the public domain, the *drogués* in Baudelaire's essays most often remain comfortably ensconced indoors and at home; if the *flâneur* by definition strolls (however slowly), the addict sits or reclines; if the *flâneur* is a man of the crowds, the hallucinator is decidedly not. Yet the defining *experiences* of these two apparently dissimilar characters—the urban spectacle and the narcotic hallucination—both turn on the crucial issue of *seeing,* and are equally characterized by "a marked preponderance of the activity of the eye over the activity of the ear" (Benjamin 38). Baudelaire's *flâneur,* as distinct from the disinterested dandy, is an "observateur passionné" who fuses detachment with a search for knowledge and an assertion of a creative intelligence to shape the otherwise ungraspable urban experience. In keeping with Balzac's definition of the *"flâneur artiste"* in *Physiologie du mariage* (1826), Baudelaire's own quintessential *flâneur* is Constantin Guys, the "peintre de la vie moderne" who is able to transform the chaotic and the arbitrary into the aesthetic and meaningful: "harnachements, scintillements, musique, regards décidés, moustaches lourdes et sérieuses, tout cela entre pêle-mêle en lui; et dans quelques minutes, le poème qui en résulte sera virtuellement composé" (2: 693).[5] Balzac's *"flâneur artiste"* is an *active* rather than a passive consumer of the urban landscape ("se promener, c'est végéter; flâner, c'est vivre" [11: 930]), who is "a writer as well as a reader of the urban text" (Ferguson 47). In a similar vein, Baudelaire's "M.G." is a man of the crowds who translates and interprets the visual signifiers into more universal truths. Whereas the dandy is "l'homme riche, oisif, et qui, même blasé, n'as pas d'autre occupation que de courir à la piste du bonheur" (2: 709), Guys, as the painter of modern life, espouses

> un but plus élevé que celui d'un pur *flâneur,* un but plus général, autre que le plaisir fugitif de la circonstance. Il cherche ce quelque chose qu'on nous permettra d'appeler la *modernité;* car il ne se présente pas de meilleur mot pour exprimer l'idée en question. Il s'agit, pour lui, de dégager de la mode ce qu'elle peut contenir de poétique dans l'historique, de tirer l'éternel du transitoire. (2: 694)

This distinction between active and passive consumption of the visual spectacle, between the idle and the artistic observer will resonate in the *Paradis artificiels* as Baudelaire posits his own *flânerie* of the landscape of the hallucinating mind. Indeed if, as Benjamin would assert, the domain of the *flâneur* is the modern no-man's land where "the street had become an *intérieur* for him, [and] now this *intérieur* turned into a street" (Benjamin 54), Baudelaire's metaphysical *flâneur* (that is, the opium eater or *haschischin*) experiences a similar porosity of boundaries. Here, however, the spatial interpenetration occurs not simply between the public sphere of the street and the private sphere of the living room, but rather between the exterior world of physical reality and the psychological "intérieur" of the perceiving consciousness.[6] The consumer of opium or hashish will become the observer of his own mental scenes and tableaux that share much with the saccadic, disjointed and ungraspable experience of the city both in form and in content. Just as Paris "entered [the] memory as a disconnected sequence of optical displays (Buck-Morss 186),"[7] the drug-induced reveries will unfold as a series of dislocated and fragmented images arising both from the memory and from the eidetic imagination. In each case, any possible "meaning" extracted from this visual experience will be the product of the shaping, creative imagination of the passionate observer.

Following the brief dedication there will be no further explicit reference to the *flâneur*, but the aesthetics of viewing, observing and consuming the spectacle unrolling before one's very eyes will dominate both *Le Poème du haschisch* and *Un Mangeur d'opium*. Accordingly, the image of the *flâneur artiste* as embodied by Guys will be a crucial model for the ultimate translation of Baudelaire's aesthetic message. And although the *flâneur* disappears, the image of painting introduced in the opening lines ("tu verras dans ce *tableau* un promeneur . . .") remains as a multifaceted metaphor for hallucination, memory, imagination and reading—indeed almost all mental functions here take on a visual form. Baudelaire describes his own experience of De Quincey's literary memoirs in terms of the author's "tableaux émouvants," characterized by "une richesse précieuse pour les yeux" (1: 515) that he hopes to translate for his own reader in a form that will retain its original, visual flavor. Thus he offers a text that "je déroulerai comme une tapisserie fantastique sous les yeux du lecteur" (1: 444). As the author transcribes his mental tableaux into verbal ones, reading perforce becomes an act of viewing in these drug-related essays.

As the best account of a tableau, according to Baudelaire, may be a sonnet or an elegy (2: 418), it is not coincidental that the first of the two essays is entitled *"Le Poème du haschisch,"* and it is on the tensions between the poetic and the narcotic in this particular essay that I will focus.[8] For intrinsic to the ultimate sense of *Les Paradis artificiels* is not only the *explicit* contrast between the artist's creations and the *drogué's*, but also the *implicit* contrast between the *haschischin*'s reception of the visual scenes as evoked by drugs, and the reader's reception of the visual scenes as evoked by drugs *via the artist*. Why this aspect of signification must perforce remain in the realm of the "non-dit" is intimately tied to Baudelaire's ultimate "Morale"; only by interpreting the repressed level of meaning will Baudelaire's full expression come to light.

As in many of his *Salons*, Baudelaire exploits the form of the interpolated prose poem within *Le Poème du haschisch* to create a linguistic equivalent to visual experience.[9] Here, as in the *Salons*, the prose poem enacts a narrative of performance through its suggestive, evocative form where meaning can only be reached by the

active assertion of the reader's eidetic imagination.[10] In other words, signification will be the product of the reader's synthesis of words into images, which in turn will lead to a meaning inscribed by the author but achieved by the reader in a dialectic movement between text and imagination. In the central section of *Le Poème du haschisch* Baudelaire incorporates a prose poem that evokes first-hand the experience of drug-induced reverie while simultaneously serving as a negative *and* a positive paradigm for the reception of a work of art. As he presents the *haschischin*'s hallucinations, Baudelaire shifts from the neutral "il" to the personal, almost accusatory "vous," transforming the reader into a direct participant in the trip. As readers we *become* the hallucinator, as Baudelaire tells us what we see and feel, his poetic prose providing an evocative experiential equivalent. The passage begins with an initial illustration of the fusion of observing subject with the object of contemplation:

> Votre oeil se fixe sur un arbre harmonieux courbé par le vent; dans quelques seconds, ce qui ne serait dans le cerveau d'un poète qu'une comparaison fort naturelle deviendra dans le vôtre une réalité. Vous prêtez d'abord à l'arbre vos passions, votre désir ou votre mélancolie; ses gémissements et ses oscillations deviennent les vôtres, et bientôt vous êtes l'arbre. (1: 419-20)

From the outset this prose poem functions as a "mise en abyme" for the entire *Poème du haschisch,* for it simultaneously presents Baudelaire's observations on drugs and on art through a series of contrasts in the creation and the reception of visual images. Thus, what would normally be a poetic metaphor (the tree as symbol for the individual), chosen and controlled by the artist, becomes a hallucinated reality in the mind of the *haschischin,* as he fuses with the object of his gaze.

Next, the prose poem expands on the two themes with an upward movement from tree to bird: "de même, l'oiseau qui plane au fond de l'azur *représente* d'abord l'immortelle envie de planer au-dessus des choses humaines; mais déjà vous êtes l'oiseau lui-même" (1: 420; original emphasis). Once again there is a movement from metaphor—the bird representing the desire to transcend human limitation—to literal identification where the tripper and the bird become (imaginatively) one. Through the *poet's* use of metaphor, however, the reader is able to *experience* the successive loss of control that drug consumption entails, while the final expansion renders the sense of the passage eminently clear. In the most striking of the three images of verticality and celestial transcendence, Baudelaire pictures the reader-cum-hallucinator smoking a pipe, watching the clouds of smoke waft upward:

> Votre attention se reposera un peu trop longtemps sur les nuages bleuâtres qui s'exhalent de votre pipe. L'idée d'une évaporation, lente, successive, éternelle, s'emparera de votre esprit, et vous appliquerez bientôt cette idée à vos propres pensées, à votre matière pensante. Par une équivoque singulière, par une espèce de transposition ou de

quiproquo intellectuel, vous vous sentirez vous
évaporant, et vous attribuerez à votre pipe (dans
laquelle vous vous sentez accroupi et ramassé
comme le tabac) l'étrange sensation de *vous fumer.*
(1: 420)

The consumer of hashish is consumed by the hashish. As
an observing subject, he not once but three times disappears within the world of narcotic fantasy, absorbed into
the object of his contemplation. Through this series of
increasingly ethereal images Baudelaire illustrates the
fatal loss of liberty and control that he will later identify
as the primary difference between the poet and the addict. But here, and throughout *Le Poème du haschisch,*
the reader's relationship to the addict is an equally significant subtext. For while openly comparing the tripper
to a poet, the passage enacts an implicit comparison between the tripper and the reader as they textually merge
into a single "vous." In order for the reader to come to
the poet's intended conclusion, she must experience the
haschischin's passive loss of control through *active* participation in the text. She must simultaneously enact the
"transpositions d'idées" while recognizing their metaphoric nature, and a second level of meaning is revealed
only through this active synthesis of signification. If
Baudelaire's prose poetic description is able to represent
the experience of a hash trip, it is only because the poet
and his audience assert their imaginative powers while
recognizing the difference between fantasy and reality. It
is through the reader's position at once inside the text, as
the hallucinating "vous," and outside of the text, recognizing the metaphoric value of the identification, that the
difference between the perception of hallucinated and
artistic tableaux becomes apparent.

Thus *Le Poème du haschisch* implicitly presents
Baudelaire's theories of artistic response in the guise of
negative example of the drug tripper. As I have indicated,
the essay is filled with direct references to both painting
and poetry, while Baudelaire's poetic descriptions of the
experience of hashish employ highly visual terms, insisting on the intensified sensations of form and color in
terms that sound remarkably close to his own theory of the
artistic "surnaturel." In a second prose poem that similarly
encodes the reader's role while ostensibly simply positing
the artist's, Baudelaire describes the *haschischin*'s experience of different forms of artistic expression.

Following his famous profile of "l'homme sensible
moderne" which includes "un tempérament moitié
nerveux, moitié bilieux . . . un esprit cultivé, exercé aux
études de la forme et la couleur . . . une grande finesse
de sens" (1: 429), thus a sensibility which shares much
not only with Baudelaire's own temperament, but with
his characterizations of Poe, Delacroix and Guys as well,
he then demonstrates what might happen to this sensitive,
implicitly artistic type, under the influence of hashish.
Once again the reader is immediately implicated in the
scene as Baudelaire shifts to the "vous" of direct address.
Beginning with the visual arts, Baudelaire demonstrates
how *everything*—good, bad, or indifferent paintings,
murals, wallpaper, indeed *any* painted surface—takes on
an intense and energetic life in the eye of the hallucinator, and the even the most trivial object "devient symbole
parlant." Hashish spreads its "vernis magique" over the
entire visual world, revealing "profondeur de l'espace,
allégorie de la profondeur du temps" (1: 430-1).[11] The
universal analogies and correspondences, normally revealed by art, are incarnate in anything the eye might fall
upon, as new allegorical depths of meaning proliferate
everywhere. The world itself takes on the aspect of a
painting.

Similarly, if the intoxicated eye should fall upon a book,
the words will take on a life of their own, becoming vivid
images and solid form, while even "l'aride grammaire
elle-même, devient quelque chose comme une sorcellerie
évocatoire." The grounds of intersection between an artistic and a narcotic experience are striking here, as
Baudelaire even endows the hallucinated reality with
"sorcellerie évocatoire"—an important element of the
artwork of genius that Baudelaire linked directly with
synaesthetic expression in his essay on Théophile
Gautier.[12] In each case, there is indeed a synaesthetic
expansion from the realm of words to the realm of visual
images: concrete, physical and chromatic. Yet here,
through the agency of hashish, *any* sentence can be transformed into a visually evocative experience, just as *any*
scene becomes an allegorical spectacle revealing the very
depths of life itself.

In the final expansion of this section, Baudelaire introduces the now familiar image of the *drogué* being consumed by the hallucination. As in the previous examples
of aesthetic experience under the influence of drugs,
there is an imbrication of sensation, and where visual
experience became a language, reading became visual,
music is perceived as *poetry.* But ultimately, the fundamental difference between the perception of art and the
perception of hallucination becomes evident. For here,
"la musique, autre langue chère . . . vous parle de vous-
même et vous raconte le poème de votre vie: elle
s'incorpore à vous et vous fondez en elle" (1: 431). The
fusion of the self with the music entails a passivity and a
self-referentiality that highlights the negative aspects of
narcotic perception while enacting once again the positive paradigm of artistic reception. The person consuming the drugs absorbs the music but gives nothing of himself, and literally melts away. The *haschischin* experiences perfect, but illusory, fusion: the gap between
perceiver and perceived, between language and ideas,
between signified and signifier is miraculously overcome and meaning is offered up on a silver platter.
The aestheticized perceptions of drug-induced reverie,
where *anything* becomes endowed with allegorical signification, which is in turn *presented* to the hallucinator to consume, as it were, ready made, can have no
real value or meaning in a Baudelairean universe. For
the precise sense of the allegorical production of
meaning lies in the *process* of translation, and in the
recognition of the fundamental alienation between
subject and object, perceiver and perceived.

Thus, as before, within the negative example of the *haschischin,* we find a positive paradigm present both at the level of the "dit" and of the "non-dit." Once again the arbitrary images of hallucination have been given *artistic* form and substance by the poet, who demonstrates his active control of production, in opposition to the hallucinator who is merely a passive spectator of his own "creations." Implicit, however, but crucial to a full understanding of the essay, is the contrast between the *perception* of art and hallucination. The reader, who presumably has *not* consumed hashish before experiencing the passage, is able through the *active* participation of the imagination and intelligence to envision and experience these same sensations and thus to reach a meaning that a passive perceiver of true hallucination could not. The active, participatory role of the artist and of the skillful reader in interpreting, translating, creating meaning out of the fragments and symbols of modern experience draws attention to the schism between them. Following the image of the *flâneur* as man of the crowd, at once part of the scene and irrevocably other, Baudelaire's artist and his ideal reader, as posited by the paradigmatic prose poems, enter into the scene via the imagination, yet never lose themselves in the fantasy of perfect harmony. Instead, the metaphysical observer synthesizes meaning as a product of a dialectic between the physical images of the scene or art work and her own personally significant images and associations, while this emblematic language makes palpable or experiential the process of allegory or fragmentation and alienation. The drug user, on the other hand, does not so much "read" as he is "read to"—meaning is presented and accepted, but not actually achieved.

Thus Baudelaire must necessarily repress direct commentary on this level of the essay, for its signification must be experienced and not merely dictated in order for it to reach its full expression. Only through the *process* of reading, interpreting and actively synthesizing meaning, can the reader come to a full understanding of the difference between the production *and* the perception of art and hallucination. If this second level of meaning had been spelled out, the reader would have been reduced to the single role of the *haschischin* as passive perceiver, without the redeeming possibility of active participation in the creation of signification.

Baudelaire highlights the dialectic nature of art and perception in the modern world, where meaning is the product of process, and even aesthetic expression is incomplete without an active perceiving intelligence to synthesize it into signification. By transforming the meaningless hallucinations into meaningful artistic expression, Baudelaire illustrates the complementary roles of artist and audience in the production of meaning out of pure aesthetic experience. The *surnaturel,* the correspondences and the analogies of the drug trip are devoid of any true meaning because they are neither shaped and controlled by an artist nor interpreted by an audience; instead they are passively produced and passively perceived. His repression of commentary on the role of the reader in the synthesis of artistic meaning allows the

reader to take an active, creative role in the text. Accordingly, in Baudelaire's aesthetics of the "non-dit," authorial repression becomes a means to readerly expression, allowing her fleeting access perhaps to the heroic realms of the *flâneur* and the artist in the assertion of individual sensibility and consciousness when faced with the annihilating spectacle of modernity.

In *Ce qu'on voit dans les rues de Paris,* Victor Fournel, a contemporary of Baudelaire's, offered the following distinction:

> N'allons pas toutefois confondre le *flâneur* avec le badaud: il y a une nuance que sentiront les adeptes. Le simple *flâneur* observe et réfléchit; il peut le faire du moins. Il est toujours en pleine possession de son individualité. Celle du badaud disparaît, au contraire, absorbé par le monde extérieur qui le ravit à lui-même, qui le frappe jusqu'à l'enivrement et l'extase. Le badaud, sous l'influence du spectacle devient en être impersonnel, ce n'est plus un homme: il est public, il est foule. (263)

The *haschischin,* as passive, intoxicated observer, mirrors the hapless *badaud* of the Parisian boulevard, absorbed by the spectacle to the point of losing his very individuality. The artist, the *flâneur* and the active reader observe and *reflect,* bringing a personal vision to the increasingly impersonal and depersonalizing scene of modern experience. Ultimately then, *Les Paradis artificiels* reflects Baudelaire's commentary not merely on drugs, but on the creation and reception of artistic meaning in the modern metropolis. The consumption of art must be as active and expressive as the production of art, inversely mirroring the passive and repressive nature of the consumption and the production of hallucination. Clearly, although the immediate experience of hashish entails an artificial paradise, the *artistic* experience of the paradisiac can lead to possible redemption not only for the artist, but also for his audience.

NOTES

[1] All subsequent reference to Baudelaire will be to the Pléiade *œuvres complètes,* ed. Claude Pichois.

[2] "Poison," "La Vie antérieure," "Rêve parisien," "L'Invitation au voyage" and the five "Vin" poems are most often cited as being thematically related to the *Paradis artificiels* in that they either address or imply states of intoxication. In a more general sense, the motifs of temptation, suffering and escape may be seen as common to both *Les Fleurs du mal* and *Les Paradis artificiels.* See Emanuel Mickel's *The Artificial Paradises in French Literature. The Influence of Opium and Hashish on French Romanticism and "Les Fleurs du mal"* for an interpretation of the entire volume of *Les Fleurs du mal* as a reflection of the poet's struggle with the purgatorial paradises of intoxication. Mickel, who presents a poem by poem analysis of possible drug allusions, sees the title as a reference both to the opium poppy and the flowering cannabis plant; the dedication to

Gautier as a reference to his role in introducing opium and hashish to the French literati of the 1840s; and "Spleen et idéal" as representative of the dual facets of drug consumption. In "Some Remarks on Baudelaire's *Poème du haschisch*" Alison Fairlie compares the architecture of *Les Fleurs du mal* to that of *Le Poème du haschisch,* which she interprets as an allegory for the sequence of human experience treated in Baudelaire's poems. See Fairlie in *The French Mind. Studies in Honor of Gustave Rudler* 291-317.

[3] In *Exposition universelle de 1855* Baudelaire describes the experience of Delacroix's paintings in terms of opium, synaesthetic sensation, the "surnaturel": "Edgar Poe dit, je ne sais pas où, que le résultat de l'opium pour les sens est de revêtir la nature entière d'un intérêt surnaturel qui donne à chaque objet un sens plus profond, plus volontaire, plus despotique. Sans avoir recours à l'opium, qui n'a connu ces admirables heures, véritables fêtes du cerveau, où les sens les plus attentifs perçoivent des sensations plus retentissantes, où le ciel d'un azur plus transparent s'enfonce comme un abîme plus infini, où les sons tintent musicalement, où les couleurs parlent, où les parfums racontent des mondes d'idées? Eh bien, la peinture de Delacroix me paraît la traduction de ces beaux jours d'esprit" (2: 596). Poe's own writings are compared to the experience of opium and the supernatural in *Edgar Poe, sa vie et ses œuvres* (1856): "Comme notre Eugène Delacroix, qui a élevé son art à la hauteur de la grande poésie, Edgar Poe aime à agiter ses figures sur des fonds violâtres et verdâtres . . . La nature dite inanimée participe de la nature des êtres vivants, et, comme eux, frissonne d'un frisson surnaturel et galvanique. L'espace est approfondi par l'opium; l'opium y donne un sens magique à toutes les teintes, et fait vibrer tous les bruits avec une plus significative sonorité" (2: 317-18). With a similar emphasis on the *experience* of the work of art, Baudelaire observes, apropos of Wagner, "il semble parfois, en écoutant cette musique ardente et despotique, qu'on retrouve peintes sur le fond des ténèbres, déchiré par la rêverie, les vertigineuses conceptions de l'opium" in *Richard Wagner* (1863) (2: 785).

[4] While I refer here to the aesthetic connotations of "volupté" as it is used within Baudelaire's lexicon to refer to pleasure in sensuous or artistic experience, the sensual implications of the word cannot be ignored. In *Le Sadisme de Baudelaire,* Georges Blin posits the poet's "dialectique d'*agonie*" where "volupté" and "cruauté," "jouissance et douleur" are inextricably linked and the sexual act becomes one of sadistic torture where "au couple de l'amant et l'aimée se substitue naturellement pour Baudelaire celui du 'bourreau' et de la 'victime'" (15). Hence the ruinous temptation of drugs, which provide momentary pleasure and transcendence, only to be followed by pain and regret, has a direct correlation to the poet's attitudes toward women, sex and suffering. Mickel has persuasively linked these two "voluptés" both through the probability that Baudelaire's introduction to opium some time around 1852 was in response to a bout of syphilis, and through recurrent images of impotence

and Satan, downfall and consolation, which he associates at once with women and drugs (137-8 and *passim*). I shall focus however on the "volupté"/narcotics/art association as it pertains to the poet's aesthetics.

[5] *Le Peintre de la vie moderne* presents Baudelaire's most extensive discussion of the *flâneur* and the dandy. Although the essay did not appear in *Le Figaro* until 1863, J. Crépet has dated its composition to late 1859-early 1860, which precisely corresponds to the period in which the *Paradis artificiels* were completed and published. On the cover of the 1860 edition of *Les Paradis artificiels* Baudelaire announced several upcoming studies, under the rubric "Réflexions sur quelques-uns de mes contemporains." One such projected study was "La Famille des Dandies."

[6] It is interesting to note that Benjamin exploited the narcotic metaphor in his own study of Baudelaire's *flâneur.* Without making specific reference to the *Paradis artificiels* or to Baudelaire's own implicit comparison of the *flâneur* and the *drogué,* he speaks of the crowd as "the latest narcotic for those abandoned. The *flâneur* is someone abandoned in the crowd . . . The intoxication to which the *flâneur* surrenders is the intoxication of the commodity around which surges the stream of customers" (55).

Gérald Froidevaux has also linked Baudelaire's theories of intoxication and modernity in "L'Ivresse comme 'chose moderne' chez Baudelaire" (335-342). Froidevaux likens Baudelaire's definition of modernity ("l'oxymoron pléonastique de la représentation du présent") to the effect of intoxicants, both of which induce a negation of time and a "présence-absence": "il y a donc entre la drogue et le moi le même rapport, à la fois de mise en valeur et de négation, qu'entre la représentation et le présent dans ce que Baudelaire conçoit comme la modernité" (340).

[7] This is in fact Susan Buck-Morss' gloss of Benjamin's analysis of Baudelaire's relationship to the city, the street and the commodity and his comparison of the experience of reading Baudelaire's poetry to that of strolling through the arcades.

[8] The second section of *Les Paradis artificiels, Un Mangeur d'opium,* presents a complementary enactment both of Baudelaire's theory of reader response and of how a work of art (specifically, a work of art about drugs) is experienced by a reader. As both a reader (of De Quincey) and author (of the translation), Baudelaire emphasizes the points of intersection between reading and hallucinating, while highlighting the crucial differences between active creation and passive consumption. Here, as in *Poème du haschisch,* the interpolated prose poem becomes the critical paradigm for the visual experience of the drug-induced reverie as it relies on the active participation of the reader in the text for the synthesis of meaning.

[9] See, for example, the section "De la couleur" in the *Salon de 1846,* a passage that Roger Shattuck considers

not only Baudelaire's first prose poem but also the first Impressionist painting (165-181).

[10] While the concept of a "narrative of/as performance" has been developed in depth by Shoshana Felman, Ross Chambers and Marie Maclean, among others, I posit the term here specifically to denote the textual postulation of active readerly participation within the fiction of the text, often in terms of imaginative visualization. Thus I focus upon the inscribed performance of the *reader* (i.e., the reader as performer on/in the text in an Iserian sense of the dialectics of response), rather than upon the text as performance or performative. Although, like Maclean, I envisage the reader as a kind of spectator, I do not draw here on the theatrical model which she applies to *Spleen de Paris* in *Narrative as Performance*.

[11] Baudelaire posits a strikingly similar definition of the supernatural in "Fusées": "dans certains états de l'âme presque surnaturels, la profondeur de la vie se révèle tout entière dans le spectacle, si ordinaire qu'il soit, qu'on a sous les yeux. Il en devient le symbole" (1: 659).

[12] See "Théophile Gautier," where Baudelaire observes "manier savamment une langue c'est pratiquer une espèce de sorcellerie évocatoire. C'est alors que la couleur parle, comme une voix profonde et vibrante; et que les monuments se dressent et font saillie sur l'espace profond . . . que le parfum provoque la pensée et le souvenir correspondants; que la passion murmure ou rugit son langage éternellement semblable" (2: 118). These same ideas, expressed with an almost identical vocabulary, are connected to the "surnaturel" in *Fusées* XI (1: 658-9).

WORKS CITED

Balzac, Honoré de. *La Comédie humaine*. Ed. P.-G. Castex et al. Bibliothèque de la Pléiade. Paris: Gallimard, 1976-81. 12 vols.

Baudelaire, Charles. *Correspondance*. Eds. Claude Pichois and Jean Ziegler. Bibliothèque de la Pléiade. Paris: Gallimard, 1973. 2 vols.

Baudelaire, Charles. *Œuvres Complètes*. Ed. Claude Pichois. Bibliothèque de la Pléiade. Paris: Gallimard, 1975-76. 2 vols.

Benjamin, Walter. *Charles Baudelaire. A Lyric Poet in the Era of High Capitalism*. Trans. Harry Zohn. London: Verso, 1989.

Blin, Georges. *Le Sadisme de Baudelaire*. Paris: Corti, 1948.

Buck-Morss, Susan. *The Dialectics of Seeing. Walter Benjamin and the Arcades Project*. Cambridge: MIT Press, 1989.

Fairlie, Alison. *The French Mind. Studies in Honor of Gustave Rudler*. Oxford: Clarendon P, 1952.

Ferguson, Priscilla Parkhurst. "The *Flâneur*: Urbanization and its Discontents." *Home and Its Dislocations in 19th-Century France*. Ed. Suzanne Nash. Albany: SUNY P, 1993.

Fournel, Victor. *Ce qu'on voit dans les rues de Paris*. Paris, 1858.

Froidevaux, Gérald. "L'Ivresse comme 'chose moderne' chez Baudelaire." *Neophilologus* 71 (1987): 335-342.

Maclean, Marie. *Narrative as Performance*. London: Routledge, 1988.

Mickel, Emanuel. *The Artificial Paradises in French Literature. The Influence of Opium and Hashish on French Romanticism and "Les Fleurs du mal."* Chapel Hill: UNC P, 1969.

Shattuck, Roger. "Vibratory Organism: Baudelaire's First Prose Poem." *The Innocent Eye: On Modern Literature and the Arts*. New York: Washington Square P, 1986. 165-181.

TWENTIETH-CENTURY LITERATURE

A. Carl Bredahl

SOURCE: "An Exploration of Power: Tom Wolfe's Acid Test," in *Critique: Studies in Modern Fiction*, Vol. XXIII, No. 2, Winter 1981-82, pp. 67-84.

[*In the following essay, Bredahl evaluates the differences between Tom Wolfe and the Merry Pranksters he wrote about in* The Electric Kool-Aid Acid Test, *noting that the Pranksters's rejection of the physical world as a hindrance to the development of perception, rather than a tool to aid in reaching a higher level of perception, was their downfall.*]

Tom Wolfe's writing is the most vivid instance of the role of the journalist in American literature, a role that has played a major part in the development of twentieth-century prose fiction. Unfortunately, even Wolfe himself, in his introduction to *The New Journalism* (1973), seems content to distinguish his work from that of novelists and to look for influences in "examples of non-fiction written by reporters." He does not but should recognize that the novel is a dynamic form, that in the hands of such journalists as Stephen Crane and Ernest Hemingway the novel has developed in this century just as it did in the eighteenth and nineteenth centuries. In the novel the imagination has always been concerned with particulars of a real world, a concern that has only been intensified in the twentieth century. The journalist, once depicted in literature as a mere observer and thus only a second-rate artist, has begun to emerge as an individual especially well trained to work with particulars. Certainly, all journalists are not suddenly novelists, but in several significant ways New Journalism is actually in the mainstream of the developing American novel. In *Green Hills of Africa* Hemingway speaks of pushing the art of writing prose fiction much further than it has ever gone before, and Wolfe, like Hemingway, is a writer who, instead of reporting facts for the consumption of a mass intelligence, is consuming the physical world as a part of his own nutriment. Like Hemingway eating the kudu's liver, this new journalist is thriving on the materials available to him: Ken Kesey and the Pranksters.

The Electric Kool-Aid Acid Test (1968) is a story of individuals keenly sensitive to the fact that they live in a new world and delighted by the prospect of exploring it. Tom Wolfe's story describes individuals anxious to say "Shazam" and draw new energies into themselves. Ultimately, however, they fail to become Captain Marvel:

> "We blew it!"
>
> " . . . just when you're beginning to think, 'I'm going to score' . . ."
>
> "We blew it!"[1]

Henry Adams dreamed of the child of power, but the twentieth-century child has discovered that power is not enough; the excitement of Eugene Gant must be combined with the cool skills of Hemingway. *The Electric Kool-Aid Acid Test* reflects Gant's exuberance in its free use of the medium, the language and syntax; but it is at the same time a carefully structured work. Neither an uncontrolled celebration of drugs nor an ordered documentary on Ken Kesey and the Pranksters, *The Electric Kool-Aid Acid Test* is an expression of a narrative imagination that sees the possibilities of the twentieth century embodied in the Pranksters. That imagination has discovered the need and ability to integrate both the exuberance and the structure if it is to function in a world characterized by electric energies.

Wolfe's values are evident in the book's opening sequence:

> That's good thinking there, Cool Breeze. Cool Breeze is a kid with three or four days' beard sitting next to me on the stamped metal bottom of the open back part of a pickup truck. Bouncing along. Dipping and rising and rolling on these rotten springs like a boat. Out of the back of the truck the city of San Francisco is bouncing down the hill, all those endless staggers of bay windows, slums with a view, bouncing and streaming down the hill. One after another, electric signs with neon martini glasses lit up on them, the San Francisco symbol of "bar"—thousands of neon-magenta martini glasses bouncing and streaming down the hill, and beneath them hundreds, thousands of people wheeling around to look at this freaking crazed truck we're in, their white faces erupting from their lapels like marshmallows.... Kneeling in the truck, facing us, also in plain view, is a

half-Ottawa Indian girl named Lois Jennings, with her head thrown back and a radiant look on her face. Also a blazing silver disk in the middle of her forehead alternately exploding with light when the sun hits it or sending off rainbows from the defraction lines on it. (1-2)

As one of several reporters covering Kesey's story, Wolfe comes to San Francisco with a pre-arranged idea of what his story will be—"Real-life Fugitive"—and interviews Kesey with all the usual questions. In spite of these limitations, Wolfe is moving, fascinated with the Pranksters, and able to focus on the details of the physical world. That world is one of objects that expode with an energy all their own. Nothing is static in the opening scene—faces erupt, lights explode, and the city bounces out of the back of the heaving, billowing truck. The description is, of course, that of the narrator Wolfe in contrast to the reporter Wolfe; but even as a reporter, Tom Wolfe is himself moving West, attracted to Kesey and the Pranksters.

"Stolid" and two years out of date as a result of being from the East, Wolfe enters a world that stimulates his senses rather than his mind. He has only a limited amount of information about Kesey, and his rational questions of what, when, and why are distinctly out of place in the world of day-glo paint and marshmallow faces—but he sees a great deal: Kesey

> has thick wrists and big forearms, and the way he has them folded makes them look gigantic. He looks taller than he really is, maybe because of his neck. He has a big neck with a pair of sternocleido-mastoid muscles that rise up out of the prison workshirt like a couple of dock ropes. His jaw and chin are massive. (6)

His first encounter with Kesey takes place in a jail, a sterile, rigid, and confined environment that contrasts sharply with the physically healthy individual who responds immediately to Wolfe's interest. That same contrast is also evident in the "conversation" between Wolfe and Kesey. Tom Wolfe, like the television reporter who later interviews Kesey but does not get the answers he is looking for, does not hear what Kesey is saying: "The ten minutes were up and I was out of there. I had gotten nothing, except my first brush with a strange phenomenon, that strange up-country charisma, the Kesey presence" (8). The early relationship between Wolfe and Kesey is imaged in the telephone they use to speak to each other:

> Then I pick up my telephone and he picks up his—and this is truly Modern Times. We are all of twenty-four inches apart, but there is a piece of plate glass as thick as a telephone directory between us. We might as well be in different continents, talking over Videophone. The telephones are very crackly and lo-fi, especially considering that they have a world of two feet to span. (7)

Physically they are close, but imaginatively they are miles apart. Wolfe is a note taker and instigator of talk, and Kesey's responses about moving and creativity lose Wolfe: "I didn't know what in the hell it was all about" (7). Little is *answered,* but Tom Wolfe has been "brushed" by Kesey's energy.

After leaving Kesey, Wolfe continues his journalistic efforts and investigates the environment of the Merry Pranksters: "Somehow my strongest memories of San Francisco are of me in a terrific rented sedan *roaring* up hills or down hills, *sliding* on and off the cable-car tracks. *Slipping* and *sliding* down to North Beach" (8, italics added). Moving enthusiastically but not with much control, Wolfe discovers that an old world is vanishing: "But it was not just North Beach that was dying. The whole old-style hip life—jazz, coffee houses, civil rights, invite a spade for dinner, Vietnam—it was all suddenly dying" (9). Wolfe's "blue silk blazer and . . . big tie with clowns on it" reflect that hip world, a world that Wolfe understands and enjoys. Now he stands on the edge of a new world and is "starting to get the trend of all this heaving and convulsing" (9); he is, however, one of the few. The straight world of the cops and the courts thinks in terms of keeping Kesey trapped and forcing him to preach their cause or be denounced by his friends—and the "heads" are unable to understand Kesey's talk about "beyond acid."

While these two groups want to "Stop Kesey," their efforts in essence directed at stopping movement, we get an insight into Kesey's values in the actions of his lawyers who are able to pull off the miracle of his release. They make things happen, in contrast to those who try to stop activity. In the best Ben Franklin sense of the word, Kesey "uses" people. The cops and heads are using Kesey as a tool to keep a structured environment rigid, but Kesey—like Ben—sees a world of continuous possibility in which individuals (and drugs and machines) can be of use to each other in realizing that possibility. The opening situation of the book, Kesey coming out of jail, thus embodies two major impulses in the narrative: the explosive activity of Kesey to make things happen and the efforts of those who fear change and wish to lock him up.

Tom Wolfe is responsive to his new world: "Well, for a start, I begin to see that people like Lois and Stewart and Black Maria are the restrained, reflective wing of the Merry Pranksters" (11). Wolfe is beginning to see actions and a world that glows; he also hears—"From out of the black hole of the garage comes the sound of a record by Bob Dylan and his raunchy harmonica and Ernest Tubb" (11)—and knows what he is hearing. Wolfe has possibilities of doing more than just recording data since he is both responsive and knowledgeable, but he is still unsure as to what is happening: "that was what Kesey had been talking to me about, I guess" (9).

"For two or three days it went like that for me in the garage with the Merry Pranksters waiting for Kesey" (15). Kesey is the unifying and stimulating ingredient; without him the Pranksters do not function. As Wolfe gets further into their life, he sees them as a gathering of individuals who, without Kesey, live amid a piled up "heap of electronic equipment" (21) and talk, however eloquently, about abstractions. Above all else, they wait.

> Through the sheet of sunlight at the doorway and down the incline into the crazy gloom comes a panel truck and in the front seat is Kesey. . . . Instead of saying anything, however, he cocks his head to one side and walks across the garage to the mass of wires, speakers, and microphones over there and makes some minute adjustment. . . . As if now everything is under control and the fine tuning begins. (22)

Kesey enters the gloom of the garage through a doorway of light, and with his fine tuning, Wolfe himself feels the electricity: "despite the skepticism I brought here, *I* am suddenly experiencing *their* feeling" (25).

> "Don't say stop plunging into the forest," Kesey says. "Don't stop being a pioneer and come back here and help these people through the door. If Leary wants to do that, that's good, it's a good thing and somebody should do it. But somebody has to be the pioneer and leave the marks for the others to follow." (27)

Kesey's drive is to keep moving, to explore new energies. He has no question about *whether* possibility exists or *whether* it is demonic; the energy is there, and Kesey wants to use it, go with its characteristics rather than impose his requirements on it. These qualities also characterize Wolfe's art, a skillful exploration of the possibilities of prose fiction. Together, the book and Kesey tremble with energy that can either transform Billy Batson into Captain Marvel or blow a fuse.

With Chapter Four Wolfe begins a flashback which carries through much of the book. We should remain aware, however, that though the focus is on Kesey, we are really seeing Wolfe "evaluate," take the strength from, Kesey and the Pranksters. The flashback is, then, a continuation of the narrative fascination with Kesey, a fascination that leads to Wolfe's own growth. Both Kesey and *The Electric Kool-Aid Acid Test* focus on physical objects that sparkle with life:

> That was the big high-school drive-in, with the huge streamlined sculpted pastel display sign with streaming streamlined superslick A-22 italic script, floodlights, clamp-on trays, car-hop girls in floppy blue slacks, hamburgers in some kind of tissuey wax paper steaming with onions pressed down and fried on the grill and mustard and catsup to squirt all over it from out plastic squirt cylinders. (34)

No corresponding attention is paid to the talk *about* life. The Perry Lane sophisticates turn "back to first principles" (31) of Greece, but Kesey is into the modern western hero who is capable of transformation into a being of superhuman energies: "A very Neon Renaissance—And the myths that actually touched you at that time—not Hercules, Orpheus, Ulysses, and Aeneas—but Superman, Plastic Man, The Flash" (35). The power of the verbal "Shazam," like the new drug LSD, sparks an electrical power surge which makes an individual begin "traveling and thinking at the speed of light" (35). Attuned to this new power, Kesey is able to see detail and movement:

> The ceiling is moving—not in a crazed swirl but along its own planes of light and shadow and surface not nearly so nice and smooth as plasterer Super Plaster Man intended with infallible carpenter level bubble sliding in dim honey Karo syrup tube not so foolproof as you thought, but, little lumps and ridges up there, bub, and lines, lines like spines on crests of waves of white desert movie sand each one with MGM shadow longshot of the ominous A-rab coming over the next crest for only the sinister Saracen can see the road and you didn't know how many subplots you left up there, Plaster man, trying to smooth it *all* out, *all* of it, with your bubble in a honey tube carpenter's level, to make us all down here look up and see nothing but ceiling, because we all know ceiling, because it has a *name,* ceiling, therefore it is nothing but a ceiling—no room for A-rabs up there in Level Land, eh, Plaster man. (36-37)

He can also see the muscles in the doctor's face or his pulse as an accurate measure of his life or Chief Broom as the key to his new novel. As his perception is altered, Kesey becomes aware of a potentially frightening world where few people want to go but which is also a place where a moving line can suddenly become a nose, "the very miracle of creation itself" (40).

Kesey's early activities after taking LSD are burstings forth of "vital energy" (41). The move to La Honda, the appearance of the intrepid traveller, and the bus trip are all forms of this eruption. The bus trip "Further," like the flashback technique Wolfe uses in his narrative, is a movement back in preparation for new directions. The bus heads *East* toward the old intellectual world of the Learyites and Europe. The trip carries the Merry Pranksters down through the pressure-cooker heat of the South, something like the first stages of a sauna bath where the body is flushed of internal poisons. The trip back culminates in "the Crypt Trip" where the pressure is of a different kind. The Pranksters expect to be received joyously, but all along the road they encounter a variety of threatening responses. When they visit the Learyites, they discover that the "Pranksters' Ancestral Mansion" (94) is not a home; rather its "sepulchral" atmosphere and "Tibetan Book of the Dead" (95) emphasize that the Pranksters have broken off from the intellectual Eastern world:

> . . . the trouble with Leary and his group is that they have turned *back*. But of course! They have turned back into that old ancient New York intellectual thing, ducked back into the Romantic past, copped out of the American trip. New York intellectuals have always looked for . . . another country, a fatherland of the mind, where it is all better and more philosophic and purer, gadget-free, and simpler and pedigreed. (100)

The Pranksters are a new group, living in a new world. They have no roots and must seek their life in constant discovery. When they emerge from the Crypt, they turn westward, but the bus now takes the cooler, Northern route. The trip ultimately integrates and unifies the Pranksters; they become a special group rather than a collection of idiosyncratic individuals.

Kesey's interest in energy and art have also been developed while on this "risk-all balls-out plunge into the unknown" (78). Simply becoming aware, sensitive to power is not enough:

> Kesey said he wanted them all to do their thing and be Pranksters, but he wanted them to be deadly competent, too. . . . They should always be alert, always alive to the moment, always deep in the whole group thing, and be deadly competent. (88)

Being alive to the moment is integrally related to Kesey's particular understanding of art. For him art is a way of getting totally into the now, a world where one experiences an event at exactly the same time it is occurring: "The whole *other world* that LSD opened your mind to existed only in the moment itself—*Now*—and any attempt to plan, compose, orchestrate, write a script, only locked you out of the moment, back in the world of conditioning and training where the brain was a reducing valve" (52). While Kesey wants to be the artist who can organize such an experience, he also wants an art form that does not determine the experience. Being trapped in the rules of syntax and the referential properties of language, while it allowed him to break through the "all-American crap" earlier, would destroy his present commitment to the now. In pointing to the bus and in creating the miracle in seven days and the acid tests, Kesey imagines an artist who can artifically create conditions but not the experience of the work. Each individual must do that—get on the bus—for himself.

"It could be scary out there in Freedom land. The Pranksters were friendly, but they glowed in the dark" (107). The frightening power of the new electricity is epitomized in the Hell's Angels:

> The Angels brought a lot of things into synch. Outlaws, by definition, were people who had moved off of dead center and were out in some kind of Edge City. The beauty of it was, the Angels had done it like the Pranksters, by choice. They had become outlaws first—to *explore,* muvva—and then got busted for it. The Angels' trip was the motorcycle and the Pranksters' was LSD, but both were in an incredible entry into orgasmic moment, *now.* (152)

As the Angels' motorcycles roar into La Honda, the energy that has been discovered and explored thus far surges forth. It is not just a test of the Pranksters; it is an event which embodies just how far the Pranksters have gone in their exploration of power. No group in America could seem more demonic than the Angels, but their tremendous energies are now being taken into the Pranksters and used by a group of highly skilled individuals. What could have been a "time bomb" (159) becomes instead a vibrating two-day party.

With all the energies of the Angels in their movie, the Pranksters are now able to achieve a "miracle in seven days." This chapter is at the center of the book and culminates the efforts of Kesey to get in tune with his environment, discover the Power that is available, and use that Power through his own art to bring others to see what it it like out on Edge City. What the conference allows Kesey to do is demonstrate that he is able to make his current fantasy work. When it is all over, "it's like all the Pranksters' theories and professed beliefs have been put to a test in the outside world, away from La Honda, and they're working now, and they have . . . Control" (170).

So that creative impulse to burst forth from the all-American crap, an impulse that is the driving force during the first part of the book, culminates in an artistic production that is non-verbal and unprogrammed. The actors and audience become one movie—but something is wrong:

> Kesey also had his court appearances to contend with and more lying, finking, framing, politicking by the constables than a body could believe—he looked like he had aged ten years in three months. He was now some indeterminate age between thirty and forty. He was taking a lot of speed and smoking a lot of grass. He looked haggard, and when he looked haggard, his face seemed lopsided. (172-73)

The final word of the chapter is "Control," and the last few pages stress "Power," but the lives of the Merry Pranksters are soon to become like a nuclear reactor that has gone beyond critical mass. The image of energy bursting forth, impulsing outward, which dominates the first half of the book, is the same image which dominates the second, but that energy is rapidly getting out of control.

Kesey's efforts have been to discover and release energy; he is beginning to find, however, that that energy may not be easily handled. Two chapters demonstrate what is happening: the one which closes the first part of the book, "The Hell's Angels," and the one which opens the second, "Cloud." In the Hell's Angels chapter the Pranksters welcome tremendous outlaw energies into their movie—"The Merry Pranksters Welcome the Hell's Angels." The situation is the same in "Cloud"—"The Merry Pranksters Welcome the Beatles"—but what had worked in the earlier chapter becomes ugly and dangerous in the second. The Beatles fantasy is an effort to continue moving, but now the vibrations are bad because the value that Kesey has been striving for—Control—is absent:

> It is like the whole thing has snapped, and the whole front section of the arena becomes a writhing, seething mass of little girls waving their arms in the air . . . and they have utter control over them—but they don't know what in the hell to do with it. (182)

Instead of energy working, the Pranksters find themselves in a pen in which "mindless amok energy" (185) threatens to become a cancer, uncontrolled and self-consuming.

The implications of that cancer are developed in the chapters after "Cloud," but one would be mistaken to suggest that the first part of the book does one thing and the second part something different. Rather, the factors that result in the blown fuse are present during the early successful activities of the Pranksters; they have just gone unrecognized by Kesey (but not by Wolfe—since they are part of his narrative). They are integral aspects of some of Kesey's major assumptions. The problem is evident in the opening of "Cloud," the chapter in which the energy becomes cancerous.

> They lie there on the mattresses, with Kesey rapping on and on and Mountain Girl trying to absorb it. Ever since Asilomar, Kesey has been deep in to the religion thing . . . on and on he talks to Mountain Girl out in the backhouse and very deep and far-out stuff it is, too. Mountain Girl tries to concentrate, but the words swim like great waves of. . . . Her mind keeps rolling and spinning over another set of data, always the same, Life—the eternal desperate calculation. In short, Mountain Girl is pregnant. (177)

Kesey has gotten so completely into his current fantasy that he has lost touch with the physical environment he is seeking to touch. Mountain Girl is pregnant, but Kesey is unaware. She is about to bring forth life, but Kesey is sensitive only to ideas.

Evidence of the difficulty appeared in Chapter Eleven when the Merry Pranksters returned from their trip East having discovered a new unity: "What they all saw in . . . a flash was the solution to the basic predicament of being *human,* the personal *I, Me,* trapped, mortal and helpless, in a vast impersonal *It,* the world around me" (114). Kesey began with the urge to create from within himself and to involve himself in his world, drives which suggest a need to experience fully what it means to be human. But in Chapter Eleven the implication is that being human has become a "predicament" that needs to be altered. At the same time, however, the movie is demanding some very human skills if it is not to become its own uncontrolled cancer:

> But the Movie was a monster . . . the sheer labor and tedium in editing forty-five hours of film was unbelievable. And besides . . . much of the film was out of focus. . . . But who needs that old Hollywood thing of long shot, medium shot, closeup, and the careful cuts and wipes and pans and dolly in and dolly out, the old bullshit. Still, plunging in on those miles of bouncing, ricocheting, blazing film with a splicer was like entering a jungle where the greeny vines grew faster than you could chop them down in front of you. (122)

The cutting needed in the jungle or in the editing of the movie *requires* a human response that is not just a submersion of the individual into the physical, a submersion that is implied in the statement, "Suddenly!—All-in-one!—flowing together, *I* into *It,* and *It* into *Me,* and in that flow I perceive a power, so near and so clear, that the whole world is blind to" (114). These words have Emersonian overtones, where the individual is in danger of losing his individuality—or where he can lose his ability to see the particular because he has become intellectual.

Chapter Eleven explores the human "predicament" as Kesey understands it, talking of Cassady:

> A person has all sorts of lags built into him, Kesey is saying. One, the most basic, is the sensory lag, the lag between the time your senses receive something and you are able to react. . . . He is a living example of how close you can come, but it can't be done. You can't go any faster than that. You can't through sheer speed overcome the lag. We are all of us doomed to spend our lives watching a movie of our lives. . . . That lag has to be overcome some other way, through some kind of total breakthrough . . . nobody can be creative without overcoming all those lags first. (129)

Kesey's statement that no one can be creative—that the creative impulse cannot burst forth and fully express itself—without overcoming this lag, this humanity, invites a potentially destructive conflict between his beliefs and the physical properties of his environment. Once the lag is ended, the individual will be completely in tune with the pattern: "one could *see* the larger pattern and move with it—Go with the flow!—and accept it and rise above one's immediate environment and even alter it by accepting the larger pattern and grooving with it" (129). However, they are left with "the great morass of a movie, with miles and miles of spiraling spliced-over film and hot splices billowing around them like so many intertwined, synched, but still chaotic and struggling human lives" (131). Such a life is Mountain Girl's and in all the theory and talk, Kesey has missed that individual. The loneliness and pregnancy of Mountain Girl, an individual who is so thoroughly a Prankster, calls attention to the dependency upon Kesey that most, if not all, the Pranksters have developed. "Kesey was essential to Mountain Girl's whole life with the Pranksters" (149) just as he was essential to the success of the party with the Hell's Angels. Kesey's initial urge had been personal, and he sought to extend his own perception while also stimulating others to begin perceiving for themselves. The Pranksters—as well as those drawn into their movie—should be developing that individuality, but their dependency on Kesey's energy has apparently limited their ability to concentrate and explore their own. What was to have stimulated the individual to discover himself has become a social enterprise where the group is dependent on a leader. If such a problem is developing, the removal of that leader ought to bring movement to a halt and perhaps to cause that tightly welded unit to disintegrate. These problems develop in the second part of the book, the section that begins with power out of control at the Beatles' concert and with the power surge in New York that blows all the city's fuses and transformers (190).

Events in the book, then, have begun to anticipate the breakup of the Merry Pranksters. In "Departures" Kesey prepares to head for Mexico, for the first time responding to the actions of others—the police—rather than initiating action himself, and Mountain Girl goes to New York to try to get herself back together. Sandy also leaves for New York, again the victim of what for him will apparently always be "the demon Speed." As if to emphasize the social thrust of their recent activities, the two chapters preceding Kesey's trip focus on the skills of the Pranksters "to extend the message to all people," with Kesey very prominently at the controls. No longer is each individual Prankster striving to become deadly competent, a functioning individual alive to the moment. Rather each is concentrating entirely on the collective enterprise of conveying their "message"—with all the verbal and social connotations of that word—to a group. Instead of the effort of the individual to go "further," the Pranksters create an authorized, organized Now.

The Mexican chapters parallel in many ways the earlier bus trip, but where the pressure cooker had then been restricted to the heat of the sun, now Kesey and those with him are subjected to disease, filth, and death. What had been an intellectual crypt trip now becomes almost too real. Wolfe's handling of the opening scene in Mexico is both a vivid description of the paranoid state into which Kesey has fallen and a major indicator of the developing difference between Kesey and Wolfe. Earlier, Wolfe had been stimulated by Kesey's skill, but now Wolfe himself is demonstrating that skill. Kesey's helpless mental state is presented with an incredibly sharp eye for detail:

> Kesey sits in this little rickety upper room with his elbow on a table and his forearm standing up perpendicular and in the palm of his hand a little mirror, so that his forearm and the mirror are like a big rear-view mirror stanchion on the side of a truck and thus he can look out the window and see them but they can't see him. . . . Kesey has Cornel Wilde Running Jacket ready hanging on the wall, a jungle-jim corduroy jacket stashed with fishing line, a knife, money, DDT, tablet, ball-points, flashlight, and grass. (200)

Kesey is seeing very little—his mind is alive largely to the details of his latest fantasy—but Wolfe is able both to focus on the reality of Kesey's world and to convey the quality of Kesey's paranoid experience, each second of which lasts no more than a minute and is agonizingly detailed and examined in the best Prankster day-glo color. Wolfe is in control, and in his hands the verbal medium comes alive.

Kesey's energies are also alive but trapped within himself—not the artificial rules of syntax. His tremendous energies are still there, and they continue to pull people back to him: Black Maria and Mountain Girl, now back with the Pranksters and eight months pregnant—as well as some Pranksters left at La Honda—begin to regroup in Mexico. What they find there is the ugly world in which

Kesey has been living: "All the vibrations outside were bad. Corpses, chiefly. Scrub cactus, brown dung dust and bloated corpses, dogs, coyotes, armadillos, a cow, all gas-bellied and dead, swollen and dead. . . . This was the flow, and it was a sickening horrible flow" (275). The intensity of the Mexican experience is epitomized in "The Red Tide," "a poison as powerful as aconitine" which is produced by the plankton in the ocean waters and which is death to the fish. That death mirrors the death on the land where the Pranksters are "stranded like flies in this 110-degree mucus of Manzanillo" (280-81). The red tide and the Mexican disaster are less efforts at journalistic accuracy than metaphors for the Prankster experience at a time when death and stagnation are as much a part of their lives as they are in the filthy pressure-cooker world of the environment. The drugs which were opening doors earlier are now only a means to escape the heat.

Under these same conditions, however, Mountain Girl has her baby, her dyed hair gradually returns to its natural state, and Kesey begins to see what is happening to them: "They have made the trip now, closed the circle, all of them, and they either emerge as Superheros, closing the door behind them and soaring through the hole in the sapling sky, or just lollygag in the loop-the-loop of the lag . . . either make this thing permanent inside of you or forever just climb draggled up into the conning tower every time for one short glimpse of the horizon" (290). The "current fantasy" has become just that, a fantasy; they have lost contact with reality. "Mommy, this movie is no fun any more, it's too *real*, Mommy" (299). That reality—in the form of the Mexican police—reaches out to capture Kesey but succeeds only in spurring him into activity: "It was time to get the Movie going on all projectors. And the bus" (301).

Kesey's return to California is a curious mixture of continuing to live in fantasy and yet wanting to get back in touch with the environment, separate values that mirror Kesey's own state of mind—"Kesey veering wildly from paranoia and hyper-security to extraordinary disregard for his own safety, one state giving way to the other in no fixed order" (312). His commitment is once again to movement, this time beyond acid and beyond the stagnant condition of the tests which have quickly become the in-thing, the sport of college students and New York intellectuals. Kesey is once again probing the "westernmost edge of experience" (323), and that scares those who are content to remain where they are. It is the Hell's Angels side of the Kesey adventure that panics the hip world because the Angels are "too freaking real. *Outlaws* . . . the heads of Haight-Asbury could never stretch their fantasy as far out as the Hell's Angels" (326).

Kesey is also having to work his imagination; at the moment he is theorizing and playing a game of cops-and-robbers with the California authorities:

> It will be a masked ball, this Test. Nobody will know which freak is who. At the midnight hour,

Kesey, masked and disguised in a Super-hero costume, on the order of Captain America of the Marvel Comics pantheon, will come up on stage and deliver his vision of the future, of the way "beyond acid." *Who is this apocalyptic*—Then he will rip off his mask—Why—it's Ken Kee-zee!—and as the law rushes for him, he will leap up on a rope hanging down from the roof at center stage and climb, hand over hand, without even using his legs, with his cape flying, straight up, up, up, up through a trap door in the roof, to where Babbs will be waiting with a helicopter, Captain Midnight of the U. S. Marines, and they will ascend into the California ozone. (328)

This seems less movement than fantasizing, less Captain Mavel than a child who is exercising his power to defy authority. Once again Kesey finds that "the current fantasy . . . this movie is too real, Mommy" (329). Appropriately, Kesey's capture is put in terms of a little boy with torn pants.

The last chapter of *The Electric Kool-Aid Acid Test* details the anticlimax of Kesey's efforts to go beyond acid; they blow it. In the final scene, the Pranksters who are striving to move are sitting on the floor of the Warehouse surrounded by too much noise and too many TV cameras. Whatever Kesey has been driving for is imaged as a much publicized stagnation: "It's like a wake" (366). Wolfe has later said that during the abstract expressionist movement of the 1950's,

> The artists themselves didn't seem to have the faintest notion of how primary Theory was becoming. I wonder if the theorists themselves did. All of them, artist and theorists, were talking as if their conscious aim was to create a totally immediate art, lucid, stripped of all the dreadful baggage of history, an art fully revealed, honest, as honest as the flat-out integral picture plane.[2]

To a Prankster as well as an abstract expressionist this passage might appear an irritatingly inaccurate evaluation of their activities, but it indicates much about Wolfe's own artistic values and does indeed point to the crucial weakness in the Prankster way of life. The emphasis in the passage is on the Word in its most sterile form: and it is this that would annoy the Pranksters because their whole effort is dedicated to going beyond an abstract verbalization which is the epitome of the distance between the event and the experiencing of it.

The desire to open oneself up to the world, not unique with the Pranksters, allows us to see them in the mainstream of American thought and literature reaching back through Hemingway, Whitehead, Melville, Thoreau, and Emerson to Franklin and the Puritans. Whitehead's emphasis on creativity and novelty illustrates the potential vitality of the Pranksters:

> "Creativity" is the principle of *novelty*. An actual occasion is a novel entity diverse from any entity in the "many" which it unifies. Thus "creativity" introduces novelty into the content of the many,

which are the universe disjunctively. The "creative advance" is the application of this ultimate principle of creativity to each novel situation which originates.[3]

The world is continually being "renewed"; there is no stasis, no biblical Garden of Eden. Kesey's concern with "beyond acid" is absolutely right, for it indicates continuing novelty; however, when he says that we are "doomed" to watch our lives and that without overcoming lag "nobody can be creative" (219), his stress is not on movement but on goal, one that is disturbingly Edenic. At such a theoretical point, the world might be moving but the individual would be carried along with it.

Kesey points to Cassady as someone "going as fast as a human can go, but even he can't overcome it. He is a living example of how close you can come, but it can't be done. You can't go any faster than that" (129). Cassady, however, is an individual who burns himself out, and Kesey's praise of Cassady should warn us of dangers implicit in Kesey's drives. When Kesey starts to talk about overcoming rather than opening, his drives become self-destructive rather than liberating. In addition, the existence of Wolfe's art indicates that, far from limiting creativity, lag is what makes creativity possible. Kesey urges the Pranksters to "go with the flow," but the danger, as any defensive tackle will verify, is always that such movement can result in being swept along. Kesey's interest is in the ability to perceive and evaluate flow so as to develop not dissolve individuality. Such perception necessitates lag. The discovery and assertion of personal skills—"The most powerful drive in the ascent of man," says Jacob Bronowski, "is the pleasure in his own skill"—is not a goal but a process that demands vision and objectivity. Kesey has all the right impulses, but when he begins to talk about overcoming lag, he is in danger either of becoming self-destructive or of being swept along by the flow.

While Kesey sees goals and ideas, Wolfe sees objects:

> But my mind is wandering. I am having a hard time listening because I am fascinated by a little plastic case with a toothbrush and toothpaste in it that Hassler has tucked under one thumb. . . . Here Hassler outlines a pyramid in the air with his hands and I watch, fascinated, as the plastic toothbrush case shiny shiny slides up one incline of the pyramid. (18)

Ultimately, the difference between Wolfe and the Pranksters is evidenced in Wolfe's ability to keep his narrative eye focused on the physical world of the Pranksters and to unify *The Electric Kool-Aid Acid Test* in contrast to the talk and endless feet of film and electrical wires that the Pranksters can never manage to bring together. Kesey worries that his experience cannot be verbalized: "But these are *words*, man! *And you couldn't put it into words.* The white Smocks liked to put it into words, like *hallucination* and *dissociative phenomena*" (40). Wolfe, however, goes for the vitality rather than the intellectual abstraction, a quality that distinguishes him from the reporters who come to cover the story of redeveloping Perry Lane:

> The papers turned up to write about the last night on Perry Lane, noble old Perry Lane, and had the old cliche at the ready, End of an Era, expecting to find some deep-thinking latter-day Thorstein Veblen intellectuals on hand with sonorous bitter statements about this machine civilization devouring its own past.
>
> Instead, there were some kind of *nuts* out there. They were up in a tree lying on a mattress, all high as coons. . . . but they managed to go back with the story they came with, End of an Era, the cliche intact. (48)

These men see with their clean, structured minds; thus the cliches. But Tom Wolfe is able to open his eyes and see the vitality of the Prankster world. His willingness to look rather than to theorize allows him to perceive "shape and pattern" in his verbal exploration of the Pranksters. The result is a functioning narrative voice in an exciting new world: "That's good thinking there, Cool Breeze. Cool Breeze is a kid with three or four days' beard sitting next to me on the stamped metal bottom of the open back part of a pickup truck. Bouncing along. Dipping and rising and rolling on these rotten springs like a boat" (1). Good thinking and movement and concrete objects—these are Tom Wolfe's values.

Kesey and Wolfe share many of the same values, but Wolfe succeeds where Kesey and the Pranksters blow it because Wolfe is able to look at physical laws as something to be used to one's advantage—evaluated—rather than as frustrations to be overcome. *The Electric Kool-Aid Acid Test* is thus a book about art, about the individual's effort to get it all together. Telling one's story and getting one's skills finely tuned are finally the same thing. Kesey has the skills to tune a piece of machinery, but he is also interested in fine tuning himself. Ultimately, he and the Pranksters fail to look at themselves or at each other as individuals (the Who Cares girl) just as they prefer to look at the physical world as metaphor rather than object. Games, roles, metaphors, and abstractions become Prankster values in spite of their talk about opening doors and going further. Tom Wolfe's uniqueness is his recognition that perception and skill must be developed together, that one can only discover his strengths by evaluating his environment.

NOTES

[1] Tom Wolfe, *The Electric Kool-Aid Acid Test* (New York: Bantam Books, 1969), p. 368. Subsequent references are to this edition.

[2] Tom Wolfe, *The Painted Word* (New York: Farrar, Straus and Giroux, 1975), p. 63.

[3] Alfred North Whitehead, *Process and Reality* (New York: The Free Press, 1969), p. 26.

Kulwant Singh Gill

SOURCE: "Aldous Huxley: The Quest for Synthetic Sainthood," in *Modern Fiction Studies,* Vol. 27, No. 4, Winter, 1981-82, pp. 601-612.

[*In the following essay, Gill discusses Aldous Huxley's experimentations with LSD as a means of reaching spiritual enlightenment, concluding that Huxley ultimately failed because of his inability to overcome his "intellectual baggage."*]

I

Aldous Huxley's Interest in psychedelics stems from his deep-rooted concern for the spiritual malaise of modern life. Though he started his literary career on a note of agnosticism,[1] adopted an attitude of "pawky playfulness" toward eternal verities,[2] and debunked mysticism as an ideal,[3] his later writings affirm his belief in the Ultimate Reality. His analysis of the human situation brought about the conviction that modern man is spiritually sick because he has alienated himself from the Divine Reality or the Godhead that, according to Huxley, is "the unmanifested principle of all manifestation" and that "to realize this supreme identity is the final end and purpose of human existence."[4] As an advocate of mysticism, Huxley suggests mediation as a method "for acquiring knowledge about the essential nature of things, a method for establishing communion between the soul and the integrating principle of the universe."[5] But his experience also showed him that contemplation, as J. B. Coates puts it, "becomes increasingly more difficult in an age whose tempo is determined by the machine."[6] So, he tried to explore the avenues of spiritual reality through psychedelics with a view to discovering an easy means to self-transcendence for modern man. He recorded his psychedelic experiences in *The Doors of Perception* (1954), which, according to Bernard S. Aaronson and Humphry Osmond, "marks the beginning of the modern psychedelic movement."[7] Because he was the first well-known writer to assert that chemicals can lead to self-transcendence, his assertions have raised the most fundamental question about the possibility of synthetic sainthood.

Laura Archera Huxley points out that "One of Aldous's chief aims in life was the extension of consciousness."[8] He experimented with mind-manifesting drugs only to ascertain their impact on consciousness. His conclusions, however, led some critics to brand him as the prophet of LSD who found God in a bottle and whose advocacy of LSD led to the promotion of hippie culture. R. E. L. Masters and Jean Houston observe that the "contemporary quest for the artificial induction of religious experiences through the use of psycho-chemicals became a controversial issue with the publication of Huxley's *Doors of Perception* in 1954."[9] This paper is an attempt to examine Huxley's assertions with regard to the spiritual nature of a chemically-induced experience and to ascertain the possibility of synthetic sainthood.

The idea that chemical means to transcendence are perhaps as good as the traditional methods of fasting and prayer also occurs in Huxley's early fiction. As an agnostic, Huxley believed that the fruit of spiritual life was ecstasy and that to induce ecstasy one need not sit on the gazelle skin and squint at the top of one's nose for hours, because ecstasy can be chemically produced. He comments on the artificial production of the state of mystical trance: "Every symptom of the trance, from the 'sense of presence' to total unconsciousness, can be produced artificially in the laboratory."[10] Miles Fanning, the central character in the story "After the Fireworks," echoes his author's idea that opium is "as good a way of becoming supernatural as looking at one's nose or one's naval, or not eating, or repeating a word over and over again."[11]

Moreover, it was Huxley's intense longing to seek enternity that made him experiment with drugs that, at least temporarily, led to some kind of self-transcendence. In *Antic Hay* (1923) Huxley raises the question: "Who lives longer; the man who takes heroin for two years and dies, or the man who lives on roast beef, water, and potatoes till ninety-five? One passes his twenty-four months in eternity. All the years of the beef-eater are lived only in time."[12] Because drugs induce a state of timelessness, bring elation to the user, and lead to an experience that shares some attributes of the mystical experience, it has been assumed by the advocates of psychedelics that these drugs lead to a genuine spiritual experience. The modern neophyte need not undergo the traditional ascetical discipline to prepare himself for the mystical experience; the pharmacist can help him seek the experience of the Divine Reality without all those physical discomforts that have been regarded by mystics as the most indispensable requirement for such experience.

Huxley goes back to the religious rites of primitive peoples to show that intoxicants had been an essential part of their religious worship. He points out that "the drug-induced experience has been regarded by primitives and even by the highly civilized as intrinsically divine."[13] R. G. Wasson and V. Wasson certify in their monumental study *Mushrooms, Russia and History* (1957) that the plants containing psychedelic substances have been a part of the religious worship of peoples belonging to cultures widely distributed over the world. There is no denying the fact that the intoxicants have been an important part of the religious rites of ancient peoples. But the drug alone was never considered sufficient to generate the required mystical experience. It merely acted as a stimulant to make the mind suggestive to religious prayers. *Soma* was, of course, used by the Aryans as a help to mystical experience, and the drug is addressed in the highest strains of adulation and veneration in the *Rigveda*. But *soma* alone was never sufficient to give them the experience of Ultimate Reality. Adolf Kaegi aptly observes that "Indra, the ruler of battles, takes no pleasure in the Soma offered without prayer; he scorns the sacrifical food prepared without a song."[14] Even in Vedic times, prayer, or the mortification of the self, was considered an essential precondition to attain a union with the *Brahman.* Moreover, the *Vedas* are a record of the mystical utterances of the ancient Aryans, and some of the sublimest utterances are mixed with the superstitious character of these archaic people. When we come to the *Upanishads,* which mark a more philosophical and speculative stage of Indian thought, we do not find any specific importance given to *soma* as a means of mystical experience. In the *Bhagavad-Gita, soma* is referred to only in a single *sloka* (IX:20),[15] and it does not enjoy any specific importance as a means of God-realization. The *Bhagavad-Gita* stresses three ways to seek the mystical experience: the *Karma Marga* (the way of action), the *jña na marga* (the way of knowledge), and the *Bhakti Marga* (the way of love). Huxley, too, in his anthology of mysticism, *The Perennial Philosophy* (1936), nowhere talks about drugs as *the* valid means of seeking salvation. No doubt the use of certain hemp derivatives such as hashish, bhang, or ganja is still prevalent in India. These intoxicants form a part of the religious worship of certain tantric cults. For instance, hashish is smoked by the Shaivites who worship Shiva, the Creator and Destroyer, Who Himself is said to have smoked hashish. Similarly, the *Nihangs,* a militant sikh sect, use bhang as a part of their daily ritual. But it is difficult to justify Masters and Houston's claim that "an estimated ninety percent of the Indian holy men use hemp, often along with other drugs."[16] And then, there is no evidence to suggest that the tantric yogis or the *Nihangs* undergo any kind of spiritual transformation by taking hashish or bhang.

II

Huxley was not the first Western intellectual to experiment with mind-changing drugs. Before him William James and Havelock Ellis had tried these drugs to learn about their impact on consciousness. Writing about his own experience under nitrous oxide, James asserts that his experience was one of reconciliation, with all conflicts melting into unity. It brought him "intense metaphysical illumination." James writes: "The centre and periphery of things seem come together. The ego and its objects, the *meum* and *tuum* are one."[17] James, however, does not try to interpret his experience in religious terms. As an empiricist, he states just facts as he finds them. Like Huxley, he does not attempt to equate his experience with the genuine mystical experience.

There are, of course, a number of important writers to whom the psychedelic experience seems of utmost spiritual significance. Allen Ginsberg insists that marijuana consciousness shifts attention from "second-hand ideological interpretations of experience to more *direct, slower, absorbing, occasionally microscopically minute, engagement with sensing phenomena* during the high moments or hours after one has smoked."[18] Alan Watts also points out that during the LSD experience he found himself "going through states of consciousness that corresponded precisely with every description of major mystical experience."[19] John W. Aiken, the founder of the Church of the Awakening, also claims that "a properly oriented psychedelic experience can be a deep and genu-

ine religious experience."[20] Walter N. Pahnke's laboratory experiments with drugs suggest that some subjects under the drug reported that they had undergone profound spiritual experience.[21] Masters and Houston also observe that "out of their total of 206 subjects, six have had the mystical experience."[22]

There are also writers who claim that the drug can never promote any genuine religious experience. It is difficult for them to accept Timothy Leary's claim that the "LSD kick is a spiritual esctasy" and the LSD trip "a religious pilgrimage."[23] For example, R. C. Zaehner does not give any credit to drug-induced experience because his own mescalin experience ushered him into "a world of non-sensical fantasy." He experienced neither esctasy nor eternity during his mescal experience. Zaechner says that "the experience was in a sense 'anti-religious' and that 'self-transcendence' of a sort did take place, but transcendence into a world of farcical meaninglessness."[24] The effort here has been made to suggest that there is no unanimity among the intelligent with regard to the nature of psychedelic experience.

III

Huxley took mescalin because it had always seemed possible to him that "by means of systematic meditation, or else by taking the appropriate drug, I might so change my ordinary mode of consciousness as to be able to know, from the inside, what the visionary, the medium, even the mystic were talking about."[25] He admits that the experience proved of infinite value to him. Under the impact of the drug, he realized that being and becoming, *nirv na* and *sams ra,* are one and the same thing. Mescalin gave him a peep into that "other world" about which he had been writing so emphatically for so many years. Huxley says, "The Beatific Vision, *Sat, Chit, Ananda,* Being-Awareness-Bliss-for the first time I understood, not by inchoate hints or at a distance, but precisely and completely what those prodigious syllables referred to" (*Doors,* p. 18).

He describes his experience under mescalin as "the sacramental vision of reality" (*Doors,* p. 22). Whereas the first experience showed no interest in human affairs, the second experience has "a human content, which the earlier solitary experience with its Other Worldly quality . . . did not possess."[26] Another mescalin experience made him realize that love is the fundamental cosmic fact, that *Nirvana* apart from the world, apart from *Mahakaruna* for sentient beings, is as terrible as the pains of hell. As his experiences under the drug increase, the generalizations about experience become more bold, and the earlier cautious attitude is replaced by confident, assertive statements. Moreover, he is more emphatic about it in his private correspondence than in his literary writings. About the psychedelic experience, he wrote to his friend Dr. Humphry Osmond: "What emerges as a general conclusion is the confirmation of the fact that mescalin does genuinely open the door and that everything including the Unknown in its purest, most comprehensive form can come through" (*Letters,* p. 771). In a letter to Victoria Ocampo, Huxley affirms that mescalin took him "beyond the realm of vision to the realm of what the mystics call 'obscure knowledge,' insight into the nature of things." He admits that the drug also brought him "the realization that, in spite of pain and tragedy, the Universe is all right, in other words that God is Love" (*Letters,* p. 802). Father Merton wrote to Huxley, raising a number of objections to the validity of the psychedelic mystical experience. Like Dean Inge,[27] Merton found it hard to accept drugs as a means to religious experience. Huxley's reply to him again affirms his positive attitude toward the drug-induced experience. He writes:

> In the course of the last five years I have taken mescalin twice and lysergic acid three or four times. My first experience was mainly aesthetic. Later experiences . . . helped me to understand many of the obscure utterances to be found in the writings of the mystics, Christian and Oriental. An unspeakable sense of gratitude for the privelege of being born into this universe. . . . A transcendence of the ordinary subject-object relationship. A transcendence of the fear of death. A sense of solidarity with the world and its spiritual principle . . . an understanding, not intellectual, but in some sort total, an understanding with the entire organism, of the affirmation that God is Love. (*Letters,* p. 863)

Similarly, in a letter to Margaret Isherwood (*Letters,* p. 874), Huxley reiterates his stand on mescalin. He tells her that he was able to go beyond vision into the genuine mystical experience. From his correspondence, it becomes quite evident that his psychedelic experiences confirmed his conviction that drugs can generate a genuine mystical experience. It is precisely for this reason that he advocates psychedelics in his "pragmatic dream," *Island,* which, according to Huxley, contains "practical instructions for the imagined and desirable harmonization of European and Indian insights become a fact" (*Letters,* p. 944). In this novel, Huxley seems to give his valedictory message to his readers. He exhorts people to try LSD, which he names "the *moksha*-medicine, the reality-revealer, the truth-and-beauty pill."[28] The inhabitants of *Island* use this *moksha*-medicine to get experience of Divine Reality, the Clear Light of the Void. Robert Macphail, the chief spokesman of the philosophy of *Island,* is, like Huxley, quite anxious to defend the use of psychedelics by the inhabitants of the island. He asserts that they are not "a set of self-indulgent dope-takers, wallowing in illusions and false *samadhis.*"[29] He urges Will Farnaby, the neurotic, Western journalist who is totally skeptical about the existence of Ultimate Reality, to try the drug to know its effect. Will takes the *moksha*-medicine and experiences a new level of consciousness. From the description of his experience, it seems that Will gets a direct, unconceptual understanding of Ultimate Reality. Such an assertion raises the most fundamental question: can we place Will Farnaby and Huxley in the category of mystics because they describe their psychedelic experiences in religious terms?

IV

Huxley's advocacy of psychedelics in *Island* has been bitterly criticized by the Establishment, which has accused him of corrupting youth. Masters and Houston observe that, to some extent, the responsibility for the seduction of the innocent lies with authors like Huxley and Alan Watts who "in their various writings imposed upon the psychedelic experience essentially Eastern ideas and terminology."[30] Huxley had absolutely no intention of misleading anybody. His chief mission in life was to dispel ignorance and to make men aware of the light within them. His refusal to appear on television in connection with drugs shows that he never wanted to be the prophet of LSD.[31] But the fact remains that he came to believe that drugs are potent enough to generate a mystical experience. To justify his claim that psychedelics really lead to a genuine religious experience, he offers a scientific explanation of the mystical experience.

Huxley accepts the Bergsonian theory of memory and perception, which states that the function of the brain and nervous system is in the main eliminative, not productive.[32] Man is at each moment capable of remembering all that has ever happened to him, and he can perceive everything that is everywhere happening in the universe. The function of the brain and nervous system is to save man from being overwhelmed by useless and irrelevant knowledge, by allowing only as much perception to come to surface as is essential for his biological survival. The enzymes regulate the supply of glucose to brain cells and enable the brain to work as an efficient reducing valve to check the full and free flow of perception. Mescalin inhibits the production of enzymes, and this lowers the amount of glucose needed by the brain and thus impairs its efficiency. The result is that strange things seem to happen to the drug-taker. Huxley says:

> In some cases there may be extra-sensory perceptions. Other persons discover a world of visionary beauty. To others again is revealed the glory, the infinite value and meaningfulness of naked existence, of the given, unconceptualized event. In the final stage of egolessness there is an "obscure knowledge" that All is in all—that All is actually each. (*Doors,* p. 26)

If rational consciousness is just a fragment of that larger consciousness, of which we become aware at certain levels—aesthetic, visionary or mystical—and if the lowering of the biological efficiency of the brain can give us entry into that larger consciousness, then the whole matter depends on the change in one's body chemistry. Huxley says that Yogic practices—fasts, prayers, flagellation, and other physical and mental austerities that the traditional mystics advocated as the most important requirements of the seeker of truth—were just the means to change body chemistry. Because drugs are available now, the novice need not undergo rigorous ascetical discipline. What he needs is a pill that will produce the required change in his body without any physical discomforts. Huxley gives a rationale of yogic breathing exercises:

Practised systematically, these exercises result, after a time, in prolonged suspensions of breath. Long suspensions of breath lead to a high concentration of carbon dioxide in the lungs and blood, and this increase in the concentration of CO^2 lowers the efficiency of the brain as a reducing valve and permits the entry into consciousness of experiences visionary or mystical, from "out there."[33]

The psalm singing of the Christians, the mantra intoning of the Buddhist monks, and the *japam* of the Hindus have one aim—to increase the concentration of carbon dioxide in the lungs and blood, which results in the lowering of the efficiency of the cerebral reducing valve, which allows the doors of perception to open wide. Huxley observes that the "way to the super-conscious is through the sub-conscious and the way . . . to the sub-conscious is through the chemistry of individual cells" (*Heaven*, p. 63). In defense of the chemically-induced experience, and as an answer to those who would not cherish a scientific explanation of fasting, hymn singing, and mental prayer, Huxley suggests:

> A similar conclusion will be reached by those whose philosophy is unduly "spiritual". God, they will insist, is a spirit and is to be worshipped in spirit. Therefore an experience which is chemically conditioned cannot be an experience of the divine. But, in one way or another, *all* our experiences are chemically conditioned, and if we imagine that some of them are purely "spiritual", purely "intellectual", purely "aesthetic", it is merely because we have never troubled to investigate the internal chemical environment at the moment of their occurrence. Furthermore, it is a matter of historical record that most contemplatives worked systematically to modify their body chemistry, with a view to creating the internal conditions favorable to spiritual insight. . . . Today we know how to lower the efficiency of the cerebral reducing valve by direct chemical action, and without the risk of inflicting serious damage on the psycho-physical organism. (*Heaven*, pp. 73-74)

If spirituality means just a change in the body chemistry, then surely the vast, degenerate majority could be brought back to the path of peace and joy. And that this is not so raises one's doubt with regard to the possibility of synthetic sainthood. Huxley's conclusions are, however, in conformity with the findings of the specialists in the fields of psychology and pharmacology. William Sargant, for instance, suggests the possibility of mechanical sainthood. He observes that if political indoctrination is a success, and if human reflexes can be reconditioned, then a lecutomy operation could bring about a religious conversion. But such conclusions are at variance with the tenets of all religions. Man is said to be superior to animal creation because he has a will, which is the true mark of his freedom. If chemical or mechanical conversion can bring about an involuntary change in man's religious beliefs, human will then loses its entire significance. Sargant stresses the point that "little scientific support has been found that any individual can resist for an indefinite period the physiological stress imposed on his body and mind." He suggests that we "only delude ourselves if we think that any but the most rare individuals can endure unchanged to the very end."[34]

To identify a psychedelic experience with a genuine mystical experience is perhaps to go too far. To justify Frank Barron's claim that "chemical technology has made available to millions the experience of transcendence of the individual ego which a century ago was available to the disciplined mystic,"[35] it is necessary to look into the nature of a genuine mystical experience. The only empirical test a student of mysticism can apply to ascertain whether a particular mystic's experience is genuine or not is to see the effect such an experience produces upon the mystic's personality. "Wherefore by their fruits Ye shall know them" (St. Matthew 7:20), not by their roots. There can be no objection to chemicals as means of transcendence if the experience under them can bring saintliness, the most coveted fruit of a mystic's pursuit. The mystical experience brings equanimity, resignation, fortitude, humility, and unbounded love and compassion to the mystic. There is no evidence to suggest that the drug user suffers such a transformation of personality. Psychedelic experience brings elation, but falls short of the ecstasy of a mystic. The drug-induced experience merely intensifies the senses, but the mystical experience is essentially supersensuous in nature. If the true test of a genuine mystical experience is the annihilation of the ego, as Huxley emphasizes in *The Perennial Philosophy*, then the psychedelic experience fails to qualify as a genuine mystical experience because it inflates the self rather than effaces it. The psychedelic experience does not prove of much value because it does not provide any new outlook on life. P. J. Saher aptly observes that mysticism "through mescalin resembles paper currency during inflation; it was valid, yet its validity was a joke for it was without value."[36]

W. T. Stace, however, employs the "principle of Causal Indifference"[37] to ascertain whether a psychedelic experience can be classed as a genuine mystical experience. According to this principle, if the phenomenological descriptions of the two experiences, the drug-induced and the mystical, are similar, then the two experiences are certainly one, and the drug-induced experience is as valid as the experience of those who have attained it after years of arduous mental and moral discipline. It has been noted earlier that the descriptions of the various drug-induced experiences are not similar. Whereas some claim that they had the experience of ineffable bliss, others brand their experiences as mere hallucinations, nonsensical fantasy. On the other hand, mystics all over the world are unanimous with regard to the outcome of *their* religious experience.

The psychedelics, it seems, are potent enough to give us a peep into the world of enhanced beauty and wonder that our senses are not accustomed to perceive in their ordinary way. At the most, these can produce a kind of visionary experience, but "visionary experience," as Huxley puts it, "is not the same as mystical experience.

Mystical experience is beyond the realm of opposites. Visionary experience is still within that realm" (*Heaven,* p. 56). Drugs, it seems, can never provide a genuine mystical experience. J. Krishnamurti questions "the necessity of taking drugs at all—drugs that promise a psychedelic expansion of the mind, great visions and intensity," and emphasizes that "no golden pill is ever going to solve our human problems."[38] To attain to a level of mystical consciousness, the disciplining of the apelike, restless mind is an imperative necessity. The effort is a costly one and requires years of mental and moral struggle. In this context S. Radhakrishnan affirms the oriental stance: "No tricks of absolution or payment by proxy, no greased paths of smooth organs and stained glass windows can help us much."[39] Surely no golden pill can take man to the City of God. It may be an aid to the goal, but it cannot be an exclusive means of attaining saintliness. Even Walter Pahnke concedes that "the drug is only a trigger, a catalyst or facilitating agent," and that "mystical experiences are hardest, certainly not automatic, even under optimal conditions."[40]

While on his death bed, Huxley took LSD, perhaps to facilitate his entry into what he often termed the Clear Light of the Void. Under the impact of LSD, Huxley, however, realized that he had been wrong in claiming that drugs can produce a genuine mystical experience. His tape-recorded conversation seems to be a confession of his failure. He was wrong when he thought that he was making an absolute "cosmic gift" (psychedelics) to the world and that he had a sort of "star role" (as the advocate of psychedelics) (*TM,* p. 268). He realized that "when *one thinks one's got beyond oneself, one hasn't*" (*TM,* p. 269). Huxley realized his error and concluded that "there must be no magic tricks," that we must learn to "come to reality without the enchanter's wand and his book of words" (*TM,* pp. 289-290). Huxley's last words, comments R. C. Zaecher, "are his recantation and his last will and testament, a warning [against the belief] . . . that psychedelic experience is not merely similar to mystical experience but is identical with it."[41] Surely, the psychedelic "magic trick" will never do, and there can be no short cut to eternity.

Huxley had never had any first-hand genuine mystical experience. Julian Huxley testifies that "Aldous was never a mystic in any exclusive or wooly sense, though he was keenly interested in the facts of mystical experience."[42] Jerome Meckier also observes, "To Huxley himself, the consciousness of being no more separate, of having attained union with the Divine Ground, probably never came."[43] He could never attain to the state of nonattachment that he advocates as the precondition for God-realization. He was never able to rise above the ordinary worldly level and was often disturbed by the failures and successes of temporal life. This is quite evident from his correspondence in later life, which expresses his professional anxiety for what early theatrical success could never gain.[44] Laurence Brander also suggests that Huxley is "like most Westerners, incapable of that 'holy indifference' to which he often refers."[45] He did genuinely knock at the doors of the Kingdom of

Heaven, but the Kingdom of Heaven never revealed its celestial glory to him. He was a pilgrim who was encumbered by heavy intellectual baggage he could never throw away to enter the straight and narrow gate of this kingdom. He could never renounce his formidable intellect, which always came between him and the Beatific Vision. Drugs simply revealed to him a world of visionary beauty, and the visionary experience affirmed his belief that beyond the visionary world there lies a world of spiritual experience. LSD is no panacea for the spiritual maladies of mankind. Huxley's quest for mystical experience through psychedelics fails, and there seems to be, for him at least, no possibility of synthetic sainthood.

[1] In the essay "One and Many" Huxley concedes that, officially speaking, he is an agnostic. Aldous Huxley, *Do What You Will,* Collected Edition (1929; rpt. London: Chatto & Windus, 1956), p. 1.

[2] Aldous Huxley, *Proper Studies,* Collected Edition (1927; rpt. London: Chatto & Windus, 1957), p. 175.

[3] In a letter (22 August 1939) to Dilipkuma Roy, Pondichey, Huxley wrote that his early interest in mysticism was "predominantly negative" and that he "read a good deal of Western and Eastern writing, always with intense interest, but always with a wish to 'debunk' them." Sirirkumar Ghose, *Aldous Huxley: A Cynical Savationist* (Bombay: Asia Publishing House, 1962), p. 187n. This letter is not found in *Letters of Aldous Huxley,* ed. Grover Smith (London: Chatto & Windus, 1969).

[4] Aldous Huxley, *Time Must Have a Stop* (1944; rpt. London: Chatto & Windus, 1946), p. 289.

[5] Aldous Huxley, *Ends and Means,* Collected Edition (1937; rpt. London: Chatto & Windus, 1957), p. 286.

[6] J. B. Coates, *The Critics of the Human Person: Some Personalist Interpretations* (London: Longmans, Green, 1949), p. 41.

[7] "Introduction," *Psychedelics: The Uses and Implications of Hallucinogenic Drugs,* ed. Bernard S. Aaronson and Humphry Osmond (London: The Hogarth Press, 1971), p. 10. Hereafter to be cited as *Psychedelics.*

[8] Laura Archera Huxley, *This Timeless Moment: A Personal View of Aldous Huxley* (London: Chatto & Windus, 1969), p. 11. Henceforth referred to parenthetically in text as *TM.*

[9] R. E. L. Masters and Jean Houston, *The Varieties of Psychedelic Experience* (London: Turnstone Books, 1973), pp. 252-253.

[10] Aldous Huxley, *Jesting Pilate,* Collected Edition (1926; rpt. London: Chatto & Windus, 1957), p. 191.

[11] Aldous Huxley, *Brief Candles: Four Stories,* Collected Edition (1930; rpt. London: Chatto & Windus, 1957), p. 246.

[12] Aldous Huxley, *Antic Hay* (1923; rpt. New York: The Modern Library, 1951), p. 293.

[13] Aldous Huxley, "Appendix," *The Devils of Loudun* (London: Chatto & Windus, 1952), p. 362.

[14] Adolf Kaegi, *The Rigveda: The Oldest Literature of the Indians,* trans. R. Arrowsmith, Indian Edition (New Delhi: Amarko Book Agency, 1972), pp. 78-79.

[15] *The Bhagavad-Gita* (Gorakhpur: Gita Press, n.d.).

[16] Masters and Houston, *The Varieties,* p. 37.

[17] William James, *The Will to Believe, Human Immortality and Other Essays on Popular Philosophy* (New York: Dover Publications, 1956), p. 295n.

[18] Allen Ginsberg, "First Manifesto to End the Bringdown," *Voices of Revelation,* ed. Nancy H. Deane (Boston, MA: Little, Brown and Company, 1970), p. 345.

[19] Alan Watts, "Psychedelics and Religious Experience," *Psychedelics,* p. 133.

[20] John W. Aiken, "The Church of the Awakening," *Psychedelics,* p. 174.

[21] Walter N. Pahnke, "Drugs and Mysticism," *Psychedelics,* p. 162.

[22] Masters and Houston, p. 307.

[23] Timothy Leary, *The Politics of Ecstasy* (London: Palladin, 1970), p. 286.

[24] R. C. Zachner, "Appendix B, *Mysticism Sacred and Profane: An Enquiry into Some Varieties of Praeternatural Experience* (Oxford: Clarendon Press, 1957), p. 226.

[25] Aldous Huxley, *The Doors of Perception* (New York: Harper & Brothers, 1954), p. 14. Hereafter to be cited parenthetically in text as *Doors.*

[26] Aldous Huxley, *Letters of Aldous Huxley,* p. 720. Hereafter to be cited parenthetically in text as *Letters.*

[27] W. R. Inge, *Mysticism in Religion* (London: Rider & Co. 1969), p. 36.

[28] Aldous Huxley, *Island* (London: Chatto & Windus, 1962), p. 136.

[29] *Island,* p. 140.

[30] Masters and Houston, p. 260.

[31] In a letter to Dr. Humphry Osmond, Huxley suggests his friend maintain secrecy about the LSD experience and its effects. See *Letters,* p. 803.

[32] Huxley accepts the Bergsonian model of the human mind. See his letter to Humphry Osmond, *Letters,* p. 668.

[33] Aldous Huxley, "Appendix I," *Heaven and Hell* (New York: Harper and Brothers, 1956), p. 62. Hereafter to be cited parenthetically in text as *Heaven.*

[34] William Sargant, *Battle for the Mind: A Physiology of Conversion and Brain Washing* (London: William Heinemann, 1957), p. 231.

[35] Frank Barron, "Motivational Patterns in LSD Usage," *LSD, Man and Society,* ed. Richard C. Debold and Russell C. Leaf (London: Faber and Faber, 1969), p. 9.

[36] P. J. Saher, *Eastern Wisdom and Western Thought: A Comparative Study In the Modern Philosophy of Religion* (London: Allen & Unwin, 1969), p. 172.

[37] W. T. Stace, *Mysticism and Philosophy* (London: Macmillan, 1961), p. 29.

[38] J. Krishnamurti, *The Only Revolution,* ed. Mary Lutyens (London: Victor Gollancz, 1970), p. 175.

[39] S. Radhakrishnan, *An Idealist View of Life,* 2nd ed. (London: George Allen & Unwin, 1957), p. 113.

[40] Walter Pahnke, "LSD and Religious Experience," *LSD, Man & Society,* p. 65.

[41] R. C. Zaechner, *Drugs, Mysticism and Make-Believe* (London: Collins, 1972), p. 109.

[42] Julian Huxley, ed., *Aldous Huxley—1894-1963: A Memorial Volume* (London: Chatto & Windus, 1965), p. 21.

[43] Jerome Meckier, *Aldous Huxley: Satire and Structure* (London: Chatto & Windus, 1969), p. 152.

[44] George Woodcock, *Dawn and the Darkest Hour: A Study of Aldous Huxley* (London: Faber and Faber, 1972), p. 265.

[45] Laurence Brander, *Aldous Huxley: A Critical Study* (London: Rupert Hart-Davis, 1969), p. 154.

Lynda S. Boren

SOURCE: "William James, Theodore Dreiser and the 'Anaesthetic Revelation,'" in *American Studies,* Vol. 24, No. 1, Spring, 1983, pp. 5-18.

[*In the following essay, Boren explores the paradox in post-Darwinian American culture between pragmatism and the pervasive sense of doom characteristic of the machine age, embodied by the respective ideas of William James and Theodore Dreiser, and the subsequent experimentations with drugs by both writers.*]

In 1874 an eccentric amateur philosopher from New York claimed that he had, at last, discovered the key to the mystery of life. The key came with a whiff of laughing gas. In a rather bizarre essay, the author insisted that he and countless others had experienced, while under the influence of nitrous oxide, a mystical revelation of eternal truth. We could, of course, regard such claims as the lunatic swan song of a table-rapping fanatism were it not for the fact that the pamphlet and its author play an intriguing role in our philosophic and literary history. As biographers and cultural historians have made clear, late nineteenth-century philosophers, writers and scientists often dipped into pseudo-scientific pursuits in an effort to harmonize the evolutionary theories of Darwin and an increasingly mechanistic view of the universe with their own peculiar desires for a spiritual redefinition of man's existence. The eccentric author in question then was not hailed as a mere fanatic. Moreover, he provides an illuminating link between two such seemingly diverse figures as William James, optimistic voice of American pragmatism, and Theodore Dreiser, tragedian of the American dream gone bad; both men knew the "Anaesthetic Revelation," and both took it seriously.

William James's obsession with mind-altering drugs, the occult and Eastern mysticism is well known, even though it was James who argued so persuasively for the necessity of empirical validation of any assumed truth. Nor does it appear out of character that Emerson's brand of mysticism in his famous essay "Nature" is paradoxically interwoven with evolutionary theories and Platonic idealism, buttressed at last by a Lockean insistance on concrete experience. Seldom is Theodore Dreiser thrown into the same basket with Emerson, James, Whitman and others as a writer or thinker deeply engrossed in spiritual questions. But from James to Dreiser we can draw a line of affinity; Benjamin Blood's "revelation" provides an interesting focus.

Caught between his need for religious solace and his defiance of absolutism, William James lived in a state of psychic limbo. A month before his death, the philosopher lamented in a memo to his son that he could not live to "round out" his system, which had become for him "too much like an arch built only on one side."[1] In his last published essay of the same month, however, James's lament exudes the passionate abandon of Nietzsche's *amor fati:* "there are no fortunes to be told," he rejoices, "no advice to be given—Farewell!"[2] Titled "A Pluralistic Mystic," this essay was in fact an enthusiastic tribute to James's life-long friendship with a little-known, self-proclaimed mystic, whose peculiar writings seem to offer the best of both religion and science. James's praise is unequivocal:

> Not for the ignoble vulgar do I write this article, but only for those dialectic-mystic souls who have an irresistible taste, acquired or native, for higher flights of metaphysics. . . . Now for years my own taste, literary as well as philosophic, has been exquisitely titillated by a writer, the name of whom I think must be unknown to the readers of this article; so I no longer continue silent about the merits of BENJAMIN PAUL BLOOD. The author's maiden adventure was the *Anaesthetic Revelation,* a pamphlet printed privately at Amsterdam in 1874. I forgot how it fell into my hands, but it fascinated me so "weirdly" that I am conscious of its having been one of the stepping-stones of my thinking ever since. (739-40)

Blood, with whom James had corresponded and argued over the years, claimed that a state of "intense illumination or philosophic perception" could be attained through the use of anaesthetic agents. Upon observing nitrous-oxide intoxication over a fourteen-year period, Blood affirmed that in every case the reaction of the patient was identical with all others: "in those brief seconds of instant recall from stupor to recognition, each patient discovers something grotesque and unutterable about his own nature, the genius of being is revealed, and the mystery of life is understood at last as but a common thing."[3] What that common thing was, however, seemed to have perplexed James in his initial encounter with the "revelation." It seems to have been nothing more than the realization, in that moment of coming to, that each person becomes vividly aware of his own uniqueness and that his "grotesque" individuality is itself an expression of God's creation. God is seen, then, not as a monistic, all-consuming One but in the diversity and change of human expression, not as the Absolute but as an ever-evolving pluralism. Under the influence of Blood's "revelation" the semi-comatose patient understands what it is to be Emerson's "Divine Man," but without the attendant monism of Emerson's absolutist position.

The "Anaesthetic Revelation" is a cosmic joke of sorts, denying heavens, hells, hierarchies and rational logic in one fell swoop. The majestic and the absurd meet with equal dignity in Blood's laughing-gas realm, which he labels the "tasteless water of souls," and the naked life, as Blood chooses to call it, does not require sanity as the basic quality of intelligence since sanity itself is a mere variable moving up or down the musical gamut like the humming of a wheel (34). Sliding back and forth from scientific observation to metaphor and poetic allusion, Blood weaves a seductive allegory of human existence, which James must have found compatible with his own paradoxical temperament:

> This thick net of space containing all worlds—this fate of being which contains both gods and men, is the capacity of the soul, and can be claimed as greater than us only by claiming a greater than the greatest, and denying God and safety. . . . The tales, whether they be true or false, are as substantial as the things of which they tell.
>
> "We are such stuff
> As dreams are made of, and our little life
> Is rounded with a sleep."
>
> (36-37)

James's initial reaction to Blood's revelation was to discard it as another Hegelian confusion, which like nitrous-oxide intoxication provided only "the immense sense of reconciliation which characterizes the 'maudlin' stage of alcoholic drunkenness."[4] In its resemblance to a whirlpool, James maintained, the vortex of Hegelian dialectic is the liveliest point, and "any one who has dipped into Hegel will recognize Mr. Blood to be one of the same tribe."[5] He also thought he recognized in Blood the characteristic orphic strains of transcendental idealism which reverberate throughout Emerson's writings, lulling us into blissful acceptance. He was perhaps also thinking of his own father's Swedenborgian mysticism, with which Blood, who had attended the elder James's lectures, was quite familiar. "I listen to the felicitously-worded concept-music circling round itself," James writes, "as on some drowsy summer noon one listens under the pines to the murmuring of leaves and insects and with as little thought of criticism."[6] What leads to James's wholehearted embracing of the "revelation" toward the end of his life is his ultimate recognition in Blood of a sort of "'left wing' voice of defiance," which breaks into "a radically pluralistic sound":

> I confess that the existence of this novel brand of mysticism has made my cowering mood depart. I feel now as if my own pluralism were not without the kind of support which mystical corroboration may confer.[7]

James's desire to "have his religion and eat it too" seems to have been realized in Blood's pluralistic mysticism, which was indeed that, as is evident in his later work, *Pluriverse: An Essay in the Philosophy of Pluralism* (1920). In this later essay Blood disparages "monism, or oneism in philosophy," as "a vision through the lens of the human ego as a pattern on which its cosmos is designed. . . . Monism is the general egotism which in idealism ends as pure solipsism."[8] Again, one gets the impression that Emerson's "transparent eyeball" has become a solipsistic metaphor to Blood's way of thinking.

To those familiar with biographies of the James family, it comes as no surprise that while drawn to supernatural phenomena, hallucinogenic drugs and mystical religions, James rejected his father's own form of empirical mysticism, which he considered a form of absolutism. His sweeping claim for Blood's genius can be best understood as another aspect of James's fluctuating temperament and as a reflection of a type of rebellion against authority that has become the hallmark of his thought and writing. James's sister Alice had aptly remarked in her journal that her brother's intellectual life was "like a blob of mercury," untouchable with the "mental finger."[9] And in spite of his apparent rebellion against "father's ideas," James demonstrated in his own brand of humanism a religiosity closely akin to James Senior's empirical mysticism. For William James, as for his father, the empirical basis of human existence was the necessary foundation of man's inner, spiritual life, and redemption was possible only in the existential realm of the living. "Every end, reason, motive, object of desire or aversion, ground of sorrow or joy that we feel," James wrote, "is in the world of finite multifariousness, for only in that world does

anything really happen, only there do events come to pass."[10] James published this statement a year before his death, and the history of his intellectual growth is recorded in the painful barriers he was forced to overcome in reaching this philosophical plateau. Bringing the rudiments of his father's mysticism to their fruition as a modern, pragmatic humanism, James carried the religious seeds of American philosophy to their predictable maturation.

Tracing the course of James's troubled life as the eldest son in a highly competitive, neurotic household, we find a pattern emerging which can be characterized as both idealistic and adolescent. Moving from mentor to mentor, from LaFarge to Agassiz to Renouvier to Bergson, vacillating between hero worship and childish petulance, James demonstrates those qualities of an eternally questing Huck, forever "lighting out for the territory ahead of the rest," ultimately resisting adoption and "sivilization," but nevertheless content to float easy on a pragmatic raft which provides conscience and religion simultaneously. Just as Huck is sheltered by Nigger Jim's superstitious but mystical faith in the signs of nature, James refused to relinquish his need for religious certitude. Experiencing the beauty of the "bright as glory" lightning against the "dark as sin" night, Huck admits (from the snugness of Jim's cave) that he "wouldn't want to be nowhere else but here. . . . Pass me along another hunk of fish and some hot cornbread," he murmurs to Jim, who rejoins,

> "Well, you wouldn't 'a' been here 'f it hadn't 'a' ben for Jim. You'd 'a' ben down dah in de woods widout any diner, en gittin' mos' drownded, too; dat you would honey. Chickens knows when it's gwyne to rain, en so do de birds, chile."[11]

James had long argued for a religious reading of his philosophical works; he too wanted the spiritual lightning along with his cornpone. In his essay on "Pragmatism and Religion," he defends pragmatism against the charge that it is a Godless system. Having completed *The Varieties of Religious Experience* (1902), James felt that his own pragmatism should be exempt from the charge of atheism: "Pragmatism can be called religious," he insisted, "if you allow that religion can be pluralistic or merely melioristic in type."[12] Blood was to complain in his *Pluriverse* that "finite sophistication keeps limiting existence to an All, or a One, not considering how these notions antagonize such an unlimited space" (73). The concept of pluralism and change had allowed James to accept the inarticulate experiences of mystical phenomena. Since the basis of his father's faith had been a negation of self in the larger selfhood of God, James survived only by asserting his will. As Gay Wilson Allen argues in his biography, for James the doctrine of free will was a "personal, intimate, fateful problem."[13] Having long resisted the "primordial chaos" of mere physical sensation as an explanation of life, James found repugnant any philosophy or theory, including Freud's, which appeared to rob man of his will and his dignity. His father's mysticism seemed little higher than vegetable bliss, while Freud's theories with their sexual base seemed to chain man to a psycho-physical treadmill. As a result, James's interest in faith-healing and psychic research was very much a desperate search for spiritual renewal.

Violent as his need was to believe in the power of mind over matter, James also believed in the strength of religious feeling and its origins in the unconscious, unreasoning elements of life. James would have it both ways, and his intellectual fence-sitting resulted in disparagement from both camps; neither pure scientist nor poet, philosopher nor theologian, James was rarely analyzed as a consistent thinker. His religious views were ignored or ridiculed as aberrational and therefore regarded in isolation from the bulk of his work. With the appearance of a popular book of animal stories, *The Varieties* was quickly retitled by a scoffing audience as "Wild Religions I have Known," *The Will to Believe* becoming "Will to Make-Believe."[14] It is fitting to see in James's final tribute to Blood a romantic dash of bravado, a leap into the unknown as a departing gesture of faith, Huck lighting out for the territory ahead. In this affirmation of mystery, James joins in Blood's exuberant claim:

> "Simply," Blood writes to me, *"we do not know."*
> But when we say, "we do not know," we are not to
> say it weakly and meekly, but with confidence. . . .
> Knowledge is and must ever be *secondary*—a
> witness rather than a principal—or a "principal"!—
> in the case. Therefore mysticism for me! (747-58)

Taking that courageous leap back into uncertainty was a spiritual victory for James. He no longer needed scientific proof of God's existence; the unknown as the all possible was the only assurance he needed. He also calls to mind the romantic heroes of his brother's fiction: Roderick Hudson tumbling over the abyss to pluck that unreachable flower for Christina Light or Hyacinth Robinson caught between two worlds, a dark shadow of frozen potential.

James's attraction to Blood and the history of their correspondence becomes even more provocative when we realize that the equally controversial writer, Theodore Dreiser, was also sufficiently intrigued with Blood's "Anaesthetic Revelation" to find in it similarities with his own satirical play that first appeared in *The Smart Set* for February, 1915. Titled *Laughing Gas,* the play dramatizes in a grimly humorous fashion the semi-conscious struggle of a patient into awareness after an almost lethal dose of nitrous oxide. The play is included with others of a similar nature in Dreiser's *Plays of the Natural and the Supernatural,* published initially in 1916 and reissued in 1926. The second impression of the 1916 printing and the 1926 reissue contain an appended gathering which includes Blood's "Revelation" and James's reference to it in *The Will to Believe.*[15] Dreiser establishes in his note of the gathering that his play was "not suggested or inspired by either of these comments. My attention was not called to them until two months after my own work had been published." The note is signed, "THE AUTHOR, New York, April, 1916" (4). Dreiser establishes the fact that he is not indebted to Blood for the subject of his play, so while it is impossible to claim the "Revelation"

as a source or an influence for *Laughing Gas,* it is significant that Dreiser took the pains to have it appended in a separate gathering.

Dreiser's source of information could have been Jacques Loeb, a physiologist and biological mechanist with whom Dreiser maintained a correspondence until the scientist's death in 1924, or Elmer Gates, an amateur scientist who had first introduced Dreiser to Loeb's physiological psychology.[16] It is more likely Loeb, however, since Gates played an active part in Dreiser's life at a much earlier period. Gates and Loeb were both proponents of a mechanistic explanation of human behavior and, as Ellen Moers illustrates in her study, highly influential forces behind the ideas inherent in *Sister Carrie* and in *An American Tragedy.*[17] Gates proposed that states of mind produced chemical changes in the body; good thoughts were beneficial physically while bad ones eventually led to mental and physical decline. Motives in human behavior were classified as arising from will or volition, the choice one makes out of habit, education or character, or from the unconscious acts that can sometimes result in tragedy, the unthinking, Pavlovian reaction to instinct.

Dreiser's concept of chemism and magnetism supplied the powerful metaphors for his fiction in which human beings in their tragic destinies are whirled like atoms in a vast machine. Dreiser hurls his own longing cry against this pitiless machine, much as James pits his will against the void, and thus mechanism functions only to cast into relief those very human qualities that Dreiser's world view denies. Hurstwood could be "but an inconspicuous drop in an ocean like New York" and "among the forces which sweep and play throughout the universe, untutored man is but a wisp in the wind."[18] Immediately the human is perceived, our sympathy is engaged, and the "terrible" lies beyond the pale of everything that *is* man, everything that denies his individuality. Dreiser has transformed James's anxiety into tragic art. The paradox works for Dreiser because it supplies the highest tension possible for an audience which can no longer view its heroes in epic dimensions but which demands something a bit more satisfying, nevertheless, than Huck's fanciful escape. Embedded in this tension is Dreiser's own desire for religious affirmation.

While James's birth in the Astor Hotel was prophetically blessed by Emerson, Theodore Dreiser's puny entrance into the world was "presided over by unearthly agents."[19] Fearing his death, his mother consulted an old German woman who reputedly possessed supernatural powers. After elaborate instructions, which included measuring him from head to toe and from finger-tip to finger-tip, chanting a solemn ritual and exposing his infant face to the light of the moon, Theodore recovered.[20] The desire to believe, one might conclude, was thus firmly implanted at the moment of Dreiser's miraculous recovery. In his introduction to *The Novels of Theodore Dreiser,* Donald Pizer tells us that Dreiser was highly responsive to the popular philosophy and religion of his day, suggesting that "his disbelief was always to be accompanied [as was James's] by a will to believe":

From his earliest *Ev'ry Month* editorials of 1895 to his death in 1945, Dreiser argued that experience was chaotic, directionless, and valueless. At the same time, though in various ways and with various degrees of self-awareness, he sought to find evidence that it had both meaning and value.[21]

As with James's philosophy, Dreiser's views of life were an expression of his "ever growing and developing personality," and just as James's arch remained unfinished so Dreiser's multiverse "required a fluctuating, wavering of the ragged-edged and the un-limited."[22] For Dreiser the psychic world and the physical world were never divided, and while described by those who knew him as "an awestruck mystic," he was nevertheless regarded by most as a "ramping materialist." Dreiser, of course, would not have seen any contradiction in two such opposing views of his character.

Dreiser's *Plays* reveal his efforts to render his speculations into artistic form. Forwarding copies of the plays to H. L. Mencken for his opinion, Dreiser assured him that he was "not turning esoteric, metaphysical or spiritualistic. These are merely an effort at drama outside the ordinary limits of dramatic interpretation."[23] Mencken did not understand what Dreiser was up to with *Laughing Gas* and dismissed it as inferior work. Reviews of the plays in this collection, however, were more sympathetic, seeing in them a strange, haunting power. In spite of Dreiser's disclaimer, his philosophical speculations do indicate a deep absorption in questions of consciousness and will. In an essay on this theme Dreiser explores the nature of the dark force that rules our being. His title for the essay that was conceived between 1911 and 1925 is simply "It."

> We say so often that we control our minds, but do we? . . .
>
> If the body complains that it cannot, that it lacks strength, It, in the subconscious where It dwells, grieves or curses, sets up a darkling mood of sorrow, a giant despair that may wreck the very machinery of the organism itself and so free It from Its bondage. . . .
>
> Dark, central force that rules in our midst, that sings whether we will or no, plays whether we will or no, decides, whether the circumstances seem propitious or no, reads, dreams, mourns. . . . It!
>
> The wonder of It![24]

In a later poem called "Machine," Dreiser gives us a lyrical rendition of man's humanistic strivings within his limitations as mere mechanism. Published in a 1926 collection titled *Moods,* this poem seems to offer a paradoxical religious synthesis without denying man his capacity for will. The logic, however, is simply that of the poem itself:

> How comes a machine to be dancing?
> Singing?
> Running?
> Playing?
> Laughing?
> Brooding?
> Weeping?
> A machine
> Most carefully
> And artfully constructed
> And yet manufactured by billions
> And that by reasons of chemicals
> And elements
> Most carefully compounded
> Goes?
> A machine that any blow will break
> And that ordinary wear and tear
> Will cause to disintegrate
> And stranger still
> That grief
> And disappointment
> If you please
> Will cause it to destroy itself![25]

Such speculations and their poetic counterparts lead quite naturally to the dramatic humor or pathos of Dreiser's philosophic plays.

Laughing Gas is a good example of Dreiser's metaphorical transformation of laboratory science into speculative drama. The protagonist, Jason Vatabeel, is an eminent physician who himself must submit to surgery. "Well, Jason, here you are, a victim of surgery after all!" Fenway Bail, the operating surgeon, gloats. As the nitrous oxide takes effect Vatabeel drifts off into the rhythm of the universe, "Om! Om! Om! Om! Om! Om!," and is transported into the realm of spirit. The forces of the universe then collect in an allegorical drama of life, accompanied always by the "Om! Om!" of the vast machine. Alcephoran is a power of physics that generates ideas ceaselessly as in a mood, without form or thought. "Deep, deep and involute are the ways and the substance of things," Alcephoran chants, "an endless sinking, an endless rising!" As Vatabeel speeds toward death (his tumor lies critically close to the carotid artery), shadows appear.

The First Shadow blames Vatabeel's decline on Valerian, "an element inimical to him. . . . It may be that he will live." Vatabeel begins to experience "a vast depression as of endless space and unutterable loneliness," and engages in a colloquy with the spirits on the meaning of life. Demyaphon, who appears only as thoughts placed in the dreamer's mind, cynically asserts, "To that which you seek there is no solution. A tool, a machine, you spin and spin on a given course through new worlds and old. Vain, vain! For you there is no great end." As the anaesthesia is increased, Vatabeel's thoughts in the character of Demyaphon become one with the laughing gas itself. A sense of something formless comes over Vatabeel, and he is conscious of a desire to smile also, though in a hopeless mechanical way. "I am laughing gas, for one thing," Demyaphon proclaims. "You will laugh with me because of me, shortly. You will not be able to help yourself. You are a mere machine run by forces which you cannot understand." Demyaphon tells Vatabeel that in order to he must create himself anew. "Round and round . . . the same difficulty, the same operation . . . your whole life repeated detail by detail. . . . Now if you live you must make an effort or die." (The gas smiles.) Vatabeel struggles desperately to assist himself to live. The struggle, of course, is against the machine. "I must live, I must try, I do not want to die. . . . Think of our being mere machines to be used by others!" (He struggles again without physically stirring.) Vatabeel struggles to establish himself on a new plane, but his greatest struggle comes with acceptance of the machine. "What if I do go round and round! I am a man! Beyond this, what? Nothing? I serve!" This ultimate acceptance of both the machine and of his own humanness thus rekindles the spark of life in Vatabeel. While the mode is comic, the gesture is the classic one of religious faith. As Vatabeel comes to life, he is vibrated by the vast machine until he becomes one with a multiverse of uncontrollable laughter. "Oh, ho! ho! ho! I see it all now! Oh, what a joke! Oh, what a trick! . . . The folly of life! . . . Ah, ha! ha! ha!" As Vatabeel leaves the hospital his face "retains a look of deep amazed abstraction."

If Vatabeel has experienced a revelation it has transformed him forever. The cosmic joke is also an affirmation; Vatabeel survives because he proclaims his own humanity in the face of annihilation, accepting a life force analogous to Dreiser's gigantic "It." Body and soul are irrevocably linked in the vast machine, and Vatabeel, like James, is forced to renounce all systems. "There is no conclusion," James insisted. "What has concluded that we might conclude in regard to it?"[26] There remains, it would seem, only the everlasting "Om" of a mystical pluriverse.

In summary, it appears that while James and Dreiser are in most instances at opposite ends of an immense ideologic gulf, their mutual realization of an impulse that can only be described accurately as religious offers insight into an important aspect of the American creative consciousness. Writing to Xenos Clark from Cambridge in 1880, James claimed that the mystical experience was an ineffable occurrence best defined by poetic language.

> I don't much expect that you will get any farther in your attempts at formulating "ø" than you have got already. . . . The attempt to state even its ineffability in your hands as well as in those of Blood only leads to metaphors and epigrams. . . . Isn't it probable that the hypnotic trance of Indian fakirs . . . induced by the syllable *om* produced your "ø" in their minds?[27]

James's question, like Vatabeel's, was answered at the end of his life with a rejection of all that is "known" or proven in favor of the "unknown."

While all of this might seem archly romantic, the origins of such an impulse can be perceived in statements such as Emerson's that "man is man by virtue of willing, not by virtue of knowing and understanding. As he is, so he sees"[28]; or even in Whitman's Vedantic belief that he is

his own creator through his Adamic re-naming of the world from a position of assumed innocence. This Edenic movement in the philosophy and literature of nineteenth-century America emphasizes the urge felt by writers to recapture innocence through negation of institutions, systems and science. But the impulse can be understood also as typifying that element in American culture which has always emphasized the inner life. As our society becomes more and more mechanized, more and more scientific, a countermovement inevitably emerges that seeks spiritual affirmation either through a return to primitivism or through an attempt to incorporate mechanism and science in the philosophy and literature of the age—to reinterpret the machine or transform it to the uses of the humanist. James's inherited belief that a man's inner world of vision is as real as the external world of fact was his synthesis of apparently incongruent forces. "To the psychologist," James insisted, "the religious propensities of man must be at least as interesting as any other of the facts pertaining to his mental constitution."[29] In his experimentation with mind-altering drugs, James most clearly reveals the deep seriousness of his attachment to vision. He never lost faith, even when denied the "mystical" euphoria described by others.

The continuation of this stream in American thinking is illustrated by Eckard Toy's recent study of the use of psychedelic drugs by the conservative strata of American society. Toy cites the movement of The Wayfarers as an example of this phenomenon. Growing out of conservative theological and political roots, the group flourished during the late fifties, sanctioning even experimentation "with drugs and psychic phenomena" in an effort to be "as scientific about religion as we are about science."[30] One of its principal members was William Mullendore, chairman of the board of Southern California Edison Company. As Toy points out,

> Although he was a conservative Republican, a moderately devout United Presbyterian, and sixty-six years old when he first tried LSD, Mullendore did not consider his actions either rebellious or deviant. He sought primarily to improve his creative intelligence and, secondarily, to enhance his spiritual awareness. Mullendore found in his experiment with LSD a partial corrective for his deepening pessimism about the future of the United States (70).

Toy's article is particularly valuable for the light it throws back on people like James and Dreiser, who also attempted to mitigate their despair by searching for new forms of spiritual expansion. Shaping "the original psychotherapy experiments with psychedelic drugs into a quasi-religious form," men like Mullendore can be seen in Toy's estimation as individualists "who longed for an elitist utopia" and who in the midst of their pessimism yet maintained a "faith that somehow man's mind would transcend and survive mankind" (75, 76).

The implications of this phenomenon for American writers, particularly those with a high degree of social awareness, are rather far reaching. In the case of William's brother Henry James, personal vision constituted a religion, and in the words of A. D. Van Nostrand, it ultimately led to "the search for a language" through which "to express it":

> In the act of expression the religion and the language to convey it are mutually dependent. . . . In these cosmologies a philosophy of God and a philosophy of composition are inseparable. If truth could be absolutely named they would never have been written.[31]

In Henry James's later work he frequently makes use of the mystical experience as a dramatic metaphor for self-understanding. As Martha Banta points out in her study of James's use of the supernatural: "the occult, the psychical and the transcendent do not refer to outside influences such as demons, nature spirits, gods, the stars or the planets. They apply solely to hidden powers of the human mind that go sufficiently beyond the 'ordinary' to grant it that metaphoric stature of the 'exceptional' that Henry James often sought for his privileged characters."[32] Perhaps the most recent culmination of this impulse in American literature can be seen in the science fiction writer, Ursula LeGuin. In her novel, *The Left Hand of Darkness,* she describes the ultimate religious experience as one of "ignorance." The high priest insists that his "business is unlearning, not learning. . . . The unknown, the unforetold, the unproven, that is what life is based on."[33] And, as if in confirmation of Huck's "lighting out" at the end of his adventures, LeGuin's priest asserts that "if it were proven that there is no God there would be no religion. . . . The only thing that makes life possible is permanent, intolerable uncertainty: not knowing what comes next" (71).

The "intolerable uncertainty" of existence might well be translated into William James's vision of a random "pluriverse" or Dreiser's sense of the vast machine. Despair with fact, with science, with progress only throws man back upon himself and ultimately produces the paradoxical amphibian of American culture: the religious pragmatist, the realist writer turned spiritualist, the materialistic mystic. When Herman Melville shocked his literary contemporaries by producing a monster of a work that dared to mix "metaphysics with chowder," he was writing out of a very old and continuing tradition. The voice of darkest pessimism often reveals a desperate need for religious affirmation in American life and letters, and writers such as Dreiser offer us much in the way of social analysis. If a "true believer" lurks beneath the mask of Theodore Dreiser while William James embraces the void with ecstasy, why shouldn't "the Chairman of the Board" take LSD?

NOTES

[1] July 26, 1910. See Gay Wilson Allen, *William James, A Biography* (New York, 1967), 496.

[2] "A Pluralistic Mystic," *The Hibbert Journal,* 8 (July, 1910), 759.

[3] *The Anaesthetic Revelation and the Gist of Philosophy* (Amsterdam, New York, 1874), 34.

[4] "Some Hegelisms," *The Will to Believe* (New York, 1897), 294-95.

[5] "A Pluralistic Mystic," 741-42.

[6] *Ibid.,* 746.

[7] *Ibid.,* 740-41.

[8] Boston, 1920, 81.

[9] November 18, 1889, in Anna Robeson Burr, *Alice James: Her Brothers, Her Journal* (New York, 1934), 112.

[10] "Monistic Idealism" in *A Pluralistic Universe* (1909; Cambridge, 1975), 28.

[11] *Adventures of Huckleberry Finn,* Sculley Bradley et al., ed. (New York, 1977), 43-44.

[12] "Pragmatism and Religion," *Pragmatism: A New Name for Some Old Ways of Thinking* (1907; Cambridge, 1975), 143-44.

[13] *William James, A Biography,* 164.

[14] See Julius Bixler's *Religion in the Philosophy of William James* (Boston, 1926), 1.

[15] See *Plays of the Natural and the Supernatural* (1916; New York, 1926), appended gathering, 1-4.

[16] While Dreiser did not correspond with Loeb until after 1919, both Ellen Moers and Donald Pizer indicate that Dreiser was undoubtedly reading Loeb much earlier, possibly as early as 1912. Dreiser himself is slightly unreliable in his recollection of when he first read Loeb, his dates ranging from 1912 to 1919. Ellen Moers believed that his knowledge of Loeb's ideas dates from 1915, a supposition confirmed in part by the frequent appearance of Loeb's names and ideas in Dreiser's unpublished essays from that point. In a letter to Loeb on May 29, 1919 (in the Library of Congress), Dreiser noted that he had read Loeb's "The Mechanistic Conception of Life" (1912) "several years ago." See Pizer's *The Novels of Theodore Dreiser* (Minnesota, 1976), 360, n. 12.

[17] See *Two Dreisers* (New York, 1969).

[18] *Sister Carrie,* edited by Donald Pizer (New York, 1970), 214, 256.

[19] See Robert Elias' *Theodore Dreiser: Apostle of Nature* (Ithaca, 1949), 3.

[20] *Ibid.,* 4.

[21] Minneapolis, 14.

[22] See John Cowper Powys' introduction to Theodore Dreiser's *Notes on Life,* edited by Marguerite Tjader and John J. McAleer (University, Alabama, 1974), xi.

[23] July 29, 1914, in *Letters of Theodore Dreiser,* Robert Elias, ed. (Philadelphia, 1959), 171.

[24] *Theodore Dreiser: A Selection of Uncollected Prose,* Donald Pizer, ed. (Detroit, 1977), 221-23.

[25] See *Selected Poems,* with introduction and notes by Robert Saalbach (New York, 1969), 192-93.

[26] "A Pluralistic Mystic," 759.

[27] December 12, 1880, in Ralph Barton Perry's *The Thought and Character of William James,* I (Boston, 1935), 727.

[28] In "Swedenborg: or, the Mystic" from *The Complete Writings of Ralph Waldo Emerson* (New York, 1929), 365.

[29] *The Varieties of Religious Experience: A Study in Human Nature* (New York, 1902), 2.

[30] "The Conservative Connection: The Chairman of the Board Took LSD Before Timothy Leary," *American Studies,* 21 (Fall, 1980), 69.

[31] *Everyman His Own Poet; Romantic Gospels in American Literature* (New York, 1968), 8.

[32] *Henry James and the Occult: The Great Extension* (Bloomington, 1972), 3.

[33] New York, 1969, 69-71.

Sue Vice

SOURCE: "The Mystique of Mezcal," in *Canadian Literature,* No. 112, Spring, 1987, pp. 197-202.

[*In the following essay, Vice examines the hallucinogenic sequences in* Under the Volcano.]

> 'If I ever start to drink that stuff, Geoffrey, you'll know I'm done for.'
>
> 'It's mescal with me . . . Tequila, no, that is healthful . . . and delightful.' (*UV* 219)
>
> On the other hand there had been until recently several drinks of mescal (why not?—the word did not intimidate him, eh?) waiting for him outside in a lemonade bottle and all these he both had and had not drunk . . . (*UV* 304)

A confusion between the drink mescal and the drug mescaline seems to lie at the bottom of *Under the Volcano,*

as if it were *con gusano,* with an agave worm in its gourd:

> The worm isn't there for looks. It is meant to be eaten. Because it is believed by many that within the worm lies the key. Some say it unlocks the door to a world of wondrous experiences. Others say it sets free a spirit of celebration. Still others say that eating the worm locks in the enchantment and excitement of Mezcal. . . . [1]*

In his article "The Place of Hallucinations in *Under the Volcano,*"[2] Thomas Gilmore suggests that the Consul's exaggerated fear of mezcal is thus explicable:

> the Consul's (and Lowry's—see *Letters,* p. 71) apparent assumption that mescal is the liquid equivalent of the hallucinogenic drug mescalin is erroneous. But the assumption explains why the Consul dreaded the great potency of mescal and why, after he begins drinking it in Section X, his hallucinations seem to increase in frequency and intensity. (287, n. 4)

However, it seems rather that the drink, with its unsubtle, smoked-tequila flavour, and high alcohol content, is a symbol to Geoffrey of the point of no return. The guilt he feels in connection with mezcal has a historical origin, when the *conquistadores* "ran out of their traditional rum, the battle-scarred fighters looked for something else to celebrate with,"* and they developed a method for obtaining mezcal out of the Aztecs' *pulque.*[3] These connotations of exploitation of indigenous culture—"' . . . no, the point is, Yvonne, that the Conquest took place in a civilization which was as good if not better than that of the conquerors, a deep-rooted structure'" (*UV* 301), as Hugh says—of over-sophistication and greedy consumerism, culminate in the bad press mezcal had in the early days of Spanish rule in Mexico as the means by which Spanish mine-owners were able to pressgang farmworkers into the mines.

As Gilmore notes, Lowry indicated the Consul's apparent inability to distinguish between alcohol and hallucinogen: "It would appear that (he) has fuddledly come to confuse the two, and he is perhaps not far wrong" (*SL* 71). In itself, such a confusion is not startling; in his essay "The Present Status of Ololiuhqui and the Other Hallucinogens of Mexico,"[4] R. Gordon Wasson explains that dried *peyotl* (commonly eroded to "peyote"), a small woolly plant of the amaryllis family, and not a cactus as is often assumed, is the hallucinogen known in the West as mescaline:

> For reasons that seem to have sprung from popular confusion, the English-speaking population of the Southwest came to call the dried *peyotl* 'mescal buttons' . . . Later, when the active agent came to be isolated, the chemists called the alkaloid 'mescaline', thus compounding the mistake. 'Mescal' comes from the Spanish of Mexico *mescal,* derived in its turn from Nahuatl *mexcalli,* the name for the agave, *maguey,* or century plant from which pulque is made, which, when distilled,

yields *mezcal. Mezcal* has nothing to do with 'mescal buttons' or 'mescaline'. (166)

It is a fortuitous coincidence in a work which extends the periphery of hallucination beyond the clinical boundaries of the alcohol-induced, that Oaxaca, site of the terrible hotel and restaurants, the very word sounding like 'the last syllables of one dying of thirst in the desert' (*UV* 53), should be at the centre[5] of the sacred mushroom cult of Mexico.[6] As Gilmore points out (285), Art Hill's discussion of *Under the Volcano* as primarily the portrait of a drunkard[7] makes little mention of the Consul's hallucinations, and Gilmore himself concentrates on Lowry's treatment of them as a means for subverting the division between sober reality and fantasy. As ever, this symbolic purpose is based firmly on a mimetic foundation, thus echoing the nature of the hallucinations themselves. Although Gilmore states that drug-induced hallucinations include abstract elements—perception of colour, geometric shapes—which are absent in alcohol-induced ones, where the emphasis is more on feelings of fear and paranoia, often leading to death, what happens to the Consul seems to fit descriptions of hallucinogenic experiences, which include:[8]

1. "changes in mood (sometimes euphoric and megalomanic, sometimes fearful, panicky, and anxiety-ridden)"—the Consul never reaches heights of unselfconscious joy, but he does experience flickers of sudden hope for his future and his salvation (cf. *UV* 88, 217), counterpointing a host of the "fearful," ranging from vindictiveness and the desire to hurt and provoke, to the longing for a mother and security, and the constant sense of being watched and spied upon.

2. "a sense of threat to the ego"—as Aldous Huxley points out in *The Doors of Perception,* this is at once the prize and the price of the mescaline experience; liberation from the self can be insupportable. In the Tibetan Book of the Dead,

> the departed soul is described as shrinking in agony from the Clear Light of the Void, and even from the lesser, tempered lights, in order to rush headlong into the comforting darkness of selfhood as reborn human being, or even as a beast, an unhappy ghost, a denizen of hell. Anything rather than the burning brightness of unmitigated Reality—anything! (*DP* 43)

3. "intensification of the other senses so that inaudible sounds become magnified or food tastes better . . ."—Geoffrey's perception of sounds becomes personalized and not quite in tune with their sources:

> *Tak: tok: help: help:* the swimming-pool ticked like a clock. (*UV* 75)

> . . . while from above, below, from the sky, and, it might be, from under the earth, came a continual sound of whistling, gnawing, rattling, even trumpeting. (*UV* 144)

Yet the place was not silent. It was filled by that

ticking: the ticking of his watch, his heart, his conscience, a clock somewhere. There was a remote sound to, from far below, of rushing water, of subterranean collapse . . . (*UV* 338)

4. " . . . or normally unnoticed aspects of things (such as the pores in concrete) become strikingly vivid"—these unnoticed aspects are, for the Consul, all fierce and unhappy ones: in Laruelle's house he notices on the wall

> a terrifying picture *he hadn't seen before,* and took at first to be a tapestry . . . Down, headlong into hades, selfish and florid-faced, into a tumult of fire-spangled fiends, Medusae, and belching monstrosities . . . plunged the drunkards. (*UV* 202, my italics)

Yet there are also moments of appreciation of a kind of newly revealed beauty:

> . . . 'how, unless you drink as I do, can you hope to understand the beauty of an old woman from Tarasco who plays dominoes at seven o'clock in the morning?' (*UV* 55)

5. "a sense of depersonalization . . ."—Huxley describes this as an awareness which is "not referred to an ego; it was, so to speak, on its own" (*DP* 41); the Consul has difficulty in separating himself as perceiver from the intensity of his visions (cf. the vision of swarming insects, *UV* 152). The fierce flora which surrounds the Consul—the accusing sunflower (*UV* 148) and phallic plantains (*UV* 70)—suggests a vision opposite to Huxley's amazed perception of some Red Hot Pokers, "so passionately alive that they seemed to be on the very brink of utterance." (*DP* 46).

6. " . . . of being simultaneously both within and without oneself, a closely related feeling of merger (dissolving) with the external world and a loss of personality"—Geoffrey contrasts the separateness of the features of his life which he enjoyed when he first met Yvonne with his present state:

> And had it not turned out that the farther down he sank, the more those features had tended to dissemble, to cloy and clutter, to become finally little better than ghastly caricatures of his dissimulating inner and outer self, or of his struggle, if struggle there were still? (*UV* 361)

which is often apparent throughout the day:

> The toilet was all of grey stone, and looked like a tomb—even the seat was cold stone. 'It is what I deserve . . . It is what I am,' thought the Consul. (*UV* 295)

> . . . he was surrounded in delirium by these phantoms of himself, the policeman, Fructuoso Sanabria, that other man who looked like a poet, the luminous skeletons, even the rabbit in the corner and the ash and sputum on the filthy floor— did not each correspond, in a way he couldn't

understand yet obscurely recognized, to some fraction of his being? (*UV* 362)

Everything he sees is deranged and doomed; he experiences the world as he experiences himself:

> The huge looping-the-loop machine . . . suggested some huge evil spirit, screaming in its lonely hell, its limbs writhing, smiting the air like flails of paddlewheels. (*UV* 224)

and it is even questionable whether much of what he sees is there at all: "Obscured by a tree, he hadn't seen it before (*UV* 224).

7. "a perception of ordinary things as if seen for the first time unstructured by perceptual 'sets'"—Huxley also mentions the cleansed, childlike vision imparted to the world by mescaline: "the percept had swallowed up the concept" (*DP* 42). Geoffrey sees things anew, glowing with menace: in his garden are

> tools, unusual tools, a murderous machete, an oddly shaped fork, somehow nakedly impaling the mind, with its twisted tines glittering in the sunlight . . . (*UV* 132)

and without perceptual sets the true nature of what is before him shines out:

> . . . on his extreme right some unusual animals resembling geese, but large as camels, and skinless men, without heads, upon stilts, whose animated entrails jerked along the ground, were issuing out of the forest path the way he had come. He shut his eyes from this and when he opened them someone who looked like a policeman was leading a horse up the path, that was all. (*UV* 342)

Huxley goes on to describe the fear of a mind confronted with a reality overwhelming in comparison with the "cosy world of symbols" (*DP* 43), "the homemade universe of common sense" (*DP* 44), which he says is the constant state of the schizophrenic.[9] In *Moksha*, Huxley points out the loss of symbolism which accompanies mescaline and is the everyday experience of the schizophrenic: "the meaningful things seem in the mescaline experience are not symbols. They do not stand for something else, do not mean anything except themselves" (*M* 63). The schizophrenic

> can't shut off the experience of a reality he isn't holy enough to live in, which he can't explain away and which, because it never permits him to look at the world with merely human eyes, scares him into interpreting its unremitting strangeness, its burning intensity of significance, as the manifestations of human or even cosmic malevolences calling for the most desperate counter-measures, from murderous violence at one end of the scale to catatonia, or psychological suicide, at the other. (*DP* 44)

This seems particularly applicable to the Consul (cf. his thoughts on the relief of madness—"psychological sui-

cide"—and his propensity for violence: the questionable fate of the German officers in his ship the *Samaritan,* his machete-wielding in the Farolito); the hallucinations he experiences function simply as intensifications of his own *angst.*

8. "hallucinations of flowers, snakes, animals, other people, etc., which subjects usually know to be hallucinations though they are powerless to stop them"—Geoffrey inhabits a veritable jungle of snakes, Hugh being one of their number (*UV* 145), which are never clearly either visions or real reptiles (e.g., *UV* 131). He almost imagines the sunflower strolling into his room (*UV* 183), and among the people he sees or speaks to when they are (probably) not there, are the dead man in the swimming-pool, Hugh in the Calle Nicaragua, and Laruelle in the Café Paris.

9. "voices commanding the user to do something"—the Consul is constantly subject to a cacophany of voices berating and mocking him, a chorus of guilt made audible, which belong to his own Good and Bad Angels as well as to the figures of his past.

10. "the release from the subconscious of repressed material, sometimes in the form of terrifying, dreamlike, visual symbols, and breakdown of conscience and superego restraints"—in some ways the whole geography of *Under the Volcano* is akin to a region of the "subconscious," and all that happens to Geoffrey in it is so elemental, so rawly powerful and significant, that it has some of the qualities of the Kafkaesque vision: the subject is placed, fully conscious and able to record literally, within his own nightmare. Huxley suggests that under certain conditions, such as after ingestion of mescaline, or following deprivation of sugar and certain vitamins, the mind gains access to a way of seeing the world which is "biologically useless," possessing "no survival value" (*DP* 12), but which "may be extremely helpful to us in so far as we are creatures capable and desirous of understanding" (*HH* 101). He shares Lowry's image of the land of the heart: "A man may be said to consist of an Old World of personal consciousness, and, on the other side of a dividing ocean, of a series of New Worlds . . . of the subconscious" (*M* 58).

In earlier drafts of *Under the Volcano,*[10] the Consul actually did take a drug—at Señora Gregorio's he "sat with his drink for a long time smoking the marihuana,"[10a] and when he sees the *pelado*'s hands trembling on the bus to Tomalín he thinks that perhaps, "like the Consul himself, he had been sampling, but not subtly, the mighty marihuana."[10b] However, no special effects follow, merely

> an opiumish clarity of vision in which each object was in its proper scenical place and touched with a supersensual significance . . . The holy virgin, the pyrene, the advertisement for the Red Cross, the jacket from less than these could a universe be constructed.[10c]

The same confusion reigns here in the Consul's mind over what is drink and what is drug—"'The first drink I ever had, Father gave me on the q.t. . . . our old man never called it anything but soma. The curious thing about it is, it's exactly the same as this mescal here, I could swear,'"[10d] but he sees more when, in the published version, he only imagines he, or likens himself to one who, has taken a psychedelic.

Markson describes mezcal as "symbolically connected with the hallucinatory drug"[11] the Consul's confusion certainly mirrors a more widespread one, allowing him to benefit from the visionary aspects of mescaline without ever taking it. Not only are his hallucinations hybrids of reality and the imaginary, in form and content, but also of drug and drink experience. This is characterized for Geoffrey by what Huxley calls "visionary hell"; for people such as he, everything in the universe,

> from the stars in the sky to the dust under their feet, is unspeakably sinister or disgusting; every event is charged with a hateful significance; every object manifests the presence of an Indwelling Horror, infinite, all-powerful, eternal. (*HH* 49)

It is in this way that the idea of entering the afterlife you deserve when you die has its full meaning: fear and anger, of themselves, make for a hell of unlovely visions. The clear light of understanding becomes a hateful spotlit glare.

References in the text are as follows:

UV: Lowry, Malcolm, *Under the Volcano*. Penguin edition, 1981 reprint.

DP: Huxley, Aldous, *Doors of Perception*. London, 1954.

HH: Huxley, Aldous, *Heaven and Hell*, London, 1956.

M: Huxley, Aldous, *Moksha*, London, 1980, ed. M. Horowitz and C. Palmer.

NOTES

[1*] This, the title, and all following quotations denoted by an asterisk, are taken from the short leaflet supplied with bottles of *Monte Alban Mezcal con Gusano*, which is *Fabricado y embotellado por Mezcal Mitla, S.A. Libertad Nol 35, Oaxaca, Oax.*

[2] Thomas B. Gilmore, "The Place of Hallucinations in *Under the Volcano*," *Contemporary Literature*, 23, no. 3 (1982).

[3] According to the *Encyclopaedia Britannica*, the Consul is in fact correct in his insistence on the healthfulness of *pulque*, it is "an important and inexpensive source of carbohydrates, amino acids, and vitamins for Mexico's low income population. Pulque may in some regions provide the major liquid intake during the dry season."

[4] R. Gordon Wasson, "Notes on the Present Status of Ololiuhqui and the Other Hallucinogens of Mexico," in *The Psychedelic Reader,* ed. Gunther M. Weil, Ralph Metzner and Timothy Leary (New Jersey, 1973).

[5] Cf. Wasson's essay, especially p. 174, and accompanying maps.

[6] Wasson's mention of an ancient mushroom religion is corroborated by Albert Hofmann's comment in his Preface to Huxley's *Moksha:* "Psychotropic substances of plant origin had already been in use for thousands of years in Mexico as sacramental drugs in religious ceremonies and as magical potions having curative effects"—it is instructive to compare abuse of such substances with the Consul's guilt over his abuse of the mystical properties of wine.

[7] Art Hill, "The Alcoholic on Alcoholism," *Canadian Literature,* no. 62 (autumn 1972).

[8] From Richard R. Lingeman, *Drugs from A to Z* (New York 1974).

[9] Richard K. Cross, in his *Malcolm Lowry: A Preface to His Fiction* (Chicago, 1980), notes Geoffrey's "acute ontological insecurity" (37), and quotes from R. D. Laing's study of schizophrenia, *The Divided Self.*

[10] This and the following four quotations are from the Malcolm Lowry Collection: University of British Columbia, The Library, Special Collections Division. The references are to box, file, and page number: (a) 22 (23) 35, (b) 23 (I) (3), (c) 23 (I)8, (d) 28(5) 18. See also 24(2) 292 and 24(5) 394.

[11] David Markson, *Malcolm Lowry's Volcano* (New York, 1980), 134.

Anna Balakian

SOURCE: "Breton and Drugs," in *Yale French Studies,* No. 50, pp. 96-107

[*In the following essay, Balakian discusses André Breton's disregard for artificial stimulants in favor of the "natural intoxicants" of the human mind and the use he made of this belief in the development of his surrealism.*]

> Chaque homme porte en lui sa dose d'opium naturel, incessamment secrétée et renouvelée.
>
> Baudelaire

Agreeing with Baudelaire that every man had a powerhouse of natural intoxicants. André Breton made of this hypothesis the apex of surrealism.

Instances of his personal disapproval[1] of all artificial stimulants can be found in the pages of *Entretiens, 1913-*

1952, avec André Parinaud (Paris: Gallimard, 1952) and in other personal accounts of his own and of his friends' experimental activities in the field of the expansion of consciousness. His quarrels with Artaud and Desnos stemmed largely from Breton's suspicions that pathological and artificial aberration of the psycho-sensory mechanism made certain of the surrealist colleagues unsuitable subjects for surrealist exploration of the human psyche.

Breton's basic departure from Freud and his alignment with Dr. Pierre Janet were based precisely on Breton's conviction that the exploration of the unconscious was not necessarily to be motivated by the desire to normalize sensual and mental deviations observed in the abnormal or pathological subject; the objective was, rather, to demolish the preestablished *norm* and to ascertain the possibility of what Baudelaire had called "l'expansion des choses infinies." Dr. Janet had indicated this new direction when he had said:

> All this teaches us that we are richer than we think, we have more ideas and sensations than we thought. . . . To limit the life of man to this clear and distinct thought process Descartes speaks about, is to suppress in my opinion, three quarters of this human life and to leave what is most attractive, the shadows and the *clair-obscur*. It is one of the merits of contemporary psychology to have tried to know the mysterious side of thought.[2]

In approval of Janet's attitude, Breton ventured on a sane man's colonization of a platform of awareness heretofore allocated only to the lunatic, hysteric, ascetic, and the narcotic. In his departure from the abnormal, he had to isolate his experiment from the other states previously involved in this form of study. Breton entered the field of psychic expansion as a neophyte medical student and with the approach of a man of science rather than as a literary escapist or a lay sensation seeker. That much for the personal circumstances!

In terms of literary history, Breton derives his concept of the "voyant" from Baudelaire and Rimbaud. In Romantic connotation the word signified intimations of otherwordly vision here on earth; in the context of Baudelaire's *Artificial Paradises* it came to mean the power of transformation of existing reality by its distortion and contorsion; the re-created dimensions of time and place, and the objectification of the subjective conveyed the sense of paradise under the effect of hashish. Although the poet as "voyant" became a "director and transformer of dreams,"[3] Baudelaire, in conclusion, minimized the attraction of such trips into evanescent eternity by balancing the ecstasy of vision against the slavery involved in the involuntary nature of the acquisition. In a parallel recital of the pleasures and agonies of drug addiction, Théophile Gautier had given still another definition of the "voyant" in his *Club des Haschischins:* an "adept who remained sober."[4] It is this definition of the nonaddicted visionary that Rimbaud conveyed in theory if not always in practice in his famous statement: "Le Poète se fait *voyant* par un long, immense et raisonné

dégèglement de *tous les sens.*"[5] Although Rimbaud underlined "dérèglement" the word that is interesting in the context of surrealism is "raisonné." Breton was to adopt *rational derangement* as the pivotal plank of his program to "remake human understanding."[6]

Regardless of what other surrealist colleagues have done with the basic premises of surrealism, Breton's own major statements were without ambiguity, and he adhered to them very closely throughout his life. Surrealism's major hypothesis was that man, in his status as everyman, was naturally endowed not merely with a *grain* of opium but with a psycho-sensory mechanism of utmost flexibility, which modern civilization had reduced more and more to rigor and uniformity of performance, thus adding to the insufferable human condition of brevity and mortality the burden of conformity and tedium. If it was futile to rebel against the mortality, he could confront the tedium of human experience: "Je n'ai jamais été porté que vers ce qui ne se tenait pas à carreau."[7]

To revive his powers of natural intoxication Breton explored dreams, automatic writing, aleatory walking, the free play of eidetic association of natural entities and man-made objects; these activities involved the auto-psychoanalysis of the non-psychotic and the non-neurotic, and aimed to recuperate the state of grace of childhood. With the drug cult Breton shared a common objective: that of provoking vertigo, which for him was synonymous with rapture. In summing himself up in the poem *Les États Généraux,* he says: "Ce que j'ai connu de plus beau c'est le vertige."[8] But he never thought that he needed drugs to achieve that state.

For him there was a stimulus much more potent than drugs, and that was the provocative power of language. All the terminology that Breton used to describe the surrealist function of language in his First Manifesto is derived from the lexicon of drug users, along with the misuse of the word "stupéfiant" or in its English equivalent of "narcotic," which technically applies to the benumbing character of drugs, whereas Breton—as well as Aragon in *Le Paysan de Paris*—uses the word as a synonym of stimulant. In fact, Breton's characterization of surrealism, surrealist language and image are in the context of "drug," "narcotic," and "hashish" not in the pharmaceutical precision of their meanings but of the general connotation reminiscent of literary descriptions of experience with drugs; it is to be noted that among the attributes which relate surrealism to drug addiction are not only the potency of effect but the habit forming character as well:

> Surrealism does not permit those who have indulged in it to drop it when they please. Everything leads us to believe that it acts on the mind in the manner of narcotics; like them it creates a state of need and can lead man to terrible revolts. . . . In many ways surrealism looms as a *new vice*. . . . Like hashish there is enough there to satisfy the most delicate systems. . . . The case of the surrealist images is very much like that of

the images of opium that man no longer evokes because they 'are offered spontaneously, despotically. He cannot dismiss them; for free will no longer has any power and does not govern his faculties.'[9]

Breton's description of the surrealist state seems to parallel so closely what Baudelaire had described as the narcotic state that Breton ends his observation with a quotation from Baudelaire's *Artificial Paradises.*

The artificial stimulant was unnecessary for Breton because of the built-in mechanism that he was cultivating to provide him with powers of provocation and reception all at once. The surrealist interest in this powerhouse is in terms of the strength and intensity of its productive energy rather than in regard to the particular quality of the resulting product, whereas all accounts of drug trips in literary context put their emphasis on the *visions* attained rather than on the *process* of the attainment. In other words, what interested Breton was not the poppy seed but the fertility of the poppy field which he situated within that inner space previously occupied by the immortal soul.

Breton's view of the expansion of consciousness and enrichment of sensory experience is the crux of the socio-ethical character of surrealism over and above any literary results it has or may have wanted to achieve. The basic metaphor of surrealism evokes intoxication, its essential definition is the natural state of hallucination attained by "the education of all the senses" and the recuperation of their primal unity with the power of perception, as Breton elaborates the doctrines of the Manifestoes in "Le Message automatique." One can go so far as to conclude from Breton's tautological and imperative warnings about the perils of depriving man of his natural opium, that this privation may indeed have resulted in acute symptoms of withdrawal in modern man, manifest in the drug cult crisis of our time.

Before Breton, the purpose of stimulants in the life of the literary man was to provoke literary inspiration and to satisfy his nostalgia for the mystical state. Breton was committed to no particular literary destiny and believed in no possible transcendence into another world. Let us remember his self-interrogation in *Nadja:*

> "Qui vive?" "Qui vive?" Est-ce vous Nadja? Est-il vrai que l'*au-delà* tout l'au-delà soit dans cette vie? Je ne vous entends pas. Qui vive? Est-ce moi seul? Est-ce moi-même.[10]

For Breton poetry was a form of epistemology as it had been at least in theory for Rimbaud and Apollinaire. Early in his career he outlined his objectives in this direction in "Les Mots sans rides":

> To restore to language its full destination . . . to make knowledge take a great step forward, and in so doing to provide life with a measure of exaltation.[11]

Poetry was a path of knowledge about man, and literature was viable only as a human science. In *Le Surréalisme et la peinture* he tells us:

When I learn where I am to see in me the end of the terrible struggle between what I have already lived and what is viable, when I lose all hope of increasing in *stupefying*[12] proportions the field of reality, heretofore extremely limited, of my endeavors, when my imagination becomes self-contained and restricted to the orbit of memory, I will consent to indulge like others in a few relative satisfactions. I will then rank myself among the embroiderers. I will forgive them. But only then and not before.[13]

The ethics of this poetry were involved not in good or evil, but in the relative extension of the spectrum of feeling and vision. As he saw no dichotomy between sensation and representation, the deepening and enlarging of the one invariably fed into its connecting vessel: not in the case only of superman but of everyman. In *Political Position of Art Today* (1935) he explains that the right to reach and utilize the forces of the unconscious is inalienable for it provides access to a common treasure.[14] Perhaps everyman's eventual recovery of the hallucinatory power will make bourgeois societies untenable and communist structures inadequate. Breton gives the impression that evil and brutality are the results of tension and of the impediment of these rights; a return to the processes of nature would restore man's benign consideration of the rights of others and the sense of freedom he would acquire would not be wasted in self-indulgence and destruction. There would result a clearer understanding of the "moi" in the perspective of the "soi" and in the elimination of the "surmoi." In other words, the cultivation of the individual essence would strengthen the existential functioning of the group. The basis of his quarrel with the communist system of the Stalin regime was his disappointment in the fact that men allegedly interested in the betterment of the socio-economic condition of everyman presumed this possible while retaining the strictures of an inhibitory rationalism inherited from previous nonegalitarian ideologies. Ironically, Breton was, at his death, light years away from having in any way affected the sensibility of everyman.

Actually, the results of his having treated surrealism as a form of stimulant to latent human energies made its impact explicit in that literature which he deemed secondary to the transformation of society. If not for everyman, then for the student of literature the textual stimulants he furnished are fertile and productive in their psychedelic effects. His lucid mind gave in its verbalization the evidences of how the literary text may be affected by its use as a channel for intensified sensory reception and a medium for hallucination. As we peruse his poetic writings from the point of view of stimulation and psychic expansion, we find some of the terminology of exaltation, convulsion, elation, and eidetic perception, but never of depression.

The sensory apparatus of Breton may be compared to an octopus, the body its transformer, the tentacles sucking into the far reaches of the natural human, vegetable, and mineral kingdoms that are intricately knit together in his ecstatic approach to reality.

Illumination, which is one of the significants of the hashish experience, is the basic key to Breton's nonpharmaceutical sharpening of vision. All the words associated with luminosity are part of his paradigmatic metaphors: étincelant, éblouissant, luisant, scintillant, flambée, phosphorescent, sphères de lucioles, verticale d'étincelles, nuit des éclairs, constellation, incandescence, maillot de lumière, lustre irisé, to name only a few of the qualifications of light, fire, crystal, all part of the extra-lucidity achieved.

Another transformation generally brought about by the drug habit is distortion. Here Breton deviates. Although closely sympathetic to Marcel Duchamp and to Cubist friends, he does not employ the dehumanization process as a feature of his metaphor; nor does he go back to the earlier distortions of perspective evidenced by De Quincey, Gautier, or Baudelaire. For him the transformational operation on reality does not occur through an alteration of proportions but through relocation or substitution, the corollary of which is incorporation. Relying on the alchemistic philosophy that all is in all, and that the arrangement of objects, and subsequently of the relation of their images to each other is an arbitrary one, he expends his creative ability on the act of subjective selection, which actually means the reception of the unconscious selection; in this way he puts his own personal ontological imprint upon the universe. An expression such as "Monde dans un baiser" is not simply an affective expression of love for Breton as it might be for Lamartine or Musset. It is a basis of reconstruction of disparate elements that his senses regroup into the chosen focus of the immediate moment. His philosophy of immanence is in fact possible because of this power to shuffle an ever wider scale of physical stimuli into a personal synthesis which constitutes the paradise of the moment. As he says in "Langue de pierres": "One finds only what one needs profoundly."[15]

The paradisiacal state of love is the chief instance of union with the universe, whose elements are redistributed to make the human pair the center of luminosity. Again the vocabulary used to describe the effect is one generally associated with the power of drugs. In his "A jour" to *Arcane 17* he says: "The act of love, on the same basis as the picture or the poem, is disqualified if the person involved does not suppose himself to be *entering into a trance*. Nowhere else is the capture of eternity so instantaneous."[16] Most illustrative of his contention that there is to be no distinction between the functions of the sensory system and the intellectual working of the mind is the erotic stimulus, which has on Breton the power of a most potent potion; in *L'Air de l'eau,* a series of poems to the "scandalously beautiful Jacqueline," whom he had just married, he compares her mouth to a hallucinatory herb: "Ta bouche est volontiers la nielle";[17] and many years later in his last series of prose poems, *Constellations,* he again puts love in the context of a stimulant when he uses the word "belladona" in the double sense of the drug and the lady who arouses him:

> Des taillis où couve une chanson ensorcelante perce par éclairs et ondule la pointe du sein de la belladone.[18]

If these are two illustrative examples of actual textual designation, the more general hallucinatory and exalted state associated with the erotic is the normal assumption for Breton: "le luxe est dans la volupté" he generalizes in another of the *Constellations* called "Femmes au bord d'un lac à la surface irisée par le passage d'un cygne."[19] But the intoxication occurs only when the sensual stimulation of sex is accompanied by the emotional one of love; one without the other remains nonintoxicating for Breton.

The hallucinatory vision or feelings of Breton, contrary to that induced by drugs, never falls into the nightmare phase; dream and hallucination are always pleasure producing agents. The need, therefore, of transcendence is overcome by the satisfaction in an immanent reality where depth and summit are points not of a vertical pattern that might range from elation to dejection, but part of a circumference of ever widening euphoria. His very vocabulary conciliates the contradictions of high and low: "elles montaient vers moi soulevées par les vapeurs d'un abîme" (*Pleine Marge*).[20] In a more general perspective we find in *Constellations:*

> Une vie protoplasmique profuse se taille dans la voie lactée, à hauteur de soupir, une amande qui germe.[21]

The image integrates several levels: the cosmic ascension to the Milky Way, the human height inherent in the sigh, and the almond at the level of germination in the soil. In the throes of the poetic trance he achieves the "certain point of the mind" which he had proposed in the *Second Manifesto* where "the high and the low cease to be perceived as contradictory."[22]

If the bird images of Breton's poetic universe are a source of ecstasy and exhilaration, so are the stones and agates that he culls from the recesses of the earth: "It is not doubtful that the obstinate pursuit of light and sign, which the 'visionary minerologist' maintains, acts on the mind like a *narcotic,*" he says in one of his final articles entitled "Langue de pierres."[23] The expression "visionary minerologist" is taken from Novalis' *Henry Ofterdingen,* where the poet seeks luminosity in the bowels of the earth, and Breton's search for stone is described in terms used by Baudelaire to depict the pharmaceutical trip. As in Baudelaire, the description has several phases: the first hallucinatory, the second extra-lucid, the last stage a total experience of dream and reality producing the "illusion of having come upon the soil of the terrestrial paradise."[24]

If Breton's self-induced qualities of the visionary do not transport him to a nonterrestrial heaven of virtue or to a burning hell of sin, it is because Breton is basically the poet of innocence, his vision benign, and the earth the terrestrial paradise. He finds here all that he needs to keep him generally "high"—or at least that is the impression he apparently wished to convey. As each vision is translated into a poem or prose, the aftermath of the dream is not a stage of attrition and self-torture as in the case of the drug addict. For the images that produce the state of euphoria are "a vital tension turned to the highest degree of health, pleasure, serenity, restored state of grace, consented practices. Its [the analogical metaphor's] mortal enemies are the deprecative and the depressant," he says in "Signe Ascendant," one of the essays collected in *La Clé des champs.*[25] Again, the qualifying adjectives have pharmaceutical connotations. Instead of the state of vacuity that follows the narcotic trip, Breton's natural one results in action and creation as the dream or hallucination, or the extra-lucid vision enter into either the personal life, as he demonstrated in *Les Vases communicants* or in *L'Amour fou,* or in the verbal image of a poem.

The early automatism of Breton's writing was a form of stimulation that was intended to launch his power of psychic association into free play much as the taking of a hallucinatory drug is supposed to achieve. His later writing was less dependent on automatic exercise of words since the practice had refined and flexed this ability sufficiently to provide evocatory association on demand.

As he grew older his need to write decreased; it had not been primarily literary but rather a very human necessity for self-illumination. The Word had been only one of his hallucinatory stimulants; the others had been people, objects, nature's manifestations. Breton's relationship with nature, a very close one, was distinctly different from that of Romantic poets. Its complicity was not the pathetic fallacy or the objective correlative, but served as a smoldering fire, the ignition, the bountiful and gratuitous replenisher of human energy.

Breton became ever more aware and more the master of his force, which made him one of that small category of writers for whom life was a state of grace and a cause for intoxication. Although it is an aphorism to say that to be a poet is to be intoxicated, few poets have had the frame of reference of intoxication so invade their linguistic code as Breton. The essential anguish—for can any man be without one?—was caused by the knowledge that the number of our years was not commensurate with the possibilities and varieties of stimulation available to the mortal senses without recourse to anything but the peaks of mountains, and the soaring of birds, and the glow of stones, charged with eternity, and the crystal iridescence of the waters of Oceania, and the vertiginous flash of lightning produced by the movement of a loved woman, and the savage eye of Breton.

Surrealism is, in fact, intoxication . . .

[1] In my own last encounter with Breton in 1964, I remember the sardonic disdain with which he explained the attempt that had been recently made to set his apartment on fire: "C'était des gens très drogués" ["They were highly drugged persons"].

[2] Pierre Janet, *L'Automatisme psychologique,* 9th ed. (Paris: Felix Alcan, 1921), p. 421. I have treated the differences in the method of Freud as opposed to that of Janet in my critical biography of Breton; my information was based on a close reading of Pierre Janet's *L'Automatisme psychologique* and of *De l'Angoisse à l'extase* in the original French; the present translation is my own. Cf. *André Breton: Magus of Surrealism* (New York and London: Oxford University Press, 1971) for development of the subject.

[3] A. Balakian, *The Symbolist Movement: A Critical Appraisal* (New York: Random House, 1967), p. 43; for detailed study of Baudelaire's treatment of the subjects of drugs, see my chapter on Baudelaire, in *Literary Origins of Surrealism* (New York: N. Y. U. Press, 1966).

[4] "Le Club des haschischins," *Revue des Deux Mondes,* ler février, 1846, p. 487 (collected in *œuvres: Romans et Contes,* [Paris: Lemerre, 1897]).

[5] In Rimbaud's letter to Paul Demeny: "The poet makes himself a seer by means of a long, immense and rational derangement of all the senses." (*œuvres complètes* [Paris: Pléiade, 1951], p. 254. In "Le Message automatique," Breton talks of the reeducation of the senses along the lines advocated by Rimbaud. Cf. "Le Message automatique," *Point du jour,* new edition (Paris: Gallimard, 1970), pp. 196-7. Original edition, 1933.)

[6] "Comète surréaliste," *La Clé des champs* (Paris: Sagittaire, 1953), p. 105.

[7] "I have never been drawn toward anything that did not throw caution to the winds." "Pleine Marge," *Poèmes* (Paris: Gallimard, 1948), p. 171. (Originally appeared as a separate work, *Salon Martigues,* 1940.)

[8] "The most beautiful thing I have ever known is vertigo." *Poèmes, op. cit.,* p. 215. "Les Etats-Généraux" was written in N.Y. in 1943.

[9] "Premier Manifeste," *Manifestes du surréalisme* (Paris: J.-J. Pauvert, 1962), p. 51. (Original edition, 1924.)

[10] "'Who is there?' 'Who is there?' Is it you Nadja? Is it true that the beyond, all the beyond is in this life? I don't hear you. Who is there? Is it I alone? Is it myself?" *Nadja* (Paris: Gallimard, 1928), p. 190.

[11] "Les Mots sans rides," *Les Pas perdus* (Paris: Idées, 1969), p. 138. (Original edition, 1924.)

[12] The underlining is mine.

[13] *Le Surréalisme et la peinture* (New York: Bretano's, 1943), p. 23. (Original edition, Paris, 1928.)

[14] Cf. "Position politique de l'art d'aujourd'hui," *Manifestes du surréalisme, op. cit.,* p. 272.

[15] "Langue de pierres," *Poésie et autre,* Gérard Legrand, ed. (Paris: Le Club du meilleur livre, 1960), p. 324. (Original printing in *Le Surréalisme même,* No. 3, Autumn 1957.)

[16] "A jour," *Arcane 17* (Paris: J. J. Pauvert, 1965), p. 148. (Original edition, N. Y., 1945.)

[17] *L'Air de l'eau* (included in *Poèmes, op. cit.,* p. 137. (Original edition, 1934.)

[18] "La Poétesse," *Constellations,* unnumbered section of *Poésie et autre, op. cit.* (Original edition, N. Y.: Pierre Matisse, 1959.)

[19] This title means: "The lady at the edge of a lake iridized by the passage of a swan." *Ibid.*

[20] " . . . they rose toward me uplifted by the vapors of an abyss"; it could also mean: "lifted by the ships of an abyss." What is important in the untranslatable Breton is the junction of the two seemingly contradictory movements of up and down. "Pleine Marge," *op. cit.,* p. 171.

[21] "A protoplasmic life cuts for itself in the Milky Way, at the level of a sigh, a germinating almond." "Femmes dans la nuit," *Constellations, op. cit.*

[22] "Second Manifeste," *Manifestes du surréalisme, op. cit.,* p. 154.

[23] "Langue de pierres." *Poésie et autre, op. cit.,* p. 320.

[24] *Ibid.,* p. 230.

[25] "Signe ascendant," *La Clé des champs, op. cit.,* p. 115.

James Campbell

SOURCE: "Alexander Trocchi: The Biggest Fiend of All," in *The Antioch Review,* Vol. 50, No. 3, Summer, 1992, pp. 458-471.

[*In the following essay, Campbell presents an overview of the works of Alexander Trocchi.*]

Cain's Book, Alexander Trocchi's drug-related master-crime, is a novel to give to minors, a book to corrupt young people. It has been banned, burned, prosecuted, refused by book-distributors everywhere, condemned for its loving descriptions of heroin use and coarse sexual content. Trocchi, a Scotsman, died in London in 1984. Since completing *Cain's Book* a quarter of a century earlier, he had written hardly anything. It's not difficult to see why. *Cain's Book* is more than a novel: it is a way of life. The book is autobiography and fiction at once, the journal of a fiend, a stage-by-stage account of the junkie's odyssey in New York, an examination of the mind under the influence, a rude gesture in the face of sexual propriety, a commentary on literary processes and critical practices, a chart for the exploration of inner space.

Trocchi accompanied Burroughs, Kerouac, Ginsberg, and others on the new roads taken in the 1950s, but he wrote with a cerebral sophistication shared by none of the other Beats. He was more fully tuned in to Literature, and therefore could refuse, and reject, its terms more conscientiously. Up in Scotland, we dipped into the mythology of the Beat Generation, borrowing and adapting what suited our brand of Celtic hip. Trocchi appeared to us as a colossus, bestriding a narrow world. He was forging his own myths—and he was one of ours. Only a Scot could formulate an epigram so calculated to outrage the native temperament as, "It is difficult to explain to the underprivileged that play is more serious than work." Or, taking different aim: "My friends will know what I mean when I say that I deplore our contemporary industrial writers. Let them dedicate a year to pinball and think again."

Even before *Cain's Book* was published in Britain, Trocchi was scheming to shock people—especially those who were well-intentioned towards him. On one famous occasion, at the 1962 Edinburgh International Writers Conference, organized by John Calder, Trocchi took command of a debate on the literature of the host country. The Scottish Nationalist poet Hugh MacDiarmid was on the platform, as usual promoting his own work, denigrating everything English, dismissing *all* contemporary fiction out of hand, proclaiming Scotland's potential as an international cultural force. The audience, or at least the Scottish part of it, had heard it all before.

When MacDiarmid had finished, a tall young man with a hawk's profile and bristly black hair got up to respond. Trocchi had published one little-read book in Britain, *Young Adam,* but some of the writers present, such as Lawrence Durrell and Norman Mailer, knew him as drug addict and a friend of Burroughs, who was sitting next to him. Trocchi answered the locally revered poet by first saying that the best modern poetry had been written by novelists anyway, then dismissed the work of MacDiarmid and his clan as "stale, cold porridge. Bible-clasping nonsense. Of what is interesting in Scottish writing in the past twenty years or so, I myself have written it all."

As a stunt to publicize a writer still unknown in Britain, it was quite a success. Trocchi's speech grabbed the front pages of the Scottish press, and he was invited on television as a "self-confessed drug addict." As the debate continued in the columns of the *New Statesman,* MacDiarmid denounced Trocchi as "cosmopolitan scum"—which only enhanced his reputation further.

I don't doubt that Trocchi saw the humor in it all. He had written altogether nine books, but most of them were "dirty books," which had been published, under pseudonyms, by Maurice Girodias's Olympia Press in Paris in the 1950s. Nonetheless, there is a finger of truth in his words to the Edinburgh Conference, for Scottish prose-writing in the period 1942-62 has nothing to rival *Cain's Book,* which was published in Britain the following year (it had come out in the United States in 1960), for style, intelligence, and formal originality.

. . . . .

Cain's Book provided a context. I first came across it in 1970, a nineteen-year-old literary minor living in the same streets where Trocchi had grown up some thirty years earlier. I refused to work, I was anti-university, I explored my "inner space" with the help of hallucinogens. Trocchi set out reasoned intellectual structures for these attitudes. Play is more serious than work. All you have to do is say it, and—well, isn't it so?

Our view of ourselves was as outsiders, escapees from society's snares, gentle outlaws. But Trocchi really was an outlaw, being a determined drug addict (there was also a rumor—true, I was to discover—that he had had to escape the U.S., and the electric chair, in disguise, being wanted on a charge of supplying narcotics to a minor). How far can a man go, he wondered, "without being obliterated?" And he put himself forward coolly as the guinea pig for his own tests.

To adopt the identity of the junkie was to refuse society's own narcotics: work, marriage, civic responsibility, family duty; it was to make oneself avant garde, the anti-man; it was to escape the bounds of social consciousness, which deadened creativity, and take up residence in inner space. Trocchi went even further. He implied that his was a moral position: "to think that a man should be allowed a gun and not a drug." Only by the way did he invoke the orthodox justifications for drug use, claiming he was "experimenting" or seeking to unlock concealed compartments of the mind. Of Aldous Huxley—the pioneer of controlled experiments—he cheekily wrote in *Cain's Book:* "He was a boyhood hero of mine, and I'm glad to see him on drugs at last." Trocchi barely countenanced the notion that his addiction could debilitate him physically, or erode his talents. On the contrary, he made heroin sound positively beneficial:

> It's somehow undignified to speak of the past or to think about the future. I don't seriously occupy myself with the question in the "here-and-now," lying on my bunk and, under the influence of heroin, inviolable. That is one of the virtues of the drug, that it empties such questions of all anguish, transports them to another region, a painless theoretical region, a play region, surprising, fertile, and unmoral. One is no longer grotesquely involved in the becoming. One simply is.

In addition to espousing original opinions on the drug laws (heroin should be placed "on the counters of all chemists . . . and sold openly") and taunting taboos in general, Trocchi was an authentic literary craftsman. This concerned us more than the drugs, which my friends and I would solemnly have described at the time as an objective correlative for alienation in the novel.

Trocchi's erudition was among his more attractive attributes. He had been properly educated (cunning old thing, he didn't let on that he took full advantage of university before opposing it); he knew Latin, read Baudelaire in the original, quoted Unamuno; he breathed out phrases like "the Aristotelian impulse to classify" as

casually as blowing smoke-rings. Trocchi's professor of philosophy at Glasgow University described him as the best student he ever taught. The junkie and pornographer Trocchi was also a philosopher, one who invites you to consider the contradictions inherent in the statement that reads: "This statement is not true." For the ingenuity of *Cain's Book,* the tease that draws you into it again and again, is that it questions its own processes at every turn, consciously undermining its own validity as a "novel," yet finally existing freely as a work of art.

On my first copy, a picture of Trocchi's tough, hollow-cheeked face glowered from the cover like a Glasgow hard-man advertising his prison memoirs. I set off on a year's travel through Europe and the Middle East, taking *Cain* with me, the alternative version, the lost Book. At every opportunity, I preached his gospel to believers in the false gods of plot and linear narrative.

> —In the pinball machine an absolute and peculiar order reigns. No scepticism is possible for the man who by a series of sharp and slight dunts tries to control the machine. It became for me a ritual act, symbolising a cosmic event. Man is serious at play. Tension, elation, frivolity, ecstasy, confirming the supra-logical nature of the human situation. Apart from jazz—probably the most vigorous and yea-saying protest of *homo ludens* in the modern world—the pinball machine seemed to me to be America's greatest contribution to culture; it rang with contemporaneity. It symbolised the rigid structural "soul" that threatened to crystallise in history, reducing man to historicity, the great mechanic monolith imposed by mass mind. The slick electric shiftings of the pinball machine, the electronic brain, the symbolical transposition of the modern Fact into the realm of play. (The distinction between the French and American attitude towards the "tilt" ("teelt"); in America and England, I have been upbraided for trying to beat the mechanism by skilful tilting; in Paris, that is the whole point.)

The early 50s in Paris—where Trocchi went after taking his finals at Glasgow University—is one of those periods that in retrospect appear particularly vital. The situation was similar to that of the 1920s: a catastrophic war had recently ended, the city was cheap for foreigners, and artists were attracted by its reputation for freedom from social and sexual restraints. London in the 50s was seeing the evolution of Angry Young Man, but in Paris there were Sartre, Camus, Cocteau, and Trocchi's idol, Beckett—not to mention Richard Wright, James Baldwin, Chester Himes, and others. Compared to this, in Trocchi's eyes, Glasgow offered religion and the work-ethic.

Basing himself in a cheap Saint-Germain hotel, Trocchi founded the literary magazine *Merlin,* publishing Ionesco, Genêt, and others. Collection Merlin, an imprint of Olympia Press, was the first publisher of Beckett's novel *Watt,* in 1953, and later issued the English version of *Molloy,* with Trocchi acting as copy editor and go-between for Beckett and Girodias.

When he quit the Left Bank scene and sailed to New York, it was ostensibly in pursuit of a woman, but the move had another significance. Greenwich Village, not Saint-Germain-des-Prés, was the proper backdrop for his new drama. His leavetaking from society was fully planned. "I reject the entire system," he wrote in a letter of the time; "I am outside your world and am no longer governed by your laws. . . . " He found a job as a scow captain, shifting cargo on the Hudson and East Rivers; now he was living on the margin both while at work—his days were spent mostly alone, on the water—and at play. It was on the scow that he drew together notes that had accumulated in Paris and elsewhere, and formed them into *Cain's Book.*

Trocchi writes of himself in the novel (as Joe Necchi) stepping between cities, luggage in hand, one suitcase packed with notes and scraps of text. Quotations are given in *Cain's Book* from "Cain's Book," passages that do not appear in the main body of the novel. It took a long time to fall into place, but in 1959 it finally did so. On the last page, Trocchi wrote as if discussing another book entirely:

> as soon as I have finished this last paragraph [I intend] to go into the next room and turn on. Later I shall phone those who have kindly intimated their willingness to publish the document and tell them that it is ready now, or as ready as it ever will be. . . .

I only wish that Trocchi's bold remarks to the Edinburgh Writers Conference could be said to be pertinent still. "Of what is interesting . . . I myself have written it all"— but he wrote nothing else of moment before his death from pneumonia in April 1984. All play and no work? It makes a dull twenty-five years, and for a writer as talented as Trocchi—"the most brilliant man I've met" Ginsberg called him—a pitiful waste.

What happened? There was the corroding effect of the drugs, of course. There was also the revolutionary movement, project sigma, to which Trocchi devoted a large part of the 1960s. The aim of sigma was "the invisible insurrection," a takeover by the culturally enlightened of the "grids of expression and the powerhouses of the mind." Based by now in a west London flat, and with a body of support that included R. D. Laing, Michael McClure, John Arden, and Robert Creeley, Trocchi plotted, not the *coup d'état* of Lenin and Trotsky, but what he called a *coup du monde,* a gradual assumption of control by "the creative ones everywhere." In his manifesto, Trocchi set out sigma's aims:

> We have already rejected any idea of a frontal attack. Mind cannot withstand matter (brute force) in open battle. It is rather a question of perceiving clearly and without prejudice what are the forces that are at work in the world and out of whose interaction tomorrow *must* come to be; and then, calmly, without indignation, by a king of mental jujitsu that is ours by virtue of intelligence, of

> modifying, of correcting, polluting, deflecting, eroding, outflanking . . . inspiring what we might call *the invisible insurrection.* It will come on the mass of men, if it comes at all, not as something they have voted for, struck for, fought for, but like the changing season. . . .

The invisible insurrection seems very much of its period, and very far-fetched now. Trocchi's prophecies—from the redundancy of the publisher ("we must eliminate the brokers") to the collapse of the nation-state—have been mocked by history. The idea of a cultural terrorist seems foppish. But if the project appears blurred by the psychedelic patterning (Trocchi envisaged "spontaneous universities" sprouting up like mushrooms across the globe), it also has a characteristic originality about it, and an intellectual and imaginative ambition that is endearing today, when underground movements mostly involve real terrorists with real guns.

Trocchi's admirers wondered why he was giving so much time to his manifestoes and so little to literature. His London publisher, John Calder (no doubt contemplating his forthcoming elimination), expressed annoyance at the failure to capitalize (*capitalize!* Trocchi would have shrieked) on *Cain's Book*'s success, and complained that no one really understood what sigma was all about anyway.

But the real question for the writer was, how to follow such a book? Trocchi's art was confessional, and you cannot make the same confessions twice. And while the novel is structured on a number of clever devices, one of them is timed to detonate at the very second at which its creator attempts to sneak back to conventional narrative: at all its stations, *Cain's Book* announces: "This novel is not a novel; such categories are hereby rendered defunct."

In short, there is a negativity implicit in *Cain's Book,* to which Trocchi could do little but succumb. "You write your future," a friend of mine once said, and the writing in *Cain's Book* is much taken up with the then-fashionable topic, the death of the novel. The novel didn't die, after all, but, following *Cain,* Trocchi's part in it did.

. . . . .

Trocchi never lost the desire to shock. Nor the ability. "If I'm not capable of satisfying my wife, for some reason, I've no objection to providing some young bull to pleasure her." Those were among the first words he ever said to me. His wife, Lyn, reading on the nearby sofa, looked up briefly from her magazine.

It was 1972 and I had lately become associated with a small magazine published from Glasgow University, called *GUM.* When the editor suggested I interview a writer for his series, I mentioned Trocchi. We got his telephone number from the publishers and on a wintry afternoon some two weeks later, Trocchi met me at the door of his Kensington flat. He was dressed in a shabby black tee-shirt with short sleeves; I suspect now that he wore it on purpose, so that I could see for myself the ski-track scars running down both snowy-white arms where the veins had collapsed. He was very tall with an enormous nose and a gray complexion, and the girl who came with me said later that she could smell evil about his person. He made her think of another notorious figure associated with Scotland, Aleister Crowley, the occultist and black-magician who was known as the Great Beast. Trocchi would not have refused the compliment.

My first impressions were more mundane. I was dismayed to learn that the Trocchis lived a fairly orderly family life. Lyn, an American, made enquiries about old friends in Glasgow. She wore dark glasses even though dusk was pressing at the windows. Trocchi himself prepared café au lait and recommended a pastry—just hot from the oven, he chimed. There were two nice boys present, Marcus and Nicky. When father told the younger one to lower the volume on the television, the instruction was quickly obeyed. Painters had recently redecorated the flat, so that the woodwork gleamed. Before leaving Glasgow, I had conferred with the editor over what to do if invited by Trocchi to shoot up with him. The editor said I must accept: "It'll look great in the interview." Fat chance. The gulf between the person I had read about and the person now before me was wide, and wrong-footed me: he was older, plumper, grayer than I had expected, and while he still liked to tickle the toes of the moral majority from time to time, he had gone soft on hard drugs.

Trocchi was still an addict—it was one of his gimmicks to ask you to wait while he gave himself a fix—but he would advise any young person against getting started, he said. I read him a passage from an article by Cyril Connolly, which had appeared in a recent *Sunday Times,* presenting the addict in a familiar way:

> A striking observation is the anti-intellectual climate that prevails in the networks. All who have known someone addicted to drugs . . . will have remarked on the increasing indifference to reality, whether to the time of day . . . or reading, or any of the pleasures and passions, food, drink, love, sex, places of art, or the acquisition of knowledge which makes life worth living.

Trocchi made a partial defense of his stance by referring to Coleridge and de Quincy: "If nothing else, they were certainly intellectuals. But up to a point, it's true what he writes. What else can one say about it?"

I learned Trocchi's own version of his flight from America, and the electric chair, in 1961. One year after the publication of the Grove Press edition of *Cain's Book,* Trocchi was arrested and charged with supplying narcotics to a minor, for which the penalty in New York State at the time was death. The evidence was strong—a prescription bearing his name had been found in the possession of a sixteen-year-old girl—and made a conviction look likely. Trocchi was bailed out of prison with the help of an old friend from Paris, but, once free, immedi-

ately got in trouble with the law again. This time it was for fixing up, with Lyn, on a station platform. Trocchi himself managed to escape, but Lyn and their child were taken to prison. Supported by people on the Greenwich Village literary scene, Trocchi obtained a false passport, slipped over the border to Canada, to be met by Leonard Cohen, and made his way back to England, where Lyn and the boy Marcus eventually joined him.

He chose London not only because of his nationality but because it was a place where heroin was available to registered addicts legally, on the National Health. In this way, in the 1960s, Britain controlled its minor drug problem. There was no need to hustle on the street, to mug or to steal, except for the few who, for some reason, could not register for prescriptions.

However, to this we must partly attribute Trocchi's demise as a literary figure in the 1960s. While the easy availability of heroin comes as a relief to the junkie, it also cuts him off from his occupation—scoring—which propels him from one day to the next. "The identity of the junkie was consciously chosen," Trocchi wrote in reference to his decision to go "far out," to make himself an outlaw in a society of conformers. But who ever heard of a state-subsidized outlaw? Much of the energy of *Cain's Book* derives from the excitement of scoring, of settling on a safe pad, of heating the spoon. . . . Legitimized, this act is deprived of its drama. Only a kind of pathetic, under-subscribed theatre remains. The junkie's determined "outsider" stance turns out to be a bit of a fake.

With Trocchi, there remained a literary style, of course. In 1972 I was much inclined to look on the bright side, but I could draw scant information from him regarding current and future projects. *Cain's Book* was well over ten years old. "You must be finding it difficult to do a follow-up," I said, "having written a book about the inability to write a book." This drew from Trocchi the comment—which I carried back to Glasgow like a coconut—that I was "quite perspicacious." He was writing something called *The Long Book,* he said, and he read a portion aloud to me. I listened hard—I really wanted to hear it—for the old brilliance.

. . . . .

Trocchi relished the notoriety that first his drug-taking and then the book had brought him—more intoxicating by far than ordinary fame. A provisional title for *Cain's Book* was "Notes towards the making of the monster" which, though charming in its way, reveals a certain deadly self-consciousness. Real monsters—like real outcasts—are not self-made. The necessary condition of the outcast is that he cannot step in. The black man (for example) in downtown New York in the 1940s and '50s, trying to find an apartment, trying to find a job, was an outcast in the way that a white, university-educated junkie can only imagine (I almost said "long for"). When a monster is self-loving, and not self-loathing, he is inhabiting what Trocchi in his early existentialist days in Paris would have called a "false consciousness." He is certainly more of a danger to others than himself. Trocchi in fact had created two monsters: one of them he could control, and he exhibited it before the public on a leash; as for the other, as time went on it turned on its master, savaging him and all around him.

Rereading *Cain's Book* after many years, I am struck by a morbidity in the relationship between sex and drugs, and sometimes death. Whereas he never waxes lyrical over women, Trocchi forges a poetic mythology of junk, which fills the space marked "Love" in the novel:

> I remember Jody saying: "When we do make love, Joe, it'll be the end!" The end-love, she meant, the ultimate.—Like an overdose, Jody?

And again:

> I thought of Jody, and of how plump she is from eating too many cakes, of the soft wad of her belly, of our thighs without urgency interlaced, of her ugly bitten hands . . . into which she drives the needle each time she fixes. "That's your cunt, Jody."

At other times, Trocchi dwells on the separate parts of women's bodies like a lecherous mortician: "the flaccid buttocks like pale meat on the stone stairs"; "this first sex shadowy and hanging colourless like a clot of spiderweb from the blunt butt of her mound"; "her belly dangling like an egg on poach"; "the skin close, odorous, opaque, yellowish, and pitted almost like pumice-stone"; "a French woman's vitals would be sweet to the taste, while with those of an Englishwoman one risked being confronted with a holy sepulchre, a repository for relics"; and plenty more in the same vein. In *Cain's Book,* from which all those quotations come, the most affectionate liaison (apart from one with a man) is with Jake, a woman with one leg cut off above the knee. Necchi desires her genuinely, but at the same time he cannot help whipping back the sheets and saying to the reader, *Look what a monster I am.*

Trocchi's "Divine Marquis" mode is even less gorgeous in his pornographic *oeuvre*. It may be that artists reveal themselves more in their moments of lowbrow frivolity than (as they like to think) at times of highbrow seriousness; in any case, what is shown up by Trocchi's obscene writings can be unappealing in the extreme.

The books were written mainly for money, which helped keep the magazine *Merlin* afloat, but Trocchi told me he considered them to be "serious enough within their own limits." Each book contains some good passages, particularly the extraordinary *My Life and Loves: Fifth Volume* by "Frank Harris" (1954), which is so stylistically convincing that it was later incorporated by mistake in a "complete" edition of Harris's opus (much to others' mirth but Trocchi's annoyance, since he received no royalties). The issue at stake is not sex, but the violence that

sex in Trocchi's obscene books often conceals. In this passage from *Thongs* (1955), sex is hardly visible at all, appearing instead in the guise of power and pain:

> My father would mark her, a small cross cut with a razor on the soft inner surface of her left thigh; his cattle. . . . Everyone knew about the mark. Fourteen women in the Gorbals had been cut already. Normally my father kept the woman for about two months afterwards. Then they were free to go. The men of the Gorbals fought each other to marry a marked woman.

The monstrosity was not confined to the printed page. Joe Necchi in *Cain's Book* does not actually say that he is responsible for turning Jody on to heroin, nor any other member of the novel's grotesquely fascinating cast of junkies, but it is a fact that in life Trocchi did just that, leading people to a "far out" place, from which many could not return.

When he met his second wife, Lyn Hicks, she was a twenty-one-year-old from Hicksville, New York—Miss Hicks from Hicksville. Photographs show her as very pretty. Within months of meeting him, she was hooked, and six months after their marriage in Mexico in 1957, she was parading herself outside the casinos on Las Vegas Boulevard, "The Strip"—Miss Hicks, the hooked hooker from Hicksville. It was just one more way to earn money for junk. In a biography of Trocchi recently published in Scotland, *The Making of the Monster,* the author Andrew Murray Scott tells us that at other times "she danced in a sleazy nightclub wearing silver spangles the size of half-dollar pieces gummed to her nipples and black satin stretched over a tiny piece of cardboard at her crotch. . . . Alex spent most of the time lying on the bed in a junk haze."

Trocchi told friends that on at least one occasion he had "cooled out of a bust" by having Lyn offer herself to a policeman in the back of a police car. Whether this is genuine monstrousness, or mere bravado, it cannot be waved away by a gesture in the direction of the famous outrageousness and charm. Lyn died in London in her thirties, having tried unsuccessfully to kick the habit many times.

If Trocchi himself seems by now about ripe for dismemberment, not only by feminists but by humanists of every sort, we might ask the question: What made the monster? What lay behind Trocchi's destructiveness? What is the key to his psychopathology? A clue can be found in an interesting diary-jotting, uncovered by Andrew Scott and quoted in his biography, concerning the funeral of Trocchi's mother, who died when Alex was sixteen:

> The last vital link with existence [was] cut. Lowered into a grave that was my extinction. Men and women in black. Brothers. Aunts. Uncles. Lingered on the green slope like quavers on a musical score. Sixteen at the time. And my father said to me, "You will never see your mother again,"

like a drain running out. But she continued to exist. Her death was my direction.

The picture has the force of a dream, a vivid summary of the dreamer's existence, which appears to him as his fate. The relatives motionless on the grass, and the insensitive father, are less alive to the boy than the corpse now underground.

This revelation about his mother connects in highly suggestive ways with self-portraits in Trocchi's published writings. For example, in *Cain's Book* there is an unexpectedly tender moment in which Joe tells how much he enjoyed "brushing my mother's hair to make it beautiful" when he was a child. "I never knew my mother when she was young and, they said, beautiful, and sometimes when I passed my hand over her hair I was invaded by a sense of outrage that she was not young and beautiful to have me."

That "have me" is awfully ambiguous, and it becomes even more troubling once it is recalled that this passage follows hard on one in which the narrator explicitly ties his liking for the red hair to subsequent revulsion at the thought of her red pubic thatch. These associations are then made concise, in a formula that links the "red sex" to a fear—which duly became a reality—of losing his mother's love: "Only the mute knowledge of her constant loving me was as vivid as the seditious thought of the red sex." This mother is both loved, for her unselfish loving, and loathed, for her private sexuality.

At this point, we turn back to Trocchi's first novel, *Young Adam,* to the part near the opening in which the narrator—also Joe, also living on water, though on a barge and not a scow—discovers a female corpse floating in the canal. As Joe describes what he has found, one detail in particular stands out:

> As I leaned over the edge of the barge with a boathook I didn't think of her as a dead woman, not even when I looked at her face. She was like some beautiful white waterfungus, a strange shining thing come up from the depths. . . . But it was the hair more than anything; it stranded away from the head like long grasses. Only it was alive, and because the body was slow, heavy, torpid, it had become a forest of antennae, caressing, feeding on the water, intricately.

If this already gives off a whiff of necrophilia, the place is positively reeking once it emerges, in the second half of the book, that Joe himself is responsible for the woman's death. Wrap it all up together with further quotations offered by Andrew Scott, such as "the conquest of a new female, especially a beautiful one, was closer to hate than to love" (from a letter to a woman Trocchi hoped to marry), and one would feel quite confident about quoting back to Trocchi his own judgment on his mother ("Her death was my direction") and concluding, "Yes, you were right."

Death was to be directed to Trocchi's house with an accuracy, and a swiftness, that he could not then have

known about. But it appeared to some people, even in Paris days, that the celebrated charisma was a toxic cloud. Sometime around 1980, hoping to spark a few illuminating anecdotes about one old Left Bank trooper by another, I mentioned his name to James Baldwin. "Trocchi?" Baldwin snapped, the nostrils flaring as the great eyes bulged. "The junkie? I hate him. *I hate him.* Tell him that from me!"

. . . . .

If I never did, it was because I still felt that one great book, while it cannot excuse everything, gets you away with quite a lot. I kept in touch with Trocchi, off and on, over the years that followed our first encounter, more than once asking him to contribute to another magazine I was involved with in Scotland. I had no success. The last time I saw him, in 1981, he again met me at the top of the stairs, sleeves rolled up. "I'm just about to give myself a fix," he said. "Can you wait?"

This time I was alone, and although it would have enhanced my sense of the occasion to have glimpsed an evil aura about his still remarkably large and hardy frame, it simply wasn't there. "My family's dying all around me," he said, a vulnerable and most affecting grin pulling at his lips. Not long after Lyn's passing, their elder son Marcus had followed, losing a three-year struggle against cancer. He was eighteen. A woman friend from New Zealand had moved in, and he spoke fondly of her attempts to impose order on his flat, though to me the place looked a shambles. "I must sort all this out," Alex murmured, gazing with the visitor's eyes at the papers and envelopes, books and wooden sculptures, paint boxes and odd detritus that littered the floor. The way he said it told you he never would.

"I am a cosmonaut of inner space," Trocchi had once proclaimed. Inner space was all that remained to him. He had few acquaintances left in the literary world. Between complaints about difficulties in getting his books relaunched in London, he spoke frustratedly, for once, of his addiction. Heroin, the young champion, had long since turned old tyrant. As much as anything, he missed the freedom to travel abroad. Alex was a Francophile, but the channel was hard to cross. "You have to make arrangements about drugs and all that. Ach, it's a drag."

By this time, Alex was running a second-hand bookshop in Kensington High Street. We went there together, and I bought three modern American first editions, sold to me for token prices. Then he took me to his afternoon drinking-club, where he ordered us the Scotsman's favorite tipple, a glass of whisky with a beer chaser. "A hauf-an-a-hauf, Jim-meh!" Alex said to the uncomprehending barman, and chuckled as if he and I were sharing a family joke.

Such moments, together with his knowledge of antiquarian books and stamps (in which he also traded), were to me curious and poignant little indicators of his "insiderness," of the tameness of the monster. He had been forgotten in Scotland, and *Cain's Book* has hardly ever been readily available in bookshops. It was while writing an article in which I mentioned *Cain's Book* in passing as one of our country's best three modern novels—the other two, Archie Hind's *Dear Green Place* and Alasdair Gray's *Lanark,* also feature artists who cannot finish their work—that I heard he was dead. Twenty months afterwards, his younger son Nicky climbed on to the roof of the empty Kensington flat and threw himself off. Like his late brother, he was eighteen.

I am horrified to discover—both because of the Trocchi tragedy and for my own failure to be "perspicacious"—that my interview with the great man for the university magazine, twenty years ago, ended with the words: "Trocchi's book is about living. . . . Most of all, that is what *he* is about: life." I know what made me put that down. Trocchi the cartographer, the flag-planter, shunning honor in his own country, opened frontiers for fellow travelers. He went far out, and then farther; he went so far that inner space swallowed him up.

Matthew Stewart

SOURCE: "Stephen Wright's Style in 'Meditations in Green'," in *Critique: Studies in Contemporary Fiction,* Vol. XXXIV, No. 2, Winter, 1993, pp. 126-36.

[*In the following essay, Stewart discusses the metaphorical implications of Stephen Wright's experimental style in* Meditations in Green.]

Stephen Wright's 1983 novel *Meditations in Green* distinguishes itself as the work of a strikingly original literary talent. Like such works as Tim O'Brien's *Going After Cacciato* (1977), Michael Herr's *Dispatches* (1978), and Gustav Hasford's *The Short-Timers* (1979) it possesses an overt sense of "literariness," of realized aesthetic intentions, not found in the majority of narratives written about the Vietnam War.[1] With a verbal virtuosity, which only occasionally overreaches, Wright transcends the type of war narrative that adheres to a more confined style of conventional realism. In so doing he is able to suggest an ample set of truths about the Vietnam War and American society with a vividness that more traditional narrative styles seldom have seemed to allow. This is not to say that Wright leaves his reader with no sense of authentic Vietnam experience. In fact *Meditations in Green* succeeds in depicting Vietnam's wastage at both a literal, descriptive level typical of traditional realism and a non-mimetic level that links the novel to more experimental fictions. When I speak of realism here, I mean to emphasize the documentary quality at the heart of much realism; I mean to specify passages and procedures whose sole or predominant import is to reflect accurately the phenomenal world—in this case "the way it was" in Vietnam. When I speak of non-mimetic passages and techniques, I mean those whose significance is to be found primarily at a metaphorical or an intratextual level,

passages whose import is not to describe phenomena representative of what actually occurred in Vietnam.[2]

Like O'Brien's *Going After Cacciato, Meditations in Green* has a three-part narrative structure. It is divided into two readily identifiable story-lines; these appear alternately in lengths of several pages and are punctuated at irregular intervals by the fifteen short "meditations", which form the narrative's third part and give the book its title. These meditations center on some aspect of plant life and refer quite frequently to the opium poppy, a particular focus of attention for the addicted protagonist of both story-lines, Spec 4 James I. Griffin. The first of these story-lines follows the doings (and undoings) in Vietnam of Griffin's unit, the 1069th Military Intelligence Group, focusing on Griffin, but by no means exclusively on him. This story-line provides an extensive exposure to the details of army life in the rear during the middle or later stages of the Vietnam War. Although there is never any evidence that allows the reader conclusively to identify this story-line's third-person narrative voice, it occasionally seems to resemble Griffin recounting his own experiences in a detached, apparently omniscient manner.

Without a doubt, Griffin does narrate the second story-line, which follows his squalid and aimless life nearly seven years after his return from Vietnam. Living in a large urban area clearly meant to resemble New York City, he is still trying to reassemble the fragments of his life, splintered by the war. He returns to the drug habit—probably heroin—which he picked up in Vietnam, spends time with his plants, his plant therapist, and his girlfriend Huey, whose name reminds Griffin of the assault helicopters used in Vietnam.[3] He also finds himself involved willy-nilly in the plot of his paranoid ex-GI buddy Trips to assassinate a man whom Trips mistakenly believes to be Sergeant Anstin, one of their noncommissioned officers in Vietnam. As Thomas Myers has pointed out, one of the thematic virtues of *Meditations* is its insistent linking of the war with already-existent features of American culture, such as the looming violence and incipient paranoia inherent in contemporary urban life. Such themes are most generously elaborated in the second story-line.

Meditations' organization is certainly nontraditional and may initially put off some readers. But it is not as difficult as it may sound at first, nor as difficult as several reviewers have claimed it to be. The meditations themselves are clearly labeled as such and are no more difficult to identify than the vignettes with which Ernest Hemingway preceded his short stories sixty years ago in *In Our Time,* a helpful literary model for reading these meditations. Undoubtedly, like Hemingway's vignettes, the meditations' function in the entire context is not without ambiguity, but that ambiguity includes a compensatory rich suggestiveness. Several of the novel's recurrent motifs, most consistently those of botany and drugs, are present in these meditations. They also call attention to the drug-influenced quality of the narrative, told by or focused upon Griffin, the self-proclaimed "genial storyteller, wreathed in a beard of smoke" (8). Nowhere is the linking of the botanical and drug motifs more direct than in the final three meditations, wherein an opium poppy is planted, harvested, and prepared for smoking.

Each story-line is also readily identifiable from its narrator (stated or implied) and setting, and neither is in itself complicated or obscure. Both are strictly chronological and episodic; the only plot involved in either is the very literal and simple plot that Trips concocts to assassinate Sergeant Anstin, and this does not even come into play until the novel's midpoint. The narrative structure of *Meditations in Green* reinforces some of Wright's themes, such as the fragmentary quality of Griffin's life and the constant intrusion of the past into his present. Vietnam remains the major fact of his daily life even though he has been back in "the world" for seven years. Wright's narrative scheme asserts that Vietnam experiences can be powerfully portrayed in nontraditional forms.

This multifaceted organization indicates the text's demands for an adaptable reader. Different sections and different events in *Meditations in Green* must be read according to a supple aesthetic, for their impact may reside at a number of different levels. In some sections, the significance lies on a realistic plane; in others, on a metaphorical level; in still others, it is the mix of realism and metaphor that is important. Certainly, there are many passages of traditional documentary realism whose main purpose is to let the reader know what it was like to be at certain places doing certain things in Vietnam, a fact that critics who condemn Wright for being too "fanciful" either overlook or dismiss. Even the military analyst and Vietnam veteran Tom Carhart interrupts his grumbling condemnations long enough to admit that Wright manages "descriptions of people, places and things [that] sometimes take one's breath away with vivid, almost electrifying imagery." Indeed, *Meditations in Green* contains passages that convey the literal experiential quality of Vietnam with graphic intensity, helping us to hear, to feel, to see what it was like to be on a mission in the jungle or to be confined to the unrelieved grind of a tedious job in a dehumanizing rear-echelon environment.

It is hard to think of a more gripping description, for example, of one soldier's physical sensations and emotions than the section in which Griffin "humps" through the jungle as a part of the mission to recover Major Quimby's and Kraft's downed helicopter. The usually very unmilitary Griffin ("I want to be a champion cringer" he declares early in the novel [23]) volunteered for this mission because "he wanted a purge, a . . . primitive sacrament if necessary" (275). But Griffin soon finds that the mission's hard physical labor dominates his thoughts, deflating his intentions to the mundane level of enduring the expedition:

> Beyond the boulders there was a second stream, swifter and deeper than the first. Two men slipped under and were carried downcurrent into a rock dam. . . . Griffin kept a careful grip on the rope and safe on the opposite bank watched his pants deflate as the water poured out onto the ground. The rest of the day his feet seemed encased in warm sponges. Accustomed now to the muscular aches, the tightening of the nerves, the suffocating air, the claustrophobic botany, the sweat slick as slime on his face, he realized . . . that he could actually take this torture, that despite his intentions he truly was a solider, a fact he had never before been able to imagine. (278-79)

In this and other passages Wright evokes the feel of taking part in a search mission in the jungles of southeast Asia with splendid clarity and vividness. At the same time, he is able to turn his descriptions to good account by combining their sheer evocative power with another textual mission. In the above excerpt, for example, we share Griffin's insight into his martial capability and the uncomfortable and unexpected sense of self-esteem accompanying this insight. The heretofore relentlessly non-gung-ho Griffin had not known about this part of himself.

Another section equally memorable for its vividness describes the unworldy Indiana boy Claypool put out on his first and only search mission, a mission which eventually leaves him in a nearly catatonic state of devastation. Not only are the rendering of individual emotions during battle itself and the quality of combat convincing and compelling—a feat which many books have attempted, and some have accomplished—but also the quieter inner battles of Claypool's reactions to learning about his assignment and the hours he spends awaiting his march and then "humping the boonies." When he does begin the mission, the soft, desk-jockey's discomfort he initially feels shortly swells into distress:

> The patrol entered the jungle. At first Claypool was grateful for the shade. Five minutes later his uniform was heavy with sweat. He had difficulty breathing. It was like being locked in a sick room with a vaporizer jammed on high. A cloud of tiny bugs swarmed about his face, flew in and out his mouth. He spit out some, swallowed the rest. Fat drops of sweat slid across the lenses of his glasses, transforming the forest into a swirling blob of shimmery green. His pack grew heavier. The straps cut into his shoulders. His back ached. His feet hurt. He was afraid to check his watch for fear the four hours his body had ticked off were only thirty minutes by the clock. (153)

Claypool is about to experience suddenly the immediate horrors of a high-tech guerrilla skirmish, but it should be remarked that Wright's evocative powers are not spent upon the fire fights alone. He is able to convey not just the terror and confusion of battle, but the full panoply of physical and mental sensation of a GI humping the boonies.

Further, Wright skillfully conveys the boredom and dispiritedness of life in the rear, the life experienced by the vast majority of American servicemen in Vietnam.

Indeed, the number of actual combat incidents depicted in the book is quite small in comparison to the number found in many novels about the war. Perhaps the unique strength of the novel's descriptive realism is its ability to portray the boredom and futility ever-present in the lives of many rear-echelon soldiers in Vietnam. In summary, there are so many nuggets of realism in *Meditations* that any accurate description of it must account for the convincing and evocative descriptions of Vietnam activities that it renders at a mimetic level.

Yet *Meditations in Green* is much more than a transcription of events, even though it renders them lifelike and palpable. Wright's larger intentions are often realized in the midst of his primarily descriptive passages; vivid depiction merges with metaphor. Certain passages assert themselves more as thematic suggestions than as accurate documentations. One such passage is woven into the search mission for which Griffin volunteers. We have seen that his boredom-inspired, romanticized hopes for a ritual cleansing are quickly knocked out from under him; he realizes almost immediately upon entering the jungle that "getting out alive was the major priority" (277). This is Griffin's first encounter with the environment he scrutinizes so closely on film as an "image interpreter" for military intelligence and his initial intimacy with the botanical world that is a central presence in the novel:

> He felt like a spy in the camp of the enemy, a judge locked into a prison of those he had condemned. . . . And there was no end to it. You pressed through one layer to arrive at another just like it and then one beyond that and another and another like passing through doors in an estate of measureless dimensions. . . . Collapse and regeneration occurred at the same moment. Buckling walls and decaying furniture were repaired automatically here in this home of the future where matter itself was perpetually pregnant. (277)

We experience the jungle as literally stifling, overwhelming and fecund; at the same time it becomes a metaphor for Vietnam and the U.S. involvement there. The image of the Asian jungle as an endless mansion suggests America's long, futile war effort. In its resilient fruitfulness, the jungle is able to "repair" itself at an insurmountable rate, just as the Vietnamese enemy seemed to Americans to absorb devastating losses without defeat. A similarly organic metaphor for Vietnam is the description of the Ho Chi Minh Trail as "a living organism of strength and guile, slithering among the damage [of bombing runs], often filled in and repaired before the landing gear of the B-52s thumped down on Okinawa" (57).

Along with the sense of futility implicit in the jungle's "measureless dimensions," we see Griffin's almost epiphanic insight into his own connectedness with the enemy and his empathy for those destroyed by the U.S. military operations. He concludes that "the effort to bring down this house, of which [he] was a part, seemed at this close distance to be both frightening and ludicrous"

(277). Griffin has only achieved this long-delayed realization by directly encountering the jungle. Previously he had been kept at a technological remove from the country, viewing it through the air reconnaissance photographs he interpreted.

The passages that are at once the most strangely suggestive and true-to-life are those that describe Griffin's drug experiences. Although these passages are divorced from ordinary experience and are narrated in highly unusual verbal combinations and a distinctive diction, their effect is to replicate Griffin's drug-induced dreams and drug-influenced perceptions of the phenomenal world:

> I rode out under urine yellow skies into a stony desert, scrub grass and dust, crumbling brick buttes and rubble canyons. Trouble on the reservation. I crept up among weeds, peered through binoculars. Indians. Teepees and Cadillacs everywhere. . . . An iron horse screeched in overhead, showering grit and sparks. A fan began to open. . . . Red dots bloomed in the cracks between objects, swelled into suns that obliterated space until all I could see was a featureless screen of bloody light. (74-75)

Here the language conveys the brilliant other-worldliness of drug-induced experience. His "consciousness was shaken in a bag," Griffin states, "dumped into pandemonium" (75). The experience is vividly surreal, and the events literally implausible in the manner of dreams, but these events are metaphorically evocative of larger issues, both formal and historical.[4]

First, drug addiction is the central facet of Griffin's Vietnam and post-Vietnam life; therefore, it is important to feel and see its quality and to be able to compare the nature of drug-altered reality with the nature of "ordinary" reality.[5] Much of our "genial storyteller's" narration is delivered, Thomas Myers reminds us, "in a hallucinatory haze," which may call into question the exactitude of Griffin's memory but "also heightens its colors and sharpens its contours" (210). Such passages make clear that the reality of Vietnam includes the fact of drug altered mind-states. Such passages also imply that verisimilitude may need to be achieved outside the bounds of a narrowly conceived realism delivered in conventional language.

Furthermore, the destruction due to addiction portrayed in the previous passage suggestively parallels the deteriorating U.S. military efforts in Southeast Asia. The apocalyptic nature of this destruction is alluded to in the imagery of the passage just quoted, as is the suggestion that the destruction is linked with archetypal American frontier experiences. Perhaps Vietnam is an extension of America's frontier-conquering spirit, complete with intrusive technology (the "iron horse") and genocidal notions of racial superiority ("trouble on the reservation" that will have to be snuffed out). That these national impulses are not only destructive of others, but reflexively destructive as well, is suggested in the drug dream's ending: "when all the images disappeared, so did I," the image-interpreter Griffin reports (75).

Many of the novel's metaphors and thematically significant images are of a piece with its large formal designs so that even in the first-person, post-Vietnam sections, the novel's most steadily realistic, Griffin's narration contributes to internal design. Some paragraphs narrated directly by Griffin concentrate on a given theme or motif that points at least as much to the structures of the text as to the phenomenal world. In the following example, Griffin is contemplating the graffiti on his apartment's walls, graffiti that he had tried to erase by painting over them:

> At night, during periods of the month when the swollen moon peered anxiously in, the letters became visible again, rose to the surface like bloated corpses. So when Huey began to practice her calligraphy on the walls I did not object. Another layer of paint might help to up the interference level, scramble communications, generate some white noise in the text. Besides, I loved to watch Huey work. Her brush arm, flowing with an orchestra conductor's grace, weaves intricacies of calm as it soon filled acres of arctic space with the bold lines and squiggles of a language I could not understand. (73)

The emphasis on the written symbol here draws attention to Griffin's role as narrator and to the narration's own status as text. Wright could have had Griffin state discursively, straightforwardly, "I wanted rid of the past, but it kept intruding on me so much that I could not make connection with anything in the present," a legitimate narrative tactic, especially with such a sensitive and self-aware narrator as Griffin. Instead, the language is allowed to lead the reader to these conclusions, echoing as it does the novel's many other references to letters, initials, acronyms, codes, slogans, signs of all sorts, the very semiotic presence of Vietnam.

The calligraphy's power to "scramble communications" would seem on the surface to be at variance with its ability simultaneously to weave "intricacies of calm" for Griffin. Griffin may be functioning here in part as Wright's alter-ego, expressing a sort of metafictional paradox that at once indicates the difficulty of signifying the reality of Vietnam, while also suggesting that there is a helpful, perhaps healing, potential found within the elusive task of (re)creation that defines the making of fictions. (We might recall here that Griffin's middle initial is *I.*) Yet, this metafictional thread, however bright, is not the primary one in *Meditations'* verbal tapestry. At the same time that this passage underscores the novel's status as a text and alludes to the difficulties of describing a seemingly incomprehensible war, it most importantly also emphasizes Griffin's predicament. Both his need for healing and his difficulty in making communicative connection are problems that relate directly to his Vietnam service. We should remember that Griffin's military job was interpretation, the "reading" of photographs. What once was literally to be a matter of war-time expertise for

Griffin, the ability to "read" Vietnam, now comprises the vehicle of the metaphor used to depict his alienation, his disconnection from the post-war world. Learning to "read" Vietnam may make it impossible to "read" back in "the world."

The recurrence of semiotic bits and allusions to semiotic matter are not the only regular leitmotif in *Meditations.* (I have already noted the steady appearance of the capital letter *O.*) The novel is also marked by a number of different opposites that sporadically contend against one another: urban versus rural, form and design versus formlessness and chaos, words versus experience, straight versus stoned. As in Michael Herr's *Dispatches,* there are many direct and indirect references to spooks, and here also to ghosts. Cameras, movie and cinematic equipment, film and photography abound. And, as the title suggests, vegetation plays a major role, with numerous botanical references—trees, plants, flowers, and the jungle—all playing a regular role not just in the meditations themselves, but in both the Vietnam and post-Vietnam storylines. Sometimes the novel's internal patterning obviously calls attention to itself, as in the example of the metafictional graffiti; at other times it is subtly woven into the text, requiring careful reading and exegesis. Wright's style, then, combines traditional documentary passages with a poetically intensive use of metaphor, and each of these aspects of his style is consistently present from beginning to end.

From page 287 onward, however, the novel's significance resides at an almost purely metaphorical level. At the same time that questions of literal truth and documentary authenticity arise with increasing frequency, these very notions become decreasingly germane to the text. This movement towards a concentratedly metaphorical level parallels one of the novel's most important themes, that of destruction. In both the Vietnam and post-Vietnam story-lines, the depiction of decline, deterioration, and disintegration is inextricably linked with Griffin's rapidly growing dependence on drugs. Griffin's ever-increasing use of drugs in Vietnam turns into abuse and eventually into the addiction with which he returns from the war. We notice that simultaneous to Griffin's personal deterioration events in the Vietnam sections grow increasingly strange to the point that they become more the stuff of fantasy, nightmare, or surrealism than of a conventionally realistic war story. Indeed, the narration reflects this increasing strangeness so that by page 260 the narrator reminds us of Griffin's illness-generated hallucinations only to remark that they never actually transpired except in his mind:

> Between spasms he would dream about winter again and a helicopter would wobble out of the whiteness and it wouldn't be like dreaming anymore but like someone shaking him awake. . . . There was a fever like a machine gun. Countryside zipped past him like film on fast forward. His blanket was the texture of a flight suit. There was a big helmet on his head he couldn't get off. He was suffocating and the visor was so darkly tinted no one could

see his face, no one knew who he was. . . . None of this ever really happened. (260)

Here, the symptoms of Griffin's illness appear in his fevered dreams in the guise of military gear and activities, including a nightmarish version of photographic interpretation, his own military specialty. But besides the impact of the surreal, febrile imagery and the brilliantly implied metaphors of the war as illness and illness as war, the passage's last sentence focuses on the question of plausibility, a question that the reader has had to entertain for some time and a question that will repeatedly assert itself in the novel's final pages.

The seemingly unexceptional statement that "none of this ever really happened," could well serve as the focal point for a central critical question raised by this novel. The word *this* apparently refers only to the events contained in Griffin's feverish dreams, none of which really did occur to him. Yet, the statement as a whole focuses attention on the status of other events depicted in the novel. To what degree are the events in *Meditations* to be taken as documentary-style realism that recreates typical actualities of Vietnam, and to what degree are they to be seen as predominantly metaphorical? No matter how one chooses to judge each event, it is worth noting here that the main accomplishment of the final chapters is to demonstrate that Griffin's overall experience of Vietnam was truly nightmarish.

As the novel draws to a close, the events it depicts seem to reside less and less at the level of documentary realism. From page 287 onward, the number of unusual, unlikely, and atypical incidents increases dramatically, especially in the Vietnam sections. The militant black GI Franklin goes AWOL, maybe even "over to the other side" if rumors can be believed, and his commanding officer is "secretly pleased"; Griffin is obviously stoned at work, but no one punishes him, helps him, or even seems to notice; eventually Griffin simply stops going to work with no apparent reprimand; a young Vietnamese is allowed to hawk drugs openly on a daily basis inside the U.S. military compound; the seriously disturbed, prize intelligence operative Kraft is left alone in a seemingly psychotic state of delusion for the final forty days of his tour because no one cares enough to bother seeking help for him; men do not know their defensive assignments during the final, apocalyptic enemy raid because their sergeant has never held any drills; Sergeant Mars coldbloodedly shoots his Vietnamese ally, Lieutenant Phan, in the face during a Vietcong attack. These events, judged against reported experiences of Vietnam, are of varying plausibility. Some of these incidents, if considered in isolation from the others, could be judged plausible if atypical. Such events did occur in Vietnam, but, even late in the war in support-oriented companies such as the 1069th of *Meditations,* these events should not be thought of as typical. Furthermore, the effect of piling them up in rapid succession ensures that their literal plausibility repeatedly will be called into question. But the significance of these events is not to be found on the literal level; in fact it scarcely matters whether or not they are typical of Vietnam.

These incidents and others like them surprise us by the straightforward manner in which they are presented. Terse and without evaluation by the narrator, they are invariably unflattering to the U.S. military in that they suggest an entire compound full of inefficient, careless, and uncommitted soldiers and officers. Because these incidents appear with such frequency and are narrated in such a matter-of-fact tone, naive readers might mistakenly believe that they are being presented as the usual experience in Vietnam. But coincident with this train of events in Griffin's burgeoning use of opiates—drugs more powerful and addicting than marijuana—a habit revealed in narrative sections that describe Griffin's feelings while stoned. We should note, too, the similarities between drug addicts and the disengaged behavior of the military men in Griffin's compound. Each is marked by a divorce from the mundane proceedings and accepted procedures and responsibilities occasioned by life's circumstances. For the drug addict this divorce is spurred by his craving for the drug and by the effects it has upon him. The men of the 1069th have been conditioned to indifference by the hopeless and meaningless environment in which they live (the very environment that has fostered the recreational or escapist use of drugs) and the pointlessly destructive enterprise of which they are a part.

The presence of the drug habit also expands rapidly in the final sections of Griffin's story in New York so that it becomes clear that the movement of both story-lines embodies exponential self-destruction. First, there is a slow erosion of Griffin and of traditional values depicted in language whose function is sometimes documentary and sometimes metaphorical; then there is an explosive sort of ruin depicted through events whose import is largely metaphorical. This is the ruin not only of Griffin but of the U.S. military and its efforts in Vietnam. To compound the disaster, Griffin repeats this destructive pattern seven years after his discharge.

Unlike more traditional Vietnam War narratives that consistently and unabatedly present themselves in the style of documentary realism, *Meditations in Green* has asked its readers to read with a dual eye, indeed with a multiple vision, from the outset. The proliferation of unusual incidents and the complete deterioration of Griffin is consistent with Wright's method. Because *Meditations in Green* has integrated traditional, descriptive realism with more experimental techniques from its outset, it has been building towards such a cluster of shocking incidents, preparing the way for our acceptance of these incidents on a metaphorical level. In great measure because of the multiple levels of reading that the novel calls for, it is able to suggest truths that the run-of-the-mill Vietnam narrative cannot render with equal power and vividness. We are ready to see the wealth of "unrealistic" incidents not as reflective of experiences necessarily typical for someone in Griffin's position in real-life Vietnam but as metaphors for the destruction wrought by military life during the Vietnam War on young men, on U.S. military institutions, and upon the countries involved in that war.

NOTES

[1] John Newman's 1988 bibliography of Vietnam War literature lists 429 novels about Vietnam; subsequently published novels will need to be added. These novels are joined by no fewer than several dozen collections of oral histories and nonfiction memoirs. Even well-written, serious narratives frequently present themselves in a "tell-it-like-it-was" realistic style that eschews experimentalism. Noteworthy exceptions (such as those named above) do exist, but the central quality of most Vietnam narratives is documentary.

[2] Among the effective narratives written along more rigidly realistic lines are *Body Count* (1973) by William Turner Huggett, *Better Times Than These* (1978) by Winston Groom, *Fields of Fire* (1978) by James Webb, and the nonfiction memoir *A Rumor of War* (1977) by Philip Caputo. Philip D. Beidler notes the strong documentary strain in Groom's and Webb's novels, their avoidance of unconventional passages and experimental prose, their impulse to demonstrate the typical "representativeness" of what their characters experience. They do not seek to "extend themselves into the domain of the 'new' novel of war as written by Heller, Vonnegut, and Pynchon" (169). What Beidler says about Groom and Webb holds equally true for Hugget and Caputo and serves as a further description of what I mean here by realism and traditional narrative styles.

[3] The drug is never identified except as being DOUBLEOGLOBE brand, and those reviewers who have hazarded an opinion have identified it as heroin. This is plausible since Griffin is seen injecting himself in the latter stages of his tour of duty in Vietnam. The way this drug is smoked and the nature and quality of the dreams it produces could also indicate opium, although a smokeable form of heroin was available in Vietnam. The inordinate number of capital letters *O* standing alone at scattered places in the text (shades of Pynchon's Vs perhaps) point to some sort of opiate.

[4] Surprisingly, such passages now call for defense against readers who have complained about the existence of a "dope and dementia" school of Vietnam literature. This phrase was coined by James C. Wilson in his 1982 study *Vietnam in Prose and Film,* and others have joined the attack on those Vietnam narratives and films that they see as residing in a "never-neverland," to use Wilson's term, that only "obscure[s] an event already obscure in the minds of most Americans" (44). Wilson sees a concentration upon drugs or other nonrational or irrational elements in texts as an "evasion" of responsibility by writers who concentrate upon such elements. Political opinions about the war aside, such critiques, it seems to me, hinge upon the belief that only a narrowly conceived realism

can tell the truth, an aesthetic principle clung to by some with a tenaciousness hard to credit in 1992. Wilson does not himself discuss *Meditations,* which was published subsequent to his study, but it has fallen prey to such categorical condemnation and will no doubt continue to do so.

[5] The ability to so compare is important because the novel, though not conclusive, leads one to believe that Griffin had overcome or held in abeyance an addiction some time subsequent to his discharge and thus chooses to risk becoming addicted once again. The reader needs such comparisons because, as Walter Kendrick rightly pointed out in his review of the novel, Wright himself offers no judgment on the matter, but leaves the reader to judge (7).

WORKS CITED

Beidler, Philip. *American Literature and the Experience of Vietnam.* Athens: U of Georgia P, 1982.

Caputo, Philip. *A Rumor of War.* New York: Ballantine, 1977.

Clute, John. "The Lie Redemptive." *Times Literary Supplement* 13 July, 1984, 791.

Groom, Winston. *Better Times Than These.* New York: Summit, 1978.

Hasford, Gustav. *The Short-Timers.* New York: Harper and Row, 1979.

Herr, Michael. *Dispatches.* New York: Knopf, 1977.

Huggett, William Turner. *Body Count.* New York: Putnam's, 1973.

Kendrick, Walter. "Drugged in Vietnam." *The New York Times Book Review* 6 November 1983: 7, 24.

Myers, Thomas. *Walking Point: American Narratives of Vietnam.* New York: Oxford UP, 1988.

Newman, John with Ann Hilfinger. *Vietnam War Literature: An Annotated Bibliography of Imaginative Works About Americans Fighting in Vietnam.* Metuchen, NJ: Scarecrow Press, 1988.

O'Brien, Tim. *Going After Cacciato.* New York: Delacort, 1978.

Webb, James. *Fields of Fire,* Englewood Cliffs, NJ: Prentice-Hall, 1978.

Wilson, James C. *Vietnam in Prose and Film.* Jefferson, NC: McFarland, 1982.

Wright, Stephen. *Meditations in Green.* New York: Scribner's, 1983.

FURTHER READING

Anthologies

Haining, Peter, ed. *The Hashish Club: An Anthology of Drug Literature.* 2 vols. London: Peter Owen Ltd., 1975, 406 p.

> Includes excerpts from works of drug literature. Volume One covers "The Founding of the Modern Tradition: From Coleridge to Crowley," while Volume Two covers "The Psychedelic Era: From Huxley to Lennon."

Secondary Sources

Abrams, Meyer Howard. *The Milk of Paradise: The Effect of Opium Visions on the Works of De Quincey, Crabbe, Francis Thompson, and Coleridge.* Cambridge, Mass.: Harvard University Press, 1934, 86 p.

> Discusses the opium addiction of four major nineteenth-century English writers and its effects on their work.

Black, Donald C., M.D. "Doyle's Drug Doggerel." *The Baker Street Journal* 31, No. 2 (June 1981): 90-103.

> Examines the marginal writings in Arthur Conan Doyle's medical school textbooks to elucidate the author's later depiction of drugs and poisons in his mystery writings.

Burress, Lee A. III. "Thoreau on Ether and Psychedelic Drugs." *American Notes and Queries* XII, No. 7 (March 1974): 99-100.

> Brief note on Thoreau's familiarity with ether as a perception-altering substance and speculation of the author's possible response to the later popularity of drugs such as marijuana and LSD.

Garren, Samuel B. "Stone's 'Porque no Tiene, Porque le Falta'." *The Explicator* 42, No. 3 (Spring 1984): 61-62.

> Briefly contrasts the experiences recounted in Robert Stone's short story "Porque no Tiene, Porque le Falta" with Tom Wolfe's characters' drug-altered perceptions of a lightning storm in *The Electric Kool-Aid Acid Test.*

Hayter, Alethea. *Opium and the Romantic Imagination.* Berkeley and Los Angeles: University of California Press, 1968, 388 p.

> Addresses the opium addiction of major Romantic writers and its effects on their work.

Marks, Jeannette. *Genius and Disaster: Studies in Drugs and Genius.* New York: Adelphi Company, 1925, 185 p.

> Examines an apparent connection between drug use, addiction, and genius, particularly among poets.

Milligan, Barry. *Pleasures and Pains: Opium and the Orient in Nineteenth-Century British Culture.* Charlottesville and London: University Press of Virginia, 1995, 156 p.

> Explicates ties between opium and orientalism in nineteenth-century Britain, with particular emphasis on the link drawn by Samuel Taylor Coleridge and Thomas De Quincey.

Platizky, Roger. "Tennyson's 'Angel in the House': Candy-Coated or Opiate-Laced?" *Victorian Poetry* 31, No. 4 (Winter 1993): 427-33.

> Questions the popular interpretation of Tennyson's heroine in his poem "Romney's Remorse" as a benign martyr to her husband's whims, instead positing that the wife's use of opiates to cure her husband of his illness is an act of open defiance.

Ramos, Juan Antonio. "Dope Themes and Other Highs." In *Images and Identities: The Puerto Rican in Two World Contexts,* edited by Asela Rodríguez de Laguna, pp. 137-43. New Brunswick and Oxford: Transaction Books, 1987.

> Discusses the emergence of the drug addict as a significant character in Puerto Rican literature after 1940.

Ronell, Avital. *Crack Wars: Literature, Addiction, Mania.* Lincoln and London: University of Nebraska Press, 1992, 175 p.

> Contains postmodernist meditations on the relationship between drugs and literature.

Schaffer, Susan C. "The Drug Experience in José Agustín's Fiction." *Mosaic: A Journal for the Interdisciplinary Study of Literature* XIX, No. 4 (Fall 1986): 133-44.

> Discusses José Agustín's place in the group of Mexican writers in the 1960s, known collectively as the Onda, who wrote about drugs.

Weinreich, Regina. "The Sinner Repents: Alan Ansen Talks to Regina Weinreich." *Review of Contemporary Fiction* 9 (Fall 1989): 199-209.

> Interview with Beat Generation poet and critic Alan Ansen that discusses drug use among the Beats as well as drugs as a literary theme.

Television and Literature

INTRODUCTION

The spectacular growth of television in the latter half of the twentieth century has had a profound effect on the ways in which many people view "literature." Small screen adaptations of literary works ranging from the classics to contemporary genre fiction now appear alongside the standard television fare of sitcoms, soap operas, and hour-long dramas. Nevertheless, a tense détente still exists between proponents of television and those of literature, with purists from the latter camp often decrying the travesties inflicted upon the classics by TV producers hoping to package literary works for mass consumption in the electronic age. At the extreme, such critics see television as an "idiot box," a means to anesthetize the minds of the viewing audience by pandering to sensationalism, cheap melodrama, and vacuous humor. They view the industry as a corrupting influence, and produce compelling evidence that television has eroded literacy. Such commentators lament the processes of simplification and abridgment required by the temporal and financial considerations of adapting lengthy works of literature for television as processes that might compromise the work itself or the imaginative spirit of its author.

At the other end of the spectrum are those who see television as simply the chief medium of popular entertainment in the present era—akin to the stage in Shakespeare's England or the novel in the Victorian era. Such commentators tend to focus on the malleability of television as a medium, and consider its substantial possibilities for literary expression. They note that, in addition to offering its own genres (the sitcom and soap opera being the most easily recognizable), television has also proved a serviceable means to introduce younger generations to the literature of the past, from works of the popular detective/mystery, horror, and romance genres to the dramas of Shakespeare. It has also been successfully used as means of education for young people, a fact demonstrated by the broad selection of programming designed to both teach and entertain children. More recent critical works have surfaced that point to a broadened acceptance of television programming as a serious topic of literary inquiry, as scholars begin to apply the tools of literary critical interpretation to contemporary video "texts."

REPRESENTATIVE WORKS*

Jane Austen
  Pride and Prejudice (television adaptation) 1995

G. K. Chesterton
  Sanctuary of Fear (television adaptation) 1979
Wilkie Collins
  The Moonstone (television adaptation) 1973
Sir Arthur Conan Doyle
  The Hound of the Baskervilles (television adaptation) 1972
Dashiell Hammett
  The Dain Curse (television adaptation) 1978
Thomas Hardy
  The Woodlanders (television adaptation) 1970
  Jude the Obscure (television adaptation) 1971
  The Mayor of Casterbridge (television adaptation) 1975
C. S. Lewis
  The Chronicles of Narnia (television adaptation) 1989
William Shakespeare
  A Midsummer Night's Dream (television adaptation) 1947
  King Lear (television adaptation) 1948
  Henry V (television adaptation) 1951
William Makepeace Thackeray
  Vanity Fair (television adaptation) 1988
Anthony Trollope
  The Warden (television adaptation) 1951
Evelyn Waugh
  Brideshead Revisited (television adaptation) 1981

*Though developed by various adaptors, these works are listed under the original authors' names.

TELEVISION AND LITERACY

Gary Burns

SOURCE: "Television and the Crisis in the Humanities," in *Journal of Popular Film and Television*, Vol. 19, No. 3, Fall, 1991, pp. 98-105.

[*In the following essay, Burns defends television against criticism that it is responsible for a decline in American cultural literacy and champions media studies as a legitimate subject of academic inquiry.*]

Comes now *TV Guide* complaining that "54 percent of Americans know that Judge [Joseph] Wapner runs *The People's Court* but only 9 percent know that Justice William Rehnquist heads the Supreme Court." Lest readers miss the point of this supposedly shocking allegation (drawn from an unidentified survey), *TV Guide* solemnly concludes: "That's a sad commentary on the public's legal savvy."[1]

Of course, one could look at it another way and say that it is a sad commentary on the Supreme Court. The "legal savvy" of Americans has probably increased as a result of *The People's Court*—more people probably know that small claims court exists and is available to anyone who wants to use it. On the other hand, the Supreme Court is remote, arcane, and (as a cynic might conclude) primarily concerned with disputes among people and groups rich enough to hire lawyers to pursue the matter that far.

This is not to say that *The People's Court* is a masterpiece of public service, entertainment, or art. Its appeal lies not in any kind of "legal savvy," however meager, but in the judge's personality and the lurid disputes he presides over. The problem with the *TV Guide* article is that it illogically implies some serious deficiency in Americans' legal knowledge, which is operationally defined as familiarity with Rehnquist. Having set up this false crisis, the article pretends to blame TV (as if *TV Guide* ever *really* blames TV) but actually blames the audience. Then the article does a pseudo-about-face and says that the solution to the alleged problem is more TV, in the form of the new cable channel Court TV, which signed on 1 July 1991, with round-the-clock legal programming, including actual courtroom proceedings from around the country (as if this will increase the percentage of Americans who can name Rehnquist, much less increase their real legal knowledge).

I begin with this example because it treats television as a site of crisis. Americans should know Rehnquist (high culture), but instead they know Wapner (low culture). The audience has failed to reach a desirable level of cultural literacy. The culprits are audience members themselves, the inferior form of television they bring about through their viewing choices, and (by implication) the educational system whose job it really is to teach people about our revered legal institutions.

In both form and function, this line of reasoning bears strong resemblance to many of the recent, well-publicized exposés of American education. The Wapner-Rehnquist comparison, although a minor part of the *TV Guide* article, is illustrative of a type of statistic widely used to sound alarm—a certain percentage of some surveyed group does not know some fact. A quarter of college seniors cannot "distinguish between the thoughts of Karl Marx and the United States Constitution." Forty-two percent "could not place the Civil War in the correct half-century." Fifty-eight percent "did not know Shakespeare wrote *The Tempest.*" Seventy-five percent of Americans could not locate the Persian Gulf on a map. And so forth.[2]

In a similar vein, William Bennett, then head of the National Endowment for the Humanities, used smoking-gun statistics from the American Council on Education to support his 1984 call for reform in humanities instruction in higher education: "a student can obtain a bachelor's degree from 75 percent of all American colleges and universities without having studied European history; from 72 percent without having studied American literature or history; and from 86 percent without having studied the civilizations of classical Greece and Rome."[3] Bennett continues with numerous other statistics, all in support of his thesis that humanities education is in a state of disarray.

Bennett's is only one voice in the strident chorus of conservative criticism aimed at higher education over the past several years. Other architects of the conservative critique include Allan Bloom, Dinesh D'Souza, Roger Kimball, Russell Kirk, Charles Sykes, Hilton Kramer, and current NEH head Lynne Cheney. This group is by no means monolithic, but there is enough agreement among them that we can give a fairly detailed and unproblematic account of what we might identify as the conservative position.

That position is that there is a crisis in the humanities or in liberal education (hence D'Souza's phrase "illiberal education").[4] The principal evidence of the crisis is the various statistics, plus anecdotal evidence, about what students do not know. This student ignorance is the effect, and conservatives make a series of assumptions, largely unsupported, about what the causes are. They include a hodgepodge curriculum; dilution of the canon of literary classics; substitution of popular culture for literature as an object of study in teaching and research; the rise of women's studies, ethnic studies, cultural studies, and other new fields; overspecialization and triviality in research (and a concomitant neglect of teaching); and overemphasis on cultural diversity, sensitivity, and multiculturalism on campus.

Above all, the conservatives blame professors. Sykes's book *ProfScam* depicts the professorate as fraught with laziness, dishonesty, and selfishness. One of Bennett's main themes in *To Reclaim a Legacy* is that it is abandonment of the humanities by professors that has landed us in our current, sorry state.[5]

In particular, the conservatives blame radical professors for the alleged decline of the humanities. Kimball's "tenured radicals,"[6] ensconced in comfortable positions, have turned their backs on supposedly timeless and universal classics of literature in favor of a politicized curriculum. According to this view, politics (i.e., the politics of radical professors) is corrupting higher education, with results not only in curricular matters, but also in such phenomena as campus speech codes that institutionalize "political correctness" and a "new McCarthyism."[7]

What's wrong with this picture? Plenty, but in order to understand its appeal, we need to examine and acknowledge the many things the conservatives get right or almost right.

To begin with, let us admit that too many students are alarmingly ignorant when they enter college, as well as when they leave. A student should learn the location of the Persian Gulf in high school or earlier, along with the dates of the Civil War, who wrote *The Tempest,* and many other facts.

But statistics about ignorance of facts are hardly an index of the gravity of the problem university teachers face. Sykes, in a rare moment of moderation, admits that the accumulation of facts in one's brain amounts to a game of Trivial Pursuit and does not make one wise or educated.[8]

Yet the conservative position typically glosses over this point. The last one-fourth of E. D. Hirsch's book *Cultural Literacy,* a favorite among conservatives despite Kimball's later rebuke of Hirsch, is little more than Trivial Pursuit in book form.[9] The idea behind the book is that an educated person should know content—that is, facts. This requires rote memorization rather than the aimless "inquiry" into methods, skills, and concepts that conservatives imagine goes on in too many college classrooms.

As I said earlier, conservatives are correct to insist that students should learn facts. Where they are wrong is to emphasize this "cultural literacy" while overlooking actual literacy. The problem is not only that students do not know facts but also that they cannot read or write.[10] As anecdotal evidence, I offer the following passage written within the past five years by a college senior in one of my classes. I use the passage with her permission. I am reproducing it, complete with mistakes, in exactly the form I received it:

> In the era we are in today, Television is doing all it could to raise controversy, since that is how the culture seems to be going. Our society is controversial about A.I.D.S., children growing up to fast, and homosexuality. In relevance to these subjects, there are shows displaying these topics. One program from the show, *The Hogan Family,* Jason Bateman's best friend dies of A.I.D.S. Then of course there is the highly rated show *Bart Simpson,* a cartoon of an obnoxious, vulgar mouth kid admired by the younger generation. The newest controversial topic shown on television, is the Madonna video displaying homosexuality. It is not allowed to be shown on air, yet when *Nightline* aired aired it to show what it was like, thousands of viewers tuned in, and millions are talking about it. The idea that in today's society controversy is strong, therefore, the media tries to capture the audiences by having strong controversial topics on television.

This is by no means the worst writing a senior has ever submitted to me—in fact, it is fairly representative, and this student had actually shown some improvement after I gave her guidance and harsh grades on three earlier papers. Still, she is incoherent and close to illiterate. Elsewhere in the paper, she plagiarizes at length because she cannot write herself. Now, I can teach this student the location of the Persian Gulf, and I can even teach her how to spell it. What I cannot do is teach her in one semester how to read, write, and think. William Bennett's

idea that everyone should read *Huckleberry Finn* is a splendid one, but this student cannot read a newspaper article, much less a serious book.

To blame professors for problems like this misses the mark. What this student needs is prolonged tutoring in remedial reading and English grammar. Of course, she will not get it, and she probably does not want it; but *these* are the subject areas that are especially in crisis, and they reflect problems in elementary and secondary education. We in higher education inherit the problems and handle them as best we can.

It is not enough to suggest, as Bennett does, that "we" raise college entrance requirements in the humanities.[11] This, according to Bennett, would have a ripple effect and cause high schools to raise their graduation requirements, or at least to increase their course offerings in the humanities. This is an unusual deviation from the conservative doctrine of local control over schools and is also pie-in-the-sky. Bennett seems to have the impression that the faculty is regularly polled about what admission requirements should be. In fifteen years in higher education, I have not once seen an issue of this sort come before the faculty. I was once involved in a decision to raise admission standards in a particular degree program, and the university administration overturned it. On another occasion, the campus faculty voted to raise graduation requirements, and the administration refused to implement the decision.

Admission and graduation requirements at all levels are very much subject to the whims of politicians and administrators. These whims lean strongly in the direction of vocational and professional training—for example, in June 1991 the Illinois legislature passed the Illinois Cooperative Work Study Program Act, which will (if signed by the governor) promote and provide funding for cooperative education at the university level. This is a curricular matter, yet the faculty has nothing to do with it. If enacted, the new program, although probably well intentioned, will certainly not have a positive impact on the humanities. It will, instead, increase the already overwhelming predominance of business and vocational concerns in student life.[12]

Bennett's conservatism will not allow him to venture into anything resembling a criticism of the business ethic. On the contrary: "To study the humanities in no way detracts from the career interests of students. Properly taught, they will enrich all."[13] Again the problem is professors, who are not teaching properly. Further,

> Conventional wisdom attributes the steep drop in the number of students who major in the humanities to a concern for finding good-paying jobs after college. Although there is some truth in this, we believe that there is another, equally important reason—namely, that we in the academy have failed to bring the humanities to life and to insist on their value. From 1970 to 1982 the number of bachelor's degrees awarded in all fields *increased*

by 11 percent from 846,110 to 952,998. But during the same period, degrees in English *dropped* not by a few percentage points, but by 57 percent, in philosophy by 41 percent, in history by 62 percent, and in modern languages by 50 percent.[14]

Let us apply a little good, old-fashioned humanistic logic to this paragraph. The uncredited statistics are quite scientific sounding, but they do not prove what Bennett would like us to think they prove, which is that there is anything wrong with "conventional wisdom" about job hunting. The statistics certainly do not support Bennett's assertion that "we in the academy have failed to bring the humanities to life and to insist on their value."

Who is "we"? Not Bennett, who gave up teaching to become an administrator and bureaucrat. Not Cheney, who left teaching to become a journalist and bureaucrat. Not Kimball, D'Souza, or Kramer, who are probably best described as gadflies with ties to conservative periodicals, foundations, and think-tanks.[15] Not Sykes, whose father was a professor but who is not a teacher himself. These "untenured conservatives" have great reverence for Homer and Dante but little respect for the teacher in the trenches, who must try to "bring the humanities to life," as Bennett puts it, in mass lectures to unruly crowds of poorly prepared and uninterested students. The students then grade the teacher through evaluation-of-instruction forms that help to determine whether the teacher will receive a 1 percent raise or a 1.5 percent raise. Low raises, poor pay and working conditions, deteriorating facilities, budget cuts, crowded classrooms, exploitation of teaching assistants and part-time faculty, low morale, and an anticipated severe shortage of qualified humanities faculty[16]—these are crises from the teacher's point of view, yet the conservatives have practically nothing to say about these issues. Similarly, from the student's perspective, the crisis lies primarily in such matters as high cost; declining availability of financial aid; balancing school, family, and career demands; and closed and cancelled classes. On these matters, too, the conservatives are silent.[17]

In fact, the crisis rhetoric of conservatives has about it the ring both of Chicken Little and of Nero fiddling. Chicken Little, because life goes on at the university with very little day-to-day evidence of the sort of crisis the conservatives have announced. Students are disgracefully illiterate, but they were equally illiterate in 1975 when I started teaching, so what we have appears to me to be more a chronic problem than a crisis. Moreover, the idea of crisis is itself chronic—we can trace it back through Philip Coombs's *World Crisis in Education* (1985), the "Literacy Crisis" of the 1970s, Charles Silberman's *Crisis in the Classroom* (1970), Christopher Dawson's *Crisis of Western Education* (1961), Bernard Iddings Bell's *Crisis in Education* (1949), Walter Moberly's *Crisis in the University* (1949), and numerous other alarmist tracts. Here is how Jacques Barzun described recent college graduates in 1959:

> . . . young men and women [who have] no knowledge that is precise and firm, no ability to

do intellectual work with thoroughness and despatch. Though here are college graduates, many of them cannot read accurately or write clearly, cannot do fractions or percentages without travail and doubt, cannot utter their thoughts with fluency or force, can rarely show a handwriting that would pass for adult, let alone legible, cannot trust themselves to use the foreign language they have studied for eight years, and can no more range conversationally over a modest gamut of intellectual topics than they can address their peers consecutively on one of the subjects they have studied.[18]

The more things change, the more they remain the same.

The conservatives also resemble Nero fiddling because, as I have noted, they ignore real problems that have better claim to the word "crisis" than do such conservative worries as political correctness, radical professors, and the inability of students to quote Shakespeare. In addition, the left has a perspective of its own about a crisis in the humanities. As Patrick Brantlinger describes it, "[t]he conservative myth that 'theory'—structuralism, deconstruction, Marxism, feminism, psychoanalysis, and so on—has *caused* the crisis in the humanities needs to be turned around: theory is a response to crisis, not its cause."[19] Viewed in this way, crisis is the discovery of illegitimate authority. There are many dimensions of crisis, including economic crisis, political crisis, and failures of institutions to serve their ostensible functions and to provide for the needs of the population. These crises and failures impinge on the humanities as intellectual dilemmas and clashes.[20]

It is at this intellectual level, rather than at the more mundane level of teachers' and students' concerns, that the conservatives concentrate their attack. In "The Real Crisis in the Humanities," the concluding chapter in *Tenured Radicals*, Kimball focuses entirely on a 1989 Williams College panel discussion called "Crisis in the Humanities?" This particular conference, or any such conference, is so far removed from the everyday experiences of most humanities teachers and students that it seems a very unlikely setting for a crisis. But in Kimball's eyes it epitomizes a widespread intellectual subterfuge:

> Here we had the most traditional of academic ceremonies, replete with academic regalia and communal singing of "My Country, 'Tis of Thee," providing the setting for a speech whose essential point was that the humanities can cut themselves off from both their foundation and their ideals and still be said to be thriving. What else are we to make of . . . the contemptuous reference to "the sanctity of the so-called canon"? Or the suggestion that "the referentiality of language" is something the humanities today could just as well do without? Or the idea that "new methods"—meaning deconstruction and its progeny—and new "subjects of inquiry"— meaning everything from pulp novels to rock videos—are fit subjects for humanistic inquiry?[21]

Recently, conservative critics have been quite concerned with free-speech issues—especially speech codes, political correctness, and instances in which conservatives have allegedly been punished for expressing their views. Here again I believe we should concede that the conservatives are correct to insist upon free speech. The problem is that, at least in one respect, they do not reciprocate. I refer particularly to Kimball's castigation of new methods and new subjects of inquiry. According to Kimball, the methods and subjects he disapproves of are not "fit subjects for humanistic inquiry." In making this assertion, he is seeking to deny the right of academic freedom to scholars who disagree with him. What is at stake in such a denial is not only the academic freedom of individuals, but also the very idea of a university as a place to study the universe. Kimball's position is also logically inconsistent in that by objecting to humanistic inquiry into rock videos, for example, he is himself, as a humanist, making a statement about rock videos. He would deny to others the right to study rock video, while reserving for himself the right to comment both about it and about anybody else's research on the subject.

As someone who has conducted humanistic inquiry into music video, television, popular music, film, and other subjects Kimball despises, I object to his attempt to restrict what I am able to say and write. He has every right to disagree with any scholar's findings about music video or some other popular culture topic, but this is not his usual tactic. What he prefers to do is ridicule the subject matter so that it becomes unnecessary to make a substantive engagement with the author. It is not that he disagrees with something I have said in one of my studies—since the subject is unfit, the study ipso facto has no value and no right to exist. As Kimball says, quoting Nietzsche: "[W]e do not refute a disease. We resist it."[22] This tidy analogy, grounded in unreason and an inflammatory use of the word "disease," overlooks the fact that in order to resist a disease, it is helpful to research it and understand it.

The condemnation of media studies (and much else) is obviously an attempt to violate academic freedom, and therefore free speech, which the conservatives claim to support.[23] Sykes finesses this inconvenient fact by latching onto half of the American Association of University Professors' "Statement of Principles on Academic Freedom and Tenure," while ignoring the other half: "The AAUP drew a careful distinction between freedom of research, which was entitled to 'full freedom,' and classroom teaching, which required professional restraint."[24] Having noted this careful distinction, Sykes proceeds to ignore it. Despite the efforts of Accuracy in Academia, it is still difficult for conservatives to document lack of professional restraint in the classrooms of radical professors. Consequently, Sykes and Kimball focus instead on incoherent curricula, silly course titles, and what they consider absurd and politically irresponsible research projects. Their critiques of the titles of courses, conference papers, and articles are usually amusing, and when they offer substantive analyses of the contents of recent scholarship, their points are often well taken. But this does not excuse or justify the conservatives' true goal, which is to prevent research that does not conform to conservative ideas about proper subject matter, methods, and political outlook. Naturally, conservatives want their agenda upheld in the classroom and curriculum as well, but their critique of research should be seen for what it is. It is not an appeal for greater professional restraint by teachers. Rather, it is an attack against the full academic freedom claimed by AAUP for researchers.

Media studies and popular culture are particularly objectionable academic pursuits, in the eyes of conservatives. One of Kimball's most virulent attacks is against E. Ann Kaplan for her book *Rocking Around the Clock,* which is a study of MTV and music video.[25] Kimball does not demonstrate, or even state, that music video is bad—he assumes it. He does not allow for the possibility that some videos may be good, or even that the entire corpus of music video may, somewhere, contain something of value. Nor does he entertain the possibility that, despite its aesthetic inferiority, there is any value whatsoever in studying music video, or that some other music video scholarship besides Kaplan's might be worth looking at. In his guerrilla-style critique of Kaplan, Kimball follows a pattern, also used by Sykes throughout *ProfScam.*[26] The pattern is this: Focus on the topic of research rather than on what the research says about the topic. In selecting research to ridicule, choose topics that can easily be portrayed as trivial (music video, TV commercials, everyday conversation, TV series, potholders, cheerleading) or sensational (masturbation, rape, phallic symbolism). Ridicule the title and subject of the study (or of a course in a college catalogue). And, sometimes, quote a few passages and make fun of them. The more ridiculous the passages, the better—and often they *are* quite ridiculous, especially when taken out of context. Interestingly, *TV Guide* was one of the pioneers of this technique in a 1988 article that poked fun at academic analyses of television.[27] It seems that anyone who wants to study television seriously needs to be prepared to withstand refutation-by-one-liner in books and magazines that reach millions of readers.

Kaplan was an attractive target for such an attack, both because of her prominent position in the humanities[28] and because of various flaws in her book. The passages selected for ridicule by Kimball use equivocation, jargon, and passive verbs to such an extent that Kaplan's meaning is often quite unclear. There is no point in trying to defend Kaplan against Kimball's substantive comments, because the comments are essentially correct. Those of us who write about popular culture should note these problems and try to avoid them in our own writing.

At the same time, we should reject Kimball's unwarranted position that music video is unworthy as an object of study. We should object not only to the position, but to the fact that Kimball arrives at it without logical argument (and in fact does so, erroneously, in the name of reason). His implied reasoning is that Kaplan's study is worthless; therefore, the study of music video is worthless. In rejecting the study of music video, Kimball is refusing to take seriously the people who create videos, the people who watch them, and the people who study them. This is anti-democratic and irresponsible, not to mention mean-spirited in the case of the attack on Kaplan.

There are good videos, good studies of music video, and viewers who exercise aesthetic judgment in watching videos. That is not to say that music video should be part of the core curriculum at universities or should fulfill general education requirements. Music video is not part of the literary canon, nor should it be, nor is anyone saying it should be. But it is part of the humanities, and it should be studied by humanists and taught in specialized courses at universities, just as we study and teach obscure painters, writers, philosophers, theologians, composers, and even the obscure filmmakers whose work has inspired music video directors.

Of course, anyone who believes that music video is now one of the most-studied subjects in the humanities is wildly mistaken. On the contrary, it has received very little serious study, and outlets for publication are extremely limited—so, again, Kimball is Chicken Little. But even a few studies of music video are too many for the conservatives. In the conservative view, there is such a thing as a corrupting "media culture," which universities should exclude and combat.

New Criterion editor Hilton Kramer makes the point in conference proceedings published in *Partisan Review:*

> [O]ur subject today is the impact of the media on the university. We know that the impact of the media as it now exists on the university has been a corrupting impact. We know that a good deal of what university teaching has to contend with is this culture of simplifications, caricatures and lies that students bring with them to the university, as if they were bringing a state of nature. For more and more students find it impossible to distinguish between media culture and outside life, what might be called "real life," because there has been so little, in their education and in their upbringing before coming to the university, that encouraged them to make the requisite distinction between culture and life itself. Such distinctions are lacking not only in the students, who are in many respects the involuntary victims of the media culture, but also in the faculty and the administration, who are more and more inclined to countenance and indeed initiate the substitution of media artifacts, media studies, media propaganda for the traditional objects of study. Indeed, they have allowed media culture to supplant humanistic culture as the basic standard of discussion.[29]

Leaving aside the question of proof, which is so often absent in conservative polemics, we find again, at the heart of the argument, the conservative distate for media studies. Elsewhere in his remarks, Kramer makes it clear that newspapers and magazines are included in what he means by "the media"—so, in the end, apparently it is only permissible to study books (the Great Books, of course), live performing arts, and museum art. In case his position is not clear enough in the preceding passage, we

may refer to an article in *New Criterion* in which Kramer states that "all forms of popular culture should be banned from courses in the arts and the humanities." This includes films, "either as objects of study or as aids to study."[30] It is safe to assume that Kramer would include television in his ban, since it is, of course, "media culture," which consists of "simplifications, caricatures and lies" (in Kramer's own simplification and caricature).

What is the "requisite distinction between culture and life itself"? Indeed, what is "life itself," and by what authority does Kramer claim to know? Kramer's life is, no doubt, quite different from that of the average student or faculty member. What is "humanistic culture," and how is it so different from "media culture," and how are these related to the "culture" that students cannot distinguish from "life itself"? Kramer does not say, but later in his remarks he provides a clue that suggests a possible interpretation of the "distinction between culture and life itself."

In a response to a "point about the ideological character of television being the result of an economically determined program," Kramer says,

> Yes, in some general way that's true. Television is a business and it's in business to make a profit. But that doesn't really address the question of what shapes its ideological content and why, from one period to another. After all, the television networks in the fifties were just as concerned with making a profit as they are in 1990, but the shift from what might loosely be called "family values" to what might loosely be called "uncontingent self-fulfillment" which dominates television today—that is, the shift to an emphasis on total autonomy of self—this is not economically determined. That's determined by the political and cultural values television shares with the elite culture of the moment—what I call the intellectual academic elite culture.[31]

It is difficult to imagine a more ill-informed view of television. First, it is not categorically true that television is a profit-oriented business enterprise. PBS is not. The BBC is not. Video art is not. Public access is not. Religious TV stations such as KNLC, St. Louis, are not. To ignore the variety of television is a grave intellectual error.

Second, it is nevertheless true that the type of TV that *is* in business to make a profit (i.e., commercial TV) is more responsive to the "economically determined program" of capitalism than to any other force in society. Todd Gitlin's *Inside Prime Time,* the most thorough recent study of the American television industry, demonstrates this convincingly.[32] This point is so undeniable that Kramer must admit it "in some general way" before moving on to his own muddled explanation.

Third, Kramer's characterization of the ideological content of both 1950s and 1990 TV is simplistic and naive, at best. There is also a logical inconsistency in his implicit nostalgia for 1950s' TV, both because 1950s' TV was part of "media culture" then, and because it still is, in the form of reruns.

Fourth, even if Kramer were right in his summary view of the change in TV's ideological content from the 1950s to 1990, he would still be wrong about the cause of change. That cause is primarily economic, rooted in the economic interests of advertisers, networks, stations, and other participants in the industry. For verification of that, one needs only to look at any good book on the history of television. A particularly instructive source is *The Sponsor,* written by Erik Barnouw, the foremost historian of American broadcasting.[33]

Fifth, Kramer's sentence about "the intellectual academic elite culture" seems to reverse his earlier position. In the previously quoted passage from *Partisan Review,* Kramer refers to the corrupting impact of "media culture" on the university. Now he blames the "political and cultural values" of "the intellectual academic elite culture" (presumably the university) for the shortcomings of television. It appears he would like to have it both ways, and perhaps his position actually is that there is a reciprocal influence—but a more plausible interpretation is that he will resort to any logical contortion necessary to keep from criticizing the commercial, "free" (and conservative) system of television. To a conservative, this system is desirable because it supports capitalism as we know it, but its content is "media culture" that must be kept out of the university and separate from "real life."

Kramer's mistaken understanding of television underscores the need for more, not less, media studies. Otherwise, how will we know the history of television? How will we have the knowledge to make intelligent responses to nonsensical polemics? (The *Partisan Review* panel participants clearly did not have sufficient knowledge.) Especially, how will we be able to evaluate, sensibly, the true contribution of television and other media to the humanities? Rather than exclude media studies, and the media themselves, from the humanities, we should include them wholeheartedly, which, conservative fears notwithstanding, has still not been done.

It is irresponsible to prate about "media culture" as if nothing worthwhile has ever appeared, or could ever appear, on television. Such a position is inconsistent with what the humanities stand for. *The Oxford English Dictionary* defines the humanities as "[l]earning or literature concerned with human culture."[34] This definition certainly encompasses television, which is human culture, and media studies, which is learning and literature concerned with it.

If it still seems unnatural to think of television as part of the humanities, it is because of deficiencies not only in television itself, but also in our understanding of it and our aspirations for it.

At the 1939 New York World's Fair demonstration of television, RCA President David Sarnoff said,

> Now we add sight to sound. It is with a feeling of humbleness that I come to this moment of announcing the birth, in this country, of a new art so important

in its implication that it is bound to affect all society. It is an art which shines like a torch in the troubled world.[35]

Today, not even an NBC executive would claim that television is a torch for the troubled world. It could have been, and it could still be, but it is not. If this is not a crisis in the humanities, it is at least a tragedy.

In his book *Theory of the Film,* Béla Balázs said,

> [A]bout fifty . . . years ago a completely new art [film] was born. Did the academies set up research groups? Did they observe, hour by hour and keeping precise records, how this embryo developed and in its development revealed the laws governing its vital process?
>
> The scholars and academies let this opportunity pass, although for many centuries it was the first chance to observe, with the naked eye so to speak, one of the rarest phenomena of the history of culture: the emergence of a new form of artistic expression, the only one born in our time. . . . [36]

We have duplicated this mistake with television, and if the conservatives have their way we will continue to do so. If this is not a crisis in the humanities, it is at least a scholarly oversight from which future generations, if not we ourselves, will suffer.

In his book *The Media Monopoly,* Ben Bagdikian demonstrates that "despite more than 25,000 outlets in the United States, twenty-three corporations control most of the business in daily newspapers, magazines, television, books, and motion pictures."[37] Five or six giant corporations dominate mass communication internationally (these include Rupert Murdoch's arch-conservative News Corporation Ltd., which owns *TV Guide*).[38] The largest media companies are increasing their integration and market shares at a rapid rate, with alarming effects on media content. If this is not a crisis in the humanities, it soon will be.

Meanwhile, it is indeed a problem, perhaps even a crisis, that many Americans are ignorant of *The Tempest,* the Civil War, the Persian Gulf, the Constitution, and Justice Rehnquist. But if humanists continue to ostracize, scorn, and ignore both media studies and the media themselves, the result will not be a return to the good old days when people read Homer and listened to Bach, but an even darker veil of ignorance, fostered for economic and political purposes by the very media that some humanists do not wish to understand. If the humanities have no use for the media, the globally monopolized media are certainly not going to have any use for the humanities—and it is the humanities, and culture itself, that will suffer the most in the ensuing Dark Age.

NOTES

[1] Neil Hickey, "Can TV Do Justice to Real-Life Courtroom Dramas?" *TV Guide,* 29 June 1991, pp. 8-9, quote on p. 9.

[2] First three statistics: Charles J. Sykes, *The Hollow Men: Politics and Corruption in Higher Education* (Washington, DC: Regnery Gateway, 1990), p. 14. Sykes is somewhat inaccurately citing Lynne V. Cheney, *50 Hours: A Core Curriculum for College Students* (Washington, DC: National Endowment for the Humanities, 1989). Cheney, in turn (p. 11) cites *A Survey of College Seniors: Knowledge of History and Literature,* conducted for the National Endowment for the Humanities (Princeton, NJ: Gallup Organization, 1989), pp. 33-56. Persian Gulf statistic: National Geographic Society/Gallup survey, reported in Philip Dine, "Geography Ignorance 'Shocking,'" *St. Louis Post-Dispatch,* 31 July 1988, pp. 1A, 9A. As of 1991, the latter survey is being used in direct mail solicitations to sell the National Geographic Society book *Exploring Your World: The Adventure of Geography.*

[3] William J. Bennett, *To Reclaim a Legacy: A Report on the Humanities in Higher Education* (Washington, DC: National Endowment for the Humanities, 1984), p. 13.

[4] Dinesh D'Souza, *Illiberal Education: The Politics of Race and Sex on Campus* (New York: Free Press, 1991).

[5] Charles J. Sykes, *ProfScam: Professors and the Demise of Higher Education* (Washington, DC: Regnery Gateway, 1988); and Bennett, *To Reclaim a Legacy,* pp. 15-17.

[6] Roger Kimball, *Tenured Radicals: How Politics Has Corrupted Our Higher Education,* paperback ed. (New York: Harper Collins, 1990).

[7] For a summary, see Laura Fraser, "The Tyranny of the Media Correct: The Assault on 'the New McCarthyism,'" *Extra!,* May/June 1991, pp. 6-8. On the politics-corruption connection, note the subtitles of Kimball's *Tenured Radicals* and Sykes's *The Hollow Men.*

[8] Sykes, *The Hollow Men,* p. 14. See also Michael C. Berthold, "*Jeopardy!,* Cultural Literacy, and the Discourse of Trivia," *Journal of American Culture* 13, No. 1 (Spring 1990), pp. 11-17.

[9] E. D. Hirsch, Jr., *Cultural Literacy: What Every American Needs to Know* (Boston: Houghton Mifflin, 1987). The follow-up volume is entirely in the Trivial Pursuit mode (E. D. Hirsch, Jr., Joseph F. Kett, and James Trefil, *The Dictionary of Cultural Literacy* [Boston: Houghton Mifflin, 1988]). For Kimball's criticism of Hirsch, see *Tenured Radicals,* pp. 7-10, 172-174.

[10] On the dimensions of this problem, see Jonathan Kozol, *Illiterate America* (Garden City, NY: Anchor Press/Doubleday, 1985).

[11] Bennett, *To Reclaim a Legacy,* pp. 21-22.

[12] For an account of the intellectual decline brought about by the policy of "career education" (former Education Commissioner Sidney Marland's euphemism for vocational education), see Ira Shor, *Culture Wars: School and Society in the Conservative Restoration 1969-1984* (Boston: Routledge & Kegan Paul, 1986), esp. pp. 30-58.

[13] Bennett, *To Reclaim a Legacy,* p. 15.

[14] Bennett, *To Reclaim a Legacy,* pp. 13-14.

[15] See Kimball, *Tenured Radicals,* p. ix; and D'Souza, *Illiberal Education,* p. ix. See also George Lipsitz, "Listening to Learn and Learning to Listen: Popular Culture, Cultural Theory, and American Studies," *American Quarterly* 42 (December 1990), pp. 615-636, esp. pp. 632, 636; Lawrence Soley, "Right Thinking Conservative Think Tanks," *Dissent* 38 (Summer 1991), pp. 418-420; and Jon Wiener, "The Olin Money Tree: Dollars for Neocon Scholars," *Nation,* 1 January 1990, pp. 12-14. Kramer is editor of the conservative journal *New Criterion.* Kimball is managing editor.

[16] "The Academic Labor Market: A Look Into the 1990s," *University Affairs,* June-July 1990, pp. 3-4.

[17] On the Reagan administration's role in financial aid cutbacks, see Svi Shapiro, *Between Capitalism and Democracy: Educational Policy and the Crisis of the Welfare State* (New York: Bergin & Garvey, 1990), p. 117.

[18] Jacques Barzun, *The House of Intellect* (New York: Harper & Brothers, 1959), pp. 98-99. Barzun is an excellent source on the history of "Intellect" and the lack thereof, through the late 1950s. A good history of the more recent "crises" in education is Shor, *Culture Wars.* The other books mentioned are Philip H. Coombs, *The World Crisis in Education: The View From the Eighties* (New York: Oxford Univ. Press, 1985); Charles E. Silberman, *Crisis in the Classroom: The Remaking of American Education* (New York: Random House, 1970); Christopher Dawson, *The Crisis of Western Education* (New York: Sheed and Ward, 1961); Bernard Iddings Bell, *Crisis in Education: A Challenge to American Complacency* (New York: Whittlesey House, 1949); and Walter Moberly, *The Crisis in the University* (London: SCM Press, 1949).

[19] Patrick Brantlinger, *Crusoe's Footprints: Cultural Studies in Britain and America* (New York: Routledge, 1990), p. 10.

[20] Brantlinger, *Crusoe's Footprints,* pp. 1-33.

[21] Kimball, *Tenured Radicals,* pp. 187-188.

[22] Kimball, *Tenured Radicals,* p. 204.

[23] To an extent, the conservatives' concentration upon free-speech issues appears to be part of a larger plan—an organized, carefully conceived campaign to "attempt to steal [the] high ground away from the left." See Sara Diamond, "Readin', Writin', and Repressin'," *Z Magazine,* February 1991, pp. 45-48, quote on p. 46.

[24] Sykes, *The Hollow Men,* p. 34.

[25] E. Ann Kaplan, *Rocking Around the Clock: Music Television, Postmodernism, and Consumer Culture* (New York: Methuen, 1987); Kimball, *Tenured Radicals,* pp. 42-45.

[26] See especially chapters 6 and 7 in Sykes, *ProfScam,* pp. 101-114. Sykes also criticizes a music video course at California State University, Los Angeles (*ProfScam,* p. 81).

[27] Merrill Panitt, "If Tom Selleck Is a 'Libidinal Spectacle' . . . Then *Miami Vice* Is a 'Confluence of Commodities,'" *TV Guide,* 5 November 1988, pp. 13-14.

[28] Kaplan, a well-known film scholar, is professor of English and director of the Humanities Institute at the State University of New York at Stony Brook.

[29] Hilton Kramer, remarks in "The Impact of the Media," panel discussion proceedings, *Partisan Review* 58 (Spring 1991), pp. 227-248, quote on pp. 229-30.

[30] Hilton Kramer, "Studying the Arts and the Humanities: What Can Be Done," *New Criterion,* February 1989, pp. 1-6, quotes on p. 4.

[31] Kramer, "Impact of the Media," pp. 233-234.

[32] Todd Gitlin, *Inside Prime Time* (New York: Pantheon, 1983).

[33] Erik Barnouw, *The Sponsor: Notes on a Modern Potentate* (Oxford and New York: Oxford Univ. Press, 1978).

[34] *The Oxford English Dictionary,* 2nd ed. (Oxford: Clarendon Press, 1989), vol. 7, p. 476. The definition actually appears under the singular form, "humanity."

[35] David Sarnoff, quoted in Harry Castleman and Walter J. Podrazik, *Watching TV: Four Decades of American Television* (New York: McGraw-Hill, 1982), p. 10.

[36] Béla Balázs, *Theory of the Film: Character and Growth of a New Art,* trans. Edith Bone (New York: Dover Publications, 1970), p. 22.

[37] Ben H. Bagdikian, *The Media Monopoly,* 3rd ed. (Boston: Beacon Press, 1990), p. 4. See also Ben H. Bagdikian, "Cornering Hearts and Minds: The Lords of the Global Village," *Nation,* 12 June 1989, pp. 805-820.

[38] Upon buying *TV Guide* in 1988, Murdoch declared the magazine "too cerebral" and promptly steered it to new depths of fatuousness, lowering the level of public discourse about television to an all-time nadir. See Katharine Seelye, "TV Guide: The Shake-Up," *Columbia Journalism Review,* November/December 1989, pp. 41-45.

Richard Poirier

SOURCE: "Literature, Technology, People," in *Daedalus: Journal of the American Academy of Arts and Sciences,* Vol. III, No. 4, Fall, 1982, pp. 61-74.

[*In the following essay, Poirier examines the perception that technology—specifically electronic media—poses a threat to the cultural position of literature.*]

From the outset, I will be involved with four terms, so large that it seems presumptuous to contend with them in an essay of this length. The terms are *Literature, Technology, People,* and, by implication, *power.* It would be foolhardy to proceed as if it were possible ever to come into firm possession of one, much less all of these words. Each has a radically different meaning in different historical periods and within different cultures. For energetic inquiry, their mere lexical definition, accompanied by lists and dates of variation, is almost useless. In addition, any one of the four wobbles in an argument whenever it approaches any of the others. Their hierarchical order is pretty much up for grabs. Indeed it soon becomes evident that it is their very instability, variability, and looseness that has made them indispensable to centuries of cultural and social controversy.

To describe this controversy in its various mutations with some degree of concision, I want to indulge in a bit of allegorization, to treat Literature, Technology, and People as persons. (I do not allegorize power because it is not an active agent; it is produced by the various interactions of the other three.) Let me begin with an observation so obvious that to ignore it, as do most pietistic devotees of Literature, is in itself an exercise of extraordinary cultural presumption: for nearly all of human history, practically no People could read. Literature included such People as subjects, compliant to the comedy and idealization in which Literature likes to indulge, but People seldom knew they were being "used," unless they happened in on a masque or a play or the oral transmission of, say, the *Iliad.* Except for an extremely small number, that is, People did not count as an *audience* for Literature. The author did not have to think of People as readers. Literature was a minority enterprise, and it exulted in its minority status. It was read and supported entirely by the economically and politically privileged classes; it was written by them, for them, and under their patronage.

As everyone knows, the situation has changed. Literature now finds itself worried about and worried by People. There are, for one thing, so many of us. Sanitation, agricultural methods, transportation, medicine, and manufacturing—all these forms of Technology have allowed a fantastic growth in the production of People and in the prolongation of life. There are now 4 billion People, and the current increase among illiterate and semiliterate peoples is approximately twice what it is among the largely literate ones. But in respect to Literature, People are different from what they were, not simply because they are more numerous, but because nearly all of them, at least in the industrialized world, can now read. It would seem to follow from this that People are at last able to assert an authority over a Literature that heretofore did not need even to speak to them.

People have acquired enormous cultural power, but they do not exercise it by reading. Their cultural power is expressed by their choosing, as they could never have done before, *not* to read, or at least, not to read Literature. This should surprise no one. The system of mass education that began to take root only about a hundred years ago was not created or motivated by a desire to make Literature more available, but to make goods and services more abundant, and as an instrument for civic regulation. The same Technology that produced billions of People also created an economy that required a mass of skilled and relatively docile labor. The literacy they acquired had nothing necessarily to do with Literature— and there is no reason it should. Literature is no more now for everyone than it ever was, at least not Literature in my sense of the term. But I want to say very directly that in being exclusive about Literature, I am not thereby being condescending to People. In fact, I would hope to see People wholly liberated from the notion that a productive relationship to Literature brings with it some moral or ethical benefit not otherwise available. Literature is a form of life, among others, and it cannot be demonstrated that it is *more* morally or ethically enhancing than, say, sports or bird-watching. Nor is it observable that those who read and write Literature, especially as a profession, are as a result in any way morally or ethically superior to those who cannot read or write at all. It often seems that the reverse is true. In my view, Literature is preeminently an activity, an example of what I have called elsewhere "the performing self" or, with respect to Frost, "the work of knowing."

The "work of knowing" can go on in many other places. In Literature, it is most successful when it creates still more work, when it leads not only from density or concealment into clarification, but out of clarification into still other densities or concealments. But there are ways of knowing that have nothing to do with the writing or reading of Literature. Literature itself says as much, for it is forever finding in these other ways analogues to its own compositional acts. It locates metaphors for literary composition in the act of love (Frost or Herbert or Donne), in farming (Thoreau), in sports (Hemingway), in exploration and scholarship (Frances Parkman), in money-making (Dreiser), in social manipulation (Henry James), in intrusions and expropriations (Wordsworth). Literature allows these analogies between itself and other activities, however, only with a proviso: the lover or explorer or athlete must be committed to his task with a dedication, a genius, a discipline worthy of a great writer. Should Literature be *more* available, say, than Thoreau's harvest of beans? "I was determined," he tells us, "to know beans." Why should not Literature in fact be a less available harvest, since we cannot ever merely watch it grow. We cannot reap it. The performance of Literature

is complete neither in the writing nor in the reading. Reading *is* writing in that it produces language; writing *is* reading in that it interprets the possibilities in what has already been written, for what can be written. The "work" required by Literature is in that sense never finished and cannot be. I would therefore define Literature, in anticipation of later discussion, as any written text whose points of clarification, whether these occur by local or by larger design, bring you only to densities always different from, but flexibly related to, those from which you have just previously emerged. Literature is that writing whose clarities bring on precipitations of density.

This can be said, I think, of the Literature of any period. But for the last hundred years or so Literature has become, to an unprecedented degree, self-conscious and defensive about its own complications. It has developed a sort of bunker mentality, and begun to insist not only on its necessary density, but on its necessary difficulty. *Moby Dick* is an obvious instance, *Bleak House,* an only somewhat less obvious one; and by the beginning of the century, Henry James directly attributes the causes to what he calls "monstrous masses." Literature, he says, cannot catch the life of the modern city or touch its inhabitants, a deduction expressed both in *The American Scene,* with respect to New York, and, with respect to London, in the Prefaces, especially to *The Altar of the Dead.* "The general black truth," he remarks, is that "London was a terrible place to die in":

> It takes space to feel, it takes time to know, and great organisms as well as small have to pause, more or less, to possess themselves and to be made aware. Monstrous masses are, by this truth, so impervious to vibration that the sharpest forces of feeling, locally applied, no more penetrate than a pin or a paper-cutter penetrates an elephant's hide. Thus the very tradition of sensibility would perish if left only to their care. It has here and there to be rescued, to be saved by independent, intelligent zeal; which type of effort, however, to avail, has to fly in the face of the conditions.

What is imagined here is not a mere standoff between "monstrous masses" and "the tradition of sensibility." James proposes some more drastic and intransigent alienation. If the "tradition" is to be saved by "independent" effort, then both the effort and the independence call for the abdication by Literature of public power in its earlier forms. Instead of applying its forces "locally"—instead, that is, of creating "vibrations" within a civilization known to be susceptible—Literature must now "fly in the face of the conditions," and these are nothing less than the civilization's "imperviousness." James's aeronautical image suggests confrontation, when in fact he and other late Edwardian writers, specifically including the line from Pater to Joyce, were to fly less in the face of, than away from, or over, these "conditions." If the "tradition of sensibility" is to be rescued, then it will be by embedding it within stylistic fortifications made intentionally and necessarily intricate. James perceived nearly twenty years before T.S. Eliot, in "The Metaphysical Poets," that

Literature "in our civilization, as it exists today, must be *difficult.*" Let it be remembered that Literature by its very nature would have excluded even a solicitous semiliterate People. But even a literate People are in James's account grown elephantine in size and thickness, and his own later novels are an instance of the stylistic release from any obligations to them.

All this suggests some reasons why in England, from about 1900 to 1914, modernist characteristics began to manifest themselves in Literature. It had happened earlier in America, during the decade before the Civil War, with Hawthorne and Melville. These are the times, significantly, when demographic and educational developments in both countries helped to produce James's "monstrous masses." In both countries—in America first, because of extraordinary growth in the economy, in compulsory education, and in land-grant universities—there emerged great numbers of People who could read and write and make unprecedented demands on cultural production. But the "tradition of sensibility," the preserve of Literature, was not necessarily a tradition for them. Literature was forced to extemporize an audience *out of itself.* The critical enterprise of F.R. Leavis and *Scrutiny* magazine was nothing less than an effort to show how this might be done. It was proposed that the Literature of "the great tradition" offered us not so much ideas as an experience of reading. The experience was to be available only to those who could enter most fully into Literature's vital, dramatic, and exploratory uses of the English language, who could reenact what it was like to have lived within "the tradition of sensibility." Reading, carried out with this particularly strenuous kind of intensity, was an implicit critique and rejection of the new civilization of People, who read, but in quite other ways. At the same time, no such reader of Literature was allowed to think that the traditions of sensibility could exist in this civilization except in remnants, redoubts, pockets of resistance. Lawrence was, and is, the necessary hero of this effort; more so, for Leavis at least, than Eliot, who was, by nationality and by the nature of his religious feeling, rendered incapable of understanding the culture Lawrence represented. More so, too, than Joyce, in the sense that Lawrence insisted that a viable culture, indigenous to the English language, still did precariously exist. But we need not here indulge in Leavisian refinements. The form of James's "tradition of sensibility" became, when it expressed itself in the twentieth century, grotesque in appearance and in sound, and it was rendered as such whether you were reading Joyce or Lawrence, Eliot or Faulkner. It was innovative, unconventional, and experimental, in order, paradoxically, that it might affirm a tradition. It was radical and reactionary.

Distortions of form and dislocations in language were meant to restore certain kinds of life that had presumably been displaced by the emergence of People. Literature was not to be a mirror of contemporary life held up to People; they would not have recognized what they saw. It was, instead, an extraordinarily difficult inquiry into certain resources for life that still existed in language and in the mythological correlations to literary form. It was

unpopular; it was ignored by People; it was read and understood only by an elite. And yet Literature was at the same time claiming for itself a degree of historical and cultural significance that it had never before, so explicitly and under such compulsion, been required to claim. Literature assumed an enormous historical mission—to record the demise of the cultural traditions that sustained it—precisely in the act of abdicating its traditional centrality, its place in the community. At the moment of its exile, Literature said to People "I banish *you,*" and then set about, as Coriolanus never could, to build another empire for itself.

Literature feels, if anything, even more embattled now. It found itself after World War II confronted with People still more indifferent, as if Literature were not there at all. Starting with radio early in the century, then with recording mechanisms, tape machines, television, and the miniaturization of these, Technology, which created vast numbers of People to begin with, provided the equipment that allowed People to become, to a degree they could never before have expected, both visible and articulate *to themselves.* Visibility and articulateness had, till recently, been exclusively in the selective giving of the literary minority, who chose to represent the illiterate classes (and the natural scene) to suit its own aesthetic and political sense of things. For the first time in history, People who in earlier centuries had no way to register their existence at all, except in church records, no way to tell anyone what it was like to be as they were day by day, could record, could re-present themselves.

Having created a new mass of People, having then removed literacy as a prerequisite for demanding a place of sustained significance in historical narrative—a prerequisite that in the past made the preterite masses, as they might be called, relatively powerless, malleable, and silent—Technology thereby induced Literature to become still more inaccessible. And this happened, remember, at exactly the time when People were disposed in any case to ignore Literature. Literature was required to re-present the consequences on People of Technology's power, to show what it is like to live under the aegis of media other than Literature, media that threaten wholly to appropriate and subvert the resources of language, and to accelerate and thereby exhaust human consciousness. What Henry Adams suspected, Thomas Pynchon was brilliantly to confirm.

Nor was this the only challenge to Literature from Technology. New processes for the reproduction and storage of sound and of video images, advanced methods for color reproduction, the proliferation of portable radios, small tape recorders, duplicating machines, and the development of word processors—by these means Technology has begun to appropriate, fracture, and disperse even the image of high culture's rarification of itself. The time was not far back when to hear one concert, to look at a single painting, even to get hold of a book—James in his study of Hawthorne gives a touching glimpse of the excitement of the arrival of books from Europe—required considerable patience, energy, money, and the time and endurance for travel. Now musical compositions are immediately on demand in the living room, played by several different orchestras and rearranged to suit the vagrant mood of the listener. On video recorders, the plays of Shakespeare and the ballets of Balanchine can be edited, put into slow motion or cut to the viewer's taste. Reproductions of paintings by a dozen artists from as many centuries can be arranged at pleasure or spliced into collages. The very idea of authorial prerogatives is under constant assault, and an undeveloped sense of plagiarism among some young people is at least in part attributable to their knowledge that the musical groups they listen to on tape are continually assisted by electronic dubbing, by the substitution of anonymous replacement performers for advertised stars, and by the ready availability of anonymously authored "soft wear" from computers. While Technology has brought to thousands of people the delights of high culture they would not otherwise have had, it can also be said to threaten the condition of relative inaccessibility on which the vitality of high culture, and especially of Literature, depends. The vast museum shows of Picasso and Matisse and Cezanne are a further instance, wherein art is deployed so that thousands of people can be force-marched at short intervals to look at several hundred works in the time insufficient for the proper appreciation of a few. What Walter Benjamin called the aura of high culture has thus been substantially reduced, and with this has gone some of the self-esteem and conviction of centrality that animates the work even of minor writers and artists. Sounds pretty grim, does it not?

But if we have arrived at a point in the story where it is possible to feel sorry for Literature, give thought, also, to a few historical contradictions and peculiarities. Before Technology struck back, or even had the capacities for doing so, it had, for the centuries before it got its growth, been the whipping boy of Literature. Consider as an instance Book II of Spenser's *The Faerie Queene.* Book II was given to the printer in 1589, but it will be important to my argument that it describes itself as an "antique" mirror of a faery land. The past for which it is an image has always been an imaginary past. Near the end of that book, Sir Guyon descends from the open fields and virgin lands of chivalric England into the Cave of Mammon. The Cave has ascribed to it the detailed horrors of what would later be called an industrial-factory system, along with many of the blandishments of finance capitalism. For one thing, it is filled with currency that reproduces its own value without in the process contributing to the growth of anything other than money, filthy lucre. The Cave is a perversion of nature in the interests of financial and industrial progress. Guyon is so appalled—or tempted—that he nearly faints when he reaches the surface. He returns to knight errantry, to the pursuit of heroic ideals that even in the sixteenth century was already recognized as antiquated, a kind of Don Quixotism.

Literature, that is, from some of its earliest and now classic instances, seems *always* to have been nostalgic for

something that has been lost. What can be the origin of a loss that was always there? It was to meet such a logistical and logical gap that Literature introduced Technology as a villain. It is obvious, again, that I am using the term Technology to describe manifestations whose early forms are quite unlike later, more familiar ones. Literature did not wait for Mark Twain or Lawrence or Pynchon before it ascribed demonic and destructive powers to what can be called Technology. Nearly from the beginnings of English literature, images of exploitative control over environment are, embryonically, images also of industrialization. Usury is an aspect of this, of money that begets only money, until, as in the opening of *Volpone,* accumulated wealth rivals the sun, the source of natural energy and generative power. In writing of this development, R.H. Tawney implies what I want directly to address—the paradoxical dependence of Literature on Technology: "Behind the genii of beauty and wisdom who were its architects"—he is speaking of the emergence of the modern from the feudal world—

> there moved a murky, but indispensable figure. It was the demon whom Dante had met muttering gibberish in the fourth circle of the Inferno, and whom Sir Guyon was to encounter three centuries later, tanned with smoke and seared with fire, in a cave adjoining the mouth of hell. His uncouth labors quarried the stones which Michael Angelo was to raise, and sank deep in the Roman clay the foundations of the walls to be adorned by Raphael.

To read Tawney is to be reminded that electronic media are, for Literature, only the most recent version of an imagined threat to cultural health and continuity. With precedents for which there are forever other precedents, Literature has always asked us to be nostalgic for some aspect of the human and the natural, whose essential purity is revealed by the very fact that it begins to perish under Technology's pressure. So much so, that it seems as if the ideal forms of the human and the natural do not in fact or in reality ever actually exist; as if when they appear, even in re-presented life, they can be no more than fleeting and pitiable remnants, like Sir Guyon, or shepherds, like Melville's Starbuck or Wordsworth's Michael, like Lawrence's Mellors or Joyce's Bloom. One might call it the Cordelia syndrome—these creations of a nostalgia for human goodness uncontaminated, a nostalgia so strong that its embodiments emerge from the doom that awaits them.

Again, why has Literature persuaded itself, and us, that this should be so? When a villain is hard to find, there is always, after all, "original sin." But original sin is one likely source of Literature itself. Original sin was probably invented to explain and relieve some feeling in each of us that we lost something, abandoned someone, betrayed our natures in the process of becoming human. We love our cats and dogs with a certain pathos, a sense that we have betrayed them, left them behind, along with other creatures, in an inarticulateness that once was ours. The Fall of Man, according to Emerson, "is the discovery we have made that we exist." We fall from the womb into the terrible consciousness of unitary existence. Literature, one of our great human creations, is in this view one compensation for the Fall. It offers consoling evidence of a community of loss but also—and this is implicit in the shaping powers of language itself—a promise of corporate creation. Without the Fall there would be, as Milton tells us, no *Paradise Lost.* What, then, has compelled Literature to invent yet another instrument of loss and call it Technology?

To ask this question is to become suspicious of Literature in a way not at all offensive to great writers and artists, though it might be so to their more pious interpreters. Literature, especially in its idealized images of the human and the natural, is a reparation for its own transgressions—this much is already admitted by and in Literature itself. I would like to go further and suggest that the transgressive nature of Literature, and Literature's own awareness of it, helps explain why it needed to displace its inevitable anxieties onto Technology. Literature's own operations are peculiarly akin to those exercises of technological power that it writes against. Like Technology, Literature appropriates, exploits, recomposes, arranges—within inherited, but constantly "modernized," mechanisms of form—materials that all the while are also said by Literature to belong mythologically to something called "life." This concern for the power of technique in Literature is especially pronounced in the English romantics—in Coleridge's "Odes" and *The Ancient Mariner,* in such poems of Wordsworth's as "Nutting" and Book I of *The Prelude,* where, as David Ferry and others have shown, human intrusions, acquisitive destructiveness, or theft, all of them visited upon an otherwise silent, aweful, and serene nature, are a metaphoric equivalent for the poet's own seizure of objects for use in poetry. Wordsworth includes in his poetry the criticism later made of him by Lawrence, that he was "impertinent."

The dialectic concern for form as against fluidity, for figuration as against fracture, for structured selves as against fragmented selves—these are not, however, original to the Romantic or modernist self-consciousness about the transgressive nature of writing. They are everywhere in Literature, expressions of a concern for order that is always—and also—an anxiety about its possibly brutal and deforming rigidities. More recent literature is especially useful for illustration, however, because it tends to treat earlier writing as if in itself it were a kind of Technology, as if it had created forms and predictable movements that have become reified and potentially deadening.

Literature's distaste for Technology reveals a squeamishness about its own operations—this is perhaps most evident in a characteristic peculiar to a species of the human that Literature tends to idealize. I refer to people who are themselves almost never interested in Literature. Here we come to a crux: in some central instances—and I realize there are many exceptions to this—the most admired and admirable characters in works of genius, especially since 1800 or so, are either unliterary or positively suspicious of Literature. The worthy rustics of pastoral poetry, no less than Faulkner's enduring Dilsey, could hardly be expected to *read* about themselves. Indeed, you might say that they are examples to the rest of us, for the very reason that they do not engage in the exploitative enterprise of reading and writing. While Leopold Bloom can, of course, read, would anyone expect him to read *Ulysses?* Literature, that is, seldom includes among its implied readers the kind of people it most admires, and when it includes literary people, they are often a shady or tortured lot. This has been the case long before such "ordinary" people were presumably corrupted by, or lost to, Literature by the TV screen. A little of such literary demography might dampen the high culturalistic bravado of, say, Anthony Burgess, who seems to assume, in his study of Joyce, that since Literature makes such redeeming use of ordinary people, it follows that ordinary people can make redeeming use of Literature.

It seems quite generally assumed that because ordinary people are available to Literature as a resource, they are also available to it as an audience, had they not been otherwise seduced. How else explain the voluble and confused disparagement visited, in the name of print culture, on television? But if critical competence in the reading of Literature requires some sort of productive engagement with difficulties made inevitable by the nature of language itself, then it requires some measure of critical *in*competence to go about complaining that Literature should or could be in competition with TV for the attention of the general public. Many avid readers of Literature spend, as I do, a great deal of time watching television, but it doesn't follow that the reverse might also be true, that inveterate watchers could care about Literature and language in ways they can rewardingly be cared about. Leaving aside the masses in the world who cannot read at all, it is evident that reading citizens, wherever they are, would not necessarily read more, or read better, if they watched television less. And much of what they do read in newspapers, magazines, and what passes for good fiction is often lacking in the nuances (because more neglectful of the human voice) that can be heard on certain TV shows, like "Kojak," or remarkable situation comedies like "Taxi," and on certain talk shows like Johnny Carson's, not to mention "Masterpiece Theater." The argument that the emergence of TV is largely responsible for the decline of reading or literacy is no more tenable than the wistful suggestions that the so-called art of conversation (never a conspicuous feature in the TV-less childhoods of people my age) disappeared from the family circle because of the intrusion of the tube. To judge from the endless conversational murmur in movie houses, which used to be much quieter, people have been convinced by TV that they can and should become more, not less, voluble before any available screen.

There is a habit of phrasing that neatly epitomizes the confusions I am trying to sort out. You may have noted how on occasion all instruments of expression *except* literature are referred to as "the media," often with the omission of such qualifiers as "electronic" or "mass." The implications are especially glaring in linked phrases like "print and media culture." What is suggested by that phrase is that video is one of "the media" and that print is not; that print, and especially literature, are exonerated from the contaminations associated with media.

The implication, not dispelled by any amount of critical theory, however ancient, is that language and literature are "natural" while all other media, like TV, are not. This is at the heart of the confusions and expectations of those who assume that Literature might compete with video for a general audience. What seems to be forgotten is that language is in itself a mediation, another point that cannot be emphasized enough, no matter how embarassingly obvious. Every word is a form of re-presentation. And Literature, by virtue of its formal conventions and the conscious struggle by which it appropriates language into poetry or the novel, is yet another, still more formidable example of media and re-presentation. It is likely that language and Literature are the most indispensable and resilient cultural resources that human beings have made available to themselves. And yet, no matter how inherent the human facility with language is judged to be, language is obviously an artifact in large part created and fashioned by all kinds of social, religious, economic, and political pressures. Perhaps the tendency to believe otherwise, to believe that language partakes of nature, is a result of the quite understandable desire to believe that language and Literature should be identical with the *kinds* of nature and humanity that they idealize and preserve. It is a very costly mistake, however, a fatal concession to vulgarians, mediacratic or literary. It concedes that culture, in its literary or high artistic manifestations, can be absorbed in the way TV is absorbed, that somehow, in its competition with popular culture, high culture has gotten not less, but more readily available than it has ever been in history.

Language is not virgin "nature," available as fully to video or to radio as it is to Literature. It is a resource that Literature, more effectively than any other media, can productively mine and develop. The cultural threat of video in its effect on the general public has been exaggerated precisely to the extent that the possible effects of Literature on the general public have been idealized. Régis Debray's recent remark that "the darkest spot in modern society is a small luminous screen," is a sample of the kind of Gallic silliness that passes for thinking on this subject. What has happened—and for a variety of reasons, whose source lies deeper than any developments in Technology—is that there have been, in the last hundred years or so, some accelerated changes and displacements in ideas of the natural, the traditional, and, especially, the human. These ideas, which are in part the invention of Literature, are essential to its prosperity and to the prospect of its being able to maintain some degree of its ancient cultural-social power. But this is not to say that Literature ought to preserve any particular image of nature, the human, or the past. The very existence of Literature, in the sense in which I have ever tried to define it, depends on its capacity to question what at the

same time it proposes, to challenge in one period—in one phrase—the images predominant in another, and to expose as a figuration any term, like "human" or "natural," that the culture at large may want, for its own political or historical convenience, to institutionalize. What is truly threatened by Technology, in the form of electronic media, is exactly that play of dialectical complication that is inseparable from the act of literary creation.

What I have been implying can now be said more directly. A feature of Literature essential to its value is quite simply its refusal to offer, in the parlance of TV, a clear image; and the obvious implication of electronic media is that Literature's kind of opacity is inessential, evasive, and obscurantist. This also, to expose the full and tortuous ironies of our cultural situation, is customarily the charge leveled against Literature itself by elements of the literary-critical establishment—who are of course extremely anxious also about the effects of TV—whenever the canon is disrupted by the appearance of experimental or theoretical work. "Inessential," "evasive," "obscurantist"—this has at some point been said of nearly every innovative writer (and critic) in recent history. Those who want Literature to be widely available, on the assumption that it is socially and morally enhancing, generally oppose TV on the grounds that it is socially and morally injurious, but their criteria are as simplistic in the one case as in the other.

We are left, nonetheless, with the task of finding some way to describe best the various ways in which Literature, unlike TV, manages to put itself out of focus, no matter how hard we try to bring it into focus. I said a bit earlier that Literature is a kind of writing whose clarities bring on precipitations of density. At other times I have used the word "difficulty,"[1] instead of density, to characterize an essential aspect, particularly of modernist literature. I want very briefly to discuss these terms and their utility in the larger argument being made here. Density is a useful term, particularly with respect to a kind of Literature that gives a more or less direct access to pleasure but that becomes, on longer acquaintance, rather strange and imponderable. Shakespeare is a good example, as is Marvell or *Paradise Lost* or *Middlemarch*. Another kind of writing may, on first encounter, seem quite bristly, resistant, difficult. If somehow, maybe with the help of notes and annotations, you master the difficulty—you cannot in the same sense master density—you may then find that there is little or no density behind it. Stephen Dedalus's tortured prose in the Proteus section of *Ulysses* is, for me, a case in point, as are the episodes like Oxen of the Sun and Ithaca, where formal mechanisms, more than any information carried by them, rather statically communicate the significance. To put it very crudely, the Joyce of "The Dead" is more dense than is the Joyce of *Ulysses,* where he is being both difficult and dense; *Ulysses,* generally speaking, is difficult, while *Women in Love* is dense; Pound is difficult, Frost is dense.

Twentieth century criticism and theory tend to prefer difficulty to density. Difficulty gives the critic a chance to strut his stuff, to treat Literature as if it really were a communication of knowledge rather than a communication of being. Difficulty also carries with it a lineage of theoretical, historical, and cultural justification. George Chapman had religious theories about the virtues of obscurity in poetry, but in this century, difficulty has been made to seem the inescapable social and political responsibility of the artist. You are already on notice that when something is hard to read, there are Big Reasons for its being so, and that *you*, reader, had better shape up. Density is another matter. No guide book will help you. It does not announce itself in Literature, anymore than it does in some of our most intimate conversations, and it can go unnoticed in either case by those who do not care to encounter it. Density is very often something that happens to the ear rather than to the eye; it is often something you hear happening to voices as they modify words and phrases that, at another point, seemed quite clear or casual. The genius of Shakespeare manifests itself in this way, as we hear one voice more or less deconstructing the vocabularies used by some other voice, and then reconstructing it for other purposes. One need only trace out, for example, what happens to the words "space," "gap," and "arch" in *Antony and Cleopatra*.

I began with one question, and have produced a couple more. At the outset the question was this: Is there a threat to literary culture posed by electronic media, this latest manifestation of Technology, Literature's ancient enemy? In response I have been arguing that the threat is in part no more than a continuing effort to secure for Literature, and for the written word generally, an immense prestige, and with it an equally immense cultural power and hegemony over the illiterate masses and over the human imagination of itself. Furthermore, I have argued that Literature often disguises its transgressive ambitions, its desire to take over where life begins and ends, and that it does so, first, by ascribing these ambitions to Technology—which it then condemns—and second, by offering, in its idealizations of the human and the natural, compensations for its own technological ambitions as manifested in acts of composition. I have then proposed that, because of these inner contradictions, and for reasons still to be explored, Literature is characterized by a degree of difficulty or density that does not allow very many People, relatively speaking, to appreciate what it does. The unavailability of Literature was not a problem, but a social and historical advantage, so long as the small minority, to whom it *was* available, was also dominant, empowered, and articulate—so much so, that it could determine the shape of culture and of its visible and audible evidences. It also determined what could *not* be seen or heard.

By this line of argument I have arrived at a position that would seem to put into question the things I regularly do as a literary person. Am I not disputing the cultural centrality of Literature and of the written word? And would it not follow that Literature has either very little historical relevance or only such relevance as would disallow most of the large claims made for it by traditional criticism?

Finally, in putting such stress on Literature's difficulty—Fielding? Thackeray? Dickens? Wordsworth? Tennyson? George Eliot?—am I not saying that it is, by and large, unyielding and obscure to nearly everyone? Can it be said that Literature pretends to send messages that it never delivers, even while thousands of people swear that they are receiving them?

I must put these questions to myself, because for twenty-five years I have given a course to all sorts of students on how best to ask questions of the classic texts of English and American literature; because the poet who is to me one of the most interesting of this century so far, Robert Frost, is also the most popular of the great poets who might be compared to him; and because I am involved in the founding and development of The Library of America, a project designed to make the best of American writing permanently available to the common reader in a form equivalent to the French Pléiade. How, it must be asked, can anyone engaged in these activities say that Literature is so essentially "difficult" or "dense" that it is somehow unavailable to the majority of People?

But these questions only arise, indeed only exist, because of prevalent assumptions, to which my opposition is already clear, about the nature of Literature and of how it is to be read. The questions are generated by humanistic traditions having to do with the way language works or ought to work in Literature. These traditions have been everywhere promoted for over a century in the teaching of Literature and in the kind of criticism that follows from that teaching. The tradition unites Arnold and Eliot, despite the latter's disclaimers; it includes Trilling along with the Southern contingent of the New Criticism, however much they may have wanted to differ; and it has set the conditions even for the challenges made to it in the past decade or so, challenges that in any case do not sufficiently acknowledge the political consequences of how one chooses or is taught to read Literature. Its emphases are epistemological, its stress is on knowledge and referentiality as essential effects of the language of Literature, and it is committed to moral and humanistic hierarchies that have proved strong enough to determine how readers, even deconstructive ones, trace out the activities of language in a text.

In opposition, I have proposed here and elsewhere that, while such hierarchies cannot be dispensed with or ignored by Literature, and are indeed its sustenance, the writer's or the reader's *proper* commitment to them is akin to the acrobat's commitment to his trapeze, the dancer's commitment to the floor or a partner, something to play against, to use opportunistically, as a candidate for office, himself a species of writer, will use language—less because *he* believes in it than because *it* is believed in: "The play's the thing / Wherein I'll catch the conscience of the King." The pleasure in Literature, whether of the writer or the reader, would thus involve, as does the pleasure of vital conversation, an attention to how words, by their interplay, their interfusions, their transformations, can, moment by moment, create and decreate structures of life and being to fit an occasion however large or small. The performing self exults in the use to which it can put the most sacrosanct or the most obscene of terms. Falstaff is one of the most obvious, Cleopatra the most subtle, of practitioners, and Shakespeare is more indifferent to sincerities than either one of them.

To read with an ear to the edifying/de-edifying movements of language in Literature is to put yourself in a position to listen, with an equivalent alertness, to the political movements of language in life, which includes the politics implicit in the making of cultural discriminations. Literature can become more, not less historically and culturally important once the reader is freed from the compulsion to treat it as a representation of life. Life already is re-presented in words, to repeat an already obvious point, and Literature is best taken as a dramatization of the career of words as they try to fulfill their impossible, their poignant and comic obligations.

Reading, in that sense, is the discovery of the movements by which certain words, including those I have been using here, like technology, life, literature, people, find a place in a hierarchy that is continually altering itself as surrounding circumstances change, as contexts evolve. I owe something here, obviously, to Kenneth Burke and, in proposing that words in a text act the way people act in life, to Leavis and his phrase, "the dramatic use of language." Initially the words are simply *there,* in a first paragraph, a first scene, an opening line, looking more innocent than they possibly can be, given the history they inescapably bring with them. Then, almost at once, they find themselves in a crowd of other words within which they discover affinities and antagonisms, the inclination to seek support or give it, the power to attract or the desire to subvert. This drama of words, as in a play by Shakespeare, can make us acutely aware of how even the most culturally revered and necessary words like "God" or "Nature" are, if you attend carefully enough, subject, even in daily usage, to extraordinary transformations, dislodgements, and jokes, no matter how unassailable they are officially meant to be.

Reading, if cultivated in this manner, can make us uncommonly attuned to the linquistic techniques outside of Literature by which social, sexual, and political hierarchies are insinuated, by which dominations are established, and by which they may possibly be resisted. However, the kind of contemporary fiction that overtly offers a self-conscious, self-referential reading of itself, carried out within the text, the kind of fiction that, in doing this, is anxious thereby to show that life and history partake of the fictional process of Literature—this kind of exercise seems to me dreary and naive. The most instructive and pleasurable occasions for reading occur, I think, when Literature is seduced by the life it proposes to create, when it half resents the fact that its powers of invention and beguilement have already been exceeded by nature's. A "classic," in Frank Kermode's sense, allows perennially for its own reformations, and it does so by *not* forcing upon us, in the manner of a Borges or a John Barth,

the proud evidence that the author has already exhausted the possibilities for analysis or is giddily overwhelmed by them. The trouble with a Literature that is intent on displaying its own hermeneutical powers is that it is too simple; it is a puzzle that drops dead when you solve it. By contrast, the most popular of what can be called great Literature is also quite often the most ordinary-seeming and the most dense, without being difficult. The Bible, Shakespeare, Dickens, Wordsworth, Lawrence, Frost— these are, at last, always interesting to return to, because they offer so much and offer it so readily that they evade analysis. Each dares to take language on trust, like a handshake before a game of some sort. They are, as it were, prompted by the platitudes of language, by its pieties, its familiar shapes and idioms. They all freely indulge in a language that makes us feel at home in the world. It is just because they do hold to a course that belongs to the natural bias of the language that they get involved in mystifications and multiplicities of meaning that threaten to cancel one another out but never quite do so.

This drama of words—this struggle by which they arrive at some only momentary stay against confusion—is really what the common reader finds exciting about Literature, and it gets expressed, too, in a taste for detective stories and the engrossing irresolutions of soap opera. Literature enacts the birth and troubled destiny of life as it is created in language, and it should remind its readers that something of the same intense obscurity can lend substance, pleasure, and promise to our daily talk. "Ordinary language is all right," Wittgenstein assures us—though of what, exactly, we cannot be sure. His sentence, like some of Thoreau's, becomes dazzlingly mysterious the more we repeat it. It is so familiar-sounding that it reverberates with tones that haphazardly pun on one another. The marvel of this, and of the writers I have mentioned, especially Shakespeare, is that ordinary discourse, the *sound* of it, is never sacrificed to the extraordinarily elusive (and allusive) movements of the words that are suspended within it. Shakespeare *is* sound, the sound of English idiom as it creates and sustains the terminological agitations and blurrings that are its essential life.

REFERENCE

[1] For particular relevance to this essay, see my article "The Difficulties of Modernism and the Modernism of Difficulty," in *Humanities and Society* Fall 1978, pp. 271-82.

READING VS. WATCHING

Robert C. Allen

SOURCE: "Reader-Oriented Criticism and Television," in *Discourse: Contemporary Criticism,* University of North Carolina Press, 1987, pp. 74-112.

[*In the following essay, Allen applies the phenomenological theory of reader-oriented criticism to the viewing of television.*]

"Reader-response criticism," "reception theory," and "reader-oriented criticism" are all names given to the variety of recent works in literary studies that foreground the role of the reader in understanding and deriving pleasure from literary texts. Traditionally, says Wolfgang Iser, a leading force in the German variant of reader-oriented studies, critics have regarded the literary text as something that possesses meaning much in the way that an oriental carpet possesses a pattern. Thus critics saw their task as finding the "figure in the carpet"—the meaning of the work that lay hidden in its structure—and relating that meaning to other readers who had not discovered it for themselves (or who did not possess the interpretative gifts of the critic).

To Iser, the presumptions of traditional literary criticism render the entire critical enterprise little more than intellectual strip mining: the critic plows through the text looking for signs of hidden meaning. When all the bits of meaning have been extracted from the textual site, the critic displays them before a suitably grateful public and then moves on to mine another text. Iser sees such an approach to criticism as fatal both for literature and for criticism, because if meaning is something that can be extracted from a text like coal from a hillside, then the act of criticism reduces literature to a pile of "used-up" texts about which there is nothing left to be said.[1]

Iser's attack on this "archeological approach" to criticism is directed at its most basic underlying assumption: that meaning is, to use Thomas Carlyle's phrase, an "open secret" waiting to be found by the insightful critic and reader. Whether the critic then ascribes that found meaning to the intention of the author, the author's unconscious motives, the "spirit" of an age, or the relationships among formal elements in the text, meaning nevertheless is seen to exist "out there," in the text, independent of the mind of the critic or reader.

All of the critics whose work I am lumping together under the category of reader-oriented criticism share with Iser the fundamental belief that this schema ignores a crucial fact of literature—namely, that works are made to mean through the process of reading. Although they disagree about many other things, literary critics and theorists as diverse as Iser, Roman Ingarden, Georges Poulet, Mikel Dufrenne, Hans Robert Jauss, Stanley Fish, Norman Holland, Jonathan Culler, and Tony Bennett would agree that literary meaning should no longer be viewed as an immutable property of a text but must be considered as the result of the confrontation between reading act and textual structure. In other words, for reader-oriented critics, what previous critics took for granted has become the central focus of critical investigation: what happens when we read a fictional narrative?

The common-sense observation that meaning does not occur except through the reading act has given rise not so much to a single approach to literature (and by extension to film, television, and other forms of cultural production) as to a field of inquiry. Critics and theorists I would call reader-oriented sometimes share little more than a common starting point for their projects—an insistence upon admitting the reading act to the critical agenda. The questions that logically flow from this starting point have hardly been answered in a single voice, perhaps because they come so close to the heart of criticism and to our relationship with those curious other worlds we call literature, or film, or television. Rather than try to disentangle the many critical skeins that go into reader-oriented criticism as a prelude to demonstrating how they might be applied to television, I will organize my discussion of this approach around what I see to be a set of key questions—keys both to the project of reader-oriented approaches in general and to their possible application to television narratives. In doing so I will necessarily emphasize the work of a few critics over that of others and gloss over philosophical and methodological differences that the proponents of the various "schools" of reader-oriented criticism delight in calling to each other's attention.[2] What is most important to the student of television is the phenomenon that reader-oriented criticism thrusts into the critical foreground—the reading act—and the questions, issues, and opportunities that arise when the text being read is televisual rather than literary or cinematic.

HOW DO WE READ A FICTIONAL NARRATIVE TEXT?

The organization of reader-oriented criticism around this central question might suggest that literary theorists did not concern themselves with it before the emergence of reader-oriented criticism in the 1960s. Like all critical approaches, however, reader-oriented criticism did not emerge from a philosophical vacuum. Despite the near irrelevance of this question for the "figure-in-the-carpet" tradition of criticism, it formed one focus of study for scholars within the branch of philosophy and literary theory called *phenomenology* decades before the publication of works by Iser and Jauss in the 1960s and 1970s.

Given its name by philosopher Edmund Husserl in the 1930s, phenomenology concerns itself with the relationship between the perceiving individual and the world of things, people, and actions that might be perceived. These are not two separate realms connected only by the passive sensory mechanisms of the individual, declared Husserl, but rather they are inextricably linked aspects of the process by which we know anything. All thought and perception involve mutually dependent subjects and objects. I cannot think but that I think *of something*. Thus to study any *thing* is to study that thing as it is experienced or conceptualized within the consciousness of a particular individual. Reality, in other words, has no meaning for us except as individually experienced phenomena.

Phenomenology provides the philosophical basis for the work of a number of literary theorists who have influenced reader-oriented criticism—Hans-Georg Gadamer,

Roman Ingarden, the so-called Geneva School of criticism of the 1930s and 1940s—and directly informs much of contemporary reader-oriented criticism itself. For the above-mentioned scholars, reading the fictional narrative text provides an especially interesting case of the more general process by which subjects (individuals) take objects into their consciousness or "intend" them, to use Husserl's term. By "intend" Husserl means not so much "to want it to be like" (as in, "He intended that things should go well") as "to direct one's conscious sensory and sense-making capacities toward."

The phenomenologist's fascination with the act of reading lies in the curious and paradoxical process by which lifeless and pitifully inadequate words on a page are not just made to mean something through the intentions of the reader but are "brought to life" in that reader's imagination. This process occurs in reading the simplest fictional narrative (a joke, folktale, or anecdote) and in the most complex literary experience (slogging through *Finnegans Wake*, for example). It occurs so quickly and so automatically that it would appear to short-circuit conscious logic. The world constructed as a result of the reading act has existence only in the mind of the reader, and yet its construction is initiated and guided by words that exist "out there" on the page. Furthermore, those words on the page were "intended" (in both senses of the term) by another consciousness—that of the author who wrote them. Geneva School critic Georges Poulet, for example, describes the reading act as an acquiescence by the reader to the thoughts of another consciousness. "Because of the strange invasion of my person by the thoughts of another, I am a self who is granted the experience of thinking thoughts foreign to him. I am the subject of thoughts other than my own."[3]

Obviously, the relationship between text and reader can be conceptualized in a number of ways—as a sort of mutually sustaining collaboration, a surrender to the thoughts of another, or even a battle of wills between the intentions of the reader and those of the author. The analogies differ according to the degree of determinancy each critic assigns the reader's intentional activity, the text, and the author's intentions. But let us take one conceptualization of the reading act and follow it through from its origins in phenomenological theory to its application to literature and television.

For Roman Ingarden, a student of Edmund Husserl, the literary text starts as an intentional act on the part of the author. Once the work has been written and published, however, it exists separately from those originating intentions. The analogy Ingarden uses is that of a musical composition. The musical text certainly has a material status as written notes on paper that have resulted from the composer's activity. At this point, however, the text is still only a set of possibilities. The musical text becomes a musical work only when a performer "concretizes" the text in performance. The text exists apart from any particular rendering of it, but the work has meaning for us only as a performance. Similarly the literary text

for Ingarden is but a "schemata," a skeletal structure of meaning possibilities awaiting concretization by the reader's own intentional activity. In a very real sense, then, each reading is a performance of meaning.[4]

As words on the page, the literary text is but one-half of the perceptual dynamic; it is an object, yet without a perceiving subject. Or, seen another way, it is the material residue of an absent, intending subject—the author. In the reading act, the fictional world represented by the words on the page is rendered within the consciousness of the reader. That world is created as the reader follows the directions for meaning construction provided by the text, but even more importantly as the reader fills in the places the text leaves vacant.

This notion of reading as "gap filling" is extremely important to Ingarden and, indeed, to the entire project of reader-oriented criticism. It is an extension of the more general phenomenological theory of perception. In making sense of the world around us we intend things, concepts, actions—that is, we impose some sense of meaning upon experiences by directing our conscious faculties toward them. When the objects of our perceptions (and hence intentions) are "real" objects, the meanings we attach to them are to some degree limited by their material qualities. The cat sitting on my lap at the moment is not just any cat, but *this* small, purring, four-year-old, female tabby named Dorothy. Still, however, I can only perceive a few of the manifold aspects of this particular cat at any given moment. Looking down at her now, I see her as a rather indistinctly shaped mass of fur with no face, feet, or tail. I can pick her up and thus reveal these hidden aspects, but in doing so I necessarily obscure others. Nothing can be perceived in all its aspects at once, and we constantly make sense of the world by extrapolating from a small number of qualities to a whole thing.

The cats we experience in literary narratives, however, have no existence in the "real" world of things. They exist only as words on a page and thus are much more indeterminate than real cats. If, for example, I read in a story: "The man sat at his computer terminal with a sleeping cat on his lap," I as the reader of this tale can imagine all sorts of qualities this fictional cat might possess. The text, as it were, leaves it up to my intentions to specify whether it is male or female; black, yellow, or multicolored; friendly or temperamental; small or large; spayed or not; and so on. In fact, the text leaves it up to me to decide how determinate a cat I want to make it at all. I can quite legitimately construct or intend whatever kind of cat I like so long as my intentions do not contradict information the text gives me. No matter how elaborately the text describes this cat, the construction of it by the reader will always be a process of making a whole cat out of an incomplete set of cat descriptors by supplying the missing parts.

One of the amazing things about the worlds we construct in reading literature is that those worlds appear to us to be fully formed and complete from the time we get our first descriptions of them on page one until after we have finished reading the final paragraph of the book. Reading a novel is not like playing "connect the dots." We don't start with an apparently random arrangement of words that take on meaning and life only at the end of the reading process. To phenomenologists this experiencing of a narrative world as fully formed from the beginning provides evidence for the crucial role of intention in our negotiation of worlds, both textual and material. Even on the basis of the tiniest scrap of information, we will provide whatever is missing until we have organized our perceptual field into objects that make sense to us.

Gap filling is also affected by our movement through the text. The confrontation between our initial expectations and the text forms a sort of provisional fictional world, on the basis of which we develop further expectations of what is likely to happen next, as well as assumptions about the relationship between any one part of this fictional world and any other. As we read further, those expectations are modified in order that we can keep a coherent world before our mind's eye at all times. Furthermore, the text keeps shifting our perspective on this world—foregrounding this aspect in one chapter; that one later on. In short, Ingarden reminds us that reading is a dynamic tension between the reader's expectations and the text's schematic instructions for meaning production. The result is a constantly changing fictional world, but one that appears to us as whole and complete at any given moment during the reading act.

Ingarden's description of the reading act becomes the starting point for Wolfgang Iser's *The Act of Reading*.[5] Iser points out that our relationship with narrative artworks is fundamentally different from that with painting or photography. A painting is available to us all at once. The only time we experience a novel or film as a whole, however, is when we have finished experiencing it—that is, when we are no longer reading it. Instead of being outside the work contemplating it as a whole, the reader of a narrative takes on what Iser calls a "wandering viewpoint": a constantly changing position within the text itself. Iser calls this relationship between dynamic reading activity and unfolding textual terrain "unique to literature." The photographic basis of the cinema (and, we may assume, television) gives it too much of an "all-at-onceness" at the level of the shot for Iser's taste. It is clear, however, that any narrative form involves the reader's (or viewer's) movement through the text, from one sentence, shot, or scene to the next.

As the term "wandering viewpoint" suggests, Iser's theory of the reading act emphasizes its diachronic (occurring over time) dimension. At every moment during the reading act, we are poised between the textual geography we have already wandered across and that we have yet to cover. This tension, between that which we have learned and that which we anticipate, occurs throughout the text and at every level of its organization. Each sentence of a literary narrative both answers questions and

asks new ones.[6] Iser describes this process as an alternation between protension (expectation or anticipation) and retention (our memory of the text to that point). Each sentence does not so much fulfill our expectations as it alters and channels them. To continue the geographic metaphor, each new "block" of text we cover provides us with a new vantage point from which to regard the landscape of the text thus far, while, at the same time, it causes us to speculate as to what lies around the next textual corner. Hence our viewpoint constantly "wanders" backwards and forwards across the text.

According to Iser, although the text can stimulate and to some degree channel protension and retention, it cannot control those processes. This is because protension and retention occur in the places where the text is silent—in the inevitable gaps between sentences, paragraphs, and chapters. It is in these holes in the textual structure that we as readers "work" on that structure. We make the connections that the text cannot make for us.

Iser's theory of reading activity as gap filling relies upon a basic semiotic distinction—discussed in Ellen Seiter's essay—between paradigmatic (associative) and syntagmatic (sequential) organization. (Perhaps the easiest way to keep straight the difference between paradigmatic and syntagmatic axes of textual organization is to think of them as the principles by which a restaurant menu is organized. Items are arranged paradigmatically, with all those having a basic affinity grouped together: appetizers with appetizers, entrées with entrées, desserts with desserts. The menu is also arranged syntagmatically according to the sequence of dishes in an ordinary meal: appetizers appear first, then soups, then fish dishes, then entrées, then desserts, etc.) The gaps Iser speaks of in the text involve the syntagmatic arrangement of textual segments—the space between one chapter and the next, for example. These gaps provide us with an opportunity to consider possible paradigmatic relationships between them as well—how might one be related to the other conceptually?

Underlying Iser's account of the reading activity is the notion of "consistency-building," which derives from Ingarden and from phenomenology in general. The connections that readers make between textual segments are those that contribute to the maintenance of a coherent textual world. Again we have the idea that, faced with an ambiguous, unconnected, or even seemingly random set of sensory experiences, we will impose some sort of coherence and order upon them. Because the fictional narrative gives us no material points of reference by which to order its world, we are continually adjusting our picture of it to fit with new information the text presents us. On the other hand, we tend to foreground that new information that fits most easily into our existing view of the text's world (our *Gestalt*) and leave on the periphery of our attention elements that cannot immediately be correlated with that which we already know. It is at the level of our totalizing view of the text's world, its *Gestalt*, that a text has meaning for us. And because this

Gestalt is imposed by the reader upon the structure of the text, it is only in the mind of the reader that a text becomes a work of literature.[7]

It is obvious from the above discussion that Iser limits his theory of the reading act to literature. In fact, as I have suggested, he seems to regard the process by which we understand films and television as inherently different. We should also note that, although the fundamentals of the reading process Iser outlines should be applicable to the experience of reading any type of fictional narrative, Iser's examples are drawn almost exclusively from "high-art" literature—*Pilgrim's Progress, Ulysses, Tristram Shandy.* Thus, Iser himself might be horrified at the prospect of someone applying his theory of reading not just to television, but to one of the most popular and least "artsy" of television narrative forms—the soap opera. Yet this is precisely what I propose to do. I believe that, regardless of the range of texts to which it was intended to be applied, the phenomenological theory of reading activity developed by Ingarden and elaborated by Iser helps to account for the relationship between soap opera viewers and the curiously structured and quite complex fictional worlds they encounter daily. (I am tempted to say it provides a guiding light into another world, but I won't.) Furthermore, given that some aspects of "reading" soap operas overlap with the processes involved in reading any narrative broadcast on commercial television, a reader-oriented account of the relationship between soap operas and their viewers might help us to understand our relationship with television narratives more generally.

Several things immediately strike us about the soap opera as a narrative structure. The first is the staggeringly large amount of text devoted, ostensibly at least, to the relating of the same story. Each year an hour-long soap opera offers its viewers 260 hours of text. Most of the soap operas currently being run on American commercial television have been on the air for at least ten years. In cinematic terms, this represents the equivalent of 1,300 feature-length films! Two soap operas, *Guiding Light* and *Search for Tomorrow,* have enjoyed continuous television runs since the early 1950s, giving them each texts that would take more than a year of nonstop viewing to "read."

Another distinctive feature of the soap opera text is its presumption of its own immortality. Although individual subplots are brought to temporary resolution, there is no point of final narrative closure toward which the soap opera narrative moves. Individual episodes advance the subplots incrementally, but no one watches a soap opera with the expectation that one day all of the conflicts and narrative entanglements will be resolved so that the entire population of Port Charles or Pine Valley can fade into happily-ever-after oblivion.

A final resolution to a soap opera's narrative seems so unlikely in part because we follow the activities of an entire community of characters rather than the fate of a few protagonists. It is not at all unusual for a soap opera to feature more than forty regularly appearing characters at any given time—not including those characters who have been consigned to the netherworld between full citizenship in the community and death: characters who are living in London, New York, or some other distant city; or whose fate is "uncertain." These large communities represent elaborate networks of character relationships, where "who" someone is is a matter of to whom he or she is related by marriage, kinship, or friendship. These complex character networks in daytime soap operas distinguish them even from their prime-time counterparts such as *Dallas* and *Dynasty*. Although the latter are serial narratives (like daytime soaps) and foreground character relationships, their networks are much smaller and are organized around a few central characters. The community of a nighttime soap consists of only twelve to fifteen regular characters at any given time.

In an attempt to account for the soap opera viewing process, we might begin by recalling Iser's point that we can never experience a narrative work in its totality while we are reading it; we are always someplace "inside" its structure rather than outside of it contemplating it as a whole. However, unlike closed narrative forms (the novel, the short story, the feature film, the made-for-TV movie), the soap opera does not give us a position after "The End" from which to look back on the entire text. The final page of a soap opera never comes, nor is it ever anticipated by the viewer. As soap opera viewers, we cannot help but be inside the narrative flow of the soap opera text. Furthermore, our "wandering" through the soap opera text as viewers is a process that can occur quite literally over the course of decades.

Even if we wished to view the entire text of *All My Children* or *General Hospital* to this point in its history we would be unable to do so. Neither could we view portions of previous textual material that we missed or wished to re-view (unless, of course, we have been videotaping each episode and saving them). Our viewing of soap operas is regulated by their being parceled out in weekday installments. Certainly, it is a characteristic of films and television programs that, unlike literature, the rate at which we "read" is a function of the text itself rather than our reading activity. Except where we manipulate the "special effects" features on videotape recorders, the images on the screen flash by at a predetermined and unalterable rate. With soap operas, and to a lesser degree with other series and serial forms of television narrative, this reading regulation is not just technological, but institutional as well—a measured portion of text is allocated for each episode and for each scene within an episode. Unlike the series form of television narrative, where a complete story is told in each episode and only the setting and characters carry through from week to week, the soap opera simply suspends the telling of its stories at the end of the hour or half-hour without any pretext of narrative resolution within a given episode. Unlike the radio soap operas of the 1930s and 1940s, the television soaps of today do not end each episode with an announcer's voice asking: "Will Mary forgive John's thoughtlessness and agree to marry him? Join us tomorrow. . . ." However, the calculated suspension of the text at the end of each episode of a television soap implicitly encourages the viewer to ask the same sort of question and provides the same answer: you'll have to tune in tomorrow to find out.

Viewed in terms of reader-oriented criticism, the time between the end of one soap opera episode and the beginning of the next constitutes an institutionally mandated gap between syntagmatic segments of the text. Iser comments on a parallel pattern of textual organization in the novels of Dickens and in serialized fiction in magazines. During Dickens's lifetime most of his readers read his novels in weekly magazine installments, rather than as chapters of a single book. In fact, says Iser, they frequently reported enjoying the serialized version of *The Old Curiosity Shop* or *Martin Chuzzlewit* more than the same work as a book. Their heightened enjoyment was a result of the protensive tension occasioned by every textual gap (What's going to happen next?) being increased by the "strategic interruption" of the narrative at crucial moments, while the delay in satisfying the reader's curiosity was prolonged. By structuring the text around the gaps between installments and by making those gaps literally days in length, the serial novel supercharged the reader's imagination and made him or her a more active reader.[8]

The relationship Iser sees between "strategic interruption" and heightened enjoyment would seem to apply with particular force to the experience of watching soap operas. It might also be responsible, in part at least, for the frequently commented-upon loyalty of many soap opera viewers and for the pleasure many viewers take in talking about their "stories" (my mother's generic term for soap operas) with other viewers. The day-long, institutionally enforced suspension of those stories increases the viewer's desire to once again join the lives of the characters the viewer has come to know over the course of years of viewing. And, because the viewer cannot induce the text to start up again, some of the energy generated by this protensive tension might get channeled into discourse about the text among fellow viewers. Furthermore, the range of protensive possibilities the viewer has to talk and wonder about is considerably wider in soap operas than in many other types of narrative. Unlike texts with a single protagonist with whom the reader identifies almost exclusively, the soap opera distributes interest among an entire community of characters, thus making any one character narratively dispensable. Even characters the viewer has known for decades may suddenly die in plane crashes, lapse into comas, or simply "leave town."

Textual gaps exist not only between soap opera episodes but within each episode as well. Each episode is planned around the placement of commercial messages, so that the scene immediately preceding a commercial raises a narrative question. For the sponsor, the soap opera narra-

tive text is but a pretext for the commercial—the "bait" that arouses the viewer's interest and prepares him or her for the delivery of the sales pitch. For the viewer, however, the commercial is an interruption of the narrative—another gap between textual segments, providing an excellent opportunity to reassess previous textual information and reformulate expectations regarding future developments. We might even argue that the repetition and predictability of commercial messages encourages this retentive and protensive activity. The Tide commercial might be novel enough to attend to the first time, but is not likely to hold the viewer's attention thereafter.

Iser theorizes that textual gaps can also be created by "cutting" between plot lines in a story. Just when the reader's interest has been secured by the characters and situation of one plot line, the text shifts perspective suddenly to another set of characters and another plot strand. In doing so, says Iser, "the reader is forced to try to find connections between the hitherto familiar story and the new, unforeseeable situations. He is faced with a whole network of possibilities, and thus begins himself to formulate missing links."[9] As regular soap opera viewers know, in any given episode there are likely to be three, four, or more major plot lines unfolding. The text "cuts" among them constantly. The action in scene I might simply be suspended for a time while we look in on another plot line. Later in the episode we might rejoin the action in scene I as if no time had elapsed in the interval, or we might join that plot line at a later moment in time.

The gaps that structure the soap opera viewing experience—between episodes, between one scene and the next, as well as those created by commercial interruptions—become all the more important when one considers the complex network of character relationships formed by the soap opera community. In a sense, the soap opera trades narrative closure for paradigmatic complexity. Anything might happen to an individual character, but, in the long run, it will not affect the community of characters as a whole. By the same token, everything that happens to an individual character affects other characters to whom he or she is related.

When I first began watching soap operas regularly I was struck by the amount of narrative redundancy within each episode. In scene I Skip tells Carol that he is calling off the wedding. Two scenes later, Carol tells Greg that Skip has called off the wedding. After the first commercial break, Greg tells Susan that Skip and Carol have broken up. This same piece of information—that Skip and Carol are not to be wed—might be repeated four or five times in the course of an hour-long episode. The repetition of information from one episode to the next can be accounted for as an attempt to keep infrequent viewers up to date, but why is the same piece of information related many times within the same episode? This is a puzzle only for the new soap opera viewer. The regular viewer, familiar with the paradigmatic structure of that particular soap (that is, its network of character relationships), will know that *who* tells *whom* is just as important as *what* is being told. The regular viewer knows that Greg still loves Carol and that Susan has schemed to keep Skip and Carol apart so that she can have Skip for herself. Each retelling of the information, "Skip has called off the wedding," is viewed against the background formed by the totality of character interrelationships. Thus the second and third retellings within the same episode are far from being *paradigmatically* redundant.

How is this paradigmatic complexity related to the structuring gaps of the soap opera text? The size of the soap opera community, the complexity of its character relationships, and the fact that soap opera characters possess both histories and memories all combine to create an almost infinite set of potential connections between one plot event and another. The syntagmatic juxtaposition of two plot lines (a scene from one following or preceding a scene from the other) arouses in the viewer the possibility of a paradigmatic connection between them. But because the connection the text makes is only a syntagmatic one, the viewer is left to imagine what sort of, if any, other connection they might have. The range of latent relationships evoked by the gaps between scenes is dependent upon the viewer's familiarity with the current community of characters and his or her historical knowledge of previous character relationships. In a very real sense, then, the better one "knows" a soap opera, the greater reason one has for wanting to watch every day. Conversely, the less involved one is in a given soap opera's textual network, the more that soap opera appears to be merely a series of plot lines that unfold so slowly that virtually nothing "happens" in any given episode and the more tiresomely redundant each episode seems.

HOW DOES THE TEXT ATTEMPT TO CONTROL THE READING ACT?

In 1961 Wayne C. Booth's book *The Rhetoric of Fiction* foregrounded a common-sensical but frequently overlooked fact of literature: every story represents not just the construction of a fictional world, but a story told from a certain perspective by certain narrational means. In other words, as Sarah Kozloff points out in her essay, every story implies a storyteller. Furthermore, the perspective from which the story is told carries with it attitudes toward the fictional world created in the story. Even in works that ostensibly give us "just the facts," inevitably there are attitudes toward those facts given as well.

Reader-oriented criticism has focused on the corollary to Booth's observation: if every story necessarily involves a storyteller, it also involves someone to whom and for whose benefit the story is being told. But before proceeding further, we need to establish the nature of the storyteller and story reader we're talking about here. Obviously, to say that a piece of narrative fiction involves a communication between addresser and addressee is to compare it to a face-to-face communication. However, reading a novel or watching a television drama differs in several key respects from talking with a friend. In the first place, the actual addresser (author) of a piece of narrative fiction is absent at the moment of reading, just

as the actual addressee (reader) is always absent at the moment of writing. Furthermore, what is being referred to in a novel or fictional television drama is only indirectly related to the immediate environment either the author or the reader inhabits (it is the fact that what we are reading does not exist that makes it fiction), so that the reader has no "real" points of reference against which to test the message being delivered in the narrative. Thus both the addresser and the addressee dealt with by narratological analysis and (with several notable exceptions to be discussed later) reader-oriented criticism are textual constructs, not flesh-and-blood human beings. To use a dangerously ambiguous term, the reader of a story constructs its teller as the "point of view" with which the values, norms, and attitudes expressed in the work are consistent.

In attempting to specify "to whom" a story is told and the role this addressee ought/might play in the reading process, reader-oriented theorists have proposed a bewildering array of readers: "fictive reader" (Iser), "model reader" (Eco), "intended reader" (Wolff), "characterized reader" (Prince), "ideal reader" (Culler and others), "inside" and "outside reader" (Sherbo), "implied reader" (Iser, Booth, Chatman, and others), and "superreader" (Riffaterre)—to name but some of the "readers" who now populate literary studies. Although each of these terms constructs a reader different in some respects from all the others, all of them refer to one of two types of readers: "implied fictional readers" and "characterized fictional readers." (Yes, I know I just added two more—and more complicated—terms to the list, but you can't very well talk about "two types of readers" without naming them in some fashion.)[10]

As anyone who has ever tried to tell an anecdote or a joke knows, every story is constructed around a set of assumptions the teller makes about his or her audience: what they know or don't know; how they are likely to feel about certain things (Republicans, college teachers, mothers-in-law); why they are willing to listen to the story to begin with; how it is likely to fit in with other stories or jokes they might already have heard; and so forth. "Model," "ideal," "super," "implied," and "intended" all refer to the composite of these assumptions as they are manifested within the narrative itself—hence the term "implied fictional reader," which I am borrowing from W. Daniel Wilson to refer to this category of reader.

For some theorists, the implied fictional reader is a projection into the text of the qualities possessed by the kind of reader the author had in mind when he or she wrote the work—hence the use of the terms "model," "ideal," and "super" to refer to this reader in the author's mind. In semiotic terms, the ideal reader would be one who fully shared the textual, lexical, cultural, and ideological codes employed by the author. As Umberto Eco describes the model reader, it is the reader "supposedly able to deal interpretively with the [text's] expressions in the same way as the author deals generatively with them." Eco's formulation reminds us that for any narrative to "work" for the reader, he or she must literally and figuratively speak something resembling the same language as the author.[11] The author must be able to presuppose certain competencies on the part of the reader if for no other reason than in order to select those things that must be made explicit in the text from those that can be left unsaid, knowing that the reader should be able to fill them in.

Some reader-oriented critics would make the correlation between the ideal reader and real readers a touchstone for interpretive validity. They would argue that the closer the reader comes to the qualities possessed by the ideal reader the author had in mind when he or she wrote the work, the closer that reader comes to fully understanding the work. As Booth puts it, "The author creates . . . an image of himself and another image of his reader; he makes the reader, as he makes his second self, and the most successful reading is one in which the created selves, author and reader, can find complete agreement."[12] Others, however, would claim that although the author might have kept before him or her the image of an ideal reader, the only real reader that could possibly fill that role is the author him- or herself! Were the author and reader to share *every* code, literary communication would be unnecessary because there would be nothing new to say.

In an attempt to avoid getting too bogged down in the ongoing debates over the nature of and name for the implied reader in the text, we might regard the implied fictional reader as a textual place or site rather than a hypothetical person. It is the position the text asks us to occupy—the preferred vantage point from which to observe the world of the text. In other words, every fiction offers not only a structure of characters, events, and settings, but a structure of attitudes, norms, and values as well. The reader is invited to take up a position relative to these structures. That "place" turns out to be the other side of the point of view that has organized the text's world—the point of view the reader is offered from which to observe that world.

One of the most obvious ways the reader's place in the text can be established is by referring directly to the reader: addressing the reader directly, confiding in the reader, appealing to the reader, describing what the reader knows or probably feels, even questioning or challenging the reader's interpretation of the text thus far. In other words, the text might create a "characterized fictional reader." Such a strategy was common in the eighteenth-century British novel (Fielding's *Tom Jones,* for example), reaching perhaps its most elaborate (and funniest) use in Laurence Sterne's novel, *Tristram Shandy.*[13]

The characterized reader was less frequently employed in nineteenth-century novels, and by the twentieth century had all but disappeared from mainstream fiction. Similarly, by the time we reach Hemingway, narrators in novels had become, if not invisible, certainly depersonalized.

The classical Hollywood cinema expends tremendous effort to hide the means by which it tells its stories. It also engages its viewers covertly, making them unseen observers of the world that always appears fully formed and autonomous. With very few exceptions (most of them comedies), the viewer of a Hollywood film is neither addressed or acknowledged. One of the cardinal sins of Hollywood acting style is looking into the lens of the camera, because doing so threatens to break the illusion of "as if it were real" by reminding viewers of the apparatus that intervenes between them and the world on the screen. This is certainly not to say that there is no implied viewer constructed by Hollywood films. In fact, if we once again consider the implied viewer as a position relative to the world of the text, it is easier to see how the viewer is located "within" the Hollywood film than is the reader within the traditional novel. Given that the viewer's knowledge of the world of the film comes through the camera, the viewer is quite literally positioned "some place" relative to the action in every shot. Furthermore, as the chapters on feminist and psychoanalytic criticism make clear, the Hollywood film carefully "writes" its viewer into the text, usually establishing its gender as male and skillfully regulating the manner by which "he" engages with the characters.

Although we would find being addressed directly by a character in a Hollywood film unusual (and perhaps discomforting), as Sarah Kozloff points out we accept the "characterized viewer" as an integral part of television. In fact, our experience of television involves two quite different modes of viewer engagement. The first, which we might call the Hollywood narrative mode, represents the adaptation to television of the classical Hollywood narrative style and its means of drawing the viewer into the text: spectator omniscience and invisibility, alternation between third- and first-person points of view and between shot and reverse shot, hiding the means by which the world of the text is created, etcetera. We find the Hollywood mode most prevalent in those television programs still shot "film style"—prime-time dramas of all sorts, (including both series and serials), made-for-TV movies, and some situation comedies. Daytime soap operas and some situation comedies have modified the Hollywood style to accommodate what is called "three-camera, live-tape" shooting; an entire scene is enacted while being shot simultaneously by three (or more) television cameras. The director electronically "cuts" between one camera and another as the scene unfolds. Live-tape production makes the shot/reverse shot and subjective point-of-view shot much more difficult to achieve than in Hollywood-style filmmaking, because repositioning the camera for the reverse shot would require penetrating the space of the scene. Hence, subjectivity in soap operas is usually rendered aurally rather than visually, by showing a close-up of a character while his or her thoughts are heard on the sound track. Despite some degree of deviation from the Hollywood cinema style, however, live-tape television style seldom, if ever, addresses the viewer and observes most other conventions of Hollywood style.

The other mode of viewer engagement on television, which we might call the rhetorical mode, derives historically from radio practice of the 1930s and 1940s and ultimately, I suppose, from the "point-to-point" communication technologies that radio superceded: the telephone and the telegraph.[14] Included in the rhetorical mode would be news programs, variety shows, talk shows, "self-help" and educational programs (cooking, exercise, and gardening shows, for example), sports, game shows, and many commercials. In the rhetorical mode, both the addresser and the addressee (what Sarah Kozloff calls the "narratee") are openly acknowledged. The former is frequently personified or "characterized" as the reporter, anchorperson, announcer, host, master of ceremonies, or quiz master. The viewer is addressed directly as characters look directly into the camera and speak to "you, the home viewer." The means of presentation, particularly the technological means of presentation, are frequently emphasized rather than hidden. David Letterman shoots rubber darts at the camera; *Jeopardy* "answers" are revealed via a bank of television monitors; local television newscasts originate from what looks to be the newsroom itself; television screens are built into the sets of news programs so that anchorpersons can talk with reporters in the field; and (in our local television market, at least) a favorite closing shot for the evening newscast is one that reveals set, cameras, and all. The "personified addresser"—host, anchor, or quiz master—manipulates this technology and mediates between the world on the other side of the screen and that in our living rooms. In doing so, he or she (it is usually a he) offers "us" a better view, more information, a dazzling technical spectacle, or, seemingly, an insider's view of how things "really work" behind the scenes.

One of the hallmarks of the rhetorical mode—and another striking difference between its method of viewer engagement and that offered by Hollywood films—is its use of characterized viewers. Direct address is but the most obvious way by which the viewer is represented on television (as the "person" Dan Rather says "good evening" to at the beginning of *CBS Evening News*). Television frequently provides us with onscreen characterized viewers—textual surrogates who "do" what real viewers cannot: interact with other characters and respond in an ideal fashion to the appeals, demands, and urgings of the addresser.

These on-screen characterized viewers abound on television commercials. An ad for *Time* magazine, for example, opens with a man sitting at his desk at home. An off-screen voice asks him, "How would you like to get *Time* delivered to your home every week for half-off the newsstand price?" The man looks into the camera as the voice speaks, but before he can respond the voice adds, "You'll also receive this pocket calculator with your paid subscription." An arm emerges from off-screen and hands the calculator to the man. He nods his acceptance of the offer, but before he can speak the voice piles on still more incentives. Finally, with not the slightest doubt remaining that the man will become a *Time* subscriber, the voice orders him to place the toll-free call. The man hesitates. "What are you waiting for?" the voice asks.

"You haven't told me the number," the man objects. The voice responds with the number and it magically appears at the bottom of the screen. The commercial ends with the man placing the phone call.

Notice that in this example the characterized addressee stands in a different relationship to the text's addresser than does the implied addressee (the "presumed" viewer at home). The man in the *Time* ad enjoys a direct, face-to-face (or, in this case at least, face-to-voice) relationship with the person who addresses him. The technology necessary to bring the commercial message "to us" disappears and is replaced by an unmediated interpersonal communication situation. In many television commercials and network and local promos, the characterized addressee is established not just to personalize and textualize the implied viewer but to make an interpersonal exchange out of a one-way, mass-communication phenomenon. The characterized addressee is established in a setting suggesting that of the implied audience: the kitchen (particularly in commercials directed at women and shown during daytime programming), the den, the family or living room. Then the addresser enters the space of the characterized addressee and talks with him or her directly. In a Drano ad, for example, we see an aproned woman standing forlornly in front of her sink while a male voice booms accusingly, "YOUR SINK'S STOPPED UP." A few years ago, at the beginning of the fall season, CBS ran a series of promotions featuring some of its schedule's most famous stars. In one vignette, a weary young woman returns to her apartment after a hard day at work, turns on the television set, and is startled to find Tom Selleck, as Magnum, standing in her living room. In a parallel scene, a young man turns on his TV set, and a television image of Loni Anderson magically is transformed into the actress herself in the man's den.

The *Time* ad illustrates another aspect of television's use of the characterized viewer—a blurring of the distinction between characterized addressee, implied addressee, and addresser. When the man responds to the voice, he does so by looking directly into the camera. Thus, he looks at "us" as if we were the source of the message. In a Hollywood film one of the principal ways of establishing identification between the viewer and a character in the film is via a strategy called "glance/object" editing. We are shown a close-up of a character as that character looks off-screen. The second shot, taken from that character's point of view, shows us what he or she sees. A third shot returns us to the close-up of the character. In the rhetorical television mode, however, glance/object editing is short-circuited, because "we" turn out to be the object of the character's glance. In the curious logic of this mode, the "voice" of the commercial is made into our voice, as the man establishes the connection between our gaze and "the" voice. At the same time "we" are characterized as the man who responds to that voice, he who acts as we "should" act. The superimposition of the telephone number at the end of the ad, however, addresses "us" rather than "him," because 1) he attends to the voice telling him the number, rather than to its appearance on the screen, and 2) even if he did notice it, it would be backwards!

This purposive collapsing of addresser, characterized addressee, and implied addressee in television's rhetorical mode creates what Robert Stam has called, with regard to news programming, "the regime of the fictive We." In the middle of *As the World Turns*, the announcer says, "We'll return in just a moment." A promo for *PM Magazine* says "Tonight on *PM Magazine* we'll journey to Rome. . . ." The examples are legion. Who is this "we"? Perhaps it merely stands for the collective "senders" of the message—the news staff, the "folks" at Procter and Gamble, and so on. But the referent of television's "we" is usually left vague enough to cover both the addresser and the implied addressee. Stam sees the "misrecognition of mirror-like images" in the fictive We to have serious political consequences:

> Shortly after the ill-fated "rescue attempt" in Iran . . . Chuck Scarborough of New York's *Channel 4 News* began his newscast, "Well, we did our best; but we didn't make it." The "We" in this case presumably included the newscaster, the president, and a few aides. It certainly did not include the majority of Americans, even if their "support" could be artfully simulated after the fact. Television news, then, claims to speak for us, and often does, but just as often it deprives us of the right to speak by deluding us into thinking that its discourse is our own.[15]

The characterized addressee plays an equally important role in two other television genres—the game show and the talk show. Whereas the commercial and the news program tend to characterize their addressees individually, game and talk shows represent their addressees as a group—the "studio audience." Also, to follow up a point made by Kozloff, in the examples above the impersonal experience of watching television was made into an interpersonal exchange by situating the action on the "viewer's" side of the television set, in the characterized addressee's living room, kitchen, etcetera. In talk and game shows, the characterized viewer is made a part of "the show." The studio audience is "there," where it really happens, able to experience the show with their own eyes rather than through the mediation of the camera lens.

Most game and talk shows carefully regulate the response of their studio audiences in order that this "actual" audience is characterized to the home viewer as an ideal audience. With the aid of "applause" signs in the studio, the audience unfailingly responds at the appropriate moment—when a new guest is introduced, when the contestant wins the big prize, when it is time for a commercial. Some game and talk shows employ someone (who usually doubles as the show's announcer) to lead the studio audience's response. Occasionally on *Late Night with David Letterman*, for example, the viewer at home can see announcer Bill Wendell standing between studio audience and set frantically waving his arms for a more

vociferous response from the studio audience. As with many talk shows, Wendell also "warms up" the studio audience before taping begins by telling a few jokes, informing the audience what to expect when taping actually begins, and quite literally telling them how to behave as a "good" audience. At a taping I attended a few years ago, Wendell admonished us, "If you chuckle silently to yourself, no one at home will think you're laughing at all. When you think something is funny, let it out!"

Game and talk shows also employ devices to individualize the studio audience. David Letterman and Johnny Carson go into the audience to play "Stump the Band" or "Ask Mr. Melman" with selected members of the audience. *Donahue* is predicated upon individual members of the studio audience asking "guests" the type of questions "we" would ask if "we" were there. Notice, however, that even when the characterized viewer is allowed to speak as an individual member of the studio audience, his or her discourse is carefully regulated and channeled. It is Phil Donahue (or his assistant) who wields the microphone and determines who is chosen to speak and for how long. The person speaking speaks to and looks at either Phil or the guests on stage. Only Phil looks directly into the camera and addresses "us." Notice also that by positioning Phil among the studio audience rather than on stage with the guests and by allowing him to serve as a spokesman for both studio and home viewers ("You'll forgive us, Mr. X, if we are just a little skeptical of your claim that all we need to do to balance the budget is . . ."), *Donahue* collapses "host," studio audience, and home audience into television's fictive "we," and covers over the means by which the responses of the characterized viewer are regulated.

In the talk show, although the studio audience is addressed and individual members are allowed to speak, the roles of host, guests, and characterized audience are demarcated, if on some shows purposefully blurred. The audience stays "in its place" on this side of the stage; guests are isolated onstage in front of the audience (at home and in the studio); the host negotiates and regulates the relationship between them and the home viewer. Except in the unlikely event that a studio audience member is called upon to speak for a few seconds (even on *Donahue* only a tiny portion of the studio audience actually speaks), his or her role is primarily that of exemplary viewer—one who listens, looks, and responds appropriately. In the game show, however, the characterized viewer crosses the line normally separating characterized "audience" from "show." This transformation of audience member into character is perhaps best exemplified by Johnny Olson's invitation to "come on down" on *The Price Is Right*. We might speculate that a large measure of the pleasure we derive from game shows stems from the fact that the contestant is more like "us" than like "them." As a characterized viewer he or she appears to us as a "real" person acting spontaneously, not an actor reading lines. (Although on many game shows the contestants are carefully screened and coached, and even if drawn at random from the studio audience, the contestant is no doubt aware of the role he or she is expected to play from having watched the show before.) In those instances in which contestants are selected from the studio audience, they are plucked from among "us."

By splitting off one or more characterized viewers from the rest of the studio audience, the game show sets up a circuit of viewer involvement. When Bob Barker asks the contestant to guess how much the travel trailer costs, we almost automatically slip into the role of contestant, guessing along with him or her. If we guess correctly along with the contestant, the bells and whistles go off for us as well as for him or her. But we can also distance ourselves from the contestants and take up the position of the studio audience as they encourage the contestants and, on *The Price Is Right,* at least, shout out what they believe to be the correct guess. As we watch a game show, we constantly shift from one viewer position to another, collapsing the distance between contestants and ourselves as we answer along with them, falling back into the role of studio audience as we assess contestant prowess and luck (or lack thereof), assuming a position superior to both when we know more than they. The viewer-positioning strategy of the game show encourages us to mimic the responses of the characterized viewer in the text. Indeed, I find it difficult to watch a game show *without* vocally responding (whether or not someone else is in the room with me). I can't resist answering the questions myself, nor can I resist commenting on a contestant's abysmal ignorance when I have the correct answer and he or she doesn't.

It is not coincidental that commercial television has developed a sophisticated rhetorical mode of viewer engagement within which so much energy is expended in giving the viewer at home an image of him or herself on the screen. The Hollywood cinema style has developed to serve a system of economic exchange in which the viewer pays "up front" for the opportunity to enjoy the cinematic experience that follows the purchase of a ticket. No further action is required of the viewer once he or she leaves the theatre to fulfill the implicit contract between institution and viewer/consumer. On the other hand, commercial television succeeds only by persuading the viewer to respond at another time, in another place, in a prescribed manner—in other words, the implicit contract the viewer has with television is fulfilled not in front of the television set, but in the grocery store. Television demands that we act; hence it is inherently rhetorical. Furthermore, that action must occur on "this" side of the television set. If the Hollywood film-viewing situation is centripetal (the one bright spot of moving light in a dark room that draws us into another world and holds us there for ninety minutes), then television is centrifugal. Its texts are not only presented for us, but directed out at us. Ironically its messages drive us away from the set, out into the "real" world of commodities and services. By conflating addresser and addressee under the regime of the fictive "we," commercial television softens the bluntness of its rhetorical thrust. By positioning "us" in "their" position, we seem to be talking ourselves into acting. By adopting

the style and mode of address of commercials, other genres of television programming rehearse "for fun" what the commercials do in earnest. Every commercial is an implicit unanswered question—"will you buy?"—that calls for action the commercial text itself cannot provide, because only "real" viewers can buy the very real commodities the commercials advertise. By offering characterized viewers within the text, commercials fictively answer their own questions with resounding affirmation. We should not be too surprised, then, when talk shows, game shows, religious programs, and other forms of commercial television programming also "write in" their own viewers and provide them with opportunities to respond and act in an affirming, if carefully regulated, manner.

In this regard, perhaps the ultimate expression of television's rhetorical mode is the television "phone-a-thon," in which appeals for financial contributions to religious groups, public television stations, or charitable causes are made. The host usually stands in front of a raised bank of tables, behind which staff members or volunteers sit answering telephones. The calls they receive are, of course, pledges phoned in from viewers who have responded to the host's plea for financial support. Obviously, it is hardly necessary that the reception of telephone pledges be done on-screen. But fund raisers realize the important function served by keeping those answered telephones in the background. Each ringing telephone is (in semiotic terminology) an indexical sign for a characterized viewer—a reminder to the audience of how they "should" act. Furthermore, by combining televisual and telephone technologies, the phone-a-thon links the sign of these characterized viewers to the responses of *real* viewers as the latter provide a material response to the text's rhetorical demand.

TO WHAT DEGREE ARE THE READER AND THE CONTEXT OF THE READING ACT DETERMINATIVE OF MEANING?

Reader-oriented approaches to literature would deprive the text of its power to enforce meaning on the reader and, at the very least, shift critical attention away from "the words on the page" to the interaction between reader and textual structure. But does this interaction result in the reader merely following the text's instructions for the assembly of meaning? Or is meaning production so dependent upon the individual reader and his or her reading activity that each reading quite literally produces a different meaning? To what degree is meaning production an individual activity at all? How is an individual reading influenced by forces external to that act—linguistic, cultural, institutional, and ideological forces of which the individual reader might not even be aware?

Any attempt to grapple with these questions requires that the critic first answer another: "What, exactly, is the reader-oriented critic analyzing?" For the traditional "figure-in-the-carpet" critic, the object of study was self-evident. Because the text's meaning was to be found within it, then obviously critics studied texts. But if we accept, with Jonathan Culler, that the study of "literature" is no longer an attempt to interpret texts but to account for "their intelligibility: the ways in which they make sense, the ways in which readers have made sense of them," then what are literary critics now supposed to study?[16] Can this sense-making process be extrapolated from the text itself? As we have seen in previous sections of this chapter, reader-oriented critics aligned with the phenomenological school of Ingarden, Iser, and Jauss would answer a qualified "yes." They would assert that we can learn a great deal about the reading act through study of the textual structures and strategies that guide and, to some degree, regulate that process.

Other reader-oriented critics would argue that the critical moves of Iser and others represent a feint rather than a shift in the orientation of literary studies. Given that Iser's "reader" is always an abstract construct, evidence for whose alleged maneuvers are always drawn from something we are supposed to recognize as "the text," how different, they ask, is Iser's analysis of the reading act from more traditional types of interpretation?[17] Has he merely replaced "the" meaning of a text with a slightly more liberal notion of "instructions for meaning production?"

Terry Eagleton, among others, points out the paradox in Iser's theory caused by his acceptance of the proposition that meaning is a product of a reader's activity at the same time he holds to the idea that evidence for that activity can be found by studying texts. "If one considers the 'text in itself' as a kind of skeleton, a set of 'schemata' waiting to be concretized in various ways by various readers, how can one discuss these schemata at all without having already concretized them? In speaking of the 'text itself,' measuring it as a norm against particular interpretations of it, is one ever dealing with anything more than one's own concretization?" Eagleton calls this a version "of the old problem of how one can know the light in the refrigerator is off when the door is closed."[18]

Iser's counter here has been to maintain a certain degree of objectivity for the textual features that guide the reader's response. Without this, he argues, the text melts away into the subjective experience of each reader's activation of it. In other words, Iser worries that if we can't agree there's something "there" in the text that at least stimulates and guides meaning production, literary scholars might as well pack up shop and find another line of work.

For several American reader-oriented critics, Iser's paradox is created by his unwillingness to accept the consequences of his own line of reasoning—even if taking that step means that literary scholars have to find something to study other than "the text." For Norman Holland, the reading act is a kind of transactional therapy and process of individual self-realization. In reading, he says, the reader uses the text "as grist with which to re-create himself, that is, to make yet another variation of his single, enduring identity."[19] This "single, enduring identity" constitutes each personality's central organizing principle

and the means by which he or she relates to the outside world. This identity changes as the individual adjusts to the flux of experience, but it also structures and reorders that flux according to its internal psychic logic. Holland uses the term "work" of literature as a verb rather than a noun. The words on the page merely initiate a process by which the reader "works on" a story, "works it over" according to his identity theme, and, finally, "works it into" his or her identity.

If we accept Holland's account of how texts (now reduced to merely words on the page) are made to mean, then the object of study for the literary critic becomes the reader's identity theme and the manner by which it "works" on texts, because it—not the text—is the stable and determining feature of the reading transaction. In *5 Readers Reading,* Holland puts his theory into practice. He identifies the identity themes of five undergraduate students through standard personality tests and other means, has them all read several stories, and then discusses their responses with them to attempt to discover signs of their individual identity themes in their interpretations of the stories. What results is, for Holland, proof of his theory of reading as self-realization. For Holland's detractors, however, *5 Readers Reading* is either a circular and self-fulfilling exercise (by establishing the "identity theme" as the independent variable in his experiment and then looking for evidence of its effect in the reader's responses, Holland is almost sure to find what he is looking for) or an inadvertent demonstration that, if Holland's theory *is* correct, the critic can do no more than reflect upon his or her own identity theme, not anyone else's. As William Ray puts it, "the subject whose self re-creation fills *5 Readers Reading* is none of the five students described, but Holland himself, whose hundreds of pages of interpretation have predigested and reformulated the raw data of the reader's responses and therefore represent the only sustained reader transaction to which we could possibly respond."[20]

For Stanley Fish, reading is not the individual and self-realizing activity Holland describes, but a fundamentally social process. In his view, the "self" is "a social construct whose operations are delimited by the systems of intelligibility that inform it."[21] Thus differences in interpretation arise from differences in the assumptions that underlie different "interpretive communities," rather than from differences between individuals. What appears to the reader as his or her individual imposition of meaning is actually the result of a system of belief and resultant interpretive strategies he or she shares (usually unknowingly) with a larger community of readers. Fish shifts the focus of literary criticism one step further away from "the text." According to him, there are no "textual structures" that exist apart from a particular interpretive strategy that looks for and values them; there is no individual reader whose activities might be isolated and theorized; both text and individual reader are social products. With Fish the very notion of a text depends upon an interpretive community that endows this set of marks with that status. The famous example Fish uses in his *Is There a Text in*

This Class? is of a reading list left on the blackboard of his classroom by a previous instructor. Told by Fish that this list was a poem, the class was able to produce analyses of it *as* a poem—thus demonstrating to Fish that the category "poetry" is a function, not of authorial intention or textual organization, but rather of a particular system of belief (in this case that which governs reading in college literature classes).[22]

What, then, does Fish suggest literary critics study? Implicit in Fish's formulation of reading is the challenge to the critic to uncover the largely unarticulated assumptions of interpretive communities, especially those that dominate the reception of texts at a particular point in history, which would presumably account for variations in reading between readers and across cultures and time. Fish is quick to point out, however, that such an exercise is also subject to the forces it attempts to explain. Unlike Holland, who would reserve some objective space within which the critic could operate, Fish fully admits that his ability to read other critics as manifestations of the beliefs of a particular interpretive community is only possible because of the beliefs that inform Fish's own work—beliefs that, in effect, sanction what Fish does as "criticism." As with other reader-oriented theories, one has to admit that there is no position "outside" reading from which one can read the responses of other readers. Fish holds out no hope to those who would adopt his metacritical strategy that the uncovering of the assumptions of another interpretive community (or even of the critic's own) will change anyone's mind or bring us closer to "the truth." He warns his readers that his theory "is not one that you (or anyone else) could live by. Its thesis is that whatever seems to you to be obvious and inescapable is only so within some institutional or conventional structure, and that means that you can never operate outside some such structure, even if you are persuaded by the thesis."[23]

Fish's emphasis on the power of interpretive communities to determine the meaning of texts (and, indeed, the power to establish what a text is) should serve as one more reminder that all reading activity, including "reading" television, occurs within larger contexts. Furthermore, although he differs with them in many other respects, Fish shares with semiotic, ideological, and psychoanalytic theorists the recognition that language, ideology, culture, and institutions to some degree "speak" us as readers and viewers. One of the "axioms" of modern critical research, says Jonathan Culler, is "that the individuality of the individual cannot function as a principle of explanation, for it is itself a complex cultural construct, a heterogeneous product rather than a unified cause."[24]

As students of television, we might also be reminded by Fish's notion of "interpretive communities" of the norms of the critical community by which television has been judged as an actual or potential art form. As I pointed out in the Introduction, one of the reasons, I believe, that so little aesthetic analysis of television has been produced over the past forty years (relative to the pervasiveness of the medium and the sheer quantity of "texts" produced over that same time) is that the dominant critical community has embraced the values of what Iser would call "traditional" criticism. In addition to the "figure-in-the-carpet" assumptions about what and how texts mean, these values would include the belief that a single artistic vision should be expressed in a work of art, that good art requires intellectual work on the part of the perceiver, and that art works should be autonomous and unified entities, among others. As I have argued elsewhere with specific reference to radio and television soap operas, it is difficult to fit many forms of broadcast programming into a critical schema that assumes these values.[25] Who is the author of a situation comedy? How can one analyze a text that, like the soap opera, refuses to end? Because critics have found it difficult to discern the textual markers of art in television, they have seen little there to analyze. Furthermore, where critics have found the exceptional program on television worthy of detailed analysis (usually a dramatic program that shares some of the qualities of literary or theatrical "art"), they have spoken of it as if its sterling qualities were inside the work itself and "found" by the perceptive critic. This strategy makes it appear that the standards the critic applies are universal and renders evaluative assessments properties of the work, not the application of critical norms by the critic. As Fish points out, however, "all aesthetics . . . are local and conventional rather than universal, reflecting a collective decision as to what will count as literature. . . . Thus criteria of evaluation (that is, criteria for identifying literature) are valid only for the aesthetic they support and reflect."[26]

Another reader-oriented critic who foregrounds the social nature of the reading act is Tony Bennett. Following on the work of Pierre Macherey, Bennett has contended that all texts come to the reader always already "encrusted" with the effects of previous readings and that it is pointless to speak of a "text" existing separate from these historically specific encrustations. Our reading of any work is inevitably conditioned by other discourses that circulate around it: advertisements for it, reviews, other works of the same genre or author, etc. For Bennett, studying the relationship between literary phenomena and society "requires that everything that has been said or written about a text, every context in which it has been inscribed by the uses to which it has been put, should, in principle, be regarded as relevant to and assigned methodological parity within such a study."[27]

Bennett cites the example of the James Bond phenomenon. Our viewing of a given James Bond film is conditioned by the previous films in the series; by the novels upon which the films are based; by the characterizations of Bond by Sean Connery and Roger Moore; by the advertisements for both novels and films; by the cover designs for the novels (featuring scantily clad women and the paraphernalia of espionage); by the songs written to accompany the films; by articles in the press about the films, their stars, Ian Fleming, "Bond" himself, British intelligence, and so forth. The film itself is merely one part of "a mobile system of circulating signifiers," a text that is activated by the reader only in relation to the reading of other texts.[28]

Commercial television might be seen as a gigantic "mobile system of circulating signifiers." Perhaps more than any other form of cultural production, television produces texts that never "stand alone." Rather, they continuously point the viewer in the direction of other texts. This is not surprising, considering the economic basis of commercial television. The viewer does not "buy" the right to view a program (as the reader buys a novel or a moviegoer buys a ticket to a film). The viewer is, in fact, sold to advertisers in lots of one thousand. The text's (program's) status in this exchange is merely that of the bait to keep the viewer watching until the commercial comes on. To the commercial networks, each program is but one device in a larger scheme designed to hold the viewer's attention throughout a block of the day.

Among television program types, the made-for-TV movie might appear to be among the more autonomous with respect to its relationship to other texts.[29] It is narratively self-contained, and, unlike the series or the serial, there are no characters or situations that carry over from one movie to the next. In fact, however, the made-for-TV movie relies heavily upon the viewer's familiarity with other texts.

Since the mid-1960s, television programmers have used the made-for-TV movie as an economical substitute for theatrical feature films. The made-for-TV movie presents a promotional problem not found with either the theatrical feature film or the television series, however. Having played in theatres a year or so before its television air date, the theatrical feature film is very much the "already read" text, bringing with it a trail of discourse that accompanied its theatrical release. Thus the audience's familiarity with the film's title, theatrical success, stars, etcetera, make the theatrical feature a known quantity by the time it reaches television screens. Carrying over its characters and setting from week to week, the series has a built-in self-promotional aspect: each episode acts as a "preview of coming attractions" for the next episode. Having no prior theatrical "life" and limited to a single airing, each made-for-TV movie presents a promotional challenge. How can an audience be built for a film whose budget usually precludes the use of big-name Hollywood stars or being based upon a popular novel, and whose single exposure on television means there can be no "word of mouth"? What is there to promote and advertise?

A number of strategies have been employed in an attempt to solve this problem, one of the most common being to make the made-for-TV movie a "problem picture." The film is based upon a current social controversy, and discourse about that controversy is used to promote the film. Over the past ten years nearly every social issue imaginable has become the basis for a made-for-TV movie:

missing children (*Adam*), spouse abuse (*The Burning Bed*), incest (*Something about Amelia*), teenage suicide (*Surviving*), and child molestation (*Kids Don't Tell*), among many others. The film then represents a narrativization of discourse about a particular social issue already circulating in newspapers, magazines, and other television programs. As Laurie Schulze and others have pointed out, the more disturbing or threatening aspects of these social problems are defused by the made-for-TV movie's reliance upon familiar genres as vehicles for their expression.[30] Typically, whether the problem is teenage prostitution or single bars, it is framed by the conventions of the family melodrama and/or the heterosexual romance. In the made-for-TV movie Schulze analyzes—*Getting Physical,* a 1984 film about female bodybuilding—this generic framing occurs even before the film is aired. One of the most important promotional devices for the made-for-TV movie is display advertising in *TV Guide.* The viewer's interest must be aroused by an ad illustrating the film's "problem" visually (usually by artwork, rather than a still from the film itself) and describing it in a few words of accompanying text. The *TV Guide* ad for *Getting Physical* showed a bikini-clad woman in a frontal bodybuilder pose, beside a photographic insert of a close-up shot of another woman and a man. The text read, "When a beautiful woman becomes a bodybuilder, the sport takes on a whole new shape, and her life new meaning." Schulze comments: "The smaller inserted photograph suggests that the benefit will have something to do with heterosexual desirability. The insert implies that the 'new meaning' given her life will involve the romantic attentions of an attractive male; bodybuilding will facilitate heterosexual romance."[31]

Made-for-TV movies are also promoted on other television programs. In fact, some television talk shows have become little more than vehicles for the promotion of other texts—books, theatrical movies, records, concert appearances, and other television programs. The stars of a forthcoming made-for-TV movie are made "available" for interviews on *Entertainment Tonight, Show Business This Week,* network morning news shows, and other such programs. The interviews may or may not center on the star's role in the made-for-TV movie, but a "plug" for it is sure to be included. Such star appearances are, of course, most likely to occur on the network showing the made-for-TV movie, and the interview's content and timing are carefully orchestrated to give maximum promotion to the movie.

In January 1986, NBC ran a made-for-TV movie entitled *Mafia Princess,* based on the memoirs of the daughter of reputed Mafia leader Sam Giancana. The film starred Tony Curtis and *All My Children* star Susan Lucci. Curtis appeared on both the *Today* show and *Late Night with David Letterman* the week before the film's airing. Curtis's remarks about the film on both programs stressed that it was "really" about a relationship between a father and a daughter, thus helping to frame it within the family melodrama genre. Interestingly, however, the interviews touched relatively briefly on *Mafia Princess,* emphasizing instead Curtis's recovery from drug abuse, his early struggles as a Hollywood actor, and his relationship with his family (particularly with his daughter, Jamie Leigh Curtis). Despite the fact that these topics did not concern *Mafia Princess* directly, they provided additional layers of discursive "encrustation." Reminded of Curtis's battle with drug abuse, the viewer might watch *Mafia Princess* for signs of the actor's rehabilitation. If the viewer had not made the connection between the film's subject matter and Curtis's sometimes stormy relationship with his own daughter before the interviews, he or she could not help but be aware of it afterwards. David Letterman even asked Curtis if he had encountered any "Mafia types" during his career in show business. He responded that he had, but coyly refused to discuss the matter further.

All of these encrustations are in addition to the most obvious—representations of organized crime the audience might have encountered in newspapers, magazine articles, other television programs, and films. Even if a viewer of *Mafia Princess* had managed to miss the ad and article in *TV Guide,* interviews with Tony Curtis and Susan Lucci, and other forms of promotion, he or she still would not have come to it as a "naive" reader. *Mafia Princess* cannot be separated from the web of other texts for which it provides a site of intersection—texts about organized crime, Italians, law and criminality, the historical personages upon whom the story was based, family relationships, and so on. Even this rather unremarkable example of textual encrustation serves to support Bennett's contention that "the text is never available for analysis except in the context of its activations."[32]

CONCLUSIONS

One major difficulty in discussing how reader-oriented criticism might relate to television analysis is the considerable theoretical and methodological diversity among critics whose work might bear the label "reader-oriented." As the section of this chapter on characterized and implied readers and viewers illustrates, there are about as many notions of what a reader is as there are critics talking about readers. Still, the strand of contemporary literary criticism that, however loosely, we can call reader-oriented has helped to at least raise a set of questions that traditional literary analysis left unasked, and in doing so has challenged us to reconsider concepts and assumptions that lie at the very heart of the critical endeavor. What is a text? How is it made to mean? What is the relationship between the world in the text and the world brought to the reading experience by the reader? To what degree is the sense-making capacity of the reader a product of external forces? In a world without texts determinative of their own meaning, what is the role of the critic? Given the fundamental nature of these questions, it should come as no surprise that reader-oriented critics fundamentally disagree about their answers.

The relationship between television and its viewers provides an excellent laboratory in which to test the insights of reader-oriented literary critics—even if, as in the case of Iser, some of those critics themselves might question the applicability of literary theory to the realm of nonliterary popular culture. The movement in reader-oriented criticism away from the notion of a stable and eternal text to that of activations of texts within historically specific conditions of reception is accelerated by the very nature of television. Television programming is inherently ephemeral—here for an hour or so and then gone, perhaps forever. Furthermore, few people in the television industry think in terms of programming as a series of autonomous and isolated texts. Because the goal of commercial television is the stimulation of habitual viewing over long periods, programs are conceived of as links in a continuous chain of programming. Raymond Williams has spoken of television programming as a "planned flow, in which the true series is not the published sequence of programme items but this sequence transformed by the inclusion of another kind of sequence, so that these sequences together compose the real flow, the real 'broadcasting.'"[33]

The insight that texts carry within them a place marked out for the hypothetical reader to occupy applies with particular force to television. Because of its economic nature (that of a vehicle for selling people to advertisers), commercial television addresses its prospective viewers much more directly than does the fictional cinema or literature. The need of advertisers to persuade viewers to become "good viewers" (to accept the arguments of the commercial messages and then purchase the product) infuses all aspects of this "flow" of programming. Viewers are not only directly addressed, they are provided with representations of themselves on the screen and embraced within the all-encompassing realm of the "fictive We."

Finally, although every reading act is "public" in the sense that it occurs within a definite social and cultural context, it is easy to overlook this fact when discussing the literary reading act. Reading a novel seems such a private and individual activity—even if, as Stanley Fish contends, that individual reader merely applies the strategies of a larger interpretive community. The public or social dimensions of television "reading" are undeniable. The simultaneity of television broadcasts, with millions of sets receiving the same images at the same time, makes watching a television program a social phenomenon even if we are "alone" while we watch. The oceanic nature of television programming, its constant references to other texts, the close connections between television and other forms of textual production, all combine to plug any individual act of television viewing into a network of other viewings and other discourses, and to link us as viewers into the larger culture.

NOTES

[1] Wolfgang Iser, *The Act of Reading: A Theory of Aesthetic Response* (Baltimore, Md.: Johns Hopkins University Press, 1978), pp. 3-5.

[2] For those interested in the finer points of these debates and in the relationship of reader-oriented criticism to other types of analysis, a good introduction is provided by Robert C. Holub, *Reception Theory: A Critical Introduction* (London: Methuen, 1984). Holub concentrates on the strand of reader-oriented criticism developed in Germany, especially that associated with Wolfgang Iser, Hans Robert Jauss, and their colleagues at the University of Constance. William Ray considers Iser, Ingarden, Holland, Bleich, Culler, and Fish as a part of his more general survey of literary interpretations since phenomenology; see *Literary Meaning: From Phenomenology to Deconstruction* (London: Basil Blackwell, 1984). Terry Eagleton discusses reception theory from a Marxist perspective in *Literary Theory: An Introduction* (Minneapolis: University of Minnesota Press, 1983). Jonathan Culler, more an actor than an observer of disputes in reader-oriented criticism, relates the project of reader-oriented criticism to semiotics in *The Pursuit of Signs: Semiotics, Literature, and Deconstruction* (London: Routledge and Kegan Paul, 1981). Two collections of reader-oriented criticism have excellent introductory essays: Susan Suleiman and Inge Crossman, eds., *The Reader in the Text: Essays on Audience and Interpretation* (Princeton, N.J.: Princeton University Press, 1980); and Jane P. Tompkins, ed., *Reader-Response Criticism: From Formalism to Post-Structuralism* (Baltimore, Md.: Johns Hopkins University Press, 1980).

[3] Georges Poulet, "Phenomenology of Reading," *New Literary History* 1 (October 1969): 56, quoted in Ray, *Literary Meaning,* p. 101.

[4] See Roman Ingarden, *The Literary Work of Art,* trans. George C. Grabowicz (Evanston, Ill.: Northwestern University Press, 1973).

[5] Iser, *The Act of Reading* (originally published in German as *Der Act Des Lesens: Theorie asthetischer Wirkung* [Munich: Wilhelm Fink, 1976]).

[6] Consider, for example, the opening sentences of Fay Weldon's novel, *Female Friends:* "Understand, and forgive. It is what my mother taught me to do, poor patient gentle Christian soul, and the discipline she herself practised, and the reason she died in poverty, alone and neglected" (*Female Friends* [London: Picador Books, 1977], p. 5). The first sentence would appear to be an injunction to "understand and forgive." But who should understand and forgive? Who is speaking these words? In what context are these admonitions meant? The following sentence answers these questions to some degree: the first-person narrator is the "speaker" of these words; they are precepts taught her by her mother. But it also asks another question: why are they the reason she "died in poverty, alone and neglected"? Obviously, we'll have to read on to find out. Perhaps the next sentence will answer this question, perhaps it will defer the answer until later, perhaps by saying nothing more about it in the following sentences the text will leave it to us to infer some causal relationship between her mother's philosophy of under-

standing and forgiving and her death. The last sentence of this very short chapter (only a few paragraphs) reads: "Such were Chloe's thoughts before she slept." Aha! Someone named Chloe "thought" what we have just read and she did so before going to sleep. Our understanding of all that we have read to this point is retrospectively altered by the information contained in this sentence. The blank paper at the bottom of that first page signals us to turn the page in the hope of discovering more about Chloe: Why is she thinking about her mother's precepts and death? And so forth. This question/answer/question chain continues throughout the novel.

[7] The above discussion of Iser's theory of the reading act is largely based on chapter 5 of *The Act of Reading,* "Grasping a Text."

[8] Iser, *The Act of Reading,* pp. 191-92.

[9] Ibid., p. 192.

[10] W. Daniel Wilson, "Readers in Texts," *PMLA* 96, no. 5 (October 1981): 848-63.

[11] Umberto Eco, *The Role of the Reader* (Bloomington: Indiana University Press, 1977), p. 7.

[12] Wayne C. Booth, *The Rhetoric of Fiction* (Chicago: University of Chicago Press, 1961), p. 138.

[13] At the beginning of chapter 4, the narrator addresses the reader: "I know there are readers in the world, as well as many other good people in it, who are no readers at all—who find themselves ill at ease, unless they are let into the whole secret from first to last, of everything which concerns you." He then goes on for a few paragraphs as to the kind of background information the reader might desire to have at the beginning of a personal history. The narrator then says:

> To such, however, as do not choose to go so far back into these things, I can give no better advice than that they skip over the remaining part of this Chapter; for I declare beforehand, 'tis wrote only for the curious and inquisitive.
>
> _____Shut the door._____
>
> I was begot in the night, betwixt the first Sunday and the first Monday in the month of March . . . (Lawrence Sterne, *Tristram Shandy* [New York: New American Library Edition, 1962], p. 12).

Note that the relationship between this characterized reader and what we might presume to be the implied reader is left unclear and that as "real" readers we're not sure whether or not we want to be identified as the "reader" the narrator addresses. Are we among those readers "who find themselves ill at ease, unless they are let into the whole secret from first to last"? We are then forced to choose what kind of reader we are; we can take the narrator's advice and "shut the door" on the rest of the chapter, or we can align ourselves with the "curious and inquisitive" and read on.

[14] Michele Hilmes discusses the "direct address" quality of television in "The Television Apparatus: Direct Address," *Journal of Film and Video* 37, no. 4 (Fall 1985): 27-36.

[15] Robert Stam, "Television News and Its Spectator," in *Regarding Television—Critical Approaches: An Anthology*, ed. E. Ann Kaplan, American Film Institute Monograph Series, vol. 2 (Frederick, Md.: University Publications of America, 1983), p. 39.

[16] Culler, *The Pursuit of Signs*, p. 50.

[17] Holub, *Reception Theory*, pp. 100-101; Eagleton, *Literary Theory*, pp. 78-85.

[18] Eagleton, *Literary Theory*, pp. 84-85.

[19] Norman Holland, *5 Readers Reading* (New Haven, Conn.: Yale University Press, 1975), pp. 28-29.

[20] Ray, *Literary Meaning*, pp. 67-68.

[21] Stanley Fish, *Is There a Text in This Class?* (Cambridge, Mass.: Harvard University Press, 1980), p. 335.

[22] Ibid., chapter 14.

[23] Ibid., p. 370.

[24] Culler, *The Pursuit of Signs*, p. 53.

[25] Robert C. Allen, *Speaking of Soap Operas* (Chapel Hill: University of North Carolina Press, 1985), pp. 11-18.

[26] Fish, *Is There a Text in This Class?* pp. 109-10.

[27] Tony Bennett, "Text and Social Process: The Case of James Bond," *Screen Education* 41 (Winter/Spring 1982): 9.

[28] Ibid., pp. 9-14.

[29] The following discussion of the made-for-TV movie is based largely on Laurie Jane Schulze, "Text/Context/Cultural Activation: The Case of the Made-for-Television Movie," M.A. thesis, University of North Carolina at Chapel Hill, 1985.

[30] Ibid., pp. 95-103.

[31] Ibid., p. 171.

[32] Bennett, "Text and Social Process," p. 14.

[33] Raymond Williams, *Television: Technology and Cultural Form* (New York: Schocken Books, 1975), p. 90.

Mariá Carrión

SOURCE: "Twin Peaks and the Circular Ruins of Fiction: Figuring (Out) the Acts of Reading," in *Literature/Film Quarterly*, Vol. 21, No. 4, 1993, pp. 240-47.

[*In the following essay, Carrión compares viewing the television series* Twin Peaks *with the act of reading a complex fictional narrative such as those written by Jorge Luis Borges.*]

> In a dream, God declared to him the secret purpose of his life and work: Dante, in wonderment, knew at last who and what he was and blessed the bitterness of his life. Tradition relates that, upon waking, he felt that he had received and lost an infinite thing, something he would not be able to recuperate or even glimpse, for the machinery of the world is much too complex for the simplicity of men.
>
> Jorge Luis Borges. *"Inferno"* 1, 32

The basic narrative structure of *Twin Peaks* had started to get as complicated as the question ABC's Programming Department was facing: should the show be discontinued or not?[1] During its first season, the Thursday-night program had a good chance to carve itself a solid niche in mainstream television and popular culture. But as it had been predicted by fans and detractors alike, the series did not last beyond the second round of episodes in the dooming "Saturday-night graveyard slot" in which it was placed (Altman 47; Corliss 86). Looking back now, those were rocky times for the fans who faithfully parked themselves in front of their sets on Saturdays expecting to follow the show and, instead, kept finding a different program on their screens. As for the concluding two-hour *solo* episode aired in June, it did not seem to offer a significant sense of an ending for *Twin Peaks*. In fact, the managerial decision to kill the show was amply parodied by the final scene, which left an unequivocal feeling of "we shall return" in the viewers' minds. Despite the problematic issues of gender and violence that convinced different audiences to condemn the series, many spectators still could not understand the network's final verdict against the program.[2]

The complexity of the stories that composed *Twin Peaks*, the replication of identities and its arrogant, self-conscious style have been blamed for its disappearance. Perhaps people got tired of self-contained sarcasm, and audiences found what Corliss calls "cliff-hanging teases" a tiring item, an obstacle to following the story line (86). By the end of the first season, however, the stuff that *Twin Peaks* was made of was not the closure of a simple murder story. By then it was obvious that just reading the plot was not an issue anymore, and that finding out who killed Laura Palmer was not at stake so much as deciphering what it was the owls (and *Twin Peaks* itself) really were (since they were not, as we know, what they seemed); or why and how was BOB going to destroy whose body next, or maybe which one of the oneiric characters in Dale Bartholomew "Coop" Cooper's fecund mind was going to give him a clue that would lead him to the assassin's path. Then, why has this difficulty of following a simple mystery-murder plot been held responsible for the extinction of a once phenomenally popular television series?

It is true that as soon as viewers lost sight of Laura Palmer's cadaver the story became an implacable search for a murderer, deceitfully like any other "Saturday Night Mysteries." But the narrative act of *Twin Peaks,* in turn, soon started to unveil various hidden agendas that break away from the canon of television detective series. The carefully staged dead body of Laura did not lead to an already familiar figure like the characters played by network favorites such as Jaclyn Smith, Angela Lansbury, Raymond Burr, or Burt Reynolds. Neither did we find, in a matter of one or two hours, a psychotic killer like the legendary Jack the Ripper or the more modern and recalcitrant Freddy, recently disappeared from the big screen. The "plot" in *Twin Peaks* opened up, before the end of the first season, to the presence of a supernatural entity whose unintelligible name ("BOB," as the viewers would learn later on) was crucial for the solution of the murder of three women. This entity, whose last name and essence remain unknown even to this day, was gradually unveiled by detective Cooper's weird attempt to decipher—via principles of oriental philosophy and strokes of chance—a number of clues: the messages left by an unknown "writer" in a set of scattered letters, the design of a mysterious map that hosted extraterrestrial entities, and the chess game on which the lives of different people depended.[3] An agent of that Greatly Respected and Feared Bureau of Intelligence enters the game, narrative and otherwise, in the middle of a dreamlike sequence; in it, places and faces seem to replicate and question the reality of the scene. Laura and Madeleine, Audrey and Donna, Bobby and James, Shelley and Norma, many of the inhabitants of Twin Peaks look a lot alike, in a suspiciously similar manner to the way in which the different logs and thick red fabrics take us—consciously or unconsciously—from the Great Northern to One-Eyed Jack's, to the local motel, or to Cooper's doubled-up dream scenario, among others. Cooper learns at a certain point that the assassin he has been chasing is not just a common outlaw, but the very same man who has taught him the art of clue-solving. What this character really wants, as Cooper will realize in time, is to see him—the detective figure—die because of a certain woman, very dear to both men, whose death was ultimately Cooper's doing because of his sin of adultery.

Syntax gets complicated when one tries to talk about *Twin Peaks.* It might have to do with the fact that one is not just trying to reveal the name of this particular entity who has put an end to somebody else's life. For *Twin Peaks'* basic narrative structure falls under the category of what John Irwin calls "pure analytic detective stories," a fictional genre that lends itself to endless acts of rereadings, "grows out of an interest in deductions and solutions rather than in love and drama [and] shows little

interest in character, managing at best to produce caricatures" (1169). Narratives tailored in this fashion, filmic or literary, put a strong emphasis on the act of reading and its processes, and not on the consummation of a discovery of a mere fact.[4] After weaning the spectator off his/her symbiotic relationship with the authority figures in the genre such as Agatha Christie, Alfred Hitchcock and, on a different level, characters such as Sherlock Holmes or Hercules Poirot, the story that Agent Cooper is trying to tell eventually turns into a seemingly pointless wander in search of the nature of the narrative driving force itself. Within the frame of pure analytic detective fiction, Cooper's development as a character is not going to be enslaved to the unveiling of the mysterious entity of the murderer. The deductive process is the goal in itself, and not the attainment of partial information (a name or a face, etc.). This wandering viewpoint, according to Wolfgang Iser, is a key element in the "act of reading," since it "permits the reader to travel through the text, thus unfolding the multiplicity of interconnecting perspectives which are offset whenever there is a switch from one to another" (118). And it is *Twin Peaks'* potential for constant substitution of identities that helps the reader create a network of connections that do not depend only on a mechanical, passive, chaining process of isolated data from these different perspectives. In other words, all the units that constitute its thick web of stories can be mixed and matched to multiply and create new stories. This, in turn, also implies a detour from the traditional detective stories: in this particular type of fiction, the author is the one responsible for the story and, hence, he or she is expected to dictate who killed the victim. Differing from this practice *Twin Peaks,* besides attempting to tell who killed Laura Palmer, represents a diverse range of social issues (drugs, prostitution, violence, incest) as well as spiritual quests (supernatural and extraterrestrial forces, the damnation of the souls of both Cooper and the beloved he attempts to rescue, belief in the self and others) and team-worked artistic invention (of which Donna-Maddy-James, Cooper-Truman-Andy-Hawk, Norma-Shelley and other recombined groups are obviously an emblem).[5] This process of switching narrative foci is, no doubt, partly what grants the act of reading its great relevance in *Twin Peaks.* The different units of its wandering viewpoint help "establish a relationship of reciprocal observation between stimulant and stimulated perspectives," which makes the reader reconsider the path of conventional one-way channels of artistic communication (Iser 118). The difficulty and danger of all this reshuffling of elements in the narrative chain is that, although the reader's network potentially encompasses the whole text, this potential can never be fully realized—in a kaleidoscopic manner.

What *Twin Peaks* seems to be attempting, then, is to conform the foundations for the process of reading, an indefinite number of selections that:

> have to be made during the reading process and which, though intersubjectively not identical—as is shown by the many different interpretations of

a single text—, nevertheless remain intersubjectively comprehensible in so far as they are all attempts to optimize the same structure. (Iser 118)[6]

Again, the potential for optimizing the text, never consummated but amply feasible by achieving as many interpretations or "readings" of it, is a double-edged sword. On the one hand it is precisely this what confers on each artistic text its beauty and richness, while at the same time it is the very element that can cause, if misused or ignored, the dismissal of a text as "incoherent," "incomplete," or, as it was mentioned before, "arrogant" or "inconsistent." Consistency is, no doubt, the most important clue for the involvement of the reader and even the writer/producer in the artistic process: "the wandering viewpoint divides the text into interacting structures, and these give raise to a grouping activity that is fundamental to the grasping of the text" (Iser 119).

In the case of *Twin Peaks* the numerous recombinants have been placed for the reader to select and group, in order to constitute a meaningful message; they have not just been preset in an obvious manner that generates artificial association of ideas and gets tiresome after the readers have mastered the basic techniques. For the process of building consistency in the act of reading, then, is not a mere "illusion-making process, but comes about through gestalt grouping, and these contain traces of illusion in so far as their closure—since it is based on selection—is not a characteristic of the text itself, but only represents a configurative meaning" (Iser 124). For Cooper, the traditionally expected center of signification in the detective story, this means that not BOB and not his former master in the Bureau, not even the weird people of his dreamland, no definite single character, can help him solve the mystery of *Twin Peaks*. For he is searching for a murderer at a literal level, but he also is seeking an understanding of himself and his own literary traces which do not fit in a clean-cut, straightforward mold of an FBI-faithful serviceman, nor in a parody of the detectivesque archetype. Ultimately, he is neither James Bond nor Max 086 (the Super-Agent); and he is not trying to recover the Pink Panther diamond with the aid of an avant-garde oriental Watson.

Then what is the actual theme of *Twin Peaks?* If it is not who killed Laura Palmer and the other three women, if it is not an attempt to reveal who is going to sacrifice Ms. Twin Peaks to the deadly chess game, what is it talking about? The bottom line, hard to digest, is that the central theme of *Twin Peaks* is whatever each one of the viewers wants to name it, because—like in any other act of reading—it is "built up by the way of the attentiveness aroused when the knowledge invoked by repertoire becomes problematic. . . . As the theme is not an end in itself, but a sign for something else, it produces an 'empty' reference, and the filling-in of this reference is what constitutes the significance" (Iser 147). Cooper's endless search for an identity, the people of Twin Peaks' drive to find out who or what BOB is, all the narrative desires of the series seem to lead its readers toward a quest for significance rather than just a mere search for an immediate meaning. This makes the viewing process,

usually quick and easy in the television environment, rather heavy and complicated. In fact, the basic element of building images out of *Twin Peaks,* fundamental to the act of reading (in) it, forces the readers to learn as much information outside of the different plots as possible: " . . . for the reader who is not fully conversant with all the elements of the repertoire . . . , there will obviously be gaps which will then prevent the theme from achieving its full significance" (Iser 145). This abyss of not achieving significance, of transcending the gap in communication, is the ultimate danger of the aesthetic response process.[7]

As the Argentinean writer Jorge Luis Borges establishes with his works in prose, the acts of writing and reading can actually turn into circular ruins, a never-ending process that confuses and exasperates the reader who does not want (or is simply not able) to see beyond the literal. It is not an artistic *capricho* that the labyrinth is a crucial narrative axis in Borges's prose, since it very significantly represents all reading processes. The world of Borges's fictions is populated by different kinds of people. It is not a pristine landscape of normal or "realistic" individuals, but a thick texture of very literary characters who inhabit a universe of reading as they always connect previously written data. In this same fashion, Cooper's relationship both with Western and Oriental traditions unveils a quest much closer to (and, paradoxically enough, distant from) home than the classic detective story. The simple reason behind this: he is, just like Jane and Johnny in any classroom of the world, learning how to read. And precisely the same as Jaromir Hladík or Erik Lönnrot, as the character named "The Man" or as Borges himself, Cooper is entangled in a difficult and painful attempt to figure out what the letters (or narrative units) really mean; not just the letters given in the story, but deeper grounds of meaning and interpretation not spelled out so clearly within the text. Well into the narrative game of *Twin Peaks,* the FBI agent pronounces BOB's name, but this literal plot wears out temporarily when the entity responding to the four-letter name flies out from the body of Leland Palmer (significantly enough, Laura's father). Likewise, the characters in some of Borges's texts (such as "The Secret Miracle," "Death and the Compass," "The Circular Ruins," and "Borges and I") find themselves uncovering puzzling sign codes, but the quest is never completed by the "author" figure. In other words, the act of reading cannot just be consummated inside the text (as a literal reading would be), but also outside of it. The true readers of both Borges's and *Twin Peaks'* narratives are not just literal consumers of texts, but characters actively engaged in a search for meaning and significance.[8] This might explain why many of the potential readers for the multiple levels of Borges's labyrinths get frustrated at the difficulty of reading (in) the textual and conceptual maze, and why they blame it on Borges. Or why many viewers have given up altogether on the "weird style" of the series and have blamed it on Lynch.

Which brings us to another step in the figuration of the act of reading in *Twin Peaks.* The text is not just an inert artifact, a static object to be approached by the reader. In order to achieve a significant moment in the communication, the text must be clearly perceived as an event, as something that is happening. The moment of contact between the text and the reader "arises out of the manner in which the strategies *disrupt* consistency-building, and by thus *opening* the potential range and interaction of gestalten, it *enables* the reader to *dwell* in the living world into which he [or she] has *transmuted* the text" (Iser 128. Emphasis mine). Notice the semantic field of all these verbs: they all converge in the common grounds of action, not just from the part of the text, but of the reader as well. In consequence, while the reader is engaged in the process of reading, he or she will react to what they have produced, that mode of reaction enabling them to experience the text as an actual event (Iser 129).

Reading as a tangible event brings us back to the concept of involvement, which is a condition of experiencing the text. Truly, the reader has to process the data in person, not allowing any other narrative entity to dictate the meaning or its significance. What do the words "Twin Peaks" signify, for example? The name of the town, the title of the series (in italics, please), the name of two mountain tops? Or maybe the pseudo-Siamese glances of the different characters at the stories? ("Are you twin-peaking tonight?" I was asked by other "freaks" on those memorable Saturdays.) The "eyes"/"I's" of the readers-viewers when watching the series? Lynch-Frost as trickster *auteurs* of the project? You name it. The firsthand, intransferable-yet-communicable involvement in the perception and interpretation process is essential to the happening of the series.[9] And these "[o]bvious textual ambiguities are like a puzzle which we have to solve ourselves" (Iser 129). This solving process, in turn, stimulates the reader to balance the contradictions emerging in it; contradictions springing out not only from the classic-styled mystery fiction plot, but also from his or her own "habitual experiences, which are now a past orientation. As such [reading] is not a passive process of acceptance, but a productive response" (Iser 133). What, then, is the task of the reader, if it is not just to think concurrently with the detective and help him or her solve the "mystery"/case, not forgetting to admire in the meantime his or her skillful and adventurous spirit? The reader is responsible for making the signs consistent, maintaining alive the possibility that those connections newly established will in turn become signs for further correlations, even if they seem not to be relevant to the traditionally central murder story. This is the actual plot of *Twin Peaks,* for the plot is "not an end in itself—it always serves a meaning, for stories are not told for their own sake but for the demonstration of something that extends beyond themselves" (Iser 123). At the risk of getting lost in the maze the true readers of this narrative *can* actually find new meanings and new significances every time they watch *Twin Peaks* again.[10] Given that, as I mentioned earlier in this article, the final two-hour episode-movie in June left us with a bittersweet and hopeful aftertaste, we can always figure out acts of reading that will offer new significant senses of an ending (other than ABC's) for *Twin Peaks.*

In my literarily-oriented mind, one reading of *Twin Peaks* would tell us that the owls are not really what they seem. Birds of the night, voices in the dark, these charming and terrifying characters of the "Ghostwood National Forest" (Lynch et al 113) are an emblematic sign of the readers. Present, yet apparently "away" or "asleep," they are very much like Cooper when he sleeps, dreams and, by the way, gets the most significant pieces of information for his job. Cooper and the owls open their eyes (*the* twin peaks?) and see in the dark; in other words, they, just like us, read.

Cooper's last dream melts with the first one; they both provide crucial information not just for the search of the murderer, but for the insides/insights of Cooper's mind, which we eventually realize that works as a mere reflection of ours. In one of the last scenes with BOB and the Master, Cooper (who, by then, we either know or at least suspect that it is a representation of ourselves) revisits Goethe's play *Faust* by selling his soul to the devil: he chooses to enter the cave in the same way Dante willingfully enters the gates of Hell, despite the warning sign. But what does this whole network of pacts and agreements mean? How is the reader represented in Cooper's heroic gesture of entering the Owl Cave, a realm in the landscape of Cooper's mental processes that supersedes and violates natural-physical laws? What does it really mean that he is driven by the love of a woman? And was it for Caroline, or for Ms. Twin Peaks? The pact of selling your soul not for your own salvation but for the sake of a loved one, brilliantly explored in Klaus Kinsky's characterization of "Nosferatu the Vampire" (in Werner Herzog's film of the same title) among others, recurs in this last scene as a way of asking the viewers the ultimate question of the act of reading: are you going to lose yourself in the process of involvement, in the experience of the text, in order to turn it into a truly aesthetic—and not just a consumerist—event? Are you going to attempt self-realization through this narrative, or are you just going to remain faithful to the tradition of simple glances at the plot, in order to consum(at)e it and eliminate it?

The moment of realization becomes evident at this point: the chess game (apparently played between Cooper and the Master) was just a trick from BOB, the until-then-ultimate-evil-character, to attract both of them to his ground of action, that hellish dreamland that Cooper dares to visit taking us inside of his mind. From there the only realization that the readers can achieve is the fact that we are all dreamed by somebody else. And then, is BOB's only motive to abort the possibility that there is some otherness above him, who is dreaming him? Then again, Borges had already told us in his "Circular Ruins," where the creator that we know throughout the story ends up being the creation of yet another being superior to him, another "father" or "master." What *Twin Peaks* tells us, beyond these circular ruins of fiction in Cooper's mind, is anybody's story. Cooper's body is released, but his soul is taken over by some other presence. In the meantime, we find out that the entity of Ms. Twin Peaks, who during the scenes in the Cave had been blurred by the appearance of the filmic persona of Caroline, seems to have returned as well. Cooper, back in his bed at the Great Northern, wonders about her and he is told that she is resting in a separate room. We would never see her again, though, which makes it impossible for us to reach the conclusion that she was truly saved, and not just spit back from hell like her beloved agent. Once he leaves his bed he realizes (and simultaneously so do we, thanks to the wonders of the mirror) that Cooper's physique looks like BOB's, in one last moment of terror. The mirror breaks, apparently by Cooper's move. And Borges, reading his passage:

> "[. . .] mirrors and copulation are abominable, because they increase the number of men. . . . *Mirrors and fatherhood are abominable because they multiply and disseminate that universe.*" (4)

make us wonder/wander: was Cooper the one who just acted out the scene, the one who has broken the looking glass in order to escape the mastery of BOB over his (id)entity? Was it actually BOB's will taking over Cooper's soul? Or is it the intensity of the moment, terrifying in its unbearable encounter between the true self of Cooper and the readers'? Or could it be Lynch and Company, breaking their young and wonderfully monstrous relationship with the world of television? Was it any, all or any combination of the above mentioned? Or was it something else?

Inevitably, Cooper's last dream brings us back to the first, that exciting and also intense moment of creativity that *Twin Peaks* offered its true readers during their television honeymoon period. The circular ruins of fiction come to an end. And yet, it is an unreal end. Because, as we know, the labyrinth only has one end: the exit. For as long as we continue reading (in) the maze of *Twin Peaks,* like in Borges's fictions, the supposed termination of the series will be as fake as the image of Cooper in the mirror and the dubious identities that inhabit the town.

NOTES

[1] From now on, whenever I mention "the basic narrative structure" of *Twin Peaks* I intentionally will be referring to the sequential units of action that many viewers followed in the small screen, and that constitute the foundations of a number of literary spin-offs such as *The Secret Diary of Laura Palmer,* written by director, writer, and actor David Lynch's daughter, Jennifer; *The Autobiography of David Cooper,* authored by Scott Frost; *Twin Peaks: Access Guide to the Town,* by David Lynch et al; and the unofficial *Welcome to Twin Peaks: A Complete Guide to Who's Who & What's What,* by Scott Knickelbine.

[2] ABC's ultimate reason to sacrifice the show should have been very simple: the fact that "the people" were not interested in it any more. The question is, however, whether this lack of interest was the *cause* for the decline of what Altman labels the "Peak Freaks" and, in turn, the

series itself, or the *effect* of ABC's obvious mismanagement. Events like the change of day for the show to be aired and a "dreadful promotional program the network put together touting the return of *Twin Peaks . . .* hosted by Alan Thicke" (Altman 53) suggest this last statement. Particularly enlightening for understanding this common problem is the phenomenon of what Eileen Meehan calls "commodity audiences" and its components of invisible economics behind the rating process (125-27) and the "people meters" system as a new way of program selectivity (129-32).

[3] These narrative units, again, are not conventional "clues" of a detectivesque game. Rather, they seem to point to the process of image-ordering and the derivation of meaning and significance. The chess game Cooper plays, for example, is not a self-contained activity, but an indicator of how, as in the work of Raúl Ruiz and Borges, "'[m]eaning,' as such, becomes a jealously guarded institution" (Richard Peña 235). This study by Peña offers a generous introduction to the significant relationship that exists between "Borges and the New Latin American Cinema."

[4] Given the enormous difficulty of achieving an effective working definition of "reading," from now on I will work within the range of what Wolfgang Iser has called "the act of reading," paying attention above all to some of the principles of this phenomenon as such: the wandering point and its correlatives (consistency-building, the text as event, involvement as a condition of experience [108-34] and the building of images) (140-51). All these narrative elements will be adequately and timely defined. The main goal of my analysis will also, for obvious reasons, assume the concept of "text" as equally applicable to the written units by Borges and other literary authors, and the filmic in *Twin Peaks* as well. The converging point will be an exploration of the issues of meaning (and its counterpart "significance"), which Frank Smith allocates in grounds not limited to one particular artistic medium: "Meaning is at a level of language where words do not belong. . . . Meaning is part of the deep structure, the semantic, cognitive level. And . . . between the surface level and the deep level of language there is no one-to-one correspondence. Meaning may always resist mere words" (185. Also quoted in Iser 120).

[5] On several occasions, different members of the *Twin Peaks* crew have expressed their awe and pleasure regarding the creative environment fostered by the whole happening of the series. Writers, actors, directors, musicians, they all have celebrated working under such fecund conditions, exceptional in a routine-making process that is so common to television productions (Altman 73-75; Knickelbine 111, 115-16, 122-23).

[6] The indefinite aspect of the act of reading that is being presented here is, then, directly related to the field of what the French psychoanalyst Jacques Lacan calls "the dialectic of intersubjectivity" (*Écrits,* 2 vols. Paris: Éditions du Seuil, 1966, 1:66. Also quoted in Irwin

1215). The central mechanism of this exchange of information is a "reciprocal imaginary objectification of self and Other found in the mirror stage" (Irwin 1212). The relevance of all this information for the process of reading "Death and the Compass," the story line closest to *Twin Peaks* among all of Borges's fictions, is analyzed brilliantly by John Irwin (1211-13). We can see that *Twin Peaks,* like Borges, utilizes a schematic geometrical shape in order to "figure the face-to-face meeting of the two men 'whose minds work in the same way' and 'who may be the same,'" as Irwin puts it (1213). This particular scheme is the reciprocal of the figure delineated by Lacan representing the mirror-doubling of two triangles (see the clear visual depiction of these geometrical shapes in Irwin 1213). The breaking of the mirror during the last scene of the final episode of *Twin Peaks* thus becomes deeply significant, since it contributes to setting the tone of the act of reading it: the formation of intersubjective, not identical, correspondence of images and what they can signify, in order to optimize the narrative structure.

[7] Or, as Herman Rapaport defines utilizing deconstructive principles, "the resistances inherent in the act of reading (itself a conflict of interpretations), which frustrate the ability to make the hermeneutical decisions that clarify the determination of meaning in a literary work. It is this critical conflict that compels one to resist a self-consistent theoretical model of a given text even as one is driven to elucidate a text's meaning or mode of signification" (139).

[8] Which, following what has already been established, is not a matter of discovering or unveiling *the* ultimate interpretation of the "plot" or story line. In this sense, Borges is legendary for his resistance to be catalogued as a systematic writer: "I reject all systematic thought because it always tends to deceive [tiende a trampear]" (Rapaport 140n). However, his texts do search for a story of their own unreadability that "can be situated in a very systematic discourse in order to demonstrate various aporias of interpretation and expose the act of reading as resisting theoretical closure and readerly identification," as Rapaport detects very precisely (141). Lynch has characterized his work-ways by a resistance to a systematization or theorizing in the same fashion as Borges: "The world is changing, and we are changing within it. As soon as you think you've got something figured out, it's different. That is what I try to do. I don't try to do anything new, or weird, or David Lynch" (quoted in Corliss 86). This, no doubt, had ample repercussions when it came to filming *Twin Peaks* and how this happening related to the written word: "[Lynch] will talk to you and give little things to say. I don't know how much in the pilot, if any, was written. We would be waiting to go, and he would come up and say, 'Say, Wrapped in plastic,' and the cameras would be rolling" (Jack Nance, as quoted in Knickelbine 116).

[9] This brings further light to the murder of the series: the disruption caused by the change of day of the week, the inconsistency of ABC when it came to air the second season individual episodes, it all comes together as an abominable attack to the very heart of the series.

[10] Critical point that contradicts yet another reason why the series was supposedly not marketable: its unfittedness for reruns. Premise that, it goes without saying, can be easily invalidated when considered under the light of how "readable" each and every one of the episodes can be.

WORKS CITED

Altman, Mark. Twin Peaks: *Behind the Scenes.* Las Vegas: Pioneer Books, 1990.

Borges, Jorge Luis. *Labyrinths.* New York: New Directions, 1962.

Corliss, Richard. "Czar of Bizarre." *Time* 1 Oct. 1990: 84-88.

Irwin, John T. "Mysteries We Reread, Mysteries of Re-reading: Poe, Borges, and the Analytic Detective Story; Also Lacan, Derrida, and Johnson." *Modern Language Notes* 101 (5) 1986: 1168-1215.

Iser, Wolfgang. *The Art of Reading: A Theory of Aesthetic Response.* Baltimore: The Johns Hopkins UP, 1978.

Knickelbine, Scott. *Welcome to* Twin Peaks: *A Complete Guide to Who's Who and What's What.* Lincoln, IL: Publications International, 1990.

Meehan, Eileen. "Why We Don't Count. The Commodity Audience." *Logics of Television: Essays in Cultural Criticism.* Ed. Patricia Mellencamp. Bloomington: Indiana UP, 1990.

Peña, Richard. "Borges and the New Latin American Cinema." *Borges and His Successors: The Borgesian Impact on Literature and the Arts.* Ed. Edna Aizenberg. Columbia: U of Missouri P, 1990. 229-43.

David Foster Wallace

SOURCE: "E Unibus Pluram: Television and U.S. Fiction," in *The Review of Contemporary Fiction,* Vol. 13, No. 2, Summer, 1993, pp. 151-94.

[*In the following essay, Wallace offers extended discussion of the relationship between television and the development of image fiction in American literature during the 1990s.*]

ACT NATURAL

Fiction writers as a species tend to be oglers. They tend to lurk and to stare. The minute fiction writers stop moving, they start lurking, and stare. They are born watchers.

They are viewers. They are the ones on the subway about whose nonchalant stare there is something creepy, somehow. Almost predatory. This is because human situations are writers' food. Fiction writers watch other humans sort of the way gapers slow down for car wrecks: they covet a vision of themselves as witnesses.

But fiction writers as a species also tend to be terribly self-conscious. Even by U.S. standards. Devoting lots of productive time to studying closely how people come across to them, fiction writers also spend lots of less productive time wondering nervously how they come across to other people. How they appear, how they seem, whether their shirttail might be hanging out their fly, whether there's maybe lipstick on their teeth, whether the people they're ogling can maybe size them up as somehow creepy, lurkers and starers.

The result is that a surprising majority of fiction writers, born watchers, tend to dislike being objects of people's attention. Being watched. The exceptions to this rule—Mailer, McInerney, Janowitz—create the misleading impression that lots of belles-lettres types like people's attention. Most don't. The few who like attention just naturally get more attention. The rest of us get less, and ogle.

Most of the fiction writers I know are Americans under forty. I don't know whether fiction writers under forty watch more television than other American species. Statisticians report that television is watched over six hours a day in the average American household. I don't know any fiction writers who live in average American households. I suspect Louise Erdrich might. Actually I have never seen an average American household. Except on TV.

So right away you can see a couple of things that look potentially great, for U.S. fiction writers, about U.S. television. First, television does a lot of our predatory human research for us. American human beings are a slippery and protean bunch, in real life, as hard to get any kind of univocal handle on as a literary territory that's gone from Darwinianly naturalistic to cybernetically postpostmodern in eighty years. But television comes equipped with just such a syncretic handle. If we want to know what American normality is—what Americans want to regard as normal—we can trust television. For television's whole *raison* is reflecting what people want to see. It's a mirror. Not the Stendhalian mirror reflecting the blue sky and mud puddle. More like the overlit bathroom mirror before which the teenager monitors his biceps and determines his better profile. This kind of window on nervous American self-perception is just invaluable, fictionwise. And writers can have faith in television. There is a lot of money at stake, after all; and television retains the best demographers applied social science has to offer, and these researchers can determine precisely what Americans in 1990 are, want, see: what we as Audience want to see ourselves *as*. Television, from the surface on down, is about *desire*. Fictionally speaking, desire is the sugar in human food.

The second great thing is that television looks to be an absolute godsend for a human subspecies that loves to watch people but hates to be watched itself. For the television screen affords access only one way. A psychic ball-check valve. We can see Them; They can't see Us. We can relax, unobserved, as we ogle. I happen to believe this is why television also appeals so much to lonely people. To voluntary shut-ins. Every lonely human I know watches way more than the average U.S. six hours a day. The lonely, like the fictional, love one-way watching. For lonely people are usually lonely not because of hideous deformity or odor or obnoxiousness—in fact there exist today social and support groups for persons with precisely these features. Lonely people tend rather to be lonely because they decline to bear the emotional costs associated with being around other humans. They are allergic to people. People affect them too strongly. Let's call the average U.S. lonely person Joe Briefcase. Joe Briefcase just loathes the strain of the self-consciousness which so oddly seems to appear only when other real human beings are around, staring, their human sense-antennae abristle. Joe B. fears how he might appear to watchers. He sits out the stressful U.S. game of appearance poker.

But lonely people, home, alone, still crave sights and scenes. Hence television. Joe can stare at Them, on the screen; They remain blind to Joe. It's almost like voyeurism. I happen to know lonely people who regard television as a veritable deus ex machina for voyeurs. And a lot of the criticism, the really rabid criticism less leveled than sprayed at networks, advertisers, and audiences alike, has to do with the charge that television has turned us into a nation of sweaty, slack-jawed voyeurs. This charge turns out to be untrue, but for weird reasons.

What classic voyeurism is is espial: watching people who don't know you're there as they go about the mundane but erotically charged little businesses of private life. It's interesting that so much classic voyeurism involves media of framed glass—windows, telescopes, etc. Maybe the framed glass is why the analogy to television is so tempting. But TV-watching is a different animal from Peeping Tomism. Because the people we're watching through TV's framed-glass screen are not really ignorant of the fact that somebody is watching them. In fact a whole *lot* of somebodies. In fact the people on television know that it is in virtue of this truly huge crowd of ogling somebodies that they are on the screen, engaging in broad non-mundane gestures, at all. Television does not afford true espial because television is performance, spectacle, which by definition requires watchers. We're not voyeurs here at all. We're just viewers. We are the Audience, megametrically many, though most often we watch alone. E unibus pluram.[1]

One reason fiction writers seem creepy in person is that by vocation they really *are* voyeurs. They need that straightforward visual theft of watching somebody without his getting to prepare a speciable watchable self. The only real illusion in espial is suffered by the voyee, who doesn't know he's giving off images and impressions. A problem with so many of us fiction writers under forty using television as a substitute for true espial, however, is that TV "voyeurism" involves a whole gorgeous orgy of illusions for the pseudo-spy, when we watch. Illusion (1) is that we're voyeurs here at all: the voyees behind the screen's glass are only pretending ignorance. They know perfectly well we're out there. And that we're there is also very much on the minds of those behind the second layer of glass, the lenses and monitors via which technicians and arrangers apply no small ingenuity to hurl the visible images at us. What we see is far from stolen; it's proffered—illusion (2). And, illusion (3), what we're seeing through the framed pane isn't people in real situations that do or even could go on without consciousness of Audience. What young writers are scanning for data on some reality to fictionalize is *already* composed of fictional characters in highly ritualized narratives. Plus, (4), we're not really even seeing "characters" at all: it's not Major Frank Burns, pathetic self-important putz from Fort Wayne, Indiana; it's Larry Linville of Ojai, California, actor stoic enough to endure thousands of letters (still coming in, even in syndication) from pseudo-voyeurs mistakenly berating him for being a putz. And, if (5) isn't too out-there for you, it's ultimately of course not even actors we're espying, not even people: it's EM-propelled analog waves and ionized streams and rear-screen chemical reactions throwing off phosphenes in grids of dots not much more lifelike than Seurat's own impressionistic "statements" on perceptual illusion. Good lord and (6) the dots are coming out of our *furniture,* all we're spying on is our own *furniture;* and our very own chairs and lamps and bookspines sit visible but unseen at our gaze's frame as we contemplate "Korea" or are "taken live to Amman, Jordan," or regard the plusher chairs and classier spines of the Huxtable "home" as illusory cues that this is some domestic interior whose membrane we have, slyly, unnoticed, violated. (7) and (8) and illusions ad inf.

Not that realities about actors and phosphenes and furniture are unknown to us. We simply choose to ignore them. For six hours a day. They are part of the belief we suspend. But we're asked to hoist such a heavy load aloft. Illusions of voyeurism and privileged access require real complicity from viewers. How can we be made so willingly to acquiesce for hours daily to the illusion that the people on the TV don't know they're being looked at, to the fantasy that we're transcending privacy and feeding on unself-conscious human activity? There might be lots of reasons why these unrealities are so swallowable, but a big one is that the performers behind the two layers of glass are—varying degrees of Thespian talent aside—absolute *geniuses* at seeming unwatched. Now, seeming unwatched in front of a TV camera is a genuine art. Take a look at how civilians act when a TV camera is pointed at them: they simply spaz out, or else go all rigor mortis. Even PR people and politicians are, camera-wise, civilians. And we love to laugh at how stiff and false non-professionals appear, on television. How *unnatural.* But if you've ever once been the object of that terrible blank round glass stare, you know all too well how self-conscious it makes you. A harried guy with earphones and a clipboard tells you to "act natural" as your face begins to leap around on your skull, struggling for a seemingly unwatched expression that feels impossible because "seeming unwatched" is, like the "act natural" which fathered it, oxymoronic. Try driving a golf ball as someone asks you whether you in- or exhale on your backswing, or getting promised lavish rewards if you can avoid thinking of a rhinoceros for ten seconds, and you'll get some idea of the truly heroic contortions of body and mind that must be required for Don Johnson to act unwatched as he's watched by a lens that's an overwhelming emblem of what Emerson, years before TV, called "the gaze of millions."

Only a certain very rare species of person, for Emerson, is "fit to stand the gaze of millions." It is not your normal, hard-working, quietly desperate species of American. The man who can stand the megagaze is a walking imago, a certain type of transcendent freak who, for Emerson, "carries the holiday in his eye."[2] The Emersonian holiday television actors' eyes carry is the potent illusion of a vacation from self-consciousness. Not worrying about how you come across. A total unallergy to gazes. It is contemporarily heroic. It is frightening and strong. It is also, of course, an *act,* a counterfeit impression—for you have to be just abnormally self-conscious and self-controlling to appear unwatched before lenses. The self-conscious appearance of unself-consciousness is the grand illusion behind TV's mirror-hall of illusions; and for us, the Audience, it is both medicine and poison.

For we gaze at these rare, highly trained, seemingly unwatched people for six hours daily. And we love these people. In terms of attributing to them true supernatural assets and desiring to emulate them, we sort of worship them. In a real Joe Briefcase-type world that shifts ever more starkly from some community of relationships to networks of strangers connected by self-interest and contest and image, the people we espy on TV offer us familiarity, community. Intimate friendship. But we split what we see. The *characters* are our "close friends"; but the *performers* are beyond strangers, they're images, demigods, and they move in a different sphere, hang out with and marry only each other, seem even as actors accessible to Audience only via the mediation of tabloids, talk show, EM signal. And yet both actors and characters, so terribly removed and filtered, seem so *natural,* when we watch.

Given how much we watch and what watching means, it's inevitable—but toxic—for those of us fictionists or Joe Briefcases who wish to be voyeurs to get the idea that these persons behind the glass, persons who are often the most colorful, attractive, animated, *alive* people in our daily experience, are also people who are oblivious to the fact that they are watched. It's toxic for allergic people because it sets up an alienating cycle, and also for writers because it replaces fiction research with a weird kind of fiction consumption. We self-conscious Americans' oversensitivity to real humans fixes us before the television and its ball-check valve in an attitude of rapt, relaxed reception. We watch various actors play various characters, etc. For 360 minutes per diem, we receive unconscious reinforcement of the deep thesis that the most significant feature of truly alive persons is watchableness, and that genuine human worth is not just identical with but rooted in the phenomenon of watching. And that the single biggest part of real watchableness is seeming to be unaware that there's any watching going on. Acting natural. The persons we young fiction writers and assorted shut-ins most study, feel for, feel *through* are, by virtue of a genius for feigned unself-consciousness, fit to stand gazes. And we, trying desperately to be nonchalant, perspire creepily, on the subway.

THE FINGER

Weighty existential predicaments aside, there's no denying that people in the U.S.A. watch so much television because it's fun. I know I watch for fun, most of the time, and that at least 51 percent of the time I do have fun when I watch. This doesn't mean I do not take television seriously. One claim of this essay is that the most dangerous thing about television for U.S. fiction writers is that we yield to the temptation not to take television seriously as both a disseminator and a definer of the cultural atmosphere we breathe and process, that many of us are so blinded by constant exposure that we regard TV the way Reagan's lame FCC chairman Mark Fowler professed to in 1981, as "just another appliance, a toaster with pictures."[3]

Television nevertheless is just plain pleasurable, though it may seem odd that so much of the pleasure my generation gets from television lies in making fun of it. But you have to remember that younger Americans grew up as much with people's disdain for TV as we did with TV itself. I knew it was a "vast wasteland" way before I knew who Newton Minow or Mark Fowler were. And it's just *fun* to laugh cynically at television—at the way the laughter from sitcoms' "live studio audience" is always suspiciously constant in pitch and duration, or at the way travel is depicted on *The Flintstones* by having the exact same cut-rate cartoon tree, rock, and house go by four times. It's fun, when a withered June Allyson comes on-screen for Depend Adult Undergarments and says "If you have a bladder-control problem, you're not alone," to hoot and shout back "Well, chances are you're alone *quite a bit,* June!"

Most scholars and critics who write about U.S. popular culture, though, seem both to take TV seriously and to suffer real pain over what they see. There's this well-known critical litany about television's vapidity, shallowness, and irrealism. The litany is often far cruder and triter than what the critics complain about, which I think is why most younger viewers find pro criticism of television far less interesting than pro television itself. I found solid examples of what I'm talking about on the first day I even looked. The *New York Times* Arts & Leisure sec-

tion for Sunday, 8/05/90, simply bulged with bitter critical derision for TV, and some of the most unhappy articles weren't about just low-quality programming so much as about how TV's become this despicable instrument of cultural decay. In a summary review of all 1990's "crash and burn" summer box-office hits in which "realism . . . seems to have gone almost entirely out of fashion," Janet Maslin locates her true anti-reality culprit: "We may be hearing about 'real life' on television shows made up of 15-second sound bites (in which 'real people' not only speak in brief, neat truisms but actually seem to think that way, perhaps as a result of having watched too much reality-molding television themselves)."[4] And one Stephen Holden, in what starts out as a mean pop music article, knows perfectly well what's behind what he hates: "Pop music is no longer a world unto itself but an adjunct of television, whose stream of commercial images projects a culture in which everything is for sale and the only things that count are fame, power, and the body beautiful."[5] This stuff just goes on and on, in the *Times.* The only Arts & Leisure piece I could find with anything upbeat to say about TV that morning was a breathless article on how lots of Ivy League graduates are now flying straight from school to New York and Los Angeles to become television writers and are clearing well over $200,000 to start and enjoying rapid advancement to harried clip-boarded production status. In this regard, 8/05's *Times* is a good example of a strange mix that's been around for a few years now: weary contempt for television as a creative product and cultural force, combined with beady-eyed fascination about the actual behind-the-glass mechanics of making that product and projecting that force.

Surely we all have friends we just hate to hear talk about TV because they so clearly loathe it—they sneer relentlessly at the hackneyed plots, the unlikely dialogue, the Cheez-Whiz resolutions, the bland condescension of the news anchors, the shrill wheedling of commercials—and yet are just as clearly obsessed with it, somehow *need* to hate their six hours a day, day in and out. Junior advertising executives, aspiring filmmakers, and graduate-school poets are in my experience especially prone to this condition where they simultaneously hate, fear, and need television, and try to disinfect themselves of whatever so much viewing might do to them by watching TV with weary irony instead of the rapt credulity most of us grew up with. (Note that most fiction writers still tend to go for the rapt credulity.)

But, since the wearily disgusted *Times* has its own demographic thumb on the pulse of news-readerly taste, it's safe to conclude that most educated, *Times*-buying Americans are wearily disgusted by television, have this weird hate-need-fear-6-hrs.-daily gestalt about it. Published TV scholarship sure reflects this mood. And the numbingly dull quality to most "literary" television analyses is due less to the turgid abstraction scholars employ to make television seem an OK object of "aesthetic" inquiry—cf. an '86 treatise: "The form of my Tuesday evening's prime-time pleasure is structured by a dialectic of elision and rift among various windows through which . . . 'flow' is more of a circumstance than a product. The real output is the quantum, the smallest maneuverable broadcast bit"[6]—than to the tired, jaded cynicism of television experts who mock and revile the very phenomenon they've chosen as scholarly vocation. It's like people who despise—I mean big-time, long-term despise—their spouses or jobs, but won't split up or quit. Critical complaint degenerates quickly into plain whining. The fecund question about U.S. television is no longer whether there are some truly nasty problems here but rather what on earth's to be done about them. On this question pop critics are mute.

In fact it's in the U.S. arts, particularly in certain strands of contemporary American fiction, that the really interesting questions about end-of-the-century TV—What is it about televisual culture that we so hate? Why are we so immersed in it if we hate it so? What implications are there in our sustained voluntary immersion in stuff we hate?—are being addressed. But they are also, weirdly, being asked and answered by television itself. This is another reason why most TV criticism seems so empty. Television's managed to become its own most profitable critic.

A.M., 8/05/90, as I was scanning and sneering at the sneering tone of the prenominate *Times* articles, a syndicated episode of *St. Elsewhere* was on the TV, cleaning up in a Sunday-morning Boston market otherwise occupied by televangelists, infomercials, and the steroid- and polyurethane-ridden *American Gladiators,* itself not charmless but definitely a low-dose show. Syndication is another new area of public fascination, not only because huge cable stations like Chicago's WGN and Atlanta's WTBS have upped the stakes from local to national, but because syndication is changing the whole creative philosophy of network television. Since it is in syndication deals (where the distributor gets both an up-front fee for a program and a percentage of the ad-slots for his own commercials) that the creators of successful television series realize truly gross profits, many new programs are designed and pitched with both immediate prime-time and down-the-road syndication audiences in mind, and are now informed less by dreams of the ten-year-beloved-TV-institution-type run—*Gunsmoke, M*A*S*H*—than of a modest three-year run that yields the seventy-eight in-can episodes required for an attractive syndication package. I, like millions of other Americans, know this stuff only because I saw a special three-part report about syndication on *Entertainment Tonight,* itself the first nationally syndicated "news" program and the first infomercial so popular that TV stations were willing to pay for it.

Sunday syndication is also intriguing because it makes for juxtapositions as eerily apposite as anything French surrealists could contrive. Lovable warlocks on *Bewitched* and commercially Satanic heavy-metal videos on *America's Top 40* run opposite airbrushed preachers decrying demonism in U.S. culture. Or, better, 8/05's *St. Elsewhere* episode 94, originally broadcast in 1988, aired on Boston's Channel 38 immediately following two back-to-back episodes of *The Mary Tyler Moore Show,* that icon of seventies pathos. The plots of the two *Mary Tyler Moore Shows* are unimportant here. But the *St. Elsewhere* episode that followed them partly concerned a cameo-role mental patient afflicted with the delusional belief that he was Mary Richards from *The Mary Tyler Moore Show.* He further believed that a fellow cameo-role mental patient was Rhoda, that Dr. Westphal was Mr. Grant, and that Dr. Auschlander was Murray. This psychiatric subplot was a one-shot; it was resolved by episode's end. The pseudo-Mary (a sad lumpy-looking guy who used to play one of Dr. Hartley's neurotic clients on the old *Bob Newhart Show*) rescues the other cameo-role mental patient, whom he believes to be Rhoda and who has been furious in his denials that he is female, much less fictional (and who is himself played by the guy who used to play Mr. Carlin, Dr. Hartley's most intractable client) from assault by a bit-part hebephrene. In gratitude, Rhoda/Mr. Carlin/mental patient declares that he'll consent to be Rhoda if that's what Mary/neurotic client/mental patient wants. At this too-real generosity, the pseudo-Mary's psychotic break breaks. The sad guy admits to Dr. Auschlander that he's not Mary Richards. He's actually just a plain old amnesiac, minus a self, existentially adrift. He has no idea who he is. He's lonely. He watches a lot of television. He figured it was "better to believe I was a TV character than not to believe I was anybody." Dr. Auschlander takes the penitent patient for a walk in the wintery Boston air and promises that he, the identityless guy, can someday find out who he really is, provided he can dispense with "the distraction of television." At this cheery prognosis, the patient removes his own fuzzy winter beret and throws it into the air. The episode ends with a freeze of the aloft hat, leaving at least one viewer credulously rapt.

This would have been just another clever low-concept eighties TV story, where the final cap-tossing and closing credits coyly undercut Dr. Auschlander's put-down of television, were it not for the countless layers of ironic, involuted TV imagery and data that whirl around this high-concept installment. Because another of this episode's cameo stars, drifting through a different subplot, is one Betty White, Sue Ann Nivens of the old *Mary Tyler Moore Show,* here playing a tortured NASA surgeon (don't ask). It is with almost tragic inevitability, then, that Ms. White, at thirty-two minutes into the episode, meets up with the TV-deluded pseudo-Mary in their respective tortured wanderings through the hospital's corridors, and that she considers the mental patient's inevitable joyful cries of "Sue Ann!" with a too-straight face and says he must have her confused with someone else. Of the convolved levels of fantasy and reality and identity here—e.g., patient simultaneously does, does not, and does have Betty White "confused" with Sue Ann Nivens—we needn't speak in detail: doubtless a Yale Contemporary Culture dissertation is underway on R. D. Laing and just this episode. But the most interesting levels of meaning here lie, and point, behind the lens. For NBC's *St. Elsewhere,* like *The Mary Tyler*

Moore Show and *The Bob Newhart Show* before it, was created, produced, and guided into syndication by MTM Studios, owned by Mary Tyler Moore and overseen by her husband, later NBC Chair Grant Tinker; and *St. Elsewhere*'s scripts and subplots are story-edited by Mark Tinker, Mary's step-, Grant's heir. The deluded mental patient, an exiled, drifting veteran of one MTM program, reaches piteously out to the exiled, drifting (literally—*NASA,* for God's sake) veteran of another MTM production, and her ironic rebuff is scripted by MTM personnel, who accomplish the parodic undercut of MTM's Dr. Auschlander with the copyrighted MTM hat-gesture of one MTM veteran who's "deluded" he's another. Dr. A.'s Fowleresque dismissal of TV as just a "distraction" is less absurd than incoherent. There is nothing *but* television on this episode; every joke and dramatic surge depends on involution, metatelevision. It is in-joke within in-joke.

So then why do I get it? Because I, the viewer, outside the glass with the rest of the Audience, am nevertheless in on the in-joke. I've seen Mary Tyler Moore's "real" toss of that fuzzy beret so often it's moved past cliché into nostalgia. I know the mental patient from *Bob Newhart,* Betty White from everywhere, *and* I know all sorts of intriguing irrelevant stuff about MTM Studios and syndication from *Entertainment Tonight.* I, the pseudo-voyeur, am indeed "behind the scenes," for in-joke purposes. But it is not I the spy who have crept inside television's boundaries. It is vice versa. Television, even the mundane little businesses of its production, have become Our interior. And we seem a jaded, jeering, but willing and *knowledgeable* Audience. This *St. Elsewhere* episode was nominated for an Emmy. For best original teleplay.

The best TV of the last five years has been about ironic self-reference like no previous species of postmodern art could have dreamed of. The colors of MTV videos, blue-black and lambently flickered, are the colors of television. *Moonlighting*'s Bruce and *Bueller*'s Ferris throw asides to the viewer every bit as bald as the old melodrama villain's monologued gloat. Segments of the new late-night glitz-news *After Hours* end with a tease that features harried headphoned guys in the production booth ordering the tease. MTV's television-trivia game show, the dry-titled *Remote Control,* got so popular it busted its own MTV-membrane and is in 1990 now syndicated band-wide. The hippest commercials, with stark computerized settings and blank beauties in mirrored shades and plastic slacks genuflecting before various forms of velocity, force, and adrenaline, seem like little more than TV's vision of how TV offers rescue to those lonely Joe Briefcases passively trapped into watching too much TV.

What explains the pointlessness of most published TV criticism is that television has become immune to charges that it lacks any meaningful connection to the world outside it. It's not that charges of nonconnection have become untrue. It's that any such connection has become otiose. Television used to point beyond itself. Those of us born in like the sixties were trained to look where it pointed, usually at versions of "real life" made prettier, sweeter, better by succumbing to a product or temptation. Today's Audience is way better trained, and TV has discarded what's not needed. A dog, if you point at something, will look only at your finger.

METAWATCHING

It's not like self-reference is new to mass entertainment. How many old radio shows—Jack Benny, Martin and Lewis, Abbott and Costello—were mostly about themselves as shows? "So, Jerry, and you said I couldn't get a big star like Miss Lucille Ball to be a guest on our show, you little twerp." Etc. But once television introduces the element of watching, and once it informs an economy and culture like radio never did, the referential stakes go way up. Six hours a day is more time than most people (consciously) do any one thing. How people who absorb such doses understand themselves changes, becomes spectatorial, self-conscious. Because the practice of watching is expansive. Exponential. We spend enough time watching, pretty soon we start watching ourselves watching. We start to "feel" ourselves feeling, yearn to experience "experiences." And that American subspecies into writing starts writing more and more about. . . .

The emergence of something called metafiction in the American sixties was and is hailed by academic critics as a radical aesthetic, a whole new literary form unshackled from the canonical cinctures of narrative and mimesis and free to plunge into reflexivity and self-conscious meditations on aboutness. Radical it may have been, but thinking that postmodern metafiction evolved unconscious of prior changes in readerly taste is about as innocent as thinking that all those students we saw on television protesting the war in southeast Asia were protesting only because they hated the war. They may have hated the war, but they also wanted to be seen protesting on television. TV was where they'd seen this war, after all. Why wouldn't they go about hating it on the very medium that made their hate possible? Metafictionists may have had aesthetic theories out the bazoo, but they were also sentient citizens of a community that was exchanging an old idea of itself as a nation of do-ers and be-ers for a new vision of the U.S.A. as an atomized mass of self-conscious watchers and appearers. Metafiction, for its time, was nothing more than a poignant hybrid of its theoretical foe, realism: if realism called it like it saw it, metafiction simply called it as it saw itself seeing itself see it. This high-cultural postmodern genre, in other words, was deeply informed by the emergence of television. And American fiction remains informed by TV . . . especially those strains of fiction with roots in postmodernism, which even at its rebellious zenith was less a "response to" televisual culture than a kind of abiding-in-TV. Even back then, the borders were starting to come down.

It's strange that it took television itself so long to wake up to watching's potent reflexivity. Television shows about television shows were rare for a long time. *The Dick Van Dyke Show* was prescient, and Mary Tyler Moore carried its insight into her own decade-long study in local-market angst. Now, of course, there's been everything from *Murphy Brown* to *Max Headroom* to *Entertainment Tonight*. And with Letterman, Arsenio, and Leno's battery of hip, sardonic, this-is-just-TV shticks, the circle back to the days of "So glad to get Miss Ball on our show" has closed and come spiral, television's power to jettison connection and castrate protest fueled by the same ironic postmodern self-consciousness it first helped fashion.

It's going to take a while, but I'm going to prove to you that the nexus where television and fiction converse and consort is self-conscious irony. Irony is, of course, a turf fictionists have long worked with zeal. And irony is important for understanding TV because "T.V.," now that it's gotten powerful enough to move from acronym to way of life, revolves off just the sorts of absurd contradictions irony's all about exposing. It is ironic that television is a syncresis that celebrates diversity. That an extremely unattractive self-consciousness is necessary to create TV performers' illusion of unconscious appeal. That products presented as helping you express individuality can afford to be advertised on television only because they sell to huge hordes. And so on.

Television regards irony the way the educated lonely regard television. Television both fears irony's capacity to expose, and needs it. It needs irony because television was practically *made* for irony. For TV is a bisensuous medium. Its displacement of radio wasn't picture displacing sound; it was picture added. Since the tension between what's said and what's seen is irony's whole sales territory, classic televisual irony works not via the juxtaposition of conflicting pictures or conflicting sounds, but with sights that undercut what's said. A scholarly article on network news describes a famous interview with a corporate guy from United Fruit on a CBS special about Guatemala: "I sure don't know of anybody being so-called 'oppressed,'" the guy in a seventies leisure suit with a tie that looks like an omelette tells Ed Rabel. "I think this is just something that some reporters have thought up."[7] The whole interview is intercut with commentless pictures of big-bellied kids in Guatemalan slums and union organizers lying there with cut throats.

Television's classic irony-function came into its own in the summer of 1974, as remorseless lenses opened to view the fertile "credibility gap" between the image of official disclaimer and the reality of high-level shenanigans. A nation was changed, as Audience. If even the president lies to you, whom are you supposed to trust to deliver the real? Television, that summer, presented itself as the earnest, worried eye on the reality behind all images. The irony that television is itself a river of image, however, was apparent even to a twelve-year-old, sitting there, rapt. There seemed to be no way out. Images and ironies all over the place. It's not a coincidence that *Saturday Night Live,* that Athens of irreverent cynicism,

specializing in parodies of (1) politics and (2) television, premiered the next fall. On television.

I'm worried when I say things like "television fears" and "television presents itself" because, even though it's an abstraction necessary to discourse, talking about television as if it were an entity can easily slip into the worst sort of anti-TV paranoia, treating of TV as some autonomous diabolical corrupter of personal agency and community gumption. I am anxious to avoid anti-TV paranoia here. Though I'm convinced that television lies, with a potency somewhere between symptom and synecdoche, behind a genuine crisis for U.S. culture and lit today, I don't share reactionary adults' vision of TV as some malignancy visited on an innocent populace, sapping IQs and compromising SAT scores while we all sit there on ever fatter bottoms with little mesmerized spirals revolving in our eyes. Because conservative critics like Samuel Huntington and Barbara Tuchman who try to claim that TV's lowering of our aesthetic standards is responsible for a "contemporary culture taken over by commercialism directed to the mass market and necessarily to mass taste"[8] can be refuted by observing that their *propter hoc* isn't even *post hoc:* by 1830 de Tocqueville had already diagnosed American culture as peculiarly devoted to easy sensation and mass-marketed entertainment, "spectacles vehement and untutored and rude" that aimed "to stir the passions more than to gratify the taste."[9]

It's undeniable that television is an example of "low" art, the sort of art that tries too hard to please. Because of the economics of nationally broadcast, advertiser-subsidized entertainment, television's one goal—never denied by anybody in or around TV since RCA first authorized field tests in 1936—is to ensure as much watching as possible. TV is the epitome of low art in its desire to appeal to and enjoy the attention of unprecedented numbers of people. But TV is not low because it is vulgar or prurient or stupid. It is often all these things, but this is a logical function of its need to please Audience. And I'm not saying that television is vulgar and dumb because the people who compose Audience are vulgar and dumb. Television is the way it is simply because people tend to be really similar in their vulgar and prurient and stupid interests and wildly different in their refined and moral and intelligent interests. It's all about syncretic diversity: neither medium nor viewers are responsible for quality. Still, for the fact that American humans consume vulgar, prurient, stupid stuff at the sobering clip of six hours a day, for this both TV and we need to answer. We are responsible basically because nobody is holding any weapons on us forcing us to spend amounts of time second only to sleep doing something that is, when you come right down to it, not good for us. Sorry to sound judgmental, but there it is: six hours a day is not good.

Television's biggest minute-by-minute appeal is that it engages without demanding. One can rest while undergoing stimulation. Receive without giving. In this respect, television resembles other things mothers call "special treats"—e.g., candy, or liquor—treats that are basically fine and fun in small amounts but bad for us in large amounts and *really* bad for us if consumed as any kind of nutritive staple. One can only guess what volume of gin or poundage of Toblerone six hours of special treat a day would convert to.

On the surface of the problem, television is responsible for our rate of its consumption only in that it's become so terribly successful at its acknowledged job of ensuring prodigious amounts of watching. Its social accountability seems sort of like that of designers of military weapons: unculpable right up until they get a little too good at their job.

But the analogy between television and liquor is best, I think. Because I'm afraid Joe Briefcase is a teleholic. Watching TV can become malignantly addictive. TV may become malignantly addictive only once a certain threshold of quantity is habitually passed, but then the same is true of whiskey. And by "malignant" and "addictive" I again do not mean evil or coercive. An activity is addictive if one's relationship to it lies on that downward-sloping continuum between liking it a little too much and downright needing it. Many addictions, from exercise to letter-writing, are pretty benign. But something is malignantly addictive if (1) it causes real problems for the addict, and (2) it offers itself as relief from the very problems it causes. A malignant addiction is also distinguished for spreading the problems of the addiction out and in in interference patterns, creating difficulties for relationships, communities, and the addict's very sense of self and soul. The hyperbole might strain the analogy for you, but concrete illustrations of malignant TV-watching cycles aren't hard to come by. If it's true that many Americans are lonely, and if it's true that many lonely people are prodigious TV-watchers, and if it's true that lonely people find in television's 2D images relief from the pain of their reluctance to be around real humans, then it's also obvious that the more time spent watching TV, the less time spent in the real human world, and the less time spent in the real human world, the harder it becomes not to feel alienated from real humans, solipsistic, lonely. It's also true that to the extent one begins to view pseudo-relationships with Bud Bundy or Jane Pauley as acceptable alternatives to relationships with real humans, one has commensurately less conscious incentive even to try to connect with real 3D persons, connections that are pretty important to mental health. For Joe Briefcase, as for many addicts, the "special treat" of TV begins to substitute for something nourishing and needed, and the original hunger subsides to a strange objectless unease.

TV-watching as a malignant cycle doesn't even require special preconditions like writerly self-consciousness or loneliness. Let's for a second imagine Joe Briefcase as now just average, relatively unlonely, adjusted, married, blessed with 2.5 apple-cheeked issue, normal, home from hard work at 5:30, starting his average six-hour stint. Since Joe B. is average, he'll shrug at pollsters' questions and say he most often watches television to "unwind" from those elements of his day and life he finds stressful. It's tempting to suppose that TV enables this "unwinding" simply because it offers an Auschlanderian distraction, something to divert the mind from quotidian troubles. But would mere distraction ensure continual massive watching? Television offers more than distraction. In lots of ways, television purveys and enables *dreams,* and most of these dreams involve some sort of transcendence of average daily life. The modes of presentation that work best for TV—stuff like "action," with shoot-outs and car wrecks, or the rapid-fire "collage" of commercials, news, and music videos, or the "hysteria" of prime-time soap and sitcom with broad gestures, high voices, too much laughter—are unsubtle in their whispers that, somewhere, life is quicker, denser, more interesting, more . . . well, *lively* than contemporary life as Joe Briefcase knows and moves through it. This might seem benign until we consider that what average Joe Briefcase does more than almost anything else in contemporary life is watch television, an activity which anyone with an average brain can see does not make for a very dense and lively life. Since television must seek to compel attention by offering a dreamy promise of escape from daily life, and since stats confirm that so grossly much of ordinary U.S. life is watching TV, TV's whispered promises must somehow undercut television-watching in theory ("Joe, Joe, there's a world where life is lively, where nobody spends six hours a day unwinding before a piece of furniture") while reinforcing television-watching in practice ("Joe, Joe, your best and only access to this world is TV").

Well, Joe Briefcase has an average, workable brain, and deep inside he knows, as we do, that there's some kind of psychic three-card monte going on in this system of conflicting whispers. But if it's so bald a delusion, why do we keep watching such doses? Part of the answer—a part which requires discretion lest it slip into anti-TV paranoia—is that the phenomenon of television somehow trains or conditions our viewership. Television has become able not only to ensure that we watch, but to inform our deepest responses to what's watched. Take jaded TV critics, or our acquaintances who sneer at the numbing sameness of all the television they sit still for. I always want to grab these unhappy guys by the lapels and shake them until their teeth rattle and point to the absence of guns to their heads and ask why the heck *they keep watching,* then. But the truth is that there's some complex high-dose psychic transaction between TV and Audience whereby Audience gets trained to respond to and then like and then *expect* trite, hackneyed, numbing television shows, and to expect them to such an extent that when networks do occasionally abandon time-tested formulas we usually punish them for it by not watching novel forms in sufficient numbers to let them get off the ground. Hence the networks' bland response to its critics that in the majority of cases—and until the rise of hip metatelevision you could count the exceptions on one hand—"different" or "high-concept" programming simply didn't get ratings. Quality television cannot stand the gaze of millions, somehow.

Now, it is true that certain PR techniques—e.g., shock, grotesquerie, or irreverence—can ease novel sorts of shows' rise to demographic viability. Examples here might be the shocking *A Current Affair,* the grotesque *Real People,* the irreverent *Married, with Children.* But these programs, like most of those touted by the industry as "fresh" or "outrageous," turn out to be just tiny transparent variations on old formulas.

But it's still not fair to blame television's shortage of originality on any lack of creativity among network talent. The truth is that we seldom get a chance to know whether anybody behind any TV show is creative, or more accurately that they seldom get a chance to show us. Despite the unquestioned assumption on the part of pop-culture critics that television's poor Audience, deep down, craves novelty, all available evidence suggests rather that the Audience really craves sameness but thinks, deep down, that it *ought* to crave novelty. Hence the mixture of devotion and sneer on viewerly faces. Hence also the weired viewer-complicity behind TV's sham "breakthrough programs": Joe Briefcase needs that PR-patina of "freshness" and "outrageousness" to quiet his conscience while he goes about getting from television what we've all been trained to want from it: some strangely American, profoundly shallow *reassurance.*

Particularly in the last decade, this tension in the Audience between what we do want and what we think we ought to want has been television's breath and bread. TV's self-mocking invitation to itself as indulgence, transgression, a glorious "giving in" (again not foreign to addictive cycles) is one of two ingenious ways it's consolidated its six-hour hold on my generation's cajones. The other is postmodern irony. The commercials for *Alf*'s Boston debut in syndicated package feature the fat, cynical, gloriously decadent puppet (so much like Snoopy, like Garfield, like Bart) advising me to "Eat a whole lot of food and stare at the TV!" His pitch is an ironic permission slip to do what I do best whenever I feel confused and guilty: assume, inside, a sort of fetal position; a pose of passive reception to escape, comfort, reassurance. The cycle is self-nourishing.

GUILTY FICTIONS

Not, again, that this cycle's root conflict is new. You can trace the opposition between what persons do and ought to desire at least as far back as Plato's chariot or the Prodigal's return. But the way entertainments appeal to and work within this conflict has been transformed in a televisual culture. This culture-of-watching's relation to the cycle of indulgence, guilt, and reassurance has important consequences for U.S. art, and though the parallels are easiest to see w/r/t Warhol's pop or Elvis's rock, the most interesting intercourse is between television and American lit.

One of the most recognizable things about this century's postmodern fiction was the movement's strategic deployment of pop-cultural references—brand names, celebri-ties, television programs—in even its loftiest high-art projects. Think of just about any example of avant-garde U.S. fiction in the last twenty-five years, from Slothrop's passion for Slippery Elm throat lozenges and his weird encounter with Mickey Rooney in *Gravity's Rainbow* to "You"'s fetish for the *New York Post*'s COMA BABY feature in *Bright Lights,* to Don DeLillo's pop-hip characters saying stuff to each other like "Elvis fulfilled the terms of the contract. Excess, deterioration, self-destructiveness, grotesque behavior, a physical bloating and a series of insults to the brain, self-delivered."[10]

The apotheosis of the pop in postwar art marked a whole new marriage between high and low culture. For the artistic viability of postmodernism is a direct consequence, again, not of any new facts about art, but of facts about the new importance of mass commercial culture. Americans seemed no longer united so much by common feelings as by common images: what binds us became what we stood witness to. No one did or does see this as a good change. In fact, pop-cultural references have become such potent metaphors in U.S. fiction not only because of how united Americans are in our exposure to mass images but also because of our guilty indulgent psychology with respect to that exposure. Put simply, the pop reference works so well in contemporary fiction because (1) we all recognize such a reference, and (2) we're all a little uneasy about how we all recognize such a reference.

The status of low-cultural images in postmodern and contemporary fiction is very different from their place in postmodernism's artistic ancestors, the "dirty realism" of a Joyce or the Ur-Dadaism of a Duchamp toilet sculpture. Duchamp's display of that vulgarest of appliances served an exclusively theoretical end: it was making statements like "The Museum is the Mausoleum is the Men's Room," etc. It was an example of what Octavio Paz calls "meta-irony,"[11] an attempt to reveal that categories we divide into superior/arty and inferior/vulgar are in fact so interdependent as to be coextensive. The use of "low" references in today's literary fiction, on the other hand, serves a less abstract agenda. It is meant (1) to help create a mood of irony and irreverence, (2) to make us uneasy and so "comment" on the vapidity of U.S. culture, and (3) most important, these days, to be just plain realistic.

Pynchon and DeLillo were ahead of their time. Today, the belief that pop images are basically just mimetic devices is one of the attitudes that separates most U.S. fiction writers under forty from the writerly generation that precedes us, reviews us, and designs our grad-school curricula. This generation-gap in conceptions of realism is, again, TV-dependent. The U.S. generation born after 1950 is the first for whom television was something to be lived with instead of just looked at. Our elders regard the set rather as the Flapper did the automobile: a curiosity turned treat turned seduction. For younger writers, TV's as much a part of reality as Toyotas and gridlock. We literally cannot imagine life without it. We're not different from our fathers insofar as television presents and defines the contemporary world. But we are different in that we have no memory of a world without such electric definition. This is why the derision so many older fictionists heap on a "Brat Pack" generation they see as insufficiently critical of mass culture is simultaneously apt and misguided. It's true that there's something sad about the fact that young lion David Leavitt's sole descriptions of certain story characters is that their T-shirts have certain brand names on them. But the fact is that, for most of the educated young readership for whom Leavitt writes, members of a generation raised and nourished on messages equating what one consumes with who one is, Leavitt's descriptions *do the job*. In our post-'50, inseparable-from-TV association pool, brand loyalty is synecdochic of identity, character.

For those U.S. writers whose ganglia were formed pre-TV, who are big on neither Duchamp nor Paz and lack the oracular foresight of a Pynchon, the mimetic deployment of pop-culture icons seems at best an annoying tic and at worst a dangerous vapidity that compromises fiction's seriousness by dating it out of the Platonic Always where it ought to reside. In one of the graduate workshops I suffered through, an earnest gray eminence kept trying to convince our class that a literary story or novel always eschews "any feature which serves to date it," because "serious fiction must be timeless." When we finally protested that, in his own well-known work, characters moved about in electrically lit rooms, drove cars, spoke not Anglo-Saxon but postwar English, inhabited a North America already separated from Africa by continental drift, he impatiently amended his proscription to those explicit references that would date a story in the frivolous "Now." When pressed for just what stuff evoked this f.N., he said of course he meant the "trendy mass-popular-media" reference. And here, at just this point, transgenerational discourse broke down. We looked at him blankly. We scratched our little heads. We didn't get it. This guy and his students just didn't imagine the "serious" world the same way. His automobiled timeless and our FCC'd own were different.

If you read the big literary supplements, you've doubtless seen the intergenerational squabble the prenominate scene explains. The plain fact is that certain key things having to do with fiction production are different for young U.S. writers now. And television is at the vortex of much of the flux. Because younger writers are not only Artists probing for the nobler interstices in what Stanley Cavell calls the reader's "willingness to be pleased"; we are also, now, self-defined parts of the great U.S. Audience, and have our own aesthetic pleasure-centers; and television has formed and trained us. It won't do, then, for the literary establishment simply to complain that, for instance, young-written characters don't have very interesting dialogues with each other, that young writers' ears seem tinny. Tinny they may be, but the truth is that in younger Americans' experience, people in the same room don't do all that much direct conversing with each other. What most of the people I know do is they all sit and face

the same direction and stare at the same thing and then structure commercial-length conversations around the sorts of questions myopic car-crash witnesses might ask each other—"Did you just see what I just saw?" And, realism-wise, the paucity of profound conversation in Brat-esque fiction seems to be mimetic of more than just our own generation. Six hours a day, in average households young and old, just how much interfacing can really be going on? So now whose literary aesthetic seems "dated"?

In terms of lit history, it's important to recognize the distinction between pop and televisual references, on the one hand, and the mere use of TV-like techniques, on the other. The latter have been around in fiction forever. The Voltaire of *Candide,* for instance, uses a bisensuous irony that would do Ed Rabel proud, having Candide and Pangloss run around smiling and saying "All for the best, the best of all worlds" amid war-dead, pogroms, rampant nastiness. Even the stream-of-consciousness guys who fathered modernism were, on a very high level, constructing the same sorts of illusions about privacy-puncturing and espial on the forbidden that television has found so fecund. And let's not even talk about Balzac.

It was in post-atomic America that pop influences on lit became something more than technical. About the time television first gasped and sucked air, mass popular U.S. culture became high-art viable as a collection of symbols and myth. The episcopate of this pop-reference movement were the post-Nabokovian black humorists, the metafictionists and assorted franc- and latinophiles only later comprised by "postmodern." The erudite, sardonic fictions of the black humorists introduced a generation of new fiction writers who saw themselves as avant-avant-garde, not only cosmopolitan and polyglot but also technologically literate, products of more than just one region, heritage, and theory, and citizens of a culture that said its most important stuff about itself via mass media. In this regard I think particularly of the Barth of *The End of the Road* and *The Sot-Weed Factor,* the Gaddis of *The Recognitions,* and the Pynchon of *The Crying of Lot 49;* but the movement toward treating of the pop as its own reservoir of mythopeia fast metastasized and has transcended both school and genre. Plucking from my bookshelves almost at random, I find poet James Cummin's 1986 *The Whole Truth,* a cycle of sestinas deconstructing Perry Mason. Here's Robert Coover's 1977 *A Public Burning,* in which Eisenhower buggers Nixon on-air, and his 1980 *A Political Fable,* in which the Cat in the Hat runs for president. I find Max Apple's 1986 *The Propheteers,* a novel-length imagining of Walt Disney's travails. Or part of poet Bill Knott's 1974 "And Other Travels":

> . . . in my hand a cat o' nine tails on every tip of
>   which was Clearasil
> I was worried because Dick Clark had told the
>   cameraman
> not to put the camera on me during the dance parts
> of the show because my skirts were too tight[12]

which serves as a lovely example because, even though this stanza appears in the poem without anything we'd normally call context or support, it is in fact self-supported by a reference we all, each of us, immediately get, conjuring as it does with *Bandstand* ritualized vanity, teenage insecurity, the management of spontaneous moments. It is the perfect pop image: at once slight and universal, soothing and discomfiting.

Recall that the phenomena of watching and consciousness of watching are by nature expansive. What distinguishes another, later wave of postmodern lit is a further shift, from television images as valid objects of literary allusion, to TV and metawatching as themselves valid *subjects*. By this I mean certain lit beginning to locate its *raison* in its commentary on, response to, a U.S. culture more and more of and for watching, illusion, and the video image. This involution of attention was first observable in academic poetry. See for instance Stephen Dobyns's 1980 "Arrested Saturday Night":

> This is how it happened: Peg and Bob had invited
> Jack and Roxanne over to their house to watch
> the TV, and on the big screen they saw Peg and
>   Bob,
> Jack and Roxanne watching themselves watch
> themselves on progressively smaller TVs. . . . [13]

or Knott's 1983 "Crash Course":

> I strap a TV monitor on my chest
> so that all who approach can see themselves
> and respond appropriately.[14]

The true prophet of this shift in U.S. fiction, though, was the prenominate Don DeLillo, a long-neglected conceptual novelist who has made signal and image his unifying topoi the way Barth and Pynchon had sculpted in paralysis and paranoia a decade earlier. DeLillo's 1985 *White Noise* sounded to fledgling fictionists a kind of televisual clarion-call. Scenelets like the following seemed especially important:

> Several days later Murray asked me about a tourist attraction known as the most photographed barn in America. We drove twenty-two miles into the country around Farmington. There were meadows and apple orchards. White fences trailed through the rolling fields. Soon the signs started appearing. THE MOST PHOTOGRAPHED BARN IN AMERICA. We counted five signs before we reached the site. . . . We walked along a cow-path to the slightly elevated spot set aside for viewing and photographing. All the people had cameras; some had tripods, telephoto lenses, filter kits. A man in a booth sold postcards and slides—pictures of the barn taken from the elevated spot. We stood near a grove of trees and watched the photographers. Murray maintained a prolonged silence, occasionally scrawling some notes in a little book.
>
> "No one sees the barn," he said finally.
>
> A long silence followed.
>
> "Once you've seen the signs about the barn, it becomes impossible to see the barn."

> He fell silent once more. People with cameras left the elevated site, replaced at once by others.
>
> "We're not here to capture an image. We're here to maintain one. Can you feel it, Jack? An accumulation of nameless energies."
>
> There was an extended silence. The man in the booth sold postcards and slides.
>
> "Being here is a kind of spiritual surrender. We see only what the others see. The thousands who were here in the past, those who will come in the future. We've agreed to be part of a collective perception. This literally colors our vision. A religious experience in a way, like all tourism."
>
> Another silence ensued.
>
> "They are taking pictures of taking pictures," he said. (12-13)

I quote this at such length not only because it's too darn good to ablate, but to draw your attention to two relevant features. The less interesting is the Dobyns-esque message here about the metastasis of watching. For not only are people watching a barn whose only claim to fame is as an object of watching, but the pop-culture scholar Murray is watching people watch a barn, and his friend Jack is watching Murray watch the watching, and we readers are pretty obviously watching Jack the narrator watch Murray watching, etc. If you leave out the reader, there's a similar regress of recordings of barn and barn-watching.

But more important are the complicated ironies at work in the scene. The scene itself is obviously absurd and absurdist. But most of the writing's parodic force is directed at Murray, the would-be transcender of spectation. Murray, by watching and analyzing, would try to figure out the how and whys of giving in to collective visions of mass images that have themselves become mass images only because they've been made the objects of collective vision. The narrator's "extended silence" in response to Murray's blather speaks volumes. But it's not to be mistaken for a silence of sympathy with the sheeplike photograph-hungry crowd. These poor Joe Briefcases are no less objects of ridicule for their "scientific" critic himself being ridiculed. The authorial tone throughout is a kind of deadpan sneer. Jack himself is utterly mute—since to speak out loud in the scene would render the narrator *part* of the farce (instead of a detached, transcendent "observer and recorder") and so vulnerable to ridicule himself. With his silence, DeLillo's alter ego Jack eloquently diagnoses the very disease from which he, Murray, barn-watchers, and readers all suffer.

I DO HAVE A THESIS

I want to convince you that irony, poker-faced silence, and fear of ridicule are distinctive of those features of contemporary U.S. culture (of which cutting-edge fiction is a part) that enjoy any significant relation to the television whose weird pretty hand has my generation by the throat. I'm going to argue that irony and ridicule are entertaining and effective, and that at the same time they are agents of a great despair and stasis in U.S. culture, and that for aspiring fictionists they pose terrifically vexing problems.

My two big premises are that, on the one hand, a certain subgenre of pop-conscious postmodern fiction, written mostly by young Americans, has lately arisen and made a real attempt to transfigure a world of and for appearance, mass appeal, and television; and that, on the other hand, televisual culture has somehow evolved to a point where it seems invulnerable to any such transfiguring assault. TV, in other words, has become able to capture and neutralize any attempt to change or even protest the attitudes of passive unease and cynicism TV requires of Audience in order to be commercially and psychologically viable at doses of several hours per day.

IMAGE-FICTION

The particular fictional subgenre I have in mind has been called by some editors "post-postmodernism" and by some critics "hyperrealism." Most of the younger readers and writers I know call it the "fiction of image." Image-fiction is basically a further involution of the relations between lit and pop that blossomed with the sixties postmodernists. If the postmodern church fathers found pop images valid *referents* and *symbols* in fiction, and if in the seventies and early eighties this appeal to the features of mass culture shifted from *use* to *mention*, certain avant-gardists starting to treat of pop and TV and watching as themselves fertile *subjects*, the new fiction of image uses the transient received myths of popular culture as a *world* in which to imagine fictions about "real," albeit pop-mediated, public characters. Early uses of imagist tactics can be seen in the DeLillo of *Great Jones Street*, the Coover of *Burning*, and in Max Apple, whose seventies short story "The Oranging of America" projected an interior life onto the figure of Howard Johnson.

But in the late eighties, despite publisher unease over the legalities of imagining private lives for public figures, a real bumper crop of this behind-the-glass stuff started appearing, authored largely by writers who didn't know or cross-fertilize one another. Apple's *Propheteers*, Jay Cantor's *Krazy Kat*, Coover's *A Night at the Movies, or You Must Remember This*, William T. Vollmann's *You Bright and Risen Angels*, Stephen Dixon's *Movies: Seventeen Stories*, and DeLillo's own fictional hologram of Oswald in *Libra* are all notable post-'85 instances. (Observe too that, in another eighties medium, the arty *Zelig*, *Purple Rose of Cairo*, and *Sex, Lies, and Videotape*, plus the low-budget *Scanners* and *Videodrome* and *Shockers*, all began to treat screens as permeable.)

It's in the last couple of years that the image-fiction scene has really taken off. A. M. Homes's 1990 *The Safety of Objects* features a stormy love affair between a boy and a Barbie doll. Vollmann's 1989 *The Rainbow*

Stories has Sonys as characters in Heideggerian parables. Michael Martone's 1990 *Fort Wayne Is Seventh on Hitler's List* is a tight cycle of stories about the Midwest's pop-culture giants—James Dean, Colonel Sanders, Dillinger—the whole project of which, spelled out in a preface about image-fiction's legal woes, involves "questioning the border between fact and fiction when in the presence of fame."[15] And Mark Leyner's 1990 campus smash *My Cousin, My Gastroenterologist*, less a novel than what the book's jacket-copy describes as "a fiction analogue of the best drug you ever took," features everything from meditations on the color of Carefree Panty Shields wrappers to "Big Squirrel, the TV kiddie-show host and kung fu mercenary," to NFL instant replays in an "X-ray vision which shows leaping skeletons in a bluish void surrounded by 75,000 roaring skulls."[16]

One thing I have to insist you realize about this new subgenre is that it's distinguished, not just by a certain neo-postmodern technique, but by a genuine socio-artistic agenda. The fiction of image is not just a use or mention of televisual culture but a *response* to it, an effort to impose some sort of accountability on a state of affairs in which more Americans get their news from television than from newspapers and in which more Americans every evening watch *Wheel of Fortune* than all three network news programs combined.

And please see that image-fiction, far from being a trendy avant-garde novelty, is almost atavistic. It's a natural adaptation of the hoary techniques of literary realism to a nineties world whose defining boundaries have been deformed by electric signal. For realistic fiction's big job used to be to afford easements across borders, to help readers leap over the walls of self and locale and show us unseen or -dreamed-of people and cultures and ways to be. Realism made the strange familiar. Today, when we can eat Tex-Mex with chopsticks while listening to reggae and watching a Soviet-satellite newscast of the Berlin Wall's fall—i.e., when darn near *everything* presents itself as familiar—it's not a surprise that some of today's most ambitious "realistic" fiction is going about trying to *make the familiar strange*. In so doing, in demanding fictional access behind lenses and screens and headlines and re-imagining what human life might truly be like over there across the chasms of illusion, mediation, demographics, marketing, image, and appearance, image-fiction is paradoxically trying to restore what's (mis)taken for "real" to three whole dimensions, to reconstruct a univocally round world out of disparate streams of flat sights.

That's the good news.

The bad news is that, almost without exception, image-fiction doesn't satisfy its own agenda. Instead, it most often degenerates into a kind of jeering, surfacy look "behind the scenes" of the very televisual front people already jeer at, and can already get behind the scenes of via *Entertainment Tonight* and *Remote Control*.

The reason why today's imagist fiction isn't the rescue from a passive, addictive TV-psychology that it tries so hard to be is that most imagist writers render their material with the same tone of irony and self-consciousness that their ancestors, the literary insurgents of Beat and postmodernism, used so effectively to rebel against their own world and context. And the reason why this irreverent postmodern approach fails to help the imagists transfigure TV is simply that TV has beaten the imagists to the punch. The fact is that for at least ten years now television has been ingeniously absorbing, homogenizing, and re-presenting the very cynical postmodern aesthetic that was once the best alternative to the appeal of low, over-easy, mass-marketed narrative. How TV's done this is blackly fascinating to see.

A quick intermission contra paranoia. By saying that the fiction of image aims to "rescue" us from TV, I again am not suggesting that television has diabolic designs, or wants souls. I'm just referring again to the kind of Audience-conditioning consequent to high doses, a conditioning so subtle it can be observed best obliquely, through examples. If a term like "conditioning" still seems either hyperbolic or empty to you, I'll ask you to consider for a moment the exemplary issue of prettiness. One of the things that makes the people on TV fit to stand the megagaze is that they are, by human standards, really pretty. I suspect that this, like most television conventions, is set up with no motive more sinister than to appeal to the largest possible Audience. Pretty people tend to be more pleasing to look at than non-pretty people. But when we're talking about television, the combination of sheer Audience size and quiet psychic intercourse between images and oglers starts a cycle that both enhances pretty images' appeal and erodes us viewers' own security in the face of gazes. Because of the way human beings relate to narrative, we tend to identify with those characters we find appealing. We try to see ourselves in them. The same I.D.-relation, however, also means that we try to see them in ourselves. When everybody we seek to identify with for six hours a day is pretty, it naturally becomes more important to us to be pretty, to be viewed as pretty. Because prettiness becomes a priority for us, the pretty people on TV become all the more attractive, a cycle which is obviously great for TV. But it's less great for us civilians, who tend to own mirrors, and who also tend not to be anywhere near as pretty as the images we try to identify with. Not only does this cause some angst personally, but the angst increases because, nationally, everybody else is absorbing six-hour doses and identifying with pretty people and valuing prettiness more, too. This very personal anxiety about our prettiness has become a national phenomenon with national consequences. The whole U.S.A. gets different about things it values and fears. The boom in diet aids, health and fitness clubs, neighborhood tanning parlors, cosmetic surgery, anorexia, bulimia, steroid use among boys, girls throwing acid at each other because one girl's hair looks more like Farrah Fawcett's than another's . . . are these supposed to be unrelated to each other? to the apotheosis of prettiness in a televisual culture?

It's not paranoid or hysterical to acknowledge that television in large doses affects people's values and self-esteem in deep ways. That televisual conditioning influences the whole psychology of one's relation to himself, his mirror, his loved ones, and a world of real people and real gazes. No one's going to claim that a culture all about watching and appearing is fatally compromised by unreal standards of beauty and fitness. But other facets of TV-training reveal themselves as more rapacious, more serious, than any irreverent fiction writer would want to take seriously.

IRONY'S AURA

It's widely recognized that television, with its horn-rimmed battery of statisticians and pollsters, is awfully good at discerning patterns in the flux of popular ideologies, absorbing them, processing them, and then re-presenting them as persuasions to watch and to buy. Commercials targeted at the eighties' upscale boomers, for example, are notorious for using processed versions of tunes from the rock culture of the sixties and seventies both to elicit the yearning that accompanies nostalgia and to yoke purchases of products with what for yuppies is a lost era of genuine conviction. Ford sport vans are advertised with "This is the dawning of the age of the Aerostar"; Ford recently litigates with Bette Midler over the theft of her old vocals on "Do You Wanna Dance"; claymation raisins dance to "Heard It Through the Grapevine"; etc. If the commercial reuse of songs and the ideals they used to symbolize seems distasteful, it's not like pop musicians are paragons of noncommercialism themselves, and anyway nobody ever said selling was pretty. The effects of any instance of TV absorbing and pablumizing cultural tokens seem innocuous. But the recycling of whole cultural trends, and the ideologies that inform them, are a different story.

U.S. pop culture is just like U.S. serious culture in that its central tension has always set the nobility of individualism on one side against the warmth of communal belonging on the other. For its first twenty or so years, it seemed as though television sought to appeal mostly to the group side of the equation. Communities and bonding were extolled on early TV, even though TV itself, and especially its advertising, has from the outset projected itself at the lone viewer, Joe Briefcase, alone. Television commercials always make their appeals to individuals, not groups, a fact that seems curious in light of the unprecedented size of TV's Audience, until one hears gifted salesmen explain how people are always most vulnerable, hence frightened, hence needy, hence persuadable, when they are approached solo.

Classic television commercials were all about the group. They took the vulnerability of Joe Briefcase, sitting there, watching, lonely, and capitalized on it by linking purchase of a given product with Joe B.'s inclusion in some attractive community. This is why those of us over twenty-one can remember all those interchangeable old commercials featuring groups of pretty people in some ecstatic context having just way more fun than anybody has a license to have, and all united as Happy Group by the conspicuous fact that they're holding a certain bottle of pop or brand of snack—and the blatant appeal here is that the relevant product can help Joe Briefcase belong. "We're the Pepsi Generation. . . ."

But since, at latest, the eighties, the individualist side of the great U.S. conversation has held sway in TV advertising. I'm not sure just why or how this happened. There are probably great connections to be traced—with Vietnam, youth cultures, Watergate and recession and the New Right's rise—but the relevant datum is that a lot of the most effective TV commercials now make their appeal to the lone viewer in a terribly different way. Products are now most often pitched as helping the viewer "express himself," assert his individuality, "stand out from the crowd." The first instance I ever saw was a perfume vividly billed in the early eighties as reacting specially with each woman's "unique body chemistry" and creating "her own individual scent," the ad depicting a cattle line of languid models waiting cramped and expressionless to get their wrists squirted one at a time, each smelling her moist individual wrist with a kind of biochemical revelation, and then moving off in what a back-pan reveals to be different directions from the squirter (we can ignore the obvious sexual connotations, squirting and all that; some tactics are changeless). Or think of that recent series of over-dreary black-and-white Cherry 7-Up ads where the only characters who get to have color and stand out from their surroundings are the pink people who become pink at the exact moment they imbibe. Examples of stand-apart ads are ubiquitous nightly, now.

Except for being sillier—products billed as distinguishing individuals from crowds sell to huge crowds of individuals—these ads aren't really any more complicated or subtle than the old join-the-fulfilling-crowd ads that now seem so quaint. But the new stand-out ads' relation to their chiaroscuro mass of lone viewers is both complex and ingenious. Today's best ads are still about the group, but they now present the group as something fearsome, something that can swallow you up, erase you, keep you from "being noticed." But noticed by whom? Crowds are still vitally important in the stand-apart ads' thesis on identity, but now a given ad's crowd, far from being more appealing, secure, and alive than the individual, functions as a mass of identical featureless eyes. The crowd is now, paradoxically, both the "herd" in contrast to which the viewer's distinctive identity is to be defined, *and* the impassive witnesses whose sight alone can confer distinctive identity. The lone viewer's isolation in front of his furniture is implicitly applauded—it's better, realer, these solipsistic ads imply, to fly solo—and yet also implicated as threatening, confusing, since after all Joe Briefcase is not an idiot, sitting here, and knows himself as a viewer to be guilty of the two big sins the ads decry: being a passive watcher (of TV) and being part of a great herd (of TV-watchers and stand-apart-product-buyers). How odd.

The surface of stand-apart ads still presents a relatively unalloyed Buy This Thing, but the deep message of television w/r/t these ads looks to be that Joe Briefcase's ontological status as just one in a reactive watching mass is in a deep way false, and that true actualization of self would ultimately consist in Joe's becoming one of the images that are the objects of this great herdlike watching. That is, TV's real pitch in these commercials is that it's better to be inside the TV than to be outside, watching.

The lonely grandeur of stand-apart advertising not only sells companies' products, then. It manages brilliantly to ensure—even in commercials that television gets paid to run—that ultimately TV, and not any specific product or service, will be regarded by Joe B. as the ultimate arbiter of human worth. An oracle, to be consulted *a lot.* Advertising scholar Mark C. Miller puts it succinctly: "TV has gone beyond the explicit celebration of commodities to the implicit reinforcement of that spectatorial posture which TV requires of us."[17] Solipsistic ads are another way television ends up pointing at itself, keeping the viewer's relation to his furniture at once alienated and anaclitic.

Maybe, though, the relation of contemporary viewer to contemporary TV is less a paradigm of infantilism and addiction than it is of the U.S.A.'s familiar relation to all the technology we equate at once with freedom and power and slavery and chaos. For, as with TV, whether we happen personally to love technology, hate it, fear it, or all three, we still look relentlessly to technology for solutions to the very problems technology seems to cause—catalysis for smog, S.D.I. for missiles, transplants for assorted rot.

And as with tech, so the gestalt of TV expands to absorb all problems associated with it. The pseudo-communities of prime-time soaps like *Knots Landing* and *thirtysomething* are viewer-soothing products of the very medium whose ambivalence about groups helps erode people's sense of connection. The staccato editing, sound bites, and summary treatment of knotty issues is network news' accommodation of an Audience whose attention-span and appetite for complexity have atrophied a bit after years of high-dose spectation. Etc.

But TV has tech-bred problems of its own. The advent of cable, often with packages of over forty channels, threatens networks and local affiliates alike. This is particularly true when the viewer is armed with a remote-control gizmo: Joe B. is still getting his six total hours of daily TV, but the amount of his retinal time devoted to any one option shrinks as he remote-scans a much wider band. Worse, the VCR, with its dreaded fast-forward and ZAP functions, threatens the very viability of commercials. Television advertisers' sensible solution? Make the ads as appealing as the shows. Or at any rate try to keep Joe from disliking the commercials enough so that he's willing to move his thumb to check out two and a half minutes of *Hazel* on the Superstation while NBC sells lip balm. Make the ads prettier, livelier, full of enough rapidly juxtaposed visual quanta that Joe's attention just doesn't get to wander, even if he remote-kills the volume. As one ad executive underputs it, "Commercials are becoming more like entertaining films."[18]

There's an obverse way to make commercials resemble programs: have programs start to resemble commercials. That way the ads seem less like interruptions than like pace-setters, metronomes, commentaries on the shows' theory. Invent a *Miami Vice,* where there's little annoying plot to interrupt an unprecedented emphasis on appearances, visuals, attitude, a certain "look."[19] Make music videos with the same amphetaminic pace and dreamy archetypal associations as ads—it doesn't hurt that videos are basically long record commercials anyway. Or introduce the sponsor-supplied "infomercial" that poses, in a light-hearted way, as a soft-news show, like *Amazing Discoveries* or those Robert Vaughn–hosted hair-loss "reports" that haunt TV's wee cheap hours.

Still, television and its commercial sponsors had a bigger long-term worry, and that was their shaky detente with the individual viewer's psyche. Given that television must revolve off antinomies about being and watching, about escape from daily life, the averagely intelligent viewer can't be all that happy about his daily life of high-dose watching. Joe Briefcase might be happy enough *when* watching, but it was hard to think he could be too terribly happy *about* watching so much. Surely, deep down, Joe was uncomfortable with being one part of the biggest crowd in human history watching images that suggest that life's meaning consists in standing visibly apart from the crowd. TV's guilt/indulgence/reassurance cycle addresses these concerns on one level. But might there not be some deeper way to keep Joe Briefcase firmly in the crowd of watchers by somehow associating his very viewership with transcendence of watching crowds? But that would be absurd.

Enter irony.

I've said, so far without support, that what makes television's hegemony so resistant to critique by the new fiction of image is that TV has co-opted the distinctive forms of the same cynical, irreverent, ironic, absurdist post–WWII literature that the imagists use as touchstones. TV's own reuse of postmodern cool has actually evolved as a grimly inspired solution to the keep-Joe-at-once-alienated-from-and-part-of-the-million-eyed-crowd problem. The solution entailed a gradual shift from oversincerity to a kind of bad-boy irreverence in the big face TV shows us. This in turn reflected a wider shift in U.S. perceptions of how art was supposed to work, a transition from art's being a creative instantiation of real values to art's being a creative instantiation of deviance from bogus values. And this wider shift in its turn paralleled both the development of the postmodern aesthetic and some deep philosophic change in how Americans chose to view concepts like authority, sincerity, and passion in terms of our willingness to be pleased. Not only are sincerity and passion now "out," TV-wise, but the very idea of pleasure has been undercut. As Mark C.

Miller puts it, contemporary television "no longer solicits our rapt absorption or hearty agreement, but—like the ads that subsidize it—actually flatters us for the very boredom and distrust it inspires in us."[20]

Miller's 1986 "Deride and Conquer," the best essay ever written on network advertising, details vividly an example of how TV's contemporary appeal to the lone viewer works. It concerns a 1985-86 ad that won Clios and still occasionally runs. It's that Pepsi commercial where a Pepsi sound van pulls up to a packed sweltering beach and the impish young guy in the van activates a lavish PA system and opens up a Pepsi and pours it into a cup up next to the microphone. And the dense glittered sound of much carbonation goes out over the beach's heat-wrinkled air, and heads turn vanward as if pulled with strings as his gulp and refreshed, spiranty sounds are broadcast; and the final shot reveals that the sound van is also a concession truck, and the whole beach's pretty population has collapsed to a clamoring mass around the truck, everybody hopping up and down and pleading to be served first, as the camera's view retreats to overhead and the slogan is flatly intoned: "Pepsi: the Choice of a New Generation." Really a stunning commercial. But need one point out, as Miller does at length, that the final slogan is here tongue-in-cheek? There's about as much "choice" at work in this commercial as there was in Pavlov's bell kennel. In fact the whole thirty-second spot is tongue-in-cheek, ironic, self-mocking. As Miller argues, it's not really choice that the commercial is "selling" Joe Briefcase on, "but the total negation of choices. Indeed, the product itself is finally incidental to the pitch. The ad does not so much extol Pepsi per se as recommend it by implying that a lot of people have been fooled into buying it. In other words, the point of this successful bit of advertising is that Pepsi has been advertised successfully."[21]

There are important things to realize here. First, this ad is deeply informed by a fear of remote gizmos, ZAPping, and viewer disdain. An ad about ads, it uses self-reference to seem too hip to hate. It protects itself from the scorn today's viewing cognoscente feels for both the fast-talking hard-sell ads Dan Akroyd parodied into oblivion on *Saturday Night Live* and the quixotic associative ads that linked soda-drinking with romance, prettiness, and group inclusion—ads today's jaded viewer finds old-fashioned and "manipulative." In contrast to a blatant Buy This Thing, this Pepsi commercial pitches parody. The ad's utterly up-front about what TV ads are popularly despised for doing: using primal, film-flam appeals to sell sugary crud to people whose identity is nothing but mass consumption. This ad manages simultaneously to make fun of itself, Pepsi, advertising, advertisers, and the great U.S. watching/consuming crowd. In fact the ad's uxorious in its flattery of only one person: the lone viewer, Joe B., who even with an average brain can't help but discern the ironic contradiction between the "choice" slogan (sound) and the Pavlovian orgy (sight). The commercial invites Joe to "see through" the manipulation the beach's horde is rabidly buying. The commercial invites complicity between its own witty irony and veteran-viewer Joe's cynical, nobody's-fool appreciation of that irony. It invites Joe into an in-joke the Audience is the butt of. It congratulates Joe Briefcase, in other words, on transcending the very crowd that defines him, here. This ad boosted Pepsi's market share through three sales quarters.

Pepsi's campaign is not unique. Isuzu Inc. hit pay dirt with its series of "Joe Isuzu" spots, featuring an oily, Satanic-looking salesman who told whoppers about Isuzus' genuine llama-skin upholstery and ability to run on tap water. Though the ads rarely said much of anything about why Isuzus are in fact good cars, sales and awards accrued. The ads succeeded as parodies of how oily and Satanic car commercials are. They invited viewers to congratulate Isuzu ads for being ironic, to congratulate themselves for getting the joke, and to congratulate Isuzu Inc. for being "fearless" and "irreverent" enough to acknowledge that car ads are ridiculous and that the Audience is dumb to believe them. The ads invite the lone viewer to drive an Isuzu as some sort of anti-advertising statement. The ads successfully associate Isuzu-purchase with fearlessness and irreverence and the capacity to see through deception. You can find successful television ads that mock TV-ad conventions almost anywhere you look, from Settlemeyer's Federal Express and Wendy's spots, with their wizened, sped-up burlesques of commercial characters, to those hip Doritos splices of commercial spokesmen and campy old clips of *Beaver* and *Mr. Ed.*

Plus you can see this tactic of heaping scorn on pretensions to those old commercial virtues of authority and sincerity—thus (1) shielding the heaper of scorn from scorn and (2) congratulating the patron of scorn for rising above the mass of people who still fall for outmoded pretensions—employed to serious advantage on many of the television programs the commercials support. Show after show, for years now, has been either a self-acknowledged blank, visual, postmodern allusion- and attitude-fest, or, even more common, an uneven battle of wits between some ineffectual spokesman for hollow authority and his precocious children, mordant spouse, or sardonic colleagues. Compare television's treatment of earnest authority figures on pre-ironic shows—*The FBI*'s Erskine, *Star Trek*'s Kirk, *Beaver*'s Ward, *Partridge Family*'s Shirley, *Five-O*'s McGarrett—to TV's depiction of Al Bundy on *Married, with Children*, Mr. Owens on *Mr. Belvedere*, Homer on *The Simpsons*, Daniels and Hunter on *Hill Street Blues*, Jason Seaver on *Growing Pains*, Dr. Craig on *St. Elsewhere*.

The modern sitcom,[22] in particular, is almost wholly dependent for laughs and tone on the *M*A*S*H*–inspired savaging of some buffoonish spokesman for hypocritical, pre-hip values at the hands of bitingly witty insurgents. As Hawkeye savaged Frank and later Charles, so Herb is savaged by Jennifer and Carlson by J. Fever on *WKRP*, Mr. Keaton by Alex on *Family Ties*, boss by typing pool on *Nine to Five*, Seaver by whole family on *Pains*, Bundy by entire planet on *Married, w/* (the ultimate sitcom parody of sitcoms). In fact,

just about the only authority figures who retain any credibility on post-eighties shows (besides those like *Hill Street*'s Furillo and *Elsewhere*'s Westphal, who are surrounded by such relentless squalor that simply hanging in there week after week makes them heroic) are those upholders of values who can communicate some irony about themselves,[23] make fun of themselves before any merciless group around them can move in for the kill—see Huxtable on *Cosby*, Belvedere on *Belvedere, Twin Peaks*' Special Agent Cooper, Fox TV's Gary Shandling (the theme to whose show goes "This is the theme to Gary's show"), and the ironic eighties' true Angel of Death, D. Letterman.

Its promulgation of cynicism about all authority works to the general advantage of television on a number of levels. First, to the extent that TV can ridicule old-fashioned conventions right off the map, it can create an authority vacuum. And then guess what fills it. The real authority on a world we now view as constructed and not depicted becomes the medium that constructs our worldview. Second, to the extent that TV can refer exclusively to itself and debunk conventional standards as hollow, it is invulnerable to critics' charges that what's on is shallow or crass or bad, since any such judgments appeal to conventional, extratelevisual standards about depth, taste, and quality. Too, the ironic tone of TV's self-reference means that no one can accuse TV of trying to put anything over on anybody: as essayist Lewis Hyde points out, all self-mocking irony is "Sincerity, with a motive."[24]

And, more to the original point, if television can invite Joe Briefcase into itself via in-gags and irony, it can ease that painful tension between Joe's need to transcend the crowd and his status as Audience member. For to the extent that TV can flatter Joe about "seeing through" the pretentiousness and hypocrisy of outdated values, it can induce in him precisely the feeling of canny superiority it's taught him to crave, and can keep him dependent on the cynical TV-watching that alone affords this feeling. And to the extent that it can train viewers to laugh at characters' unending put-downs of one another, to view ridicule as both the mode of social intercourse and the ultimate art form, television can reinforce its own queer ontology of appearance: the most frightening prospect, for the well-conditioned viewer, becomes leaving oneself open to others' ridicule by betraying passé expressions of value, emotion, or vulnerability. Other people become judges; the crime is naïveté. The well-trained lonely viewer becomes even more allergic to people. Lonelier. Joe B.'s exhaustive TV-training in how to worry about how he might come across, seem to other eyes, makes riskily genuine human encounters seem even scarier. But televisual irony has the solution (to the problem it's aggravated): further viewing begins to seem almost like required research, lessons in the blank, bored, too-wise expression that Joe must learn how to wear for tomorrow's excruciating ride on the brightly lit subway, where crowds of blank, bored-looking people have little to look at but each other.

What does TV's institutionalization of hip irony have to do with U.S. fiction? Well, for one thing, American literary fiction tends to be about U.S. culture and the people who inhabit it. Culture-wise, shall I spend much of your time pointing out the degree to which televisual values influence the contemporary mood of jaded weltschmerz, self-mocking materialism, blank indifference, and the delusion that cynicism and naïveté are mutually exclusive? Can we deny connections between an unprecedentedly powerful consensual medium that suggests no real difference between image and substance and the rise of Teflon presidencies, the establishment of nationwide tanning and liposuction industries, the popularity of "vogueing" to a bad Marilyn-imitator's synthesized command to "strike a pose"? Or, in serious contemporary art, that televisual disdain for "hypocritical" retrovalues like originality, depth, and integrity has no truck with those recombinant "appropriation" styles of art and architecture in which past becomes pastiche,[25] or with the tuneless solmization of a Glass or a Reich, or with the self-conscious catatonia of a platoon of Raymond Carver wannabes?

In fact the numb blank bored demeanor—what my best friend calls the "girl-who's-dancing-with-you-but-would-obviously-rather-be-dancing-with-somebody-else" expression—that has become my generation's version of cool is all about TV. "Television," after all, literally means "seeing far"; and our 6 hrs. daily not only helps us feel up-close and personal at like the Pan Am Games or Operation Desert Shield but, obversely, trains us to see real-life personal up-close stuff the same way we relate to the distant and exotic, as if separated from us by physics and glass, extant only as performance, awaiting our cool review. Indifference is actually just the contemporary version of frugality, for U.S. young people: wooed several gorgeous hours a day for nothing but our attention, we regard that attention as our chief commodity, our social capital, and we are loath to fritter it. In the same regard, see that in 1990, flatness, numbness, and cynicism in one's demeanor are clear ways to transmit the televisual attitude of standout transcendence—flatness is a transcendence of melodrama, numbness transcends sentimentality, and cynicism announces that one knows the score, was last naive about something at maybe like age four.

Whether or not 1990s youth culture seems as grim to you as it does to me, surely we can agree that the culture's TV-defined pop ethic has pulled a marvelous touché on the postmodern aesthetic that originally sought to co-opt and redeem the pop. Television has pulled the old dynamics of reference and redemption inside-out: it is now *television* that takes elements of the *postmodern*—the involution, the absurdity, the sardonic fatigue, the iconoclasm and rebellion—and bends them to the ends of spectation and consumption. As early as '84, critics of capitalism were warning that "What began as a mood of the avant-garde has surged into mass culture."[26]

But postmodernism didn't just all of a sudden "surge" into television in 1984. Nor have the vectors of influence between the postmodern and the televisual been one-way. The chief connection between today's television and

today's fiction is historical. The two share roots. For postmodern fiction—written almost exclusively by young white males—clearly evolved as an intellectual expression of the "rebellious youth culture" of the sixties and early seventies. And since the whole gestalt of youthful U.S. rebellion was made possible by a national medium that erased communicative boundaries between regions and replaced a society segmented by location and ethnicity with what rock music critics have called "a national self-consciousness stratified by generation,"[27] the phenomenon of TV had as much to do with postmodernism's rebellious irony as it did with peaceniks' protest rallies.

In fact, by offering young, overeducated fiction writers a comprehensive view of how hypocritically the U.S.A. saw itself circa 1960, early television helped legitimize absurdism and irony as not just literary devices but sensible responses to an unrealistic world. For irony—exploiting gaps between what's said and what's meant, between how things try to appear and how they really are—is the time-honored way artists seek to illuminate and explode hypocrisy. And the television of lone-gunman Westerns, paternalistic sitcoms, and jut-jawed law enforcement circa 1960 celebrated a deeply hypocritical American self-image. Miller describes nicely how the 1960s sitcom, like the Westerns that preceded them, "negated the increasing powerlessness of white-collar males with images of paternal strength and manly individualism. Yet by the time these sit-coms were produced, the world of small business [whose virtues were the Hugh Beaumontish ones of 'self-possession, probity, and sound judgment'] had long since been . . . superseded by what C. Wright Mills called 'the managerial demiurge,' and the virtues personified by . . . Dad were in fact passé."[28]

In other words, early U.S. TV was a hypocritical apologist for values whose reality had become attenuated in a period of corporate ascendancy, bureaucratic entrenchment, foreign adventurism, racial conflict, secret bombing, assassination, wiretaps, etc. It's not one bit accidental that postmodern fiction aimed its ironic cross hairs at the banal, the naive, the sentimental and simplistic and conservative, for these qualities were *just* what sixties TV seemed to celebrate as "American."

And the rebellious irony in the best postmodern fiction wasn't only credible as art; it seemed downright socially useful in its capacity for what counterculture critics call "a *critical negation* that would make it self-evident to everyone that the world is not as it seems."[29] Kesey's dark parody of asylums suggested that our arbiters of sanity were maybe crazier than their patients; Pynchon reoriented our view of paranoia from deviant psychic fringe to central thread in the corporo-bureaucratic weave; DeLillo exposed image, signal, data, and tech as agents of spiritual chaos and not social order. Burroughs's icky explorations of American narcosis exploded hypocrisy; Gaddis's exposure of abstract capital as dehumanizing exploded hypocrisy; Coover's repulsive political farces exploded hypocrisy. Irony in sixties art and culture started out the same way youthful rebellion did. It was difficult and painful, and *productive*—a grim diagnosis of a long-denied disease. The assumptions behind this early postmodern irony, on the other hand, were still frankly idealistic: that etiology and diagnosis pointed toward cure; that revelation of imprisonment yielded freedom.

So then how have irony, irreverence, and rebellion come to be not liberating but enfeebling in the culture today's avant-garde tries to write about? One clue's to be found in the fact that irony is *still around,* bigger than ever after thirty long years as the dominant mode of hip expression. It's not a mode that wears especially well. As Hyde puts it, "Irony has only emergency use. Carried over time, it is the voice of the trapped who have come to enjoy their cage." This is because irony, entertaining as it is, serves an exclusively negative function. It's critical and destructive, a ground-clearing. Surely this is the way our postmodern fathers saw it. But irony's singularly unuseful when it comes to constructing anything to replace the hypocrisies it debunks. This is why Hyde seems right about persistent irony being tiresome. It is unmeaty. Even gifted ironists work best in sound bites. I find them sort of wickedly fun to listen to at parties, but I always walk away feeling like I've had several radical surgical procedures. And as for actually driving cross-country with a gifted ironist, or sitting through a 300-page novel full of nothing but trendy sardonic exhaustion, one ends up feeling not only empty but somehow . . . oppressed.

Think, if you will for a moment, of Third World rebels and coups. Rebels are great at exposing and overthrowing corrupt hypocritical regimes, but seem noticeably less great at the mundane, non-negative tasks of then establishing a superior governing alternative. Victorious rebels, in fact, seem best at using their tough cynical rebel skills to avoid being rebelled against themselves—in other words they just become better tyrants.

And make no mistake: irony tyrannizes us. The reason why our pervasive cultural irony is at once so powerful and so unsatisfying is that an ironist is *impossible to pin down.* All irony is a variation on a sort of existential poker-face. All U.S. irony is based on an implicit "I don't really mean what I say." So what *does* irony as a cultural norm mean to say? That it's impossible to mean what you say? That maybe it's too bad it's impossible, but wake up and smell the coffee already? Most likely, I think, today's irony ends up saying: "How very *banal* to ask what I mean." Anyone with the heretical gall to ask an ironist what he actually stands for ends up looking like a hysteric or a prig. And herein lies the oppressiveness of institutionalized irony, the too-successful rebel: the ability to interdict the *question* without attending to its *content* is tyranny. It is the new junta, using the very tool that exposed its enemy to insulate itself.

This is why our educated teleholic friends' use of weary cynicism to try to seem superior to TV is so pathetic. And this is why the fiction-writing citizen of our

televisual culture is in such deep doo. What do you do when postmodern rebellion becomes a pop-cultural institution? For this of course is the second clue to why avant-garde irony and rebellion have become dilute and malign. They have been absorbed, emptied, and redeployed by the very televisual establishment they had originally set themselves athwart.

Not that television is culpable for true evil, here. Just for immoderate success. This is, after all, what TV *does:* it discerns, decocts, and represents what it thinks U.S. culture wants to see and hear about itself. No one and everyone is at fault for the fact that television started gleaning rebellion and cynicism as the hip, upscale, baby-boomer *imago populi.* But the harvest has been dark: the forms of our best rebellious art have become mere gestures, shticks, not only sterile but perversely enslaving. How can even the idea of rebellion against corporate culture stay meaningful when Chrysler Inc. advertises trucks by invoking "The Dodge Rebellion"? How is one to be a bona fide iconoclast when Burger King sells onion rings with "Sometimes You Gotta Break the Rules"? How can a new image-fiction writer hope to make people more critical of televisual culture by parodying television as a self-serving commercial enterprise when Pepsi and Isuzu and Fed Ex parodies of self-serving commercials are already big business? It's almost a history lesson: I'm starting to see just why turn-of-the-century America's biggest fear was of anarchists and anarchy. For if anarchy actually *wins,* if rulelessness becomes the rule, then protest and change become not just impossible but incoherent. It'd be like casting ballots for Stalin—how do you vote for no more voting?

So here's the stumper for the 1990 U.S. fictionist who both breaths out cultural atmosphere and sees himself heir to whatever was neat and valuable in postmodern lit. How to rebel against TV's aesthetic of rebellion. How to snap readers awake to the fact that our TV-culture has become a cynical, narcissistic, essentially empty phenomenon, when television regularly *celebrates* just these features in itself and its viewers? These are the very questions DeLillo's poor schmuck of a popologist was asking back in '85 about America, that most photographed of barns:

> "What was the barn like before it was photographed?" he said. "What did it look like, how was it different from other barns, how was it similar to other barns? We can't answer these questions because we've read the signs, seen the people snapping the pictures. We can't get outside the aura. We're part of the aura. We're here, we're now."
>
> He seemed immensely pleased by this.[30]

END OF THE END OF THE LINE

What responses to television's commercialization of the modes of literary protest seem possible, then, today? One obvious option is for the fiction writer to become reactionary, fundamentalist. Declare contemporary television evil and contemporary culture evil and turn one's back on the whole Spandexed mess and genuflect instead to good old pre-sixties Hugh Beaumontish virtues and literal readings of the Testaments and be pro-Life, anti-Fluoride, antediluvian. The problem with this is that Americans who've opted for this tack seem to have one eyebrow straight across their forehead and knuckles that drag on the ground and just seem like an *excellent* crowd to want to transcend. Besides, the rise of Reagan/Bush showed that hypocritical nostalgia for a kinder, gentler, more Christian pseudo-past is no less susceptible to manipulation in the interests of corporate commercialism and PR image. Most of us will still take nihilism over neanderthalism.

Another option is to adopt a somewhat more enlightened political conservatism that exempts viewer and networks alike from any complicity in the bitter stasis of televisual culture, and instead blames all TV-related problems on certain correctable defects in broadcasting technology. Enter media futurologist George Gilder, a Hudson Institute Senior Fellow and author of 1990's *Life after Television: The Coming Transformation of Media and American Life*. The single most fascinating thing about *Life after Television* is that it's a book with *commercials*. Published in something called "The Larger Agenda Series" by a "Whittle Direct Books" in Federal Express Inc.'s Knoxville headquarters, the book sells for only $11.00 hard, including postage, is big and thin enough to look great on executive coffee tables, and has really pretty full-page ads for Federal Express on every fifth page. The book's also largely a work of fiction, plus is a heart-rending dramatization of why anti-TV conservatives, motivated by simple convictions like "Television is at heart a totalitarian medium" whose "system is an alien and corrosive force in democratic capitalism"[31] are going to be of little help with our ultraradical TV problems, attached as conservative intellectuals still are to their twin tired remedies for all U.S. ills: the beliefs that (1) the discerning consumer instincts of the little guy would correct all imbalances if only big systems would quit stifling his freedom to choose, and that (2) tech-bred problems can be resolved technologically.

Gilder's basic report and forecast run thus: television as we know and suffer it is "a technology with supreme powers but deadly flaws." The really fatal flaw is that the whole structure of television programming broadcasting, and reception is still informed by the technological limitations of the old vacuum tubes that first enabled TV. The "expense and complexity of these tubes used in television sets meant that most of the processing of signals would have to be done at the" networks, a state of affair that "dictated that television would be a top-down system—in electronic terms, a 'master-slave' architecture. A few broadcasting centers would originate programs for millions of passive receivers, or 'dumb terminals.'" By the time the transistor (which does essentially what vacuum tubes do but in less space at lower cost) found commercial applications, the top-down TV system was already entrenched and petrified, dooming viewers to

docile reception of programs they were dependent on a very few networks to provide, and creating a "psychology of the masses" in which a trio of programming alternatives aimed to appeal to millions and millions of Joe B.s. The passive plight of the viewer was aggravated by the fact that the EM pulses used to broadcast TV signals are analog waves. Analogs were once the required medium, since "with little storage or processing available at the set, the signals . . . would have to be directly displayable waves," and "analog waves directly simulate sound, brightness, and color." But analog waves can't be saved or edited by their recipient. They're too much like life: there in gorgeous toto one instant and then gone. What the poor TV viewer gets is only what he sees. With cultural consequences Gilder describes in apocalyptic detail. Even High Definition Television (HDTV), touted by the industry as the next big advance in entertainment-furniture, will, according to Gilder, be just the same vacuuous emperor in a snazzier suit.

But in 1990, TV, still clinging to the crowd-binding and hierarchical technologies of yesterdecade, is for Gilder now doomed by the advances in microchip and fiber-optic technology of the last couple years. The user-friendly microchip, which consolidates the activities of millions of transistors on one 49¢ wafer, and whose capacities will get even more attractive as controlled-electron conduction approaches the geodesic paradigm of efficiency, will allow receivers—TV sets—to do much of the image-processing that has hitherto been done "for" the viewer by the broadcaster. In another happy development, transporting images through glass fibers rather than the EM spectrum will allow people's TV sets to be hooked up with each other in a kind of interactive net instead of all feeding passively at the transmitting teat of a single broadcaster. And fiber-optic transmissions have the further advantage that they conduct characters of information digitally. Since "digital signals have an advantage over analog signals in that they can be stored and manipulated without deterioration," as well as being crisp and interferenceless as quality CDs, they'll allow the microchip'd television receiver (and thus the TV viewer) to enjoy much of the discretion over selection, manipulation, and recombination of video images that is now restricted to the director's booth.

For Gilder, the new piece of furniture that will free Joe Briefcase from passive dependence on his furniture will be "the telecomputer, a personal computer adapted for video processing and connected by fiber-optic threads to other telecomputers around the world." The fibrous TC "will forever break the broadcast bottleneck" of television's one-active-many-passive structure of image-propagation. Now everybody'll get to be his own harried guy with headphones and clipboard. In the new millennium, U.S. television will finally become ideally, GOPishly democratic: egalitarian, interactive, and "profitable without being exploitative."

Boy, does Gilder know his "Larger Agenda" audience. You can just see saliva overflowing lower lips in boardrooms as Gilder forecasts that the consumer's whole complicated fuzzy inconveniently transient world will become broadcastable, manipulable, storable, and viewable in the comfort of his own condo. "With artful programming of telecomputers, you could spend a day interacting on the screen with Henry Kissinger, Kim Basinger, or Billy Graham." Rather ghastly interactions to contemplate, but then in Gilderland *to each his own:* "Celebrities could produce and sell their own software. You could view the Super Bowl from any point in the stadium you choose, or soar above the basket with Michael Jordan. Visit your family on the other side of the world with moving pictures hardly distinguishable from real-life images. Give a birthday party for Grandma in her nursing home in Florida, bringing her descendents from all over the country to the foot of her bed in living color."

And not just warm 2D images of family: *any* experience will be transferrable to image and marketable, manipulable, consumable. People will be able to "go comfortably sight-seeing from their living room through high-resolution screens, visiting Third-World countries without having to worry about air fares or exchange rates . . . you could fly an airplane over the Alps or climb Mount Everest—all on a powerful high-resolution display."

We will, in short, be able to engineer our own dreams.

In sum, then, a conservative tech writer offers a really attractive way of looking at viewer passivity and TV's institutionalization of irony, narcissism, nihilism, stasis. It's not our fault! It's outmoded technology's fault! If TV-dissemination were up to date, it would be impossible for it to "institutionalize" anything through its demonic "mass psychology"! Let's let Joe B., the little lonely guy, be his *own* manipulator of video-bits! Once all experience is finally reduced to marketable image, once the receiving user of user-friendly receivers can choose freely, Americanly, from an Americanly infinite variety of moving images *hardly distinguishable from real-life images,* and can then choose further just how he wishes to store, enhance, edit, recombine, and present those images to himself, in the privacy of his very own home and skull, TV's ironic, totalitarian grip on the American psychic cajones will be broken!

Note that Gilder's semiconducted vision of a free, orderly video future is way more upbeat than postmodernism's old view of image and data. The seminal novels of Pynchon and DeLillo revolve metaphorically off the concept of interference: the more connections, the more chaos, and the harder it is to cull any meaning from the seas of signal. Gilder would call their gloom outmoded, their metaphor infected with the deficiencies of the transistor: "In all networks of wires and switches, except for those on the microchip, complexity tends to grow exponentially as the number of interconnections rises, [but] in the silicon maze of microchip technology . . . efficiency, not complexity, grows as the square of the number of interconnections to be organized." Rather than a vacuous TV-culture smothering in

cruddy images, Gilder foresees a TC-culture redeemed by a whole lot more to choose from and a whole lot more control over what you choose to . . . umm . . . see? pseudo-experience? dream?

It'd be unrealistic to think that expanded choices alone could resolve our televisual bind. The advent of cable upped choices from four or five to forty-plus synchronic alternatives, with little apparent loosening of television's grip on mass attitudes and aesthetics. It seems rather that Gilder sees the nineties' impending breakthrough as U.S. viewers' graduation from passive reception of facsimiles of experience to active manipulation of facsimiles of experience.

It's worth questioning Gilder's definition of televisual "passivity," though. His new tech would indeed end "the passivity of mere reception." But the passivity of Audience, the acquiescence inherent in a whole culture of and about watching, looks unaffected by TCs.

The appeal of watching television has always involved fantasy. Contemporary TV, I've claimed, has gotten vastly better at enabling the viewer's fantasy that he can transcend the limitations of individual human experience, that he can be inside the set, imago'd, "anyone, anywhere."[32] Since the limitations of being one human being involve certain restrictions on the number of different experiences possible to us in a given period of time, it's arguable that the biggest TV-tech "advances" of recent years have done little but abet this fantasy of escape from the defining limits of being human. Cable expands our choices of evening realities; hand-held gizmos let us leap instantly from one to another; VCRs let us commit experiences to an eidetic memory that permits re-experience at any time without loss or alteration. These advances sold briskly and upped average viewing-doses, but they sure haven't made U.S. televisual culture any less passive or cynical.

The downside of TV's big fantasy is that it's just a fantasy. As a special treat, my escape from the limits of genuine experience is neato. As my steady diet, though, it can't help but render my own reality less attractive (because in it I'm just one Dave, with limits and restrictions all over the place), render me less fit to make the most of it (because I spend all my time pretending I'm not in it), and render me dependent on the device that affords escape from just what my escapism makes unpleasant.

It's tough to see how Gilder's soteriological vision of having more "control" over the arrangement of high-quality fantasy-bits is going to ease either the dependency that is part of my relation to TV or the impotent irony I must use to pretend I'm not dependent. Whether passive or active as viewer, I must still cynically pretend, because I'm still dependent, because my real dependency here is not on the single show or few networks any more than the hophead's is on the Turkish florist or the Marseilles refiner. My real dependency is on the *fanta-*

sies and the *images* that enable them, and thus on any *technology* that can make images fantastic. Make no mistake. We are dependent on image-technology; and the better the tech, the harder we're hooked.

The paradox in Gilder's rosy forecast is the same as in all forms of artificial enhancement. The more enhancing the mediation—see for instance binoculars, amplifiers, graphic equalizers, or "high-resolution pictures hardly distinguishable from real-life images"—the more direct, vivid, and real the experience *seems,* which is to say the more direct, vivid, and real the fantasy and dependence *are.*

An exponential surge in the mass of televisual images, and a commensurate increase in my ability to cut, paste, magnify, and combine them to suit my own fancy, can do nothing but render my interactive TC a more powerful enhancer and enabler of fantasy, my attraction to that fantasy stronger, the real experiences of which my TC offers more engaging and controllable simulacra paler and more frustrating to deal with, and me just a *whole* lot more dependent on my furniture. Jacking the number of choices and options up with better tech will remedy exactly nothing, so long as no sources of insight on comparative worth, no guides to *why* and *how* to choose among experiences, fantasies, beliefs, and predilections, are permitted serious consideration in U.S. culture. Insights and guides to human value used to be among literature's jobs, didn't they? But then who's going to want to take such stuff seriously in ecstatic post-TV life, with Kim Basinger waiting to be interacted with?

My God, I've just reread my heartfelt criticisms of Gilder. That he is naive. That he is an apologist for cynical corporate self-interest. That his book has commercials. That under its futuristic novelty is just the same old American same-old that got us into this televisual mess. That Gilder vastly underestimates the intractability of the mess. Its hopelessness. Our fatigue. My attitude, reading Gilder, is sardonic, aloof, jaded. My reading of Gilder is televisual. I am in the aura.

Well, but at least Gilder is unironic. In this respect he's like a cool summer breeze compared to Mark Leyner, the young New Jersey writer whose 1990 *My Cousin, My Gastroenterologist* is the biggest thing for campus hipsters since *The Dharma Bums.* Leyner's ironic cyberpunk novel exemplifies a third kind of literary response to our problem. For of course young U.S. writers can "resolve" the problem of being trapped in the televisual aura the same way French poststructuralists "resolve" their being enmeshed in the logos. We can solve the problem by celebrating it. Transcend feelings of mass-defined angst by genuflecting to them. We can be *reverently ironic.*

My Cousin, My Gastroenterologist is new not so much in kind as in degree. It is a methedrine compound of pop pastiche, offhand high tech, and dazzling televisual parody, formed with surreal juxtapositions and grammarless monologues and flash-cut editing, and

framed with a relentless irony designed to make its frantic tone seem irreverent instead of repulsive. You want sendups of commercial culture?

> I had just been fired from McDonald's for refusing to wear a kilt during production launch week for their new McHaggis sandwich. (18)

> he picks up a copy of *das plumpe denken* new england's most disreputable german-language newsmagazine blast in egg cream factory kills philatelist he turns the page radioactive glow-in-the-dark semen found in canada he turns the page modern-day hottentots carry young in resealable sandwich bags he turns the page wayne newton calls mother's womb single-occupancy garden of eden morgan fairchild calls sally struthers loni anderson. (37)

> what color is your mozzarella? i asked the waitress it's pink—it's the same color as the top of a mennen lady speed stick dispenser, y'know that color? no, maam I said it's the same color they use for the gillette daisy disposable razors for women . . . y'know that color? nope well, it's the same pink as pepto-bismol, y'know that color oh yeah, i said, well do you have spaghetti? (144)

You want mordant sendups of television?

> Muriel got the *TV Guide,* flipped to Tuesday 8 P.M., and read aloud: . . . There's a show called "A Tumult of Pubic Hair and Bobbing Flaccid Penises as Sweaty Naked Chubby Men Run From the Sauna Screaming Snake! Snake!" . . . It also stars Brian Keith, Buddy Ebsen, Nipsey Russell, and Lesley Ann Warren. (98-99)

You like mocking self-reference? The novel's whole last chapter is a parody of its own "About the Author" page. Or maybe you're into hip identitylessness?

> Grandma rolled up a magazine and hit Buzz on the side of the head. . . . Buzz's mask was knocked loose. There was no skin beneath that mask. There were two white eyeballs protruding on stems from a mass of oozing blood-red musculature. (98)

> I can't tell if she's human or a fifth-generation gynemorphic android and I don't care. (6)

Parodic meditations on the boundaryless flux of televisual monoculture?

> I'm stirring a pitcher of Tanqueray martinis with one hand and sliding a tray of frozen clams *oreganata* into the oven with my foot. God, these methedrine suppositories that Yogi Vithaldas gave me are good! As I iron a pair of tennis shorts I dictate a haiku into the tape recorder and then . . . do three minutes on the speedbag before making an origami praying mantis and then reading an article in *High Fidelity* magazine as I stir the coq au vin. (49)

The decay of both the limits and the integrity of the single human self?

There was a woman with the shrunken, wrinkled face of an eighty- or ninety-year-old. And this withered hag, this apparent octogenarian, had the body of a male Olympic swimmer. The long lean sinewy arms, the powerful V-shaped upper torso, without a single ounce of fat. . . . (120)

to install your replacement head place the head assembly on neck housing and insert guide pins through mounting holes . . . if, after installing new head, you are unable to discern the contradictions in capitalist modes of production, you have either installed your head improperly or head is defective (142-43)

In fact, one of *My Cousin, My Gastroenterologist*'s unifying obsessions is this latter juxtaposition of parts of selves, people and machines, human subjects and discrete objects. Leyner's fiction is, in this regard, an eloquent reply to Gilder's prediction that our TV-culture problems can be resolved by the dismantling of images into discrete chunks we can recombine as we fancy. Leyner's world is a Gilder-esque dystopia. The passivity and schizoid decay still endure for Leyner in his characters' reception of images and waves of data. The ability to *combine* them only adds a layer of disorientation: when all experience can be deconstructed and reconfigured, there become simply too many choices. And in the absence of any credible, noncommercial guides for living, the freedom to choose is about as "liberating" as a bad acid trip: each quantum is as good as the next, and the only standard of an assembly's quality is its weirdness, incongruity, its ability to stand out from a crowd of other image-constructs and wow some Audience.

Leyner's novel, in its amphetaminic eagerness to wow the reader, marks the far dark frontier of the fiction of image—literature's absorption of not just the icons, techniques, and phenomena of television, but of television's whole *objective*. *My Cousin, My Gastroenterologist*'s sole aim is, finally, to wow, to ensure that the reader is pleased and continues to read. The book does this by (1) flattering the reader with appeals to his erudite postmodern weltschmerz, and (2) relentlessly reminding the reader that the author is smart and funny. The book itself is extremely funny, but it's not funny the way funny stories are funny. It's not that funny things happen here; it's that funny things are self-consciously imagined and pointed out, like the comedian's stock "You ever notice how . . . ?" or "Ever wonder what would happen if . . . ?"

Actually, Leyner's whole high-imagist style most often resembles a kind of lapidary stand-up comedy:

Suddenly Bob couldn't speak properly. He had suffered some form of spontaneous aphasia. But it wasn't total aphasia. He could speak, but only in a staccato telegraphic style. Here's how he described driving through the Midwest on Interstate 80: "Corn corn corn corn Stuckeys. Corn corn corn corn Stuckeys." (20)

there's a bar on the highway which caters almost exclusively to authority figures and the only drink

it serves is lite beer and the only food it serves is surf and turf and the place is filled with cops and state troopers and gym teachers and green berets and toll attendants and game wardens and crossing guards and umpires. (89-90)

Leyner's fictional response to television is less a novel than a piece of witty, erudite, extremely high-quality prose television. Velocity and vividness—the wow—replace the literary hmm of actual development. People flicker in and out; events are garishly there and then gone and never referred to. There's a brashly irreverent rejection of "outmoded" concepts like integrated plot or enduring character. Instead there's a series of dazzlingly creative parodic vignettes, designed to appeal to the forty-five seconds of near-Zen concentration we call the TV attention span. Unifying the vignettes in the absence of plot are moods—antic anxiety, the over-stimulated stasis of too many choices and no chooser's manual, irreverent brashness toward televisual reality—and, after the manner of pop films, music videos, dreams, and television programs, recurring "key images"—here exotic drugs, exotic technology, exotic food, exotic bowel dysfunctions. It's no accident that *My Cousin, My Gastroenterologist*'s central preoccupation is with digestion and elimination. Its mocking challenge to the reader is the same as television's flood of realities and choices: ABSORB ME—PROVE YOU'RE CONSUMER ENOUGH.

Leyner's work, the best image-fiction yet, is both amazing and forgettable, wonderful and oddly hollow. I'm finishing up by talking about it at length because, in its masterful reabsorption of the very features TV had absorbed from postmodern lit, it seems as of now the ultimate union of U.S. television and fiction. It seems also to limn the qualities of image-fiction itself in stark relief: the best stuff the subgenre's produced to date is hilarious, upsetting, sophisticated, and extremely shallow—and just plain doomed by its desire to ridicule a TV-culture whose ironic mockery of itself and all "outdated" value absorbs all ridicule. Leyner's attempt to "respond" to television via ironic genuflection is all too easily subsumed into the tired televisual ritual of mock worship.

Entirely possible that my plangent cries about the impossibility of rebelling against an aura that promotes and attenuates all rebellion says more about my residency inside that aura, my own lack of vision, than it does about any exhaustion of U.S. fiction's possibilities. The next real literary "rebels" in this country might well emerge as some weird bunch of "anti-rebels," born oglers who dare to back away from ironic watching, who have the childish gall actually to endorse single-entendre values. Who treat old untrendy human troubles and emotions in U.S. life with reverence and conviction. Who eschew self-consciousness and fatigue. These anti-rebels would be outdated, of course, before they even started. Too sincere. Clearly repressed. Backward, quaint, naive, anachronistic. Maybe that'll be the point, why they'll be the next real rebels. Real rebels, as far as I can see, risk things. Risk disapproval. The old postmodern insurgents risked the gasp and squeal: shock, disgust, outrage, censorship, accusations of socialism, anarchism, nihilism. The new rebels might be the ones willing to risk the yawn, the rolled eyes, the cool smile, the nudged ribs, the parody of gifted ironists, the "How banal." Accusations of sentimentality, melodrama. Credulity. Willingness to be suckered by a world of lurkers and starers who fear gaze and ridicule above imprisonment without law. Who knows. Today's most engaged young fiction does seem like some kind of line's end's end. I guess that means we all get to draw our own conclusions. Have to. Are you immensely pleased.

—For M. M. Karr

NOTES FOR EDITOR, WHICH EDITOR, FOR REASONS KNOWN ONLY TO HIM, WANTS TO RUN W/ESSAY.

[1] This, and thus the title, is from a toss-off in Michael Sorkin's "Faking It," published in Todd Gitlin, ed., *Watching Television,* Pantheon, 1987.

[2] Quoted by Stanley Cavell in *Pursuits of Happiness,* Harvard U. Press, 1981, epigraph.

[3] Bernard Nossiter, "The FCC's Big Giveaway Show," *The Nation,* 10/26/85, p. 402.

[4] Janet Maslin, "It's Tough for Movies to Get Real," *NYT* Arts & Leisure, 8/05/90, p. 9.

[5] Stephen Holden, "Strike the Pose: When Music Is Skin-Deep," ibid., p. 1.

[6] Michael Sorkin, p. 163.

[7] Daniel Hallin, "We Keep America on Top of the World," in Gitlin anthology.

[8] Barbara Tuchman, "The Decline of Quality," *NYT Magazine,* 11/02/80.

[9] Alexis de Tocqueville, *Democracy in America,* Vintage, 1945, pp. 57 and 73.

[10] Don DeLillo, *White Noise,* Viking, 1985, p. 72

[11] Octavio Paz, *Children of the Mire,* Harvard U. Press, 1974, pp. 103-18.

[12] Bill Knott, "And Other Travels," in *Love Poems to Myself, Book One,* Barn Dream Press, 1974.

[13] Stephen Dobyns, "Arrested Saturday Night," in *Heat Death,* McClelland and Stewart, 1980.

[14] Bill Knott, "Crash Course," in *Becos,* Vintage, 1983.

[15] Michael Martone, *Fort Wayne Is Seventh On Hitler's List,* Indiana U. Press, 1990, p. ix.

[16] Mark Leyner, *My Cousin, My Gastroenterologist,* Harmony/Crown, 1990, p. 82.

[17] Mark C. Miller, "Deride and Conquer," in Gitlin anthology.

[18] At Foote, Cone and Belding, quoted by Miller (somewhere I can't find in notes).

[19] There's a similar point made about *Miami Vice* in Todd Gitlin's "We Build Excitement" in his anthology.

[20] Miller, p. 194.

[21] Miller, p. 187.

[22] Miller's "Deride" has a similar analysis of sitcoms (in fact my whole discussion of TV irony leans heavily on Gitlin's, Sorkin's, and Miller's essays in Gitlin's anthology), but anyway w/r/t sitcoms Miller is talking about some weird Freudian patricide in how TV comedy views The Father—strange but very cool.

[23] Miller's "Deride" makes pretty much this same point about Cosby.

[24] Lewis Hyde, "Alcohol and Poetry: John Berryman and the Booze Talking," *American Poetry Review,* reprinted in the *Pushcart Prize* anthology for '87.

[25] I liberated this from somewhere in *Watching Television;* can't find just where.

[26] Fredric Jameson, "Postmodernism, or the Cultural Logic of Late Capitalism," *New Left Review* 146, Summer '84, pp. 60-66.

[27] Pat Auferhode, "The Look of the Sound," in Gitlin anthology, p. 113.

[28] Miller, p. 199.

ADAPTATIONS

J. Roger Osterholm

SOURCE: "Michener's Space, the Novel and Miniseries," in *Journal of Popular Culture,* Vol. 23, No. 3, Winter, 1989, pp. 51-64.

[*In the following essay, Osterholm considers alterations of characterization, thematic emphasis, and plot incidents in the television miniseries adaptation of James Michener's novel* Space *(1982).*]

James Michener's 1982 novel *Space* and its adaptation as a thirteen-hour television miniseries provide excellent material for a case study on the styles and trappings of major productions for the popular American culture. The miniseries cost $32 million and was broadcast on the CBS television network April 14 to 18, 1985, with a nine-hour abridgement broadcast in July 1987. Significant alterations in characterization, plot, and themes for the miniseries reflect popular interests and obsessions, at least as well as the experienced producer, writers, and directors for television could both identify and further popularize them. Michener's novel, although popular itself, is clearly more refined and advanced, more demanding of its audience, than the broadcast version—as the novelist has himself suggested in a letter to this writer.

The miniseries was produced by Dick Berg (who produced the earlier miniseries *Wallenberg: A Hero's Story*), written by Stirling Silliphant and Dick Berg, and directed by Joseph Sargent and Lee Philips. Silliphant wrote the first nine hours, leaving Berg to complete the script, which had been expanded from a projected eight hours as production neared (Dougan A5). The television characters have a different ranking from those in the novel, with Senator Norman Grant (played by James Garner) eclipsing the role of Stanley Mott (played by Bruce Dern), a brilliant engineer based on Christopher C. Kraft, Jr., (Watson) a noted rocket pioneer. Mott rescues German scientists and manages much of the American space program.

The senator is a Navy war hero turned politician and champion of the space program, a role inflated to suit the stature of James Garner. Penny Pope (played by Blair Brown) is an intelligent small-town girl who marries a man destined to become an astronaut as she becomes the leading counselor to the Senate Committee on Space. Dieter Kolff (Michael York) is a brilliant mechanic and technician who designs much of the equipment for German rockets and becomes the leading American rocket designer. Randy Claggett (Beau Bridges) is a Marine pilot who becomes the greatest astronaut; John Pope (Harry Hamlin) is a "straight arrow" John Glenn–type of Naval aviator and astronaut who marries Penny. Both are based on Richard F. Gordon, Jr., the astronaut who piloted Apollo 12 for the second manned lunar landing, served as a technical consultant on the miniseries, and took an acting role in it (Boxer). These are Navy or Marine Corps pilots, the type that dominates nearly all of Michener's early fiction, from 1947 to *Sayonara* of 1955, in which the ace fighter pilot is Air Force.

Leopold Strabismus, born Martin Scorcella, is the confidence man (played by David Dukes) who turns from writing plagiarized doctoral dissertations to running a clearing house for information on visitors from outer space and progresses to excelling as a hypocritical television evangelist in an America suspicious of science. Elinor Grant (Susan Anspach) is the senator's gullible wife; Rachel Mott (Melinda Dillon) is the intelligent and sophisticated wife of the engineer; Liesl Kolff (Barbara Sukowa) is the simple wife of the German technician—obese in the novel but trim in the miniseries; and Senator

Glancey (Martin Balsam) is an older politician and space advocate who hires Penny Hardesty before she marries John Pope.

In addition to magnifying the role of Senator Grant over Stanley Mott, the miniseries also expands the roles of Randy Claggett and Cindy Rhee (Maggie Han), the Korean New Journalist. The reason for the first two changes is the stature of actors Garner and Bridges; the reason for the third is clearly salacious. Further demands for erotic incidents produce other alterations in the plot and characterizations while many thoughtful and demanding themes are minimized or eliminated.

One critical axiom is that most television productions are popular, not examples of high culture, and most serious novels are less popular. The seriousness of the five-part miniseries of *Space* as a superior television production is indicated by the media critic Stanley Marcus, writing in *TV Guide* for April 13, 1985, who avowed that it offers "an acting team second to none. With characterizations that jump out of the screen, they will keep you aloft all week. What more can one say? Order up a dozen Emmys" (A-4). Although it won no awards, the television network repeated the production, omitting four hours, on Saturdays in July 1987. Writing elsewhere, Andrew J. Edelstein notes that the miniseries transcends the "campiness" of similar productions, although television is bound to emphasize "the romantic and family relationships of its characters" rather than action (4). The importance of the novel is suggested by its dominance of the *New York Times* Bestseller List for six months in 1982 and 1983 and the eminence of the paperback edition the last two months of 1983.

One line to separate popular works from those of high culture may be drawn between the common and the unusual and between the traditional and the experimental. Morse Peckham has established such a distinction in his 1965 study *Man's Rage for Chaos* (see 72, 261, 285, 291, 311), which he summarizes in his *Art and Pornography* (77-80, 90-94). Observing that "art has survival value" for the individual and society from experiencing unsatisfied expectations, "psychic insulation," and the inherent resistance or difficulty of the medium, Peckham explains: "The higher the cultural level the greater the discontinuity, the greater the psychic insulation, and the more difficult the problems offered by the semantic aspect and the more uncertain their solution" (*Art* 79). The form or content or both may be pressed to extremes, but hardly in popular works. A few examples of possible cultural survival values in advanced literature are in novels by Kafka, Joyce, Faulkner, Sartre, and Samuel Beckett.

A test pilot is dedicated to experiences with the unknown and, as Tom Wolfe explains it, with "pushing the outside of the envelope" (the limits of an aircraft's performance) and with "the ability to go up in a hurtling piece of machinery and put his hide on the line and then have the moxie, the reflexes, the experience, the coolness, to pull it back in the last yawning moment—and then go up again *the next day,* and the next . . ." (8-9, 18-19). High culture lives at the edges, popular culture at the more comfortable center. The artist may push his craft onto destruction in nihilism, the absurd, and postmodernism. In the analogy with aviation, Michener's *Space* is a jumbo jetliner connecting distant but popular destinations, neither testing a new machine nor a new course, while the televised version is an even smaller airliner traversing an even more popular route. The former, in effect, transports us from one end of the earth to the other, the latter merely from Chicago to Hollywood.

We may observe high culture in the arts generally in the order in which they repudiated Victorian prudishness— loosely from painting, sculpture, music, literature, the theater, the cinema, and then to television—from the least popular media to the most popular. Of course, along with an increased blatancy in the popular arts came a diminished decency, earnestness, and respectfulness. As novels go, Michener's are demanding and respectable popular works, never debased or pornographic even when titillating.

The novelist himself has explained in his letter that he is "quietly amused" at a "condescending classification of my novels as cheap popular fiction. Popular they certainly are. . . . [T]here will be something like ten million readers of the book." Michener goes on:

> My heavy mail divides into three categories: one-third comes from people who obviously don't read widely; one-third comes from people who would fit apparently into the [d]ead middle of our society; and one-third comes from scholars in all parts of the world who want to discuss in more detail subjects I've touched upon. I'll accept that mix, especially when one-third of ten million means that some three million readers with relatively good sense have bothered with what I've written.

> I think, however, that the denigrating phrase 'merely popular writer,' does apply justly to me, because when I write something I intuitively go back and knock out all the fancy passages. I eliminate the heavy-handed symbolism. I think that may be why all of my books are still in print— except one erudite one on politics—and why none has ever been remaindered, the only instance of its kind, [from] a study concluded some years back. My search for the pure statement seems to work.

> I enjoyed your letter and the accompanying essay. I'm proud that someone took the trouble to make the comparison. . . .

> Congenially,
> [signed] James A. Michener

"The accompanying essay" Michener refers to is a draft of this article, which did not classify the novelist as anything but a demanding and excellent popular writer. What makes *Space* a popular novel rather than one of high culture is an intriguing question; moreover, what makes the miniseries even more centrally popular than the novel

is blatantly obvious and more indicative of popular American values, at least in the popular arts and entertainment, which, even when perverse or debased, are yet only conventionally so.

Edelstein's notion that popular television is more interested in romance than action is dubious, for car chases, murders, rapes, and other examples of violence are common incidents. His idea that "campiness" is a common trait is sound, especially if we extend the idea of "camp" to include not only amusing outlandishness and the sense of the 1930s of "exaggerated effeminate mannerisms" of homosexuals (as *Webster's Ninth New Collegiate Dictionary* defines the term) but also lust, the bizarre, gratuitous titillation, hedonism, sentimentality, youth and physical vigor, patriotism, luxury, and sometimes profound love as common television themes. Daytime and prime-time melodramas reveal that campiness includes deviant psychology, sexual obsessions, escapism, immature social defiance, occasional heroism, success, and fantasies. It is sometimes even tender and sweet, but, then, *campiness* becomes synonymous with *popular.*

The paradox that popular culture can emphasize deviance and defiance and yet fail to become high culture is resolved by recognizing that such portrayals reflect only popular and even naive values without primarily attempting to refine or challenge them. O. Henry–type surprise endings are similarly popular because the discontinuity is superficial, even artificial—merely clipping the tail of the dog rather than inventing a mythical beast. The essential distinction between popular and high cultural plots and other literary traits is remarkably similar to that posed by Coleridge between the Fancy and Imagination, in which "fancy is indeed no other than a mode of memory emancipated from the order of time and space," while imagination "dissolves, diffuses, dissipates, in order to recreate; or . . . it struggles to idealize and to unify" (Ch. 13, 263).

What, then, is popular in both Michener's novel and in the miniseries? There are the themes of major historical events and human problems, social leaders and talented professionals, heroism, patriotism, lust, television evangelism, space flight, feminism, Germans, blacks, Jews, and marriage. The novel, however, emphasizes drugs, defiant children, social criticism, civil rights, religion, education, military waste, interservice rivalry, New Journalism, capitalism, politics, and homosexuality more than does the televised version, which completely ignores the issues of drugs, violent children, theology (except for televangelism), education, and military waste. Both versions equally emphasize themes on science and research, marriage, and feminism, but the long miniseries exaggerates lust, incest, physical attractiveness, the Democratic Party, Jewishness, social deviance, and sexual liberation far beyond the scope of the novel, although of these the novel ignores only incest and mutes the Democratic Party almost into nonexistence. This even though Michener has been an active Democrat and an apologist of sorts for rebellious youths, short of accepting violence (Day 138, 144-45). Clearly, some of the major revisions for television avoid major themes (like drugs, violent children, and religious piety) and exaggerate cheap romantic elements of sexual affairs, sexual liberation, and seduction. One newspaper critic writes that the miniseries "is a paean to the human libido. . . . Silliphant certainly immersed himself in the obvious symbolism of the towering Apollo rocket" ("Booster" B1).

Marcus states that Michener probably told Dick Berg that the technical focus could be suppressed, Wernher von Braun omitted, and that the characters "can get into bed as often as you feel is necessary," but the novelist disputes any such conversation. In his letter Michener begins:

Austin, Texas

16 January 1986

Dear Dr. Osterholm,

You do me the honor and courtesy in sending me a copy of your well thought-out and written article comparing the television show SPACE and my original novel on which it was based. I read your pages with pleasure and a frequent nod of my head in assent.

I found only one serious error, and it was not chargeable to you. It was, however, distasteful to me, but in such matters I rarely express any concern about what has been said about me in print. I let such things fall to their own level, and here I am merely pointing out the problem.

. . . you quote Stanley Marcus as [understanding] from Dick Berg that I gave him, Berg, authority to 'get the characters into bed as often as you feel necessary.' I never said that. It's the type of statement I doubt I would ever make. I met Berg, a fine director, briefly at a big bash in Hollywood and told him: 'I wrote a novel. You're making a television series. They're different.' Certainly, by implication I not only invited him but encouraged him to go his own way, and he did.

I never discussed the series with anyone beyond that brief statement, never saw any scripts, never had any input in any way, and certainly never had any censorship authority. I did not even know who the actors were to be nor how the series was to be constructed. At a press conference in Washington it was stated that I'd read and approved the scripts; I did not bother to correct the error, as I take little notice in my life of such errors.

However, I liked the series, judged the technical work to be exceptionally good and the actors to be even better. . . . I thought the frequent sex interpolations sometimes gratuitous and even unnecessary, and unrelated to the idea of the book. I had no objection to the dropping of the idea-rich last 150 pages; they would not have fitted well into the series as Hollywood conceived it. My attitude has always been: 'If the book is on the shelf the way I wanted it, there it stands, year after year.'

Unlike the miniseries, the novel is intelligent, credible, and realistic. It is panoramic, like most of Michener's work, with incidents too numerous for even a thirteen-hour dramatization and with characters that are recognizable, like those in one of his earliest novels, the brief *The Bridges at Toko-ri,* published in 1953, five years after he won the Pulitzer Prize for fiction with *Tales of the South Pacific,* published in 1947. *Space* is largely an answer to the question raised by Admiral George Tarrant at the end of *Bridges:* "Why is America lucky enough to have such men? . . . Where did we get such men?" (126). He is referring to Lieutenant Harry Brubaker, who, like Randy Claggett, is the pilot of a Banshee jet and fights because the duty has fallen on him. Having himself served in the U.S. Navy during World War II, Michener often emphasizes that branch. He wrote "The Forgotten Heroes of Korea" on Navy fighter pilots for the May 10, 1952, issue of *The Saturday Evening Post,* which became the inspiration for the 1954 film *Men of the Fighting Lady,* which features Louis Calhern playing the novelist on a yuletide visit to an aircraft carrier. His *Bridges* is a minor masterpiece of plotting and characterization, with the filmed version appearing in 1954.

In *Space* Senator Norman Grant, his wife, and both John and Penny are natives of the state of Fremont, a lightly disguised Colorado, and both men are Navy men. The occasional slapstick comedy of *Bridges,* however, disappears into the somber gullibility of Elinor Grant and into the bizarre confidence schemes of Leopold Strabismus, who bilks no one more than Elinor. *Strabismus,* the name assumed by the "visionary," of course, is the medical term for being cross-eyed or having a "wandering eye."

Christopher Mott, the second son of the scientist and brother to the homosexual Millard, is one character omitted from the miniseries, perhaps because his involvement with drugs in elementary school and as a pusher is too subtle for television. He dies at thirty attempting to smuggle $11 million worth of Colombian cocaine into the West Palm Beach airport at night in a stolen Lear jet without using lights or the radio (736-40). Early in the previous chapter Michener produces the most penetrating social criticism of the book as he editorializes on the son's defiance, a note ignored in television:

> The songs of his day, the patterns of dress, television's idealization of the illiterate rowdy who disrupts the classroom, sleazy newspaper stories and the dreadful pressure of one's peers, all had conspired to put [Rachel Mott's] son on trial, and she and Stanley had been too preoccupied with society's business to combat the destructive influences. (660)

Michener provokes mature thought, and television does provide some social criticism as well. The miniseries portrays homosexual Millard and draft evasion over the Vietnam War, but when television depicts misguided youths and corrupted adults, it hardly ever includes itself or the other media as part of the problem.

The novel elaborates on many popular concerns, like feelings toward science, humanism, confidence men, education, visions of space flight, and communication skills. It touches on the culture of Swedes in Worcester, Massachusetts, (125-28, 348-49) and the sleaziness of California (336-38, 354-59). Much more than the miniseries, the novel depicts a growing anti-intellectuality in a populace of backward thinkers with anti-scientific and anti-humanistic attitudes. It emphasizes a devotion to modern art, classical music, and Swedish folk art as valuable contributions to a household (129-34). It also stresses the importance placed on the humanities by the German scientists (141-42), debates on contemporary theater and films by fighter pilots in Korea, with Claggett instructing Pope on an interpretation of Shakespeare's *Othello* (191-96), and Pope's early dedication to astronomy (60-65). Pope becomes a professor of astronomy as his mentor, Professor Anderssen, is denounced by the masses as an irreligious scientist, targeted in the anti-humanistic crusade of Dr. Strabismus, while the aged professor explains to his former students that education depends upon willing and eager minds and souls (701, 707-09). English instructors would profit from passages in which Claggett explains to Pope that two-thirds of a test pilot's skills are clear communication (283-84, 286, 294, 296, 298) and from another in which a counselor explains that verbal skills may be the decisive factor in selecting astronauts (403). The one skill devalued in a test pilot in Tom Wolfe's *The Right Stuff* is the verbal (96, 119). Education, like the Orient and brotherhood, is another staple of Michener.

The novel exposes anti-humanistic values, especially in Leopold Strabismus, who turns late in the book into a scheming evangelist in support of a simpler life opposed to the terrifying challenges of progress (677-83, 702-07, 753-61, 775-83). Strabismus denounces humanism, the idea of evolution, and all he calls "atheistic humanism," while practicing book burnings and attempting to ban science, with success in a few states (656, 676-83, 702-07, 734-35, 752-61, 774-81, 796, 801-03). Although the miniseries develops this theme well, it ignores the nuances, such as the evangelist's actual respect for science and Darwin and Stanley Mott's increasing understanding that Strabismus is partly correct (758-60, 800-05). The finest portrayal in the novel is that of the scientist, son of a Methodist minister, accepting the limits of science as the proper concern of society and the beginning of religion. Again, this is all too subtle for the superficialities of television drama.

Michener is more devoted to reportage and didacticism than to art. His friend Professor Day even compares him to muckrackers and crusaders like Jack London and Upton Sinclair (17, 33, 165). One reporter quotes the novelist as saying that NASA officials were not happy with his portrayal of the astronauts at the Bali Hai Motel in Cocoa Beach, but he had to be honest even as an advocate of the space program (Watson). Yet, behind Michener's realism wafts the scent of a distant Bali Hai calling his reader to a more compassionate life, an odor that turns rancid in television.

In the miniseries Strabismus is merely a debased hypocrite, and the Democratic Party, Jewish-Americans, and

sensuality are inflated. It is insignificant that the miniseries places Pope and Claggett in the same Navy flight class and that it omits the extension of the novel into other NASA programs following the death of Claggett on the far side of the moon and into the political demise of Senator Grant in 1982 with the election of Penny Pope, even though these concerns cover the final fifth or 150 pages of the novel. One of the major alterations is depicting jet flying as a mere matter of skill and raw courage, while the novel captures its ecstasy that approaches religion (180-98). Another is that Liesl proposes marriage in Germany to Dieter, but he proposes in the book (83). Grant becomes more powerful and has a continuing affair with Penny Pope, which she dismisses as a "wrestle in the mud like animals," but this baseness is competely absent from the novel, where Penny remains faithful and the marriage secure, although there is a difficult moment after her husband spends three harmless days in Australia with Cindy Rhee (663-76). Television also invents a long estrangement for the Popes. Silliphant changes the character of Grant because he is "too consistently nice" in the novel and good television needs villains (Boxer). In the miniseries Penny is nearly raped by her stepfather, but there is no such character in the book. Some television writers, it seems, project their own obsessive sexuality onto the home screen, perhaps in the attempt to liberate public standards to suit their own tastes or interests.

Senator Grant is a Republican in the book but a Democrat in television, apparently an accommodation to the personal political persuasion of James Garner, according to Andy Meisler (10). Penny becomes not only more sexually liberated and looser in television, she becomes the strength of a weaker husband. Perhaps the images of strong women and weak men are popular, as Penny needs men less and uses them more, although she does come to feel a bit guilty. The Korean journalist who writes for a Japanese newspaper has more affairs in the novel, and John Pope escapes her in both versions, but in television she brazenly tells Claggett that she might not only try to sleep with each of the Solid Six astronauts, she would please them all simultaneously if Claggett wishes.

In the miniseries Strabismus (when he was Martin Scorcella) has sexual romps with the daughter of the dean of a university in New York and with the wife of a professor at Yale before going to California, events not in the novel at all, where this period is covered in barely two pages (245-46). These scenes also appear much earlier in the miniseries, as Silliphant hastened to invent them. In the novel all of Strabismus' sexual escapades occur in California, where he founds the Universal Space Associates, gulls Elinor Grant, and leads her daughter, Marcia (Jennifer Runyon), into bed. He plays fast and loose with Marcia in the novel, changed in the miniseries apparently because the popular mind could not abide her living so long in a tenuous relationship. In the book she shares the mastermind with sixteen-year-olds for years and endures a terrifying abortion before they marry (315-19, 334-38, 478-82, 580-85, 676-79). The miniseries also omits Strabismus' intermediate institutes, the University of Space and Aviation and the University of Spiritual Americans, formed after the Universal Space Associates (obsessed with flying saucers) and prior to the United Scripture Alliance (which is, for some reason, "Scriptures" in television) (245, 678, 702, 753). The University of Space and Aviation in the novel issues phony advanced degrees, one to Dieter Kolff (334-35, 349-50). The confidence man is both clearer and more subtle in the novel, where he seeks power and vengeance on Yale-type students and professors who condescend toward him (705-06), but in television his superficial motives are merely sensuality and wealth.

The sexual inventions for the miniseries are astounding. Others include the love-making by Sam Cottage (Robbie Weaver), a student at the Sun Study Center in Boulder, Colorado, with his demanding girlfriend and the rape of Liesl Kolff by General Helmut Funkhauser (Wolf Kohler) as he interrogates her toward the end of the war. In television the general is soon shot by Liesl as she, Dieter, and the general try to reach the American lines, but in the book Funkhauser is more principled and becomes another German expert in the American space effort, albeit as an executive for a private corporation, Allied Aviation.

As the televised version is anti-German, it is also somewhat pro-Jewish, for the novel has no Jewish characters other than the secretly half-Jewish Strabismus. Television invents an interview between Dieter Kolff and Himmler (Hitler in the novel), who is portrayed as a bumbler in a badly cut uniform supplied by Albert Speer. It also invents an elaborate Jewish wedding in which Stanley Kolff (Dieter's son Magnus in the novel) marries a Jewish girl, a wife unidentified in the novel. In television Liesl tells her new daughter-in-law that she is loved, but no one tells the Germans they are loved. However justifiable it is to emphasize favorable attitudes toward Jews in our popular culture, which yet contains traces of anti-Semitism, it is an overt manipulation of the novel somewhat at the expense of the Germans. Many Americans denigrate Germans, especially any soldier of World War II. On the *Donahue* discussion show televised April 18, 1985, the morning of the final installment of the miniseries, many in the audience stated, concerning President Reagan's controversial intentions of laying a wreath at the German military cemetery at Bitburg, that honoring any German soldier honors the Nazi Party and the despicable SS.

Blacks also get short shrift in television compared to the novel, for the third astronaut (Jonathan Goldsmith) on the voyage to the far side of the moon is in the novel an important black scientist, Dr. Paul Linley, "whitened" and diminished in television. Both versions, however, have one significant black character: Gawain Butler (Dick Anthony Williams), another Navy shipmate of Grant's and later a Detroit educator and adviser to the senator (40, 120, 203-05, 464-67). One excellent scene in the miniseries has Richard Gordon, playing the Capsule

Communicator (CapCom) from earth to the fictional Apollo 18, crying when the two astronauts on the surface of the moon die, in a performance that touched Bruce Dern (Durden F14).

The miniseries exaggerates voyeurism, luxury, and hedonism beyond the scope of the novel, in which many leaders are at least dedicated and more deserving of their honors. The video version, on the other hand, abounds in simplicities and the ill-formed notions that fame is importance, wealth is success, and pleasure is happiness. Michener's themes on humanism and brotherhood lie wanting. From the miniseries we have evidence that popular television is, at least in these ideas, juvenile and simple-minded. Such immaturity is reinforced by trivializing pseudorealism. Michener's novel rises in intelligence to the top of the popular culture from where the wide expanse of high culture may at least be surveyed.

Michener's ambitious popular novel, then, is more important and more realistic than the miniseries and its emphasis on escapism, lust, and puerile themes. The television production does do its public duty in briefly advocating civil rights, scientific research, feminism, and education, especially in a final speech supporting such values delivered by Laurence Luckinbill, the narrator, but these themes are undercut by the sensual portrayals and mindless characters of the dramatization. The happy or uplifting stock ending remains superficial.

Michener's novel has modernist traits of ruthless realism and absurdities. General Funkhauser, for example, twice orders Dieter Kolff shot, but both times rescinds the orders, to his ultimate benefit as he uses Kolff to escape the Russians to the American lines (76-80, 99-102). When Norman Grant first campaigns for the Senate in 1946, his father-in-law (a supportive Ralph Bellamy in television) and his wife refuse to campaign for him (117-18). His campaign manager, Tim Finnerty (James Sutorius), the former yeoman of Grant's ill-fated destroyer escort during the war, is an Irish Catholic Democrat from Boston (shades of John F. Kennedy) for a Republican campaign in a Waspish Western state (24, 119). Later Dieter and Liesl defend Funkhauser against charges of being a Nazi, of illegally employing his large automobile as a taxicab, and of transporting prostitutes across the Mexican border. The Kolffs proclaim his value to the space program and his high character (153-60). One good line comparing the American and Soviet space programs in the novel has Grant telling Penny in 1958 that "our Germans are as good as their Germans" (327), words given to Mott in television.

The novel has a few errors. Paul Stidham, Elinor's father, is first called Frank (113, 117), and the novelist calls a half-track a "semi-tank" and alters the pilot's common phrase for dying in a crash from "buying the farm" to the uncommon "buying the ranch" (107, 289, 636). He overuses the word *elegant* (e.g., 389, 572, 598, 709), and challenges credibility a few times, as with Funkhauser's belief that he needs Dieter only to approach the American lines but not for American acceptance. Another is with the super-intelligent Stanley Mott, the aeronautical engineer who has mastered both atomic power and rocketry, who expects Dieter to abscond with papers on the German atomic bomb (7, 10, 101, 104, 108). The miniseries is more credible on this point as Mott is amazed to learn the Dieter has stolen the plans to the A-10, a rocket larger than the A-4 (or V-2). Tucker Thompson (Thomas in television, played by G. D. Spradlin), the editor of a magazine with an exclusive on the Solid Six astronauts, as *Life* had with the seven Mercury astronauts, is ludicrously convinced that competing magazines would delight in scandals on only the Solid Six to diminish the value of his contract without tarnishing the reputations of other astronauts (380-81, 410, 547, 645, 668, 673). The novel offers the lame solution of loosening bolts that fasten a dosimeter to an orbiting satellite by squirting oil on them (516)—in the heatless conditions of space that would turn any oil to stone.

Such are a few momentary lapses in the novel that may establish the legends of early space explorations. Michener reflects his own expansive style when he describes the Korean journalist's technique of writing as imitating the laborious "underpainting" of exquisite Korean ceramics (489, 609)—Michener is also a popularizer of Oriental art (Day 22, 126-27). The novelist studies his subjects minutely, which serves as his "underpainting," and produces informative and intricate novels. The television miniseries suffers from the absence of depth and scarcely creates any legend at all, primarily just ephemeral titillation. Television resides in the realm of "Single vision," to allude to the "double vision" of Michener's Strabismus and to the phrase in William Blake's poem "With Happiness Stretch'd Across the Hills" (see line 27-28, 57, 83-88).

John and Penny Pope would sing another song by Blake on their cross-country automobile trips in the novel, with lines on "Arrows of desire" and "Chariots of fire." Identified by Michener (304-05, 563), the lines are from Blake's "And Did Those Feet" (lines 9-12) from his Preface to *Milton*. The succeeding and concluding quatrain expresses Michener's own vision:

> I will not cease from Mental Fight,
> Nor shall my Sword sleep in my hand,
> Till we have built Jerusalem
> In England's green & pleasant Land.

Michener and Blake celebrate a larger and eternal vision of religion, with the novelist generally achieving the "threefold" vision of poetic insight in *Space*. That Michener even contemplates Blake's "fourfold" vision (with stages from materialism and rationality, to experience and sexuality, to pastoral innocence, up to imaginative integration with the universe) is intriguing and revealing for one with a theme that is essentially humanistic, hardly mystical. The miniseries settles for triteness, campiness, which is average television, but the novel, although popular and not a work secure in high culture, is excellent. And even fair television is surpassed by even a mediocre novel.

The nine-hour version of the miniseries telecast by CBS-TV on Saturdays through July 1987 improves the miniseries by excluding the first three hours and one of the remaining ten. The abbreviation loses the roots of the story in World War II, but it also omits the inventions of Penny's stepfather, a debased General Funkhauser, Strabismus' early affairs, and some of the Grant—Penny Pope affair. The revision emphasizes her sense of remorse and further focuses the story on the space program.

One final comment by Michener in his letter on the miniseries:

> Specifically, I thought Television did much better for my novel than the movies did for Tom Wolfe's excellent non-fiction book. Certainly Television handled the Washington scenes better than the Movies handled President Johnson—more accurately, I mean—and my [story on] Television helped create a more honest picture of the astronauts than the Movies did when doing the tremendous damage they did to John Glenn.

James Michener is nothing if not a pursuer of brotherhood, truth, and accuracy in their wayward forms and elusive flights, and these are captured securely in the novel, hardly in the trivialized miniseries. If the miniseries does not grossly distort Washington politics, it is because it is already simple-minded enough. If the miniseries does not grossly distort the Solid Six astronauts, it is because they are already popular enough. The televised version certainly demeans intelligent experience and morality. Honest novels and titillating network television are the common natures of the popular beasts, and with this novel and miniseries we see the former at its best and the latter near its standard vacuousness.

WORKS CITED

Blake, William. "And Did Those Feet" and "With Happiness Stretch'd Across the Hills." *Complete Writings,* Ed. Geoffrey Keynes. Rev. London: Oxford UP, 1971. 480-81, 816-18.

"Booster Rockets Prevent 'Space' from Fizzling Out." *Atlanta Journal* April 12, 1985. Newsbank: Film and TV 1984-85, 11:116 B1-2.

Boxer, Tim. "Tube Launches Space Program." *New York Post* April 10, 1985. Newsbank: Film and TV 1984-85, 11:105 F11.

Coleridge, Samuel Taylor. *Biographia Literaria. Selected Poetry and Prose.* Ed. Donald A. Stauffer. New York: Modern, 1951. 109-428.

Day, A. Grove. *James Michener.* 2nd ed. Boston: Twayne, 1977.

Dougan, Michael. "Space." *San Francisco Examiner* April 14, 1985. Newsbank: Film and TV 1984-85, 11:116 A4-6.

Durden, Douglas. "Dern Carves Out 'Space' on TV." *Richmond* (Va.) *Times-Dispatch* April 12, 1985. Newsbank: Film and TV 1984-85, 11:105 F13-14.

Edelstein, Andrew J. "Can 'Space' Bring Minis Back to Earth?" Daytona Beach, Fla., *Sunday News-Journal TV Log* April 14, 1985: 4.

Marcus, Stanley. "News and Previews." *TV Guide* April 13, 1985: A4.

Meisler, Andy. "Will This Colossus Fly?" *TV Guide* April 13, 1985: 8-11.

Michener, James A. *The Bridges at Toko-ri.* 1953. New York: Fawcett Crest, n.d.

———*Space.* 1982. New York: Fawcett Crest, 1983.

———Letter to the author. Jan. 16, 1986.

Peckham, Morse. *Man's Rage for Chaos: Biology, Behavior, and the Arts.* 1965. New York: Schocken, 1967.

———*Art and Pornography: An Experiment in Explanation.* 1969. New York: Harper, 1971.

Space. CBS-TV. April 14-18, 1985. Abridged July 1987.

Watson, Keith. "Seeking Their Own Sense of Space." *Houston Post* April 9, 1985. Newsbank: Film and TV 1984-85, 11:105 F12.

Wolfe, Tom. *The Right Stuff.* 1979. New York: Bantam, 1980.

Charles H. Helmetag

SOURCE: "The Lost Honor of Kathryn Beck: A German Story on American Television," in *Literature/Film Quarterly,* Vol. 13, No. 4, 1985, pp. 240-44.
[*In the following essay, Helmetag examines the American television adaptation of Heinrich Böll's* Die verlorene Ehre der Katharina Blum *(1974) as* The Lost Honor of Kathryn Beck *(1984).*]

Heinrich Böll's story *Die verlorene Ehre der Katharina Blum* was published in German in 1974.[1] According to the author, the book was inspired by the treatment of Peter Brückner, a professor in Hannover, because of his alleged association with the Baader-Meinhof group.[2] An English translation by Leila Vennewitz appeared in 1975.[3] The work gained an even wider audience with the release of Volker Schlöndorff's film adaptation that same year.[4] The Schlöndorff film has been the subject of several scholarly articles.[5] On Tuesday, January 24, 1984 *The Lost Honor of Kathryn Beck,* an American adaptation made expressly for television, was shown on the CBS television network, giving Böll's story its widest exposure to date.

In Böll's story Katharina Blum is a decent, industrious young housekeeper living in West Berlin who attends a party where she meets a young man named Ludwig Götten, who she later learns is wanted by the police. Katherina and Götten spend the night together in her apartment. The next morning police storm the apartment and, when they discover Götten has fled, treat Katharina as if she herself were a criminal. She is interrogated repeatedly by the police and slandered by the newspaper *Die Zeitung.* Within a few short days her life is destroyed. She agrees to meet with the unscrupulous *Zeitung* reporter Tötges, calmly shoots him and turns herself over to the authorities.

As in *Ende einer Dienstfahrt* (1966) and *Gruppenbild mit Dame* (1971), Böll uses here the device of the objective narrator who has pieced his report together from various, sometimes conflicting sources.[6] In order to prove the veracity and objectivity of his information, the *Katharina Blum* narrator lists his sources in the first paragraph. The presentation of the story's events on film is "necessarily more direct" than Böll's narrative, to borrow a phrase from William and Joan Magretta's analysis of Schlöndorff's film version of *Katharina Blum*[7] Both the German film and the American television version present the bulk of the events in strict chronological order. Both permit us, literally, to see Katharina, who is never directly described in the story, and to witness the things that happen to her, some of which are dispensed with in a few sentences in the story. The reporter is also more visually present in the two film versions, while in Böll's story he was more of an abstraction, an allegorical representative of the media at their most ruthless.[8] Most of these differences stem from the essential difference in medium: prose narrative and film.

Böll's story attacked the brutal destructiveness of yellow journalism of the *Bild-Zeitung* school and indicted West German society for failing to protect the dignity of the individual. The Schlöndorff film expands the themes of the story (or at least makes them more obvious) to include the "terrorism of institutions"[9] not just the press, but also the police, the judiciary, business, the Church and, "formed by them, public opinion."[10] Moreover, since the victim of this terrorism is not Peter Brückner but a woman and her persecutors are all men, the film also served as an example of the modern feminist film.

The feminist outlook is even more central in the American television adaptation. *The Lost Honor of Kathryn Beck* was produced by Marlo Thomas, who also stars in the title role. Thomas, one of the leading feminists in the American entertainment industry, suggested the story to CBS and personally recruited Kris Kristofferson to play the role of the suspected terrorist called Ben Cole in the American production, a part considerably smaller than that of the reporter or the police interrogator. Thomas' goals in producing the film, according to a newspaper report, were "to demonstrate that witnesses like Beck, who may or may not have relevant information to supply, are not granted the same full legal rights as suspects like Cole" and to show that female witnesses are particularly vulnerable.[11]

The *Karneval* atmosphere and the pointed reference to the *Bild-Zeitung* make Böll's story and the Schlöndorff film peculiarly German, as does the portrayal of the strong West German reaction to terrorism. The American television adaptation written by Karl Miller changes the names of all the characters and transfers the setting from mid-1970s Berlin to a small midwestern American town in the 1980s (judging by Kathryn's late model automobile, which is ravaged by the police in their search for evidence). Whereas Götten was allegedly associated with the Baader-Meinhof group, there is a vague reference to the underground Weathermen organization in connection with Cole. Given these changes, the film is surprisingly effective, thanks to excellent acting and the direction of Simon Langton,[12] which in keeping with the style of Böll's story leans toward a documentary approach. Schlöndorff portrays the events of the story more subjectively from Katharina's point of view, a technique evident in departures from the novel such as her presence on the scene of Götten's capture and the emotional meeting of the lovers as prisoners.[13] Langton, however, strives for the impression of greater objectivity (seen in his frequent use of medium and full shots), showing the heroine and what happens to her from the outside.

Both the Schlöndorff film and the American television movie make certain departures from Böll's story while remaining quite faithful to the spirit of the book. Schlöndorff introduces four new sequences: the opening scenes involving the filming of Götten's activities by police photographers, the rendezvous between Katharina and the businessman arranged by Pater Urbanus (designed to show the collusion of capitalism and the Church), the meeting between Katharina and Götten as they are being taken to jail and the epilogue which portrays the reporter's funeral. Although the television version Americanizes the setting and characters, it invents no major new episodes. There are a few new, economical early scenes to establish Kathryn's occupation, her industriousness and her loneliness and reserve as well as some very effective scenes from the perspective of the police before they storm her apartment. The TV movie also has the police enter while she is still nude and in bed rather than in the kitchen in her bathrobe, and it adds some symbolic American popular music at her cousin's party.[14]

Like the German film, the American version presents in some detail scenes which the book only mentions. One is the reporter's "interview" with Katharina's mother in the hospital. The scene is presented more abruptly by Schlöndorff with no preliminary establishing shot, underscoring the heartlessness of Tötges' behavior. The TV version leads up to the "interview" by showing Catton trying and eventually succeeding in getting into the old woman's room. In Böll's story the reporter claims to have used "the simplest trick in the book," namely disguising himself as a painter; the American version retains this costume while Schlöndorff's reporter opts for a more obvious surgical gown.

Both films allow several shots for the "terrorist's" capture by the police, an event only mentioned by Böll. In both film versions the massive array of military equipment and personnel dispatched to capture a single man recalls the SWAT team which invaded the heroine's little apartment and the helplessness of the individual against seemingly anonymous authorities.

In both the Schlöndorff film and the television version the police are portrayed even more clearly than in the written work as the heroine's unjust persecutors. In both productions, however, steps were taken to portray the police with reasonable accuracy. The eerie, helmeted military uniforms worn by the men who storm Katharina's apartment in the German film, for example, are authentic, bought from the same company that supplies them for the police.[15] To satisfy the network, Marlo Thomas obtained an affadavit from state officials in Illinois, the setting for the TV movie, stating that what happens to the heroine could actually take place there. Thomas also had police present as advisors for the scenes involving police.[16] The storming of Kathryn's apartment and the surrounding of the summer house where her lover is hiding are both effectively staged, somewhat reminiscent of the scene where helmeted scientists invade the house where the incapacitated extraterrestrial being has been located in *E.T.* and the combing of Karen Silkwood's house by similarly dressed plant investigators in *Silkwood*. These are the anonymous authorities who outnumber, dwarf and intimidate the individual, not only in the 1980s, but even in stories of Böll's 1950 collection of stories *Wanderer, kommst du nach Spa. . . .*

It is, however, the dry, detached modus operandi of the police, the politicians and, above all, the reporter Catton which make the television film so frightening—and so frighteningly real. The police interrogate and subtly threaten Kathryn in an unfeeling monotone. They order sandwiches and coffee in the same tone of voice as they sit in their car eavesdropping on the woman's lovemaking by means of an electronic listening device.

An important departure from Böll's story in the TV version deals with the reporter's character. Catton, though still unscrupulous in pursuing a story, is somehow less obnoxious than his conterpart Tötges in the book and the Schlöndorff film. Surprisingly, the TV version barely suggests that the reporter tries to seduce Kathryn, while his proposition in both the book and the German film inspires a grotesque pun on Katharina's part, which almost implies that he has driven her over the brink:

> Er sagte: "Na, Blümchen, was machen wir zwei denn jetzt? . . . Was guckst du mich denn so entgeistert an, mein Blümelein—ich schlage vor, daß wir jetzt erst einmal bumsen." Nun, inzwischen war ich bei meiner Handtasche, und er ging mir an die Kledage, und ich dachte: "Bumsen, meinetwegen," und ich hab die Pistole rausgenommen und sofort auf ihn geschossen.[17]

Considering the preceding scenes, it seems unlikely that the American adaptors were making concessions in the murder scene to meet network guidelines of taste.[18] Perhaps it was simply the difficulty of finding a decent translation which caused the Americans to settle for Catton's merely toying verbally with Kathryn. Leila Vennewitz' translation of the passage does not seem appropriate for the Catton character:

> He said: "Well, Blumikins, what'll we do now, you and me? . . . Why do you look at me like that, Blumikins, as if you're scared out of your wits? How about us having a bang for a start?" Well, by this time I had my hand in my purse, and as he went for my dress I thought: "Bang, if that's what you want," and I pulled out the pistol and shot him then and there.[19]

The omission weakens the final scene, since the reporter's blunt advances to Katharina in Böll's story underscore his complete lack of respect for her as an individual. In his view, women have significance only as news stories or as sexual prey.

In both the story and the Schlöndorff film the reporter Tötges appears as Katharina's principal antagonist. Just as the police regard the need to break a case as justification for their treatment of Katharina, the reporter thinks nothing of hounding the woman and her dying mother and distorting the truth for the sake of a story. In Americanizing Böll's book, the TV version foregoes associating the reporter with one of the tabloids sold in super markets and replaces the nationally sold *Bild-Zeitung* with a local newspaper called ironically (since it pillories an innocent bystander) the *Ledger-Citizen.*[20] In this age of electronic media when wars, assassinations and grieving loved ones are presented close-up on the evening television news, it might not have distorted the novel to make Catton a TV reporter, but here again the TV film is faithful to the novel. Böll's reporter uses the written word to distort the facts. In literary works, essays and interviews Böll has often expressed his respect for language and his disdain for those who misuse it,[21] for, as the German name of the *Zeitung* reporter suggests and both film versions demonstrate, in unscrupulous hands the written word becomes a deadly weapon.

Böll's story ends with Katharina's own detailed written account of Tötges's murder. The Schlönderff film, on the other hand, ends with a eulogy at the reporter's funeral defending freedom of the press and with an ironic "disclaimer" about the *Bild-Zeitung* which Böll placed at the beginning of his book. The final scene of the American television film, in contrast to both the book and the German film, shows Kathryn surrounded by police and media representatives as she arrives at the police station. The scene ends with a slow zoom in to a grainy image of her anguished face, a freeze-frame which goes to the black-and-white of a newspaper photograph. This final tightly framed shot graphically summarizes in cinematic terms the basic theme of Böll's story: an innocent bystander trapped and robbed of her human dignity by the authorities and the press.

NOTES

[1] Heinrich Böll, *Die verlorene Ehre der Katharina Blum oder Wie Gewalt entstehen und wohin sie führen kann* (Cologne: Kiepenheuer & Witsch, 1974).

[2] Dieter Zilligen, "Interview Heinrich Böll," in *Bücherjournal*, NDR Television, October 19, 1974, quoted in Hanno Beth, "Rufmord und Mord: die publizistische Dimension der Gewalt. Zu Heinrich Bölls Erzählung 'Die verlorene Ehre der Katharina Blum'," in *Heinrich Böll. Eine Einführung in das Gesamtwerk in Einzelinterpretationen,* ed. Hanno Beth. 2nd edition (Königstein: Scriptor, 1974), pp. 71-72.

[3] Heinrich Böll, *The Lost Honor of Katharina Blum or: How Violence Develops and Where It Can Lead,* translated by Leila Vennewitz (New York: McGraw-Hill, 1975).

[4] The film was directed by Schlöndorff and Margarethe von Trotta from a screenplay by Schlöndorff.

[5] E.g., Lester D. Friedman, "Cinematic Techniques in *The Lost Honor of Katharina Blum,*" *Literature/Film Quarterly,* 7 (1979), 244-52: David Head, "'Der Autor muss respektiert werden'—Schlöndorff/Trotta's *Die verlorene Ehre der Katharina Blum* and Brecht's Critique of Film Adaptation," *German Life and Letters,* 32 (1979), 248-64; William R. Magretta and Joan Magretta, "Story and Discourse. Schlöndorff and von Trotta's *The Lost Honor of Katharina Blum* (1975). From the Novel by Heinrich Böll," in *Modern European Filmmakers and the Art of Adaptation,* ed. Andrew Horton and Joan Magretta (New York: Frederick Ungar, 1981), pp. 278-94.

[6] Böll has used the concept of an artist's pattern ("Malvorlage") in connection with the form of *Katharina Blum.* Heinrich Böll/Christian Linder, *Drei Tage im März: Ein Gespräch* (Cologne: Kiepenheuer & Witsch, 1975), p. 67. Cf. *Handbuch der deutschen Erzählung,* ed. Karl Konrad Polheim (Düsseldorf: Bagel, 1981), p. 540.

[7] Magretta, p. 285.

[8] For a more detailed discussion of the Tötges character in the Schlöndorff film, see Magretta, pp. 285-286.

[9] Volker Schlöndorff, "De Toerless à Katharina Blum," *Juene Cinéma,* No. 94, April 1976, p. 11. Quoted in Magretta, p. 280.

[10] *Idem.*

[11] Lee Winfrey, "Telemovie Tells Story of a Lost Reputation," *Philadelphia Inquirer,* January 24, 1984, p. 6-C. On the feminist concerns raised by the German film version, see Magretta, p. 281.

[12] Langton is best known as the director of the television miniseries *Smiley's People, Kathryn Beck* is also distinguished as the first television film of cinematographer Gordon Willis.

[13] For a discussion of Schlöndorff's use of visual symbolism and imagery, see the article by Friedman in note 5.

[14] Kathryn and Cole dance to a recording of Roberta Flack's "Making Love to You" and Kathryn observes that she likes the singer's other record "Killing Me Softly." The dance serves as foreplay for the couple's lovemaking while the reference to the other song provides those familiar with the lyrics ("Killing me softly with his songs, Telling my whole life with his words. . . .") with an ironic foreshadowing of the reporter's exploitation of the heroine.

[15] Magretta, p. 290.

[16] Winfrey.

[17] *Die verlorene Ehre der Katharina Blum*, p. 185.

[18] Not surprisingly, the police interrogator's first question to Katharina: "Hat er dich gefickt?" has been toned down to "Did you sleep with him?" This alteration, however, does not seriously lessen the question's impact on Katharina or the authorities' assault on the privacy of an innocent person.

[19] *The Lost Honor of Katharina Blum*, p. 137.

[20] A key to Katharina's guilt or innocence in Böll's eyes is to be found in a statement which the author made in an interview which predates the publication of Katharina Blum. Here he maintained that someone who conceals another person from the authorities may have committed a punishable act and be subject to the law, but he is by no means a criminal. *Stern*, February 17, 1972, p. 190. For another view of Katharina's innocence, see J. C. Franklin. "Alienation and the Retention of the Self: The Heroines of *Der gute Mensch von Sezuan, Abschied von Gestern,* and *Die verlorene Ehre der Katharina Blum,*" *Mosaic*, 12 (1979), iv, 87-98.

[21] Cf. Theodore Ziolkowski, "The Inner Veracity of Form," *Books Abroad,* 47 (1973), p. 22.

Derek Paget

SOURCE: "Screening *The Mill on the Floss*: David Edgar and Peter Hall's George Eliot," in *Critical Survey*, Vol. 3, No. 3, 1991, pp. 275-82.

[In the following essay, Paget discusses preparations for a television adaptation of George Eliot's The Mill on the Floss, *noting particularly issues relating to the development of the script, the collaboration of the writer and director, and financial and technical aspects of production.]*

INTRODUCTION—ADAPTATIONS AIN'T WHAT THEY USED T'BE

When I began work on this article, my intention was to follow the process by which a front-rank modern dramatist (David Edgar) and a key post-war theatre director (Sir Peter Hall) adapted a major nineteenth-century novelist's work (George Eliot's *The Mill on the Floss*), then televised it via the agency of a national broadcasting institution (the BBC). My presuppositions were two-fold: the first was that the article would essentially be about the *reading* of a novel inevitably offered through adaptation. If all readings of novels involve mental *prioritising* of meanings disclosed to the reader, 'transformation artists'[1] engaged in the translation of one medium into another visualise, indeed physicalise, their priorities in their eventual re-production. When texts shift into performances, all hint of possibility, all interpretative hedging, must necessarily give way to the achieved reality of the final product. Anything critically *un*certain must be made certain; on the subject of Tom and Maggie's demise in the Floss flood, for example, David Edgar observed:

> As an adaptor, you can't take the view that the flood is a mistake, as David Lodge does, without rewriting the end.[2]

Although much of the subsequent debate about adaptations tends to concern their 'truth to the original', this matters not so much, perhaps, as the continuation of an ongoing debate about the meanings inherent in the 'host text'.

My second presupposition was that the project was going to become one more example of a minor genre, the Televised Classic Serial, which from the 1950s onwards has been a feature of our cultural life. Tending historically to occupy a hallowed 'family slot' (often early on Sunday evenings), its scheduling always carried more than a hint of Sunday solemnity—as well as being 'entertainment', it was also profoundly *serious*. What was being taken seriously was, after all, the literary part of our English 'heritage'. Looking back, those Sunday evenings watching *David Copperfield, Pride and Prejudice* and the rest were Preliminary Courses in canonical works of the Victorian period. If Hall/Edgar's two-part adaptation had reached our television screens by Christmas 1990 (which seemed possible), I was confident that readers of this periodical who were studying *The Mill on the Floss* would encounter it as their teachers strove to make the text accessible. After all, what better way of 'getting to know the story' of a long book has there ever been?

The project to make a television version of *The Mill on the Floss* was Hall's idea. His choice of David Edgar as adapter was the result of an interest in the playwright's 1985 Dorchester 'community play' *Entertaining Strangers* (performed by the National Theatre at the Cottesloe in 1987). The BBC were initially favourable to the idea, and Edgar's first draft of the adaptation, in two ninety-minute episodes, was with them by March 1990. Hall hoped to receive their go-ahead in time for autumn filming, and was aiming for the Christmas 1990 schedules. By summer 1990, however, the project was stalled because the BBC had turned the treatment down; the cold winds of economic change meant, in Edgar's words, that 'the BBC's present plans did not include expensive two-part adaptations of long nineteenth century novels'. *The Mill on the Floss* project is now dormant, although in an interview in the *Observer* on 12 August 1990, Hall mentioned it as one of several possible *film* ventures vaguely scheduled for 'the next two years' (Edgar has 'cobbled together a single-episode version, just to show it can be done as a film'). Having seemed an institution which time could not make mortal, the 'market place' has intervened and Classic Serial adaptations (of George Eliot anyway) are surplus to requirements.

The reasons for this high-level 'editing' of George Eliot are worthy of scrutiny, disclosing as they do the symbiotic relationship between the economic and the aesthetic. The pun on 'screen' in my title has therefore taken on a different, and wider, dimension from the obvious one (the thing onto which a film or programme is 'projected' / that which is 'sorted' or 'selected' in adaptation). For George Eliot has been 'screened off', or 'screened out' in a far more drastic selection process. While the project may yet see the light of day, it also seems that television adaptations, like nostalgia in the famous joke, are not what they used to be.

PARADISE LOST?—HALL, EDGAR AND THE COMMUNITY PAST

Amongst the items marking out Sir Peter Hall's career is a film he made in 1974 called *Akenfield.* Adapted from Ronald Blythe's 1969 'oral history' of an East Anglian village community, this film was a kind of personal homage from Hall to his own past. The film articulates two interconnected myths which resonate with *The Mill on the Floss,* and which also drew Hall to the community-inflected *Entertaining Strangers* and its author. There is the myth of an idealised 'rural past' always already disappearing under the inexorable pressure of technological and industrial 'progress'. In *The Mill on the Floss,* for example, Mr Tulliver's folk-craft world is under pressure from the enterprise culture of St Oggs, a culture through which his son Tom, wheeler-dealing successfully with Bob Jakin, ironically repossesses the Mill in Book 7, chapter 1. In *Akenfield,* Blythe remarks that the testimony contained in his book 'covers half a century of farming slump and the beginning of what is being called the second agricultural revolution'. Blythe presents a nuanced view of this world, acknowledging 'a conservatism as heavy as the clay lands themselves' under pressure from the 'new villagers' and from new farming methods.[3]

The other, interconnected, myth is of personal 'roots' which are somehow recoverable through quasi-ritualistic acts of homage to precise *localities.* Like the phenomenon of the community play itself, these artistic imperatives represent an interest in the past as the repository of certain *values* which are threatened by the galvanic forces of historical shifts.[4] 'Communities', it is argued, shape us and we *need* to return to them from time to time to renew ourselves. Change from the outside threatens them, and by extension *us.* Part of the semi-autobiographical dimension of *The Mill on the Floss* is an articulation of this myth, which paradoxically speaks of *belonging* as it simultaneously asserts alienated *difference.* Blythe is equally strong on this idea, claiming that the

newcomer 'never becomes joined' to the village, but that 'the atavistic thread, whether he likes it or not, remains unbroken for the [old] village man'. Blythe's use of *individuals* (different from characters) and their testimony about a twentieth-century community/paradise lost marks a privileging of semi-documentary authenticity over fictional invention, and this tendency was accentuated in Hall's film.

For Hall, the past is a railwayman's cottage in a remote East Anglian village not unlike the one in Blythe's book. He talked about this recently, and at length, on Anthony Clare's radio programme *In the Psychiatrist's Chair.* Hall's personal story can be read as a representative history of the postwar experiment with class boundaries; it discloses the parameters of its success and failure. As the classic achieving working-class child of postwar reconstruction, educated into a new élite, Hall is an alienated figure of *class translation* pulled both towards and away from 'origins' which, like ghosts, must be exorcised from time to time. Such alienation inevitably makes for a confused attitude towards Self (individual fulfilment) and Others (social responsibility). In this he is not unlike George Eliot herself, or rather, like Maggie in *The Mill on the Floss.*

Hall's created Self (successful, indeed revolutionary, shaper of postwar British theatre) is inscribed with these contradictions. His art has always been his business, and his recently published diary bears frequent testimony to how hard-up he thinks himself. He is in the market place with only his talent to sell, and has had (literally) to 'sell' his name. He has endorsed products, for example—much as John Cleese now endorses American Express, Hall once helped sell wallpaper in an advertisement. The existence of this entrepreneurial Hall illustrates the historical necessity for even the most 'creative' to *commodify* their fame in a capitalist society. In the *Observer* interview, he quantified the current saleability of his name, claiming that 'in marketing terms there are 40-50,000 people who will think seriously about coming to see a play I do'. This, clearly, was a bargaining counter used in the attempt to finance *The Mill on the Floss.*

David Edgar, by contrast, is a committed *left*-wing playwright, where the diaries reveal Hall to have drifted *rightwards*. Edgar's commitment has been less obviously to the development of a personalised talent and an entrepreneurial 'trading' on a recognisable identity, more to *collectivities* increasingly under threat through the 1980s (especially since the collapse of Eastern European socialism). His career as a dramatist has been built around overtly political plays, the most recent being the 1990 *The Shape of the Table* (about Czechoslovakia's 'velvet revolution'). But he too has had to 'make his name', so to speak, as a political playwright in a capitalist world.

But the Edgar *oeuvre* has another strand which answers to the old 1960s phrase 'the personal is political', and which resonates with Hall's more conservative desire to explore his past. Plays in this category include adaptations like the 1978 *The Jail Diary of Albie Sachs.* Some dramatists can be more than slightly sniffy about adapting, but Edgar has always viewed the exercise positively, and perhaps his biggest success to date has been the 1980 stage adaptation of *Nicholas Nickleby* for the RSC (televised on Channel 4 in 1982). Crucially, Edgar sees adaptations as 'in part about the author of the original work' (Edgar, p. 146), and it is possible to see his script for *The Mill on the Floss* as partly about the character 'George Eliot' and her articulation of the contradictory pull of rootedness (responsibility) against detachment (self-fulfilment). If, for Hall, the novel's repeated tropes of passion and repression, duty and self-fulfilment, transgression and reconciliation are bisected by the soft-focus, semi-documentary sense of loss evident in his film of *Akenfield,* the process for Edgar has been slightly different. His meeting-ground with Hall may be defined through the concept of the 'community' as an arena in which the personal-political may yet be meaningfully expressed in a 'post-socialist' world.

GEORGE/MARY AND MARY/MAGGIE—THE DOUBLE PRESENCE

In the Victorian novel, it has been argued, there is a 'hierarchy of discourses' which produces realism as an 'effect of language'. In reading, we are made aware that some 'voices' are to be trusted more than others. Our 'knowing subjectivity' as readers (or our view as privileged observers outside a 'real' action) is assured by *technical,* as opposed to natural, strategies. The figure of the Narrator him/herself is usually at the apex of the discourse hierarchy.[5] In George Eliot's work, this figure has the kind of lofty intelligence which induces implicit trust on the part of a reader. Her authority ultimately underwrites our 'knowingness' and, as Roger Ebbatson has noted, the 'unity of the experience . . . is that of the author, not of the character'.[6] But the narrator in *The Mill on the Floss* has a *double*—Maggie Tulliver.

Ebbatson defines the double authorial presence in *The Mill on the Floss* as an ' "impersonal" narrator/historian' and an 'authorial "second self"' (p. 35). The first is standard procedure in a Victorian novel; in *The Mill on the Floss,* there is authorial commentary on, among other things, economic shifts in a provincial community which is being inflected inexorably with 'modern' industrial/business and legal/financial meanings. But the second authorial presence is what often draws readers to *The Mill on the Floss* as a kind of *autobiographical* work. In this presence, we might understand some of the reasons why Mary Ann Evans became 'George Eliot'. We certainly see how the psychological forces of 'character' or 'nature' drive Maggie towards personal fulfilment, then contradictorily towards repression (especially sexual repression). Over and against this force, there is 'causation' or 'nurture', conditioning social being (and a sense of 'duty' and 'responsibility') and producing (in Tom's case) economic activity.

Mary Ann Evans became 'George Eliot' in order to become economically active. That is, to get her material

accepted, typeset, printed, published and distributed—to gain access to the means of literary production in the Victorian period—she had to take a *male* identity. In doing so, she recognised that 'the only gender that can presume to speak as if ungendered and for all genders is the dominant gender', which was, and is, male.[7] It is interesting to see how Edgar mediates this Narrator in his script, and how the mediation addresses the novel-narrator's gender (which is far from clear from the text alone).

A lone middle-aged female figure is glimpsed in the opening frames of Episode One, observing Dorlcote Mill and the young Maggie Tulliver from a distance. This figure is the filmic equivalent of the 'dreaming narrator' of the novel's first chapter. The figure links up gradually with a *female* 'voice-over', supplying narration. Figure and voice are one by the end of the episode, but the ambiguity of Eliot's 'simultaneous . . . endorse[ment] and subver[sion of] the norm of patriarchal dominance' (Ebbatson, p. 70) is partly mediated by the 'male companion' who questions her on the significance of the river in the final dialogue sequence of the episode:

MAN: So what's the river?

WOMAN: Well, I suppose, it is the unpredictable. That which lies beyond our control or understanding.

MAN: What, accident? Or fate?

WOMAN: That is the question.

At the conclusion of Episode Two, these 'framing' characters debate the problematic deaths of Tom and Maggie:

MAN: How will you end it?

WOMAN: They drown.

MAN: They *drown?*

WOMAN: In a mighty flood. Hence the river. Hence the mill.

MAN: I see.

Because the drowning *precedes* the discussion in film-time, Edgar can underscore his reading of Eliot's message. He has, in fact, killed his Tom and Maggie with a 'huge part of *the Mill itself*' (my italics), thus making their past catch up with them—both literally and metaphorically.

Finally, George Eliot and George Henry Lewes (only the 'stage directions' use the names) get into a horse-drawn trap which sets off down the road away from the now-deserted mill. The dialogue continues:

MAN: Don't you think—that we'd like to know how they'd grow up? Or marry? or not marry? Bring up children? And grow old?

Pause.

WOMAN: I don't know if she could. Perhaps that's work for other minds.

Slight pause.

WOMAN: Or perhaps it's better as it is.

The adaptation concludes with Maggie in voice-over repeating the last part of the legend of St Ogg as the trap bearing 'Eliot' and 'Lewes' disappears into the distance. Ogg, the son of Beorl, is, of course, the ferryman of 'the heart's need' (see Book 1, chapter 12); Edgar may not exactly 'change the ending' of the novel, but he undoubtedly endorses the heart's need to escape the heavy clay of origin.

In one of his earlier 'readerly' interpolations, Edgar again equates yet differentiates Maggie and Mary Ann. Following Maggie's seduction-that-isn't by Stephen Guest (Book 6, chapters 13 and 14), Edgar tidies up the confused itinerary by which she returns to St Oggs, and has her almost board a coach to London:

> MAGGIE: And this coach? Where does this coach go?
>
> INNKEEPER: O, this 'un's London, Miss. No good for you.
>
> *The Innkeepeer carries on loading. Maggie looks at him, and the coach.*

Edgar *shows* a 'real' London coach, which Maggie does not board, but *connotes* a mythic 'London coach', which took Mary Ann Evans away from Warwickshire, and from obscurity to fame. This fame was superintended by a male (Lewes), and protected, at least initially, by a male identity (George Eliot).

CONCLUSION—'CONTESTABLE AREAS'

Having read all Eliot's novels as part of his background research for adapting *The Mill on the Floss*, Edgar was particularly drawn to this passage from *Daniel Deronda*:

> A human life, I think, should be well rooted in some spot of a native land, where it may get the love of tender kinship . . . for whatever will give that early home a familiar unmistakable difference amidst the future widening of knowledge . . . (Book 1, chapter 3)

In common with the left as a whole, Edgar has had to take stock of an altered situation in the late 1980s. As part of his own, and a wider, reappraisal, he made connections between

> this question of *her* and her treatment of her own life [and] notions of place and issues of responsibility to the collectivities in which you grow up, and to notions of *alignment.*

These questions, Edgar believes, are 'crucial for socialists in a post-socialist period'. Ideas (like personal re-

sponsibility) seized by the right, must be 'contestable areas' for the left in the future.

The classic 'nature/nurture' argument is at the heart of the contest. Edgar was particularly interested in the implicit decision by the author to destroy her younger self. His female narrator and her implied 'act of leaving' signified to him a *rite de passage,* her nature finally able (unlike Maggie's) to break the bonds of nurture. He dramatises the narrator accordingly, leaving the 'historian' figure largely in the hands of *mise-en-scène* and camera work. The dialectical pull between self-denial and self-fulfilment is achieved by juxtaposing the gypsy in Maggie ('a code for her desire to let it all hang out') with the repressive determinism she draws particularly from her reading of Thomas à Kempis ('a code for her will to keep it all in').

Edgar's newly differentiated view of the individual's struggle between competing notions of duty and responsibility, on the one hand, and personal fulfilment on the other, contrasts with his own much starker earlier views:

> I'm quite admiring of Tom's settling down and lashing himself to the wheel and getting his father's mill back. I would have been more dismissive of that twenty years ago, and less ambiguously critical of Maggie's repression of herself. I think I'd want to view the contradictions as being more painful today.

The essential collectivity found in the theatre has become for him an emblem of that politics-of-the-personal which can harness the energies of the individual to the common good:

> the theatre challenges the notion that people's basic work motivation is material advantage, and gives some support to the idea that within the right environment people of individuality and talent can function collectively, collaboratively and efficiently.[8]

However, another version of the theatre industry might see conditions not unlike an old-fashioned agricultural hiring fair, and collectivity still tending to suffer in the search for that 'right environment'.

In the environment of television, a costume drama such as *The Mill on the Floss* would probably cost £3-4 million (a film would require twice that). *The Mill on the Floss* was, and is, *Hall's* project, and his name is crucial to its financing. That may have been one of his problems; his stock is low at present (especially following *Born Again,* his musical version of Ionesco's *Rhinoceros*). But the marketing problem goes further; classic serialisations have always tended to be of *some* novels (and writers) rather than others. George Eliot has never been quite so marketable as, for example, Dickens. *Silas Marner,* her one significant 'success' on TV, in 1985, had the notable advantage of being short and easily convertible into a ninety-minute film drama. There was also a beefy role for a star name (Ben Kingsley as the eponymous hero), and the winter scenes were tailor-made for the Christmas schedules. Finally, the novel can be read as a classic tearjerker in which everything ends up happily; it is (and perhaps this says it all) the least 'George-Eliotic' of Mary Ann Evans's novels. It has even been made into a *cartoon* version, as have a number of Dickens's novels; it is unimaginable that any other of George Eliot's works could be so treated.

Although Edgar makes the most of the book's Christmas scene (Book 2, chapter 2), *The Mill on the Floss* fails the rest of the above criteria. As a result, we must wait to see whether *The Mill on the Floss* does eventually get screened through the 'open market', or whether it has been completely 'screened out'.

[1] See 'Adapting *Nicholas Nickleby*', in David Edgar, *The Second Time As Farce* (Lawrence & Wishart, 1988), p. 143.

[2] Unless stated otherwise, quotations are from an interview of 6 June 1990. I am also grateful to David Edgar for permission to quote from his draft adaptation of *The Mill on the Floss*.

[3] See Ronald Blythe, *Akenfield: Portrait of an English Village* (Penguin, 1972), p. 19.

[4] For further information, see Ann Jellicoe, *Community Plays* (Methuen, 1987).

[5] See Catherine Belsey, *Critical Practice* (Methuen, 1980).

[6] Roger Ebbatson, *The Mill on the Floss—Penguin Critical Study* (Penguin, 1985), p. 46.

[7] Nancy Armstrong and Lawrence Tennenhouse (eds.), *The Violence of Representation* (Routledge, 1989), p. 3.

[8] David Edgar, 'Stage Left', in *Marxism Today,* December 1990, p. 3.

Martin Esslin

SOURCE: "The Art of Television Drama," in *The Boston Review,* Vol. IX, No. 4, July/August, 1984, pp. 12-14.

[*In the following essay, Esslin discusses the abandonment of literary drama by American commercial and public television programmers.*]

There is an immense amount of "drama" on American television—situation comedy, police and detective series, soap operas. Yet "television drama"—in the sense, that is, of serious drama specially conceived for the medium—is to all intents and purposes extinct in the United States. There was, once upon a time, a golden age of it in the 1950s, when writers like Rod Serling and Paddy Chayefsky produced a series of near-masterpieces in the genre, plays like Chayefsky's *Marty* (1953) or Serling's *Requiem for a Heavyweight* (1957). But that time has long since gone. (Serling, for example, gave up writing serious television drama in 1959, when he denounced censorship by sponsors and declared that "It's a crime, but scripts with a social significance can't get done on TV.") The sponsors gradually abandoned the series of "play-houses" and "theatres of the air" in the 1960s, and today's occasional blockbuster "dramas" like *The Day After* are, by their very nature, simply feature films made for television and certainly cannot aspire to be regarded as works of art.

Most of what little television drama with literary aspirations there still is tends to appear on the "public" network under the idiotic label of "Masterpiece Theatre," which covers an incongruous medley of imports from England. These range from adaptations of classic and not so classic novels, to soap operas like *Upstairs Downstairs,* to the occasional detective story, with introductions designed for illiterates by a "host" (the unfortunate, charming and intelligent Alistair Cooke) who has to explain, for example, that there was such a thing as a First World War from 1914 to 1918, or who Dickens or Trollope might have been. Genuine television drama, as it exists on the continent of Europe (and for that matter, in Canada), hardly ever gets a showing on American television. Some of the best works of major writers like Samuel Beckett, Harold Pinter, Tom Stoppard, David Mercer, and others have thus remained unknown on this side of the Atlantic.

Nevertheless, television drama is a powerful art form in its own right, poised somewhere between the stage and the cinema, with the advantages, and some of the liabilities, of each. At first glance, television drama is obviously closer to film than to live theater: here, as in the cinema, the spectator can see the story only through the viewpoint dictated by the director's use of shots and camera angles. Yet television is not just film on a small screen.

The most significant basic difference between film and television drama lies in the conditions under which the work is watched. The film happens not only on a large screen, but in a theater that has been darkened and is filled by a crowd. The television viewer, on the other hand, is usually sitting in his own home, with the lights on, alone, or with very few people. Moreover, he is in control of his set. If he is bored, he can switch it off or go to another channel. The need to keep the viewer riveted to the screen is thus far greater in television than in the cinema, with its captive audience securely settled into their seats and determined to get a ticket's worth of performance. Television drama has to capture the audience's attention immediately and hold it relentlessly, which has led to the false assumption that the viewer must, in the very first minute, be overwhelmed by events so exciting and mysterious that he is simply compelled to go on watching. (Hence the medleys of violent stunts and tantalizing sex scenes that precede the American police or adventure series installments as trailers or "appetizers.")

In fact, however, the intimacy of the television screen is so great that the relatively slow establishment of a milieu or atmosphere can indeed become hypnotically riveting and intriguing enough to hold the viewer. Pinter's television play *Tea Party,* to give just one example, opens with a long surrealistic travelling shot of rows of sanitary appliances displayed in glass cabinets, establishing that the principal character is a rich manufacturer of toilet bowls and washbasins. This seemingly surrealistic, and yet completely real opening sequence demonstrates that the need to capture the viewer's attention from the very beginning can be met by imaginative visuals that endow everyday objects with mystery, suspense, wit, and the promise of intriguing events to come.

On the other hand, television drama cannot, like the cinema, offer the viewer vast and spectacular vistas. Television drama does not work well in the long shot, and is at its best in close-up. And indeed, to the viewer sitting at home in his living room, only a few feet away from the screen, such close-ups of faces will appear on a human scale, barely different in size from the faces of the people he would see in the room itself. (On the large screens of today's cinema, however, the close-up has to be used sparingly: a face blown up to gigantic size easily becomes grotesque.) Thus, the most effective scenes in television drama involve only two or three people, whose emotions and reactions will register in the minutest detail in their features, no further away from the viewer than those of people with whom he interacts in real life. Television drama is thus the ideal chamber play, as postulated by Strindberg and the early naturalists.

Another of the specific characteristics of television drama (which derives from its affinity with the other, and even more intimate electronic medium, radio) is that the spoken word registers more intimately at low volume in a living room than at high volume in a theater. Some of the finest effects of television drama derive from the use of narration that ironically contrasts with the images being shown. (For example, a voice reciting a letter describing the wonderful place the writer is in, contrasted with shots of the sordid reality of the place.) Internal monologue and the visualization of the daydream and fantasy are also much more effective on television than in film or live drama.

Intimacy and closeness to the characters, which television drama shares with the radio play, are thus the special strengths of the best of serious television drama. On the other hand, this intimacy and closeness also allow television drama to exploit to the hilt a quality it shares with the cinema: the ability of the director to control the point of view from which the action is seen. In the rich literature of British television drama, for example, there are a number of major works that make use of this special strength of the medium. John Hopkins's famous television tetralogy *Talking to a Stranger* (1966), for example, showed the same family reunion from the different points of view of four different members of the family. The late David Mercer—one of the most important television dramatists to have emerged in the short history of the genre—repeatedly dramatized case histories of mental breakdown (for example in his *A Suitable Case for Treatment,* which later became a feature film). In Peter Nichols's classic television play *The George* (1965), the variation of points of view was made even more complex: it showed a family viewing a home movie of an outing to the country and contrasted the clumsy, cliched images of a happy family occasion with what had actually happened during the excursion—at least as remembered by one of the principal people involved in the events, the young son of the family.

This tendency to "internalize" the action is balanced by television's ability to represent the real world with photographic accuracy. Moreover, perhaps the most characteristic feature of television as against the cinema is its essential nature as a continuous, never-ending stream of images. Television is perceived by the viewer as a continuum of virtually undifferentiated "real" events (the news, sports) and fiction. The faces appearing on the screen are at one moment those of actors, at the next those of real people, and then again, in the person of anchormen and women and announcers, those of real but entirely artificial "personalities." Contemporary television drama often exploits this characteristic of the medium by using semi-documentary techniques, mixing actors with real people and even, as in the outstandingly interesting work of directors like Mike Leigh, improvising dialogue and action in the rehearsal process. Directors like Ken Loach, writers like Colin Welland (who won an academy award for his screenplay for *Chariots of Fire,* but had written many television plays in the preceding decade) have produced an impressive body of this type of documentary-realistic drama.

Many other writers have kept within the area of psychological realism, which, of course, involves the fantasy and dream life of the characters as well as the realities of their environment. In plays like Harold Pinter's *The Lover,* for example, we are given a glimpse of a married couple whose erotic life is based on their playing the parts of a prostitute and her client. The situation is real enough, yet at the same time we are taken into the fantasy life of the couple. Another way in which fantasy and reality can be merged in this most intimate of all media is that of the lyrical play of reminiscence, of which perhaps Laurie Lee's *Cider With Rosie* is a classic example—an evocation of childhood memories halfway between reality and dream-like, nostalgic reminiscence.

The impact of television drama in a country like Britain is immense. While it is true that it cannot rival situation comedy or major sports events in attracting the largest mass audiences, its viewing figures are still impressive. An average television play on BBC1 or on the major commercial channel in Britain can attract between six and ten million viewers; the most successful plays have reached audiences of up to 15 million. (British audience research is carried out by an independent body for the BBC and the commercial TV companies, and is far more thorough than the "ratings" research in the United States, being based daily on a far larger sample. These figures represent percentages of the total adult population of the United Kingdom. Thus 15 million is 30 per cent of the total adult population.) On the "minority" channels, BBC2 and the commercial "Channel 4," the more intellectually demanding plays still attract audiences around three million. (It must be stressed here that in Britain even the commercial channel can show advertisements *only* in "natural breaks between programmes," hence even in commercial television serious drama is possible.)

No wonder, then, that British television drama attracts the best playwrights: it offers them an audience much larger than they could ever reach with a stage play, while sparing them the humiliations suffered by writers in the film industry. Harold Pinter, Tom Stoppard, John Osborne, Trevor Griffiths, David Hare, Simon Gray, Howard Brenton, Michael Frayn, Peter Nichols, John Mortimer, and a host of others have written some of their best work for television.

The sheer quantity of serious drama on British television has an important impact on the cultural life of the nation. Playwrights can make a steady living by regularly providing material for the continuous demand constituted by the programming needs of three national radio and four national television channels, which, between them, need many hundreds of hours of television drama each year. Adaptations of novels and short stories can, in this context, be seen as preliminary steps towards the mastering of the techniques that will come to full fruition in original plays. Moreover, the existence of the BBC as a public service (and not, as most Americans tend erroneously to assume, a government-controlled organization), creates an ideal training ground: many writers start with short radio plays, progress to longer and more complex radio work, and gradually enter television; when they have established themselves there, the step to the live theatre and the cinema becomes much easier.

The flowering of dramatic writing in Britain since the late 1950s is undoubtedly a consequence, in part, of the opportunities the mass media have offered to new writers to acquire polish and professional experience. The situation in countries like France, Germany, Norway, Sweden, Denmark, and Italy is similar. It is surely no coincidence that even major world figures like Ingmar Bergman choose to produce some of their best work for the television medium. Bergman's *Portrait of a Marriage,* for example was ideal television material and he made it for television. Nor is it a coincidence that one of the greatest playwrights of this century, Samuel Beckett, has been experimenting with television drama since 1966 (when the BBC produced his first play specifically written for television, *Eh Joe!*) and has since written four more plays specifically conceived for television and unthinkable in any other medium—*Ghost Trio* (1976), " . . . *but the clouds . . .*" (1976), *Quad 1 1/3 2* (1981) and *Nacht und Traeume* (1982). In these haunting pieces Beckett uses the television's capacity for intimacy, for a dialectic be-

tween word and image, and, above all, its ability to turn simple objects into profound metaphoric images, to create what amounts to a new kind of visual poetry.

These short plays (none longer than about twenty minutes) are very difficult to describe. Their scripts, insofar as they have been published, cannot give even a faint idea of their impact, simply because they were conceived as images and only work as such. In *Ghost Trio,* for example, the faint voice of a woman is heard describing the familiar Beckett chamber—bare walls, one window, one mirror, a door, a pallet (or mattress) on the floor. The faint woman's voice comments on the actions of an old man with gray hair who is sitting holding an unidentifiable object on his lap. From time to time music, a passage from Beethoven's fifth piano trio ("The Ghost"), is heard. The old man is waiting for someone, a woman, to appear; he goes to the window to look out, to the door, when he thinks he has heard someone approaching. But there is nothing there. Eventually steps are heard—there is a knock at the door. Outside stands a small boy in a plastic rain coat. Drenched by the rain, he looks up at the old man and faintly shakes his head in a denying gesture, then departs. The old man remains alone; we realize that the object in his hands is a small cassette recorder on which he has turned the phrase from Beethoven's trio on and off. The play ends with a shot of his tired, sad old face.

This short play does not tell a story. It is merely an image, a visual metaphor for the human condition, compressed in to its most concise form. The waiting man, the little boy with his negative message recall *Waiting for Godot,* but here the image is even more telling, more concise. As in Beckett's other late television plays, which are a new form of visual poetry, everything depends on scale. Blown up to the size of a cinema screen these images would lose their power; live theatre, on the other hand, would not be able to provide the extreme precision of timing and gesture, the subtle interplay of voice-over and music, they require.

It is unfortunate that these masterpieces of a new art form have hitherto been denied to American viewers. What has caused the virtual death of television drama in the United States? The short answer is: the prevailing system, which makes one of the most powerful media of communication and culture ever available to mankind subject to the control of advertisers. Serious drama, undoubtedly, is not among the most popular of entertainments for a mass audience and will thus never get the highest ratings. It can be harrowing and intellectually demanding; above all, it requires a degree of concentration that cannot be attained in a medium subject to incessant interruptions by commercials which are not only trivial and ugly but are bound to destroy any sustained emotional tension or mood. Serious drama is, in fact, impossible under the conditions of American commercial television.

But advertising is not the only culprit. The public television service (insofar as it can be said to exist at all), hardly ever carries serious drama, written specifically for television, as distinct from adaptations of novels and short stories, or studio reproductions of stage performances. This is due not only to public television's poverty. After all, it would cost no more to buy an original work by Beckett or Stoppard than six episodes of Dorothy Sayers or a soap opera about Edward VIII. The reason seems to be that the television industry is convinced that American audiences, used as they are to the fare they are offered by the commercial networks, are not capable of watching any serious work on the television screen. The industry also seems to believe that the American audience has become so accustomed to the series format that a play, which stands by itself, has no chance of being watched. Television executives reason that a series can be advertised and will have a chance to establish itself; it forms a habit of being viewed at set times on set days of the week. In the serial form of situation comedies and police and detective series, moreover, the need for an exposition that has to be followed with concentration is eliminated by the familiarity of milieu and characters. The same is even more true of the endless serial form of the soap operas which dominate the afternoon hours.

The "single play," on the other hand, lacks these advantages and will simply disappear in the vast amorphous mass of programming. The consequence is that on commercial television adaptations of novels in several installments have to be dubbed "mini-series," from which it would follow that a play standing by itself like *Hamlet* or *Hedda Gabler* would have to be described as a "mini-mini-series" consisting of only one installment! This concept has also seeped into "public" service. And here, moreover, the organization of the network as a federation of independent units that have to be separately persuaded to carry programs, is so complex that scheduling an isolated program is in itself far too difficult to be considered worth the effort.

A television drama which explores and opens up new frontiers of expression that have become available through new technology is obviously of immense importance. Unfortunately, it is now under constant threat everywhere. As screens become bigger, as video cassettes make the whole past output of the classic cinema accessible, as more and more feature films are being produced with television in mind, the intimate form of the television play concentrating on the subtle interplay of a few characters and their dreams and fantasies is being assailed from many sides. Television has become, and will increasingly become, a huge industry relying, for the enormous demand of hundreds of new channels, on more and more industrialized methods of mass production. It would be a sad loss if this outlet for the creative imagination were lost in Europe, where it still flourishes, as it has already been lost in the United States. It would be even more wonderful if ways could be found to make this body of work accessible here. Perhaps the new forms of distribution—cable, and video-cassettes—will make that possible. Let us hope so.

Stuart Laing

SOURCE: "The Three Small Worlds of David Lodge," in *Critical Survey,* Vol. 3, No. 3, 1991, pp. 324-30.

[*In the following essay, Laing discusses the plot, themes, and techniques of David Lodge's novel* Small World *(1985), considers alterations including a shift in point of view and compression of events in the serial adaptation for British commercial television in 1988, and examines issues of the television medium central to Lodge's 1987 documentary "Big Words: Small World."*]

David Lodge's novel *Small World* was published in hardback in 1984, put into paperback in 1985 and turned into a six-part television serialisation in 1988 by the ITV company Granada. In this essay I consider first the main narrative structure and issues of the novel, then the changes made in the process of transforming the story into television serial drama, and finally some further issues of television form arising out of a documentary on a literary conference ('Big Words: Small World') presented by David Lodge on Channel Four in November 1987.

SMALL WORLD—THE NOVEL

Small World, the novel, presents events occurring during the annual round of international literary critical conferences in the year of 1979. In particular the exploits of three figures are followed. Both Philip Swallow (a middle-aged and traditionalist English literary critic) and Morris Zapp (an ambitious American post-structuralist) are characters resurrected from Lodge's earlier novel, *Changing Places* (1975); their past personal and professional histories become factors in this novel. By contrast Persse McGarrigle, the main protagonist, is a young naïve scholar ('a conference virgin', as Morris Zapp calls him during the conference at Rummidge which opens the book) from a rural Irish Catholic background whose initiation into the complexities both of literary critical theory and politics and of sexual desire, love and romance run in parallel through the novel. The events of the novel follow the conference / international lecture circuit from April to mid-winter, moving from Rummidge (a thinly disguised Birmingham) to Amsterdam, Geneva, Lausanne, Turkey, Greece, Jerusalem, Hawaii, Seoul and finally the MLA conference (the 'Big Daddy of conferences') at New York.

While the adventures of these three characters form the main forward narrative movement of the novel they do not constitute its exclusive centre. The narrative mode is that of an omniscient author deploying a range of characters situated across the globe. Thus the story of events at the Rummidge conference is followed by a lengthy thirty-page section (in which Persse plays no part at all) evoking the characteristic world of the modern literary international network—a world linked by telephones, fax machines and international travel. In a typically modernist device Lodge shows us a number of his characters

(Morris Zapp in England *en route* for Italy, Wainwright in Australia preparing his conference paper for Jerusalem, Désirée Zapp asleep at her writer's retreat in New Hampshire, Fulvia Morgana, Italian Marxist professor, and the Ringbaums *en route* for London—and other academics in Chicago, Berlin, Paris, Turkey and Tokyo) all simultaneously acting, planning and scheming as part of a single system of which at best they have only partial knowledge.

The novel's dominant attitude is, however, not that of modernist writing, nor even of campus novel comic realism; rather Lodge uses the notion of 'romance' (the book is sub-titled 'An Academic Romance') in a particular formal sense. As Cheryl Summerbee explains to Persse: 'Real romance is a pre-novelistic kind of narrative. It's full of adventure and coincidence and surprises and marvels, and has lots of characters who are lost or enchanted or wandering about looking for each other, or for the Grail, or something like that. Of course, they're often in love too . . .' (p. 258).[1] Persse (whose surname means 'Son of Super-valour') spends the novel looking (mostly in vain) for the brilliant and beautiful Angelica Pabst; his quest is impeded by the existence of Angelica's 'bad' twin sister Lily and aided by the visionary Miss Maiden (a retired scholar from Girton College and a former pupil of Jessie Weston's who shares Persse's deep interest in Eliot's *The Waste Land*). Morris's kidnapping (by Italian revolutionaries seeking his ex-wife's money) and Philip's apparently miraculous rediscovery of Joy, a lost love he thought dead, also add to the romance elements of the various plots. The novel's climax comes at the MLA conference when the elder statesman of international literary criticism, Arthur Kingfisher (having just been awarded the UNESCO chair of literary criticism, for which the various characters have been competing throughout the novel) is revealed to be the father of Angelica and Lily—their mother being Miss Maiden.

Lodge's adoption of a free-wheeling romance plot structure is a major source of the novel's comedy (in addition to the numerous parodies of academic literary discourse and behaviour). However it also serves as a way of placing some of the many positions on literature and criticism which characters adopt in the novel. The definition of romance used by Cheryl is in fact learnt from Angelica and the latter's ideas on romance, including her analogies between various literary forms and forms of sexuality, constitute one position which Lodge has to offer against various kinds of reductionism as offered by critical theorists (Marxist or post-structuralist) or computer stylistics (exemplified in the novel by the character of Dempsey). However, ultimately the novel offers a balance between romance and realism as its particular vision. All three central characters are shown as experiencing certain professional, personal and sexual adventures in parallel—although largely unknown to each other. In each case an extreme philosophical or romantic view of the world is undercut by their experiences. Morris's kidnapping leads him to have 'lost faith in deconstruction . . . death is the one concept you can't deconstruct. Work back from there and you end up with the old idea of an autonomous self.

I can die, therefore I am. I realized that when those wop radicals threatened to deconstruct me.' (p. 328). Philip's recognition of family responsibilities leads him to have 'failed in the role of romantic hero . . . My nerve failed me at a crucial moment' (p. 336); he rejects Joy to stay with his wife Hilary and to support her in her new career as a marriage counsellor. Finally, Persse realises, through making love with Lily while thinking she is Angelica, that his 'love' for Angelica is a fantasy; he discovers instead that he is really in love with Cheryl, the girl at the Heathrow Information desk, and the novel ends with his setting out on a new search for her.

SMALL WORLD—THE TELEVISION SERIAL

In adapting any novel for television a number of broad constraints immediately present themselves. From the adapter's point of view the most significant is the amount of time available and the shape of that time. This may vary from the single play (average ninety minutes) to the multi-episodic serial (traditionally thirteen in the case of the BBC Sunday afternoon Dickens of the early sixties—twenty-six for *War and Peace*). *Small World* was accorded a reasonably generous amount of air-time—six episodes of an hour long (or rather around fifty-three minutes allowing for advertising). This decision then posed three further issues about the shape of the adaptation. Firstly, even with well over five hours' script-time it was unlikely that all the novel's events could be included. Secondly, the material needed to be rendered into six reasonably discrete portions; and finally, a form of narration needed to be adopted which could hold the material together. This could have been a televisual version of the novelistic omniscient voice—an all-seeing camera going far beyond the knowledge of any individual character accompanied, when required, by an unseen narrative voice-over.

In fact the adaptation chose to deal with all three problems at once by radically recasting the way the story is told. Each of the six episodes opens with the figure of Persse in the underground chapel at Heathrow telling the tale of his adventures into a miniature tape-recorder as a form of confession (a variant of an actual Catholic confession) to Professor McCreedy, his departmental head at the University of Limerick who has financed his conference globe-trotting. The whole story is then told in flashback and at any point in any episode Persse's voice-over can be introduced to carry the narrative forward plausibly as part of his confession. This device allows a good deal of disparate material to be unified by being passed through the consciousness of Persse—thus events which are told as free-standing components in the novel are now converted into letters or stories told to Persse. The drawback, however, to this re-rendering of a third-person novel as in effect an autobiographical narrative is that now everything that happens must first come to be known to Persse. He moves firmly to the centre of the story, altering that balance between the fate of individuals and the construction of a general conference world which the novel carefully preserves.

This decision then dictates the inevitable compression of events and detail which occurs in the serial. Certain minor characters disappear. The Australian dimension is excised altogether. The (admittedly rather unpleasant) character of Wainwright and the story of his never to be finished conference paper with its unanswered question 'how can literary criticism maintain its Arnoldian function of identifying the best which has been thought and said, when literary discourse itself has been decentred by deconstructing the traditional concept of the author, of authority?' (p. 84)—both disappear. So too do the Ringbaums—even more minor characters, although Thelma plays an important part in the novel's ending, as part of Morris's return to a belief in human relations, rather than deconstruction and professional ambition, as a personal goal. Another minor figure to be dropped is Akira Sakazaki, the Japanese translator of the English 'Angry' novelist Frobisher; his main role in the novel is to serve as the butt of various linguistic jokes about the difficulty of translating English idioms—material which would in any case have had no visual equivalent.

This reduction, within the serial, of concern with specifically linguistic literary issues is reflected also in the greatly diminished role of Dempsey who now only figures in the first episode as one of those used by Angelica to fuel Persse's jealousy and desire. In the novel a powerful and depressing sub-plot turns on his obsession with computerising the stylistic study of literature at his new University of Darlington; this leads by turns to Frobisher's blockage as a creative writer (on being told that his favourite word is 'greasy') and to Dempsey's breakdown as he comes to look to the computer to solve his personal problems. Another character with a greatly reduced role is Philip's Turkish host Akbil Borak; as with the Japanese component of the novel (reduced in the serial to Persse and Frobisher singing 'Hey Jude' in a karaoke bar), this attempt to render something of the complexity and absurdity of how 'English Literature' is understood in a quite different culture is largely deleted.

In fact in the serial the implications of the idea of 'small world' change—not absolutely, but as a matter of degree. The novel's emphasis on the existence of a particular invisible, but powerful, literary academic network which functions through the most modern communications systems shifts more towards the idea of a romance world of symbolic coincidences, interconnections and identities as a smaller cast of characters are more explicitly linked to each other in a multiplicity of ways. In particular the plot narrows considerably to become much more dominantly the sentimental education of Persse, closely and directly interwoven now with the two stories of his friends and mentors Philip Swallow and Morris Zapp. Their relationship is explicitly denoted as fellow knight-errants on a quest, and is even more strikingly described by Persse (when Philip and Morris become lost in their own rivalry for the UNESCO chair) in romance terms—'My surrogate fathers were lost to ego and competition with no time for their surrogate son'. From the first episode a closeness of relationship between the three is firmly established.

In the case of Philip it is now he rather than Dempsey who is tricked by Angelica into waiting in bed for her at the Rummidge conference. Persse's discovery of Philip leads to a shared sense of disappointment and to Philip's sharing with Persse his memories of Euphoria and his desire for 'intensity of experience'; this is followed by his telling both Persse and Morris (not just Morris as in the novel) the story of his brief encounter with Joy. Later, in a café in Amsterdam, he again tells them both of his rediscovery of Joy in Turkey. In the novel, Persse has no knowledge of Joy and indeed, after Rummidge, has no further contact at all with Philip until the end of the novel. Similarly with Morris, Persse is now on hand in Geneva to hear from Désirée of Morris's kidnapping, is present at Désirée's apartment when his release is arranged and accompanies Philip to rescue Morris from the abandoned villa where he has been held. In the novel Persse has no knowledge of these events, being on the other side of the world at the time.

Such perhaps plausible interweaving is supplemented by an intensification of more overt romance elements. Miss Maiden's role as a seer becomes more important as she becomes used indiscriminately to keep the plot moving (as when she turns up beside the Lake Isle of Innisfree to give Persse further instructions) without the need to provide much explanation. In one of the more imaginative uses of the television form, the novel's central mystery—the fact and origins of the identical Pabst twins—is replicated at another level by the casting of the same actresses in the parts of Philip's wife and mistress (Hilary and Joy) and of Morris's ex-wife and mistress (Désirée and Fulvia). This derives perhaps from a hint in the novel where Joy is seen by Philip as a younger version of Hilary, but, while visually striking and adding to the sense of play in the whole serial, this device contributes to some confusion in the way the closure of the various plot lines is handled. In particular the pairing off of Morris with Fulvia at the end (rather than with the essentially cipher-like Thelma) loses the novel's implication of Morris's abandonment of radical theory. The final scene sees the whole cast involved in a dance whose general celebratory quality implies the victory of a comic and romantic view of the world from which Persse removes himself only to seek to rejoin it again by a renewed quest for Cheryl.

BIG WORDS: SMALL WORLD

Adapting *Small World* for television posed one further problem in addition to those present with any novel. Lodge's novel is itself concerned with questions of literature, literary criticism and literary form. Its comments on these issues are moreover made not only via the thoughts, speeches and actions of the characters or even the ruminations of the narrative voice, but also by the very form of the book itself—the particular mix of romance and realism and the implicit assumptions about the relations between literature and life which underlie the novel's mode of writing. As the example of *The French Lieutenant's Woman* shows, this creates an extra level of difficulty—solved in that case by the device of replacing a novel about writing a novel with that of a film about making a film. *Small World* is not such a clearcut example of a metafictional novel and it is unlikely there was ever any question of developing a form for the serial in which self-consciousness about formal televisual questions would play any significant part, although clearly some thought was given as to how to convert the emphasis on romance conventions into televisual form (as in the double-casting discussed above). Nevertheless it is clear that the adaptation resulted in a considerable loss in the range and depth of implication of the specifically literary issues with which the novel was concerned. For an example of the kinds of questions which would have arisen had there been some attempt to produce a televisual equivalent of such issues it is worth considering the Channel Four documentary *Big Words: Small World* on the subject of a literature and linguistics conference held at the University of Strathclyde in the summer of 1986.

This documentary, presented by Lodge, was a collaborative production involving also some of the conference organisers (including Nigel Fabb, Alan Durant and Colin MacCabe), and at certain points explicitly invoked a parallel with Lodge's novel in its attempt to explain what goes on at literary conferences and in what terms they can be understood. Without giving anything like a full account of the programme, I will note a few of the issues with which it attempted to deal, especially those concerning televisual form. One general point of comparison between the serial and the documentary is that of their use of the typical 'look' or mode of presentation of their particular genre. Whatever its leanings towards romance the basic narrative mode of the *Small World* serial was that television version of theatre naturalism which is the staple of popular television drama. Characters address each other (not the camera) and play across our line of vision; the writing and editing are designed to allow us to close each scene as part of a fixed sequence of events. As against this the typical documentary mode is a series of more disparate items—'descriptive' shots of the general social or natural environment involved, the presenter talking to camera, and other talking heads talking to a seen or unseen interviewer or sometimes directly to the camera itself. We rely predominantly on the unifying presenter or the voice-over to provide us with the significance of much of what we see, and to keep the sequence and argument moving.

Much of the first part of *Big Words: Small World* works like this with Lodge setting the scene both directly to camera and as voice-over. Part of his task here is to discuss the subject matter of the conference; an attempt is made to explain structuralism to the viewer (in much the same terms as it is explained to Persse and to the reader/viewer during the Rummidge conference) and reference is made to Derrida's view that 'all our discourse is founded on the void'. The arrival of the American critic Stanley Fish is shown (with reference to the commonly held view that he provided the model for Morris Zapp). Part Two opens with Lodge's own paper on Bakhtin (his

commentary refers to *Small World* as itself a Bakhtinian 'carnivalesque novel about literary conferences') which turns on a paradox that while ideally we should favour the dialogic above the monologic in our discourse, literary criticism must perhaps necessarily be monologic in its attempt to persuade and to assert authority. The most we can hope for, Lodge suggests, in our critical discourse is that it should display 'openness about its closure'. Resuming his position as narrator, Lodge comments that the documentary too is a form of monologic discourse, which is the cue for the camera to pan back revealing that Lodge's 'office' is in fact a television studio and for Colin MacCabe to enter from the side asking that Lodge's control over the material be broken. After a short debate they agree that Lodge's narrative should continue but should be interrupted by other voices commenting on the conference as seems appropriate to MacCabe. These other voices (inserted by superimposing framed talking heads over the main shots of the conference) include many non-participants (such as Stuart Hall, Terry Eagleton, Fredric Jameson, Rosalind Coward) as well as, later, ordinary conference members who feel that their concerns have been excluded from the main conference business. This disruption of the single line of the documentary narrative is parallelled by the story Lodge's narrative goes on to tell. By the final day of the conference many participants began to complain about the lack of social and political contextual issues (concerning both English as an international language and the specific regional concerns of Glasgow) and even about the effect of the presence of the television cameras themselves. Such comments are partly contained by Lodge's narrative through seeing them as typical of the way in which conferences themselves tend to become their own subject matter and the documentary concludes with Lodge and MacCabe continuing to debate and disagree over the best form for the programme itself.

In however obviously staged a way, this debate over documentary form within the programme is an attempt to parallel the arguments within the conference itself over the kinds of discourse which were possible or desirable within literary critical practice, and over the very nature of the conference event. In this sense there was an effort to effect a translation of the issues of the conference into another medium (television) by taking account of the distinctive features of that other medium, rather than simply by regarding that medium as a potentially neutral channel for the presentation of ideas. The television serial of *Small World* was certainly not unaware of this problem. It sought to select certain key ideas and issues, dropping those which could not easily be translated into a television serial format, and using televisual opportunities to develop the romance elements and to stress close parallels between the three heroes. The use of unusually explicit sexual scenes for prime-time main channel television (prompting the prior warning each week that an 'adult' comedy was to follow) emphasised the argument that the link between literary forms and sexual desire (suggested by Angelica, Morris and others) offered one way of seeing how literature did relate to practical questions of how to live, as well as stressing the importance of primary sensuous experience (as against the various theories which sought to place literature, language or even criticism as of greater value). Within the confines of its received form the serial did all that was reasonable to ask of it; it would have been a different and much more radical project to have taken the novel's underlying issues of representation, creativity, criticism and the new international order of academic life and asked how they could best be televised in fictional form. Both may be seen as worthwhile projects and neither should be seen as fully substitutable for the other; there is of course no reason why, in any rationally ordered culture and television service, we could not and should not be able to have both.

[1] David Lodge, *Small World* (London, 1984; Penguin edition, 1985). All page numbers refer to the paperback edition.

LITERARY GENRES AND TELEVISION

Steve Fore

SOURCE: "Same Old Others: The Western, *Lonesome Dove,* and the Lingering Difficulty of Difference," in *The Velvet Light Trap,* Vol. 27, Spring, 1991, pp. 49-62.

[*In the following essay, Fore examines the ways in which the television adaptation of Larry McMurtry's novel* Lonesome Dove *perpetuates racist and sexist stereotypes and endorses the myth of manifest destiny.*]

> The Red Indians who have been fortunate enough to secure permanent engagements with the several Western film companies are paid a salary that keeps them well provided with tobacco and their worshipped "firewater". . . . They put their heart and soul in the work, especially in battles with the whites, and it is necessary to have armed guards watch over their movements for the least sign of treachery. They naturally object to acting in pictures where they are defeated, and it requires a good deal of coaxing to induce them to take on such objectionable parts. . . . With all the precautions that are taken, the Redskins occasionally manage to smuggle real bullets into action; but happily they have always been detected in the nick of time. . . .
>
> (Dench 92-3)

It is as if you accept the heroes and stories of Western society, not voluntarily, but because of the social and political forces you are caught up in. In fact, as kids, we tried to act out the things we had seen in the movies. We used to play cowboys and indians in the mountains around Gondar [Ethiopia]. . . . We acted out the roles of these heroes, identifying with the cowboys conquering the indians. We didn't identify with the indians at all and we never wanted the indians

to win. Even in Tarzan movies, we would become totally galvanized by the activities of the hero and follow the story from his point of view, completely caught up in the structure of the story. Whenever Africans sneaked up behind Tarzan, we would scream our heads off, trying to warn him that "they" were coming.

(Haile Gerima, quoted in Roy Armes, 44)

In the weeks following the unexpected ratings and critical success of *Lonesome Dove* in February 1989, the CBS miniseries was accorded something approaching mythic status in the popular press and media industry trade papers. The story went something like this: Suzanne de Passe, president of the fitfully successful film and television arm of Motown, Inc., optioned Larry McMurtry's epic novel of the first cattle drive to Montana (the 1,500-page pre-publication manuscript carted into de Passe's office in a wheelbarrow) for $50,000 in 1985 after every major television production house in Hollywood had turned it down.[1] The miniseries was a dying breed, went the conventional wisdom, and the television and movie western's corpse had been cold for years. The novel proceeded to win a Pulitzer Prize, and suddenly the project was a go; CBS bit for $16 million of the $20-million budget, with the Australian communications and resorts company Qintex, Ltd., picking up the difference in exchange for distribution and ancillary rights. The eight-hour, four-night broadcast of *Lonesome Dove* then surprised just about everybody, as noted in *Variety,* by winning its time slot with the best ratings (26.1 rating/39 share) for any miniseries since 1984 (Gelman 85). It turned a profit for CBS in its initial airing, a rare occurrence for a miniseries, and it was estimated that it would eventually generate an estimated $30 million in advertising revenue for the network over three broadcasts. Qintex, meanwhile, was expected to clear another $20 million in exchange for foreign, cable, videocassette, and syndication rights, while Motown walked away with a million-dollar fee from Qintex, a cool 2,000% return on its initial investment (Carter). Once again, television history was made at night.

But what kind of history? What does it mean when a genre as apparently moribund as the western is resurrected, or at least refurbished, so successfully? Why did it decline in the first place? And what are the consequences of its revival, in the specific instance of *Lonesome Dove?*

One could approach these questions from many angles. In this essay, I will deal with them primarily from the perspective of the representation of race, with supplemental commentary on the representation of gender ("supplemental" not because the latter is of secondary concern, but because the question of gender in connection with this program and the so-called revisionist western in general warrants a full-scale investigation beyond the scope of this project). This focus seems appropriate in relation to *Lonesome Dove* given the project's genesis at Motown, one of the United States's most successful black-owned companies at the time of its sale to MCA Inc. (with which Motown had signed a national record distribution deal in 1982) in June 1988 for $61 million (Castro 51). In a more general sense, a decision to consider the narrative and thematic proclivities of the western in terms of its representation of race is almost necessarily also a decision to look at the genre from a nontraditional perspective. The issue of race *always* has been *implicitly* central to literary, cinematic, televisual, and historical accounts of the conquest of the North American continent. At an *explicit* level, however, these interpretive narratives typically have suppressed, marginalized, grotesquely distorted, or ignored it.[2]

Nelson George has attributed the gradual decline in the Motown Record Corporation's creative influence and commercial clout since its heyday in the 1960s and early 1970s to a combination of factors. These include a general squeeze on independent record companies by the large corporate labels (Motown was the last significant holdout), defection from Motown by most of its major talent (e.g., Marvin Gaye, Diana Ross, Michael Jackson) coupled with an inability to nurture successful new acts with the same consistency, and a general loss of drive and focused sense of purpose. The company's ventures into movie and television production in the 1970s and 1980s perhaps may be indicative of scattershot corporate goal-making, but Motown's attempts to establish a cross-media base of operations mirrors on a smaller scale the accelerating trend toward diversified ownership among the giant media conglomerates (a trend accelerated, of course, by the Reagan administration's acknowledgment that existing antitrust statutes would be tacitly ignored).

Still, *Lonesome Dove* represented something of a new direction for Motown. Not only had the company not had a substantial commercial success in the realm of feature filmmaking since 1972's *Lady Sings the Blues,* but, as George notes, most of its other sporadic productions had leaned thematically and narratively toward explorations of aspects of the African-American experience (e.g., *Mahogany, The Bingo Long Traveling All-Stars and Motor Kings, Scott Joplin: King of Ragtime, Thank God It's Friday,* and *The Wiz*). *Lonesome Dove,* in contrast, was a novel by a white Texan featuring an ensemble of predominantly white characters who undergo experiences viewed from perspectives historically characteristic of white-male mythologies of the American West. According to Gelman, Suzanne de Passe says that "Motown maintained creative control of *Dove*" (101). Nevertheless, it is unclear just what this control entailed, as the adaptation of the novel for television by Bill Wittliff (another white Texan) was remarkably faithful to the letter and spirit of McMurtry's novel. By no means am I suggesting that this choice of projects or the subsequent fidelity of the miniseries to the source novel was a "betrayal" of Motown's deep roots in the African-American experience. Rather, it seems primarily to indicate a new direction in corporate strategy, a signal to the Hollywood establishment that Motown intended to position itself as a broad-based, general interest production company. I do, however, want to explore some of the ramifications for the representation of race and gender implicit in the act

of renovating this particular genre in the context of American culture and society in the late 1980s.

The western, of course, is one of the most venerable and resilient genres in American popular literature. In the field of film studies, it has also been one of the most exhaustively researched.[3] Significantly, however, academic scholarship dealing with the western has slowed to a trickle since the late 1970s. This decline roughly coincided with the purported "death" of the genre as a commercially viable product within the American film and television industry. None of the few large-scale cinematic westerns produced by Hollywood in the 1980s (*Pale Rider, Silverado, Young Guns,* and a handful of others), has been more than a marginally bright star at the box office. It has been observed that some of the traditional thematic and narrative concerns of the western have been transposed to generic forms more currently in favor with movie audiences, such as the science fiction film (e.g., *The Road Warrior, Star Wars*) and the cop film. (The miscellaneous Dirty Harry films have all outgrossed *Pale Rider,* suggesting that viewers prefer Clint Eastwood brandishing a .44 Magnum rather than a Colt Peacemaker.)

It is generally agreed that the western is the Hollywood genre most overtly and fundamentally concerned with mythologies surrounding the geographic and cultural expansion of the United States. It traditionally charts the struggle of the forces of (European-derived) civilization against the forces of the wilderness (both natural elements and non-European peoples), ultimately celebrating the promised manifest destiny of a new order consisting of representative democracy and a free market economy. Early in its cinematic and literary history, the western also developed a tendency to be elegiac in tone. By the time Owen Wister's Virginian announced (the novel, set in the 1880s, was published in 1902), "We are getting ready for the change . . . [w]hen the natural pasture is eaten off" (362), the American west already had been declared officially closed, and the Virginian himself was planning to shift his prosperous livelihood from the cattle business to the coal industry.

Individual cowboys like the Virginian were the primary shock troops of Anglo civilization in these mythic representations, subsequently personified in the movies by reverberatingly iconic figures such as William S. Hart, Tom Mix, Gary Cooper (the most famous cinematic Virginian), John Wayne, Randolph Scott, and Clint Eastwood. Like the protagonists of other genres, the white male western hero lived according to a relatively inflexible moral code that placed him as a mediating figure between "civilization" and "savagery," community and the individual. A romanticized perpetual wanderer, he stood firm with the forces of the new social order, even though he himself would never be comfortably "civilized" (hence civilization's door slamming on Ethan Edwards' backside as he trudges alone back into Monument Valley at the end of *The Searchers*). As Robert Warshow wrote of "The Westerner" in 1954,

[i]f justice and order did not continually demand his protection, he would be without a calling. Indeed, we come upon him often in just that situation, as the reign of law settles over the West and he is forced to see that his day is over; those are the pictures which end with his death or with his departure to some more remote frontier.... The Westerner is the last gentleman, and the movies which over and over again tell his story are probably the last art form in which the concept of honor retains its strength. (140)

But whose "honor" is this? "Justice and order" for whom? Whose story is being told here, in these chronicles of American expansionism into a vast but finite frontier? If, as Thomas Schatz suggests, the processes of cultural mythmaking constitute "a basic human activity which structures human experience—whether social or personal, whether physical or metaphysical—in a distinct and consistent fashion" (262), it is important to remember that individual myths are designed and acceded to not just to explain events and patterns of behavior but to justify them in order to preserve a society's political and economic equilibrium. Roland Barthes' famous observation will suffice in this connection:

> Myth hides nothing and flaunts nothing: it distorts; myth is neither a lie nor a confession: it is an inflexion.... Entrusted with "glossing over" an intentional concept, . . . [myth,] driven to having either to unveil or to liquidate the concept . . . will *naturalize* it. We reach here the very principle of myth: it transforms history into nature. We now understand why, *in the eyes of the myth-consumer,* the intention . . . of the concept can remain manifest without however appearing to have an interest in the matter: what causes mythical speech to be uttered is perfectly explicit, but it is immediately frozen into something natural; it is not read as a motive, but as a reason. (original emphasis, 129)

Thus, for instance, when Frederick Jackson Turner in 1893 wrote his famous, influential, and much-debated essay, "The Significance of the Frontier in American History," he was offering a summary analysis of a geographical and social phenomenon—the westward expansion of the United States—that was by then already receding into history. Turner articulated a thesis that provided a justification of expansionism for his contemporaries and served, in conjunction with other complementary ideas voiced in the same era, to establish the philosophical basis of much subsequent policy and action by American public and private interests throughout the twentieth century. He saw the fact and idea of the frontier as the force propelling and guiding all over significant events and movements in American history, from the growth of industry to the Civil War. The American frontier, for Turner, was historically cyclical. Significantly, we always lived on the edge of it, in a perpetual tension between the settled metropolis and the verdant wilderness, and this tension generated in turn a constant urge to expand, to move forward (and always *from* the metropolis *to* the wilderness).

American social development has been continually beginning over again on the frontier. This perennial rebirth, this fluidity of American life, this expansion westward with its new opportunities, its continuous touch with the simplicity of primitive society, furnish the forces dominating American character. (1-2)

Seen as a mythical narrative, Turner's thesis is as interesting for what (and whom) it leaves out as it is for what it includes in its explanation of the American national identity. It "naturalizes" the phenomenon of geographical and economic expansion across the continent on the part of white European settlers as a positive and, in any case, inevitable occurrence. It privileges the wilderness, with its wide open spaces, as a land of unfettered economic opportunity and personal freedom—especially in comparison with the city's hyperregulated and hypercongested environment. Yet at the same time, suggests historian Richard Slotkin, the goal of Turner's and other traditional versions of the myth is less to celebrate the frontier than to "function as rationalizer of the processes of capitalist development in America" (34). The version of American history celebrated in Turner's thesis and in most other conventional renderings of the myth of the frontier, says Slotkin,

> became part of a nascent national ideology and mythology. The economic patterns it rationalized and the individual virtues it celebrated were only exotic and melodramatic versions of the characteristic processes of capitalist development—notably the boom/bust business cycle—and the social types thrown up by an expanding middle class. Thus the story of the Frontier and the materials of local folklore were taken up by the literary and ideological spokesmen of "the nation"—a group that had its own localistic loyalties, but which projected from them an ideology capable of organizing America as a unified nation-state. . . . [I]f the Frontier was at once a magic locus of potential wealth, it was also a mirror of its Metropolitan past, and the platform on which future Metropolitan centers would be erected. (39)

If we begin to reconceptualize the ideological agenda of the western story form as an artifact of American popular culture along these lines, it becomes increasingly clear that the narrative conventions of the genre were designed to serve the interests of society's status quo—and the racial, ethnic, and social groups most directly served by that status quo. It also becomes clearer why the genre—and the frontier myth itself—specifically excluded those groups who were traditionally marginalized within American culture as a whole. Hollywood's version of the West must, like Turner's, be scrutinized in recognition of its implicit acknowledgment and its particularized interpretation of the history of power relations in the United States. That is, the western typically speaks the myth of the American West in terms most conducive to placing the interests of market capitalism and white male entrepreneurs in a favorable light. The genre has traditionally celebrated the unfettered expansionist ambitions of the ruggedly individual Anglo cowboy, whether those ambitions are expressed as a generalized lust for the wide-open spaces (themselves symbolizing the supposed limitlessly exploitable potential of the free market) or as the violent seizure of a specific, and usually substantial, piece of turf. *Red River,* by overtly making the cowboy a capitalist, is a good example of the ideological framework of cinematic six-gun expansionism. When John Wayne's Tom Dunson shoots the Mexican range-riders in cold blood at the beginning of the film and declares that the entire landscape he is scanning now belongs to Tom Dunson, his act becomes an exercise in an explicitly mercantile manifest destiny. Dunson may be portrayed as a half-mad Captain Bligh in much of *Red River,* but he comes to his senses in the end (thanks to Montgomery Clift's steady Matthew Garth/Fletcher Christian, the junior partner in the firm), and in any case the film's narrative trajectory is very much in keeping with Frederick Jackson Turner's principles of the "inevitability" of westward expansion and of the unquestioned worth of the end result for society as a whole. Ruthlessness pays both emotionally and monetarily, and the film never so much as glances back at those dead Mexicans.

The decline of the western as a commercially viable film and television genre in the 1970s and 1980s is not tied only to its traditional association with white male supremacy, however. After all, other currently popular action genres, including those that have absorbed some of the western's traditional thematic concerns, are similarly dominated by white male protagonists (e.g., the science fiction film: *The Road Warrior* "solves" the problem of the vanished wilderness by blowing up the world and starting from scratch, placing Mad Max as the reluctant and cynical avatar of a new civilization in a post-apocalyptic frontier). Rather, the western was rendered obsolete primarily because of its close ties with the nineteenth- and early twentieth-century myth of free-enterprise capitalism. In the present postindustrial era, as more and more people find themselves permanently un- or underemployed and underpaid, as distinctions among social groups along race, gender, and class lines grow ever wider and more apparent, as the United States' decline as a world political and economic power grows more and more undeniable, America and Americans are increasingly concerned with keeping pace in this ominous new environment rather than dominating it. In *The Rise and Fall of the Great Powers,* Paul Kennedy alludes to the lingering appeal within the realm of popular culture of the notion of an ironclad American hegemony in world affairs. He suggests that the United States' ability "to reformulate its grand strategy in the light of the larger, uncontrollable changes taking place" is hindered by, among other things, "The still-powerful 'escapist' urges in the American social culture, which may be understandable in terms of the nation's 'frontier' past but [are] a hindrance to coming to terms with today's more complex, integrated world and with *other* cultures and ideologies" (524).[4]

How, then, can we correlate the popular success of *Lonesome Dove* with its appropriation of a generic vehicle characterized by such a blatant and ostensibly out-of-

fashion celebration of American expansionism? First of all, as a cultural document of the late Reagan era, *Lonesome Dove*'s relatively faithful adherence to generic conventions as they existed in the pre–*Little Big Man* era of the western marks it as a "return to traditionalism" in keeping with Reaganite ideology's willful conflation of history with myth in its rereading of America's past. (In this framework, for instance, the invasions of Grenada and Panama and the bombing of Libya become strategic and tactical triumphs reminiscent of World War II—the "Good War"—and the Nicaraguan Contras become the moral equivalent of America's "founding fathers.") If "Reaganite entertainment" is characterized by an attempt to reassure the viewer that such phenomena as the civil-rights and women's movements have been beaten into submission, then *Lonesome Dove* to a degree fits within the axis of desire defined most successfully by the self-consciously old-fashioned films of the *Star Wars* and *Indiana Jones* series, minus the neurotic irony of the Lucas-Spielberg factory.[5] It celebrates expansionism, the expansiveness of the wilderness, and masculine individuality to a greater degree than any Hollywood-generated western of the last generation or so.

Of course, the circle is never quite joined under these circumstances. In significant ways, we do not, cannot, buy into the frontier myth through means appropriate for audiences of earlier generations. Too much history (Vietnam, Watergate, the decline of America's industrial economy) has intervened between the myth and its material referents. Crucially, though, *Lonesome Dove* preserves the western's elegiac, nostalgic celebration of a way of life that exists no longer (and, of course, at all times existed only within the limited and orderly parameters of the myth. Characters and events are scaled at a level of epic grandness and historical self-consciousness unavailable within almost any other generic framework. In fact, the world created in this miniseries is rather hermetically sealed in the past. While steeped in the muted mourning for a passing era characteristic of many 60s and 70s westerns, we see in *Lonesome Dove* none of the markers of Progress that dot the landscape of movies like *The Wild Bunch* and *The Shootist*—no automobiles, no electric lights, not even the railroad.

Again, this is not the naively unambiguous celebration of the American West mummified in, for example, 1962's Cinerama spectacular *How the West Was Won* (considered a pretty stale cookie even by contemporary critics, much less those of succeeding generations). To the contrary, *Lonesome Dove* is characteristic of the "new traditionalism" in some contemporary American mass media storytelling in its calculated blending of the stately, linear logic of myth and the messy, nonlinear randomness of quotidian realism. In order to buy into a story form as oft-told as the western, to accept the premises of its internal logic, present-day viewers (like viewers in any era) have required the form to retool itself in accordance with current cultural norms, including in this instance a recognition and acknowledgment of the unpredictable nature of human existence. Consequently, the *Time* review of *Lone-*

some Dove was able to applaud the miniseries both for its adherence to fictional traditions *and* its gritty realism.

> *Lonesome Dove* is surprisingly nonrevisionist in its picture of the West. The good guys still perform stunning heroics with six-shooters, and Indians are faceless villains who whoop when they ride. Yet in its everyday details—the dust and the spit, the casual conversations about whoring, the pain of a man getting a mesquite thorn removed from his thumb—this may be the most vividly rendered old West in TV history. (Zoglin 78)

Newsweek, meanwhile, used the program's realistic touches as a convenient and cliched means of censuring television's supposedly usual mode of discourse: "In a medium built on cheap, prefab, illusion, *Lonesome Dove* drips with authenticity" (Waters 55).

In fact, the program's recurrent and deliberate obfuscation of the gap between historical myth and historical reality constitutes a narrative trope entirely characteristic of the fiction of Larry McMurtry. In his novels, McMurtry self-consciously engages in an ongoing comparison of the "old" West with the "new," stirring the ashes of the former until they spark a connection with the latter. His perspective is typically disillusioned, even fatalistic, betraying a nostalgic and sentimental longing to make the myth live and breathe in the here and now. McMurtry himself indirectly acknowledges this contradiction in an essay from *In a Narrow Grave.* In this essay he describes the down-to-earth "realism" of the working cowboy while continuing to conflate reality and myth. He moves effortlessly between broad descriptions in the abstract—as below—and concrete anecdotes involving his own relatives, who in turn become mythic figures by association. (Incidentally, the description here could also serve as a character sketch of *Lonesome Dove*'s cowboy philosopher Gus McCrae):

> The view is often proffered by worshippers of the cowboy that he is a realist of the first order, but that view is an extravagant and imperceptive fiction. Cowboys are romantics, extreme romantics, and ninety-nine out of a hundred of them are sentimental to the core. . . . People who think cowboys are realists generally think so because the cowboy's speech is salty and apparently straight-forward, replete with the wisdom of natural men. What that generally means is that cowboy talk sounds shrewd and perceptive, and so it does. In fact, however, both the effect and the intention of much cowboy talk is literary: cowboys are aphorists. . . . It is a realism in tone only: its insights are either wildly romantic, mock-cynical, or solemnly sentimental. . . . (149)

In his novels, McMurtry is obsessed with the fragility and preciousness of life and with the ways in which people cope with death, which in McMurtry-land typically arrives unpredictably, without prior narrative warning or motivation. The suddenness and apparent arbitrariness of death in a McMurtry novel send a shock through the surviving characters, who learn in succeeding chapters to cope with their loss. They also send a shock through the reader, who continues to follow the narrative and, on another level, is invited to perceive this story as more "authentic" and more "real" than other stories of the same generic lineage. The insertion of apparently random events (such as deaths) into an otherwise conventionally linear and generically archetypal storyline customarily connotes within the Western (as opposed to western) literary tradition a heightened realism, a closer connection between the fictional construct and reality itself.

This literary trope is absolutely central to *Lonesome Dove,* both as novel and as miniseries. The story is propelled as much by a series of sudden, random deaths (the Irish boy Sean's horrible poisoning by swarming water moccasins, Joe's, Janey's, and Roscoe's murders at the hands of Blue Duck, etc.) and terrifying misfortunes (Lorena's kidnapping) as it is by the cattle drive to Montana. McMurtry's philosophical perspective on life is embedded in these deaths, and he entrusts various characters—most often Gus McCrae—with verbalizing that perspective. In the television version of the story, for instance, McCrae and his partner Woodrow Call comment in tandem on Sean's tragic and violent demise: "This was a good, brave boy," says McCrae. "Had a fine tenor voice and we'll miss him. There's accidents in life and he met with a bad one. Now we may all do the same if we ain't careful. Ashes to ashes, dust to dust. Now let's the rest of us go on to Montana." The more taciturn and unreflective Call adds, "He's right, boys. The best thing you can do with death is to ride off from it."

In their blend of straightforward sentiment with masculine stoicism, these are the kinds of cowboy aphorisms McMurtry finds so profound. And well they may be. Viewers may indeed be sobered by the randomness of Sean's death and by its graphic depiction—and moved to assume on that basis that *Lonesome Dove* is more "realistic" than most westerns because the world it depicts is as disordered as the world in which we live. The narrative construction of the story thus tends to diminish or conceal its status as fiction, although the world of *Lonesome Dove* can lay no stronger claim to "truth" or "reality" than any other fictional story. In fact, like all narratives, it shapes its world so that some points of view are directly acknowledged and voiced, while others are not; in any reading of this story, as with all stories, we must, as Robert Stam and Louise Spence have argued, "distinguish . . . between realism as a goal—Brecht's 'laying bare the causal network'—and realism as a style or constellation of strategies aimed at producing an illusionistic 'reality effect' (8). The narrative strategies of *Lonesome Dove,* then, are deployed in part to convince the viewer that this is not "just" a western; by appropriating "realism as a style" and the emotional jolts generated through that style, the program obscures to a degree its ties to this "obsolete" genre. It "naturalizes" the traditional world of the western no less than *Stagecoach*, say, did in 1939. Differences in the specific articulation of that world in the context of the late 1980s occur because the rhetorical means of reaching that goal must be reformulated in accordance with generalized shifts in historical perspective since the hey-day of the genre.

It seems likely also that *Lonesome Dove* appealed to viewers because its narrative strategies are specifically geared to the discursive demands of the medium in which it appeared. That is, this is a *television* western, not a movie western. In *TV: The Most Popular Art,* Horace Newcomb observes that the classic television westerns of the 1950s and 1960s, such as *Gunsmoke* and *Bonanza,* moved "away from the classical problems of the western frontier toward the more human and individualistic aspects of those problems," and that the process of adapting the western for the world of television was marked both by an adherence to much of the genre's conventional iconography and by an infusion of new conventions and emphases, "the elements of family and psychology common to the more domestic types of television" (74-5). The need for these changes was perceived because series television demands repetition and a permanent deferral of ultimate resolution in ways that the movies do not. If the hero rides off into the sunset at the end of the first episode, what do you do next week? Consequently, says Newcomb, rigid fidelity to the narrative patterns of the novelist or cinematic westerns would have ensured that on television "the classic issues of western adventure would have played themselves out long ago. In order to avoid this the producers have applied the western vision to a host of other problems" (82). This redirection of the genre, its scaling down from the epic to the intimate, stems also from the technology of the medium. In "Toward a Television Aesthetic," Newcomb argues that the small size of the television screen and the relatively poor quality of the image muffles the visual possibilities for grandeur and expansiveness (617).

If the western was to survive on television, then, it had to tell and sell itself in new ways, and *Lonesome Dove* is simply a recent manifestation of lessons first learned by writers and producers more than three decades ago. As grand as the scope of the program seems, this expansiveness is informed more by the historical and mythic baggage carried by the western genre itself than by what we actually see on our television sets. This sense of sweep is also suggested by the geographic and temporal trajectory of the narrative and by the form of the miniseries itself (a story so large it must be spread across four evenings and eight hours). Within those thousands of miles and several hundred minutes of story, we witness primarily small-scale events involving various combinations of the ensemble of characters, and these are engaged primarily in conversation, not "action." Despite the attention paid by critics to the amount of blood spilled over the course of *Lonesome Dove*'s cattle drive, the program's most significant and emotionally charged moments are not gunfights, stampedes, or other violently cathartic events usually associated with the western. Rather, the program's fireworks occur mainly in the aftermaths of these events (e.g., the several funerals steeped in Gus's cowboy proverbs, finally including his own deathbed scene) and in intimate conversations, usually involving only two characters at a time,

which have little direct lineage to the narrative patterns and thematic concerns of the movie western.

Exemplary here is the sequence early in the drive in which Gus and Woodrow find themselves by a creek outside of San Antonio. This creek holds such powerful and bittersweet memories for Gus in relation to the torch he's been carrying for Clara Allen, the great love of his life, who's now living on a ranch in Kansas with her husband and kids. At the scene's beginning Gus waxes nostalgic over the happy times spent with Clara by this creek (he even openly weeps). The scene's end with him haranguing Call over Call's mistreatment of a former lover, the long-deceased prostitute Maggie, and over Call's subsequent refusal to acknowledge that he is the father of Maggie's son Newt (the young initiate cowhand of the story). In the studied contrast (here and throughout the story) between Gus's loquaciousness and unashamed externalizing of emotion and Woodrow's taciturnity and repression of feeling, *Lonesome Dove* explores turf upon which the western does not ordinarily tread. Richard Campbell has suggested, in fact, that McCrae's privileging of interpersonal relationships and of the idea of community over the westerner's (and Call's) more conventional isolation and individualism marks Gus as a uniquely "feminized" western hero. Campbell contends that the program as a whole stands as "a stern critique of the perils of rugged individualism and its impulse to cut us off from genuine emotion, from the self, and from our responsibilities for others" (29-32). Campbell's argument is provocative and illuminating, but he doesn't adequately consider the incorporation of "claw-back" strategies within the text that work to blunt the effect of this critique. After all, McCrae "compensates" for his feminine characteristics by wielding his shooting iron with a deadly and unrepentent efficiency. Moreover, unlike the women in the story, he remains free to ride off into whatever sunset he chooses. That is, it can be argued that the character of McCrae does little more than pay convenient lip service to historical and social changes that helped render the western passé. As David Thorburn has suggested, Gus's extended bouts of self-reflection and moralizing

> have no impact on McCrae's behavior. They complicate his character for the audience, as they are no doubt intended to do, but they remain essentially irrelevant to the momentum of the action, and represent a characteristic habit or gesture of self-indulgence wherein the story confesses to crimes or failings which it then proceeds to reenact anyway. (16-17)

Still, it is true that *Lonesome Dove,* like many contemporary male-buddy narratives, is centrally concerned with the process of redefining a (white) masculinity in crisis, pressured on all sides by "threats" to its hegemony. The series emphasizes a melodramatic limning of the masculine mystique characteristic of television ensemble dramas such as *Magnum P.I., Hill Street Blues,* and *St. Elsewhere.* John Fiske suggests that these televisual rituals of male bonding develop a goal-centered, rather than relationship-centered (i.e., conventionally feminine), intimacy. Fiske adds, "The hero team also compensates for male insecurity: any inadequacies of one member are compensated by the strengths of another, so the teams become composite constructions of masculinity" (263).

Male melodrama sandwiched between layers of iconography characteristic of the movie and television western, then, constitutes *Lonesome Dove*'s operative mode. It is the narrative and ideological strategies of the western which are of most immediate concern in a consideration of the representation of race. From its mythic perch, the genre traditionally has scanned a landscape dominated by white, male patriarchal culture. In another context, Stuart Hall has identified this slant as characteristic of colonialist literatures in general and has noted the ubiquitous presence of

> the "absent" but imperializing "white eye"; the unmarked position from which all these observations are made and from which, alone, they make sense. This is the history of slavery and conquest, written, seen, drawn and photographed by The Winners. They cannot be *read* and made sense of from any other position. The "white eye" is always outside the frame—but seeing and positioning everything within it. (38-9)

This is Hollywood's West: it is the West seen from the point of view of the colonizers rather than that of the colonized. The western becomes, that is, a rhetorical means of explaining and justifying the forcible Anglo expansion into non-Anglo lands, and the obliteration by Anglo culture of non-Anglo ways of life, not to mention non-Anglo peoples. The genre is articulated in ways that deliberately control and limit the terms of debate over the issues confronted in the historical act of westward expansion. Working from a different but analogous imperial paradigm, Edward Said also establishes this assertion of linguistic control as the ideological basis of scholarly and literary discussions of "the Orient" by European writers during the period of European colonization of the Middle East:

> . . . Orientalism can be discussed and analyzed as the corporate institution for dealing with the Orient—dealing with it by making statements about it, authorizing views of it, describing it, by teaching it, settling it, ruling over it: in short, Orientalism as a Western style for dominating, restructuring, and having authority over the Orient. (3)

The conventions of plot, character, and setting within the Hollywood western, then, generally work to forward this goal of "having authority over" a geographic and cultural Other by portraying white expansionism in the North American frontier as an epic adventure with generally positive historical ramifications. In Tom Engelhardt's words, "the viewer is forced behind the barrel of [the Westerner's] repeating rifle and it is from that position . . . that he receives a picture history of Western colonialism and imperialism" (270). In an essay on race and American culture, Michael Omi notes the appropriateness of Engelhardt's extended metaphor, arguing:

Westerns have indeed become the prototype for European and American excursions throughout the Third World. . . . The "humanity" of whites is contrasted with the brutality and treachery of non-whites, brave (i.e., white) souls are pitted against the merciless hordes in conflicts ranging from Indians against the British Lancers to Zulus against the Boers. What Stuart Hall refers to as the imperializing "white eye" provides the framework for these films, lurking outside the frame and yet seeing and positioning everything within. . . . (116)

Richard Dyer also addresses this generic agenda in the course of discussing the narrative parameters of British-produced films dealing with the British colonial experience in black Africa.

> The colonial landscape is expansive, enabling the hero to roam and giving us the entertainment of action; it is unexplored, giving him the task of discovery and us the pleasures of mystery; it is uncivilised, needing taming, providing the spectacle of power; it is difficult and dangerous, testing his machismo, providing us with suspense. In other words, the colonial landscape provides the occasion for the realisation of white male virtues, which are not qualities of being but of doing—acting, discovering, taming, conquering. At the same time, colonialism, as a social, political and economic system, even in fictions, also carries with it challenges of responsibility, of the establishment and maintenance of order, of the application of reason and authority to situations. These, too, are qualities of white manhood that are realised in the process of the colonial text. . . . (52)

This symbiotic relationship between landscape and male protagonist is, of course, also very much a part of the western. As an American colonial spectacle, it offers, in Steve Neale's words, "maximum scope for variations and permutations on the relations of the male figure to space, light, texture, colour and so on, as well as for variations and permutations on the speed and mode of its movements" (59). To this I would add only that this central figure is almost always a *white* male. Even in the so-called anti-westerns of the late 1960s and early 1970s (e.g., *The Wild Bunch, Little Big Man, A Man Called Horse*), most reversals and negations of generic conventions that historically "speak" the perspective of the white establishment in fact only shift the dominant point of view from the white establishment to the white counterculture. This perspective is more sympathetic to (especially) Native Americans' position on white westward expansion, but even here the colonized people have no authentic voice. Instead, their words and actions are witnessed and interpreted by a white intermediary who is the central protagonist of the film (Dustin Hoffman in *Little Big Man,* Richard Harris in *A Man Called Horse*). Virtually all westerns, then, whether "traditional" or "revisionist," are locked into a colonialist mode of enunciation. As Mikhail Bakhtin suggested:

> Language for the individual consciousness, lies on the borderline between oneself and the other. The

word in language is half someone else's. It becomes "one's own" only when the speaker populates it with his own intention, his own accent, when he appropriates the word, adapting it to his own semantic and expressive intention. Prior to this moment of appropriation, the word does not exist in a neutral and impersonal language (it is not, after all, out of a dictionary that the speaker gets his words!), but rather it exists in other people's mouths, in other people's contexts, serving other people's intentions: it is from there that one must take the word, and make it one's own. (293-4)

Access to one's "own accent" traditionally has been denied to racial minorities and women in the western. Thus, the western—not unlike other literary, film, and television genres—reproduces and naturalizes historical reality: those groups who are traditionally marginalized and oppressed in the real world of social relations in the United States are similarly marginalized and oppressed in the fictive world of the cowboy movie. This hegemonic relationship leaks within the world of the western as much as within other genres, producing revisionist representations such as those described above, but, again, the western has never completely escaped a mode of discourse in which "the intruder exchanges places in our eyes with the intruded upon" (Engelhardt 270).

What I find unfortunate about *Lonesome Dove,* then, is the way the creators of the series deal with the ideological baggage it inevitably carries. Whatever else it might be talking about, the western tells a story of imperialism from the perspective of the imperialist, who almost always happens to be a white male of European heritage. In order for this perspective to remain ascendant, all potential "competitors" for the westerner's turf—Native Americans, Mexicans, African-Americans, women of all racial and ethnic backgrounds—must be neutralized or eradicated. This activity is carried out in *Lonesome Dove* no less than in the average Gene Autry film. The women of the story either are domesticated or want to be. While the cowboys are trekking thousands of miles and engaging in miscellaneous rites of ruggedly individualistic manhood, the women are tied to a parcel of land and/or a man—they're looking for roots. Even July Johnson's wife Ellie, the one woman in the story who wanders as footloose as the male characters, only does so in obsessive pursuit of her ex-lover; if he hadn't been hanged just after she found him, she probably would have settled down, too. As it is, Ellie's wander lust becomes in the context of this story a deeply neurotic flight from a woman's true calling as nurturer of home and hearth. When she abandons her own newborn (male) baby (who is immediately adopted by Clara, the resident earth mother in a ten-gallon hat), that tears it—Ellie turns up gruesomely dead within the space of two commercial breaks.[6]

The narrative space apportioned to *Lonesome Dove*'s minority characters (all of whom are male) is no less problematic. All are connected by a mutually mystical and mystified closeness to Nature and a metaphysical version of reality. Deets, the black cowhand, is the drive's chief scout and guide—he can smell a storm brewing or a tank of water from 80 miles off. Po Campo, the drive's Mexican cook, is the group's second-rank philosopher (behind Gus) and eventually its seer when he accurately foretells Gus's death. The "half-breed" Blue Duck apparently ranges over the Southwest filling a role as the frontier's demonic id, melting out of and into the landscape at will.

Of these characters, Blue Duck carries the most narrative weight—he is even accorded his own recurrent musical theme, an ominous "Indian-sounding" trill on a flute that modulates into a wail evoking the howl of a wolf. He is the story's most significant manifestation of human evil, an enemy dating from McCrae's and Call's past as Texas Rangers ridding the territory of outlaws and Indians, returned now to terrorize them anew. Menacingly and charismatically portrayed in the miniseries by Frederick Forrest, Blue Duck robs, kidnaps, and murders with no compunction and no explanations—he exists as the unknowable and lethal Other of which civilized folks are justifiably terrified. He is also a racist caricature worthy of a Cecil B. DeMille epic. When he kidnaps the beautiful-yet-innocent prostitute Lorena, he trots her through a tour of the most horrible psychological and physical tortures he can dream up. Even before he sells her to a band of depraved (and, eventually, yes, drunken) Indians and a couple of white buffalo hunters reminiscent of the street scum who get shot full of holes in the average Charles Bronson movie, he tells the petrified girl, in graphically visual images, what he'll do to her if she tries to escape:

> I got a treatment for women that try to run away. I cut a little hole in their stomachs, pull out a gut, and wrap it around a limb. I drag 'em thirty or forty feet and tie 'em down. Then I watch what the coyotes are havin' for supper.[7]

While Gus rides to Lorena's rescue in this instance, efficiently dispatching all of the Indians and street scum with one bullet each, Blue Duck escapes. We expect a climactic confrontation and shoot-out between him and the ex-Rangers, but this would be out of step with *Lonesome Dove*'s messily "realistic" version of the Wild West. Instead, Call encounters Blue Duck entirely by accident near the end of the story, in the course of his journey back to Texas with McCrae's pickled body. The indian has been captured and is about to be hanged by the good people of Santa Rosa, New Mexico Territory. The curious Call visits Blue Duck in the local jail, where the "breed" is wrapped in chains and guarded by a battalion of lawmen. He is also utterly unrepentant. After declaring that he should have "caught . . . and cooked" Gus when he had the chance, he states with considerable pride, "I raped women, stole children, burned houses and shot men, and run off horses and killed cattle, and robbed who I pleased all over your territory and you never even had a good look at me until today." Then, as he is being escorted from his cell to be hanged, Blue Duck breaks free and, taking a hapless deputy with him, plunges spectacularly out of a fourth floor window to his (and the deputy's) death on the street below. Even here, he successfully eludes the letter of the white man's law. But this is no defiant gesture characteristic of 70s revisionist westerns, symbolically asserting the strength and character of the Native American way of life. Within the world of *Lonesome Dove,* Blue Duck is not a revisionist hero—he deserved to be hanged, and the circumstances of his demise evoke only a renewed wonder and fear of the nonwhite Other he represents.

The characterization of Deets (played by Danny Glover) is in a way more perplexing than that of Blue Duck, who is at least unambiguously and flamboyantly portrayed as evil incarnate. Deets is one of the good guys—a veritable saint among men, in fact. And here lies the "problem" with Deets—there's no "there" there, no personality to speak of except for his unfailing kindness, sunny disposition, generosity, and competence. In a narrative environment full of prickly, rounded, strikingly individualized characters, Deets is distinctive only in his utter blandness. The western still doesn't know how to fit an African-American cowboy into its generic framework, although Deets' presence does implicitly acknowledge the fact that approximately 25% of all ranch hands and cowboys during the period of American expansion across the western plains and mountains were black.[8] The genre does, of course, have a racial agenda, but this agenda usually has been directed toward rationalizing the eradication of Native Americans by whites. Movie and television westerns generally have been content simply to ignore the fact of black people in the Wild West except as an occasional novelty, typically in stories specifically focusing on the issue of race (e.g., *The Legend of Nigger Charley, Blazing Saddles,* single episodes of *Lawman* and *The Rifleman,* the late 60s series *The Outcasts*).[9]

Lonesome Dove makes a valiant effort to normalize Deets' presence by not calling attention to his racial heritage, by making him one of the boys, but no narratively or thematically significant niche is ever found for him in the story. A moral leader by example, he never seeks to usurp the worldly power of Call and McCrae. He engages in little banter with the other cowboys (although he does sit at the same table), and he is forever riding on ahead. He thus drifts into the periphery of the story, progressively becoming just another invisible man. Deets' most spectacular scene is the one in which he meets his shockingly violent and irony-laden death, skewered by a lance wielded by a starving Native American boy (who is in turn shot dead by Call and McCrae) who apparently reads hostile intent in Deets' kindly concern for the welfare of another child, "Take him, Captain," whispers the dying man as he holds the baby out to the others. "Don't want him to fall."

But even here Deets is marginalized. His death, which concludes the third part of the miniseries, and his funeral, which begins part four, become in tandem just another vehicle through which the central characters conduct further explorations of the capriciousness of existence. McCrae, as usual, says some plain but eloquent words and gets a little choked up. The usually stoic Call carves

a eulogy into a wooden grave marker. Young Newt flashes back to Deets waving him, in slow motion, a final, smiling farewell. The music swells. The sheer quantity of emotion poured out through these scenes seems out of proportion to Deets' previously peripheral presence in and importance to the story. Everybody likes and respects him, but until he dies we don't see much significant interaction between him and the other characters. Newt's teary remembrance rings especially false; not only is it overwrought, but we've never really had a clue that he felt so deeply about Deets. As a result of all this melodrama, *Lonesome Dove*'s treatment of Deets, and especially his death, smacks uncomfortably of paternalism. The program wants to present a "positive image" of an African-American person in the context of a semitraditional western, but the strategy for doing so involves bleaching him of all markings of a distinctive identity. Robert Stam and Louise Spence have forcefully addressed the problem with this strategy.

> Much of the work on racism in the cinema, like early work on the representation of women, has stressed the issue of the "positive image." This reductionism, though not wrong, is inadequate and fraught with methodological dangers. The exact nature of "positive," first of all, is somewhat relative: black incarnations of patience and gradualism, for example, have always been more pleasing to whites than to blacks. A cinema dominated by positive images, characterised by a bending-over-backwards-not-to-be-racist attitude, might ultimately betray a lack of confidence in the group portrayed, which usually has no illusions concerning its own perfection. . . . We should be equally suspicious of a naive integrationism which simply inserts new heroes and heroines, this time drawn from the ranks of the oppressed, into the old functional roles that were themselves oppressive, much as colonialism invited a few assimilated "natives" to join the club of the "elite." (9)

Lonesome Dove treads very nervously and delicately on the issue of race; clearly, its creators would prefer to tiptoe around it altogether. They apparently fail to grasp, however, that using the voice of America's most overtly imperial storytelling genre to tell their tale not only inherently weaves the issue of race into the fabric of the narrative, but also makes it extraordinarily difficult to eradicate racist notions from that narrative. It is inexcusable that the characterization of Blue Duck resorts to priming the pump of an undifferentiated fear of (cultural, racial) difference that pollutes most cinematic and televisual representations of Native Americans. It is in a way no more defensible to "naively integrate" the character of Deets into the world of the western without ever acknowledging the historically problematic nature of his presence there. Consequently, an attempt to ferret out the preferred meanings within this miniseries' narrative strategies would probably stamp *Lonesome Dove,* in the context of late-Reagan/early-Bush era cultural production, as a mainstream liberal tract. That is, its views on race and gender, communicated obliquely through deliberate and often thoughtful disruptions of the conventions of the western genre (Gus's "feminine" attributes, Clara's strength and managerial ability, the matter-of-fact presence of Deets as an equal member of the team), are more enlightened than those of Ed Meese, the Rehnquist court, or certainly the Great Communicator himself or his successor. But *Lonesome Dove* (as liberals will) also makes a series of narrative, thematic, and political compromises. While it is willing to stretch the boundaries of the western ever so gently, it finally adheres to and embraces the more sexist and racist connotations of the genre (e.g., through the celebration—ambiguous, admittedly—of a specifically masculine rootlessness and individuality, as well as the disingenuous martyring of Deets).

Is this genre therefore by definition incapable of expressing a more progressive, egalitarian point of view? Is there some way out of the prison house of the western? I think so, but it will involve rewriting the genre by first rewriting the history that informs it. In his BBC television series *The Day the Universe Changed,* James Burke tells of the peasants in eighteenth-century France who informed scientists working for Louis XVI of their repeated sightings of rocks that seemed to fall from the sky. This news was immediately discounted by the scientists, since it had come from the mouths of noncredible sources, i.e., peasants. Come the Revolution, whereupon the voice of the peasant commanded a new and unprecedented respect, *et voilà*, these rocks were quickly identified as meteorites. The key is, as Stuart Hall puts it, to make "visible what is usually invisible; the assumptions on which current practices depend" (47). A truly "progressive" *and* popular movie or television western, then, is possible, but its realization depends on a radical reconceptualization of our mainstream notions of "difference" and "otherness"—and that will happen only when historically marginalized voices within American culture find the means of seizing and holding center stage without resorting to debilitating assimilationist strategies, when it becomes possible to "populate" that rock with a "new intention" and call it a meteorite.

NOTES

[1] Very briefly summarized, *Lonesome Dove* chronicles the adventures of Augustus McCrae (Robert Duvall) and Woodrow Call (Tommy Lee Jones), former Texas Rangers who at the beginning of the story are marking time with some haphazard ranching in the tiny, isolated south Texas settlement of Lonesome Dove. When their former Ranger compadre Jake Spoon (Robert Urich) rides into town after an absence of several years with tales of wide-open spaces in Montana, Call's insatiable wanderlust and sense of adventure are stimulated. He decides to embark on an epic cattle drive to the new territories, taking Lonesome Dove's miscellaneous ranchhands and a reluctant McCrae (he's by nature more philosopher and raconteur than man of action) along for the ride. The important supporting characters introduced here include: Newt (Ricky Schroeder), an ingenuous and promising teenaged hand for whom the drive serves as an initiation into manhood and who, it develops, may be Call's illegitimate

son; Deets (Danny Glover), also a longtime compatriot of Call and McCrae and the most competent cowboy on the drive; and Lorena (Diane Lane), the young town prostitute, who tags along with the irresponsible, footloose Jake because he promises to take her to San Francisco. Most of the rest of the miniseries is an episodic account of adventures encountered over the course of the drive, including: the kidnaping of Lorena by the evil "half-breed" Blue Duck (Frederic Forrest) and her subsequent rescue by McCrae; the bittersweet reunion of McCrae and his former lover Clara (Anjelica Huston), who is now the matriarch of a ranch in Nebraska tending to a herd of horses, two young daughters, and a comatose husband; and the death by various ironic means of several members of the party, including Spoon, Deets, and McCrae. Miscellaneous other supporting characters weave in and out of the story through interactions with members of the drive; most significant among them are July Johnson (Chris Cooper), a young sheriff from Arkansas, and his wayward wife Ellie (Glenn Headly), who abandons her husband and embarks on her own ill-fated trek in search of a long-lost lover. Finally, Call and the remaining hands reach Montana and stake out a new homestead. The last section of the story describes Call's solitary trek back to Texas to bury the body of his old friend McCrae. For a good general account of themes and narrative strategies in *Lonesome Dove,* see Richard Campbell and Jimmie L. Reeves, "Resurrecting the TV Western: The Cowboy, the Frontier, and *Lonesome Dove*," *Television Quarterly* 24.3 (1990): 33-44.

[2] For a very useful single-volume summary of much recent revisionist work on the various mythologies of the American West, see Patricia Nelson Limerick, *The Legacy of Conquest* (New York: Norton, 1987).

[3] See books by the following authors: John Cawelti, *The Six Gun Mystique,* 2d ed. (Bowling Green: Bowling Green State University Popular Press, 1984); George N. Fenin and William K. Everson, *The Western: From Silents to the Seventies* (New York: Penguin, 1977); William T. Pilkington and Don Graham, eds., *Western Movies* (Albuquerque: University of New Mexico Press, 1979); Jim Kitses, *Horizons West* (Bloomington: Indiana University Press, 1969); John H. Lenihan, *Showdown* (Urbana: University of Illinois Press, 1980); and Will Wright, *Sixguns and Society* (Berkeley: University of California Press, 1975).

[4] Among recently popular Hollywood films, *Black Rain,* with its extremes of paranoia and schizophrenic racism, is an especially interesting genre-based attempt to work out the new rules of the game.

[5] See Andrew Britton, "Blissing Out: The Politics of Reaganite Entertainment," *Movie* 31/32 (1986): 1-42; and Robin Wood, "Papering the Cracks: Fantasy and Ideology in the Reagan Era," in *Hollywood from Vietnam to Reagan* (New York: Columbia University Press, 1986): 162-88.

[6] For an overview and bibliography of women in the historical American West, see Limerick above. For an ex-

tremely provocative and useful recent interpretation of women's place in the literature of the West, see Jane Tompkins, "West of Everything," *South Atlantic Quarterly* 86.4 (Fall 1987): 357-77.

[7] This speech is lifted verbatim from the novel except for the last line which was apparently considered inappropriate for family viewing. In McMurtry's novel, the last line reads: "That way they can watch the coyotes come and eat their guts" (419).

[8] See Philip Durham and Everett L. Jones, *The Negro Cowboys* (New York: Dodd, Mead, 1965); Kenneth W. Porter, *The Negro on the American Frontier* (New York: Arno Press, 1971); William Loren Katz, *The Black West*, rev. ed. (Garden City, NY: Anchor Press, 1973); and W. Sherman Savage, *Blacks in the West* (Westport, CT: Greenwood Press, 1976).

[9] For information on African Americans in television westerns, see J. Fred MacDonald, *Blacks and White TV* (Chicago: Nelson-Hall, 1983).

WORKS CITED

Armes, Roy. *Third World Film Making and the West.* Berkeley: University of California Press, 1987.

Bakhtin, M. M. "Discourse in the Novel." *The Dialogic Imagination.* Austin: University of Texas Press, 1981. 259-422.

Barthes, Roland. *Mythologies.* New York: Hill and Wang, 1972.

Campbell, Richard. "*Lonesome Dove* and the Re-Invention of the Western Hero." Speech Communication Association Convention. November, 1989.

Carter, Bill. "A Big Playoff for *Lonesome Dove.*" *New York Times* 6 Mar. 1989: D1, D8.

Castro, Janice. "Hitsville Goes Hollywood." *Time* 30 Jan. 1989:51.

Dench, Ernest A. "The Dangers of Employing Redskins as Movie Actors" in *Making Movies.* New York: Macmillan, 1915.

Dyer, Richard. "White." *Screen* 29.4 (Autumn 1988): 44-64.

Engelhardt, Tom. "Ambush at Kamikaze Pass." *Counterpoint Perspectives on Asian America.* Ed. Emma Gee. Los Angeles: University of California Asian American Study Center, 1976. 269-79.

Fiske, John. "British Cultural Studies and Television." *Channels of Discourse.* Ed. Robert C. Allen. Chapel Hill: University of North Carolina Press, 1987. 254-89.

Gelman, Morrie. "*Dove*'s High Scores Fly in the Face of Conventional Wisdom. *Variety* 15-21 Feb. 1989: 85.

————. "Motown's *Lonesome Dove* Gamble Pays Off: de Passe Declares Herself Vindicated." *Variety* 15-21 Feb. 1989: 85.

George, Nelson. *The Death of Rhythm and Blues,* New York: Pantheon, 1988.

————. *Where Did Our Love Go?* New York: St. Martin's Press, 195.

Hall, Stuart. "The Whites of Their Eyes: Racist Ideologies and the Media." *Silver Linings.* Eds. George Bridges and Rosalind Brunt. London: Lawrence and Wishart, 1981.

Kennedy, Paul. *The Rise and Fall of the Great Powers.* New York: Random House, 1987.

McMurtry, Larry. *In a Narrow Grave.* New York: Touchstone, 1968.

————. *Lonesome Dove.* New York: Pocket Books, 1985.

Newcomb, Horace. "Toward a Television Aesthetic." *Television: The Critical View,* 4th ed. Ed. Horace Newcomb. New York: Oxford, 1987. 613-27.

Omi, Michael. "In Living Color: Race and American Culture." *Cultural Politics in Contemporary America.* Eds. Ian Angus and Sut Jhally. New York: Routledge, 1989. 111-22.

Said, Edward. *Orientialism.* New York: Vintage, 1979.

Schatz, Thomas. *Hollywood Genres.* New York: Random House, 1981.

Slotkin, Richard. *The Fatal Environment.* New York: Atheneum, 1985.

Stam, Robert and Louise Spence. "Colonialism, Racism and Representation." *Screen* 24.2 (Mar./Apr. 1983): 2-20.

Thorburn, David. "Reading *Lonesome Dove.*" Speech Communication Association Convention. November, 1989.

Turner, Frederick Jackson. "The Significance of the Frontier in American History." *The Turner Thesis.* Ed. George Rogers Taylor. Boston: D. C. Heath, 1949. 1-2.

Warshow, Robert. "Movie Chronicle: The Westerner." *The Immediate Experience.* Garden City: Doubleday, 1962.

Waters, Harry F. "How the West Was Once." *Newsweek* 6 Feb. 1989: 55.

Wister, Owen. *The Virginian.* New York: Pocket Books, 1956.

Zoglin, Richard. "Poetry on the Prairie." *Time* 6 Feb. 1989: 78.

Catherine Nickerson

SOURCE: "Serial Detection and Serial Killers in *Twin Peaks*," in *Literature Film Quarterly,* Vol. 21, No. 4, 1993, pp. 271-76.

[*In the following essay, Nickerson discusses ways in which* Twin Peaks *both embodies and subverts the conventions of detective fiction while employing characteristics of the literary gothic tradition.*]

During its first season, *Twin Peaks* invited us to watch as if we were reading a detective novel. The narrative began with—or at—a dead body, as all proper detective stories do, then unfolded into a series of investigative responses to the murder of a young woman: the arrival of a heroic detective, the evaluation of physical and forensic evidence, the interrogation of suspects and witnesses. But as many people have observed, the series seemed, in the second season—if not even earlier—to become something quite other than a televised detective novel. *Twin Peaks* asks us to compare it with the literary detective novel in both its parody of the genre and its celebration of detective conventions, but, at the same time, the series slyly disassembles the narrative structure that undergirds detective fiction. This subversion is precisely what makes the show so simultaneously like and unlike a detective novel.

The parody and celebration begin with the arrival of the FBI agent, Dale Cooper. Cooper is a "Special Agent" in many senses; all the qualities that immediately mark him as special or extraordinary—his perceptions of what is unusual about Twin Peaks; his attention to correct FBI procedures and protocol; his ability and willingness to look with cool suspicion past social standing and social performances—are those of the hero-detective of both the British classic style and the American hard-boiled school. Cooper quickly establishes his investigative authority—not only directly (telling Truman, "the Bureau gets called in, Bureau's in charge; you're going to be working for me"), but also by deed, proving his genius when he points out that the picnic videotape captures the reflection of James Hurley's motorcycle in the iris of Laura Palmer's eye ("holy smoke," we chorus with Truman and Lucy). Cooper's virtuosity suggests that the game being laid out is an evidentiary one, one in which we can participate by close attention and reasoned speculation based on the facts gathered by the sheriff's deputies and by Albert Rosenfeld's examination of the body. Even when the investigative methodologies get weird—interpretation of dreams and mind-body coordination—the guiding principle Cooper declares allegiance to is "break the code, solve the crime" (episode four). This cryptological tenet is one that has been fundamental to detective fiction since Poe, whose tales of ratiocination celebrate the "mind that *disentangles*" and whose "The Gold-Bug" makes explicit an analogy between the search for the truth and the deciphering of codes.[1]

Like all heroic detectives, Cooper is an indefatigable truth seeker. In an impulse shared by the Op of Dashiell Hammett's *Red Harvest* who continues investigating the goings-on in Poisonville even after his client fires him, Cooper keeps working (as a sheriff's deputy) toward the truth after he is relieved of his duties by the Bureau. Detectives, as detective fiction has created them, are not innocent men and women: they are cynical, they understand the methods and thought processes of criminals, and some—especially in the hard-boiled school—cross the line into extralegal behavior in more or less serious ways (as when Sue Grafton's Kinsey Millhone picks the locks of suspects' apartments or Cooper crosses the border into Canada). But, while the detective-hero is not innocent or without moral weakness, he or she is, in the ways that really matter, an incorruptible agent of truth and justice. Cooper establishes his particular brand of morality early in the first season when he cuts off Albert's necrophagous zeal and allows the Palmer family to bury Laura's body, and when he refuses to help Albert file a complaint against Sheriff Truman, citing the "decency, honor and dignity" of the "good people" of Twin Peaks, where "life has meaning . . . every life" (episode four).

Especially important is the question of Cooper's sexual morality. We know that Cooper is attracted to Audrey, but he refuses to take advantage of her youthful infatuation. Even when Audrey plants herself in his bed, Cooper sticks to the straight and narrow: "Audrey, you're a high-school girl. I'm an agent of the FBI. . . . When a man joins the FBI, he swears to uphold certain values" (episode seven). The crucial moment in this scene—which works so hard to establish Cooper as a superior moral being—comes at the end, when Cooper tells Audrey that "secrets are dangerous things." He verbalizes something we understand as a given of detective fiction: the difference between the epistemological role of the object of a criminal investigation ("Laura had a lot of secrets," notes Audrey) and that of the detective ("my job is to find those out," responds Cooper). For all his quirks, Cooper is in this first season a simple character: he has, as he assures Audrey in the scene above, no past and no secrets. He investigates the secrets of others, but he is, like classic British and hard-boiled American detectives, not himself a person to be investigated.

However, the second season offers a fundamental readjustment of that depiction of Cooper; the shift of focus from Laura Palmer's past to Dale Cooper's past signals a number of other changes in both the epistemological and the narrative structures of *Twin Peaks*. The shift can be quite precisely located, in another conversation between Cooper and Audrey in episode eighteen, a scene that is—significantly—a revision of the one in which Cooper discovers Audrey in his bed. As Cooper prepares to leave Twin Peaks, Audrey comes to his hotel room to say goodbye; the first indication that something is about to change is Cooper's statement that he is "going fishing," an exact repetition of the declaration with which Pete Martell opens the show's verbal narrative. This scene is part of the episode in which *Twin Peaks* seems to start all over again; having more or less solved the murder of Laura Palmer, the show must find a new object of investigation. At least one of those objects—as FBI Agent Roger Hardy announces later in this episode—will be Cooper himself.

The bedroom conversation that ensues when Audrey comes to say goodbye is one that rewrites their earlier exchange concerning Cooper's past. Previously, Cooper insisted that he had no secrets; here he tells us that he does, in fact, have a skeleton in the closet. When Cooper reminds Audrey that he has a "personal policy" against romantic entanglements with women who have been involved in his cases, Audrey says, "someone must have hurt you once really badly." Cooper drops a narrative bombshell when he answers:

> COOPER: No, someone was hurt by me. And I'll never let that happen again.
>
> AUDREY: What happened? Did she die or something?
>
> COOPER: As a matter of fact, she did. Wanna know how? . . . We were supposed to protect her. . . . And when the attempt on her life was finally made, I wasn't ready because I loved her. She died in my arms. I was badly injured and my partner lost his mind. Need to hear anymore?

Of course, we do need to hear more, because Cooper is leaving out some crucial facts about this tragic love affair. But for the moment, we think we have heard enough—that Cooper was in love with a woman involved in a case, that he was supposed to protect her and failed to do so—largely because we have heard it all before. Specifically, we heard this conversation in a bedroom in Roman Polanski's *Chinatown*, when Evelyn Mulwray questions Jake Gittes about the experiences in Chinatown that he prefers not to speak of:

> JAKE: I was trying to keep someone from being hurt. I ended up making sure that she was hurt.
>
> EVELYN: *Cherchez la femme*. Was there a woman involved?
>
> JAKE: Of course.
>
> EVELYN: Dead?

The reference to *Chinatown* resonates from this point forward to the end of the series, for in *Twin Peaks* as in *Chinatown* the past is determined to repeat itself. This scene warns us that any woman Cooper becomes involved with is at serious risk, though the specific shape

of Windom Earle's revenge is still unforeseeable. The shift is one of narrative structure and, paradoxically, the more we learn about Cooper's past, the stronger the forward pull of the story becomes. What has happened in restarting *Twin Peaks* after the solution of Laura Palmer's murder is an important disruption of the paradigmatic narrative structure of the detective novel.

The basic narrative structure of the detective novel is a double, and doubled, one.[2] One strand of the narrative is the story of the investigation: the discovery of the body, the search for and interpretation of physical evidence, the interrogation of witnesses and surveillance of suspects, and the apprehension of the murderer. The second strand is the story of the actual murder: how and why it was committed, who was involved, and how the murderer concealed his or her identity. This second story is a submerged and secret one—one that has been deliberately rendered unreadable by a murderer who figuratively and literally attempts to cover his or her tracks. The story of investigation, then, is also a story of construction or reconstruction of fragments into narrative coherency. Detective fiction has two sets of contradictory impulses, both of which reveal their connections to the more general gothic mode from which they evolved. Detective fiction contains—in the murderer's story—a narrative of concealment *and*—in the detective's investigation—a narrative of disclosure. Oscillation between the urge to repress knowledge into secrecy and the compulsion to reveal what is concealed is one of the central features of Gothic narrative;[3] in detective fiction that oscillation is largely—but not entirely—stabilized by the privileging of investigation and resolution. Detective fiction also contains opposing trajectories of narrative time. While the criminal investigation moves forward in time toward the goal of identification and apprehension, the reconstruction of the story of murder is a movement backward in narrative time.

In the detective novel, the solution of the crime is also a recuperation—a retrieval and a resolution—of the past. In the first season, that retrieval is the underlying goal of both Cooper and the Sheriff's department and of the amateur team of James, Donna, and Maddy; we see it in the attention paid to alibis, to ways that physical evidence links certain people to the crime scene, and to the stories people tell about their relationships to the murder victim. Much is done to gather and interpret the fragmented traces that Laura Palmer has left behind—the secret and incomplete diaries, the audio- and videotapes, the broken heart, the cash and cocaine, the chocolate bunnies—that might constitute a coherent narrative of her life, if not her murder. However, *Twin Peaks* evades and subverts that structure in several ways. The more visible emblems of the way that the show resists the paradigm of retrieval-as-recuperation include Major Briggs's mysterious journey backwards and/or forward in time and the fact that the killer BOB exists outside the space-time continuum. The sense of time is so fragmented and chaotic that it is entirely possible to believe that the killer BOB and the spirit Mike are actually the future manifestations of

Bobby Briggs and *his* sidekick Mike Nelson (who claim to have killed someone in the period before the show begins).[4]

More important, however, is the renovation of the narrative structure of *Twin Peaks*—a show which seems at first to be in the tradition of the magazine detective serial—that is announced in the second bedroom conversation between Audrey and Cooper cited above. From this point on, *Twin Peaks* becomes increasingly removed from the double structure of a detective novel and closer to a purely forward-moving serial narrative. The key, paradoxically, is the introduction of material about Cooper's past. The difference between this exposure of the past and the kind of retrieval of the past that completes the detective novel is that the story of Cooper's past tells a story of revenge against him in the future. Like Jake Gittes's, Cooper's tale is a *disclosure* of certain facts—a woman in danger, a detective in love—but is emphatically not a gesture of *closure*. Cooper's past is only introduced as the context in which to understand the last nine episodes of the show.

Earlier I stated that one of the objects of investigation in the renovated or restarted narrative of those last nine episodes is Cooper himself. One of the others is Windom Earle, and his arrival in Twin Peaks initiates a further disruption and dismantling of the detective-fiction narrative structure that seemed to be operative—if not predominant—in the first season. Windom Earle is so disruptive because he—even more than BOB—is a radically *serial* killer. His murders don't remain in a retrievable or recuperative past because they are only understandable as parts of a chain of events that stretch into the future as well as into the past. We might state it even more strongly, describing Earle as a *narrative* killer, whose crimes are so closely woven together that they constitute a sustained act of story telling. To be sure, BOB is a repetitive killer (murdering both Laura and her double) with a sense of linguistic sequence (his "signature" action is the insertion of the letters of his name under the fingernails of his victims). But where BOB simply spells his name, Earle writes a novel, one that includes himself, Caroline, Cooper, and Annie Blackburne as the main characters. His narrative style is both more grandiose than BOB's—he writes the initial "C" of Caroline on an enormous scale by sending parts of her wedding outfit to police stations over a large area of the country—and more ludicrous. His narrative is both stylistically and thematically based on chess: he likes to make Cooper think four or five moves ahead, and he wants to literalize the game by clearing away the pawns and capturing Cooper's queen. Cooper's response—to enlist Pete Martell in finding moves that will not allow Earle to remove a piece from the chessboard—is one that enmeshes him in Earle's criminal narrative to the detriment of his ability to investigate it. Cooper slips from the role of the gifted reader of criminal narratives into the less powerful role of a character in one; if the detective seems sometimes to be author of a narrative about the fragmentary made coherent, Cooper has lost that status by capitulating to Earle's rivaling authorship.

Earle's narrative is one that connects the past to the future (by, for example, stabbing a drifter exactly the way that he stabbed Caroline) in ways that are diseased, but not disorganized. There is, one might argue, too *much* coherence and unity to Earle's story. Once Cooper relinquishes his status as an outsider to the criminal narratives operating in Twin Peaks (beginning at or before the moment he becomes a sheriff's deputy instead of a Federal agent), he—and the entire show—are pulled seaward by the narrative undertow of Earle's revenge plot. That current is one that pulls the events of the past through the present, sweeping both past and present into the future. The world of the last nine episodes of the show is such that one expects to find one's past before one; in the sense that Earle's plot is a vengeful return of the repressed, Twin Peaks is a gothic place.

In fact, *Twin Peaks* is laced with gothic figurations and gestures, revealing a preoccupation with gothicism that goes beyond its engagement with detective fiction. We see the mark of the gothic in the opening shot of Josie painting her lips in the mirror; Lynch tropes the Orientalism so prevalent in the traditional gothic mode to make her face the emblem not only of mystery but of knowingness. The show is filled with gothic touches: secret passageways, mirrors, disguises and masks, eavesdropping, secret paternity, invalidism, and the threat of incest. One of the most striking features of the gothic mode is that secrets are always revealed, no matter how vehemently they are repressed, and this is certainly true of *Twin Peaks*. There is a compulsion to confess—always paired with a desire to conceal—that runs through the gothic, and we see it operating when Catherine keeps double books on the mill and when Laura Palmer keeps double books on her life. There are other emblems of the inevitability of disclosure, including Waldo, the talking bird who saw and heard it all, and the Log Lady's log, who has "something to say" about the night of Laura Palmer's death, and the letters BOB leaves under his victims' fingernails.[5]

The most significant gothic convention at work—and in play—in *Twin Peaks* is that of the double. Not only do we have the complex and puzzling resemblance of Laura Palmer and Maddy Ferguson, the grotesque doubles of the dwarf and the giant, and the double consciousness of Philip Gerard and Mike, but also we have a principle of doubling at work in the plot of the show, especially in the last nine episodes. Windom Earle is, of course, Dale Cooper's double—his alienated partner and teacher, his sexual rival, and his moral and criminal opposite. A confrontation between them becomes inevitable; the narrative undertow pulls us toward the future in general and toward the victory of one of these agents over the other. The discovery of the existence of a white lodge and a black lodge only reinforces the sense that the narrative is shifting into uncanny oppositions and repetitions, patterns that seem to point to disastrous, but definitive, endings. The ending of Twin Peaks is this kind of disaster, as it is the merger of Cooper with his shadow self. He is, in the black lodge, overtaken by an alternate version of himself, who may be BOB or simply the intermediary that allows BOB to invade the host. In any case, that merger of the morally superior Cooper with the depraved and chaotic BOB is a gesture of firm, if disturbing closure.

The ending of *Twin Peaks* is strictly antithetical to the plot structure of classic British and even hard-boiled detective fiction. It is a commonplace to say that the detective novel begins with a sense of innocence violated by the discovery of a murder and works to restore that sense of innocence and order by rooting out and abolishing the murderer.[6] *Twin Peaks,* of course, begins with a sense of innocence violated, but ends with the complete destruction of the detective-hero who was supposed to restore the goodness and stability of the social order. In hard-boiled detective fiction, investigation may temporarily make things worse—not better—as it puts pressure on a desperate murderer who may kill again to silence a potential witness. In *Twin Peaks,* the suspicion that the detective may do more harm than good is articulated as a direct accusation against Cooper by Jean Renault:

> Before you came, Twin Peaks was a simple place. . . . Quiet people lived a quiet life. Then a pretty girl die, and you arrive, and everything change. . . . Suddenly the simple dream become the nightmare. So if you die, maybe you will be the last to die. Maybe you brought the nightmare with you, and maybe the nightmare will die with you. (episode twenty-one)

Cooper, listening, seems to take Jean's words to heart, and perhaps we should also. The scene ends with Cooper shooting and killing Jean Renault, and the episode ends with the discovery of a corpse bearing the signature of Windom Earle and demonstrating the nightmarish content of the "baggage" Cooper admits bringing to town (episode twenty-two).

So, while *Twin Peaks* contains many elements of detective fiction, it ultimately subverts the narrative structures and intentions of the genre. Like *Chinatown,* it leaves us with the image of the detective defeated and even vilified. The failure of the investigative narrative to master the criminal narrative or to recuperate the past suggests that *Twin Peaks* may be best understood not as hardboiled detective fiction, but as hard-boiled gothic. As Lynch tells us, in the guise of Cooper's supervisor Gordon Cole, "I believe in secrecy" (episode fourteen); since we know that "secrets are dangerous things," we know that *Twin Peaks* believes in danger even more strongly than it believes in Special Agent Cooper.

NOTES

[1] Edgar Allan Poe, "The Murders in the Rue Morgue," *The Complete Tales and Poems* (New York: Random House, 1975) 141.

[2] My sense of the doubled narrative of detective fiction is based on the analysis of the narrative structure of the genre by Tstevan Todorov in *The Poetics of Prose,* trans. Richard Howard (Ithaca: Cornell UP, 1977) 45.

[3] See Eve Kosofsky Sedgwick, *The Coherence of Gothic Conventions* (New York: Methuen, 1986) 19-20.

[4] Truman's reaction upon hearing the names "Mike and Bob" in Cooper's account of his dream is a surprised "Mike and Bobby?" My thanks to Bruce Covey for sharing this interpretation with me.

[5] However, in *Twin Peaks,* even more than in most detective novels, the narrative privileges the act of knowing over the act of telling; one of Cooper's most impressive gifts is his ability to discern, on the basis of almost no information whatsoever, who is sleeping with whom in Twin Peaks.

[6] The source of this commonplace is an essay—perhaps overly tidy, but nevertheless important—by W.H. Auden from 1948: "The Guilty Vicarage" in *Detective Fiction: A Collection of Critical Essays,* ed. Robin Winks (Englewood Cliffs, NJ: Prentice Hall, 1980).

Frank W. Oglesbee

SOURCE: "Doctor Who: Televised Science Fiction as Contemporary Melodrama," in *Extrapolation,* Vol. 30, No. 2, Summer, 1989, pp. 176-87.

[*In the following essay, Oglesbee details how conventions of science fiction and literary melodrama are utilized in* Dr. Who.]

Science fiction television programs have one thing in common with all other genres—more fail than succeed. And, given the comparatively high cost and low audience figures, science fiction is less common than, for example, situation comedies. In 1988, however, the longest running prime-time drama series in the world is *Doctor Who,* in production since 1963. It has become an international success, whose audience includes as many adults as children. In 1983, ten thousand people attended a twentieth-birthday party for the series in Chicago; forty thousand attended a similar event in England (Tulloch and Alvarado, 5, 11).

The program, successful in itself, has given rise to ancillary elements familiar in popular culture: paperback novelizations, tee shirts, and other memorabilia—one catalog lists over eight hundred items (*Star Tech*). Numerous fan clubs have been organized, the largest being the Doctor Who Appreciation Society (Great Britain) and the Doctor Who Fan Club of America. Three magazines, *Doctor Who Monthly, Fantasy Empire,* and *The Doctor Who Magazine,* center on the series.

Lofficier (1981) has written two guide books to the series: the first summarizing stories; the second indexing characters and places mentioned in the series. Haining

(1983, 1984) has also written two books: the first, an overview with interviews and essays by actors, writers, and producers; the second, a summary of events in the series' history through the first half of 1984, which draws on English and Australian newspapers, parliamentary records, fan magazines, etc. The longest scholarly study to date, by Tulloch and Alvarado (1984), examines the program in terms of the "industrial, institutional, . . . and other practices which have shaped it" (2).

None of the writers mentioned here noted *Doctor Who*'s relation to melodrama, in the better sense of the word. This science fiction series is a modern romantic melodrama, carrying out a classical comedy function, within a tight aesthetic and budgetary framework. It resembles soap opera in structure, with science fiction plots and special effects, but has unique features.

Further, *Doctor Who*'s accessibility makes over twenty years of a popular culture text available for study: many PBS stations play it, and the BBC is releasing videotapes for sale to the public.

The remainder of the essay summarizes concepts of science fiction and melodrama, briefly describes the nature of the series, and shows, through two detailed examples, how the program applies the theories of science fiction and melodrama in a practical manner.

SCIENCE FICTION

Butor says the best science fiction treats "the interface between man and machine" (177). It is a form which speculates on "the human experience of science and its resultant technologies" (Bretnor 150). It provides a "sense of novelty" and has "a dislocation in time or space" (Warwick 82). Constant factors include either "a world in some respect different from our own," or "the impact of some strange element on our world" (Rose 3). Its themes include: time travel, alien encounters, questing scientists, dystopian satires, post-apocalyptic scenes, or evolutionary fables (Rose 2). Science fiction film, and by extension television—together the "art of the moving image, the only art that is truly of our time," (Bettleheim 80)—can show a "visual play of man's fears and symbols in the twentieth century" (Zebrowski 48).

The limits of science fiction on television are not limits of science fiction alone, but those of televised drama. The question is not whether drama is unreal; it must be. The question is whether the unreality is acceptably done. In television, it is often acceptably done as melodrama, a term often used pejoratively, but recent criticism takes exception to this.

MELODRAMA

Kehr says the term melodrama "conjures visions of mustache-twirling villains and virginal heroines strapped to sawmills, and the term is usually reserved for the crudest work in the field (that is, we seem capable of recognizing

melodrama only when it fails)" (43-44). But, he holds, when "understood as a genre rather than as a negative judgment on style, it is clearly no worse (and no better) than any other ritual form" (44).

Conversely, when melodrama succeeds—when we accept a melodramatic unreality—we do not recognize it as "melodrama," that quaint form from the last century. In the 1980s, the virgin, the sawmill, the deed to the farm seem a ludicrous set of concerns. But rape, actual or metaphorical, by an evil *persona* is still a valid premise. Threats to life, property, honor are symbolized differently across time but still exist. In science fiction, a villain may threaten to hurl the heroine into the vacuum of space unless he gets the device needed for his plan of galactic conquest: the virgin, the deed, and the sawmill reinvented.

Audiences accept and enjoy certain conventions as long as they do not interfere with the central thrust of science fiction, "more concerned with the conduct of human society than with its techniques" (Merrill 59)—as is melodrama.

Gowans holds that "television is the last and finest representative of traditional melodrama" (174) Thorburn writes in more detail that television is often contemporary melodrama: ritualistic, cunning, adaptable, optimistic (529-546). Melodrama has important functions with which science fiction can be congruent. It enacts a "fantasy of reassurance" (531). It says that ordinary people matter; that their problems and concerns are worthy of attention; that goodness and decency are preferable to evil and cruelty (Thorburn 531-532, Kehr 43-44). Rahill classifies it as "conventionally moral and humanitarian in point of view, and sentimental and optimistic in temper, concluding its fable happily with virtue rewarded after many trials and vice punished" (xiv).

Lastly, melodrama and science fiction are often Romantic, as Romance has at its core "a Manichean vision of the universe as a struggle between good and bad magic" (Nicholls 180-181). Many interested in science fiction will recall Arthur C. Clarke's Third Law: "Any sufficiently advanced technology is indistinguishable from magic" (Briggs 35).

A science fiction series might, if it ran long enough, show examples of dystopias, time and space travel, worlds impacted, aliens, blessings and curses of technology, apocalypse and the aftermath, and questing scientists. If melodramatic, it would do this with Manichean tones, yet offer a fantasy of reassurance, arguing the human race will survive. All of this to be done within the aesthetic and budget limits of television, "the rectangle and the dollar," as choreographer Twyla Tharp puts it.

No other science fiction series has so determinedly carried out the melodramatic themes within such a tight budget as *Doctor Who*. The *Buck Rogers* and *Battlestar Galactica* series of the late 1970s cost as much as a million dollars an episode, while *Doctor Who* cost about $150,000—less than a typical situation comedy made for commercial television in the USA.

Doctor Who also includes elements which no other science fiction series does. An exposition on the series will precede examples concentrating on two principal recurring villains, the dehumanized Daleks and the humanoid master.

THE SERIES

The series centers on the picaresque adventures of "the Doctor," a time-and-space traveling, questing, humanitarian, scientific individualist. Mister Spock, a major character in *Star Trek,* was half-human; the Doctor is fully alien, a two-hearted native of the planet Gallifrey, a somewhat dystopic, stagnant and conservative society. The Doctor's temperament was unsuited to this, so he left, "borrowing" a Tardis, a vehicle named for its ability to move in "Time and Relative Dimensions in Space." Not all Gallifreyans have access to a Tardis; the planet is ruled by Time Lords, those Gallifreyans who, after arduous study at the Academy, qualify.

The above exemplifies the cunning adaptability of melodrama. Originally, the Doctor was an outcast for unknown reasons from an unnamed planet. As the series continued, a history was invented. Time Lords were not mentioned until the sixth season ("War Games" 1969); their planet, first seen in "The Three Doctors" (1973), was not named until the next year, in "The Time Warrior."

One of the program's unique elements also arose from necessity. William Hartnell, who originated the role of the Doctor, was stricken with multiple sclerosis and had to retire. While it is not unknown for a new actor to take over a part, what makes the series unique is that the change was explained as "regeneration." Time Lords regenerate into new bodies twelve times before they die; this may be normal or brought on by severe trauma, which is the case with the Doctor, because of his risky lifestyle. The practical result of the premise is that every few years a new actor plays the role, bringing a new perspective, and considerable publicity, to the series.

To assist in continuity, and to provide further new faces and characters, the series features Companions, major supporting roles who join the Doctor for one or two seasons; the longer terms are for those who carry over after a regeneration. Companions carry out the traditional functions of the hero's or heroes' side-kicks. Their dialogue aids in exposition; they rescue, or are rescued by, the Doctor; they provide a contrast in *persona*. Don Quixote needs Sancho Panza, and the Lone Ranger needs Tonto; the audience needs them too—it would be quite tiresome if the Don and the Lone Ranger explained everything to their horses. As the Doctor has always been played by a male, the majority of Companions have been female. Beginning with the third Doctor, these roles have reflected social changes, with increasing feminism. This

is not unique to the series, but helps to explain its appeal. Apart from the Companions, females are often scientists, military officers, starship captains, or planetary rulers.

A second characteristic unique to the series is a continuous sense of humor, rather than the intermittent examples seen in *Star Trek* or the *Twilight Zone.* Faced with a villain announcing a plan to rule the world (or universe), the Doctor's reaction is likely to be, "Oh—that again," or "But that would take up all your time." Asked by a Companion if they should interfere in some dispute he says, "Of course we should interfere. Always do what you're best at." He tells another that if you show people you're unarmed and mean them no harm, they won't harm you. "It always works—nine times out of ten. Well, seven times out of ten."

The third unusual difference in *Doctor Who* is that its stories are told in episodic serial form. Unlike the commonest series arrangement (self-contained storylines in every episode) or soap opera (one or more storylines running until exhausting audience interest or writers' invention), an episodic serial tells a story in a pre-determined number of episodes. Unlike a miniseries, the serial continues and tells another story. The typical *Doctor Who* adventure, as the stories are called, takes four or six twenty-five minute episodes, allowing more complex plots, and more importantly, more time for character interaction, than a half-hour or hour episode.

Character interaction is a major strength of the series. As one of its producers explains, *Doctor Who,* lacking the budget to compete with the technological slickness of a *Star Trek,* relies on a British "television strength . . . building and creating character . . . and pretty quirky character at that" (Tulloch and Alvarado 159).

Doctor Who, then, deliberately uses the limit of televised drama to present ideas through characters. Such science fiction drama "frequently treats the ethical behavior of scientists as its major theme. . . . We expect the story to contain either explicit or implicit statements of ethical postulates, and we expect to see the coherent working out of a morally right course of action" (Butrym 55).

The Doctor, the central character of the series, is a scientist who argues and strives for the morally right choice. In the rare instance when he makes the wrong choice, and then by accident, he corrects it. In "Face of Evil" (1977), the Doctor finds that in trying, centuries ago, to repair the main computer of a wrecked spaceship, he started the evolution of a new form of life, a machine-creature. Unfortunately, it became a paranoid schizophrenic, which set itself up as the god Xoanon, putting the tribes descended from the ship's personnel at war. Not for the first time in the series, a failed technology becomes religion, in a story which warns against giving godlike properties to machinery. The Doctor, in a brief session of reality therapy, shows it the mistake. It repairs itself, and offers atonement through service to the uniting tribes. To give a melodramatic flourish appropriate to the series, in the final scenes the leaders of the tribes argue loudly (but nonviolently) over rights and duties. "Ah, gentlemen, democracy at work, I see," says the Doctor, and takes his leave.

The attitude toward technology is firmly on the middle ground; technology may be used for good or ill. This contrasts with two points of view from earlier periods of science fiction. American science fiction in particular, from 1879-1930, was largely optimistic about the benefits of technology. Stories were often imperialistic in thrust; and racist, or at least chauvinistic, in tone; with American scientists overcoming foreign/alien perils, as in Serviss's *Edison's Conquest of Mars,* written in reaction to Wells's *War of the Worlds.* (For a detailed exposition of this view, see Clareson.)

The Second World War and the start of the nuclear age increased the incidence of another science fiction theme— the mad or amoral scientist. In films—which as drama require characters to personalize abstractions—such scientists and their allies, the technocrats, became prominent from the late 1940s through about 1965. (For critical reviews of several films on the nuclear threat, see Shaheen.)

The Doctor, then, represents Good, and frequently opposes Evil scientists and their work—exemplified by the Daleks and the Master.

THE DALEKS

The Daleks, bent on ruling the universe, are responsible for the series' early success. *Dr. Who* drew a small audience in its first weeks and was an unlikely candidate for renewal (Road 28-29). The Daleks quadrupled the audience. They were also the first merchandising venture for the series, their image appearing on punching bags, wallpaper, lapel pins, as wind-up toys, and so forth (Bentham 38-44).

Daleks were invented by Terry Nation, script editor of the series, who wanted to do a monster "that wasn't a man dressed up" (Interviewho: 5). He invented Daleks to "represent government, officialdom, that unhearing unthinking, blanked-out face of authority that will destroy you because it *wants* to" (Haining, *Key to Time,* 21).

The result is a shape like a polygonal salt shaker, over five-and-a-half feet tall, moving on wheels, hidden by the metal hem of its metallic body. It has one arm, one electronic eye, a deadly ray gun and a harsh, mechanical voice. Operational Daleks are maneuvered by men hidden inside. Usually only three of these are used, to save costs. This dollar limit problem is minimized by the TV rectangle's limit: a small number of anything fills the screen. Shooting from different angles, editing in stock footage, and using shells of Daleks—or only shadows cast by cardboard cutouts—gives the impression of an army of monsters.

The Dalek character is a familiar science fiction premise—creatures devoid of human emotion. They rep-

resent both chaos (destruction of desirable order) and control (totalitarian rule). As with Time Lords and Gallifrey, they were not explained until long after they entered the series, in the eleventh Dalek story, "Genesis of the Daleks" (1975). The story opens on a harsh, fog-swept landscape where, to ominous slow-paced music in minor chords, soldiers in gas masks move slowly, their uniforms and weapons odd mixtures from different centuries. The Kaleds and Thals, at war for a thousand years, near the end of their resources. The Kaleds' jackboots, decorations, and salutes are modeled on those of the Third Reich. The Doctor begs them to stop the experiments of their chief scientist, Davros, who is developing Daleks, whose name "for a thousand generations . . . will bring fear and terror."

The story shows modern fears as a panoply of science fiction elements fills the small screen. The Doctor is sent by the Time Lords to a severely dystopic planet where people are abused, and a mad scientist creates a perverted man-machine interface.

Crippled by radiation, Davros is confined to an elaborate wheelchair, a design echoed in the Daleks, as are his electronic eye, his one usable arm, and his moral limitations. As the Doctor warns, Davros, "one of the finest scientific minds in existence," is "without conscience, without soul, without pity, and his machines are equally devoid of these qualities."

The Doctor is right: Davros has altered Kaled genetics, evolving a small octopus-shaped being, which cannot survive outside its incubator or its traveling machine. This man-machine interface is the Dalek. The Doctor hesitates to destroy the incubation chamber. Has he the right to kill an intelligent species? What is the proper moral choice?

Davros has no such dilemma. The obligatory confrontation scene shows the ethical dissonance. Would he, asks the Doctor, loose a virus that could kill every living thing in the universe? He would. "To know that life and death on such a scale was my choice. . . . That power would set me above the gods—and through the Daleks *I will have that power.*"

Now the Doctor destroys the incubation chamber, but Daleks are already assembled. They are delayed for many years, but will thrive. "Out of their evil must come something good," he declares, which within the fact is a so far unsupported optimism.

Outside the fact, it is just the ending that fans of the series want. The Daleks' origin is explained; a new and satisfying villain is introduced; and the Daleks can return, as in "Destiny of the Daleks" (1979), to be met by the Doctor and a Time Lord Companion, Romana, whose introduction to the continual threat was reviewed thus: "She found herself in a time-honored role. Horror struck and backed against a wall by who else but the Daleks. It bodes well" (Haining, *Key to Time,* 191).

THE MASTER

During 1970-1974, the Doctor spent most of his time on Earth, his Tardis disabled for breaking the rules of the Time Lords High Council. The actual reason, during a time of tight budgets at the BBC, was to save costs by using available sets and costumes. Scriptwriter Malcolm Hulke summed up the result, "right, you have only two stories, invasion from outer space and mad scientist" (Dicks 23). Both themes are science fiction staples and within these limits the series continued to employ melodramatic cunning. The most successful example is the combination of invasion and mad scientist, in the person of the Master.

Sedately dapper, exuding charm, the Master conceals ruthless ambition and hubric vanity. His ambition is a science fiction ambition—to rule the universe—and his crimes are science fiction crimes, involving magical technology and alien forces. The principal humanoid villain of the series, like its hero, is an individual. The less humanoid the villains, like the Daleks, the more likely they are to be corporate, working in teams, obeying orders. Part of *Doctor Who*'s attraction for American audiences is its similarity to the American tradition of the individualistic hero, e.g., the Lone Ranger, or Tom Swift, the independent inventor.

In "Terror of the Autons" (1971), the Master, new to the series, is spoken of as an old foe. He plans to help the Autons conquer Earth, then betray them and use Earth as a base for his own ambition. "Vicious, complicated, and inefficient," says the Doctor, "typical of your thinking."

So it is, and sets a pattern. The Master, often in disguise, compels innocents, aligns with villains, or uses deception (or all three), to carry out schemes made needlessly complex by his pride and by his thirst for revenge. He has no friends and betrays any ally. In his vanity, he is surprised when they betray him, and he must defeat his own scheme (sometimes with the Doctor's help) and escape.

Examples from two stories, ten years apart, illustrate the consistent differences between the Holmes and Moriarty of science fiction. In "Colony in Space" (1971), they are captured by a tribe of primitive humanoids and taken to the ruins of a technologically advanced city, now a place of sacrifice—once again, failed technology made into a brutal religion. The Master knows the planet was the home of a great civilization, where "by genetic engineering they developed a super race." The Doctor wonders why "the super race became priests of a lunatic religion, worshipping machines instead of gods." The Master has a more pragmatic goal, to find the super race's Doomsday weapon, as "the very threat of its use could hold the galaxy to ransom"; a "sawmill" of cosmic proportions.

With his grudging respect for the Doctor—"I admire him in many ways . . . I have so few worthy opponents" ("Time Monster" 1972)—he makes, perhaps seriously for once, an offer of alliance. "We're both Time Lords. Both Renegades. We could be masters of the galaxy. *Absolute* power—power for Good." No, says the Doctor, "absolute power is evil."

This familiar ritualistic discourse is interrupted by the arrival of the Guardian of the weapon, the last survivor of humanoid evolution on the planet. The Master asks that the weapon be released, "it could build a *new* empire." Did it bring the Guardian's people any good? asks the Doctor, and the answer speaks to a familiar fear in our time: "Once the weapon was built our race began to decay. Radiation from the weapon's power source poisons our planet."

The Master aruges, "We could be *gods*." "You are not fit to be a god," replies the Guardian, and tells the Doctor how to activate the Destruct mechanism. The city collapses, in another example of low cost special effects: quick zooming in and out, accompanied by de-focusing, shifting the color balance, and shaking the camera. The weapon is destroyed and the Master temporarily frustrated.

The final example, "Logopolis" (1981), celebrates the human mind in the age of computers, despite the sin of pride and the dangers of technology. Logopolis is on a planet located at the edge of our universe. Its inhabitants live a life of mathematics, using computers only for basic calculation. Their glory is Block Transfer Computation, mathematics so sophisticated that it alters the structure of matter. ("Logopolis" is replete with the jargon that endears science fiction to some and drives others away). Computers would be affected; the living brain is immune. The Master, believing a valuable secret to be hidden there, stops the workings of Logopolis to deliver an ultimatum. Unknowingly, he commits "the most dangerous crime in the universe." Because of entropy, the universe is past the point of total collapse; Block Transfer Computation has created temporary Charged Vacuum Emboitments, drawing energy from other universes. Logopolis starts to disappear: the miniature city set crumbles, large stones fall in narrow streets in full-size sets, citizens vanish piece by piece through electronic special effects.

The Master finds himself among the virgins in the path of the sawmill's teeth. Again, the two Time Lords form a necessary alliance. The Master, in a burst of jargon, suggests they "reconfigure both Tardeses into time cone invertors and apply temporal inversion to as much of space/time as we can isolate." But entropy is too advanced; they must use the radio telescope of the Pharos Project on Earth to send the program to the edge of the universe, accelerated by using the "light speed overdrive" from the Master's Tardis. The Master, still himself, threatens to cancel the program unless all planets submit to his rule. The Doctor thwarts the scheme, but falls from the telescope. The Master escapes.

This story is the final one of the eighteenth season. Tom Baker, who had played the Doctor since 1974, was ready to leave. His exit, the end of the season, and the promise of the series' continuance were blended into a satisfying melodramatic closing scene. The Doctor lies on the ground, visions of enemies and former Companions flashing before his eyes. His current Companions gather around as he says, "It's the end. But the moment has been prepared for." Through the familiar technique of multiple exposures the Doctor regenerates: Tom Baker fades away, Peter Davison fades in, and the fifth Doctor blinks, smiles, and sits up. The closing theme comes in full, and the closing credits roll, listing both Baker and Davison as the Doctor. Villainy is defeated, but lurks; a new Doctor is ready for the next season; and three Companions are on hand to carry through the transition.

Again, a melodramatic ritual has been enacted. Despite death and destruction, the universe is saved. Despite technology, humanity is paramount. Despite danger, Good triumphs, if narrowly, over Evil.

CONCLUSION

Any television genre can, but not necessarily will, function as melodrama, as a ritualized comedy in cautionary celebration of ordinary human character. Situation comedies concentrate on humorous approaches to small-group interpersonal relationships. Their tactics vary with the times, as the success in recent years of "irregular families" shows, for example, the single-parent sitcom (*One Day At A Time, Kate and Allie*).

Police and private detective series speak to the urban fears of the times, replacing the lone hero and public servant westerns (from *Have Gun Will Travel* to *Magnum, P.I.*; from *Gunsmoke* and *Lawman* to *Kojak* and *Cagney and Lacey*).

The televised drama of science fiction differs from other forms in its tension between the sometimes literally universal scope of a danger to the proper order and the limits of the rectangle and the dollar in bringing that story to the small screen. A world, galaxy, or universe tied to a railroad track is saved by an effort that fits that screen, carried out by a public servant or servants (the crew of the Enterprise), or in the case of *Doctor Who*, a free individual spirit who goes on his way after solving the problem.

Cawelti argues that to keep culture shaped by "rational humanistic discourse" it is vital to include criticism of the media along with the exploration of "other areas which constitute the major expressions of the human imagination" (377). The writer's argument, backed by the descriptive passages of this essay, is that one approach to such criticism is to find television texts of unusual interest, and that *Doctor Who* is one of these. Marc found that a problem with television is that "its texts are generally unavailable on demand" (12). In the case of *Doctor Who*, with the printed materials available (especially Tulloch and Alvarado), and the growing number of stories available on video cassette, the problem does not exist.

Replying to the criticism that television tends to pander to popular taste, Crinkley writes that "popular taste, in its continuing need for order and hope and resolution in its experience is worthy of respect" (32). Perhaps this search for order, hope and resolution in a universe of technological wonders is the key to *Doctor Who*'s success, and a reason to use it in exemplifying media criticism. The series is not only an example of an unusually enduring television vehicle, but, in its insistence on character over impressive effects, is an example of its own message: humanity need neither reject technology nor be a slave to it. More than any other television series to date, *Doctor Who*, for over twenty years, has dramatized the hopeful caution expression by Barzun "there is no getting away from the machine. It is only the use of it that is in your control" (3).

NOTES

The writer gratefully acknowledges the assistance of John Nathan-Turner, producer of *Doctor Who*, for allowing access to scripts and tapes; and to Nathan-Turner's secretary, Sara Lee, for assembling the materials and arranging for a quiet viewing room at the BBC.

WORKS CITED

Barzun, J., and Saunders, J. R. *Art in Basic Education.* Washington: Council for Basic Education, 1979.

Bentham, J. J. "Dalekmania." *Fantasy Empire* (Special Summer Issue 1983): 38-44.

Bettleheim, B. "The Art of the Moving Picture." *Harper's* (October 1981): 80-83.

Bretnor, R., ed. "Science Fiction in the Age of Space." *Science Fiction, Today and Tomorrow.* Cambridge: MIT P, 1974. 150-78.

Briggs, P. "Three Styles of Arthur C. Clarke: The Projector, the Wit and the Mystic." *Arthur C. Clarke.* Eds. J. C. Olander and M. H. Greenberg. New York: Taplinger Publishing Company, 1977.

Butor, M. "Science Fiction: The Crisis of its Growth." *SF the Other Side of Realism: Essays on Modern Fantasy and Science Fiction.* Ed. T. D. Clareson. Bowling Green: Popular Press, 1977. 157-65.

Butrym, A. J. "For Suffering Humanity: The Ethics of Science in Science Fiction." *The Transcendent Adventure: Studies of Religion in Science Fiction Fantasy.* Ed. R. Reilly. Westport: Greenwood Press, 1985. 55-70.

Cawelti, J. G. "With the Benefit to Hindsight: Popular Culture Criticism." *Critical Studies in Mass Communication* 2. 4 (1985): 363-77.

Clareson, T. O. *Some Kind of Paradise: The Emergence of American Science Fiction.* Westport: Greenwood Press, 1985.

Crinkley, R. "Looking at Nuclear Aesthetics." *National Review* (24 August 1984): 28-35.

Dicks, Terrance. Interview by J. M. Lofficier and R. Lofficier. *Official Doctor Who Magazine,* No. 95. (December 1984): 22-25.

Gowans, A. *Learning to See: Historical Perspectives on Modern Popular/Commercial Arts.* Bowling Green: Popular Press, 1981.

Haining, P. *Doctor Who: A Celebration.* London: W. H. Allen & Co., 1983.

———. ed. *Doctor Who: The Key to Time.* London: W. H. Allen & Co., 1984.

Interviewho: Terry Nation. *Whovian Times* 7 (1984): 5.

Kehr, D. "The New American Melodrama." *American Film* (April 1983): 42-47.

Lofficier, J. M. *The Doctor Who Programme Guide:* Vol. 1, *The Programmes,* and Vol. 2, *What's What and Who's Who.* London: Target Books, 1981.

Marc, D. *Demographic Vistas: Television in American Culture.* Philadelphia: U of P Press, 1984.

Marsden, M. T. "Television Viewing as Ritual." *Rituals and Ceremonies in Popular Culture.* Ed. R. B. Brown. Bowling Green: Popular Press, 1980. 120-24.

Merrill, J. "What Do You Mean: Science? Fiction?" *SF: The Other Side of Realism: Essays on Modern Fantasy and Science Fiction.* Ed. T. D. Clareson. Bowling Green: Popular Press, 1977. 53-95.

Nicholls, P., ed. *The Encyclopedia of Science Fiction, an Illustrated A to Z.* London: Granada, 1979.

Rahill, F. *The World of Melodrama.* University Park: Pennsylvania State UP, 1967.

Road, A. *Doctor Who: The Making of a Television Series.* London: Andre Deutsch, Ltd., 1982.

Rose, M. *Anatomy of Science Fiction.* London, Cambridge: Harvard UP, 1981.

Serviss, G. P. *Edison's Conquest of Mars.* Los Angeles: Carcosa House, 1947. (First published serially in the *New York Evening Journal,* 1898).

Shaheen, J. G., ed. *Nuclear War Films.* Carbonadale: Southern Illinois UP, 1979.

Star Tech Catalog. Dunlap: Star Tech, 1986.

Tulloch, J. and Alvarado, M. *Doctor Who: The Unfolding Text.* London: MacMillan Press, 1984.

Thorburn, D. "Television Melodrama." *Television: The Critical View* 3rd ed. Ed. H. Newcomb. New York: Oxford UP, 1982. 529-46.

Warwick, P. *The Cybernetic Imagination in Science Fiction.* Cambridge, Massachusetts: MIT Press, 1982. 82.

Zebrowski, G. "Science Fiction and the Visual Media." *Science Fiction, Today and Tomorrow.* Ed. R. Bretnor. New York: Harper & Row, 1974. 46-64.

April Selley

SOURCE: "'I Have Been, and Ever Shall Be, Your Friend': *Star Trek, The Deerslayer* and the American Romance," in *Journal of Popular Culture,* Vol. 20, No. 1, Summer, 1986, pp. 89-104.

[*In the following essay, Selley focuses on the relationship between Captain Kirk and Dr. Spock in the television, film, and literary series* Star Trek, *identifying it in the tradition of mythic male friendship initiated in American literature by Natty Bumppo and Chingachgook in James Fenimore Cooper's* Leatherstocking Tales.]

D. H. Lawrence and Leslie Fiedler have noted that the most enduring and respected American "classics" revolve around the friendships of two males, usually of two different races—Natty and Chingachgook, Ishmael and Queequeg, Huck and Jim.[1] It is thus appropriate that the classic television series *Star Trek* and the three films it has spawned also focus upon the friendship between an American, white male, Captain Kirk, and the alien, green-blooded Mr. Spock. Their personalities and their adventures in the unknown form the backbone and backdrop of their friendship, which especially resembles that of Natty Bumppo and Chingachgook in *The Deerslayer.* In conjunction with the other Leatherstocking Tales, *The Deerslayer* provides the first significant portrayal of close male friendships in American literature. In both *The Deerslayer* and *Star Trek,* the male friendships do not constitute an escape from responsibility toward others, but rather an escape from time and its limitations—from the burdens of the past and ancestors and the complications of the future and descendants. Ultimately, both *Star Trek* and *The Deerslayer* are American romances as characterized by Joel Porte in *The Romance in America* and Leslie Fiedler in *Love and Death in the American Novel.*

In *Love and Death in the American Novel,* Fiedler describes the mythic friendship which is so familiar to Cooper's—and to *Star Trek's*—audiences

Two mythic figures have detached themselves from the text of Cooper's books and have entered the free domain of our dreams: Natty Bumppo, the hunter and enemy of cities; and Chingachgook, nature's nobleman and Vanishing American. But these two between them postulate a third myth, an archetypal relationship which also haunts the American psyche: two lonely men, one dark-skinned, one white, bent together over a carefully guarded fire in the virgin heart of the American wilderness; they have forsaken all others for the sake of the austere, almost inarticulate, but unquestioned love which binds them to each other and to the world of nature which they have preferred to civilization.[2]

Although Kirk and Spock bend over their computer consoles aboard the starship *Enterprise* rather than over campfires, they too have forsaken the comfortable world of the safe and the civilized for (as the opening of each episode says) "space, the final frontier" in order "to explore strange new worlds, to seek out new life and new civilizations, to boldly go where no man has gone before." The *Star Trek* series presented an exploratory five-year space mission in which Captain Kirk, like Natty Bumppo, was the romantic hero, the scout in the wilderness preparing the way for those who would follow.

In the novel version of *Star Trek: The Motion Picture*, series creator Gene Roddenberry "quotes" a Captain Kirk who bears a striking resemblance to Natty Bumppo in his independence and conservatism. In "Admiral Kirk's Preface" Kirk writes of himself and his fellow Starfleet captains:

> We are a highly conservative and strongly individualistic group. The old customs die hard with us. We submit ourselves to starship discipline because we know it is made necessary by the realities of deep-space exploration. We are proud that each of us has accepted this discipline voluntarily—and doubly proud when neither temptation nor jeopardy is able to shake our obedience to the oath we have taken.[3]

"Temptation" (from the passions, usually incited by women) and "jeopardy" (from the unknown) present the greatest dangers to Kirk and Natty, and their self-discipline seems harsh when viewed by softer, more self-indulgent people in "civilization." Thus Kirk notes that some critics characterize the members of Starfleet as "primitives'." He readily admits that Starfleet's officers

> resemble our forebears of a couple of centuries ago more than they resemble most people today. We are not part of those increasingly large numbers of humans who seem willing to submerge their own identities into the groups to which they belong.[4]

The latter breed of human being, according to Kirk, "makes a poor space traveler,"[5] however.

And yet both Natty and Kirk are modest about their "gifts." Kirk protests that he has been "painted somewhat larger than life,"[6] as Natty might protest to Cooper, especially about Natty's portrayal in the last two Leatherstocking novels which critics have noted as the most mythic. Natty and Kirk are modest not only because it is seemly for heroes to be so, but also because they both feel like outsiders and have a humble perception of their intellectual abilities. The "lack of intellectual agility"[7] of which Kirk speaks and the "simplicity of mind"[8] with which Cooper endows the illiterate Natty place them squarely in the American tradition of self-reliant heroes who are honest and forthright because excessive education has not made them artful and deceptive. Both Kirk and Natty are guided by experience and intuition on their

respective frontiers, where they have acquired common sense and manly courage, but not the foolhardiness of a Hurry Harry. As Kirk says, "I have never happily invited injury; I have disliked in the extreme every duty circumstance which required me to risk my life."[9] Yet, since both Natty and Kirk can more effectively prove their loyalty, integrity, strength, endurance, agility and stoicism in combat, both *The Deerslayer* and *Star Trek* are filled with violent action. Moreover, both Natty and Kirk must constantly confront death, the frontier beyond even the vast forest and limitless space. The possibility of death subtly reminds the heroes (and the reader) that something always remains mysterious and unconquerable. This awareness keeps the heroes' abilities in perspective—their constant cheating of death endows them with self-reliance and mythic stature, yet their ultimate susceptibility to death as human beings keeps them humble and emotionally sensitive to their own and their friends' transience.

But it is through their friendships—Kirk's with Mr. Spock and Natty's with Chingachgook—that the heroes most effectively demonstrate both their manly independence and emotional sensitivity. Kirk's and Spock's relationship parallels that which D. H. Lawrence describes between Natty and Chingachgook in *The Deerslayer:* "Each obeys the other when the moment arrives. And each is stark and dumb in the other's presence, starkly himself, without illusion created."[10] Although Kirk is Spock's superior officer, Kirk relies upon Spock for the purely logical advice which Spock's Vulcan heritage makes possible. Kirk—like Natty, who praises "white man's reason" over instinct[11] admires Spock's stoic unemotionalism. This unemotionalism, if it doesn't allow for softness, also does not allow for the revenge and the other meannesses associated with violent emotion, meannesses which Kirk finds contemptible. Captain Kirk's code, like Natty's, "does not allow him to plunder, exploit, or kill in hate."[12] Kirk is humane, like the United Federation of Planets to which he owes allegiance. However, as Richard Chase points out about Natty Bumppo, "the ideal American image" is that "of a man who is a killer but *nevertheless* has natural piety."[13]

Thus Kirk and Bumppo must retain their passionate, killer instinct; it is all the more to their credit if they can control this instinct and utilize it constructively. In *The Deerslayer* Natty Bumppo demonstrates his killer instinct by wantonly shooting the eagle, which symbolically illustrates, as Joel Porte notes, Bumppo's "mastery over the American wilderness."[14] But Natty is sorely repentant afterwards, not only because his natural piety tells him to respect all life, but because killing the eagle demonstrates loss of control over his lower instincts, such as pride.

Similarly, *Star Trek* calls attention to Kirk's ability to control his "killer" instincts. In "The Enemy Within" episode, Kirk is divided into his "good" and "evil" sides, and he discovers that his "animal" side gives him the power of command. Spock tells Kirk's "good" side, which is marginally and indecisively in command of the

Enterprise, "Your negative energy was removed from you by that duplication process. Thus, the power of command has begun to fail you."[15] In "Mirror, Mirror," several crewmembers from the *Enterprise* are accidentally exchanged with their brutal counterparts in a parallel universe. When the *Enterprise* crewmembers are finally returned, Spock tells Kirk that "It was much easier for you, as civilized men, to act as barbarians, than it was for them, as barbarians, to act as civilized men." Spock then looks at Kirk, as if to say he knows how much Kirk enjoyed the barbarian role. So there is still the barbarian in Kirk, which also allows him to subdue an alien commander in "Arena" in order to save the lives of his crew (although Kirk significantly spares the commander's life). Interestingly, Kirk's antagonist in "Arena" is a huge reptile, thus placing Kirk in the role of archangel slaying the dragon-devil.[16] So Kirk is also involved in the cosmic struggle between good and evil; like Natty he is aware

> that he can maintain his goodness in a fallen world only by means of a strict moral code, devilish cunning, and a deadly weapon. His is a goodness that takes evil tacitly into account, a militant goodness that protects its purity by being always on guard against the enemy.[17]

Kirk's self-defensive actions parallel Natty's when Natty must kill the two treacherous Hurons.

Kirk's and Natty's actions are of a distinctively American character. Chase points out that "The novelty in the conception of Natty Bumppo and his descendants is the irony of their double personality, and it is this that sets Cooper's hero apart from the softer, less ironic natural piety of a Rousseauistic or Wordsworthian man."[18] The American Romantic hero has "The 'hard, isolate, stoic,' or 'Indian' quality" which "gives the image uniqueness." As Chase explains, "The romantic individual or solitary hero of nineteenth-century European literature had never been exposed to New England Puritanism or to frontier conditions, and this makes a difference."[19]

Natty admires Chingachgook for his stoic qualities and tries to emulate them as far as his "gifts allow," as Kirk tries to emulate Spock without imitating him. While the frontier, whether on earth or in space, tests men's stoic qualities, it also preserves those qualities by keeping the hero and his companion away from domestic entanglements which might separate them from each other. "Nature undefiled . . . is the inevitable setting of the Sacred Marriage of males."[20] Fiedler notes that this "Sacred Marriage" "blends with the myth of running away to sea, of running the great river down to the sea."[21] And, of course, most of *The Deerslayer* takes place on the wide and long Glimmerglass. On *Star Trek,* "voyages" are made on a star *ship* and Captain Kirk identifies himself with ships' captains of old (on one episode, Kirk even quotes from John Masefield's poem "Sea Fever"). Moreover, most of the starships introduced on *Star Trek*—the *Enterprise,* the *Vigilant,* the *Columbia,* the *Defiant*—bear the names of America's Cup Defenders.

But the "ocean of space" is not merely parallel to oceans on earth; the two are intrinsically related. R.W.B. Lewis explains the metaphoric relationship between the two oceans when he speaks about the evolution of the American Adamic hero:

> The evolution of the hero as Adam in the fiction of the New World—an evolution which coincides precisely, as I believe, with the evolution of *the* hero of American fiction generally—begins rightly with Natty Bumppo. I call such a figure the hero in *space,* in two senses of the word. First, the hero seems to take his start outside time, or on the very outer edges of it, so that his location is essentially in space alone; and, second, his initial habitat is space as spaciousness, as the unbounded, the area of total possibility. The Adamic hero is discovered, as an old stage direction might have it, "surrounded, detached in *measureless oceans* of space."[22]

Gene Roddenberry placed his heroes in a third kind of space, outer space, and outer space has even more direct affinities with the ocean. Man evolved from creatures in the sea, but before that, earth was formed from the materials of space. *Star Trek* essentially affirms that space was the common mother of all. The *Enterprise* crew not only discover "humanoids" throughout the galaxy, but civilizations parallel to earth civilizations as well: to the Greeks' in "Plato's Stepchildren"; to the Romans' in "Bread and Circuses"; to the American Indians' in "The Paradise Syndrome." But the *Enterprise* crew also discovers that Eden does not exist on any planet.

The planet on *Star Trek,* like the shore for Cooper, Melville and Twain, represents civilization, corruption and stagnation. Even planets which appear to be paradisiacal turn out to be otherwise. In "This Way to Eden," a band of space "hippies" finally find an uninhabited, garden-like planet, only to discover that all of its vegetation is poisonous. In "The Apple," the people on Gamma Trianguli VI are cared for by the godlike Vaal. They never have to work and are completely innocent, but they are dull-witted and accomplish and produce nothing—neither the food they eat nor children. They are thus completely susceptible to Vaal's whims—and to any changes in the environment which Vaal proves unable to control.

But "This Side of Paradise" provides *Star Trek*'s best illustration that paradise cannot be attained by settling on a planet. In this episode, plant spores produce a blissful high in the planet's colonists and in Kirk's mutinied crew, including Spock. The episode ends with Dr. McCoy (*Star Trek*'s foil to Mr. Spock, since McCoy relies primarily on emotion when making judgments) commenting: "That's the second time that Man has been thrown out of Paradise." Kirk replies:

> No—this time we walked out on our own. Maybe we don't belong in Paradise, Bones. Maybe we're meant to fight our way through. Struggle. Claw our way up, fighting every inch of the way. Maybe we can't stroll to the music of lutes, Bones—we must march to the sound of drums.[23]

Of course Kirk and Spock, like Natty and Chingachgook, would eventually become bored in Paradise.

Kirk is cynical about the spores throughout the episode: "No wants or needs? We weren't meant for that, any of us. A man stagnates and goes sour if he has no ambition, no desire to be more than he is." Sandoval, the leader of the expedition, protests, "We have what we need," but Kirk merely reiterates his position more vehemently: "Except a challenge! You haven't made a bit of progress here. You're not creating or learning, Sandoval. You're backsliding—rotting away in your paradise."[24] Later, when released from the spores' influence, Sandoval laments, "We do nothing here," and after talking of the lost years, he tells Kirk, "I'd—we'd—like to get some work done." Man must struggle, produce, achieve. Similarly, Cooper's Chingachgook looks forward to hunting and fishing in Paradise after death.[25]

In "This Side of Paradise," Sandoval's enthusiasm for release from the spores' influence is not shared by botanist Leila Kalomi, who represents another corrupting influence on planets and in civilization—women. Leila had fallen in love with Spock years before. Now, with the spores that she originally discovered, she has released Spock's human half, and, for the first time on the *Star Trek* series, has compelled him to fall in love. Spock is almost killed by the spores' initial aftereffects (thus demonstrating women's capacity for destruction, which will be handled in more detail later). But he is finally subdued, almost literally domesticated, and walks around the settlement like everyone else—contented but seemingly lobotomized.

Kirk is initially angered by Spock's abandonment of his duties, and later by the desertion of his crew; this anger allows him to resist the spores himself. The hard, stoic, killer American quality emerges in Kirk. In the words of James Blish's adaptation of the screenplay, "As peace and love and tranquility settled around him like a soggy blanket, he was blazing."[26] Kirk begins reclaiming his crew by provoking the killer instinct in Spock, and he succeeds admirably: "Spock was striking out with killer force, and with all the science of his once-warrior race."[27] Interestingly, when Spock's old self is restored, he has no desire to return to his euphoric state. Together, Kirk and Spock resourcefully build a subsonic transmitter to negate the spores' influence on everyone else. The episode ends, as nearly all *Star Trek* episodes end, with the *Enterprise* heading out into the freedom—and comparative security—of space.

Leila is just one of many aggressive females portrayed in *Star Trek,* all of whom come from outside the *Enterprise*'s crew and disappear after one episode. The female crew members do not present the same threats as outsiders because they are part of the world of the "sea" rather than the "shore." Indeed, Gene Roddenberry originally wanted the Spock role to be played by a woman. However, NBC executives in the late 1960s claimed that a woman would not be accepted as commanding and unemotional. The only regular female characters retained on the bridge of the *Enterprise* were the businesslike and efficient, but feminine, communications officer, Lt. Uhura, and Capt. Kirk's secretary, the young blond with a very obvious crush on the captain, Yeoman Rand.[28]

With their positions of responsibility, the women on board the *Enterprise* were way ahead of their time for prime-time television. But other women intruded into the *Enterprise* world only to entice Kirk, Spock and other crew members away from their work. Kirk and Spock are consistently rescuing each other from the romantic Dark Lady, so like Judith Hutter in *The Deerslayer,*[29] whose worldly experience has resulted in her becoming "cautious, rational and practiced in her handling of men. [She exemplifies] resourcefulness, . . . pragmatic intelligence, . . . and frank sexuality."[30] Judith offers Natty paradise when she asks him, after her father's death, to take possession of her heart, the ark, the castle and the lake. But Natty refuses, of course. And although much of *The Deerslayer* concerns Chingachgook's rescue of his beloved Hist, he, too, is solitary at the end of the book. Hist "slumbers beneath the pines of the Delawares,"[31] apparently having lived only long enough to give Chingachgook a son who becomes the inseparable companion of Natty and Chingachgook, assuming the role of the child in their celibate "marriage."

Similarly, Kirk and Spock resist restrictive marriages with women in episodes which allow them to prove their loyalty to one another. In the first episode shown in *Star Trek*'s second season, "Amok Time," Spock is compelled by primordial drives to return to the planet Vulcan or die, and to marry T'pring, to whom he has been betrothed since childhood. Kirk, disregarding Starfleet's orders to the contrary ("He [Spock] has saved my life a dozen times. Isn't that worth a career?"), takes Spock to Vulcan, where the treacherous T'pring, as is her right, compels Spock to battle for her hand. She selects Kirk as Spock's opponent. Kirk is willing to give his life for Spock, and when Spock believes that he has killed Kirk, his desire for T'pring (Spock later calls it "madness") is gone. When the distraught Spock bids farewell to a Vulcan elder and is told to "Live long and prosper," he declares, "I will do neither, for I have killed my captain, and my friend."[32] Of course Kirk is alive, and star trekking continues.

In "The Paradise Syndrome" shown during *Star Trek*'s third season, Spock saves Kirk. Kirk loses his memory on a planet whose inhabitants resemble American Indians. They assume that Kirk is a god, and he is told by Miramanee, the daughter of the chief, that custom decrees they should be married. When the *Enterprise* returns two months later, Miramanee is pregnant and Kirk is deliriously happy. In order to restore Kirk's memory, Spock uses the Vulcan mind meld, a telepathic fusion of minds which makes literally possible "the marriage of true minds," the fleshless, Sacred Marriage of which Fiedler speaks. Once his memory is restored, Kirk does not wish to return to his idyll, and Miramanee dies from internal injuries sustained when she and Kirk were stoned earlier. (Curiously, Miramanee's fate, for being the only woman to marry Kirk and to compromise the relationship between him and Spock, is to die by the ancient Hebrew method of punishing women taken in adultery.)

Miramanee's love for Kirk cannot save her, and her fate parallels that of another gentle, beautiful woman, Edith Keeler, in one of *Star Trek*'s most popular episodes, "The City on the Edge of Forever." Kirk falls in love with Keeler, who runs a soup kitchen during the American Depression, where Kirk and Spock find themselves. Keeler is listed in the episode's credits as "Sister" Edith Keeler, probably to emphasize her pure, almost nunlike, quality. She resembles Hetty Hutter in *The Deerslayer,* whom Cooper characterizes as "one of those mysterious links between the material and immaterial world . . . [who] offer so beautiful an illustration of the truth, purity, and simplicity of another."[33] Kirk's admiration for Keeler's optimism and altruism reveals Kirk's own deep humanity, despite his job of making life and death decisions in harsh situations, as Natty's respect for Hetty demonstrates his own spiritual side. Although Kirk is romantically attracted to Keeler, his chivalrous affection is reminiscent of Deerslayer's for Hetty.

But, like Hetty, Edith cannot survive in a corrupt "civilization"—one headed for World War Two. And, like Hetty, Edith dies. She is hit by a car, the quintessential symbol, as Fitzgerald so eloquently portrays it in *The Great Gatsby,* of careless, corrupt power.[34] Coincidentally, it is Spock (in order to restore history to its original sequence and save millions of lives) who urges Kirk not to save Keeler when they see the car coming.

Thus the non-crew women on *Star Trek* are either angels, who must die like Stowe's little Eva and other romantic secular saints, or, what is more commonly the case, demons. *Star Trek* presented a plethora of these artful and intelligent seductresses; Elaan in "Elaan of Troyius," Lenore in "The Conscience of the King," and Sylvia in "Catspaw" even try to murder Kirk. But it is the last episode aired during *Star Trek*'s third season, "Turnabout Intruder," which has remained an embarrassment to those associated with the series.[35] Based on a story by Gene Roddenberry, "Turnabout Intruder" is about Janice Lester, a woman scientist who was once in love with Kirk. Feeling that she never became a starship captain only because she was a woman (admittedly *Star Trek* never *has* presented a female starship captain), Lester engineers a machine to switch her mind into Kirk's body, and vice-versa. As Captain, she proves to be emotionally volatile to the point of irrationality, viciously ordering the executions of all who would mutiny against her. Thus, what Chase says about the portrayal of women in Cooper's novels is true of the characterization of non-crew women on *Star Trek:* women tend "to be seen obliquely and with a rather covert displeasure, or unhappy fascination, or secret vindictiveness."[36]

It is women's intelligence which makes them dangerous, thus reflecting Natty's observation about Judith that "the

Evil Spirit delights more to dwell in an artful body than in one that has no cunning to work upon." Commenting on this remark, Porte explains why intelligent women in American fiction are associated with evil:

> Here Cooper not only institutes an association of sex with the head that was to become standard in the American romance, but also combines in Natty's reaction our national ambivalence toward sexuality and what many observers consider our native anti-intellectualism.[37]

Yet the conniving woman serves an important purpose in both *The Deerslayer* and *Star Trek.* As the pure woman allows Natty and Kirk to see and to show the goodness within themselves, the dark lady forces the hero to face "his own duplex nature—the light and darkness within himself—and the duplex nature of experience generally."[38] If Kirk, like Natty, is to combine "prelapsarian virtue with postlapsarian knowledge,"[39] he must confront Janice Lesters as well as Edith Keelers, Judiths as well as Hettys.[40]

But it is in the *Star Trek* films that Admiral Kirk and Capt. Spock come closest to losing all faults, attaining prelapsarian virtue and postlapsarian knowledge, and becoming most like Natty and Chingachgook. Neither Kirk nor Spock become romantically involved with anyone in the *Star Trek* films, nor does any woman attempt to seduce them. Their celibacy makes them purer and more mythic;[41] "the real mythic action is the ritual reassertion of celibacy, the purification and escape from the taint of sex."[42] Indeed, in the novel *Star Trek: The Motion Picture,* Roddenberry even takes pains to establish that Kirk and Spock are not homosexual lovers, ending with the reminder that Spock comes "into sexual heat only once every seven years."[43]

In *Star Trek II: The Wrath of Khan,* Kirk's former lover, Dr. Carol Marcus, and their son, David, are introduced. However, there are no longer any sparks between Carol and Kirk; indeed, Kirk stands at a distance from Carol whenever they are together. Like Chingachgook at the end of *The Deerslayer* and Natty at the end of *The Pathfinder,* Kirk has apparently put romance behind him. Kirk's emotional responses are reserved for Spock. Spock "dies" in the film, giving his life to save Kirk, Carol, David and the *Enterprise* crew. Although the dying Spock states that "the needs of the many outweigh the needs of the few, or the one," his last words are for Kirk alone: "I have been, and ever shall be, your friend." Shortly afterwards, David tells Kirk, with whom David has had an uneasy relationship throughout the film, that he is proud to be Kirk's son. But Kirk's response to David is nowhere near as emotional as Kirk's response to Spock's death, indicating that the most intense relationship in the film is not that between father and son but between friend and friend.

In *Star Trek III: The Search for Spock,* David dies, giving his life for Spock and Lt. Saavik, a half Vulcan, half Romulan woman with whom David has been exploring the planet Genesis. David's fate is especially relevant to this essay. He is Kirk's only family. But American mythic heroes, like Kirk and Natty Bumppo, have no family ties and only vague origins. Lewis explains why this is so:

> The new habits to be engendered on the new American scene were suggested by the image of a radically new personality, the hero of the new adventure: an individual emancipated from history, happily bereft of ancestry, untouched and undefiled by the usual inheritances of family and race; an individual standing alone, self-reliant and self-propelling, ready to confront whatever awaited him with the aid of his own unique and inherent resources.[44]

Indeed, *Star Trek* shrouded Kirk's family in mystery. The only family members seen on the series, Kirk's brother and his wife and children, were introduced and died in "Operation—Annihilate."

David also parallels Chingachgook's son, Uncas. But of course Uncas dies in *The Last of the Mohicans.* When Chingachgook mourns that he has been left alone by the death of his son, Natty reassures him:

> "No, no, no, Sagamore, not alone. The gifts of our colors may be different, but God hath so placed us as to journey in the same path. I have no kin, and I may also say, like you, no people. . . . The boy has left us for a time; but, Sagamore, you are not alone."[45]

Similarly, Kirk is "not alone" at the end of *The Search for Spock* because his best friend has been restored to him. Both the opening and closing words of the film reiterate Spock's friendship with Kirk: "I have been, and ever shall be, your friend."

Of course, Spock does have a family. His father, Sarek, and his mother, Amanda, were introduced in "Journey to Babel." Yet Sarek's and Amanda's roles serve more to illustrate Spock's devotion to Kirk, and vice versa, than Spock's devotion to his parents, since Vulcan logic prevents any display of sentimental filial emotion. When Amanda tells Kirk that Sarek and Spock have not spoken for eighteen years, Kirk replies that Spock is his best friend. Thus the bond between Kirk and Spock appears even closer by contrast with the relationship between Spock and his father. Amanda is reassured by Kirk's and Spock's friendship as she goes on to establish Spock's position as the outsider (the Chingachgook-Jim-Queequeg figure): "I am glad he has such a friend. It hasn't been easy for Spock—neither Vulcan nor human; at home nowhere, except Starfleet"[46]—and one might add, with Capt. Kirk. In "The Ultimate Computer," Spock tells Kirk why M-5, although "practical," is not a "desirable" starship captain: "A Starship, Captain, also runs on loyalty, loyalty to a man—one man. Nothing can replace it. Nor him."[47]

Sarek appears again in *The Search for Spock,* and he tells Kirk that the cost of Spock's rescue has been Kirk's son

and his ship. Kirk replies, "If I hadn't tried, the cost would have been my soul." When the resurrected Spock asks why Kirk went to such lengths to rescue him, Kirk replies that "the needs of the one outweigh the needs of the many." The individual, and his relationships, have highest priority. At the end of the film, Kirk and Spock are left together, surrounded by the bridge crew of the *Enterprise,* and Sarek is conspicuously excluded from the circle.

It is important that the heroes Kirk and Spock are not left alone immediately at the end of the film. The American myth does elevate male friendships—in the works of authors from Cooper to Melville and Twain to Fitzgerald to Hemingway. But the American myth is not one of perennial carefree boyhood, as some critics have suggested. The representative American hero is not the self-seeking and dangerous Tom Sawyer, as it is not Tom Hutter or Tom Buchanan. Rather, our representative hero is the moral, sad, conscientious Natty Bumppo, Huck Finn, Nick Carroway and Capt. Kirk. If the American hero is plagued by anything, it is precisely the curse and blessing of prelapsarian virtue in a postlapsarian world in which the hero has attained postlapsarian knowledge. The hero's virtue combined with his knowledge produce the sensitive intelligence which alone makes compassion possible. This compassion compels the American hero to be the most responsible of men—the man who is his brother's keeper, but who must continually leave the world of the shore or planet because he finds it too painful to watch others' selfishness. At the end of *The Search for Spock,* the American, the Vulcan, the Scotsman, the Russian, the Oriental and the Black stand together in the harmony of mutual esteem, loyalty and responsibility, all second Adams, "American" Adams, who have shown their willingness to lay down their careers and their lives for their friends.

Thus *The Search for Spock* shows more than the closeness of Kirk's and Spock's friendship. It illustrates that the closest thing to paradise is man's harmony with his friends, achieved in a world where, as in Eden, time does not seem to exist since one has no parents or children whose aging reminds one of one's own mortality. As if to reiterate that Eden must be found in relationships, not in a place or time, *The Search for Spock* proves once again that paradise cannot exist on a planet. With his mother, Kirk's son David has "created" the planet Genesis from nonliving matter. At the end of *The Wrath of Khan,* Genesis looks like the wilderness celebrated in *The Deerslayer.* But the intrusion of "rational" beings leads to the corruption of both the Genesis and Glimmerglass wildernesses. David and Saavik, like Adam and Eve before the fall, explore Genesis, but there is a snake in the Garden. The Klingons, who resemble traditional portraits of Satan, want the secret of Genesis to use as an ultimate weapon.

The Klingons and their Romulan allies are *Star Trek*'s version of the warlike Hurons. Both Klingons and Romulans share ancestors with the now-peaceful Vulcans as the Huron Indians do with the peaceful Delawares, to whose tribe Chingachgook belongs. Klingons do everything for the greater glory of their Empire. No individual loyalties take priority over the Empire's rules. Indeed, at the beginning of *The Search for Spock,* Kruge, a Klingon commander, illustrates that the "needs of the many outweigh the needs of the one" by unhesitatingly destroying his lover's spaceship in order to maintain security. The conformist Klingons contrast in every way with the members of the Federation. David brought life from non-life (indeed, following in his father's footsteps, he even broke some rules to do so). But the Klingons, the greedy and exploitative Tom Hutters and Hurry Hurrys of space, bring non-life from life. They commit the first murder on Genesis by killing David/Adam. But the idyllic Genesis cannot last once it is corrupted. The planet begins to disintegrate as Kirk and Kruge fight until Kirk must kill Kruge in self-defense. At the point of the planet's dissolution, Spock, whose resurrected body has been growing from infancy as the planet aged, reaches maturity. He is a Christ figure (his burial clothes are left in his casket like the Shroud of Turin), the second Adam who comes to restore the lost Eden through friendship and caring. Like Christ's, his relationships after his resurrection are with his friends rather than with his family.

At the end of *The Search for Spock,* all vestiges of man's presence are absorbed into space with the disintegration of Genesis and of the *Enterprise.* Similarly, at the end of *The Deerslayer* Tom Hutter's ark and castle and other reminders of man's intrusion are being absorbed back into nature. Yet *The Deerslayer,* although it deals with the earliest period of Natty Bumppo's life as recorded in the Leatherstocking novels, was the last of the tales to be written. Thus not only Cooper, but his readers as well, knew that the wilderness around the Glimmerglass was already vanishing in reality.[48] Indeed, in order to find the true wilderness, Natty and Chingachgook must, in Huck Finn's words, "light out for the territory" at the end of *The Deerslayer,* as they do at the end of each of the Leatherstocking novels until Natty, in his old age, lights out for the final territory of death in *The Prairie.*

Cooper calls attention to the exploitation of the wilderness in the last sentence of *The Deerslayer:* "We live in a world of transgressions and selfishness, and no pictures that represent us otherwise can be true." But he qualifies this melancholy thought by saying "though happily for human nature, gleamings of that pure spirit in whose likeness man has been fashioned are to be seen, relieving its deformities and mitigating if not excusing his crimes."[49] Cooper is not only referring to the "pure spirit" of the fragile and ephemeral Hetty Hutters, but to the resilient Nattys and Chingachgooks, Kirks and Spocks, whose friendships are harmonious with the wilderness. *The Search for Spock* ends with the words "The adventure continues." Like Christ, who ascended into heaven after 40 days, Kirk and Spock, we are to assume, return to space, for the last shot in the movie is of the sky above Vulcan. But wherever the adventure continues, *Star Trek* is a quintessential American romance, and that may well be the principal reason for its enormous appeal.

NOTES

[1] See further comments on the relationship between Natty Bumppo and Chingachgook in Leslie Fiedler, "Come Back to the Raft Ag'in, Huck Honey!" in Leslie Fiedler, *A Fiedler Reader* (New York: Stein and Day, 1977), p. 6; D. H. Lawrence, *Studies in Classic American Literature* (New York: Viking, 1969), pp. 47-63; and Leslie Fiedler, *Love and Death in the American Novel* (New York: Stein and Day, 1975), pp. 162-214.

[2] Fiedler, *Love and Death,* p. 192.

[3] Gene Roddenberry, *Star Trek: The Motion Picture* (New York: Pocket Books, 1979), pp. 5-6.

[4] *Ibid.,* p. 6.

[5] *Ibid.,* p. 6.

[6] *Ibid.,* p. 7.

[7] *Ibid.,* p. 7.

[8] James Fenimore Cooper, *The Deerslayer* (New York: New American Library, 1963), p. 136.

[9] Roddenberry, p. 8.

[10] Lawrence, p. 44.

[11] Cooper, p. 136.

[12] Richard Chase, *The American Novel and Its Tradition* (Garden City: Doubleday Anchor Books, 1957), p. 62.

[13] *Ibid.,* p. 63.

[14] Joel Porte, *The Romance in America* (Middletown, Ct.: Wesleyan University Press, 1969), p. 5. See pp. 3-5 for more on the significance of shooting the eagle.

[15] James Blish, *Star Trek 8* (New York: Bantam, 1972), p. 47. After repeated viewings of every *Star Trek* episode and film, I can quote many lines from memory and will do so in the text. When I cannot remember a line verbatim, I will refer to James Blish's adaptations of the scripts, except when Blish's words differ radically from the scripts as I recall them.

[16] The name "James Tiberius Kirk" itself has religious significance. There are a number of Jameses in the New Testament, including James, the "brother" of Jesus, who became the leader of the Christian Church in Jerusalem. Another James wrote the General Epistle of James, which declares that "faith without works is dead" (Jas. 2:17-26), a sentiment which would be shared by Capt. Kirk and Natty Bumppo. "Tiberius" was the Roman emperor who ruled in the lifetime of Christ. And "kirk" of course means "church." Although not a member of any established church, Capt. Kirk has a name which establishes

his "natural piety." (Of course, Tiberius was a good, and then a ruthless, ruler.)

[17] Porte, p. 27.

[18] Chase, p. 63.

[19] *Ibid.,* p. 63.

[20] Fiedler, "Come Back," p. 9.

[21] *Ibid.,* p. 9.

[22] R.W.B. Lewis, *The American Adam* (Chicago: University of Chicago Press, 1955), p. 91.

[23] James Blish, *Star Trek 5* (New York: Bantam, 1972), pp. 71-2.

[24] *Ibid.,* p. 68.

[25] Cooper, p. 423.

[26] Blish, *Star Trek 5,* p. 65.

[27] Blish, *Star Trek 5,* p. 70.

[28] The Yeoman Rand character was dropped after *Star Trek*'s first season, probably because Kirk's character could not fall in love with her and retain his position of respect. On the other hand, if Rand lost her crush on Kirk, her character presented no plot possibilities.

[29] For an in-depth study of the romantic "dark lady" see Mario Praz, *The Romantic Agony,* trans. by Angus Davidson (Cleveland: World Publishing Co., 1951), Chapter 4. The seductive women in *Star Trek* are not always dark-haired. It is interesting that in James Blish's adaptation of "This Side of Paradise," Leila Kalomi is Eurasian, although Leila was played on the episode by ' 'ond, blue-eyed Jill Ireland. Blish says in his "Preface" to *Star Trek 12* that although he adapts theoretically shooting scripts, those scripts do not reflect last-minute changes made during filming.

On *Star Trek,* almost all women from outside the *Enterprise* crew are dark ladies, not necessarily in coloring, but certainly in their power over men. Even the most gentle one among them, like Nathaniel Hawthorne's Hilda in *The Marble Faun,* is capable of becoming what Porte calls "a worse and more subtle tyrant: not only the gentle guardian of religion and culture, but simultaneously an incitement to licence and desire—at once demanding respectful love and obedience and inspiring lust" (p. 101).

[30] David Brion Davis, "The Deerslayer, A Democratic Knight of the Wilderness: Cooper, 1841," in *Twelve Original Essays on Great American novels,* ed., Charles Shapiro (Detroit: Wayne State Univ. Press, 1958), p. 7.

[31] Cooper, p. 532.

[32] According to Leonard Nimoy, who plays Spock, this line "defined the essence of that relationship [between Kirk and Spock] for me." See William Shatner, Sondra Marshak and Myrna Culbreath, *Shatner: Where No Man* (New York: Grosset and Dunlap, 1979), p. 190.

[33] Cooper, p. 521.

[34] Interestingly enough, Edith Keeler was played by actress Joan Collins, who before this role had, and since has, always portrayed a vamp.

[35] See Gene Roddenberry's and Leonard Nimoy's comments on "Turnabout Intruder" in Shatner, Marshak and Culbreath, p. 194.

[36] Chase, p. 64.

[37] Porte, p. 23.

[38] *Ibid.,* p. 10.

[39] *Ibid.,* p. 27.

[40] Cooper has a harsh attitude toward Judith Hutter, since he implies at the end of *The Deerslayer* that she becomes the mistress of the reprehensible Capt. Warley. However, the twentieth-century reader is more likely to regard Judith as Cooper's most interesting, complex and ultimately admirable heroine.

[41] The *Star Trek* series, no doubt restricted by censors in 1966-69, usually was vague about the actual consummation of male-female relationships. In "Wink of an Eye," there is a brief scene in Kirk's quarters when he is pulling on his boots and Deela is brushing her hair, and in "Bread and Circuses," a beautiful woman is sent into Kirk's bedroom before he is scheduled to be put to death. Otherwise, Kirk's and Spock's relationships with women, to borrow from Oscar Wilde, appear to have been "passionately celibate."

[42] Chase, p. 55.

[43] Roddenberry, p. 22.

[44] Lewis, p. 5.

[45] As quoted by Fiedler in *Love and Death,* pp. 211-12.

[46] James Blish, *Star Trek 4* (New York: Bantam, 1971), p. 48.

[47] James Blish, *Star Trek 9* (New York: Bantam, 1973), p. 44.

[48] For further reflections on the end of *The Deerslayer* see Donald Ringe, *James Fenimore Cooper* (New York: Twayne, 1962), p. 88.

[49] Cooper, p. 534.

TELEVISION GENRES AND LITERATURE

Pearl G. Aldrich

SOURCE: "Daniel Defoe: The Father of the Soap Opera," in *Journal of Popular Culture,* Vol. VIII, No. 4, Spring, 1975, pp. 767-74.

[*In the following essay, Aldrich identifies similarities of plot, character, theme, and language between the modern television serial drama and the novels of Daniel Defoe.*]

Should one mention Defoe and soap opera in the same breath, theoretically he is dealing with two extremes—literature and non-literature written for the mass media—but actually he is not. In his own day, Defoe wrote for the mass media and his five novels, mined from the enormous paper mountain his great productivity piled up, are now called literature because they show, in retrospect, qualities that became identified as artistic during the novel's development into an art form. Whether soap opera, in retrospect, will show qualities of a yet-to-be-named art form is impossible to predict, but we can make some relationships between past and present with existing material. One will be to show that structures underlying popular and elite art are essentially the same. Another, that in the novels he wrote for mass consumption, Daniel Defoe fathered soap opera. Who was the mother? Why, *Moll Flanders,* of course.

Twentieth-century soap opera and eighteenth-century prose narratives such as Defoe's all come under the standard definition of fiction; i.e., a false story invented by the writer, although in both centuries great effort has been made to convince the public that all the stories were and are true, taken with photographic accuracy from "real life." The great popularity of both the soaps and Defoe's narratives does not need documentation here, but the foundation upon which this popularity was built does. According to John J. Richetti,

> [Fiction] depends for its effectiveness as popular entertainment upon its exploitation of what I will choose to call an 'ideology' . . . a body of assumptions and attitudes which commands immediate, emotional and inarticulate assent, as opposed to a set of ideas which requires self-conscious and deliberate intellectual formulation. Fiction, in general, depends upon a community of such belief; the novelist (any storyteller) ruthlessly selects and inescapably shapes events when he presents them to his audience. This process of selection required by the act of narration itself expresses value judgments. . . . The great appeal of fiction at the popular level was its ability to provide an over-simplification of the structure of society and the moral universe which allowed the reader to place himself in a world of intelligible values where right and wrong were clearly and unmistakably labelled. To read these popular narratives was, at least for the moment of belief and participation that even the most inept narrator

can induce, to submit to an ideology, a neatly comprehensible . . . pattern of reality.[1]

Richetti was writing about the eighteenth century, but this explanation also applies to popular fiction today, particularly soap opera. In Defoe's time, the hidden assumptions that commanded immediate, emotional and inarticulate assent were religious; today, they are psychological. *Moll Flanders,* therefore, can be called fictional religious biography; the soaps, psychological biography.

The technique employed by writers of both is based upon isolating one motivating factor of life—religious in the eighteenth century, psychological in the twentieth—then magnifying the importance and pervasiveness of this factor to represent all of life. Within this technical structure, the working of each element of the religious and psychological motivation is presented one at a time, as though each operates in isolation from all other elements of life, so that the audience can understand without confusion.

The audience for mass media offerings in both centuries seems to be similar—non-analytical people, mostly women, who accept passivity as a way of life and believe unexamined, generally fragmented, over-simplified, socially accepted, popular mythology. Popular mythology in this context means ideas that are not true, but are believed by large numbers of people. The male counterpart, incidentally, is the spectator sportsman; the watcher of all the football, basketball, and baseball games. Soap opera's audience cannot and does not live by these ideas; real life could never be so simple, but the fictional people who do and, as a result, receive the rewards and punishment such mythology establishes, provide vicarious thrills and deep satisfaction for their audience. Such popular and superficial fiction, by reflecting and enhancing the simplest common denominators of cultural mythology, not only makes all its readers' and viewers' dreams come true, but also reinforces these beliefs.

When Ian Watt wrote that, in the early eighteenth century, emphasis in the whole culture of England had shifted to the "great power and self-confidence of the middle class as a whole," to whom Defoe was able to appeal because he was one of them, expressing their "needs from the inside much more freely than would previously have been possible,"[2] Watt was ostensibly talking about Defoe as a middle-class tradesman, but Watt's comment can be applied to Defoe's religious beliefs also. They were those of the ultra-conservative, orthodox Puritan, which, according to Maximillian Novak, "was good Calvinistic theology, but it was in distinct opposition to the thought of his time."[3] However, it was just this aspect that appealed to Defoe's readers, to what Richetti has called "the deeply reactionary wisdom of the masses."[4] Richetti further explains the importance of the traditional religious theme to those people at that time:

> The reiteration of the key theme that Providence is behind natural and human events points to one source of the ideological tensions of the day; the defence of the traditional religious view of man

against the new secularism of the Enlightenment, the encroaching forces of infidelity.

> . . . the ideological key of the narratives . . . is fairly limited and definable in its larger outlines . . . this structure tends to take the form of a dramatic confrontation between two opposing attitudes to experience. I will choose to call these two ways of existing in the imaginary worlds the narratives put before their readers 'secular' and 'religious'. . . . In eighteenth-century popular narratives, that is, action itself tends to be depicted as impious aggression against the natural or social order or against innocent and therefore virtuously passive characters.[5]

When Defoe stated in the Preface to *Moll Flanders,* that

> . . . this work is chiefly recommended to those who know how to read it, and how to make good the uses of it which the story all along recommends to them; so it is to be hop'd that such readers will be much more pleas'd with the moral than the fable, with the application than with the relation, and with the end of the writer than with the life of the person written on. . . .
>
> In a word, as the whole relation is carefully garbled of all the levity and looseness that was in it, so it is applied, and with the utmost care, to vertuous and religious uses,[6]

he is very carefully setting the stage to work out the moral equation that sin + suffering = repentance to avoid eternal damnation which evoked the immediate, emotional, and inarticulate assent. He is saying to his readers, in effect, "Beware! This may happen to you," and promotes reader identification with Moll by limiting the motivation for her separate sins to consideration of one at a time—for example, Moll's vanity as the reason for the success of the elder brother's seduction.

"Thus I gave up my self to ruin without the least concern," Moll tells her readers, "and am a fair memento to all young women whose vanity prevails over their virtue," (p. 24) a thought they all shared because, after all, Moll is a member of her own audience.

Moll's actions throughout most of the narrative are impious aggression, not only because they were dishonest, immoral, and taboo, but also because they were *actions,* an outspoken lack of submission that thrilled Defoe's religiously submissive readers. Their enjoyment was increased because they knew that Moll would suffer for her sins and repent, finally, to avoid damnation.

Every time Moll stole and, by stealing successfully hardened in sin according to orthodox Puritan doctrine, her readers nonetheless partook of her courage, defiance, and impious aggression; comfortable, though, in the knowledge that the moral equation would work out. In fact, Defoe, through Moll, keeps reminding the reader that it is going to work out. One episode is typical of the many: As a thief, Moll usually worked alone, then decided to learn to work as part of a team. After several practice sessions for small gain, Moll and her partner pull off a fairly big job, and Moll says,

> This was my first adventure in company . . . and thus I was enter'd a compleat thief, harden'd to a pitch above all the reflections of conscience or modesty, and to a degree which I had never thought possible in me.
>
> Thus the devil who began, by the help of an irresistible poverty, to push me into this wickedness, brought me on to a height beyond the common rate. . . . (pp. 175-76)

She reflects upon what could happen to her if she continues with the gang in this criminal life even though she is getting rich, but avarice would not let her stop—and here Defoe is concentrating on the consequences of the sin of avarice. Moll then says that once a "kind spirit" suggested she get out while she was ahead of the game,

> This was doubtless the happy minute, when, if I had hearken'd to the blessed hint from whatsoever hand it came, I had still a [chance] for an easie life; but my fate was otherwise determin'd, the busie devil that drew me in had too fast hold of me to let me go back. . . . (p. 176)

And every one of Defoe's readers knew exactly what happens to people held fast by the busy devil. How was she going to get out of it? The next chapter would tell.

If the two opposing attitudes to experience then were secular and religious, the two opposing attitudes now are psychological happiness and unhappiness. If the repeated exhortation in the eighteenth century was "repent and ye'll be saved," today's must be "search for happiness and you'll find it." If, in the eighteenth century, the unifying theme of the mass media for which Defoe wrote was ultra-conservative religious doctrine, the unifying theme of twentieth century soap opera is ultra-conservative Freudian psychology with neither Freud's subtleties nor Jung's, Adler's, Horney's, or anyone else's modifications. Freud's early statement that sex is the central driving force of all man's activities has been accepted *in toto* by literal, non-analytical minds. Sex, however, in the soaps, is purged of vulgarity and dressed in gentility. It's called "loving" in the same euphemistic way Moll referred to sex as her "correspondence" with a man.

In the soaps, "love" is the all-purpose universal solvent in a one-dimensional world of people either happy or unhappy. If they have "love," they are happy until disaster removes it. Where Moll can be seduced because of the sin of vanity, Lisa, Jane, Lynn, and their ilk can be seduced because they are "searching for Happiness" according to the following orthodox morality in the soaps: Love is the only motivating element in life. One cannot lie about love. Once it is admitted, the admission requires action. Love is beyond control. (It wasn't anything we wanted, Joanne; it just happened.) No woman who is really in love with a man should give him up easily. (I'll stay right here, Father, and fight for him.) Happily married women spend most of their time in the kitchen—a very reactionary idea—and, in one popular soap opera, the kitchen is decorated in Early American furniture. Only bad women who are alone and unhappy decorate their apartments in Swedish modern while searching for happiness. Money can't buy happiness; only loneliness.

The obvious logical step that would resolve a problem is slow to be observed because the people involved are not logical; they are giving the immediate, emotional, and inarticulate assent to the moral equation they all believe in—that is, loving + mating = happiness to avoid loneliness. In soap opera, we have double-barrelled reinforcement of this mythology. The woman who sought happiness successfully and stayed married to one man gets the deep satisfaction of seeing the "impious aggressor" get her just punishment—loss of her man. Yet the divorcee is reinforced, too. She and "the impious aggressor" on the TV screen are still searching for happiness, and that's fine because it's what real life is supposedly all about.

In addition to these similarities of thematic structure, the soaps and *Moll Flanders* are similar in plot. Each consists of a string of disasters crowding one after another upon the main character.

> The soap opera's plot invariably turned on some excruciating crisis in the life of one of its characters. This might be a financial or marital crisis, but on most occasions it was something a good deal more dire. . . . In the small towns which dotted the map of soap opera land, there were, on the average, perhaps 300 per cent more automobile accidents, sudden onslaughts of exotic ailments, and murders for which the wrong person was put on trial than there were in any comparable group of small towns in the real world.[7]

Although this comment is about radio soap opera, television offers the same ingredients to its viewers.

In *Moll Flanders,* just the statement of the book's full title is sufficient to place it securely within soap opera plot requirements: *The Fortunes and Misfortunes of the Famous Moll Flanders, Who was Born in Newgate, and during a Life of continu'd Variety for Three-score Years, besides her Childhood, was Twelve Year a Whore, five times a Wife (whereof once to her own Brother) Twelve Year a Thief, Eight Year a Transported Felon in Virginia, at last grew Rich, live'd Honest and died a Penitent.*

When the book ended, Moll died rich and penitent, which was happy and successful in eighteenth century Puritan terms. When a serial ends, each character is mated, which is happy and successful in soap opera terms. For example, in the last episode of *Secret Storm,* the lump on Joanna Morrison's leg proves to be benign, and she and Robert Landers plan a happy future together. Amy is reunited with Kevin, who can now walk again, and the two plan a happy future together. In the last episode of *Love is a Many Splendored Thing,* Angel Chernak,

though dying, plans a happy future with her husband and children of the little time she has left. Betsy and Joe marry and plan a happy future together.

In the early eighteenth century prose narratives that are now considered the first novels, such as *Moll Flanders, Pamela* and *Clarissa,* as well as the hundreds that were not of sufficiently high quality to survive, the suffering main character is a woman, as the early titles indicate. So, too, in the soaps. Even though, when transplanted to television, more men entered the plot, the main, superior, and relentless sufferer is a woman.

The string of disasters that afflict Moll, Claire, Ellen, Lisa, Sandy, Joanne, *et al.,* are contained in self-enclosed, almost independent, episodes. In *Moll Flanders,* though Defoe conscientiously recorded her age at intervals, many episodes could have changed places in the text. Moll could have married the linen draper after her affair with the gentleman at Bath and the result would have been the same. Moll's courtship and short-lived marriage with Jemmy could have occurred between episodes of thievery, and they could still have been reunited in Newgate. She could have met and lived with the Captain's widow before or after her marriage to the banker and still been in the same difficulty when the Captain's widow remarried. Moll could have had another illegitimate child after her banker husband died, even at the advanced age of eight and forty, and disposed of it through her "governess" to the same woman in Hertford, then faced her next disaster.

In the soaps, the same episodic independence is evident. In "As the World Turns," the episode in which Dr. Dan learns that Ellen is his real mother could have taken place even before the episode in which Ellen accidently kills the housekeeper who threatened to tell Dan the truth. Ellen would not have known that Dan knew the truth and would have hit the housekeeper with that statue under the same stress. The ripple effect would have touched the other characters with the same impact, triggering other catastrophes.

In "Days of Our Lives," it would have mattered very little when Bill's father discovered Kitty's tape recording—before or after her heart attack and death—because of the explosive quality of its content which proved that Laura's husband was not the father of Laura's child. Bill's father would have had to keep it secret as much before Bill's conviction for Kitty's alleged murder as after.

Another Defoe characteristic demonstrated in *Moll Flanders* that is matched in soap opera is use of language. Literary analysts have called Defoe's style pedestrian, vulgar, repetitious, clumsy, lumbering, yet it was the non-literary everyday language of his audience in the same way the style of soap opera is the contemporary voice of the same audience. Banal comments and trite expressions are uttered slowly, with great significance, as, indeed, they must be to an audience that gives immediate, emotional, and inarticulate assent to the underlying idea that, psychologically, everyday phrases *are* significant. "You never really know what's going to happen, do you?" is a frequently used philosophical comment. "We all have to do what we think best" and "Everyone is an individual" are psychological truisms based on as total an acceptance of the mythology of individual self-determinism as it was rejected in Defoe's day.

In *Moll Flanders,* Moll's voice as the narrator looking back over her life and pointing the morals echoes Defoe echoing pulpit oratory. In soap opera, every character is a working psychologist. Twentieth century psychological mythology says that any two or more "individuals" are capable of "helping each other solve their problems;" therefore, the morals are presented in dialogue using question—Is that what you *really* want? Will marrying Scott make you happy?—and summary—"You're still in love with Scott—not with the Scott that is, but the Scott that could be." While Moll cried out in Puritan agony after that particularly lucrative con job on the mercer, "O! Had I even now had the grace of repentance. . . . I had still leisure to have look'd back upon my follies. . . ." (p. 220)

Another major objection of literary analysts through the years has been to the set, unchanging, one-dimensional characterization of Moll Flanders. However, soap opera viewers would recognize her immediately as one of their own—people in soap opera are clearly, permanently, identified by a set, unchanging, one-dimensional characterization.

In soap opera, the intricacies of family relationships duplicate in quality, if not in quantity, those of eighteenth-century prose narratives. The modern reader who is shocked by Moll's many illegal marriages and other relationships with men, including the incestuous one with her own brother, the number and fate of her ten (or was it twelve?) children should visit among the soaps for a week or two. In one, the illegitimate son adopted and reared by a close friend, grows up, becomes a doctor, and on the day he is to operate on a woman, is told that she is his mother. In another, a man, blinded by flying glass, faces eye surgery on the day his wife runs away from home because she lost custody of her son, Jimmy, born in prison while she was doing time for helping her first husband rob a store. In still another, Dr. Bill is the father of one of his sister-in-law's children because her husband, his brother, is sterile, but the brother doesn't know it.

In the small enclosed world of the soaps, major political and economic events come and go without remark. Neither atomic blasts, hurricanes, nor political scandal slow the relentless search for happiness; neither war, revolution, fire nor plague intruded into Moll's stylized progress to religious stability.

In the same way that Moll's impious aggression thrilled and excited readers who would never be other than religiously submissive, so the continuous search for happiness thrills and excites women who will remain married to the same man for the rest of their lives.

To be sinful and not repent was the worst fate within the eighteenth century conservative Puritan ideology. To be alone and not be unhappy is the worst psychological sin a woman can commit in the twentieth-century soaps.

Defoe used the jargon of popular religion to command the immediate, emotional, and inarticulate assent; contemporary soap opera writers use the jargon of popular psychology. Defoe dramatized the popular religious equation that sin + suffering = repentance to avoid damnation; contemporary soap opera writers dramatize the popular psychological equation of loving + mating = happiness to avoid loneliness. Defoe tried to create religious symbols and gave us memorable people. The soaps try to create memorable people and give us psychological symbols. The relationship between the two, however, points out that, indeed, the underlying structures of popular and elite art are essentially the same.

In the eighteenth century, the religious-passive-virtuous were the mythologically successful, although a casual glance around the population would have exploded that myth. Today, substitute married-passive-happy for the mythologically successful, and the parallel between Defoe's *Moll Flanders* and twentieth-century soap opera becomes clear. Similarities of theme, structure, plot, characterization, and language firmly establish both that Daniel Defoe was the father of soap opera and that yesterday's popular art is often today's elite art.

NOTES

[1] *Popular Fiction Before Richardson: Narrative Patterns 1700-1739* (London: Oxford University Press, 1969), p. 11.

[2] *Rise of the Novel, Studies in Defoe, Richardson and Fielding* (1957; rpt. Berkeley and Los Angeles: University of California Press, 1967), p. 59.

[3] *Defoe and the Nature of Man* (London: Oxford University Press, 1963), p. 10.

[4] *Ibid.,* p. 44.

[5] *Ibid.,* pp. 15-16, 13.

[6] Introduction and Notes by James Sutherland, Riverside Edition (Boston: Houghton, Mifflin, 1959), p. 4. All subsequent page references noted within the text of this paper are from this edition.

[7] Thomas Meehan, "The 'Soaps' Fade but Do Not Die," *New York Times Magazine,* 4 December 1960, p. 27.

Deborah D. Rogers

SOURCE: "Guiding Blight: The Soap Opera and the Eighteenth-Century Novel," in *The Centennial Review,* Vol. XXXIV, No. 1, Winter, 1990, pp. 73-91.

[In the following essay, Rogers views daytime serial dramas within the literary framework originating in such eighteenth-century English novels as Samuel Richardson's Pamela, or Virtue Rewarded.*]*

Contemporary soap operas (here defined as televised morning or daytime serial drama, as distinct from the prime-time serial and mini-series) contain sentiments so deep-rooted as to have much in common with various literary predecessors. For example, soap opera philosophy could, with some justice, be traced back to the medieval wheel of fortune. And not only does the passive, submissive soap heroine have roots that reach at least as far back in English literature as Chaucer's Griselda, but the aggressive, manipulative, lustful soap villainess can find an ancestor in Chaucer's Wife of Bath if not in Shakespeare's Goneril and Regan. Of course, Grendel's mother, the first female character in English literature, is a witch. In fact, the resemblances between soap characters and their literary forebears are endless, so fixed are these types in Western civilization.

One recent study compared soap plots and characters to Renaissance tragedies (Morton and Morton). Soaps have also been linked to the prose narratives of Defoe (Aldrich) and, somewhat casually, to the novel of manners of Burney (Modleski 15). Sentimental and heroic drama could be added to the list. Although other eighteenth-century precursors have been mentioned whimsically or in passing, the usual connection is with the nineteenth-century novel (Keeler; Modleski; Cantor and Pingree 20-22; Allen, *Speaking* 140-51; Stedman 284-91; Weibel; Cantor, "Popular Culture" 193).

While all these links are valid—indeed, they testify to how deeply ingrained soaps are in our culture—the particular fantasies and anxieties of the soap opera relate most directly to the eighteenth-century sentimental novel. Such similarities as the theme of seduction (*Clarissa*) or the reformed-rake plot (*Pamela; Love in Excess*) come immediately to mind. (Recently, for example, one soap ex-bad boy announced, " . . . there are a lot of good girls out there who want to find a bad boy they can reform and bring home to Mama.") But the connection is much more profound. Although literary critics may differ about the origins and founders of the novel (Watt; McKeon; Spender; Spencer), one thing is certain: without the development of the extended narrative form of the novel and its serialization, both eighteenth-century phenomena, the soap opera is inconceivable.

The novel shifted the attention of literature to the romances and family lives of ordinary people, who reflected a new middle-class audience of readers. This focus is understandable since the genesis of the novel is itself associated with the Industrial Revolution, which virtually created the middle class, with its new emphases on "affective individualism," romantic love within a marriage, a new female stereotype, and the nuclear family (Stone; Utter and Needham; Watt). Although the exact nature of these changes is much debated among scholars

(see below), they are all central to soaps and are expressive of an ideology embodied in what is, I argue, their most direct antecedent, the eighteenth-century sentimental novel, historically a feminine genre. Like the early novel, soap operas, which are directed to women, are governed by conventions of realism and broadcast conservative messages that reinforce the status quo. Given these circumstances, it is important to examine cardinal soap beliefs in a historical context that invites analysis.

It is by now a commonplace that the increased amount of feminine leisure time that came with economic specialization was a major contributing factor to the growth of eighteenth-century literacy. Encouraged by the establishment of the circulating library, women became the primary audience for the sentimental novel (Watt 42-49; Altick ch. 2; Leavis 133ff). This new genre followed Richardson in separating the "two spheres" and addressing what are culturally (though not, perhaps, naturally) considered to be feminine preoccupations. The Richardsonian novel is concerned almost exclusively with what is appropriate to the passive, private sphere, including the (overlapping) concerns of home, family, childbearing and rearing, morals, romantic love, courtship, marriage, emotions, interpersonal relationships, and personal dilemmas. Deemphasized is the public "male" realm of action along with "male topics," which are, according to our cultural orientation, usually thought to include law, business, government, news, and politics. Social problems and concerns of the world at large appear only in terms of the personal, which, of course, as the saying goes, is political. The takeover of the Jabot Company on "The Young and the Restless" is important for its effect on the Abbott family, not for its effect on the Dow. According to Charlotte Brunsdon, the soap opera "*colonizes* the public masculine sphere," representing it from a personal perspective (78). If gender is translated into these terms, this model of the feminine subverting or co-opting the masculine is complicated: Television and the press, both powerful agents for the dissemination of culture, are part of the public sphere that colonizes—by commercializing—the personal. Soap operas are brought to us through the agency of big business, which sponsors these programs. Similarly, Richardson and other eighteenth-century printers in their enterpreneurial roles helped disseminate "the feminine."

Soaps continue to emphasize feminine preoccupations. Like the sentimental novel, the soap opera has been and continues to be a form of women's fiction. Of the various types of feminine texts such as Gothics, magazine serials, and romances, soaps are unique in that they are the only fiction on television, that most popular of mass cultural media, that is specifically created for women, especially those who are at home during the day, many of whom are homemakers. One has only to examine commercials aired during the soaps—from which, after all, the genre derives its name—to perceive the target audience: women at home who are potential customers for everything from cleaning products to makeup. Missing are the prime-time commercials for "big-ticket" items such as cars or even washers and dryers, which implicitly require some male decisions for purchase.

Although fewer women are full-time homemakers as more join the labor force, women, mostly between the ages of eighteen and forty-nine, still constitute over eighty percent of the twenty-five million viewers who tune in to soaps daily (Cantor and Pingree 11, 23). These statistics may, however, be changing with the advent of the VCR. Indeed, recent commercials for products like diapers for incontinent adults may indicate a geriatric audience, if not a (female?) audience that must tend to older parents.

This is not to say that men cannot be soap fans. Indeed, some of the new adventure stories (previously unusual in the soap world, especially insofar as they contain physical violence) seem to speak to a male audience, which may be increasing, due to rises in both unemployment and early retirement. Yet these adventure plots, shot for the most part on location, are still relatively rare. Instead, aimed at a female audience, soaps follow Richardson in his "keyhole" presentation of "to-the-moment" emotions.

Samuel Johnson long ago warned against reading Richardson for his tediously discriminated plot: " . . . if you were to read Richardson for the story, your impatience would be so much fretted that you would hang yourself. But you must read him for the sentiment . . ." (Boswell 480). Similarly, soaps are for the most part all talk and no action. In fact, at their inception, televised soap operas were considered to be "radio with pictures" (Cantor and Pingree 48). Although this may have been true of most early television, it continues to be much the case with today's soaps, where with the exception of the rare adventure plot mentioned above, physical movement is minimal. Since talk, whether dialogue or interior monologue, predominates, camera shots are mostly close-ups of faces, allowing for intimate views of every nuance of feeling. This emphasis on emotions and words (as well as the repetitive structure and slow pacing—also characteristic of the Richardsonian novel) enables women to do household chores that require some degree of visual attention (such as ironing or sewing) while watching their soaps. It has been suggested that the fact that action on soaps is reported rather than portrayed makes them popular with workers who listen on television-band radios and with the blind (Liss cited in Cantor and Pingree 24). This same feature, which allows for lapses in visual attention, may appeal to homemakers.

In both the Richardsonian novel and the soap, a multitude of details slowly unfolds in a realistic time scheme. As opposed to prime-time, where weeks, months, and even years are compressed into single episodes, soap time is expanded (one day may take a week to unfold) or it approximates real time (Cantor and Pingree 70). When holidays occur on weekdays, unless programs are preempted by parades or sporting events, they are invariably celebrated in a soap world that parallels our own. In this way the soaps seem to go along with or keep up with our lives. Although soap time may be protracted, in another sense soap time is our time. The effect of realism on the soaps is enhanced by daily serialization, as the soaps become a (much-discussed) part of everyday lives. In addition, as Horace Newcomb suggests, the ongoing nature of soap stories allows for characters to grow old and get wrinkled along with the audience (177, 179).

As should by this time be obvious, realism, the defining characteristic of the early novel, the feature that distinguishes it from previous fiction (Watt 9-34; McKeon), is also the governing convention of the soaps. The realism of both the novel and the soap resides in the fiction that they are actual accounts of real experiences in the daily lives of ordinary individuals. (This emphasis depends on a new ethos that may have developed with the Industrial Revolution, the valuing of individualism, as the everyday lives of average people became sufficiently interesting to merit and sustain attention; Watt). Like the Richardsonian novel, most soaps take place in familiar (if interior) territory such as living rooms. As the early novel addresses concerns that may be more real to the middle-class reader than concerns addressed in other literature, the soap deals with problems that come closer to those of the middle-class viewer than do problems on prime time. Just as it is likely that eighteenth-century readers found the problems of family authority in *Clarissa* much more like their own than Belinda's problems at Hampton Court, so it is likely that the contemporary viewer is more familiar with infidelity or divorce than with the problems inherent in marrying the Prince of Moldavia or in figuring out who shot J.R.

The Richardsonian novel and the soap, then, may approximate experienced reality. Yet realism is still a convention, even if its references, alluding as they do to the everyday world, are easily understood. The soap population hardly reflects today's society: soaps almost entirely ignore the working class. They exaggerate the number of people divorced and the number of people employed in general and employed in professional occupations in particular. Ninety-seven percent of soap characters are Caucasian, less than sixteen percent are over fifty-five, and more than twenty-five percent are fairly rich (Cantor and Pingree 85-90). Although no comparable statistics are available for the eighteenth century, we can be fairly certain that the world depicted in *Pamela* is no more realistic. For one thing, we know that when many young girls migrated to the city, where they were cut off from traditional systems of support such as family, community, and church, they became prostitutes (Tilly, Scott, Cohen).

To understand how fictional the world of apparently realistic eighteenth-century prose fiction is, one has only to think of the full title of *Moll Flanders: The Fortunes and Misfortunes of the Famous Moll Flanders, &c who was Born in Newgate, and during a Life of Continu'd Variety for Three-score Years, besides her Childhood, was Twelve Year a Whore, Five Times a Wife (whereof once to her own Brother) Twelve Year a Thief, Eight Year a*

Transported Felon in Virginia, at Last Grew Rich, Liv'd Honest, and Died a Penitent. Consider the following brief outline of the adventures of "One Life to Live's" Victoria Buchanan, which is equally unbelievable: Soon after Viki marries Joe Riley, he is "killed" in a car accident. She then marries Steve Burke, only to find that Joe actually survived the crash although he has that favorite soap illness, amnesia (a rare disease in real life). After divorcing Steve, Viki remarries Joe. When Joe really dies, Viki marries Clint Buchanan and reverts to her alter ego, Nikki Smith. Fearing that, as Nikki, she may have kidnapped her own daughter, Viki finally comes to her senses only to get amnesia and fall in love with Tom Dennison, Joe Riley's previously nonexistent identical twin. Later, she discovers another husband and daughter who had slipped her mind.

Accepting such sensational stories as true seems to depend on a unique viewer or reader response based on an understanding between audience and author that is similar to a "gentleman's agreement". In effect, the audience must "see double". This phenomenon is common in the eighteenth century. Much eighteenth-century satire, especially Swift's, depends upon this mechanism, as does the whole rollercoaster concept of "sublime" feelings, which are evoked in a frightening or, even better, seemingly life-threatening situation, when one knows one is safe. Richardson's audience was accustomed to seeing double, to believing that his accounts were true, while knowing at heart that they were fictitious. In his serially published novels Richardson uses elaborate textual apparatus, including an editorial pose, to insist that his accounts are factual. The audience in turn becomes intensely concerned with the fate of his heroines, as if they were real people, but at the same time writes letters to Richardson asking him to transform the situations of his characters. Perhaps the only other genre to elicit this bifurcated response is the soap opera. Soap characters regularly receive letters of advice and everything from wedding presents to baby booties, as the occasion demands, from an audience that delights in discussing them as if they are actual people. If eighteenth-century villagers attending a reading of *Pamela* rushed out to ring church bells to celebrate her nuptials, all over America students cut classes to watch "General Hospital" when Luke and Laura tied the knot.

Like the early novel, then, soap fantasies are directed to women and are governed by conventions of realism. As Ian Watt has observed of eighteenth-century novels—and the same could be applied to soap operas—realism makes them "capable of . . . a thorough subversion of psychological and social reality" (206), giving them, in the words of another critic, a "formative influence on the expectations and aspirations of modern consciousness." In this connection, the messages of the early novel are so deep rooted—if not indelible—in our culture that they are still promoted today, especially in the soap opera.

Perhaps nothing is more central to both the eighteenth-century novel and the soap opera than the family. Much scholarly debate surrounds the historical, sociological, and cultural development of this institution. Some contend that for economic reasons, the eighteenth-century nuclear family may have been unstable (Wrigley; Laslett, *World* and *Family*). Lawrence Stone argues that the nuclear family was firmly established by the sixteenth century and that "affective individualism," an eighteenth-century phenomenon, was unrelated to the Industrial Revolution. The eighteenth-century family may have developed from an unemotional structure in the Middle Ages to a patriarchal nuclear family with emotional bonds due to several related factors. These include the increase in marriages for affective rather than economic reasons, the lowered infant mortality rate, which allowed for more emotional relationships between parents and children, the increased power of the state, and the decreased importance of the extended family. Towards the end of the seventeenth century, these changes, which must have had different effects on different classes, began to manifest themselves in more affectionate family behavior such as the jettisoning of restrictive swaddling clothes, less severe beating of children, and breastfeeding by mothers instead of by wet-nurses. Parental love came to focus on children, as more marriages were based on affection rather than property (Stone). Others insist that in the eighteenth century the family may have been in a state of transition as the breakdown of cottage industry led to a migration to the city and an increased emphasis on the nuclear family rather than on extended kinship (Watt 139-41). Indeed, it is difficult to imagine how the shift in human feelings described by Stone could be unconnected to the growing commercialization of eighteenth-century England. New prosperity may have allowed for time to devote to emotional considerations.

Although we may never know the exact nature of the family in the eighteenth century, this much is clear: domesticity, emotional ties, love, sex, romance, and marriage, all in relation to the nuclear family, received an emphasis unknown in previous literature. This preoccupation with the family may reflect the difficulty of the novel's first audience, eighteenth-century women, in dealing with the hierarchical power structure of this institution. Equating the family's desires with those of the father, our collective myth of family unity, which dates back to the eighteenth century, reinforces male dominance. It is therefore not surprising that much eighteenth-century writing is concerned with the anxiety of working out a new model of family relationships. For example, Eliza Haywood's guides, *The Wife* (1756) and *The Husband, in Answer to the Wife* (1756), outline the duties and moral behavior of spouses. Daniel Defoe's didactic works, *The Family Instructor* (1715-27), *Religious Courtship* (1722), and *Conjugal Lewdness* (1727), are conduct books for the middle class. As such, they provide domestic instruction for relationships between and among husbands and wives, parents and children, and couples, taking up issues ranging from premarital sex to love, sex, and marriage to disobedient children. Such concerns are central to much eighteenth-century prose fiction. Albeit in widely different ways, love, sex, marriage, and the family are focal to such diverse eighteenth-century novels as Delariviere Manley's *The New Atalantas* (c. 1710), Eliza Haywood's *Love in Excess* (1719) and *The History of Miss Betsy Thoughtless* (1751), Daniel Defoe's *Moll Flanders* (1722), Henry Fielding's *Tom Jones* (1749), Charlotte Lennox's *The Female Quixote* (1752), Frances Sheridan's *Memoirs of Miss Sidney Biddulph* (1761), Oliver Goldsmith's *Vicar of Wakefield* (1766), Elizabeth Inchbald's *Simple Story* (1791), and Charlotte Smith's *Emmeline* (1788), *Desmond* (1792), and *The Old Manor House* (1793). In perhaps the best known example, *Pamela* goes on for almost 150 pages after the marriage to spell out all the facets of a marriage and family based on affective ties. A two-volume continuation chronicles in great detail her widely praised domestic "family management". And in different ways, both Robinson Crusoe and Clarissa challenge the authority of their fathers, only to accept the authority of God, the Father.

As a form of popular culture targeted specifically to women, soap operas similarly provoke considerable anxiety about the family. If soap operas endorse the family, they also undercut in with a subtext that reflects the difficulty women experience living in a male-centered structure that institutionalizes female subordination. At the same time, however, soaps may themselves substitute for the family, allaying anxiety by meeting fundamental psychological needs unsatisfied by their real-life counterpart.

Soap operas often appear to value the family obsessively. Characters yearn for "the kind of security that a family has that has deep roots" and urge that "family means giving and sharing." Indeed one soap, "All My Children," begins every daily episode with a shot of the family album. Defining family as "the big enchilada," soap characters come to eloquent realizations like "Family is important—it's damn important" or "Family is all we've got—and we must never ever lose sight of that, ever." They manage to get through all their trials and tribulations only because they are sustained by their families. In difficult situations, characters repeatedly identify the family as "the one thing that kept me going." Consider, for example, the apotheosis of the family in the following exchange from "The Young and the Restless" between Nellie, a bag lady, and Jack Abbott, scion of the wealthy Abbott clan, concerning his estrangement from his father:

> N: Mothers and fathers always forgive their children. . . . Isn't that why most religions call God our Father? Hmm? Because if we're truly sorry, he always forgives us?
>
> J: Yeah, but you're talking about a supreme being, not a human being.
>
> N: I'm talking about parent-child, mother-daughter, father-son. That kind of love lasts forever.

While all this may seem fairly straightforward, it would be a mistake to take these metaphors that have been imposed on the family at face value. The explicit message of the soaps is the glorification of the family, but a different message is implicit in the way the family is actually depicted. Even as the family is deified, it is always in chaos, which insures its centrality. For example, in the present instance, the reason for the antagonism between Jack and his father is that Jack slept with his father's second wife. If the family is enshrined, it is also embroiled in massive and nasty problems such as adultery, divorce, incest, alcoholism, illegitimacy, and babynapping. Not pretty. Although the breakdown of the family is criticized, and deviations from the view of the family as central are punished, as in the early novel, in the soaps considerable tension is inherent in the difference between what is said about the family and what is shown (Rogers, *Monitor*).

It may be tempting to follow feminists such as Elaine Showalter and Tania Modleski and read this subtext as a competing discourse, submerged subversively beneath the orthodox discourse to express covert feminine anger, hostility, protest against patriarchy, and desire for power. While all this may be true, it may nonetheless escape typical viewers, who probably do not approach television programs as texts. In fact, since the fragmentation of soap operas encourages the suspension of critical processes, viewers probably never analyze (and may be unaware of) the underlying tension. Instead, they may turn around and cling all the more tenaciously to the conservative message, which endorses the patriarchal family, as the only explicit solution that has been offered. The subtext that emphasizes the very instability of the patriarchal nuclear family is probably not coded as protest, which might lead to questioning the institution of the nuclear family, but instead goes unrecognized, generating considerable anxiety, especially since the contradictions may be exactly those that are central to women.

The ideological basis of these contradictions may be simultaneous anxiety about the breakdown of the patriarchal nuclear family and deep-rooted female ambivalence about an institution that dates at least as far back as the eighteenth century. Feminists have located the valorization of motherhood as women's chief identity in the Industrial Revolution, when production was transferred out of the home, which ceased functioning as the major manufacturing unit. No longer economically useful at home, women came to accept motherhood as a full-time (selfless) vocation that dominated their lives. The sanctification of this form of motherhood and the gradual dissolution of the extended family were attended by increased sexual division of labor and its consequent inequality for women. Sexual stratification was constituted in the model for the patriarchal nuclear family, the King-subject analogy. With the breakup of cottage industry and of the extended family, as adult relatives as well as nonfamily members (boarders, servants) who could help take care of children left the home, child care became the exclusive domain of the mother.

Ironically, however, many soaps do not primarily reflect the nuclear family (Pingree and Thompson). Often they hark back to the extended family, as adult children marry and have children of their own without moving out of the family home. This nostalgic leapfrogging may indicate dissatisfaction with the nuclear family, which may fail to provide sufficient emotional sustenance for women, whose lives sometimes become circumscribed by economic dependence and child-care demands. On the soaps, where there's a child, there is usually an extended family (or, at the very least, servants) to help with care. Whether aunt, uncle, parent, grandparent, or servant, somebody is always on hand to take care of little Clint.

This is a situation unavailable to most women—or, perhaps available only via the soaps themselves, which can come to function as a replacement for extended kinship. Like the respondents in a recent survey I conducted, many viewers regard soap characters as "family" or "friends". If women must move away from traditional systems of support like family, friends, community, and church or synagogue, they can always "take along" their soaps. Assuming a quasi-familial role, soaps may diffuse a need created by the development of the nuclear family, providing isolated mothers with what may be their only mature "conversation" and "company" throughout the day.

Simultaneously embracing and undercutting the nuclear family, even as they function as a substitute for it, soap operas may both stimulate and contain our anxieties. By providing vicarious relief from the solitude created by patriarchal institutions, soaps may inhibit women from actively transforming their lives, leaving unquestioned the large inequalities and insufficiencies of the male-dominated nuclear family.

Since at least on the surface both the soaps and the early novel exalt the family, neither genre can tolerate behavior that threatens this institution. Within this context, it is necessary for women to remain virtuous. In his prefaces Richardson outlines his admittedly didactic purposes. (Indeed, Sylvia Kasey Marks convincingly reads Richardson's novels as conduct books. The soaps could, of course, be read in the same manner.) In *Pamela* Richardson would

> . . . inculcate *religion* and *morality* . . . set forth in the most exemplary lights, the *parental,* the *filial,* and the *social* duties . . . paint VICE in its proper colours . . . set VIRTUE in its own amiable light . . . [and] give *practical* examples, worthy to be followed in the most *critical* and *affecting* cases, by the *virgin,* the *bride,* and the *wife* . . . (31).

To this end, Richardson epitomized an important new feminine stereotype that has persisted in literature until the twentieth century and continues unabated on the soaps. Reflective of the new cultural and economic developments that came with the Industrial Revolution, this highly influential female role model was, above all, virtuous. With the increased importance of property came an increased emphasis on female chastity, so husbands could be sure that their sons were their rightful heirs. For Pamela's parents, death is preferable to the loss of "that jewel" (46). They warn their daughter, " . . . resolve to lose your life rather than your virtue" (52). This equation of sex and death, which Richardson explores more fully in *Clarissa,* his next novel, foreshadows the treatment of AIDS on the soaps, where a disease primarily of drug abusers and of male homosexuals serves to punish female promiscuity (Rogers, *Times*).

Like the forever-fainting Pamela, the new female was inexperienced, delicate, passive, and immune to passion until she was married (Watt 157-161; Utter and Needham). Despite immediate appearances to the contrary, this stereotype persists in soap operas, where sexual purity for women is still highly valued. For example, the most important thing about Caroline Spenser of "The Bold and the Beautiful" at the program's inception is that she is saving herself for marriage. She is "a virgin—untouched, unblemished, a challenge." Like the attempts on Pamela and the rape of Clarissa and countless other eighteenth-century virgins, Caroline's rape may subversively demonstrate how provocative this female model is.

Most of the time, however, the persistence of the Richardsonian female stereotype on the soaps, while true, is not this apparent. In fact, soaps are often criticized for condoning immorality. And it is obvious that premarital and extramarital sex is rampant on the soaps (and certainly more prevalent than in the Richardsonian novel). Yet the soaps illustrate on a regular basis that sexual transgressions are invariably punished in the end,[1] often in the form of pregnancy, which, in typical eighteenth-century fashion, is double-edged.

Not only does Western culture enshrine motherhood as women's destiny, if not their greatest "achievement," it also devalues pregnancy as ploy, punishment, illness, and, as it is categorized by some insurance companies, disability. (Anna Quindlen was recently amused when an insurance form asked whether her disability occurred on the job or in a car.) Perhaps nowhere are these contradictions perpetuated more than on the soaps. Characterizing babies as "miracles" and motherhood as "instinctive," soap heroines commonly desire "a little house full of children . . ." Invoked with regularity is the traditional fantasy that procreation is a vehicle for secular (male) immortality, that " . . . any man . . . would just go crazy to have a son that would carry on your name and follow in your footsteps."

At the same time that pregnancy is idealized, it is devalued, presented stereotypically as a female ploy to trap a man. Soap heroes endlessly accuse women of being "too smart to get pregnant . . . unless you wanted to" and voice sentiments like "I've never known a woman yet . . . who got pregnant without an ulterior motive." Using what is regularly referred to as "the oldest trick in the book," female characters with amazing frequency get men drunk in order to seduce them. Since on the soaps sex always has consequences, these women routinely become pregnant by these unconscious (read blameless) men.

Unfortunately, all this may seem unremarkable, but what is perhaps less obvious is that if pregnancy functions as a woman's greatest reward, it also becomes her supreme punishment, all in the service of male domination. The ideological basis of this contradiction is deep-rooted.

Used to justify male dominance, this duality was introduced in popular culture almost 250 years ago in *Pamela,* which cites Biblical authority for these notions. In *Pamela* pregnancy is valorized, albeit negatively, in terms of "how uneasy many women are, not to be in this circumstance (my good Lady Davers particularly, at times), and Rachel and Hannah in holy writ; and how a childless estate might lessen one in the esteem of one's husband" (*Pamela* 3:282). Yet even as pregnancy is privileged, the agony of childbirth is interpreted as a special punishment meted out for female sexuality. In Pamela's paraphrase the whole serves as a pretext for female subordination:

> . . . the apostle . . . says, That *he suffers not a woman to teach, nor to usurp authority over the man, but to be in silence.*—And what is the reason he gives? Why a reason that is a natural consequence of the curse on the first disobedience, that she shall be in subjection to her husband.— For, says he, *Adam was NOT deceived; but the woman, being deceived, was in the transgression.* As much as to say, "had it not been for the woman, Adam had kept his integrity, and therefore her punishment shall be, as it is said, *I will greatly multiply thy sorrow in thy conception: in sorrow shalt thou bring forth children,—and thy husband shall rule over thee* (*Pamela* 3:281).

These cultural pieties, which dictate that a woman's natural role is one of suffering and subordination, bear repeating: the doctrine of Original Sin, which brings sex and death into the world, stipulates that the woman never "*usurp authority over the man, but . . . be in silence . . .* in subjection to her husband. . . ." It also connects this male dominance to female pain at delivery, defining both causally as punishment for female sexuality: woman's "*punishment shall be . . . in sorrow shalt thou bring forth children,—and thy husband shall rule over thee.*"

This long tradition of reading pregnancy as punishment for female sexuality continues tenaciously in the soap opera. For example, on "The Young and the Restless" one unwed mother experiences life-threatening complications in childbirth. For weeks she is in a coma, suspended precariously between life and death. (As previously mentioned, the equation of female sexuality and death is elaborated in the Richardsonian novel.) On the same soap an adulterous affair results in pregnancy, and, in short order, abortion, and institutionalization. (Note that abortion is read literally as insanity.) In general, upholding standards of conventional morality, soaps support the status quo, reinforcing the virtuous female stereotype of the early novel from Melliora (*Love in Excess*) to Pamela and Clarissa.

Identified with moral failure and sexual pollution, an unmarried pregnant woman becomes in this scheme a text in which sexuality is made visible. Pregnancy is, of course, a particularly appropriate punishment since the "crime" or causality is unambiguous. (It is possible to impose all these metaphoric equivalences on pregnancy because personal aspects of women's lives simply *show* more than men's and are therefore more open to public scrutiny. Although in the case of pregnancy, this has a biological foundation, it is difficult to see why sexual asymmetry extends in this way to such public tokens of private relationship as engagement rings or the title "Mrs." which have no male equivalent).

The punitive notion of pregnancy, where unmarried pregnant women are standard tropes for sexual transgression, is not confined to "The Young and the Restless," but is pervasive on the soaps. Of a piece with the stories of her eighteenth-century sisters like the evil, aggressive Alovisa, who is killed (*Love in Excess*), or the sexually passionate Lady Elmwood, who dies after an extramarital affair (*Simple Story*), is the situation of Pine Valley's resident femme fatale and self-styled feminist, the much-married Erica Kane Martin Brent Cudahy Chandler (soon to be Montgomery). Immediately after she denounces the institution of marriage, declaring her "liberation" from having "fallen into the cultural trap of thinking I needed marriage to be happy," Erica receives a call from her physician, who informs her that she is expecting. Some months later when the cat is out of the bag—although the cookie is still in the oven—Erica is hospitalized, in danger of losing both her baby and her life. At this point she explicitly connects previous moral lapses with her current danger: "My baby—I'm losing my baby. . . . This is my punishment." Convinced that she is now "paying the price," Erica reflects, "God is punishing me. . . . That's why I'm hooked up to all these machines."

Reinforcing the notion that female sexuality is punished by pregnancy, which may be fatal, the soaps help perpetuate the eighteenth-century double bind for women: bearing children and continuing a male line are enshrined as a woman's greatest achievement, even as exercising her sexuality is punished by the pain of pregnancy and domination. (This dichotomy extends to menstruation, which women variously nickname "the curse" or "my friend" and even to the—hormonally induced—happy "glow" of pregnancy, which may nevertheless be attended by morning sickness, heartburn, constipation, and hemorrhoids.)

To "hook" and keep a man, women are supposed to be sexually alluring, but realizing female sexuality, even within a monogamous relationship, may lead to pregnancy and pain. Physiologically vulnerable during gestation and labor, pregnant women are additionally subjected to ideological confusion that enforces female subordination. So tenacious is this double message that, as indicated, it was first articulated in popular culture in the early novel and persists in today's soap operas. In both genres pregnancy is endorsed, even as the subtext reflects women's anxieties and fears about pain and mortality, calling into question the happiness women are supposed to experience in a condition that is surrounded by the rhetoric of punishment and subordination.

Since these notions are so deep-rooted in our culture, it may be worthwhile to re-examine them, especially as they find expression in our current ideas about natural childbirth. Today some obstetricians limit their practices to natural childbirth, allowing women no choice. Other physicians administer anesthesia only at the last stage of delivery, after most of the pain has subsided. But so deeply are our views about parturition inscribed in popular culture that the issue may be one of ideology as much as medical necessity, which may serve as a pretext for enforcing female punishment and subordination.

Like the early novel, the soap opera reconciles women to traditional feminine roles and relationships, reinforcing patriarchal stereotypes and structures. Like the sentimental novel, soap fantasies address themselves to women and are governed by a realism that, as one critic wrote of the early novel, "gives authenticity to the deceptions of romance." For all these reasons, soap beliefs—such as those about the family and pregnancy—are a vehicle for our profoundly ambivalent attitude towards women and female sexuality, which not only causes pain but also justifies the "ideal" Western family structure in which males dominate. The stories we have been telling ourselves on soap operas represent a deeply inscribed, enduring potential danger that can best be understood by tracing them back to past literature. Only then can we fully understand their impact and critique them in a way that frees us from oppression.

NOTE

[1] Moral violations on the soaps (the most frequent of which are deceit, murder, and premarital/extramarital sex) are normally not condoned and the offenders are usually punished (Sutherland and Siniawsky).

WORKS CITED

Aldrich, Pearl. "Defoe: The Father of Soap Opera." *Journal of Popular Culture* 8 (1975): 767-74.

Allen, Robert C. *Speaking of Soap Operas.* Chapel Hill: U of North Carolina P, 1985.

Altick, Richard. *The English Common Reader: A Social History of the Mass Reading Public, 1800-1900.* Chicago: U of Chicago P, 1957.

Boswell, James. *Life of Johnson.* Edited by R. W. Chapman. 3rd ed., corrected by J. D. Fleeman. New York: Oxford UP, 1970.

Brunsdon, Charlotte. "*Crossroads:* Notes on Soap Opera." In *Regarding Television: Critical Approaches— an Anthology,* edited by E. Ann Kaplan. Frederick, Maryland: University Publications of America, 1983: 76-83.

Cantor, Muriel G. "Popular Culture and the Portrayal of Women: Content and Control." In *Analyzing Gender: A Handbook of Social Science Research,* edited by Beth Hess and Myra Marx Ferree. Beverly Hills: Sage Publications, 1987.

Cantor, Muriel G. and Suzanne Pingree. *The Soap Opera.* Beverly Hills: Sage Publications, 1983.

Keeler, J. "Soaps: Counterpart to the 18th Century's Quasi-Moral Novel." *The New York Times,* 16 March 1980.

Laslett, Peter. *Family Life and Illicit Love in Earlier Generations: Essays in Historical Sociology.* New York: Cambridge UP, 1977.

Laslett, Peter. *The World We Have Lost.* London: Methuen, 1965.

Leavis, Q. D. *Fiction and the Reading Public.* 1932. London: Chatto and Windus, 1965.

McKeon, Michael. *The Origins of the English Novel, 1600-1740.* Baltimore: Johns Hopkins UP, 1987.

Marks, Sylvia Kasey. "*Clarissa* as Conduct Book." *South Atlantic Review* 51 (1986): 3-16.

———. *Sir Charles Grandison: The Compleat Conduct Book.* London: Associated University Presses, 1986.

Modleski, Tania. *Loving with a Vengeance: Mass-Produced Fantasies for Women.* 1982. New York: Methuen, 1984.

Morton, Gerald and Claire Morton. "Three Hundred Years of Reruns." *Markham Review* 11 (1982): 32-36.

Newcomb, Horace. *TV: The Most Popular Art.* New York: Anchor, 1974.

Pingree, Suzanne and Margaret Thompson. "The Family in Daytime Serials." In *Television and the American Family,* edited by J. Bryant. Hillsdale, NJ: Lawrence Erlbaum Associates, forthcoming.

Richardson, Samuel. *Pamela or, Virtue Rewarded.* Edited by Peter Sabor. New York: Penguin, 1980.

———. *Pamela or Virtue Rewarded.* 4 vols. In *The Complete Novels of Mr. Samuel Richardson* introduced by Austin Dobson and William Lyon Phelps. London: William Heinemann, 1902. Vols. 3 and 4.

Rogers, Deborah D. "The Afternoons of Our Lives." 23 September 1988, *The Christian Science Monitor.*

———. "AIDS Spreads to the Soaps." *The New York Times,* 28 August 1988.

Spencer, Jane. *The Rise of the Woman Novelist.* NY: Basil Blackwell, 1986.

Spender, Dale. *Mothers of the Novel.* New York: Pandora P, 1986.

Stedman, Raymond William. *The Serials: Suspense and Drama by Installment.* 1971. Norman: U of Oaklahoma P, 1977.

Stone, Lawrence. *The Family, Sex and Marriage in England, 1500-1800.* New York: Harper, 1977.

Sutherland, John and Shelley Siniawsky. "The Treatment and Resolution of Moral Violations on Soap Operas." *Journal of Communication* 32 (1982): 67-74.

Tilly, Louise, Joan Scott, and Miriam Cohen. "Women's Work and European Fertility Patterns." *Journal of Interdisciplinary History* 6 (1976): 447-76.

Utter, Robert and Gwendolyn Needham. *Pamela's Daughters.* New York: Macmillan, 1936.

Watt, Ian. *The Rise of the Novel.* 1957. Berkeley: U of California P, 1974.

Weibel, Kathryn. *Mirror Mirror: Images of Women Reflected in Popular Culture.* NY: Anchor Books, 1977.

Wrigley, Edward. *Population and History.* New York: McGraw-Hill, 1969.

David Konstan

SOURCE: "The Premises of Comedy: Functions of Dramatic Space in an Ancient and Modern Art Form," in *Journal of Popular Film and Television,* Vol. 15, No. 4, Winter, 1988, pp. 180-90.

[*In the following essay, Konstan focuses on such workplace situation comedies as* Barney Miller *and* Archie Bunker's Place *in a discussion of the function of place in classical Greek New Comedy and the television comedy series.*]

In this paper, I shall examine the function of place, in the sense of the scene or site of dramatic action, in two comic traditions, one ancient, the other recent and still lively.[1] These traditions are the so-called New Comedy of the classical Greek dramatists and their Roman imitators or adapters and the contemporary situation comedies of television. Comparison of sitcoms with the classical form will help reveal the ways in which the settings of comedy, both ancient and modern, are specific to their respective cultures, and to the ideological problematics that they generate.

The contrast between the place where the comedies of Menander, Plautus, and Terence were located and the scene of TV comedy is extreme. Classical drama in general did not represent interior scenes. The action took place out-of-doors, and in New Comedy normally on a city street, whether in Athens or another Greek town, that ran before the façades of two or three houses. The houses were drawn on the wall, or *skene,* behind the stage, in which doors gave access to the dressing area. Characters entered and exited by means of the doors, if their business took them inside one of the houses, or else by the wings if there were downtown or country visits. Remote events, or whatever happened indoors, might be reported by characters, but they were not enacted directly on stage.[2]

Television sitcoms are dramas of interiors. There is usually a single indoor set in which all or most of the action occurs, either the parlor of a home, or else an office, eatery, or other situation where the characters primarily interact. (*Gilligan's Island,* located on a desert island, is the kind of exception that proves the rule; it has an ancient analogue in Plautus' *Rudens,* situated on a barren seashore.) As many commentators have remarked, television as a medium is best suited to small, intimate scenes rather than to panoramic vistas.[3] It is good at closeups, and the backdrop is generally sparse, schematic, and familiar, the kind of set that is characteristic of soap operas. Partly, this is a function of the small screen and low resolution of TV, as opposed to the cinema; partly too, of budgetary constraints, where weekly episodes must be filmed, though an inexpensive outdoor set of the antique kind is quite feasible, and is employed, interestingly, on the children's show *Sesame Street.*[4] In addition, the interior scene corresponds to the circumstances of the viewer, who alone, or among a small, intimate group clustered in the living room, will find his or her own reflection in the settings of domestic comedies or in the family-like context of a local pub or the collegial environment of professional associates.

Correspondingly, the open-air theaters of the Greeks and Romans favored public scenes exposed to the gaze of the entire community gathered for the festival occasion of the drama. But I should like to argue further that the communal character of the Greek theater and the public locus of the dramatic action have to do also with the nature of Greek social life, or, more particularly, with the arena projected by Greek city-state ideology as the place where the tensions of that ideology were situated and dramatically explored.[5] Greek ideology emphasized the interaction among the several households that comprised the city-state. In turn, it has been suggested that the private setting of TV drama, which is in many ways the heir of parlor plays of Chekhov and Ibsen, is a manifestation of the relative isolation of the family in modern capitalist society.[6] The family or affiliated group is treated, or perhaps it is better to say fantasized, as the primary scene of personal identity and fulfillment.[7]

In what follows, I shall expand briefly upon the characteristics of Greek society and ideology that find their image and their problematic in the street setting of Greco-Roman New Comedy, then discuss how modern ideology and social arrangements find expression in the enclosed spaces of the TV sitcoms.[8] After this general and more or less abstract preamble, I shall turn to specific plays or episodes, and indicate how the dramatic issue in each may be understood as a potential displacement, a breach in the confines of the privileged space where action and interaction occur, and, correspondingly, how the denouement serves to restabilize the public space in ancient comedy, the private space in modern, as the proper place for the narrative to occur. Finally, I shall consider how this restabilization is itself an ideological strategy by which the drama seeks to exclude or deny, though never with perfect success, the presence of another order of social relations that impinges upon and interferes with the communal vision of the ancient city-state, or, in the case of the sitcoms, with the ideal of a natural, familial association that is safe and secure from the competitive and impersonal relations of production and exchange in the outside world.

With respect to sitcoms, I shall concentrate particularly on the type that is located in what may be described as a place of business rather than in a family setting. The locales for such sitcoms may be, for example, a detectives' room, as in *Barney Miller,* or a tavern, as in *Archie Bunker's Place.* A hospital is the setting in *House Calls;* a radio station in *WKRP in Cincinnati;* there is the newsroom in *The Mary Tyler Moore Show;* a fire station in the short-lived *A Star in the Family;* the dispatcher's headquarters in *Taxi;* law offices in *The Associates,* which had a run of a little over a month; a school in *Welcome Back Kotter* and *The Facts of Life* (if education counts as business); an unemployment office in *Calluci's Dept.* (another failure); restaurants or bars again in *Alice* and in *Cheers;* another police station in *Carter Country;* the New York Garment District in *Pins and Needles;* and, perhaps at the margins of the type, a prison (*On the Rocks*), a military detention camp (*Hogan's Heroes*), a submarine (*Operation Petticoat*), and, in general, the army, beginning way back with *Sergeant Bilko* and continuing strong with *M*A*S*H* and *Private Benjamin*—though it may be, as Horace Newcomb has suggested, that the military comedies constitute a subgenre of their own.[9]

Partly, this restriction in the choice of sitcoms is a matter of convenience, but it is also motivated by two special considerations. First, comedies situated in a place of business, that is, a public locale, are a better analogue than strictly domestic comedy to the civic drama of antiquity. In the office or tavern, there is a wide variety of social relations including, but not limited to, conflict between generations and tensions within marriage. The second reason for focusing on sitcoms of the workplace goes beyond the specific scope of this paper. TV sitcoms are, I believe, the first comic genre to make the workplace the primary locus of the drama (there is a precedent of sorts in some of the cinema comedies of the 1930s, but the emphasis on the place of business was never so exclusive). It is one of the special contributions of TV sitcoms to the history of drama and has been pretty well ignored by critics, so far as I know. But it is, I think, of great importance. To take only a single aspect, everyone in the workplace is, by definition, self-supporting. Thus, whatever the conventional stereotyping of women's roles, for instance, as domestic or subordinate, there will always be

at least the implicit suggestion that relations between the sexes are based on mutual economic independence. This is new, and it justifies special attention, even if I must reserve a full discussion of this aspect for a future occasion.

Of the hundreds and hundreds of comedies produced in Athens in the fourth and third centuries B.C., when New Comedy flourished, we possess only one in its entirety, the *Dyscolus* or *Grouch* of Menander, who was the best esteemed playwright in the genre. But we know from the testimony of Plutarch and Ovid, for example, that all of Menander's comedies—he wrote more than 100 of them—involved romantic passion, or *er s.*[10] Now, love has perhaps a natural comic appeal, but its pervasiveness, not only in the work of Menander but in New Comedy generally, invites interpretation. Indeed, precisely because of its omnipresence in the genre, it seems, the function of passion has rarely been questioned or analyzed; most often, it is simply noted as a convention. What fascination was exercised by the numberless young lovers scheming to outwit stern fathers or bombastic rivals for the possession of their sweethearts?

To approach an answer to this question, we may consider the image of society in ancient literature and oratory, and more especially in Aristotle's *Politics,* which is a kind of dictionary of middle-class common sense views on the polis. Aristotle observes that "the first form of association . . . is . . . the family"[11]; next comes the village; and, at the highest level, the city-state, which is also a natural entity, Aristotle says, "because it is the completion of associations existing by nature" (1.2.8). Aristotle adds that the polis is logically prior to the household in the same way that the body is logically prior to a foot or a hand (1.2.13). The household itself, or *oikos,* was understood to include, under the authority of its male head, his wife, children, slaves, and property—for ownership of property in the polis was, on the whole, both a right and a requirement of citizenship. The several households out of which the city was constituted as a natural association aspired to an ideal of economic autonomy or autarky, though they were related to one another by a certain elementary division of labor and exchange of goods, as well as by common responsibilities for the defense of their territory and the management of the state and its possessions abroad. Finally, the households were related by connubial exchange as the basis of social reproduction. Such, in broad outline, is the ancient society's own theory of itself. In Menander's time, and for the century and a half preceding, citizens might marry only citizens at Athens, and citizens were the offspring of citizen parents on both sides, mother's and father's. Athens was, then, a closed descent group. Marriage took place beyond the household but within the set of households that constituted the polis.

We may construe the marriage code as a set of bonds uniting the individual households out of which the ancient society seemed to be, and in part really was, made up. In a society of this sort, characterized by an elaborated ideology of kinship and by a relatively low level of the division of labor—in Durkheim's terminology, by mechanical rather than organic solidarity—that allowed at least the fiction or ideal of the household as a self-sufficient unit, marriage ties were an important expression of social cohesion. They identified the society as a community, excluding those who were outside the citizen body and binding into the social texture the potentially independent family estates. The interest in love and marriage, from this point of view, related not so much to the individual home as a locus of unity and security as to the production of links among the households, the creation or expression of a social space defined by their integration into a polis.

The impulse toward integration was, we may say, formulated as *eros,* the desire that drove beyond the bounds of the autonomous home and pressed for union with another. That the object of *eros* was commonly a woman ineligible as a partner in marriage, a slave or foreigner, for instance, means that the passionate basis of connubial association was perceived as a natural rather than as a social impulse: It was the task of comedy to reveal the social form that governs the natural impulse (itself, of course, a socially constructed category) by arranging the notorious recognition scenes and other coincidences by which the citizen credentials of the parties involved were confirmed. And the space in which the revelation of the socialized *er s* took place, the scene of the verification of the community of citizen households, was precisely the public street onto which the individual houses faced, which might seem to unite them physically, like a cord through beads, into the social structure characteristic of the polis and its ideology.

Modern urban society seems at the opposite extreme from the ancient city-state in respect to individual autarky. Households make no pretense of self-sufficiency, despite the vogue of suburban gardening. Their implication in the universal division of labor, where each unit is bound by relations of exchange to all others, is taken for granted. According to the ideal conception of the modern economy, the office or workplace is constituted simply as a nodal point in the system of production, where people are related as participants in a common enterprise based not on personal feelings, much less kinship, but on standards of performance. At work, people of different ethnicity, religion, gender, or sexual orientation cooperate and coexist for the sake of a service or a product, that is, for the job. At the same time, every enclosed space is treated as a nucleus of personal relations in the sitcoms, a refuge of the affections encapsulated or encysted within the impersonal order of economic life.

In modern society, the family is the model for every sort of unmediated solidarity (witness the formulas of sisterhood and brotherhood in feminist, labor, and religious movements), and the group at work or in the tavern is conceived of as a domestic unit. The representation of relations in the workplace as a kind of family is in part a reflex of the same impulse that inspires identification within ethnic groups, fraternal orders, and other forms of

association based on likeness or essential solidarity, the collective sense of unity over and against the functional and provisional form of association based on performance and competition.[12] It is a response to the radical equality of the market whose essence, like that of the commodity, is to respect no qualities at all, an equality that reduces all personal attributes to time and competence on the job, which is to say, to labor power.

The private sphere of home or office—to the extent that the office is treated as a private sphere—stands against the world outside, while, in ancient drama, the interior domain was held within the social nexus by liaisons and contracts managed on public streets. In the modern sitcoms, rationalized forms of life press upon the personal and must be repeatedly expelled or controlled. In both genres alike, interior and exterior exist in a dynamic stasis, and the space of the drama is continually recorroborated through the narrative tactics of the plot. Space is not the passive locus of dramatic action; it is defined by the social relations it contains or excludes, challenged or defended as a symbol of social structure.

With this bare sketch of a theory of place in comedy ancient and modern, and the way in which it encodes social tensions that are enacted and resolved in the drama, I shall turn to the examination of a few specific comedies in which the defense of place is thematic. Clearly, my choices are not disinterested, and not every drama, I am sure, can be shown to operate in these terms. But through specific cases it is, I think, possible to see how the defense of the dramatic space is a strategy of comedy, more or less foregrounded or thematized as the complex of issues in the story demands, but always, or almost always, there in the deep structure of the narrative.

Plautus' *Aulularia* is about a man who has discovered a buried pot of gold in his house and, as a result, dotes on his hoard to the exclusion of all other concerns. From miserliness, he refuses to provide a dowry for his daughter, and thus removes himself simultaneously from both processes of exchange that constituted the ancient city-state, according to its own ideology: commerce and kinship. His wealth is stolen when he removes it from the temple of Good Faith, which he distrusts, to a wild precinct sacred to the woodland god Silvanus, beyond the city walls. As it happens, his daughter is pregnant as a result of rape (there is thus a double assault on the old man's substance); but the youth who violated her has a sudden change of heart and accepts the girl in marriage, at the same time restoring the stolen treasure, which he had recovered from his slave. The play ends with the marriage agreement, and no doubt the miser's gold, or part of it, made up the dowry (the last act of the *Aulularia* is mutilated).[13]

Let us consider the spatial dynamics of the play. It begins with the miser driving his much-abused maid out of the house, suspicious that she may be snooping out his treasure. He dashes inside again to check on his gold, and announces to the audience the wish that he might never leave his house at all. His reason for emerging now is that a public donation is to be distributed, and the miser fears that his absence may draw attention to himself and suggest that he is harboring a secret hoard. The ironies here are evident: The miser's obsession is such that entering public space even to increase his private wealth is odious, and his sole motive for doing so is to insure the inviolability of his cache. When he returns, he is reluctantly drawn into dialogue with a rich neighbor, who requests his daughter's hand in marriage. The miser interrupts the discourse twice by rushing into his house before he finally departs for the market to purchase provisions for the wedding feast. On his return, he discovers a cook at work inside his home, commissioned by the would-be groom next door, and he expels the cook violently.

The interior of the house, then, is represented as the locus of the miser's fixation and of his social isolation. By charging repeatedly into his house, he disrupts the marriage negotiations—albeit vain ones, since the young assailant rather than the rich neighbor is destined for the girl—and thus the bond between his household and another that can integrate him morally, economically, and by kinship into the civic community. The negotiations take place in the street, the area between the houses of the father and the suitor. The interior is thus presented as the potential negation of the solidarity of civic relations. Correspondingly, the miser's venture outside the city limits leaves him at the mercy of mere theft (itself an analogue of the rape that occurred, as often in New Comedy, during a ritual festival). Only in the civic spaces of the city, on its public ways, are the transactions that symbolize its communal identity carried out. Against the withdrawal of the miser into his private domain and his sally into the wilderness outside the city walls, the street that passes by the housefronts is reasserted as the proper place of citizen association.

In an episode of *Archie Bunker's Place*—the successor to *All in the Family*—one of the regular patrons of the tavern, a ne'er-do-well called Barney with a nincompoop's charm, enjoys a winning streak at the races, which, he believes, is due to an elaborate number system. As a result, Barney is addicted. In his initial flush of wealth, he enters the tavern sporting bright new clothes and affecting expensive and sophisticated tastes (e.g., for caviar) to the indignation of his old friends who express their resentment of his big-spender manner by ridiculing his pretensions. At the same time, Barney is asked to pay up arrears on his tab. This demand points, on the one hand, to Archie's distrust of his friend's unearned and chancy fortune: He wants the bill cleared before Barney's luck changes. On the other hand, Archie's demand is a kind of ostracism, a refusal to extend the credit that makes relations of good faith among the tavern crowd. The breach of solidarity represented by the gambler's new style, his racy, *grand homme* demeanor jars with the cautious morality of the tavern's proprietors and regular customers. The breach between Barney and the rest is both widened and symbolized when he roots for the out-of-town team in a basketball game on the bar's TV.

Barney has money on the opponents of the home team, and he is guided by interest, not by sentimental loyalties. The local favorites win, but Barney is treated as a traitor, and he takes refuge from his friends' scorn in a neighboring topless establishment where, as Barney puts it, the owner has class.

We can easily see what defines the social space of Archie Bunker's tavern. Its membership is bound by shared symbols, such as support for the home team and by commitment to a kind of moral economy, in E. P. Thompson's phrase, an economy that allows credit to temporarily hard-up patrons but draws the line at subsidizing high-risk speculation that seeks gain without reference to the symbols of group solidarity. With the mention of the topless bar, there is a suggestion of libertinism that fills out the picture of easy virtue, loose money, and the casual trade of old for new acquaintances that Barney has bought into.

Outside Archie's place is a network of vice in love and finance, against which Archie and his friends endorse the traditional wisdom of business, to be sure, but a less aggressive sort of business that leaves room for solidarity based on personal rapport, the petit-bourgeois nostalgia for a natural community of values. In the sitcom model, where the interior space represents an enclave within the free-for-all competition of the market place, rather than, as in the ancient comedy, a withdrawal from the public arena of civic reciprocity, the hoarder of the latter form is restyled as a gambler. Rather than secreting his wealth in a private location, he risks it constantly in the mysterious, foreign, and shady world of big gains and sudden losses. Whereas the miser feared to leave his house, the bettor's transactions draw him outside, until the tavern becomes merely a base, and his new style and aspirations make of him a stranger. It may be worth noting that halfway between the miser and the gambler, in the history of the fetishization of money, is the usurer, and in Molière's *L'Avare,* based in large part on the *Aulularia,* Harpagon guards his money-chest indoors, but negotiates his loans—as it happens, with his own son—on a public street; correspondingly, marriage for the usurer is conceived as a means of making a profit.

In the episode of *Archie Bunker's Place,* as in Plautus' *Aulularia,* greed is humbled through loss, which prepares the outcast for his reintegration into the community. Barney's winning streak comes to an end, and he is left penniless and heavily in debt to loan sharks. In his pride he refuses charity, and goes into hiding when the mob comes to collect. Archie feigns unconcern, in part through that stubborn selfishness that lends the character his charm, but finally as a lesson by intimidation on the wages of gambling. Archie finds Barney at home, sharing a last can of food with his dog before hanging himself.[14] Barney, in his desperation, at last begs for help; Archie treats himself to a beer from Barney's refrigerator, signifying the restoration of solidarity by the publican's version of communion, and offers to make good on Barney's debt just as the gangsters enter with a hearty "buona sera." The leader offers a wry sermon on how the underworld exists to instruct mankind on the advantages of sober self-control.

There is a peculiar and disturbing symmetry between the morality of Archie's tavern society and that of the stylized mafiosi. The cohesion of Archie's world is guaranteed by the danger of transactions outside. At the same time, Archie and his partner, who also helps to bail out Barney by insuring payment of the loans, implicitly sanction the idea that the fault for falling into debt lies with the borrower and not with the conditions of the loan. This is the same lesson, though more brutal, that is taught when Archie demands payment of Barney's bill at the bar. There is a continuity between the principles of commerce inside and outside the tavern, despite the show of mutuality among friends. Moreover, the ethnic stereotyping of the gangsters gives to their association the same appearance of natural loyalty that the community of friends in the tavern enjoys, albeit the latter is a product of sentiment rather than of national affiliation. The image of the mafiosi imports into the drama a hint of the dangers associated with a purely essentialist mode of solidarity, a mode that is represented by Archie's prejudices as well (when Barney, still ahead, contemplates retiring on his new riches to Florida, Archie quips that he will probably start betting on how many Cubans will make it swimming to the United States' shores; earlier, Barney's display of wealth evokes for Archie the image of an Arab sheikh). But despite a certain blurring of the lines between the inner and outer domains, an overall opposition subsists between the personal society of companions and the harsh transactions of the greater world. Against the cold greed and inexorable reprisals of the game of cash and credit, the space of the tavern is defended as the locus of natural fellowship. Even when the gangsters come into Archie's place in search of Barney, they do not step forward from the threshold, as though acknowledging the perimeter of a sanctuary.

Although Cubans and Arabs, and perhaps Italians as well, signify the presence or penetration within the society of foreign populations, remote lands—the territories beyond the boundaries of the nation state—are not figured in our episode of *Archie Bunker's Place* as the scene of lawlessness or presocial behavior. The very category of nationality presupposes social entities beyond the borders, as opposed to the grove of Silvanus in Plautus' play, where the combination of wilderness and sacred space suggests an antithesis with civil society as such. The streets themselves, in the sitcom, are the arena in which theft, or at least extortion, prevails; as does sexual violation too, intimidated here in the reference to the topless bar with its suggestion of commercial sex, a suggestion that is further developed in the sitcom we shall consider presently. It is not that the city streets in *Archie Bunker's Place* are precisely analogous to the territory beyond the city walls in the *Aulularia,* for extortion and the gambling practices upon which it is parasitical are systematic and quasi-social structures. This is, on one level, the meaning of their incorporation into the society, as this is

represented by the public order (or disorder) of the neighborhood outside. There is a difference, that is, between plunder and racketeering; the latter is contained within the perimeters of the community. The prominent place of gangsterism in the sitcom is, I am suggesting, part of the implicit social vision of the episode (and of the series as well) in which the space outside the tavern represents in a socially determinate form one pole of the opposition between solidarity and aggression. It is precisely at the moment when accumulation seems violent and unproductive, and yet at the same time systematic, that the world outside one's private space—a world at once alien and yet one's own—will be a place of threat and danger.[15]

There is a hint, as we have seen, in the episode from *Archie Bunker's Place* of a different locale, also private but diminished: the home of Barney, which he shares with his dog. It serves in this instance more as a symbol of Barney's isolation from the society of the tavern than as a place of refuge, or as a symbolic space in its own right, but the possibility of a ternary spatial structure is, of course, available to comic drama. I shall discuss two examples, one from antiquity, the other from TV, in order to show that also in the case of such structures, space functions as a sign of ideological processes that are conditioned by the character of social formations.

In an episode from *Barney Miller,* a man in ecclesiastical habit enters the police station to report that a novice, who was being escorted with a group of boys to a rural monastery, is missing. The cleric belongs to a monastic order; he is not a priest, and responds irritably when addressed as Father rather than as Brother. The cause of his defensiveness is a barely disguised sense of inferiority, which is exposed by the tactless remark of a detective: Not everyone can make it as a priest. His anxiety for the boy betrays a streak of authoritarianism, which compensates for his sense of injury. The theme of oppressive paternalism emerges also among the detectives. When Officer Wojo, who is taking the monk's testimony, is interrupted, Captain Barney Miller intervenes, and is admonished for his officiousness. Wojo asserts that the men will never grow up and become good detectives if Barney intrudes upon their responsibilities. Abashed, Barney retreats to his office—the only private space in the squad room.

There is a symmetry between the structure of the monastic order and that of the detective force: both are fraternal associations, exclusively male, presided over by a paternal authority figure. The monastic life, however, is presented as escapist and repressive, escapist in its idyllic tranquility and detachment, a veritable golden age in the part wistful, part ironic description of Officer Harris, and repressive for the strain of moral coercion that is conspicuous in the monk's reaction to the runaway novice Joseph. Joseph, during his brief parole, fell in with a prostitute for whose attentions he was prepared to pay with a credit card lifted from the monk himself. At the end of the episode, Wojo, on his own initiative, grants Joseph, who has been rounded up along with the hooker, a day's reprieve from the monastic life by rigorously applying paperwork rules that delay his release. Barney Miller disapproves, but refrains from interfering.

Thus the monastery is represented as a realm from which desire is banished, holy but more than human in its rigors. The boy's own desire is at the mercy of a world where commerce rules all transactions, even those of the heart. Between is the society of the policemen, who acknowledge desire but enforce its restriction to contexts and practices that are deemed legitimate. At one point the prostitute draws the lines neatly: "I break laws, not commandments."

The prostitute, released without charges, is expelled to the streets. The monk departs for his retreat with his boys in tow, save Joseph, who remains with the detectives. Between the carnal attractions of the city outside and the spirituality of the religious order, the police station appears as a locus of humane association that is appropriate to its mission of containing illegal and exploitative commerce without aspiring to enforce subjective moral sanctity. To a certain extent, this mediate structure is modelled on the family, with Barney Miller as father and the other detectives as sons, like the monastic structure, as we have seen. But it is different from the monastic order in its functionality, which is reflected, for example, in the conditions of membership in the group. In fact, there is a novice of a kind among the detectives as well, in this case Officer Leavitt who serves as a part-time detective when need arises, but is otherwise assigned downstairs among the uniformed policemen. Leavitt's desire to be fully part of the detectives' group is the reverse of Joseph's reluctance. But Leavitt's eagerness and commitment are not sufficient; he must also demonstrate competence, and there must be an open position on the squad. Promotion on the force is not simply a reflex of the state of one's soul. It is determined by social constraints.

The authoritarian aspect of the hierarchy of the detectives' squad is modified further by the role of the old inspector whose lugubrious anticipations of his own death, combined with a paternal if slightly macabre display of affection for Barney Miller, reduce the captain to helpless confusion. The inspector's control over Barney is as much a personal matter as the privilege of rank. This mixing of the personal and the official, which, as we have seen, informs Barney's relationship to his men as well, defines the interior space of the sitcom. The workplace is both business-like and familial, marked off from the cold transactions of the streets and from the segregated communion of monastic withdrawal. It has about it the quality of a club—a men's club, more precisely—yet it is a public institution charged with enforcement of laws. The enclosed space of the detectives' room contains and asserts this complex of relations.

Such a structuring of relations, with one form privileged as the locus of mediation, shapes the narrative in certain plays of ancient New Comedy as well, with the difference that the scene of mediation is a public rather than a private space. A common pattern involves a hetaera, loosely an independent call girl. Her house has some of the moral irregularity that attaches to the streetwalker's occupation in the *Barney Miller* episode, allowing, of course, for the considerable difference between the ancient Greek and our own, post-Victorian attitudes to such a calling. The chief danger in the association with a hetaera, in comedy, at least, was financial, and a father feared more for his purse than for propriety when his son showed signs of passion for a woman of that sort. Whereas in marriage alliances wealth was put in social circulation, with meretricious love it was imagined that the resources of the ancestral estate poured endlessly into the lady's coffers like rivers into the ocean. In the city-state ideology, paying money to a hetaera removed wealth from the domain of social exchange just like buried treasure (or like donations to a temple, where, however, the consecration of wealth to a divinity gave special sanction to the sequestering).[16]

At the same time, the undifferentiated sensuality of the whorehouse could be valorized as a form of carnival communion, an ecstatic moment of union not entirely unconnected with rituals of collective identification in cult and festival. In Plautus' *Bacchides,* two women named Bacchis—the association with the rites of Dionysus is underscored by explicit puns and allusion—seduce into their establishment not only a pair of youths, but, in the finale, their fathers as well. The brothel thus has witty overtones of a ritual orgy, and is a symbol of all-round reconciliation (like the wedding feast at the end of the *Dyscolus,* which takes place inside a grotto sacred to Pan and the Nymphs). We may compare the drawing of a bedroom shade at the end of a movie, or, in the sitcom mode, a couple exiting from office or tavern with a significant glance backwards through the open door. The sexual intimacy of the house of the Bacchis twins mocks social and public norms, but it is also a symbol of solidarity, just as the spiritual monastic community of the *Barney Miller* episode serves in part as a metaphor for the familial solidarity of the detectives. Such unity may be valorized, but only as a temporary or special state. The primary scene of social relations remains the place on stage.

Plautus' *Bacchides* is based on two misunderstandings, the first accidental, the second contrived by an intriguing slave. In the first half of the play, a young man, infatuated with Bacchis, is jealous of his friend's attention to her, until he discovers that the object of his friend's passion is another lady of the same name. The confusion is dispelled and friendship between the youths restored: Nowhere in New Comedy is there a real and permanent rivalry between friends and fellow-citizens, and even the suggestion of such competition is rare. Thus, in the *Bacchides,* the association between citizen households is represented not through marriage ties but through the more diffuse bond of comradeship, the value of which was discussed extensively by Plato, Aristotle, and in literature generally.

Friendship is reasserted against the potentially divisive force of natural passions, or *eros.* The friendship between the two young men seems analogous to the idea of fraternity in sit-coms of the workplace. Just as the collegial association among the detectives in *Barney Miller* mediates between religious community and the commercial relations of the outside world, so the bond of friendship in the *Bacchides* stands between the formal conventions of exchange that are constitutive of the polis and the immediacy of ritual communion, here comically encoded as the experience of the brothel. Friendship, then, is to the public mode of the classical comedy what the familial model of the workplace is to the modern sitcom, the personalized aspect of formal social relations.

In the second half of the *Bacchides,* the youths inveigle money from one of the fathers, persuading the old man (on the advice of a clever slave) that his son has been caught with the wife of a mercenary soldier, and that his life is in danger unless he pays compensation. Fearful for his son, the father promptly surrenders the money. The sentimental solidarity of the father with his son, like the friendship between the two youths, personalizes the conventional and legal authority of the head of the household. At the same time, it asserts the bond among respectable citizen families against the threat of the professional soldier, whose ties with the city-state community were relatively weak. Seduction of a married woman was not normally done in New Comedy; that it might be brought in even hypothetically, as here, in the case of a soldier suggests his distance from the code that obtains among the citizen body (compare also the trick played upon the mercenary in the *Miles Gloriosus;* in the *Amphitryo,* the seducer is a god, which is another matter).

We may sharpen the contrast between the values of public and private space in the two works under consideration, and also disclose more clearly the structuring function of social forms of exchange, by attending more specifically to the place of the women in each. We have seen that the prostitute in the *Barney Miller* episode is relegated to the streets, while the hetaerae in the *Bacchides* work out of a house, into which they draw their customers. In both situations, to be sure, the women make their bodies available for money; in both, the cash transaction is covered by at least the illusion of infatuation on the part of the buyers. Moreover, the commodification of sexual passion is equally a theme in each; and in each, again, the cash expended upon women is acquired by theft or trickery: It must be set loose from the normal process of economic circulation by a violation of the code of commerce. But the precise nature of the commerce, and consequently of its counter-image in the parallel market of prostitution, differs in the two contexts. That the novice Joseph uses a stolen credit card exposes the penetration of the modern credit system into both the brotherhood of the religious order, where by a comic anachronism it serves also to enable the monk to function without needing to handle ordinary lucre, and into the sublegal world of streetwalkers. The profession of prostitution is thereby assimilated to the fluid motion of value that is characteristic of modern capitalist exchange. However much the individual hooker may act as a private entrepreneur, she is part of a system, in much the way the loan sharks in the episode of *Archie Bunker's Place* function both as renegade profiteers and emblems of the risks of high finance.

There is a subordinate theme in the *Barney Miller* episode that I have so far neglected to discuss and that reveals further the ambiguous characterization of the urban street as the place of violence and desire. One officer, Dietrich by name, has drawn duty as a decoy. This entails walking the streets dressed as a woman, to trap would-be muggers and rapists. In this moment of life on the outside, sex is intimately attached to violence. The streets are the locus of arbitrary force or appropriation, like the wilderness or the sea in ancient (or renaissance) comic imagery. But Dietrich, who is eager to succeed at the assignment, cannot, despite his primping, present himself as a passably attractive female. His wish to do so, together with his failure, produce a brief burlesque on gender roles, but also intimate the detective's transgressive desire to operate in the arena of illicit passion. Because Dietrich is cast in the show as a kind of intellectual, with an encyclopedic knowledge of odd facts and an air of superiority, it is comically appropriate that he be the vehicle of a disguised urge to go slumming. More generally, however, the closed world of the police precinct is shown to be permeable by the lusty, if illicit, spirit of the city outside. In this respect, Dietrich's vulnerability, manifested in his preening transvestism, is not unlike the suceptibility of the two fathers in the *Bacchides* to the lures of the hetaerae. But, in Plautus' play, the attraction is open and aboveboard; in *Barney Miller* it is manifested in a displaced or repressed fashion.

For the detectives, the streets are the place where the lawless violence of the presocial world intersects with shady practices that image, and are tangential to, the commodified exchange of the market. This is the space against which the squad room is defined as lawful and communal simultaneously. In the ancient city-state, hetaerae too were in principle foreign: most commonly, in Athens, resident aliens or metics, who had special rights and privileges within the polis, but were excluded from citizenship. They are, thus, partially integrated into the city-state community. But, in the *Bacchides,* their mediate status is figured not by their association with the streets but rather with the removed space of the house. They represent not the universalization of commodity relations of modern capitalism but luxury items imported into the home. The eroticized dimension of Greek cultic life, as opposed to the delibidinized character of Christian monasticism, allows the interior space of the brothel to do service as a carnival domain: It is limited and contained, a place for special occasions. But their off-the-street position indicates as well, I would argue, that the hetaerae are not a metaphor for the real relations of the city-state, which are grounded in kinship, at least in the imagery of classical New Comedy. Once again, the topography of the comedies, ancient and modern, appears as socially constructed.

I shall conclude with one more illustration from a sitcom, in which the street is the scene of theft and the reversal of gender roles. It is a simple case, but is useful for the clarity with which the interior and exterior spaces are initially defined, then compromised by the action of the narrative, and finally reaffirmed, though not with complete success. An episode of the sitcom *Alice* opens with an attack upon Mel, the owner of the diner that is the location for the series. The mugger is an elderly woman who blackjacks Mel from behind. Mel pretends, in his embarrassment, that his attackers are several toughs, and is humiliated when the true villain is brought into the restaurant by a policeman. As Alice, a waitress for whom the show is named, comforts Mel, Vera, another waitress, has her purse stolen outside the restaurant. Mel comforts Vera by assuring her that money is not important, but when he discovers that her purse contained the restaurant's receipts for the previous two days he is furious. Jostled by a customer—not one of the regulars—on his way out, Mel feels for his wallet and finds it missing. Together with Vera and Alice, he assaults the fellow outside, recovers the wallet—or what he thinks is his wallet, until it is revealed that Mel had put his own wallet in the office safe. General consternation: The policeman returns with the battered customer; explanations are accepted, and all follow the poor man outside to press apologies upon him, along with hearty denunciations of the spirit of suspicion that led them to violence. A well-dressed, elderly man inside, left alone at his table, locks the rest out, and proceeds to empty the till as Mel and the waitresses stare helplessly through the glass door.

The spatial structure is obvious. Inside is safe territory, opposed to theft and violence on the street outside. But public disorder affects the interior domain, and the victims become violent in turn. Their assault also occurs in the street in front of the restaurant. Only in the final scene are the valences of inside and outside reversed: The thief is secure within while the proprietor and his staff are locked out. The small-time personal establishment of the diner is permeable to the corruption of the outer world, but it seeks to retain the sense of trust that marks it as a haven of traditional values. This communal character is in part achieved by implicating Vera and Alice in robbing the innocent customer. Although the narrative makes it clear that the proceeds of the restaurant are Mel's alone, and that he cares more for his cash than his employees' welfare, their identification with him reasserts the bonding of the diner people against the perfidy of the outside world.

To point up the contrast between sitcoms and ancient New Comedy, we may compare the scene in Terence's *Brothers* in which a passionate young man, having abducted a slave-girl from a brothel, threatens the brothel-keeper on the threshold of his own establishment. It is a particularly violent scene for the genre, and one that has been introduced into the Menandrian model for the *Brothers* by Terence himself, according to the practice known anciently as contamination. The keeper is intimidated and withdraws, but not without threatening legal action for violence against a citizen. Save for its contribution to the characterization of the youth, the scene has

no consequences in the drama. But the young man, who has stolen the girl not for his own sake but for his brother's, is later disclosed to have formed an irregular liaison with a citizen woman next door, who has borne his child. The play ends with the union of the two households through a double wedding—the youth's father is shamed into accepting the young lady's mother in marriage as well—arranged and consented to on stage. The offense against the brothel-keeper, which drives him out of the public space and back into his off-stage domain, is compensated for, in a sublimated way, by the regularization of citizen relations in the civic arena.

In *A Grammar of Motives,* Kenneth Burke cites "a tiny drama enacted in real life" to illustrate the way in which the scene may be shaped to an action.

> The occasion: a committee-meeting. The setting: a group of committee members bunched about a desk in an office, after hours. Not far from the desk was a railing; but despite the crowding, all the members were bunched about the chairman at the desk, inside the railing. . . . [A]s the discussion continued, one member quietly arose, and opened the gate in the railing. She picked up her coat, laid it across her arm, and stood waiting. A few minutes later, when there was a pause in the discussion, she asked for the floor. After being recognized by the chairman, she very haltingly, in embarrassment, announced with regret that she would have to resign from the committee.

Burke concludes: "She had strategically modified the arrangement of the scene in such a way that it implicitly (ambiguously) contained the quality of her act."[17]

This anecdote follows upon Burke's brilliant analysis of the spaces in Ibsen's *An Enemy of the People,* the finale of O'Neill's *Mourning Becomes Electra,* and other moments in drama. In and of itself, the little real-life episode is too bare of context to yield much more to further speculation. Were there other women on the committee? one is tempted to ask; is the barrier significant with respect to gender? Why is the woman so halting and embarrassed, when her action seems rhetorically so forceful? There is no way to tell. But in well-formed literary genres, which encode social patterns in their conventions, including conventions of scene or space, the relation between interior and exterior is not simply an abstract metaphor for belonging or exclusion, a sign of psychological isolation or community. Space is structured according to ideological commitments characteristic of an age or social formation: commitments that are informed by radical tensions, to be sure, or they would not be the stuff of drama, but which, all the same, have a certain stability. Comedy, in the tradition inaugurated by Greek New Comedy, is especially interesting to examine for the social structuring of its spatial and other elements, because it is the single most conservative literary form in the western tradition. Devices of plot and wit are remarkably consistent, and the formal connection between TV sitcoms and the plays of Menander has no parallel in, say, the history of tragedy, lyric, or the novel. The genre is, accordingly, a kind of laboratory model for revealing the way in which a social content inheres in apparently neutral structural relations.

I have attempted to reveal the content of the place of action in ancient comedy and modern sitcoms. Clearly, this content is not uniform in either genre. It is subject to various constructions and emphases; it may be set off against a single complementary domain or situated in a complex of alternative social spaces. But the location of ancient comedy in the public street, as against the interior scene of the sitcoms, seems a significant fact and not merely a matter of convention or a reflection of the difference between life in a Mediterranean town on the one hand and in a northern climate on the other. For all their staying power, conventions are generated and sustained by a relation to social life. Where public space was in antiquity perceived as a primary arena of social life, it has, in the comedies of television, come to seem impersonal and dangerous, the place where worship of money and the commodification of everything else reigns supreme. In such a world, the spaces that are cherished are havens of personal and sympathetic relations, even if they simultaneously serve the needs of the wider economy. In modern as in ancient comedy, talented writers constantly expand the range of meanings and symbols. But comparison of the two genres, despite the many signs of their continuity, suggests that history has transformed their premises.

NOTES

[1] The present paper is a much expanded version of a talk presented to the conference on Themes in Drama, on the topic "The Theatrical Space," held at the University of California at Riverside, 16-18 February 1985. On the popularity of situation comedies or sitcoms in the 1970s, it is enough to observe that they held twelve out of the top twenty places in the Nielsen ratings in 1978-79; Alex McNeil, *Total Television: A Comprehensive Guide to Programming from 1948 to 1980* (Harmondsworth: Penguin, 1980). After a brief slump in the early 1980s, it is clear that sitcoms again dominate TV programming.

[2] On ancient stage conventions, see Peter D. Arnott, *The Ancient Greek and Roman Theatre* (New York: Random House, 1971); Harold C. Baldry, "Theatre and Society in Greek and Roman Antiquity," in *Drama and Society [Themes in Drama 1]* (Cambridge: Cambridge University Press, 1979), pp. 1-21.

[3] See, for example, Martin Esslin, "The Art of Television Drama," *Boston Review,* 9, No. 4 (August 1984), 12-14.

[4] It is significant that this show represents poor, urban children at play; compare also the early sitcom *The Goldbergs,* with its characteristic scene of conversation through open windows, and the current British show *Good Neighbors.*

[5] For a sensitive and scholarly analysis of the role of public space in ancient Greek life and the tendency to veil the private domain from view, see Paul A. Rahe, "The Primacy of Politics in Classical Greece," *American Historical Review,* 89 (1984), 265-293. Rahe's approach is indebted to that of Hannah Arendt, *The Human Condition* (Chicago: University of Chicago Press, 1958), and differs substantially from my own in its frankly positive assessment of the Greek ideology. See also Jürgen Habermas, *Strukturwandel der Öffentlichkeit* (Neuwied: H. Luchterhand, 1962 [*Politica,* Vol. 4] and the discussion in Terry Eagleton, *The Function of Criticism* (London: Verso, 1984), pp. 115-124. On setting as a social signifier, see Anne Ubersfeld, *Lire le Théâtre* (Paris: Éditions sociales, 1978), pp. 169-170, 188-189. That the semantic function of the setting is not usually invoked through explicit, figured oppositions is a feature of the realistic mode of New Comedy and the situation comedies, but it is no less effective for that; see Norman Bryson, *Word and Image: French Painting of the Ancien Régime* (Cambridge: Cambridge University Press, 1981), Ch. I, "Discourse, Figure," pp. 1-28.

[6] See Raymond Williams, *Television: Technology and Cultural Form* (New York: Schocken, 1974), p. 27.

[7] See Christopher Lasch, *Haven in a Heartless World: The Family Besieged* (New York: Basic Books, 1977).

[8] For a penetrating social analysis of a single sitcom series, see Robert Goldman, "Hegemony and Managed Critique in Prime-Time Television: A Critical Reading of 'Mork and Mindy,'" *Theory and Society,* 11 (1982), 363-388.

[9] See Horace Newcomb, *TV: The Most Popular Art* (Garden City: Doubleday, 1974), pp. 1-52, for a discussion of TV genres.

[10] Plutarch, fr. 134 Sandbach (Loeb Library); Ovid *Amores* 1.15.17-18. Ovid emphasizes the structural roles of the passionate youth, deceived father, and clever slave (cf. *Ars Amatoria* 3.332); contrast the rectangle described by Emmanuel Le Roy Ladurie for courtship in eighteenth-century southern France, in *Love, Death and Money in the Pays d'Or,* trans. Alan Sheridan (New York: George Braziller, 1982).

[11] *Politics* 1.2.5; the translation is that of Ernest Barker, *The Politics of Aristotle* (New York and London: Oxford University Press, 1958).

[12] On the tension between the values of "home" and "work" in modern capitalist ideology, see Steve Barnett and Martin G. Silverman, *Ideology and Everyday Life: Anthropology, Neomarxist Thought, and the Problem of Ideology and the Social Whole* (Ann Arbor: University of Michigan Press, 1979), pp. 41-81. It is worth noting that the popular series such as *Dallas, Falconcrest,* and *Dynasty* represent an alternative tension of business and family values, here situated in the home (more often, mansion), where the corrosive effects of a competitive or performance-based ethos is exhibited. (I am indebted for

this observation to my friend, Jonathan Haynes of Benington College.)

[13] I have discussed the *Aulularia* in *Roman Comedy* (Ithaca, NY: Cornell University Press, 1983), pp. 33-46.

[14] Focus on the society of pub or workplace often entails a corresponding reduction in the quality of home life; so too, in the new format, Archie's wife of *All in the Family* is deceased. In the 1970s, domestic sitcoms increasingly, indeed almost exclusively, featured families that were broken or irregular.

[15] In an article on corporate crime entitled "White-Collar Crime Is Big Business," Mark Green and John F. Berry observe: "The criminologists downplay it. In the introduction to his influential book *Thinking about Crime,* James Q. Wilson writes that the public is correct in fearing crime in the streets more than crime in the suites because 'economic violators don't make difficult or impossible *the maintenance of basic human communities*'" (my emphasis). They go on to quote from an editorial in *The Wall Street Journal:* "It isn't very helpful to suggest that white-collar crime is a more serious threat . . . than predatory street crime, which inspires fear right across the board" (*The Nation,* 240, No. 22, 8 June 1985, pp. 689, 704). Corporate crime, in these descriptions, occupies an unstable and ambiguous position between lawlessness, characterized by violence, and social behavior; in sitcoms, the streets are the site of this ambiguity. See also the poll reported in *The New York Times,* 9 June 1985, section 3, p. 1, indicating that 55 percent of those interviewed believed that American corporate executives are not honest.

[16] See Laurence Kahn, *Hermès passe ou les ambiguités de la communication* (Paris: Maspero, 1978), pp. 70-71, on temple donations vs. the circulation of wealth.

[17] Kenneth Burke, *A Grammar of Motives* (Berkeley and Los Angeles: University of California Press, 1969, orig. 1945), p. 11.

CHILDREN'S LITERATURE/ CHILDREN'S TELEVISION

Kimberley Reynolds

SOURCE: "Books on the Box: The BBC Chronicles of Narnia," in *Critical Survey,* Vol. 3, No. 3, 1991, pp. 313-23.

[*In the following essay, Reynolds centers on the BBC adaptation of C. S. Lewis's Chronicles of Narnia in a broader examination of issues and assumptions about the translation of children's books into television.*]

It is rare to find parents and educators actively promoting a television series (other than the specifically didactic 'schools' broadcasts) and treating it as a cultural event.

This reflects a deeply rooted ambivalence about television as entertainment which is directly linked to attitudes surrounding children's reading. Watching television is inevitably regarded as an activity less worthwhile than reading, and for long has been accused of seducing children away from books. Nevertheless, when in 1989 the BBC launched its three-year serialisation of C. S. Lewis's Chronicles of Narnia, families around the country regularly settled down to an early Sunday evening's viewing, and the whir of institutional video recorders switching themselves on was almost audible. The ongoing adaptation of the Narnia books for television (at the time of writing *The Silver Chair* is being screened in the six weeks leading up to Christmas 1990) raises a number of key issues about children's literature and television. These have primarily to do with status, audience, and the construction of narrative. In particular, the 'made-for-TV' nature of the series (as compared with the many film adaptations of children's texts such as *Black Beauty, National Velvet, The Secret Garden* and *Treasure Island*) created problems and possibilities which need to be explored. In this article I shall be less concerned with the specific adaptation of Lewis's books than with the attitudes toward televised versions of children's books the series highlights. In particular, I want to question long-held assumptions about the fugitive and reductionist nature of visual renditions now that the video recorder has come of age.

SCREENED STORIES: SCEPTICS, STATUS, AND SKILLS

C. S. Lewis belonged to a well-established school of thought which holds that books are infinitely superior to films and (especially) television, and that any attempt to make a filmed version of a 'good' book is doomed to fail. He identified some of the reasons for this failure in a brief analysis of a filmed version of Rider Haggard's *King Solomon's Mines.*

> Of its many sins—not least the introduction of a totally irrelevant young woman in shorts who accompanied the adventurers wherever they went—only one here concerns us. At the end of Haggard's book . . . the heroes are awaiting death entombed in a rock chamber and surrounded by the mummified kings of that land. The maker of the film version, however, apparently thought this tame. He substituted a subterranean volcanic eruption, and then went one better by adding an earthquake. Perhaps we should not blame him. Perhaps the scene in the original was not 'cinematic' and the man was right, by the canons of his own art, in altering it. But it would have been better not to have chosen in the first place a story which could be adapted to the screen only by being ruined.[1]

Lewis goes on to say that the story is ruined not because one ending is necessarily better than another, but because they create entirely different feelings in the reader/spectator. This difference in feeling he attributes to two causes. First, the dictates of cinematic conventions and expectations (his prejudices against which are not denied), and second, the lack of understanding on the part of the film's director of what constitutes a good story. The educated élite, Lewis argues, tend to disparage the power of narratives which concern themselves more with plot than character development or portraits of society, and particularly those plots which involve excursions into other worlds or 'shadow lands'. The kind of literary snobbishness which dismisses genres such as children's fiction or science fiction as all plot and no substance misses an important point, for to a certain kind of reader such writing has the power to convey 'profound experiences, which are . . . not acceptable in any other form.'[2]

Lewis's defence of literature characterised by powerful plots is based entirely on the subjective nature of the *reading* experience. It is unique, personal, private and capable of enabling the reader to transcend mundane reality. Because of these qualities the written text is supremely able to adapt to the needs of the individual reader and to do this at different stages in his/her development. Lewis believed utterly in the power of the written word, be it poetry for the educated or adventure stories for the masses, and likewise deprecated filmed narratives. 'Nothing', he wrote, 'can be more disastrous than the view that cinema can and should replace popular written fictions. The elements which it excludes are precisely those which give the untrained mind its only access to the imaginative world. There is a death in the cinema.'[3]

In such passages Lewis is articulating the fear held by many that television and films would do two things; especially with regard to the juvenile population. First, that they would prove so seductive that children would abandon, or fail to acquire, the habit of reading. Second, that filmed versions of texts would make even the best stories mechanical: each viewing would be identical to the one before; the child would not be free to change emphases; the viewer would become a passive spectator, as all the 'work' (e.g. the animation of the text) had been done, etc. All in all, the viewing process was protrayed as an entirely impoverished one when compared to that of reading. It was believed that the child would develop no analytical skills through watching rather than reading. Perhaps most important of all, Lewis is suggesting that watching a film prevented the child from making the complex series of unconscious identifications with characters and situations which make fantasy literature useful for psychological development.

However valid some of these arguments may be, they must also be understood as typical of attitudes toward popular culture throughout the ages. Ironically, Lewis was at great pains to defend the virtues of popular forms of literature (including children's fiction) precisely because of their appeal to less experienced or sophisticated readers. It needs also to be remembered that at the time that Lewis was writing his defence of popular texts (1947), television ownership was not widespread, prolonged daily viewing was impossible, the VCR had yet to be invented, and no research had yet been done into the viewing process.

Since Lewis's death in 1963 a considerable amount of research into the effects of television on the child has been conducted, and much of it can be used to debate the objections outlined above. In particular, it is now recognised that children are not necessarily passive and indiscriminate viewers, but may instead develop 'visual literacy' skills which can complement those acquired through reading. The ability to decode a complex visual narrative often precedes but does not necessarily preclude a similar degree of sophistication and facility with written texts. Despite frequent media discussion of these issues, there has long remained a distrust of television and filmed versions of classic children's books, and the advent of cable and satellite TV seems bound to provoke a reactionary revival of those parents who announce that they have no television as if this were a virtue. (Funnily enough, such behaviour is closely related to the non-smoking, teetotalling, vegetarian adults Lewis repeatedly mocks in the Narnia books.) Recently, however, there has been a *volte-face* on the part of many adults who previously deplored filmed versions of children's books as at best inevitably disappointing and at worst travesties of the original. There seem to be two key reasons for this U-turn. The first is that far from discouraging children from reading, television and films have given birth to a vigorous new publishing activity—the book of the film/programme. Children's book sales have increased by 170 per cent over the last five years, precisely the period over which domestic sales of VCRs have also rocketed.[4] Through TV tie-ins young readers are introduced to an eclectic range of writing, from Ghostbusters to Adrian Mole and back to such classics as *A Little Princess* and, of course, the Chronicles of Narnia. More importantly, the viewing and reading processes have increasingly been recognised to be complementary rather than mutually exclusive.

The second and in some ways more interesting reason for the new acceptability of filmed versions of juvenile texts, also based on the widespread use of VCRs in homes and schools, is the growth of a children's video library. Much work needs to be done to raise the overall quality of material readily available on video for children, and this is important. Video's are not just 're-usable resources', useful for keeping children quietly entertained; they have the potential to make the viewing process more analogous to reading and so for developing analytical skills useful for both activities. VCRs make it possible to review, to skim, to watch selected scenes repeatedly, to omit sections and pause over others—all of which make viewing more personal, more creative, and potentially more intellectually demanding. They also mean that greater care has to be taken over the translation of complex texts into videos, as re-viewing, like re-reading, demands that there be something new to discover at different stages in the young viewer's development.

The ramifications of this degree of control over the presentation of video material are many. For the older child it enables very detailed interaction between the written and visual texts. By encouraging visual decoding, videos may enhance understanding of the director's version of a text and so the potential for comparison with the reader's own interpretation. Repeated watching of a visual version of a text with which the child is familiar can highlight differences in the narrative functioning and capabilities of the two media. Even a young child will notice and understand adjustments to the way in which a story is told; for instance, the need to make the narrator a character in the action or to substitute descriptions of events (as in a letter) with enactment. By comparing the narrative organisation of printed and visual versions of a text a great deal can be learned about the relationship between structure, form and meaning.

Re-viewing is undoubtedly the most important aspect of video material. According to Lewis, the desire to re-read indicated that a story was not just being read to find out what happened or whodunnit; indeed, his criterion for a good book was that it became more pleasurable on subsequent readings. Particularly in the young child it is not aesthetic qualities which are being sought through repeated readings, listenings, or tellings but (as the psychologist Bruno Bettelheim has observed) the satisfaction of having resolved difficult emotional problems. The same applies equally to the viewing process, which additionally has the reassuring property of never forgetting or changing what comes next.

For all of these reasons videos have the potential both to complement printed versions of juvenile texts and to raise the standard and status of televised adaptations. If they are to do this effectively it is necessary to overcome established attitudes to children's literature itself and, just as importantly, habitualised practices in the adaptation process. To render the narrative complexity of texts (and particularly those which were not originally intended for reading aloud), those involved in making adaptations must be encouraged to exploit the medium of television to its full potential. At present most books which are adapted for television make unhappy compromises as to how far they are prepared to 'adapt' the original text, and as a consequence generally leave the viewer dissatisfied. In a recent article for *Screen,* Paul Kerr identifies the principal cause of this dissatisfaction as the tendency for televised versions to 'flatten' a text so that, 'it is less a "novel" as such that is being adapted than its plot, characters, setting [and] dialogue'.[5] The reason for this flattening is a direct consequence of the elevation of the written text over the film (and especially over TV). Tradition has enshrined the practice of trying to be entirely faithful to the original, which means treating film or television as a transparent medium purely concerned with showing what the writer has written.[6] The irony is that a great deal of most literary texts (as opposed to sensational stories) *cannot* be shown in the conventional sense, as they tend to be concerned with exploring internal states, providing ancillary information, and generally digressing from the main action of the text. At present a limited range of visual conventions is used to render the most crucial of these (voice-overs, flashbacks, etc.), but too much experimentation is avoided as this is deemed to

call attention to the fact that what is being watched is television rather than an animated book. This is surely ironic as it is only through interpretation—the translation from literary to visual language—that the 'flattening' process can be minimised and the complexity of the original restored.

This debate is concerned equally with the adaptation of novels for adults and those intended to be read primarily by children, but because juvenile fiction is generally regarded as inferior to and of less importance than adult fiction it could be in this area that the break with traditional ways of approaching the adaptation process could most readily be challenged. As well, the narrative structures of most children's books are necessarily less sophisticated than those for more experienced readers, thus simplifying the problems of recreating their effects visually.

C. S. Lewis was convinced that a strong plot was crucial to a book's success in stimulating the young reader to the point where entertainment became a form of spiritual enlightenment. The Narnia books were designed to be read aloud as well as for private reading (each chapter is a satisfyingly complete episode but is short enough to make a good 'bed-time' story) and so have an in-built sensitivity to the needs of interrupted performance. With their high status in the juvenile canon (which means the ability to attract funds but not necessarily the same level of constraints on the adaptation process experienced by those working on adult texts), their emphasis on plot, their adherence to classic-realist narrative conventions, and yet their dependence on fantasy lands, images, and experiences, Lewis's books seem ideal for television adaptation. The Paul Stone / Alan Seymour adaptations of the Chronicles of Narnia for the BBC thus provide a useful indication of how much work has been done to date to release the potential of the text-to-television transition, not least because the production and viewing processes have been spread over three years, thus allowing comparison of earlier and later episodes.

WITCHES AND WARDROBES: WHY, WHEN, AND FOR WHOM

The Chronicles of Narnia are among those few children's texts which adults take seriously. The reason for this is not based primarily in nostalgia, for those books which are given to children by adults are not necessarily those which adults most enjoyed when children themselves, but generally comprise a canon of those works of juvenile fiction deemed to have literary merit. This means in essence that the texts are capable of appealing simultaneously to readers at a variety of intellectual levels. Thus the very young readers of the Narnia stories may be primarily interested in the events which befall the children, while older readers may respond more to the ways in which Lewis has blended allegory, myth, legend, and children's fantasy to tell his story. At the primary level the stories are both exciting and also deal with problems such as separation, which frequently trouble young children. For the more mature reader, the most striking feature of the first book in the series, *The Lion, the Witch and the Wardrobe* (1950), may be the way in which Lewis manages successfully to defamiliarise the Christian Passion story through the self-sacrifice of the lion, Aslan.

Lewis began writing the Narnia books in 1950, producing one annually for seven years. The books were immediately successful and have grown in popularity and critical stature over the decades. *The Lion, the Witch and the Wardrobe* has frequently been adapted for the stage, and there has been at least one previous attempt to adapt the series: an animated version for US television. None has so far succeeded in winning the vast popularity and approval accorded the books. Paradoxically, the principal reason for this failure is a consequence of the books' prestige. The tendency to 'flatten' texts through insistence on textual fidelity increases with a text's cultural status.[7] It is in the adaptation of what are now called 'classic texts' that accuracy to the original is most insisted upon. In the children's canon at least, the Chronicles of Narnia have been designated modern 'classics', a status reflected in the transmission of the BBC adaptations. Each of the series is aired early on Sunday evenings (the institutionalised day for 'classic serials') and always in the six weeks before Christmas (a significant time in the television year and the battle for ratings). More important to this discussion is that the books were also *treated* as classics. Great care was taken to be true to the originals and to maintain those characteristics which contributed to the high regard in which they are held. This includes carefully reproducing the war-time, upper-middle-class setting, which is known to appeal to critics and sponsors.[8]

Such concern with literal fidelity creates problems of expectation. The production team had to cope with the imaginative projections and prejudices of a large proportion (those who had already read the books) of the 10 million UK viewers who have regularly watched the current Narnia adaptations. Additionally, they were faced with the problem that there was not one but seven texts to be considered, not all of which were felt to be equally suitable for filmed adaptation. (I will argue that this 'lack of suitability' is largely a consequence of traditional expectations of adaptations of classic texts.) Even when it was decided not to dramatise three of the books in the series, the size of the original Chronicles meant that the adaptation had to straddle two different television categories: the serial (usually associated with the action which makes up a single text) and the series (in which continuity is derived primarily from the characters), each with its own conventions and constraints.[9]

The scale of the project has been enormous, spanning three years and costing in excess of £7 million. It has nonetheless required substantial adjustments to Lewis's original series. The most obvious change is that the BBC adaptations are based on only four of the original seven Narnia books: *The Lion, the Witch and the Wardrobe* (1950), *Prince Caspian* (1951), *The Voyage of the Dawn Treader* (1952), and *The Silver Chair* (1953). Those fa-

miliar with the Narnia books will know that while these were the first four books about Narnia which Lewis wrote, they do not follow the internal chronology of Narnian history, which technically begins with *The Magician's Nephew* (1955). *The Horse and His Boy* (1954) properly belongs to the period when Peter was High King of Narnia and so should follow *The Lion, the Witch and the Wardrobe*. It was decided not to try to telescope these later embellishments into the original tales in the televised version for a number of reasons. First it was felt that they would disrupt the continuity and coherence which exists between the first four tales. In the first two books the four Pevensie children all appear; in the third only Lucy and Edmund return to Narnia (Peter and Susan are now too old), but they are joined by their despicable cousin, Eustace. In *The Silver Chair* it is Eustace and his schoolmate Jill Pole who journey into Narnia. The two later books introduce a range of characters and events which do not advance the overall plot of the four original stories about Narnia.

The logic behind the decision to drop the books about the creation and history of Narnia is perfectly clear and could at this stage be defended on the grounds that the original readers of the series would not have had the information and material they contain as they first read the Narnia stories. Their exclusion, which is based on facilitating comprehension of the central plot, highlights one of the major differences between the viewing and reading processes. The BBC Chronicles of Narnia will have been shown over a period of three years, each annual screening spanning six weekly slots. While a good proportion of the audience will have read the books before watching the adaptations (though perhaps not for some years), there are also a large number of very young and first-time viewers. It is rare to find as widely mixed an audience for reading or even listening to a text as needs to be catered for in these television broadcasts, and it inevitably has led to constant simplification. The episodic viewing pattern in which the adaptations are originally broadcast demands that all the connections necessary to the advancement of the plot are made very clear and that most of the loose ends are tied up at the end of each week's instalment. The degree of simplification could perhaps have been minimised by relying on the young viewer's familiarity with a range of basic viewing conventions (significant music, who is in/excluded from a particular shot, pace, flashbacks, montage, significant looks in close-up, voice-overs, etc.) which help to encode meanings and reduce the flattening effects of literal adaptations, but frequent reliance on such devices is deemed to be antipathetic to the concerns of the classic serial.

In fact, imaginative use of the medium to build up layers of meaning is necessary if a visual version of a text is actually to be truthful to the original and to retain its ability to appeal to viewers of different ages and stages in their development. For example, while Lewis's narratives have very strong plots, they also use a number of juxtapositions and narrative delays. In the books such devices are crucial to understanding internal processes within the characters. For the first-time viewer, however (and particularly when a week intervenes between episodes), they could be confusing. This, together with the dictates of the thirty-minute time constraints on each episode, has necessitated simplifying and sometimes reorganising events. The result is that, particularly on first viewing, many of the levels on which the texts work appear to be missing. While the plots are essentially intact, the 'dual address' which has given the printed texts their status has been seriously diminished. The most obvious example is in *Prince Caspian,* certainly the least successful adaptation of those so far screened. Six half-hour slots were allotted to both *The Lion, the Witch and the Wardrobe* and *The Silver Chair,* and four to *The Voyage of the Dawn Treader. Prince Caspian,* however, was condensed into two thirty-minute episodes. While the bare bones of the plot were included, this meant that the televised *Prince Caspian* served primarily to introduce *The Voyage of the Dawn Treader.* The ways in which the story tried and tested individual characters were almost completely lost, and without them it is extremely difficult to understand why only Lucy can see Aslan at first and why Peter and Susan are told they can never return to Narnia.

Prince Caspian is a more wordy and in some ways more reflective book than the other three which have been serialised. It is more overtly concerned with character development and emotional resolutions than the other texts, and perhaps for this reason was deemed to make less good children's TV. Such truncating and changing of an original text, however, both violates the code of the 'classic serial' and exaggerates the 'flattening' effect. While the plot is essentially unchanged, the feeling and effect of the Stone/Seymour *Caspian* is very different from the original. For example, in the original text the pace of events is often slow, and realisation dawns on individual characters gradually over a range of incidents. The reader, from the privileged vantage point provided by the omniscient narrator, often knows more than the characters, yet also learns with them. The marvellous stages by which, for instance, the Pevensie children realise that they have returned to Cair Paravel hundreds of years after their reign (but only a year in their own lives), and the mixed emotions this knowledge engenders are completely lost in the televised version. The pace is too rapid and the gaze too external. The incident is rendered trivial to those who have not read the book, but brutalises those who have. Unfortunately, in this case departure from the orthodoxy of the 'classic serial' was neither innovative nor helpful in reproducing the meaning of the original. Moreover, the amount of condensing which has had to go on has resulted in a lack of clarity at times, and though for most of the series it is not necessary to have read the books in order to understand the televised version, this is not true of the BBC *Prince Caspian.* In particular, the book spends a considerable amount of time explaining the damaging effects of Miraz's rule. All of the best and most beautiful facets of the land have gone into a permanent state of hibernation—a living death—to await Aslan's coming. Just as in *The Lion, the Witch and the Wardrobe* Aslan's

presence thaws the White Witch's eternal winter, so in *Prince Caspian* he recalls to life the dormant dryads, nymphs, giants and other 'mythical' creatures. The televised version of this waking is unsuccessful largely because who or what is being wakened is never explained. The activities of Aslan and the girls are seen as entirely separate from those of Caspian and the Pevensie boys (and of less importance), while they are meant to be simultaneous and complementary.

The adaptation of *Prince Caspian* highlights many of the weaknesses of the Stone/Seymour Chronicles (and especially the refusal to engage with those aspects of the texts which are not directly related to plot), but it would be unfair to judge the series as a whole by its weakest part. If it has been some time since you have read the books, many of the subtleties of this dramatisation may be lost, but if (as is true of many of the children in the audience) you read the books in tandem with the broadcasts, the thought and attention to detail lavished on the series become evident. Close viewing shows that the adaptations are not as passive as they may appear on first viewing when, as with a first reading, concerns of plot are all-important. For instance, Lewis drew on a range of myths, legends, sagas and earlier romance, epic and fantasy material in the construction of his stories. These sources are reflected in the costuming of the adaptations which reflects a wide range of influences and periods but nevertheless manages to make a unified world, as Lewis does in his texts. A more radical element is provided in the enactment of certain scenes. For instance, Lewis has often been criticised for making his characters conform to sex-role stereotypes. In his books boys are always active, publicly tested heroes, while the girls are associated with passivity and spirituality. The televised versions do not alter the plots or adjust the boys' roles, but they do show the girls taking active roles in some of the battles—not only fighting, but actually killing enemies. They are also allowed to give vent to anger and frustration more forcefully than they do in the originals. A good example of this is in the opening of *Prince Caspian* when the children are shown to be waiting for trains which will take them to various destinations. Susan is going to America, which marks her out as the most changed of the children (she is the only one never to return to Narnia), and she quarrels spitefully with Lucy.

Another useful change is made in *The Silver Chair.* In the book, when the children first met Prince Rilian in the Underworld, they noticed that though he was 'handsome and looked both bold and kind . . . there was something about his face that didn't seem quite right'.[10] The error in his visage is repeatedly registered in the children's thoughts until the Prince is finally released from his enchantment through the destruction of the silver chair:

> 'Lie there, vile engine of sorcery,' he said, 'lest your mistress should ever use you for another victim.' Then he turned and surveyed his rescuers; and the something wrong, whatever it was, had vanished from his face.[11]

In the Stone/Seymour version the abstract 'something wrong' is rendered concrete: the Prince's face is partially encased in an ornate metal helmet which he removes and crushes once he has broken the spell. This device works as effectively visually as the narrator's remarks do verbally. Both require interpretation; we are never told why his face was wrong or what the mask represents. More of this kind of translation of verbal to visual meanings would have greatly enhanced the series.

The final element of the BBC Chronicles I want to discuss in relation to children's reading and viewing habits is that of the problems surrounding any attempt to visualise an alternative world and the enactment of events which are impossible in our own. Narnia is like Never Never Land: some of its characteristics are described but much of it is the product of the unconscious—collective and individual. All of the events which take place there work on a variety of levels. For instance, *The Lion, the Witch and the Wardrobe* is certainly a religious allegory, but it is also a story about the child's need to deal with separation (boarding schools and war-time evacuation being the specific causes which promote anxiety in the children's real world[12]), and the problems of believing in the love of a person (or deity) who cannot be physically present. The alternative world is thus evoked not only to deal with the problems of Christian faith, but also to comment on contemporary social problems and individual emotional needs.

There is a danger that if the alternative world is made too real in enactment then the viewer's capacity to project aspects of the self into the events may be diminished. It was therefore in the creation of Narnia itself that most care needed to be taken and most thought given to the potential of the medium to imply and create feelings rather than always to show what was happening. This presented a paradox for the production team, for one facet of the appeal to those devising and creating the televised Narnia was that the stories required the kind of 'high-tech' interpretation usually associated with films such as *Superman* and *Star Wars* while also operating on a more complex level. The televised versions of the Chronicles relied on a vast range of special effects to help create an acceptable Narnia, including mixing animation with 'live' action. Perhaps inadvertently this mixture of real people and cartoons proved a successful way of presenting an alternative world for two reasons. First, it provided a metaphor for the relationship between reality and fantasy in the individual's life. Second, because the mixture was often crude, the viewer was regularly made aware that this was in fact *not* the 'real' Narnia but only television. The other world thus remained intact for readers and viewers alike. However, the point is not so much whether the television Narnia ultimately worked as that the production team felt compelled to make their Narnia look as much as possible like that described by Lewis and drawn by his illustrator, Pauline Baynes, rather than attempting to use television imaginatively. Surely there are ways of suggesting states of mind when journeying endlessly underground that don't depend entirely on dialogue, or to imply the *existence* of giants without reverting to the 'camera magic' which seemed dated when *Land of the Giants* was first broadcast more than two decades ago.

It was this reluctance to deal with states of mind (which is what the Narnia books are really about) rather than actions which led to the decision not to include *The Last Battle* in the BBC series. This is the final volume of Lewis's saga and the one for which he was awarded the Carnegie Medal in 1955, but it is also a book filled with problems for the adapter who is concerned with making 'good' children's television (that is programmes characterised by exciting action and external achievements). The images and events in the text are predominantly prophetic and visionary and, as in *Prince Caspian,* the plot is in many ways subordinate to internal development. Since the producer and dramatist conceived the BBC Chronicles as an extended classic serial, it is not surprising that they fell at *The Last Battle*. If, however, they had conceived their task throughout the series as developing and accommodating their audience to a new language for viewing that did not simply imitate but actually translated words and narrative devices into images, then by the time this final text had been reached the viewing audience would have been able to make the transition in the same way that the reader does. Indeed, by far the majority of viewers have read, are reading, or will soon read the Narnia books, and since this series has ultimately been designed for commercial video release as well as one-off viewing, by this time in the series the relationship between readers and viewers could have been made a strength.

Classic texts and their adapters rarely exploit the strengths of their relationship, and this is largely because to date adaptations have succumbed to the flattening process and pretended to *be* books. This pattern is deeply entrenched with adult fiction, particularly since most adults do not re-read and re-view with the same frequency and intensity as children. But as all the statistics prove, there is a high level of interaction between children, their books, and television adaptations. Added to this is the fact that children's books are not guarded with the same ferocity as are adult texts. Rather than slavishly aping adult television adaptation practices it would be exciting to see producers and dramatists of books for children capitalising on the unique qualities of children's reading/viewing habits to tackle the adaptation process in a more imaginative way. This can only stimulate further children's interest in the original texts, and in the process develop links between verbal and visual literacy in the next generation.

NOTES

[1] Cited in *The Cool Web: The Pattern of Children's Reading,* ed. M. Meek, A. Warlow, and G. Barton (Bodley Head, 1977), p. 78.

[2] *The Cool Web,* p. 86.

[3] *The Cool Web,* p. 86.

[4] *Young Telegraph,* no. 1 (6 October 1990), p. 1.

[5] Paul Kerr, 'Classic Serials—To Be Continued', *Screen,* vol. 23, no. 1 (May-June 1982), p. 11.

[6] Kerr, p. 12.

[7] For a comprehensive discussion of the tendency of visual texts to 'flatten' novels see Kerr's article.

[8] Kerr, pp. 17-19.

[9] Kerr, p. 7.

[10] C. S. Lewis, *The Silver Chair* (Puffin Books, 1953), p. 132.

[11] *The Silver Chair,* p. 143.

[12] M. and M. Rustin, 'Narnia: An Imaginary Land as Container of Moral and Emotional Adventure', in *Narratives of Love and Loss: Studies in Modern Children's Fiction* (Verso, 1987), p. 55.

The author would like to thank Paul Stone (the producer of the BBC series) for discussing the process of making *The Chronicles of Narnia.*

Susan Drain

SOURCE: "'Too Much Love-Making': *Anne of Green Gables* on Television," in *The Lion and the Unicorn: A Critical Journal of Children's Literature,* Vol. 11, No. 2, October, 1987, pp. 63-72.

[*In the following essay, Drain discusses the manner in which plot alterations in the television adaptation of Lucy Maud Montgomery's* Anne of Green Gables *shifted focus from Anne's maturation to her romance with Gilbert Blythe.*]

> "Ruby Gillis . . . put too much love-making into her stories and you know too much is worse than too little."
>
> —(Chapter 26)

Lucy Maud Montgomery's *Anne of Green Gables* has been a popular book since it first appeared in 1908. Generations of girls have followed Anne's misadventures with love and sympathy, recognizing beneath the regional colour and the particular details the aspirations and periods of loneliness which are part of all growing up. It is one of the few books still commonly read that emerged from the nineteenth-century tradition of "orphan" books: *Pollyanna* is perhaps the only other example, and even she, after her reincarnation in Walt Disney's film, has faded again from view. Although *Anne*'s appeal has been more enduring, it has been limited by its reputation as a

girl's book. It is a rare boy who identifies with the dreamy, excitable, bookish, romantic Anne. However, Kevin Sullivan's translation of *Anne* to the small screen in his 1985 film version for the Canadian Broadcasting Corporation has finally made Anne known to a wider audience, not just outside Canada, but also beyond its female readership.

Curiously, the television version both brings the story to life and distances it. On the screen we see the places and the costumes which help make the story seem more real: the fabrics and the furnishings, the buildings and the landscape bring the past reassuringly before our eyes. But at the same time as the setting becomes vivid, the immediacy is lost. It is all there, but it is outside us. It is a convincing Green Gables, but it is not ours. We are visitors to this world, not co-creators of it. The same distancing affects our response to Anne. The reader's Anne is seen from the inside out; the reader identifies with her, and participates in her adventures. Though the identification is not complete—the narrative is not first-person, for example, and from time to time the reader shares the perspective of other characters, or even the occasionally ironic stance of the narrator—it is closer than is possible on the screen. Those images are seen from the outside; however sympathetic the camera, its eye settles on exteriors. Intimacy and identification are replaced by interpretation: we watch actions and expressions, we listen to words, but we remain outside.

Despite this distancing, however, the television version of *Anne of Green Gables* was a tremendous success—an Oscar is popular proof of that. Perversely, however, the success has been achieved only by sacrifice. Beautiful and moving as it is, the film *Anne* is yet a lesser accomplishment. It succeeds by reducing to predictability the leisurely complexities of character development and the gradual accommodation of individual and community that are the deeper patterns of Montgomery's original.

Admittedly, television is a special medium and its story-telling functions under certain constraints. For one thing the usual pattern of a television film is that of an extended viewing period, uninterrupted except perhaps by commercials. Even a mini-series, spread out over several days, is viewed in large chunks. The episodic quality of the novel is at odds with this pattern. The novel requires that the reader meet and accept Anne; then it proceeds in a leisurely way through a score of episodic incidents. Many a chapter is self-contained, and the book lends itself, after the initial half-dozen introductory chapters, to interruption and resumption. That is not to deny the book's unity, but only to say that its unity is chiefly on the level of theme and character, rather than plot. The expectation is, however, that television productions must compel attention for the duration of the broadcast, and it is plot that must compel. The episodic structure will not serve, and so the viewer who knows the novel will notice some major structural changes.

In fact, the story line is broken into two sub-stories, which we can briefly identify as "The Trial" and "The

Love Story." "The Trial" is the story of Anne's adoption: will she or won't she be able to stay at Green Gables? "The Love Story" is the thread which ties together all Anne's subsequent adventures: will she or won't she be reconciled with Gilbert? These two sub-stories are unequal in length, approximately one-third, two-thirds rather than half-and-half, yet the broadcast requirement is for two equal sections. The scriptwriters' solution to this difficulty is to bridge the gap with the plot complication of Anne's friendship with Diana. The growth of their friendship is intertwined with the early development of the love story, but the last minutes of the first broadcast are devoted entirely to the crisis which occurs when Mrs. Barry accuses Anne of "getting Diana drunk" and forbids their meeting. The program closes with the girls' swearing an oath of friendship before they part. The viewer is left in suspense until the broadcast resumes: will Anne's innocence be proven and her friend restored to her?

When the broadcast does continue, a new school year has begun and Anne is taken up by the new school teacher, Miss Stacey, but these events are intercut with glimpses of Anne's estrangement from Diana. The viewer is not allowed to forget Anne's suffering, until at length Anne is restored to Mrs. Barry's good graces after saving Diana's baby sister during an attack of the croup. Immediately thereafter, the love story, temporarily overshadowed by the severed friendship, is resumed. The bridge succeeds in keeping the viewer's interest over the intermission in a way that the only gradually unfolding love story could not.

It is worth examining exactly how the scriptwriters have restructured the episodic narrative of the novel into the two sub-stories whose conflicts give direction and unity to the film. For instance, the opening third of the film ("The Trial") includes not only the opening scenes of the book, in which the Cuthberts are surprised by the outcome of their request for a boy to adopt, but also scenes of Anne's life before her adoption, a life only briefly described, in retrospect, in the novel. Furthermore, the first part includes most of Anne's early adventures in Avonlea, such as the affront to Mrs. Lynde and the loss of the amethyst brooch. What binds these incidents is the viewer's anxiety about Anne's fate, for the script writers have imposed a trial period of Anne's adoption. "You may not be happy here with two old grumps like us," says Marilla, though the viewer has no doubt about Anne's allegiance. It is purely a plot device, instituted to give an edge—will they send her back?—to the viewer's reaction to Anne's scrapes.

That edge is sharpened by a further rearrangement of episodes. Immediately after Anne's apology to Mrs. Lynde, Anne is sent to school, even though there are only a few weeks left before vacation. Marilla is prompt to warn Anne that going to school does not mean that the trial is over: "It's just as easy to take you out of school as to put you in." The novel's Marilla, however, had explicitly decided against Anne's going to school for such a brief period: "You must go to school; but it's only

a fortnight till vacation so it isn't worth while for you to start before it opens again in September" (Chapter 8). This alteration allows the film version to include within the Trial section the "Tempest in the School Teapot" episode (Chapter 15), in which Anne cracks her slate over Gilbert's head, though in the novel Gilbert does not appear until school resumes in the fall. Nor is it enough to add this episode; the scriptwriters link it immediately with a scrape from much later in the book—Anne's disastrous attempt to dye her hair (Chapter 27). It does follow aptly enough that Gilbert's taunt of "Carrots" should have provoked her to buy the peddlar's dye, but the cumulative effect of all this trouble is to plunge Anne into the depths of despair and to raise the viewer to the peak of anxiety. At this very point, however, Marilla announces that the trial is over. Apparently, Anne is staying at Green Gables because of, rather than in spite of, her penchant for trouble. To her own surprise, Marilla recognizes that she prefers the tumultuous Anne to the well-behaved child she had thought she wanted. "Did you really crack the slate?" she asks. The question seals her acceptance of Anne: "I think you may be a kindred spirit after all." In accepting Anne, Marilla is realigning herself, siding with Anne against the larger community, who might justly see Anne's behavior as something to be punished rather than condoned. This realignment is slightly but significantly different from its depiction in the novel.

The novel opens by introducing the reader to the chief members of the community of Avonlea long before the stranger Anne appears. The film, however, opens with Anne some time before she reaches Avonlea. She is shown in the squalor and the emotional and physical isolation of life with the Hammonds, and we watch as she is dispossessed of even these unsympathetic companions, and is returned to the orphanage, unwelcome even there. The only constant in her life, we see, is loneliness, and the imaginary companion her loneliness has made for her in her own reflection in a piece of glass. The scenes where Anne talks to her own reflection are glimpses of something dangerously close to madness: she is living in a dream-world, as the matron tells her, and that dream-world must be shattered if the child is to be saved.
Thus, by the time Anne reaches Avonlea, the viewer's anxiety on Anne's behalf is heightened by our awareness of Anne's fate if she does not survive the trial. Marilla is unaware that sending Anne back to the orphanage means condemning her to misery and madness. But the viewer is firmly allied with Anne—and in due course, with Matthew—because it is clear that she is in need—"we might be some good to her" (Chapter 3).

Once the trial is over, another plot complication must develop to carry the viewer through to the end. The relationship between Anne and Gilbert Blythe provides the conflict which gives shape to the remainder of the story. From the hints and possibilities in the novel, the scriptwriters have woven a love story—almost, in fact, two love stories.

We have already noted that Gilbert appears several months earlier in the film version than he does in the novel, but in fact, he has already been glimpsed at a distance. The Sunday-school picnic has shown us Anne and Diana in competition with Gilbert and Moody in the three-legged race—a pure invention. The race, however, foreshadows the academic competition between Anne and Gilbert, and also allows for an exchange of glances between the two. Although Anne declares to Diana that Gilbert is bold to have winked at her, the possibility of something other than a mere playground rivalry has been raised already, especially as Diana hints that Gilbert is a desirable object of romantic interest.

Even more curious is the way a second love-story is adumbrated. Very early, when her amethyst brooch has vanished, Marilla declares, "That brooch meant a great deal to me, more than any picnic," but she does not explain why, though Anne's imagination is quick to supply a reason. "Was it a keepsake from a tragic romance?" she asks. The novel permits no romantic mystery about this "treasured possession. A seafaring uncle had given it to [Marilla's] mother who in turn had bequeathed it to Marilla" (Chapter 13). But the scriptwriters suppress that explanation and invent new details to deepen the mystery. Immediately after Marilla has announced the end of Anne's trial, Diana reports to Anne a conversation she has overheard, in which Marilla is described as having a temper similar to Anne's. Here, we are to understand, is the basis for that statement, somewhat startling to readers of the novel, that Marilla and Anne may be kindred spirits after all. But that is not all; the eavesdropper had also heard that Marilla's temper had caused her to break her engagement. Anne's imagination, of course, immediately seizes on this news: Marilla is bathed in the glamour of those who have been disappointed in love. What the scene also does is to draw the parallel between Anne's fight with Gilbert and Marilla's lover's quarrel, thus confirming what we have already suspected, that there is a romantic tension in the classroom squabbles.

From this point on, Gilbert is omnipresent. In the book his role during these years is essentially as an academic rival to Anne—a rival she will not acknowledge; the rest of her life is related without reference to him. The scriptwriters, however, have worked Gilbert into several other episodes: the spruce-gum scene, for instance, has been rewritten as an episode in which the boys tease the girls, and Anne chases Gilbert like an avenging fury. Thus Gilbert becomes not only the punishment (when Anne is sent to sit with him in class), but also the occasion, of Anne's trangression. Again, a series of picturesque scenes, used to indicate the passage of time, concludes with the sight of Gilbert languishing behind a tree, following Anne and Diana with ardent eyes.

To speed up the plot, several episodes are ingeniously linked: the teacher's departure is honored with a party, at which Anne responds to Josie's dare to walk the ridgepole of the kitchen roof. She is not allowed to break her ankle, however, for she is to return from the party through the Haunted Wood. In the novel, these last are two self-contained episodes, "Anne Comes to Grief in an Affair of Honour" (Chapter 23) and "A Good Imagination Gone Wrong" (Chapter 20). Gilbert, of course, is made to link them all. By this time, Josie Pye's jealousy of Gilbert's attention has been established in an invented schoolyard scene, so that her daring of Anne implies her wish to diminish Anne in Gilbert's eyes. In the novel, daring was simply "the fashionable amusement among the Avonlea small fry . . . that summer" (Chapter 23). On screen, it is an exchange of glances with Gilbert that confirms Anne's determination to carry out the dare. After Anne's fall, Josie's triumph is short-lived, for we see Gilbert snub Josie, even though he is smarting from Anne's refusal of his help to get home. It is because of this stiff-necked refusal, then, that Anne and Diana choose the shortcut home through the woods, where they terrify each other with tales of ghosts. In the novel, these scenes are part of the gradual maturing process Anne goes through; her early scrapes have shown her her faults, such as temper and absent-mindedness; these two later episodes show Anne learning that even virtues— imagination, honor, and courage—may be faults if exercised without moderation. All this careful characterbuilding has been sacrificed to the television love story.

To recognize this change is to realize why it is wrong to shift the hair-dye episode to the beginning of the story. In the novel, that chapter begins with Marilla comfortably looking forward to "a briskly snapping fire and a table nicely spread for tea, instead of to the cold comfort of old Aid meeting evenings before Anne had come to Green Gables" (Chapter 27). Thus Anne's dereliction of duty is seen to be an unusual back-sliding, for she is clearly much more steady and reliable than she used to be. Despite her improvement she is no paragon, and it is not by chance that her fall from grace is caused by vanity. That fault has not been her most apparent, though it is her most persistent—and it must be subdued before she can go on to real achievements. Anne suffers her "vexation of spirit" in confronting her own vanity, and in learning to distinguish true from meretricious qualities: to reduce this vexation to a mere petulant reaction against a schoolboy's taunt is to obliterate the moral subtleties of the novel.

It is not moral subtlety that concerns the scriptwriters, however, as much as "boy meets girl," and as soon as the estrangement between Anne and Diana is over, Gilbert resumes his role as romantic interest. Hitherto, no major changes have been necessary, but from this point forward, the scriptwriters take increasing liberties with the text in order to make the romance prominent. The school's Christmas concert, for instance, is transmogrified into a Christmas ball to which Anne is invited by the Barrys as part of their renewed kindness to her. A ball serves as well as a concert to allow Matthew to insist on puffed sleeves and to precede the girls' latenight leap onto Aunt Josephine in the spare-room bed, but a ball also has dancing, and thus provides the scriptwriters with a chance to complicate the romance. Anne tries to demonstrate her power over Gilbert, but he spurns her. Lest we think he has lost interest, however, we are shown his secretly pocketing Anne's dance card. The scene is pure fabrication, but we see that Anne's interest in Gilbert is sparked by his snubbing of her.

The linking of scenes, again, tightens the plot as self-contained episodes from the novel are integrated with others, but it also produces certain incongruities. For example, it is harder to accept that the Anne who co-quettes, even unsuccessfully, at the ball is the same person as the madcap who dives into the spare-room bed. In the novel, the leap takes place ten months before the Christmas of the puffed sleeves, and during those months episodes such as tea at the manse show Anne becoming somewhat steadier.

The ensuing scenes of school and entrance exams are shadowed by Anne's awareness of Gilbert; even her teacher urges Anne to reconcile. Anne, however, is ada-mant, though clearly miserable. By the time Gilbert res-cues her after the sinking of the lily maid's barge, her hurt pride compels her to return his Christmas-time snub. The chronology has again been altered here: in the novel, "The Unfortunate Lily Maid" (Chapter 28) takes place before "The Queen's Class is Organized" (Chapter 30), whereas the film makes the adventure coincide with the announcement of the Queen's entrance-exam results. Thus the film's Anne swings even more wildly between childhood and young womanhood than does the novel's. Though in both, Anne's near-drowning leads to her renunciation of romance ("Today's mistake is going to cure me of being romantic"), in the film the word "romance" is clearly in-tended to include any relationship with Gilbert, as well as the attempt to recreate "towered Camelot" in Avonlea.

Thus far, those who are familiar with the novel will rec-ognize shifts of emphasis, changes in chronology, and some small inventions, but here begins a series of events that departs drastically from the novel and leaves no doubt in the reader's mind that the love story is the new heart of the television *Anne*.

Marilla meets Gilbert by chance, and warns him away from Anne: "She has the talent to make something of herself," she tells him, "but she's still very young." De-spite her warning, Gilbert makes another overture, an offer of a ride home to an Anne laden with parcels. Anne apologizes and Gilbert renounces any grudge, but it is hardly a reconciliation. Both are touchy, and Anne is quick to take offense. Nevertheless, they are looking for-ward to each other's company at the White Sands Hotel concert. Any chance of this truce mellowing into friend-ship is destroyed by Marilla's angry reaction to Mrs. Lynde's report of Anne's buggy ride with Gilbert. Marilla's motives are unclear, here, except that she is anticipating the unhappy separation when Anne goes to Queen's. She doesn't want Anne "making any ties she'll regret," she says; in attacking Gilbert, she is able to voice her own fear that Anne may outgrow both Avonlea and her guardians. Fortunately Anne is sensitive to Marilla's real anxiety, declaring she will always be "Anne of Green Gables."

Nevertheless, events conspire to thwart the relationship with Gilbert: first Marilla's disapproval, and then the acclaim Anne receives after her recitation at the concert (a portent of Anne's outgrowing Avonlea). As a result, Anne and Gilbert spend their Queen's year in unhappy isolation from each other. Gilbert appears unconscious of her, but Anne is clearly preoccupied with him. Certainly, very little of Anne's life at Queen's is shown except when it reveals the tension over Gilbert. Even crusty Aunt Josephine is drawn into the love story: recognizing Anne's dreams and ambitions, she nevertheless urges her to "make room in your plans for romance." The alternative, she warns, is a cantankerous old-maidhood like her own.

The place of Gilbert in Anne's thoughts is quite different from the one assigned him in the novel. There, when Gilbert accompanies Ruby, Anne "could not help think-ing . . . that it would be very pleasant to have such a friend as Gilbert to jest and chatter with and exchange ideas about books and studies and ambitions. Gilbert had ambitions, she knew." In case the reader suspects that Anne is merely fooling herself about the nature of her interest in Gilbert, the narrator explicitly pronounces upon Anne's state of heart: "There was no silly sentiment in Anne's ideas concerning Gilbert. Boys were to her, when she thought about them at all, merely possible good comrades" (Chapter 35). The film-makers have no such scruples about sentiment, silly or otherwise. Nor do they hesitate to complicate the love story even further, making Gilbert the price Anne must be willing to pay for her ambitions. Discussing her four years ahead at the univer-sity on her newly won scholarship, Anne is dismayed to learn that Diana is in love with Gilbert. She confesses only because she is convinced by Anne's denial of inter-est. Anne is caught in a trap of her own making, her loyalty to her friend in conflict with her own inclination.

Now events rush to their close: catastrophe strikes, with-out the novel's foreshadowing. A deeper understanding with Marilla is achieved, as in the novel, and the secret of Marilla's broken engagement to Gilbert's father is revealed. This revelation, a surprise in the novel, ends the speculation that was raised with the amethyst-brooch story and fed by Avonlea's gossip. Marilla's sense of loss is greater in the film than in the book: "Everybody has forgot about me and John. I'd forgotten myself," says the novel's Marilla. "But it all came back to me when I saw Gilbert last Sunday" (Chapter 38). It is more as if Marilla's life had lost a potential richness when she lost romance, than that it was blighted. By making this loss more prominent, the film-makers reinforce Aunt Josephine's im-plied equation of fulfillment with romance.

So the scene is set for the reconciliation with Gilbert which is clearly the climax of the film. In the novel, Mrs. Lynde tells Anne of Gilbert's giving up the Avonlea school for her, and it is by chance that Anne meets Gil-bert and is moved to hold out her hand to him, but the film brings Gilbert to deliver the news of his magnanim-ity himself. The situation is thus profoundly different, in that, by coming in person, Gilbert assumes control. His power to compel Anne's gratitude, and her acknowledgment of him, are symbolized in the horse that he rides. His assertion that her help with his studies will be a fair exchange for his sacrifice sounds almost condescending, and his descent from his horse to walk her home underlines the fundamental inequality in this reconciliation. Ambition vanishes in the glow of sunset; the restoration of romance is the film's culmination.

The novel ends, as it began, on a different note: "Anne sat long at her window that night companioned by a glad content." Her thoughts embrace the landscape before her eyes, her future, and indeed, the whole world; her happiness is multi-faceted, and Gilbert only a part of it. "The joys of sincere work and worthy aspiration and congenial friendship were to be hers" (Chapter 38).

Whether Montgomery is not so much delicate as uncomfortable in handling romance is another question. What is clear is that the script-writers' version of *Anne of Green Gables* is profoundly different from Montgomery's. Their added complication of the love story is fascinating to watch, and is so skillfully interwoven with the original fabric of the novel that the full import of their changes almost evades the viewer who knows the book.

Certainly, the film has many virtues: its handling of moods is deft; it is visually heart-stealing, and it avoids the sentimentality which would have been as stickily treacherous as Anne's raspberry cordial. Furthermore, its acting is superb: henceforward no one will ever imagine Marilla except as Colleen Dewhurst. But the film, by concentrating on the love story, is in some ways more old-fashioned, or even narrower, than the book. The film is an exquisite romance, but the novel is a *Bildungsroman*. That reduction is, finally, a loss.

Perry Nodelman

SOURCE: "Not Much More Than Once upon a Classic," in *Children's Literature Association Quarterly*, Vol. 7, No. 3, Fall, 1982, pp. 27-30.
[*In the following essay, Nodelman presents a negative appraisal of* Once upon a Classic, *a PBS series which adapted nineteenth-century novels into television for children.*]

This is not so much a review as it is a confession. I did try to watch *Once Upon a Classic.* Lord knows I tried. I wrote it down on my list of things to remember: "Watch *Once Upon a Classic.*" But somehow, Sunday at twelve thirty passed, and I had not watched *Once Upon a Classic.*

Yes, Sunday at twelve thirty. That was part of the problem. Half past noon on Sunday, when sensible people are eating their lunch and yelling at their husbands to turn off that TV and get in here immediately or else: that's when my local PBS station shows *Once Upon a Classic.* Well, I turned off that TV and I got in there at once, and made plans for next week. I told sensible people about the

serious nature of my project. Sensible people pretended to understand. She planned to delay lunch next week. I wrote it down on my list of things to remember, and underlined it twice, and added two exclamation marks: "Watch *Once Upon a Classic:* DON'T FORGET!!"

I forgot. So I told my son, who is seven and impressionable, that if he forgot to remember to remind me to watch *Once Upon a Classic* next Sunday, I would lock him in his room for a whole week and feed him nothing but tomatoes and asparagus, both of which he hates. He remembered. I forgot.

On succeeding Sundays, I made complicated soups for lunch, tidied my desk, changed the filter on the furnace, and wrote letters to old friends I had been meaning to write for years but had never got around to. One Sunday I even read some student essays. In the seven months that I've been planning to write this article, I've actually managed to watch *Once Upon a Classic* four times. I probably shouldn't be writing the article; I can't guarantee those four episodes are representative.

But I suspect they are. They were so much alike in the ways that made me so inventive about not watching the program that they suggest a horrifying consistency. To put it plainly, *Once Upon a Classic* is boring. Very boring. It is boring enough to actually deserve being shown to the three people who watch PBS at half past noon on Sunday. It is boring enough that anyone who does watch it even only four times in seven months has undeniably earned the right to tell the rest of the world how very boring it is.

Produced in Pittsburgh, *Once Upon a Classic* consists for the most part of adaptations of well known nineteenth-century novels, divided into half-hour segments. The shows were originally produced in Britian. *Once Upon a Classic* is a sort of mini–*Masterpiece Theatre*. It even has a host who explains everything at the beginning and the end of each show, just like the maxi–*Masterpiece Theatre*. The mini–Alistair Cooke is Bill Bixby, an American actor who is much better known for playing the meek, mild-mannered guy who turns into the Incredible Hulk when he gets angry on commercial TV. On PBS, we get Bixby very much without the Hulk. He's a meek, mild-mannered guy wearing these tasteful two hundred dollar sweaters and standing in front of this tasteful fireplace in what may be the only tastefully understated British room in Pittsburgh. He looks as though if he ever did get angry it would probably be at the unBritish tastelessness of the rest of Pittsburgh; and his anger would probably transform him from a meek mild-mannered guy into a meek, mild-mannered guy with a frown. There's just no way anything as macho and as energetic as a green former Mr. America would ever show up in that quiet room, and it would be criminal for expanding green muscles to rip up those wonderful sweaters.

During the months I planned to watch *Once Upon a Classic,* the show presented adaptations of three novels:

Dickens' *A Tale of Two Cities,* Scott's *The Talisman,* and George Eliot's *The Mill on the Floss.* These are the sorts of novels they used to make us read in high school literature courses, before relevance and self-image building became more important considerations for curriculum planners than the fact that we've done it ever since 1892, have copies for everyone, and if it was good enough for me when I was your age then it's good enough for you, punk. I don't mean to suggest that these aren't good novels. They're all at least pretty good, and *A Tale of Two Cities* is particularly good, as melodramatic now as it ever was and a tremendous amount of fun because of it.

But these are not the sort of novels that many children nowadays do read; and I don't think they're the sort of novels most children should read. Pleasure in them depends on knowledge of their genre and of the idiosyncrasies of nineteenth century prose, and few children nowadays possess that competence. Better they shouldn't read these books at all than that they should be bored by them! For those lucky few bookish enough to develop a taste for such things, Scott and Dickens and Eliot will be as pleasureful as they ever were; for those who aren't, obviously, there is *Once Upon a Classic.* It's clearly meant to provide painless culture for those who don't want to waste their valuable time on cultural monuments: this is a TV version of those Classic Comics of my youth, the ones you couldn't trade for a Superman no matter how hard you tried.

Dickens and Eliot, and particularly Scott, were pretty good storytellers. That is, they invented interesting, suspenseful plots. But when it comes right down to it, none of them were as good at inventing *things* to write about as they were at finding interesting *ways* to write about those things. They are novelists, dealers in words, not inventors of action-filled scenarios. In those old Classic Comics, and in *Once Upon a Classic,* the events these novelists describe so well in their novels get divorced from the novelists' descriptions and become just scenarios. And the worst thing about the scripts based on these scenarios is that they deprive Dickens and Eliot and Scott of their wonderful, distinct styles, and make them all come out the same. *Once Upon a Classic* is an appropriate title in more ways than one: in these TV versions, all these classics are the same classic.

Part of their sameness derives from the inevitable limitations of TV production. For one thing, each novel must be divided into segments of equal length, like swatches of yard goods. The episodes I saw of both *The Talisman* and *A Tale of Two Cities* were bad television mostly because they were opening chapters, and therefore, mostly exposition. Now, you can get away with presenting lots of information at the beginning of a novel because your readers know it'll lead to some exciting action later on; but we expect each of the episodes of a TV series to have its own developing action and climax—as well we might, since we have to wait a whole week between episodes. Viewers, therefore, expect a more immediate return on the attention invested than something that is going to

happen two or three months in the future. But no matter how hard they tried, the script writers of these adaptations simply could not find a suspense-building shape in the events of any episodes based on an early chapter of the novel. In the Dickens I saw, the characters nattered about people who weren't even on screen, and most of the Scott episode consisted of a bunch of people in mediaeval robes sitting around a table and explaining the history of the crusades to each other, like a graduate seminar in drag. I suppose it all amounted to something three or four episodes later, but by then, for some reason, the furnace filter seemed to promise more adventure.

Even if good novels could easily make good TV, the unfailingly consistent production values of *Once Upon a Classic* would probably murder it. There appears to be a confusion in the minds of British TV producers between fiction and history. These books were historical novels in their own time, and they are all historical novels to us. But there's a big difference between historical fiction and history. Scott wanted to capture the romance, the exuberance, the excitement of the crusades; Dickens felt much the same about the French revolution. But the *Once Upon a Classic* productions invest so much effort on historical detail that all those indubitably correct sets are more interesting than the things happening on them, and I found myself thinking about how clever the costumes were instead of becoming involved with the characters wearing them. Not only is the atmosphere accurate, it's quite astonishingly beautiful, just like *Masterpiece Theatre* is; but the beauty inhibits the actions like a frame around a picture. Watching these shows is like looking at those "authentic" rooms in museums with a rope in front of them. The characters are so clearly part of a detailed and beautiful past that they sink into a fog of nostalgia, a dense atmosphere of historicity that even the best of actors would have trouble cutting through. These are *not* always the best of actors, even if they do have British accents.

At least part of that historical atmosphere is actually physically present, created by what I've come to think of as PBS lighting. PBS lighting is white light only, and lots of it, coming from discrete sources that create a chiaroscuro of many different browns and a lot of white, and not much else. Characters frequently appear in front of windows filled with white light; they almost always have haloes of white light on their hair. This is lighting that deliberately avoids the atmospheric effects of colored light but it is not without atmosphere. In fact, the mood PBS lighting creates supports the feeling of accuracy in the sets and costumes. It is a mood of documentary, of seeing things as they actually might have been, uncolored by the eccentricities of fictional style.

Enmeshed by all this low-key accuracy, the characters seem odd, very odd indeed. They talk like characters in Dickens and Scott and Eliot; and when they do it, they sound silly. Surely people wearing these highly unfictional clothes and walking in these real-life rooms under this ever-so-natural lighting did not talk in this eccentric way. The fact is, Dickens' characters are caricatures; Scott's are made out of cardboard, and even Eliot's are larger than you and me. They all need a more distinctly colored, more one-sided atmosphere to feel at home in, and when they don't get it, they seem objectionably self-indulgent even when their authors intended us to like them. When a Dickens' character says, "I have no imagination, none whatsoever," it's not the truthful statement it is in the book: either he's teasing, or self-congratulatory. And when Richard the Lionheart in *The Talisman* says, "Ah, my sweet Berengaria, how fares she?" it is to upchuck. No human being in real life ever talked like that, at least not in a gray room with accurate smoke from a naturalistic fire.

In the long run, it's the feeling of documentary they all convey that makes these *Once Upon a Classics,* set in such different times and places, seem much like one another. They become a sort of seamless classic running forever on PBS, convincing us yet again that classics, like all the other monuments we know we ought to respect, are actually monumentally boring.

But not quite. I did see *one* episode that was interesting: and my children, who fled like startled robins from the other *Once Upon a Classics,* watched this one with great involvement and much enthusiasm. It was the final episode of something called *Black Island.* You've probably never heard of it, and that's instructive. *Black Island* was "based on a story by Peter Van Praagh." Peter Van Who? It's hardly a classic.

In fact, *Black Island* turned out to be quite unclassically exciting, a typical adventure story, the sort that gets by on lots of action and no style at all. Michael and Joe, stuck on a deserted island, end up being kept as hostages by a pair of escaped convicts. Since the setting is contemporary, the people talk like people—mostly in grunts and hesitations, not like characters in novels at all. Since the story this was based on seems to have been filled with action, we got good, action-filled television. In the episode I saw, after a few harrowing *Once Upon a Classic* moments at the beginning during which it seemed to take four days for a kid to bandage his fingers and stare at an old man, who stared back, we had twenty good minutes of almost hair's-breadth escapes, recaptures, a scavenging trip to the mainland to steal food, scenes of impending starvation and the joyful discovery of wild potatoes, a house on fire and near escape from death by burning, and finally, rescue in the nick of time. Now that's exciting, a lot more exciting than I'd come to expect from *Once Upon a Classic!*

But it was obviously the non-classic status of the material that allowed it to be exciting. There was no good or even distinctive writing to contradict or to dissipate, no novel-length plot to break into wrong-sized equal segments, no historical period to overaccurately represent, and no distinct style of speech for characters to seem silly speaking. *Black Island* is good TV because it is no classic.

Once Upon a Classic proudly announces on each show that it's been honored by Action for Children's Televi-sion as an outstanding program for children and their parents. Sure, as we used to say when I was young, out standing in the rain. *Once Upon a Classic* is too tasteful to be interesting; even worse, it makes classics dull by misrepresenting what it was that made them classics. If the Incredible Hulk ever did show up in front of that tasteful fireplace with the remnants of one of those snazzy sweaters dripping from his biceps, he'd know what to do: give those British videotapes a big squeeze, until the weak tea that runs in their veins spilled onto that tasteful British floor, and they could inflict their numbness upon us no more.

Perry Nodelman

SOURCE: "The Objectionable Other, or Walter de la Mare Meets My Little Pony," in *Children's Literature Association Quarterly,* Vol. 12, No. 2, Summer, 1987, pp. 58-60.

[*In the following essay, Nodelman addresses the ways in which the enjoyment of television negatively affects the enjoyment of literature among children.*]

The articles in the special section of this issue deal with aspects of the lives of children that experts in children's literature often feel superior to. For educated adults of good sense and good taste, the most obvious response to a book with wheels attached to it or a Walt Disney image of love's young dream is horror. "This," we say, "This is what the world has come to? This is what we feed the tender imaginations of our young with? This pap? This garbage? This insult to good sense and good taste?"

But despite our own smug invulnerability to such insultingly vulgar objects, we nevertheless believe that the real trouble with them is not just their bad taste; it is the fact that children do like them so much. Surely something so obviously silly and vulgar should not be so enjoyable. Surely something so enjoyable must be bad for those who enjoy it. So we view aspects of popular culture for children with great alarm—and then, most likely, we turn our backs upon the offending objects, dismiss them from our thoughts, and purify our minds of the tainting stench by immersing ourselves in that which is truly great and truly inspiring; we imbibe a poem by de la Mare or a novel by Eleanor Cameron not because they are inherently enjoyable but as Peewee Herman antidotes. If we think at all about popular literature for children or about the mass culture of toys and television and such, it is merely to point out how inferior they are in relation to that which is truly worthwhile.

In this we are not alone—it is a common habit of high-minded people to attack the artifacts of popular culture in defense of real excellence. Tania Modleski speaks of "the tendency of critics and theorists to make mass culture into the 'other' of whatever, at any given moment, they happen to be championing—and moreover, to denigrate the other primarily because it allegedly provides pleasure to the consumer" (*Studies in Entertainment* [Bloomington: Indiana Universty Press, 1986] 157).

These are dangerous attitudes, I think. They depend on two assumptions, one arrogant and one silly. The silly assumption is the puritanical one that pleasure is always a bad thing, a sign of dangerously unproductive self-indulgence; any worthwhile work of art has to be important, serious, and therefore, obviously, no fun at all. The arrogant assumption is the elitist one that what most people most easily like is inevitably both bad art and bad for them—that they aren't smart enough to know what's not good for them. Both assumptions are wrong.

The main (maybe the only) thing art has to offer is pleasure. The only good reason for reading Walter de la Mare or Eleanor Cameron is that they are a pleasure to read. Even art that makes us think is merely offering us the pleasure of thinking. It's surely not the intention of artists to be educational, to teach us important things about important subjects; in my own experience, what people say they've learned from a work of art is always in fact something they already knew, and in any case, what a novel or a painting might actually happen to teach us could always be learned more easily in less circuitous ways—if Shakespeare had merely wanted us to understand that he who hesitates is lost, a simple five word statement would have been more efficacious than *Hamlet.* Those who really don't like to think but force themselves to experience serious art because it's good for them, because they'll learn to be better people from it, are rather missing the point; and as for the theory that great art can ennoble us and lift us above ourselves, I believe it was George Steiner who once pointed out how that theory was contradicted for eternity by those high-minded Nazi officials who read poetry and listened to Beethoven recordings before they went off to inspect the gas chambers.

As for the second, dangerous assumption: to feel superior to those who enjoy what's popular is to deny the obvious fact that much of what gives us pleasure in high culture resides in what it shares with popular culture. In addition to what is essentially Picasso-like, Picasso offers us the same basic sensual enjoyment of line and shape and color that we find in Superman comics; at the heart of *King Lear* is a satisfying fairy tale about a youngest sister who does better in a contest than her two older sisters; and the profiles of nuclear physicists that appear in the *New Yorker* offer the joys of gossip, just as do the profiles in *People.* Which is to say, merely, that high art is not the opposite of popular art—not its "other" at all, but merely an extension of it, a variation on the same basic patterns and pleasures. Neither high culture nor popular culture is particularly good for us; both have the main purpose of offering us pleasure.

The main difference between popular art and high art is that high art is harder to learn to appreciate—and therefore, harder to take pleasure from. By definition, popular culture appeals to a lowest common denominator ability

to enjoy; it offers pleasures we all (or at least the largest number of us) can share, usually by giving us exactly what we expect in a form just superficially different enough to seem new—for instance, another situation comedy about a family that is eccentric in a slightly different way than were the families in the other situation comedies we've already seen. Indeed, the inherent widely-based enjoyability of popular art is neatly confirmed by the fact that most of us who actually do enjoy high art nevertheless have our secret trashy vices, indulged in moments when comfort is required: those of us who are honest will surely have to admit to a secret passion for romances, perhaps, or slasher movies, or super-hero comics (I am myself a sucker for TV beauty contests). But high art offers less immediate comfort, for the differences in it are more than superficial; high art tends to refer to familiar patterns or archetypes in order to undercut or to change them, so that what emerges is less significantly familiar than different. High culture offers not just the pleasures of the familiar but also the pleasures of distinctiveness—it gives us something we did not expect rather than merely confirming our expectations. It gives us Picasso as well as basic form, unique poetry as well as a fairy tale.

Now it is possible to read *King Lear* as a fairy tale, and to enjoy it as such—and to miss what is distinct and most specifically pleasurable about it. It is possible to read *New Yorker* profiles of nuclear physicists in order to get the dirt about famous people, and to enjoy them as such—and to miss pleasurable insights into science and culture that distinguish such profiles from those in *People* magazine. And it is possible, never having read anything but Choose Your Own Adventures, to expect all novels to have the exciting plots of Choose Your Own Adventures—and to quickly get bogged down in *A la Recherche du Temps Perdu.* Taking pleasure in that which is distinct as well as in that which is expectable is a learned skill, and it is arrogant indeed to feel superior to those who have not learned it—especially if we know that nobody has tried to teach it to them. It is especially arrogant when it is an attitude expressed towards children who enjoy Punky Brewster on TV instead of reading novels by Virginia Hamilton: if we believe that Virginia Hamilton can be pleasurable too, then we need to teach younger readers *how* to take pleasure in her work.

That is why it is dangerous to dismiss the mass culture designed to appeal to children from our consideration when we think about children's literature. If we want to help children to a greater enjoyment of good children's books, we need to understand what they know already, and we need to use our understanding to develop ways of showing them how to extend that knowledge into new and alien territories. Because Saturday morning cartoons and the imaginative world implied by the advertising for My Little Pony form the context in which children read literature, we need to understand the meaning, the characteristic structures and implications of the Saturday morning cartoons and the My Little Ponies before we can hope to understand how children read literature. If we do not understand the contexts which define children's literature for most young readers, then we will not be able to find ways of teaching them how to develop other contexts.

In choosing the relationships between popular culture and children's literature as the topic for this issue's special section, the *Quarterly* editors had hoped for articles that would consider the ways in which things like Saturday morning cartoons and My Little Pony might influence a child's reading of literature. While the articles you will find here do not always spell out the connections, they do indeed offer some understanding of some popular cultural contexts past and present into which the "good" literature for children fits. We rejected many other submissions, however, not because they were not competent discussions of popular culture, but because so few of them tried to analyze relationships between popular culture and so-called "good" children's literature. That's not particularly surprising—a glance through any journal of popular culture quickly reveals that those interested in writing about it are often rather mindless celebrants of its joys, and just as dismissive of the elitism of "good" literature as the proponents of good literature are dismissive of popular culture. When it comes to the culture of childhood, apparently, popular culture and good literature continue to be each other's "other"—the alien evoked merely to be dismissed.

I hope the articles in this issue will help to lessen the distance between these two "others," which are obviously less distant in the lives of real children than they are in the minds of most scholars. And I hope this issue will stimulate thinking that will encourage the writing of more articles in this important area.

Before that will happen, however, a lot more specialists in children's literature will need to be persuaded that popular culture is more than just offensive trash to be avoided—that it has meanings and patterns that can and do significantly influence both the adults and the children who enjoy it, and that those patterns and meanings are therefore worthy of analysis. For those who need to be so persuaded, I suggest a fascinating book. *Studies in Entertainment: Critical Approaches to Mass Culture* is a collection of essays edited by Tania Modleski that offers a number of subtle analyses of various aspects of popular culture—or mass culture, as these essays perhaps more accurately call it—from fashion to the *I Love Lucy* show. The critics represented in this volume are working at trying to understand popular entertainment in the context of contemporary literary, social, and psychoanalytical theory; their arguments are often based in the work of thoughtful commentators like Roland Barthes and Jacques Lacan. They never talk about popular entertainment specifically directed at children; but what they do talk about is provocative indeed—and suggests much that might well stimulate further thinking about the relationship between popular culture and children's literature.

To take one example: television is the aspect of popular culture that probably bulks largest in the lives of most children. Many of the essays in *Studies in Entertainment* refer to and grow out of Raymond Williams' concept of television as flow—as a continuous sequence of events rather than the discrete unities we expect of other forms of narrative. Television programming continues uninterrupted all day; and emerging as it does from the context of that continuous flow of information, each separate program lacks the discrete wholeness, the sense of a separate beginning and ending, that we expect and demand of novels and poems. Furthermore, the narrative structures of individual TV programs are themselves constantly interrupted by commercials and news breaks and such, so that each segment of a story becomes part of a continuous flow of other kinds of information. That television characteristically structures events in this way suggests much about the narrative expectations that children who watch a lot of television are most comfortable with, and therefore, I suspect, approach literature with.

Since TV offers a continuous uninterrupted flow of information, we cannot and do not always give it our complete attention—we tend to watch intensely only that which specifically interests us, and learn to be inattentive to parts of its continuing message that we shove into the background—the commercials, perhaps, or the promos for other shows, or even parts of shows that don't interest us. In an essay called "Television/Sound" in *Studies in Entertainment,* Rick Altman says that " . . . there is a growing body of data suggesting that intermittent attention is in fact the dominant mode of television viewing" (42). Programmers who understand that take it into account; Altman describes how various aspects of TV sound are designed to attract our attention back to a TV set that may be on but not closely watched. One significant result is a characteristic narrative structure that does not require our full and continuing attention; we may, for instance, watch segments of a weekly situation comedy in random order, or we may understand that we can watch a few minutes of the *Tonight* show without being confused as to the shape of the whole; and, as Altman says, "*Dallas* does not expect to subordinate all our attention to the linearity, directionality, and teleology of a goal-oriented plot. Instead, it recognizes from the start our desire to choose the objects of our attention on other grounds as well"—those grounds being our individual interest in specific characters or sub-plots (44-5). Children used to the flow of TV might well have trouble giving certain kinds of novels the close attention they demand and deserve; such children might well need to be taught a different form of attentiveness as they approach written fiction.

That seems particularly true if we consider Altman's assertion that the ultimate message of TV, in constantly offering us messages on the sound track that request our attention to the picture, is "that the TV image is manufactured and broadcast just for me, at precisely the time that I need it" (51). Such a message might well encourage TV-watching children into a misleadingly solipsistic reading of written fiction. Instead of bewailing the shallow egocentricity of the young, we might better understand that TV has taught it to them, and, understanding that, work to find ways of moving them beyond egocentric reading into the less self-centered dividing of attention among a number of different characters required by most serious fiction.

In an essay called "Brief Encounters: Mass Culture and the Evacuation of Sense," Dana Polan suggests another way in which television flow might affect the attitude of TV-watching children towards reading. Polan believes that the mixture of varying kinds of information in the sequential flow of TV makes it similar to experimental art, "which works through an interplay, a kind of montage, of moments that vaguely hint at meanings and moments that disavow posited meanings, engage in contradiction, undercut every sense by a subsequent or coincident non-sense" (182). Polan offers as an example the varying messages and non-messages of the series of interviews and other segments on any given *Tonight* show; he might equally have suggested *Sesame Street,* which also offers isolated bits of meanings with no relationship to each other, and for which the "whole effect of the show comes from the incongruous confrontation of each bit with the other, the ongoing flow that forces each scene to give way to the next" (182). For Polan, "Flow involves the transcendence of meaningful units by a system whose only meaning is the fact of its global non-meaning," and that results in a particular attitude of cynical powerlessness for viewers: "powerlessness in postmodern mass culture now comes from a situation in which the montage of elements calls into question each and every role that one might care to adopt. There is no position except that of alienated cynicism" (183). Whether cynical or not, young TV viewers might have need of special training in coming to grips with written narrative forms that do in fact imply global meaning.

In a third essay, "Situation Comedy, Feminism and Freud: Discourses of Gracie and Lucy," Patricia Mellencamp suggests yet another way in which TV viewers may have developed narrative expectations quite at odds with much serious fiction. She says, "Situation comedy, with 'gaps' of performance and discontinuities, *use* narrative offhandedly. The hermeneutic code is not replete with expectation, not in need of decipherment, not ensnaring us or lying to us" (91). If TV narrative is at odds with our usual fictional expectations in all these central ways, then an inexperienced reader who knows mainly TV narrative will not understand the reader's obligation to decipher, and to enjoy being ensnared and lied to as conventional fictional plots always do.

Other essays in *Studies in Entertainment,* on topics such as the characteristics of TV news, the relationship between femininity and colonization in advertising, and contemporary horror films, have a less immediate relevance for those interested in the culture of childhood— but throughout the book, these commentators offer interesting insights that might well stimulate further thinking about children and literature. Margaret Morse's discussion of the news makes the fascinating point that all the visual images in news broadcasts are symbolic rather than representational—even the actual White House becomes a symbol when used as a backdrop for any story about the presidency. Such a focus on the visual as symbolic rather than representational might well run through all TV programming, and might explain much about what children expect to see when they look at picture books. And in a discussion of romances, Jean Franco suggests how the plots of fiction relate to the plots we impose on life itself—how conventional fictional narratives relate to the societally-engendered narratives about our expectations, our national values, and so on that help to define us; her comment on comic-strip novels intended for Mexican women might well apply to certain kinds of narratives for children: "Often this moral and ending are so arbitrary in relation to the sequence of events that they highlight the arbitrary nature of all narratives, including the master narrative of nationalism with its appeal to rootedness, to place, to community" (135).

Popular culture is too powerful—and often, too enjoyable—to be merely dismissable. It needs our attention, not just as an example of what we disdain, and not just as an example of what we can uncritically immerse ourselves in. If we could persuade ourselves that the objectionable other were less objectionable, perhaps we could find a way of seeing it as less "other"—and then, maybe, we could find ways of helping minds filled with the life history of My Little Ponies to enjoy Walter de la Mare.

FURTHER READING

Criticism

Giddings, Robert, Keith Selby, and Chris Wensley. *Screening the Novel: The Theory and Practice of Literary Dramatization.* New York: St. Martin's Press, 1990, 174 p.

> In-depth study of the problems and concerns associated with producing screen adaptations of literary classics. The authors focus primarily on two case study examples, Charles Dickens's *Great Expectations* and William Thackeray's *Vanity Fair.*

Heath, Stephen, and Gillian Skirrow. "An Interview with Raymond Williams." In *Studies in Entertainment: Critical Approaches to Mass Culture,* edited by Tania Modleski, pp. 3-17. Bloomington: Indiana University Press, 1986.

> Interview with the author of *Television: Technology and Cultural Form* on the relation of television to the concepts of "mass" and "popular culture" and on the significance of the medium to the organization of modern society.

Holderness, Graham, and Christopher McCullough. "Shakespeare on the Screen: A Selective Filmography." *Shakespeare Survey: An Annual Survey of Shakespearean*

Study and Production 39 (1987): 13-37.
Lists "complete, straightforward versions of Shakespeare's plays in film, television, and video form."

Jameson, Fredric. "Reading without Interpretation: Postmodernism and the Video-Text." In *The Linguistics of Writing: Arguments between Language and Literature*, edited by Nigel Fabb, Derek Attridge, Alan Durant and Colin MacCabe, pp. 199-223. New York: Methuen, 1987.
Interprets the medium of video art as one that produces postmodern texts—those which resist traditional thematic interpretation.

Klaver, Elizabeth. "Samuel Beckett's *Ohio Impromptu*, *Quad*, and *What Where*: How It Is in the Matrix of Text and Television." *Contemporary Literature* 32, No. 3 (Fall 1991): 366-82.
Concentrates on the semiotic "tension between visual and verbal" associated with the translation of Beckett's narrative texts into video images.

Lachman, Marvin. "Prime Time Crime." *The Armchair Detective* 19, No. 4 (Fall 1986): 362-72.
Catalogues television series and adaptations based on mystery and detective fiction.

Larson, Randall D. *Films into Books: An Analytical Bibliography of Film Novelizations, Movie, and TV Tie-Ins*. Metuchen, N.J.: The Scarecrow Press, 1995, 608 p.
Bibliography of original novels derived from film and television. Larson includes an extensive introduction on the creation of novelizations and transcribes viewpoints offered by dozens of well-known authors of such works.

Stoneback, H. R. "Jeopardy in the Evening: For Whom the Telly Tolls." *The Hemingway Review* VIII, No. 2 (Spring 1989): 66-7.
Notes the appearance of questions pertaining to the life and works of Ernest Hemingway on the popular television game show *Jeopardy!*

Traub, James. "Intrigues of the Story Trade: How Mega-Books Become Mini-Series." *Channels of Communication* 4, No. 6 (March/April 1985): 22-6.
Investigates the big business of adapting popular contemporary novels for television's mass audiences.

Wade, David. "The Limits of the Electronic Media." *Times Literary Supplement* 71 (5 May 1972): 515-16.
Recounts the possible detrimental effects on literature of television and radio adaptation.

Widdowson, Peter. "'Tragedies of Modern Life'? Thomas Hardy on Radio, TV, and Film." In *Hardy in History: A Study of Literary Sociology*, pp. 93-126. London: Routledge, 1989.
Offers an interpretation of television and film versions of Hardy's works. Widdowson sees many of these as impressive pieces of historical realism that nevertheless fail to authentically re-create Hardy's "historical myth of Wessex."

Wright, Andrew. "Trollope Transformed; Or, The Disguises of Mr. Harding and Others." In *Victorian Literature and Society*, edited by James R. Kincaid and Albert J. Kuhn, pp. 315-30. Columbus: Ohio State University Press, 1984.
Evaluates the process of abridging and simplifying literary texts for mass consumption as television and film adaptations.

Twentieth-Century
Literary Criticism

Cumulative Indexes
Volumes 1-78

How to Use This Index

The main references

Calvino, Italo
1923–1985 .... CLC 5, 8, 11, 22, 33, 39,
73; SSC 3

list all author entries in the following Gale Literary Criticism series:

BLC = Black Literature Criticism
CLC = Contemporary Literary Criticism
CLR = Children's Literature Review
CMLC = Classical and Medieval Literature Criticism
DA = DISCovering Authors
DAB = DISCovering Authors: British
DAC = DISCovering Authors: Canadian
DAM = DISCovering Authors: Modules
    DRAM: Dramatists Module; MST: Most-Studied Authors Module;
    MULT: Multicultural Authors Module; NOV: Novelists Module;
    POET: Poets Module; POP: Popular Fiction and Genre Authors Module
DC = Drama Criticism
HLC = Hispanic Literature Criticism
LC = Literature Criticism from 1400 to 1800
NCLC = Nineteenth-Century Literature Criticism
PC = Poetry Criticism
SSC = Short Story Criticism
TCLC = Twentieth-Century Literary Criticism
WLC = World Literature Criticism, 1500 to the Present

The cross-references

See also CANR 23; CA 85-88;
  obituary CA116

list all author entries in the following Gale biographical and literary sources:

AAYA = Authors & Artists for Young Adults
AITN = Authors in the News
BEST = Bestsellers
BW = Black Writers
CA = Contemporary Authors
CAAS = Contemporary Authors Autobiography Series
CABS = Contemporary Authors Bibliographical Series
CANR = Contemporary Authors New Revision Series
CAP = Contemporary Authors Permanent Series
CDALB = Concise Dictionary of American Literary Biography
CDBLB = Concise Dictionary of British Literary Biography
DLB = Dictionary of Literary Biography
DLBD = Dictionary of Literary Biography Documentary Series
DLBY = Dictionary of Literary Biography Yearbook
HW = Hispanic Writers
JRDA = Junior DISCovering Authors
MAICYA = Major Authors and Illustrators for Children and Young Adults
MTCW = Major 20th-Century Writers
NNAL = Native North American Literature
SAAS = Something about the Author Autobiography Series
SATA = Something about the Author
YABC = Yesterday's Authors of Books for Children

Literary Criticism Series
Cumulative Author Index

Abasiyanik, Sait Faik 1906-1954
See Sait Faik
See also CA 123

Abbey, Edward 1927-1989 .... **CLC 36, 59**
See also CA 45-48; 128; CANR 2, 41

Abbott, Lee K(ittredge) 1947- .... **CLC 48**
See also CA 124; CANR 51; DLB 130

Abe, Kobo 1924-1993**CLC 8, 22, 53, 81; DAM NOV**
See also CA 65-68; 140; CANR 24, 60; DLB 182; MTCW

Abelard, Peter c. 1079-c. 1142 ...... **CMLC 11**
See also DLB 115

Abell, Kjeld 1901-1961 .... **CLC 15**
See also CA 111

Abish, Walter 1931- .... **CLC 22**
See also CA 101; CANR 37; DLB 130

Abrahams, Peter (Henry) 1919- .... **CLC 4**
See also BW 1; CA 57-60; CANR 26; DLB 117; MTCW

Abrams, M(eyer) H(oward) 1912- .... **CLC 24**
See also CA 57-60; CANR 13, 33; DLB 67

Abse, Dannie 1923- . **CLC 7, 29; DAB; DAM POET**
See also CA 53-56; CAAS 1; CANR 4, 46; DLB 27

Achebe, (Albert) Chinua(lumogu) 1930-**C L C 1, 3, 5, 7, 11, 26, 51, 75; BLC; DA; DAB; DAC; DAM MST, MULT, NOV; WLC**
See also AAYA 15; BW 2; CA 1-4R; CANR 6, 26, 47; CLR 20; DLB 117; MAICYA; MTCW; SATA 40; SATA-Brief 38

Acker, Kathy 1948- .... **CLC 45**
See also CA 117; 122; CANR 55

Ackroyd, Peter 1949-.................... **CLC 34, 52**
See also CA 123; 127; CANR 51; DLB 155; INT 127

Acorn, Milton 1923- .... **CLC 15; DAC**
See also CA 103; DLB 53; INT 103

Adamov, Arthur 1908-1970**CLC 4, 25; DAM DRAM**
See also CA 17-18; 25-28R; CAP 2; MTCW

Adams, Alice (Boyd) 1926-**CLC 6, 13, 46; SSC 24**
See also CA 81-84; CANR 26, 53; DLBY 86; INT CANR-26; MTCW

Adams, Andy 1859-1935 .... **TCLC 56**
See also YABC 1

Adams, Douglas (Noel) 1952- .... **CLC 27, 60; DAM POP**
See also AAYA 4; BEST 89:3; CA 106; CANR 34, 64; DLBY 83; JRDA

Adams, Francis 1862-1893 .... **NCLC 33**

Adams, Henry (Brooks) 1838-1918 **TCLC 4, 52; DA; DAB; DAC; DAM MST**
See also CA 104; 133; DLB 12, 47

Adams, Richard (George) 1920-**CLC 4, 5, 18; DAM NOV**
See also AAYA 16; AITN 1, 2; CA 49-52; CANR 3, 35; CLR 20; JRDA; MAICYA; MTCW; SATA 7, 69

Adamson, Joy(-Friederike Victoria) 1910-1980 **CLC 17**
See also CA 69-72; 93-96; CANR 22; MTCW; SATA 11; SATA-Obit 22

Adcock, Fleur 1934- .... **CLC 41**
See also CA 25-28R; CAAS 23; CANR 11, 34; DLB 40

Addams, Charles (Samuel) 1912-1988**CLC 30**
See also CA 61-64; 126; CANR 12

Addams, Jane 1860-1935 .... **TCLC 76**

Addison, Joseph 1672-1719 .... **LC 18**
See also CDBLB 1660-1789; DLB 101

Adler, Alfred (F.) 1870-1937 .... **TCLC 61**
See also CA 119; 159

Adler, C(arole) S(chwerdtfeger) 1932- . **C L C 35**
See also AAYA 4; CA 89-92; CANR 19, 40; JRDA; MAICYA; SAAS 15; SATA 26, 63

Adler, Renata 1938- .... **CLC 8, 31**
See also CA 49-52; CANR 5, 22, 52; MTCW

Ady, Endre 1877-1919 .... **TCLC 11**
See also CA 107

A.E. 1867-1935 .... **TCLC 3, 10**
See also Russell, George William

Aeschylus 525B.C.-456B.C. ..**CMLC 11; DA; DAB; DAC; DAM DRAM, MST; DC 8; WLCS**
See also DLB 176

Africa, Ben
See Bosman, Herman Charles

Afton, Effie
See Harper, Frances Ellen Watkins

Agapida, Fray Antonio
See Irving, Washington

Agee, James (Rufus) 1909-1955 **TCLC 1, 19; DAM NOV**
See also AITN 1; CA 108; 148; CDALB 1941-1968; DLB 2, 26, 152

Aghill, Gordon
See Silverberg, Robert

Agnon, S(hmuel) Y(osef Halevi) 1888-1970 **CLC 4, 8, 14; SSC 29**
See also CA 17-18; 25-28R; CANR 60; CAP 2; MTCW

Agrippa von Nettesheim, Henry Cornelius 1486-1535 .... **LC 27**

Aherne, Owen
See Cassill, R(onald) V(erlin)

Ai 1947- .... **CLC 4, 14, 69**
See also CA 85-88; CAAS 13; DLB 120

Aickman, Robert (Fordyce) 1914-1981 **C L C 57**
See also CA 5-8R; CANR 3

Aiken, Conrad (Potter) 1889-1973**CLC 1, 3, 5, 10, 52; DAM NOV, POET; SSC 9**
See also CA 5-8R; 45-48; CANR 4, 60; CDALB 1929-1941; DLB 9, 45, 102; MTCW; SATA 3, 30

Aiken, Joan (Delano) 1924- .... **CLC 35**
See also AAYA 1; CA 9-12R; CANR 4, 23, 34, 64; CLR 1, 19; DLB 161; JRDA; MAICYA; MTCW; SAAS 1; SATA 2, 30, 73

Ainsworth, William Harrison 1805-1882 **NCLC 13**
See also DLB 21; SATA 24

Aitmatov, Chingiz (Torekulovich) 1928-**C L C 71**
See also CA 103; CANR 38; MTCW; SATA 56

Akers, Floyd
See Baum, L(yman) Frank

Akhmadulina, Bella Akhatovna 1937-**CLC 53; DAM POET**
See also CA 65-68

Akhmatova, Anna 1888-1966**CLC 11, 25, 64; DAM POET; PC 2**
See also CA 19-20; 25-28R; CANR 35; CAP 1; MTCW

Aksakov, Sergei Timofeyvich 1791-1859 **NCLC 2**

Aksenov, Vassily
See Aksyonov, Vassily (Pavlovich)

Aksyonov, Vassily (Pavlovich) 1932-**CLC 22, 37, 101**
See also CA 53-56; CANR 12, 48

Akutagawa, Ryunosuke 1892-1927 **TCLC 16**
See also CA 117; 154

Alain 1868-1951 .... **TCLC 41**

Alain-Fournier .... **TCLC 6**
See also Fournier, Henri Alban
See also DLB 65

Alarcon, Pedro Antonio de 1833-1891**NCLC 1**

Alas (y Urena), Leopoldo (Enrique Garcia) 1852-1901 .... **TCLC 29**
See also CA 113; 131; HW

Albee, Edward (Franklin III) 1928-**CLC 1, 2, 3, 5, 9, 11, 13, 25, 53, 86; DA; DAB; DAC; DAM DRAM, MST; WLC**
See also AITN 1; CA 5-8R; CABS 3; CANR 8, 54; CDALB 1941-1968; DLB 7; INT CANR-8; MTCW

Alberti, Rafael 1902- .... **CLC 7**
See also CA 85-88; DLB 108

Albert the Great 1200(?)-1280 ...... **CMLC 16**
See also DLB 115

Alcala-Galiano, Juan Valera y
See Valera y Alcala-Galiano, Juan

Alcott, Amos Bronson 1799-1888 .... **NCLC 1**
See also DLB 1

Alcott, Louisa May 1832-1888 . **NCLC 6, 58; DA; DAB; DAC; DAM MST, NOV; SSC 27; WLC**
See also AAYA 20; CDALB 1865-1917; CLR 1, 38; DLB 1, 42, 79; DLBD 14; JRDA;

MAICYA; YABC 1

Aldanov, M. A.
See Aldanov, Mark (Alexandrovich)

Aldanov, Mark (Alexandrovich) 1886(?)-1957
TCLC 23
See also CA 118

Aldington, Richard 1892-1962 .... **CLC 49**
See also CA 85-88; CANR 45; DLB 20, 36, 100, 149

Aldiss, Brian W(ilson) 1925- . **CLC 5, 14, 40; DAM NOV**
See also CA 5-8R; CAAS 2; CANR 5, 28, 64; DLB 14; MTCW; SATA 34

Alegria, Claribel 1924- **CLC 75; DAM MULT**
See also CA 131; CAAS 15; DLB 145; HW

Alegria, Fernando 1918- .... **CLC 57**
See also CA 9-12R; CANR 5, 32; HW

Aleichem, Sholom .... **TCLC 1, 35**
See also Rabinovitch, Sholem

Aleixandre, Vicente 1898-1984 ... **CLC 9, 36; DAM POET; PC 15**
See also CA 85-88; 114; CANR 26; DLB 108; HW; MTCW

Alepoudelis, Odysseus
See Elytis, Odysseus

Aleshkovsky, Joseph 1929-
See Aleshkovsky, Yuz
See also CA 121; 128

Aleshkovsky, Yuz .... **CLC 44**
See also Aleshkovsky, Joseph

Alexander, Lloyd (Chudley) 1924- ... **CLC 35**
See also AAYA 1; CA 1-4R; CANR 1, 24, 38, 55; CLR 1, 5, 48; DLB 52; JRDA; MAICYA; MTCW; SAAS 19; SATA 3, 49, 81

Alexander, Samuel 1859-1938 .... **TCLC 77**

Alexie, Sherman (Joseph, Jr.) 1966- **CLC 96; DAM MULT**
See also CA 138; DLB 175; NNAL

Alfau, Felipe 1902- .... **CLC 66**
See also CA 137

Alger, Horatio, Jr. 1832-1899 .... **NCLC 8**
See also DLB 42; SATA 16

Algren, Nelson 1909-1981 .... **CLC 4, 10, 33**
See also CA 13-16R; 103; CANR 20, 61; CDALB 1941-1968; DLB 9; DLBY 81, 82; MTCW

Ali, Ahmed 1910- .... **CLC 69**
See also CA 25-28R; CANR 15, 34

Alighieri, Dante
See Dante

Allan, John B.
See Westlake, Donald E(dwin)

Allan, Sidney
See Hartmann, Sadakichi

Allan, Sydney
See Hartmann, Sadakichi

Allen, Edward 1948- .... **CLC 59**

Allen, Paula Gunn 1939- .... **CLC 84; DAM MULT**
See also CA 112; 143; CANR 63; DLB 175; NNAL

Allen, Roland
See Ayckbourn, Alan

Allen, Sarah A.
See Hopkins, Pauline Elizabeth

Allen, Sidney H.
See Hartmann, Sadakichi

Allen, Woody 1935- **CLC 16, 52; DAM POP**
See also AAYA 10; CA 33-36R; CANR 27, 38, 63; DLB 44; MTCW

Allende, Isabel 1942- . **CLC 39, 57, 97; DAM MULT, NOV; HLC; WLCS**
See also AAYA 18; CA 125; 130; CANR 51;

DLB 145; HW; INT 130; MTCW

Alleyn, Ellen
See Rossetti, Christina (Georgina)

Allingham, Margery (Louise) 1904-1966 **CLC 19**
See also CA 5-8R; 25-28R; CANR 4, 58; DLB 77; MTCW

Allingham, William 1824-1889 ...... **NCLC 25**
See also DLB 35

Allison, Dorothy E. 1949- .... **CLC 78**
See also CA 140

Allston, Washington 1779-1843 .... **NCLC 2**
See also DLB 1

Almedingen, E. M. .... **CLC 12**
See also Almedingen, Martha Edith von
See also SATA 3

Almedingen, Martha Edith von 1898-1971
See Almedingen, E. M.
See also CA 1-4R; CANR 1

Almqvist, Carl Jonas Love 1793-1866 **NCLC 42**

Alonso, Damaso 1898-1990 .... **CLC 14**
See also CA 110; 131; 130; DLB 108; HW

Alov
See Gogol, Nikolai (Vasilyevich)

Alta 1942- .... **CLC 19**
See also CA 57-60

Alter, Robert B(ernard) 1935- .... **CLC 34**
See also CA 49-52; CANR 1, 47

Alther, Lisa 1944- .... **CLC 7, 41**
See also CA 65-68; CANR 12, 30, 51; MTCW

Althusser, L.
See Althusser, Louis

Althusser, Louis 1918-1990 .... **CLC 106**
See also CA 131; 132

Altman, Robert 1925- .... **CLC 16**
See also CA 73-76; CANR 43

Alvarez, A(lfred) 1929- .... **CLC 5, 13**
See also CA 1-4R; CANR 3, 33, 63; DLB 14, 40

Alvarez, Alejandro Rodriguez 1903-1965
See Casona, Alejandro
See also CA 131; 93-96; HW

Alvarez, Julia 1950- .... **CLC 93**
See also CA 147

Alvaro, Corrado 1896-1956 .... **TCLC 60**

Amado, Jorge 1912- **CLC 13, 40, 106; DAM MULT, NOV; HLC**
See also CA 77-80; CANR 35; DLB 113; MTCW

Ambler, Eric 1909- .... **CLC 4, 6, 9**
See also CA 9-12R; CANR 7, 38; DLB 77; MTCW

Amichai, Yehuda 1924- .... **CLC 9, 22, 57**
See also CA 85-88; CANR 46, 60; MTCW

Amichai, Yehudah
See Amichai, Yehuda

Amiel, Henri Frederic 1821-1881 .... **NCLC 4**

Amis, Kingsley (William) 1922-1995 **CLC 1, 2, 3, 5, 8, 13, 40, 44; DA; DAB; DAC; DAM MST, NOV**
See also AITN 2; CA 9-12R; 150; CANR 8, 28, 54; CDBLB 1945-1960; DLB 15, 27, 100, 139; DLBY 96; INT CANR-8; MTCW

Amis, Martin (Louis) 1949- **CLC 4, 9, 38, 62, 101**
See also BEST 90:3; CA 65-68; CANR 8, 27, 54; DLB 14; INT CANR-27

Ammons, A(rchie) R(andolph) 1926- **CLC 2, 3, 5, 8, 9, 25, 57, 108; DAM POET; PC 16**
See also AITN 1; CA 9-12R; CANR 6, 36, 51; DLB 5, 165; MTCW

Amo, Tauraatua i

See Adams, Henry (Brooks)

Anand, Mulk Raj 1905- .. **CLC 23, 93; DAM NOV**
See also CA 65-68; CANR 32, 64; MTCW

Anatol
See Schnitzler, Arthur

Anaximander c. 610B.C.-c. 546B.C. **CMLC 22**

Anaya, Rudolfo A(lfonso) 1937- ..... **CLC 23; DAM MULT, NOV; HLC**
See also AAYA 20; CA 45-48; CAAS 4; CANR 1, 32, 51; DLB 82; HW 1; MTCW

Andersen, Hans Christian 1805-1875 **NCLC 7; DA; DAB; DAC; DAM MST, POP; SSC 6; WLC**
See also CLR 6; MAICYA; YABC 1

Anderson, C. Farley
See Mencken, H(enry) L(ouis); Nathan, George Jean

Anderson, Jessica (Margaret) Queale 1916-
CLC 37
See also CA 9-12R; CANR 4, 62

Anderson, Jon (Victor) 1940- .. **CLC 9; DAM POET**
See also CA 25-28R; CANR 20

Anderson, Lindsay (Gordon) 1923-1994 **CLC 20**
See also CA 125; 128; 146

Anderson, Maxwell 1888-1959 **TCLC 2; DAM DRAM**
See also CA 105; 152; DLB 7

Anderson, Poul (William) 1926- .... **CLC 15**
See also AAYA 5; CA 1-4R; CAAS 2; CANR 2, 15, 34, 64; DLB 8; INT CANR-15; MTCW; SATA 90; SATA-Brief 39

Anderson, Robert (Woodruff) 1917- **CLC 23; DAM DRAM**
See also AITN 1; CA 21-24R; CANR 32; DLB 7

Anderson, Sherwood 1876-1941 **TCLC 1, 10, 24; DA; DAB; DAC; DAM MST, NOV; SSC 1; WLC**
See also CA 104; 121; CANR 61; CDALB 1917-1929; DLB 4, 9, 86; DLBD 1; MTCW

Andier, Pierre
See Desnos, Robert

Andouard
See Giraudoux, (Hippolyte) Jean

Andrade, Carlos Drummond de .... **CLC 18**
See also Drummond de Andrade, Carlos

Andrade, Mario de 1893-1945 .... **TCLC 43**

Andreae, Johann V(alentin) 1586-1654 **LC 32**
See also DLB 164

Andreas-Salome, Lou 1861-1937 ... **TCLC 56**
See also DLB 66

Andress, Lesley
See Sanders, Lawrence

Andrewes, Lancelot 1555-1626 .... **LC 5**
See also DLB 151, 172

Andrews, Cicily Fairfield
See West, Rebecca

Andrews, Elton V.
See Pohl, Frederik

Andreyev, Leonid (Nikolaevich) 1871-1919
TCLC 3
See also CA 104

Andric, Ivo 1892-1975 .... **CLC 8**
See also CA 81-84; 57-60; CANR 43, 60; DLB 147; MTCW

Androvar
See Prado (Calvo), Pedro

Angelique, Pierre
See Bataille, Georges

Angell, Roger 1920- .... **CLC 26**

See also CA 57-60; CANR 13, 44; DLB 171

Angelou, Maya 1928-**CLC 12, 35, 64, 77; BLC; DA; DAB; DAC; DAM MST, MULT, POET, POP; WLCS**
See also AAYA 7, 20; BW 2; CA 65-68; CANR 19, 42; DLB 38; MTCW; SATA 49

Anna Comnena 1083-1153 .... **CMLC 25**

Annensky, Innokenty (Fyodorovich) 1856-1909 **TCLC 14**
See also CA 110; 155

Annunzio, Gabriele d'
See D'Annunzio, Gabriele

Anodos
See Coleridge, Mary E(lizabeth)

Anon, Charles Robert
See Pessoa, Fernando (Antonio Nogueira)

Anouilh, Jean (Marie Lucien Pierre) 1910-1987 **CLC 1, 3, 8, 13, 40, 50; DAM DRAM; DC 8**
See also CA 17-20R; 123; CANR 32; MTCW

Anthony, Florence
See Ai

Anthony, John
See Ciardi, John (Anthony)

Anthony, Peter
See Shaffer, Anthony (Joshua); Shaffer, Peter (Levin)

Anthony, Piers 1934- .... **CLC 35; DAM POP**
See also AAYA 11; CA 21-24R; CANR 28, 56; DLB 8; MTCW; SAAS 22; SATA 84

Antoine, Marc
See Proust, (Valentin-Louis-George-Eugene-) Marcel

Antoninus, Brother
See Everson, William (Oliver)

Antonioni, Michelangelo 1912- .... **CLC 20**
See also CA 73-76; CANR 45

Antschel, Paul 1920-1970
See Celan, Paul
See also CA 85-88; CANR 33, 61; MTCW

Anwar, Chairil 1922-1949 .... **TCLC 22**
See also CA 121

Apollinaire, Guillaume 1880-1918**TCLC 3, 8, 51; DAM POET; PC 7**
See also Kostrowitzki, Wilhelm Apollinaris de
See also CA 152

Appelfeld, Aharon 1932- .... **CLC 23, 47**
See also CA 112; 133

Apple, Max (Isaac) 1941-............... **CLC 9, 33**
See also CA 81-84; CANR 19, 54; DLB 130

Appleman, Philip (Dean) 1926- .... **CLC 51**
See also CA 13-16R; CAAS 18; CANR 6, 29, 56

Appleton, Lawrence
See Lovecraft, H(oward) P(hillips)

Apteryx
See Eliot, T(homas) S(tearns)

Apuleius, (Lucius Madaurensis) 125(?)-175(?) **CMLC 1**

Aquin, Hubert 1929-1977 .... **CLC 15**
See also CA 105; DLB 53

Aragon, Louis 1897-1982 .. **CLC 3, 22; DAM NOV, POET**
See also CA 69-72; 108; CANR 28; DLB 72; MTCW

Arany, Janos 1817-1882 .... **NCLC 34**

Arbuthnot, John 1667-1735 .... **LC 1**
See also DLB 101

Archer, Herbert Winslow
See Mencken, H(enry) L(ouis)

Archer, Jeffrey (Howard) 1940- ..... **CLC 28; DAM POP**
See also AAYA 16; BEST 89:3; CA 77-80;

CANR 22, 52; INT CANR-22

Archer, Jules 1915- .... **CLC 12**
See also CA 9-12R; CANR 6; SAAS 5; SATA 4, 85

Archer, Lee
See Ellison, Harlan (Jay)

Arden, John 1930-**CLC 6, 13, 15; DAM DRAM**
See also CA 13-16R; CAAS 4; CANR 31; DLB 13; MTCW

Arenas, Reinaldo 1943-1990 . **CLC 41; DAM MULT; HLC**
See also CA 124; 128; 133; DLB 145; HW

Arendt, Hannah 1906-1975 .... **CLC 66, 98**
See also CA 17-20R; 61-64; CANR 26, 60; MTCW

Aretino, Pietro 1492-1556 ....**LC 12**

Arghezi, Tudor ....**CLC 80**
See also Theodorescu, Ion N.

Arguedas, Jose Maria 1911-1969 **CLC 10, 18**
See also CA 89-92; DLB 113; HW

Argueta, Manlio 1936- .... **CLC 31**
See also CA 131; DLB 145; HW

Ariosto, Ludovico 1474-1533 .... **LC 6**

Aristides
See Epstein, Joseph

Aristophanes 450B.C.-385B.C.**CMLC 4; DA; DAB; DAC; DAM DRAM, MST; DC 2; WLCS**
See also DLB 176

Arlt, Roberto (Godofredo Christophersen) 1900-1942**TCLC 29; DAM MULT; HLC**
See also CA 123; 131; HW

Armah, Ayi Kwei 1939-**CLC 5, 33; BLC; DAM MULT, POET**
See also BW 1; CA 61-64; CANR 21, 64; DLB 117; MTCW

Armatrading, Joan 1950- .... **CLC 17**
See also CA 114

Arnette, Robert
See Silverberg, Robert

Arnim, Achim von (Ludwig Joachim von Arnim) 1781-1831 ...... **NCLC 5; SSC 29**
See also DLB 90

Arnim, Bettina von 1785-1859 .... **NCLC 38**
See also DLB 90

Arnold, Matthew 1822-1888**NCLC 6, 29; DA; DAB; DAC; DAM MST, POET; PC 5; WLC**
See also CDBLB 1832-1890; DLB 32, 57

Arnold, Thomas 1795-1842 .... **NCLC 18**
See also DLB 55

Arnow, Harriette (Louisa) Simpson 1908-1986 **CLC 2, 7, 18**
See also CA 9-12R; 118; CANR 14; DLB 6; MTCW; SATA 42; SATA-Obit 47

Arp, Hans
See Arp, Jean

Arp, Jean 1887-1966 .... **CLC 5**
See also CA 81-84; 25-28R; CANR 42

Arrabal
See Arrabal, Fernando

Arrabal, Fernando 1932-.... **CLC 2, 9, 18, 58**
See also CA 9-12R; CANR 15

Arrick, Fran .... **CLC 30**
See also Gaberman, Judie Angell

Artaud, Antonin (Marie Joseph) 1896-1948 **TCLC 3, 36; DAM DRAM**
See also CA 104; 149

Arthur, Ruth M(abel) 1905-1979 ...... **CLC 12**
See also CA 9-12R; 85-88; CANR 4; SATA 7, 26

Artsybashev, Mikhail (Petrovich) 1878-1927 **TCLC 31**

Arundel, Honor (Morfydd) 1919-1973**CLC 17**
See also CA 21-22; 41-44R; CAP 2; CLR 35; SATA 4; SATA-Obit 24

Arzner, Dorothy 1897-1979 .... **CLC 98**

Asch, Sholem 1880-1957 .... **TCLC 3**
See also CA 105

Ash, Shalom
See Asch, Sholem

Ashbery, John (Lawrence) 1927-**CLC 2, 3, 4, 6, 9, 13, 15, 25, 41, 77; DAM POET**
See also CA 5-8R; CANR 9, 37; DLB 5, 165; DLBY 81; INT CANR-9; MTCW

Ashdown, Clifford
See Freeman, R(ichard) Austin

Ashe, Gordon
See Creasey, John

Ashton-Warner, Sylvia (Constance) 1908-1984 **CLC 19**
See also CA 69-72; 112; CANR 29; MTCW

Asimov, Isaac 1920-1992 **CLC 1, 3, 9, 19, 26, 76, 92; DAM POP**
See also AAYA 13; BEST 90:2; CA 1-4R; 137; CANR 2, 19, 36, 60; CLR 12; DLB 8; DLBY 92; INT CANR-19; JRDA; MAICYA; MTCW; SATA 1, 26, 74

Assis, Joaquim Maria Machado de
See Machado de Assis, Joaquim Maria

Astley, Thea (Beatrice May) 1925- ... **CLC 41**
See also CA 65-68; CANR 11, 43

Aston, James
See White, T(erence) H(anbury)

Asturias, Miguel Angel 1899-1974 **CLC 3, 8, 13; DAM MULT, NOV; HLC**
See also CA 25-28; 49-52; CANR 32; CAP 2; DLB 113; HW; MTCW

Atares, Carlos Saura
See Saura (Atares), Carlos

Atheling, William
See Pound, Ezra (Weston Loomis)

Atheling, William, Jr.
See Blish, James (Benjamin)

Atherton, Gertrude (Franklin Horn) 1857-1948 **TCLC 2**
See also CA 104; 155; DLB 9, 78, 186

Atherton, Lucius
See Masters, Edgar Lee

Atkins, Jack
See Harris, Mark

Atkinson, Kate .... **CLC 99**

Attaway, William (Alexander) 1911-1986 **CLC 92; BLC; DAM MULT**
See also BW 2; CA 143; DLB 76

Atticus
See Fleming, Ian (Lancaster)

Atwood, Margaret (Eleanor) 1939-**CLC 2, 3, 4, 8, 13, 15, 25, 44, 84; DA; DAB; DAC; DAM MST, NOV, POET; PC 8; SSC 2; WLC**
See also AAYA 12; BEST 89:2; CA 49-52; CANR 3, 24, 33, 59; DLB 53; INT CANR-24; MTCW; SATA 50

Aubigny, Pierre d'
See Mencken, H(enry) L(ouis)

Aubin, Penelope 1685-1731(?) .... **LC 9**
See also DLB 39

Auchincloss, Louis (Stanton) 1917-**CLC 4, 6, 9, 18, 45; DAM NOV; SSC 22**
See also CA 1-4R; CANR 6, 29, 55; DLB 2; DLBY 80; INT CANR-29; MTCW

Auden, W(ystan) H(ugh) 1907-1973**CLC 1, 2, 3, 4, 6, 9, 11, 14, 43; DA; DAB; DAC; DAM DRAM, MST, POET; PC 1; WLC**
See also AAYA 18; CA 9-12R; 45-48; CANR

5, 61; CDBLB 1914-1945; DLB 10, 20; MTCW

Audiberti, Jacques 1900-1965 **CLC 38; DAM DRAM**
See also CA 25-28R

Audubon, John James 1785-1851 .. **NCLC 47**

Auel, Jean M(arie) 1936- **CLC 31, 107; DAM POP**
See also AAYA 7; BEST 90:4; CA 103; CANR 21, 64; INT CANR-21; SATA 91

Auerbach, Erich 1892-1957 .... **TCLC 43**
See also CA 118; 155

Augier, Emile 1820-1889 .... **NCLC 31**

August, John
See De Voto, Bernard (Augustine)

Augustine, St. 354-430 .... **CMLC 6; DAB**

Aurelius
See Bourne, Randolph S(illiman)

Aurobindo, Sri 1872-1950 .... **TCLC 63**

Austen, Jane 1775-1817 **NCLC 1, 13, 19, 33, 51; DA; DAB; DAC; DAM MST, NOV; WLC**
See also AAYA 19; CDBLB 1789-1832; DLB 116

Auster, Paul 1947- .... **CLC 47**
See also CA 69-72; CANR 23, 52

Austin, Frank
See Faust, Frederick (Schiller)

Austin, Mary (Hunter) 1868-1934 . **TCLC 25**
See also CA 109; DLB 9, 78

Autran Dourado, Waldomiro
See Dourado, (Waldomiro Freitas) Autran

Averroes 1126-1198 .... **CMLC 7**
See also DLB 115

Avicenna 980-1037 .... **CMLC 16**
See also DLB 115

Avison, Margaret 1918- **CLC 2, 4, 97; DAC; DAM POET**
See also CA 17-20R; DLB 53; MTCW

Axton, David
See Koontz, Dean R(ay)

Ayckbourn, Alan 1939- **CLC 5, 8, 18, 33, 74; DAB; DAM DRAM**
See also CA 21-24R; CANR 31, 59; DLB 13; MTCW

Aydy, Catherine
See Tennant, Emma (Christina)

Ayme, Marcel (Andre) 1902-1967 .... **CLC 11**
See also CA 89-92; CLR 25; DLB 72; SATA 91

Ayrton, Michael 1921-1975 .... **CLC 7**
See also CA 5-8R; 61-64; CANR 9, 21

Azorin .... **CLC 11**
See also Martinez Ruiz, Jose

Azuela, Mariano 1873-1952 . **TCLC 3; DAM MULT; HLC**
See also CA 104; 131; HW; MTCW

Baastad, Babbis Friis
See Friis-Baastad, Babbis Ellinor

Bab
See Gilbert, W(illiam) S(chwenck)

Babbis, Eleanor
See Friis-Baastad, Babbis Ellinor

Babel, Isaac
See Babel, Isaak (Emmanuilovich)

Babel, Isaak (Emmanuilovich) 1894-1941(?) **TCLC 2, 13; SSC 16**
See also CA 104; 155

Babits, Mihaly 1883-1941 .... **TCLC 14**
See also CA 114

Babur 1483-1530 .... **LC 18**

Bacchelli, Riccardo 1891-1985 .... **CLC 19**
See also CA 29-32R; 117

Bach, Richard (David) 1936- **CLC 14; DAM**

NOV, POP
See also AITN 1; BEST 89:2; CA 9-12R; CANR 18; MTCW; SATA 13

Bachman, Richard
See King, Stephen (Edwin)

Bachmann, Ingeborg 1926-1973 .... **CLC 69**
See also CA 93-96; 45-48; DLB 85

Bacon, Francis 1561-1626 .... **LC 18, 32**
See also CDBLB Before 1660; DLB 151

Bacon, Roger 1214(?)-1292 .... **CMLC 14**
See also DLB 115

Bacovia, George .... **TCLC 24**
See also Vasiliu, Gheorghe

Badanes, Jerome 1937- .... **CLC 59**

Bagehot, Walter 1826-1877 .... **NCLC 10**
See also DLB 55

Bagnold, Enid 1889-1981 .... **CLC 25; DAM DRAM**
See also CA 5-8R; 103; CANR 5, 40; DLB 13, 160; MAICYA; SATA 1, 25

Bagritsky, Eduard 1895-1934 .... **TCLC 60**

Bagrjana, Elisaveta
See Belcheva, Elisaveta

Bagryana, Elisaveta .... **CLC 10**
See also Belcheva, Elisaveta
See also DLB 147

Bailey, Paul 1937- .... **CLC 45**
See also CA 21-24R; CANR 16, 62; DLB 14

Baillie, Joanna 1762-1851 .... **NCLC 2**
See also DLB 93

Bainbridge, Beryl (Margaret) 1933- **CLC 4, 5, 8, 10, 14, 18, 22, 62; DAM NOV**
See also CA 21-24R; CANR 24, 55; DLB 14; MTCW

Baker, Elliott 1922- .... **CLC 8**
See also CA 45-48; CANR 2, 63

Baker, Jean H. .... **TCLC 3, 10**
See also Russell, George William

Baker, Nicholson 1957- **CLC 61; DAM POP**
See also CA 135; CANR 63

Baker, Ray Stannard 1870-1946 .... **TCLC 47**
See also CA 118

Baker, Russell (Wayne) 1925- .... **CLC 31**
See also BEST 89:4; CA 57-60; CANR 11, 41, 59; MTCW

Bakhtin, M.
See Bakhtin, Mikhail Mikhailovich

Bakhtin, M. M.
See Bakhtin, Mikhail Mikhailovich

Bakhtin, Mikhail
See Bakhtin, Mikhail Mikhailovich

Bakhtin, Mikhail Mikhailovich 1895-1975 **CLC 83**
See also CA 128; 113

Bakshi, Ralph 1938(?)- .... **CLC 26**
See also CA 112; 138

Bakunin, Mikhail (Alexandrovich) 1814-1876 **NCLC 25, 58**

Baldwin, James (Arthur) 1924-1987 **CLC 1, 2, 3, 4, 5, 8, 13, 15, 17, 42, 50, 67, 90; BLC; DA; DAB; DAC; DAM MST, MULT, NOV, POP; DC 1; SSC 10; WLC**
See also AAYA 4; BW 1; CA 1-4R; 124; CABS 1; CANR 3, 24; CDALB 1941-1968; DLB 2, 7, 33; DLBY 87; MTCW; SATA 9; SATA-Obit 54

Ballard, J(ames) G(raham) 1930- **CLC 3, 6, 14, 36; DAM NOV, POP; SSC 1**
See also AAYA 3; CA 5-8R; CANR 15, 39; DLB 14; MTCW; SATA 93

Balmont, Konstantin (Dmitriyevich) 1867-1943 **TCLC 11**
See also CA 109; 155

Balzac, Honore de 1799-1850 **NCLC 5, 35, 53; DA; DAB; DAC; DAM MST, NOV; SSC 5; WLC**
See also DLB 119

Bambara, Toni Cade 1939-1995 **CLC 19, 88; BLC; DA; DAC; DAM MST, MULT; WLCS**
See also AAYA 5; BW 2; CA 29-32R; 150; CANR 24, 49; DLB 38; MTCW

Bamdad, A.
See Shamlu, Ahmad

Banat, D. R.
See Bradbury, Ray (Douglas)

Bancroft, Laura
See Baum, L(yman) Frank

Banim, John 1798-1842 .... **NCLC 13**
See also DLB 116, 158, 159

Banim, Michael 1796-1874 .... **NCLC 13**
See also DLB 158, 159

Banjo, The
See Paterson, A(ndrew) B(arton)

Banks, Iain
See Banks, Iain M(enzies)

Banks, Iain M(enzies) 1954- .... **CLC 34**
See also CA 123; 128; CANR 61; INT 128

Banks, Lynne Reid .... **CLC 23**
See also Reid Banks, Lynne
See also AAYA 6

Banks, Russell 1940- .... **CLC 37, 72**
See also CA 65-68; CAAS 15; CANR 19, 52; DLB 130

Banville, John 1945- .... **CLC 46**
See also CA 117; 128; DLB 14; INT 128

Banville, Theodore (Faullain) de 1832-1891 **NCLC 9**

Baraka, Amiri 1934- **CLC 1, 2, 3, 5, 10, 14, 33; BLC; DA; DAC; DAM MST, MULT, POET, POP; DC 6; PC 4; WLCS**
See also Jones, LeRoi
See also BW 2; CA 21-24R; CABS 3; CANR 27, 38, 61; CDALB 1941-1968; DLB 5, 7, 16, 38; DLBD 8; MTCW

Barbauld, Anna Laetitia 1743-1825 **NCLC 50**
See also DLB 107, 109, 142, 158

Barbellion, W. N. P. .... **TCLC 24**
See also Cummings, Bruce F(rederick)

Barbera, Jack (Vincent) 1945- .... **CLC 44**
See also CA 110; CANR 45

Barbey d'Aurevilly, Jules Amedee 1808-1889 **NCLC 1; SSC 17**
See also DLB 119

Barbusse, Henri 1873-1935 .... **TCLC 5**
See also CA 105; 154; DLB 65

Barclay, Bill
See Moorcock, Michael (John)

Barclay, William Ewert
See Moorcock, Michael (John)

Barea, Arturo 1897-1957 .... **TCLC 14**
See also CA 111

Barfoot, Joan 1946- .... **CLC 18**
See also CA 105

Baring, Maurice 1874-1945 .... **TCLC 8**
See also CA 105; DLB 34

Barker, Clive 1952- .... **CLC 52; DAM POP**
See also AAYA 10; BEST 90:3; CA 121; 129; INT 129; MTCW

Barker, George Granville 1913-1991 **CLC 8, 48; DAM POET**
See also CA 9-12R; 135; CANR 7, 38; DLB 20; MTCW

Barker, Harley Granville
See Granville-Barker, Harley
See also DLB 10

Barker, Howard 1946- .... **CLC 37**
     See also CA 102; DLB 13
Barker, Pat(ricia) 1943- .... **CLC 32, 94**
     See also CA 117; 122; CANR 50; INT 122
Barlow, Joel 1754-1812 .... **NCLC 23**
     See also DLB 37
Barnard, Mary (Ethel) 1909- .... **CLC 48**
     See also CA 21-22; CAP 2
Barnes, Djuna 1892-1982 **CLC 3, 4, 8, 11, 29;**
     SSC 3
     See also CA 9-12R; 107; CANR 16, 55; DLB
     4, 9, 45; MTCW
Barnes, Julian (Patrick) 1946- **CLC 42; DAB**
     See also CA 102; CANR 19, 54; DLBY 93
Barnes, Peter 1931- .... **CLC 5, 56**
     See also CA 65-68; CAAS 12; CANR 33, 34,
     64; DLB 13; MTCW
Baroja (y Nessi), Pio 1872-1956 **TCLC 8; HLC**
     See also CA 104
Baron, David
     See Pinter, Harold
Baron Corvo
     See Rolfe, Frederick (William Serafino Austin
     Lewis Mary)
Barondess, Sue K(aufman) 1926-1977 **CLC 8**
     See also Kaufman, Sue
     See also CA 1-4R; 69-72; CANR 1
Baron de Teive
     See Pessoa, Fernando (Antonio Nogueira)
Barres, Maurice 1862-1923 .... **TCLC 47**
     See also DLB 123
Barreto, Afonso Henrique de Lima
     See Lima Barreto, Afonso Henrique de
Barrett, (Roger) Syd 1946- .... **CLC 35**
Barrett, William (Christopher) 1913-1992
     CLC 27
     See also CA 13-16R; 139; CANR 11; INT
     CANR-11
Barrie, J(ames) M(atthew) 1860-1937 **T C L C**
     2; DAB; DAM DRAM
     See also CA 104; 136; CDBLB 1890-1914;
     CLR 16; DLB 10, 141, 156; MAICYA;
     YABC 1
Barrington, Michael
     See Moorcock, Michael (John)
Barrol, Grady
     See Bograd, Larry
Barry, Mike
     See Malzberg, Barry N(athaniel)
Barry, Philip 1896-1949 .... **TCLC 11**
     See also CA 109; DLB 7
Bart, Andre Schwarz
     See Schwarz-Bart, Andre
Barth, John (Simmons) 1930- **CLC 1, 2, 3, 5, 7,**
     9, 10, 14, 27, 51, 89; DAM NOV; SSC 10
     See also AITN 1, 2; CA 1-4R; CABS 1; CANR
     5, 23, 49, 64; DLB 2; MTCW
Barthelme, Donald 1931-1989 **CLC 1, 2, 3, 5, 6,**
     8, 13, 23, 46, 59; DAM NOV; SSC 2
     See also CA 21-24R; 129; CANR 20, 58; DLB
     2; DLBY 80, 89; MTCW; SATA 7; SATA-
     Obit 62
Barthelme, Frederick 1943- .... **CLC 36**
     See also CA 114; 122; DLBY 85; INT 122
Barthes, Roland (Gerard) 1915-1980 **CLC 24,**
     83
     See also CA 130; 97-100; MTCW
Barzun, Jacques (Martin) 1907- .... **CLC 51**
     See also CA 61-64; CANR 22
Bashevis, Isaac
     See Singer, Isaac Bashevis
Bashkirtseff, Marie 1859-1884 ...... **NCLC 27**
Basho

See Matsuo Basho
Bass, Kingsley B., Jr.
     See Bullins, Ed
Bass, Rick 1958- .... **CLC 79**
     See also CA 126; CANR 53
Bassani, Giorgio 1916- .... **CLC 9**
     See also CA 65-68; CANR 33; DLB 128, 177;
     MTCW
Bastos, Augusto (Antonio) Roa
     See Roa Bastos, Augusto (Antonio)
Bataille, Georges 1897-1962 .... **CLC 29**
     See also CA 101; 89-92
Bates, H(erbert) E(rnest) 1905-1974 **CLC 46;**
     DAB; DAM POP; SSC 10
     See also CA 93-96; 45-48; CANR 34; DLB 162;
     MTCW
Bauchart
     See Camus, Albert
Baudelaire, Charles 1821-1867 . **NCLC 6, 29,**
     55; DA; DAB; DAC; DAM MST, POET;
     PC 1; SSC 18; WLC
Baudrillard, Jean 1929- .... **CLC 60**
Baum, L(yman) Frank 1856-1919 ... **TCLC 7**
     See also CA 108; 133; CLR 15; DLB 22; JRDA;
     MAICYA; MTCW; SATA 18
Baum, Louis F.
     See Baum, L(yman) Frank
Baumbach, Jonathan 1933- .... **CLC 6, 23**
     See also CA 13-16R; CAAS 5; CANR 12;
     DLBY 80; INT CANR-12; MTCW
Bausch, Richard (Carl) 1945- .... **CLC 51**
     See also CA 101; CAAS 14; CANR 43, 61; DLB
     130
Baxter, Charles (Morley) 1947- **CLC 45, 78;**
     DAM POP
     See also CA 57-60; CANR 40, 64; DLB 130
Baxter, George Owen
     See Faust, Frederick (Schiller)
Baxter, James K(eir) 1926-1972 .... **CLC 14**
     See also CA 77-80
Baxter, John
     See Hunt, E(verette) Howard, (Jr.)
Bayer, Sylvia
     See Glassco, John
Baynton, Barbara 1857-1929 .... **TCLC 57**
Beagle, Peter S(oyer) 1939- .... **CLC 7, 104**
     See also CA 9-12R; CANR 4, 51; DLBY 80;
     INT CANR-4; SATA 60
Bean, Normal
     See Burroughs, Edgar Rice
Beard, Charles A(ustin) 1874-1948 **TCLC 15**
     See also CA 115; DLB 17; SATA 18
Beardsley, Aubrey 1872-1898 .... **NCLC 6**
Beattie, Ann 1947- **CLC 8, 13, 18, 40, 63; DAM**
     NOV, POP; SSC 11
     See also BEST 90:2; CA 81-84; CANR 53;
     DLBY 82; MTCW
Beattie, James 1735-1803 .... **NCLC 25**
     See also DLB 109
Beauchamp, Kathleen Mansfield 1888-1923
     See Mansfield, Katherine
     See also CA 104; 134; DA; DAC; DAM MST
Beaumarchais, Pierre-Augustin Caron de 1732-
     1799 .... **DC 4**
     See also DAM DRAM
Beaumont, Francis 1584(?)-1616 **LC 33; DC 6**
     See also CDBLB Before 1660; DLB 58, 121
Beauvoir, Simone (Lucie Ernestine Marie
     Bertrand) de 1908-1986 **CLC 1, 2, 4, 8, 14,**
     31, 44, 50, 71; DA; DAB; DAC; DAM MST,
     NOV; WLC
     See also CA 9-12R; 118; CANR 28, 61; DLB
     72; DLBY 86; MTCW

Becker, Carl (Lotus) 1873-1945 ..... **TCLC 63**
     See also CA 157; DLB 17
Becker, Jurek 1937-1997 .... **CLC 7, 19**
     See also CA 85-88; 157; CANR 60; DLB 75
Becker, Walter 1950- .... **CLC 26**
Beckett, Samuel (Barclay) 1906-1989 **CLC 1,**
     2, 3, 4, 6, 9, 10, 11, 14, 18, 29, 57, 59, 83;
     DA; DAB; DAC; DAM DRAM, MST,
     NOV; SSC 16; WLC
     See also CA 5-8R; 130; CANR 33, 61; CDBLB
     1945-1960; DLB 13, 15; DLBY 90; MTCW
Beckford, William 1760-1844 .... **NCLC 16**
     See also DLB 39
Beckman, Gunnel 1910- .... **CLC 26**
     See also CA 33-36R; CANR 15; CLR 25;
     MAICYA; SAAS 9; SATA 6
Becque, Henri 1837-1899 .... **NCLC 3**
Beddoes, Thomas Lovell 1803-1849 **NCLC 3**
     See also DLB 96
Bede c. 673-735 .... **CMLC 20**
     See also DLB 146
Bedford, Donald F.
     See Fearing, Kenneth (Flexner)
Beecher, Catharine Esther 1800-1878 **N C L C**
     30
     See also DLB 1
Beecher, John 1904-1980 .... **CLC 6**
     See also AITN 1; CA 5-8R; 105; CANR 8
Beer, Johann 1655-1700 .... **LC 5**
     See also DLB 168
Beer, Patricia 1924- .... **CLC 58**
     See also CA 61-64; CANR 13, 46; DLB 40
Beerbohm, Max
     See Beerbohm, (Henry) Max(imilian)
Beerbohm, (Henry) Max(imilian) 1872-1956
     TCLC 1, 24
     See also CA 104; 154; DLB 34, 100
Beer-Hofmann, Richard 1866-1945 **TCLC 60**
     See also CA 160; DLB 81
Begiebing, Robert J(ohn) 1946- .... **CLC 70**
     See also CA 122; CANR 40
Behan, Brendan 1923-1964 **CLC 1, 8, 11, 15,**
     79; DAM DRAM
     See also CA 73-76; CANR 33; CDBLB 1945-
     1960; DLB 13; MTCW
Behn, Aphra 1640(?)-1689 **LC 1, 30; DA; DAB;**
     DAC; DAM DRAM, MST, NOV, POET;
     DC 4; PC 13; WLC
     See also DLB 39, 80, 131
Behrman, S(amuel) N(athaniel) 1893-1973
     CLC 40
     See also CA 13-16; 45-48; CAP 1; DLB 7, 44
Belasco, David 1853-1931 .... **TCLC 3**
     See also CA 104; DLB 7
Belcheva, Elisaveta 1893- .... **CLC 10**
     See also Bagryana, Elisaveta
Beldone, Phil "Cheech"
     See Ellison, Harlan (Jay)
Beleno
     See Azuela, Mariano
Belinski, Vissarion Grigoryevich 1811-1848
     NCLC 5
Belitt, Ben 1911- .... **CLC 22**
     See also CA 13-16R; CAAS 4; CANR 7; DLB
     5
Bell, Gertrude 1868-1926 .... **TCLC 67**
     See also DLB 174
Bell, James Madison 1826-1902 ... **TCLC 43;**
     BLC; DAM MULT
     See also BW 1; CA 122; 124; DLB 50
Bell, Madison Smartt 1957- ...... **CLC 41, 102**
     See also CA 111; CANR 28, 54
Bell, Marvin (Hartley) 1937- **CLC 8, 31; DAM**

POET
See also CA 21-24R; CAAS 14; CANR 59; DLB 5; MTCW

Bell, W. L. D.
See Mencken, H(enry) L(ouis)

Bellamy, Atwood C.
See Mencken, H(enry) L(ouis)

Bellamy, Edward 1850-1898 .... NCLC 4
See also DLB 12

Bellin, Edward J.
See Kuttner, Henry

Belloc, (Joseph) Hilaire (Pierre Sebastien Rene Swanton) 1870-1953 TCLC 7, 18; DAM POET
See also CA 106; 152; DLB 19, 100, 141, 174; YABC 1

Belloc, Joseph Peter Rene Hilaire
See Belloc, (Joseph) Hilaire (Pierre Sebastien Rene Swanton)

Belloc, Joseph Pierre Hilaire
See Belloc, (Joseph) Hilaire (Pierre Sebastien Rene Swanton)

Belloc, M. A.
See Lowndes, Marie Adelaide (Belloc)

Bellow, Saul 1915-CLC 1, 2, 3, 6, 8, 10, 13, 15, 25, 33, 34, 63, 79; DA; DAB; DAC; DAM MST, NOV, POP; SSC 14; WLC
See also AITN 2; BEST 89:3; CA 5-8R; CABS 1; CANR 29, 53; CDALB 1941-1968; DLB 2, 28; DLBD 3; DLBY 82; MTCW

Belser, Reimond Karel Maria de 1929-
See Ruyslinck, Ward
See also CA 152

Bely, Andrey .... TCLC 7; PC 11
See also Bugayev, Boris Nikolayevich

Benary, Margot
See Benary-Isbert, Margot

Benary-Isbert, Margot 1889-1979 .... CLC 12
See also CA 5-8R; 89-92; CANR 4; CLR 12; MAICYA; SATA 2; SATA-Obit 21

Benavente (y Martinez), Jacinto 1866-1954 TCLC 3; DAM DRAM, MULT
See also CA 106; 131; HW; MTCW

Benchley, Peter (Bradford) 1940- CLC 4, 8; DAM NOV, POP
See also AAYA 14; AITN 2; CA 17-20R; CANR 12, 35; MTCW; SATA 3, 89

Benchley, Robert (Charles) 1889-1945 T C L C 1, 55
See also CA 105; 153; DLB 11

Benda, Julien 1867-1956 .... TCLC 60
See also CA 120; 154

Benedict, Ruth (Fulton) 1887-1948 TCLC 60
See also CA 158

Benedikt, Michael 1935- .... CLC 4, 14
See also CA 13-16R; CANR 7; DLB 5

Benet, Juan 1927- .... CLC 28
See also CA 143

Benet, Stephen Vincent 1898-1943 . TCLC 7; DAM POET; SSC 10
See also CA 104; 152; DLB 4, 48, 102; YABC 1

Benet, William Rose 1886-1950 .... TCLC 28; DAM POET
See also CA 118; 152; DLB 45

Benford, Gregory (Albert) 1941- ...... CLC 52
See also CA 69-72; CAAS 27; CANR 12, 24, 49; DLBY 82

Bengtsson, Frans (Gunnar) 1894-1954 T C L C 48

Benjamin, David
See Slavitt, David R(ytman)

Benjamin, Lois

See Gould, Lois

Benjamin, Walter 1892-1940 .... TCLC 39

Benn, Gottfried 1886-1956 .... TCLC 3
See also CA 106; 153; DLB 56

Bennett, Alan 1934-CLC 45, 77; DAB; DAM MST
See also CA 103; CANR 35, 55; MTCW

Bennett, (Enoch) Arnold 1867-1931 TCLC 5, 20
See also CA 106; 155; CDBLB 1890-1914; DLB 10, 34, 98, 135

Bennett, Elizabeth
See Mitchell, Margaret (Munnerlyn)

Bennett, George Harold 1930-
See Bennett, Hal
See also BW 1; CA 97-100

Bennett, Hal .... CLC 5
See also Bennett, George Harold
See also DLB 33

Bennett, Jay 1912- .... CLC 35
See also AAYA 10; CA 69-72; CANR 11, 42; JRDA; SAAS 4; SATA 41, 87; SATA-Brief 27

Bennett, Louise (Simone) 1919-CLC 28; BLC; DAM MULT
See also BW 2; CA 151; DLB 117

Benson, E(dward) F(rederic) 1867-1940 TCLC 27
See also CA 114; 157; DLB 135, 153

Benson, Jackson J. 1930- .... CLC 34
See also CA 25-28R; DLB 111

Benson, Sally 1900-1972 .... CLC 17
See also CA 19-20; 37-40R; CAP 1; SATA 1, 35; SATA-Obit 27

Benson, Stella 1892-1933 .... TCLC 17
See also CA 117; 155; DLB 36, 162

Bentham, Jeremy 1748-1832 .... NCLC 38
See also DLB 107, 158

Bentley, E(dmund) C(lerihew) 1875-1956 TCLC 12
See also CA 108; DLB 70

Bentley, Eric (Russell) 1916- .... CLC 24
See also CA 5-8R; CANR 6; INT CANR-6

Beranger, Pierre Jean de 1780-1857 NCLC 34

Berdyaev, Nicolas
See Berdyaev, Nikolai (Aleksandrovich)

Berdyaev, Nikolai (Aleksandrovich) 1874-1948 TCLC 67
See also CA 120; 157

Berdyayev, Nikolai (Aleksandrovich)
See Berdyaev, Nikolai (Aleksandrovich)

Berendt, John (Lawrence) 1939- ...... CLC 86
See also CA 146

Berger, Colonel
See Malraux, (Georges-)Andre

Berger, John (Peter) 1926- .... CLC 2, 19
See also CA 81-84; CANR 51; DLB 14

Berger, Melvin H. 1927- .... CLC 12
See also CA 5-8R; CANR 4; CLR 32; SAAS 2; SATA 5, 88

Berger, Thomas (Louis) 1924-CLC 3, 5, 8, 11, 18, 38; DAM NOV
See also CA 1-4R; CANR 5, 28, 51; DLB 2; DLBY 80; INT CANR-28; MTCW

Bergman, (Ernst) Ingmar 1918- CLC 16, 72
See also CA 81-84; CANR 33

Bergson, Henri 1859-1941 .... TCLC 32

Bergstein, Eleanor 1938- .... CLC 4
See also CA 53-56; CANR 5

Berkoff, Steven 1937- .... CLC 56
See also CA 104

Bermant, Chaim (Icyk) 1929- .... CLC 40
See also CA 57-60; CANR 6, 31, 57

Bern, Victoria
See Fisher, M(ary) F(rances) K(ennedy)

Bernanos, (Paul Louis) Georges 1888-1948 TCLC 3
See also CA 104; 130; DLB 72

Bernard, April 1956- .... CLC 59
See also CA 131

Berne, Victoria
See Fisher, M(ary) F(rances) K(ennedy)

Bernhard, Thomas 1931-1989 CLC 3, 32, 61
See also CA 85-88; 127; CANR 32, 57; DLB 85, 124; MTCW

Bernhardt, Sarah (Henriette Rosine) 1844-1923 TCLC 75
See also CA 157

Berriault, Gina 1926- .... CLC 54
See also CA 116; 129; DLB 130

Berrigan, Daniel 1921- .... CLC 4
See also CA 33-36R; CAAS 1; CANR 11, 43; DLB 5

Berrigan, Edmund Joseph Michael, Jr. 1934-1983
See Berrigan, Ted
See also CA 61-64; 110; CANR 14

Berrigan, Ted .... CLC 37
See also Berrigan, Edmund Joseph Michael, Jr.
See also DLB 5, 169

Berry, Charles Edward Anderson 1931-
See Berry, Chuck
See also CA 115

Berry, Chuck .... CLC 17
See also Berry, Charles Edward Anderson

Berry, Jonas
See Ashbery, John (Lawrence)

Berry, Wendell (Erdman) 1934- CLC 4, 6, 8, 27, 46; DAM POET
See also AITN 1; CA 73-76; CANR 50; DLB 5, 6

Berryman, John 1914-1972 CLC 1, 2, 3, 4, 6, 8, 10, 13, 25, 62; DAM POET
See also CA 13-16; 33-36R; CABS 2; CANR 35; CAP 1; CDALB 1941-1968; DLB 48; MTCW

Bertolucci, Bernardo 1940- .... CLC 16
See also CA 106

Berton, Pierre (Francis De Marigny) 1920- CLC 104
See also CA 1-4R; CANR 2, 56; DLB 68

Bertrand, Aloysius 1807-1841 .... NCLC 31

Bertran de Born c. 1140-1215 .... CMLC 5

Besant, Annie (Wood) 1847-1933 .... TCLC 9
See also CA 105

Bessie, Alvah 1904-1985 .... CLC 23
See also CA 5-8R; 116; CANR 2; DLB 26

Bethlen, T. D.
See Silverberg, Robert

Beti, Mongo ...... CLC 27; BLC; DAM MULT
See also Biyidi, Alexandre

Betjeman, John 1906-1984 CLC 2, 6, 10, 34, 43; DAB; DAM MST, POET
See also CA 9-12R; 112; CANR 33, 56; CDBLB 1945-1960; DLB 20; DLBY 84; MTCW

Bettelheim, Bruno 1903-1990 .... CLC 79
See also CA 81-84; 131; CANR 23, 61; MTCW

Betti, Ugo 1892-1953 .... TCLC 5
See also CA 104; 155

Betts, Doris (Waugh) 1932- ...... CLC 3, 6, 28
See also CA 13-16R; CANR 9; DLBY 82; INT CANR-9

Bevan, Alistair
See Roberts, Keith (John Kingston)

Bialik, Chaim Nachman 1873-1934 TCLC 25

Bickerstaff, Isaac

See Swift, Jonathan
Bidart, Frank 1939- .... **CLC 33**
See also CA 140
Bienek, Horst 1930- .... **CLC 7, 11**
See also CA 73-76; DLB 75
Bierce, Ambrose (Gwinett) 1842-1914(?)
**TCLC 1, 7, 44; DA; DAC; DAM MST; SSC
9; WLC**
See also CA 104; 139; CDALB 1865-1917;
DLB 11, 12, 23, 71, 74, 186
Biggers, Earl Derr 1884-1933 .... **TCLC 65**
See also CA 108; 153
Billings, Josh
See Shaw, Henry Wheeler
Billington, (Lady) Rachel (Mary) 1942- **C L C
43**
See also AITN 2; CA 33-36R; CANR 44
Binyon, T(imothy) J(ohn) 1936- .... **CLC 34**
See also CA 111; CANR 28
Bioy Casares, Adolfo 1914-1984**CLC 4, 8, 13,
88; DAM MULT; HLC; SSC 17**
See also CA 29-32R; CANR 19, 43; DLB 113;
HW; MTCW
Bird, Cordwainer
See Ellison, Harlan (Jay)
Bird, Robert Montgomery 1806-1854**NCLC 1**
Birney, (Alfred) Earle 1904-1995**CLC 1, 4, 6,
11; DAC; DAM MST, POET**
See also CA 1-4R; CANR 5, 20; DLB 88;
MTCW
Bishop, Elizabeth 1911-1979 **CLC 1, 4, 9, 13,
15, 32; DA; DAC; DAM MST, POET; PC
3**
See also CA 5-8R; 89-92; CABS 2; CANR 26,
61; CDALB 1968-1988; DLB 5, 169;
MTCW; SATA-Obit 24
Bishop, John 1935- .... **CLC 10**
See also CA 105
Bissett, Bill 1939- .... **CLC 18; PC 14**
See also CA 69-72; CAAS 19; CANR 15; DLB
53; MTCW
Bitov, Andrei (Georgievich) 1937- ... **CLC 57**
See also CA 142
Biyidi, Alexandre 1932-
See Beti, Mongo
See also BW 1; CA 114; 124; MTCW
Bjarme, Brynjolf
See Ibsen, Henrik (Johan)
Bjornson, Bjornstjerne (Martinius) 1832-1910
TCLC 7, 37
See also CA 104
Black, Robert
See Holdstock, Robert P.
Blackburn, Paul 1926-1971 .... **CLC 9, 43**
See also CA 81-84; 33-36R; CANR 34; DLB
16; DLBY 81
Black Elk 1863-1950**TCLC 33; DAM MULT**
See also CA 144; NNAL
Black Hobart
See Sanders, (James) Ed(ward)
Blacklin, Malcolm
See Chambers, Aidan
Blackmore, R(ichard) D(oddridge) 1825-1900
TCLC 27
See also CA 120; DLB 18
Blackmur, R(ichard) P(almer) 1904-1965
CLC 2, 24
See also CA 11-12; 25-28R; CAP 1; DLB 63
Black Tarantula
See Acker, Kathy
Blackwood, Algernon (Henry) 1869-1951
TCLC 5
See also CA 105; 150; DLB 153, 156, 178

Blackwood, Caroline 1931-1996**CLC 6, 9, 100**
See also CA 85-88; 151; CANR 32, 61; DLB
14; MTCW
Blade, Alexander
See Hamilton, Edmond; Silverberg, Robert
Blaga, Lucian 1895-1961 .... **CLC 75**
Blair, Eric (Arthur) 1903-1950
See Orwell, George
See also CA 104; 132; DA; DAB; DAC; DAM
MST, NOV; MTCW; SATA 29
Blais, Marie-Claire 1939-**CLC 2, 4, 6, 13, 22;
DAC; DAM MST**
See also CA 21-24R; CAAS 4; CANR 38; DLB
53; MTCW
Blaise, Clark 1940- .... **CLC 29**
See also AITN 2; CA 53-56; CAAS 3; CANR
5; DLB 53
Blake, Fairley
See De Voto, Bernard (Augustine)
Blake, Nicholas
See Day Lewis, C(ecil)
See also DLB 77
Blake, William 1757-1827 . **NCLC 13, 37, 57;
DA; DAB; DAC; DAM MST, POET; PC
12; WLC**
See also CDBLB 1789-1832; DLB 93, 163;
MAICYA; SATA 30
Blasco Ibanez, Vicente 1867-1928 **TCLC 12;
DAM NOV**
See also CA 110; 131; HW; MTCW
Blatty, William Peter 1928-**CLC 2; DAM POP**
See also CA 5-8R; CANR 9
Bleeck, Oliver
See Thomas, Ross (Elmore)
Blessing, Lee 1949- .... **CLC 54**
Blish, James (Benjamin) 1921-1975 . **CLC 14**
See also CA 1-4R; 57-60; CANR 3; DLB 8;
MTCW; SATA 66
Bliss, Reginald
See Wells, H(erbert) G(eorge)
Blixen, Karen (Christentze Dinesen) 1885-1962
See Dinesen, Isak
See also CA 25-28; CANR 22, 50; CAP 2;
MTCW; SATA 44
Bloch, Robert (Albert) 1917-1994 .... **CLC 33**
See also CA 5-8R; 146; CAAS 20; CANR 5;
DLB 44; INT CANR-5; SATA 12; SATA-Obit
82
Blok, Alexander (Alexandrovich) 1880-1921
TCLC 5; PC 21
See also CA 104
Blom, Jan
See Breytenbach, Breyten
Bloom, Harold 1930- .... **CLC 24, 103**
See also CA 13-16R; CANR 39; DLB 67
Bloomfield, Aurelius
See Bourne, Randolph S(illiman)
Blount, Roy (Alton), Jr. 1941- .... **CLC 38**
See also CA 53-56; CANR 10, 28, 61; INT
CANR-28; MTCW
Bloy, Leon 1846-1917 .... **TCLC 22**
See also CA 121; DLB 123
Blume, Judy (Sussman) 1938- ... **CLC 12, 30;
DAM NOV, POP**
See also AAYA 3; CA 29-32R; CANR 13, 37;
CLR 2, 15; DLB 52; JRDA; MAICYA;
MTCW; SATA 2, 31, 79
Blunden, Edmund (Charles) 1896-1974 **C L C
2, 56**
See also CA 17-18; 45-48; CANR 54; CAP 2;
DLB 20, 100, 155; MTCW
Bly, Robert (Elwood) 1926-**CLC 1, 2, 5, 10, 15,
38; DAM POET**

See also CA 5-8R; CANR 41; DLB 5; MTCW
Boas, Franz 1858-1942 .... **TCLC 56**
See also CA 115
Bobette
See Simenon, Georges (Jacques Christian)
Boccaccio, Giovanni 1313-1375 ...**CMLC 13;
SSC 10**
Bochco, Steven 1943- .... **CLC 35**
See also AAYA 11; CA 124; 138
Bodenheim, Maxwell 1892-1954 .... **TCLC 44**
See also CA 110; DLB 9, 45
Bodker, Cecil 1927- .... **CLC 21**
See also CA 73-76; CANR 13, 44; CLR 23;
MAICYA; SATA 14
Boell, Heinrich (Theodor) 1917-1985 **CLC 2,
3, 6, 9, 11, 15, 27, 32, 72; DA; DAB; DAC;
DAM MST, NOV; SSC 23; WLC**
See also CA 21-24R; 116; CANR 24; DLB 69;
DLBY 85; MTCW
Boerne, Alfred
See Doeblin, Alfred
Boethius 480(?)-524(?) .... **CMLC 15**
See also DLB 115
Bogan, Louise 1897-1970 . **CLC 4, 39, 46, 93;
DAM POET; PC 12**
See also CA 73-76; 25-28R; CANR 33; DLB
45, 169; MTCW
Bogarde, Dirk .... **CLC 19**
See also Van Den Bogarde, Derek Jules Gaspard
Ulric Niven
See also DLB 14
Bogosian, Eric 1953- .... **CLC 45**
See also CA 138
Bograd, Larry 1953- .... **CLC 35**
See also CA 93-96; CANR 57; SAAS 21; SATA
33, 89
Boiardo, Matteo Maria 1441-1494 .... **LC 6**
Boileau-Despreaux, Nicolas 1636-1711 . **LC 3**
Bojer, Johan 1872-1959 .... **TCLC 64**
Boland, Eavan (Aisling) 1944- .. **CLC 40, 67;
DAM POET**
See also CA 143; CANR 61; DLB 40
Bolt, Lee
See Faust, Frederick (Schiller)
Bolt, Robert (Oxton) 1924-1995 ..... **CLC 14;
DAM DRAM**
See also CA 17-20R; 147; CANR 35; DLB 13;
MTCW
Bombet, Louis-Alexandre-Cesar
See Stendhal
Bomkauf
See Kaufman, Bob (Garnell)
Bonaventura .... **NCLC 35**
See also DLB 90
Bond, Edward 1934- **CLC 4, 6, 13, 23; DAM
DRAM**
See also CA 25-28R; CANR 38; DLB 13;
MTCW
Bonham, Frank 1914-1989 .... **CLC 12**
See also AAYA 1; CA 9-12R; CANR 4, 36;
JRDA; MAICYA; SAAS 3; SATA 1, 49;
SATA-Obit 62
Bonnefoy, Yves 1923-... **CLC 9, 15, 58; DAM
MST, POET**
See also CA 85-88; CANR 33; MTCW
Bontemps, Arna(ud Wendell) 1902-1973**C L C
1, 18; BLC; DAM MULT, NOV, POET**
See also BW 1; CA 1-4R; 41-44R; CANR 4,
35; CLR 6; DLB 48, 51; JRDA; MAICYA;
MTCW; SATA 2, 44; SATA-Obit 24
Booth, Martin 1944- .... **CLC 13**
See also CA 93-96; CAAS 2
Booth, Philip 1925- .... **CLC 23**

See also CA 5-8R; CANR 5; DLBY 82

Booth, Wayne C(layson) 1921- .... **CLC 24**
See also CA 1-4R; CAAS 5; CANR 3, 43; DLB 67

Borchert, Wolfgang 1921-1947 .... **TCLC 5**
See also CA 104; DLB 69, 124

Borel, Petrus 1809-1859 .... **NCLC 41**

Borges, Jorge Luis 1899-1986**CLC 1, 2, 3, 4, 6, 8, 9, 10, 13, 19, 44, 48, 83; DA; DAB; DAC; DAM MST, MULT; HLC; SSC 4; WLC**
See also AAYA 19; CA 21-24R; CANR 19, 33; DLB 113; DLBY 86; HW; MTCW

Borowski, Tadeusz 1922-1951 .... **TCLC 9**
See also CA 106; 154

Borrow, George (Henry) 1803-1881 **NCLC 9**
See also DLB 21, 55, 166

Bosman, Herman Charles 1905-1951 **T C L C 49**
See also Malan, Herman
See also CA 160

Bosschere, Jean de 1878(?)-1953 ... **TCLC 19**
See also CA 115

Boswell, James 1740-1795 . **LC 4; DA; DAB; DAC; DAM MST; WLC**
See also CDBLB 1660-1789; DLB 104, 142

Bottoms, David 1949- .... **CLC 53**
See also CA 105; CANR 22; DLB 120; DLBY 83

Boucicault, Dion 1820-1890 .... **NCLC 41**

Boucolon, Maryse 1937(?)-
See Conde, Maryse
See also CA 110; CANR 30, 53

Bourget, Paul (Charles Joseph) 1852-1935 **TCLC 12**
See also CA 107; DLB 123

Bourjaily, Vance (Nye) 1922- .... **CLC 8, 62**
See also CA 1-4R; CAAS 1; CANR 2; DLB 2, 143

Bourne, Randolph S(illiman) 1886-1918 **TCLC 16**
See also CA 117; 155; DLB 63

Bova, Ben(jamin William) 1932- ...... **CLC 45**
See also AAYA 16; CA 5-8R; CAAS 18; CANR 11, 56; CLR 3; DLBY 81; INT CANR-11; MAICYA; MTCW; SATA 6, 68

Bowen, Elizabeth (Dorothea Cole) 1899-1973 **CLC 1, 3, 6, 11, 15, 22; DAM NOV; SSC 3, 28**
See also CA 17-18; 41-44R; CANR 35; CAP 2; CDBLB 1945-1960; DLB 15, 162; MTCW

Bowering, George 1935- .... **CLC 15, 47**
See also CA 21-24R; CAAS 16; CANR 10; DLB 53

Bowering, Marilyn R(uthe) 1949- .... **CLC 32**
See also CA 101; CANR 49

Bowers, Edgar 1924- .... **CLC 9**
See also CA 5-8R; CANR 24; DLB 5

Bowie, David .... **CLC 17**
See also Jones, David Robert

Bowles, Jane (Sydney) 1917-1973 **CLC 3, 68**
See also CA 19-20; 41-44R; CAP 2

Bowles, Paul (Frederick) 1910-1986**CLC 1, 2, 19, 53; SSC 3**
See also CA 1-4R; CAAS 1; CANR 1, 19, 50; DLB 5, 6; MTCW

Box, Edgar
See Vidal, Gore

Boyd, Nancy
See Millay, Edna St. Vincent

Boyd, William 1952- .... **CLC 28, 53, 70**
See also CA 114; 120; CANR 51

Boyle, Kay 1902-1992**CLC 1, 5, 19, 58; SSC 5**
See also CA 13-16R; 140; CAAS 1; CANR 29,

61; DLB 4, 9, 48, 86; DLBY 93; MTCW

Boyle, Mark
See Kienzle, William X(avier)

Boyle, Patrick 1905-1982 .... **CLC 19**
See also CA 127

Boyle, T. C. 1948-
See Boyle, T(homas) Coraghessan

Boyle, T(homas) Coraghessan 1948-**CLC 36, 55, 90; DAM POP; SSC 16**
See also BEST 90:4; CA 120; CANR 44; DLBY 86

Boz
See Dickens, Charles (John Huffam)

Brackenridge, Hugh Henry 1748-1816**N C L C 7**
See also DLB 11, 37

Bradbury, Edward P.
See Moorcock, Michael (John)

Bradbury, Malcolm (Stanley) 1932- **CLC 32, 61; DAM NOV**
See also CA 1-4R; CANR 1, 33; DLB 14; MTCW

Bradbury, Ray (Douglas) 1920-**CLC 1, 3, 10, 15, 42, 98; DA; DAB; DAC; DAM MST, NOV, POP; SSC 29; WLC**
See also AAYA 15; AITN 1, 2; CA 1-4R; CANR 2, 30; CDALB 1968-1988; DLB 2, 8; MTCW; SATA 11, 64

Bradford, Gamaliel 1863-1932 ...... **TCLC 36**
See also CA 160; DLB 17

Bradley, David (Henry, Jr.) 1950- .. **CLC 23; BLC; DAM MULT**
See also BW 1; CA 104; CANR 26; DLB 33

Bradley, John Ed(mund, Jr.) 1958- .. **CLC 55**
See also CA 139

Bradley, Marion Zimmer 1930-**CLC 30; DAM POP**
See also AAYA 9; CA 57-60; CAAS 10; CANR 7, 31, 51; DLB 8; MTCW; SATA 90

Bradstreet, Anne 1612(?)-1672**LC 4, 30; DA; DAC; DAM MST, POET; PC 10**
See also CDALB 1640-1865; DLB 24

Brady, Joan 1939- .... **CLC 86**
See also CA 141

Bragg, Melvyn 1939- .... **CLC 10**
See also BEST 89:3; CA 57-60; CANR 10, 48; DLB 14

Braine, John (Gerard) 1922-1986**CLC 1, 3, 41**
See also CA 1-4R; 120; CANR 1, 33; CDBLB 1945-1960; DLB 15; DLBY 86; MTCW

Bramah, Ernest 1868-1942 .... **TCLC 72**
See also CA 156; DLB 70

Brammer, William 1930(?)-1978 .... **CLC 31**
See also CA 77-80

Brancati, Vitaliano 1907-1954 .... **TCLC 12**
See also CA 109

Brancato, Robin F(idler) 1936- .... **CLC 35**
See also AAYA 9; CA 69-72; CANR 11, 45; CLR 32; JRDA; SAAS 9; SATA 23

Brand, Max
See Faust, Frederick (Schiller)

Brand, Millen 1906-1980 .... **CLC 7**
See also CA 21-24R; 97-100

Branden, Barbara .... **CLC 44**
See also CA 148

Brandes, Georg (Morris Cohen) 1842-1927 **TCLC 10**
See also CA 105

Brandys, Kazimierz 1916- .... **CLC 62**

Branley, Franklyn M(ansfield) 1915-**CLC 21**
See also CA 33-36R; CANR 14, 39; CLR 13; MAICYA; SAAS 16; SATA 4, 68

Brathwaite, Edward Kamau 1930- . **CLC 11;**

DAM POET
See also BW 2; CA 25-28R; CANR 11, 26, 47; DLB 125

Brautigan, Richard (Gary) 1935-1984**CLC 1, 3, 5, 9, 12, 34, 42; DAM NOV**
See also CA 53-56; 113; CANR 34; DLB 2, 5; DLBY 80, 84; MTCW; SATA 56

Brave Bird, Mary 1953-
See Crow Dog, Mary (Ellen)
See also NNAL

Braverman, Kate 1950- .... **CLC 67**
See also CA 89-92

Brecht, (Eugen) Bertolt (Friedrich) 1898-1956 **TCLC 1, 6, 13, 35; DA; DAB; DAC; DAM DRAM, MST; DC 3; WLC**
See also CA 104; 133; CANR 62; DLB 56, 124; MTCW

Brecht, Eugen Berthold Friedrich
See Brecht, (Eugen) Bertolt (Friedrich)

Bremer, Fredrika 1801-1865 .... **NCLC 11**

Brennan, Christopher John 1870-1932**T C L C 17**
See also CA 117

Brennan, Maeve 1917- .... **CLC 5**
See also CA 81-84

Brent, Linda
See Jacobs, Harriet

Brentano, Clemens (Maria) 1778-1842**N C L C 1**
See also DLB 90

Brent of Bin Bin
See Franklin, (Stella Maraia Sarah) Miles

Brenton, Howard 1942- .... **CLC 31**
See also CA 69-72; CANR 33; DLB 13; MTCW

Breslin, James 1930-1996
See Breslin, Jimmy
See also CA 73-76; CANR 31; DAM NOV; MTCW

Breslin, Jimmy .... **CLC 4, 43**
See also Breslin, James
See also AITN 1

Bresson, Robert 1901- .... **CLC 16**
See also CA 110; CANR 49

Breton, Andre 1896-1966**CLC 2, 9, 15, 54; PC 15**
See also CA 19-20; 25-28R; CANR 40, 60; CAP 2; DLB 65; MTCW

Breytenbach, Breyten 1939(?)- . **CLC 23, 37; DAM POET**
See also CA 113; 129; CANR 61

Bridgers, Sue Ellen 1942- .... **CLC 26**
See also AAYA 8; CA 65-68; CANR 11, 36; CLR 18; DLB 52; JRDA; MAICYA; SAAS 1; SATA 22, 90

Bridges, Robert (Seymour) 1844-1930**T C L C 1; DAM POET**
See also CA 104; 152; CDBLB 1890-1914; DLB 19, 98

Bridie, James .... **TCLC 3**
See also Mavor, Osborne Henry
See also DLB 10

Brin, David 1950- .... **CLC 34**
See also AAYA 21; CA 102; CANR 24; INT CANR-24; SATA 65

Brink, Andre (Philippus) 1935- **CLC 18, 36, 106**
See also CA 104; CANR 39, 62; INT 103; MTCW

Brinsmead, H(esba) F(ay) 1922- .... **CLC 21**
See also CA 21-24R; CANR 10; CLR 47; MAICYA; SAAS 5; SATA 18, 78

Brittain, Vera (Mary) 1893(?)-1970 . **CLC 23**
See also CA 13-16; 25-28R; CANR 58; CAP 1;

MTCW
Broch, Hermann 1886-1951 .... **TCLC 20**
See also CA 117; DLB 85, 124
Brock, Rose
See Hansen, Joseph
Brodkey, Harold (Roy) 1930-1996 .... **CLC 56**
See also CA 111; 151; DLB 130
Brodsky, Iosif Alexandrovich 1940-1996
See Brodsky, Joseph
See also AITN 1; CA 41-44R; 151; CANR 37;
DAM POET; MTCW
Brodsky, Joseph 1940-1996 **CLC 4, 6, 13, 36,
100; PC 9**
See also Brodsky, Iosif Alexandrovich
Brodsky, Michael (Mark) 1948- .... **CLC 19**
See also CA 102; CANR 18, 41, 58
Bromell, Henry 1947- .... **CLC 5**
See also CA 53-56; CANR 9
Bromfield, Louis (Brucker) 1896-1956 **T C L C
11**
See also CA 107; 155; DLB 4, 9, 86
Broner, E(sther) M(asserman) 1930- **CLC 19**
See also CA 17-20R; CANR 8, 25; DLB 28
Bronk, William 1918- .... **CLC 10**
See also CA 89-92; CANR 23; DLB 165
Bronstein, Lev Davidovich
See Trotsky, Leon
Bronte, Anne 1820-1849 .... **NCLC 4**
See also DLB 21
Bronte, Charlotte 1816-1855 **NCLC 3, 8, 33,
58; DA; DAB; DAC; DAM MST, NOV;
WLC**
See also AAYA 17; CDBLB 1832-1890; DLB
21, 159
Bronte, Emily (Jane) 1818-1848 **NCLC 16, 35;
DA; DAB; DAC; DAM MST, NOV, POET;
PC 8; WLC**
See also AAYA 17; CDBLB 1832-1890; DLB
21, 32
Brooke, Frances 1724-1789 .... **LC 6**
See also DLB 39, 99
Brooke, Henry 1703(?)-1783 .... **LC 1**
See also DLB 39
Brooke, Rupert (Chawner) 1887-1915 **T C L C
2, 7; DA; DAB; DAC; DAM MST, POET;
WLC**
See also CA 104; 132; CANR 61; CDBLB
1914-1945; DLB 19; MTCW
Brooke-Haven, P.
See Wodehouse, P(elham) G(renville)
Brooke-Rose, Christine 1926(?)- .... **CLC 40**
See also CA 13-16R; CANR 58; DLB 14
Brookner, Anita 1928- **CLC 32, 34, 51; DAB;
DAM POP**
See also CA 114; 120; CANR 37, 56; DLBY
87; MTCW
Brooks, Cleanth 1906-1994 .... **CLC 24, 86**
See also CA 17-20R; 145; CANR 33, 35; DLB
63; DLBY 94; INT CANR-35; MTCW
Brooks, George
See Baum, L(yman) Frank
Brooks, Gwendolyn 1917- **CLC 1, 2, 4, 5, 15,
49; BLC; DA; DAC; DAM MST, MULT,
POET; PC 7; WLC**
See also AAYA 20; AITN 1; BW 2; CA 1-4R;
CANR 1, 27, 52; CDALB 1941-1968; CLR
27; DLB 5, 76, 165; MTCW; SATA 6
Brooks, Mel .... **CLC 12**
See also Kaminsky, Melvin
See also AAYA 13; DLB 26
Brooks, Peter 1938- .... **CLC 34**
See also CA 45-48; CANR 1
Brooks, Van Wyck 1886-1963 .... **CLC 29**

See also CA 1-4R; CANR 6; DLB 45, 63, 103
Brophy, Brigid (Antonia) 1929-1995 **CLC 6,
11, 29, 105**
See also CA 5-8R; 149; CAAS 4; CANR 25,
53; DLB 14; MTCW
Brosman, Catharine Savage 1934- ..... **CLC 9**
See also CA 61-64; CANR 21, 46
Brother Antoninus
See Everson, William (Oliver)
The Brothers Quay
See Quay, Stephen; Quay, Timothy
Broughton, T(homas) Alan 1936- ..... **CLC 19**
See also CA 45-48; CANR 2, 23, 48
Broumas, Olga 1949- .... **CLC 10, 73**
See also CA 85-88; CANR 20
Brown, Alan 1951- .... **CLC 99**
Brown, Charles Brockden 1771-1810 **N C L C
22**
See also CDALB 1640-1865; DLB 37, 59, 73
Brown, Christy 1932-1981 .... **CLC 63**
See also CA 105; 104; DLB 14
Brown, Claude 1937- ... **CLC 30; BLC; DAM
MULT**
See also AAYA 7; BW 1; CA 73-76
Brown, Dee (Alexander) 1908- .. **CLC 18, 47;
DAM POP**
See also CA 13-16R; CAAS 6; CANR 11, 45,
60; DLBY 80; MTCW; SATA 5
Brown, George
See Wertmueller, Lina
Brown, George Douglas 1869-1902 **TCLC 28**
Brown, George Mackay 1921-1996 **CLC 5, 48,
100**
See also CA 21-24R; 151; CAAS 6; CANR 12,
37, 62; DLB 14, 27, 139; MTCW; SATA 35
Brown, (William) Larry 1951- .... **CLC 73**
See also CA 130; 134; INT 133
Brown, Moses
See Barrett, William (Christopher)
Brown, Rita Mae 1944- **CLC 18, 43, 79; DAM
NOV, POP**
See also CA 45-48; CANR 2, 11, 35, 62; INT
CANR-11; MTCW
Brown, Roderick (Langmere) Haig-
See Haig-Brown, Roderick (Langmere)
Brown, Rosellen 1939- .... **CLC 32**
See also CA 77-80; CAAS 10; CANR 14, 44
Brown, Sterling Allen 1901-1989 **CLC 1, 23,
59; BLC; DAM MULT, POET**
See also BW 1; CA 85-88; 127; CANR 26; DLB
48, 51, 63; MTCW
Brown, Will
See Ainsworth, William Harrison
Brown, William Wells 1813-1884 ... **NCLC 2;
BLC; DAM MULT; DC 1**
See also DLB 3, 50
Browne, (Clyde) Jackson 1948(?)- .... **CLC 21**
See also CA 120
Browning, Elizabeth Barrett 1806-1861
**NCLC 1, 16, 61, 66; DA; DAB; DAC; DAM
MST, POET; PC 6; WLC**
See also CDBLB 1832-1890; DLB 32
Browning, Robert 1812-1889 **NCLC 19; DA;
DAB; DAC; DAM MST, POET; PC 2;
WLCS**
See also CDBLB 1832-1890; DLB 32, 163;
YABC 1
Browning, Tod 1882-1962 .... **CLC 16**
See also CA 141; 117
Brownson, Orestes (Augustus) 1803-1876
NCLC 50
Bruccoli, Matthew J(oseph) 1931- ... **CLC 34**
See also CA 9-12R; CANR 7; DLB 103

Bruce, Lenny .... **CLC 21**
See also Schneider, Leonard Alfred
Bruin, John
See Brutus, Dennis
Brulard, Henri
See Stendhal
Brulls, Christian
See Simenon, Georges (Jacques Christian)
Brunner, John (Kilian Houston) 1934-1995
CLC 8, 10; DAM POP
See also CA 1-4R; 149; CAAS 8; CANR 2, 37;
MTCW
Bruno, Giordano 1548-1600 .... **LC 27**
Brutus, Dennis 1924- ... **CLC 43; BLC; DAM
MULT, POET**
See also BW 2; CA 49-52; CAAS 14; CANR 2,
27, 42; DLB 117
Bryan, C(ourtlandt) D(ixon) B(arnes) 1936-
CLC 29
See also CA 73-76; CANR 13; INT CANR-13
Bryan, Michael
See Moore, Brian
Bryant, William Cullen 1794-1878 . **NCLC 6,
46; DA; DAB; DAC; DAM MST, POET;
PC 20**
See also CDALB 1640-1865; DLB 3, 43, 59
Bryusov, Valery Yakovlevich 1873-1924
TCLC 10
See also CA 107; 155
Buchan, John 1875-1940 ..... **TCLC 41; DAB;
DAM POP**
See also CA 108; 145; DLB 34, 70, 156; YABC
2
Buchanan, George 1506-1582 .... **LC 4**
Buchheim, Lothar-Guenther 1918- .... **CLC 6**
See also CA 85-88
Buchner, (Karl) Georg 1813-1837 . **NCLC 26**
Buchwald, Art(hur) 1925- .... **CLC 33**
See also AITN 1; CA 5-8R; CANR 21; MTCW;
SATA 10
Buck, Pearl S(ydenstricker) 1892-1973 **CLC 7,
11, 18; DA; DAB; DAC; DAM MST, NOV**
See also AITN 1; CA 1-4R; 41-44R; CANR 1,
34; DLB 9, 102; MTCW; SATA 1, 25
Buckler, Ernest 1908-1984 .... **CLC 13; DAC;
DAM MST**
See also CA 11-12; 114; CAP 1; DLB 68; SATA
47
Buckley, Vincent (Thomas) 1925-1988 **CLC 57**
See also CA 101
Buckley, William F(rank), Jr. 1925- **CLC 7, 18,
37; DAM POP**
See also AITN 1; CA 1-4R; CANR 1, 24, 53;
DLB 137; DLBY 80; INT CANR-24; MTCW
Buechner, (Carl) Frederick 1926- **CLC 2, 4, 6,
9; DAM NOV**
See also CA 13-16R; CANR 11, 39, 64; DLBY
80; INT CANR-11; MTCW
Buell, John (Edward) 1927- .... **CLC 10**
See also CA 1-4R; DLB 53
Buero Vallejo, Antonio 1916- ..... **CLC 15, 46**
See also CA 106; CANR 24, 49; HW; MTCW
Bufalino, Gesualdo 1920(?)- .... **CLC 74**
Bugayev, Boris Nikolayevich 1880-1934
See Bely, Andrey
See also CA 104
Bukowski, Charles 1920-1994 **CLC 2, 5, 9, 41,
82, 108; DAM NOV, POET; PC 18**
See also CA 17-20R; 144; CANR 40, 62; DLB
5, 130, 169; MTCW
Bulgakov, Mikhail (Afanas'evich) 1891-1940
TCLC 2, 16; DAM DRAM, NOV; SSC 18
See also CA 105; 152

Bulgya, Alexander Alexandrovich 1901-1956
TCLC 53
See also Fadeyev, Alexander
See also CA 117

Bullins, Ed 1935-... **CLC 1, 5, 7; BLC; DAM
DRAM, MULT; DC 6**
See also BW 2; CA 49-52; CAAS 16; CANR
24, 46; DLB 7, 38; MTCW

Bulwer-Lytton, Edward (George Earle Lytton)
1803-1873 .... NCLC 1, 45
See also DLB 21

Bunin, Ivan Alexeyevich 1870-1953 TCLC 6;
SSC 5
See also CA 104

Bunting, Basil 1900-1985 ..... CLC 10, 39, 47;
DAM POET
See also CA 53-56; 115; CANR 7; DLB 20

Bunuel, Luis 1900-1983 .. CLC 16, 80; DAM
MULT; HLC
See also CA 101; 110; CANR 32; HW

Bunyan, John 1628-1688 ... LC 4; DA; DAB;
DAC; DAM MST; WLC
See also CDBLB 1660-1789; DLB 39

Burckhardt, Jacob (Christoph) 1818-1897
NCLC 49

Burford, Eleanor
See Hibbert, Eleanor Alice Burford

Burgess, Anthony CLC 1, 2, 4, 5, 8, 10, 13, 15,
22, 40, 62, 81, 94; DAB
See also Wilson, John (Anthony) Burgess
See also AITN 1; CDBLB 1960 to Present; DLB
14

Burke, Edmund 1729(?)-1797 LC 7, 36; DA;
DAB; DAC; DAM MST; WLC
See also DLB 104

Burke, Kenneth (Duva) 1897-1993 CLC 2, 24
See also CA 5-8R; 143; CANR 39; DLB 45,
63; MTCW

Burke, Leda
See Garnett, David

Burke, Ralph
See Silverberg, Robert

Burke, Thomas 1886-1945 .... TCLC 63
See also CA 113; 155

Burney, Fanny 1752-1840 .... NCLC 12, 54
See also DLB 39

Burns, Robert 1759-1796 .... PC 6
See also CDBLB 1789-1832; DA; DAB; DAC;
DAM MST, POET; DLB 109; WLC

Burns, Tex
See L'Amour, Louis (Dearborn)

Burnshaw, Stanley 1906- .... CLC 3, 13, 44
See also CA 9-12R; DLB 48

Burr, Anne 1937- .... CLC 6
See also CA 25-28R

Burroughs, Edgar Rice 1875-1950 . TCLC 2,
32; DAM NOV
See also AAYA 11; CA 104; 132; DLB 8;
MTCW; SATA 41

Burroughs, William S(eward) 1914-1997 CLC
1, 2, 5, 15, 22, 42, 75; DA; DAB; DAC;
DAM MST, NOV, POP; WLC
See also AITN 2; CA 9-12R; 160; CANR 20,
52; DLB 2, 8, 16, 152; DLBY 81; MTCW

Burton, Richard F. 1821-1890 .... NCLC 42
See also DLB 55, 184

Busch, Frederick 1941- ..... CLC 7, 10, 18, 47
See also CA 33-36R; CAAS 1; CANR 45; DLB
6

Bush, Ronald 1946- .... CLC 34
See also CA 136

Bustos, F(rancisco)
See Borges, Jorge Luis

Bustos Domecq, H(onorio)
See Bioy Casares, Adolfo; Borges, Jorge Luis

Butler, Octavia E(stelle) 1947- CLC 38; DAM
MULT, POP
See also AAYA 18; BW 2; CA 73-76; CANR
12, 24, 38; DLB 33; MTCW; SATA 84

Butler, Robert Olen (Jr.) 1945- CLC 81; DAM
POP
See also CA 112; DLB 173; INT 112

Butler, Samuel 1612-1680 .... LC 16
See also DLB 101, 126

Butler, Samuel 1835-1902 . TCLC 1, 33; DA;
DAB; DAC; DAM MST, NOV; WLC
See also CA 143; CDBLB 1890-1914; DLB 18,
57, 174

Butler, Walter C.
See Faust, Frederick (Schiller)

Butor, Michel (Marie Francois) 1926- CLC 1,
3, 8, 11, 15
See also CA 9-12R; CANR 33; DLB 83; MTCW

Butts, Mary 1892(?)-1937 .... TCLC 77
See also CA 148

Buzo, Alexander (John) 1944- .... CLC 61
See also CA 97-100; CANR 17, 39

Buzzati, Dino 1906-1972 .... CLC 36
See also CA 160; 33-36R; DLB 177

Byars, Betsy (Cromer) 1928-.............. CLC 35
See also AAYA 19; CA 33-36R; CANR 18, 36,
57; CLR 1, 16; DLB 52; INT CANR-18;
JRDA; MAICYA; MTCW; SAAS 1; SATA
4, 46, 80

Byatt, A(ntonia) S(usan Drabble) 1936- C L C
19, 65; DAM NOV, POP
See also CA 13-16R; CANR 13, 33, 50; DLB
14; MTCW

Byrne, David 1952- .... CLC 26
See also CA 127

Byrne, John Keyes 1926-
See Leonard, Hugh
See also CA 102; INT 102

Byron, George Gordon (Noel) 1788-1824
NCLC 2, 12; DA; DAB; DAC; DAM MST,
POET; PC 16; WLC
See also CDBLB 1789-1832; DLB 96, 110

Byron, Robert 1905-1941 .... TCLC 67
See also CA 160

C. 3. 3.
See Wilde, Oscar (Fingal O'Flahertie Wills)

Caballero, Fernan 1796-1877 .... NCLC 10

Cabell, Branch
See Cabell, James Branch

Cabell, James Branch 1879-1958 .... TCLC 6
See also CA 105; 152; DLB 9, 78

Cable, George Washington 1844-1925 T C L C
4; SSC 4
See also CA 104; 155; DLB 12, 74; DLBD 13

Cabral de Melo Neto, Joao 1920- ... CLC 76;
DAM MULT
See also CA 151

Cabrera Infante, G(uillermo) 1929- CLC 5, 25,
45; DAM MULT; HLC
See also CA 85-88; CANR 29; DLB 113; HW;
MTCW

Cade, Toni
See Bambara, Toni Cade

Cadmus and Harmonia
See Buchan, John

Caedmon fl. 658-680 .... CMLC 7
See also DLB 146

Caeiro, Alberto
See Pessoa, Fernando (Antonio Nogueira)

Cage, John (Milton, Jr.) 1912- .... CLC 41
See also CA 13-16R; CANR 9; INT CANR-9

Cahan, Abraham 1860-1951 .... TCLC 71
See also CA 108; 154; DLB 9, 25, 28

Cain, G.
See Cabrera Infante, G(uillermo)

Cain, Guillermo
See Cabrera Infante, G(uillermo)

Cain, James M(allahan) 1892-1977 CLC 3, 11,
28
See also AITN 1; CA 17-20R; 73-76; CANR 8,
34, 61; MTCW

Caine, Mark
See Raphael, Frederic (Michael)

Calasso, Roberto 1941- .... CLC 81
See also CA 143

Calderon de la Barca, Pedro 1600-1681 .. L C
23; DC 3

Caldwell, Erskine (Preston) 1903-1987 CLC 1,
8, 14, 50, 60; DAM NOV; SSC 19
See also AITN 1; CA 1-4R; 121; CAAS 1;
CANR 2, 33; DLB 9, 86; MTCW

Caldwell, (Janet Miriam) Taylor (Holland)
1900-1985 CLC 2, 28, 39; DAM NOV, POP
See also CA 5-8R; 116; CANR 5

Calhoun, John Caldwell 1782-1850 NCLC 15
See also DLB 3

Calisher, Hortense 1911- CLC 2, 4, 8, 38; DAM
NOV; SSC 15
See also CA 1-4R; CANR 1, 22; DLB 2; INT
CANR-22; MTCW

Callaghan, Morley Edward 1903-1990 CLC 3,
14, 41, 65; DAC; DAM MST
See also CA 9-12R; 132; CANR 33; DLB 68;
MTCW

Callimachus c. 305B.C.-c. 240B.C. CMLC 18
See also DLB 176

Calvin, John 1509-1564 .... LC 37

Calvino, Italo 1923-1985 CLC 5, 8, 11, 22, 33,
39, 73; DAM NOV; SSC 3
See also CA 85-88; 116; CANR 23, 61; MTCW

Cameron, Carey 1952- .... CLC 59
See also CA 135

Cameron, Peter 1959- .... CLC 44
See also CA 125; CANR 50

Campana, Dino 1885-1932 .... TCLC 20
See also CA 117; DLB 114

Campanella, Tommaso 1568-1639 .... LC 32

Campbell, John W(ood, Jr.) 1910-1971 C L C
32
See also CA 21-22; 29-32R; CANR 34; CAP 2;
DLB 8; MTCW

Campbell, Joseph 1904-1987 .... CLC 69
See also AAYA 3; BEST 89:2; CA 1-4R; 124;
CANR 3, 28, 61; MTCW

Campbell, Maria 1940- .... CLC 85; DAC
See also CA 102; CANR 54; NNAL

Campbell, (John) Ramsey 1946- CLC 42; SSC
19
See also CA 57-60; CANR 7; INT CANR-7

Campbell, (Ignatius) Roy (Dunnachie) 1901-
1957 .... TCLC 5
See also CA 104; 155; DLB 20

Campbell, Thomas 1777-1844 .... NCLC 19
See also DLB 93; 144

Campbell, Wilfred .... TCLC 9
See also Campbell, William

Campbell, William 1858(?)-1918
See Campbell, Wilfred
See also CA 106; DLB 92

Campion, Jane .... CLC 95
See also CA 138

Campos, Alvaro de
See Pessoa, Fernando (Antonio Nogueira)

Camus, Albert 1913-1960 CLC 1, 2, 4, 9, 11, 14,

32, 63, 69; DA; DAB; DAC; DAM DRAM, MST, NOV; DC 2; SSC 9; WLC
See also CA 89-92; DLB 72; MTCW

Canby, Vincent 1924- .... **CLC 13**
See also CA 81-84

Cancale
See Desnos, Robert

Canetti, Elias 1905-1994 **CLC 3, 14, 25, 75, 86**
See also CA 21-24R; 146; CANR 23, 61; DLB 85, 124; MTCW

Canin, Ethan 1960- .... **CLC 55**
See also CA 131; 135

Cannon, Curt
See Hunter, Evan

Cape, Judith
See Page, P(atricia) K(athleen)

Capek, Karel 1890-1938 ... **TCLC 6, 37; DA; DAB; DAC; DAM DRAM, MST, NOV; DC 1; WLC**
See also CA 104; 140

Capote, Truman 1924-1984 **CLC 1, 3, 8, 13, 19, 34, 38, 58; DA; DAB; DAC; DAM MST, NOV, POP; SSC 2; WLC**
See also CA 5-8R; 113; CANR 18, 62; CDALB 1941-1968; DLB 2; DLBY 80, 84; MTCW; SATA 91

Capra, Frank 1897-1991 .... **CLC 16**
See also CA 61-64; 135

Caputo, Philip 1941- .... **CLC 32**
See also CA 73-76; CANR 40

Caragiale, Ion Luca 1852-1912 ..... **TCLC 76**
See also CA 157

Card, Orson Scott 1951- **CLC 44, 47, 50; DAM POP**
See also AAYA 11; CA 102; CANR 27, 47; INT CANR-27; MTCW; SATA 83

Cardenal, Ernesto 1925- .... **CLC 31; DAM MULT, POET; HLC**
See also CA 49-52; CANR 2, 32; HW; MTCW

Cardozo, Benjamin N(athan) 1870-1938
TCLC 65
See also CA 117

Carducci, Giosue (Alessandro Giuseppe) 1835-1907 .... **TCLC 32**

Carew, Thomas 1595(?)-1640 .... **LC 13**
See also DLB 126

Carey, Ernestine Gilbreth 1908- .... **CLC 17**
See also CA 5-8R; SATA 2

Carey, Peter 1943- .... **CLC 40, 55, 96**
See also CA 123; 127; CANR 53; INT 127; MTCW; SATA 94

Carleton, William 1794-1869 .... **NCLC 3**
See also DLB 159

Carlisle, Henry (Coffin) 1926- .... **CLC 33**
See also CA 13-16R; CANR 15

Carlsen, Chris
See Holdstock, Robert P.

Carlson, Ron(ald F.) 1947- .... **CLC 54**
See also CA 105; CANR 27

Carlyle, Thomas 1795-1881 . **NCLC 22; DA; DAB; DAC; DAM MST**
See also CDBLB 1789-1832; DLB 55; 144

Carman, (William) Bliss 1861-1929 **TCLC 7; DAC**
See also CA 104; 152; DLB 92

Carnegie, Dale 1888-1955 .... **TCLC 53**

Carossa, Hans 1878-1956 .... **TCLC 48**
See also DLB 66

Carpenter, Don(ald Richard) 1931-1995 **C L C 41**
See also CA 45-48; 149; CANR 1

Carpentier (y Valmont), Alejo 1904-1980 **CLC 8, 11, 38; DAM MULT; HLC**

See also CA 65-68; 97-100; CANR 11; DLB 113; HW

Carr, Caleb 1955(?)- .... **CLC 86**
See also CA 147

Carr, Emily 1871-1945 .... **TCLC 32**
See also CA 159; DLB 68

Carr, John Dickson 1906-1977 .... **CLC 3**
See also Fairbairn, Roger
See also CA 49-52; 69-72; CANR 3, 33, 60; MTCW

Carr, Philippa
See Hibbert, Eleanor Alice Burford

Carr, Virginia Spencer 1929- .... **CLC 34**
See also CA 61-64; DLB 111

Carrere, Emmanuel 1957- .... **CLC 89**

Carrier, Roch 1937- **CLC 13, 78; DAC; DAM MST**
See also CA 130; CANR 61; DLB 53

Carroll, James P. 1943(?)- .... **CLC 38**
See also CA 81-84

Carroll, Jim 1951- .... **CLC 35**
See also AAYA 17; CA 45-48; CANR 42

Carroll, Lewis ..... **NCLC 2, 53; PC 18; WLC**
See also Dodgson, Charles Lutwidge
See also CDBLB 1832-1890; CLR 2, 18; DLB 18, 163, 178; JRDA

Carroll, Paul Vincent 1900-1968 ...... **CLC 10**
See also CA 9-12R; 25-28R; DLB 10

Carruth, Hayden 1921- **CLC 4, 7, 10, 18, 84; PC 10**
See also CA 9-12R; CANR 4, 38, 59; DLB 5, 165; INT CANR-4; MTCW; SATA 47

Carson, Rachel Louise 1907-1964 .. **CLC 71; DAM POP**
See also CA 77-80; CANR 35; MTCW; SATA 23

Carter, Angela (Olive) 1940-1992 **CLC 5, 41, 76; SSC 13**
See also CA 53-56; 136; CANR 12, 36, 61; DLB 14; MTCW; SATA 66; SATA-Obit 70

Carter, Nick
See Smith, Martin Cruz

Carver, Raymond 1938-1988 **CLC 22, 36, 53, 55; DAM NOV; SSC 8**
See also CA 33-36R; 126; CANR 17, 34, 61; DLB 130; DLBY 84, 88; MTCW

Cary, Elizabeth, Lady Falkland 1585-1639
LC 30

Cary, (Arthur) Joyce (Lunel) 1888-1957
TCLC 1, 29
See also CA 104; CDBLB 1914-1945; DLB 15, 100

Casanova de Seingalt, Giovanni Jacopo 1725-1798 .... **LC 13**

Casares, Adolfo Bioy
See Bioy Casares, Adolfo

Casely-Hayford, J(oseph) E(phraim) 1866-1930
TCLC 24; BLC; DAM MULT
See also BW 2; CA 123; 152

Casey, John (Dudley) 1939- .... **CLC 59**
See also BEST 90:2; CA 69-72; CANR 23

Casey, Michael 1947- .... **CLC 2**
See also CA 65-68; DLB 5

Casey, Patrick
See Thurman, Wallace (Henry)

Casey, Warren (Peter) 1935-1988 ..... **CLC 12**
See also CA 101; 127; INT 101

Casona, Alejandro .... **CLC 49**
See also Alvarez, Alejandro Rodriguez

Cassavetes, John 1929-1989 .... **CLC 20**
See also CA 85-88; 127

Cassian, Nina 1924- .... **PC 17**

Cassill, R(onald) V(erlin) 1919- .... **CLC 4, 23**

See also CA 9-12R; CAAS 1; CANR 7, 45; DLB 113; HW

Cassirer, Ernst 1874-1945 .... **TCLC 61**
See also CA 157

Cassity, (Allen) Turner 1929- .... **CLC 6, 42**
See also CA 17-20R; CAAS 8; CANR 11; DLB 105

Castaneda, Carlos 1931(?)- .... **CLC 12**
See also CA 25-28R; CANR 32; HW; MTCW

Castedo, Elena 1937- .... **CLC 65**
See also CA 132

Castedo-Ellerman, Elena
See Castedo, Elena

Castellanos, Rosario 1925-1974 **CLC 66; DAM MULT; HLC**
See also CA 131; 53-56; CANR 58; DLB 113; HW

Castelvetro, Lodovico 1505-1571 .... **LC 12**

Castiglione, Baldassare 1478-1529 ...... **LC 12**

Castle, Robert
See Hamilton, Edmond

Castro, Guillen de 1569-1631 .... **LC 19**

Castro, Rosalia de 1837-1885 **NCLC 3; DAM MULT**

Cather, Willa
See Cather, Willa Sibert

Cather, Willa Sibert 1873-1947 **TCLC 1, 11, 31; DA; DAB; DAC; DAM MST, NOV; SSC 2; WLC**
See also CA 104; 128; CDALB 1865-1917; DLB 9, 54, 78; DLBD 1; MTCW; SATA 30

Cato, Marcus Porcius 234B.C.-149B.C.
CMLC 21

Catton, (Charles) Bruce 1899-1978 .. **CLC 35**
See also AITN 1; CA 5-8R; 81-84; CANR 7; DLB 17; SATA 2; SATA-Obit 24

Catullus c. 84B.C.-c. 54B.C. .... **CMLC 18**

Cauldwell, Frank
See King, Francis (Henry)

Caunitz, William J. 1933-1996 .... **CLC 34**
See also BEST 89:3; CA 125; 130; 152; INT 130

Causley, Charles (Stanley) 1917- .... **CLC 7**
See also CA 9-12R; CANR 5, 35; CLR 30; DLB 27; MTCW; SATA 3, 66

Caute, (John) David 1936- ..... **CLC 29; DAM NOV**
See also CA 1-4R; CAAS 4; CANR 1, 33, 64; DLB 14

Cavafy, C(onstantine) P(eter) 1863-1933
TCLC 2, 7; DAM POET
See also Kavafis, Konstantinos Petrou
See also CA 148

Cavallo, Evelyn
See Spark, Muriel (Sarah)

Cavanna, Betty .... **CLC 12**
See also Harrison, Elizabeth Cavanna
See also JRDA; MAICYA; SAAS 4; SATA 1, 30

Cavendish, Margaret Lucas 1623-1673 **LC 30**
See also DLB 131

Caxton, William 1421(?)-1491(?) .... **LC 17**
See also DLB 170

Cayrol, Jean 1911- .... **CLC 11**
See also CA 89-92; DLB 83

Cela, Camilo Jose 1916- **CLC 4, 13, 59; DAM MULT; HLC**
See also BEST 90:2; CA 21-24R; CAAS 10; CANR 21, 32; DLBY 89; HW; MTCW

Celan, Paul .... **CLC 10, 19, 53, 82; PC 10**
See also Antschel, Paul
See also DLB 69

Celine, Louis-Ferdinand **CLC 1, 3, 4, 7, 9, 15,**

47
See also Destouches, Louis-Ferdinand
See also DLB 72
Cellini, Benvenuto 1500-1571 .... **LC 7**
Cendrars, Blaise 1887-1961 ..... **CLC 18, 106**
See also Sauser-Hall, Frederic
Cernuda (y Bidon), Luis 1902-1963 **CLC 54;**
DAM POET
See also CA 131; 89-92; DLB 134; HW
Cervantes (Saavedra), Miguel de 1547-1616
LC 6, 23; DA; DAB; DAC; DAM MST,
NOV; SSC 12; WLC
Cesaire, Aime (Fernand) 1913- . **CLC 19, 32;**
BLC; DAM MULT, POET
See also BW 2; CA 65-68; CANR 24, 43;
MTCW
Chabon, Michael 1963- .... **CLC 55**
See also CA 139; CANR 57
Chabrol, Claude 1930- .... **CLC 16**
See also CA 110
Challans, Mary 1905-1983
See Renault, Mary
See also CA 81-84; 111; SATA 23; SATA-Obit
36
Challis, George
See Faust, Frederick (Schiller)
Chambers, Aidan 1934- .... **CLC 35**
See also CA 25-28R; CANR 12, 31, 58; JRDA;
MAICYA; SAAS 12; SATA 1, 69
Chambers, James 1948-
See Cliff, Jimmy
See also CA 124
Chambers, Jessie
See Lawrence, D(avid) H(erbert Richards)
Chambers, Robert W. 1865-1933 ... **TCLC 41**
Chandler, Raymond (Thornton) 1888-1959
TCLC 1, 7; SSC 23
See also CA 104; 129; CANR 60; CDALB
1929-1941; DLBD 6; MTCW
Chang, Eileen 1921- .... **SSC 28**
Chang, Jung 1952- .... **CLC 71**
See also CA 142
Channing, William Ellery 1780-1842 **NCLC**
17
See also DLB 1, 59
Chaplin, Charles Spencer 1889-1977 **CLC 16**
See also Chaplin, Charlie
See also CA 81-84; 73-76
Chaplin, Charlie
See Chaplin, Charles Spencer
See also DLB 44
Chapman, George 1559(?)-1634 **LC 22; DAM**
DRAM
See also DLB 62, 121
Chapman, Graham 1941-1989 .... **CLC 21**
See also Monty Python
See also CA 116; 129; CANR 35
Chapman, John Jay 1862-1933 .... **TCLC 7**
See also CA 104
Chapman, Lee
See Bradley, Marion Zimmer
Chapman, Walker
See Silverberg, Robert
Chappell, Fred (Davis) 1936- ..... **CLC 40, 78**
See also CA 5-8R; CAAS 4; CANR 8, 33; DLB
6, 105
Char, Rene(-Emile) 1907-1988 **CLC 9, 11, 14,**
55; DAM POET
See also CA 13-16R; 124; CANR 32; MTCW
Charby, Jay
See Ellison, Harlan (Jay)
Chardin, Pierre Teilhard de
See Teilhard de Chardin, (Marie Joseph) Pierre

Charles I 1600-1649 .... **LC 13**
Charriere, Isabelle de 1740-1805 .. **NCLC 66**
Charyn, Jerome 1937- .... **CLC 5, 8, 18**
See also CA 5-8R; CAAS 1; CANR 7, 61;
DLBY 83; MTCW
Chase, Mary (Coyle) 1907-1981 .... **DC 1**
See also CA 77-80; 105; SATA 17; SATA-Obit
29
Chase, Mary Ellen 1887-1973 .... **CLC 2**
See also CA 13-16; 41-44R; CAP 1; SATA 10
Chase, Nicholas
See Hyde, Anthony
Chateaubriand, Francois Rene de 1768-1848
NCLC 3
See also DLB 119
Chatterje, Sarat Chandra 1876-1936(?)
See Chatterji, Saratchandra
See also CA 109
Chatterji, Bankim Chandra 1838-1894 **NCLC**
19
Chatterji, Saratchandra .... **TCLC 13**
See also Chatterje, Sarat Chandra
Chatterton, Thomas 1752-1770 . **LC 3; DAM**
POET
See also DLB 109
Chatwin, (Charles) Bruce 1940-1989 **CLC 28,**
57, 59; DAM POP
See also AAYA 4; BEST 90:1; CA 85-88; 127
Chaucer, Daniel
See Ford, Ford Madox
Chaucer, Geoffrey 1340(?)-1400 **LC 17; DA;**
DAB; DAC; DAM MST, POET; PC 19;
WLCS
See also CDBLB Before 1660; DLB 146
Chaviaras, Strates 1935-
See Haviaras, Stratis
See also CA 105
Chayefsky, Paddy .... **CLC 23**
See also Chayefsky, Sidney
See also DLB 7, 44; DLBY 81
Chayefsky, Sidney 1923-1981
See Chayefsky, Paddy
See also CA 9-12R; 104; CANR 18; DAM
DRAM
Chedid, Andree 1920- .... **CLC 47**
See also CA 145
Cheever, John 1912-1982 **CLC 3, 7, 8, 11, 15,**
25, 64; DA; DAB; DAC; DAM MST, NOV,
POP; SSC 1; WLC
See also CA 5-8R; 106; CABS 1; CANR 5, 27;
CDALB 1941-1968; DLB 2, 102; DLBY 80,
82; INT CANR-5; MTCW
Cheever, Susan 1943- .... **CLC 18, 48**
See also CA 103; CANR 27, 51; DLBY 82; INT
CANR-27
Chekhonte, Antosha
See Chekhov, Anton (Pavlovich)
Chekhov, Anton (Pavlovich) 1860-1904 **TCLC**
3, 10, 31, 55; DA; DAB; DAC; DAM
DRAM, MST; SSC 2, 28; WLC
See also CA 104; 124; SATA 90
Chernyshevsky, Nikolay Gavrilovich 1828-1889
NCLC 1
Cherry, Carolyn Janice 1942-
See Cherryh, C. J.
See also CA 65-68; CANR 10
Cherryh, C. J. .... **CLC 35**
See also Cherry, Carolyn Janice
See also DLBY 80; SATA 93
Chesnutt, Charles W(addell) 1858-1932
TCLC 5, 39; BLC; DAM MULT; SSC 7
See also BW 1; CA 106; 125; DLB 12, 50, 78;
MTCW

Chester, Alfred 1929(?)-1971 .... **CLC 49**
See also CA 33-36R; DLB 130
Chesterton, G(ilbert) K(eith) 1874-1936
TCLC 1, 6, 64; DAM NOV, POET; SSC 1
See also CA 104; 132; CDBLB 1914-1945;
DLB 10, 19, 34, 70, 98, 149, 178; MTCW;
SATA 27
Chiang Pin-chin 1904-1986
See Ding Ling
See also CA 118
Ch'ien Chung-shu 1910- .... **CLC 22**
See also CA 130; MTCW
Child, L. Maria
See Child, Lydia Maria
Child, Lydia Maria 1802-1880 .... **NCLC 6**
See also DLB 1, 74; SATA 67
Child, Mrs.
See Child, Lydia Maria
Child, Philip 1898-1978 .... **CLC 19, 68**
See also CA 13-14; CAP 1; SATA 47
Childers, (Robert) Erskine 1870-1922 **TCLC**
65
See also CA 113; 153; DLB 70
Childress, Alice 1920-1994 **CLC 12, 15, 86, 96;**
BLC; DAM DRAM, MULT, NOV; DC 4
See also AAYA 8; BW 2; CA 45-48; 146; CANR
3, 27, 50; CLR 14; DLB 7, 38; JRDA;
MAICYA; MTCW; SATA 7, 48, 81
Chin, Frank (Chew, Jr.) 1940- .... **DC 7**
See also CA 33-36R; DAM MULT
Chislett, (Margaret) Anne 1943- ...... **CLC 34**
See also CA 151
Chitty, Thomas Willes 1926- .... **CLC 11**
See also Hinde, Thomas
See also CA 5-8R
Chivers, Thomas Holley 1809-1858 **NCLC 49**
See also DLB 3
Chomette, Rene Lucien 1898-1981
See Clair, Rene
See also CA 103
Chopin, Kate **TCLC 5, 14; DA; DAB; SSC 8;**
WLCS
See also Chopin, Katherine
See also CDALB 1865-1917; DLB 12, 78
Chopin, Katherine 1851-1904
See Chopin, Kate
See also CA 104; 122; DAC; DAM MST, NOV
Chretien de Troyes c. 12th cent. -.. **CMLC 10**
Christie
See Ichikawa, Kon
Christie, Agatha (Mary Clarissa) 1890-1976
CLC 1, 6, 8, 12, 39, 48; DAB; DAC; DAM
NOV
See also AAYA 9; AITN 1, 2; CA 17-20R; 61-
64; CANR 10, 37; CDBLB 1914-1945; DLB
13, 77; MTCW; SATA 36
Christie, (Ann) Philippa
See Pearce, Philippa
See also CA 5-8R; CANR 4
Christine de Pizan 1365(?)-1431(?) .... **LC 9**
Chubb, Elmer
See Masters, Edgar Lee
Chulkov, Mikhail Dmitrievich 1743-1792 **LC 2**
See also DLB 150
Churchill, Caryl 1938- ..... **CLC 31, 55; DC 5**
See also CA 102; CANR 22, 46; DLB 13;
MTCW
Churchill, Charles 1731-1764 .... **LC 3**
See also DLB 109
Chute, Carolyn 1947- .... **CLC 39**
See also CA 123
Ciardi, John (Anthony) 1916-1986 . **CLC 10,**
40, 44; DAM POET

See also CA 5-8R; 118; CAAS 2; CANR 5, 33;
　CLR 19; DLB 5; DLBY 86; INT CANR-5;
　MAICYA; MTCW; SATA 1, 65; SATA-Obit
　46
Cicero, Marcus Tullius　106B.C.-43B.C.
　CMLC 3
Cimino, Michael　1943- .... **CLC 16**
　See also CA 105
Cioran, E(mil) M.　1911-1995 .... **CLC 64**
　See also CA 25-28R; 149
Cisneros, Sandra　1954-**CLC 69; DAM MULT;**
　HLC
　See also AAYA 9; CA 131; CANR 64; DLB 122,
　152; HW
Cixous, Helene　1937- .... **CLC 92**
　See also CA 126; CANR 55; DLB 83; MTCW
Clair, Rene　.. **CLC 20**
　See also Chomette, Rene Lucien
Clampitt, Amy　1920-1994 ..... **CLC 32; PC 19**
　See also CA 110; 146; CANR 29; DLB 105
Clancy, Thomas L., Jr.　1947-
　See Clancy, Tom
　See also CA 125; 131; CANR 62; INT 131;
　MTCW
Clancy, Tom　.......... **CLC 45; DAM NOV, POP**
　See also Clancy, Thomas L., Jr.
　See also AAYA 9; BEST 89:1, 90:1
Clare, John　1793-1864　**NCLC 9; DAB; DAM**
　POET
　See also DLB 55, 96
Clarin
　See Alas (y Urena), Leopoldo (Enrique Garcia)
Clark, Al C.
　See Goines, Donald
Clark, (Robert) Brian　1932- .... **CLC 29**
　See also CA 41-44R
Clark, Curt
　See Westlake, Donald E(dwin)
Clark, Eleanor　1913-1996 .... **CLC 5, 19**
　See also CA 9-12R; 151; CANR 41; DLB 6
Clark, J. P.
　See Clark, John Pepper
　See also DLB 117
Clark, John Pepper　1935- ...... **CLC 38; BLC;**
　DAM DRAM, MULT; DC 5
　See also Clark, J. P.
　See also BW 1; CA 65-68; CANR 16
Clark, M. R.
　See Clark, Mavis Thorpe
Clark, Mavis Thorpe　1909- .... **CLC 12**
　See also CA 57-60; CANR 8, 37; CLR 30;
　MAICYA; SAAS 5; SATA 8, 74
Clark, Walter Van Tilburg　1909-1971**CLC 28**
　See also CA 9-12R; 33-36R; CANR 63; DLB
　9; SATA 8
Clarke, Arthur C(harles)　1917-**CLC 1, 4, 13,**
　18, 35; DAM POP; SSC 3
　See also AAYA 4; CA 1-4R; CANR 2, 28, 55;
　JRDA; MAICYA; MTCW; SATA 13, 70
Clarke, Austin　1896-1974 .... **CLC 6, 9; DAM**
　POET
　See also CA 29-32; 49-52; CAP 2; DLB 10, 20
Clarke, Austin C(hesterfield)　1934-**CLC 8, 53;**
　BLC; DAC; DAM MULT
　See also BW 1; CA 25-28R; CAAS 16; CANR
　14, 32; DLB 53, 125
Clarke, Gillian　1937- .... **CLC 61**
　See also CA 106; DLB 40
Clarke, Marcus (Andrew Hislop)　1846-1881
　NCLC 19
Clarke, Shirley　1925- .... **CLC 16**
Clash, The
　See Headon, (Nicky) Topper; Jones, Mick;

　Simonon, Paul; Strummer, Joe
Claudel, Paul (Louis Charles Marie)　1868-1955
　TCLC 2, 10
　See also CA 104
Clavell, James (duMaresq)　1925-1994**CLC 6,**
　25, 87; DAM NOV, POP
　See also CA 25-28R; 146; CANR 26, 48;
　MTCW
Cleaver, (Leroy) Eldridge　1935- ..... **CLC 30;**
　BLC; DAM MULT
　See also BW 1; CA 21-24R; CANR 16
Cleese, John (Marwood)　1939- .... **CLC 21**
　See also Monty Python
　See also CA 112; 116; CANR 35; MTCW
Cleishbotham, Jebediah
　See Scott, Walter
Cleland, John　1710-1789 .... **LC 2**
　See also DLB 39
Clemens, Samuel Langhorne　1835-1910
　See Twain, Mark
　See also CA 104; 135; CDALB 1865-1917; DA;
　DAB; DAC; DAM MST, NOV; DLB 11, 12,
　23, 64, 74, 186; JRDA; MAICYA; YABC 2
Cleophil
　See Congreve, William
Clerihew, E.
　See Bentley, E(dmund) C(lerihew)
Clerk, N. W.
　See Lewis, C(live) S(taples)
Cliff, Jimmy　.. **CLC 21**
　See also Chambers, James
Clifton, (Thelma) Lucille　1936- **CLC 19, 66;**
　BLC; DAM MULT, POET; PC 17
　See also BW 2; CA 49-52; CANR 2, 24, 42;
　CLR 5; DLB 5, 41; MAICYA; MTCW; SATA
　20, 69
Clinton, Dirk
　See Silverberg, Robert
Clough, Arthur Hugh　1819-1861 ... **NCLC 27**
　See also DLB 32
Clutha, Janet Paterson Frame　1924-
　See Frame, Janet
　See also CA 1-4R; CANR 2, 36; MTCW
Clyne, Terence
　See Blatty, William Peter
Cobalt, Martin
　See Mayne, William (James Carter)
Cobb, Irvin S.　1876-1944 .... **TCLC 77**
　See also DLB 11, 25, 86
Cobbett, William　1763-1835 .... **NCLC 49**
　See also DLB 43, 107, 158
Coburn, D(onald) L(ee)　1938- .... **CLC 10**
　See also CA 89-92
Cocteau, Jean (Maurice Eugene Clement)　1889-
　1963**CLC 1, 8, 15, 16, 43; DA; DAB; DAC;**
　DAM DRAM, MST, NOV; WLC
　See also CA 25-28; CANR 40; CAP 2; DLB
　65; MTCW
Codrescu, Andrei　1946-**CLC 46; DAM POET**
　See also CA 33-36R; CAAS 19; CANR 13, 34,
　53
Coe, Max
　See Bourne, Randolph S(illiman)
Coe, Tucker
　See Westlake, Donald E(dwin)
Coen, Ethan　1958- .... **CLC 108**
　See also CA 126
Coen, Joel　1955- .... **CLC 108**
　See also CA 126
Coetzee, J(ohn) M(ichael)　1940- **CLC 23, 33,**
　66; DAM NOV
　See also CA 77-80; CANR 41, 54; MTCW
Coffey, Brian

　See Koontz, Dean R(ay)
Cohan, George M(ichael)　1878-1942**TCLC 60**
　See also CA 157
Cohen, Arthur A(llen)　1928-1986 . **CLC 7, 31**
　See also CA 1-4R; 120; CANR 1, 17, 42; DLB
　28
Cohen, Leonard (Norman)　1934- **CLC 3, 38;**
　DAC; DAM MST
　See also CA 21-24R; CANR 14; DLB 53;
　MTCW
Cohen, Matt　1942- .... **CLC 19; DAC**
　See also CA 61-64; CAAS 18; CANR 40; DLB
　53
Cohen-Solal, Annie　19(?)- .... **CLC 50**
Colegate, Isabel　1931- .... **CLC 36**
　See also CA 17-20R; CANR 8, 22; DLB 14;
　INT CANR-22; MTCW
Coleman, Emmett
　See Reed, Ishmael
Coleridge, M. E.
　See Coleridge, Mary E(lizabeth)
Coleridge, Mary E(lizabeth)　1861-1907**TCLC**
　73
　See also CA 116; DLB 19, 98
Coleridge, Samuel Taylor　1772-1834**NCLC 9,**
　54; DA; DAB; DAC; DAM MST, POET;
　PC 11; WLC
　See also CDBLB 1789-1832; DLB 93, 107
Coleridge, Sara　1802-1852 .... **NCLC 31**
Coles, Don　1928- .... **CLC 46**
　See also CA 115; CANR 38
Coles, Robert (Martin)　1929- .... **CLC 108**
　See also CA 45-48; CANR 3, 32; INT CANR-
　32; SATA 23
Colette, (Sidonie-Gabrielle)　1873-1954**T C L C**
　1, 5, 16; DAM NOV; SSC 10
　See also CA 104; 131; DLB 65; MTCW
Collett, (Jacobine) Camilla (Wergeland)　1813-
　1895 .... **NCLC 22**
Collier, Christopher　1930- .... **CLC 30**
　See also AAYA 13; CA 33-36R; CANR 13, 33;
　JRDA; MAICYA; SATA 16, 70
Collier, James L(incoln)　1928-**CLC 30; DAM**
　POP
　See also AAYA 13; CA 9-12R; CANR 4, 33,
　60; CLR 3; JRDA; MAICYA; SAAS 21;
　SATA 8, 70
Collier, Jeremy　1650-1726 .... **LC 6**
Collier, John　1901-1980 .... **SSC 19**
　See also CA 65-68; 97-100; CANR 10; DLB
　77
Collingwood, R(obin) G(eorge)　1889(?)-1943
　TCLC 67
　See also CA 117; 155
Collins, Hunt
　See Hunter, Evan
Collins, Linda　1931- .... **CLC 44**
　See also CA 125
Collins, (William) Wilkie　1824-1889**NCLC 1,**
　18
　See also CDBLB 1832-1890; DLB 18, 70, 159
Collins, William　1721-1759 . **LC 4, 40; DAM**
　POET
　See also DLB 109
Collodi, Carlo　1826-1890 .... **NCLC 54**
　See also Lorenzini, Carlo
　See also CLR 5
Colman, George
　See Glassco, John
Colt, Winchester Remington
　See Hubbard, L(afayette) Ron(ald)
Colter, Cyrus　1910- .... **CLC 58**
　See also BW 1; CA 65-68; CANR 10; DLB 33

Colton, James
See Hansen, Joseph
Colum, Padraic 1881-1972 .... **CLC 28**
See also CA 73-76; 33-36R; CANR 35; CLR
36; MAICYA; MTCW; SATA 15
Colvin, James
See Moorcock, Michael (John)
Colwin, Laurie (E.) 1944-1992 **CLC 5, 13, 23,
84**
See also CA 89-92; 139; CANR 20, 46; DLBY
80; MTCW
Comfort, Alex(ander) 1920- **CLC 7; DAM POP**
See also CA 1-4R; CANR 1, 45
Comfort, Montgomery
See Campbell, (John) Ramsey
Compton-Burnett, I(vy) 1884(?)-1969 **CLC 1,
3, 10, 15, 34; DAM NOV**
See also CA 1-4R; 25-28R; CANR 4; DLB 36;
MTCW
Comstock, Anthony 1844-1915 ...... **TCLC 13**
See also CA 110
Comte, Auguste 1798-1857 .... **NCLC 54**
Conan Doyle, Arthur
See Doyle, Arthur Conan
Conde, Maryse 1937- ...... **CLC 52, 92; DAM
MULT**
See also Boucolon, Maryse
See also BW 2
Condillac, Etienne Bonnot de 1714-1780 **L C
26**
Condon, Richard (Thomas) 1915-1996 **CLC 4,
6, 8, 10, 45, 100; DAM NOV**
See also BEST 90:3; CA 1-4R; 151; CAAS 1;
CANR 2, 23; INT CANR-23; MTCW
Confucius 551B.C.-479B.C. .. **CMLC 19; DA;
DAB; DAC; DAM MST; WLCS**
Congreve, William 1670-1729 **LC 5, 21; DA;
DAB; DAC; DAM DRAM, MST, POET;
DC 2; WLC**
See also CDBLB 1660-1789; DLB 39, 84
Connell, Evan S(helby), Jr. 1924- **CLC 4, 6, 45;
DAM NOV**
See also AAYA 7; CA 1-4R; CAAS 2; CANR
2, 39; DLB 2; DLBY 81; MTCW
Connelly, Marc(us Cook) 1890-1980 .. **CLC 7**
See also CA 85-88; 102; CANR 30; DLB 7;
DLBY 80; SATA-Obit 25
Connor, Ralph .... **TCLC 31**
See also Gordon, Charles William
See also DLB 92
Conrad, Joseph 1857-1924 **TCLC 1, 6, 13, 25,
43, 57; DA; DAB; DAC; DAM MST, NOV;
SSC 9; WLC**
See also CA 104; 131; CANR 60; CDBLB
1890-1914; DLB 10, 34, 98, 156; MTCW;
SATA 27
Conrad, Robert Arnold
See Hart, Moss
Conroy, Donald Pat(rick) 1945- **CLC 30, 74;
DAM NOV, POP**
See also AAYA 8; AITN 1; CA 85-88; CANR
24, 53; DLB 6; MTCW
Constant (de Rebecque), (Henri) Benjamin
1767-1830 .... **NCLC 6**
See also DLB 119
Conybeare, Charles Augustus
See Eliot, T(homas) S(tearns)
Cook, Michael 1933- .... **CLC 58**
See also CA 93-96; DLB 53
Cook, Robin 1940- .... **CLC 14; DAM POP**
See also BEST 90:2; CA 108; 111; CANR 41;
INT 111
Cook, Roy

See Silverberg, Robert
Cooke, Elizabeth 1948- .... **CLC 55**
See also CA 129
Cooke, John Esten 1830-1886 .... **NCLC 5**
See also DLB 3
Cooke, John Estes
See Baum, L(yman) Frank
Cooke, M. E.
See Creasey, John
Cooke, Margaret
See Creasey, John
Cook-Lynn, Elizabeth 1930- .. **CLC 93; DAM
MULT**
See also CA 133; DLB 175; NNAL
Cooney, Ray .... **CLC 62**
Cooper, Douglas 1960- .... **CLC 86**
Cooper, Henry St. John
See Creasey, John
Cooper, J(oan) California .... **CLC 56; DAM
MULT**
See also AAYA 12; BW 1; CA 125; CANR 55
Cooper, James Fenimore 1789-1851 **NCLC 1,
27, 54**
See also AAYA 22; CDALB 1640-1865; DLB
3; SATA 19
Coover, Robert (Lowell) 1932- **CLC 3, 7, 15,
32, 46, 87; DAM NOV; SSC 15**
See also CA 45-48; CANR 3, 37, 58; DLB 2;
DLBY 81; MTCW
Copeland, Stewart (Armstrong) 1952- **CLC 26**
Coppard, A(lfred) E(dgar) 1878-1957 **T C L C
5; SSC 21**
See also CA 114; DLB 162; YABC 1
Coppee, Francois 1842-1908 .... **TCLC 25**
Coppola, Francis Ford 1939- .... **CLC 16**
See also CA 77-80; CANR 40; DLB 44
Corbiere, Tristan 1845-1875 .... **NCLC 43**
Corcoran, Barbara 1911- .... **CLC 17**
See also AAYA 14; CA 21-24R; CAAS 2;
CANR 11, 28, 48; DLB 52; JRDA; SAAS
20; SATA 3, 77
Cordelier, Maurice
See Giraudoux, (Hippolyte) Jean
Corelli, Marie 1855-1924 .... **TCLC 51**
See also Mackay, Mary
See also DLB 34, 156
Corman, Cid .... **CLC 9**
See also Corman, Sidney
See also CAAS 2; DLB 5
Corman, Sidney 1924-
See Corman, Cid
See also CA 85-88; CANR 44; DAM POET
Cormier, Robert (Edmund) 1925- **CLC 12, 30;
DA; DAB; DAC; DAM MST, NOV**
See also AAYA 3, 19; CA 1-4R; CANR 5, 23;
CDALB 1968-1988; CLR 12; DLB 52; INT
CANR-23; JRDA; MAICYA; MTCW; SATA
10, 45, 83
Corn, Alfred (DeWitt III) 1943- .... **CLC 33**
See also CA 104; CAAS 25; CANR 44; DLB
120; DLBY 80
Corneille, Pierre 1606-1684 .... **LC 28; DAB;
DAM MST**
Cornwell, David (John Moore) 1931- **CLC 9,
15; DAM POP**
See also le Carre, John
See also CA 5-8R; CANR 13, 33, 59; MTCW
Corso, (Nunzio) Gregory 1930- .... **CLC 1, 11**
See also CA 5-8R; CANR 41; DLB 5, 16;
MTCW
Cortazar, Julio 1914-1984 **CLC 2, 3, 5, 10, 13,
15, 33, 34, 92; DAM MULT, NOV; HLC;
SSC 7**

See also CA 21-24R; CANR 12, 32; DLB 113;
HW; MTCW
CORTES, HERNAN 1484-1547 .... **LC 31**
Corwin, Cecil
See Kornbluth, C(yril) M.
Cosic, Dobrica 1921- .... **CLC 14**
See also CA 122; 138; DLB 181
Costain, Thomas B(ertram) 1885-1965 **C L C
30**
See also CA 5-8R; 25-28R; DLB 9
Costantini, Humberto 1924(?)-1987 . **CLC 49**
See also CA 131; 122; HW
Costello, Elvis 1955- .... **CLC 21**
Cotes, Cecil V.
See Duncan, Sara Jeannette
Cotter, Joseph Seamon Sr. 1861-1949 **T C L C
28; BLC; DAM MULT**
See also BW 1; CA 124; DLB 50
Couch, Arthur Thomas Quiller
See Quiller-Couch, Arthur Thomas
Coulton, James
See Hansen, Joseph
Couperus, Louis (Marie Anne) 1863-1923
TCLC 15
See also CA 115
Coupland, Douglas 1961- **CLC 85; DAC; DAM
POP**
See also CA 142; CANR 57
Court, Wesli
See Turco, Lewis (Putnam)
Courtenay, Bryce 1933- .... **CLC 59**
See also CA 138
Courtney, Robert
See Ellison, Harlan (Jay)
Cousteau, Jacques-Yves 1910-1997 .. **CLC 30**
See also CA 65-68; 159; CANR 15; MTCW;
SATA 38
Cowan, Peter (Walkinshaw) 1914- .... **SSC 28**
See also CA 21-24R; CANR 9, 25, 50
Coward, Noel (Peirce) 1899-1973 **CLC 1, 9, 29,
51; DAM DRAM**
See also AITN 1; CA 17-18; 41-44R; CANR
35; CAP 2; CDBLB 1914-1945; DLB 10;
MTCW
Cowley, Malcolm 1898-1989 .... **CLC 39**
See also CA 5-8R; 128; CANR 3, 55; DLB 4,
48; DLBY 81, 89; MTCW
Cowper, William 1731-1800 . **NCLC 8; DAM
POET**
See also DLB 104, 109
Cox, William Trevor 1928- .... **CLC 9, 14, 71;
DAM NOV**
See also Trevor, William
See also CA 9-12R; CANR 4, 37, 55; DLB 14;
INT CANR-37; MTCW
Coyne, P. J.
See Masters, Hilary
Cozzens, James Gould 1903-1978 **CLC 1, 4, 11,
92**
See also CA 9-12R; 81-84; CANR 19; CDALB
1941-1968; DLB 9; DLBD 2; DLBY 84;
MTCW
Crabbe, George 1754-1832 .... **NCLC 26**
See also DLB 93
Craddock, Charles Egbert
See Murfree, Mary Noailles
Craig, A. A.
See Anderson, Poul (William)
Craik, Dinah Maria (Mulock) 1826-1887
NCLC 38
See also DLB 35, 163; MAICYA; SATA 34
Cram, Ralph Adams 1863-1942 ..... **TCLC 45**
See also CA 160

Crane, (Harold) Hart 1899-1932 **TCLC 2, 5;
    DA; DAB; DAC; DAM MST, POET; PC
    3; WLC**
    See also CA 104; 127; CDALB 1917-1929;
    DLB 4, 48; MTCW
Crane, R(onald) S(almon) 1886-1967**CLC 27**
    See also CA 85-88; DLB 63
Crane, Stephen (Townley) 1871-1900 **T C L C
    11, 17, 32; DA; DAB; DAC; DAM MST,
    NOV, POET; SSC 7; WLC**
    See also AAYA 21; CA 109; 140; CDALB 1865-
    1917; DLB 12, 54, 78; YABC 2
Crase, Douglas 1944- .... **CLC 58**
    See also CA 106
Crashaw, Richard 1612(?)-1649 .... **LC 24**
    See also DLB 126
Craven, Margaret 1901-1980 . **CLC 17; DAC**
    See also CA 103
Crawford, F(rancis) Marion 1854-1909**TCLC
    10**
    See also CA 107; DLB 71
Crawford, Isabella Valancy 1850-1887**N CLC
    12**
    See also DLB 92
Crayon, Geoffrey
    See Irving, Washington
Creasey, John 1908-1973 .... **CLC 11**
    See also CA 5-8R; 41-44R; CANR 8, 59; DLB
    77; MTCW
Crebillon, Claude Prosper Jolyot de (fils) 1707-
    1777 .... **LC 28**
Credo
    See Creasey, John
Credo, Alvaro J. de
    See Prado (Calvo), Pedro
Creeley, Robert (White) 1926-**CLC 1, 2, 4, 8,
    11, 15, 36, 78; DAM POET**
    See also CA 1-4R; CAAS 10; CANR 23, 43;
    DLB 5, 16, 169; MTCW
Crews, Harry (Eugene) 1935- **CLC 6, 23, 49**
    See also AITN 1; CA 25-28R; CANR 20, 57;
    DLB 6, 143; MTCW
Crichton, (John) Michael 1942-**CLC 2, 6, 54,
    90; DAM NOV, POP**
    See also AAYA 10; AITN 2; CA 25-28R; CANR
    13, 40, 54; DLBY 81; INT CANR-13; JRDA;
    MTCW; SATA 9, 88
Crispin, Edmund .... **CLC 22**
    See also Montgomery, (Robert) Bruce
    See also DLB 87
Cristofer, Michael 1945(?)- .... **CLC 28; DAM
    DRAM**
    See also CA 110; 152; DLB 7
Croce, Benedetto 1866-1952 .... **TCLC 37**
    See also CA 120; 155
Crockett, David 1786-1836 .... **NCLC 8**
    See also DLB 3, 11
Crockett, Davy
    See Crockett, David
Crofts, Freeman Wills 1879-1957 .. **TCLC 55**
    See also CA 115; DLB 77
Croker, John Wilson 1780-1857 .... **NCLC 10**
    See also DLB 110
Crommelynck, Fernand 1885-1970 .. **CLC 75**
    See also CA 89-92
Cronin, A(rchibald) J(oseph) 1896-1981**C L C
    32**
    See also CA 1-4R; 102; CANR 5; SATA 47;
    SATA-Obit 25
Cross, Amanda
    See Heilbrun, Carolyn G(old)
Crothers, Rachel 1878(?)-1958 ...... **TCLC 19**
    See also CA 113; DLB 7

Croves, Hal
    See Traven, B.
Crow Dog, Mary (Ellen) (?)- .... **CLC 93**
    See also Brave Bird, Mary
    See also CA 154
Crowfield, Christopher
    See Stowe, Harriet (Elizabeth) Beecher
Crowley, Aleister .... **TCLC 7**
    See also Crowley, Edward Alexander
Crowley, Edward Alexander 1875-1947
    See Crowley, Aleister
    See also CA 104
Crowley, John 1942- .... **CLC 57**
    See also CA 61-64; CANR 43; DLBY 82; SATA
    65
Crud
    See Crumb, R(obert)
Crumarums
    See Crumb, R(obert)
Crumb, R(obert) 1943- .... **CLC 17**
    See also CA 106
Crumbum
    See Crumb, R(obert)
Crumski
    See Crumb, R(obert)
Crum the Bum
    See Crumb, R(obert)
Crunk
    See Crumb, R(obert)
Crustt
    See Crumb, R(obert)
Cryer, Gretchen (Kiger) 1935- .... **CLC 21**
    See also CA 114; 123
Csath, Geza 1887-1919 .... **TCLC 13**
    See also CA 111
Cudlip, David 1933- .... **CLC 34**
Cullen, Countee 1903-1946**TCLC 4, 37; BLC;
    DA; DAC; DAM MST, MULT, POET; PC
    20; WLCS**
    See also BW 1; CA 108; 124; CDALB 1917-
    1929; DLB 4, 48, 51; MTCW; SATA 18
Cum, R.
    See Crumb, R(obert)
Cummings, Bruce F(rederick) 1889-1919
    See Barbellion, W. N. P.
    See also CA 123
Cummings, E(dward) E(stlin) 1894-1962**CLC
    1, 3, 8, 12, 15, 68; DA; DAB; DAC; DAM
    MST, POET; PC 5; WLC 2**
    See also CA 73-76; CANR 31; CDALB 1929-
    1941; DLB 4, 48; MTCW
Cunha, Euclides (Rodrigues Pimenta) da 1866-
    1909 .... **TCLC 24**
    See also CA 123
Cunningham, E. V.
    See Fast, Howard (Melvin)
Cunningham, J(ames) V(incent) 1911-1985
    CLC 3, 31
    See also CA 1-4R; 115; CANR 1; DLB 5
Cunningham, Julia (Woolfolk) 1916-**CLC 12**
    See also CA 9-12R; CANR 4, 19, 36; JRDA;
    MAICYA; SAAS 2; SATA 1, 26
Cunningham, Michael 1952- .... **CLC 34**
    See also CA 136
Cunninghame Graham, R(obert) B(ontine)
    1852-1936 .... **TCLC 19**
    See also Graham, R(obert) B(ontine)
    Cunninghame
    See also CA 119; DLB 98
Currie, Ellen 19(?)- .... **CLC 44**
Curtin, Philip
    See Lowndes, Marie Adelaide (Belloc)
Curtis, Price

    See Ellison, Harlan (Jay)
Cutrate, Joe
    See Spiegelman, Art
Cynewulf c. 770-c. 840 .... **CMLC 23**
Czaczkes, Shmuel Yosef
    See Agnon, S(hmuel) Y(osef Halevi)
Dabrowska, Maria (Szumska) 1889-1965**CLC
    15**
    See also CA 106
Dabydeen, David 1955- .... **CLC 34**
    See also BW 1; CA 125; CANR 56
Dacey, Philip 1939- .... **CLC 51**
    See also CA 37-40R; CAAS 17; CANR 14, 32,
    64; DLB 105
Dagerman, Stig (Halvard) 1923-1954 **T C L C
    17**
    See also CA 117; 155
Dahl, Roald 1916-1990**CLC 1, 6, 18, 79; DAB;
    DAC; DAM MST, NOV, POP**
    See also AAYA 15; CA 1-4R; 133; CANR 6,
    32, 37, 62; CLR 1, 7, 41; DLB 139; JRDA;
    MAICYA; MTCW; SATA 1, 26, 73; SATA-
    Obit 65
Dahlberg, Edward 1900-1977 .. **CLC 1, 7, 14**
    See also CA 9-12R; 69-72; CANR 31, 62; DLB
    48; MTCW
Daitch, Susan 1954- .... **CLC 103**
    See also CA 161
Dale, Colin .... **TCLC 18**
    See also Lawrence, T(homas) E(dward)
Dale, George E.
    See Asimov, Isaac
Daly, Elizabeth 1878-1967 .... **CLC 52**
    See also CA 23-24; 25-28R; CANR 60; CAP 2
Daly, Maureen 1921- .... **CLC 17**
    See also AAYA 5; CANR 37; JRDA; MAICYA;
    SAAS 1; SATA 2
Damas, Leon-Gontran 1912-1978 .... **CLC 84**
    See also BW 1; CA 125; 73-76
Dana, Richard Henry Sr. 1787-1879**NCLC 53**
Daniel, Samuel 1562(?)-1619 .... **LC 24**
    See also DLB 62
Daniels, Brett
    See Adler, Renata
Dannay, Frederic 1905-1982 . **CLC 11; DAM
    POP**
    See also Queen, Ellery
    See also CA 1-4R; 107; CANR 1, 39; DLB 137;
    MTCW
D'Annunzio, Gabriele 1863-1938**TCLC 6, 40**
    See also CA 104; 155
Danois, N. le
    See Gourmont, Remy (-Marie-Charles) de
Dante 1265-1321 .... **CMLC 3, 18; DA; DAB;
    DAC; DAM MST, POET; PC 21; WLCS**
d'Antibes, Germain
    See Simenon, Georges (Jacques Christian)
Danticat, Edwidge 1969- .... **CLC 94**
    See also CA 152
Danvers, Dennis 1947- .... **CLC 70**
Danziger, Paula 1944- .... **CLC 21**
    See also AAYA 4; CA 112; 115; CANR 37; CLR
    20; JRDA; MAICYA; SATA 36, 63; SATA-
    Brief 30
Da Ponte, Lorenzo 1749-1838 .... **NCLC 50**
Dario, Ruben 1867-1916 .... **TCLC 4; DAM
    MULT; HLC; PC 15**
    See also CA 131; HW; MTCW
Darley, George 1795-1846 .... **NCLC 2**
    See also DLB 96
Darwin, Charles 1809-1882 .... **NCLC 57**
    See also DLB 57, 166
Daryush, Elizabeth 1887-1977 ...... **CLC 6, 19**

See also CA 49-52; CANR 3; DLB 20
Dashwood, Edmee Elizabeth Monica de la Pasture 1890-1943
See Delafield, E. M.
See also CA 119; 154
Daudet, (Louis Marie) Alphonse 1840-1897
NCLC 1
See also DLB 123
Daumal, Rene 1908-1944 .... **TCLC 14**
See also CA 114
Davenport, Guy (Mattison, Jr.) 1927-**CLC 6, 14, 38; SSC 16**
See also CA 33-36R; CANR 23; DLB 130
Davidson, Avram 1923-
See Queen, Ellery
See also CA 101; CANR 26; DLB 8
Davidson, Donald (Grady) 1893-1968**CLC 2, 13, 19**
See also CA 5-8R; 25-28R; CANR 4; DLB 45
Davidson, Hugh
See Hamilton, Edmond
Davidson, John 1857-1909 .... **TCLC 24**
See also CA 118; DLB 19
Davidson, Sara 1943- .... **CLC 9**
See also CA 81-84; CANR 44
Davie, Donald (Alfred) 1922-1995 . **CLC 5, 8, 10, 31**
See also CA 1-4R; 149; CAAS 3; CANR 1, 44; DLB 27; MTCW
Davies, Ray(mond Douglas) 1944- ... **CLC 21**
See also CA 116; 146
Davies, Rhys 1903-1978 .... **CLC 23**
See also CA 9-12R; 81-84; CANR 4; DLB 139
Davies, (William) Robertson 1913-1995 **C L C 2, 7, 13, 25, 42, 75, 91; DA; DAB; DAC; DAM MST, NOV, POP; WLC**
See also BEST 89:2; CA 33-36R; 150; CANR 17, 42; DLB 68; INT CANR-17; MTCW
Davies, W(illiam) H(enry) 1871-1940**TCLC 5**
See also CA 104; DLB 19, 174
Davies, Walter C.
See Kornbluth, C(yril) M.
Davis, Angela (Yvonne) 1944- **CLC 77; DAM MULT**
See also BW 2; CA 57-60; CANR 10
Davis, B. Lynch
See Bioy Casares, Adolfo; Borges, Jorge Luis
Davis, Gordon
See Hunt, E(verette) Howard, (Jr.)
Davis, Harold Lenoir 1896-1960 ...... **CLC 49**
See also CA 89-92; DLB 9
Davis, Rebecca (Blaine) Harding 1831-1910
TCLC 6
See also CA 104; DLB 74
Davis, Richard Harding 1864-1916**TCLC 24**
See also CA 114; DLB 12, 23, 78, 79; DLBD 13
Davison, Frank Dalby 1893-1970 ..... **CLC 15**
See also CA 116
Davison, Lawrence H.
See Lawrence, D(avid) H(erbert Richards)
Davison, Peter (Hubert) 1928- .... **CLC 28**
See also CA 9-12R; CAAS 4; CANR 3, 43; DLB 5
Davys, Mary 1674-1732 .... **LC 1**
See also DLB 39
Dawson, Fielding 1930-........................ **CLC 6**
See also CA 85-88; DLB 130
Dawson, Peter
See Faust, Frederick (Schiller)
Day, Clarence (Shepard, Jr.) 1874-1935
TCLC 25
See also CA 108; DLB 11

Day, Thomas 1748-1789 .... **LC 1**
See also DLB 39; YABC 1
Day Lewis, C(ecil) 1904-1972 . **CLC 1, 6, 10; DAM POET; PC 11**
See also Blake, Nicholas
See also CA 13-16; 33-36R; CANR 34; CAP 1; DLB 15, 20; MTCW
Dazai, Osamu .... **TCLC 11**
See also Tsushima, Shuji
See also DLB 182
de Andrade, Carlos Drummond
See Drummond de Andrade, Carlos
Deane, Norman
See Creasey, John
de Beauvoir, Simone (Lucie Ernestine Marie Bertrand)
See Beauvoir, Simone (Lucie Ernestine Marie Bertrand) de
de Beer, P.
See Bosman, Herman Charles
de Brissac, Malcolm
See Dickinson, Peter (Malcolm)
de Chardin, Pierre Teilhard
See Teilhard de Chardin, (Marie Joseph) Pierre
Dee, John 1527-1608 .... **LC 20**
Deer, Sandra 1940- .... **CLC 45**
De Ferrari, Gabriella 1941- .... **CLC 65**
See also CA 146
Defoe, Daniel 1660(?)-1731 **LC 1; DA; DAB; DAC; DAM MST, NOV; WLC**
See also CDBLB 1660-1789; DLB 39, 95, 101; JRDA; MAICYA; SATA 22
de Gourmont, Remy(-Marie-Charles)
See Gourmont, Remy (-Marie-Charles) de
de Hartog, Jan 1914- .... **CLC 19**
See also CA 1-4R; CANR 1
de Hostos, E. M.
See Hostos (y Bonilla), Eugenio Maria de
de Hostos, Eugenio M.
See Hostos (y Bonilla), Eugenio Maria de
Deighton, Len .... **CLC 4, 7, 22, 46**
See also Deighton, Leonard Cyril
See also AAYA 6; BEST 89:2; CDBLB 1960 to Present; DLB 87
Deighton, Leonard Cyril 1929-
See Deighton, Len
See also CA 9-12R; CANR 19, 33; DAM NOV, POP; MTCW
Dekker, Thomas 1572(?)-1632 .. **LC 22; DAM DRAM**
See also CDBLB Before 1660; DLB 62, 172
Delafield, E. M. 1890-1943 .... **TCLC 61**
See also Dashwood, Edmee Elizabeth Monica de la Pasture
See also DLB 34
de la Mare, Walter (John) 1873-1956**TCLC 4, 53; DAB; DAC; DAM MST, POET; SSC 14; WLC**
See also CDBLB 1914-1945; CLR 23; DLB 162; SATA 16
Delaney, Franey
See O'Hara, John (Henry)
Delaney, Shelagh 1939-**CLC 29; DAM DRAM**
See also CA 17-20R; CANR 30; CDBLB 1960 to Present; DLB 13; MTCW
Delany, Mary (Granville Pendarves) 1700-1788
LC 12
Delany, Samuel R(ay, Jr.) 1942-**CLC 8, 14, 38; BLC; DAM MULT**
See also BW 2; CA 81-84; CANR 27, 43; DLB 8, 33; MTCW
De La Ramee, (Marie) Louise 1839-1908
See Ouida

See also SATA 20
de la Roche, Mazo 1879-1961 .... **CLC 14**
See also CA 85-88; CANR 30; DLB 68; SATA 64
De La Salle, Innocent
See Hartmann, Sadakichi
Delbanco, Nicholas (Franklin) 1942- **CLC 6, 13**
See also CA 17-20R; CAAS 2; CANR 29, 55; DLB 6
del Castillo, Michel 1933- .... **CLC 38**
See also CA 109
Deledda, Grazia (Cosima) 1875(?)-1936
TCLC 23
See also CA 123
Delibes, Miguel .... **CLC 8, 18**
See also Delibes Setien, Miguel
Delibes Setien, Miguel 1920-
See Delibes, Miguel
See also CA 45-48; CANR 1, 32; HW; MTCW
DeLillo, Don 1936- **CLC 8, 10, 13, 27, 39, 54, 76; DAM NOV, POP**
See also BEST 89:1; CA 81-84; CANR 21; DLB 6, 173; MTCW
de Lisser, H. G.
See De Lisser, H(erbert) G(eorge)
See also DLB 117
De Lisser, H(erbert) G(eorge) 1878-1944
TCLC 12
See also de Lisser, H. G.
See also BW 2; CA 109; 152
Deloney, Thomas 1560-1600................. **LC 41**
Deloria, Vine (Victor), Jr. 1933- ..... **CLC 21; DAM MULT**
See also CA 53-56; CANR 5, 20, 48; DLB 175; MTCW; NNAL; SATA 21
Del Vecchio, John M(ichael) 1947- ... **CLC 29**
See also CA 110; DLBD 9
de Man, Paul (Adolph Michel) 1919-1983
CLC 55
See also CA 128; 111; CANR 61; DLB 67; MTCW
De Marinis, Rick 1934- .... **CLC 54**
See also CA 57-60; CAAS 24; CANR 9, 25, 50
Dembry, R. Emmet
See Murfree, Mary Noailles
Demby, William 1922- . **CLC 53; BLC; DAM MULT**
See also BW 1; CA 81-84; DLB 33
de Menton, Francisco
See Chin, Frank (Chew, Jr.)
Demijohn, Thom
See Disch, Thomas M(ichael)
de Montherlant, Henry (Milon)
See Montherlant, Henry (Milon) de
Demosthenes 384B.C.-322B.C. .... **CMLC 13**
See also DLB 176
de Natale, Francine
See Malzberg, Barry N(athaniel)
Denby, Edwin (Orr) 1903-1983 .... **CLC 48**
See also CA 138; 110
Denis, Julio
See Cortazar, Julio
Denmark, Harrison
See Zelazny, Roger (Joseph)
Dennis, John 1658-1734 .... **LC 11**
See also DLB 101
Dennis, Nigel (Forbes) 1912-1989....... **CLC 8**
See also CA 25-28R; 129; DLB 13, 15; MTCW
Dent, Lester 1904(?)-1959............... **TCLC 72**
See also CA 112; 161
De Palma, Brian (Russell) 1940-....... **CLC 20**
See also CA 109

De Quincey, Thomas 1785-1859 ...... **NCLC 4**
  See also CDBLB 1789-1832; DLB 110; 144
Deren, Eleanora 1908(?)-1961
  See Deren, Maya
  See also CA 111
Deren, Maya 1917-1961 .... **CLC 16, 102**
  See also Deren, Eleanora
Derleth, August (William) 1909-1971**CLC 31**
  See also CA 1-4R; 29-32R; CANR 4; DLB 9;
  SATA 5
Der Nister 1884-1950 .... **TCLC 56**
de Routisie, Albert
  See Aragon, Louis
Derrida, Jacques 1930- .... **CLC 24, 87**
  See also CA 124; 127
Derry Down Derry
  See Lear, Edward
Dersonnes, Jacques
  See Simenon, Georges (Jacques Christian)
Desai, Anita 1937-**CLC 19, 37, 97; DAB; DAM
  NOV**
  See also CA 81-84; CANR 33, 53; MTCW;
  SATA 63
de Saint-Luc, Jean
  See Glassco, John
de Saint Roman, Arnaud
  See Aragon, Louis
Descartes, Rene 1596-1650 .... **LC 20, 35**
De Sica, Vittorio 1901(?)-1974 .... **CLC 20**
  See also CA 117
Desnos, Robert 1900-1945 .... **TCLC 22**
  See also CA 121; 151
Destouches, Louis-Ferdinand 1894-1961**C L C
  9, 15**
  See also Celine, Louis-Ferdinand
  See also CA 85-88; CANR 28; MTCW
de Tolignac, Gaston
  See Griffith, D(avid Lewelyn) W(ark)
Deutsch, Babette 1895-1982 .... **CLC 18**
  See also CA 1-4R; 108; CANR 4; DLB 45;
  SATA 1; SATA-Obit 33
Devenant, William 1606-1649 .... **LC 13**
Devkota, Laxmiprasad 1909-1959 . **TCLC 23**
  See also CA 123
De Voto, Bernard (Augustine) 1897-1955
  TCLC 29
  See also CA 113; 160; DLB 9
De Vries, Peter 1910-1993 **CLC 1, 2, 3, 7, 10,
  28, 46; DAM NOV**
  See also CA 17-20R; 142; CANR 41; DLB 6;
  DLBY 82; MTCW
Dexter, John
  See Bradley, Marion Zimmer
Dexter, Martin
  See Faust, Frederick (Schiller)
Dexter, Pete 1943- ... **CLC 34, 55; DAM POP**
  See also BEST 89:2; CA 127; 131; INT 131;
  MTCW
Diamano, Silmang
  See Senghor, Leopold Sedar
Diamond, Neil 1941- .... **CLC 30**
  See also CA 108
Diaz del Castillo, Bernal 1496-1584 .... **LC 31**
di Bassetto, Corno
  See Shaw, George Bernard
Dick, Philip K(indred) 1928-1982**CLC 10, 30,
  72; DAM NOV, POP**
  See also CA 49-52; 106; CANR 2, 16; DLB 8;
  MTCW
Dickens, Charles (John Huffam) 1812-1870
  **NCLC 3, 8, 18, 26, 37, 50; DA; DAB; DAC;
  DAM MST, NOV; SSC 17; WLC**
  See also CDBLB 1832-1890; DLB 21, 55, 70,

159, 166; JRDA; MAICYA; SATA 15
Dickey, James (Lafayette) 1923-1997 **CLC 1,
  2, 4, 7, 10, 15, 47; DAM NOV, POET, POP**
  See also AITN 1, 2; CA 9-12R; 156; CABS 2;
  CANR 10, 48, 61; CDALB 1968-1988; DLB
  5; DLBD 7; DLBY 82, 93, 96; INT CANR-
  10; MTCW
Dickey, William 1928-1994 .... **CLC 3, 28**
  See also CA 9-12R; 145; CANR 24; DLB 5
Dickinson, Charles 1951- .... **CLC 49**
  See also CA 128
Dickinson, Emily (Elizabeth) 1830-1886
  **NCLC 21; DA; DAB; DAC; DAM MST,
  POET; PC 1; WLC**
  See also AAYA 22; CDALB 1865-1917; DLB
  1; SATA 29
Dickinson, Peter (Malcolm) 1927-**CLC 12, 35**
  See also AAYA 9; CA 41-44R; CANR 31, 58;
  CLR 29; DLB 87, 161; JRDA; MAICYA;
  SATA 5, 62, 95
Dickson, Carr
  See Carr, John Dickson
Dickson, Carter
  See Carr, John Dickson
Diderot, Denis 1713-1784 .... **LC 26**
Didion, Joan 1934-**CLC 1, 3, 8, 14, 32; DAM
  NOV**
  See also AITN 1; CA 5-8R; CANR 14, 52;
  CDALB 1968-1988; DLB 2, 173; DLBY 81,
  86; MTCW
Dietrich, Robert
  See Hunt, E(verette) Howard, (Jr.)
Dillard, Annie 1945- **CLC 9, 60; DAM NOV**
  See also AAYA 6; CA 49-52; CANR 3, 43, 62;
  DLBY 80; MTCW; SATA 10
Dillard, R(ichard) H(enry) W(ilde) 1937-
  CLC 5
  See also CA 21-24R; CAAS 7; CANR 10; DLB
  5
Dillon, Eilis 1920-1994 .... **CLC 17**
  See also CA 9-12R; 147; CAAS 3; CANR 4,
  38; CLR 26; MAICYA; SATA 2, 74; SATA-
  Obit 83
Dimont, Penelope
  See Mortimer, Penelope (Ruth)
Dinesen, Isak .... **CLC 10, 29, 95; SSC 7**
  See also Blixen, Karen (Christentze Dinesen)
Ding Ling .... **CLC 68**
  See also Chiang Pin-chin
Disch, Thomas M(ichael) 1940- ....**CLC 7, 36**
  See also AAYA 17; CA 21-24R; CAAS 4;
  CANR 17, 36, 54; CLR 18; DLB 8;
  MAICYA; MTCW; SAAS 15; SATA 92
Disch, Tom
  See Disch, Thomas M(ichael)
d'Isly, Georges
  See Simenon, Georges (Jacques Christian)
Disraeli, Benjamin 1804-1881 .... **NCLC 2, 39**
  See also DLB 21, 55
Ditcum, Steve
  See Crumb, R(obert)
Dixon, Paige
  See Corcoran, Barbara
Dixon, Stephen 1936- .... **CLC 52; SSC 16**
  See also CA 89-92; CANR 17, 40, 54; DLB 130
Doak, Annie
  See Dillard, Annie
Dobell, Sydney Thompson 1824-1874 **N C L C
  43**
  See also DLB 32
Doblin, Alfred .... **TCLC 13**
  See also Doeblin, Alfred
Dobrolyubov, Nikolai Alexandrovich 1836-1861

NCLC 5
Dobson, Austin 1840-1921 .... **TCLC 79**
  See also DLB 35; 144
Dobyns, Stephen 1941- .... **CLC 37**
  See also CA 45-48; CANR 2, 18
Doctorow, E(dgar) L(aurence) 1931- **CLC 6,
  11, 15, 18, 37, 44, 65; DAM NOV, POP**
  See also AAYA 22; AITN 2; BEST 89:3; CA
  45-48; CANR 2, 33, 51; CDALB 1968-1988;
  DLB 2, 28, 173; DLBY 80; MTCW
Dodgson, Charles Lutwidge 1832-1898
  See Carroll, Lewis
  See also CLR 2; DA; DAB; DAC; DAM MST,
  NOV, POET; MAICYA; YABC 2
Dodson, Owen (Vincent) 1914-1983 **CLC 79;
  BLC; DAM MULT**
  See also BW 1; CA 65-68; 110; CANR 24; DLB
  76
Doeblin, Alfred 1878-1957 .... **TCLC 13**
  See also Doblin, Alfred
  See also CA 110; 141; DLB 66
Doerr, Harriet 1910- .... **CLC 34**
  See also CA 117; 122; CANR 47; INT 122
Domecq, H(onorio) Bustos
  See Bioy Casares, Adolfo; Borges, Jorge Luis
Domini, Rey
  See Lorde, Audre (Geraldine)
Dominique
  See Proust, (Valentin-Louis-George-Eugene-)
  Marcel
Don, A
  See Stephen, Leslie
Donaldson, Stephen R. 1947- **CLC 46; DAM
  POP**
  See also CA 89-92; CANR 13, 55; INT CANR-
  13
Donleavy, J(ames) P(atrick) 1926-**CLC 1, 4, 6,
  10, 45**
  See also AITN 2; CA 9-12R; CANR 24, 49, 62;
  DLB 6, 173; INT CANR-24; MTCW
Donne, John 1572-1631**LC 10, 24; DA; DAB;
  DAC; DAM MST, POET; PC 1**
  See also CDBLB Before 1660; DLB 121, 151
Donnell, David 1939(?)- .... **CLC 34**
Donoghue, P. S.
  See Hunt, E(verette) Howard, (Jr.)
Donoso (Yanez), Jose 1924-1996**CLC 4, 8, 11,
  32, 99; DAM MULT; HLC**
  See also CA 81-84; 155; CANR 32; DLB 113;
  HW; MTCW
Donovan, John 1928-1992 .... **CLC 35**
  See also AAYA 20; CA 97-100; 137; CLR 3;
  MAICYA; SATA 72; SATA-Brief 29
Don Roberto
  See Cunninghame Graham, R(obert) B(ontine)
Doolittle, Hilda 1886-1961**CLC 3, 8, 14, 31, 34,
  73; DA; DAC; DAM MST, POET; PC 5;
  WLC**
  See also H. D.
  See also CA 97-100; CANR 35; DLB 4, 45;
  MTCW
Dorfman, Ariel 1942- ...... **CLC 48, 77; DAM
  MULT; HLC**
  See also CA 124; 130; HW; INT 130
Dorn, Edward (Merton) 1929- ... **CLC 10, 18**
  See also CA 93-96; CANR 42; DLB 5; INT 93-
  96
Dorsan, Luc
  See Simenon, Georges (Jacques Christian)
Dorsange, Jean
  See Simenon, Georges (Jacques Christian)
Dos Passos, John (Roderigo) 1896-1970 **C L C
  1, 4, 8, 11, 15, 25, 34, 82; DA; DAB; DAC;**

DAM MST, NOV; WLC
See also CA 1-4R; 29-32R; CANR 3; CDALB
1929-1941; DLB 4, 9; DLBD 1, 15; DLBY
96; MTCW

Dossage, Jean
See Simenon, Georges (Jacques Christian)

Dostoevsky, Fedor Mikhailovich 1821-1881
NCLC 2, 7, 21, 33, 43; DA; DAB; DAC;
DAM MST, NOV; SSC 2; WLC

Doughty, Charles M(ontagu) 1843-1926
TCLC 27
See also CA 115; DLB 19, 57, 174

Douglas, Ellen .... CLC 73
See also Haxton, Josephine Ayres; Williamson,
Ellen Douglas

Douglas, Gavin 1475(?)-1522 .... LC 20

Douglas, Keith (Castellain) 1920-1944 T C L C
40
See also CA 160; DLB 27

Douglas, Leonard
See Bradbury, Ray (Douglas)

Douglas, Michael
See Crichton, (John) Michael

Douglas, Norman 1868-1952 .... TCLC 68

Douglass, Frederick 1817(?)-1895 NCLC 7, 55;
BLC; DA; DAC; DAM MST, MULT; WLC
See also CDALB 1640-1865; DLB 1, 43, 50,
79; SATA 29

Dourado, (Waldomiro Freitas) Autran 1926-
CLC 23, 60
See also CA 25-28R; CANR 34

Dourado, Waldomiro Autran
See Dourado, (Waldomiro Freitas) Autran

Dove, Rita (Frances) 1952- CLC 50, 81; DAM
MULT, POET; PC 6
See also BW 2; CA 109; CAAS 19; CANR 27,
42; DLB 120

Dowell, Coleman 1925-1985 .... CLC 60
See also CA 25-28R; 117; CANR 10; DLB 130

Dowson, Ernest (Christopher) 1867-1900
TCLC 4
See also CA 105; 150; DLB 19, 135

Doyle, A. Conan
See Doyle, Arthur Conan

Doyle, Arthur Conan 1859-1930 TCLC 7; DA;
DAB; DAC; DAM MST, NOV; SSC 12;
WLC
See also AAYA 14; CA 104; 122; CDBLB 1890-
1914; DLB 18, 70, 156, 178; MTCW; SATA
24

Doyle, Conan
See Doyle, Arthur Conan

Doyle, John
See Graves, Robert (von Ranke)

Doyle, Roddy 1958(?)- .... CLC 81
See also AAYA 14; CA 143

Doyle, Sir A. Conan
See Doyle, Arthur Conan

Doyle, Sir Arthur Conan
See Doyle, Arthur Conan

Dr. A
See Asimov, Isaac; Silverstein, Alvin

Drabble, Margaret 1939- CLC 2, 3, 5, 8, 10, 22,
53; DAB; DAC; DAM MST, NOV, POP
See also CA 13-16R; CANR 18, 35, 63; CDBLB
1960 to Present; DLB 14, 155; MTCW;
SATA 48

Drapier, M. B.
See Swift, Jonathan

Drayham, James
See Mencken, H(enry) L(ouis)

Drayton, Michael 1563-1631 .... LC 8

Dreadstone, Carl
See Campbell, (John) Ramsey

Dreiser, Theodore (Herman Albert) 1871-1945
TCLC 10, 18, 35; DA; DAC; DAM MST,
NOV; WLC
See also CA 106; 132; CDALB 1865-1917;
DLB 9, 12, 102, 137; DLBD 1; MTCW

Drexler, Rosalyn 1926- .... CLC 2, 6
See also CA 81-84

Dreyer, Carl Theodor 1889-1968 ...... CLC 16
See also CA 116

Drieu la Rochelle, Pierre(-Eugene) 1893-1945
TCLC 21
See also CA 117; DLB 72

Drinkwater, John 1882-1937 .... TCLC 57
See also CA 109; 149; DLB 10, 19, 149

Drop Shot
See Cable, George Washington

Droste-Hulshoff, Annette Freiin von 1797-1848
NCLC 3
See also DLB 133

Drummond, Walter
See Silverberg, Robert

Drummond, William Henry 1854-1907 T C L C
25
See also CA 160; DLB 92

Drummond de Andrade, Carlos 1902-1987
CLC 18
See also Andrade, Carlos Drummond de
See also CA 132; 123

Drury, Allen (Stuart) 1918- .... CLC 37
See also CA 57-60; CANR 18, 52; INT CANR-
18

Dryden, John 1631-1700 LC 3, 21; DA; DAB;
DAC; DAM DRAM, MST, POET; DC 3;
WLC
See also CDBLB 1660-1789; DLB 80, 101, 131

Duberman, Martin (Bauml) 1930- ..... CLC 8
See also CA 1-4R; CANR 2, 63

Dubie, Norman (Evans) 1945- .... CLC 36
See also CA 69-72; CANR 12; DLB 120

Du Bois, W(illiam) E(dward) B(urghardt) 1868-
1963 CLC 1, 2, 13, 64, 96; BLC; DA; DAC;
DAM MST, MULT, NOV; WLC
See also BW 1; CA 85-88; CANR 34; CDALB
1865-1917; DLB 47, 50, 91; MTCW; SATA
42

Dubus, Andre 1936- CLC 13, 36, 97; SSC 15
See also CA 21-24R; CANR 17; DLB 130; INT
CANR-17

Duca Minimo
See D'Annunzio, Gabriele

Ducharme, Rejean 1941- .... CLC 74
See also DLB 60

Duclos, Charles Pinot 1704-1772 .... LC 1

Dudek, Louis 1918- .... CLC 11, 19
See also CA 45-48; CAAS 14; CANR 1; DLB
88

Duerrenmatt, Friedrich 1921-1990 CLC 1, 4,
8, 11, 15, 43, 102; DAM DRAM
See also CA 17-20R; CANR 33; DLB 69, 124;
MTCW

Duffy, Bruce (?)- .... CLC 50

Duffy, Maureen 1933- .... CLC 37
See also CA 25-28R; CANR 33; DLB 14;
MTCW

Dugan, Alan 1923- .... CLC 2, 6
See also CA 81-84; DLB 5

du Gard, Roger Martin
See Martin du Gard, Roger

Duhamel, Georges 1884-1966 .... CLC 8
See also CA 81-84; 25-28R; CANR 35; DLB
65; MTCW

Dujardin, Edouard (Emile Louis) 1861-1949

TCLC 13
See also CA 109; DLB 123

Dulles, John Foster 1888-1959 .... TCLC 72
See also CA 115; 149

Dumas, Alexandre (Davy de la Pailleterie)
1802-1870 .. NCLC 11; DA; DAB; DAC;
DAM MST, NOV; WLC
See also DLB 119; SATA 18

Dumas, Alexandre 1824-1895 NCLC 9; DC 1
See also AAYA 22

Dumas, Claudine
See Malzberg, Barry N(athaniel)

Dumas, Henry L. 1934-1968 .... CLC 6, 62
See also BW 1; CA 85-88; DLB 41

du Maurier, Daphne 1907-1989 CLC 6, 11, 59;
DAB; DAC; DAM MST, POP; SSC 18
See also CA 5-8R; 128; CANR 6, 55; MTCW;
SATA 27; SATA-Obit 60

Dunbar, Paul Laurence 1872-1906 . TCLC 2,
12; BLC; DA; DAC; DAM MST, MULT,
POET; PC 5; SSC 8; WLC
See also BW 1; CA 104; 124; CDALB 1865-
1917; DLB 50, 54, 78; SATA 34

Dunbar, William 1460(?)-1530(?) .... LC 20
See also DLB 132, 146

Duncan, Dora Angela
See Duncan, Isadora

Duncan, Isadora 1877(?)-1927 .... TCLC 68
See also CA 118; 149

Duncan, Lois 1934- .... CLC 26
See also AAYA 4; CA 1-4R; CANR 2, 23, 36;
CLR 29; JRDA; MAICYA; SAAS 2; SATA
1, 36, 75

Duncan, Robert (Edward) 1919-1988 CLC 1,
2, 4, 7, 15, 41, 55; DAM POET; PC 2
See also CA 9-12R; 124; CANR 28, 62; DLB
5, 16; MTCW

Duncan, Sara Jeannette 1861-1922 TCLC 60
See also CA 157; DLB 92

Dunlap, William 1766-1839 .... NCLC 2
See also DLB 30, 37, 59

Dunn, Douglas (Eaglesham) 1942- CLC 6, 40
See also CA 45-48; CANR 2, 33; DLB 40;
MTCW

Dunn, Katherine (Karen) 1945- .... CLC 71
See also CA 33-36R

Dunn, Stephen 1939- .... CLC 36
See also CA 33-36R; CANR 12, 48, 53; DLB
105

Dunne, Finley Peter 1867-1936 ...... TCLC 28
See also CA 108; DLB 11, 23

Dunne, John Gregory 1932- .... CLC 28
See also CA 25-28R; CANR 14, 50; DLBY 80

Dunsany, Edward John Moreton Drax Plunkett
1878-1957
See Dunsany, Lord
See also CA 104; 148; DLB 10

Dunsany, Lord .... TCLC 2, 59
See also Dunsany, Edward John Moreton Drax
Plunkett
See also DLB 77, 153, 156

du Perry, Jean
See Simenon, Georges (Jacques Christian)

Durang, Christopher (Ferdinand) 1949-C L C
27, 38
See also CA 105; CANR 50

Duras, Marguerite 1914-1996 CLC 3, 6, 11, 20,
34, 40, 68, 100
See also CA 25-28R; 151; CANR 50; DLB 83;
MTCW

Durban, (Rosa) Pam 1947- .... CLC 39
See also CA 123

Durcan, Paul 1944- CLC 43, 70; DAM POET

See also CA 134

Durkheim, Emile 1858-1917 .... **TCLC 55**

Durrell, Lawrence (George) 1912-1990 **C L C 1, 4, 6, 8, 13, 27, 41; DAM NOV**
See also CA 9-12R; 132; CANR 40; CDBLB 1945-1960; DLB 15, 27; DLBY 90; MTCW

Durrenmatt, Friedrich
See Duerrenmatt, Friedrich

Dutt, Toru 1856-1877 .... **NCLC 29**

Dwight, Timothy 1752-1817 .... **NCLC 13**
See also DLB 37

Dworkin, Andrea 1946- .... **CLC 43**
See also CA 77-80; CAAS 21; CANR 16, 39; INT CANR-16; MTCW

Dwyer, Deanna
See Koontz, Dean R(ay)

Dwyer, K. R.
See Koontz, Dean R(ay)

Dye, Richard
See De Voto, Bernard (Augustine)

Dylan, Bob 1941- .... **CLC 3, 4, 6, 12, 77**
See also CA 41-44R; DLB 16

Eagleton, Terence (Francis) 1943-
See Eagleton, Terry
See also CA 57-60; CANR 7, 23; MTCW

Eagleton, Terry .... **CLC 63**
See also Eagleton, Terence (Francis)

Early, Jack
See Scoppettone, Sandra

East, Michael
See West, Morris L(anglo)

Eastaway, Edward
See Thomas, (Philip) Edward

Eastlake, William (Derry) 1917-1997 **CLC 8**
See also CA 5-8R; 158; CAAS 1; CANR 5, 63; DLB 6; INT CANR-5

Eastman, Charles A(lexander) 1858-1939 **TCLC 55; DAM MULT**
See also DLB 175; NNAL; YABC 1

Eberhart, Richard (Ghormley) 1904- **CLC 3, 11, 19, 56; DAM POET**
See also CA 1-4R; CANR 2; CDALB 1941-1968; DLB 48; MTCW

Eberstadt, Fernanda 1960- .... **CLC 39**
See also CA 136

Echegaray (y Eizaguirre), Jose (Maria Waldo) 1832-1916 .... **TCLC 4**
See also CA 104; CANR 32; HW; MTCW

Echeverria, (Jose) Esteban (Antonino) 1805-1851 .... **NCLC 18**

Echo
See Proust, (Valentin-Louis-George-Eugene-) Marcel

Eckert, Allan W. 1931- .... **CLC 17**
See also AAYA 18; CA 13-16R; CANR 14, 45; INT CANR-14; SAAS 21; SATA 29, 91; SATA-Brief 27

Eckhart, Meister 1260(?)-1328(?) ... **CMLC 9**
See also DLB 115

Eckmar, F. R.
See de Hartog, Jan

Eco, Umberto 1932- **CLC 28, 60; DAM NOV, POP**
See also BEST 90:1; CA 77-80; CANR 12, 33, 55; MTCW

Eddison, E(ric) R(ucker) 1882-1945 **TCLC 15**
See also CA 109; 156

Eddy, Mary (Morse) Baker 1821-1910 **T C L C 71**
See also CA 113

Edel, (Joseph) Leon 1907-1997 .. **CLC 29, 34**
See also CA 1-4R; 161; CANR 1, 22; DLB 103; INT CANR-22

Eden, Emily 1797-1869 .... **NCLC 10**

Edgar, David 1948- ... **CLC 42; DAM DRAM**
See also CA 57-60; CANR 12, 61; DLB 13; MTCW

Edgerton, Clyde (Carlyle) 1944- ...... **CLC 39**
See also AAYA 17; CA 118; 134; CANR 64; INT 134

Edgeworth, Maria 1768-1849 .... **NCLC 1, 51**
See also DLB 116, 159, 163; SATA 21

Edmonds, Paul
See Kuttner, Henry

Edmonds, Walter D(umaux) 1903- ... **CLC 35**
See also CA 5-8R; CANR 2; DLB 9; MAICYA; SAAS 4; SATA 1, 27

Edmondson, Wallace
See Ellison, Harlan (Jay)

Edson, Russell .... **CLC 13**
See also CA 33-36R

Edwards, Bronwen Elizabeth
See Rose, Wendy

Edwards, G(erald) B(asil) 1899-1976 **CLC 25**
See also CA 110

Edwards, Gus 1939- .... **CLC 43**
See also CA 108; INT 108

Edwards, Jonathan 1703-1758 .... **LC 7; DA; DAC; DAM MST**
See also DLB 24

Efron, Marina Ivanovna Tsvetaeva
See Tsvetaeva (Efron), Marina (Ivanovna)

Ehle, John (Marsden, Jr.) 1925- .... **CLC 27**
See also CA 9-12R

Ehrenbourg, Ilya (Grigoryevich)
See Ehrenburg, Ilya (Grigoryevich)

Ehrenburg, Ilya (Grigoryevich) 1891-1967 **CLC 18, 34, 62**
See also CA 102; 25-28R

Ehrenburg, Ilyo (Grigoryevich)
See Ehrenburg, Ilya (Grigoryevich)

Eich, Guenter 1907-1972 .... **CLC 15**
See also CA 111; 93-96; DLB 69, 124

Eichendorff, Joseph Freiherr von 1788-1857 **NCLC 8**
See also DLB 90

Eigner, Larry .... **CLC 9**
See also Eigner, Laurence (Joel)
See also CAAS 23; DLB 5

Eigner, Laurence (Joel) 1927-1996
See Eigner, Larry
See also CA 9-12R; 151; CANR 6

Einstein, Albert 1879-1955 .... **TCLC 65**
See also CA 121; 133; MTCW

Eiseley, Loren Corey 1907-1977 .... **CLC 7**
See also AAYA 5; CA 1-4R; 73-76; CANR 6

Eisenstadt, Jill 1963- .... **CLC 50**
See also CA 140

Eisenstein, Sergei (Mikhailovich) 1898-1948 **TCLC 57**
See also CA 114; 149

Eisner, Simon
See Kornbluth, C(yril) M.

Ekeloef, (Bengt) Gunnar 1907-1968 **CLC 27; DAM POET**
See also CA 123; 25-28R

Ekelof, (Bengt) Gunnar
See Ekeloef, (Bengt) Gunnar

Ekelund, Vilhelm 1880-1949 .... **TCLC 75**

Ekwensi, C. O. D.
See Ekwensi, Cyprian (Odiatu Duaka)

Ekwensi, Cyprian (Odiatu Duaka) 1921- **CLC 4; BLC; DAM MULT**
See also BW 2; CA 29-32R; CANR 18, 42; DLB 117; MTCW; SATA 66

Elaine .... **TCLC 18**

See also Leverson, Ada

El Crummo
See Crumb, R(obert)

Elder, Lonne III 1931-1996 .... **DC 8**
See also BLC; BW 1; CA 81-84; 152; CANR 25; DAM MULT; DLB 7, 38, 44

Elia
See Lamb, Charles

Eliade, Mircea 1907-1986 .... **CLC 19**
See also CA 65-68; 119; CANR 30, 62; MTCW

Eliot, A. D.
See Jewett, (Theodora) Sarah Orne

Eliot, Alice
See Jewett, (Theodora) Sarah Orne

Eliot, Dan
See Silverberg, Robert

Eliot, George 1819-1880 **NCLC 4, 13, 23, 41, 49; DA; DAB; DAC; DAM MST, NOV; PC 20; WLC**
See also CDBLB 1832-1890; DLB 21, 35, 55

Eliot, John 1604-1690 .... **LC 5**
See also DLB 24

Eliot, T(homas) S(tearns) 1888-1965 **CLC 1, 2, 3, 6, 9, 10, 13, 15, 24, 34, 41, 55, 57; DA; DAB; DAC; DAM DRAM, MST, POET; PC 5; WLC 2**
See also CA 5-8R; 25-28R; CANR 41; CDALB 1929-1941; DLB 7, 10, 45, 63; DLBY 88; MTCW

Elizabeth 1866-1941 .... **TCLC 41**

Elkin, Stanley L(awrence) 1930-1995 **CLC 4, 6, 9, 14, 27, 51, 91; DAM NOV, POP; SSC 12**
See also CA 9-12R; 148; CANR 8, 46; DLB 2, 28; DLBY 80; INT CANR-8; MTCW

Elledge, Scott .... **CLC 34**

Elliot, Don
See Silverberg, Robert

Elliott, Don
See Silverberg, Robert

Elliott, George P(aul) 1918-1980 .... **CLC 2**
See also CA 1-4R; 97-100; CANR 2

Elliott, Janice 1931- .... **CLC 47**
See also CA 13-16R; CANR 8, 29; DLB 14

Elliott, Sumner Locke 1917-1991 ..... **CLC 38**
See also CA 5-8R; 134; CANR 2, 21

Elliott, William
See Bradbury, Ray (Douglas)

Ellis, A. E. .... **CLC 7**

Ellis, Alice Thomas .... **CLC 40**
See also Haycraft, Anna

Ellis, Bret Easton 1964- .. **CLC 39, 71; DAM POP**
See also AAYA 2; CA 118; 123; CANR 51; INT 123

Ellis, (Henry) Havelock 1859-1939 **TCLC 14**
See also CA 109

Ellis, Landon
See Ellison, Harlan (Jay)

Ellis, Trey 1962- .... **CLC 55**
See also CA 146

Ellison, Harlan (Jay) 1934- ... **CLC 1, 13, 42; DAM POP; SSC 14**
See also CA 5-8R; CANR 5, 46; DLB 8; INT CANR-5; MTCW

Ellison, Ralph (Waldo) 1914-1994 . **CLC 1, 3, 11, 54, 86; BLC; DA; DAB; DAC; DAM MST, MULT, NOV; SSC 26; WLC**
See also AAYA 19; BW 1; CA 9-12R; 145; CANR 24, 53; CDALB 1941-1968; DLB 2, 76; DLBY 94; MTCW

Ellmann, Lucy (Elizabeth) 1956- ...... **CLC 61**
See also CA 128

Ellmann, Richard (David) 1918-1987**CLC 50**
See also BEST 89:2; CA 1-4R; 122; CANR 2, 28, 61; DLB 103; DLBY 87; MTCW

Elman, Richard 1934- .... **CLC 19**
See also CA 17-20R; CAAS 3; CANR 47

Elron
See Hubbard, L(afayette) Ron(ald)

Eluard, Paul .... **TCLC 7, 41**
See also Grindel, Eugene

Elyot, Sir Thomas 1490(?)-1546 .... **LC 11**

Elytis, Odysseus 1911-1996 **CLC 15, 49, 100; DAM POET; PC 21**
See also CA 102; 151; MTCW

Emecheta, (Florence Onye) Buchi 1944-**C L C 14, 48; BLC; DAM MULT**
See also BW 2; CA 81-84; CANR 27; DLB 117; MTCW; SATA 66

Emerson, Mary Moody 1774-1863 **NCLC 66**

Emerson, Ralph Waldo 1803-1882 . **NCLC 1, 38; DA; DAB; DAC; DAM MST, POET; PC 18; WLC**
See also CDALB 1640-1865; DLB 1, 59, 73

Eminescu, Mihail 1850-1889 .... **NCLC 33**

Empson, William 1906-1984**CLC 3, 8, 19, 33, 34**
See also CA 17-20R; 112; CANR 31, 61; DLB 20; MTCW

Enchi Fumiko (Ueda) 1905-1986 ...... **CLC 31**
See also CA 129; 121

Ende, Michael (Andreas Helmuth) 1929-1995 **CLC 31**
See also CA 118; 124; 149; CANR 36; CLR 14; DLB 75; MAICYA; SATA 61; SATA-Brief 42; SATA-Obit 86

Endo, Shusaku 1923-1996 **CLC 7, 14, 19, 54, 99; DAM NOV**
See also CA 29-32R; 153; CANR 21, 54; DLB 182; MTCW

Engel, Marian 1933-1985 .... **CLC 36**
See also CA 25-28R; CANR 12; DLB 53; INT CANR-12

Engelhardt, Frederick
See Hubbard, L(afayette) Ron(ald)

Enright, D(ennis) J(oseph) 1920-**CLC 4, 8, 31**
See also CA 1-4R; CANR 1, 42; DLB 27; SATA 25

Enzensberger, Hans Magnus 1929- .. **CLC 43**
See also CA 116; 119

Ephron, Nora 1941- .... **CLC 17, 31**
See also AITN 2; CA 65-68; CANR 12, 39

Epicurus 341B.C.-270B.C. .... **CMLC 21**
See also DLB 176

Epsilon
See Betjeman, John

Epstein, Daniel Mark 1948- .... **CLC 7**
See also CA 49-52; CANR 2, 53

Epstein, Jacob 1956- .... **CLC 19**
See also CA 114

Epstein, Joseph 1937-......................... **CLC 39**
See also CA 112; 119; CANR 50

Epstein, Leslie 1938- .... **CLC 27**
See also CA 73-76; CAAS 12; CANR 23

Equiano, Olaudah 1745(?)-1797**LC 16; BLC; DAM MULT**
See also DLB 37, 50

ER .... **TCLC 33**
See also CA 160; DLB 85

Erasmus, Desiderius 1469(?)-1536 ...... **LC 16**

Erdman, Paul E(mil) 1932- .... **CLC 25**
See also AITN 1; CA 61-64; CANR 13, 43

Erdrich, Louise 1954- ..... **CLC 39, 54; DAM MULT, NOV, POP**
See also AAYA 10; BEST 89:1; CA 114; CANR 41, 62; DLB 152, 175; MTCW; NNAL; SATA 94

Erenburg, Ilya (Grigoryevich)
See Ehrenburg, Ilya (Grigoryevich)

Erickson, Stephen Michael 1950-
See Erickson, Steve
See also CA 129

Erickson, Steve 1950- .... **CLC 64**
See also Erickson, Stephen Michael
See also CANR 60

Ericson, Walter
See Fast, Howard (Melvin)

Eriksson, Buntel
See Bergman, (Ernst) Ingmar

Ernaux, Annie 1940- .... **CLC 88**
See also CA 147

Eschenbach, Wolfram von
See Wolfram von Eschenbach

Eseki, Bruno
See Mphahlele, Ezekiel

Esenin, Sergei (Alexandrovich) 1895-1925 **TCLC 4**
See also CA 104

Eshleman, Clayton 1935- .... **CLC 7**
See also CA 33-36R; CAAS 6; DLB 5

Espriella, Don Manuel Alvarez
See Southey, Robert

Espriu, Salvador 1913-1985 .... **CLC 9**
See also CA 154; 115; DLB 134

Espronceda, Jose de 1808-1842 ..... **NCLC 39**

Esse, James
See Stephens, James

Esterbrook, Tom
See Hubbard, L(afayette) Ron(ald)

Estleman, Loren D. 1952-**CLC 48; DAM NOV, POP**
See also CA 85-88; CANR 27; INT CANR-27; MTCW

Euclid 306B.C.-283B.C. .... **CMLC 25**

Eugenides, Jeffrey 1960(?)- .... **CLC 81**
See also CA 144

Euripides c. 485B.C.-406B.C.**CMLC 23; DA; DAB; DAC; DAM DRAM, MST; DC 4; WLCS**
See also DLB 176

Evan, Evin
See Faust, Frederick (Schiller)

Evans, Evan
See Faust, Frederick (Schiller)

Evans, Marian
See Eliot, George

Evans, Mary Ann
See Eliot, George

Evarts, Esther
See Benson, Sally

Everett, Percival L. 1956- .... **CLC 57**
See also BW 2; CA 129

Everson, R(onald) G(ilmour) 1903- . **CLC 27**
See also CA 17-20R; DLB 88

Everson, William (Oliver) 1912-1994 **CLC 1, 5, 14**
See also CA 9-12R; 145; CANR 20; DLB 5, 16; MTCW

Evtushenko, Evgenii Aleksandrovich
See Yevtushenko, Yevgeny (Alexandrovich)

Ewart, Gavin (Buchanan) 1916-1995**CLC 13, 46**
See also CA 89-92; 150; CANR 17, 46; DLB 40; MTCW

Ewers, Hanns Heinz 1871-1943 ..... **TCLC 12**
See also CA 109; 149

Ewing, Frederick R.
See Sturgeon, Theodore (Hamilton)

Exley, Frederick (Earl) 1929-1992 **CLC 6, 11**
See also AITN 2; CA 81-84; 138; DLB 143; DLBY 81

Eynhardt, Guillermo
See Quiroga, Horacio (Sylvestre)

Ezekiel, Nissim 1924- .... **CLC 61**
See also CA 61-64

Ezekiel, Tish O'Dowd 1943- .... **CLC 34**
See also CA 129

Fadeyev, A.
See Bulgya, Alexander Alexandrovich

Fadeyev, Alexander .... **TCLC 53**
See also Bulgya, Alexander Alexandrovich

Fagen, Donald 1948- .... **CLC 26**

Fainzilberg, Ilya Arnoldovich 1897-1937
See Ilf, Ilya
See also CA 120

Fair, Ronald L. 1932- .... **CLC 18**
See also BW 1; CA 69-72; CANR 25; DLB 33

Fairbairn, Roger
See Carr, John Dickson

Fairbairns, Zoe (Ann) 1948- .... **CLC 32**
See also CA 103; CANR 21

Falco, Gian
See Papini, Giovanni

Falconer, James
See Kirkup, James

Falconer, Kenneth
See Kornbluth, C(yril) M.

Falkland, Samuel
See Heijermans, Herman

Fallaci, Oriana 1930- .... **CLC 11**
See also CA 77-80; CANR 15, 58; MTCW

Faludy, George 1913- .... **CLC 42**
See also CA 21-24R

Faludy, Gyoergy
See Faludy, George

Fanon, Frantz 1925-1961**CLC 74; BLC; DAM MULT**
See also BW 1; CA 116; 89-92

Fanshawe, Ann 1625-1680 .... **LC 11**

Fante, John (Thomas) 1911-1983 ..... **CLC 60**
See also CA 69-72; 109; CANR 23; DLB 130; DLBY 83

Farah, Nuruddin 1945- **CLC 53; BLC; DAM MULT**
See also BW 2; CA 106; DLB 125

Fargue, Leon-Paul 1876(?)-1947 ... **TCLC 11**
See also CA 109

Farigoule, Louis
See Romains, Jules

Farina, Richard 1936(?)-1966 .... **CLC 9**
See also CA 81-84; 25-28R

Farley, Walter (Lorimer) 1915-1989 **CLC 17**
See also CA 17-20R; CANR 8, 29; DLB 22; JRDA; MAICYA; SATA 2, 43

Farmer, Philip Jose 1918- .... **CLC 1, 19**
See also CA 1-4R; CANR 4, 35; DLB 8; MTCW; SATA 93

Farquhar, George 1677-1707 ...**LC 21; DAM DRAM**
See also DLB 84

Farrell, J(ames) G(ordon) 1935-1979 **CLC 6**
See also CA 73-76; 89-92; CANR 36; DLB 14; MTCW

Farrell, James T(homas) 1904-1979**CLC 1, 4, 8, 11, 66; SSC 28**
See also CA 5-8R; 89-92; CANR 9, 61; DLB 4, 9, 86; DLBD 2; MTCW

Farren, Richard J.
See Betjeman, John

Farren, Richard M.
See Betjeman, John

Fassbinder, Rainer Werner 1946-1982 **CLC 20**
　　See also CA 93-96; 106; CANR 31
Fast, Howard (Melvin) 1914- **CLC 23; DAM NOV**
　　See also AAYA 16; CA 1-4R; CAAS 18; CANR 1, 33, 54; DLB 9; INT CANR-33; SATA 7
Faulcon, Robert
　　See Holdstock, Robert P.
Faulkner, William (Cuthbert) 1897-1962 **CLC 1, 3, 6, 8, 9, 11, 14, 18, 28, 52, 68; DA; DAB; DAC; DAM MST, NOV; SSC 1; WLC**
　　See also AAYA 7; CA 81-84; CANR 33; CDALB 1929-1941; DLB 9, 11, 44, 102; DLBD 2; DLBY 86; MTCW
Fauset, Jessie Redmon 1884(?)-1961 **CLC 19, 54; BLC; DAM MULT**
　　See also BW 1; CA 109; DLB 51
Faust, Frederick (Schiller) 1892-1944(?) **TCLC 49; DAM POP**
　　See also CA 108; 152
Faust, Irvin 1924- .... **CLC 8**
　　See also CA 33-36R; CANR 28; DLB 2, 28; DLBY 80
Fawkes, Guy
　　See Benchley, Robert (Charles)
Fearing, Kenneth (Flexner) 1902-1961 . **C L C 51**
　　See also CA 93-96; CANR 59; DLB 9
Fecamps, Elise
　　See Creasey, John
Federman, Raymond 1928- .... **CLC 6, 47**
　　See also CA 17-20R; CAAS 8; CANR 10, 43; DLBY 80
Federspiel, J(uerg) F. 1931- .... **CLC 42**
　　See also CA 146
Feiffer, Jules (Ralph) 1929- ..... **CLC 2, 8, 64; DAM DRAM**
　　See also AAYA 3; CA 17-20R; CANR 30, 59; DLB 7, 44; INT CANR-30; MTCW; SATA 8, 61
Feige, Hermann Albert Otto Maximilian
　　See Traven, B.
Feinberg, David B. 1956-1994 .... **CLC 59**
　　See also CA 135; 147
Feinstein, Elaine 1930- .... **CLC 36**
　　See also CA 69-72; CAAS 1; CANR 31; DLB 14, 40; MTCW
Feldman, Irving (Mordecai) 1928- ..... **CLC 7**
　　See also CA 1-4R; CANR 1; DLB 169
Felix-Tchicaya, Gerald
　　See Tchicaya, Gerald Felix
Fellini, Federico 1920-1993 .... **CLC 16, 85**
　　See also CA 65-68; 143; CANR 33
Felsen, Henry Gregor 1916- .... **CLC 17**
　　See also CA 1-4R; CANR 1; SAAS 2; SATA 1
Fenno, Jack
　　See Calisher, Hortense
Fenton, James Martin 1949- .... **CLC 32**
　　See also CA 102; DLB 40
Ferber, Edna 1887-1968 .... **CLC 18, 93**
　　See also AITN 1; CA 5-8R; 25-28R; DLB 9, 28, 86; MTCW; SATA 7
Ferguson, Helen
　　See Kavan, Anna
Ferguson, Samuel 1810-1886 .... **NCLC 33**
　　See also DLB 32
Fergusson, Robert 1750-1774 .... **LC 29**
　　See also DLB 109
Ferling, Lawrence
　　See Ferlinghetti, Lawrence (Monsanto)
Ferlinghetti, Lawrence (Monsanto) 1919(?)- **CLC 2, 6, 10, 27; DAM POET; PC 1**
　　See also CA 5-8R; CANR 3, 41; CDALB 1941-

1968; DLB 5, 16; MTCW
Fernandez, Vicente Garcia Huidobro
　　See Huidobro Fernandez, Vicente Garcia
Ferrer, Gabriel (Francisco Victor) Miro
　　See Miro (Ferrer), Gabriel (Francisco Victor)
Ferrier, Susan (Edmonstone) 1782-1854 **NCLC 8**
　　See also DLB 116
Ferrigno, Robert 1948(?)- .... **CLC 65**
　　See also CA 140
Ferron, Jacques 1921-1985 .... **CLC 94; DAC**
　　See also CA 117; 129; DLB 60
Feuchtwanger, Lion 1884-1958 .... **TCLC 3**
　　See also CA 104; DLB 66
Feuillet, Octave 1821-1890 .... **NCLC 45**
Feydeau, Georges (Leon Jules Marie) 1862-1921 .... **TCLC 22; DAM DRAM**
　　See also CA 113; 152
Fichte, Johann Gottlieb 1762-1814 **NCLC 62**
　　See also DLB 90
Ficino, Marsilio 1433-1499 .... **LC 12**
Fiedeler, Hans
　　See Doeblin, Alfred
Fiedler, Leslie A(aron) 1917- . **CLC 4, 13, 24**
　　See also CA 9-12R; CANR 7, 63; DLB 28, 67; MTCW
Field, Andrew 1938- .... **CLC 44**
　　See also CA 97-100; CANR 25
Field, Eugene 1850-1895 .... **NCLC 3**
　　See also DLB 23, 42, 140; DLBD 13; MAICYA; SATA 16
Field, Gans T.
　　See Wellman, Manly Wade
Field, Michael .... **TCLC 43**
Field, Peter
　　See Hobson, Laura Z(ametkin)
Fielding, Henry 1707-1754 **LC 1; DA; DAB; DAC; DAM DRAM, MST, NOV; WLC**
　　See also CDBLB 1660-1789; DLB 39, 84, 101
Fielding, Sarah 1710-1768 .... **LC 1**
　　See also DLB 39
Fierstein, Harvey (Forbes) 1954- ... **CLC 33; DAM DRAM, POP**
　　See also CA 123; 129
Figes, Eva 1932- .... **CLC 31**
　　See also CA 53-56; CANR 4, 44; DLB 14
Finch, Anne 1661-1720 .... **LC 3; PC 21**
　　See also DLB 95
Finch, Robert (Duer Claydon) 1900- **CLC 18**
　　See also CA 57-60; CANR 9, 24, 49; DLB 88
Findley, Timothy 1930- . **CLC 27, 102; DAC; DAM MST**
　　See also CA 25-28R; CANR 12, 42; DLB 53
Fink, William
　　See Mencken, H(enry) L(ouis)
Firbank, Louis 1942-
　　See Reed, Lou
　　See also CA 117
Firbank, (Arthur Annesley) Ronald 1886-1926 **TCLC 1**
　　See also CA 104; DLB 36
Fisher, M(ary) F(rances) K(ennedy) 1908-1992 **CLC 76, 87**
　　See also CA 77-80; 138; CANR 44
Fisher, Roy 1930- .... **CLC 25**
　　See also CA 81-84; CAAS 10; CANR 16; DLB 40
Fisher, Rudolph 1897-1934 . **TCLC 11; BLC; DAM MULT; SSC 25**
　　See also BW 1; CA 107; 124; DLB 51, 102
Fisher, Vardis (Alvero) 1895-1968 ...... **CLC 7**
　　See also CA 5-8R; 25-28R; DLB 9
Fiske, Tarleton

See Bloch, Robert (Albert)
Fitch, Clarke
　　See Sinclair, Upton (Beall)
Fitch, John IV
　　See Cormier, Robert (Edmund)
Fitzgerald, Captain Hugh
　　See Baum, L(yman) Frank
FitzGerald, Edward 1809-1883 .... **NCLC 9**
　　See also DLB 32
Fitzgerald, F(rancis) Scott (Key) 1896-1940 **TCLC 1, 6, 14, 28, 55; DA; DAB; DAC; DAM MST, NOV; SSC 6; WLC**
　　See also AITN 1; CA 110; 123; CDALB 1917-1929; DLB 4, 9, 86; DLBD 1, 15, 16; DLBY 81, 96; MTCW
Fitzgerald, Penelope 1916- ... **CLC 19, 51, 61**
　　See also CA 85-88; CAAS 10; CANR 56; DLB 14
Fitzgerald, Robert (Stuart) 1910-1985 **CLC 39**
　　See also CA 1-4R; 114; CANR 1; DLBY 80
FitzGerald, Robert D(avid) 1902-1987 **CLC 19**
　　See also CA 17-20R
Fitzgerald, Zelda (Sayre) 1900-1948 **TCLC 52**
　　See also CA 117; 126; DLBY 84
Flanagan, Thomas (James Bonner) 1923- **CLC 25, 52**
　　See also CA 108; CANR 55; DLBY 80; INT 108; MTCW
Flaubert, Gustave 1821-1880 **NCLC 2, 10, 19, 62, 66; DA; DAB; DAC; DAM MST, NOV; SSC 11; WLC**
　　See also DLB 119
Flecker, Herman Elroy
　　See Flecker, (Herman) James Elroy
Flecker, (Herman) James Elroy 1884-1915 **TCLC 43**
　　See also CA 109; 150; DLB 10, 19
Fleming, Ian (Lancaster) 1908-1964 . **CLC 3, 30; DAM POP**
　　See also CA 5-8R; CANR 59; CDBLB 1945-1960; DLB 87; MTCW; SATA 9
Fleming, Thomas (James) 1927- .... **CLC 37**
　　See also CA 5-8R; CANR 10; INT CANR-10; SATA 8
Fletcher, John 1579-1625 .... **LC 33; DC 6**
　　See also CDBLB Before 1660; DLB 58
Fletcher, John Gould 1886-1950 .... **TCLC 35**
　　See also CA 107; DLB 4, 45
Fleur, Paul
　　See Pohl, Frederik
Flooglebuckle, Al
　　See Spiegelman, Art
Flying Officer X
　　See Bates, H(erbert) E(rnest)
Fo, Dario 1926- .... **CLC 32; DAM DRAM**
　　See also CA 116; 128; MTCW
Fogarty, Jonathan Titulescu Esq.
　　See Farrell, James T(homas)
Folke, Will
　　See Bloch, Robert (Albert)
Follett, Ken(neth Martin) 1949- ..... **CLC 18; DAM NOV, POP**
　　See also AAYA 6; BEST 89:4; CA 81-84; CANR 13, 33, 54; DLB 87; DLBY 81; INT CANR-33; MTCW
Fontane, Theodor 1819-1898 .... **NCLC 26**
　　See also DLB 129
Foote, Horton 1916- **CLC 51, 91; DAM DRAM**
　　See also CA 73-76; CANR 34, 51; DLB 26; INT CANR-34
Foote, Shelby 1916- **CLC 75; DAM NOV, POP**
　　See also CA 5-8R; CANR 3, 45; DLB 2, 17
Forbes, Esther 1891-1967 .... **CLC 12**

See also AAYA 17; CA 13-14; 25-28R; CAP 1; CLR 27; DLB 22; JRDA; MAICYA; SATA 2

Forche, Carolyn (Louise) 1950- **CLC 25, 83, 86; DAM POET; PC 10**
See also CA 109; 117; CANR 50; DLB 5; INT 117

Ford, Elbur
See Hibbert, Eleanor Alice Burford

Ford, Ford Madox 1873-1939 **TCLC 1, 15, 39, 57; DAM NOV**
See also CA 104; 132; CDBLB 1914-1945; DLB 162; MTCW

Ford, Henry 1863-1947 .... **TCLC 73**
See also CA 115; 148

Ford, John 1586-(?) .... **DC 8**
See also CDBLB Before 1660; DAM DRAM; DLB 58

Ford, John 1895-1973 .... **CLC 16**
See also CA 45-48

Ford, Richard .... **CLC 99**

Ford, Richard 1944- .... **CLC 46**
See also CA 69-72; CANR 11, 47

Ford, Webster
See Masters, Edgar Lee

Foreman, Richard 1937- .... **CLC 50**
See also CA 65-68; CANR 32, 63

Forester, C(ecil) S(cott) 1899-1966 ... **CLC 35**
See also CA 73-76; 25-28R; SATA 13

Forez
See Mauriac, Francois (Charles)

Forman, James Douglas 1932- .... **CLC 21**
See also AAYA 17; CA 9-12R; CANR 4, 19, 42; JRDA; MAICYA; SATA 8, 70

Fornes, Maria Irene 1930- .... **CLC 39, 61**
See also CA 25-28R; CANR 28; DLB 7; HW; INT CANR-28; MTCW

Forrest, Leon 1937- .... **CLC 4**
See also BW 2; CA 89-92; CAAS 7; CANR 25, 52; DLB 33

Forster, E(dward) M(organ) 1879-1970 **C L C 1, 2, 3, 4, 9, 10, 13, 15, 22, 45, 77; DA; DAB; DAC; DAM MST, NOV; SSC 27; WLC**
See also AAYA 2; CA 13-14; 25-28R; CANR 45; CAP 1; CDBLB 1914-1945; DLB 34, 98, 162, 178; DLBD 10; MTCW; SATA 57

Forster, John 1812-1876 .... **NCLC 11**
See also DLB 144, 184

Forsyth, Frederick 1938- **CLC 2, 5, 36; DAM NOV, POP**
See also BEST 89:4; CA 85-88; CANR 38, 62; DLB 87; MTCW

Forten, Charlotte L. .... **TCLC 16; BLC**
See also Grimke, Charlotte L(ottie) Forten
See also DLB 50

Foscolo, Ugo 1778-1827 .... **NCLC 8**

Fosse, Bob .... **CLC 20**
See also Fosse, Robert Louis

Fosse, Robert Louis 1927-1987
See Fosse, Bob
See also CA 110; 123

Foster, Stephen Collins 1826-1864 **NCLC 26**

Foucault, Michel 1926-1984 . **CLC 31, 34, 69**
See also CA 105; 113; CANR 34; MTCW

Fouque, Friedrich (Heinrich Karl) de la Motte 1777-1843 .... **NCLC 2**
See also DLB 90

Fourier, Charles 1772-1837 .... **NCLC 51**

Fournier, Henri Alban 1886-1914
See Alain-Fournier
See also CA 104

Fournier, Pierre 1916- .... **CLC 11**
See also Gascar, Pierre
See also CA 89-92; CANR 16, 40

Fowles, John 1926- **CLC 1, 2, 3, 4, 6, 9, 10, 15, 33, 87; DAB; DAC; DAM MST**
See also CA 5-8R; CANR 25; CDBLB 1960 to Present; DLB 14, 139; MTCW; SATA 22

Fox, Paula 1923- .... **CLC 2, 8**
See also AAYA 3; CA 73-76; CANR 20, 36, 62; CLR 1, 44; DLB 52; JRDA; MAICYA; MTCW; SATA 17, 60

Fox, William Price (Jr.) 1926- .... **CLC 22**
See also CA 17-20R; CAAS 19; CANR 11; DLB 2; DLBY 81

Foxe, John 1516(?)-1587 .... **LC 14**

Frame, Janet 1924- **CLC 2, 3, 6, 22, 66, 96; SSC 29**
See also Clutha, Janet Paterson Frame

France, Anatole .... **TCLC 9**
See also Thibault, Jacques Anatole Francois
See also DLB 123

Francis, Claude 19(?)- .... **CLC 50**

Francis, Dick 1920- **CLC 2, 22, 42, 102; DAM POP**
See also AAYA 5, 21; BEST 89:3; CA 5-8R; CANR 9, 42; CDBLB 1960 to Present; DLB 87; INT CANR-9; MTCW

Francis, Robert (Churchill) 1901-1987 **C L C 15**
See also CA 1-4R; 123; CANR 1

Frank, Anne(lies Marie) 1929-1945 **TCLC 17; DA; DAB; DAC; DAM MST; WLC**
See also AAYA 12; CA 113; 133; MTCW; SATA 87; SATA-Brief 42

Frank, Elizabeth 1945- .... **CLC 39**
See also CA 121; 126; INT 126

Frankl, Viktor E(mil) 1905-1997 ...... **CLC 93**
See also CA 65-68; 161

Franklin, Benjamin
See Hasek, Jaroslav (Matej Frantisek)

Franklin, Benjamin 1706-1790 .. **LC 25; DA; DAB; DAC; DAM MST; WLCS**
See also CDALB 1640-1865; DLB 24, 43, 73

Franklin, (Stella Maraia Sarah) Miles 1879-1954 .... **TCLC 7**
See also CA 104

Fraser, (Lady) Antonia (Pakenham) 1932- **CLC 32, 107**
See also CA 85-88; CANR 44; MTCW; SATA-Brief 32

Fraser, George MacDonald 1925- ...... **CLC 7**
See also CA 45-48; CANR 2, 48

Fraser, Sylvia 1935- .... **CLC 64**
See also CA 45-48; CANR 1, 16, 60

Frayn, Michael 1933- **CLC 3, 7, 31, 47; DAM DRAM, NOV**
See also CA 5-8R; CANR 30; DLB 13, 14; MTCW

Fraze, Candida (Merrill) 1945- .... **CLC 50**
See also CA 126

Frazer, J(ames) G(eorge) 1854-1941 **TCLC 32**
See also CA 118

Frazer, Robert Caine
See Creasey, John

Frazer, Sir James George
See Frazer, J(ames) G(eorge)

Frazier, Ian 1951- .... **CLC 46**
See also CA 130; CANR 54

Frederic, Harold 1856-1898 .... **NCLC 10**
See also DLB 12, 23; DLBD 13

Frederick, John
See Faust, Frederick (Schiller)

Frederick the Great 1712-1786 .... **LC 14**

Fredro, Aleksander 1793-1876 .... **NCLC 8**

Freeling, Nicolas 1927- .... **CLC 38**
See also CA 49-52; CAAS 12; CANR 1, 17, 50; DLB 87

Freeman, Douglas Southall 1886-1953 **T C L C 11**
See also CA 109; DLB 17

Freeman, Judith 1946- .... **CLC 55**
See also CA 148

Freeman, Mary Eleanor Wilkins 1852-1930 **TCLC 9; SSC 1**
See also CA 106; DLB 12, 78

Freeman, R(ichard) Austin 1862-1943 **T C L C 21**
See also CA 113; DLB 70

French, Albert 1943- .... **CLC 86**

French, Marilyn 1929- **CLC 10, 18, 60; DAM DRAM, NOV, POP**
See also CA 69-72; CANR 3, 31; INT CANR-31; MTCW

French, Paul
See Asimov, Isaac

Freneau, Philip Morin 1752-1832 ... **NCLC 1**
See also DLB 37, 43

Freud, Sigmund 1856-1939 .... **TCLC 52**
See also CA 115; 133; MTCW

Friedan, Betty (Naomi) 1921- .... **CLC 74**
See also CA 65-68; CANR 18, 45; MTCW

Friedlander, Saul 1932- .... **CLC 90**
See also CA 117; 130

Friedman, B(ernard) H(arper) 1926- **CLC 7**
See also CA 1-4R; CANR 3, 48

Friedman, Bruce Jay 1930- ...... **CLC 3, 5, 56**
See also CA 9-12R; CANR 25, 52; DLB 2, 28; INT CANR-25

Friel, Brian 1929- .... **CLC 5, 42, 59; DC 8**
See also CA 21-24R; CANR 33; DLB 13; MTCW

Friis-Baastad, Babbis Ellinor 1921-1970 **CLC 12**
See also CA 17-20R; 134; SATA 7

Frisch, Max (Rudolf) 1911-1991 **CLC 3, 9, 14, 18, 32, 44; DAM DRAM, NOV**
See also CA 85-88; 134; CANR 32; DLB 69, 124; MTCW

Fromentin, Eugene (Samuel Auguste) 1820-1876 .... **NCLC 10**
See also DLB 123

Frost, Frederick
See Faust, Frederick (Schiller)

Frost, Robert (Lee) 1874-1963 **CLC 1, 3, 4, 9, 10, 13, 15, 26, 34, 44; DA; DAB; DAC; DAM MST, POET; PC 1; WLC**
See also AAYA 21; CA 89-92; CANR 33; CDALB 1917-1929; DLB 54; DLBD 7; MTCW; SATA 14

Froude, James Anthony 1818-1894 **NCLC 43**
See also DLB 18, 57, 144

Froy, Herald
See Waterhouse, Keith (Spencer)

Fry, Christopher 1907- **CLC 2, 10, 14; DAM DRAM**
See also CA 17-20R; CAAS 23; CANR 9, 30; DLB 13; MTCW; SATA 66

Frye, (Herman) Northrop 1912-1991 **CLC 24, 70**
See also CA 5-8R; 133; CANR 8, 37; DLB 67, 68; MTCW

Fuchs, Daniel 1909-1993 .... **CLC 8, 22**
See also CA 81-84; 142; CAAS 5; CANR 40; DLB 9, 26, 28; DLBY 93

Fuchs, Daniel 1934- .... **CLC 34**
See also CA 37-40R; CANR 14, 48

Fuentes, Carlos 1928- **CLC 3, 8, 10, 13, 22, 41, 60; DA; DAB; DAC; DAM MST, MULT, NOV; HLC; SSC 24; WLC**

See also AAYA 4; AITN 2; CA 69-72; CANR 10, 32; DLB 113; HW; MTCW

Fuentes, Gregorio Lopez y
See Lopez y Fuentes, Gregorio

Fugard, (Harold) Athol 1932-**CLC 5, 9, 14, 25, 40, 80; DAM DRAM; DC 3**
See also AAYA 17; CA 85-88; CANR 32, 54; MTCW

Fugard, Sheila 1932- .... **CLC 48**
See also CA 125

Fuller, Charles (H., Jr.) 1939- **CLC 25; BLC; DAM DRAM, MULT; DC 1**
See also BW 2; CA 108; 112; DLB 38; INT 112; MTCW

Fuller, John (Leopold) 1937-............. **CLC 62**
See also CA 21-24R; CANR 9, 44; DLB 40

Fuller, Margaret .... **NCLC 5, 50**
See also Ossoli, Sarah Margaret (Fuller marchesa d')

Fuller, Roy (Broadbent) 1912-1991**CLC 4, 28**
See also CA 5-8R; 135; CAAS 10; CANR 53; DLB 15, 20; SATA 87

Fulton, Alice 1952- .... **CLC 52**
See also CA 116; CANR 57

Furphy, Joseph 1843-1912 .... **TCLC 25**

Fussell, Paul 1924- .... **CLC 74**
See also BEST 90:1; CA 17-20R; CANR 8, 21, 35; INT CANR-21; MTCW

Futabatei, Shimei 1864-1909 .... **TCLC 44**
See also DLB 180

Futrelle, Jacques 1875-1912 .... **TCLC 19**
See also CA 113; 155

Gaboriau, Emile 1835-1873 .... **NCLC 14**

Gadda, Carlo Emilio 1893-1973 .... **CLC 11**
See also CA 89-92; DLB 177

Gaddis, William 1922- **CLC 1, 3, 6, 8, 10, 19, 43, 86**
See also CA 17-20R; CANR 21, 48; DLB 2; MTCW

Gage, Walter
See Inge, William (Motter)

Gaines, Ernest J(ames) 1933- **CLC 3, 11, 18, 86; BLC; DAM MULT**
See also AAYA 18; AITN 1; BW 2; CA 9-12R; CANR 6, 24, 42; CDALB 1968-1988; DLB 2, 33, 152; DLBY 80; MTCW; SATA 86

Gaitskill, Mary 1954- .... **CLC 69**
See also CA 128; CANR 61

Galdos, Benito Perez
See Perez Galdos, Benito

Gale, Zona 1874-1938**TCLC 7; DAM DRAM**
See also CA 105; 153; DLB 9, 78

Galeano, Eduardo (Hughes) 1940-... **CLC 72**
See also CA 29-32R; CANR 13, 32; HW

Galiano, Juan Valera y Alcala
See Valera y Alcala-Galiano, Juan

Gallagher, Tess 1943- ...... **CLC 18, 63; DAM POET; PC 9**
See also CA 106; DLB 120

Gallant, Mavis 1922-... **CLC 7, 18, 38; DAC; DAM MST; SSC 5**
See also CA 69-72; CANR 29; DLB 53; MTCW

Gallant, Roy A(rthur) 1924- .... **CLC 17**
See also CA 5-8R; CANR 4, 29, 54; CLR 30; MAICYA; SATA 4, 68

Gallico, Paul (William) 1897-1976 ..... **CLC 2**
See also AITN 1; CA 5-8R; 69-72; CANR 23; DLB 9, 171; MAICYA; SATA 13

Gallo, Max Louis 1932- .... **CLC 95**
See also CA 85-88

Gallois, Lucien
See Desnos, Robert

Gallup, Ralph

See Whitemore, Hugh (John)

Galsworthy, John 1867-1933**TCLC 1, 45; DA; DAB; DAC; DAM DRAM, MST, NOV; SSC 22; WLC 2**
See also CA 104; 141; CDBLB 1890-1914; DLB 10, 34, 98, 162; DLBD 16

Galt, John 1779-1839 .... **NCLC 1**
See also DLB 99, 116, 159

Galvin, James 1951- .... **CLC 38**
See also CA 108; CANR 26

Gamboa, Federico 1864-1939 .... **TCLC 36**

Gandhi, M. K.
See Gandhi, Mohandas Karamchand

Gandhi, Mahatma
See Gandhi, Mohandas Karamchand

Gandhi, Mohandas Karamchand 1869-1948 **TCLC 59; DAM MULT**
See also CA 121; 132; MTCW

Gann, Ernest Kellogg 1910-1991 ...... **CLC 23**
See also AITN 1; CA 1-4R; 136; CANR 1

Garcia, Cristina 1958- .... **CLC 76**
See also CA 141

Garcia Lorca, Federico 1898-1936**TCLC 1, 7, 49; DA; DAB; DAC; DAM DRAM, MST, MULT, POET; DC 2; HLC; PC 3; WLC**
See also CA 104; 131; DLB 108; HW; MTCW

Garcia Marquez, Gabriel (Jose) 1928-**CLC 2, 3, 8, 10, 15, 27, 47, 55, 68; DA; DAB; DAC; DAM MST, MULT, NOV, POP; HLC; SSC 8; WLC**
See also AAYA 3; BEST 89:1, 90:4; CA 33-36R; CANR 10, 28, 50; DLB 113; HW; MTCW

Gard, Janice
See Latham, Jean Lee

Gard, Roger Martin du
See Martin du Gard, Roger

Gardam, Jane 1928- .... **CLC 43**
See also CA 49-52; CANR 2, 18, 33, 54; CLR 12; DLB 14, 161; MAICYA; MTCW; SAAS 9; SATA 39, 76; SATA-Brief 28

Gardner, Herb(ert) 1934- .... **CLC 44**
See also CA 149

Gardner, John (Champlin), Jr. 1933-1982 **CLC 2, 3, 5, 7, 8, 10, 18, 28, 34; DAM NOV, POP; SSC 7**
See also AITN 1; CA 65-68; 107; CANR 33; DLB 2; DLBY 82; MTCW; SATA 40; SATA-Obit 31

Gardner, John (Edmund) 1926-**CLC 30; DAM POP**
See also CA 103; CANR 15; MTCW

Gardner, Miriam
See Bradley, Marion Zimmer

Gardner, Noel
See Kuttner, Henry

Gardons, S. S.
See Snodgrass, W(illiam) D(e Witt)

Garfield, Leon 1921-1996 .... **CLC 12**
See also AAYA 8; CA 17-20R; 152; CANR 38, 41; CLR 21; DLB 161; JRDA; MAICYA; SATA 1, 32, 76; SATA-Obit 90

Garland, (Hannibal) Hamlin 1860-1940 **TCLC 3; SSC 18**
See also CA 104; DLB 12, 71, 78

Garneau, (Hector de) Saint-Denys 1912-1943 **TCLC 13**
See also CA 111; DLB 88

Garner, Alan 1934-**CLC 17; DAB; DAM POP**
See also AAYA 18; CA 73-76; CANR 15, 64; CLR 20; DLB 161; MAICYA; MTCW; SATA 18, 69

Garner, Hugh 1913-1979 .... **CLC 13**

See also CA 69-72; CANR 31; DLB 68

Garnett, David 1892-1981 .... **CLC 3**
See also CA 5-8R; 103; CANR 17; DLB 34

Garos, Stephanie
See Katz, Steve

Garrett, George (Palmer) 1929-**CLC 3, 11, 51**
See also CA 1-4R; CAAS 5; CANR 1, 42; DLB 2, 5, 130, 152; DLBY 83

Garrick, David 1717-1779 ....**LC 15; DAM DRAM**
See also DLB 84

Garrigue, Jean 1914-1972 .... **CLC 2, 8**
See also CA 5-8R; 37-40R; CANR 20

Garrison, Frederick
See Sinclair, Upton (Beall)

Garth, Will
See Hamilton, Edmond; Kuttner, Henry

Garvey, Marcus (Moziah, Jr.) 1887-1940 **TCLC 41; BLC; DAM MULT**
See also BW 1; CA 120; 124

Gary, Romain .... **CLC 25**
See also Kacew, Romain
See also DLB 83

Gascar, Pierre .... **CLC 11**
See also Fournier, Pierre

Gascoyne, David (Emery) 1916- .... **CLC 45**
See also CA 65-68; CANR 10, 28, 54; DLB 20; MTCW

Gaskell, Elizabeth Cleghorn 1810-1865**NCLC 5; DAB; DAM MST; SSC 25**
See also CDBLB 1832-1890; DLB 21, 144, 159

Gass, William H(oward) 1924-**CLC 1, 2, 8, 11, 15, 39; SSC 12**
See also CA 17-20R; CANR 30; DLB 2; MTCW

Gasset, Jose Ortega y
See Ortega y Gasset, Jose

Gates, Henry Louis, Jr. 1950-**CLC 65; DAM MULT**
See also BW 2; CA 109; CANR 25, 53; DLB 67

Gautier, Theophile 1811-1872 .. **NCLC 1, 59; DAM POET; PC 18; SSC 20**
See also DLB 119

Gawsworth, John
See Bates, H(erbert) E(rnest)

Gay, Oliver
See Gogarty, Oliver St. John

Gaye, Marvin (Penze) 1939-1984 ..... **CLC 26**
See also CA 112

Gebler, Carlo (Ernest) 1954- .... **CLC 39**
See also CA 119; 133

Gee, Maggie (Mary) 1948- .... **CLC 57**
See also CA 130

Gee, Maurice (Gough) 1931- .... **CLC 29**
See also CA 97-100; SATA 46

Gelbart, Larry (Simon) 1923- .... **CLC 21, 61**
See also CA 73-76; CANR 45

Gelber, Jack 1932- .... **CLC 1, 6, 14, 79**
See also CA 1-4R; CANR 2; DLB 7

Gellhorn, Martha (Ellis) 1908- .. **CLC 14, 60**
See also CA 77-80; CANR 44; DLBY 82

Genet, Jean 1910-1986**CLC 1, 2, 5, 10, 14, 44, 46; DAM DRAM**
See also CA 13-16R; CANR 18; DLB 72; DLBY 86; MTCW

Gent, Peter 1942- .... **CLC 29**
See also AITN 1; CA 89-92; DLBY 82

Gentlewoman in New England, A
See Bradstreet, Anne

Gentlewoman in Those Parts, A
See Bradstreet, Anne

George, Jean Craighead 1919- .... **CLC 35**
See also AAYA 8; CA 5-8R; CANR 25; CLR 1;

DLB 52; JRDA; MAICYA; SATA 2, 68
George, Stefan (Anton) 1868-1933**TCLC 2, 14**
See also CA 104
Georges, Georges Martin
See Simenon, Georges (Jacques Christian)
Gerhardi, William Alexander
See Gerhardie, William Alexander
Gerhardie, William Alexander 1895-1977
CLC 5
See also CA 25-28R; 73-76; CANR 18; DLB
36
Gerstler, Amy 1956- .... **CLC 70**
See also CA 146
Gertler, T. .... **CLC 34**
See also CA 116; 121; INT 121
Ghalib .... **NCLC 39**
See also Ghalib, Hsadullah Khan
Ghalib, Hsadullah Khan 1797-1869
See Ghalib
See also DAM POET
Ghelderode, Michel de 1898-1962**CLC 6, 11;**
DAM DRAM
See also CA 85-88; CANR 40
Ghiselin, Brewster 1903- .... **CLC 23**
See also CA 13-16R; CAAS 10; CANR 13
Ghose, Zulfikar 1935- .... **CLC 42**
See also CA 65-68
Ghosh, Amitav 1956- .... **CLC 44**
See also CA 147
Giacosa, Giuseppe 1847-1906 .... **TCLC 7**
See also CA 104
Gibb, Lee
See Waterhouse, Keith (Spencer)
Gibbon, Lewis Grassic .... **TCLC 4**
See also Mitchell, James Leslie
Gibbons, Kaye 1960-**CLC 50, 88; DAM POP**
See also CA 151
Gibran, Kahlil 1883-1931 . **TCLC 1, 9; DAM**
POET, POP; PC 9
See also CA 104; 150
Gibran, Khalil
See Gibran, Kahlil
Gibson, William 1914- .. **CLC 23; DA; DAB;**
DAC; DAM DRAM, MST
See also CA 9-12R; CANR 9, 42; DLB 7; SATA
66
Gibson, William (Ford) 1948- ... **CLC 39, 63;**
DAM POP
See also AAYA 12; CA 126; 133; CANR 52
Gide, Andre (Paul Guillaume) 1869-1951
TCLC 5, 12, 36; DA; DAB; DAC; DAM
MST, NOV; SSC 13; WLC
See also CA 104; 124; DLB 65; MTCW
Gifford, Barry (Colby) 1946- .... **CLC 34**
See also CA 65-68; CANR 9, 30, 40
Gilbert, Frank
See De Voto, Bernard (Augustine)
Gilbert, W(illiam) S(chwenck) 1836-1911
TCLC 3; DAM DRAM, POET
See also CA 104; SATA 36
Gilbreth, Frank B., Jr. 1911- .... **CLC 17**
See also CA 9-12R; SATA 2
Gilchrist, Ellen 1935-**CLC 34, 48; DAM POP;**
SSC 14
See also CA 113; 116; CANR 41, 61; DLB 130;
MTCW
Giles, Molly 1942- .... **CLC 39**
See also CA 126
Gill, Patrick
See Creasey, John
Gilliam, Terry (Vance) 1940- .... **CLC 21**
See also Monty Python
See also AAYA 19; CA 108; 113; CANR 35;

INT 113
Gillian, Jerry
See Gilliam, Terry (Vance)
Gilliatt, Penelope (Ann Douglass) 1932-1993
CLC 2, 10, 13, 53
See also AITN 2; CA 13-16R; 141; CANR 49;
DLB 14
Gilman, Charlotte (Anna) Perkins (Stetson)
1860-1935 .... **TCLC 9, 37; SSC 13**
See also CA 106; 150
Gilmour, David 1949- .... **CLC 35**
See also CA 138, 147
Gilpin, William 1724-1804 .... **NCLC 30**
Gilray, J. D.
See Mencken, H(enry) L(ouis)
Gilroy, Frank D(aniel) 1925- .... **CLC 2**
See also CA 81-84; CANR 32, 64; DLB 7
Gilstrap, John 1957(?)- .... **CLC 99**
See also CA 160
Ginsberg, Allen 1926-1997**CLC 1, 2, 3, 4, 6, 13,**
36, 69; DA; DAB; DAC; DAM MST,
POET; PC 4; WLC 3
See also AITN 1; CA 1-4R; 157; CANR 2, 41,
63; CDALB 1941-1968; DLB 5, 16, 169;
MTCW
Ginzburg, Natalia 1916-1991**CLC 5, 11, 54, 70**
See also CA 85-88; 135; CANR 33; DLB 177;
MTCW
Giono, Jean 1895-1970 .... **CLC 4, 11**
See also CA 45-48; 29-32R; CANR 2, 35; DLB
72; MTCW
Giovanni, Nikki 1943-**CLC 2, 4, 19, 64; BLC;**
DA; DAB; DAC; DAM MST, MULT,
POET; PC 19; WLCS
See also AAYA 22; AITN 1; BW 2; CA 29-32R;
CAAS 6; CANR 18, 41, 60; CLR 6; DLB 5,
41; INT CANR-18; MAICYA; MTCW; SATA
24
Giovene, Andrea 1904- .... **CLC 7**
See also CA 85-88
Gippius, Zinaida (Nikolayevna) 1869-1945
See Hippius, Zinaida
See also CA 106
Giraudoux, (Hippolyte) Jean 1882-1944
TCLC 2, 7; DAM DRAM
See also CA 104; DLB 65
Gironella, Jose Maria 1917- .... **CLC 11**
See also CA 101
Gissing, George (Robert) 1857-1903**TCLC 3,**
24, 47
See also CA 105; DLB 18, 135, 184
Giurlani, Aldo
See Palazzeschi, Aldo
Gladkov, Fyodor (Vasilyevich) 1883-1958
TCLC 27
Glanville, Brian (Lester) 1931- .... **CLC 6**
See also CA 5-8R; CAAS 9; CANR 3; DLB 15,
139; SATA 42
Glasgow, Ellen (Anderson Gholson) 1873(?)-
1945 .... **TCLC 2, 7**
See also CA 104; DLB 9, 12
Glaspell, Susan 1882(?)-1948 .... **TCLC 55**
See also CA 110; 154; DLB 7, 9, 78; YABC 2
Glassco, John 1909-1981 .... **CLC 9**
See also CA 13-16R; 102; CANR 15; DLB 68
Glasscock, Amnesia
See Steinbeck, John (Ernst)
Glasser, Ronald J. 1940(?)- .... **CLC 37**
Glassman, Joyce
See Johnson, Joyce
Glendinning, Victoria 1937- .... **CLC 50**
See also CA 120; 127; CANR 59; DLB 155
Glissant, Edouard 1928- . **CLC 10, 68; DAM**

MULT
See also CA 153
Gloag, Julian 1930- .... **CLC 40**
See also AITN 1; CA 65-68; CANR 10
Glowacki, Aleksander
See Prus, Boleslaw
Gluck, Louise (Elisabeth) 1943-**CLC 7, 22, 44,**
81; DAM POET; PC 16
See also CA 33-36R; CANR 40; DLB 5
Glyn, Elinor 1864-1943 .... **TCLC 72**
See also DLB 153
Gobineau, Joseph Arthur (Comte) de 1816-
1882 .... **NCLC 17**
See also DLB 123
Godard, Jean-Luc 1930- .... **CLC 20**
See also CA 93-96
Godden, (Margaret) Rumer 1907- ... **CLC 53**
See also AAYA 6; CA 5-8R; CANR 4, 27, 36,
55; CLR 20; DLB 161; MAICYA; SAAS 12;
SATA 3, 36
Godoy Alcayaga, Lucila 1889-1957
See Mistral, Gabriela
See also BW 2; CA 104; 131; DAM MULT;
HW; MTCW
Godwin, Gail (Kathleen) 1937- **CLC 5, 8, 22,**
31, 69; DAM POP
See also CA 29-32R; CANR 15, 43; DLB 6;
INT CANR-15; MTCW
Godwin, William 1756-1836 .... **NCLC 14**
See also CDBLB 1789-1832; DLB 39, 104, 142,
158, 163
Goebbels, Josef
See Goebbels, (Paul) Joseph
Goebbels, (Paul) Joseph 1897-1945**TCLC 68**
See also CA 115; 148
Goebbels, Joseph Paul
See Goebbels, (Paul) Joseph
Goethe, Johann Wolfgang von 1749-1832
NCLC 4, 22, 34; DA; DAB; DAC; DAM
DRAM, MST, POET; PC 5; WLC 3
See also DLB 94
Gogarty, Oliver St. John 1878-1957**TCLC 15**
See also CA 109; 150; DLB 15, 19
Gogol, Nikolai (Vasilyevich) 1809-1852**NCLC**
5, 15, 31; DA; DAB; DAC; DAM DRAM,
MST; DC 1; SSC 4, 29; WLC
Goines, Donald 1937(?)-1974 **CLC 80; BLC;**
DAM MULT
See also AITN 1; BW 1; CA 124; 114; DLB 33
Gold, Herbert 1924- .... **CLC 4, 7, 14, 42**
See also CA 9-12R; CANR 17, 45; DLB 2;
DLBY 81
Goldbarth, Albert 1948- .... **CLC 5, 38**
See also CA 53-56; CANR 6, 40; DLB 120
Goldberg, Anatol 1910-1982 .... **CLC 34**
See also CA 131; 117
Goldemberg, Isaac 1945- .... **CLC 52**
See also CA 69-72; CAAS 12; CANR 11, 32;
HW
Golding, William (Gerald) 1911-1993**CLC 1,**
2, 3, 8, 10, 17, 27, 58, 81; DA; DAB; DAC;
DAM MST, NOV; WLC
See also AAYA 5; CA 5-8R; 141; CANR 13,
33, 54; CDBLB 1945-1960; DLB 15, 100;
MTCW
Goldman, Emma 1869-1940 .... **TCLC 13**
See also CA 110; 150
Goldman, Francisco 1955- .... **CLC 76**
Goldman, William (W.) 1931- .... **CLC 1, 48**
See also CA 9-12R; CANR 29; DLB 44
Goldmann, Lucien 1913-1970 .... **CLC 24**
See also CA 25-28; CAP 2
Goldoni, Carlo 1707-1793**LC 4; DAM DRAM**

Goldsberry, Steven 1949- .... **CLC 34**
  See also CA 131
Goldsmith, Oliver 1728-1774**LC 2; DA; DAB; DAC; DAM DRAM, MST, NOV, POET; DC 8; WLC**
  See also CDBLB 1660-1789; DLB 39, 89, 104, 109, 142; SATA 26
Goldsmith, Peter
  See Priestley, J(ohn) B(oynton)
Gombrowicz, Witold 1904-1969**CLC 4, 7, 11, 49; DAM DRAM**
  See also CA 19-20; 25-28R; CAP 2
Gomez de la Serna, Ramon 1888-1963**CLC 9**
  See also CA 153; 116; HW
Goncharov, Ivan Alexandrovich 1812-1891 **NCLC 1, 63**
Goncourt, Edmond (Louis Antoine Huot) de 1822-1896 .... **NCLC 7**
  See also DLB 123
Goncourt, Jules (Alfred Huot) de 1830-1870 **NCLC 7**
  See also DLB 123
Gontier, Fernande 19(?)- .... **CLC 50**
Gonzalez Martinez, Enrique 1871-1952 **TCLC 72**
  See also HW
Goodman, Paul 1911-1972 ...... **CLC 1, 2, 4, 7**
  See also CA 19-20; 37-40R; CANR 34; CAP 2; DLB 130; MTCW
Gordimer, Nadine 1923-**CLC 3, 5, 7, 10, 18, 33, 51, 70; DA; DAB; DAC; DAM MST, NOV; SSC 17; WLCS**
  See also CA 5-8R; CANR 3, 28, 56; INT CANR-28; MTCW
Gordon, Adam Lindsay 1833-1870 **NCLC 21**
Gordon, Caroline 1895-1981**CLC 6, 13, 29, 83; SSC 15**
  See also CA 11-12; 103; CANR 36; CAP 1; DLB 4, 9, 102; DLBY 81; MTCW
Gordon, Charles William 1860-1937
  See Connor, Ralph
  See also CA 109
Gordon, Mary (Catherine) 1949- **CLC 13, 22**
  See also CA 102; CANR 44; DLB 6; DLBY 81; INT 102; MTCW
Gordon, N. J.
  See Bosman, Herman Charles
Gordon, Sol 1923- .... **CLC 26**
  See also CA 53-56; CANR 4; SATA 11
Gordone, Charles 1925-1995**CLC 1, 4; DAM DRAM; DC 8**
  See also BW 1; CA 93-96; 150; CANR 55; DLB 7; INT 93-96; MTCW
Gore, Catherine 1800-1861 .... **NCLC 65**
  See also DLB 116
Gorenko, Anna Andreevna
  See Akhmatova, Anna
Gorky, Maxim 1868-1936**TCLC 8; DAB; SSC 28; WLC**
  See also Peshkov, Alexei Maximovich
Goryan, Sirak
  See Saroyan, William
Gosse, Edmund (William) 1849-1928**TCLC 28**
  See also CA 117; DLB 57, 144, 184
Gotlieb, Phyllis Fay (Bloom) 1926- .. **CLC 18**
  See also CA 13-16R; CANR 7; DLB 88
Gottesman, S. D.
  See Kornbluth, C(yril) M.; Pohl, Frederik
Gottfried von Strassburg fl. c. 1210- **CMLC 10**
  See also DLB 138
Gould, Lois ....**CLC 4, 10**
  See also CA 77-80; CANR 29; MTCW

Gourmont, Remy (-Marie-Charles) de 1858-1915 .... **TCLC 17**
  See also CA 109; 150
Govier, Katherine 1948- .... **CLC 51**
  See also CA 101; CANR 18, 40
Goyen, (Charles) William 1915-1983**CLC 5, 8, 14, 40**
  See also AITN 2; CA 5-8R; 110; CANR 6; DLB 2; DLBY 83; INT CANR-6
Goytisolo, Juan 1931- . **CLC 5, 10, 23; DAM MULT; HLC**
  See also CA 85-88; CANR 32, 61; HW; MTCW
Gozzano, Guido 1883-1916 .... **PC 10**
  See also CA 154; DLB 114
Gozzi, (Conte) Carlo 1720-1806 .... **NCLC 23**
Grabbe, Christian Dietrich 1801-1836**NCLC 2**
  See also DLB 133
Grace, Patricia 1937- .... **CLC 56**
Gracian y Morales, Baltasar 1601-1658**LC 15**
Gracq, Julien .... **CLC 11, 48**
  See also Poirier, Louis
  See also DLB 83
Grade, Chaim 1910-1982 .... **CLC 10**
  See also CA 93-96; 107
Graduate of Oxford, A
  See Ruskin, John
Grafton, Garth
  See Duncan, Sara Jeannette
Graham, John
  See Phillips, David Graham
Graham, Jorie 1951- .... **CLC 48**
  See also CA 111; CANR 63; DLB 120
Graham, R(obert) B(ontine) Cunninghame
  See Cunninghame Graham, R(obert) B(ontine)
  See also DLB 98, 135, 174
Graham, Robert
  See Haldeman, Joe (William)
Graham, Tom
  See Lewis, (Harry) Sinclair
Graham, W(illiam) S(ydney) 1918-1986**CLC 29**
  See also CA 73-76; 118; DLB 20
Graham, Winston (Mawdsley) 1910- **CLC 23**
  See also CA 49-52; CANR 2, 22, 45; DLB 77
Grahame, Kenneth 1859-1932**TCLC 64; DAB**
  See also CA 108; 136; CLR 5; DLB 34, 141, 178; MAICYA; YABC 1
Grant, Skeeter
  See Spiegelman, Art
Granville-Barker, Harley 1877-1946**TCLC 2; DAM DRAM**
  See also Barker, Harley Granville
  See also CA 104
Grass, Guenter (Wilhelm) 1927-**CLC 1, 2, 4, 6, 11, 15, 22, 32, 49, 88; DA; DAB; DAC; DAM MST, NOV; WLC**
  See also CA 13-16R; CANR 20; DLB 75, 124; MTCW
Gratton, Thomas
  See Hulme, T(homas) E(rnest)
Grau, Shirley Ann 1929- .. **CLC 4, 9; SSC 15**
  See also CA 89-92; CANR 22; DLB 2; INT CANR-22; MTCW
Gravel, Fern
  See Hall, James Norman
Graver, Elizabeth 1964- .... **CLC 70**
  See also CA 135
Graves, Richard Perceval 1945- .... **CLC 44**
  See also CA 65-68; CANR 9, 26, 51
Graves, Robert (von Ranke) 1895-1985 **CLC 1, 2, 6, 11, 39, 44, 45; DAB; DAC; DAM MST, POET; PC 6**

  See also CA 5-8R; 117; CANR 5, 36; CDBLB 1914-1945; DLB 20, 100; DLBY 85; MTCW; SATA 45
Graves, Valerie
  See Bradley, Marion Zimmer
Gray, Alasdair (James) 1934- .... **CLC 41**
  See also CA 126; CANR 47; INT 126; MTCW
Gray, Amlin 1946- .... **CLC 29**
  See also CA 138
Gray, Francine du Plessix 1930- ..... **CLC 22; DAM NOV**
  See also BEST 90:3; CA 61-64; CAAS 2; CANR 11, 33; INT CANR-11; MTCW
Gray, John (Henry) 1866-1934 ...... **TCLC 19**
  See also CA 119
Gray, Simon (James Holliday) 1936- **CLC 9, 14, 36**
  See also AITN 1; CA 21-24R; CAAS 3; CANR 32; DLB 13; MTCW
Gray, Spalding 1941-**CLC 49; DAM POP; DC 7**
  See also CA 128
Gray, Thomas 1716-1771**LC 4, 40; DA; DAB; DAC; DAM MST; PC 2; WLC**
  See also CDBLB 1660-1789; DLB 109
Grayson, David
  See Baker, Ray Stannard
Grayson, Richard (A.) 1951- .... **CLC 38**
  See also CA 85-88; CANR 14, 31, 57
Greeley, Andrew M(oran) 1928- ..... **CLC 28; DAM POP**
  See also CA 5-8R; CAAS 7; CANR 7, 43; MTCW
Green, Anna Katharine 1846-1935 **TCLC 63**
  See also CA 112; 159
Green, Brian
  See Card, Orson Scott
Green, Hannah
  See Greenberg, Joanne (Goldenberg)
Green, Hannah 1927(?)-1996 .... **CLC 3**
  See also CA 73-76; CANR 59
Green, Henry 1905-1973 .... **CLC 2, 13, 97**
  See also Yorke, Henry Vincent
  See also DLB 15
Green, Julian (Hartridge) 1900-
  See Green, Julien
  See also CA 21-24R; CANR 33; DLB 4, 72; MTCW
Green, Julien .... **CLC 3, 11, 77**
  See also Green, Julian (Hartridge)
Green, Paul (Eliot) 1894-1981**CLC 25; DAM DRAM**
  See also AITN 1; CA 5-8R; 103; CANR 3; DLB 7, 9; DLBY 81
Greenberg, Ivan 1908-1973
  See Rahv, Philip
  See also CA 85-88
Greenberg, Joanne (Goldenberg) 1932- **CLC 7, 30**
  See also AAYA 12; CA 5-8R; CANR 14, 32; SATA 25
Greenberg, Richard 1959(?)- .... **CLC 57**
  See also CA 138
Greene, Bette 1934- .... **CLC 30**
  See also AAYA 7; CA 53-56; CANR 4; CLR 2; JRDA; MAICYA; SAAS 16; SATA 8
Greene, Gael .... **CLC 8**
  See also CA 13-16R; CANR 10
Greene, Graham (Henry) 1904-1991**CLC 1, 3, 6, 9, 14, 18, 27, 37, 70, 72; DA; DAB; DAC; DAM MST, NOV; SSC 29; WLC**
  See also AITN 2; CA 13-16R; 133; CANR 35, 61; CDBLB 1945-1960; DLB 13, 15, 77,

Author Index

100, 162; DLBY 91; MTCW; SATA 20

Greene, Robert 1558-1592 .... **LC 41**

Greer, Richard
See Silverberg, Robert

Gregor, Arthur 1923- .... **CLC 9**
See also CA 25-28R; CAAS 10; CANR 11;
SATA 36

Gregor, Lee
See Pohl, Frederik

Gregory, Isabella Augusta (Persse) 1852-1932
TCLC 1
See also CA 104; DLB 10

Gregory, J. Dennis
See Williams, John A(lfred)

Grendon, Stephen
See Derleth, August (William)

Grenville, Kate 1950- .... **CLC 61**
See also CA 118; CANR 53

Grenville, Pelham
See Wodehouse, P(elham) G(renville)

Greve, Felix Paul (Berthold Friedrich) 1879-
1948
See Grove, Frederick Philip
See also CA 104; 141; DAC; DAM MST

Grey, Zane 1872-1939 .. **TCLC 6; DAM POP**
See also CA 104; 132; DLB 9; MTCW

Grieg, (Johan) Nordahl (Brun) 1902-1943
TCLC 10
See also CA 107

Grieve, C(hristopher) M(urray) 1892-1978
CLC 11, 19; DAM POET
See MacDiarmid, Hugh; Pteleon
See also CA 5-8R; 85-88; CANR 33; MTCW

Griffin, Gerald 1803-1840 .... **NCLC 7**
See also DLB 159

Griffin, John Howard 1920-1980 ..... **CLC 68**
See also AITN 1; CA 1-4R; 101; CANR 2

Griffin, Peter 1942- .... **CLC 39**
See also CA 136

Griffith, D(avid Lewelyn) W(ark) 1875(?)-1948
TCLC 68
See also CA 119; 150

Griffith, Lawrence
See Griffith, D(avid Lewelyn) W(ark)

Griffiths, Trevor 1935- .... **CLC 13, 52**
See also CA 97-100; CANR 45; DLB 13

Griggs, Sutton Elbert 1872-1930(?)**TCLC 77**
See also CA 123; DLB 50

Grigson, Geoffrey (Edward Harvey) 1905-1985
CLC 7, 39
See also CA 25-28R; 118; CANR 20, 33; DLB
27; MTCW

Grillparzer, Franz 1791-1872 .... **NCLC 1**
See also DLB 133

Grimble, Reverend Charles James
See Eliot, T(homas) S(tearns)

Grimke, Charlotte L(ottie) Forten 1837(?)-1914
See Forten, Charlotte L.
See also BW 1; CA 117; 124; DAM MULT,
POET

Grimm, Jacob Ludwig Karl 1785-1863**NCLC
3**
See also DLB 90; MAICYA; SATA 22

Grimm, Wilhelm Karl 1786-1859 .... **NCLC 3**
See also DLB 90; MAICYA; SATA 22

Grimmelshausen, Johann Jakob Christoffel von
1621-1676 .... **LC 6**
See also DLB 168

Grindel, Eugene 1895-1952
See Eluard, Paul
See also CA 104

Grisham, John 1955- .... **CLC 84; DAM POP**
See also AAYA 14; CA 138; CANR 47

Grossman, David 1954- .... **CLC 67**
See also CA 138

Grossman, Vasily (Semenovich) 1905-1964
CLC 41
See also CA 124; 130; MTCW

Grove, Frederick Philip .... **TCLC 4**
See also Greve, Felix Paul (Berthold Friedrich)
See also DLB 92

Grubb
See Crumb, R(obert)

Grumbach, Doris (Isaac) 1918-**CLC 13, 22, 64**
See also CA 5-8R; CAAS 2; CANR 9, 42; INT
CANR-9

Grundtvig, Nicolai Frederik Severin 1783-1872
NCLC 1

Grunge
See Crumb, R(obert)

Grunwald, Lisa 1959- .... **CLC 44**
See also CA 120

Guare, John 1938- . **CLC 8, 14, 29, 67; DAM
DRAM**
See also CA 73-76; CANR 21; DLB 7; MTCW

Gudjonsson, Halldor Kiljan 1902-
See Laxness, Halldor
See also CA 103

Guenter, Erich
See Eich, Guenter

Guest, Barbara 1920- .... **CLC 34**
See also CA 25-28R; CANR 11, 44; DLB 5

Guest, Judith (Ann) 1936- **CLC 8, 30; DAM
NOV, POP**
See also AAYA 7; CA 77-80; CANR 15; INT
CANR-15; MTCW

Guevara, Che .... **CLC 87; HLC**
See also Guevara (Serna), Ernesto

Guevara (Serna), Ernesto 1928-1967
See Guevara, Che
See also CA 127; 111; CANR 56; DAM MULT;
HW

Guild, Nicholas M. 1944- .... **CLC 33**
See also CA 93-96

Guillemin, Jacques
See Sartre, Jean-Paul

Guillen, Jorge 1893-1984 .... **CLC 11; DAM
MULT, POET**
See also CA 89-92; 112; DLB 108; HW

Guillen, Nicolas (Cristobal) 1902-1989 **CLC
48, 79; BLC; DAM MST, MULT, POET;
HLC**
See also BW 2; CA 116; 125; 129; HW

Guillevic, (Eugene) 1907- .... **CLC 33**
See also CA 93-96

Guillois
See Desnos, Robert

Guillois, Valentin
See Desnos, Robert

Guiney, Louise Imogen 1861-1920 **TCLC 41**
See also CA 160; DLB 54

Guiraldes, Ricardo (Guillermo) 1886-1927
TCLC 39
See also CA 131; HW; MTCW

Gumilev, Nikolai Stephanovich 1886-1921
TCLC 60

Gunesekera, Romesh 1954- .... **CLC 91**
See also CA 159

Gunn, Bill .... **CLC 5**
See also Gunn, William Harrison
See also DLB 38

Gunn, Thom(son William) 1929-**CLC 3, 6, 18,
32, 81; DAM POET**
See also CA 17-20R; CANR 9, 33; CDBLB
1960 to Present; DLB 27; INT CANR-33;
MTCW

Gunn, William Harrison 1934(?)-1989
See Gunn, Bill
See also AITN 1; BW 1; CA 13-16R; 128;
CANR 12, 25

Gunnars, Kristjana 1948- .... **CLC 69**
See also CA 113; DLB 60

Gurdjieff, G(eorgei) I(vanovich) 1877(?)-1949
TCLC 71
See also CA 157

Gurganus, Allan 1947- . **CLC 70; DAM POP**
See also BEST 90:1; CA 135

Gurney, A(lbert) R(amsdell), Jr. 1930-. **C L C
32, 50, 54; DAM DRAM**
See also CA 77-80; CANR 32, 64

Gurney, Ivor (Bertie) 1890-1937 ... **TCLC 33**

Gurney, Peter
See Gurney, A(lbert) R(amsdell), Jr.

Guro, Elena 1877-1913 .... **TCLC 56**

Gustafson, James M(oody) 1925- ... **CLC 100**
See also CA 25-28R; CANR 37

Gustafson, Ralph (Barker) 1909- ..... **CLC 36**
See also CA 21-24R; CANR 8, 45; DLB 88

Gut, Gom
See Simenon, Georges (Jacques Christian)

Guterson, David 1956- .... **CLC 91**
See also CA 132

Guthrie, A(lfred) B(ertram), Jr. 1901-1991
CLC 23
See also CA 57-60; 134; CANR 24; DLB 6;
SATA 62; SATA-Obit 67

Guthrie, Isobel
See Grieve, C(hristopher) M(urray)

Guthrie, Woodrow Wilson 1912-1967
See Guthrie, Woody
See also CA 113; 93-96

Guthrie, Woody .... **CLC 35**
See also Guthrie, Woodrow Wilson

Guy, Rosa (Cuthbert) 1928- .... **CLC 26**
See also AAYA 4; BW 2; CA 17-20R; CANR
14, 34; CLR 13; DLB 33; JRDA; MAICYA;
SATA 14, 62

Gwendolyn
See Bennett, (Enoch) Arnold

H. D. .... **CLC 3, 8, 14, 31, 34, 73; PC 5**
See also Doolittle, Hilda

H. de V.
See Buchan, John

Haavikko, Paavo Juhani 1931- .. **CLC 18, 34**
See also CA 106

Habbema, Koos
See Heijermans, Herman

Habermas, Juergen 1929- .... **CLC 104**
See also CA 109

Habermas, Jurgen
See Habermas, Juergen

Hacker, Marilyn 1942- **CLC 5, 9, 23, 72, 91;
DAM POET**
See also CA 77-80; DLB 120

Haggard, H(enry) Rider 1856-1925**TCLC 11**
See also CA 108; 148; DLB 70, 156, 174, 178;
SATA 16

Hagiosy, L.
See Larbaud, Valery (Nicolas)

Hagiwara Sakutaro 1886-1942**TCLC 60; PC
18**

Haig, Fenil
See Ford, Ford Madox

Haig-Brown, Roderick (Langmere) 1908-1976
CLC 21
See also CA 5-8R; 69-72; CANR 4, 38; CLR
31; DLB 88; MAICYA; SATA 12

Hailey, Arthur 1920-**CLC 5; DAM NOV, POP**
See also AITN 2; BEST 90:3; CA 1-4R; CANR

2, 36; DLB 88; DLBY 82; MTCW

Hailey, Elizabeth Forsythe 1938- ..... **CLC 40**
See also CA 93-96; CAAS 1; CANR 15, 48; INT CANR-15

Haines, John (Meade) 1924- .... **CLC 58**
See also CA 17-20R; CANR 13, 34; DLB 5

Hakluyt, Richard 1552-1616 .... **LC 31**

Haldeman, Joe (William) 1943- .... **CLC 61**
See also CA 53-56; CAAS 25; CANR 6; DLB 8; INT CANR-6

Haley, Alex(ander Murray Palmer) 1921-1992
CLC 8, 12, 76; BLC; DA; DAB; DAC; DAM MST, MULT, POP
See also BW 2; CA 77-80; 136; CANR 61; DLB 38; MTCW

Haliburton, Thomas Chandler 1796-1865
NCLC 15
See also DLB 11, 99

Hall, Donald (Andrew, Jr.) 1928- **CLC 1, 13, 37, 59; DAM POET**
See also CA 5-8R; CAAS 7; CANR 2, 44, 64; DLB 5; SATA 23

Hall, Frederic Sauser
See Sauser-Hall, Frederic

Hall, James
See Kuttner, Henry

Hall, James Norman 1887-1951 ..... **TCLC 23**
See also CA 123; SATA 21

Hall, (Marguerite) Radclyffe 1886-1943
TCLC 12
See also CA 110; 150

Hall, Rodney 1935- .... **CLC 51**
See also CA 109

Halleck, Fitz-Greene 1790-1867 .... **NCLC 47**
See also DLB 3

Halliday, Michael
See Creasey, John

Halpern, Daniel 1945- .... **CLC 14**
See also CA 33-36R

Hamburger, Michael (Peter Leopold) 1924-
CLC 5, 14
See also CA 5-8R; CAAS 4; CANR 2, 47; DLB 27

Hamill, Pete 1935- .... **CLC 10**
See also CA 25-28R; CANR 18

Hamilton, Alexander 1755(?)-1804 **NCLC 49**
See also DLB 37

Hamilton, Clive
See Lewis, C(live) S(taples)

Hamilton, Edmond 1904-1977 .... **CLC 1**
See also CA 1-4R; CANR 3; DLB 8

Hamilton, Eugene (Jacob) Lee
See Lee-Hamilton, Eugene (Jacob)

Hamilton, Franklin
See Silverberg, Robert

Hamilton, Gail
See Corcoran, Barbara

Hamilton, Mollie
See Kaye, M(ary) M(argaret)

Hamilton, (Anthony Walter) Patrick 1904-1962
CLC 51
See also CA 113; DLB 10

Hamilton, Virginia 1936- .... **CLC 26; DAM MULT**
See also AAYA 2, 21; BW 2; CA 25-28R; CANR 20, 37; CLR 1, 11, 40; DLB 33, 52; INT CANR-20; JRDA; MAICYA; MTCW; SATA 4, 56, 79

Hammett, (Samuel) Dashiell 1894-1961 **C L C 3, 5, 10, 19, 47; SSC 17**
See also AITN 1; CA 81-84; CANR 42; CDALB 1929-1941; DLBD 6; DLBY 96; MTCW

Hammon, Jupiter 1711(?)-1800(?) .. **NCLC 5;**

BLC; DAM MULT, POET; PC 16
See also DLB 31, 50

Hammond, Keith
See Kuttner, Henry

Hamner, Earl (Henry), Jr. 1923- ...... **CLC 12**
See also AITN 2; CA 73-76; DLB 6

Hampton, Christopher (James) 1946- **CLC 4**
See also CA 25-28R; DLB 13; MTCW

Hamsun, Knut .... **TCLC 2, 14, 49**
See also Pedersen, Knut

Handke, Peter 1942- **CLC 5, 8, 10, 15, 38; DAM DRAM, NOV**
See also CA 77-80; CANR 33; DLB 85, 124; MTCW

Hanley, James 1901-1985 ..... **CLC 3, 5, 8, 13**
See also CA 73-76; 117; CANR 36; MTCW

Hannah, Barry 1942- .... **CLC 23, 38, 90**
See also CA 108; 110; CANR 43; DLB 6; INT 110; MTCW

Hannon, Ezra
See Hunter, Evan

Hansberry, Lorraine (Vivian) 1930-1965 **CLC 17, 62; BLC; DA; DAB; DAC; DAM DRAM, MST, MULT; DC 2**
See also BW 1; CA 109; 25-28R; CABS 3; CANR 58; CDALB 1941-1968; DLB 7, 38; MTCW

Hansen, Joseph 1923- .... **CLC 38**
See also CA 29-32R; CAAS 17; CANR 16, 44; INT CANR-16

Hansen, Martin A. 1909-1955 .... **TCLC 32**

Hanson, Kenneth O(stlin) 1922- .... **CLC 13**
See also CA 53-56; CANR 7

Hardwick, Elizabeth 1916- .... **CLC 13; DAM NOV**
See also CA 5-8R; CANR 3, 32; DLB 6; MTCW

Hardy, Thomas 1840-1928 **TCLC 4, 10, 18, 32, 48, 53, 72; DA; DAB; DAC; DAM MST, NOV, POET; PC 8; SSC 2; WLC**
See also CA 104; 123; CDBLB 1890-1914; DLB 18, 19, 135; MTCW

Hare, David 1947- .... **CLC 29, 58**
See also CA 97-100; CANR 39; DLB 13; MTCW

Harewood, John
See Van Druten, John (William)

Harford, Henry
See Hudson, W(illiam) H(enry)

Hargrave, Leonie
See Disch, Thomas M(ichael)

Harjo, Joy 1951- .... **CLC 83; DAM MULT**
See also CA 114; CANR 35; DLB 120, 175; NNAL

Harlan, Louis R(udolph) 1922- .... **CLC 34**
See also CA 21-24R; CANR 25, 55

Harling, Robert 1951(?)- .... **CLC 53**
See also CA 147

Harmon, William (Ruth) 1938- .... **CLC 38**
See also CA 33-36R; CANR 14, 32, 35; SATA 65

Harper, F. E. W.
See Harper, Frances Ellen Watkins

Harper, Frances E. W.
See Harper, Frances Ellen Watkins

Harper, Frances E. Watkins
See Harper, Frances Ellen Watkins

Harper, Frances Ellen
See Harper, Frances Ellen Watkins

Harper, Frances Ellen Watkins 1825-1911
TCLC 14; BLC; DAM MULT, POET; PC 21
See also BW 1; CA 111; 125; DLB 50

Harper, Michael S(teven) 1938- .... **CLC 7, 22**

See also BW 1; CA 33-36R; CANR 24; DLB 41

Harper, Mrs. F. E. W.
See Harper, Frances Ellen Watkins

Harris, Christie (Lucy) Irwin 1907- **CLC 12**
See also CA 5-8R; CANR 6; CLR 47; DLB 88; JRDA; MAICYA; SAAS 10; SATA 6, 74

Harris, Frank 1856-1931 .... **TCLC 24**
See also CA 109; 150; DLB 156

Harris, George Washington 1814-1869 **NCLC 23**
See also DLB 3, 11

Harris, Joel Chandler 1848-1908 ... **TCLC 2; SSC 19**
See also CA 104; 137; DLB 11, 23, 42, 78, 91; MAICYA; YABC 1

Harris, John (Wyndham Parkes Lucas) Beynon 1903-1969
See Wyndham, John
See also CA 102; 89-92

Harris, MacDonald .... **CLC 9**
See also Heiney, Donald (William)

Harris, Mark 1922- .... **CLC 19**
See also CA 5-8R; CAAS 3; CANR 2, 55; DLB 2; DLBY 80

Harris, (Theodore) Wilson 1921- ... **CLC 25**
See also BW 2; CA 65-68; CAAS 16; CANR 11, 27; DLB 117; MTCW

Harrison, Elizabeth Cavanna 1909-
See Cavanna, Betty
See also CA 9-12R; CANR 6, 27

Harrison, Harry (Max) 1925- .... **CLC 42**
See also CA 1-4R; CANR 5, 21; DLB 8; SATA 4

Harrison, James (Thomas) 1937- **CLC 6, 14, 33, 66; SSC 19**
See also CA 13-16R; CANR 8, 51; DLBY 82; INT CANR-8

Harrison, Jim
See Harrison, James (Thomas)

Harrison, Kathryn 1961- .... **CLC 70**
See also CA 144

Harrison, Tony 1937- .... **CLC 43**
See also CA 65-68; CANR 44; DLB 40; MTCW

Harriss, Will(ard Irvin) 1922- .... **CLC 34**
See also CA 111

Harson, Sley
See Ellison, Harlan (Jay)

Hart, Ellis
See Ellison, Harlan (Jay)

Hart, Josephine 1942(?)- **CLC 70; DAM POP**
See also CA 138

Hart, Moss 1904-1961 **CLC 66; DAM DRAM**
See also CA 109; 89-92; DLB 7

Harte, (Francis) Bret(t) 1836(?)-1902 **TCLC 1, 25; DA; DAC; DAM MST; SSC 8; WLC**
See also CA 104; 140; CDALB 1865-1917; DLB 12, 64, 74, 79; SATA 26

Hartley, L(eslie) P(oles) 1895-1972 **CLC 2, 22**
See also CA 45-48; 37-40R; CANR 33; DLB 15, 139; MTCW

Hartman, Geoffrey H. 1929- .... **CLC 27**
See also CA 117; 125; DLB 67

Hartmann, Sadakichi 1867-1944 ... **TCLC 73**
See also CA 157; DLB 54

Hartmann von Aue c. 1160-c. 1205 **CMLC 15**
See also DLB 138

Hartmann von Aue 1170-1210 ...... **CMLC 15**

Haruf, Kent 1943- .... **CLC 34**
See also CA 149

Harwood, Ronald 1934- .... **CLC 32; DAM DRAM, MST**
See also CA 1-4R; CANR 4, 55; DLB 13

Hasek, Jaroslav (Matej Frantisek) 1883-1923
  TCLC 4
  See also CA 104; 129; MTCW
Hass, Robert 1941- ... CLC 18, 39, 99; PC 16
  See also CA 111; CANR 30, 50; DLB 105;
  SATA 94
Hastings, Hudson
  See Kuttner, Henry
Hastings, Selina .... CLC 44
Hathorne, John 1641-1717 .... LC 38
Hatteras, Amelia
  See Mencken, H(enry) L(ouis)
Hatteras, Owen .... TCLC 18
  See also Mencken, H(enry) L(ouis); Nathan,
  George Jean
Hauptmann, Gerhart (Johann Robert) 1862-
  1946 .... TCLC 4; DAM DRAM
  See also CA 104; 153; DLB 66, 118
Havel, Vaclav 1936- ... CLC 25, 58, 65; DAM
  DRAM; DC 6
  See also CA 104; CANR 36, 63; MTCW
Haviaras, Stratis .... CLC 33
  See also Chaviaras, Strates
Hawes, Stephen 1475(?)-1523(?) .... LC 17
Hawkes, John (Clendennin Burne, Jr.) 1925-
  CLC 1, 2, 3, 4, 7, 9, 14, 15, 27, 49
  See also CA 1-4R; CANR 2, 47, 64; DLB 2, 7;
  DLBY 80; MTCW
Hawking, S. W.
  See Hawking, Stephen W(illiam)
Hawking, Stephen W(illiam) 1942- . CLC 63,
  105
  See also AAYA 13; BEST 89:1; CA 126; 129;
  CANR 48
Hawthorne, Julian 1846-1934 .... TCLC 25
Hawthorne, Nathaniel 1804-1864 NCLC 39;
  DA; DAB; DAC; DAM MST, NOV; SSC
  3, 29; WLC
  See also AAYA 18; CDALB 1640-1865; DLB
  1, 74; YABC 2
Haxton, Josephine Ayres 1921-
  See Douglas, Ellen
  See also CA 115; CANR 41
Hayaseca y Eizaguirre, Jorge
  See Echegaray (y Eizaguirre), Jose (Maria
  Waldo)
Hayashi Fumiko 1904-1951 .... TCLC 27
  See also CA 161; DLB 180
Haycraft, Anna
  See Ellis, Alice Thomas
  See also CA 122
Hayden, Robert E(arl) 1913-1980 . CLC 5, 9,
  14, 37; BLC; DA; DAC; DAM MST,
  MULT, POET; PC 6
  See also BW 1; CA 69-72; 97-100; CABS 2;
  CANR 24; CDALB 1941-1968; DLB 5, 76;
  MTCW; SATA 19; SATA-Obit 26
Hayford, J(oseph) E(phraim) Casely
  See Casely-Hayford, J(oseph) E(phraim)
Hayman, Ronald 1932- .... CLC 44
  See also CA 25-28R; CANR 18, 50; DLB 155
Haywood, Eliza (Fowler) 1693(?)-1756 LC 1
Hazlitt, William 1778-1830 .... NCLC 29
  See also DLB 110, 158
Hazzard, Shirley 1931- .... CLC 18
  See also CA 9-12R; CANR 4; DLBY 82;
  MTCW
Head, Bessie 1937-1986 ... CLC 25, 67; BLC;
  DAM MULT
  See also BW 2; CA 29-32R; 119; CANR 25;
  DLB 117; MTCW
Headon, (Nicky) Topper 1956(?)- ..... CLC 30
Heaney, Seamus (Justin) 1939- CLC 5, 7, 14,

25, 37, 74, 91; DAB; DAM POET; PC 18;
  WLCS
  See also CA 85-88; CANR 25, 48; CDBLB
  1960 to Present; DLB 40; DLBY 95; MTCW
Hearn, (Patricio) Lafcadio (Tessima Carlos)
  1850-1904 .... TCLC 9
  See also CA 105; DLB 12, 78
Hearne, Vicki 1946- .... CLC 56
  See also CA 139
Hearon, Shelby 1931- .... CLC 63
  See also AITN 2; CA 25-28R; CANR 18, 48
Heat-Moon, William Least .... CLC 29
  See also Trogdon, William (Lewis)
  See also AAYA 9
Hebbel, Friedrich 1813-1863 NCLC 43; DAM
  DRAM
  See also DLB 129
Hebert, Anne 1916- CLC 4, 13, 29; DAC; DAM
  MST, POET
  See also CA 85-88; DLB 68; MTCW
Hecht, Anthony (Evan) 1923- CLC 8, 13, 19;
  DAM POET
  See also CA 9-12R; CANR 6; DLB 5, 169
Hecht, Ben 1894-1964 .... CLC 8
  See also CA 85-88; DLB 7, 9, 25, 26, 28, 86
Hedayat, Sadeq 1903-1951 .... TCLC 21
  See also CA 120
Hegel, Georg Wilhelm Friedrich 1770-1831
  NCLC 46
  See also DLB 90
Heidegger, Martin 1889-1976 .... CLC 24
  See also CA 81-84; 65-68; CANR 34; MTCW
Heidenstam, (Carl Gustaf) Verner von 1859-
  1940 .... TCLC 5
  See also CA 104
Heifner, Jack 1946- .... CLC 11
  See also CA 105; CANR 47
Heijermans, Herman 1864-1924 .... TCLC 24
  See also CA 123
Heilbrun, Carolyn G(old) 1926- .... CLC 25
  See also CA 45-48; CANR 1, 28, 58
Heine, Heinrich 1797-1856 .... NCLC 4, 54
  See also DLB 90
Heinemann, Larry (Curtiss) 1944- ... CLC 50
  See also CA 110; CAAS 21; CANR 31; DLBD
  9; INT CANR-31
Heiney, Donald (William) 1921-1993
  See Harris, MacDonald
  See also CA 1-4R; 142; CANR 3, 58
Heinlein, Robert A(nson) 1907-1988 CLC 1, 3,
  8, 14, 26, 55; DAM POP
  See also AAYA 17; CA 1-4R; 125; CANR 1,
  20, 53; DLB 8; JRDA; MAICYA; MTCW;
  SATA 9, 69; SATA-Obit 56
Helforth, John
  See Doolittle, Hilda
Hellenhofferu, Vojtech Kapristian z
  See Hasek, Jaroslav (Matej Frantisek)
Heller, Joseph 1923- CLC 1, 3, 5, 8, 11, 36, 63;
  DA; DAB; DAC; DAM MST, NOV, POP;
  WLC
  See also AITN 1; CA 5-8R; CABS 1; CANR 8,
  42; DLB 2, 28; DLBY 80; INT CANR-8;
  MTCW
Hellman, Lillian (Florence) 1906-1984 CLC 2,
  4, 8, 14, 18, 34, 44, 52; DAM DRAM; DC 1
  See also AITN 1, 2; CA 13-16R; 112; CANR
  33; DLB 7; DLBY 84; MTCW
Helprin, Mark 1947- CLC 7, 10, 22, 32; DAM
  NOV, POP
  See also CA 81-84; CANR 47, 64; DLBY 85;
  MTCW
Helvetius, Claude-Adrien 1715-1771 .. LC 26

Helyar, Jane Penelope Josephine 1933-
  See Poole, Josephine
  See also CA 21-24R; CANR 10, 26; SATA 82
Hemans, Felicia 1793-1835 .... NCLC 29
  See also DLB 96
Hemingway, Ernest (Miller) 1899-1961 C L C
  1, 3, 6, 8, 10, 13, 19, 30, 34, 39, 41, 44, 50,
  61, 80; DA; DAB; DAC; DAM MST, NOV;
  SSC 25; WLC
  See also AAYA 19; CA 77-80; CANR 34;
  CDALB 1917-1929; DLB 4, 9, 102; DLBD
  1, 15, 16; DLBY 81, 87, 96; MTCW
Hempel, Amy 1951- .... CLC 39
  See also CA 118; 137
Henderson, F. C.
  See Mencken, H(enry) L(ouis)
Henderson, Sylvia
  See Ashton-Warner, Sylvia (Constance)
Henderson, Zenna (Chlarson) 1917-1983 S S C
  29
  See also CA 1-4R; 133; CANR 1; DLB 8; SATA
  5
Henley, Beth .... CLC 23; DC 6
  See also Henley, Elizabeth Becker
  See also CABS 3; DLBY 86
Henley, Elizabeth Becker 1952-
  See Henley, Beth
  See also CA 107; CANR 32; DAM DRAM,
  MST; MTCW
Henley, William Ernest 1849-1903 .. TCLC 8
  See also CA 105; DLB 19
Hennissart, Martha
  See Lathen, Emma
  See also CA 85-88; CANR 64
Henry, O. .... TCLC 1, 19; SSC 5; WLC
  See also Porter, William Sydney
Henry, Patrick 1736-1799 .... LC 25
Henryson, Robert 1430(?)-1506(?) ...... LC 20
  See also DLB 146
Henry VIII 1491-1547 .... LC 10
Henschke, Alfred
  See Klabund
Hentoff, Nat(han Irving) 1925- .... CLC 26
  See also AAYA 4; CA 1-4R; CAAS 6; CANR
  5, 25; CLR 1; INT CANR-25; JRDA;
  MAICYA; SATA 42, 69; SATA-Brief 27
Heppenstall, (John) Rayner 1911-1981 C L C
  10
  See also CA 1-4R; 103; CANR 29
Heraclitus c. 540B.C.-c. 450B.C. .. CMLC 22
  See also DLB 176
Herbert, Frank (Patrick) 1920-1986 CLC 12,
  23, 35, 44, 85; DAM POP
  See also AAYA 21; CA 53-56; 118; CANR 5,
  43; DLB 8; INT CANR-5; MTCW; SATA 9,
  37; SATA-Obit 47
Herbert, George 1593-1633 ..... LC 24; DAB;
  DAM POET; PC 4
  See also CDBLB Before 1660; DLB 126
Herbert, Zbigniew 1924- .. CLC 9, 43; DAM
  POET
  See also CA 89-92; CANR 36; MTCW
Herbst, Josephine (Frey) 1897-1969 CLC 34
  See also CA 5-8R; 25-28R; DLB 9
Hergesheimer, Joseph 1880-1954 .. TCLC 11
  See also CA 109; DLB 102, 9
Herlihy, James Leo 1927-1993 .... CLC 6
  See also CA 1-4R; 143; CANR 2
Hermogenes fl. c. 175- .... CMLC 6
Hernandez, Jose 1834-1886 .... NCLC 17
Herodotus c. 484B.C.-429B.C. ...... CMLC 17
  See also DLB 176
Herrick, Robert 1591-1674 LC 13; DA; DAB;

DAC; DAM MST, POP; PC 9
See also DLB 126
Herring, Guilles
See Somerville, Edith
Herriot, James 1916-1995**CLC 12; DAM POP**
See also Wight, James Alfred
See also AAYA 1; CA 148; CANR 40; SATA
86
Herrmann, Dorothy 1941- .... **CLC 44**
See also CA 107
Herrmann, Taffy
See Herrmann, Dorothy
Hersey, John (Richard) 1914-1993**CLC 1, 2, 7,
9, 40, 81, 97; DAM POP**
See also CA 17-20R; 140; CANR 33; DLB 6;
MTCW; SATA 25; SATA-Obit 76
Herzen, Aleksandr Ivanovich 1812-1870
NCLC 10, 61
Herzl, Theodor 1860-1904 .... **TCLC 36**
Herzog, Werner 1942- .... **CLC 16**
See also CA 89-92
Hesiod c. 8th cent. B.C.- .... **CMLC 5**
See also DLB 176
Hesse, Hermann 1877-1962**CLC 1, 2, 3, 6, 11,
17, 25, 69; DA; DAB; DAC; DAM MST,
NOV; SSC 9; WLC**
See also CA 17-18; CAP 2; DLB 66; MTCW;
SATA 50
Hewes, Cady
See De Voto, Bernard (Augustine)
Heyen, William 1940- .... **CLC 13, 18**
See also CA 33-36R; CAAS 9; DLB 5
Heyerdahl, Thor 1914- .... **CLC 26**
See also CA 5-8R; CANR 5, 22; MTCW; SATA
2, 52
Heym, Georg (Theodor Franz Arthur) 1887-
1912 .... **TCLC 9**
See also CA 106
Heym, Stefan 1913- .... **CLC 41**
See also CA 9-12R; CANR 4; DLB 69
Heyse, Paul (Johann Ludwig von) 1830-1914
TCLC 8
See also CA 104; DLB 129
Heyward, (Edwin) DuBose 1885-1940 **T C L C
59**
See also CA 108; 157; DLB 7, 9, 45; SATA 21
Hibbert, Eleanor Alice Burford 1906-1993
CLC 7; DAM POP
See also BEST 90:4; CA 17-20R; 140; CANR
9, 28, 59; SATA 2; SATA-Obit 74
Hichens, Robert (Smythe) 1864-1950 **T C L C
64**
See also CA 162; DLB 153
Higgins, George V(incent) 1939-**CLC 4, 7, 10,
18**
See also CA 77-80; CAAS 5; CANR 17, 51;
DLB 2; DLBY 81; INT CANR-17; MTCW
Higginson, Thomas Wentworth 1823-1911
TCLC 36
See also DLB 1, 64
Highet, Helen
See MacInnes, Helen (Clark)
Highsmith, (Mary) Patricia 1921-1995**CLC 2,
4, 14, 42, 102; DAM NOV, POP**
See also CA 1-4R; 147; CANR 1, 20, 48, 62;
MTCW
Highwater, Jamake (Mamake) 1942(?)- **C L C
12**
See also AAYA 7; CA 65-68; CAAS 7; CANR
10, 34; CLR 17; DLB 52; DLBY 85; JRDA;
MAICYA; SATA 32, 69; SATA-Brief 30
Highway, Tomson 1951-**CLC 92; DAC; DAM
MULT**

See also CA 151; NNAL
Higuchi, Ichiyo 1872-1896 .... **NCLC 49**
Hijuelos, Oscar 1951- **CLC 65; DAM MULT,
POP; HLC**
See also BEST 90:1; CA 123; CANR 50; DLB
145; HW
Hikmet, Nazim 1902(?)-1963 .... **CLC 40**
See also CA 141; 93-96
Hildegard von Bingen 1098-1179 . **CMLC 20**
See also DLB 148
Hildesheimer, Wolfgang 1916-1991 .. **CLC 49**
See also CA 101; 135; DLB 69, 124
Hill, Geoffrey (William) 1932- **CLC 5, 8, 18,
45; DAM POET**
See also CA 81-84; CANR 21; CDBLB 1960
to Present; DLB 40; MTCW
Hill, George Roy 1921- .... **CLC 26**
See also CA 110; 122
Hill, John
See Koontz, Dean R(ay)
Hill, Susan (Elizabeth) 1942- . **CLC 4; DAB;
DAM MST, NOV**
See also CA 33-36R; CANR 29; DLB 14, 139;
MTCW
Hillerman, Tony 1925- . **CLC 62; DAM POP**
See also AAYA 6; BEST 89:1; CA 29-32R;
CANR 21, 42; SATA 6
Hillesum, Etty 1914-1943 .... **TCLC 49**
See also CA 137
Hilliard, Noel (Harvey) 1929- .... **CLC 15**
See also CA 9-12R; CANR 7
Hillis, Rick 1956- .... **CLC 66**
See also CA 134
Hilton, James 1900-1954 .... **TCLC 21**
See also CA 108; DLB 34, 77; SATA 34
Himes, Chester (Bomar) 1909-1984**CLC 2, 4,
7, 18, 58, 108; BLC; DAM MULT**
See also BW 2; CA 25-28R; 114; CANR 22;
DLB 2, 76, 143; MTCW
Hinde, Thomas .... **CLC 6, 11**
See also Chitty, Thomas Willes
Hindin, Nathan
See Bloch, Robert (Albert)
Hine, (William) Daryl 1936- .... **CLC 15**
See also CA 1-4R; CAAS 15; CANR 1, 20; DLB
60
Hinkson, Katharine Tynan
See Tynan, Katharine
Hinton, S(usan) E(loise) 1950- **CLC 30; DA;
DAB; DAC; DAM MST, NOV**
See also AAYA 2; CA 81-84; CANR 32, 62;
CLR 3, 23; JRDA; MAICYA; MTCW; SATA
19, 58
Hippius, Zinaida .... **TCLC 9**
See also Gippius, Zinaida (Nikolayevna)
Hiraoka, Kimitake 1925-1970
See Mishima, Yukio
See also CA 97-100; 29-32R; DAM DRAM;
MTCW
Hirsch, E(ric) D(onald), Jr. 1928- .... **CLC 79**
See also CA 25-28R; CANR 27, 51; DLB 67;
INT CANR-27; MTCW
Hirsch, Edward 1950- .... **CLC 31, 50**
See also CA 104; CANR 20, 42; DLB 120
Hitchcock, Alfred (Joseph) 1899-1980**CLC 16**
See also AAYA 22; CA 159; 97-100; SATA 27;
SATA-Obit 24
Hitler, Adolf 1889-1945 .... **TCLC 53**
See also CA 117; 147
Hoagland, Edward 1932-................... **CLC 28**
See also CA 1-4R; CANR 2, 31, 57; DLB 6;
SATA 51
Hoban, Russell (Conwell) 1925- . **CLC 7, 25;**

DAM NOV
See also CA 5-8R; CANR 23, 37; CLR 3; DLB
52; MAICYA; MTCW; SATA 1, 40, 78
Hobbes, Thomas 1588-1679 .... **LC 36**
See also DLB 151
Hobbs, Perry
See Blackmur, R(ichard) P(almer)
Hobson, Laura Z(ametkin) 1900-1986**CLC 7,
25**
See also CA 17-20R; 118; CANR 55; DLB 28;
SATA 52
Hochhuth, Rolf 1931- .. **CLC 4, 11, 18; DAM
DRAM**
See also CA 5-8R; CANR 33; DLB 124; MTCW
Hochman, Sandra 1936- .... **CLC 3, 8**
See also CA 5-8R; DLB 5
Hochwaelder, Fritz 1911-1986**CLC 36; DAM
DRAM**
See also CA 29-32R; 120; CANR 42; MTCW
Hochwalder, Fritz
See Hochwaelder, Fritz
Hocking, Mary (Eunice) 1921-.......... **CLC 13**
See also CA 101; CANR 18, 40
Hodgins, Jack 1938- .... **CLC 23**
See also CA 93-96; DLB 60
Hodgson, William Hope 1877(?)-1918 **T C L C
13**
See also CA 111; DLB 70, 153, 156, 178
Hoeg, Peter 1957- .... **CLC 95**
See also CA 151
Hoffman, Alice 1952- ... **CLC 51; DAM NOV**
See also CA 77-80; CANR 34; MTCW
Hoffman, Daniel (Gerard) 1923-**CLC 6, 13, 23**
See also CA 1-4R; CANR 4; DLB 5
Hoffman, Stanley 1944- .... **CLC 5**
See also CA 77-80
Hoffman, William M(oses) 1939-...... **CLC 40**
See also CA 57-60; CANR 11
Hoffmann, E(rnst) T(heodor) A(madeus) 1776-
1822 .... **NCLC 2; SSC 13**
See also DLB 90; SATA 27
Hofmann, Gert 1931- .... **CLC 54**
See also CA 128
Hofmannsthal, Hugo von 1874-1929**TCLC 11;
DAM DRAM; DC 4**
See also CA 106; 153; DLB 81, 118
Hogan, Linda 1947- ... **CLC 73; DAM MULT**
See also CA 120; CANR 45; DLB 175; NNAL
Hogarth, Charles
See Creasey, John
Hogarth, Emmett
See Polonsky, Abraham (Lincoln)
Hogg, James 1770-1835 .... **NCLC 4**
See also DLB 93, 116, 159
Holbach, Paul Henri Thiry Baron 1723-1789
LC 14
Holberg, Ludvig 1684-1754 .... **LC 6**
Holden, Ursula 1921- .... **CLC 18**
See also CA 101; CAAS 8; CANR 22
Holderlin, (Johann Christian) Friedrich 1770-
1843 .... **NCLC 16; PC 4**
Holdstock, Robert
See Holdstock, Robert P.
Holdstock, Robert P. 1948- .... **CLC 39**
See also CA 131
Holland, Isabelle 1920- .... **CLC 21**
See also AAYA 11; CA 21-24R; CANR 10, 25,
47; JRDA; MAICYA; SATA 8, 70
Holland, Marcus
See Caldwell, (Janet Miriam) Taylor (Holland)
Hollander, John 1929- .... **CLC 2, 5, 8, 14**
See also CA 1-4R; CANR 1, 52; DLB 5; SATA
13

Hollander, Paul
See Silverberg, Robert
Holleran, Andrew 1943(?)- .... **CLC 38**
See also CA 144
Hollinghurst, Alan 1954- .... **CLC 55, 91**
See also CA 114
Hollis, Jim
See Summers, Hollis (Spurgeon, Jr.)
Holly, Buddy 1936-1959 .... **TCLC 65**
Holmes, Gordon
See Shiel, M(atthew) P(hipps)
Holmes, John
See Souster, (Holmes) Raymond
Holmes, John Clellon 1926-1988 ...... **CLC 56**
See also CA 9-12R; 125; CANR 4; DLB 16
Holmes, Oliver Wendell, Jr. 1841-1935T C L C
77
See also CA 114
Holmes, Oliver Wendell 1809-1894 NCLC 14
See also CDALB 1640-1865; DLB 1; SATA 34
Holmes, Raymond
See Souster, (Holmes) Raymond
Holt, Victoria
See Hibbert, Eleanor Alice Burford
Holub, Miroslav 1923- .... **CLC 4**
See also CA 21-24R; CANR 10
Homer c. 8th cent. B.C.- ... **CMLC 1, 16; DA;**
DAB; DAC; DAM MST, POET; WLCS
See also DLB 176
Honig, Edwin 1919- .... **CLC 33**
See also CA 5-8R; CAAS 8; CANR 4, 45; DLB
5
Hood, Hugh (John Blagdon) 1928- CLC 15, 28
See also CA 49-52; CAAS 17; CANR 1, 33;
DLB 53
Hood, Thomas 1799-1845 .... **NCLC 16**
See also DLB 96
Hooker, (Peter) Jeremy 1941- .... **CLC 43**
See also CA 77-80; CANR 22; DLB 40
hooks, bell .... **CLC 94**
See also Watkins, Gloria
Hope, A(lec) D(erwent) 1907- .... **CLC 3, 51**
See also CA 21-24R; CANR 33; MTCW
Hope, Brian
See Creasey, John
Hope, Christopher (David Tully) 1944- C L C
52
See also CA 106; CANR 47; SATA 62
Hopkins, Gerard Manley 1844-1889 .. N C L C
17; DA; DAB; DAC; DAM MST, POET;
PC 15; WLC
See also CDBLB 1890-1914; DLB 35, 57
Hopkins, John (Richard) 1931- .... **CLC 4**
See also CA 85-88
Hopkins, Pauline Elizabeth 1859-1930T C L C
28; BLC; DAM MULT
See also BW 2; CA 141; DLB 50
Hopkinson, Francis 1737-1791 .... **LC 25**
See also DLB 31
Hopley-Woolrich, Cornell George 1903-1968
See Woolrich, Cornell
See also CA 13-14; CANR 58; CAP 1
Horatio
See Proust, (Valentin-Louis-George-Eugene-)
Marcel
Horgan, Paul (George Vincent O'Shaughnessy)
1903-1995 .... **CLC 9, 53; DAM NOV**
See also CA 13-16R; 147; CANR 9, 35; DLB
102; DLBY 85; INT CANR-9; MTCW;
SATA 13; SATA-Obit 84
Horn, Peter
See Kuttner, Henry
Hornem, Horace Esq.

See Byron, George Gordon (Noel)
Horney, Karen (Clementine Theodore
Danielsen) 1885-1952 .... **TCLC 71**
See also CA 114
Hornung, E(rnest) W(illiam) 1866-1921
TCLC 59
See also CA 108; 160; DLB 70
Horovitz, Israel (Arthur) 1939-CLC 56; DAM
DRAM
See also CA 33-36R; CANR 46, 59; DLB 7
Horvath, Odon von
See Horvath, Oedoen von
See also DLB 85, 124
Horvath, Oedoen von 1901-1938 ... **TCLC 45**
See also Horvath, Odon von
See also CA 118
Horwitz, Julius 1920-1986 .... **CLC 14**
See also CA 9-12R; 119; CANR 12
Hospital, Janette Turner 1942- .... **CLC 42**
See also CA 108; CANR 48
Hostos, E. M. de
See Hostos (y Bonilla), Eugenio Maria de
Hostos, Eugenio M. de
See Hostos (y Bonilla), Eugenio Maria de
Hostos, Eugenio Maria
See Hostos (y Bonilla), Eugenio Maria de
Hostos (y Bonilla), Eugenio Maria de 1839-1903
TCLC 24
See also CA 123; 131; HW
Houdini
See Lovecraft, H(oward) P(hillips)
Hougan, Carolyn 1943- .... **CLC 34**
See also CA 139
Household, Geoffrey (Edward West) 1900-1988
CLC 11
See also CA 77-80; 126; CANR 58; DLB 87;
SATA 14; SATA-Obit 59
Housman, A(lfred) E(dward) 1859-1936
TCLC 1, 10; DA; DAB; DAC; DAM MST,
POET; PC 2; WLCS
See also CA 104; 125; DLB 19; MTCW
Housman, Laurence 1865-1959 .... **TCLC 7**
See also CA 106; 155; DLB 10; SATA 25
Howard, Elizabeth Jane 1923- ..... **CLC 7, 29**
See also CA 5-8R; CANR 8, 62
Howard, Maureen 1930- .... **CLC 5, 14, 46**
See also CA 53-56; CANR 31; DLBY 83; INT
CANR-31; MTCW
Howard, Richard 1929- .... **CLC 7, 10, 47**
See also AITN 1; CA 85-88; CANR 25; DLB 5;
INT CANR-25
Howard, Robert E(rvin) 1906-1936 **TCLC 8**
See also CA 105; 157
Howard, Warren F.
See Pohl, Frederik
Howe, Fanny 1940- .... **CLC 47**
See also CA 117; CAAS 27; SATA-Brief 52
Howe, Irving 1920-1993 .... **CLC 85**
See also CA 9-12R; 141; CANR 21, 50; DLB
67; MTCW
Howe, Julia Ward 1819-1910 .... **TCLC 21**
See also CA 117; DLB 1
Howe, Susan 1937- .... **CLC 72**
See also CA 160; DLB 120
Howe, Tina 1937- .... **CLC 48**
See also CA 109
Howell, James 1594(?)-1666 .... **LC 13**
See also DLB 151
Howells, W. D.
See Howells, William Dean
Howells, William D.
See Howells, William Dean
Howells, William Dean 1837-1920TCLC 7, 17,

41
See also CA 104; 134; CDALB 1865-1917;
DLB 12, 64, 74, 79
Howes, Barbara 1914-1996 .... **CLC 15**
See also CA 9-12R; 151; CAAS 3; CANR 53;
SATA 5
Hrabal, Bohumil 1914-1997 .... **CLC 13, 67**
See also CA 106; 156; CAAS 12; CANR 57
Hsun, Lu
See Lu Hsun
Hubbard, L(afayette) Ron(ald) 1911-1986
CLC 43; DAM POP
See also CA 77-80; 118; CANR 52
Huch, Ricarda (Octavia) 1864-1947TCLC 13
See also CA 111; DLB 66
Huddle, David 1942- .... **CLC 49**
See also CA 57-60; CAAS 20; DLB 130
Hudson, Jeffrey
See Crichton, (John) Michael
Hudson, W(illiam) H(enry) 1841-1922T C L C
29
See also CA 115; DLB 98, 153, 174; SATA 35
Hueffer, Ford Madox
See Ford, Ford Madox
Hughart, Barry 1934- .... **CLC 39**
See also CA 137
Hughes, Colin
See Creasey, John
Hughes, David (John) 1930- .... **CLC 48**
See also CA 116; 129; DLB 14
Hughes, Edward James
See Hughes, Ted
See also DAM MST, POET
Hughes, (James) Langston 1902-1967CLC 1,
5, 10, 15, 35, 44, 108; BLC; DA; DAB;
DAC; DAM DRAM, MST, MULT, POET;
DC 3; PC 1; SSC 6; WLC
See also AAYA 12; BW 1; CA 1-4R; 25-28R;
CANR 1, 34; CDALB 1929-1941; CLR 17;
DLB 4, 7, 48, 51, 86; JRDA; MAICYA;
MTCW; SATA 4, 33
Hughes, Richard (Arthur Warren) 1900-1976
CLC 1, 11; DAM NOV
See also CA 5-8R; 65-68; CANR 4; DLB 15,
161; MTCW; SATA 8; SATA-Obit 25
Hughes, Ted 1930- CLC 2, 4, 9, 14, 37; DAB;
DAC; PC 7
See also Hughes, Edward James
See also CA 1-4R; CANR 1, 33; CLR 3; DLB
40, 161; MAICYA; MTCW; SATA 49; SATA-
Brief 27
Hugo, Richard F(ranklin) 1923-1982 CLC 6,
18, 32; DAM POET
See also CA 49-52; 108; CANR 3; DLB 5
Hugo, Victor (Marie) 1802-1885NCLC 3, 10,
21; DA; DAB; DAC; DAM DRAM, MST,
NOV, POET; PC 17; WLC
See also DLB 119; SATA 47
Huidobro, Vicente
See Huidobro Fernandez, Vicente Garcia
Huidobro Fernandez, Vicente Garcia 1893-
1948 .... **TCLC 31**
See also CA 131; HW
Hulme, Keri 1947- .... **CLC 39**
See also CA 125; INT 125
Hulme, T(homas) E(rnest) 1883-1917 T C L C
21
See also CA 117; DLB 19
Hume, David 1711-1776 .... **LC 7**
See also DLB 104
Humphrey, William 1924-1997 .... **CLC 45**
See also CA 77-80; 160; DLB 6
Humphreys, Emyr Owen 1919- .... **CLC 47**

See also CA 5-8R; CANR 3, 24; DLB 15
Humphreys, Josephine 1945- ..... **CLC 34, 57**
See also CA 121; 127; INT 127
Huneker, James Gibbons 1857-1921**TCLC 65**
See also DLB 71
Hungerford, Pixie
See Brinsmead, H(esba) F(ay)
Hunt, E(verette) Howard, (Jr.) 1918-. **CLC 3**
See also AITN 1; CA 45-48; CANR 2, 47
Hunt, Kyle
See Creasey, John
Hunt, (James Henry) Leigh 1784-1859**N C L C 1; DAM POET**
Hunt, Marsha 1946- .... **CLC 70**
See also BW 2; CA 143
Hunt, Violet 1866-1942 .... **TCLC 53**
See also DLB 162
Hunter, E. Waldo
See Sturgeon, Theodore (Hamilton)
Hunter, Evan 1926-. **CLC 11, 31; DAM POP**
See also CA 5-8R; CANR 5, 38, 62; DLBY 82;
INT CANR-5; MTCW; SATA 25
Hunter, Kristin (Eggleston) 1931- .... **CLC 35**
See also AITN 1; BW 1; CA 13-16R; CANR
13; CLR 3; DLB 33; INT CANR-13;
MAICYA; SAAS 10; SATA 12
Hunter, Mollie 1922- .... **CLC 21**
See also McIlwraith, Maureen Mollie Hunter
See also AAYA 13; CANR 37; CLR 25; DLB
161; JRDA; MAICYA; SAAS 7; SATA 54
Hunter, Robert (?)-1734 .... **LC 7**
Hurston, Zora Neale 1903-1960**CLC 7, 30, 61;
BLC; DA; DAC; DAM MST, MULT, NOV;
SSC 4; WLCS**
See also AAYA 15; BW 1; CA 85-88; CANR
61; DLB 51, 86; MTCW
Huston, John (Marcellus) 1906-1987**CLC 20**
See also CA 73-76; 123; CANR 34; DLB 26
Hustvedt, Siri 1955- .... **CLC 76**
See also CA 137
Hutten, Ulrich von 1488-1523 .... **LC 16**
See also DLB 179
Huxley, Aldous (Leonard) 1894-1963**CLC 1,
3, 4, 5, 8, 11, 18, 35, 79; DA; DAB; DAC;
DAM MST, NOV; WLC**
See also AAYA 11; CA 85-88; CANR 44;
CDBLB 1914-1945; DLB 36, 100, 162;
MTCW; SATA 63
Huxley, T. H. 1825-1895 .... **NCLC 67**
See also DLB 57
Huysmans, Charles Marie Georges 1848-1907
See Huysmans, Joris-Karl
See also CA 104
Huysmans, Joris-Karl .... **TCLC 7, 69**
See also Huysmans, Charles Marie Georges
See also DLB 123
Hwang, David Henry 1957-... **CLC 55; DAM
DRAM; DC 4**
See also CA 127; 132; INT 132
Hyde, Anthony 1946- .... **CLC 42**
See also CA 136
Hyde, Margaret O(ldroyd) 1917- ..... **CLC 21**
See also CA 1-4R; CANR 1, 36; CLR 23; JRDA;
MAICYA; SAAS 8; SATA 1, 42, 76
Hynes, James 1956(?)- .... **CLC 65**
Ian, Janis 1951- .... **CLC 21**
See also CA 105
Ibanez, Vicente Blasco
See Blasco Ibanez, Vicente
Ibarguengoitia, Jorge 1928-1983 ..... **CLC 37**
See also CA 124; 113; HW
Ibsen, Henrik (Johan) 1828-1906 **TCLC 2, 8,
16, 37, 52; DA; DAB; DAC; DAM DRAM,**

MST; DC 2; WLC
See also CA 104; 141
Ibuse Masuji 1898-1993 .... **CLC 22**
See also CA 127; 141; DLB 180
Ichikawa, Kon 1915- .... **CLC 20**
See also CA 121
Idle, Eric 1943-................................. **CLC 21**
See also Monty Python
See also CA 116; CANR 35
Ignatow, David 1914- .... **CLC 4, 7, 14, 40**
See also CA 9-12R; CAAS 3; CANR 31, 57;
DLB 5
Ihimaera, Witi 1944- .... **CLC 46**
See also CA 77-80
Ilf, Ilya .... **TCLC 21**
See also Fainzilberg, Ilya Arnoldovich
Illyes, Gyula 1902-1983 .... **PC 16**
See also CA 114; 109
Immermann, Karl (Lebrecht) 1796-1840
NCLC 4, 49
See also DLB 133
Inchbald, Elizabeth 1753-1821 ...... **NCLC 62**
See also DLB 39, 89
Inclan, Ramon (Maria) del Valle
See Valle-Inclan, Ramon (Maria) del
Infante, G(uillermo) Cabrera
See Cabrera Infante, G(uillermo)
Ingalls, Rachel (Holmes) 1940- .... **CLC 42**
See also CA 123; 127
Ingamells, Rex 1913-1955 .... **TCLC 35**
Inge, William (Motter) 1913-1973 . **CLC 1, 8,
19; DAM DRAM**
See also CA 9-12R; CDALB 1941-1968; DLB
7; MTCW
Ingelow, Jean 1820-1897 .... **NCLC 39**
See also DLB 35, 163; SATA 33
Ingram, Willis J.
See Harris, Mark
Innaurato, Albert (F.) 1948(?)- .. **CLC 21, 60**
See also CA 115; 122; INT 122
Innes, Michael
See Stewart, J(ohn) I(nnes) M(ackintosh)
Innis, Harold Adams 1894-1952 .... **TCLC 77**
See also DLB 88
Ionesco, Eugene 1909-1994**CLC 1, 4, 6, 9, 11,
15, 41, 86; DA; DAB; DAC; DAM DRAM,
MST; WLC**
See also CA 9-12R; 144; CANR 55; MTCW;
SATA 7; SATA-Obit 79
Iqbal, Muhammad 1873-1938 .... **TCLC 28**
Ireland, Patrick
See O'Doherty, Brian
Iron, Ralph
See Schreiner, Olive (Emilie Albertina)
Irving, John (Winslow) 1942-**CLC 13, 23, 38;
DAM NOV, POP**
See also AAYA 8; BEST 89:3; CA 25-28R;
CANR 28; DLB 6; DLBY 82; MTCW
Irving, Washington 1783-1859 . **NCLC 2, 19;
DA; DAB; DAM MST; SSC 2; WLC**
See also CDALB 1640-1865; DLB 3, 11, 30,
59, 73, 74; YABC 2
Irwin, P. K.
See Page, P(atricia) K(athleen)
Isaacs, Susan 1943- .... **CLC 32; DAM POP**
See also BEST 89:1; CA 89-92; CANR 20, 41;
INT CANR-20; MTCW
Isherwood, Christopher (William Bradshaw)
1904-1986 .... **CLC 1, 9, 11, 14, 44; DAM
DRAM, NOV**
See also CA 13-16R; 117; CANR 35; DLB 15;
DLBY 86; MTCW
Ishiguro, Kazuo 1954-**CLC 27, 56, 59; DAM**

NOV
See also BEST 90:2; CA 120; CANR 49;
MTCW
Ishikawa, Hakuhin
See Ishikawa, Takuboku
Ishikawa, Takuboku 1886(?)-1912 **TCLC 15;
DAM POET; PC 10**
See also CA 113; 153
Iskander, Fazil 1929- .... **CLC 47**
See also CA 102
Isler, Alan (David) 1934- .... **CLC 91**
See also CA 156
Ivan IV 1530-1584 .... **LC 17**
Ivanov, Vyacheslav Ivanovich 1866-1949
TCLC 33
See also CA 122
Ivask, Ivar Vidrik 1927-1992 .... **CLC 14**
See also CA 37-40R; 139; CANR 24
Ives, Morgan
See Bradley, Marion Zimmer
J. R. S.
See Gogarty, Oliver St. John
Jabran, Kahlil
See Gibran, Kahlil
Jabran, Khalil
See Gibran, Kahlil
Jackson, Daniel
See Wingrove, David (John)
Jackson, Jesse 1908-1983 .... **CLC 12**
See also BW 1; CA 25-28R; 109; CANR 27;
CLR 28; MAICYA; SATA 2, 29; SATA-Obit
48
Jackson, Laura (Riding) 1901-1991
See Riding, Laura
See also CA 65-68; 135; CANR 28; DLB 48
Jackson, Sam
See Trumbo, Dalton
Jackson, Sara
See Wingrove, David (John)
Jackson, Shirley 1919-1965 . **CLC 11, 60, 87;
DA; DAC; DAM MST; SSC 9; WLC**
See also AAYA 9; CA 1-4R; 25-28R; CANR 4,
52; CDALB 1941-1968; DLB 6; SATA 2
Jacob, (Cyprien-)Max 1876-1944 .... **TCLC 6**
See also CA 104
Jacobs, Harriet 1813(?)-1897 .... **NCLC 67**
Jacobs, Jim 1942- .... **CLC 12**
See also CA 97-100; INT 97-100
Jacobs, W(illiam) W(ymark) 1863-1943
TCLC 22
See also CA 121; DLB 135
Jacobsen, Jens Peter 1847-1885 .... **NCLC 34**
Jacobsen, Josephine 1908-........ **CLC 48, 102**
See also CA 33-36R; CAAS 18; CANR 23, 48
Jacobson, Dan 1929- .... **CLC 4, 14**
See also CA 1-4R; CANR 2, 25; DLB 14;
MTCW
Jacqueline
See Carpentier (y Valmont), Alejo
Jagger, Mick 1944- .... **CLC 17**
Jahiz, Al- c. 776-869 .... **CMLC 25**
Jakes, John (William) 1932- .. **CLC 29; DAM
NOV, POP**
See also BEST 89:4; CA 57-60; CANR 10, 43;
DLBY 83; INT CANR-10; MTCW; SATA 62
James, Andrew
See Kirkup, James
James, C(yril) L(ionel) R(obert) 1901-1989
CLC 33
See also BW 2; CA 117; 125; 128; CANR 62;
DLB 125; MTCW
James, Daniel (Lewis) 1911-1988
See Santiago, Danny

See also CA 125

James, Dynely
See Mayne, William (James Carter)

James, Henry Sr. 1811-1882 .... **NCLC 53**

James, Henry 1843-1916 **TCLC 2, 11, 24, 40,
47, 64; DA; DAB; DAC; DAM MST, NOV;
SSC 8; WLC**
See also CA 104; 132; CDALB 1865-1917;
DLB 12, 71, 74; DLBD 13; MTCW

James, M. R.
See James, Montague (Rhodes)
See also DLB 156

James, Montague (Rhodes) 1862-1936 **T C L C
6; SSC 16**
See also CA 104

James, P. D. .... **CLC 18, 46**
See also White, Phyllis Dorothy James
See also BEST 90:2; CDBLB 1960 to Present;
DLB 87

James, Philip
See Moorcock, Michael (John)

James, William 1842-1910 .... **TCLC 15, 32**
See also CA 109

James I 1394-1437 .... **LC 20**

Jameson, Anna 1794-1860 .... **NCLC 43**
See also DLB 99, 166

Jami, Nur al-Din 'Abd al-Rahman 1414-1492
LC 9

Jammes, Francis 1868-1938 .... **TCLC 75**

Jandl, Ernst 1925- .... **CLC 34**

Janowitz, Tama 1957- .. **CLC 43; DAM POP**
See also CA 106; CANR 52

Japrisot, Sebastien 1931- .... **CLC 90**

Jarrell, Randall 1914-1965 **CLC 1, 2, 6, 9, 13,
49; DAM POET**
See also CA 5-8R; 25-28R; CABS 2; CANR 6,
34; CDALB 1941-1968; CLR 6; DLB 48, 52;
MAICYA; MTCW; SATA 7

Jarry, Alfred 1873-1907 .. **TCLC 2, 14; DAM
DRAM; SSC 20**
See also CA 104; 153

Jarvis, E. K.
See Bloch, Robert (Albert); Ellison, Harlan
(Jay); Silverberg, Robert

Jeake, Samuel, Jr.
See Aiken, Conrad (Potter)

Jean Paul 1763-1825 .... **NCLC 7**

Jefferies, (John) Richard 1848-1887 **NCLC 47**
See also DLB 98, 141; SATA 16

Jeffers, (John) Robinson 1887-1962 **CLC 2, 3,
11, 15, 54; DA; DAC; DAM MST, POET;
PC 17; WLC**
See also CA 85-88; CANR 35; CDALB 1917-
1929; DLB 45; MTCW

Jefferson, Janet
See Mencken, H(enry) L(ouis)

Jefferson, Thomas 1743-1826 .... **NCLC 11**
See also CDALB 1640-1865; DLB 31

Jeffrey, Francis 1773-1850 .... **NCLC 33**
See also DLB 107

Jelakowitch, Ivan
See Heijermans, Herman

Jellicoe, (Patricia) Ann 1927- .... **CLC 27**
See also CA 85-88; DLB 13

Jen, Gish .... **CLC 70**
See also Jen, Lillian

Jen, Lillian 1956(?)-
See Jen, Gish
See also CA 135

Jenkins, (John) Robin 1912- .... **CLC 52**
See also CA 1-4R; CANR 1; DLB 14

Jennings, Elizabeth (Joan) 1926- . **CLC 5, 14**
See also CA 61-64; CAAS 5; CANR 8, 39; DLB

27; MTCW; SATA 66

Jennings, Waylon 1937- .... **CLC 21**

Jensen, Johannes V. 1873-1950 ...... **TCLC 41**

Jensen, Laura (Linnea) 1948- .... **CLC 37**
See also CA 103

Jerome, Jerome K(lapka) 1859-1927 **TCLC 23**
See also CA 119; DLB 10, 34, 135

Jerrold, Douglas William 1803-1857 **NCLC 2**
See also DLB 158, 159

Jewett, (Theodora) Sarah Orne 1849-1909
TCLC 1, 22; SSC 6
See also CA 108; 127; DLB 12, 74; SATA 15

Jewsbury, Geraldine (Endsor) 1812-1880
NCLC 22
See also DLB 21

Jhabvala, Ruth Prawer 1927- **CLC 4, 8, 29, 94;
DAB; DAM NOV**
See also CA 1-4R; CANR 2, 29, 51; DLB 139;
INT CANR-29; MTCW

Jibran, Kahlil
See Gibran, Kahlil

Jibran, Khalil
See Gibran, Kahlil

Jiles, Paulette 1943- .... **CLC 13, 58**
See also CA 101

Jimenez (Mantecon), Juan Ramon 1881-1958
**TCLC 4; DAM MULT, POET; HLC; PC
7**
See also CA 104; 131; DLB 134; HW; MTCW

Jimenez, Ramon
See Jimenez (Mantecon), Juan Ramon

Jimenez Mantecon, Juan
See Jimenez (Mantecon), Juan Ramon

Joel, Billy .... **CLC 26**
See also Joel, William Martin

Joel, William Martin 1949-
See Joel, Billy
See also CA 108

John of the Cross, St. 1542-1591 .... **LC 18**

Johnson, B(ryan) S(tanley William) 1933-1973
CLC 6, 9
See also CA 9-12R; 53-56; CANR 9; DLB 14,
40

Johnson, Benj. F. of Boo
See Riley, James Whitcomb

Johnson, Benjamin F. of Boo
See Riley, James Whitcomb

Johnson, Charles (Richard) 1948- **CLC 7, 51,
65; BLC; DAM MULT**
See also BW 2; CA 116; CAAS 18; CANR 42;
DLB 33

Johnson, Denis 1949- .... **CLC 52**
See also CA 117; 121; DLB 120

Johnson, Diane 1934- .... **CLC 5, 13, 48**
See also CA 41-44R; CANR 17, 40, 62; DLBY
80; INT CANR-17; MTCW

Johnson, Eyvind (Olof Verner) 1900-1976
CLC 14
See also CA 73-76; 69-72; CANR 34

Johnson, J. R.
See James, C(yril) L(ionel) R(obert)

Johnson, James Weldon 1871-1938 **TCLC 3,
19; BLC; DAM MULT, POET**
See also BW 1; CA 104; 125; CDALB 1917-
1929; CLR 32; DLB 51; MTCW; SATA 31

Johnson, Joyce 1935- .... **CLC 58**
See also CA 125; 129

Johnson, Lionel (Pigot) 1867-1902 **TCLC 19**
See also CA 117; DLB 19

Johnson, Mel
See Malzberg, Barry N(athaniel)

Johnson, Pamela Hansford 1912-1981 **CLC 1,
7, 27**

See also CA 1-4R; 104; CANR 2, 28; DLB 15;
MTCW

Johnson, Robert 1911(?)-1938 .... **TCLC 69**

Johnson, Samuel 1709-1784 **LC 15; DA; DAB;
DAC; DAM MST; WLC**
See also CDBLB 1660-1789; DLB 39, 95, 104,
142

Johnson, Uwe 1934-1984 .. **CLC 5, 10, 15, 40**
See also CA 1-4R; 112; CANR 1, 39; DLB 75;
MTCW

Johnston, George (Benson) 1913- ..... **CLC 51**
See also CA 1-4R; CANR 5, 20; DLB 88

Johnston, Jennifer 1930- .... **CLC 7**
See also CA 85-88; DLB 14

Jolley, (Monica) Elizabeth 1923- **CLC 46; SSC
19**
See also CA 127; CAAS 13; CANR 59

Jones, Arthur Llewellyn 1863-1947
See Machen, Arthur
See also CA 104

Jones, D(ouglas) G(ordon) 1929- ...... **CLC 10**
See also CA 29-32R; CANR 13; DLB 53

Jones, David (Michael) 1895-1974 **CLC 2, 4, 7,
13, 42**
See also CA 9-12R; 53-56; CANR 28; CDBLB
1945-1960; DLB 20, 100; MTCW

Jones, David Robert 1947-
See Bowie, David
See also CA 103

Jones, Diana Wynne 1934- .... **CLC 26**
See also AAYA 12; CA 49-52; CANR 4, 26,
56; CLR 23; DLB 161; JRDA; MAICYA;
SAAS 7; SATA 9, 70

Jones, Edward P. 1950- .... **CLC 76**
See also BW 2; CA 142

Jones, Gayl 1949- .... **CLC 6, 9; BLC; DAM
MULT**
See also BW 2; CA 77-80; CANR 27; DLB 33;
MTCW

Jones, James 1921-1977 ...... **CLC 1, 3, 10, 39**
See also AITN 1, 2; CA 1-4R; 69-72; CANR 6;
DLB 2, 143; MTCW

Jones, John J.
See Lovecraft, H(oward) P(hillips)

Jones, LeRoi .... **CLC 1, 2, 3, 5, 10, 14**
See also Baraka, Amiri

Jones, Louis B. .... **CLC 65**
See also CA 141

Jones, Madison (Percy, Jr.) 1925- .... **CLC 4**
See also CA 13-16R; CAAS 11; CANR 7, 54;
DLB 152

Jones, Mervyn 1922- .... **CLC 10, 52**
See also CA 45-48; CAAS 5; CANR 1; MTCW

Jones, Mick 1956(?)- .... **CLC 30**

Jones, Nettie (Pearl) 1941- .... **CLC 34**
See also BW 2; CA 137; CAAS 20

Jones, Preston 1936-1979 .... **CLC 10**
See also CA 73-76; 89-92; DLB 7

Jones, Robert F(rancis) 1934- .... **CLC 7**
See also CA 49-52; CANR 2, 61

Jones, Rod 1953- .... **CLC 50**
See also CA 128

Jones, Terence Graham Parry 1942- **CLC 21**
See also Jones, Terry; Monty Python
See also CA 112; 116; CANR 35; INT 116

Jones, Terry
See Jones, Terence Graham Parry
See also SATA 67; SATA-Brief 51

Jones, Thom 1945(?)- .... **CLC 81**
See also CA 157

Jong, Erica 1942- . **CLC 4, 6, 8, 18, 83; DAM
NOV, POP**
See also AITN 1; BEST 90:2; CA 73-76; CANR

26, 52; DLB 2, 5, 28, 152; INT CANR-26; MTCW

Jonson, Ben(jamin) 1572(?)-1637 .. **LC 6, 33; DA; DAB; DAC; DAM DRAM, MST, POET; DC 4; PC 17; WLC**
See also CDBLB Before 1660; DLB 62, 121

Jordan, June 1936- ...... **CLC 5, 11, 23; DAM MULT, POET**
See also AAYA 2; BW 2; CA 33-36R; CANR 25; CLR 10; DLB 38; MAICYA; MTCW; SATA 4

Jordan, Pat(rick M.) 1941- .... **CLC 37**
See also CA 33-36R

Jorgensen, Ivar
See Ellison, Harlan (Jay)

Jorgenson, Ivar
See Silverberg, Robert

Josephus, Flavius c. 37-100 .... **CMLC 13**

Josipovici, Gabriel 1940- .... **CLC 6, 43**
See also CA 37-40R; CAAS 8; CANR 47; DLB 14

Joubert, Joseph 1754-1824 .... **NCLC 9**

Jouve, Pierre Jean 1887-1976 .... **CLC 47**
See also CA 65-68

Jovine, Francesco 1902-1950 .... **TCLC 79**

Joyce, James (Augustine Aloysius) 1882-1941 **TCLC 3, 8, 16, 35, 52; DA; DAB; DAC; DAM MST, NOV, POET; SSC 3, 26; WLC**
See also CA 104; 126; CDBLB 1914-1945; DLB 10, 19, 36, 162; MTCW

Jozsef, Attila 1905-1937 .... **TCLC 22**
See also CA 116

Juana Ines de la Cruz 1651(?)-1695 ...... **LC 5**

Judd, Cyril
See Kornbluth, C(yril) M.; Pohl, Frederik

Julian of Norwich 1342(?)-1416(?) .... **LC 6**
See also DLB 146

Juniper, Alex
See Hospital, Janette Turner

Junius
See Luxemburg, Rosa

Just, Ward (Swift) 1935- .... **CLC 4, 27**
See also CA 25-28R; CANR 32; INT CANR-32

Justice, Donald (Rodney) 1925- .. **CLC 6, 19, 102; DAM POET**
See also CA 5-8R; CANR 26, 54; DLBY 83; INT CANR-26

Juvenal c. 55-c. 127 .... **CMLC 8**

Juvenis
See Bourne, Randolph S(illiman)

Kacew, Romain 1914-1980
See Gary, Romain
See also CA 108; 102

Kadare, Ismail 1936- .... **CLC 52**
See also CA 161

Kadohata, Cynthia .... **CLC 59**
See also CA 140

Kafka, Franz 1883-1924 **TCLC 2, 6, 13, 29, 47, 53; DA; DAB; DAC; DAM MST, NOV; SSC 5, 29; WLC**
See also CA 105; 126; DLB 81; MTCW

Kahanovitsch, Pinkhes
See Der Nister

Kahn, Roger 1927- .... **CLC 30**
See also CA 25-28R; CANR 44; DLB 171; SATA 37

Kain, Saul
See Sassoon, Siegfried (Lorraine)

Kaiser, Georg 1878-1945 .... **TCLC 9**
See also CA 106; DLB 124

Kaletski, Alexander 1946- .... **CLC 39**
See also CA 118; 143

Kalidasa fl. c. 400- .... **CMLC 9**

Kallman, Chester (Simon) 1921-1975 **CLC 2**
See also CA 45-48; 53-56; CANR 3

Kaminsky, Melvin 1926-
See Brooks, Mel
See also CA 65-68; CANR 16

Kaminsky, Stuart M(elvin) 1934- ..... **CLC 59**
See also CA 73-76; CANR 29, 53

Kane, Francis
See Robbins, Harold

Kane, Paul
See Simon, Paul (Frederick)

Kane, Wilson
See Bloch, Robert (Albert)

Kanin, Garson 1912- .... **CLC 22**
See also AITN 1; CA 5-8R; CANR 7; DLB 7

Kaniuk, Yoram 1930- .... **CLC 19**
See also CA 134

Kant, Immanuel 1724-1804 ...... **NCLC 27, 67**
See also DLB 94

Kantor, MacKinlay 1904-1977 .... **CLC 7**
See also CA 61-64; 73-76; CANR 60, 63; DLB 9, 102

Kaplan, David Michael 1946- .... **CLC 50**

Kaplan, James 1951- .... **CLC 59**
See also CA 135

Karageorge, Michael
See Anderson, Poul (William)

Karamzin, Nikolai Mikhailovich 1766-1826 **NCLC 3**
See also DLB 150

Karapanou, Margarita 1946- .... **CLC 13**
See also CA 101

Karinthy, Frigyes 1887-1938 .... **TCLC 47**

Karl, Frederick R(obert) 1927- .... **CLC 34**
See also CA 5-8R; CANR 3, 44

Kastel, Warren
See Silverberg, Robert

Kataev, Evgeny Petrovich 1903-1942
See Petrov, Evgeny
See also CA 120

Kataphusin
See Ruskin, John

Katz, Steve 1935- .... **CLC 47**
See also CA 25-28R; CAAS 14, 64; CANR 12; DLBY 83

Kauffman, Janet 1945- .... **CLC 42**
See also CA 117; CANR 43; DLBY 86

Kaufman, Bob (Garnell) 1925-1986 . **CLC 49**
See also BW 1; CA 41-44R; 118; CANR 22; DLB 16, 41

Kaufman, George S. 1889-1961 **CLC 38; DAM DRAM**
See also CA 108; 93-96; DLB 7; INT 108

Kaufman, Sue .... **CLC 3, 8**
See also Barondess, Sue K(aufman)

Kavafis, Konstantinos Petrou 1863-1933
See Cavafy, C(onstantine) P(eter)
See also CA 104

Kavan, Anna 1901-1968 .... **CLC 5, 13, 82**
See also CA 5-8R; CANR 6, 57; MTCW

Kavanagh, Dan
See Barnes, Julian (Patrick)

Kavanagh, Patrick (Joseph) 1904-1967 **C L C 22**
See also CA 123; 25-28R; DLB 15, 20; MTCW

Kawabata, Yasunari 1899-1972 **CLC 2, 5, 9, 18, 107; DAM MULT; SSC 17**
See also CA 93-96; 33-36R; DLB 180

Kaye, M(ary) M(argaret) 1909- .... **CLC 28**
See also CA 89-92; CANR 24, 60; MTCW; SATA 62

Kaye, Mollie

See Kaye, M(ary) M(argaret)

Kaye-Smith, Sheila 1887-1956 .... **TCLC 20**
See also CA 118; DLB 36

Kaymor, Patrice Maguilene
See Senghor, Leopold Sedar

Kazan, Elia 1909- .... **CLC 6, 16, 63**
See also CA 21-24R; CANR 32

Kazantzakis, Nikos 1883(?)-1957 **TCLC 2, 5, 33**
See also CA 105; 132; MTCW

Kazin, Alfred 1915- .... **CLC 34, 38**
See also CA 1-4R; CAAS 7; CANR 1, 45; DLB 67

Keane, Mary Nesta (Skrine) 1904-1996
See Keane, Molly
See also CA 108; 114; 151

Keane, Molly .... **CLC 31**
See also Keane, Mary Nesta (Skrine)
See also INT 114

Keates, Jonathan 19(?)- .... **CLC 34**

Keaton, Buster 1895-1966 .... **CLC 20**

Keats, John 1795-1821 . **NCLC 8; DA; DAB; DAC; DAM MST, POET; PC 1; WLC**
See also CDBLB 1789-1832; DLB 96, 110

Keene, Donald 1922- .... **CLC 34**
See also CA 1-4R; CANR 5

Keillor, Garrison .... **CLC 40**
See also Keillor, Gary (Edward)
See also AAYA 2; BEST 89:3; DLBY 87; SATA 58

Keillor, Gary (Edward) 1942-
See Keillor, Garrison
See also CA 111; 117; CANR 36, 59; DAM POP; MTCW

Keith, Michael
See Hubbard, L(afayette) Ron(ald)

Keller, Gottfried 1819-1890 **NCLC 2; SSC 26**
See also DLB 129

Kellerman, Jonathan 1949- ... **CLC 44; DAM POP**
See also BEST 90:1; CA 106; CANR 29, 51; INT CANR-29

Kelley, William Melvin 1937- .... **CLC 22**
See also BW 1; CA 77-80; CANR 27; DLB 33

Kellogg, Marjorie 1922- .... **CLC 2**
See also CA 81-84

Kellow, Kathleen
See Hibbert, Eleanor Alice Burford

Kelly, M(ilton) T(erry) 1947- .... **CLC 55**
See also CA 97-100; CAAS 22; CANR 19, 43

Kelman, James 1946- .... **CLC 58, 86**
See also CA 148

Kemal, Yashar 1923- .... **CLC 14, 29**
See also CA 89-92; CANR 44

Kemble, Fanny 1809-1893 .... **NCLC 18**
See also DLB 32

Kemelman, Harry 1908-1996 .... **CLC 2**
See also AITN 1; CA 9-12R; 155; CANR 6; DLB 28

Kempe, Margery 1373(?)-1440(?) .... **LC 6**
See also DLB 146

Kempis, Thomas a 1380-1471 .... **LC 11**

Kendall, Henry 1839-1882 .... **NCLC 12**

Keneally, Thomas (Michael) 1935- **CLC 5, 8, 10, 14, 19, 27, 43; DAM NOV**
See also CA 85-88; CANR 10, 50; MTCW

Kennedy, Adrienne (Lita) 1931- ..... **CLC 66; BLC; DAM MULT; DC 5**
See also BW 2; CA 103; CAAS 20; CABS 3; CANR 26, 53; DLB 38

Kennedy, John Pendleton 1795-1870 **NCLC 2**
See also DLB 3

Kennedy, Joseph Charles 1929-

See Kennedy, X. J.
See also CA 1-4R; CANR 4, 30, 40; SATA 14, 86

Kennedy, William 1928- ..**CLC 6, 28, 34, 53; DAM NOV**
See also AAYA 1; CA 85-88; CANR 14, 31; DLB 143; DLBY 85; INT CANR-31; MTCW; SATA 57

Kennedy, X. J. ....**CLC 8, 42**
See also Kennedy, Joseph Charles
See also CAAS 9; CLR 27; DLB 5; SAAS 22

Kenny, Maurice (Francis) 1929- .....**CLC 87; DAM MULT**
See also CA 144; CAAS 22; DLB 175; NNAL

Kent, Kelvin
See Kuttner, Henry

Kenton, Maxwell
See Southern, Terry

Kenyon, Robert O.
See Kuttner, Henry

Kerouac, Jack ...... **CLC 1, 2, 3, 5, 14, 29, 61**
See also Kerouac, Jean-Louis Lebris de
See also CDALB 1941-1968; DLB 2, 16; DLBD 3; DLBY 95

Kerouac, Jean-Louis Lebris de 1922-1969
See Kerouac, Jack
See also AITN 1; CA 5-8R; 25-28R; CANR 26, 54; DA; DAB; DAC; DAM MST, NOV, POET, POP; MTCW; WLC

Kerr, Jean 1923- ....**CLC 22**
See also CA 5-8R; CANR 7; INT CANR-7

Kerr, M. E. .... **CLC 12, 35**
See also Meaker, Marijane (Agnes)
See also AAYA 2; CLR 29; SAAS 1

Kerr, Robert ....**CLC 55**

Kerrigan, (Thomas) Anthony 1918-**CLC 4, 6**
See also CA 49-52; CAAS 11; CANR 4

Kerry, Lois
See Duncan, Lois

Kesey, Ken (Elton) 1935- **CLC 1, 3, 6, 11, 46, 64; DA; DAB; DAC; DAM MST, NOV, POP; WLC**
See also CA 1-4R; CANR 22, 38; CDALB 1968-1988; DLB 2, 16; MTCW; SATA 66

Kesselring, Joseph (Otto) 1902-1967**CLC 45; DAM DRAM, MST**
See also CA 150

Kessler, Jascha (Frederick) 1929- ...... **CLC 4**
See also CA 17-20R; CANR 8, 48

Kettelkamp, Larry (Dale) 1933- .... **CLC 12**
See also CA 29-32R; CANR 16; SAAS 3; SATA 2

Key, Ellen 1849-1926 .... **TCLC 65**

Keyber, Conny
See Fielding, Henry

Keyes, Daniel 1927-**CLC 80; DA; DAC; DAM MST, NOV**
See also CA 17-20R; CANR 10, 26, 54; SATA 37

Keynes, John Maynard 1883-1946 **TCLC 64**
See also CA 114; DLBD 10

Khanshendel, Chiron
See Rose, Wendy

Khayyam, Omar 1048-1131**CMLC 11; DAM POET; PC 8**

Kherdian, David 1931-......................**CLC 6, 9**
See also CA 21-24R; CAAS 2; CANR 39; CLR 24; JRDA; MAICYA; SATA 16, 74

Khlebnikov, Velimir .... **TCLC 20**
See also Khlebnikov, Viktor Vladimirovich

Khlebnikov, Viktor Vladimirovich 1885-1922
See Khlebnikov, Velimir
See also CA 117

Khodasevich, Vladislav (Felitsianovich) 1886-1939 .... **TCLC 15**
See also CA 115

Kielland, Alexander Lange 1849-1906**T C L C 5**
See also CA 104

Kiely, Benedict 1919- .... **CLC 23, 43**
See also CA 1-4R; CANR 2; DLB 15

Kienzle, William X(avier) 1928- ..... **CLC 25; DAM POP**
See also CA 93-96; CAAS 1; CANR 9, 31, 59; INT CANR-31; MTCW

Kierkegaard, Soren 1813-1855 ...... **NCLC 34**

Killens, John Oliver 1916-1987 .... **CLC 10**
See also BW 2; CA 77-80; 123; CAAS 2; CANR 26; DLB 33

Killigrew, Anne 1660-1685 .... **LC 4**
See also DLB 131

Kim
See Simenon, Georges (Jacques Christian)

Kincaid, Jamaica 1949- .. **CLC 43, 68; BLC; DAM MULT, NOV**
See also AAYA 13; BW 2; CA 125; CANR 47, 59; DLB 157

King, Francis (Henry) 1923-**CLC 8, 53; DAM NOV**
See also CA 1-4R; CANR 1, 33; DLB 15, 139; MTCW

King, Martin Luther, Jr. 1929-1968 **CLC 83; BLC; DA; DAB; DAC; DAM MST, MULT; WLCS**
See also BW 2; CA 25-28; CANR 27, 44; CAP 2; MTCW; SATA 14

King, Stephen (Edwin) 1947-**CLC 12, 26, 37, 61; DAM NOV, POP; SSC 17**
See also AAYA 1, 17; BEST 90:1; CA 61-64; CANR 1, 30, 52; DLB 143; DLBY 80; JRDA; MTCW; SATA 9, 55

King, Steve
See King, Stephen (Edwin)

King, Thomas 1943- ... **CLC 89; DAC; DAM MULT**
See also CA 144; DLB 175; NNAL; SATA 96

Kingman, Lee .... **CLC 17**
See also Natti, (Mary) Lee
See also SAAS 3; SATA 1, 67

Kingsley, Charles 1819-1875 .... **NCLC 35**
See also DLB 21, 32, 163; YABC 2

Kingsley, Sidney 1906-1995 .... **CLC 44**
See also CA 85-88; 147; DLB 7

Kingsolver, Barbara 1955-**CLC 55, 81; DAM POP**
See also AAYA 15; CA 129; 134; CANR 60; INT 134

Kingston, Maxine (Ting Ting) Hong 1940-**CLC 12, 19, 58; DAM MULT, NOV; WLCS**
See also AAYA 8; CA 69-72; CANR 13, 38; DLB 173; DLBY 80; INT CANR-13; MTCW; SATA 53

Kinnell, Galway 1927- **CLC 1, 2, 3, 5, 13, 29**
See also CA 9-12R; CANR 10, 34; DLB 5; DLBY 87; INT CANR-34; MTCW

Kinsella, Thomas 1928- ....**CLC 4, 19**
See also CA 17-20R; CANR 15; DLB 27; MTCW

Kinsella, W(illiam) P(atrick) 1935- .**CLC 27, 43; DAC; DAM NOV, POP**
See also AAYA 7; CA 97-100; CAAS 7; CANR 21, 35; INT CANR-21; MTCW

Kipling, (Joseph) Rudyard 1865-1936 **T C L C 8, 17; DA; DAB; DAC; DAM MST, POET; PC 3; SSC 5; WLC**

See also CA 105; 120; CANR 33; CDBLB 1890-1914; CLR 39; DLB 19, 34, 141, 156; MAICYA; MTCW; YABC 2

Kirkup, James 1918- .... **CLC 1**
See also CA 1-4R; CAAS 4; CANR 2; DLB 27; SATA 12

Kirkwood, James 1930(?)-1989 .... **CLC 9**
See also AITN 2; CA 1-4R; 128; CANR 6, 40

Kirshner, Sidney
See Kingsley, Sidney

Kis, Danilo 1935-1989 .... **CLC 57**
See also CA 109; 118; 129; CANR 61; DLB 181; MTCW

Kivi, Aleksis 1834-1872 .... **NCLC 30**

Kizer, Carolyn (Ashley) 1925-**CLC 15, 39, 80; DAM POET**
See also CA 65-68; CAAS 5; CANR 24; DLB 5, 169

Klabund 1890-1928 .... **TCLC 44**
See also DLB 66

Klappert, Peter 1942-........................ **CLC 57**
See also CA 33-36R; DLB 5

Klein, A(braham) M(oses) 1909-1972**CLC 19; DAB; DAC; DAM MST**
See also CA 101; 37-40R; DLB 68

Klein, Norma 1938-1989 .... **CLC 30**
See also AAYA 2; CA 41-44R; 128; CANR 15, 37; CLR 2, 19; INT CANR-15; JRDA; MAICYA; SAAS 1; SATA 7, 57

Klein, T(heodore) E(ibon) D(onald) 1947-**CLC 34**
See also CA 119; CANR 44

Kleist, Heinrich von 1777-1811 **NCLC 2, 37; DAM DRAM; SSC 22**
See also DLB 90

Klima, Ivan 1931- .... **CLC 56; DAM NOV**
See also CA 25-28R; CANR 17, 50

Klimentov, Andrei Platonovich 1899-1951
See Platonov, Andrei
See also CA 108

Klinger, Friedrich Maximilian von 1752-1831 **NCLC 1**
See also DLB 94

Klingsor the Magician
See Hartmann, Sadakichi

Klopstock, Friedrich Gottlieb 1724-1803 **NCLC 11**
See also DLB 97

Knapp, Caroline 1959-...................... **CLC 99**
See also CA 154

Knebel, Fletcher 1911-1993 .... **CLC 14**
See also AITN 1; CA 1-4R; 140; CAAS 3; CANR 1, 36; SATA 36; SATA-Obit 75

Knickerbocker, Diedrich
See Irving, Washington

Knight, Etheridge 1931-1991 **CLC 40; BLC; DAM POET; PC 14**
See also BW 1; CA 21-24R; 133; CANR 23; DLB 41

Knight, Sarah Kemble 1666-1727 .... **LC 7**
See also DLB 24

Knister, Raymond 1899-1932 .... **TCLC 56**
See also DLB 68

Knowles, John 1926- . **CLC 1, 4, 10, 26; DA; DAC; DAM MST, NOV**
See also AAYA 10; CA 17-20R; CANR 40; CDALB 1968-1988; DLB 6; MTCW; SATA 8, 89

Knox, Calvin M.
See Silverberg, Robert

Knox, John c. 1505-1572 .... **LC 37**
See also DLB 132

Knye, Cassandra

See Disch, Thomas M(ichael)

Koch, C(hristopher) J(ohn) 1932- .... **CLC 42**
See also CA 127

Koch, Christopher
See Koch, C(hristopher) J(ohn)

Koch, Kenneth 1925- ..... **CLC 5, 8, 44; DAM POET**
See also CA 1-4R; CANR 6, 36, 57; DLB 5; INT CANR-36; SATA 65

Kochanowski, Jan 1530-1584 .... **LC 10**

Kock, Charles Paul de 1794-1871 . **NCLC 16**

Koda Shigeyuki 1867-1947
See Rohan, Koda
See also CA 121

Koestler, Arthur 1905-1983 **CLC 1, 3, 6, 8, 15, 33**
See also CA 1-4R; 109; CANR 1, 33; CDBLB 1945-1960; DLBY 83; MTCW

Kogawa, Joy Nozomi 1935- .. **CLC 78; DAC; DAM MST, MULT**
See also CA 101; CANR 19, 62

Kohout, Pavel 1928- .... **CLC 13**
See also CA 45-48; CANR 3

Koizumi, Yakumo
See Hearn, (Patricio) Lafcadio (Tessima Carlos)

Kolmar, Gertrud 1894-1943 .... **TCLC 40**

Komunyakaa, Yusef 1947- .... **CLC 86, 94**
See also CA 147; DLB 120

Konrad, George
See Konrad, Gyoergy

Konrad, Gyoergy 1933- .... **CLC 4, 10, 73**
See also CA 85-88

Konwicki, Tadeusz 1926- .... **CLC 8, 28, 54**
See also CA 101; CAAS 9; CANR 39, 59; MTCW

Koontz, Dean R(ay) 1945- ..... **CLC 78; DAM NOV, POP**
See also AAYA 9; BEST 89:3, 90:2; CA 108; CANR 19, 36, 52; MTCW; SATA 92

Kopit, Arthur (Lee) 1937- **CLC 1, 18, 33; DAM DRAM**
See also AITN 1; CA 81-84; CABS 3; DLB 7; MTCW

Kops, Bernard 1926- .... **CLC 4**
See also CA 5-8R; DLB 13

Kornbluth, C(yril) M. 1923-1958 .... **TCLC 8**
See also CA 105; 160; DLB 8

Korolenko, V. G.
See Korolenko, Vladimir Galaktionovich

Korolenko, Vladimir
See Korolenko, Vladimir Galaktionovich

Korolenko, Vladimir G.
See Korolenko, Vladimir Galaktionovich

Korolenko, Vladimir Galaktionovich 1853-1921 .... **TCLC 22**
See also CA 121

Korzybski, Alfred (Habdank Skarbek) 1879-1950 .... **TCLC 61**
See also CA 123; 160

Kosinski, Jerzy (Nikodem) 1933-1991 **CLC 1, 2, 3, 6, 10, 15, 53, 70; DAM NOV**
See also CA 17-20R; 134; CANR 9, 46; DLB 2; DLBY 82; MTCW

Kostelanetz, Richard (Cory) 1940- .. **CLC 28**
See also CA 13-16R; CAAS 8; CANR 38

Kostrowitzki, Wilhelm Apollinaris de 1880-1918
See Apollinaire, Guillaume
See also CA 104

Kotlowitz, Robert 1924- .... **CLC 4**
See also CA 33-36R; CANR 36

Kotzebue, August (Friedrich Ferdinand) von 1761-1819 .... **NCLC 25**

See also DLB 94

Kotzwinkle, William 1938- ..... **CLC 5, 14, 35**
See also CA 45-48; CANR 3, 44; CLR 6; DLB 173; MAICYA; SATA 24, 70

Kowna, Stancy
See Szymborska, Wislawa

Kozol, Jonathan 1936- .... **CLC 17**
See also CA 61-64; CANR 16, 45

Kozoll, Michael 1940(?)- .... **CLC 35**

Kramer, Kathryn 19(?)- .... **CLC 34**

Kramer, Larry 1935- **CLC 42; DAM POP; DC 8**
See also CA 124; 126; CANR 60

Krasicki, Ignacy 1735-1801 .... **NCLC 8**

Krasinski, Zygmunt 1812-1859 .... **NCLC 4**

Kraus, Karl 1874-1936 .... **TCLC 5**
See also CA 104; DLB 118

Kreve (Mickevicius), Vincas 1882-1954 **TCLC 27**

Kristeva, Julia 1941- .... **CLC 77**
See also CA 154

Kristofferson, Kris 1936- .... **CLC 26**
See also CA 104

Krizanc, John 1956- .... **CLC 57**

Krleza, Miroslav 1893-1981 .... **CLC 8**
See also CA 97-100; 105; CANR 50; DLB 147

Kroetsch, Robert 1927- **CLC 5, 23, 57; DAC; DAM POET**
See also CA 17-20R; CANR 8, 38; DLB 53; MTCW

Kroetz, Franz
See Kroetz, Franz Xaver

Kroetz, Franz Xaver 1946- .... **CLC 41**
See also CA 130

Kroker, Arthur (W.) 1945- .... **CLC 77**
See also CA 161

Kropotkin, Peter (Alekseievich) 1842-1921 **TCLC 36**
See also CA 119

Krotkov, Yuri 1917- .... **CLC 19**
See also CA 102

Krumb
See Crumb, R(obert)

Krumgold, Joseph (Quincy) 1908-1980 **C L C 12**
See also CA 9-12R; 101; CANR 7; MAICYA; SATA 1, 48; SATA-Obit 23

Krumwitz
See Crumb, R(obert)

Krutch, Joseph Wood 1893-1970 ...... **CLC 24**
See also CA 1-4R; 25-28R; CANR 4; DLB 63

Krutzch, Gus
See Eliot, T(homas) S(tearns)

Krylov, Ivan Andreevich 1768(?)-1844 **N C L C 1**
See also DLB 150

Kubin, Alfred (Leopold Isidor) 1877-1959 **TCLC 23**
See also CA 112; 149; DLB 81

Kubrick, Stanley 1928- .... **CLC 16**
See also CA 81-84; CANR 33; DLB 26

Kumin, Maxine (Winokur) 1925- **CLC 5, 13, 28; DAM POET; PC 15**
See also AITN 2; CA 1-4R; CAAS 8; CANR 1, 21; DLB 5; MTCW; SATA 12

Kundera, Milan 1929- . **CLC 4, 9, 19, 32, 68; DAM NOV; SSC 24**
See also AAYA 2; CA 85-88; CANR 19, 52; MTCW

Kunene, Mazisi (Raymond) 1930- .... **CLC 85**
See also BW 1; CA 125; DLB 117

Kunitz, Stanley (Jasspon) 1905- **CLC 6, 11, 14; PC 19**

See also CA 41-44R; CANR 26, 57; DLB 48; INT CANR-26; MTCW

Kunze, Reiner 1933- .... **CLC 10**
See also CA 93-96; DLB 75

Kuprin, Aleksandr Ivanovich 1870-1938 **TCLC 5**
See also CA 104

Kureishi, Hanif 1954(?)- .... **CLC 64**
See also CA 139

Kurosawa, Akira 1910- **CLC 16; DAM MULT**
See also AAYA 11; CA 101; CANR 46

Kushner, Tony 1957(?)- **CLC 81; DAM DRAM**
See also CA 144

Kuttner, Henry 1915-1958 .... **TCLC 10**
See also Vance, Jack
See also CA 107; 157; DLB 8

Kuzma, Greg 1944- .... **CLC 7**
See also CA 33-36R

Kuzmin, Mikhail 1872(?)-1936 ...... **TCLC 40**

Kyd, Thomas 1558-1594 **LC 22; DAM DRAM; DC 3**
See also DLB 62

Kyprianos, Iossif
See Samarakis, Antonis

La Bruyere, Jean de 1645-1696 .... **LC 17**

Lacan, Jacques (Marie Emile) 1901-1981 **CLC 75**
See also CA 121; 104

Laclos, Pierre Ambroise Francois Choderlos de 1741-1803 .... **NCLC 4**

La Colere, Francois
See Aragon, Louis

Lacolere, Francois
See Aragon, Louis

La Deshabilleuse
See Simenon, Georges (Jacques Christian)

Lady Gregory
See Gregory, Isabella Augusta (Persse)

Lady of Quality, A
See Bagnold, Enid

La Fayette, Marie (Madelaine Pioche de la Vergne Comtes 1634-1693 .... **LC 2**

Lafayette, Rene
See Hubbard, L(afayette) Ron(ald)

Laforgue, Jules 1860-1887 **NCLC 5, 53; PC 14; SSC 20**

Lagerkvist, Paer (Fabian) 1891-1974 **CLC 7, 10, 13, 54; DAM DRAM, NOV**
See also Lagerkvist, Par
See also CA 85-88; 49-52; MTCW

Lagerkvist, Par .... **SSC 12**
See also Lagerkvist, Paer (Fabian)

Lagerloef, Selma (Ottiliana Lovisa) 1858-1940 **TCLC 4, 36**
See also Lagerlof, Selma (Ottiliana Lovisa)
See also CA 108; SATA 15

Lagerlof, Selma (Ottiliana Lovisa)
See Lagerloef, Selma (Ottiliana Lovisa)
See also CLR 7; SATA 15

La Guma, (Justin) Alex(ander) 1925-1985 **CLC 19; DAM NOV**
See also BW 1; CA 49-52; 118; CANR 25; DLB 117; MTCW

Laidlaw, A. K.
See Grieve, C(hristopher) M(urray)

Lainez, Manuel Mujica
See Mujica Lainez, Manuel
See also HW

Laing, R(onald) D(avid) 1927-1989 .. **CLC 95**
See also CA 107; 129; CANR 34; MTCW

Lamartine, Alphonse (Marie Louis Prat) de 1790-1869 **NCLC 11; DAM POET; PC 16**

Lamb, Charles 1775-1834 ..... **NCLC 10; DA;**

DAB; DAC; DAM MST; WLC
See also CDBLB 1789-1832; DLB 93, 107, 163;
SATA 17
Lamb, Lady Caroline 1785-1828 ... **NCLC 38**
See also DLB 116
Lamming, George (William) 1927- **CLC 2, 4,
66; BLC; DAM MULT**
See also BW 2; CA 85-88; CANR 26; DLB 125;
MTCW
L'Amour, Louis (Dearborn) 1908-1988 **C L C
25, 55; DAM NOV, POP**
See also AAYA 16; AITN 2; BEST 89:2; CA 1-
4R; 125; CANR 3, 25, 40; DLBY 80; MTCW
Lampedusa, Giuseppe (Tomasi) di 1896-1957
TCLC 13
See also Tomasi di Lampedusa, Giuseppe
See also DLB 177
Lampman, Archibald 1861-1899 ... **NCLC 25**
See also DLB 92
Lancaster, Bruce 1896-1963 .... **CLC 36**
See also CA 9-10; CAP 1; SATA 9
Lanchester, John .... **CLC 99**
Landau, Mark Alexandrovich
See Aldanov, Mark (Alexandrovich)
Landau-Aldanov, Mark Alexandrovich
See Aldanov, Mark (Alexandrovich)
Landis, Jerry
See Simon, Paul (Frederick)
Landis, John 1950- .... **CLC 26**
See also CA 112; 122
Landolfi, Tommaso 1908-1979 .... **CLC 11, 49**
See also CA 127; 117; DLB 177
Landon, Letitia Elizabeth 1802-1838 **N C L C
15**
See also DLB 96
Landor, Walter Savage 1775-1864 **NCLC 14**
See also DLB 93, 107
Landwirth, Heinz 1927-
See Lind, Jakov
See also CA 9-12R; CANR 7
Lane, Patrick 1939- ... **CLC 25; DAM POET**
See also CA 97-100; CANR 54; DLB 53; INT
97-100
Lang, Andrew 1844-1912 .... **TCLC 16**
See also CA 114; 137; DLB 98, 141, 184;
MAICYA; SATA 16
Lang, Fritz 1890-1976 .... **CLC 20, 103**
See also CA 77-80; 69-72; CANR 30
Lange, John
See Crichton, (John) Michael
Langer, Elinor 1939- .... **CLC 34**
See also CA 121
Langland, William 1330(?)-1400(?) ... **LC 19;
DA; DAB; DAC; DAM MST, POET**
See also DLB 146
Langstaff, Launcelot
See Irving, Washington
Lanier, Sidney 1842-1881 ..... **NCLC 6; DAM
POET**
See also DLB 64; DLBD 13; MAICYA; SATA
18
Lanyer, Aemilia 1569-1645............ **LC 10, 30**
See also DLB 121
Lao Tzu .... **CMLC 7**
Lapine, James (Elliot) 1949- .... **CLC 39**
See also CA 123; 130; CANR 54; INT 130
Larbaud, Valery (Nicolas) 1881-1957**TCLC 9**
See also CA 106; 152
Lardner, Ring
See Lardner, Ring(gold) W(ilmer)
Lardner, Ring W., Jr.
See Lardner, Ring(gold) W(ilmer)
Lardner, Ring(gold) W(ilmer) 1885-1933

TCLC 2, 14
See also CA 104; 131; CDALB 1917-1929;
DLB 11, 25, 86; DLBD 16; MTCW
Laredo, Betty
See Codrescu, Andrei
Larkin, Maia
See Wojciechowska, Maia (Teresa)
Larkin, Philip (Arthur) 1922-1985**CLC 3, 5, 8,
9, 13, 18, 33, 39, 64; DAB; DAM MST,
POET; PC 21**
See also CA 5-8R; 117; CANR 24, 62; CDBLB
1960 to Present; DLB 27; MTCW
Larra (y Sanchez de Castro), Mariano Jose de
1809-1837 .... **NCLC 17**
Larsen, Eric 1941- .... **CLC 55**
See also CA 132
Larsen, Nella 1891-1964**CLC 37; BLC; DAM
MULT**
See also BW 1; CA 125; DLB 51
Larson, Charles R(aymond) 1938- ... **CLC 31**
See also CA 53-56; CANR 4
Larson, Jonathan 1961-1996............. **CLC 99**
See also CA 156
Las Casas, Bartolome de 1474-1566 ... **LC 31**
Lasch, Christopher 1932-1994 .... **CLC 102**
See also CA 73-76; 144; CANR 25; MTCW
Lasker-Schueler, Else 1869-1945 ... **TCLC 57**
See also DLB 66, 124
Laski, Harold 1893-1950 .... **TCLC 79**
Latham, Jean Lee 1902- .... **CLC 12**
See also AITN 1; CA 5-8R; CANR 7; MAICYA;
SATA 2, 68
Latham, Mavis
See Clark, Mavis Thorpe
Lathen, Emma .... **CLC 2**
See also Hennissart, Martha; Latsis, Mary J(ane)
Lathrop, Francis
See Leiber, Fritz (Reuter, Jr.)
Latsis, Mary J(ane)
See Lathen, Emma
See also CA 85-88
Lattimore, Richmond (Alexander) 1906-1984
CLC 3
See also CA 1-4R; 112; CANR 1
Laughlin, James 1914- .... **CLC 49**
See also CA 21-24R; CAAS 22; CANR 9, 47;
DLB 48; DLBY 96
Laurence, (Jean) Margaret (Wemyss) 1926-
1987 .. **CLC 3, 6, 13, 50, 62; DAC; DAM
MST; SSC 7**
See also CA 5-8R; 121; CANR 33; DLB 53;
MTCW; SATA-Obit 50
Laurent, Antoine 1952- .... **CLC 50**
Lauscher, Hermann
See Hesse, Hermann
Lautreamont, Comte de 1846-1870**NCLC 12;
SSC 14**
Laverty, Donald
See Blish, James (Benjamin)
Lavin, Mary 1912-1996**CLC 4, 18, 99; SSC 4**
See also CA 9-12R; 151; CANR 33; DLB 15;
MTCW
Lavond, Paul Dennis
See Kornbluth, C(yril) M.; Pohl, Frederik
Lawler, Raymond Evenor 1922- .... **CLC 58**
See also CA 103
Lawrence, D(avid) H(erbert Richards) 1885-
1930**TCLC 2, 9, 16, 33, 48, 61; DA; DAB;
DAC; DAM MST, NOV, POET; SSC 4, 19;
WLC**
See also CA 104; 121; CDBLB 1914-1945;
DLB 10, 19, 36, 98, 162; MTCW
Lawrence, T(homas) E(dward) 1888-1935

TCLC 18
See also Dale, Colin
See also CA 115
Lawrence of Arabia
See Lawrence, T(homas) E(dward)
Lawson, Henry (Archibald Hertzberg) 1867-
1922 .... **TCLC 27; SSC 18**
See also CA 120
Lawton, Dennis
See Faust, Frederick (Schiller)
Laxness, Halldor .... **CLC 25**
See also Gudjonsson, Halldor Kiljan
Layamon fl. c. 1200- .... **CMLC 10**
See also DLB 146
Laye, Camara 1928-1980 .. **CLC 4, 38; BLC;
DAM MULT**
See also BW 1; CA 85-88; 97-100; CANR 25;
MTCW
Layton, Irving (Peter) 1912-**CLC 2, 15; DAC;
DAM MST, POET**
See also CA 1-4R; CANR 2, 33, 43; DLB 88;
MTCW
Lazarus, Emma 1849-1887 .... **NCLC 8**
Lazarus, Felix
See Cable, George Washington
Lazarus, Henry
See Slavitt, David R(ytman)
Lea, Joan
See Neufeld, John (Arthur)
Leacock, Stephen (Butler) 1869-1944**TCLC 2;
DAC; DAM MST**
See also CA 104; 141; DLB 92
Lear, Edward 1812-1888 .... **NCLC 3**
See also CLR 1; DLB 32, 163, 166; MAICYA;
SATA 18
Lear, Norman (Milton) 1922- .... **CLC 12**
See also CA 73-76
Leavis, F(rank) R(aymond) 1895-1978**CLC 24**
See also CA 21-24R; 77-80; CANR 44; MTCW
Leavitt, David 1961- ..... **CLC 34; DAM POP**
See also CA 116; 122; CANR 50, 62; DLB 130;
INT 122
Leblanc, Maurice (Marie Emile) 1864-1941
TCLC 49
See also CA 110
Lebowitz, Fran(ces Ann) 1951(?)-**CLC 11, 36**
See also CA 81-84; CANR 14, 60; INT CANR-
14; MTCW
Lebrecht, Peter
See Tieck, (Johann) Ludwig
le Carre, John .... **CLC 3, 5, 9, 15, 28**
See also Cornwell, David (John Moore)
See also BEST 89:4; CDBLB 1960 to Present;
DLB 87
Le Clezio, J(ean) M(arie) G(ustave) 1940-
CLC 31
See also CA 116; 128; DLB 83
Leconte de Lisle, Charles-Marie-Rene 1818-
1894 .... **NCLC 29**
Le Coq, Monsieur
See Simenon, Georges (Jacques Christian)
Leduc, Violette 1907-1972 .... **CLC 22**
See also CA 13-14; 33-36R; CAP 1
Ledwidge, Francis 1887(?)-1917 .... **TCLC 23**
See also CA 123; DLB 20
Lee, Andrea 1953-**CLC 36; BLC; DAM MULT**
See also BW 1; CA 125
Lee, Andrew
See Auchincloss, Louis (Stanton)
Lee, Chang-rae 1965- .... **CLC 91**
See also CA 148
Lee, Don L. .... **CLC 2**
See also Madhubuti, Haki R.

Lee, George W(ashington) 1894-1976 CLC 52;
    BLC; DAM MULT
    See also BW 1; CA 125; DLB 51
Lee, (Nelle) Harper 1926- .. CLC 12, 60; DA;
    DAB; DAC; DAM MST, NOV; WLC
    See also AAYA 13; CA 13-16R; CANR 51;
    CDALB 1941-1968; DLB 6; MTCW; SATA
    11
Lee, Helen Elaine 1959(?)- .... CLC 86
    See also CA 148
Lee, Julian
    See Latham, Jean Lee
Lee, Larry
    See Lee, Lawrence
Lee, Laurie 1914-1997 CLC 90; DAB; DAM
    POP
    See also CA 77-80; 158; CANR 33; DLB 27;
    MTCW
Lee, Lawrence 1941-1990 .... CLC 34
    See also CA 131; CANR 43
Lee, Manfred B(ennington) 1905-1971 CLC 11
    See also Queen, Ellery
    See also CA 1-4R; 29-32R; CANR 2; DLB 137
Lee, Shelton Jackson 1957(?)- CLC 105; DAM
    MULT
    See also Lee, Spike
    See also BW 2; CA 125; CANR 42
Lee, Spike
    See Lee, Shelton Jackson
    See also AAYA 4
Lee, Stan 1922- .... CLC 17
    See also AAYA 5; CA 108; 111; INT 111
Lee, Tanith 1947- .... CLC 46
    See also AAYA 15; CA 37-40R; CANR 53;
    SATA 8, 88
Lee, Vernon .... TCLC 5
    See also Paget, Violet
    See also DLB 57, 153, 156, 174, 178
Lee, William
    See Burroughs, William S(eward)
Lee, Willy
    See Burroughs, William S(eward)
Lee-Hamilton, Eugene (Jacob) 1845-1907
    TCLC 22
    See also CA 117
Leet, Judith 1935- .... CLC 11
Le Fanu, Joseph Sheridan 1814-1873 NCLC 9,
    58; DAM POP; SSC 14
    See also DLB 21, 70, 159, 178
Leffland, Ella 1931- .... CLC 19
    See also CA 29-32R; CANR 35; DLBY 84; INT
    CANR-35; SATA 65
Leger, Alexis
    See Leger, (Marie-Rene Auguste) Alexis Saint-
    Leger
Leger, (Marie-Rene Auguste) Alexis Saint-
    Leger 1887-1975 CLC 11; DAM POET
    See also Perse, St.-John
    See also CA 13-16R; 61-64; CANR 43; MTCW
Leger, Saintleger
    See Leger, (Marie-Rene Auguste) Alexis Saint-
    Leger
Le Guin, Ursula K(roeber) 1929- CLC 8, 13,
    22, 45, 71; DAB; DAC; DAM MST, POP;
    SSC 12
    See also AAYA 9; AITN 1; CA 21-24R; CANR
    9, 32, 52; CDALB 1968-1988; CLR 3, 28;
    DLB 8, 52; INT CANR-32; JRDA; MAICYA;
    MTCW; SATA 4, 52
Lehmann, Rosamond (Nina) 1901-1990 CLC 5
    See also CA 77-80; 131; CANR 8; DLB 15
Leiber, Fritz (Reuter, Jr.) 1910-1992 CLC 25
    See also CA 45-48; 139; CANR 2, 40; DLB 8;

MTCW; SATA 45; SATA-Obit 73
Leibniz, Gottfried Wilhelm von 1646-1716 LC
    35
    See also DLB 168
Leimbach, Martha 1963-
    See Leimbach, Marti
    See also CA 130
Leimbach, Marti .... CLC 65
    See also Leimbach, Martha
Leino, Eino .... TCLC 24
    See also Loennbohm, Armas Eino Leopold
Leiris, Michel (Julien) 1901-1990 ..... CLC 61
    See also CA 119; 128; 132
Leithauser, Brad 1953- .... CLC 27
    See also CA 107; CANR 27; DLB 120
Lelchuk, Alan 1938- .... CLC 5
    See also CA 45-48; CAAS 20; CANR 1
Lem, Stanislaw 1921- .... CLC 8, 15, 40
    See also CA 105; CAAS 1; CANR 32; MTCW
Lemann, Nancy 1956- .... CLC 39
    See also CA 118; 136
Lemonnier, (Antoine Louis) Camille 1844-1913
    TCLC 22
    See also CA 121
Lenau, Nikolaus 1802-1850 .... NCLC 16
L'Engle, Madeleine (Camp Franklin) 1918-
    CLC 12; DAM POP
    See also AAYA 1; AITN 2; CA 1-4R; CANR 3,
    21, 39; CLR 1, 14; DLB 52; JRDA;
    MAICYA; MTCW; SAAS 15; SATA 1, 27,
    75
Lengyel, Jozsef 1896-1975 .... CLC 7
    See also CA 85-88; 57-60
Lenin 1870-1924
    See Lenin, V. I.
    See also CA 121
Lenin, V. I. .... TCLC 67
    See also Lenin
Lennon, John (Ono) 1940-1980 . CLC 12, 35
    See also CA 102
Lennox, Charlotte Ramsay 1729(?)-1804
    NCLC 23
    See also DLB 39
Lentricchia, Frank (Jr.) 1940- .... CLC 34
    See also CA 25-28R; CANR 19
Lenz, Siegfried 1926- .... CLC 27
    See also CA 89-92; DLB 75
Leonard, Elmore (John, Jr.) 1925- CLC 28, 34,
    71; DAM POP
    See also AAYA 22; AITN 1; BEST 89:1, 90:4;
    CA 81-84; CANR 12, 28, 53; DLB 173; INT
    CANR-28; MTCW
Leonard, Hugh .... CLC 19
    See also Byrne, John Keyes
    See also DLB 13
Leonov, Leonid (Maximovich) 1899-1994
    CLC 92; DAM NOV
    See also CA 129; MTCW
Leopardi, (Conte) Giacomo 1798-1837 NCLC
    22
Le Reveler
    See Artaud, Antonin (Marie Joseph)
Lerman, Eleanor 1952- .... CLC 9
    See also CA 85-88
Lerman, Rhoda 1936- .... CLC 56
    See also CA 49-52
Lermontov, Mikhail Yuryevich 1814-1841
    NCLC 47; PC 18
Leroux, Gaston 1868-1927 .... TCLC 25
    See also CA 108; 136; SATA 65
Lesage, Alain-Rene 1668-1747 .... LC 28
Leskov, Nikolai (Semyonovich) 1831-1895
    NCLC 25

Lessing, Doris (May) 1919- CLC 1, 2, 3, 6, 10,
    15, 22, 40, 94; DA; DAB; DAC; DAM MST,
    NOV; SSC 6; WLCS
    See also CA 9-12R; CAAS 14; CANR 33, 54;
    CDBLB 1960 to Present; DLB 15, 139;
    DLBY 85; MTCW
Lessing, Gotthold Ephraim 1729-1781 . LC 8
    See also DLB 97
Lester, Richard 1932- .... CLC 20
Lever, Charles (James) 1806-1872 NCLC 23
    See also DLB 21
Leverson, Ada 1865(?)-1936(?) ...... TCLC 18
    See also Elaine
    See also CA 117; DLB 153
Levertov, Denise 1923- CLC 1, 2, 3, 5, 8, 15, 28,
    66; DAM POET; PC 11
    See also CA 1-4R; CAAS 19; CANR 3, 29, 50;
    DLB 5, 165; INT CANR-29; MTCW
Levi, Jonathan .... CLC 76
Levi, Peter (Chad Tigar) 1931- .... CLC 41
    See also CA 5-8R; CANR 34; DLB 40
Levi, Primo 1919-1987 . CLC 37, 50; SSC 12
    See also CA 13-16R; 122; CANR 12, 33, 61;
    DLB 177; MTCW
Levin, Ira 1929- .... CLC 3, 6; DAM POP
    See also CA 21-24R; CANR 17, 44; MTCW;
    SATA 66
Levin, Meyer 1905-1981 . CLC 7; DAM POP
    See also AITN 1; CA 9-12R; 104; CANR 15;
    DLB 9, 28; DLBY 81; SATA 21; SATA-Obit
    27
Levine, Norman 1924- .... CLC 54
    See also CA 73-76; CAAS 23; CANR 14; DLB
    88
Levine, Philip 1928- ... CLC 2, 4, 5, 9, 14, 33;
    DAM POET
    See also CA 9-12R; CANR 9, 37, 52; DLB 5
Levinson, Deirdre 1931- .... CLC 49
    See also CA 73-76
Levi-Strauss, Claude 1908- .... CLC 38
    See also CA 1-4R; CANR 6, 32, 57; MTCW
Levitin, Sonia (Wolff) 1934- .... CLC 17
    See also AAYA 13; CA 29-32R; CANR 14, 32;
    JRDA; MAICYA; SAAS 2; SATA 4, 68
Levon, O. U.
    See Kesey, Ken (Elton)
Levy, Amy 1861-1889 .... NCLC 59
    See also DLB 156
Lewes, George Henry 1817-1878 ... NCLC 25
    See also DLB 55, 144
Lewis, Alun 1915-1944 .... TCLC 3
    See also CA 104; DLB 20, 162
Lewis, C. Day
    See Day Lewis, C(ecil)
Lewis, C(live) S(taples) 1898-1963 CLC 1, 3, 6,
    14, 27; DA; DAB; DAC; DAM MST, NOV,
    POP; WLC
    See also AAYA 3; CA 81-84; CANR 33;
    CDBLB 1945-1960; CLR 3, 27; DLB 15,
    100, 160; JRDA; MAICYA; MTCW; SATA
    13
Lewis, Janet 1899- .... CLC 41
    See also Winters, Janet Lewis
    See also CA 9-12R; CANR 29, 63; CAP 1;
    DLBY 87
Lewis, Matthew Gregory 1775-1818 NCLC 11,
    62
    See also DLB 39, 158, 178
Lewis, (Harry) Sinclair 1885-1951 . TCLC 4,
    13, 23, 39; DA; DAB; DAC; DAM MST,
    NOV; WLC
    See also CA 104; 133; CDALB 1917-1929;
    DLB 9, 102; DLBD 1; MTCW

Lewis, (Percy) Wyndham 1882(?)-1957 **TCLC 2, 9**
See also CA 104; 157; DLB 15
Lewisohn, Ludwig 1883-1955 .... **TCLC 19**
See also CA 107; DLB 4, 9, 28, 102
Lewton, Val 1904-1951 .... **TCLC 76**
Leyner, Mark 1956- .... **CLC 92**
See also CA 110; CANR 28, 53
Lezama Lima, Jose 1910-1976 **CLC 4, 10, 101; DAM MULT**
See also CA 77-80; DLB 113; HW
L'Heureux, John (Clarke) 1934- .... **CLC 52**
See also CA 13-16R; CANR 23, 45
Liddell, C. H.
See Kuttner, Henry
Lie, Jonas (Lauritz Idemil) 1833-1908(?)
TCLC 5
See also CA 115
Lieber, Joel 1937-1971 .... **CLC 6**
See also CA 73-76; 29-32R
Lieber, Stanley Martin
See Lee, Stan
Lieberman, Laurence (James) 1935- **CLC 4, 36**
See also CA 17-20R; CANR 8, 36
Lieksman, Anders
See Haavikko, Paavo Juhani
Li Fei-kan 1904-
See Pa Chin
See also CA 105
Lifton, Robert Jay 1926- .... **CLC 67**
See also CA 17-20R; CANR 27; INT CANR-
27; SATA 66
Lightfoot, Gordon 1938- .... **CLC 26**
See also CA 109
Lightman, Alan P(aige) 1948- .... **CLC 81**
See also CA 141; CANR 63
Ligotti, Thomas (Robert) 1953- **CLC 44; SSC 16**
See also CA 123; CANR 49
Li Ho 791-817 .... **PC 13**
Liliencron, (Friedrich Adolf Axel) Detlev von 1844-1909 .... **TCLC 18**
See also CA 117
Lilly, William 1602-1681 .... **LC 27**
Lima, Jose Lezama
See Lezama Lima, Jose
Lima Barreto, Afonso Henrique de 1881-1922
TCLC 23
See also CA 117
Limonov, Edward 1944- .... **CLC 67**
See also CA 137
Lin, Frank
See Atherton, Gertrude (Franklin Horn)
Lincoln, Abraham 1809-1865 .... **NCLC 18**
Lind, Jakov .... **CLC 1, 2, 4, 27, 82**
See also Landwirth, Heinz
See also CAAS 4
Lindbergh, Anne (Spencer) Morrow 1906-
CLC 82; DAM NOV
See also CA 17-20R; CANR 16; MTCW; SATA 33
Lindsay, David 1878-1945 .... **TCLC 15**
See also CA 113
Lindsay, (Nicholas) Vachel 1879-1931 **TCLC 17; DA; DAC; DAM MST, POET; WLC**
See also CA 114; 135; CDALB 1865-1917; DLB 54; SATA 40
Linke-Poot
See Doeblin, Alfred
Linney, Romulus 1930- .... **CLC 51**
See also CA 1-4R; CANR 40, 44
Linton, Eliza Lynn 1822-1898 .... **NCLC 41**

See also DLB 18
Li Po 701-763 .... **CMLC 2**
Lipsius, Justus 1547-1606 .... **LC 16**
Lipsyte, Robert (Michael) 1938- **CLC 21; DA; DAC; DAM MST, NOV**
See also AAYA 7; CA 17-20R; CANR 8, 57; CLR 23; JRDA; MAICYA; SATA 5, 68
Lish, Gordon (Jay) 1934- ... **CLC 45; SSC 18**
See also CA 113; 117; DLB 130; INT 117
Lispector, Clarice 1925-1977 .... **CLC 43**
See also CA 139; 116; DLB 113
Littell, Robert 1935(?)- .... **CLC 42**
See also CA 109; 112; CANR 64
Little, Malcolm 1925-1965
See Malcolm X
See also BW 1; CA 125; 111; DA; DAB; DAC; DAM MST, MULT; MTCW
Littlewit, Humphrey Gent.
See Lovecraft, H(oward) P(hillips)
Litwos
See Sienkiewicz, Henryk (Adam Alexander Pius)
Liu E 1857-1909 .... **TCLC 15**
See also CA 115
Lively, Penelope (Margaret) 1933- .. **CLC 32, 50; DAM NOV**
See also CA 41-44R; CANR 29; CLR 7; DLB 14, 161; JRDA; MAICYA; MTCW; SATA 7, 60
Livesay, Dorothy (Kathleen) 1909- **CLC 4, 15, 79; DAC; DAM MST, POET**
See also AITN 2; CA 25-28R; CAAS 8; CANR 36; DLB 68; MTCW
Livy c. 59B.C.-c. 17 .... **CMLC 11**
Lizardi, Jose Joaquin Fernandez de 1776-1827
NCLC 30
Llewellyn, Richard
See Llewellyn Lloyd, Richard Dafydd Vivian
See also DLB 15
Llewellyn Lloyd, Richard Dafydd Vivian 1906-
1983 .... **CLC 7, 80**
See also Llewellyn, Richard
See also CA 53-56; 111; CANR 7; SATA 11; SATA-Obit 37
Llosa, (Jorge) Mario (Pedro) Vargas
See Vargas Llosa, (Jorge) Mario (Pedro)
Lloyd Webber, Andrew 1948-
See Webber, Andrew Lloyd
See also AAYA 1; CA 116; 149; DAM DRAM; SATA 56
Llull, Ramon c. 1235-c. 1316 .... **CMLC 12**
Locke, Alain (Le Roy) 1886-1954 .. **TCLC 43**
See also BW 1; CA 106; 124; DLB 51
Locke, John 1632-1704 .... **LC 7, 35**
See also DLB 101
Locke-Elliott, Sumner
See Elliott, Sumner Locke
Lockhart, John Gibson 1794-1854 .. **NCLC 6**
See also DLB 110, 116, 144
Lodge, David (John) 1935- **CLC 36; DAM POP**
See also BEST 90:1; CA 17-20R; CANR 19, 53; DLB 14; INT CANR-19; MTCW
Lodge, Thomas 1558-1625 .... **LC 41**
Loennbohm, Armas Eino Leopold 1878-1926
See Leino, Eino
See also CA 123
Loewinsohn, Ron(ald William) 1937- **CLC 52**
See also CA 25-28R
Logan, Jake
See Smith, Martin Cruz
Logan, John (Burton) 1923-1987 .... **CLC 5**
See also CA 77-80; 124; CANR 45; DLB 5
Lo Kuan-chung 1330(?)-1400(?) .... **LC 12**

Lombard, Nap
See Johnson, Pamela Hansford
London, Jack . **TCLC 9, 15, 39; SSC 4; WLC**
See also London, John Griffith
See also AAYA 13; AITN 2; CDALB 1865-
1917; DLB 8, 12, 78; SATA 18
London, John Griffith 1876-1916
See London, Jack
See also CA 110; 119; DA; DAB; DAC; DAM MST, NOV; JRDA; MAICYA; MTCW
Long, Emmett
See Leonard, Elmore (John, Jr.)
Longbaugh, Harry
See Goldman, William (W.)
Longfellow, Henry Wadsworth 1807-1882
NCLC 2, 45; DA; DAB; DAC; DAM MST, POET; WLCS
See also CDALB 1640-1865; DLB 1, 59; SATA 19
Longley, Michael 1939- .... **CLC 29**
See also CA 102; DLB 40
Longus fl. c. 2nd cent. - .... **CMLC 7**
Longway, A. Hugh
See Lang, Andrew
Lonnrot, Elias 1802-1884 .... **NCLC 53**
Lopate, Phillip 1943- .... **CLC 29**
See also CA 97-100; DLBY 80; INT 97-100
Lopez Portillo (y Pacheco), Jose 1920- . **CLC 46**
See also CA 129; HW
Lopez y Fuentes, Gregorio 1897(?)-1966 **CLC 32**
See also CA 131; HW
Lorca, Federico Garcia
See Garcia Lorca, Federico
Lord, Bette Bao 1938- .... **CLC 23**
See also BEST 90:3; CA 107; CANR 41; INT 107; SATA 58
Lord Auch
See Bataille, Georges
Lord Byron
See Byron, George Gordon (Noel)
Lorde, Audre (Geraldine) 1934-1992 **CLC 18, 71; BLC; DAM MULT, POET; PC 12**
See also BW 1; CA 25-28R; 142; CANR 16, 26, 46; DLB 41; MTCW
Lord Houghton
See Milnes, Richard Monckton
Lord Jeffrey
See Jeffrey, Francis
Lorenzini, Carlo 1826-1890
See Collodi, Carlo
See also MAICYA; SATA 29
Lorenzo, Heberto Padilla
See Padilla (Lorenzo), Heberto
Loris
See Hofmannsthal, Hugo von
Loti, Pierre .... **TCLC 11**
See also Viaud, (Louis Marie) Julien
See also DLB 123
Louie, David Wong 1954- .... **CLC 70**
See also CA 139
Louis, Father M.
See Merton, Thomas
Lovecraft, H(oward) P(hillips) 1890-1937
TCLC 4, 22; DAM POP; SSC 3
See also AAYA 14; CA 104; 133; MTCW
Lovelace, Earl 1935- .... **CLC 51**
See also BW 2; CA 77-80; CANR 41; DLB 125; MTCW
Lovelace, Richard 1618-1657 .... **LC 24**
See also DLB 131
Lowell, Amy 1874-1925 .... **TCLC 1, 8; DAM**

POET; PC 13
See also CA 104; 151; DLB 54, 140
Lowell, James Russell 1819-1891 .... NCLC 2
See also CDALB 1640-1865; DLB 1, 11, 64, 79
Lowell, Robert (Traill Spence, Jr.) 1917-1977 CLC 1, 2, 3, 4, 5, 8, 9, 11, 15, 37; DA; DAB; DAC; DAM MST, NOV; PC 3; WLC
See also CA 9-12R; 73-76; CABS 2; CANR 26, 60; DLB 5, 169; MTCW
Lowndes, Marie Adelaide (Belloc) 1868-1947 TCLC 12
See also CA 107; DLB 70
Lowry, (Clarence) Malcolm 1909-1957 T C L C 6, 40
See also CA 105; 131; CANR 62; CDBLB 1945-1960; DLB 15; MTCW
Lowry, Mina Gertrude 1882-1966
See Loy, Mina
See also CA 113
Loxsmith, John
See Brunner, John (Kilian Houston)
Loy, Mina .... CLC 28; DAM POET; PC 16
See also Lowry, Mina Gertrude
See also DLB 4, 54
Loyson-Bridet
See Schwob, (Mayer Andre) Marcel
Lucas, Craig 1951- .... CLC 64
See also CA 137
Lucas, E(dward) V(errall) 1868-1938 T C L C 73
See also DLB 98, 149, 153; SATA 20
Lucas, George 1944- .... CLC 16
See also AAYA 1; CA 77-80; CANR 30; SATA 56
Lucas, Hans
See Godard, Jean-Luc
Lucas, Victoria
See Plath, Sylvia
Ludlam, Charles 1943-1987 .... CLC 46, 50
See also CA 85-88; 122
Ludlum, Robert 1927- CLC 22, 43; DAM NOV, POP
See also AAYA 10; BEST 89:1, 90:3; CA 33-36R; CANR 25, 41; DLBY 82; MTCW
Ludwig, Ken .... CLC 60
Ludwig, Otto 1813-1865 .... NCLC 4
See also DLB 129
Lugones, Leopoldo 1874-1938 .... TCLC 15
See also CA 116; 131; HW
Lu Hsun 1881-1936 .... TCLC 3; SSC 20
See also Shu-Jen, Chou
Lukacs, George .... CLC 24
See also Lukacs, Gyorgy (Szegeny von)
Lukacs, Gyorgy (Szegeny von) 1885-1971
See Lukacs, George
See also CA 101; 29-32R; CANR 62
Luke, Peter (Ambrose Cyprian) 1919-1995 CLC 38
See also CA 81-84; 147; DLB 13
Lunar, Dennis
See Mungo, Raymond
Lurie, Alison 1926- .... CLC 4, 5, 18, 39
See also CA 1-4R; CANR 2, 17, 50; DLB 2; MTCW; SATA 46
Lustig, Arnost 1926- .... CLC 56
See also AAYA 3; CA 69-72; CANR 47; SATA 56
Luther, Martin 1483-1546 .... LC 9, 37
See also DLB 179
Luxemburg, Rosa 1870(?)-1919 ..... TCLC 63
See also CA 118
Luzi, Mario 1914- .... CLC 13

See also CA 61-64; CANR 9; DLB 128
Lyly, John 1554(?)-1606 LC 41; DAM DRAM; DC 7
See also DLB 62, 167
L'Ymagier
See Gourmont, Remy (-Marie-Charles) de
Lynch, B. Suarez
See Bioy Casares, Adolfo; Borges, Jorge Luis
Lynch, David (K.) 1946- .... CLC 66
See also CA 124; 129
Lynch, James
See Andreyev, Leonid (Nikolaevich)
Lynch Davis, B.
See Bioy Casares, Adolfo; Borges, Jorge Luis
Lyndsay, Sir David 1490-1555 .... LC 20
Lynn, Kenneth S(chuyler) 1923- .... CLC 50
See also CA 1-4R; CANR 3, 27
Lynx
See West, Rebecca
Lyons, Marcus
See Blish, James (Benjamin)
Lyre, Pinchbeck
See Sassoon, Siegfried (Lorraine)
Lytle, Andrew (Nelson) 1902-1995 ... CLC 22
See also CA 9-12R; 150; DLB 6; DLBY 95
Lyttelton, George 1709-1773 .... LC 10
Maas, Peter 1929- .... CLC 29
See also CA 93-96; INT 93-96
Macaulay, Rose 1881-1958 .... TCLC 7, 44
See also CA 104; DLB 36
Macaulay, Thomas Babington 1800-1859 NCLC 42
See also CDBLB 1832-1890; DLB 32, 55
MacBeth, George (Mann) 1932-1992 CLC 2, 5, 9
See also CA 25-28R; 136; CANR 61; DLB 40; MTCW; SATA 4; SATA-Obit 70
MacCaig, Norman (Alexander) 1910- CLC 36; DAB; DAM POET
See also CA 9-12R; CANR 3, 34; DLB 27
MacCarthy, (Sir Charles Otto) Desmond 1877-1952 .... TCLC 36
MacDiarmid, Hugh CLC 2, 4, 11, 19, 63; PC 9
See also Grieve, C(hristopher) M(urray)
See also CDBLB 1945-1960; DLB 20
MacDonald, Anson
See Heinlein, Robert A(nson)
Macdonald, Cynthia 1928- .... CLC 13, 19
See also CA 49-52; CANR 4, 44; DLB 105
MacDonald, George 1824-1905 .... TCLC 9
See also CA 106; 137; DLB 18, 163, 178; MAICYA; SATA 33
Macdonald, John
See Millar, Kenneth
MacDonald, John D(ann) 1916-1986 CLC 3, 27, 44; DAM NOV, POP
See also CA 1-4R; 121; CANR 1, 19, 60; DLB 8; DLBY 86; MTCW
Macdonald, John Ross
See Millar, Kenneth
Macdonald, Ross .... CLC 1, 2, 3, 14, 34, 41
See also Millar, Kenneth
See also DLBD 6
MacDougal, John
See Blish, James (Benjamin)
MacEwen, Gwendolyn (Margaret) 1941-1987 CLC 13, 55
See also CA 9-12R; 124; CANR 7, 22; DLB 53; SATA 50; SATA-Obit 55
Macha, Karel Hynek 1810-1846 .... NCLC 46
Machado (y Ruiz), Antonio 1875-1939 T C L C 3
See also CA 104; DLB 108

Machado de Assis, Joaquim Maria 1839-1908 TCLC 10; BLC; SSC 24
See also CA 107; 153
Machen, Arthur .... TCLC 4; SSC 20
See also Jones, Arthur Llewellyn
See also DLB 36, 156, 178
Machiavelli, Niccolo 1469-1527 LC 8, 36; DA; DAB; DAC; DAM MST; WLCS
MacInnes, Colin 1914-1976 .... CLC 4, 23
See also CA 69-72; 65-68; CANR 21; DLB 14; MTCW
MacInnes, Helen (Clark) 1907-1985 CLC 27, 39; DAM POP
See also CA 1-4R; 117; CANR 1, 28, 58; DLB 87; MTCW; SATA 22; SATA-Obit 44
Mackay, Mary 1855-1924
See Corelli, Marie
See also CA 118
Mackenzie, Compton (Edward Montague) 1883-1972 .... CLC 18
See also CA 21-22; 37-40R; CAP 2; DLB 34, 100
Mackenzie, Henry 1745-1831 .... NCLC 41
See also DLB 39
Mackintosh, Elizabeth 1896(?)-1952
See Tey, Josephine
See also CA 110
MacLaren, James
See Grieve, C(hristopher) M(urray)
Mac Laverty, Bernard 1942- .... CLC 31
See also CA 116; 118; CANR 43; INT 118
MacLean, Alistair (Stuart) 1922(?)-1987 C L C 3, 13, 50, 63; DAM POP
See also CA 57-60; 121; CANR 28, 61; MTCW; SATA 23; SATA-Obit 50
Maclean, Norman (Fitzroy) 1902-1990 C L C 78; DAM POP; SSC 13
See also CA 102; 132; CANR 49
MacLeish, Archibald 1892-1982 CLC 3, 8, 14, 68; DAM POET
See also CA 9-12R; 106; CANR 33, 63; DLB 4, 7, 45; DLBY 82; MTCW
MacLennan, (John) Hugh 1907-1990 CLC 2, 14, 92; DAC; DAM MST
See also CA 5-8R; 142; CANR 33; DLB 68; MTCW
MacLeod, Alistair 1936- CLC 56; DAC; DAM MST
See also CA 123; DLB 60
Macleod, Fiona
See Sharp, William
MacNeice, (Frederick) Louis 1907-1963 C L C 1, 4, 10, 53; DAB; DAM POET
See also CA 85-88; CANR 61; DLB 10, 20; MTCW
MacNeill, Dand
See Fraser, George MacDonald
Macpherson, James 1736-1796 .... LC 29
See also DLB 109
Macpherson, (Jean) Jay 1931- .... CLC 14
See also CA 5-8R; DLB 53
MacShane, Frank 1927- .... CLC 39
See also CA 9-12R; CANR 3, 33; DLB 111
Macumber, Mari
See Sandoz, Mari(e Susette)
Madach, Imre 1823-1864 .... NCLC 19
Madden, (Jerry) David 1933- .... CLC 5, 15
See also CA 1-4R; CAAS 3; CANR 4, 45; DLB 6; MTCW
Maddern, Al(an)
See Ellison, Harlan (Jay)
Madhubuti, Haki R. 1942- CLC 6, 73; BLC; DAM MULT, POET; PC 5

See also Lee, Don L.
See also BW 2; CA 73-76; CANR 24, 51; DLB 5, 41; DLBD 8
Maepenn, Hugh
See Kuttner, Henry
Maepenn, K. H.
See Kuttner, Henry
Maeterlinck, Maurice 1862-1949 ... **TCLC 3; DAM DRAM**
See also CA 104; 136; SATA 66
Maginn, William 1794-1842 .... **NCLC 8**
See also DLB 110, 159
Mahapatra, Jayanta 1928- .... **CLC 33; DAM MULT**
See also CA 73-76; CAAS 9; CANR 15, 33
Mahfouz, Naguib (Abdel Aziz Al-Sabilgi) 1911(?)-
See Mahfuz, Najib
See also BEST 89:2; CA 128; CANR 55; DAM NOV; MTCW
Mahfuz, Najib .... **CLC 52, 55**
See also Mahfouz, Naguib (Abdel Aziz Al-Sabilgi)
See also DLBY 88
Mahon, Derek 1941- .... **CLC 27**
See also CA 113; 128; DLB 40
Mailer, Norman 1923-**CLC 1, 2, 3, 4, 5, 8, 11, 14, 28, 39, 74; DA; DAB; DAC; DAM MST, NOV, POP**
See also AITN 2; CA 9-12R; CABS 1; CANR 28; CDALB 1968-1988; DLB 2, 16, 28; DLBD 3; DLBY 80, 83; MTCW
Maillet, Antonine 1929- .... **CLC 54; DAC**
See also CA 115; 120; CANR 46; DLB 60; INT 120
Mais, Roger 1905-1955 .... **TCLC 8**
See also BW 1; CA 105; 124; DLB 125; MTCW
Maistre, Joseph de 1753-1821 .... **NCLC 37**
Maitland, Frederic 1850-1906 .... **TCLC 65**
Maitland, Sara (Louise) 1950- .... **CLC 49**
See also CA 69-72; CANR 13, 59
Major, Clarence 1936- **CLC 3, 19, 48; BLC; DAM MULT**
See also BW 2; CA 21-24R; CAAS 6; CANR 13, 25, 53; DLB 33
Major, Kevin (Gerald) 1949-..**CLC 26; DAC**
See also AAYA 16; CA 97-100; CANR 21, 38; CLR 11; DLB 60; INT CANR-21; JRDA; MAICYA; SATA 32, 82
Maki, James
See Ozu, Yasujiro
Malabaila, Damiano
See Levi, Primo
Malamud, Bernard 1914-1986**CLC 1, 2, 3, 5, 8, 9, 11, 18, 27, 44, 78, 85; DA; DAB; DAC; DAM MST, NOV, POP; SSC 15; WLC**
See also AAYA 16; CA 5-8R; 118; CABS 1; CANR 28, 62; CDALB 1941-1968; DLB 2, 28, 152; DLBY 80, 86; MTCW
Malan, Herman
See Bosman, Herman Charles; Bosman, Herman Charles
Malaparte, Curzio 1898-1957 .... **TCLC 52**
Malcolm, Dan
See Silverberg, Robert
Malcolm X .... **CLC 82; BLC; WLCS**
See also Little, Malcolm
Malherbe, Francois de 1555-1628 .... **LC 5**
Mallarme, Stephane 1842-1898 **NCLC 4, 41; DAM POET; PC 4**
Mallet-Joris, Francoise 1930- .... **CLC 11**
See also CA 65-68; CANR 17; DLB 83
Malley, Ern

See McAuley, James Phillip
Mallowan, Agatha Christie
See Christie, Agatha (Mary Clarissa)
Maloff, Saul 1922- .... **CLC 5**
See also CA 33-36R
Malone, Louis
See MacNeice, (Frederick) Louis
Malone, Michael (Christopher) 1942-**CLC 43**
See also CA 77-80; CANR 14, 32, 57
Malory, (Sir) Thomas 1410(?)-1471(?)**LC 11; DA; DAB; DAC; DAM MST; WLCS**
See also CDBLB Before 1660; DLB 146; SATA 59; SATA-Brief 33
Malouf, (George Joseph) David 1934-**CLC 28, 86**
See also CA 124; CANR 50
Malraux, (Georges-)Andre 1901-1976**CLC 1, 4, 9, 13, 15, 57; DAM NOV**
See also CA 21-22; 69-72; CANR 34, 58; CAP 2; DLB 72; MTCW
Malzberg, Barry N(athaniel) 1939- ... **CLC 7**
See also CA 61-64; CAAS 4; CANR 16; DLB 8
Mamet, David (Alan) 1947-**CLC 9, 15, 34, 46, 91; DAM DRAM; DC 4**
See also AAYA 3; CA 81-84; CABS 3; CANR 15, 41; DLB 7; MTCW
Mamoulian, Rouben (Zachary) 1897-1987 **CLC 16**
See also CA 25-28R; 124
Mandelstam, Osip (Emilievich) 1891(?)-1938(?) **TCLC 2, 6; PC 14**
See also CA 104; 150
Mander, (Mary) Jane 1877-1949 ... **TCLC 31**
Mandeville, John fl. 1350- .... **CMLC 19**
See also DLB 146
Mandiargues, Andre Pieyre de .... **CLC 41**
See also Pieyre de Mandiargues, Andre
See also DLB 83
Mandrake, Ethel Belle
See Thurman, Wallace (Henry)
Mangan, James Clarence 1803-1849**NCLC 27**
Maniere, J.-E.
See Giraudoux, (Hippolyte) Jean
Manley, (Mary) Delariviere 1672(?)-1724**LC 1**
See also DLB 39, 80
Mann, Abel
See Creasey, John
Mann, Emily 1952- .... **DC 7**
See also CA 130; CANR 55
Mann, (Luiz) Heinrich 1871-1950 ... **TCLC 9**
See also CA 106; DLB 66
Mann, (Paul) Thomas 1875-1955 **TCLC 2, 8, 14, 21, 35, 44, 60; DA; DAB; DAC; DAM MST, NOV; SSC 5; WLC**
See also CA 104; 128; DLB 66; MTCW
Mannheim, Karl 1893-1947 .... **TCLC 65**
Manning, David
See Faust, Frederick (Schiller)
Manning, Frederic 1887(?)-1935 ... **TCLC 25**
See also CA 124
Manning, Olivia 1915-1980 .... **CLC 5, 19**
See also CA 5-8R; 101; CANR 29; MTCW
Mano, D. Keith 1942- .... **CLC 2, 10**
See also CA 25-28R; CAAS 6; CANR 26, 57; DLB 6
Mansfield, KatherineTCLC 2, 8, 39; DAB; SSC 9, 23; WLC**
See also Beauchamp, Kathleen Mansfield
See also DLB 162
Manso, Peter 1940- .... **CLC 39**
See also CA 29-32R; CANR 44
Mantecon, Juan Jimenez

See Jimenez (Mantecon), Juan Ramon
Manton, Peter
See Creasey, John
Man Without a Spleen, A
See Chekhov, Anton (Pavlovich)
Manzoni, Alessandro 1785-1873 .... **NCLC 29**
Mapu, Abraham (ben Jekutiel) 1808-1867 **NCLC 18**
Mara, Sally
See Queneau, Raymond
Marat, Jean Paul 1743-1793 .... **LC 10**
Marcel, Gabriel Honore 1889-1973 . **CLC 15**
See also CA 102; 45-48; MTCW
Marchbanks, Samuel
See Davies, (William) Robertson
Marchi, Giacomo
See Bassani, Giorgio
Margulies, Donald .... **CLC 76**
Marie de France c. 12th cent. - .... **CMLC 8**
Marie de l'Incarnation 1599-1672 ...... **LC 10**
Marier, Captain Victor
See Griffith, D(avid Lewelyn) W(ark)
Mariner, Scott
See Pohl, Frederik
Marinetti, Filippo Tommaso 1876-1944**TCLC 10**
See also CA 107; DLB 114
Marivaux, Pierre Carlet de Chamblain de 1688-1763 .... **LC 4; DC 7**
Markandaya, Kamala .... **CLC 8, 38**
See also Taylor, Kamala (Purnaiya)
Markfield, Wallace 1926- .... **CLC 8**
See also CA 69-72; CAAS 3; DLB 2, 28
Markham, Edwin 1852-1940 .... **TCLC 47**
See also CA 160; DLB 54
Markham, Robert
See Amis, Kingsley (William)
Marks, J
See Highwater, Jamake (Mamake)
Marks-Highwater, J
See Highwater, Jamake (Mamake)
Markson, David M(errill) 1927- .... **CLC 67**
See also CA 49-52; CANR 1
Marley, Bob .... **CLC 17**
See also Marley, Robert Nesta
Marley, Robert Nesta 1945-1981
See Marley, Bob
See also CA 107; 103
Marlowe, Christopher 1564-1593**LC 22; DA; DAB; DAC; DAM DRAM, MST; DC 1; WLC**
See also CDBLB Before 1660; DLB 62
Marlowe, Stephen 1928-
See Queen, Ellery
See also CA 13-16R; CANR 6, 55
Marmontel, Jean-Francois 1723-1799 ..**LC 2**
Marquand, John P(hillips) 1893-1960**CLC 2, 10**
See also CA 85-88; DLB 9, 102
Marques, Rene 1919-1979 ..... **CLC 96; DAM MULT; HLC**
See also CA 97-100; 85-88; DLB 113; HW
Marquez, Gabriel (Jose) Garcia
See Garcia Marquez, Gabriel (Jose)
Marquis, Don(ald Robert Perry) 1878-1937 **TCLC 7**
See also CA 104; DLB 11, 25
Marric, J. J.
See Creasey, John
Marryat, Frederick 1792-1848 .... **NCLC 3**
See also DLB 21, 163
Marsden, James
See Creasey, John

Marsh, (Edith) Ngaio 1899-1982 **CLC 7, 53; DAM POP**
See also CA 9-12R; CANR 6, 58; DLB 77; MTCW

Marshall, Garry 1934- .... **CLC 17**
See also AAYA 3; CA 111; SATA 60

Marshall, Paule 1929-**CLC 27, 72; BLC; DAM MULT; SSC 3**
See also BW 2; CA 77-80; CANR 25; DLB 157; MTCW

Marsten, Richard
See Hunter, Evan

Marston, John 1576-1634**LC 33; DAM DRAM**
See also DLB 58, 172

Martha, Henry
See Harris, Mark

Marti, Jose 1853-1895**NCLC 63; DAM MULT; HLC**

Martial c. 40-c. 104 .... **PC 10**

Martin, Ken
See Hubbard, L(afayette) Ron(ald)

Martin, Richard
See Creasey, John

Martin, Steve 1945- .... **CLC 30**
See also CA 97-100; CANR 30; MTCW

Martin, Valerie 1948- .... **CLC 89**
See also BEST 90:2; CA 85-88; CANR 49

Martin, Violet Florence 1862-1915 **TCLC 51**

Martin, Webber
See Silverberg, Robert

Martindale, Patrick Victor
See White, Patrick (Victor Martindale)

Martin du Gard, Roger 1881-1958 **TCLC 24**
See also CA 118; DLB 65

Martineau, Harriet 1802-1876 .... **NCLC 26**
See also DLB 21, 55, 159, 163, 166; YABC 2

Martines, Julia
See O'Faolain, Julia

Martinez, Enrique Gonzalez
See Gonzalez Martinez, Enrique

Martinez, Jacinto Benavente y
See Benavente (y Martinez), Jacinto

Martinez Ruiz, Jose 1873-1967
See Azorin; Ruiz, Jose Martinez
See also CA 93-96; HW

Martinez Sierra, Gregorio 1881-1947**TCLC 6**
See also CA 115

Martinez Sierra, Maria (de la O'LeJarraga) 1874-1974 .... **TCLC 6**
See also CA 115

Martinsen, Martin
See Follett, Ken(neth Martin)

Martinson, Harry (Edmund) 1904-1978**CLC 14**
See also CA 77-80; CANR 34

Marut, Ret
See Traven, B.

Marut, Robert
See Traven, B.

Marvell, Andrew 1621-1678**LC 4; DA; DAB; DAC; DAM MST, POET; PC 10; WLC**
See also CDBLB 1660-1789; DLB 131

Marx, Karl (Heinrich) 1818-1883 . **NCLC 17**
See also DLB 129

Masaoka Shiki .... **TCLC 18**
See also Masaoka Tsunenori

Masaoka Tsunenori 1867-1902
See Masaoka Shiki
See also CA 117

Masefield, John (Edward) 1878-1967**CLC 11, 47; DAM POET**
See also CA 19-20; 25-28R; CANR 33; CAP 2; CDBLB 1890-1914; DLB 10, 19, 153, 160;

MTCW; SATA 19

Maso, Carole 19(?)- .... **CLC 44**

Mason, Bobbie Ann 1940-**CLC 28, 43, 82; SSC 4**
See also AAYA 5; CA 53-56; CANR 11, 31, 58; DLB 173; DLBY 87; INT CANR-31; MTCW

Mason, Ernst
See Pohl, Frederik

Mason, Lee W.
See Malzberg, Barry N(athaniel)

Mason, Nick 1945- .... **CLC 35**

Mason, Tally
See Derleth, August (William)

Mass, William
See Gibson, William

Masters, Edgar Lee 1868-1950 **TCLC 2, 25; DA; DAC; DAM MST, POET; PC 1; WLCS**
See also CA 104; 133; CDALB 1865-1917; DLB 54; MTCW

Masters, Hilary 1928- .... **CLC 48**
See also CA 25-28R; CANR 13, 47

Mastrosimone, William 19(?)- .... **CLC 36**

Mathe, Albert
See Camus, Albert

Mather, Cotton 1663-1728 .... **LC 38**
See also CDALB 1640-1865; DLB 24, 30, 140

Mather, Increase 1639-1723 .... **LC 38**
See also DLB 24

Matheson, Richard Burton 1926- ..... **CLC 37**
See also CA 97-100; DLB 8, 44; INT 97-100

Mathews, Harry 1930- .... **CLC 6, 52**
See also CA 21-24R; CAAS 6; CANR 18, 40

Mathews, John Joseph 1894-1979 .. **CLC 84; DAM MULT**
See also CA 19-20; 142; CANR 45; CAP 2; DLB 175; NNAL

Mathias, Roland (Glyn) 1915- .... **CLC 45**
See also CA 97-100; CANR 19, 41; DLB 27

Matsuo Basho 1644-1694 .... **PC 3**
See also DAM POET

Mattheson, Rodney
See Creasey, John

Matthews, Greg 1949- .... **CLC 45**
See also CA 135

Matthews, William 1942- .... **CLC 40**
See also CA 29-32R; CAAS 18; CANR 12, 57; DLB 5

Matthias, John (Edward) 1941- .... **CLC 9**
See also CA 33-36R; CANR 56

Matthiessen, Peter 1927-**CLC 5, 7, 11, 32, 64; DAM NOV**
See also AAYA 6; BEST 90:4; CA 9-12R; CANR 21, 50; DLB 6, 173; MTCW; SATA 27

Maturin, Charles Robert 1780(?)-1824**NCLC 6**
See also DLB 178

Matute (Ausejo), Ana Maria 1925- .. **CLC 11**
See also CA 89-92; MTCW

Maugham, W. S.
See Maugham, W(illiam) Somerset

Maugham, W(illiam) Somerset 1874-1965 **CLC 1, 11, 15, 67, 93; DA; DAB; DAC; DAM DRAM, MST, NOV; SSC 8; WLC**
See also CA 5-8R; 25-28R; CANR 40; CDBLB 1914-1945; DLB 10, 36, 77, 100, 162; MTCW; SATA 54

Maugham, William Somerset
See Maugham, W(illiam) Somerset

Maupassant, (Henri Rene Albert) Guy de 1850-1893**NCLC 1, 42; DA; DAB; DAC; DAM**

MST; SSC 1; WLC
See also DLB 123

Maupin, Armistead 1944-**CLC 95; DAM POP**
See also CA 125; 130; CANR 58; INT 130

Maurhut, Richard
See Traven, B.

Mauriac, Claude 1914-1996 .... **CLC 9**
See also CA 89-92; 152; DLB 83

Mauriac, Francois (Charles) 1885-1970 **CLC 4, 9, 56; SSC 24**
See also CA 25-28; CAP 2; DLB 65; MTCW

Mavor, Osborne Henry 1888-1951
See Bridie, James
See also CA 104

Maxwell, William (Keepers, Jr.) 1908-**CLC 19**
See also CA 93-96; CANR 54; DLBY 80; INT 93-96

May, Elaine 1932- .... **CLC 16**
See also CA 124; 142; DLB 44

Mayakovski, Vladimir (Vladimirovich) 1893-1930 .... **TCLC 4, 18**
See also CA 104; 158

Mayhew, Henry 1812-1887 .... **NCLC 31**
See also DLB 18, 55

Mayle, Peter 1939(?)- .... **CLC 89**
See also CA 139; CANR 64

Maynard, Joyce 1953- .... **CLC 23**
See also CA 111; 129; CANR 64

Mayne, William (James Carter) 1928-**CLC 12**
See also AAYA 20; CA 9-12R; CANR 37; CLR 25; JRDA; MAICYA; SAAS 11; SATA 6, 68

Mayo, Jim
See L'Amour, Louis (Dearborn)

Maysles, Albert 1926- .... **CLC 16**
See also CA 29-32R

Maysles, David 1932- .... **CLC 16**

Mazer, Norma Fox 1931- .... **CLC 26**
See also AAYA 5; CA 69-72; CANR 12, 32; CLR 23; JRDA; MAICYA; SAAS 1; SATA 24, 67

Mazzini, Guiseppe 1805-1872 .... **NCLC 34**

McAuley, James Phillip 1917-1976 .. **CLC 45**
See also CA 97-100

McBain, Ed
See Hunter, Evan

McBrien, William Augustine 1930- .. **CLC 44**
See also CA 107

McCaffrey, Anne (Inez) 1926-**CLC 17; DAM NOV, POP**
See also AAYA 6; AITN 2; BEST 89:2; CA 25-28R; CANR 15, 35, 55; DLB 8; JRDA; MAICYA; MTCW; SAAS 11; SATA 8, 70

McCall, Nathan 1955(?)- .... **CLC 86**
See also CA 146

McCann, Arthur
See Campbell, John W(ood, Jr.)

McCann, Edson
See Pohl, Frederik

McCarthy, Charles, Jr. 1933-
See McCarthy, Cormac
See also CANR 42; DAM POP

McCarthy, Cormac 1933- **CLC 4, 57, 59, 101**
See also McCarthy, Charles, Jr.
See also DLB 6, 143

McCarthy, Mary (Therese) 1912-1989**CLC 1, 3, 5, 14, 24, 39, 59; SSC 24**
See also CA 5-8R; 129; CANR 16, 50, 64; DLB 2; DLBY 81; INT CANR-16; MTCW

McCartney, (James) Paul 1942- **CLC 12, 35**
See also CA 146

McCauley, Stephen (D.) 1955- .... **CLC 50**
See also CA 141

McClure, Michael (Thomas) 1932-**CLC 6, 10**

See also CA 21-24R; CANR 17, 46; DLB 16
McCorkle, Jill (Collins) 1958- .... **CLC 51**
See also CA 121; DLBY 87
McCourt, James 1941- .... **CLC 5**
See also CA 57-60
McCoy, Horace (Stanley) 1897-1955TCLC 28
See also CA 108; 155; DLB 9
McCrae, John 1872-1918 .... **TCLC 12**
See also CA 109; DLB 92
McCreigh, James
See Pohl, Frederik
McCullers, (Lula) Carson (Smith) 1917-1967
CLC 1, 4, 10, 12, 48, 100; DA; DAB; DAC;
DAM MST, NOV; SSC 9, 24; WLC
See also AAYA 21; CA 5-8R; 25-28R; CABS
1, 3; CANR 18; CDALB 1941-1968; DLB
2, 7, 173; MTCW; SATA 27
McCulloch, John Tyler
See Burroughs, Edgar Rice
McCullough, Colleen 1938(?)- **CLC 27, 107;**
DAM NOV, POP
See also CA 81-84; CANR 17, 46; MTCW
McDermott, Alice 1953- .... **CLC 90**
See also CA 109; CANR 40
McElroy, Joseph 1930-................**CLC 5, 47**
See also CA 17-20R
McEwan, Ian (Russell) 1948- .... **CLC 13, 66;**
DAM NOV
See also BEST 90:4; CA 61-64; CANR 14, 41;
DLB 14; MTCW
McFadden, David 1940- .... **CLC 48**
See also CA 104; DLB 60; INT 104
McFarland, Dennis 1950- .... **CLC 65**
McGahern, John 1934-**CLC 5, 9, 48; SSC 17**
See also CA 17-20R; CANR 29; DLB 14;
MTCW
McGinley, Patrick (Anthony) 1937- . **CLC 41**
See also CA 120; 127; CANR 56; INT 127
McGinley, Phyllis 1905-1978 .... **CLC 14**
See also CA 9-12R; 77-80; CANR 19; DLB 11,
48; SATA 2, 44; SATA-Obit 24
McGinniss, Joe 1942- .... **CLC 32**
See also AITN 2; BEST 89:2; CA 25-28R;
CANR 26; INT CANR-26
McGivern, Maureen Daly
See Daly, Maureen
McGrath, Patrick 1950- .... **CLC 55**
See also CA 136
McGrath, Thomas (Matthew) 1916-1990CLC
28, 59; DAM POET
See also CA 9-12R; 132; CANR 6, 33; MTCW;
SATA 41; SATA-Obit 66
McGuane, Thomas (Francis III) 1939-**CLC 3,**
7, 18, 45
See also AITN 2; CA 49-52; CANR 5, 24, 49;
DLB 2; DLBY 80; INT CANR-24; MTCW
McGuckian, Medbh 1950- ..... **CLC 48; DAM**
POET
See also CA 143; DLB 40
McHale, Tom 1942(?)-1982 .... **CLC 3, 5**
See also AITN 1; CA 77-80; 106
McIlvanney, William 1936- .... **CLC 42**
See also CA 25-28R; CANR 61; DLB 14
McIlwraith, Maureen Mollie Hunter
See Hunter, Mollie
See also SATA 2
McInerney, Jay 1955- ... **CLC 34; DAM POP**
See also AAYA 18; CA 116; 123; CANR 45;
INT 123
McIntyre, Vonda N(eel) 1948- .... **CLC 18**
See also CA 81-84; CANR 17, 34; MTCW
McKay, ClaudeTCLC 7, 41; BLC; DAB; PC 2
See also McKay, Festus Claudius

See also DLB 4, 45, 51, 117
McKay, Festus Claudius 1889-1948
See McKay, Claude
See also BW 1; CA 104; 124; DA; DAC; DAM
MST, MULT, NOV, POET; MTCW; WLC
McKuen, Rod 1933-......................... **CLC 1, 3**
See also AITN 1; CA 41-44R; CANR 40
McLoughlin, R. B.
See Mencken, H(enry) L(ouis)
McLuhan, (Herbert) Marshall 1911-1980
CLC 37, 83
See also CA 9-12R; 102; CANR 12, 34, 61;
DLB 88; INT CANR-12; MTCW
McMillan, Terry (L.) 1951-**CLC 50, 61; DAM**
MULT, NOV, POP
See also AAYA 21; BW 2; CA 140; CANR 60
McMurtry, Larry (Jeff) 1936-**CLC 2, 3, 7, 11,**
27, 44; DAM NOV, POP
See also AAYA 15; AITN 2; BEST 89:2; CA 5-
8R; CANR 19, 43, 64; CDALB 1968-1988;
DLB 2, 143; DLBY 80, 87; MTCW
McNally, T. M. 1961- .... **CLC 82**
McNally, Terrence 1939-....**CLC 4, 7, 41, 91;**
DAM DRAM
See also CA 45-48; CANR 2, 56; DLB 7
McNamer, Deirdre 1950- .... **CLC 70**
McNeile, Herman Cyril 1888-1937
See Sapper
See also DLB 77
McNickle, (William) D'Arcy 1904-1977 **C L C**
89; DAM MULT
See also CA 9-12R; 85-88; CANR 5, 45; DLB
175; NNAL; SATA-Obit 22
McPhee, John (Angus) 1931- .... **CLC 36**
See also BEST 90:1; CA 65-68; CANR 20, 46,
64; MTCW
McPherson, James Alan 1943-... **CLC 19, 77**
See also BW 1; CA 25-28R; CAAS 17; CANR
24; DLB 38; MTCW
McPherson, William (Alexander) 1933- **C L C**
34
See also CA 69-72; CANR 28; INT CANR-28
Mead, Margaret 1901-1978 .... **CLC 37**
See also AITN 1; CA 1-4R; 81-84; CANR 4;
MTCW; SATA-Obit 20
Meaker, Marijane (Agnes) 1927-
See Kerr, M. E.
See also CA 107; CANR 37, 63; INT 107;
JRDA; MAICYA; MTCW; SATA 20, 61
Medoff, Mark (Howard) 1940- ... **CLC 6, 23;**
DAM DRAM
See also AITN 1; CA 53-56; CANR 5; DLB 7;
INT CANR-5
Medvedev, P. N.
See Bakhtin, Mikhail Mikhailovich
Meged, Aharon
See Megged, Aharon
Meged, Aron
See Megged, Aharon
Megged, Aharon 1920- .... **CLC 9**
See also CA 49-52; CAAS 13; CANR 1
Mehta, Ved (Parkash) 1934- .... **CLC 37**
See also CA 1-4R; CANR 2, 23; MTCW
Melanter
See Blackmore, R(ichard) D(oddridge)
Melikow, Loris
See Hofmannsthal, Hugo von
Melmoth, Sebastian
See Wilde, Oscar (Fingal O'Flahertie Wills)
Meltzer, Milton 1915- .... **CLC 26**
See also AAYA 8; CA 13-16R; CANR 38; CLR
13; DLB 61; JRDA; MAICYA; SAAS 1;
SATA 1, 50, 80

Melville, Herman 1819-1891NCLC 3, 12, 29,
45, 49; DA; DAB; DAC; DAM MST, NOV;
SSC 1, 17; WLC
See also CDALB 1640-1865; DLB 3, 74; SATA
59
Menander c. 342B.C.-c. 292B.C. ..... **CMLC 9;**
DAM DRAM; DC 3
See also DLB 176
Mencken, H(enry) L(ouis) 1880-1956 **T C L C**
13
See also CA 105; 125; CDALB 1917-1929;
DLB 11, 29, 63, 137; MTCW
Mendelsohn, Jane 1965(?)- .... **CLC 99**
See also CA 154
Mercer, David 1928-1980**CLC 5; DAM DRAM**
See also CA 9-12R; 102; CANR 23; DLB 13;
MTCW
Merchant, Paul
See Ellison, Harlan (Jay)
Meredith, George 1828-1909 . **TCLC 17, 43;**
DAM POET
See also CA 117; 153; CDBLB 1832-1890;
DLB 18, 35, 57, 159
Meredith, William (Morris) 1919-**CLC 4, 13,**
22, 55; DAM POET
See also CA 9-12R; CAAS 14; CANR 6, 40;
DLB 5
Merezhkovsky, Dmitry Sergeyevich 1865-1941
TCLC 29
Merimee, Prosper 1803-1870NCLC 6, 65; SSC
7
See also DLB 119
Merkin, Daphne 1954- .... **CLC 44**
See also CA 123
Merlin, Arthur
See Blish, James (Benjamin)
Merrill, James (Ingram) 1926-1995**CLC 2, 3,**
6, 8, 13, 18, 34, 91; DAM POET
See also CA 13-16R; 147; CANR 10, 49, 63;
DLB 5, 165; DLBY 85; INT CANR-10;
MTCW
Merriman, Alex
See Silverberg, Robert
Merritt, E. B.
See Waddington, Miriam
Merton, Thomas 1915-1968**CLC 1, 3, 11, 34,**
83; PC 10
See also CA 5-8R; 25-28R; CANR 22, 53; DLB
48; DLBY 81; MTCW
Merwin, W(illiam) S(tanley) 1927- **CLC 1, 2,**
3, 5, 8, 13, 18, 45, 88; DAM POET
See also CA 13-16R; CANR 15, 51; DLB 5,
169; INT CANR-15; MTCW
Metcalf, John 1938- .... **CLC 37**
See also CA 113; DLB 60
Metcalf, Suzanne
See Baum, L(yman) Frank
Mew, Charlotte (Mary) 1870-1928 .. **TCLC 8**
See also CA 105; DLB 19, 135
Mewshaw, Michael 1943- .... **CLC 9**
See also CA 53-56; CANR 7, 47; DLBY 80
Meyer, June
See Jordan, June
Meyer, Lynn
See Slavitt, David R(ytman)
Meyer-Meyrink, Gustav 1868-1932
See Meyrink, Gustav
See also CA 117
Meyers, Jeffrey 1939-......................... **CLC 39**
See also CA 73-76; CANR 54; DLB 111
Meynell, Alice (Christina Gertrude Thompson)
1847-1922 .... **TCLC 6**
See also CA 104; DLB 19, 98

Meyrink, Gustav .... **TCLC 21**
    See also Meyer-Meyrink, Gustav
    See also DLB 81
Michaels, Leonard 1933- **CLC 6, 25; SSC 16**
    See also CA 61-64; CANR 21, 62; DLB 130;
    MTCW
Michaux, Henri 1899-1984 .... **CLC 8, 19**
    See also CA 85-88; 114
Micheaux, Oscar 1884-1951 .... **TCLC 76**
    See also DLB 50
Michelangelo 1475-1564 .... **LC 12**
Michelet, Jules 1798-1874 .... **NCLC 31**
Michener, James A(lbert) 1907(?)-1997 **C L C
    1, 5, 11, 29, 60; DAM NOV, POP**
    See also AITN 1; BEST 90:1; CA 5-8R; 161;
    CANR 21, 45; DLB 6; MTCW
Mickiewicz, Adam 1798-1855 .... **NCLC 3**
Middleton, Christopher 1926- .... **CLC 13**
    See also CA 13-16R; CANR 29, 54; DLB 40
Middleton, Richard (Barham) 1882-1911
    TCLC 56
    See also DLB 156
Middleton, Stanley 1919- .... **CLC 7, 38**
    See also CA 25-28R; CAAS 23; CANR 21, 46;
    DLB 14
Middleton, Thomas 1580-1627 **LC 33; DAM
    DRAM, MST; DC 5**
    See also DLB 58
Migueis, Jose Rodrigues 1901- .... **CLC 10**
Mikszath, Kalman 1847-1910 .... **TCLC 31**
Miles, Jack .... **CLC 100**
Miles, Josephine (Louise) 1911-1985**CLC 1, 2,
    14, 34, 39; DAM POET**
    See also CA 1-4R; 116; CANR 2, 55; DLB 48
Militant
    See Sandburg, Carl (August)
Mill, John Stuart 1806-1873 .... **NCLC 11, 58**
    See also CDBLB 1832-1890; DLB 55
Millar, Kenneth 1915-1983 .... **CLC 14; DAM
    POP**
    See also Macdonald, Ross
    See also CA 9-12R; 110; CANR 16, 63; DLB
    2; DLBD 6; DLBY 83; MTCW
Millay, E. Vincent
    See Millay, Edna St. Vincent
Millay, Edna St. Vincent 1892-1950**TCLC 4,
    49; DA; DAB; DAC; DAM MST, POET;
    PC 6; WLCS**
    See also CA 104; 130; CDALB 1917-1929;
    DLB 45; MTCW
Miller, Arthur 1915-**CLC 1, 2, 6, 10, 15, 26, 47,
    78; DA; DAB; DAC; DAM DRAM, MST;
    DC 1; WLC**
    See also AAYA 15; AITN 1; CA 1-4R; CABS
    3; CANR 2, 30, 54; CDALB 1941-1968;
    DLB 7; MTCW
Miller, Henry (Valentine) 1891-1980**CLC 1, 2,
    4, 9, 14, 43, 84; DA; DAB; DAC; DAM
    MST, NOV; WLC**
    See also CA 9-12R; 97-100; CANR 33, 64;
    CDALB 1929-1941; DLB 4, 9; DLBY 80;
    MTCW
Miller, Jason 1939(?)- .... **CLC 2**
    See also AITN 1; CA 73-76; DLB 7
Miller, Sue 1943- .... **CLC 44; DAM POP**
    See also BEST 90:3; CA 139; CANR 59; DLB
    143
Miller, Walter M(ichael, Jr.) 1923-**CLC 4, 30**
    See also CA 85-88; DLB 8
Millett, Kate 1934- .... **CLC 67**
    See also AITN 1; CA 73-76; CANR 32, 53;
    MTCW
Millhauser, Steven (Lewis) 1943- **CLC 21, 54**

See also CA 110; 111; CANR 63; DLB 2; INT
    111
Millin, Sarah Gertrude 1889-1968 ... **CLC 49**
    See also CA 102; 93-96
Milne, A(lan) A(lexander) 1882-1956**TCLC 6;
    DAB; DAC; DAM MST**
    See also CA 104; 133; CLR 1, 26; DLB 10, 77,
    100, 160; MAICYA; MTCW; YABC 1
Milner, Ron(ald) 1938- **CLC 56; BLC; DAM
    MULT**
    See also AITN 1; BW 1; CA 73-76; CANR 24;
    DLB 38; MTCW
Milnes, Richard Monckton 1809-1885**N C L C
    61**
    See also DLB 32, 184
Milosz, Czeslaw 1911- **CLC 5, 11, 22, 31, 56,
    82; DAM MST, POET; PC 8; WLCS**
    See also CA 81-84; CANR 23, 51; MTCW
Milton, John 1608-1674 ..... **LC 9; DA; DAB;
    DAC; DAM MST, POET; PC 19; WLC**
    See also CDBLB 1660-1789; DLB 131, 151
Min, Anchee 1957- .... **CLC 86**
    See also CA 146
Minehaha, Cornelius
    See Wedekind, (Benjamin) Frank(lin)
Miner, Valerie 1947- .... **CLC 40**
    See also CA 97-100; CANR 59
Minimo, Duca
    See D'Annunzio, Gabriele
Minot, Susan 1956- .... **CLC 44**
    See also CA 134
Minus, Ed 1938- .... **CLC 39**
Miranda, Javier
    See Bioy Casares, Adolfo
Mirbeau, Octave 1848-1917 .... **TCLC 55**
    See also DLB 123
Miro (Ferrer), Gabriel (Francisco Victor) 1879-
    1930 .... **TCLC 5**
    See also CA 104
Mishima, Yukio 1925-1970**CLC 2, 4, 6, 9, 27;
    DC 1; SSC 4**
    See also Hiraoka, Kimitake
    See also DLB 182
Mistral, Frederic 1830-1914 .... **TCLC 51**
    See also CA 122
Mistral, Gabriela .... **TCLC 2; HLC**
    See also Godoy Alcayaga, Lucila
Mistry, Rohinton 1952- .... **CLC 71; DAC**
    See also CA 141
Mitchell, Clyde
    See Ellison, Harlan (Jay); Silverberg, Robert
Mitchell, James Leslie 1901-1935
    See Gibbon, Lewis Grassic
    See also CA 104; DLB 15
Mitchell, Joni 1943- .... **CLC 12**
    See also CA 112
Mitchell, Joseph (Quincy) 1908-1996**CLC 98**
    See also CA 77-80; 152; DLBY 96
Mitchell, Margaret (Munnerlyn) 1900-1949
    TCLC 11; DAM NOV, POP
    See also CA 109; 125; CANR 55; DLB 9;
    MTCW
Mitchell, Peggy
    See Mitchell, Margaret (Munnerlyn)
Mitchell, S(ilas) Weir 1829-1914 ... **TCLC 36**
Mitchell, W(illiam) O(rmond) 1914-**CLC 25;
    DAC; DAM MST**
    See also CA 77-80; CANR 15, 43; DLB 88
Mitford, Mary Russell 1787-1855 ... **NCLC 4**
    See also DLB 110, 116
Mitford, Nancy 1904-1973 .... **CLC 44**
    See also CA 9-12R
Miyamoto, Yuriko 1899-1951 .... **TCLC 37**

See also DLB 180
Miyazawa Kenji 1896-1933 .... **TCLC 76**
    See also CA 157
Mizoguchi, Kenji 1898-1956 .... **TCLC 72**
Mo, Timothy (Peter) 1950(?)- .... **CLC 46**
    See also CA 117; MTCW
Modarressi, Taghi (M.) 1931- .... **CLC 44**
    See also CA 121; 134; INT 134
Modiano, Patrick (Jean) 1945- .... **CLC 18**
    See also CA 85-88; CANR 17, 40; DLB 83
Moerck, Paal
    See Roelvaag, O(le) E(dvart)
Mofolo, Thomas (Mokopu) 1875(?)-1948
    TCLC 22; BLC; DAM MULT
    See also CA 121; 153
Mohr, Nicholasa 1938-**CLC 12; DAM MULT;
    HLC**
    See also AAYA 8; CA 49-52; CANR 1, 32, 64;
    CLR 22; DLB 145; HW; JRDA; SAAS 8;
    SATA 8
Mojtabai, A(nn) G(race) 1938- **CLC 5, 9, 15,
    29**
    See also CA 85-88
Moliere 1622-1673 . **LC 28; DA; DAB; DAC;
    DAM DRAM, MST; WLC**
Molin, Charles
    See Mayne, William (James Carter)
Molnar, Ferenc 1878-1952 .. **TCLC 20; DAM
    DRAM**
    See also CA 109; 153
Momaday, N(avarre) Scott 1934- **CLC 2, 19,
    85, 95; DA; DAB; DAC; DAM MST,
    MULT, NOV, POP; WLCS**
    See also AAYA 11; CA 25-28R; CANR 14, 34;
    DLB 143, 175; INT CANR-14; MTCW;
    NNAL; SATA 48; SATA-Brief 30
Monette, Paul 1945-1995 .... **CLC 82**
    See also CA 139; 147
Monroe, Harriet 1860-1936 .... **TCLC 12**
    See also CA 109; DLB 54, 91
Monroe, Lyle
    See Heinlein, Robert A(nson)
Montagu, Elizabeth 1917- .... **NCLC 7**
    See also CA 9-12R
Montagu, Mary (Pierrepont) Wortley 1689-
    1762 .... **LC 9; PC 16**
    See also DLB 95, 101
Montagu, W. H.
    See Coleridge, Samuel Taylor
Montague, John (Patrick) 1929- **CLC 13, 46**
    See also CA 9-12R; CANR 9; DLB 40; MTCW
Montaigne, Michel (Eyquem) de 1533-1592
    LC 8; DA; DAB; DAC; DAM MST; WLC
Montale, Eugenio 1896-1981**CLC 7, 9, 18; PC
    13**
    See also CA 17-20R; 104; CANR 30; DLB 114;
    MTCW
Montesquieu, Charles-Louis de Secondat 1689-
    1755 .... **LC 7**
Montgomery, (Robert) Bruce 1921-1978
    See Crispin, Edmund
    See also CA 104
Montgomery, L(ucy) M(aud) 1874-1942
    TCLC 51; DAC; DAM MST
    See also AAYA 12; CA 108; 137; CLR 8; DLB
    92; DLBD 14; JRDA; MAICYA; YABC 1
Montgomery, Marion H., Jr. 1925- .... **CLC 7**
    See also AITN 1; CA 1-4R; CANR 3, 48; DLB
    6
Montgomery, Max
    See Davenport, Guy (Mattison, Jr.)
Montherlant, Henry (Milon) de 1896-1972
    CLC 8, 19; DAM DRAM

See also CA 85-88; 37-40R; DLB 72; MTCW

Monty Python
See Chapman, Graham; Cleese, John (Marwood); Gilliam, Terry (Vance); Idle, Eric; Jones, Terence Graham Parry; Palin, Michael (Edward)
See also AAYA 7

Moodie, Susanna (Strickland) 1803-1885 **NCLC 14**
See also DLB 99

Mooney, Edward 1951-
See Mooney, Ted
See also CA 130

Mooney, Ted .... **CLC 25**
See also Mooney, Edward

Moorcock, Michael (John) 1939-**CLC 5, 27, 58**
See also CA 45-48; CAAS 5; CANR 2, 17, 38, 64; DLB 14; MTCW; SATA 93

Moore, Brian 1921- **CLC 1, 3, 5, 7, 8, 19, 32, 90; DAB; DAC; DAM MST**
See also CA 1-4R; CANR 1, 25, 42, 63; MTCW

Moore, Edward
See Muir, Edwin

Moore, George Augustus 1852-1933**TCLC 7; SSC 19**
See also CA 104; DLB 10, 18, 57, 135

Moore, Lorrie .... **CLC 39, 45, 68**
See also Moore, Marie Lorena

Moore, Marianne (Craig) 1887-1972**CLC 1, 2, 4, 8, 10, 13, 19, 47; DA; DAB; DAC; DAM MST, POET; PC 4; WLCS**
See also CA 1-4R; 33-36R; CANR 3, 61; CDALB 1929-1941; DLB 45; DLBD 7; MTCW; SATA 20

Moore, Marie Lorena 1957-
See Moore, Lorrie
See also CA 116; CANR 39

Moore, Thomas 1779-1852 .... **NCLC 6**
See also DLB 96, 144

Morand, Paul 1888-1976 .... **CLC 41; SSC 22**
See also CA 69-72; DLB 65

Morante, Elsa 1918-1985 .... **CLC 8, 47**
See also CA 85-88; 117; CANR 35; DLB 177; MTCW

Moravia, Alberto 1907-1990**CLC 2, 7, 11, 27, 46; SSC 26**
See Pincherle, Alberto
See also DLB 177

More, Hannah 1745-1833 .... **NCLC 27**
See also DLB 107, 109, 116, 158

More, Henry 1614-1687 .... **LC 9**
See also DLB 126

More, Sir Thomas 1478-1535 .... **LC 10, 32**

Moreas, Jean .... **TCLC 18**
See also Papadiamantopoulos, Johannes

Morgan, Berry 1919-............................ **CLC 6**
See also CA 49-52; DLB 6

Morgan, Claire
See Highsmith, (Mary) Patricia

Morgan, Edwin (George) 1920- .... **CLC 31**
See also CA 5-8R; CANR 3, 43; DLB 27

Morgan, (George) Frederick 1922- .. **CLC 23**
See also CA 17-20R; CANR 21

Morgan, Harriet
See Mencken, H(enry) L(ouis)

Morgan, Jane
See Cooper, James Fenimore

Morgan, Janet 1945- .... **CLC 39**
See also CA 65-68

Morgan, Lady 1776(?)-1859 .... **NCLC 29**
See also DLB 116, 158

Morgan, Robin 1941- .... **CLC 2**
See also CA 69-72; CANR 29; MTCW; SATA 80

Morgan, Scott
See Kuttner, Henry

Morgan, Seth 1949(?)-1990 .... **CLC 65**
See also CA 132

Morgenstern, Christian 1871-1914 . **TCLC 8**
See also CA 105

Morgenstern, S.
See Goldman, William (W.)

Moricz, Zsigmond 1879-1942 .... **TCLC 33**

Morike, Eduard (Friedrich) 1804-1875**NCLC 10**
See also DLB 133

Mori Ogai .... **TCLC 14**
See also Mori Rintaro

Mori Rintaro 1862-1922
See Mori Ogai
See also CA 110

Moritz, Karl Philipp 1756-1793 .... **LC 2**
See also DLB 94

Morland, Peter Henry
See Faust, Frederick (Schiller)

Morren, Theophil
See Hofmannsthal, Hugo von

Morris, Bill 1952- .... **CLC 76**

Morris, Julian
See West, Morris L(anglo)

Morris, Steveland Judkins 1950(?)-
See Wonder, Stevie
See also CA 111

Morris, William 1834-1896 .... **NCLC 4**
See also CDBLB 1832-1890; DLB 18, 35, 57, 156, 178, 184

Morris, Wright 1910- ...... **CLC 1, 3, 7, 18, 37**
See also CA 9-12R; CANR 21; DLB 2; DLBY 81; MTCW

Morrison, Arthur 1863-1945 .... **TCLC 72**
See also CA 120; 157; DLB 70, 135

Morrison, Chloe Anthony Wofford
See Morrison, Toni

Morrison, James Douglas 1943-1971
See Morrison, Jim
See also CA 73-76; CANR 40

Morrison, Jim .... **CLC 17**
See also Morrison, James Douglas

Morrison, Toni 1931-**CLC 4, 10, 22, 55, 81, 87; BLC; DA; DAB; DAC; DAM MST, MULT, NOV, POP**
See also AAYA 1, 22; BW 2; CA 29-32R; CANR 27, 42; CDALB 1968-1988; DLB 6, 33, 143; DLBY 81; MTCW; SATA 57

Morrison, Van 1945- .... **CLC 21**
See also CA 116

Morrissy, Mary 1958- .... **CLC 99**

Mortimer, John (Clifford) 1923-**CLC 28, 43; DAM DRAM, POP**
See also CA 13-16R; CANR 21; CDBLB 1960 to Present; DLB 13; INT CANR-21; MTCW

Mortimer, Penelope (Ruth) 1918-....... **CLC 5**
See also CA 57-60; CANR 45

Morton, Anthony
See Creasey, John

Mosca, Gaetano 1858-1941 .... **TCLC 75**

Mosher, Howard Frank 1943- .... **CLC 62**
See also CA 139

Mosley, Nicholas 1923- .... **CLC 43, 70**
See also CA 69-72; CANR 41, 60; DLB 14

Mosley, Walter 1952- **CLC 97; DAM MULT, POP**
See also AAYA 17; BW 2; CA 142; CANR 57

Moss, Howard 1922-1987 **CLC 7, 14, 45, 50; DAM POET**
See also CA 1-4R; 123; CANR 1, 44; DLB 5

Mossgiel, Rab
See Burns, Robert

Motion, Andrew (Peter) 1952- .... **CLC 47**
See also CA 146; DLB 40

Motley, Willard (Francis) 1909-1965 **CLC 18**
See also BW 1; CA 117; 106; DLB 76, 143

Motoori, Norinaga 1730-1801 .... **NCLC 45**

Mott, Michael (Charles Alston) 1930-**CLC 15, 34**
See also CA 5-8R; CAAS 7; CANR 7, 29

Mountain Wolf Woman 1884-1960 .. **CLC 92**
See also CA 144; NNAL

Moure, Erin 1955- .... **CLC 88**
See also CA 113; DLB 60

Mowat, Farley (McGill) 1921-**CLC 26; DAC; DAM MST**
See also AAYA 1; CA 1-4R; CANR 4, 24, 42; CLR 20; DLB 68; INT CANR-24; JRDA; MAICYA; MTCW; SATA 3, 55

Moyers, Bill 1934- .... **CLC 74**
See also AITN 2; CA 61-64; CANR 31, 52

Mphahlele, Es'kia
See Mphahlele, Ezekiel
See also DLB 125

Mphahlele, Ezekiel 1919-1983**CLC 25; BLC; DAM MULT**
See also Mphahlele, Es'kia
See also BW 2; CA 81-84; CANR 26

Mqhayi, S(amuel) E(dward) K(rune Loliwe) 1875-1945**TCLC 25; BLC; DAM MULT**
See also CA 153

Mrozek, Slawomir 1930-................. **CLC 3, 13**
See also CA 13-16R; CAAS 10; CANR 29; MTCW

Mrs. Belloc-Lowndes
See Lowndes, Marie Adelaide (Belloc)

Mtwa, Percy (?)- .... **CLC 47**

Mueller, Lisel 1924- .... **CLC 13, 51**
See also CA 93-96; DLB 105

Muir, Edwin 1887-1959 .... **TCLC 2**
See also CA 104; DLB 20, 100

Muir, John 1838-1914 .... **TCLC 28**

Mujica Lainez, Manuel 1910-1984 ... **CLC 31**
See also Lainez, Manuel Mujica
See also CA 81-84; 112; CANR 32; HW

Mukherjee, Bharati 1940-**CLC 53; DAM NOV**
See also BEST 89:2; CA 107; CANR 45; DLB 60; MTCW

Muldoon, Paul 1951-**CLC 32, 72; DAM POET**
See also CA 113; 129; CANR 52; DLB 40; INT 129

Mulisch, Harry 1927- .... **CLC 42**
See also CA 9-12R; CANR 6, 26, 56

Mull, Martin 1943- .... **CLC 17**
See also CA 105

Mulock, Dinah Maria
See Craik, Dinah Maria (Mulock)

Munford, Robert 1737(?)-1783 .... **LC 5**
See also DLB 31

Mungo, Raymond 1946-..................... **CLC 72**
See also CA 49-52; CANR 2

Munro, Alice 1931- .... **CLC 6, 10, 19, 50, 95; DAC; DAM MST, NOV; SSC 3; WLCS**
See also AITN 2; CA 33-36R; CANR 33, 53; DLB 53; MTCW; SATA 29

Munro, H(ector) H(ugh) 1870-1916
See Saki
See also CA 104; 130; CDBLB 1890-1914; DA; DAB; DAC; DAM MST, NOV; DLB 34, 162; MTCW; WLC

Murasaki, Lady .... **CMLC 1**

Murdoch, (Jean) Iris 1919-**CLC 1, 2, 3, 4, 6, 8, 11, 15, 22, 31, 51; DAB; DAC; DAM MST,**

NOV
See also CA 13-16R; CANR 8, 43; CDBLB
1960 to Present; DLB 14; INT CANR-8;
MTCW
Murfree, Mary Noailles 1850-1922 ... **SSC 22**
See also CA 122; DLB 12, 74
Murnau, Friedrich Wilhelm
See Plumpe, Friedrich Wilhelm
Murphy, Richard 1927- .... **CLC 41**
See also CA 29-32R; DLB 40
Murphy, Sylvia 1937- .... **CLC 34**
See also CA 121
Murphy, Thomas (Bernard) 1935- ... **CLC 51**
See also CA 101
Murray, Albert L. 1916- .... **CLC 73**
See also BW 2; CA 49-52; CANR 26, 52; DLB
38
Murray, Judith Sargent 1751-1820 **NCLC 63**
See also DLB 37
Murray, Les(lie) A(llan) 1938- **CLC 40; DAM**
POET
See also CA 21-24R; CANR 11, 27, 56
Murry, J. Middleton
See Murry, John Middleton
Murry, John Middleton 1889-1957 **TCLC 16**
See also CA 118; DLB 149
Musgrave, Susan 1951- .... **CLC 13, 54**
See also CA 69-72; CANR 45
Musil, Robert (Edler von) 1880-1942 **T C L C**
12, 68; SSC 18
See also CA 109; CANR 55; DLB 81, 124
Muske, Carol 1945- .... **CLC 90**
See also Muske-Dukes, Carol (Anne)
Muske-Dukes, Carol (Anne) 1945-
See Muske, Carol
See also CA 65-68; CANR 32
Musset, (Louis Charles) Alfred de 1810-1857
NCLC 7
My Brother's Brother
See Chekhov, Anton (Pavlovich)
Myers, L(eopold) H(amilton) 1881-1944
TCLC 59
See also CA 157; DLB 15
Myers, Walter Dean 1937- ..... **CLC 35; BLC;**
DAM MULT, NOV
See also AAYA 4; BW 2; CA 33-36R; CANR
20, 42; CLR 4, 16, 35; DLB 33; INT CANR-
20; JRDA; MAICYA; SAAS 2; SATA 41, 71;
SATA-Brief 27
Myers, Walter M.
See Myers, Walter Dean
Myles, Symon
See Follett, Ken(neth Martin)
Nabokov, Vladimir (Vladimirovich) 1899-1977
CLC 1, 2, 3, 6, 8, 11, 15, 23, 44, 46, 64;
DA; DAB; DAC; DAM MST, NOV; SSC
11; WLC
See also CA 5-8R; 69-72; CANR 20; CDALB
1941-1968; DLB 2; DLBD 3; DLBY 80, 91;
MTCW
Nagai Kafu 1879-1959 .... **TCLC 51**
See also Nagai Sokichi
See also DLB 180
Nagai Sokichi 1879-1959
See Nagai Kafu
See also CA 117
Nagy, Laszlo 1925-1978 .... **CLC 7**
See also CA 129; 112
Naipaul, Shiva(dhar Srinivasa) 1945-1985
CLC 32, 39; DAM NOV
See also CA 110; 112; 116; CANR 33; DLB
157; DLBY 85; MTCW
Naipaul, V(idiadhar) S(urajprasad) 1932-

CLC 4, 7, 9, 13, 18, 37, 105; DAB; DAC;
DAM MST, NOV
See also CA 1-4R; CANR 1, 33, 51; CDBLB
1960 to Present; DLB 125; DLBY 85;
MTCW
Nakos, Lilika 1899(?)- .... **CLC 29**
Narayan, R(asipuram) K(rishnaswami) 1906-
CLC 7, 28, 47; DAM NOV; SSC 25
See also CA 81-84; CANR 33, 61; MTCW;
SATA 62
Nash, (Frediric) Ogden 1902-1971 . **CLC 23;**
DAM POET; PC 21
See also CA 13-14; 29-32R; CANR 34, 61; CAP
1; DLB 11; MAICYA; MTCW; SATA 2, 46
Nashe, Thomas 1567-1601 .... **LC 41**
Nathan, Daniel
See Dannay, Frederic
Nathan, George Jean 1882-1958 .... **TCLC 18**
See also Hatteras, Owen
See also CA 114; DLB 137
Natsume, Kinnosuke 1867-1916
See Natsume, Soseki
See also CA 104
Natsume, Soseki 1867-1916 .... **TCLC 2, 10**
See also Natsume, Kinnosuke
See also DLB 180
Natti, (Mary) Lee 1919-
See Kingman, Lee
See also CA 5-8R; CANR 2
Naylor, Gloria 1950- **CLC 28, 52; BLC; DA;**
DAC; DAM MST, MULT, NOV, POP;
WLCS
See also AAYA 6; BW 2; CA 107; CANR 27,
51; DLB 173; MTCW
Neihardt, John Gneisenau 1881-1973 **CLC 32**
See also CA 13-14; CAP 1; DLB 9, 54
Nekrasov, Nikolai Alekseevich 1821-1878
NCLC 11
Nelligan, Emile 1879-1941 .... **TCLC 14**
See also CA 114; DLB 92
Nelson, Willie 1933- .... **CLC 17**
See also CA 107
Nemerov, Howard (Stanley) 1920-1991 **CLC 2,**
6, 9, 36; DAM POET
See also CA 1-4R; 134; CABS 2; CANR 1, 27,
53; DLB 5, 6; DLBY 83; INT CANR-27;
MTCW
Neruda, Pablo 1904-1973 **CLC 1, 2, 5, 7, 9, 28,**
62; DA; DAB; DAC; DAM MST, MULT,
POET; HLC; PC 4; WLC
See also CA 19-20; 45-48; CAP 2; HW; MTCW
Nerval, Gerard de 1808-1855 **NCLC 1, 67; PC**
13; SSC 18
Nervo, (Jose) Amado (Ruiz de) 1870-1919
TCLC 11
See also CA 109; 131; HW
Nessi, Pio Baroja y
See Baroja (y Nessi), Pio
Nestroy, Johann 1801-1862 .... **NCLC 42**
See also DLB 133
Netterville, Luke
See O'Grady, Standish (James)
Neufeld, John (Arthur) 1938- .... **CLC 17**
See also AAYA 11; CA 25-28R; CANR 11, 37,
56; MAICYA; SAAS 3; SATA 6, 81
Neville, Emily Cheney 1919- .... **CLC 12**
See also CA 5-8R; CANR 3, 37; JRDA;
MAICYA; SAAS 2; SATA 1
Newbound, Bernard Slade 1930-
See Slade, Bernard
See also CA 81-84; CANR 49; DAM DRAM
Newby, P(ercy) H(oward) 1918-1997 **CLC 2,**
13; DAM NOV

See also CA 5-8R; 161; CANR 32; DLB 15;
MTCW
Newlove, Donald 1928- .... **CLC 6**
See also CA 29-32R; CANR 25
Newlove, John (Herbert) 1938- .... **CLC 14**
See also CA 21-24R; CANR 9, 25
Newman, Charles 1938- .... **CLC 2, 8**
See also CA 21-24R
Newman, Edwin (Harold) 1919- .... **CLC 14**
See also AITN 1; CA 69-72; CANR 5
Newman, John Henry 1801-1890 .. **NCLC 38**
See also DLB 18, 32, 55
Newton, Suzanne 1936- .... **CLC 35**
See also CA 41-44R; CANR 14; JRDA; SATA
5, 77
Nexo, Martin Andersen 1869-1954 **TCLC 43**
Nezval, Vitezslav 1900-1958 .... **TCLC 44**
See also CA 123
Ng, Fae Myenne 1957(?)- .... **CLC 81**
See also CA 146
Ngema, Mbongeni 1955- .... **CLC 57**
See also BW 2; CA 143
Ngugi, James T(hiong'o) .... **CLC 3, 7, 13**
See also Ngugi wa Thiong'o
Ngugi wa Thiong'o 1938- **CLC 36; BLC; DAM**
MULT, NOV
See also Ngugi, James T(hiong'o)
See also BW 2; CA 81-84; CANR 27, 58; DLB
125; MTCW
Nichol, B(arrie) P(hillip) 1944-1988 **CLC 18**
See also CA 53-56; DLB 53; SATA 66
Nichols, John (Treadwell) 1940- .... **CLC 38**
See also CA 9-12R; CAAS 2; CANR 6; DLBY
82
Nichols, Leigh
See Koontz, Dean R(ay)
Nichols, Peter (Richard) 1927- **CLC 5, 36, 65**
See also CA 104; CANR 33; DLB 13; MTCW
Nicolas, F. R. E.
See Freeling, Nicolas
Niedecker, Lorine 1903-1970 .... **CLC 10, 42;**
DAM POET
See also CA 25-28; CAP 2; DLB 48
Nietzsche, Friedrich (Wilhelm) 1844-1900
TCLC 10, 18, 55
See also CA 107; 121; DLB 129
Nievo, Ippolito 1831-1861 .... **NCLC 22**
Nightingale, Anne Redmon 1943-
See Redmon, Anne
See also CA 103
Nik. T. O.
See Annensky, Innokenty (Fyodorovich)
Nin, Anais 1903-1977 **CLC 1, 4, 8, 11, 14, 60;**
DAM NOV, POP; SSC 10
See also AITN 2; CA 13-16R; 69-72; CANR
22, 53; DLB 2, 4, 152; MTCW
Nishiwaki, Junzaburo 1894-1982 .... **PC 15**
See also CA 107
Nissenson, Hugh 1933- .... **CLC 4, 9**
See also CA 17-20R; CANR 27; DLB 28
Niven, Larry .... **CLC 8**
See also Niven, Laurence Van Cott
See also DLB 8
Niven, Laurence Van Cott 1938-
See Niven, Larry
See also CA 21-24R; CAAS 12; CANR 14, 44;
DAM POP; MTCW; SATA 95
Nixon, Agnes Eckhardt 1927- .... **CLC 21**
See also CA 110
Nizan, Paul 1905-1940 .... **TCLC 40**
See also CA 161; DLB 72
Nkosi, Lewis 1936- .... **CLC 45; BLC; DAM**
MULT

See also BW 1; CA 65-68; CANR 27; DLB 157
Nodier, (Jean) Charles (Emmanuel) 1780-1844
NCLC 19
See also DLB 119
Nolan, Christopher 1965- .... **CLC 58**
See also CA 111
Noon, Jeff 1957- .... **CLC 91**
See also CA 148
Norden, Charles
See Durrell, Lawrence (George)
Nordhoff, Charles (Bernard) 1887-1947
TCLC 23
See also CA 108; DLB 9; SATA 23
Norfolk, Lawrence 1963- .... **CLC 76**
See also CA 144
Norman, Marsha 1947-**CLC 28; DAM DRAM;**
DC 8
See also CA 105; CABS 3; CANR 41; DLBY
84
Norris, Frank 1870-1902 .... **SSC 28**
See also Norris, (Benjamin) Frank(lin, Jr.)
See also CDALB 1865-1917; DLB 12, 71
Norris, (Benjamin) Frank(lin, Jr.) 1870-1902
TCLC 24
See also Norris, Frank
See also CA 110; 160
Norris, Leslie 1921- .... **CLC 14**
See also CA 11-12; CANR 14; CAP 1; DLB 27
North, Andrew
See Norton, Andre
North, Anthony
See Koontz, Dean R(ay)
North, Captain George
See Stevenson, Robert Louis (Balfour)
North, Milou
See Erdrich, Louise
Northrup, B. A.
See Hubbard, L(afayette) Ron(ald)
North Staffs
See Hulme, T(homas) E(rnest)
Norton, Alice Mary
See Norton, Andre
See also MAICYA; SATA 1, 43
Norton, Andre 1912- .... **CLC 12**
See also Norton, Alice Mary
See also AAYA 14; CA 1-4R; CANR 2, 31; DLB
8, 52; JRDA; MTCW; SATA 91
Norton, Caroline 1808-1877 .... **NCLC 47**
See also DLB 21, 159
Norway, Nevil Shute 1899-1960
See Shute, Nevil
See also CA 102; 93-96
Norwid, Cyprian Kamil 1821-1883 **NCLC 17**
Nosille, Nabrah
See Ellison, Harlan (Jay)
Nossack, Hans Erich 1901-1978 .... **CLC 6**
See also CA 93-96; 85-88; DLB 69
Nostradamus 1503-1566 .... **LC 27**
Nosu, Chuji
See Ozu, Yasujiro
Notenburg, Eleanora (Genrikhovna) von
See Guro, Elena
Nova, Craig 1945- .... **CLC 7, 31**
See also CA 45-48; CANR 2, 53
Novak, Joseph
See Kosinski, Jerzy (Nikodem)
Novalis 1772-1801 .... **NCLC 13**
See also DLB 90
Novis, Emile
See Weil, Simone (Adolphine)
Nowlan, Alden (Albert) 1933-1983 **CLC 15;**
DAC; DAM MST
See also CA 9-12R; CANR 5; DLB 53

Noyes, Alfred 1880-1958 .... **TCLC 7**
See also CA 104; DLB 20
Nunn, Kem .... **CLC 34**
See also CA 159
Nye, Robert 1939- .. **CLC 13, 42; DAM NOV**
See also CA 33-36R; CANR 29; DLB 14;
MTCW; SATA 6
Nyro, Laura 1947- .... **CLC 17**
Oates, Joyce Carol 1938-**CLC 1, 2, 3, 6, 9, 11,**
15, 19, 33, 52, 108; DA; DAB; DAC; DAM
MST, NOV, POP; SSC 6; WLC
See also AAYA 15; AITN 1; BEST 89:2; CA 5-
8R; CANR 25, 45; CDALB 1968-1988; DLB
2, 5, 130; DLBY 81; INT CANR-25; MTCW
O'Brien, Darcy 1939- .... **CLC 11**
See also CA 21-24R; CANR 8, 59
O'Brien, E. G.
See Clarke, Arthur C(harles)
O'Brien, Edna 1936- **CLC 3, 5, 8, 13, 36, 65;**
DAM NOV; SSC 10
See also CA 1-4R; CANR 6, 41; CDBLB 1960
to Present; DLB 14; MTCW
O'Brien, Fitz-James 1828-1862 ..... **NCLC 21**
See also DLB 74
O'Brien, Flann .... **CLC 1, 4, 5, 7, 10, 47**
See also O Nuallain, Brian
O'Brien, Richard 1942- .... **CLC 17**
See also CA 124
O'Brien, (William) Tim(othy) 1946- . **CLC 7,**
19, 40, 103; DAM POP
See also AAYA 16; CA 85-88; CANR 40, 58;
DLB 152; DLBD 9; DLBY 80
Obstfelder, Sigbjoern 1866-1900 ... **TCLC 23**
See also CA 123
O'Casey, Sean 1880-1964**CLC 1, 5, 9, 11, 15,**
88; DAB; DAC; DAM DRAM, MST;
WLCS
See also CA 89-92; CANR 62; CDBLB 1914-
1945; DLB 10; MTCW
O'Cathasaigh, Sean
See O'Casey, Sean
Ochs, Phil 1940-1976 .... **CLC 17**
See also CA 65-68
O'Connor, Edwin (Greene) 1918-1968**CLC 14**
See also CA 93-96; 25-28R
O'Connor, (Mary) Flannery 1925-1964 **C L C**
1, 2, 3, 6, 10, 13, 15, 21, 66, 104; DA; DAB;
DAC; DAM MST, NOV; SSC 1, 23; WLC
See also AAYA 7; CA 1-4R; CANR 3, 41;
CDALB 1941-1968; DLB 2, 152; DLBD 12;
DLBY 80; MTCW
O'Connor, Frank .... **CLC 23; SSC 5**
See also O'Donovan, Michael John
See also DLB 162
O'Dell, Scott 1898-1989 .... **CLC 30**
See also AAYA 3; CA 61-64; 129; CANR 12,
30; CLR 1, 16; DLB 52; JRDA; MAICYA;
SATA 12, 60
Odets, Clifford 1906-1963**CLC 2, 28, 98; DAM**
DRAM; DC 6
See also CA 85-88; CANR 62; DLB 7, 26;
MTCW
O'Doherty, Brian 1934- .... **CLC 76**
See also CA 105
O'Donnell, K. M.
See Malzberg, Barry N(athaniel)
O'Donnell, Lawrence
See Kuttner, Henry
O'Donovan, Michael John 1903-1966**CLC 14**
See also O'Connor, Frank
See also CA 93-96
Oe, Kenzaburo 1935- **CLC 10, 36, 86; DAM**
NOV; SSC 20

See also CA 97-100; CANR 36, 50; DLB 182;
DLBY 94; MTCW
O'Faolain, Julia 1932- .... **CLC 6, 19, 47, 108**
See also CA 81-84; CAAS 2; CANR 12, 61;
DLB 14; MTCW
O'Faolain, Sean 1900-1991 **CLC 1, 7, 14, 32,**
70; SSC 13
See also CA 61-64; 134; CANR 12; DLB 15,
162; MTCW
O'Flaherty, Liam 1896-1984**CLC 5, 34; SSC 6**
See also CA 101; 113; CANR 35; DLB 36, 162;
DLBY 84; MTCW
Ogilvy, Gavin
See Barrie, J(ames) M(atthew)
O'Grady, Standish (James) 1846-1928**T C L C**
5
See also CA 104; 157
O'Grady, Timothy 1951- .... **CLC 59**
See also CA 138
O'Hara, Frank 1926-1966 . **CLC 2, 5, 13, 78;**
DAM POET
See also CA 9-12R; 25-28R; CANR 33; DLB
5, 16; MTCW
O'Hara, John (Henry) 1905-1970**CLC 1, 2, 3,**
6, 11, 42; DAM NOV; SSC 15
See also CA 5-8R; 25-28R; CANR 31, 60;
CDALB 1929-1941; DLB 9, 86; DLBD 2;
MTCW
O Hehir, Diana 1922- .... **CLC 41**
See also CA 93-96
Okigbo, Christopher (Ifenayichukwu) 1932-
1967 .... **CLC 25, 84; BLC; DAM MULT,**
POET; PC 7
See also BW 1; CA 77-80; DLB 125; MTCW
Okri, Ben 1959- .... **CLC 87**
See also BW 2; CA 130; 138; DLB 157; INT
138
Olds, Sharon 1942- .... **CLC 32, 39, 85; DAM**
POET
See also CA 101; CANR 18, 41; DLB 120
Oldstyle, Jonathan
See Irving, Washington
Olesha, Yuri (Karlovich) 1899-1960 .. **CLC 8**
See also CA 85-88
Oliphant, Laurence 1829(?)-1888 .. **NCLC 47**
See also DLB 18, 166
Oliphant, Margaret (Oliphant Wilson) 1828-
1897 .... **NCLC 11, 61; SSC 25**
See also DLB 18, 159
Oliver, Mary 1935- .... **CLC 19, 34, 98**
See also CA 21-24R; CANR 9, 43; DLB 5
Olivier, Laurence (Kerr) 1907-1989 . **CLC 20**
See also CA 111; 150; 129
Olsen, Tillie 1913-**CLC 4, 13; DA; DAB; DAC;**
DAM MST; SSC 11
See also CA 1-4R; CANR 1, 43; DLB 28; DLBY
80; MTCW
Olson, Charles (John) 1910-1970**CLC 1, 2, 5,**
6, 9, 11, 29; DAM POET; PC 19
See also CA 13-16; 25-28R; CABS 2; CANR
35, 61; CAP 1; DLB 5, 16; MTCW
Olson, Toby 1937- .... **CLC 28**
See also CA 65-68; CANR 9, 31
Olyesha, Yuri
See Olesha, Yuri (Karlovich)
Ondaatje, (Philip) Michael 1943-**CLC 14, 29,**
51, 76; DAB; DAC; DAM MST
See also CA 77-80; CANR 42; DLB 60
Oneal, Elizabeth 1934-
See Oneal, Zibby
See also CA 106; CANR 28; MAICYA; SATA
30, 82
Oneal, Zibby .... **CLC 30**

See also Oneal, Elizabeth
See also AAYA 5; CLR 13; JRDA
O'Neill, Eugene (Gladstone) 1888-1953**TCLC
   1, 6, 27, 49; DA; DAB; DAC; DAM DRAM,
   MST; WLC**
   See also AITN 1; CA 110; 132; CDALB 1929-
   1941; DLB 7; MTCW
Onetti, Juan Carlos 1909-1994 ... **CLC 7, 10;
   DAM MULT, NOV; SSC 23**
   See also CA 85-88; 145; CANR 32, 63; DLB
   113; HW; MTCW
O Nuallain, Brian 1911-1966
   See O'Brien, Flann
   See also CA 21-22; 25-28R; CAP 2
Ophuls, Max 1902-1957 .... **TCLC 79**
   See also CA 113
Opie, Amelia 1769-1853 .... **NCLC 65**
   See also DLB 116, 159
Oppen, George 1908-1984 ...... **CLC 7, 13, 34**
   See also CA 13-16R; 113; CANR 8; DLB 5,
   165
Oppenheim, E(dward) Phillips 1866-1946
   TCLC 45
   See also CA 111; DLB 70
Opuls, Max
   See Ophuls, Max
Origen c. 185-c. 254 .... **CMLC 19**
Orlovitz, Gil 1918-1973 .... **CLC 22**
   See also CA 77-80; 45-48; DLB 2, 5
Orris
   See Ingelow, Jean
Ortega y Gasset, Jose 1883-1955 .... **TCLC 9;
   DAM MULT; HLC**
   See also CA 106; 130; HW; MTCW
Ortese, Anna Maria 1914- .... **CLC 89**
   See also DLB 177
Ortiz, Simon J(oseph) 1941-.. **CLC 45; DAM
   MULT, POET; PC 17**
   See also CA 134; DLB 120, 175; NNAL
Orton, Joe .... **CLC 4, 13, 43; DC 3**
   See also Orton, John Kingsley
   See also CDBLB 1960 to Present; DLB 13
Orton, John Kingsley 1933-1967
   See Orton, Joe
   See also CA 85-88; CANR 35; DAM DRAM;
   MTCW
Orwell, George . **TCLC 2, 6, 15, 31, 51; DAB;
   WLC**
   See also Blair, Eric (Arthur)
   See also CDBLB 1945-1960; DLB 15, 98
Osborne, David
   See Silverberg, Robert
Osborne, George
   See Silverberg, Robert
Osborne, John (James) 1929-1994**CLC 1, 2, 5,
   11, 45; DA; DAB; DAC; DAM DRAM,
   MST; WLC**
   See also CA 13-16R; 147; CANR 21, 56;
   CDBLB 1945-1960; DLB 13; MTCW
Osborne, Lawrence 1958- .... **CLC 50**
Oshima, Nagisa 1932- .... **CLC 20**
   See also CA 116; 121
Oskison, John Milton 1874-1947 .. **TCLC 35;
   DAM MULT**
   See also CA 144; DLB 175; NNAL
Ossoli, Sarah Margaret (Fuller marchesa d')
   1810-1850
   See Fuller, Margaret
   See also SATA 25
Ostrovsky, Alexander 1823-1886**NCLC 30, 57**
Otero, Blas de 1916-1979 .... **CLC 11**
   See also CA 89-92; DLB 134
Otto, Whitney 1955- .... **CLC 70**

See also CA 140
Ouida .... **TCLC 43**
   See also De La Ramee, (Marie) Louise
   See also DLB 18, 156
Ousmane, Sembene 1923- .... **CLC 66; BLC**
   See also BW 1; CA 117; 125; MTCW
Ovid 43B.C.-18(?)**CMLC 7; DAM POET; PC
   2**
Owen, Hugh
   See Faust, Frederick (Schiller)
Owen, Wilfred (Edward Salter) 1893-1918
   **TCLC 5, 27; DA; DAB; DAC; DAM MST,
   POET; PC 19; WLC**
   See also CA 104; 141; CDBLB 1914-1945;
   DLB 20
Owens, Rochelle 1936- .... **CLC 8**
   See also CA 17-20R; CAAS 2; CANR 39
Oz, Amos 1939-**CLC 5, 8, 11, 27, 33, 54; DAM
   NOV**
   See also CA 53-56; CANR 27, 47; MTCW
Ozick, Cynthia 1928-**CLC 3, 7, 28, 62; DAM
   NOV, POP; SSC 15**
   See also BEST 90:1; CA 17-20R; CANR 23,
   58; DLB 28, 152; DLBY 82; INT CANR-
   23; MTCW
Ozu, Yasujiro 1903-1963 .... **CLC 16**
   See also CA 112
Pacheco, C.
   See Pessoa, Fernando (Antonio Nogueira)
Pa Chin .... **CLC 18**
   See also Li Fei-kan
Pack, Robert 1929- .... **CLC 13**
   See also CA 1-4R; CANR 3, 44; DLB 5
Padgett, Lewis
   See Kuttner, Henry
Padilla (Lorenzo), Heberto 1932- ..... **CLC 38**
   See also AITN 1; CA 123; 131; HW
Page, Jimmy 1944- .... **CLC 12**
Page, Louise 1955- .... **CLC 40**
   See also CA 140
Page, P(atricia) K(athleen) 1916- **CLC 7, 18;
   DAC; DAM MST; PC 12**
   See also CA 53-56; CANR 4, 22; DLB 68;
   MTCW
Page, Thomas Nelson 1853-1922 .... **SSC 23**
   See also CA 118; DLB 12, 78; DLBD 13
Pagels, Elaine Hiesey 1943- .... **CLC 104**
   See also CA 45-48; CANR 2, 24, 51
Paget, Violet 1856-1935
   See Lee, Vernon
   See also CA 104
Paget-Lowe, Henry
   See Lovecraft, H(oward) P(hillips)
Paglia, Camille (Anna) 1947- .... **CLC 68**
   See also CA 140
Paige, Richard
   See Koontz, Dean R(ay)
Paine, Thomas 1737-1809 .... **NCLC 62**
   See also CDALB 1640-1865; DLB 31, 43, 73,
   158
Pakenham, Antonia
   See Fraser, (Lady) Antonia (Pakenham)
Palamas, Kostes 1859-1943 .... **TCLC 5**
   See also CA 105
Palazzeschi, Aldo 1885-1974 .... **CLC 11**
   See also CA 89-92; 53-56; DLB 114
Paley, Grace 1922-**CLC 4, 6, 37; DAM POP;
   SSC 8**
   See also CA 25-28R; CANR 13, 46; DLB 28;
   INT CANR-13; MTCW
Palin, Michael (Edward) 1943- .... **CLC 21**
   See also Monty Python
   See also CA 107; CANR 35; SATA 67

Palliser, Charles 1947- .... **CLC 65**
   See also CA 136
Palma, Ricardo 1833-1919 .... **TCLC 29**
Pancake, Breece Dexter 1952-1979
   See Pancake, Breece D'J
   See also CA 123; 109
Pancake, Breece D'J .... **CLC 29**
   See also Pancake, Breece Dexter
   See also DLB 130
Panko, Rudy
   See Gogol, Nikolai (Vasilyevich)
Papadiamantis, Alexandros 1851-1911**TCLC
   29**
Papadiamantopoulos, Johannes 1856-1910
   See Moreas, Jean
   See also CA 117
Papini, Giovanni 1881-1956 .... **TCLC 22**
   See also CA 121
Paracelsus 1493-1541 .... **LC 14**
   See also DLB 179
Parasol, Peter
   See Stevens, Wallace
Pareto, Vilfredo 1848-1923 .... **TCLC 69**
Parfenie, Maria
   See Codrescu, Andrei
Parini, Jay (Lee) 1948- .... **CLC 54**
   See also CA 97-100; CAAS 16; CANR 32
Park, Jordan
   See Kornbluth, C(yril) M.; Pohl, Frederik
Park, Robert E(zra) 1864-1944 ...... **TCLC 73**
   See also CA 122
Parker, Bert
   See Ellison, Harlan (Jay)
Parker, Dorothy (Rothschild) 1893-1967**CLC
   15, 68; DAM POET; SSC 2**
   See also CA 19-20; 25-28R; CAP 2; DLB 11,
   45, 86; MTCW
Parker, Robert B(rown) 1932-**CLC 27; DAM
   NOV, POP**
   See also BEST 89:4; CA 49-52; CANR 1, 26,
   52; INT CANR-26; MTCW
Parkin, Frank 1940- .... **CLC 43**
   See also CA 147
Parkman, Francis, Jr. 1823-1893 .. **NCLC 12**
   See also DLB 1, 30
Parks, Gordon (Alexander Buchanan) 1912-
   CLC 1, 16; BLC; DAM MULT
   See also AITN 2; BW 2; CA 41-44R; CANR
   26; DLB 33; SATA 8
Parmenides c. 515B.C.-c. 450B.C. **CMLC 22**
   See also DLB 176
Parnell, Thomas 1679-1718 .... **LC 3**
   See also DLB 94
Parra, Nicanor 1914- ...... **CLC 2, 102; DAM
   MULT; HLC**
   See also CA 85-88; CANR 32; HW; MTCW
Parrish, Mary Frances
   See Fisher, M(ary) F(rances) K(ennedy)
Parson
   See Coleridge, Samuel Taylor
Parson Lot
   See Kingsley, Charles
Partridge, Anthony
   See Oppenheim, E(dward) Phillips
Pascal, Blaise 1623-1662 .... **LC 35**
Pascoli, Giovanni 1855-1912 .... **TCLC 45**
Pasolini, Pier Paolo 1922-1975 . **CLC 20, 37,
   106; PC 17**
   See also CA 93-96; 61-64; CANR 63; DLB 128,
   177; MTCW
Pasquini
   See Silone, Ignazio
Pastan, Linda (Olenik) 1932- **CLC 27; DAM**

POET
See also CA 61-64; CANR 18, 40, 61; DLB 5

Pasternak, Boris (Leonidovich) 1890-1960 **CLC 7, 10, 18, 63; DA; DAB; DAC; DAM MST, NOV, POET; PC 6; WLC**
See also CA 127; 116; MTCW

Patchen, Kenneth 1911-1972 ... **CLC 1, 2, 18; DAM POET**
See also CA 1-4R; 33-36R; CANR 3, 35; DLB 16, 48; MTCW

Pater, Walter (Horatio) 1839-1894 .. **NCLC 7**
See also CDBLB 1832-1890; DLB 57, 156

Paterson, A(ndrew) B(arton) 1864-1941 **TCLC 32**
See also CA 155

Paterson, Katherine (Womeldorf) 1932-**C L C 12, 30**
See also AAYA 1; CA 21-24R; CANR 28, 59; CLR 7; DLB 52; JRDA; MAICYA; MTCW; SATA 13, 53, 92

Patmore, Coventry Kersey Dighton 1823-1896 **NCLC 9**
See also DLB 35, 98

Paton, Alan (Stewart) 1903-1988 **CLC 4, 10, 25, 55, 106; DA; DAB; DAC; DAM MST, NOV; WLC**
See also CA 13-16; 125; CANR 22; CAP 1; MTCW; SATA 11; SATA-Obit 56

Paton Walsh, Gillian 1937-
See Walsh, Jill Paton
See also CANR 38; JRDA; MAICYA; SAAS 3; SATA 4, 72

Patton, George S. 1885-1945 .... **TCLC 79**

Paulding, James Kirke 1778-1860 ... **NCLC 2**
See also DLB 3, 59, 74

Paulin, Thomas Neilson 1949-
See Paulin, Tom
See also CA 123; 128

Paulin, Tom .... **CLC 37**
See also Paulin, Thomas Neilson
See also DLB 40

Paustovsky, Konstantin (Georgievich) 1892-1968 .... **CLC 40**
See also CA 93-96; 25-28R

Pavese, Cesare 1908-1950 ... **TCLC 3; PC 13; SSC 19**
See also CA 104; DLB 128, 177

Pavic, Milorad 1929- .... **CLC 60**
See also CA 136; DLB 181

Payne, Alan
See Jakes, John (William)

Paz, Gil
See Lugones, Leopoldo

Paz, Octavio 1914-**CLC 3, 4, 6, 10, 19, 51, 65; DA; DAB; DAC; DAM MST, MULT, POET; HLC; PC 1; WLC**
See also CA 73-76; CANR 32; DLBY 90; HW; MTCW

p'Bitek, Okot 1931-1982**CLC 96; BLC; DAM MULT**
See also BW 2; CA 124; 107; DLB 125; MTCW

Peacock, Molly 1947- .... **CLC 60**
See also CA 103; CAAS 21; CANR 52; DLB 120

Peacock, Thomas Love 1785-1866 . **NCLC 22**
See also DLB 96, 116

Peake, Mervyn 1911-1968 .... **CLC 7, 54**
See also CA 5-8R; 25-28R; CANR 3; DLB 15, 160; MTCW; SATA 23

Pearce, Philippa .... **CLC 21**
See also Christie, (Ann) Philippa
See also CLR 9; DLB 161; MAICYA; SATA 1, 67

Pearl, Eric
See Elman, Richard

Pearson, T(homas) R(eid) 1956- .... **CLC 39**
See also CA 120; 130; INT 130

Peck, Dale 1967- .... **CLC 81**
See also CA 146

Peck, John 1941- .... **CLC 3**
See also CA 49-52; CANR 3

Peck, Richard (Wayne) 1934- .... **CLC 21**
See also AAYA 1; CA 85-88; CANR 19, 38; CLR 15; INT CANR-19; JRDA; MAICYA; SAAS 2; SATA 18, 55

Peck, Robert Newton 1928- ..... **CLC 17; DA; DAC; DAM MST**
See also AAYA 3; CA 81-84; CANR 31, 63; CLR 45; JRDA; MAICYA; SAAS 1; SATA 21, 62

Peckinpah, (David) Sam(uel) 1925-1984**C L C 20**
See also CA 109; 114

Pedersen, Knut 1859-1952
See Hamsun, Knut
See also CA 104; 119; CANR 63; MTCW

Peeslake, Gaffer
See Durrell, Lawrence (George)

Peguy, Charles Pierre 1873-1914 .. **TCLC 10**
See also CA 107

Pena, Ramon del Valle y
See Valle-Inclan, Ramon (Maria) del

Pendennis, Arthur Esquir
See Thackeray, William Makepeace

Penn, William 1644-1718 .... **LC 25**
See also DLB 24

PEPECE
See Prado (Calvo), Pedro

Pepys, Samuel 1633-1703 **LC 11; DA; DAB; DAC; DAM MST; WLC**
See also CDBLB 1660-1789; DLB 101

Percy, Walker 1916-1990**CLC 2, 3, 6, 8, 14, 18, 47, 65; DAM NOV, POP**
See also CA 1-4R; 131; CANR 1, 23, 64; DLB 2; DLBY 80, 90; MTCW

Perec, Georges 1936-1982 .... **CLC 56**
See also CA 141; DLB 83

Pereda (y Sanchez de Porrua), Jose Maria de 1833-1906 .... **TCLC 16**
See also CA 117

Pereda y Porrua, Jose Maria de
See Pereda (y Sanchez de Porrua), Jose Maria de

Peregoy, George Weems
See Mencken, H(enry) L(ouis)

Perelman, S(idney) J(oseph) 1904-1979 **C L C 3, 5, 9, 15, 23, 44, 49; DAM DRAM**
See also AITN 1, 2; CA 73-76; 89-92; CANR 18; DLB 11, 44; MTCW

Peret, Benjamin 1899-1959 .... **TCLC 20**
See also CA 117

Peretz, Isaac Loeb 1851(?)-1915 ... **TCLC 16; SSC 26**
See also CA 109

Peretz, Yitzhok Leibush
See Peretz, Isaac Loeb

Perez Galdos, Benito 1843-1920 .... **TCLC 27**
See also CA 125; 153; HW

Perrault, Charles 1628-1703 .... **LC 2**
See also MAICYA; SATA 25

Perry, Brighton
See Sherwood, Robert E(mmet)

Perse, St.-John .... **CLC 4, 11, 46**
See also Leger, (Marie-Rene Auguste) Alexis Saint-Leger

Perutz, Leo 1882-1957 .... **TCLC 60**

See also DLB 81

Peseenz, Tulio F.
See Lopez y Fuentes, Gregorio

Pesetsky, Bette 1932- .... **CLC 28**
See also CA 133; DLB 130

Peshkov, Alexei Maximovich 1868-1936
See Gorky, Maxim
See also CA 105; 141; DA; DAC; DAM DRAM, MST, NOV

Pessoa, Fernando (Antonio Nogueira) 1888-1935 .... **TCLC 27; HLC; PC 20**
See also CA 125

Peterkin, Julia Mood 1880-1961 .... **CLC 31**
See also CA 102; DLB 9

Peters, Joan K(aren) 1945- .... **CLC 39**
See also CA 158

Peters, Robert L(ouis) 1924- .... **CLC 7**
See also CA 13-16R; CAAS 8; DLB 105

Petofi, Sandor 1823-1849 .... **NCLC 21**

Petrakis, Harry Mark 1923- .... **CLC 3**
See also CA 9-12R; CANR 4, 30

Petrarch 1304-1374 **CMLC 20; DAM POET; PC 8**

Petrov, Evgeny .... **TCLC 21**
See also Kataev, Evgeny Petrovich

Petry, Ann (Lane) 1908-1997 ... **CLC 1, 7, 18**
See also BW 1; CA 5-8R; 157; CAAS 6; CANR 4, 46; CLR 12; DLB 76; JRDA; MAICYA; MTCW; SATA 5; SATA-Obit 94

Petursson, Halligrimur 1614-1674 .... **LC 8**

Phaedrus 18(?)B.C.-55(?) .... **CMLC 25**

Philips, Katherine 1632-1664 .... **LC 30**
See also DLB 131

Philipson, Morris H. 1926- .... **CLC 53**
See also CA 1-4R; CANR 4

Phillips, Caryl 1958- .. **CLC 96; DAM MULT**
See also BW 2; CA 141; CANR 63; DLB 157

Phillips, David Graham 1867-1911 **TCLC 44**
See also CA 108; DLB 9, 12

Phillips, Jack
See Sandburg, Carl (August)

Phillips, Jayne Anne 1952-**CLC 15, 33; SSC 16**
See also CA 101; CANR 24, 50; DLBY 80; INT CANR-24; MTCW

Phillips, Richard
See Dick, Philip K(indred)

Phillips, Robert (Schaeffer) 1938- .... **CLC 28**
See also CA 17-20R; CAAS 13; CANR 8; DLB 105

Phillips, Ward
See Lovecraft, H(oward) P(hillips)

Piccolo, Lucio 1901-1969 .... **CLC 13**
See also CA 97-100; DLB 114

Pickthall, Marjorie L(owry) C(hristie) 1883-1922 .... **TCLC 21**
See also CA 107; DLB 92

Pico della Mirandola, Giovanni 1463-1494**LC 15**

Piercy, Marge 1936- **CLC 3, 6, 14, 18, 27, 62**
See also CA 21-24R; CAAS 1; CANR 13, 43; DLB 120; MTCW

Piers, Robert
See Anthony, Piers

Pieyre de Mandiargues, Andre 1909-1991
See Mandiargues, Andre Pieyre de
See also CA 103; 136; CANR 22

Pilnyak, Boris .... **TCLC 23**
See also Vogau, Boris Andreyevich

Pincherle, Alberto 1907-1990 ... **CLC 11, 18; DAM NOV**
See also Moravia, Alberto
See also CA 25-28R; 132; CANR 33, 63; MTCW

Pinckney, Darryl 1953- .... **CLC 76**
 See also BW 2; CA 143
Pindar 518B.C.-446B.C. ..... **CMLC 12; PC 19**
 See also DLB 176
Pineda, Cecile 1942- .... **CLC 39**
 See also CA 118
Pinero, Arthur Wing 1855-1934 ... **TCLC 32;**
 DAM DRAM
 See also CA 110; 153; DLB 10
Pinero, Miguel (Antonio Gomez) 1946-1988
 CLC 4, 55
 See also CA 61-64; 125; CANR 29; HW
Pinget, Robert 1919-1997 .... **CLC 7, 13, 37**
 See also CA 85-88; 160; DLB 83
Pink Floyd
 See Barrett, (Roger) Syd; Gilmour, David; Ma-
 son, Nick; Waters, Roger; Wright, Rick
Pinkney, Edward 1802-1828 .... **NCLC 31**
Pinkwater, Daniel Manus 1941- .... **CLC 35**
 See also Pinkwater, Manus
 See also AAYA 1; CA 29-32R; CANR 12, 38;
 CLR 4; JRDA; MAICYA; SAAS 3; SATA 46,
 76
Pinkwater, Manus
 See Pinkwater, Daniel Manus
 See also SATA 8
Pinsky, Robert 1940-**CLC 9, 19, 38, 94; DAM**
 POET
 See also CA 29-32R; CAAS 4; CANR 58;
 DLBY 82
Pinta, Harold
 See Pinter, Harold
Pinter, Harold 1930-**CLC 1, 3, 6, 9, 11, 15, 27,**
 58, 73; DA; DAB; DAC; DAM DRAM,
 MST; WLC
 See also CA 5-8R; CANR 33; CDBLB 1960 to
 Present; DLB 13; MTCW
Piozzi, Hester Lynch (Thrale) 1741-1821
 NCLC 57
 See also DLB 104, 142
Pirandello, Luigi 1867-1936**TCLC 4, 29; DA;**
 DAB; DAC; DAM DRAM, MST; DC 5;
 SSC 22; WLC
 See also CA 104; 153
Pirsig, Robert M(aynard) 1928-**CLC 4, 6, 73;**
 DAM POP
 See also CA 53-56; CANR 42; MTCW; SATA
 39
Pisarev, Dmitry Ivanovich 1840-1868 **N C L C**
 25
Pix, Mary (Griffith) 1666-1709 .... **LC 8**
 See also DLB 80
Pixerecourt, Guilbert de 1773-1844**NCLC 39**
Plaatje, Sol(omon) T(shekisho) 1876-1932
 TCLC 73
 See also BW 2; CA 141
Plaidy, Jean
 See Hibbert, Eleanor Alice Burford
Planche, James Robinson 1796-1880**NCLC 42**
Plant, Robert 1948- .... **CLC 12**
Plante, David (Robert) 1940- **CLC 7, 23, 38;**
 DAM NOV
 See also CA 37-40R; CANR 12, 36, 58; DLBY
 83; INT CANR-12; MTCW
Plath, Sylvia 1932-1963 **CLC 1, 2, 3, 5, 9, 11,**
 14, 17, 50, 51, 62; DA; DAB; DAC; DAM
 MST, POET; PC 1; WLC
 See also AAYA 13; CA 19-20; CANR 34; CAP
 2; CDALB 1941-1968; DLB 5, 6, 152;
 MTCW; SATA 96
Plato 428(?)B.C.-348(?)B.C. .... **CMLC 8; DA;**
 DAB; DAC; DAM MST; WLCS
 See also DLB 176

Platonov, Andrei .... **TCLC 14**
 See also Klimentov, Andrei Platonovich
Platt, Kin 1911- .... **CLC 26**
 See also AAYA 11; CA 17-20R; CANR 11;
 JRDA; SAAS 17; SATA 21, 86
Plautus c. 251B.C.-184B.C. .... **DC 6**
Plick et Plock
 See Simenon, Georges (Jacques Christian)
Plimpton, George (Ames) 1927- .... **CLC 36**
 See also AITN 1; CA 21-24R; CANR 32;
 MTCW; SATA 10
Pliny the Elder c. 23-79 .... **CMLC 23**
Plomer, William Charles Franklin 1903-1973
 CLC 4, 8
 See also CA 21-22; CANR 34; CAP 2; DLB
 20, 162; MTCW; SATA 24
Plowman, Piers
 See Kavanagh, Patrick (Joseph)
Plum, J.
 See Wodehouse, P(elham) G(renville)
Plumly, Stanley (Ross) 1939- .... **CLC 33**
 See also CA 108; 110; DLB 5; INT 110
Plumpe, Friedrich Wilhelm 1888-1931**T C L C**
 53
 See also CA 112
Po Chu-i 772-846 .... **CMLC 24**
Poe, Edgar Allan 1809-1849**NCLC 1, 16, 55;**
 DA; DAB; DAC; DAM MST, POET; PC
 1; SSC 1, 22; WLC
 See also AAYA 14; CDALB 1640-1865; DLB
 3, 59, 73, 74; SATA 23
Poet of Titchfield Street, The
 See Pound, Ezra (Weston Loomis)
Pohl, Frederik 1919- .... **CLC 18; SSC 25**
 See also CA 61-64; CAAS 1; CANR 11, 37;
 DLB 8; INT CANR-11; MTCW; SATA 24
Poirier, Louis 1910-
 See Gracq, Julien
 See also CA 122; 126
Poitier, Sidney 1927- .... **CLC 26**
 See also BW 1; CA 117
Polanski, Roman 1933- .... **CLC 16**
 See also CA 77-80
Poliakoff, Stephen 1952- .... **CLC 38**
 See also CA 106; DLB 13
Police, The
 See Copeland, Stewart (Armstrong); Summers,
 Andrew James; Sumner, Gordon Matthew
Polidori, John William 1795-1821 . **NCLC 51**
 See also DLB 116
Pollitt, Katha 1949- .... **CLC 28**
 See also CA 120; 122; MTCW
Pollock, (Mary) Sharon 1936-**CLC 50; DAC;**
 DAM DRAM, MST
 See also CA 141; DLB 60
Polo, Marco 1254-1324 .... **CMLC 15**
Polonsky, Abraham (Lincoln) 1910- **CLC 92**
 See also CA 104; DLB 26; INT 104
Polybius c. 200B.C.-c. 118B.C. ...... **CMLC 17**
 See also DLB 176
Pomerance, Bernard 1940-.... **CLC 13; DAM**
 DRAM
 See also CA 101; CANR 49
Ponge, Francis (Jean Gaston Alfred) 1899-1988
 CLC 6, 18; DAM POET
 See also CA 85-88; 126; CANR 40
Pontoppidan, Henrik 1857-1943 .... **TCLC 29**
Poole, Josephine .... **CLC 17**
 See also Helyar, Jane Penelope Josephine
 See also SAAS 2; SATA 5
Popa, Vasko 1922-1991 .... **CLC 19**
 See also CA 112; 148; DLB 181
Pope, Alexander 1688-1744 **LC 3; DA; DAB;**

 DAC; DAM MST, POET; WLC
 See also CDBLB 1660-1789; DLB 95, 101
Porter, Connie (Rose) 1959(?)- .... **CLC 70**
 See also BW 2; CA 142; SATA 81
Porter, Gene(va Grace) Stratton 1863(?)-1924
 TCLC 21
 See also CA 112
Porter, Katherine Anne 1890-1980**CLC 1, 3, 7,**
 10, 13, 15, 27, 101; DA; DAB; DAC; DAM
 MST, NOV; SSC 4
 See also AITN 2; CA 1-4R; 101; CANR 1; DLB
 4, 9, 102; DLBD 12; DLBY 80; MTCW;
 SATA 39; SATA-Obit 23
Porter, Peter (Neville Frederick) 1929-**CLC 5,**
 13, 33
 See also CA 85-88; DLB 40
Porter, William Sydney 1862-1910
 See Henry, O.
 See also CA 104; 131; CDALB 1865-1917; DA;
 DAB; DAC; DAM MST; DLB 12, 78, 79;
 MTCW; YABC 2
Portillo (y Pacheco), Jose Lopez
 See Lopez Portillo (y Pacheco), Jose
Post, Melville Davisson 1869-1930 **TCLC 39**
 See also CA 110
Potok, Chaim 1929- . **CLC 2, 7, 14, 26; DAM**
 NOV
 See also AAYA 15; AITN 1, 2; CA 17-20R;
 CANR 19, 35, 64; DLB 28, 152; INT CANR-
 19; MTCW; SATA 33
Potter, (Helen) Beatrix 1866-1943
 See Webb, (Martha) Beatrice (Potter)
 See also MAICYA
Potter, Dennis (Christopher George) 1935-1994
 CLC 58, 86
 See also CA 107; 145; CANR 33, 61; MTCW
Pound, Ezra (Weston Loomis) 1885-1972
 CLC 1, 2, 3, 4, 5, 7, 10, 13, 18, 34, 48, 50;
 DA; DAB; DAC; DAM MST, POET; PC
 4; WLC
 See also CA 5-8R; 37-40R; CANR 40; CDALB
 1917-1929; DLB 4, 45, 63; DLBD 15;
 MTCW
Povod, Reinaldo 1959-1994 .... **CLC 44**
 See also CA 136; 146
Powell, Adam Clayton, Jr. 1908-1972**CLC 89;**
 BLC; DAM MULT
 See also BW 1; CA 102; 33-36R
Powell, Anthony (Dymoke) 1905-**CLC 1, 3, 7,**
 9, 10, 31
 See also CA 1-4R; CANR 1, 32, 62; CDBLB
 1945-1960; DLB 15; MTCW
Powell, Dawn 1897-1965 .... **CLC 66**
 See also CA 5-8R
Powell, Padgett 1952- .... **CLC 34**
 See also CA 126; CANR 63
Power, Susan 1961- .... **CLC 91**
Powers, J(ames) F(arl) 1917-**CLC 1, 4, 8, 57;**
 SSC 4
 See also CA 1-4R; CANR 2, 61; DLB 130;
 MTCW
Powers, John J(ames) 1945-
 See Powers, John R.
 See also CA 69-72
Powers, John R. .... **CLC 66**
 See also Powers, John J(ames)
Powers, Richard (S.) 1957- .... **CLC 93**
 See also CA 148
Pownall, David 1938- .... **CLC 10**
 See also CA 89-92; CAAS 18; CANR 49; DLB
 14
Powys, John Cowper 1872-1963**CLC 7, 9, 15,**
 46

See also CA 85-88; DLB 15; MTCW
Powys, T(heodore) F(rancis) 1875-1953
    TCLC 9
    See also CA 106; DLB 36, 162
Prado (Calvo), Pedro 1886-1952 ... TCLC 75
    See also CA 131; HW
Prager, Emily 1952- .... CLC 56
Pratt, E(dwin) J(ohn) 1883(?)-1964 CLC 19;
    DAC; DAM POET
    See also CA 141; 93-96; DLB 92
Premchand .... TCLC 21
    See also Srivastava, Dhanpat Rai
Preussler, Otfried 1923- .... CLC 17
    See also CA 77-80; SATA 24
Prevert, Jacques (Henri Marie) 1900-1977
    CLC 15
    See also CA 77-80; 69-72; CANR 29, 61;
    MTCW; SATA-Obit 30
Prevost, Abbe (Antoine Francois) 1697-1763
    LC 1
Price, (Edward) Reynolds 1933-CLC 3, 6, 13,
    43, 50, 63; DAM NOV; SSC 22
    See also CA 1-4R; CANR 1, 37, 57; DLB 2;
    INT CANR-37
Price, Richard 1949- .... CLC 6, 12
    See also CA 49-52; CANR 3; DLBY 81
Prichard, Katharine Susannah 1883-1969
    CLC 46
    See also CA 11-12; CANR 33; CAP 1; MTCW;
    SATA 66
Priestley, J(ohn) B(oynton) 1894-1984CLC 2,
    5, 9, 34; DAM DRAM, NOV
    See also CA 9-12R; 113; CANR 33; CDBLB
    1914-1945; DLB 10, 34, 77, 100, 139; DLBY
    84; MTCW
Prince 1958(?)- .... CLC 35
Prince, F(rank) T(empleton) 1912- .. CLC 22
    See also CA 101; CANR 43; DLB 20
Prince Kropotkin
    See Kropotkin, Peter (Aleksieevich)
Prior, Matthew 1664-1721 .... LC 4
    See also DLB 95
Prishvin, Mikhail 1873-1954 .... TCLC 75
Pritchard, William H(arrison) 1932-CLC 34
    See also CA 65-68; CANR 23; DLB 111
Pritchett, V(ictor) S(awdon) 1900-1997 C L C
    5, 13, 15, 41; DAM NOV; SSC 14
    See also CA 61-64; 157; CANR 31, 63; DLB
    15, 139; MTCW
Private 19022
    See Manning, Frederic
Probst, Mark 1925- .... CLC 59
    See also CA 130
Prokosch, Frederic 1908-1989 ...... CLC 4, 48
    See also CA 73-76; 128; DLB 48
Prophet, The
    See Dreiser, Theodore (Herman Albert)
Prose, Francine 1947- .... CLC 45
    See also CA 109; 112; CANR 46
Proudhon
    See Cunha, Euclides (Rodrigues Pimenta) da
Proulx, E. Annie 1935- .... CLC 81
Proust, (Valentin-Louis-George-Eugene-)
    Marcel 1871-1922 TCLC 7, 13, 33; DA;
    DAB; DAC; DAM MST, NOV; WLC
    See also CA 104; 120; DLB 65; MTCW
Prowler, Harley
    See Masters, Edgar Lee
Prus, Boleslaw 1845-1912 .... TCLC 48
Pryor, Richard (Franklin Lenox Thomas) 1940-
    CLC 26
    See also CA 122
Przybyszewski, Stanislaw 1868-1927TCLC 36

See also CA 160; DLB 66
Pteleon
    See Grieve, C(hristopher) M(urray)
    See also DAM POET
Puckett, Lute
    See Masters, Edgar Lee
Puig, Manuel 1932-1990CLC 3, 5, 10, 28, 65;
    DAM MULT; HLC
    See also CA 45-48; CANR 2, 32, 63; DLB 113;
    HW; MTCW
Pulitzer, Joseph 1847-1911 .... TCLC 76
    See also CA 114; DLB 23
Purdy, Al(fred Wellington) 1918-CLC 3, 6, 14,
    50; DAC; DAM MST, POET
    See also CA 81-84; CAAS 17; CANR 42; DLB
    88
Purdy, James (Amos) 1923- CLC 2, 4, 10, 28,
    52
    See also CA 33-36R; CAAS 1; CANR 19, 51;
    DLB 2; INT CANR-19; MTCW
Pure, Simon
    See Swinnerton, Frank Arthur
Pushkin, Alexander (Sergeyevich) 1799-1837
    NCLC 3, 27; DA; DAB; DAC; DAM
    DRAM, MST, POET; PC 10; SSC 27;
    WLC
    See also SATA 61
P'u Sung-ling 1640-1715 .... LC 3
Putnam, Arthur Lee
    See Alger, Horatio, Jr.
Puzo, Mario 1920-CLC 1, 2, 6, 36, 107; DAM
    NOV, POP
    See also CA 65-68; CANR 4, 42; DLB 6;
    MTCW
Pygge, Edward
    See Barnes, Julian (Patrick)
Pyle, Ernest Taylor 1900-1945
    See Pyle, Ernie
    See also CA 115; 160
Pyle, Ernie 1900-1945 .... TCLC 75
    See also Pyle, Ernest Taylor
    See also DLB 29
Pym, Barbara (Mary Crampton) 1913-1980
    CLC 13, 19, 37
    See also CA 13-14; 97-100; CANR 13, 34; CAP
    1; DLB 14; DLBY 87; MTCW
Pynchon, Thomas (Ruggles, Jr.) 1937-CLC 2,
    3, 6, 9, 11, 18, 33, 62, 72; DA; DAB; DAC;
    DAM MST, NOV, POP; SSC 14; WLC
    See also BEST 90:2; CA 17-20R; CANR 22,
    46; DLB 2, 173; MTCW
Pythagoras c. 570B.C.-c. 500B.C.. CMLC 22
    See also DLB 176
Qian Zhongshu
    See Ch'ien Chung-shu
Qroll
    See Dagerman, Stig (Halvard)
Quarrington, Paul (Lewis) 1953- ..... CLC 65
    See also CA 129; CANR 62
Quasimodo, Salvatore 1901-1968 ..... CLC 10
    See also CA 13-16; 25-28R; CAP 1; DLB 114;
    MTCW
Quay, Stephen 1947- .... CLC 95
Quay, Timothy 1947- .... CLC 95
Queen, Ellery .... CLC 3, 11
    See also Dannay, Frederic; Davidson, Avram;
    Lee, Manfred B(ennington); Marlowe,
    Stephen; Sturgeon, Theodore (Hamilton);
    Vance, John Holbrook
Queen, Ellery, Jr.
    See Dannay, Frederic; Lee, Manfred
    B(ennington)
Queneau, Raymond 1903-1976 CLC 2, 5, 10,

42
    See also CA 77-80; 69-72; CANR 32; DLB 72;
    MTCW
Quevedo, Francisco de 1580-1645 .... LC 23
Quiller-Couch, Arthur Thomas 1863-1944
    TCLC 53
    See also CA 118; DLB 135, 153
Quin, Ann (Marie) 1936-1973 .... CLC 6
    See also CA 9-12R; 45-48; DLB 14
Quinn, Martin
    See Smith, Martin Cruz
Quinn, Peter 1947- .... CLC 91
Quinn, Simon
    See Smith, Martin Cruz
Quiroga, Horacio (Sylvestre) 1878-1937
    TCLC 20; DAM MULT; HLC
    See also CA 117; 131; HW; MTCW
Quoirez, Francoise 1935- .... CLC 9
    See also Sagan, Francoise
    See also CA 49-52; CANR 6, 39; MTCW
Raabe, Wilhelm 1831-1910 .... TCLC 45
    See also DLB 129
Rabe, David (William) 1940- ... CLC 4, 8, 33;
    DAM DRAM
    See also CA 85-88; CABS 3; CANR 59; DLB 7
Rabelais, Francois 1483-1553LC 5; DA; DAB;
    DAC; DAM MST; WLC
Rabinovitch, Sholem 1859-1916
    See Aleichem, Sholom
    See also CA 104
Rachilde 1860-1953 .... TCLC 67
    See also DLB 123
Racine, Jean 1639-1699 . LC 28; DAB; DAM
    MST
Radcliffe, Ann (Ward) 1764-1823NCLC 6, 55
    See also DLB 39, 178
Radiguet, Raymond 1903-1923 ...... TCLC 29
    See also DLB 65
Radnoti, Miklos 1909-1944 .... TCLC 16
    See also CA 118
Rado, James 1939- .... CLC 17
    See also CA 105
Radvanyi, Netty 1900-1983
    See Seghers, Anna
    See also CA 85-88; 110
Rae, Ben
    See Griffiths, Trevor
Raeburn, John (Hay) 1941- .... CLC 34
    See also CA 57-60
Ragni, Gerome 1942-1991 .... CLC 17
    See also CA 105; 134
Rahv, Philip 1908-1973 .... CLC 24
    See also Greenberg, Ivan
    See also DLB 137
Raine, Craig 1944- .... CLC 32, 103
    See also CA 108; CANR 29, 51; DLB 40
Raine, Kathleen (Jessie) 1908- ...... CLC 7, 45
    See also CA 85-88; CANR 46; DLB 20; MTCW
Rainis, Janis 1865-1929 .... TCLC 29
Rakosi, Carl .... CLC 47
    See also Rawley, Callman
    See also CAAS 5
Raleigh, Richard
    See Lovecraft, H(oward) P(hillips)
Raleigh, Sir Walter 1554(?)-1618 . LC 31, 39
    See also CDBLB Before 1660; DLB 172
Rallentando, H. P.
    See Sayers, Dorothy L(eigh)
Ramal, Walter
    See de la Mare, Walter (John)
Ramon, Juan
    See Jimenez (Mantecon), Juan Ramon
Ramos, Graciliano 1892-1953 .... TCLC 32

Rampersad, Arnold 1941- .... **CLC 44**
  See also BW 2; CA 127; 133; DLB 111; INT
    133
Rampling, Anne
  See Rice, Anne
Ramsay, Allan 1684(?)-1758 .... **LC 29**
  See also DLB 95
Ramuz, Charles-Ferdinand 1878-1947T C L C
    33
Rand, Ayn 1905-1982**CLC 3, 30, 44, 79; DA;**
    DAC; DAM MST, NOV, POP; WLC
  See also AAYA 10; CA 13-16R; 105; CANR
    27; MTCW
Randall, Dudley (Felker) 1914-**CLC 1; BLC;**
    DAM MULT
  See also BW 1; CA 25-28R; CANR 23; DLB
    41
Randall, Robert
  See Silverberg, Robert
Ranger, Ken
  See Creasey, John
Ransom, John Crowe 1888-1974**CLC 2, 4, 5,**
    11, 24; DAM POET
  See also CA 5-8R; 49-52; CANR 6, 34; DLB
    45, 63; MTCW
Rao, Raja 1909- ...... **CLC 25, 56; DAM NOV**
  See also CA 73-76; CANR 51; MTCW
Raphael, Frederic (Michael) 1931-**CLC 2, 14**
  See also CA 1-4R; CANR 1; DLB 14
Ratcliffe, James P.
  See Mencken, H(enry) L(ouis)
Rathbone, Julian 1935- .... **CLC 41**
  See also CA 101; CANR 34
Rattigan, Terence (Mervyn) 1911-1977**CLC 7;**
    DAM DRAM
  See also CA 85-88; 73-76; CDBLB 1945-1960;
    DLB 13; MTCW
Ratushinskaya, Irina 1954- .... **CLC 54**
  See also CA 129
Raven, Simon (Arthur Noel) 1927- .. **CLC 14**
  See also CA 81-84
Rawley, Callman 1903-
  See Rakosi, Carl
  See also CA 21-24R; CANR 12, 32
Rawlings, Marjorie Kinnan 1896-1953T C L C
    4
  See also AAYA 20; CA 104; 137; DLB 9, 22,
    102; JRDA; MAICYA; YABC 1
Ray, Satyajit 1921-1992 .. **CLC 16, 76; DAM**
    MULT
  See also CA 114; 137
Read, Herbert Edward 1893-1968 ..... **CLC 4**
  See also CA 85-88; 25-28R; DLB 20, 149
Read, Piers Paul 1941- .... **CLC 4, 10, 25**
  See also CA 21-24R; CANR 38; DLB 14; SATA
    21
Reade, Charles 1814-1884 .... **NCLC 2**
  See also DLB 21
Reade, Hamish
  See Gray, Simon (James Holliday)
Reading, Peter 1946- .... **CLC 47**
  See also CA 103; CANR 46; DLB 40
Reaney, James 1926- .. **CLC 13; DAC; DAM**
    MST
  See also CA 41-44R; CAAS 15; CANR 42; DLB
    68; SATA 43
Rebreanu, Liviu 1885-1944 .... **TCLC 28**
Rechy, John (Francisco) 1934- **CLC 1, 7, 14,**
    18, 107; DAM MULT; HLC
  See also CA 5-8R; CAAS 4; CANR 6, 32, 64;
    DLB 122; DLBY 82; HW; INT CANR-6
Redcam, Tom 1870-1933 .... **TCLC 25**
Reddin, Keith .... **CLC 67**

Redgrove, Peter (William) 1932- .. **CLC 6, 41**
  See also CA 1-4R; CANR 3, 39; DLB 40
Redmon, Anne .... **CLC 22**
  See also Nightingale, Anne Redmon
  See also DLBY 86
Reed, Eliot
  See Ambler, Eric
Reed, Ishmael 1938-**CLC 2, 3, 5, 6, 13, 32, 60;**
    BLC; DAM MULT
  See also BW 2; CA 21-24R; CANR 25, 48; DLB
    2, 5, 33, 169; DLBD 8; MTCW
Reed, John (Silas) 1887-1920 .... **TCLC 9**
  See also CA 106
Reed, Lou .... **CLC 21**
  See also Firbank, Louis
Reeve, Clara 1729-1807 .... **NCLC 19**
  See also DLB 39
Reich, Wilhelm 1897-1957 .... **TCLC 57**
Reid, Christopher (John) 1949- .... **CLC 33**
  See also CA 140; DLB 40
Reid, Desmond
  See Moorcock, Michael (John)
Reid Banks, Lynne 1929-
  See Banks, Lynne Reid
  See also CA 1-4R; CANR 6, 22, 38; CLR 24;
    JRDA; MAICYA; SATA 22, 75
Reilly, William K.
  See Creasey, John
Reiner, Max
  See Caldwell, (Janet Miriam) Taylor (Holland)
Reis, Ricardo
  See Pessoa, Fernando (Antonio Nogueira)
Remarque, Erich Maria 1898-1970 **CLC 21;**
    DA; DAB; DAC; DAM MST, NOV
  See also CA 77-80; 29-32R; DLB 56; MTCW
Remizov, A.
  See Remizov, Aleksei (Mikhailovich)
Remizov, A. M.
  See Remizov, Aleksei (Mikhailovich)
Remizov, Aleksei (Mikhailovich) 1877-1957
    TCLC 27
  See also CA 125; 133
Renan, Joseph Ernest 1823-1892 .. **NCLC 26**
Renard, Jules 1864-1910 .... **TCLC 17**
  See also CA 117
Renault, Mary .... **CLC 3, 11, 17**
  See also Challans, Mary
  See also DLBY 83
Rendell, Ruth (Barbara) 1930- . **CLC 28, 48;**
    DAM POP
  See also Vine, Barbara
  See also CA 109; CANR 32, 52; DLB 87; INT
    CANR-32; MTCW
Renoir, Jean 1894-1979 .... **CLC 20**
  See also CA 129; 85-88
Resnais, Alain 1922- .... **CLC 16**
Reverdy, Pierre 1889-1960 .... **CLC 53**
  See also CA 97-100; 89-92
Rexroth, Kenneth 1905-1982**CLC 1, 2, 6, 11,**
    22, 49; DAM POET; PC 20
  See also CA 5-8R; 107; CANR 14, 34, 63;
    CDALB 1941-1968; DLB 16, 48, 165;
    DLBY 82; INT CANR-14; MTCW
Reyes, Alfonso 1889-1959 .... **TCLC 33**
  See also CA 131; HW
Reyes y Basoalto, Ricardo Eliecer Neftali
  See Neruda, Pablo
Reymont, Wladyslaw (Stanislaw) 1868(?)-1925
    TCLC 5
  See also CA 104
Reynolds, Jonathan 1942- .... **CLC 6, 38**
  See also CA 65-68; CANR 28
Reynolds, Joshua 1723-1792 .... **LC 15**

  See also DLB 104
Reynolds, Michael Shane 1937- .... **CLC 44**
  See also CA 65-68; CANR 9
Reznikoff, Charles 1894-1976 .... **CLC 9**
  See also CA 33-36; 61-64; CAP 2; DLB 28, 45
Rezzori (d'Arezzo), Gregor von 1914-**CLC 25**
  See also CA 122; 136
Rhine, Richard
  See Silverstein, Alvin
Rhodes, Eugene Manlove 1869-1934**TCLC 53**
R'hoone
  See Balzac, Honore de
Rhys, Jean 1890(?)-1979 **CLC 2, 4, 6, 14, 19,**
    51; DAM NOV; SSC 21
  See also CA 25-28R; 85-88; CANR 35, 62;
    CDBLB 1945-1960; DLB 36, 117, 162;
    MTCW
Ribeiro, Darcy 1922-1997 .... **CLC 34**
  See also CA 33-36R; 156
Ribeiro, Joao Ubaldo (Osorio Pimentel) 1941-
    CLC 10, 67
  See also CA 81-84
Ribman, Ronald (Burt) 1932- .... **CLC 7**
  See also CA 21-24R; CANR 46
Ricci, Nino 1959-................................. **CLC 70**
  See also CA 137
Rice, Anne 1941- .... **CLC 41; DAM POP**
  See also AAYA 9; BEST 89:2; CA 65-68; CANR
    12, 36, 53
Rice, Elmer (Leopold) 1892-1967 **CLC 7, 49;**
    DAM DRAM
  See also CA 21-22; 25-28R; CAP 2; DLB 4, 7;
    MTCW
Rice, Tim(othy Miles Bindon) 1944- **CLC 21**
  See also CA 103; CANR 46
Rich, Adrienne (Cecile) 1929-**CLC 3, 6, 7, 11,**
    18, 36, 73, 76; DAM POET; PC 5
  See also CA 9-12R; CANR 20, 53; DLB 5, 67;
    MTCW
Rich, Barbara
  See Graves, Robert (von Ranke)
Rich, Robert
  See Trumbo, Dalton
Richard, Keith .... **CLC 17**
  See also Richards, Keith
Richards, David Adams 1950- **CLC 59; DAC**
  See also CA 93-96; CANR 60; DLB 53
Richards, I(vor) A(rmstrong) 1893-1979**C L C**
    14, 24
  See also CA 41-44R; 89-92; CANR 34; DLB
    27
Richards, Keith 1943-
  See Richard, Keith
  See also CA 107
Richardson, Anne
  See Roiphe, Anne (Richardson)
Richardson, Dorothy Miller 1873-1957**TCLC**
    3
  See also CA 104; DLB 36
Richardson, Ethel Florence (Lindesay) 1870-
    1946
  See Richardson, Henry Handel
  See also CA 105
Richardson, Henry Handel .... **TCLC 4**
  See also Richardson, Ethel Florence (Lindesay)
Richardson, John 1796-1852**NCLC 55; DAC**
  See also DLB 99
Richardson, Samuel 1689-1761 ... **LC 1; DA;**
    DAB; DAC; DAM MST, NOV; WLC
  See also CDBLB 1660-1789; DLB 39
Richler, Mordecai 1931-**CLC 3, 5, 9, 13, 18, 46,**
    70; DAC; DAM MST, NOV
  See also AITN 1; CA 65-68; CANR 31, 62; CLR

17; DLB 53; MAICYA; MTCW; SATA 44;
SATA-Brief 27
Richter, Conrad (Michael) 1890-1968**CLC 30**
See also AAYA 21; CA 5-8R; 25-28R; CANR
23; DLB 9; MTCW; SATA 3
Ricostranza, Tom
See Ellis, Trey
Riddell, J. H. 1832-1906 .... **TCLC 40**
Riding, Laura .... **CLC 3, 7**
See also Jackson, Laura (Riding)
Riefenstahl, Berta Helene Amalia 1902-
See Riefenstahl, Leni
See also CA 108
Riefenstahl, Leni .... **CLC 16**
See also Riefenstahl, Berta Helene Amalia
Riffe, Ernest
See Bergman, (Ernst) Ingmar
Riggs, (Rolla) Lynn 1899-1954 ..... **TCLC 56;
DAM MULT**
See also CA 144; DLB 175; NNAL
Riley, James Whitcomb 1849-1916**TCLC 51;
DAM POET**
See also CA 118; 137; MAICYA; SATA 17
Riley, Tex
See Creasey, John
Rilke, Rainer Maria 1875-1926**TCLC 1, 6, 19;
DAM POET; PC 2**
See also CA 104; 132; CANR 62; DLB 81;
MTCW
Rimbaud, (Jean Nicolas) Arthur 1854-1891
**NCLC 4, 35; DA; DAB; DAC; DAM MST,
POET; PC 3; WLC**
Rinehart, Mary Roberts 1876-1958**TCLC 52**
See also CA 108
Ringmaster, The
See Mencken, H(enry) L(ouis)
Ringwood, Gwen(dolyn Margaret) Pharis
1910-1984 .... **CLC 48**
See also CA 148; 112; DLB 88
Rio, Michel 19(?)- .... **CLC 43**
Ritsos, Giannes
See Ritsos, Yannis
Ritsos, Yannis 1909-1990 .... **CLC 6, 13, 31**
See also CA 77-80; 133; CANR 39, 61; MTCW
Ritter, Erika 1948(?)- .... **CLC 52**
Rivera, Jose Eustasio 1889-1928 ... **TCLC 35**
See also HW
Rivers, Conrad Kent 1933-1968 .... **CLC 1**
See also BW 1; CA 85-88; DLB 41
Rivers, Elfrida
See Bradley, Marion Zimmer
Riverside, John
See Heinlein, Robert A(nson)
Rizal, Jose 1861-1896 .... **NCLC 27**
Roa Bastos, Augusto (Antonio) 1917-**CLC 45;
DAM MULT; HLC**
See also CA 131; DLB 113; HW
Robbe-Grillet, Alain 1922- **CLC 1, 2, 4, 6, 8,
10, 14, 43**
See also CA 9-12R; CANR 33; DLB 83; MTCW
Robbins, Harold 1916-1997 ..... **CLC 5; DAM
NOV**
See also CA 73-76; CANR 26, 54; MTCW
Robbins, Thomas Eugene 1936-
See Robbins, Tom
See also CA 81-84; CANR 29, 59; DAM NOV,
POP; MTCW
Robbins, Tom .... **CLC 9, 32, 64**
See also Robbins, Thomas Eugene
See also BEST 90:3; DLBY 80
Robbins, Trina 1938- .... **CLC 21**
See also CA 128
Roberts, Charles G(eorge) D(ouglas) 1860-1943

TCLC 8
See also CA 105; CLR 33; DLB 92; SATA 88;
SATA-Brief 29
Roberts, Elizabeth Madox 1886-1941 **T C L C
68**
See also CA 111; DLB 9, 54, 102; SATA 33;
SATA-Brief 27
Roberts, Kate 1891-1985 .... **CLC 15**
See also CA 107; 116
Roberts, Keith (John Kingston) 1935-**CLC 14**
See also CA 25-28R; CANR 46
Roberts, Kenneth (Lewis) 1885-1957**TCLC 23**
See also CA 109; DLB 9
Roberts, Michele (B.) 1949- .... **CLC 48**
See also CA 115; CANR 58
Robertson, Ellis
See Ellison, Harlan (Jay); Silverberg, Robert
Robertson, Thomas William 1829-1871**NCLC
35; DAM DRAM**
Robeson, Kenneth
See Dent, Lester
Robinson, Edwin Arlington 1869-1935**T C L C
5; DA; DAC; DAM MST, POET; PC 1**
See also CA 104; 133; CDALB 1865-1917;
DLB 54; MTCW
Robinson, Henry Crabb 1775-1867**NCLC 15**
See also DLB 107
Robinson, Jill 1936- .... **CLC 10**
See also CA 102; INT 102
Robinson, Kim Stanley 1952- .... **CLC 34**
See also CA 126
Robinson, Lloyd
See Silverberg, Robert
Robinson, Marilynne 1944- .... **CLC 25**
See also CA 116
Robinson, Smokey .... **CLC 21**
See also Robinson, William, Jr.
Robinson, William, Jr. 1940-
See Robinson, Smokey
See also CA 116
Robison, Mary 1949- .... **CLC 42, 98**
See also CA 113; 116; DLB 130; INT 116
Rod, Edouard 1857-1910 .... **TCLC 52**
Roddenberry, Eugene Wesley 1921-1991
See Roddenberry, Gene
See also CA 110; 135; CANR 37; SATA 45;
SATA-Obit 69
Roddenberry, Gene .... **CLC 17**
See also Roddenberry, Eugene Wesley
See also AAYA 5; SATA-Obit 69
Rodgers, Mary 1931- .... **CLC 12**
See also CA 49-52; CANR 8, 55; CLR 20; INT
CANR-8; JRDA; MAICYA; SATA 8
Rodgers, W(illiam) R(obert) 1909-1969**CLC 7**
See also CA 85-88; DLB 20
Rodman, Eric
See Silverberg, Robert
Rodman, Howard 1920(?)-1985 .... **CLC 65**
See also CA 118
Rodman, Maia
See Wojciechowska, Maia (Teresa)
Rodriguez, Claudio 1934- .... **CLC 10**
See also DLB 134
Roelvaag, O(le) E(dvart) 1876-1931**TCLC 17**
See also CA 117; DLB 9
Roethke, Theodore (Huebner) 1908-1963**CLC
1, 3, 8, 11, 19, 46, 101; DAM POET; PC 15**
See also CA 81-84; CABS 2; CDALB 1941-
1968; DLB 5; MTCW
Rogers, Thomas Hunton 1927- .... **CLC 57**
See also CA 89-92; INT 89-92
Rogers, Will(iam Penn Adair) 1879-1935
TCLC 8, 71; DAM MULT

See also CA 105; 144; DLB 11; NNAL
Rogin, Gilbert 1929- .... **CLC 18**
See also CA 65-68; CANR 15
Rohan, Koda .... **TCLC 22**
See also Koda Shigeyuki
Rohlfs, Anna Katharine Green
See Green, Anna Katharine
Rohmer, Eric .... **CLC 16**
See also Scherer, Jean-Marie Maurice
Rohmer, Sax .... **TCLC 28**
See also Ward, Arthur Henry Sarsfield
See also DLB 70
Roiphe, Anne (Richardson) 1935- ..**CLC 3, 9**
See also CA 89-92; CANR 45; DLBY 80; INT
89-92
Rojas, Fernando de 1465-1541 .... **LC 23**
**Rolfe, Frederick (William Serafino Austin
Lewis Mary)** 1860-1913 .... **TCLC 12**
See also CA 107; DLB 34, 156
Rolland, Romain 1866-1944 .... **TCLC 23**
See also CA 118; DLB 65
Rolle, Richard c. 1300-c. 1349 ...... **CMLC 21**
See also DLB 146
Rolvaag, O(le) E(dvart)
See Roelvaag, O(le) E(dvart)
Romain Arnaud, Saint
See Aragon, Louis
Romains, Jules 1885-1972 .... **CLC 7**
See also CA 85-88; CANR 34; DLB 65; MTCW
Romero, Jose Ruben 1890-1952 .... **TCLC 14**
See also CA 114; 131; HW
Ronsard, Pierre de 1524-1585 ... **LC 6; PC 11**
Rooke, Leon 1934- .. **CLC 25, 34; DAM POP**
See also CA 25-28R; CANR 23, 53
Roosevelt, Theodore 1858-1919 ..... **TCLC 69**
See also CA 115; DLB 47
Roper, William 1498-1578 .... **LC 10**
Roquelaure, A. N.
See Rice, Anne
Rosa, Joao Guimaraes 1908-1967 .... **CLC 23**
See also CA 89-92; DLB 113
Rose, Wendy 1948-**CLC 85; DAM MULT; PC
13**
See also CA 53-56; CANR 5, 51; DLB 175;
NNAL; SATA 12
Rosen, R. D.
See Rosen, Richard (Dean)
Rosen, Richard (Dean) 1949- .... **CLC 39**
See also CA 77-80; CANR 62; INT CANR-30
Rosenberg, Isaac 1890-1918 .... **TCLC 12**
See also CA 107; DLB 20
Rosenblatt, Joe .... **CLC 15**
See also Rosenblatt, Joseph
Rosenblatt, Joseph 1933-
See Rosenblatt, Joe
See also CA 89-92; INT 89-92
Rosenfeld, Samuel
See Tzara, Tristan
Rosenstock, Sami
See Tzara, Tristan
Rosenstock, Samuel
See Tzara, Tristan
Rosenthal, M(acha) L(ouis) 1917-1996 . **C L C
28**
See also CA 1-4R; 152; CAAS 6; CANR 4, 51;
DLB 5; SATA 59
Ross, Barnaby
See Dannay, Frederic
Ross, Bernard L.
See Follett, Ken(neth Martin)
Ross, J. H.
See Lawrence, T(homas) E(dward)
Ross, Martin

See Martin, Violet Florence
See also DLB 135
Ross, (James) Sinclair 1908- **CLC 13; DAC; DAM MST; SSC 24**
See also CA 73-76; DLB 88
Rossetti, Christina (Georgina) 1830-1894 **NCLC 2, 50, 66; DA; DAB; DAC; DAM MST, POET; PC 7; WLC**
See also DLB 35, 163; MAICYA; SATA 20
Rossetti, Dante Gabriel 1828-1882. **NCLC 4; DA; DAB; DAC; DAM MST, POET; WLC**
See also CDBLB 1832-1890; DLB 35
Rossner, Judith (Perelman) 1935-**CLC 6, 9, 29**
See also AITN 2; BEST 90:3; CA 17-20R; CANR 18, 51; DLB 6; INT CANR-18; MTCW
Rostand, Edmond (Eugene Alexis) 1868-1918 **TCLC 6, 37; DA; DAB; DAC; DAM DRAM, MST**
See also CA 104; 126; MTCW
Roth, Henry 1906-1995 ..... **CLC 2, 6, 11, 104**
See also CA 11-12; 149; CANR 38, 63; CAP 1; DLB 28; MTCW
Roth, Philip (Milton) 1933-**CLC 1, 2, 3, 4, 6, 9, 15, 22, 31, 47, 66, 86; DA; DAB; DAC; DAM MST, NOV, POP; SSC 26; WLC**
See also BEST 90:3; CA 1-4R; CANR 1, 22, 36, 55; CDALB 1968-1988; DLB 2, 28, 173; DLBY 82; MTCW
Rothenberg, Jerome 1931- .... **CLC 6, 57**
See also CA 45-48; CANR 1; DLB 5
Roumain, Jacques (Jean Baptiste) 1907-1944 **TCLC 19; BLC; DAM MULT**
See also BW 1; CA 117; 125
Rourke, Constance (Mayfield) 1885-1941 **TCLC 12**
See also CA 107; YABC 1
Rousseau, Jean-Baptiste 1671-1741 ...... **LC 9**
Rousseau, Jean-Jacques 1712-1778**LC 14, 36; DA; DAB; DAC; DAM MST; WLC**
Roussel, Raymond 1877-1933 .... **TCLC 20**
See also CA 117
Rovit, Earl (Herbert) 1927- .... **CLC 7**
See also CA 5-8R; CANR 12
Rowe, Nicholas 1674-1718 .... **LC 8**
See also DLB 84
Rowley, Ames Dorrance
See Lovecraft, H(oward) P(hillips)
Rowson, Susanna Haswell 1762(?)-1824 **NCLC 5**
See also DLB 37
Roy, Gabrielle 1909-1983 **CLC 10, 14; DAB; DAC; DAM MST**
See also CA 53-56; 110; CANR 5, 61; DLB 68; MTCW
Rozewicz, Tadeusz 1921- .. **CLC 9, 23; DAM POET**
See also CA 108; CANR 36; MTCW
Ruark, Gibbons 1941- .... **CLC 3**
See also CA 33-36R; CAAS 23; CANR 14, 31, 57; DLB 120
Rubens, Bernice (Ruth) 1923- .... **CLC 19, 31**
See also CA 25-28R; CANR 33; DLB 14; MTCW
Rubin, Harold
See Robbins, Harold
Rudkin, (James) David 1936- .... **CLC 14**
See also CA 89-92; DLB 13
Rudnik, Raphael 1933- .... **CLC 7**
See also CA 29-32R
Ruffian, M.
See Hasek, Jaroslav (Matej Frantisek)
Ruiz, Jose Martinez .... **CLC 11**

See also Martinez Ruiz, Jose
Rukeyser, Muriel 1913-1980**CLC 6, 10, 15, 27; DAM POET; PC 12**
See also CA 5-8R; 93-96; CANR 26, 60; DLB 48; MTCW; SATA-Obit 22
Rule, Jane (Vance) 1931- .... **CLC 27**
See also CA 25-28R; CAAS 18; CANR 12; DLB 60
Rulfo, Juan 1918-1986 ...... **CLC 8, 80; DAM MULT; HLC; SSC 25**
See also CA 85-88; 118; CANR 26; DLB 113; HW; MTCW
Rumi, Jalal al-Din 1297-1373 .... **CMLC 20**
Runeberg, Johan 1804-1877 .... **NCLC 41**
Runyon, (Alfred) Damon 1884(?)-1946**TCLC 10**
See also CA 107; DLB 11, 86, 171
Rush, Norman 1933- .... **CLC 44**
See also CA 121; 126; INT 126
Rushdie, (Ahmed) Salman 1947-**CLC 23, 31, 55, 100; DAB; DAC; DAM MST, NOV, POP; WLCS**
See also BEST 89:3; CA 108; 111; CANR 33, 56; INT 111; MTCW
Rushforth, Peter (Scott) 1945- .... **CLC 19**
See also CA 101
Ruskin, John 1819-1900 .... **TCLC 63**
See also CA 114; 129; CDBLB 1832-1890; DLB 55, 163; SATA 24
Russ, Joanna 1937- .... **CLC 15**
See also CA 25-28R; CANR 11, 31; DLB 8; MTCW
Russell, George William 1867-1935
See Baker, Jean H.
See also CA 104; 153; CDBLB 1890-1914; DAM POET
Russell, (Henry) Ken(neth Alfred) 1927-**CLC 16**
See also CA 105
Russell, Willy 1947- .... **CLC 60**
Rutherford, Mark .... **TCLC 25**
See also White, William Hale
See also DLB 18
Ruyslinck, Ward 1929- .... **CLC 14**
See also Belser, Reimond Karel Maria de
Ryan, Cornelius (John) 1920-1974 ..... **CLC 7**
See also CA 69-72; 53-56; CANR 38
Ryan, Michael 1946- .... **CLC 65**
See also CA 49-52; DLBY 82
Ryan, Tim
See Dent, Lester
Rybakov, Anatoli (Naumovich) 1911-**CLC 23, 53**
See also CA 126; 135; SATA 79
Ryder, Jonathan
See Ludlum, Robert
Ryga, George 1932-1987**CLC 14; DAC; DAM MST**
See also CA 101; 124; CANR 43; DLB 60
S. H.
See Hartmann, Sadakichi
S. S.
See Sassoon, Siegfried (Lorraine)
Saba, Umberto 1883-1957 .... **TCLC 33**
See also CA 144; DLB 114
Sabatini, Rafael 1875-1950 .... **TCLC 47**
Sabato, Ernesto (R.) 1911-**CLC 10, 23; DAM MULT; HLC**
See also CA 97-100; CANR 32; DLB 145; HW; MTCW
Sacastru, Martin
See Bioy Casares, Adolfo
Sacher-Masoch, Leopold von 1836(?)-1895

NCLC 31
Sachs, Marilyn (Stickle) 1927- .... **CLC 35**
See also AAYA 2; CA 17-20R; CANR 13, 47; CLR 2; JRDA; MAICYA; SAAS 2; SATA 3, 68
Sachs, Nelly 1891-1970 .... **CLC 14, 98**
See also CA 17-18; 25-28R; CAP 2
Sackler, Howard (Oliver) 1929-1982 **CLC 14**
See also CA 61-64; 108; CANR 30; DLB 7
Sacks, Oliver (Wolf) 1933- .... **CLC 67**
See also CA 53-56; CANR 28, 50; INT CANR-28; MTCW
Sadakichi
See Hartmann, Sadakichi
Sade, Donatien Alphonse Francois Comte 1740-1814 .... **NCLC 47**
Sadoff, Ira 1945- .... **CLC 9**
See also CA 53-56; CANR 5, 21; DLB 120
Saetone
See Camus, Albert
Safire, William 1929- .... **CLC 10**
See also CA 17-20R; CANR 31, 54
Sagan, Carl (Edward) 1934-1996 ..... **CLC 30**
See also AAYA 2; CA 25-28R; 155; CANR 11, 36; MTCW; SATA 58; SATA-Obit 94
Sagan, Francoise .... **CLC 3, 6, 9, 17, 36**
See also Quoirez, Francoise
See also DLB 83
Sahgal, Nayantara (Pandit) 1927- .... **CLC 41**
See also CA 9-12R; CANR 11
Saint, H(arry) F. 1941- .... **CLC 50**
See also CA 127
St. Aubin de Teran, Lisa 1953-
See Teran, Lisa St. Aubin de
See also CA 118; 126; INT 126
Saint Birgitta of Sweden c. 1303-1373**CMLC 24**
Sainte-Beuve, Charles Augustin 1804-1869 **NCLC 5**
Saint-Exupery, Antoine (Jean Baptiste Marie Roger) de 1900-1944**TCLC 2, 56; DAM NOV; WLC**
See also CA 108; 132; CLR 10; DLB 72; MAICYA; MTCW; SATA 20
St. John, David
See Hunt, E(verette) Howard, (Jr.)
Saint-John Perse
See Leger, (Marie-Rene Auguste) Alexis Saint-Leger
Saintsbury, George (Edward Bateman) 1845-1933 .... **TCLC 31**
See also CA 160; DLB 57, 149
Sait Faik .... **TCLC 23**
See also Abasiyanik, Sait Faik
Saki .... **TCLC 3; SSC 12**
See also Munro, H(ector) H(ugh)
Sala, George Augustus .... **NCLC 46**
Salama, Hannu 1936- .... **CLC 18**
Salamanca, J(ack) R(ichard) 1922-**CLC 4, 15**
See also CA 25-28R
Sale, J. Kirkpatrick
See Sale, Kirkpatrick
Sale, Kirkpatrick 1937- .... **CLC 68**
See also CA 13-16R; CANR 10
Salinas, Luis Omar 1937- ...... **CLC 90; DAM MULT; HLC**
See also CA 131; DLB 82; HW
Salinas (y Serrano), Pedro 1891(?)-1951 **TCLC 17**
See also CA 117; DLB 134
Salinger, J(erome) D(avid) 1919-**CLC 1, 3, 8, 12, 55, 56; DA; DAB; DAC; DAM MST, NOV, POP; SSC 2, 28; WLC**

See also AAYA 2; CA 5-8R; CANR 39; CDALB
1941-1968; CLR 18; DLB 2, 102, 173;
MAICYA; MTCW; SATA 67
Salisbury, John
See Caute, (John) David
Salter, James 1925- .... **CLC 7, 52, 59**
See also CA 73-76; DLB 130
Saltus, Edgar (Everton) 1855-1921 . **TCLC 8**
See also CA 105
Saltykov, Mikhail Evgrafovich 1826-1889
NCLC 16
Samarakis, Antonis 1919- .... **CLC 5**
See also CA 25-28R; CAAS 16; CANR 36
Sanchez, Florencio 1875-1910........ **TCLC 37**
See also CA 153; HW
Sanchez, Luis Rafael 1936- .... **CLC 23**
See also CA 128; DLB 145; HW
Sanchez, Sonia 1934- ..... **CLC 5; BLC; DAM
MULT; PC 9**
See also BW 2; CA 33-36R; CANR 24, 49; CLR
18; DLB 41; DLBD 8; MAICYA; MTCW;
SATA 22
Sand, George 1804-1876**NCLC 2, 42, 57; DA;
DAB; DAC; DAM MST, NOV; WLC**
See also DLB 119
Sandburg, Carl (August) 1878-1967**CLC 1, 4,
10, 15, 35; DA; DAB; DAC; DAM MST,
POET; PC 2; WLC**
See also CA 5-8R; 25-28R; CANR 35; CDALB
1865-1917; DLB 17, 54; MAICYA; MTCW;
SATA 8
Sandburg, Charles
See Sandburg, Carl (August)
Sandburg, Charles A.
See Sandburg, Carl (August)
Sanders, (James) Ed(ward) 1939- .... **CLC 53**
See also CA 13-16R; CAAS 21; CANR 13, 44;
DLB 16
Sanders, Lawrence 1920-1998**CLC 41; DAM
POP**
See also BEST 89:4; CA 81-84; CANR 33, 62;
MTCW
Sanders, Noah
See Blount, Roy (Alton), Jr.
Sanders, Winston P.
See Anderson, Poul (William)
Sandoz, Mari(e Susette) 1896-1966 .. **CLC 28**
See also CA 1-4R; 25-28R; CANR 17, 64; DLB
9; MTCW; SATA 5
Saner, Reg(inald Anthony) 1931- .... **CLC 9**
See also CA 65-68
Sannazaro, Jacopo 1456(?)-1530 .... **LC 8**
Sansom, William 1912-1976 **CLC 2, 6; DAM
NOV; SSC 21**
See also CA 5-8R; 65-68; CANR 42; DLB 139;
MTCW
Santayana, George 1863-1952 .... **TCLC 40**
See also CA 115; DLB 54, 71; DLBD 13
Santiago, Danny .... **CLC 33**
See also James, Daniel (Lewis)
See also DLB 122
Santmyer, Helen Hoover 1895-1986 . **CLC 33**
See also CA 1-4R; 118; CANR 15, 33; DLBY
84; MTCW
Santoka, Taneda 1882-1940 .... **TCLC 72**
Santos, Bienvenido N(uqui) 1911-1996 . **C L C
22; DAM MULT**
See also CA 101; 151; CANR 19, 46
Sapper .... **TCLC 44**
See also McNeile, Herman Cyril
Sapphire 1950- .... **CLC 99**
Sappho fl. 6th cent. B.C.- ...... **CMLC 3; DAM
POET; PC 5**

See also DLB 176
Sarduy, Severo 1937-1993 .... **CLC 6, 97**
See also CA 89-92; 142; CANR 58; DLB 113;
HW
Sargeson, Frank 1903-1982 .... **CLC 31**
See also CA 25-28R; 106; CANR 38
Sarmiento, Felix Ruben Garcia
See Dario, Ruben
Saroyan, William 1908-1981**CLC 1, 8, 10, 29,
34, 56; DA; DAB; DAC; DAM DRAM,
MST, NOV; SSC 21; WLC**
See also CA 5-8R; 103; CANR 30; DLB 7, 9,
86; DLBY 81; MTCW; SATA 23; SATA-Obit
24
Sarraute, Nathalie 1900-**CLC 1, 2, 4, 8, 10, 31,
80**
See also CA 9-12R; CANR 23; DLB 83; MTCW
Sarton, (Eleanor) May 1912-1995**CLC 4, 14,
49, 91; DAM POET**
See also CA 1-4R; 149; CANR 1, 34, 55; DLB
48; DLBY 81; INT CANR-34; MTCW;
SATA 36; SATA-Obit 86
Sartre, Jean-Paul 1905-1980**CLC 1, 4, 7, 9, 13,
18, 24, 44, 50, 52; DA; DAB; DAC; DAM
DRAM, MST, NOV; DC 3; WLC**
See also CA 9-12R; 97-100; CANR 21; DLB
72; MTCW
Sassoon, Siegfried (Lorraine) 1886-1967**C L C
36; DAB; DAM MST, NOV, POET; PC 12**
See also CA 104; 25-28R; CANR 36; DLB 20;
MTCW
Satterfield, Charles
See Pohl, Frederik
Saul, John (W. III) 1942-**CLC 46; DAM NOV,
POP**
See also AAYA 10; BEST 90:4; CA 81-84;
CANR 16, 40
Saunders, Caleb
See Heinlein, Robert A(nson)
Saura (Atares), Carlos 1932- .... **CLC 20**
See also CA 114; 131; HW
Sauser-Hall, Frederic 1887-1961 ...... **CLC 18**
See also Cendrars, Blaise
See also CA 102; 93-96; CANR 36, 62; MTCW
Saussure, Ferdinand de 1857-1913 **TCLC 49**
Savage, Catharine
See Brosman, Catharine Savage
Savage, Thomas 1915- .... **CLC 40**
See also CA 126; 132; CAAS 15; INT 132
Savan, Glenn 19(?)- .... **CLC 50**
Sayers, Dorothy L(eigh) 1893-1957 **TCLC 2,
15; DAM POP**
See also CA 104; 119; CANR 60; CDBLB 1914-
1945; DLB 10, 36, 77, 100; MTCW
Sayers, Valerie 1952- .... **CLC 50**
See also CA 134; CANR 61
Sayles, John (Thomas) 1950- . **CLC 7, 10, 14**
See also CA 57-60; CANR 41; DLB 44
Scammell, Michael 1935- .... **CLC 34**
See also CA 156
Scannell, Vernon 1922- .... **CLC 49**
See also CA 5-8R; CANR 8, 24, 57; DLB 27;
SATA 59
Scarlett, Susan
See Streatfeild, (Mary) Noel
Schaeffer, Susan Fromberg 1941- **CLC 6, 11,
22**
See also CA 49-52; CANR 18; DLB 28; MTCW;
SATA 22
Schary, Jill
See Robinson, Jill
Schell, Jonathan 1943- .... **CLC 35**
See also CA 73-76; CANR 12

Schelling, Friedrich Wilhelm Joseph von 1775-
1854 .... **NCLC 30**
See also DLB 90
Schendel, Arthur van 1874-1946 ... **TCLC 56**
Scherer, Jean-Marie Maurice 1920-
See Rohmer, Eric
See also CA 110
Schevill, James (Erwin) 1920- .... **CLC 7**
See also CA 5-8R; CAAS 12
Schiller, Friedrich 1759-1805**NCLC 39; DAM
DRAM**
See also DLB 94
Schisgal, Murray (Joseph) 1926- .... **CLC 6**
See also CA 21-24R; CANR 48
Schlee, Ann 1934- .... **CLC 35**
See also CA 101; CANR 29; SATA 44; SATA-
Brief 36
Schlegel, August Wilhelm von 1767-1845
NCLC 15
See also DLB 94
Schlegel, Friedrich 1772-1829 .... **NCLC 45**
See also DLB 90
Schlegel, Johann Elias (von) 1719(?)-1749**L C
5**
Schlesinger, Arthur M(eier), Jr. 1917-**CLC 84**
See also AITN 1; CA 1-4R; CANR 1, 28, 58;
DLB 17; INT CANR-28; MTCW; SATA 61
Schmidt, Arno (Otto) 1914-1979 ...... **CLC 56**
See also CA 128; 109; DLB 69
Schmitz, Aron Hector 1861-1928
See Svevo, Italo
See also CA 104; 122; MTCW
Schnackenberg, Gjertrud 1953- .... **CLC 40**
See also CA 116; DLB 120
Schneider, Leonard Alfred 1925-1966
See Bruce, Lenny
See also CA 89-92
Schnitzler, Arthur 1862-1931**TCLC 4; SSC 15**
See also CA 104; DLB 81, 118
Schoenberg, Arnold 1874-1951 ...... **TCLC 75**
See also CA 109
Schonberg, Arnold
See Schoenberg, Arnold
Schopenhauer, Arthur 1788-1860 . **NCLC 51**
See also DLB 90
Schor, Sandra (M.) 1932(?)-1990 ...... **CLC 65**
See also CA 132
Schorer, Mark 1908-1977 .... **CLC 9**
See also CA 5-8R; 73-76; CANR 7; DLB 103
Schrader, Paul (Joseph) 1946- .... **CLC 26**
See also CA 37-40R; CANR 41; DLB 44
Schreiner, Olive (Emilie Albertina) 1855-1920
TCLC 9
See also CA 105; DLB 18, 156
Schulberg, Budd (Wilson) 1914- ... **CLC 7, 48**
See also CA 25-28R; CANR 19; DLB 6, 26,
28; DLBY 81
Schulz, Bruno 1892-1942**TCLC 5, 51; SSC 13**
See also CA 115; 123
Schulz, Charles M(onroe) 1922- .... **CLC 12**
See also CA 9-12R; CANR 6; INT CANR-6;
SATA 10
Schumacher, E(rnst) F(riedrich) 1911-1977
CLC 80
See also CA 81-84; 73-76; CANR 34
Schuyler, James Marcus 1923-1991**CLC 5, 23;
DAM POET**
See also CA 101; 134; DLB 5, 169; INT 101
Schwartz, Delmore (David) 1913-1966**CLC 2,
4, 10, 45, 87; PC 8**
See also CA 17-18; 25-28R; CANR 35; CAP 2;
DLB 28, 48; MTCW
Schwartz, Ernst

See Ozu, Yasujiro

Schwartz, John Burnham 1965- .... **CLC 59**
See also CA 132

Schwartz, Lynne Sharon 1939- .... **CLC 31**
See also CA 103; CANR 44

Schwartz, Muriel A.
See Eliot, T(homas) S(tearns)

Schwarz-Bart, Andre 1928- .... **CLC 2, 4**
See also CA 89-92

Schwarz-Bart, Simone 1938- .... **CLC 7**
See also BW 2; CA 97-100

Schwob, (Mayer Andre) Marcel 1867-1905
TCLC 20
See also CA 117; DLB 123

Sciascia, Leonardo 1921-1989 . **CLC 8, 9, 41**
See also CA 85-88; 130; CANR 35; DLB 177;
MTCW

Scoppettone, Sandra 1936- .... **CLC 26**
See also AAYA 11; CA 5-8R; CANR 41; SATA
9, 92

Scorsese, Martin 1942- .... **CLC 20, 89**
See also CA 110; 114; CANR 46

Scotland, Jay
See Jakes, John (William)

Scott, Duncan Campbell 1862-1947 **TCLC 6;**
DAC
See also CA 104; 153; DLB 92

Scott, Evelyn 1893-1963 .... **CLC 43**
See also CA 104; 112; CANR 64; DLB 9, 48

Scott, F(rancis) R(eginald) 1899-1985 **CLC 22**
See also CA 101; 114; DLB 88; INT 101

Scott, Frank
See Scott, F(rancis) R(eginald)

Scott, Joanna 1960- .... **CLC 50**
See also CA 126; CANR 53

Scott, Paul (Mark) 1920-1978 .... **CLC 9, 60**
See also CA 81-84; 77-80; CANR 33; DLB 14;
MTCW

Scott, Walter 1771-1832 **NCLC 15; DA; DAB;**
DAC; DAM MST, NOV, POET; PC 13;
WLC
See also AAYA 22; CDBLB 1789-1832; DLB
93, 107, 116, 144, 159; YABC 2

Scribe, (Augustin) Eugene 1791-1861 **NCLC**
16; DAM DRAM; DC 5

Scrum, R.
See Crumb, R(obert)

Scudery, Madeleine de 1607-1701 .... **LC 2**

Scum
See Crumb, R(obert)

Scumbag, Little Bobby
See Crumb, R(obert)

Seabrook, John
See Hubbard, L(afayette) Ron(ald)

Sealy, I. Allan 1951- .... **CLC 55**

Search, Alexander
See Pessoa, Fernando (Antonio Nogueira)

Sebastian, Lee
See Silverberg, Robert

Sebastian Owl
See Thompson, Hunter S(tockton)

Sebestyen, Ouida 1924- .... **CLC 30**
See also AAYA 8; CA 107; CANR 40; CLR 17;
JRDA; MAICYA; SAAS 10; SATA 39

Secundus, H. Scriblerus
See Fielding, Henry

Sedges, John
See Buck, Pearl S(ydenstricker)

Sedgwick, Catharine Maria 1789-1867 **NCLC**
19
See also DLB 1, 74

Seelye, John 1931- .... **CLC 7**

Seferiades, Giorgos Stylianou 1900-1971

See Seferis, George
See also CA 5-8R; 33-36R; CANR 5, 36;
MTCW

Seferis, George .... **CLC 5, 11**
See also Seferiades, Giorgos Stylianou

Segal, Erich (Wolf) 1937- . **CLC 3, 10; DAM**
POP
See also BEST 89:1; CA 25-28R; CANR 20,
36; DLBY 86; INT CANR-20; MTCW

Seger, Bob 1945- .... **CLC 35**

Seghers, Anna .... **CLC 7**
See Radvanyi, Netty
See also DLB 69

Seidel, Frederick (Lewis) 1936- .... **CLC 18**
See also CA 13-16R; CANR 8; DLBY 84

Seifert, Jaroslav 1901-1986 .. **CLC 34, 44, 93**
See also CA 127; MTCW

Sei Shonagon c. 966-1017(?) .... **CMLC 6**

Selby, Hubert, Jr. 1928- **CLC 1, 2, 4, 8; SSC 20**
See also CA 13-16R; CANR 33; DLB 2

Selzer, Richard 1928- .... **CLC 74**
See also CA 65-68; CANR 14

Sembene, Ousmane
See Ousmane, Sembene

Senancour, Etienne Pivert de 1770-1846
NCLC 16
See also DLB 119

Sender, Ramon (Jose) 1902-1982 **CLC 8; DAM**
MULT; HLC
See also CA 5-8R; 105; CANR 8; HW; MTCW

Seneca, Lucius Annaeus 4B.C.-65 . **CMLC 6;**
DAM DRAM; DC 5

Senghor, Leopold Sedar 1906- **CLC 54; BLC;**
DAM MULT, POET
See also BW 2; CA 116; 125; CANR 47; MTCW

Serling, (Edward) Rod(man) 1924-1975 **CLC**
30
See also AAYA 14; AITN 1; CA 65-68; 57-60;
DLB 26

Serna, Ramon Gomez de la
See Gomez de la Serna, Ramon

Serpieres
See Guillevic, (Eugene)

Service, Robert
See Service, Robert W(illiam)
See also DAB; DLB 92

Service, Robert W(illiam) 1874(?)-1958 **TCLC**
15; DA; DAC; DAM MST, POET; WLC
See also Service, Robert
See also CA 115; 140; SATA 20

Seth, Vikram 1952- **CLC 43, 90; DAM MULT**
See also CA 121; 127; CANR 50; DLB 120;
INT 127

Seton, Cynthia Propper 1926-1982 .. **CLC 27**
See also CA 5-8R; 108; CANR 7

Seton, Ernest (Evan) Thompson 1860-1946
TCLC 31
See also CA 109; DLB 92; DLBD 13; JRDA;
SATA 18

Seton-Thompson, Ernest
See Seton, Ernest (Evan) Thompson

Settle, Mary Lee 1918- .... **CLC 19, 61**
See also CA 89-92; CAAS 1; CANR 44; DLB
6; INT 89-92

Seuphor, Michel
See Arp, Jean

Sevigne, Marie (de Rabutin-Chantal) Marquise
de 1626-1696 .... **LC 11**

Sewall, Samuel 1652-1730 .... **LC 38**
See also DLB 24

Sexton, Anne (Harvey) 1928-1974 **CLC 2, 4, 6,**
8, 10, 15, 53; DA; DAB; DAC; DAM MST,
POET; PC 2; WLC

See also CA 1-4R; 53-56; CABS 2; CANR 3,
36; CDALB 1941-1968; DLB 5, 169;
MTCW; SATA 10

Shaara, Michael (Joseph, Jr.) 1929-1988 **CLC**
15; DAM POP
See also AITN 1; CA 102; 125; CANR 52;
DLBY 83

Shackleton, C. C.
See Aldiss, Brian W(ilson)

Shacochis, Bob .... **CLC 39**
See also Shacochis, Robert G.

Shacochis, Robert G. 1951-
See Shacochis, Bob
See also CA 119; 124; INT 124

Shaffer, Anthony (Joshua) 1926- .... **CLC 19;**
DAM DRAM
See also CA 110; 116; DLB 13

Shaffer, Peter (Levin) 1926- **CLC 5, 14, 18, 37,**
60; DAB; DAM DRAM, MST; DC 7
See also CA 25-28R; CANR 25, 47; CDBLB
1960 to Present; DLB 13; MTCW

Shakey, Bernard
See Young, Neil

Shalamov, Varlam (Tikhonovich) 1907(?)-1982
CLC 18
See also CA 129; 105

Shamlu, Ahmad 1925- .... **CLC 10**

Shammas, Anton 1951- .... **CLC 55**

Shange, Ntozake 1948- **CLC 8, 25, 38, 74; BLC;**
DAM DRAM, MULT; DC 3
See also AAYA 9; BW 2; CA 85-88; CABS 3;
CANR 27, 48; DLB 38; MTCW

Shanley, John Patrick 1950- .... **CLC 75**
See also CA 128; 133

Shapcott, Thomas W(illiam) 1935- ... **CLC 38**
See also CA 69-72; CANR 49

Shapiro, Jane .... **CLC 76**

Shapiro, Karl (Jay) 1913- ... **CLC 4, 8, 15, 53**
See also CA 1-4R; CAAS 6; CANR 1, 36; DLB
48; MTCW

Sharp, William 1855-1905 .... **TCLC 39**
See also CA 160; DLB 156

Sharpe, Thomas Ridley 1928-
See Sharpe, Tom
See also CA 114; 122; INT 122

Sharpe, Tom .... **CLC 36**
See also Sharpe, Thomas Ridley
See also DLB 14

Shaw, Bernard .... **TCLC 45**
See also Shaw, George Bernard
See also BW 1

Shaw, G. Bernard
See Shaw, George Bernard

Shaw, George Bernard 1856-1950 **TCLC 3, 9,**
21; DA; DAB; DAC; DAM DRAM, MST;
WLC
See also Shaw, Bernard
See also CA 104; 128; CDBLB 1914-1945;
DLB 10, 57; MTCW

Shaw, Henry Wheeler 1818-1885 .. **NCLC 15**
See also DLB 11

Shaw, Irwin 1913-1984 **CLC 7, 23, 34; DAM**
DRAM, POP
See also AITN 1; CA 13-16R; 112; CANR 21;
CDALB 1941-1968; DLB 6, 102; DLBY 84;
MTCW

Shaw, Robert 1927-1978 .... **CLC 5**
See also AITN 1; CA 1-4R; 81-84; CANR 4;
DLB 13, 14

Shaw, T. E.
See Lawrence, T(homas) E(dward)

Shawn, Wallace 1943- .... **CLC 41**
See also CA 112

Shea, Lisa 1953- .... **CLC 86**
See also CA 147
Sheed, Wilfrid (John Joseph) 1930-**CLC 2, 4, 10, 53**
See also CA 65-68; CANR 30; DLB 6; MTCW
Sheldon, Alice Hastings Bradley 1915(?)-1987
See Tiptree, James, Jr.
See also CA 108; 122; CANR 34; INT 108; MTCW
Sheldon, John
See Bloch, Robert (Albert)
Shelley, Mary Wollstonecraft (Godwin) 1797-1851**NCLC 14, 59; DA; DAB; DAC; DAM MST, NOV; WLC**
See also AAYA 20; CDBLB 1789-1832; DLB 110, 116, 159, 178; SATA 29
Shelley, Percy Bysshe 1792-1822 . **NCLC 18; DA; DAB; DAC; DAM MST, POET; PC 14; WLC**
See also CDBLB 1789-1832; DLB 96, 110, 158
Shepard, Jim 1956- .... **CLC 36**
See also CA 137; CANR 59; SATA 90
Shepard, Lucius 1947- .... **CLC 34**
See also CA 128; 141
Shepard, Sam 1943- **CLC 4, 6, 17, 34, 41, 44; DAM DRAM; DC 5**
See also AAYA 1; CA 69-72; CABS 3; CANR 22; DLB 7; MTCW
Shepherd, Michael
See Ludlum, Robert
Sherburne, Zoa (Morin) 1912- .... **CLC 30**
See also AAYA 13; CA 1-4R; CANR 3, 37; MAICYA; SAAS 18; SATA 3
Sheridan, Frances 1724-1766 .... **LC 7**
See also DLB 39, 84
Sheridan, Richard Brinsley 1751-1816**NCLC 5; DA; DAB; DAC; DAM DRAM, MST; DC 1; WLC**
See also CDBLB 1660-1789; DLB 89
Sherman, Jonathan Marc .... **CLC 55**
Sherman, Martin 1941(?)- .... **CLC 19**
See also CA 116; 123
Sherwin, Judith Johnson 1936- .... **CLC 7, 15**
See also CA 25-28R; CANR 34
Sherwood, Frances 1940- .... **CLC 81**
See also CA 146
Sherwood, Robert E(mmet) 1896-1955**TCLC 3; DAM DRAM**
See also CA 104; 153; DLB 7, 26
Shestov, Lev 1866-1938 .... **TCLC 56**
Shevchenko, Taras 1814-1861 .... **NCLC 54**
Shiel, M(atthew) P(hipps) 1865-1947**TCLC 8**
See also Holmes, Gordon
See also CA 106; 160; DLB 153
Shields, Carol 1935- .... **CLC 91; DAC**
See also CA 81-84; CANR 51
Shields, David 1956- .... **CLC 97**
See also CA 124; CANR 48
Shiga, Naoya 1883-1971 ...... **CLC 33; SSC 23**
See also CA 101; 33-36R; DLB 180
Shilts, Randy 1951-1994 .... **CLC 85**
See also AAYA 19; CA 115; 127; 144; CANR 45; INT 127
Shimazaki, Haruki 1872-1943
See Shimazaki Toson
See also CA 105; 134
Shimazaki Toson 1872-1943 .... **TCLC 5**
See also Shimazaki, Haruki
See also DLB 180
Sholokhov, Mikhail (Aleksandrovich) 1905-1984 .... **CLC 7, 15**
See also CA 101; 112; MTCW; SATA-Obit 36
Shone, Patric

See Hanley, James
Shreve, Susan Richards 1939- .... **CLC 23**
See also CA 49-52; CAAS 5; CANR 5, 38; MAICYA; SATA 46, 95; SATA-Brief 41
Shue, Larry 1946-1985**CLC 52; DAM DRAM**
See also CA 145; 117
Shu-Jen, Chou 1881-1936
See Lu Hsun
See also CA 104
Shulman, Alix Kates 1932- .... **CLC 2, 10**
See also CA 29-32R; CANR 43; SATA 7
Shuster, Joe 1914- .... **CLC 21**
Shute, Nevil .... **CLC 30**
See also Norway, Nevil Shute
Shuttle, Penelope (Diane) 1947- .... **CLC 7**
See also CA 93-96; CANR 39; DLB 14, 40
Sidney, Mary 1561-1621 .... **LC 19, 39**
Sidney, Sir Philip 1554-1586 **LC 19, 39; DA; DAB; DAC; DAM MST, POET**
See also CDBLB Before 1660; DLB 167
Siegel, Jerome 1914-1996 .... **CLC 21**
See also CA 116; 151
Siegel, Jerry
See Siegel, Jerome
Sienkiewicz, Henryk (Adam Alexander Pius) 1846-1916 .... **TCLC 3**
See also CA 104; 134
Sierra, Gregorio Martinez
See Martinez Sierra, Gregorio
Sierra, Maria (de la O'LeJarraga) Martinez
See Martinez Sierra, Maria (de la O'LeJarraga)
Sigal, Clancy 1926- .... **CLC 7**
See also CA 1-4R
Sigourney, Lydia Howard (Huntley) 1791-1865 **NCLC 21**
See also DLB 1, 42, 73
Siguenza y Gongora, Carlos de 1645-1700**LC 8**
Sigurjonsson, Johann 1880-1919 ... **TCLC 27**
Sikelianos, Angelos 1884-1951 .... **TCLC 39**
Silkin, Jon 1930- .... **CLC 2, 6, 43**
See also CA 5-8R; CAAS 5; DLB 27
Silko, Leslie (Marmon) 1948-**CLC 23, 74; DA; DAC; DAM MST, MULT, POP; WLCS**
See also AAYA 14; CA 115; 122; CANR 45; DLB 143, 175; NNAL
Sillanpaa, Frans Eemil 1888-1964 ... **CLC 19**
See also CA 129; 93-96; MTCW
Sillitoe, Alan 1928- ... **CLC 1, 3, 6, 10, 19, 57**
See also AITN 1; CA 9-12R; CAAS 2; CANR 8, 26, 55; CDBLB 1960 to Present; DLB 14, 139; MTCW; SATA 61
Silone, Ignazio 1900-1978 .... **CLC 4**
See also CA 25-28; 81-84; CANR 34; CAP 2; MTCW
Silver, Joan Micklin 1935- .... **CLC 20**
See also CA 114; 121; INT 121
Silver, Nicholas
See Faust, Frederick (Schiller)
Silverberg, Robert 1935- **CLC 7; DAM POP**
See also CA 1-4R; CAAS 3; CANR 1, 20, 36; DLB 8; INT CANR-20; MAICYA; MTCW; SATA 13, 91
Silverstein, Alvin 1933- .... **CLC 17**
See also CA 49-52; CANR 2; CLR 25; JRDA; MAICYA; SATA 8, 69
Silverstein, Virginia B(arbara Opshelor) 1937- **CLC 17**
See also CA 49-52; CANR 2; CLR 25; JRDA; MAICYA; SATA 8, 69
Sim, Georges
See Simenon, Georges (Jacques Christian)
Simak, Clifford D(onald) 1904-1988**CLC 1, 55**

See also CA 1-4R; 125; CANR 1, 35; DLB 8; MTCW; SATA-Obit 56
Simenon, Georges (Jacques Christian) 1903-1989 .. **CLC 1, 2, 3, 8, 18, 47; DAM POP**
See also CA 85-88; 129; CANR 35; DLB 72; DLBY 89; MTCW
Simic, Charles 1938-.... **CLC 6, 9, 22, 49, 68; DAM POET**
See also CA 29-32R; CAAS 4; CANR 12, 33, 52, 61; DLB 105
Simmel, Georg 1858-1918 .... **TCLC 64**
See also CA 157
Simmons, Charles (Paul) 1924- .... **CLC 57**
See also CA 89-92; INT 89-92
Simmons, Dan 1948- ..... **CLC 44; DAM POP**
See also AAYA 16; CA 138; CANR 53
Simmons, James (Stewart Alexander) 1933-**CLC 43**
See also CA 105; CAAS 21; DLB 40
Simms, William Gilmore 1806-1870 **NCLC 3**
See also DLB 3, 30, 59, 73
Simon, Carly 1945-........................... **CLC 26**
See also CA 105
Simon, Claude 1913-1984 .. **CLC 4, 9, 15, 39; DAM NOV**
See also CA 89-92; CANR 33; DLB 83; MTCW
Simon, (Marvin) Neil 1927-**CLC 6, 11, 31, 39, 70; DAM DRAM**
See also AITN 1; CA 21-24R; CANR 26, 54; DLB 7; MTCW
Simon, Paul (Frederick) 1941(?)- ..... **CLC 17**
See also CA 116; 153
Simonon, Paul 1956(?)- .... **CLC 30**
Simpson, Harriette
See Arnow, Harriette (Louisa) Simpson
Simpson, Louis (Aston Marantz) 1923-**CLC 4, 7, 9, 32; DAM POET**
See also CA 1-4R; CAAS 4; CANR 1, 61; DLB 5; MTCW
Simpson, Mona (Elizabeth) 1957- .... **CLC 44**
See also CA 122; 135
Simpson, N(orman) F(rederick) 1919-**CLC 29**
See also CA 13-16R; DLB 13
Sinclair, Andrew (Annandale) 1935-. **CLC 2, 14**
See also CA 9-12R; CAAS 5; CANR 14, 38; DLB 14; MTCW
Sinclair, Emil
See Hesse, Hermann
Sinclair, Iain 1943- .... **CLC 76**
See also CA 132
Sinclair, Iain MacGregor
See Sinclair, Iain
Sinclair, Irene
See Griffith, D(avid Lewelyn) W(ark)
Sinclair, Mary Amelia St. Clair 1865(?)-1946
See Sinclair, May
See also CA 104
Sinclair, May .... **TCLC 3, 11**
See also Sinclair, Mary Amelia St. Clair
See also DLB 36, 135
Sinclair, Roy
See Griffith, D(avid Lewelyn) W(ark)
Sinclair, Upton (Beall) 1878-1968 **CLC 1, 11, 15, 63; DA; DAB; DAC; DAM MST, NOV; WLC**
See also CA 5-8R; 25-28R; CANR 7; CDALB 1929-1941; DLB 9; INT CANR-7; MTCW; SATA 9
Singer, Isaac
See Singer, Isaac Bashevis
Singer, Isaac Bashevis 1904-1991**CLC 1, 3, 6, 9, 11, 15, 23, 38, 69; DA; DAB; DAC; DAM**

MST, NOV; SSC 3; WLC
See also AITN 1, 2; CA 1-4R; 134; CANR 1, 39; CDALB 1941-1968; CLR 1; DLB 6, 28, 52; DLBY 91; JRDA; MAICYA; MTCW; SATA 3, 27; SATA-Obit 68
Singer, Israel Joshua 1893-1944 .... **TCLC 33**
Singh, Khushwant 1915- .... **CLC 11**
See also CA 9-12R; CAAS 9; CANR 6
Singleton, Ann
See Benedict, Ruth (Fulton)
Sinjohn, John
See Galsworthy, John
Sinyavsky, Andrei (Donatevich) 1925-1997
CLC 8
See also CA 85-88; 159
Sirin, V.
See Nabokov, Vladimir (Vladimirovich)
Sissman, L(ouis) E(dward) 1928-1976 **CLC 9, 18**
See also CA 21-24R; 65-68; CANR 13; DLB 5
Sisson, C(harles) H(ubert) 1914- .... **CLC 8**
See also CA 1-4R; CAAS 3; CANR 3, 48; DLB 27
Sitwell, Dame Edith 1887-1964 **CLC 2, 9, 67; DAM POET; PC 3**
See also CA 9-12R; CANR 35; CDBLB 1945-1960; DLB 20; MTCW
Siwaarmill, H. P.
See Sharp, William
Sjoewall, Maj 1935- .... **CLC 7**
See also CA 65-68
Sjowall, Maj
See Sjoewall, Maj
Skelton, Robin 1925-1997 .... **CLC 13**
See also AITN 2; CA 5-8R; 160; CAAS 5; CANR 28; DLB 27, 53
Skolimowski, Jerzy 1938- .... **CLC 20**
See also CA 128
Skram, Amalie (Bertha) 1847-1905 **TCLC 25**
Skvorecky, Josef (Vaclav) 1924- **CLC 15, 39, 69; DAC; DAM NOV**
See also CA 61-64; CAAS 1; CANR 10, 34, 63; MTCW
Slade, Bernard .... **CLC 11, 46**
See also Newbound, Bernard Slade
See also CAAS 9; DLB 53
Slaughter, Carolyn 1946- .... **CLC 56**
See also CA 85-88
Slaughter, Frank G(ill) 1908- .... **CLC 29**
See also AITN 2; CA 5-8R; CANR 5; INT CANR-5
Slavitt, David R(ytman) 1935- ...... **CLC 5, 14**
See also CA 21-24R; CAAS 3; CANR 41; DLB 5, 6
Slesinger, Tess 1905-1945 .... **TCLC 10**
See also CA 107; DLB 102
Slessor, Kenneth 1901-1971 .... **CLC 14**
See also CA 102; 89-92
Slowacki, Juliusz 1809-1849 .... **NCLC 15**
Smart, Christopher 1722-1771 .. **LC 3; DAM POET; PC 13**
See also DLB 109
Smart, Elizabeth 1913-1986 .... **CLC 54**
See also CA 81-84; 118; DLB 88
Smiley, Jane (Graves) 1949- **CLC 53, 76; DAM POP**
See also CA 104; CANR 30, 50; INT CANR-30
Smith, A(rthur) J(ames) M(arshall) 1902-1980
CLC 15; DAC
See also CA 1-4R; 102; CANR 4; DLB 88
Smith, Adam 1723-1790 .... **LC 36**
See also DLB 104

Smith, Alexander 1829-1867 .... **NCLC 59**
See also DLB 32, 55
Smith, Anna Deavere 1950- .... **CLC 86**
See also CA 133
Smith, Betty (Wehner) 1896-1972 .... **CLC 19**
See also CA 5-8R; 33-36R; DLBY 82; SATA 6
Smith, Charlotte (Turner) 1749-1806 **NCLC 23**
See also DLB 39, 109
Smith, Clark Ashton 1893-1961 .... **CLC 43**
See also CA 143
Smith, Dave .... **CLC 22, 42**
See also Smith, David (Jeddie)
See also CAAS 7; DLB 5
Smith, David (Jeddie) 1942-
See Smith, Dave
See also CA 49-52; CANR 1, 59; DAM POET
Smith, Florence Margaret 1902-1971
See Smith, Stevie
See also CA 17-18; 29-32R; CANR 35; CAP 2; DAM POET; MTCW
Smith, Iain Crichton 1928- .... **CLC 64**
See also CA 21-24R; DLB 40, 139
Smith, John 1580(?)-1631 .... **LC 9**
Smith, Johnston
See Crane, Stephen (Townley)
Smith, Joseph, Jr. 1805-1844 .... **NCLC 53**
Smith, Lee 1944- .... **CLC 25, 73**
See also CA 114; 119; CANR 46; DLB 143; DLBY 83; INT 119
Smith, Martin
See Smith, Martin Cruz
Smith, Martin Cruz 1942- ..... **CLC 25; DAM MULT, POP**
See also BEST 89:4; CA 85-88; CANR 6, 23, 43; INT CANR-23; NNAL
Smith, Mary-Ann Tirone 1944- .... **CLC 39**
See also CA 118; 136
Smith, Patti 1946- .... **CLC 12**
See also CA 93-96; CANR 63
Smith, Pauline (Urmson) 1882-1959 **TCLC 25**
Smith, Rosamond
See Oates, Joyce Carol
Smith, Sheila Kaye
See Kaye-Smith, Sheila
Smith, Stevie .... **CLC 3, 8, 25, 44; PC 12**
See also Smith, Florence Margaret
See also DLB 20
Smith, Wilbur (Addison) 1933- .... **CLC 33**
See also CA 13-16R; CANR 7, 46; MTCW
Smith, William Jay 1918- .... **CLC 6**
See also CA 5-8R; CANR 44; DLB 5; MAICYA; SAAS 22; SATA 2, 68
Smith, Woodrow Wilson
See Kuttner, Henry
Smolenskin, Peretz 1842-1885 .... **NCLC 30**
Smollett, Tobias (George) 1721-1771 .... **LC 2**
See also CDBLB 1660-1789; DLB 39, 104
Snodgrass, W(illiam) D(e Witt) 1926- **CLC 2, 6, 10, 18, 68; DAM POET**
See also CA 1-4R; CANR 6, 36; DLB 5; MTCW
Snow, C(harles) P(ercy) 1905-1980 **CLC 1, 4, 6, 9, 13, 19; DAM NOV**
See also CA 5-8R; 101; CANR 28; CDBLB 1945-1960; DLB 15, 77; MTCW
Snow, Frances Compton
See Adams, Henry (Brooks)
Snyder, Gary (Sherman) 1930- **CLC 1, 2, 5, 9, 32; DAM POET; PC 21**
See also CA 17-20R; CANR 30, 60; DLB 5, 16, 165
Snyder, Zilpha Keatley 1927- .... **CLC 17**
See also AAYA 15; CA 9-12R; CANR 38; CLR

31; JRDA; MAICYA; SAAS 2; SATA 1, 28, 75
Soares, Bernardo
See Pessoa, Fernando (Antonio Nogueira)
Sobh, A.
See Shamlu, Ahmad
Sobol, Joshua .... **CLC 60**
Soderberg, Hjalmar 1869-1941 ..... **TCLC 39**
Sodergran, Edith (Irene)
See Soedergran, Edith (Irene)
Soedergran, Edith (Irene) 1892-1923 **T C L C 31**
Softly, Edgar
See Lovecraft, H(oward) P(hillips)
Softly, Edward
See Lovecraft, H(oward) P(hillips)
Sokolov, Raymond 1941- .... **CLC 7**
See also CA 85-88
Solo, Jay
See Ellison, Harlan (Jay)
Sologub, Fyodor .... **TCLC 9**
See also Teternikov, Fyodor Kuzmich
Solomons, Ikey Esquir
See Thackeray, William Makepeace
Solomos, Dionysios 1798-1857 .... **NCLC 15**
Solwoska, Mara
See French, Marilyn
Solzhenitsyn, Aleksandr I(sayevich) 1918-
CLC 1, 2, 4, 7, 9, 10, 18, 26, 34, 78; DA; DAB; DAC; DAM MST, NOV; WLC
See also AITN 1; CA 69-72; CANR 40; MTCW
Somers, Jane
See Lessing, Doris (May)
Somerville, Edith 1858-1949 .... **TCLC 51**
See also DLB 135
Somerville & Ross
See Martin, Violet Florence; Somerville, Edith
Sommer, Scott 1951- .... **CLC 25**
See also CA 106
Sondheim, Stephen (Joshua) 1930- . **CLC 30, 39; DAM DRAM**
See also AAYA 11; CA 103; CANR 47
Song, Cathy 1955- .... **PC 21**
See also CA 154; DLB 169
Sontag, Susan 1933- **CLC 1, 2, 10, 13, 31, 105; DAM POP**
See also CA 17-20R; CANR 25, 51; DLB 2, 67; MTCW
Sophocles 496(?)B.C.-406(?)B.C. .. **CMLC 2; DA; DAB; DAC; DAM DRAM, MST; DC 1; WLCS**
See also DLB 176
Sordello 1189-1269 .... **CMLC 15**
Sorel, Julia
See Drexler, Rosalyn
Sorrentino, Gilbert 1929- **CLC 3, 7, 14, 22, 40**
See also CA 77-80; CANR 14, 33; DLB 5, 173; DLBY 80; INT CANR-14
Soto, Gary 1952- **CLC 32, 80; DAM MULT; HLC**
See also AAYA 10; CA 119; 125; CANR 50; CLR 38; DLB 82; HW; INT 125; JRDA; SATA 80
Soupault, Philippe 1897-1990 .... **CLC 68**
See also CA 116; 147; 131
Souster, (Holmes) Raymond 1921- **CLC 5, 14; DAC; DAM POET**
See also CA 13-16R; CAAS 14; CANR 13, 29, 53; DLB 88; SATA 63
Southern, Terry 1924(?)-1995 .... **CLC 7**
See also CA 1-4R; 150; CANR 1, 55; DLB 2
Southey, Robert 1774-1843 .... **NCLC 8**
See also DLB 93, 107, 142; SATA 54

Southworth, Emma Dorothy Eliza Nevitte 1819-1899 .... NCLC 26

Souza, Ernest
See Scott, Evelyn

Soyinka, Wole 1934-CLC 3, 5, 14, 36, 44; BLC; DA; DAB; DAC; DAM DRAM, MST, MULT; DC 2; WLC
See also BW 2; CA 13-16R; CANR 27, 39; DLB 125; MTCW

Spackman, W(illiam) M(ode) 1905-1990C L C 46
See also CA 81-84; 132

Spacks, Barry (Bernard) 1931- .... CLC 14
See also CA 154; CANR 33; DLB 105

Spanidou, Irini 1946- .... CLC 44

Spark, Muriel (Sarah) 1918-CLC 2, 3, 5, 8, 13, 18, 40, 94; DAB; DAC; DAM MST, NOV; SSC 10
See also CA 5-8R; CANR 12, 36; CDBLB 1945-1960; DLB 15, 139; INT CANR-12; MTCW

Spaulding, Douglas
See Bradbury, Ray (Douglas)

Spaulding, Leonard
See Bradbury, Ray (Douglas)

Spence, J. A. D.
See Eliot, T(homas) S(tearns)

Spencer, Elizabeth 1921- .... CLC 22
See also CA 13-16R; CANR 32; DLB 6; MTCW; SATA 14

Spencer, Leonard G.
See Silverberg, Robert

Spencer, Scott 1945- .... CLC 30
See also CA 113; CANR 51; DLBY 86

Spender, Stephen (Harold) 1909-1995CLC 1, 2, 5, 10, 41, 91; DAM POET
See also CA 9-12R; 149; CANR 31, 54; CDBLB 1945-1960; DLB 20; MTCW

Spengler, Oswald (Arnold Gottfried) 1880-1936 TCLC 25
See also CA 118

Spenser, Edmund 1552(?)-1599LC 5, 39; DA; DAB; DAC; DAM MST, POET; PC 8; WLC
See also CDBLB Before 1660; DLB 167

Spicer, Jack 1925-1965 CLC 8, 18, 72; DAM POET
See also CA 85-88; DLB 5, 16

Spiegelman, Art 1948- .... CLC 76
See also AAYA 10; CA 125; CANR 41, 55

Spielberg, Peter 1929- .... CLC 6
See also CA 5-8R; CANR 4, 48; DLBY 81

Spielberg, Steven 1947- .... CLC 20
See also AAYA 8; CA 77-80; CANR 32; SATA 32

Spillane, Frank Morrison 1918-
See Spillane, Mickey
See also CA 25-28R; CANR 28, 63; MTCW; SATA 66

Spillane, Mickey .... CLC 3, 13
See also Spillane, Frank Morrison

Spinoza, Benedictus de 1632-1677 .... LC 9

Spinrad, Norman (Richard) 1940- ... CLC 46
See also CA 37-40R; CAAS 19; CANR 20; DLB 8; INT CANR-20

Spitteler, Carl (Friedrich Georg) 1845-1924 TCLC 12
See also CA 109; DLB 129

Spivack, Kathleen (Romola Drucker) 1938- CLC 6
See also CA 49-52

Spoto, Donald 1941- .... CLC 39
See also CA 65-68; CANR 11, 57

Springsteen, Bruce (F.) 1949- .... CLC 17

See also CA 111

Spurling, Hilary 1940- .... CLC 34
See also CA 104; CANR 25, 52

Spyker, John Howland
See Elman, Richard

Squires, (James) Radcliffe 1917-1993CLC 51
See also CA 1-4R; 140; CANR 6, 21

Srivastava, Dhanpat Rai 1880(?)-1936
See Premchand
See also CA 118

Stacy, Donald
See Pohl, Frederik

Stael, Germaine de
See Stael-Holstein, Anne Louise Germaine Necker Baronn
See also DLB 119

Stael-Holstein, Anne Louise Germaine Necker Baronn 1766-1817 .... NCLC 3
See also Stael, Germaine de

Stafford, Jean 1915-1979CLC 4, 7, 19, 68; SSC 26
See also CA 1-4R; 85-88; CANR 3; DLB 2, 173; MTCW; SATA-Obit 22

Stafford, William (Edgar) 1914-1993 CLC 4, 7, 29; DAM POET
See also CA 5-8R; 142; CAAS 3; CANR 5, 22; DLB 5; INT CANR-22

Stagnelius, Eric Johan 1793-1823 . NCLC 61

Staines, Trevor
See Brunner, John (Kilian Houston)

Stairs, Gordon
See Austin, Mary (Hunter)

Stannard, Martin 1947- .... CLC 44
See also CA 142; DLB 155

Stanton, Elizabeth Cady 1815-1902TCLC 73
See also DLB 79

Stanton, Maura 1946- .... CLC 9
See also CA 89-92; CANR 15; DLB 120

Stanton, Schuyler
See Baum, L(yman) Frank

Stapledon, (William) Olaf 1886-1950 T C L C 22
See also CA 111; DLB 15

Starbuck, George (Edwin) 1931-1996CLC 53; DAM POET
See also CA 21-24R; 153; CANR 23

Stark, Richard
See Westlake, Donald E(dwin)

Staunton, Schuyler
See Baum, L(yman) Frank

Stead, Christina (Ellen) 1902-1983 CLC 2, 5, 8, 32, 80
See also CA 13-16R; 109; CANR 33, 40; MTCW

Stead, William Thomas 1849-1912 TCLC 48

Steele, Richard 1672-1729 .... LC 18
See also CDBLB 1660-1789; DLB 84, 101

Steele, Timothy (Reid) 1948- .... CLC 45
See also CA 93-96; CANR 16, 50; DLB 120

Steffens, (Joseph) Lincoln 1866-1936 T C L C 20
See also CA 117

Stegner, Wallace (Earle) 1909-1993CLC 9, 49, 81; DAM NOV; SSC 27
See also AITN 1; BEST 90:3; CA 1-4R; 141; CAAS 9; CANR 1, 21, 46; DLB 9; DLBY 93; MTCW

Stein, Gertrude 1874-1946TCLC 1, 6, 28, 48; DA; DAB; DAC; DAM MST, NOV, POET; PC 18; WLC
See also CA 104; 132; CDALB 1917-1929; DLB 4, 54, 86; DLBD 15; MTCW

Steinbeck, John (Ernst) 1902-1968CLC 1, 5, 9, 13, 21, 34, 45, 75; DA; DAB; DAC; DAM DRAM, MST, NOV; SSC 11; WLC
See also AAYA 12; CA 1-4R; 25-28R; CANR 1, 35; CDALB 1929-1941; DLB 7, 9; DLBD 2; MTCW; SATA 9

Steinem, Gloria 1934- .... CLC 63
See also CA 53-56; CANR 28, 51; MTCW

Steiner, George 1929- ... CLC 24; DAM NOV
See also CA 73-76; CANR 31; DLB 67; MTCW; SATA 62

Steiner, K. Leslie
See Delany, Samuel R(ay, Jr.)

Steiner, Rudolf 1861-1925 .... TCLC 13
See also CA 107

Stendhal 1783-1842NCLC 23, 46; DA; DAB; DAC; DAM MST, NOV; SSC 27; WLC
See also DLB 119

Stephen, Adeline Virginia
See Woolf, (Adeline) Virginia

Stephen, Leslie 1832-1904 .... TCLC 23
See also CA 123; DLB 57, 144

Stephen, Sir Leslie
See Stephen, Leslie

Stephen, Virginia
See Woolf, (Adeline) Virginia

Stephens, James 1882(?)-1950 .... TCLC 4
See also CA 104; DLB 19, 153, 162

Stephens, Reed
See Donaldson, Stephen R.

Steptoe, Lydia
See Barnes, Djuna

Sterchi, Beat 1949- .... CLC 65

Sterling, Brett
See Bradbury, Ray (Douglas); Hamilton, Edmond

Sterling, Bruce 1954- .... CLC 72
See also CA 119; CANR 44

Sterling, George 1869-1926 .... TCLC 20
See also CA 117; DLB 54

Stern, Gerald 1925- .... CLC 40, 100
See also CA 81-84; CANR 28; DLB 105

Stern, Richard (Gustave) 1928- .... CLC 4, 39
See also CA 1-4R; CANR 1, 25, 52; DLBY 87; INT CANR-25

Sternberg, Josef von 1894-1969 .... CLC 20
See also CA 81-84

Sterne, Laurence 1713-1768LC 2; DA; DAB; DAC; DAM MST, NOV; WLC
See also CDBLB 1660-1789; DLB 39

Sternheim, (William Adolf) Carl 1878-1942 TCLC 8
See also CA 105; DLB 56, 118

Stevens, Mark 1951- .... CLC 34
See also CA 122

Stevens, Wallace 1879-1955 TCLC 3, 12, 45; DA; DAB; DAC; DAM MST, POET; PC 6; WLC
See also CA 104; 124; CDALB 1929-1941; DLB 54; MTCW

Stevenson, Anne (Katharine) 1933-CLC 7, 33
See also CA 17-20R; CAAS 9; CANR 9, 33; DLB 40; MTCW

Stevenson, Robert Louis (Balfour) 1850-1894 NCLC 5, 14, 63; DA; DAB; DAC; DAM MST, NOV; SSC 11; WLC
See also CDBLB 1890-1914; CLR 10, 11; DLB 18, 57, 141, 156, 174; DLBD 13; JRDA; MAICYA; YABC 2

Stewart, J(ohn) I(nnes) M(ackintosh) 1906-1994 .... CLC 7, 14, 32
See also CA 85-88; 147; CAAS 3; CANR 47; MTCW

Stewart, Mary (Florence Elinor) 1916-CLC 7,

35; DAB
See also CA 1-4R; CANR 1, 59; SATA 12

Stewart, Mary Rainbow
See Stewart, Mary (Florence Elinor)

Stifle, June
See Campbell, Maria

Stifter, Adalbert 1805-1868NCLC 41; SSC 28
See also DLB 133

Still, James 1906- .... **CLC 49**
See also CA 65-68; CAAS 17; CANR 10, 26;
DLB 9; SATA 29

Sting
See Sumner, Gordon Matthew

Stirling, Arthur
See Sinclair, Upton (Beall)

Stitt, Milan 1941- .... **CLC 29**
See also CA 69-72

Stockton, Francis Richard 1834-1902
See Stockton, Frank R.
See also CA 108; 137; MAICYA; SATA 44

Stockton, Frank R. .... **TCLC 47**
See also Stockton, Francis Richard
See also DLB 42, 74; DLBD 13; SATA-Brief 32

Stoddard, Charles
See Kuttner, Henry

Stoker, Abraham 1847-1912
See Stoker, Bram
See also CA 105; DA; DAC; DAM MST, NOV;
SATA 29

Stoker, Bram 1847-1912TCLC 8; DAB; WLC
See also Stoker, Abraham
See also CA 150; CDBLB 1890-1914; DLB 36,
70, 178

Stolz, Mary (Slattery) 1920- .... **CLC 12**
See also AAYA 8; AITN 1; CA 5-8R; CANR
13, 41; JRDA; MAICYA; SAAS 3; SATA 10,
71

Stone, Irving 1903-1989 .. CLC 7; DAM POP
See also AITN 1; CA 1-4R; 129; CAAS 3;
CANR 1, 23; INT CANR-23; MTCW; SATA
3; SATA-Obit 64

Stone, Oliver (William) 1946- .... **CLC 73**
See also AAYA 15; CA 110; CANR 55

Stone, Robert (Anthony) 1937-CLC 5, 23, 42
See also CA 85-88; CANR 23; DLB 152; INT
CANR-23; MTCW

Stone, Zachary
See Follett, Ken(neth Martin)

Stoppard, Tom 1937-CLC 1, 3, 4, 5, 8, 15, 29,
34, 63, 91; DA; DAB; DAC; DAM DRAM,
MST; DC 6; WLC
See also CA 81-84; CANR 39; CDBLB 1960
to Present; DLB 13; DLBY 85; MTCW

Storey, David (Malcolm) 1933-CLC 2, 4, 5, 8;
DAM DRAM
See also CA 81-84; CANR 36; DLB 13, 14;
MTCW

Storm, Hyemeyohsts 1935- ...... CLC 3; DAM
MULT
See also CA 81-84; CANR 45; NNAL

Storm, (Hans) Theodor (Woldsen) 1817-1888
NCLC 1; SSC 27

Storni, Alfonsina 1892-1938 . TCLC 5; DAM
MULT; HLC
See also CA 104; 131; HW

Stoughton, William 1631-1701 .... LC 38
See also DLB 24

Stout, Rex (Todhunter) 1886-1975 ..... CLC 3
See also AITN 2; CA 61-64

Stow, (Julian) Randolph 1935- .. CLC 23, 48
See also CA 13-16R; CANR 33; MTCW

Stowe, Harriet (Elizabeth) Beecher 1811-1896

NCLC 3, 50; DA; DAB; DAC; DAM MST,
NOV; WLC
See also CDALB 1865-1917; DLB 1, 12, 42,
74; JRDA; MAICYA; YABC 1

Strachey, (Giles) Lytton 1880-1932 TCLC 12
See also CA 110; DLB 149; DLBD 10

Strand, Mark 1934- CLC 6, 18, 41, 71; DAM
POET
See also CA 21-24R; CANR 40; DLB 5; SATA
41

Straub, Peter (Francis) 1943- . CLC 28, 107;
DAM POP
See also BEST 89:1; CA 85-88; CANR 28;
DLBY 84; MTCW

Strauss, Botho 1944-........................... CLC 22
See also CA 157; DLB 124

Streatfeild, (Mary) Noel 1895(?)-1986CLC 21
See also CA 81-84; 120; CANR 31; CLR 17;
DLB 160; MAICYA; SATA 20; SATA-Obit
48

Stribling, T(homas) S(igismund) 1881-1965
CLC 23
See also CA 107; DLB 9

Strindberg, (Johan) August 1849-1912T C L C
1, 8, 21, 47; DA; DAB; DAC; DAM DRAM,
MST; WLC
See also CA 104; 135

Stringer, Arthur 1874-1950 .... TCLC 37
See also CA 161; DLB 92

Stringer, David
See Roberts, Keith (John Kingston)

Stroheim, Erich von 1885-1957 ..... TCLC 71

Strugatskii, Arkadii (Natanovich) 1925-1991
CLC 27
See also CA 106; 135

Strugatskii, Boris (Natanovich) 1933-CLC 27
See also CA 106

Strummer, Joe 1953(?)- .... CLC 30

Stuart, Don A.
See Campbell, John W(ood, Jr.)

Stuart, Ian
See MacLean, Alistair (Stuart)

Stuart, Jesse (Hilton) 1906-1984CLC 1, 8, 11,
14, 34
See also CA 5-8R; 112; CANR 31; DLB 9, 48,
102; DLBY 84; SATA 2; SATA-Obit 36

Sturgeon, Theodore (Hamilton) 1918-1985
CLC 22, 39
See also Queen, Ellery
See also CA 81-84; 116; CANR 32; DLB 8;
DLBY 85; MTCW

Sturges, Preston 1898-1959 .... TCLC 48
See also CA 114; 149; DLB 26

Styron, William 1925-CLC 1, 3, 5, 11, 15, 60;
DAM NOV, POP; SSC 25
See also BEST 90:4; CA 5-8R; CANR 6, 33;
CDALB 1968-1988; DLB 2, 143; DLBY 80;
INT CANR-6; MTCW

Suarez Lynch, B.
See Bioy Casares, Adolfo; Borges, Jorge Luis

Su Chien 1884-1918
See Su Man-shu
See also CA 123

Suckow, Ruth 1892-1960 .... SSC 18
See also CA 113; DLB 9, 102

Sudermann, Hermann 1857-1928 .. TCLC 15
See also CA 107; DLB 118

Sue, Eugene 1804-1857 .... NCLC 1
See also DLB 119

Sueskind, Patrick 1949- .... CLC 44
See also Suskind, Patrick

Sukenick, Ronald 1932- .... CLC 3, 4, 6, 48
See also CA 25-28R; CAAS 8; CANR 32; DLB

173; DLBY 81

Suknaski, Andrew 1942- .... **CLC 19**
See also CA 101; DLB 53

Sullivan, Vernon
See Vian, Boris

Sully Prudhomme 1839-1907 .... **TCLC 31**

Su Man-shu .... **TCLC 24**
See also Su Chien

Summerforest, Ivy B.
See Kirkup, James

Summers, Andrew James 1942- .... **CLC 26**

Summers, Andy
See Summers, Andrew James

Summers, Hollis (Spurgeon, Jr.) 1916-CLC 10
See also CA 5-8R; CANR 3; DLB 6

**Summers, (Alphonsus Joseph-Mary Augustus)
Montague** 1880-1948 .... **TCLC 16**
See also CA 118

Sumner, Gordon Matthew 1951- ...... **CLC 26**

Surtees, Robert Smith 1803-1864 .. NCLC 14
See also DLB 21

Susann, Jacqueline 1921-1974 .... **CLC 3**
See also AITN 1; CA 65-68; 53-56; MTCW

Su Shih 1036-1101 .... **CMLC 15**

Suskind, Patrick
See Sueskind, Patrick
See also CA 145

Sutcliff, Rosemary 1920-1992CLC 26; DAB;
DAC; DAM MST, POP
See also AAYA 10; CA 5-8R; 139; CANR 37;
CLR 1, 37; JRDA; MAICYA; SATA 6, 44,
78; SATA-Obit 73

Sutro, Alfred 1863-1933 .... **TCLC 6**
See also CA 105; DLB 10

Sutton, Henry
See Slavitt, David R(ytman)

Svevo, Italo 1861-1928 . TCLC 2, 35; SSC 25
See also Schmitz, Aron Hector

Swados, Elizabeth (A.) 1951- .... **CLC 12**
See also CA 97-100; CANR 49; INT 97-100

Swados, Harvey 1920-1972 .... **CLC 5**
See also CA 5-8R; 37-40R; CANR 6; DLB 2

Swan, Gladys 1934- .... **CLC 69**
See also CA 101; CANR 17, 39

Swarthout, Glendon (Fred) 1918-1992CLC 35
See also CA 1-4R; 139; CANR 1, 47; SATA 26

Sweet, Sarah C.
See Jewett, (Theodora) Sarah Orne

Swenson, May 1919-1989CLC 4, 14, 61, 106;
DA; DAB; DAC; DAM MST, POET; PC
14
See also CA 5-8R; 130; CANR 36, 61; DLB 5;
MTCW; SATA 15

Swift, Augustus
See Lovecraft, H(oward) P(hillips)

Swift, Graham (Colin) 1949- ...... CLC 41, 88
See also CA 117; 122; CANR 46

Swift, Jonathan 1667-1745 LC 1; DA; DAB;
DAC; DAM MST, NOV, POET; PC 9;
WLC
See also CDBLB 1660-1789; DLB 39, 95, 101;
SATA 19

Swinburne, Algernon Charles 1837-1909
TCLC 8, 36; DA; DAB; DAC; DAM MST,
POET; WLC
See also CA 105; 140; CDBLB 1832-1890;
DLB 35, 57

Swinfen, Ann .... **CLC 34**

Swinnerton, Frank Arthur 1884-1982CLC 31
See also CA 108; DLB 34

Swithen, John
See King, Stephen (Edwin)

Sylvia

See Ashton-Warner, Sylvia (Constance)

Symmes, Robert Edward
See Duncan, Robert (Edward)

Symonds, John Addington 1840-1893 N C L C 34
See also DLB 57, 144

Symons, Arthur 1865-1945 .... **TCLC 11**
See also CA 107; DLB 19, 57, 149

Symons, Julian (Gustave) 1912-1994 **CLC 2, 14, 32**
See also CA 49-52; 147; CAAS 3; CANR 3, 33, 59; DLB 87, 155; DLBY 92; MTCW

Synge, (Edmund) J(ohn) M(illington) 1871-1909 ... **TCLC 6, 37; DAM DRAM; DC 2**
See also CA 104; 141; CDBLB 1890-1914; DLB 10, 19

Syruc, J.
See Milosz, Czeslaw

Szirtes, George 1948- .... **CLC 46**
See also CA 109; CANR 27, 61

Szymborska, Wislawa 1923-............... **CLC 99**
See also CA 154; DLBY 96

T. O., Nik
See Annensky, Innokenty (Fyodorovich)

Tabori, George 1914- .... **CLC 19**
See also CA 49-52; CANR 4

Tagore, Rabindranath 1861-1941 **TCLC 3, 53; DAM DRAM, POET; PC 8**
See also CA 104; 120; MTCW

Taine, Hippolyte Adolphe 1828-1893 . N C L C 15

Talese, Gay 1932- .... **CLC 37**
See also AITN 1; CA 1-4R; CANR 9, 58; INT CANR-9; MTCW

Tallent, Elizabeth (Ann) 1954- .... **CLC 45**
See also CA 117; DLB 130

Tally, Ted 1952- :............................... **CLC 42**
See also CA 120; 124; INT 124

Tamayo y Baus, Manuel 1829-1898 **NCLC 1**

Tammsaare, A(nton) H(ansen) 1878-1940 **TCLC 27**

Tam'si, Tchicaya U
See Tchicaya, Gerald Felix

Tan, Amy (Ruth) 1952- **CLC 59; DAM MULT, NOV, POP**
See also AAYA 9; BEST 89:3; CA 136; CANR 54; DLB 173; SATA 75

Tandem, Felix
See Spitteler, Carl (Friedrich Georg)

Tanizaki, Jun'ichiro 1886-1965 **CLC 8, 14, 28; SSC 21**
See also CA 93-96; 25-28R; DLB 180

Tanner, William
See Amis, Kingsley (William)

Tao Lao
See Storni, Alfonsina

Tarassoff, Lev
See Troyat, Henri

Tarbell, Ida M(inerva) 1857-1944 . **TCLC 40**
See also CA 122; DLB 47

Tarkington, (Newton) Booth 1869-1946 **TCLC 9**
See also CA 110; 143; DLB 9, 102; SATA 17

Tarkovsky, Andrei (Arsenyevich) 1932-1986 **CLC 75**
See also CA 127

Tartt, Donna 1964(?)- .... **CLC 76**
See also CA 142

Tasso, Torquato 1544-1595 .... **LC 5**

Tate, (John Orley) Allen 1899-1979 **CLC 2, 6, 9, 11, 14, 24**
See also CA 5-8R; 85-88; CANR 32; DLB 4, 45, 63; MTCW

Tate, Ellalice
See Hibbert, Eleanor Alice Burford

Tate, James (Vincent) 1943- ..... **CLC 2, 6, 25**
See also CA 21-24R; CANR 29, 57; DLB 5, 169

Tavel, Ronald 1940- .... **CLC 6**
See also CA 21-24R; CANR 33

Taylor, C(ecil) P(hilip) 1929-1981 .... **CLC 27**
See also CA 25-28R; 105; CANR 47

Taylor, Edward 1642(?)-1729 ..... **LC 11; DA; DAB; DAC; DAM MST, POET**
See also DLB 24

Taylor, Eleanor Ross 1920- .... **CLC 5**
See also CA 81-84

Taylor, Elizabeth 1912-1975 ..... **CLC 2, 4, 29**
See also CA 13-16R; CANR 9; DLB 139; MTCW; SATA 13

Taylor, Frederick Winslow 1856-1915 **T C L C 76**

Taylor, Henry (Splawn) 1942- .... **CLC 44**
See also CA 33-36R; CAAS 7; CANR 31; DLB 5

Taylor, Kamala (Purnaiya) 1924-
See Markandaya, Kamala
See also CA 77-80

Taylor, Mildred D. .... **CLC 21**
See also AAYA 10; BW 1; CA 85-88; CANR 25; CLR 9; DLB 52; JRDA; MAICYA; SAAS 5; SATA 15, 70

Taylor, Peter (Hillsman) 1917-1994 **CLC 1, 4, 18, 37, 44, 50, 71; SSC 10**
See also CA 13-16R; 147; CANR 9, 50; DLBY 81, 94; INT CANR-9; MTCW

Taylor, Robert Lewis 1912- .... **CLC 14**
See also CA 1-4R; CANR 3, 64; SATA 10

Tchekhov, Anton
See Chekhov, Anton (Pavlovich)

Tchicaya, Gerald Felix 1931-1988 .. **CLC 101**
See also CA 129; 125

Tchicaya U Tam'si
See Tchicaya, Gerald Felix

Teasdale, Sara 1884-1933 .... **TCLC 4**
See also CA 104; DLB 45; SATA 32

Tegner, Esaias 1782-1846 .... **NCLC 2**

Teilhard de Chardin, (Marie Joseph) Pierre 1881-1955 .... **TCLC 9**
See also CA 105

Temple, Ann
See Mortimer, Penelope (Ruth)

Tennant, Emma (Christina) 1937- **CLC 13, 52**
See also CA 65-68; CAAS 9; CANR 10, 38, 59; DLB 14

Tenneshaw, S. M.
See Silverberg, Robert

Tennyson, Alfred 1809-1892 ... **NCLC 30, 65; DA; DAB; DAC; DAM MST, POET; PC 6; WLC**
See also CDBLB 1832-1890; DLB 32

Teran, Lisa St. Aubin de .... **CLC 36**
See also St. Aubin de Teran, Lisa

Terence 195(?)B.C.-159B.C. **CMLC 14; DC 7**

Teresa de Jesus, St. 1515-1582 .... **LC 18**

Terkel, Louis 1912-
See Terkel, Studs
See also CA 57-60; CANR 18, 45; MTCW

Terkel, Studs .... **CLC 38**
See also Terkel, Louis
See also AITN 1

Terry, C. V.
See Slaughter, Frank G(ill)

Terry, Megan 1932- .... **CLC 19**
See also CA 77-80; CABS 3; CANR 43; DLB 7

Tertz, Abram

See Sinyavsky, Andrei (Donatevich)

Tesich, Steve 1943(?)-1996 .... **CLC 40, 69**
See also CA 105; 152; DLBY 83

Teternikov, Fyodor Kuzmich 1863-1927
See Sologub, Fyodor
See also CA 104

Tevis, Walter 1928-1984 .... **CLC 42**
See also CA 113

Tey, Josephine .... **TCLC 14**
See also Mackintosh, Elizabeth
See also DLB 77

Thackeray, William Makepeace 1811-1863 **NCLC 5, 14, 22, 43; DA; DAB; DAC; DAM MST, NOV; WLC**
See also CDBLB 1832-1890; DLB 21, 55, 159, 163; SATA 23

Thakura, Ravindranatha
See Tagore, Rabindranath

Tharoor, Shashi 1956- .... **CLC 70**
See also CA 141

Thelwell, Michael Miles 1939- .... **CLC 22**
See also BW 2; CA 101

Theobald, Lewis, Jr.
See Lovecraft, H(oward) P(hillips)

Theodorescu, Ion N. 1880-1967
See Arghezi, Tudor
See also CA 116

Theriault, Yves 1915-1983 .... **CLC 79; DAC; DAM MST**
See also CA 102; DLB 88

Theroux, Alexander (Louis) 1939- **CLC 2, 25**
See also CA 85-88; CANR 20, 63

Theroux, Paul (Edward) 1941- **CLC 5, 8, 11, 15, 28, 46; DAM POP**
See also BEST 89:4; CA 33-36R; CANR 20, 45; DLB 2; MTCW; SATA 44

Thesen, Sharon 1946- .... **CLC 56**

Thevenin, Denis
See Duhamel, Georges

Thibault, Jacques Anatole Francois 1844-1924
See France, Anatole
See also CA 106; 127; DAM NOV; MTCW

Thiele, Colin (Milton) 1920-............. **CLC 17**
See also CA 29-32R; CANR 12, 28, 53; CLR 27; MAICYA; SAAS 2; SATA 14, 72

Thomas, Audrey (Callahan) 1935- **CLC 7, 13, 37, 107; SSC 20**
See also AITN 2; CA 21-24R; CAAS 19; CANR 36, 58; DLB 60; MTCW

Thomas, D(onald) M(ichael) 1935- . **CLC 13, 22, 31**
See also CA 61-64; CAAS 11; CANR 17, 45; CDBLB 1960 to Present; DLB 40; INT CANR-17; MTCW

Thomas, Dylan (Marlais) 1914-1953 **TCLC 1, 8, 45; DA; DAB; DAC; DAM DRAM, MST, POET; PC 2; SSC 3; WLC**
See also CA 104; 120; CDBLB 1945-1960; DLB 13, 20, 139; MTCW; SATA 60

Thomas, (Philip) Edward 1878-1917 . **T C L C 10; DAM POET**
See also CA 106; 153; DLB 19

Thomas, Joyce Carol 1938- .... **CLC 35**
See also AAYA 12; BW 2; CA 113; 116; CANR 48; CLR 19; DLB 33; INT 116; JRDA; MAICYA; MTCW; SAAS 7; SATA 40, 78

Thomas, Lewis 1913-1993 .... **CLC 35**
See also CA 85-88; 143; CANR 38, 60; MTCW

Thomas, Paul
See Mann, (Paul) Thomas

Thomas, Piri 1928- .... **CLC 17**
See also CA 73-76; HW

Thomas, R(onald) S(tuart) 1913- **CLC 6, 13,**

48; DAB; DAM POET
See also CA 89-92; CAAS 4; CANR 30;
CDBLB 1960 to Present; DLB 27; MTCW

Thomas, Ross (Elmore) 1926-1995 ... **CLC 39**
See also CA 33-36R; 150; CANR 22, 63

Thompson, Francis Clegg
See Mencken, H(enry) L(ouis)

Thompson, Francis Joseph 1859-1907**TCLC 4**
See also CA 104; CDBLB 1890-1914; DLB 19

Thompson, Hunter S(tockton) 1939-. **CLC 9,**
17, 40, 104; DAM POP
See also BEST 89:1; CA 17-20R; CANR 23,
46; MTCW

Thompson, James Myers
See Thompson, Jim (Myers)

Thompson, Jim (Myers) 1906-1977(?)**CLC 69**
See also CA 140

Thompson, Judith .... **CLC 39**

Thomson, James 1700-1748 ... **LC 16, 29, 40;**
DAM POET
See also DLB 95

Thomson, James 1834-1882 **NCLC 18; DAM**
POET
See also DLB 35

Thoreau, Henry David 1817-1862**NCLC 7, 21,**
61; DA; DAB; DAC; DAM MST; WLC
See also CDALB 1640-1865; DLB 1

Thornton, Hall
See Silverberg, Robert

Thucydides c. 455B.C.-399B.C. .... **CMLC 17**
See also DLB 176

Thurber, James (Grover) 1894-1961. **CLC 5,**
11, 25; DA; DAB; DAC; DAM DRAM,
MST, NOV; SSC 1
See also CA 73-76; CANR 17, 39; CDALB
1929-1941; DLB 4, 11, 22, 102; MAICYA;
MTCW; SATA 13

Thurman, Wallace (Henry) 1902-1934**T C L C**
6; BLC; DAM MULT
See also BW 1; CA 104; 124; DLB 51

Ticheburn, Cheviot
See Ainsworth, William Harrison

Tieck, (Johann) Ludwig 1773-1853 **NCLC 5,**
46
See also DLB 90

Tiger, Derry
See Ellison, Harlan (Jay)

Tilghman, Christopher 1948(?)- .... **CLC 65**
See also CA 159

Tillinghast, Richard (Williford) 1940-**CLC 29**
See also CA 29-32R; CAAS 23; CANR 26, 51

Timrod, Henry 1828-1867 .... **NCLC 25**
See also DLB 3

Tindall, Gillian (Elizabeth) 1938- ...... **CLC 7**
See also CA 21-24R; CANR 11

Tiptree, James, Jr. .... **CLC 48, 50**
See also Sheldon, Alice Hastings Bradley
See also DLB 8

Titmarsh, Michael Angelo
See Thackeray, William Makepeace

Tocqueville, Alexis (Charles Henri Maurice
Clerel Comte) 1805-1859 ...**NCLC 7, 63**

Tolkien, J(ohn) R(onald) R(euel) 1892-1973
CLC 1, 2, 3, 8, 12, 38; DA; DAB; DAC;
DAM MST, NOV, POP; WLC
See also AAYA 10; AITN 1; CA 17-18; 45-48;
CANR 36; CAP 2; CDBLB 1914-1945; DLB
15, 160; JRDA; MAICYA; MTCW; SATA 2,
32; SATA-Obit 24

Toller, Ernst 1893-1939 .... **TCLC 10**
See also CA 107; DLB 124

Tolson, M. B.
See Tolson, Melvin B(eaunorus)

Tolson, Melvin B(eaunorus) 1898(?)-1966
CLC 36, 105; BLC; DAM MULT, POET
See also BW 1; CA 124; 89-92; DLB 48, 76

Tolstoi, Aleksei Nikolaevich
See Tolstoy, Alexey Nikolaevich

Tolstoy, Alexey Nikolaevich 1882-1945**T C L C**
18
See also CA 107; 158

Tolstoy, Count Leo
See Tolstoy, Leo (Nikolaevich)

Tolstoy, Leo (Nikolaevich) 1828-1910**TCLC 4,**
11, 17, 28, 44, 79; DA; DAB; DAC; DAM
MST, NOV; SSC 9; WLC
See also CA 104; 123; SATA 26

Tomasi di Lampedusa, Giuseppe 1896-1957
See Lampedusa, Giuseppe (Tomasi) di
See also CA 111

Tomlin, Lily .... **CLC 17**
See also Tomlin, Mary Jean

Tomlin, Mary Jean 1939(?)-
See Tomlin, Lily
See also CA 117

Tomlinson, (Alfred) Charles 1927-**CLC 2, 4, 6,**
13, 45; DAM POET; PC 17
See also CA 5-8R; CANR 33; DLB 40

Tomlinson, H(enry) M(ajor) 1873-1958**TCLC**
71
See also CA 118; 161; DLB 36, 100

Tonson, Jacob
See Bennett, (Enoch) Arnold

Toole, John Kennedy 1937-1969 **CLC 19, 64**
See also CA 104; DLBY 81

Toomer, Jean 1894-1967 .... **CLC 1, 4, 13, 22;**
BLC; DAM MULT; PC 7; SSC 1; WLCS
See also BW 1; CA 85-88; CDALB 1917-1929;
DLB 45, 51; MTCW

Torley, Luke
See Blish, James (Benjamin)

Tornimparte, Alessandra
See Ginzburg, Natalia

Torre, Raoul della
See Mencken, H(enry) L(ouis)

Torrey, E(dwin) Fuller 1937- .... **CLC 34**
See also CA 119

Torsvan, Ben Traven
See Traven, B.

Torsvan, Benno Traven
See Traven, B.

Torsvan, Berick Traven
See Traven, B.

Torsvan, Berwick Traven
See Traven, B.

Torsvan, Bruno Traven
See Traven, B.

Torsvan, Traven
See Traven, B.

Tournier, Michel (Edouard) 1924-**CLC 6, 23,**
36, 95
See also CA 49-52; CANR 3, 36; DLB 83;
MTCW; SATA 23

Tournimparte, Alessandra
See Ginzburg, Natalia

Towers, Ivar
See Kornbluth, C(yril) M.

Towne, Robert (Burton) 1936(?)- ..... **CLC 87**
See also CA 108; DLB 44

Townsend, Sue .... **CLC 61**
See also Townsend, Susan Elaine
See also SATA 55, 93; SATA-Brief 48

Townsend, Susan Elaine 1946-
See Townsend, Sue
See also CA 119; 127; DAB; DAC; DAM MST

Townshend, Peter (Dennis Blandford) 1945-

CLC 17, 42
See also CA 107

Tozzi, Federigo 1883-1920 .... **TCLC 31**
See also CA 160

Traill, Catharine Parr 1802-1899 .. **NCLC 31**
See also DLB 99

Trakl, Georg 1887-1914 .... **TCLC 5; PC 20**
See also CA 104

Transtroemer, Tomas (Goesta) 1931-**CLC 52,**
65; DAM POET
See also CA 117; 129; CAAS 17

Transtromer, Tomas Gosta
See Transtroemer, Tomas (Goesta)

Traven, B. (?)-1969 .... **CLC 8, 11**
See also CA 19-20; 25-28R; CAP 2; DLB 9,
56; MTCW

Treitel, Jonathan 1959- .... **CLC 70**

Tremain, Rose 1943- .... **CLC 42**
See also CA 97-100; CANR 44; DLB 14

Tremblay, Michel 1942- **CLC 29, 102; DAC;**
DAM MST
See also CA 116; 128; DLB 60; MTCW

Trevanian .... **CLC 29**
See also Whitaker, Rod(ney)

Trevor, Glen
See Hilton, James

Trevor, William 1928- . **CLC 7, 9, 14, 25, 71;**
SSC 21
See also Cox, William Trevor
See also DLB 14, 139

Trifonov, Yuri (Valentinovich) 1925-1981
CLC 45
See also CA 126; 103; MTCW

Trilling, Lionel 1905-1975 ...... **CLC 9, 11, 24**
See also CA 9-12R; 61-64; CANR 10; DLB 28,
63; INT CANR-10; MTCW

Trimball, W. H.
See Mencken, H(enry) L(ouis)

Tristan
See Gomez de la Serna, Ramon

Tristram
See Housman, A(lfred) E(dward)

Trogdon, William (Lewis) 1939-
See Heat-Moon, William Least
See also CA 115; 119; CANR 47; INT 119

Trollope, Anthony 1815-1882**NCLC 6, 33; DA;**
DAB; DAC; DAM MST, NOV; SSC 28;
WLC
See also CDBLB 1832-1890; DLB 21, 57, 159;
SATA 22

Trollope, Frances 1779-1863 .... **NCLC 30**
See also DLB 21, 166

Trotsky, Leon 1879-1940 .... **TCLC 22**
See also CA 118

Trotter (Cockburn), Catharine 1679-1749**L C**
8
See also DLB 84

Trout, Kilgore
See Farmer, Philip Jose

Trow, George W. S. 1943- .... **CLC 52**
See also CA 126

Troyat, Henri 1911- .... **CLC 23**
See also CA 45-48; CANR 2, 33; MTCW

Trudeau, G(arretson) B(eekman) 1948-
See Trudeau, Garry B.
See also CA 81-84; CANR 31; SATA 35

Trudeau, Garry B. .... **CLC 12**
See also Trudeau, G(arretson) B(eekman)
See also AAYA 10; AITN 2

Truffaut, Francois 1932-1984 .. **CLC 20, 101**
See also CA 81-84; 113; CANR 34

Trumbo, Dalton 1905-1976 .... **CLC 19**
See also CA 21-24R; 69-72; CANR 10; DLB

26

Trumbull, John 1750-1831 .... **NCLC 30**
See also DLB 31

Trundlett, Helen B.
See Eliot, T(homas) S(tearns)

Tryon, Thomas 1926-1991 . **CLC 3, 11; DAM POP**
See also AITN 1; CA 29-32R; 135; CANR 32; MTCW

Tryon, Tom
See Tryon, Thomas

Ts'ao Hsueh-ch'in 1715(?)-1763 .... **LC 1**

Tsushima, Shuji 1909-1948
See Dazai, Osamu
See also CA 107

Tsvetaeva (Efron), Marina (Ivanovna) 1892-1941 .... **TCLC 7, 35; PC 14**
See also CA 104; 128; MTCW

Tuck, Lily 1938- .... **CLC 70**
See also CA 139

Tu Fu 712-770 .... **PC 9**
See also DAM MULT

Tunis, John R(oberts) 1889-1975 ...... **CLC 12**
See also CA 61-64; CANR 62; DLB 22, 171; JRDA; MAICYA; SATA 37; SATA-Brief 30

Tuohy, Frank .... **CLC 37**
See also Tuohy, John Francis
See also DLB 14, 139

Tuohy, John Francis 1925-
See Tuohy, Frank
See also CA 5-8R; CANR 3, 47

Turco, Lewis (Putnam) 1934- ...... **CLC 11, 63**
See also CA 13-16R; CAAS 22; CANR 24, 51; DLBY 84

Turgenev, Ivan 1818-1883 .... **NCLC 21; DA; DAB; DAC; DAM MST, NOV; DC 7; SSC 7; WLC**

Turgot, Anne-Robert-Jacques 1727-1781 **L C 26**

Turner, Frederick 1943- .... **CLC 48**
See also CA 73-76; CAAS 10; CANR 12, 30, 56; DLB 40

Tutu, Desmond M(pilo) 1931- **CLC 80; BLC; DAM MULT**
See also BW 1; CA 125

Tutuola, Amos 1920-1997 **CLC 5, 14, 29; BLC; DAM MULT**
See also BW 2; CA 9-12R; 159; CANR 27; DLB 125; MTCW

Twain, Mark TCLC 6, 12, 19, 36, 48, 59; SSC 26; WLC
See also Clemens, Samuel Langhorne
See also AAYA 20; DLB 11, 12, 23, 64, 74

Tyler, Anne 1941- . **CLC 7, 11, 18, 28, 44, 59, 103; DAM NOV, POP**
See also AAYA 18; BEST 89:1; CA 9-12R; CANR 11, 33, 53; DLB 6, 143; DLBY 82; MTCW; SATA 7, 90

Tyler, Royall 1757-1826 .... **NCLC 3**
See also DLB 37

Tynan, Katharine 1861-1931 .... **TCLC 3**
See also CA 104; DLB 153

Tyutchev, Fyodor 1803-1873 .... **NCLC 34**

Tzara, Tristan 1896-1963 ...... **CLC 47; DAM POET**
See also CA 153; 89-92

Uhry, Alfred 1936- ... **CLC 55; DAM DRAM, POP**
See also CA 127; 133; INT 133

Ulf, Haerved
See Strindberg, (Johan) August

Ulf, Harved
See Strindberg, (Johan) August

Ulibarri, Sabine R(eyes) 1919-**CLC 83; DAM MULT**
See also CA 131; DLB 82; HW

Unamuno (y Jugo), Miguel de 1864-1936 **TCLC 2, 9; DAM MULT, NOV; HLC; SSC 11**
See also CA 104; 131; DLB 108; HW; MTCW

Undercliffe, Errol
See Campbell, (John) Ramsey

Underwood, Miles
See Glassco, John

Undset, Sigrid 1882-1949**TCLC 3; DA; DAB; DAC; DAM MST, NOV; WLC**
See also CA 104; 129; MTCW

Ungaretti, Giuseppe 1888-1970**CLC 7, 11, 15**
See also CA 19-20; 25-28R; CAP 2; DLB 114

Unger, Douglas 1952- .... **CLC 34**
See also CA 130

Unsworth, Barry (Forster) 1930- ..... **CLC 76**
See also CA 25-28R; CANR 30, 54

Updike, John (Hoyer) 1932-**CLC 1, 2, 3, 5, 7, 9, 13, 15, 23, 34, 43, 70; DA; DAB; DAC; DAM MST, NOV, POET, POP; SSC 13, 27; WLC**
See also CA 1-4R; CABS 1; CANR 4, 33, 51; CDALB 1968-1988; DLB 2, 5, 143; DLBD 3; DLBY 80, 82; MTCW

Upshaw, Margaret Mitchell
See Mitchell, Margaret (Munnerlyn)

Upton, Mark
See Sanders, Lawrence

Urdang, Constance (Henriette) 1922-**CLC 47**
See also CA 21-24R; CANR 9, 24

Uriel, Henry
See Faust, Frederick (Schiller)

Uris, Leon (Marcus) 1924- **CLC 7, 32; DAM NOV, POP**
See also AITN 1, 2; BEST 89:2; CA 1-4R; CANR 1, 40; MTCW; SATA 49

Urmuz
See Codrescu, Andrei

Urquhart, Jane 1949- .... **CLC 90; DAC**
See also CA 113; CANR 32

Ustinov, Peter (Alexander) 1921- .... **CLC 1**
See also AITN 1; CA 13-16R; CANR 25, 51; DLB 13

U Tam'si, Gerald Felix Tchicaya
See Tchicaya, Gerald Felix

U Tam'si, Tchicaya
See Tchicaya, Gerald Felix

Vachss, Andrew (Henry) 1942- .... **CLC 106**
See also CA 118; CANR 44

Vachss, Andrew H.
See Vachss, Andrew (Henry)

Vaculik, Ludvik 1926- .... **CLC 7**
See also CA 53-56

Vaihinger, Hans 1852-1933 .... **TCLC 71**
See also CA 116

Valdez, Luis (Miguel) 1940- .. **CLC 84; DAM MULT; HLC**
See also CA 101; CANR 32; DLB 122; HW

Valenzuela, Luisa 1938- **CLC 31, 104; DAM MULT; SSC 14**
See also CA 101; CANR 32; DLB 113; HW

Valera y Alcala-Galiano, Juan 1824-1905 **TCLC 10**
See also CA 106

Valery, (Ambroise) Paul (Toussaint Jules) 1871-1945 ..... **TCLC 4, 15; DAM POET; PC 9**
See also CA 104; 122; MTCW

Valle-Inclan, Ramon (Maria) del 1866-1936 **TCLC 5; DAM MULT; HLC**
See also CA 106; 153; DLB 134

Vallejo, Antonio Buero
See Buero Vallejo, Antonio

Vallejo, Cesar (Abraham) 1892-1938**TCLC 3, 56; DAM MULT; HLC**
See also CA 105; 153; HW

Vallette, Marguerite Eymery
See Rachilde

Valle Y Pena, Ramon del
See Valle-Inclan, Ramon (Maria) del

Van Ash, Cay 1918- .... **CLC 34**

Vanbrugh, Sir John 1664-1726 **LC 21; DAM DRAM**
See also DLB 80

Van Campen, Karl
See Campbell, John W(ood, Jr.)

Vance, Gerald
See Silverberg, Robert

Vance, Jack .... **CLC 35**
See also Kuttner, Henry; Vance, John Holbrook
See also DLB 8

Vance, John Holbrook 1916-
See Queen, Ellery; Vance, Jack
See also CA 29-32R; CANR 17; MTCW

Van Den Bogarde, Derek Jules Gaspard Ulric Niven 1921-
See Bogarde, Dirk
See also CA 77-80

Vandenburgh, Jane .... **CLC 59**

Vanderhaeghe, Guy 1951- .... **CLC 41**
See also CA 113

van der Post, Laurens (Jan) 1906-1996**CLC 5**
See also CA 5-8R; 155; CANR 35

van de Wetering, Janwillem 1931- ... **CLC 47**
See also CA 49-52; CANR 4, 62

Van Dine, S. S. .... **TCLC 23**
See also Wright, Willard Huntington

Van Doren, Carl (Clinton) 1885-1950 **T C L C 18**
See also CA 111

Van Doren, Mark 1894-1972 .... **CLC 6, 10**
See also CA 1-4R; 37-40R; CANR 3; DLB 45; MTCW

Van Druten, John (William) 1901-1957**TCLC 2**
See also CA 104; 161; DLB 10

Van Duyn, Mona (Jane) 1921- **CLC 3, 7, 63; DAM POET**
See also CA 9-12R; CANR 7, 38, 60; DLB 5

Van Dyne, Edith
See Baum, L(yman) Frank

van Itallie, Jean-Claude 1936- .... **CLC 3**
See also CA 45-48; CAAS 2; CANR 1, 48; DLB 7

van Ostaijen, Paul 1896-1928 .... **TCLC 33**

Van Peebles, Melvin 1932- **CLC 2, 20; DAM MULT**
See also BW 2; CA 85-88; CANR 27

Vansittart, Peter 1920- .... **CLC 42**
See also CA 1-4R; CANR 3, 49

Van Vechten, Carl 1880-1964 .... **CLC 33**
See also CA 89-92; DLB 4, 9, 51

Van Vogt, A(lfred) E(lton) 1912- .... **CLC 1**
See also CA 21-24R; CANR 28; DLB 8; SATA 14

Varda, Agnes 1928-............................. **CLC 16**
See also CA 116; 122

Vargas Llosa, (Jorge) Mario (Pedro) 1936-**CLC 3, 6, 9, 10, 15, 31, 42, 85; DA; DAB; DAC; DAM MST, MULT, NOV; HLC**
See also CA 73-76; CANR 18, 32, 42; DLB 145; HW; MTCW

Vasiliu, Gheorghe 1881-1957
See Bacovia, George

See also CA 123

Vassa, Gustavus
See Equiano, Olaudah

Vassilikos, Vassilis 1933- .... **CLC 4, 8**
See also CA 81-84

Vaughan, Henry 1621-1695 .... **LC 27**
See also DLB 131

Vaughn, Stephanie .... **CLC 62**

Vazov, Ivan (Minchov) 1850-1921 . **TCLC 25**
See also CA 121; DLB 147

Veblen, Thorstein (Bunde) 1857-1929 **T C L C 31**
See also CA 115

Vega, Lope de 1562-1635 .... **LC 23**

Venison, Alfred
See Pound, Ezra (Weston Loomis)

Verdi, Marie de
See Mencken, H(enry) L(ouis)

Verdu, Matilde
See Cela, Camilo Jose

Verga, Giovanni (Carmelo) 1840-1922**T C L C 3; SSC 21**
See also CA 104; 123

Vergil 70B.C.-19B.C. ... **CMLC 9; DA; DAB; DAC; DAM MST, POET; PC 12; WLCS**

Verhaeren, Emile (Adolphe Gustave) 1855-1916 **TCLC 12**
See also CA 109

Verlaine, Paul (Marie) 1844-1896**NCLC 2, 51; DAM POET; PC 2**

Verne, Jules (Gabriel) 1828-1905**TCLC 6, 52**
See also AAYA 16; CA 110; 131; DLB 123; JRDA; MAICYA; SATA 21

Very, Jones 1813-1880 .... **NCLC 9**
See also DLB 1

Vesaas, Tarjei 1897-1970 .... **CLC 48**
See also CA 29-32R

Vialis, Gaston
See Simenon, Georges (Jacques Christian)

Vian, Boris 1920-1959 .... **TCLC 9**
See also CA 106; DLB 72

Viaud, (Louis Marie) Julien 1850-1923
See Loti, Pierre
See also CA 107

Vicar, Henry
See Felsen, Henry Gregor

Vicker, Angus
See Felsen, Henry Gregor

Vidal, Gore 1925-**CLC 2, 4, 6, 8, 10, 22, 33, 72; DAM NOV, POP**
See also AITN 1; BEST 90:2; CA 5-8R; CANR 13, 45; DLB 6, 152; INT CANR-13; MTCW

Viereck, Peter (Robert Edwin) 1916- . **CLC 4**
See also CA 1-4R; CANR 1, 47; DLB 5

Vigny, Alfred (Victor) de 1797-1863**NCLC 7; DAM POET**
See also DLB 119

Vilakazi, Benedict Wallet 1906-1947**TCLC 37**

Villiers de l'Isle Adam, Jean Marie Mathias Philippe Auguste Comte 1838-1889 **NCLC 3; SSC 14**
See also DLB 123

Villon, Francois 1431-1463(?) .... **PC 13**

Vinci, Leonardo da 1452-1519 ....**LC 12**

Vine, Barbara .... **CLC 50**
See also Rendell, Ruth (Barbara)
See also BEST 90:4

Vinge, Joan D(ennison) 1948-**CLC 30; SSC 24**
See also CA 93-96; SATA 36

Violis, G.
See Simenon, Georges (Jacques Christian)

Visconti, Luchino 1906-1976 .... **CLC 16**
See also CA 81-84; 65-68; CANR 39

Vittorini, Elio 1908-1966 .... **CLC 6, 9, 14**
See also CA 133; 25-28R

Vizenor, Gerald Robert 1934-**CLC 103; DAM MULT**
See also CA 13-16R; CAAS 22; CANR 5, 21, 44; DLB 175; NNAL

Vizinczey, Stephen 1933- .... **CLC 40**
See also CA 128; INT 128

Vliet, R(ussell) G(ordon) 1929-1984 **CLC 22**
See also CA 37-40R; 112; CANR 18

Vogau, Boris Andreyevich 1894-1937(?)
See Pilnyak, Boris
See also CA 123

Vogel, Paula A(nne) 1951- .... **CLC 76**
See also CA 108

Voight, Ellen Bryant 1943- .... **CLC 54**
See also CA 69-72; CANR 11, 29, 55; DLB 120

Voigt, Cynthia 1942-......................... **CLC 30**
See also AAYA 3; CA 106; CANR 18, 37, 40; CLR 13,48; INT CANR-18; JRDA; MAICYA; SATA 48, 79; SATA-Brief 33

Voinovich, Vladimir (Nikolaevich) 1932-**CLC 10, 49**
See also CA 81-84; CAAS 12; CANR 33; MTCW

Vollmann, William T. 1959-... **CLC 89; DAM NOV, POP**
See also CA 134

Voloshinov, V. N.
See Bakhtin, Mikhail Mikhailovich

Voltaire 1694-1778 . **LC 14; DA; DAB; DAC; DAM DRAM, MST; SSC 12; WLC**

von Daeniken, Erich 1935- .... **CLC 30**
See also AITN 1; CA 37-40R; CANR 17, 44

von Daniken, Erich
See von Daeniken, Erich

von Heidenstam, (Carl Gustaf) Verner
See Heidenstam, (Carl Gustaf) Verner von

von Heyse, Paul (Johann Ludwig)
See Heyse, Paul (Johann Ludwig von)

von Hofmannsthal, Hugo
See Hofmannsthal, Hugo von

von Horvath, Odon
See Horvath, Oedoen von

von Horvath, Oedoen
See Horvath, Oedoen von

von Liliencron, (Friedrich Adolf Axel) Detlev
See Liliencron, (Friedrich Adolf Axel) Detlev von

Vonnegut, Kurt, Jr. 1922-**CLC 1, 2, 3, 4, 5, 8, 12, 22, 40, 60; DA; DAB; DAC; DAM MST, NOV, POP; SSC 8; WLC**
See also AAYA 6; AITN 1; BEST 90:4; CA 1-4R; CANR 1, 25, 49; CDALB 1968-1988; DLB 2, 8, 152; DLBD 3; DLBY 80; MTCW

Von Rachen, Kurt
See Hubbard, L(afayette) Ron(ald)

von Rezzori (d'Arezzo), Gregor
See Rezzori (d'Arezzo), Gregor von

von Sternberg, Josef
See Sternberg, Josef von

Vorster, Gordon 1924-......................... **CLC 34**
See also CA 133

Vosce, Trudie
See Ozick, Cynthia

Voznesensky, Andrei (Andreievich) 1933-**CLC 1, 15, 57; DAM POET**
See also CA 89-92; CANR 37; MTCW

Waddington, Miriam 1917- .... **CLC 28**
See also CA 21-24R; CANR 12, 30; DLB 68

Wagman, Fredrica 1937- .... **CLC 7**
See also CA 97-100; INT 97-100

Wagner, Linda W.

See Wagner-Martin, Linda (C.)

Wagner, Linda Welshimer
See Wagner-Martin, Linda (C.)

Wagner, Richard 1813-1883 .... **NCLC 9**
See also DLB 129

Wagner-Martin, Linda (C.) 1936- .... **CLC 50**
See also CA 159

Wagoner, David (Russell) 1926- **CLC 3, 5, 15**
See also CA 1-4R; CAAS 3; CANR 2; DLB 5; SATA 14

Wah, Fred(erick James) 1939- .... **CLC 44**
See also CA 107; 141; DLB 60

Wahloo, Per 1926-1975 .... **CLC 7**
See also CA 61-64

Wahloo, Peter
See Wahloo, Per

Wain, John (Barrington) 1925-1994 . **CLC 2, 11, 15, 46**
See also CA 5-8R; 145; CAAS 4; CANR 23, 54; CDBLB 1960 to Present; DLB 15, 27, 139, 155; MTCW

Wajda, Andrzej 1926- .... **CLC 16**
See also CA 102

Wakefield, Dan 1932- .... **CLC 7**
See also CA 21-24R; CAAS 7

Wakoski, Diane 1937- **CLC 2, 4, 7, 9, 11, 40; DAM POET; PC 15**
See also CA 13-16R; CAAS 1; CANR 9, 60; DLB 5; INT CANR-9

Wakoski-Sherbell, Diane
See Wakoski, Diane

Walcott, Derek (Alton) 1930-**CLC 2, 4, 9, 14, 25, 42, 67, 76; BLC; DAB; DAC; DAM MST, MULT, POET; DC 7**
See also BW 2; CA 89-92; CANR 26, 47; DLB 117; DLBY 81; MTCW

Waldman, Anne 1945- .... **CLC 7**
See also CA 37-40R; CAAS 17; CANR 34; DLB 16

Waldo, E. Hunter
See Sturgeon, Theodore (Hamilton)

Waldo, Edward Hamilton
See Sturgeon, Theodore (Hamilton)

Walker, Alice (Malsenior) 1944- **CLC 5, 6, 9, 19, 27, 46, 58, 103; BLC; DA; DAB; DAC; DAM MST, MULT, NOV, POET, POP; SSC 5; WLCS**
See also AAYA 3; BEST 89:4; BW 2; CA 37-40R; CANR 9, 27, 49; CDALB 1968-1988; DLB 6, 33, 143; INT CANR-27; MTCW; SATA 31

Walker, David Harry 1911-1992 .... **CLC 14**
See also CA 1-4R; 137; CANR 1; SATA 8; SATA-Obit 71

Walker, Edward Joseph 1934-
See Walker, Ted
See also CA 21-24R; CANR 12, 28, 53

Walker, George F. 1947- . **CLC 44, 61; DAB; DAC; DAM MST**
See also CA 103; CANR 21, 43, 59; DLB 60

Walker, Joseph A. 1935- .... **CLC 19; DAM DRAM, MST**
See also BW 1; CA 89-92; CANR 26; DLB 38

Walker, Margaret (Abigail) 1915- **CLC 1, 6; BLC; DAM MULT; PC 20**
See also BW 2; CA 73-76; CANR 26, 54; DLB 76, 152; MTCW

Walker, Ted .... **CLC 13**
See also Walker, Edward Joseph
See also DLB 40

Wallace, David Foster 1962- .... **CLC 50**
See also CA 132; CANR 59

Wallace, Dexter

See Masters, Edgar Lee

Wallace, (Richard Horatio) Edgar 1875-1932
TCLC 57
See also CA 115; DLB 70

Wallace, Irving 1916-1990 **CLC 7, 13; DAM
NOV, POP**
See also AITN 1; CA 1-4R; 132; CAAS 1;
CANR 1, 27; INT CANR-27; MTCW

Wallant, Edward Lewis 1926-1962 **CLC 5, 10**
See also CA 1-4R; CANR 22; DLB 2, 28, 143;
MTCW

Walley, Byron
See Card, Orson Scott

Walpole, Horace 1717-1797 .... **LC 2**
See also DLB 39, 104

Walpole, Hugh (Seymour) 1884-1941 **TCLC 5**
See also CA 104; DLB 34

Walser, Martin 1927- .... **CLC 27**
See also CA 57-60; CANR 8, 46; DLB 75, 124

Walser, Robert 1878-1956 **TCLC 18; SSC 20**
See also CA 118; DLB 66

Walsh, Jill Paton .... **CLC 35**
See also Paton Walsh, Gillian
See also AAYA 11; CLR 2; DLB 161; SAAS 3

Walter, William Christian
See Andersen, Hans Christian

Wambaugh, Joseph (Aloysius, Jr.) 1937- **C L C
3, 18; DAM NOV, POP**
See also AITN 1; BEST 89:3; CA 33-36R;
CANR 42; DLB 6; DLBY 83; MTCW

Wang Wei 699(?)-761(?) .... **PC 18**

Ward, Arthur Henry Sarsfield 1883-1959
See Rohmer, Sax
See also CA 108

Ward, Douglas Turner 1930- .... **CLC 19**
See also BW 1; CA 81-84; CANR 27; DLB 7,
38

Ward, Mary Augusta
See Ward, Mrs. Humphry

Ward, Mrs. Humphry 1851-1920 .. **TCLC 55**
See also DLB 18

Ward, Peter
See Faust, Frederick (Schiller)

Warhol, Andy 1928(?)-1987 .... **CLC 20**
See also AAYA 12; BEST 89:4; CA 89-92; 121;
CANR 34

Warner, Francis (Robert le Plastrier) 1937-
CLC 14
See also CA 53-56; CANR 11

Warner, Marina 1946- .... **CLC 59**
See also CA 65-68; CANR 21, 55

Warner, Rex (Ernest) 1905-1986 ...... **CLC 45**
See also CA 89-92; 119; DLB 15

Warner, Susan (Bogert) 1819-1885 **NCLC 31**
See also DLB 3, 42

Warner, Sylvia (Constance) Ashton
See Ashton-Warner, Sylvia (Constance)

Warner, Sylvia Townsend 1893-1978 **CLC 7,
19; SSC 23**
See also CA 61-64; 77-80; CANR 16, 60; DLB
34, 139; MTCW

Warren, Mercy Otis 1728-1814 ..... **NCLC 13**
See also DLB 31

Warren, Robert Penn 1905-1989 **CLC 1, 4, 6,
8, 10, 13, 18, 39, 53, 59; DA; DAB; DAC;
DAM MST, NOV, POET; SSC 4; WLC**
See also AITN 1; CA 13-16R; 129; CANR 10,
47; CDALB 1968-1988; DLB 2, 48, 152;
DLBY 80, 89; INT CANR-10; MTCW; SATA
46; SATA-Obit 63

Warshofsky, Isaac
See Singer, Isaac Bashevis

Warton, Thomas 1728-1790 ..... **LC 15; DAM
POET**
See also DLB 104, 109

Waruk, Kona
See Harris, (Theodore) Wilson

Warung, Price 1855-1911 .... **TCLC 45**

Warwick, Jarvis
See Garner, Hugh

Washington, Alex
See Harris, Mark

Washington, Booker T(aliaferro) 1856-1915
TCLC 10; BLC; DAM MULT
See also BW 1; CA 114; 125; SATA 28

Washington, George 1732-1799 .... **LC 25**
See also DLB 31

Wassermann, (Karl) Jakob 1873-1934 **T C L C
6**
See also CA 104; DLB 66

Wasserstein, Wendy 1950- ... **CLC 32, 59, 90;
DAM DRAM; DC 4**
See also CA 121; 129; CABS 3; CANR 53; INT
129; SATA 94

Waterhouse, Keith (Spencer) 1929- . **CLC 47**
See also CA 5-8R; CANR 38; DLB 13, 15;
MTCW

Waters, Frank (Joseph) 1902-1995 .. **CLC 88**
See also CA 5-8R; 149; CAAS 13; CANR 3,
18, 63; DLBY 86

Waters, Roger 1944- .... **CLC 35**

Watkins, Frances Ellen
See Harper, Frances Ellen Watkins

Watkins, Gerrold
See Malzberg, Barry N(athaniel)

Watkins, Gloria 1955(?)-
See hooks, bell
See also BW 2; CA 143

Watkins, Paul 1964- .... **CLC 55**
See also CA 132; CANR 62

Watkins, Vernon Phillips 1906-1967 **CLC 43**
See also CA 9-10; 25-28R; CAP 1; DLB 20

Watson, Irving S.
See Mencken, H(enry) L(ouis)

Watson, John H.
See Farmer, Philip Jose

Watson, Richard F.
See Silverberg, Robert

Waugh, Auberon (Alexander) 1939- .. **CLC 7**
See also CA 45-48; CANR 6, 22; DLB 14

Waugh, Evelyn (Arthur St. John) 1903-1966
**CLC 1, 3, 8, 13, 19, 27, 44, 107; DA; DAB;
DAC; DAM MST, NOV, POP; WLC**
See also CA 85-88; 25-28R; CANR 22; CDBLB
1914-1945; DLB 15, 162; MTCW

Waugh, Harriet 1944- .... **CLC 6**
See also CA 85-88; CANR 22

Ways, C. R.
See Blount, Roy (Alton), Jr.

Waystaff, Simon
See Swift, Jonathan

Webb, (Martha) Beatrice (Potter) 1858-1943
TCLC 22
See Potter, (Helen) Beatrix
See also CA 117

Webb, Charles (Richard) 1939- .... **CLC 7**
See also CA 25-28R

Webb, James H(enry), Jr. 1946- .... **CLC 22**
See also CA 81-84

Webb, Mary (Gladys Meredith) 1881-1927
TCLC 24
See also CA 123; DLB 34

Webb, Mrs. Sidney
See Webb, (Martha) Beatrice (Potter)

Webb, Phyllis 1927- .... **CLC 18**
See also CA 104; CANR 23; DLB 53

Webb, Sidney (James) 1859-1947 .. **TCLC 22**
See also CA 117

Webber, Andrew Lloyd .... **CLC 21**
See also Lloyd Webber, Andrew

Weber, Lenora Mattingly 1895-1971 **CLC 12**
See also CA 19-20; 29-32R; CAP 1; SATA 2;
SATA-Obit 26

Weber, Max 1864-1920 .... **TCLC 69**
See also CA 109

Webster, John 1579(?)-1634(?) ... **LC 33; DA;
DAB; DAC; DAM DRAM, MST; DC 2;
WLC**
See also CDBLB Before 1660; DLB 58

Webster, Noah 1758-1843 .... **NCLC 30**

Wedekind, (Benjamin) Frank(lin) 1864-1918
TCLC 7; DAM DRAM
See also CA 104; 153; DLB 118

Weidman, Jerome 1913- .... **CLC 7**
See also AITN 2; CA 1-4R; CANR 1; DLB 28

Weil, Simone (Adolphine) 1909-1943 **TCLC 23**
See also CA 117; 159

Weinstein, Nathan
See West, Nathanael

Weinstein, Nathan von Wallenstein
See West, Nathanael

Weir, Peter (Lindsay) 1944- .... **CLC 20**
See also CA 113; 123

Weiss, Peter (Ulrich) 1916-1982 **CLC 3, 15, 51;
DAM DRAM**
See also CA 45-48; 106; CANR 3; DLB 69, 124

Weiss, Theodore (Russell) 1916- **CLC 3, 8, 14**
See also CA 9-12R; CAAS 2; CANR 46; DLB
5

Welch, (Maurice) Denton 1915-1948 **TCLC 22**
See also CA 121; 148

Welch, James 1940- ..... **CLC 6, 14, 52; DAM
MULT, POP**
See also CA 85-88; CANR 42; DLB 175; NNAL

Weldon, Fay 1931- . **CLC 6, 9, 11, 19, 36, 59;
DAM POP**
See also CA 21-24R; CANR 16, 46, 63; CDBLB
1960 to Present; DLB 14; INT CANR-16;
MTCW

Wellek, Rene 1903-1995 .... **CLC 28**
See also CA 5-8R; 150; CAAS 7; CANR 8; DLB
63; INT CANR-8

Weller, Michael 1942- .... **CLC 10, 53**
See also CA 85-88

Weller, Paul 1958- .... **CLC 26**

Wellershoff, Dieter 1925- .... **CLC 46**
See also CA 89-92; CANR 16, 37

Welles, (George) Orson 1915-1985 **CLC 20, 80**
See also CA 93-96; 117

Wellman, Mac 1945- .... **CLC 65**

Wellman, Manly Wade 1903-1986 .... **CLC 49**
See also CA 1-4R; 118; CANR 6, 16, 44; SATA
6; SATA-Obit 47

Wells, Carolyn 1869(?)-1942 .... **TCLC 35**
See also CA 113; DLB 11

Wells, H(erbert) G(eorge) 1866-1946 **TCLC 6,
12, 19; DA; DAB; DAC; DAM MST, NOV;
SSC 6; WLC**
See also AAYA 18; CA 110; 121; CDBLB 1914-
1945; DLB 34, 70, 156, 178; MTCW; SATA
20

Wells, Rosemary 1943- .... **CLC 12**
See also AAYA 13; CA 85-88; CANR 48; CLR
16; MAICYA; SAAS 1; SATA 18, 69

Welty, Eudora 1909- **CLC 1, 2, 5, 14, 22, 33,
105; DA; DAB; DAC; DAM MST, NOV;
SSC 1, 27; WLC**
See also CA 9-12R; CABS 1; CANR 32;
CDALB 1941-1968; DLB 2, 102, 143;

DLBD 12; DLBY 87; MTCW
Wen I-to 1899-1946 .... **TCLC 28**
Wentworth, Robert
See Hamilton, Edmond
Werfel, Franz (Viktor) 1890-1945 ... **TCLC 8**
See also CA 104; 161; DLB 81, 124
Wergeland, Henrik Arnold 1808-1845 **N C L C 5**
Wersba, Barbara 1932- .... **CLC 30**
See also AAYA 2; CA 29-32R; CANR 16, 38;
CLR 3; DLB 52; JRDA; MAICYA; SAAS 2;
SATA 1, 58
Wertmueller, Lina 1928- .... **CLC 16**
See also CA 97-100; CANR 39
Wescott, Glenway 1901-1987 .... **CLC 13**
See also CA 13-16R; 121; CANR 23; DLB 4,
9, 102
Wesker, Arnold 1932- .... **CLC 3, 5, 42; DAB; DAM DRAM**
See also CA 1-4R; CAAS 7; CANR 1, 33;
CDBLB 1960 to Present; DLB 13; MTCW
Wesley, Richard (Errol) 1945- .... **CLC 7**
See also BW 1; CA 57-60; CANR 27; DLB 38
Wessel, Johan Herman 1742-1785 .... **LC 7**
West, Anthony (Panther) 1914-1987 **CLC 50**
See also CA 45-48; 124; CANR 3, 19; DLB 15
West, C. P.
See Wodehouse, P(elham) G(renville)
West, (Mary) Jessamyn 1902-1984 **CLC 7, 17**
See also CA 9-12R; 112; CANR 27; DLB 6;
DLBY 84; MTCW; SATA-Obit 37
West, Morris L(anglo) 1916- .... **CLC 6, 33**
See also CA 5-8R; CANR 24, 49, 64; MTCW
West, Nathanael 1903-1940 **TCLC 1, 14, 44; SSC 16**
See also CA 104; 125; CDALB 1929-1941;
DLB 4, 9, 28; MTCW
West, Owen
See Koontz, Dean R(ay)
West, Paul 1930- .... **CLC 7, 14, 96**
See also CA 13-16R; CAAS 7; CANR 22, 53;
DLB 14; INT CANR-22
West, Rebecca 1892-1983 .... **CLC 7, 9, 31, 50**
See also CA 5-8R; 109; CANR 19; DLB 36;
DLBY 83; MTCW
Westall, Robert (Atkinson) 1929-1993 **CLC 17**
See also AAYA 12; CA 69-72; 141; CANR 18;
CLR 13; JRDA; MAICYA; SAAS 2; SATA
23, 69; SATA-Obit 75
Westlake, Donald E(dwin) 1933- **CLC 7, 33; DAM POP**
See also CA 17-20R; CAAS 13; CANR 16, 44;
INT CANR-16
Westmacott, Mary
See Christie, Agatha (Mary Clarissa)
Weston, Allen
See Norton, Andre
Wetcheek, J. L.
See Feuchtwanger, Lion
Wetering, Janwillem van de
See van de Wetering, Janwillem
Wetherell, Elizabeth
See Warner, Susan (Bogert)
Whale, James 1889-1957 .... **TCLC 63**
Whalen, Philip 1923- .... **CLC 6, 29**
See also CA 9-12R; CANR 5, 39; DLB 16
Wharton, Edith (Newbold Jones) 1862-1937
TCLC 3, 9, 27, 53; DA; DAB; DAC; DAM MST, NOV; SSC 6; WLC
See also CA 104; 132; CDALB 1865-1917;
DLB 4, 9, 12, 78; DLBD 13; MTCW
Wharton, James
See Mencken, H(enry) L(ouis)

Wharton, William (a pseudonym) **CLC 18, 37**
See also CA 93-96; DLBY 80; INT 93-96
Wheatley (Peters), Phillis 1754(?)-1784 **LC 3; BLC; DA; DAC; DAM MST, MULT, POET; PC 3; WLC**
See also CDALB 1640-1865; DLB 31, 50
Wheelock, John Hall 1886-1978 .... **CLC 14**
See also CA 13-16R; 77-80; CANR 14; DLB
45
White, E(lwyn) B(rooks) 1899-1985 **CLC 10, 34, 39; DAM POP**
See also AITN 2; CA 13-16R; 116; CANR 16,
37; CLR 1, 21; DLB 11, 22; MAICYA;
MTCW; SATA 2, 29; SATA-Obit 44
White, Edmund (Valentine III) 1940- **CLC 27; DAM POP**
See also AAYA 7; CA 45-48; CANR 3, 19, 36,
62; MTCW
White, Patrick (Victor Martindale) 1912-1990
CLC 3, 4, 5, 7, 9, 18, 65, 69
See also CA 81-84; 132; CANR 43; MTCW
White, Phyllis Dorothy James 1920-
See James, P. D.
See also CA 21-24R; CANR 17, 43; DAM POP;
MTCW
White, T(erence) H(anbury) 1906-1964 **C L C 30**
See also AAYA 22; CA 73-76; CANR 37; DLB
160; JRDA; MAICYA; SATA 12
White, Terence de Vere 1912-1994 ... **CLC 49**
See also CA 49-52; 145; CANR 3
White, Walter F(rancis) 1893-1955 **TCLC 15**
See also White, Walter
See also BW 1; CA 115; 124; DLB 51
White, William Hale 1831-1913
See Rutherford, Mark
See also CA 121
Whitehead, E(dward) A(nthony) 1933- **CLC 5**
See also CA 65-68; CANR 58
Whitemore, Hugh (John) 1936- .... **CLC 37**
See also CA 132; INT 132
Whitman, Sarah Helen (Power) 1803-1878
NCLC 19
See also DLB 1
Whitman, Walt(er) 1819-1892 . **NCLC 4, 31; DA; DAB; DAC; DAM MST, POET; PC 3; WLC**
See also CDALB 1640-1865; DLB 3, 64; SATA
20
Whitney, Phyllis A(yame) 1903- ..... **CLC 42; DAM POP**
See also AITN 2; BEST 90:3; CA 1-4R; CANR
3, 25, 38, 60; JRDA; MAICYA; SATA 1, 30
Whittemore, (Edward) Reed (Jr.) 1919- **CLC 4**
See also CA 9-12R; CAAS 8; CANR 4; DLB 5
Whittier, John Greenleaf 1807-1892 **NCLC 8, 59**
See also DLB 1
Whittlebot, Hernia
See Coward, Noel (Peirce)
Wicker, Thomas Grey 1926-
See Wicker, Tom
See also CA 65-68; CANR 21, 46
Wicker, Tom .... **CLC 7**
See also Wicker, Thomas Grey
Wideman, John Edgar 1941- **CLC 5, 34, 36, 67; BLC; DAM MULT**
See also BW 2; CA 85-88; CANR 14, 42; DLB
33, 143
Wiebe, Rudy (Henry) 1934- .. **CLC 6, 11, 14; DAC; DAM MST**
See also CA 37-40R; CANR 42; DLB 60
Wieland, Christoph Martin 1733-1813 **N C L C
17**
See also DLB 97
Wiene, Robert 1881-1938 .... **TCLC 56**
Wieners, John 1934- .... **CLC 7**
See also CA 13-16R; DLB 16
Wiesel, Elie(zer) 1928- **CLC 3, 5, 11, 37; DA; DAB; DAC; DAM MST, NOV; WLCS 2**
See also AAYA 7; AITN 1; CA 5-8R; CAAS 4;
CANR 8, 40; DLB 83; DLBY 87; INT
CANR-8; MTCW; SATA 56
Wiggins, Marianne 1947- .... **CLC 57**
See also BEST 89:3; CA 130; CANR 60
Wight, James Alfred 1916-
See Herriot, James
See also CA 77-80; SATA 55; SATA-Brief 44
Wilbur, Richard (Purdy) 1921- **CLC 3, 6, 9, 14, 53; DA; DAB; DAC; DAM MST, POET**
See also CA 1-4R; CABS 2; CANR 2, 29; DLB
5, 169; INT CANR-29; MTCW; SATA 9
Wild, Peter 1940- .... **CLC 14**
See also CA 37-40R; DLB 5
Wilde, Oscar (Fingal O'Flahertie Wills)
1854(?)-1900 **TCLC 1, 8, 23, 41; DA; DAB; DAC; DAM DRAM, MST, NOV; SSC 11; WLC**
See also CA 104; 119; CDBLB 1890-1914;
DLB 10, 19, 34, 57, 141, 156; SATA 24
Wilder, Billy .... **CLC 20**
See also Wilder, Samuel
See also DLB 26
Wilder, Samuel 1906-
See Wilder, Billy
See also CA 89-92
Wilder, Thornton (Niven) 1897-1975 **CLC 1, 5, 6, 10, 15, 35, 82; DA; DAB; DAC; DAM DRAM, MST, NOV; DC 1; WLC**
See also AITN 2; CA 13-16R; 61-64; CANR
40; DLB 4, 7, 9; MTCW
Wilding, Michael 1942- .... **CLC 73**
See also CA 104; CANR 24, 49
Wiley, Richard 1944- .... **CLC 44**
See also CA 121; 129
Wilhelm, Kate .... **CLC 7**
See also Wilhelm, Katie Gertrude
See also AAYA 20; CAAS 5; DLB 8; INT
CANR-17
Wilhelm, Katie Gertrude 1928-
See Wilhelm, Kate
See also CA 37-40R; CANR 17, 36, 60; MTCW
Wilkins, Mary
See Freeman, Mary Eleanor Wilkins
Willard, Nancy 1936- .... **CLC 7, 37**
See also CA 89-92; CANR 10, 39; CLR 5; DLB
5, 52; MAICYA; MTCW; SATA 37, 71;
SATA-Brief 30
Williams, C(harles) K(enneth) 1936- **CLC 33, 56; DAM POET**
See also CA 37-40R; CAAS 26; CANR 57; DLB
5
Williams, Charles
See Collier, James L(incoln)
Williams, Charles (Walter Stansby) 1886-1945
TCLC 1, 11
See also CA 104; DLB 100, 153
Williams, (George) Emlyn 1905-1987 **CLC 15; DAM DRAM**
See also CA 104; 123; CANR 36; DLB 10, 77;
MTCW
Williams, Hugo 1942- .... **CLC 42**
See also CA 17-20R; CANR 45; DLB 40
Williams, J. Walker
See Wodehouse, P(elham) G(renville)
Williams, John A(lfred) 1925- ..... **CLC 5, 13;**

BLC; DAM MULT
See also BW 2; CA 53-56; CAAS 3; CANR 6,
26, 51; DLB 2, 33; INT CANR-6

Williams, Jonathan (Chamberlain) 1929-
CLC 13
See also CA 9-12R; CAAS 12; CANR 8; DLB
5

Williams, Joy 1944- .... CLC 31
See also CA 41-44R; CANR 22, 48

Williams, Norman 1952- .... CLC 39
See also CA 118

Williams, Sherley Anne 1944-CLC 89; BLC;
DAM MULT, POET
See also BW 2; CA 73-76; CANR 25; DLB 41;
INT CANR-25; SATA 78

Williams, Shirley
See Williams, Sherley Anne

Williams, Tennessee 1911-1983CLC 1, 2, 5, 7,
8, 11, 15, 19, 30, 39, 45, 71; DA; DAB;
DAC; DAM DRAM, MST; DC 4; WLC
See also AITN 1, 2; CA 5-8R; 108; CABS 3;
CANR 31; CDALB 1941-1968; DLB 7;
DLBD 4; DLBY 83; MTCW

Williams, Thomas (Alonzo) 1926-1990CLC 14
See also CA 1-4R; 132; CANR 2

Williams, William C.
See Williams, William Carlos

Williams, William Carlos 1883-1963CLC 1, 2,
5, 9, 13, 22, 42, 67; DA; DAB; DAC; DAM
MST, POET; PC 7
See also CA 89-92; CANR 34; CDALB 1917-
1929; DLB 4, 16, 54, 86; MTCW

Williamson, David (Keith) 1942- ...... CLC 56
See also CA 103; CANR 41

Williamson, Ellen Douglas 1905-1984
See Douglas, Ellen
See also CA 17-20R; 114; CANR 39

Williamson, Jack .... CLC 29
See also Williamson, John Stewart
See also CAAS 8; DLB 8

Williamson, John Stewart 1908-
See Williamson, Jack
See also CA 17-20R; CANR 23

Willie, Frederick
See Lovecraft, H(oward) P(hillips)

Willingham, Calder (Baynard, Jr.) 1922-1995
CLC 5, 51
See also CA 5-8R; 147; CANR 3; DLB 2, 44;
MTCW

Willis, Charles
See Clarke, Arthur C(harles)

Willy
See Colette, (Sidonie-Gabrielle)

Willy, Colette
See Colette, (Sidonie-Gabrielle)

Wilson, A(ndrew) N(orman) 1950- ... CLC 33
See also CA 112; 122; DLB 14, 155

Wilson, Angus (Frank Johnstone) 1913-1991
CLC 2, 3, 5, 25, 34; SSC 21
See also CA 5-8R; 134; CANR 21; DLB 15,
139, 155; MTCW

Wilson, August 1945- CLC 39, 50, 63; BLC;
DA; DAB; DAC; DAM DRAM, MST,
MULT; DC 2; WLCS
See also AAYA 16; BW 2; CA 115; 122; CANR
42, 54; MTCW

Wilson, Brian 1942- .... CLC 12

Wilson, Colin 1931- .... CLC 3, 14
See also CA 1-4R; CAAS 5; CANR 1, 22, 33;
DLB 14; MTCW

Wilson, Dirk
See Pohl, Frederik

Wilson, Edmund 1895-1972CLC 1, 2, 3, 8, 24

See also CA 1-4R; 37-40R; CANR 1, 46; DLB
63; MTCW

Wilson, Ethel Davis (Bryant) 1888(?)-1980
CLC 13; DAC; DAM POET
See also CA 102; DLB 68; MTCW

Wilson, John 1785-1854 .... NCLC 5

Wilson, John (Anthony) Burgess 1917-1993
See Burgess, Anthony
See also CA 1-4R; 143; CANR 2, 46; DAC;
DAM NOV; MTCW

Wilson, Lanford 1937- CLC 7, 14, 36; DAM
DRAM
See also CA 17-20R; CABS 3; CANR 45; DLB
7

Wilson, Robert M. 1944- .... CLC 7, 9
See also CA 49-52; CANR 2, 41; MTCW

Wilson, Robert McLiam 1964- .... CLC 59
See also CA 132

Wilson, Sloan 1920- .... CLC 32
See also CA 1-4R; CANR 1, 44

Wilson, Snoo 1948- .... CLC 33
See also CA 69-72

Wilson, William S(mith) 1932- .... CLC 49
See also CA 81-84

Wilson, Woodrow 1856-1924 .... TCLC 73
See also DLB 47

Winchilsea, Anne (Kingsmill) Finch Counte
1661-1720
See Finch, Anne

Windham, Basil
See Wodehouse, P(elham) G(renville)

Wingrove, David (John) 1954- .... CLC 68
See also CA 133

Wintergreen, Jane
See Duncan, Sara Jeannette

Winters, Janet Lewis .... CLC 41
See also Lewis, Janet
See also DLBY 87

Winters, (Arthur) Yvor 1900-1968 CLC 4, 8,
32
See also CA 11-12; 25-28R; CAP 1; DLB 48;
MTCW

Winterson, Jeanette 1959-CLC 64; DAM POP
See also CA 136; CANR 58

Winthrop, John 1588-1649 .... LC 31
See also DLB 24, 30

Wiseman, Frederick 1930- .... CLC 20
See also CA 159

Wister, Owen 1860-1938 .... TCLC 21
See also CA 108; DLB 9, 78; SATA 62

Witkacy
See Witkiewicz, Stanislaw Ignacy

Witkiewicz, Stanislaw Ignacy 1885-1939
TCLC 8
See also CA 105

Wittgenstein, Ludwig (Josef Johann) 1889-1951
TCLC 59
See also CA 113

Wittig, Monique 1935(?)- .... CLC 22
See also CA 116; 135; DLB 83

Wittlin, Jozef 1896-1976 .... CLC 25
See also CA 49-52; 65-68; CANR 3

Wodehouse, P(elham) G(renville) 1881-1975
CLC 1, 2, 5, 10, 22; DAB; DAC; DAM
NOV; SSC 2
See also AITN 2; CA 45-48; 57-60; CANR 3,
33; CDBLB 1914-1945; DLB 34, 162;
MTCW; SATA 22

Woiwode, L.
See Woiwode, Larry (Alfred)

Woiwode, Larry (Alfred) 1941- ....CLC 6, 10
See also CA 73-76; CANR 16; DLB 6; INT
CANR-16

Wojciechowska, Maia (Teresa) 1927-CLC 26
See also AAYA 8; CA 9-12R; CANR 4, 41; CLR
1; JRDA; MAICYA; SAAS 1; SATA 1, 28,
83

Wolf, Christa 1929- .... CLC 14, 29, 58
See also CA 85-88; CANR 45; DLB 75; MTCW

Wolfe, Gene (Rodman) 1931- CLC 25; DAM
POP
See also CA 57-60; CAAS 9; CANR 6, 32, 60;
DLB 8

Wolfe, George C. 1954- .... CLC 49
See also CA 149

Wolfe, Thomas (Clayton) 1900-1938TCLC 4,
13, 29, 61; DA; DAB; DAC; DAM MST,
NOV; WLC
See also CA 104; 132; CDALB 1929-1941;
DLB 9, 102; DLBD 2, 16; DLBY 85; MTCW

Wolfe, Thomas Kennerly, Jr. 1931-
See Wolfe, Tom
See also CA 13-16R; CANR 9, 33; DAM POP;
INT CANR-9; MTCW

Wolfe, Tom .... CLC 1, 2, 9, 15, 35, 51
See also Wolfe, Thomas Kennerly, Jr.
See also AAYA 8; AITN 2; BEST 89:1; DLB
152

Wolff, Geoffrey (Ansell) 1937- .... CLC 41
See also CA 29-32R; CANR 29, 43

Wolff, Sonia
See Levitin, Sonia (Wolff)

Wolff, Tobias (Jonathan Ansell) 1945- . C L C
39, 64
See also AAYA 16; BEST 90:2; CA 114; 117;
CAAS 22; CANR 54; DLB 130; INT 117

Wolfram von Eschenbach c. 1170-c. 1220
CMLC 5
See also DLB 138

Wolitzer, Hilma 1930- .... CLC 17
See also CA 65-68; CANR 18, 40; INT CANR-
18; SATA 31

Wollstonecraft, Mary 1759-1797 .... LC 5
See also CDBLB 1789-1832; DLB 39, 104, 158

Wonder, Stevie .... CLC 12
See also Morris, Steveland Judkins

Wong, Jade Snow 1922- .... CLC 17
See also CA 109

Woodberry, George Edward 1855-1930
TCLC 73
See also DLB 71, 103

Woodcott, Keith
See Brunner, John (Kilian Houston)

Woodruff, Robert W.
See Mencken, H(enry) L(ouis)

Woolf, (Adeline) Virginia 1882-1941TCLC 1,
5, 20, 43, 56; DA; DAB; DAC; DAM MST,
NOV; SSC 7; WLC
See also CA 104; 130; CANR 64; CDBLB
1914-1945; DLB 36, 100, 162; DLBD 10;
MTCW

Woolf, Virginia Adeline
See Woolf, (Adeline) Virginia

Woollcott, Alexander (Humphreys) 1887-1943
TCLC 5
See also CA 105; 161; DLB 29

Woolrich, Cornell 1903-1968 .... CLC 77
See also Hopley-Woolrich, Cornell George

Wordsworth, Dorothy 1771-1855 .. NCLC 25
See also DLB 107

Wordsworth, William 1770-1850 .. NCLC 12,
38; DA; DAB; DAC; DAM MST, POET;
PC 4; WLC
See also CDBLB 1789-1832; DLB 93, 107

Wouk, Herman 1915-CLC 1, 9, 38; DAM NOV,
POP

See also CA 5-8R; CANR 6, 33; DLBY 82; INT CANR-6; MTCW
Wright, Charles (Penzel, Jr.) 1935-**CLC 6, 13, 28**
See also CA 29-32R; CAAS 7; CANR 23, 36, 62; DLB 165; DLBY 82; MTCW
Wright, Charles Stevenson 1932- ... **CLC 49; BLC 3; DAM MULT, POET**
See also BW 1; CA 9-12R; CANR 26; DLB 33
Wright, Jack R.
See Harris, Mark
Wright, James (Arlington) 1927-1980**CLC 3, 5, 10, 28; DAM POET**
See also AITN 2; CA 49-52; 97-100; CANR 4, 34, 64; DLB 5, 169; MTCW
Wright, Judith (Arandell) 1915- **CLC 11, 53; PC 14**
See also CA 13-16R; CANR 31; MTCW; SATA 14
Wright, L(aurali) R. 1939- .... **CLC 44**
See also CA 138
Wright, Richard (Nathaniel) 1908-1960 **C L C 1, 3, 4, 9, 14, 21, 48, 74; BLC; DA; DAB; DAC; DAM MST, MULT, NOV; SSC 2; WLC**
See also AAYA 5; BW 1; CA 108; CANR 64; CDALB 1929-1941; DLB 76, 102; DLBD 2; MTCW
Wright, Richard B(ruce) 1937- .... **CLC 6**
See also CA 85-88; DLB 53
Wright, Rick 1945- .... **CLC 35**
Wright, Rowland
See Wells, Carolyn
Wright, Stephen 1946- .... **CLC 33**
Wright, Willard Huntington 1888-1939
See Van Dine, S. S.
See also CA 115; DLBD 16
Wright, William 1930- .... **CLC 44**
See also CA 53-56; CANR 7, 23
Wroth, LadyMary 1587-1653(?) .... **LC 30**
See also DLB 121
Wu Ch'eng-en 1500(?)-1582(?) .... **LC 7**
Wu Ching-tzu 1701-1754 .... **LC 2**
Wurlitzer, Rudolph 1938(?)- .... **CLC 2, 4, 15**
See also CA 85-88; DLB 173
Wycherley, William 1641-1715**LC 8, 21; DAM DRAM**
See also CDBLB 1660-1789; DLB 80
Wylie, Elinor (Morton Hoyt) 1885-1928 **TCLC 8**
See also CA 105; DLB 9, 45
Wylie, Philip (Gordon) 1902-1971 ... **CLC 43**
See also CA 21-22; 33-36R; CAP 2; DLB 9
Wyndham, John .... **CLC 19**
See also Harris, John (Wyndham Parkes Lucas) Beynon
Wyss, Johann David Von 1743-1818**NCLC 10**
See also JRDA; MAICYA; SATA 29; SATA-Brief 27
Xenophon c. 430B.C.-c. 354B.C. ... **CMLC 17**
See also DLB 176
Yakumo Koizumi
See Hearn, (Patricio) Lafcadio (Tessima Carlos)
Yanez, Jose Donoso
See Donoso (Yanez), Jose
Yanovsky, Basile S.
See Yanovsky, V(assily) S(emenovich)
Yanovsky, V(assily) S(emenovich) 1906-1989 **CLC 2, 18**
See also CA 97-100; 129

Yates, Richard 1926-1992 .... **CLC 7, 8, 23**
See also CA 5-8R; 139; CANR 10, 43; DLB 2; DLBY 81, 92; INT CANR-10
Yeats, W. B.
See Yeats, William Butler
Yeats, William Butler 1865-1939**TCLC 1, 11, 18, 31; DA; DAB; DAC; DAM DRAM, MST, POET; PC 20; WLC**
See also CA 104; 127; CANR 45; CDBLB 1890-1914; DLB 10, 19, 98, 156; MTCW
Yehoshua, A(braham) B. 1936- .. **CLC 13, 31**
See also CA 33-36R; CANR 43
Yep, Laurence Michael 1948-............ **CLC 35**
See also AAYA 5; CA 49-52; CANR 1, 46; CLR 3, 17; DLB 52; JRDA; MAICYA; SATA 7, 69
Yerby, Frank G(arvin) 1916-1991 .**CLC 1, 7, 22; BLC; DAM MULT**
See also BW 1; CA 9-12R; CANR 16, 52; DLB 76; INT CANR-16; MTCW
Yesenin, Sergei Alexandrovich
See Esenin, Sergei (Alexandrovich)
Yevtushenko, Yevgeny (Alexandrovich) 1933-**CLC 1, 3, 13, 26, 51; DAM POET**
See also CA 81-84; CANR 33, 54; MTCW
Yezierska, Anzia 1885(?)-1970 .... **CLC 46**
See also CA 126; 89-92; DLB 28; MTCW
Yglesias, Helen 1915- .... **CLC 7, 22**
See also CA 37-40R; CAAS 20; CANR 15; INT CANR-15; MTCW
Yokomitsu Riichi 1898-1947 .... **TCLC 47**
Yonge, Charlotte (Mary) 1823-1901**TCLC 48**
See also CA 109; DLB 18, 163; SATA 17
York, Jeremy
See Creasey, John
York, Simon
See Heinlein, Robert A(nson)
Yorke, Henry Vincent 1905-1974 ...... **CLC 13**
See also Green, Henry
See also CA 85-88; 49-52
Yosano Akiko 1878-1942 .... **TCLC 59; PC 11**
See also CA 161
Yoshimoto, Banana .... **CLC 84**
See also Yoshimoto, Mahoko
Yoshimoto, Mahoko 1964-
See Yoshimoto, Banana
See also CA 144
Young, Al(bert James) 1939- .**CLC 19; BLC; DAM MULT**
See also BW 2; CA 29-32R; CANR 26; DLB 33
Young, Andrew (John) 1885-1971 ...... **CLC 5**
See also CA 5-8R; CANR 7, 29
Young, Collier
See Bloch, Robert (Albert)
Young, Edward 1683-1765 .... **LC 3, 40**
See also DLB 95
Young, Marguerite (Vivian) 1909-1995 **C L C 82**
See also CA 13-16; 150; CAP 1
Young, Neil 1945- .... **CLC 17**
See also CA 110
Young Bear, Ray A. 1950-...... **CLC 94; DAM MULT**
See also CA 146; DLB 175; NNAL
Yourcenar, Marguerite 1903-1987**CLC 19, 38, 50, 87; DAM NOV**
See also CA 69-72; CANR 23, 60; DLB 72; DLBY 88; MTCW
Yurick, Sol 1925- .... **CLC 6**

See also CA 13-16R; CANR 25
Zabolotskii, Nikolai Alekseevich 1903-1958 **TCLC 52**
See also CA 116
Zamiatin, Yevgenii
See Zamyatin, Evgeny Ivanovich
Zamora, Bernice (B. Ortiz) 1938- .. **CLC 89; DAM MULT; HLC**
See also CA 151; DLB 82; HW
Zamyatin, Evgeny Ivanovich 1884-1937 **TCLC 8, 37**
See also CA 105
Zangwill, Israel 1864-1926 .... **TCLC 16**
See also CA 109; DLB 10, 135
Zappa, Francis Vincent, Jr. 1940-1993
See Zappa, Frank
See also CA 108; 143; CANR 57
Zappa, Frank .... **CLC 17**
See also Zappa, Francis Vincent, Jr.
Zaturenska, Marya 1902-1982 ...... **CLC 6, 11**
See also CA 13-16R; 105; CANR 22
Zeami 1363-1443 .... **DC 7**
Zelazny, Roger (Joseph) 1937-1995 . **CLC 21**
See also AAYA 7; CA 21-24R; 148; CANR 26, 60; DLB 8; MTCW; SATA 57; SATA-Brief 39
Zhdanov, Andrei A(lexandrovich) 1896-1948 **TCLC 18**
See also CA 117
Zhukovsky, Vasily 1783-1852 .... **NCLC 35**
Ziegenhagen, Eric .... **CLC 55**
Zimmer, Jill Schary
See Robinson, Jill
Zimmerman, Robert
See Dylan, Bob
Zindel, Paul 1936-**CLC 6, 26; DA; DAB; DAC; DAM DRAM, MST, NOV; DC 5**
See also AAYA 2; CA 73-76; CANR 31; CLR 3, 45; DLB 7, 52; JRDA; MAICYA; MTCW; SATA 16, 58
Zinov'Ev, A. A.
See Zinoviev, Alexander (Aleksandrovich)
Zinoviev, Alexander (Aleksandrovich) 1922-**CLC 19**
See also CA 116; 133; CAAS 10
Zoilus
See Lovecraft, H(oward) P(hillips)
Zola, Emile (Edouard Charles Antoine) 1840-1902**TCLC 1, 6, 21, 41; DA; DAB; DAC; DAM MST, NOV; WLC**
See also CA 104; 138; DLB 123
Zoline, Pamela 1941- .... **CLC 62**
See also CA 161
Zorrilla y Moral, Jose 1817-1893 .... **NCLC 6**
Zoshchenko, Mikhail (Mikhailovich) 1895-1958 **TCLC 15; SSC 15**
See also CA 115; 160
Zuckmayer, Carl 1896-1977 .... **CLC 18**
See also CA 69-72; DLB 56, 124
Zuk, Georges
See Skelton, Robin
Zukofsky, Louis 1904-1978**CLC 1, 2, 4, 7, 11, 18; DAM POET; PC 11**
See also CA 9-12R; 77-80; CANR 39; DLB 5, 165; MTCW
Zweig, Paul 1935-1984 .... **CLC 34, 42**
See also CA 85-88; 113
Zweig, Stefan 1881-1942 .... **TCLC 17**
See also CA 112; DLB 81, 118
Zwingli, Huldreich 1484-1531 ....**LC 37**
See also DLB 179

Literary Criticism Series
Cumulative Topic Index

This index lists all topic entries in Gale's *Classical and Medieval Literature Criticism, Contemporary Literary Criticism, Literature Criticism from 1400 to 1800, Nineteenth-Century Literature Criticism,* and *Twentieth-Century Literary Criticism.*

Age of Johnson LC 15: 1-87
Johnson's London, 3-15
aesthetics of neoclassicism, 15-36
"age of prose and reason," 36-45
clubmen and bluestockings, 45-56
printing technology, 56-62
periodicals: "a map of busy life," 62-74
transition, 74-86

Age of Spenser LC 39: 1-70
Overviews, 2-21
Literary Style, 22-34
Poets and the Crown, 34-70

AIDS in Literature CLC 81: 365-416

Alcohol and Literature TCLC 70: 1-58
overview, 2-8
fiction, 8-48
poetry and drama, 48-58

American Abolitionism NCLC 44: 1-73
overviews, 2-26
abolitionist ideals, 26-46
the literature of abolitionism, 46-72

American Black Humor Fiction TCLC 54: 1-85
characteristics of black humor, 2-13
origins and development, 13-38
black humor distinguished from related literary trends, 38-60
black humor and society, 60-75
black humor reconsidered, 75-83

American Civil War in Literature NCLC 32: 1-109
overviews, 2-20
regional perspectives, 20-54
fiction popular during the war, 54-79
the historical novel, 79-108

American Frontier in Literature NCLC 28: 1-103
definitions, 2-12
development, 12-17

nonfiction writing about the frontier, 17-30
frontier fiction, 30-45
frontier protagonists, 45-66
portrayals of Native Americans, 66-86
feminist readings, 86-98
twentieth-century reaction against frontier literature, 98-100

American Humor Writing NCLC 52: 1-59
overviews, 2-12
the Old Southwest, 12-42
broader impacts, 42-5
women humorists, 45-58

American Mercury, The TCLC 74: 1-80

American Popular Song, Golden Age of TCLC 42: 1-49
background and major figures, 2-34
the lyrics of popular songs, 34-47

American Proletarian Literature TCLC 54: 86-175
overviews, 87-95
American proletarian literature and the American Communist Party, 95-111
ideology and literary merit, 111-7
novels, 117-36
Gastonia, 136-48
drama, 148-54
journalism, 154-9
proletarian literature in the United States, 159-74

American Romanticism NCLC 44: 74-138
overviews, 74-84
sociopolitical influences, 84-104
Romanticism and the American frontier, 104-15
thematic concerns, 115-37

American Western Literature TCLC 46: 1-100
definition and development of American Western literature, 2-7

characteristics of the Western novel, 8-23
Westerns as history and fiction, 23-34
critical reception of American Western literature, 34-41
the Western hero, 41-73
women in Western fiction, 73-91
later Western fiction, 91-9

Art and Literature TCLC 54: 176-248
overviews, 176-93
definitions, 193-219
influence of visual arts on literature, 219-31
spatial form in literature, 231-47

Arthurian Literature CMLC 10: 1-127
historical context and literary beginnings, 2-27
development of the legend through Malory, 27-64
development of the legend from Malory to the Victorian Age, 65-81
themes and motifs, 81-95
principal characters, 95-125

Arthurian Revival NCLC 36: 1-77
overviews, 2-12
Tennyson and his influence, 12-43
other leading figures, 43-73
the Arthurian legend in the visual arts, 73-6

Australian Literature TCLC 50: 1-94
origins and development, 2-21
characteristics of Australian literature, 21-33
historical and critical perspectives, 33-41
poetry, 41-58
fiction, 58-76
drama, 76-82
Aboriginal literature, 82-91

Beat Generation, Literature of the TCLC 42: 50-102
overviews, 51-9
the Beat generation as a social phenomenon, 59-62

development, 62-5
Beat literature, 66-96
influence, 97-100

The Bell Curve Controversy CLC 91:
281-330

Bildungsroman **in Nineteenth-Century
Literature** NCLC 20: 92-168
surveys, 93-113
in Germany, 113-40
in England, 140-56
female *Bildungsroman,* 156-67

Bloomsbury Group TCLC 34: 1-73
history and major figures, 2-13
definitions, 13-7
influences, 17-27
thought, 27-40
prose, 40-52
and literary criticism, 52-4
political ideals, 54-61
response to, 61-71

Bly, Robert, *Iron John: A Book about
Men and Men's Work* **CLC 70: 414-62**

The Book of J **CLC 65: 289-311**

Buddhism and Literature TCLC 70: 59-
164
eastern literature, 60-113
western literature, 113-63

Businessman in American Literature
TCLC 26: 1-48
portrayal of the businessman, 1-32
themes and techniques in business
fiction, 32-47

**Catholicism in Nineteenth-Century
American Literature** NCLC 64: 1-58
overviews, 3-14
polemical literature, 14-46
Catholicism in literature, 47-57

Celtic Mythology CMLC 26: 1-111
overviews, 2-22
Celtic myth as literature and history, 22-
48
Celtic religion: Druids and divinities, 48-
80
Fionn MacCuhaill and the Fenian cycle,
80-111

Celtic Twilight
See Irish Literary Renaissance

Chartist Movement and Literature, The
NCLC 60: 1-84

overview: nineteenth-century working-
class fiction, 2-19
Chartist fiction and poetry, 19-73
the Chartist press, 73-84

**Children's Literature, Nineteenth-
Century** NCLC 52: 60-135
overviews, 61-72
moral tales, 72-89
fairy tales and fantasy, 90-119
making men/making women, 119-34

Civic Critics, Russian NCLC 20: 402-46
principal figures and background, 402-9
and Russian Nihilism, 410-6
aesthetic and critical views, 416-45

The Cockney School NCLC 68: 1-64
overview, 2-7
Blackwood's Magazine and the
contemporary critical response, 7-24
the political and social import of the
Cockneys and their critics, 24-63

**Colonial America: The Intellectual
Background** LC 25: 1-98
overviews, 2-17
philosophy and politics, 17-31
early religious influences in Colonial
America, 31-60
consequences of the Revolution, 60-78
religious influences in post-revolutionary
America, 78-87
colonial literary genres, 87-97

**Colonialism in Victorian English
Literature** NCLC 56: 1-77
overviews, 2-34
colonialism and gender, 34-51
monsters and the occult, 51-76

**Columbus, Christopher, Books on the
Quincentennial of His Arrival in the New
World** CLC 70: 329-60

Comic Books TCLC 66: 1-139
historical and critical perspectives, 2-48
superheroes, 48-67
underground comix, 67-88
comic books and society, 88-122
adult comics and graphic novels, 122-36

Connecticut Wits NCLC 48: 1-95
general overviews, 2-40
major works, 40-76
intellectual context, 76-95

Crime in Literature TCLC 54: 249-307
evolution of the criminal figure in
literature, 250-61

crime and society, 261-77
literary perspectives on crime and
punishment, 277-88
writings by criminals, 288-306

**Czechoslovakian Literature of the
Twentieth Century** TCLC 42: 103-96
through World War II, 104-35
de-Stalinization, the Prague Spring, and
contemporary literature, 135-72
Slovak literature, 172-85
Czech science fiction, 185-93

Dadaism TCLC 46: 101-71
background and major figures, 102-16
definitions, 116-26
manifestos and commentary by Dadaists,
126-40
theater and film, 140-58
nature and characteristics of Dadaist
writing, 158-70

Darwinism and Literature NCLC 32: 110-
206
background, 110-31
direct responses to Darwin, 131-71
collateral effects of Darwinism, 171-205

**Death in Nineteenth-Century British
Literature** NCLC 68: 65-142
overviews, 66-92
responses to death, 92-102
feminist perspectives, 103-17
striving for immortality, 117-41

Death in Literature TCLC 78:1-183
fiction, 2-115
poetry, 115-46
drama, 146-81

de Man, Paul, Wartime Journalism of
CLC 55: 382-424

Detective Fiction, Nineteenth-Century
NCLC 36: 78-148
origins of the genre, 79-100
history of nineteenth-century detective
fiction, 101-33
significance of nineteenth-century
detective fiction, 133-46

Detective Fiction, Twentieth-Century
TCLC 38: 1-96
genesis and history of the detective
story, 3-22
defining detective fiction, 22-32
evolution and varieties, 32-77
the appeal of detective fiction, 77-90

Disease and Literature TCLC 66: 140-283

overviews, 141-65
disease in nineteenth-century literature,
    165-81
tuberculosis and literature, 181-94
women and disease in literature, 194-221
plague literature, 221-53
AIDS in literature, 253-82

**The Double in Nineteenth-Century
Literature** NCLC 40: 1-95
    genesis and development of the theme,
        2-15
    the double and Romanticism, 16-27
    sociological views, 27-52
    psychological interpretations, 52-87
    philosophical considerations, 87-95

Dramatic Realism NCLC 44: 139-202
    overviews, 140-50
    origins and definitions, 150-66
    impact and influence, 166-93
    realist drama and tragedy, 193-201

Drugs and Literature TCLC 78: 184-282
    overviews, 185-201
    pre-twentieth-century literature, 201-42
    twentieth-century literature, 242-82

Eastern Mythology CMLC 26: 112-92
    heroes and kings, 113-51
    cross-cultural perspective, 151-69
    relations to history and society, 169-92

**Electronic "Books": Hypertext and
Hyperfiction** CLC 86: 367-404
    books vs. CD-ROMS, 367-76
    hypertext and hyperfiction, 376-95
    implications for publishing, libraries, and
        the public, 395-403

Eliot, T. S., Centenary of Birth CLC 55:
345-75

Elizabethan Drama LC 22: 140-240
    origins and influences, 142-67
    characteristics and conventions, 167-83
    theatrical production, 184-200
    histories, 200-12
    comedy, 213-20
    tragedy, 220-30

Elizabethan Prose Fiction LC 41: 1-70
    overviews, 1-15
    origins and influences, 15-43
    style and structure, 43-69

The Encyclopedists LC 26: 172-253
    overviews, 173-210
    intellectual background, 210-32
    views on esthetics, 232-41

views on women, 241-52

English Caroline Literature LC 13: 221-
307
    background, 222-41
    evolution and varieties, 241-62
    the Cavalier mode, 262-75
    court and society, 275-91
    politics and religion, 291-306

**English Decadent Literature of the
1890s** NCLC 28: 104-200
    fin de siècle: the Decadent period, 105-
        19
    definitions, 120-37
    major figures: "the tragic generation,"
        137-50
    French literature and English literary
        Decadence, 150-7
    themes, 157-61
    poetry, 161-82
    periodicals, 182-96

English Essay, Rise of the LC 18: 238-
308
    definitions and origins, 236-54
    influence on the essay, 254-69
    historical background, 269-78
    the essay in the seventeenth century,
        279-93
    the essay in the eighteenth century, 293-
        307

English Mystery Cycle Dramas LC 34: 1-
88
    overviews, 1-27
    the nature of dramatic performances,
        27-42
    the medieval worldview and the mystery
        cycles, 43-67
    the doctrine of repentance and the
        mystery cycles, 67-76
    the fall from grace in the mystery cycles,
        76-88

English Romantic Hellenism NCLC 68:
143-250
    overviews, 144-69
    historical development of English
        Romantic Hellenism, 169-91
    inflience of Greek mythology on the
        Romantics, 191-229
    influence of Greek literature, art, and
        culture on the Romantics, 229-50

English Romantic Poetry NCLC 28: 201-
327
    overviews and reputation, 202-37
    major subjects and themes, 237-67
    forms of Romantic poetry, 267-78

politics, society, and Romantic poetry,
    278-99
philosophy, religion, and Romantic poetry,
    299-324

Espionage Literature TCLC 50: 95-159
    overviews, 96-113
    espionage fiction/formula fiction, 113-26
    spies in fact and fiction, 126-38
    the female spy, 138-44
    social and psychological perspectives,
        144-58

European Romanticism NCLC 36: 149-
284
    definitions, 149-77
    origins of the movement, 177-82
    Romantic theory, 182-200
    themes and techniques, 200-23
    Romanticism in Germany, 223-39
    Romanticism in France, 240-61
    Romanticism in Italy, 261-4
    Romanticism in Spain, 264-8
    impact and legacy, 268-82

Existentialism and Literature TCLC 42:
197-268
    overviews and definitions, 198-209
    history and influences, 209-19
    Existentialism critiqued and defended,
        220-35
    philosophical and religious perspectives,
        235-41
    Existentialist fiction and drama, 241-67

Familiar Essay NCLC 48: 96-211
    definitions and origins, 97-130
    overview of the genre, 130-43
    elements of form and style, 143-59
    elements of content, 159-73
    the Cockneys: Hazlitt, Lamb, and Hunt,
        173-91
    status of the genre, 191-210

Fear in Literature TCLC 74: 81-258
    overviews, 81
    pre-twentieth-century literature, 123
    twentieth-century literature, 182

**Feminism in the 1990s: Commentary on
Works by Naomi Wolf, Susan Faludi, and
Camille Paglia** CLC 76: 377-415

Feminist Criticism in 1990 CLC 65: 312-
60

Fifteenth-Century English Literature
LC 17: 248-334
    background, 249-72
    poetry, 272-315

drama, 315-23
prose, 323-33

Film and Literature TCLC 38: 97-226
overviews, 97-119
film and theater, 119-34
film and the novel, 134-45
the art of the screenplay, 145-66
genre literature/genre film, 167-79
the writer and the film industry, 179-90
authors on film adaptations of their
works, 190-200
fiction into film: comparative essays,
200-23

French Drama in the Age of Louis XIV
LC 28: 94-185
overview, 95-127
tragedy, 127-46
comedy, 146-66
tragicomedy, 166-84

French Enlightenment LC 14: 81-145
the question of definition, 82-9
Le siècle des lumières, 89-94
women and the salons, 94-105
censorship, 105-15
the philosophy of reason, 115-31
influence and legacy, 131-44

French Realism NCLC 52: 136-216
origins and definitions, 137-70
issues and influence, 170-98
realism and representation, 198-215

French Revolution and English Litera-
ture NCLC 40: 96-195
history and theory, 96-123
romantic poetry, 123-50
the novel, 150-81
drama, 181-92
children's literature, 192-5

Futurism, Italian TCLC 42: 269-354
principles and formative influences, 271-9
manifestos, 279-88
literature, 288-303
theater, 303-19
art, 320-30
music, 330-6
architecture, 336-9
and politics, 339-46
reputation and significance, 346-51

Gaelic Revival
See **Irish Literary Renaissance**

Gates, Henry Louis, Jr., and African-
American Literary Criticism CLC 65:
361-405

Gay and Lesbian Literature CLC 76:
416-39

German Exile Literature TCLC 30: 1-58
the writer and the Nazi state, 1-10
definition of, 10-4
life in exile, 14-32
surveys, 32-50
Austrian literature in exile, 50-2
German publishing in the United States,
52-7

German Expressionism TCLC 34: 74-160
history and major figures, 76-85
aesthetic theories, 85-109
drama, 109-26
poetry, 126-38
film, 138-42
painting, 142-7
music, 147-53
and politics, 153-8

***Glasnost* and Contemporary Soviet**
Literature CLC 59: 355-97

Gothic Novel NCLC 28: 328-402
development and major works, 328-34
definitions, 334-50
themes and techniques, 350-78
in America, 378-85
in Scotland, 385-91
influence and legacy, 391-400

Graphic Narratives CLC 86: 405-32
history and overviews, 406-21
the "Classics Illustrated" series, 421-2
reviews of recent works, 422-32

Greek Historiography CMLC 17: 1-49

Greek Mythology CMLC-26 193-320
overviews, 194-209
origins and development of Greek
mythology, 209-29
cosmogonies and divinities in Greek
mythology, 229-54
heroes and heroines in Greek mythology,
254-80
women in Greek mythology, 280-320

Harlem Renaissance TCLC 26: 49-125
principal issues and figures, 50-67
the literature and its audience, 67-74
theme and technique in poetry, fiction,
and drama, 74-115
and American society, 115-21
achievement and influence, 121-2

Havel, Václav, Playwright and President
CLC 65: 406-63

Historical Fiction, Nineteenth-Century
NCLC 48: 212-307
definitions and characteristics, 213-36
Victorian historical fiction, 236-65
American historical fiction, 265-88
realism in historical fiction, 288-306

Holocaust and the Atomic Bomb: Fifty
Years Later CLC 91: 331-82
the Holocaust remembered, 333-52
Anne Frank revisited, 352-62
the atomic bomb and American memory,
362-81

Holocaust Denial Literature TCLC 58: 1-110
overviews, 1-30
Robert Faurisson and Noam Chomsky,
30-52
Holocaust denial literature in America,
52-71
library access to Holocaust denial
literature, 72-5
the authenticity of Anne Frank's diary,
76-90
David Irving and the "normalization" of
Hitler, 90-109

Holocaust, Literature of the TCLC 42:
355-450
historical overview, 357-61
critical overview, 361-70
diaries and memoirs, 370-95
novels and short stories, 395-425
poetry, 425-41
drama, 441-8

Homosexuality in Nineteenth-Century
Literature NCLC 56: 78-182
defining homosexuality, 80-111
Greek love, 111-44
trial and danger, 144-81

Hungarian Literature of the Twentieth
Century TCLC 26: 126-88
surveys of, 126-47
Nyugat and early twentieth-century
literature, 147-56
mid-century literature, 156-68
and politics, 168-78
since the 1956 revolt, 178-87

Hysteria in Nineteenth-Century Litera-
ture NCLC 64: 59-184
the history of hysteria, 60-75
the gender of hysteria, 75-103
hysteria and women's narratives, 103-57
hysteria in nineteenth-century poetry,
157-83

Imagism TCLC 74: 259-454

history and development, 260
major figures, 288
sources and influences, 352
Imagism and other movements, 397
influence and legacy, 431

Indian Literature in English TCLC 54: 308-406
overview, 309-13
origins and major figures, 313-25
the Indo-English novel, 325-55
Indo-English poetry, 355-67
Indo-English drama, 367-72
critical perspectives on Indo-English literature, 372-80
modern Indo-English literature, 380-9
Indo-English authors on their work, 389-404

Industrial Revolution in Literature, The NCLC 56: 183-273
historical and cultural perspectives, 184-201
contemporary reactions to the machine, 201-21
themes and symbols in literature, 221-73

The Irish Famine as Represented in Nineteenth-Century Literature NCLC 64: 185-261
overviews, 187-98
historical background, 198-212
famine novels, 212-34
famine poetry, 234-44
famine letters and eye-witness accounts, 245-61

Irish Literary Renaissance TCLC 46: 172-287
overview, 173-83
development and major figures, 184-202
influence of Irish folklore and mythology, 202-22
Irish poetry, 222-34
Irish drama and the Abbey Theatre, 234-56
Irish fiction, 256-86

Irish Nationalism and Literature NCLC 44: 203-73
the Celtic element in literature, 203-19
anti-Irish sentiment and the Celtic response, 219-34
literary ideals in Ireland, 234-45
literary expressions, 245-73

Italian Futurism
See **Futurism, Italian**

Italian Humanism LC 12: 205-77

origins and early development, 206-18
revival of classical letters, 218-23
humanism and other philosophies, 224-39
humanisms and humanists, 239-46
the plastic arts, 246-57
achievement and significance, 258-76

Italian Romanticism NCLC 60: 85-145
origins and overviews, 86-101
Italian Romantic theory, 101-25
the language of Romanticism, 125-45

Jacobean Drama LC 33: 1-37
the Jacobean worldview: an era of transition, 2-14
the moral vision of Jacobean drama, 14-22
Jacobean tragedy, 22-3
the Jacobean masque, 23-36

Jewish-American Fiction TCLC 62: 1-181
overviews, 2-24
major figures, 24-48
Jewish writers and American life, 48-78
Jewish characters in American fiction, 78-108
themes in Jewish-American fiction, 108-43
Jewish-American women writers, 143-59
the Holocaust and Jewish-American fiction, 159-81

Knickerbocker Group, The NCLC 56: 274-341
overviews, 276-314
Knickerbocker periodicals, 314-26
writers and artists, 326-40

Lake Poets, The NCLC 52: 217-304
characteristics of the Lake Poets and their works, 218-27
literary influences and collaborations, 227-66
defining and developing Romantic ideals, 266-84
embracing Conservatism, 284-303

Larkin, Philip, Controversy CLC 81: 417-64

Latin American Literature, Twentieth-Century TCLC 58: 111-98
historical and critical perspectives, 112-36
the novel, 136-45
the short story, 145-9
drama, 149-60
poetry, 160-7
the writer and society, 167-86

Native Americans in Latin American literature, 186-97

Madness in Twentieth-Century Literature TCLC 50: 160-225
overviews, 161-71
madness and the creative process, 171-86
suicide, 186-91
madness in American literature, 191-207
madness in German literature, 207-13
madness and feminist artists, 213-24

Memoirs of Trauma CLC 109: 419-466

Metaphysical Poets LC 24: 356-439
early definitions, 358-67
surveys and overviews, 367-92
cultural and social influences, 392-406
stylistic and thematic variations, 407-38

Modern Essay, The TCLC 58: 199-273
overview, 200-7
the essay in the early twentieth century, 207-19
characteristics of the modern essay, 219-32
modern essayists, 232-45
the essay as a literary genre, 245-73

Modern Japanese Literature TCLC 66: 284-389
poetry, 285-305
drama, 305-29
fiction, 329-61
western influences, 361-87

Modernism TCLC 70: 165-275
definitions, 166-184
Modernism and earlier influences, 184-200
stylistic and thematic traits, 200-229
poetry and drama, 229-242
redefining Modernism, 242-275

Muckraking Movement in American Journalism TCLC 34: 161-242
development, principles, and major figures, 162-70
publications, 170-9
social and political ideas, 179-86
targets, 186-208
fiction, 208-19
decline, 219-29
impact and accomplishments, 229-40

Multiculturalism in Literature and Education CLC 70: 361-413

Music and Modern Literature TCLC 62:

182-329
    overviews, 182-211
    musical form/literary form, 211-32
    music in literature, 232-50
    the influence of music on literature, 250-
        73
    literature and popular music, 273-303
    jazz and poetry, 303-28

Native American Literature CLC 76:
440-76

Natural School, Russian NCLC 24: 205-
40
    history and characteristics, 205-25
    contemporary criticism, 225-40

Naturalism NCLC 36: 285-382
    definitions and theories, 286-305
    critical debates on Naturalism, 305-16
    Naturalism in theater, 316-32
    European Naturalism, 332-61
    American Naturalism, 361-72
    the legacy of Naturalism, 372-81

Negritude TCLC 50: 226-361
    origins and evolution, 227-56
    definitions, 256-91
    Negritude in literature, 291-343
    Negritude reconsidered, 343-58

New Criticism TCLC 34: 243-318
    development and ideas, 244-70
    debate and defense, 270-99
    influence and legacy, 299-315

The New World in Renaissance Litera-
ture LC 31: 1-51
    overview, 1-18
    utopia vs. terror, 18-31
    explorers and Native Americans, 31-51

New York Intellectuals and *Partisan*
Review TCLC 30: 117-98
    development and major figures, 118-28
    influence of Judaism, 128-39
    Partisan Review, 139-57
    literary philosophy and practice, 157-75
    political philosophy, 175-87
    achievement and significance, 187-97

The New Yorker TCLC 58: 274-357
    overviews, 274-95
    major figures, 295-304
    New Yorker style, 304-33
    fiction, journalism, and humor at *The*
        New Yorker, 333-48
    the new *New Yorker,* 348-56

Newgate Novel NCLC 24: 166-204

development of Newgate literature, 166-
    73
Newgate Calendar, 173-7
Newgate fiction, 177-95
Newgate drama, 195-204

Nigerian Literature of the Twentieth
Century TCLC 30: 199-265
    surveys of, 199-227
    English language and African life, 227-
        45
    politics and the Nigerian writer, 245-54
    Nigerian writers and society, 255-62

Nineteenth-Century Native American
Autobiography NCLC 64: 262-389
    overview, 263-8
    problems of authorship, 268-81
    the evolution of Native American
        autobiography, 281-304
    political issues, 304-15
    gender and autobiography, 316-62
    autobiographical works during the turn of
        the century, 362-88

Norse Mythology CMLC-26: 321-85
    history and mythological tradition, 322-44
    Eddic poetry, 344-74
    Norse mythology and other traditions,
        374-85

Northern Humanism LC 16: 281-356
    background, 282-305
    precursor of the Reformation, 305-14
    the Brethren of the Common Life, the
        Devotio Moderna, and education,
        314-40
    the impact of printing, 340-56

Novel of Manners, The NCLC 56: 342-96
    social and political order, 343-53
    domestic order, 353-73
    depictions of gender, 373-83
    the American novel of manners, 383-95

Nuclear Literature: Writings and
Criticism in the Nuclear Age TCLC 46:
288-390
    overviews, 290-301
    fiction, 301-35
    poetry, 335-8
    nuclear war in Russo-Japanese
        literature, 338-55
    nuclear war and women writers, 355-67
    the nuclear referent and literary
        criticism, 367-88

Occultism in Modern Literature TCLC
50: 362-406
    influence of occultism on literature, 363-72

occultism, literature, and society, 372-87
fiction, 387-96
drama, 396-405

Opium and the Nineteenth-Century
Literary Imagination NCLC 20: 250-301
    original sources, 250-62
    historical background, 262-71
    and literary society, 271-9
    and literary creativity, 279-300

Periodicals, Nineteenth-Century British
NCLC 24: 100-65
    overviews, 100-30
    in the Romantic Age, 130-41
    in the Victorian era, 142-54
    and the reviewer, 154-64

Plath, Sylvia, and the Nature of Biogra-
phy CLC 86: 433-62
    the nature of biography, 433-52
    reviews of *The Silent Woman,* 452-61

Political Theory from the 15th to the
18th Century LC 36: 1-55
    <Overview, 1-26
    Natural Law, 26-42
    Empiricism, 42-55

Polish Romanticism NCLC 52: 305-71
    overviews, 306-26
    major figures, 326-40
    Polish Romantic drama, 340-62
    influences, 362-71

Popular Literature TCLC 70: 279-382
    overviews, 280-324
    "formula" fiction, 324-336
    readers of popular literature, 336-351
    evolution of popular literature, 351-382

Pre-Raphaelite Movement NCLC 20:
302-401
    overview, 302-4
    genesis, 304-12
    Germ and *Oxford and Cambridge*
        Magazine, 312-20
    Robert Buchanan and the "Fleshly
        School of Poetry," 320-31
    satires and parodies, 331-4
    surveys, 334-51
    aesthetics, 351-75
    sister arts of poetry and painting, 375-94
    influence, 394-9

Preromanticism LC 40: 1-56
    overviews, 2-14
    defining the period, 14-23
    new directions in poetry and prose, 23-
        45

the focus on the self, 45-56

Presocratic Philosophy CMLC 22: 1-56
overviews, 3-24
the Ionians and the Pythagoreans, 25-35
Heraclitus, the Eleatics, and the
Atomists, 36-47
the Sophists, 47-55

**Protestant Reformation, Literature of
the** LC 37: 1-83
overviews, 1-49
humanism and scholasticism, 49-69
the reformation and literature, 69-82

Psychoanalysis and Literature TCLC 38:
227-338
overviews, 227-46
Freud on literature, 246-51
psychoanalytic views of the literary
process, 251-61
psychoanalytic theories of response to
literature, 261-88
psychoanalysis and literary criticism,
288-312
psychoanalysis as literature/literature as
psychoanalysis, 313-34

Rap Music CLC 76: 477-50

Renaissance Natural Philosophy LC 27:
201-87
cosmology, 201-28
astrology, 228-54
magic, 254-86

Restoration Drama LC 21: 184-275
general overviews, 185-230
Jeremy Collier stage controversy, 230-9
other critical interpretations, 240-75

Revising the Literary Canon CLC 81:
465-509

Robin Hood, Legend of LC 19: 205-58
origins and development of the Robin
Hood legend, 206-20
representations of Robin Hood, 220-44
Robin Hood as hero, 244-56

Rushdie, Salman, *Satanic Verses* **Controversy** CLC 55 214-63; 59: 404-56

Russian Nihilism NCLC 28: 403-47
definitions and overviews, 404-17
women and Nihilism, 417-27
literature as reform: the Civic Critics,
427-33
Nihilism and the Russian novel:
Turgenev and Dostoevsky, 433-47

Russian Thaw TCLC 26: 189-247
literary history of the period, 190-206
theoretical debate of socialist realism,
206-11
Novy Mir, 211-7
Literary Moscow, 217-24
Pasternak, *Zhivago,* and the Nobel
Prize, 224-7
poetry of liberation, 228-31
Brodsky trial and the end of the Thaw,
231-6
achievement and influence, 236-46

Salem Witch Trials LC-38: 1-145
overviews, 2-30
historical background, 30-65
judicial background, 65-78
the search for causes, 78-115
the role of women in the trials, 115-44

Salinger, J. D., Controversy Surrounding
In Search of J. D. Salinger CLC 55: 325-
44

Science Fiction, Nineteenth-Century
NCLC 24: 241-306
background, 242-50
definitions of the genre, 251-6
representative works and writers, 256-75
themes and conventions, 276-305

Scottish Chaucerians LC 20: 363-412

Scottish Poetry, Eighteenth-Century LC
29: 95-167
overviews, 96-114
the Scottish Augustans, 114-28
the Scots Vernacular Revival, 132-63
Scottish poetry after Burns, 163-6

Sentimental Novel, The NCLC 60: 146-
245
overviews, 147-58
the politics of domestic fiction, 158-79
a literature of resistance and repression,
179-212
the reception of sentimental fiction, 213-
44

Sherlock Holmes Centenary TCLC 26:
248-310
Doyle's life and the composition of the
Holmes stories, 248-59
life and character of Holmes, 259-78
method, 278-9
Holmes and the Victorian world, 279-92
Sherlockian scholarship, 292-301
Doyle and the development of the
detective story, 301-7
Holmes's continuing popularity, 307-9

Slave Narratives, American NCLC 20: 1-91
background, 2-9
overviews, 9-24
contemporary responses, 24-7
language, theme, and technique, 27-70
historical authenticity, 70-5
antecedents, 75-83
role in development of Black American
literature, 83-8

Spanish Civil War Literature TCLC 26:
311-85
topics in, 312-33
British and American literature, 333-59
French literature, 359-62
Spanish literature, 362-73
German literature, 373-5
political idealism and war literature, 375-
83

Spanish Golden Age Literature LC 23:
262-332
overviews, 263-81
verse drama, 281-304
prose fiction, 304-19
lyric poetry, 319-31

Spasmodic School of Poetry NCLC 24:
307-52
history and major figures, 307-21
the Spasmodics on poetry, 321-7
Firmilian and critical disfavor, 327-39
theme and technique, 339-47
influence, 347-51

Steinbeck, John, Fiftieth Anniversary of
The Grapes of Wrath CLC 59: 311-54

Sturm und Drang NCLC 40: 196-276
definitions, 197-238
poetry and poetics, 238-58
drama, 258-75

**Supernatural Fiction in the Nineteenth
Century** NCLC 32: 207-87
major figures and influences, 208-35
the Victorian ghost story, 236-54
the influence of science and occultism,
254-66
supernatural fiction and society, 266-86

Supernatural Fiction, Modern TCLC 30:
59-116
evolution and varieties, 60-74
"decline" of the ghost story, 74-86
as a literary genre, 86-92
technique, 92-101
nature and appeal, 101-15

Surrealism TCLC 30: 334-406

history and formative influences, 335-43
manifestos, 343-54
philosophic, aesthetic, and political
    principles, 354-75
poetry, 375-81
novel, 381-6
drama, 386-92
film, 392-8
painting and sculpture, 398-403
achievement, 403-5

Symbolism, Russian TCLC 30: 266-333
doctrines and major figures, 267-92
theories, 293-8
and French Symbolism, 298-310
themes in poetry, 310-4
theater, 314-20
and the fine arts, 320-32

Symbolist Movement, French NCLC 20:
169-249
background and characteristics, 170-86
principles, 186-91
attacked and defended, 191-7
influences and predecessors, 197-211
and Decadence, 211-6
theater, 216-26
prose, 226-33
decline and influence, 233-47

Television and Literature TCLC 78: 283-
426
television and literacy, 283-98
reading vs. watching, 298-341
adaptations, 341-62
literary genres and television, 362-90
television genres and literature, 390-410
children's literature/children's television,
    410-25

Theater of the Absurd TCLC 38: 339-415
"The Theater of the Absurd," 340-7
major plays and playwrights, 347-58
and the concept of the absurd, 358-86
theatrical techniques, 386-94
predecessors of, 394-402
influence of, 402-13

Tin Pan Alley
See **American Popular Song, Golden Age
of**

Transcendentalism, American NCLC 24:
1-99
overviews, 3-23
contemporary documents, 23-41
theological aspects of, 42-52
and social issues, 52-74
literature of, 74-96

**Travel Writing in the Nineteenth
Century** NCLC 44: 274-392
the European grand tour, 275-303
the Orient, 303-47
North America, 347-91

Travel Writing in the Twentieth Century
TCLC 30: 407-56
conventions and traditions, 407-27
and fiction writing, 427-43
comparative essays on travel writers,
    443-54

True-Crime Literature CLC 99: 333-433
history and analysis, 334-407
reviews of true-crime publications, 407-
    23
writing instruction, 424-29
author profiles, 429-33

Ulysses **and the Process of Textual
Reconstruction** TCLC 26: 386-416
evaluations of the new *Ulysses,* 386-94
editorial principles and procedures, 394-
    401
theoretical issues, 401-16

Utopian Literature, Nineteenth-Century
NCLC 24: 353-473
definitions, 354-74
overviews, 374-88
theory, 388-408
communities, 409-26
fiction, 426-53
women and fiction, 454-71

Utopian Literature, Renaissance LC-32:
1-63
overviews, 2-25
classical background, 25-33
utopia and the social contract, 33-9
origins in mythology, 39-48
utopia and the Renaissance country
    house, 48-52
influence of millenarianism, 52-62

Vampire in Literature TCLC 46: 391-454
origins and evolution, 392-412
social and psychological perspectives,
    413-44
vampire fiction and science fiction, 445-
    53

Victorian Autobiography NCLC 40: 277-
363
development and major characteristics,
    278-88
themes and techniques, 289-313
the autobiographical tendency in
    Victorian prose and poetry, 313-47

Victorian women's autobiographies, 347-
    62

Victorian Fantasy Literature NCLC 60:
246-384
overviews, 247-91
major figures, 292-366
women in Victorian fantasy literature,
    366-83

Victorian Hellenism NCLC 68: 251-376
overviews, 252-78
the meanings of Hellenism, 278-335
the literary influence, 335-75

Victorian Novel NCLC 32: 288-454
development and major characteristics,
    290-310
themes and techniques, 310-58
social criticism in the Victorian novel,
    359-97
urban and rural life in the Victorian
    novel, 397-406
women in the Victorian novel, 406-25
Mudie's Circulating Library, 425-34
the late-Victorian novel, 434-51

Vietnam War in Literature and Film CLC
91: 383-437
overview, 384-8
prose, 388-412
film and drama, 412-24
poetry, 424-35

Vorticism TCLC 62: 330-426
Wyndham Lewis and Vorticism, 330-8
characteristics and principles of
    Vorticism, 338-65
Lewis and Pound, 365-82
Vorticist writing, 382-416
Vorticist painting, 416-26

Women's Diaries, Nineteenth-Century
NCLC 48: 308-54
overview, 308-13
diary as history, 314-25
sociology of diaries, 325-34
diaries as psychological scholarship, 334-
    43
diary as autobiography, 343-8
diary as literature, 348-53

Women Writers, Seventeenth-Century
LC 30: 2-58
overview, 2-15
women and education, 15-9

Topic Index

women and autobiography, 19-31
women's diaries, 31-9
early feminists, 39-58

World War I Literature TCLC 34: 392-486
overview, 393-403
English, 403-27
German, 427-50
American, 450-66
French, 466-74
and modern history, 474-82

Yellow Journalism NCLC 36: 383-456
overviews, 384-96
major figures, 396-413

Young Playwrights Festival
1988—CLC 55: 376-81
1989—CLC 59: 398-403
1990—CLC 65: 444-8

Twentieth-Century Literary Criticism
Cumulative Nationality Index

AMERICAN

Adams, Andy **56**
Adams, Henry (Brooks) **4, 52**
Addams, Jane **76**
Agee, James (Rufus) **1, 19**
Anderson, Maxwell **2**
Anderson, Sherwood **1, 10, 24**
Atherton, Gertrude (Franklin Horn) **2**
Austin, Mary (Hunter) **25**
Baker, Ray Stannard **47**
Barry, Philip **11**
Baum, L(yman) Frank **7**
Beard, Charles A(ustin) **15**
Becker, Carl (Lotus) **63**
Belasco, David **3**
Bell, James Madison **43**
Benchley, Robert (Charles) **1, 55**
Benedict, Ruth (Fulton) **60**
Benet, Stephen Vincent **7**
Benet, William Rose **28**
Bierce, Ambrose (Gwinett) **1, 7, 44**
Biggers, Earl Derr **65**
Black Elk **33**
Boas, Franz **56**
Bodenheim, Maxwell **44**
Bourne, Randolph S(illiman) **16**
Bradford, Gamaliel **36**
Brennan, Christopher John **17**
Bromfield, Louis (Brucker) **11**
Burroughs, Edgar Rice **2, 32**
Cabell, James Branch **6**
Cable, George Washington **4**
Cahan, Abraham **71**
Cardozo, Benjamin N(athan) **65**
Carnegie, Dale **53**
Cather, Willa Sibert **1, 11, 31**
Chambers, Robert W. **41**
Chandler, Raymond (Thornton) **1, 7**
Chapman, John Jay **7**
Chesnutt, Charles W(addell) **5, 39**
Chopin, Kate **5, 14**
Cobb, Irvin S. **77**
Cohan, George M(ichael) **60**
Comstock, Anthony **13**
Cotter, Joseph Seamon Sr. **28**
Cram, Ralph Adams **45**
Crane, (Harold) Hart **2, 5**
Crane, Stephen (Townley) **11, 17, 32**
Crawford, F(rancis) Marion **10**
Crothers, Rachel **19**
Cullen, Countee **4, 37**
Davis, Rebecca (Blaine) Harding **6**
Davis, Richard Harding **24**
Day, Clarence (Shepard Jr.) **25**
Dent, Lester **72**
De Voto, Bernard (Augustine) **29**
Dreiser, Theodore (Herman Albert) **10, 18, 35**
Dulles, John Foster **72**

Dunbar, Paul Laurence **2, 12**
Duncan, Isadora **68**
Dunne, Finley Peter **28**
Eastman, Charles A(lexander) **55**
Eddy, Mary (Morse) Baker **71**
Einstein, Albert **65**
Faust, Frederick (Schiller) **49**
Fisher, Rudolph **11**
Fitzgerald, F(rancis) Scott (Key) **1, 6, 14, 28, 55**
Fitzgerald, Zelda (Sayre) **52**
Flecker, (Herman) James Elroy **43**
Fletcher, John Gould **35**
Ford, Henry **73**
Forten, Charlotte L. **16**
Freeman, Douglas Southall **11**
Freeman, Mary Eleanor Wilkins **9**
Futrelle, Jacques **19**
Gale, Zona **7**
Garland, (Hannibal) Hamlin **3**
Gilman, Charlotte (Anna) Perkins (Stetson) **9, 37**
Glasgow, Ellen (Anderson Gholson) **2, 7**
Glaspell, Susan **55**
Goldman, Emma **13**
Green, Anna Katharine **63**
Grey, Zane **6**
Griffith, D(avid Lewelyn) W(ark) **68**
Griggs, Sutton Elbert **77**
Guiney, Louise Imogen **41**
Hall, James Norman **23**
Harper, Frances Ellen Watkins **14**
Harris, Joel Chandler **2**
Harte, (Francis) Bret(t) **1, 25**
Hartmann, Sadakichi **73**
Hatteras, Owen **18**
Hawthorne, Julian **25**
Hearn, (Patricio) Lafcadio (Tessima Carlos) **9**
Henry, O. **1, 19**
Hergesheimer, Joseph **11**
Higginson, Thomas Wentworth **36**
Holly, Buddy **65**
Holmes, Oliver Wendell Jr. **77**
Hopkins, Pauline Elizabeth **28**
Horney, Karen (Clementine Theodore Danielsen) **71**
Howard, Robert E(rvin) **8**
Howe, Julia Ward **21**
Howells, William Dean **7, 17, 41**
Huneker, James Gibbons **65**
James, Henry **2, 11, 24, 40, 47, 64**
James, William **15, 32**
Jewett, (Theodora) Sarah Orne **1, 22**
Johnson, James Weldon **3, 19**
Johnson, Robert **69**
Kornbluth, C(yril) M. **8**
Korzybski, Alfred (Habdank Skarbek) **61**
Kuttner, Henry **10**

Lardner, Ring(gold) W(ilmer) **2, 14**
Lewis, (Harry) Sinclair **4, 13, 23, 39**
Lewisohn, Ludwig **19**
Lewton, Val **76**
Lindsay, (Nicholas) Vachel **17**
Locke, Alain (Le Roy) **43**
London, Jack **9, 15, 39**
Lovecraft, H(oward) P(hillips) **4, 22**
Lowell, Amy **1, 8**
Markham, Edwin **47**
Marquis, Don(ald Robert Perry) **7**
Masters, Edgar Lee **2, 25**
McCoy, Horace (Stanley) **28**
McKay, Claude **7, 41**
Mencken, H(enry) L(ouis) **13**
Micheaux, Oscar **76**
Millay, Edna St. Vincent **4, 49**
Mitchell, Margaret (Munnerlyn) **11**
Mitchell, S(ilas) Weir **36**
Monroe, Harriet **12**
Muir, John **28**
Nathan, George Jean **18**
Nordhoff, Charles (Bernard) **23**
Norris, (Benjamin) Frank(lin Jr.) **24**
O'Neill, Eugene (Gladstone) **1, 6, 27, 49**
Oskison, John Milton **35**
Park, Robert E(zra) **73**
Patton, George S. **79**
Phillips, David Graham **44**
Porter, Gene(va Grace) Stratton **21**
Post, Melville Davisson **39**
Pulitzer, Joseph **76**
Pyle, Ernie **75**
Rawlings, Marjorie Kinnan **4**
Reed, John (Silas) **9**
Reich, Wilhelm **57**
Rhodes, Eugene Manlove **53**
Riggs, (Rolla) Lynn **56**
Riley, James Whitcomb **51**
Rinehart, Mary Roberts **52**
Roberts, Elizabeth Madox **68**
Roberts, Kenneth (Lewis) **23**
Robinson, Edwin Arlington **5**
Roelvaag, O(le) E(dvart) **17**
Rogers, Will(iam Penn Adair) **8, 71**
Roosevelt, Theodore **69**
Rourke, Constance (Mayfield) **12**
Runyon, (Alfred) Damon **10**
Saltus, Edgar (Everton) **8**
Santayana, George **40**
Schoenberg, Arnold **75**
Sherwood, Robert E(mmet) **3**
Slesinger, Tess **10**
Stanton, Elizabeth Cady **73**
Steffens, (Joseph) Lincoln **20**
Stein, Gertrude **1, 6, 28, 48**
Sterling, George **20**
Stevens, Wallace **3, 12, 45**

Stockton, Frank R. 47
Stroheim, Erich von 71
Sturges, Preston 48
Tarbell, Ida M(inerva) 40
Tarkington, (Newton) Booth 9
Taylor, Frederick Winslow 76
Teasdale, Sara 4
Thurman, Wallace (Henry) 6
Twain, Mark 6, 12, 19, 36, 48, 59
Van Dine, S. S. 23
Van Doren, Carl (Clinton) 18
Veblen, Thorstein (Bunde) 31
Washington, Booker T(aliaferro) 10
Wells, Carolyn 35
West, Nathanael 1, 14, 44
Whale, James 63
Wharton, Edith (Newbold Jones) 3, 9, 27, 53
White, Walter F(rancis) 15
Wilson, Woodrow 73
Wister, Owen 21
Wolfe, Thomas (Clayton) 4, 13, 29, 61
Woodberry, George Edward 73
Woollcott, Alexander (Humphreys) 5
Wylie, Elinor (Morton Hoyt) 8

ARGENTINIAN
Arlt, Roberto (Godofredo Christophersen) 29
Guiraldes, Ricardo (Guillermo) 39
Lugones, Leopoldo 15
Storni, Alfonsina 5

AUSTRALIAN
Baynton, Barbara 57
Franklin, (Stella Maraia Sarah) Miles 7
Furphy, Joseph 25
Ingamells, Rex 35
Lawson, Henry (Archibald Hertzberg) 27
Paterson, A(ndrew) B(arton) 32
Richardson, Henry Handel 4
Warung, Price 45

AUSTRIAN
Beer-Hofmann, Richard 60
Broch, Hermann 20
Freud, Sigmund 52
Hofmannsthal, Hugo von 11
Kafka, Franz 2, 6, 13, 29, 47, 53
Kraus, Karl 5
Kubin, Alfred (Leopold Isidor) 23
Meyrink, Gustav 21
Musil, Robert (Edler von) 12, 68
Perutz, Leo 60
Roth, (Moses) Joseph 33
Schnitzler, Arthur 4
Steiner, Rudolf 13
Stroheim, Erich von 71
Trakl, Georg 5
Werfel, Franz (Viktor) 8
Zweig, Stefan 17

BELGIAN
Bosschere, Jean de 19
Lemonnier, (Antoine Louis) Camille 22
Maeterlinck, Maurice 3
van Ostaijen, Paul 33
Verhaeren, Emile (Adolphe Gustave) 12

BRAZILIAN
Andrade, Mario de 43
Cunha, Euclides (Rodrigues Pimenta) da 24
Lima Barreto, Afonso Henrique de 23
Machado de Assis, Joaquim Maria 10
Ramos, Graciliano 32

BULGARIAN
Vazov, Ivan (Minchov) 25

CANADIAN
Campbell, Wilfred 9
Carman, (William) Bliss 7
Carr, Emily 32
Connor, Ralph 31
Drummond, William Henry 25
Duncan, Sara Jeannette 60
Garneau, (Hector de) Saint-Denys 13
Grove, Frederick Philip 4
Innis, Harold Adams 77
Knister, Raymond 56
Leacock, Stephen (Butler) 2
McCrae, John 12
Montgomery, L(ucy) M(aud) 51
Nelligan, Emile 14
Pickthall, Marjorie L(owry) C(hristie) 21
Roberts, Charles G(eorge) D(ouglas) 8
Scott, Duncan Campbell 6
Service, Robert W(illiam) 15
Seton, Ernest (Evan) Thompson 31
Stringer, Arthur 37

CHILEAN
Huidobro Fernandez, Vicente Garcia 31
Mistral, Gabriela 2
Prado (Calvo), Pedro 75

CHINESE
Liu E 15
Lu Hsun 3
Su Man-shu 24
Wen I-to 28

COLOMBIAN
Rivera, Jose Eustasio 35

CZECH
Capek, Karel 6, 37
Freud, Sigmund 52
Hasek, Jaroslav (Matej Frantisek) 4
Kafka, Franz 2, 6, 13, 29, 47, 53
Nezval, Vitezslav 44

DANISH
Brandes, Georg (Morris Cohen) 10
Hansen, Martin A. 32
Jensen, Johannes V. 41
Nexo, Martin Andersen 43
Pontoppidan, Henrik 29

DUTCH
Couperus, Louis (Marie Anne) 15
Frank, Anne(lies Marie) 17
Heijermans, Herman 24
Hillesum, Etty 49
Schendel, Arthur van 56

ENGLISH
Alexander, Samuel 77
Barbellion, W. N. P. 24
Baring, Maurice 8
Beerbohm, (Henry) Max(imilian) 1, 24
Bell, Gertrude 67
Belloc, (Joseph) Hilaire (Pierre Sebastien Rene
    Swanton) 7, 18
Bennett, (Enoch) Arnold 5, 20
Benson, E(dward) F(rederic) 27
Benson, Stella 17
Bentley, E(dmund) C(lerihew) 12

Besant, Annie (Wood) 9
Blackmore, R(ichard) D(oddridge) 27
Blackwood, Algernon (Henry) 5
Bramah, Ernest 72
Bridges, Robert (Seymour) 1
Brooke, Rupert (Chawner) 2, 7
Burke, Thomas 63
Butler, Samuel 1, 33
Butts, Mary 77
Byron, Robert 67
Chesterton, G(ilbert) K(eith) 1, 6, 64
Childers, (Robert) Erskine 65
Coleridge, Mary E(lizabeth) 73
Collingwood, R(obin) G(eorge) 67
Conrad, Joseph 1, 6, 13, 25, 43, 57
Coppard, A(lfred) E(dgar) 5
Corelli, Marie 51
Crofts, Freeman Wills 55
Crowley, Aleister 7
Dale, Colin 18
Delafield, E. M. 61
de la Mare, Walter (John) 4, 53
Dobson, Austin 79
Doughty, Charles M(ontagu) 27
Douglas, Keith (Castellain) 40
Douglas, Norman 68
Dowson, Ernest (Christopher) 4
Doyle, Arthur Conan 7
Drinkwater, John 57
Eddison, E(ric) R(ucker) 15
Elaine 18
Elizabeth 41
Ellis, (Henry) Havelock 14
Field, Michael 43
Firbank, (Arthur Annesley) Ronald 1
Ford, Ford Madox 1, 15, 39, 57
Freeman, R(ichard) Austin 21
Galsworthy, John 1, 45
Gilbert, W(illiam) S(chwenck) 3
Gissing, George (Robert) 3, 24, 47
Glyn, Elinor 72
Gosse, Edmund (William) 28
Grahame, Kenneth 64
Granville-Barker, Harley 2
Gray, John (Henry) 19
Gurney, Ivor (Bertie) 33
Haggard, H(enry) Rider 11
Hall, (Marguerite) Radclyffe 12
Hardy, Thomas 4, 10, 18, 32, 48, 53, 72
Henley, William Ernest 8
Hilton, James 21
Hodgson, William Hope 13
Housman, A(lfred) E(dward) 1, 10
Housman, Laurence 7
Hudson, W(illiam) H(enry) 29
Hulme, T(homas) E(rnest) 21
Hunt, Violet 53
Jacobs, W(illiam) W(ymark) 22
James, Montague (Rhodes) 6
Jerome, Jerome K(lapka) 23
Johnson, Lionel (Pigot) 19
Kaye-Smith, Sheila 20
Keynes, John Maynard 64
Kipling, (Joseph) Rudyard 8, 17
Laski, Harold 79
Lawrence, D(avid) H(erbert Richards) 2, 9,
    16, 33, 48, 61
Lawrence, T(homas) E(dward) 18
Lee, Vernon 5
Lee-Hamilton, Eugene (Jacob) 22
Leverson, Ada 18
Lewis, (Percy) Wyndham 2, 9
Lindsay, David 15

Lowndes, Marie Adelaide (Belloc) 12
Lowry, (Clarence) Malcolm 6, 40
Lucas, E(dward) V(errall) 73
Macaulay, Rose 7, 44
MacCarthy, (Sir Charles Otto) Desmond 36
Maitland, Frederic 65
Manning, Frederic 25
Meredith, George 17, 43
Mew, Charlotte (Mary) 8
Meynell, Alice (Christina Gertrude Thompson)
   6
Middleton, Richard (Barham) 56
Milne, A(lan) A(lexander) 6
Morrison, Arthur 72
Murry, John Middleton 16
Noyes, Alfred 7
Oppenheim, E(dward) Phillips 45
Orwell, George 2, 6, 15, 31, 51
Ouida 43
Owen, Wilfred (Edward Salter) 5, 27
Pinero, Arthur Wing 32
Powys, T(heodore) F(rancis) 9
Quiller-Couch, Arthur Thomas 53
Richardson, Dorothy Miller 3
Rohmer, Sax 28
Rolfe, Frederick (William Serafino Austin Lewis
   Mary) 12
Rosenberg, Isaac 12
Ruskin, John 20
Rutherford, Mark 25
Sabatini, Rafael 47
Saintsbury, George (Edward Bateman) 31
Saki 3
Sapper 44
Sayers, Dorothy L(eigh) 2, 15
Shiel, M(atthew) P(hipps) 8
Sinclair, May 3, 11
Stapledon, (William) Olaf 22
Stead, William Thomas 48
Stephen, Leslie 23
Strachey, (Giles) Lytton 12
Summers, (Alphonsus Joseph-Mary Augustus)
   Montague 16
Sutro, Alfred 6
Swinburne, Algernon Charles 8, 36
Symons, Arthur 11
Thomas, (Philip) Edward 10
Thompson, Francis Joseph 4
Tomlinson, H(enry) M(ajor) 71
Van Druten, John (William) 2
Wallace, (Richard Horatio) Edgar 57
Walpole, Hugh (Seymour) 5
Ward, Mrs. Humphry 55
Warung, Price 45
Webb, (Martha) Beatrice (Potter) 22
Webb, Mary (Gladys Meredith) 24
Webb, Sidney (James) 22
Welch, (Maurice) Denton 22
Wells, H(erbert) G(eorge) 6, 12, 19
Williams, Charles (Walter Stansby) 1, 11
Woolf, (Adeline) Virginia 1, 5, 20, 43, 56
Yonge, Charlotte (Mary) 48
Zangwill, Israel 16

ESTONIAN
Tammsaare, A(nton) H(ansen) 27

FINNISH
Leino, Eino 24
Soedergran, Edith (Irene) 31

FRENCH
Alain 41
Alain-Fournier 6
Apollinaire, Guillaume 3, 8, 51
Artaud, Antonin (Marie Joseph) 3, 36
Barbusse, Henri 5
Barres, Maurice 47
Benda, Julien 60
Bergson, Henri 32
Bernanos, (Paul Louis) Georges 3
Bernhardt, Sarah (Henriette Rosine) 75
Bloy, Leon 22
Bourget, Paul (Charles Joseph) 12
Claudel, Paul (Louis Charles Marie) 2, 10
Colette, (Sidonie-Gabrielle) 1, 5, 16
Coppee, Francois 25
Daumal, Rene 14
Desnos, Robert 22
Drieu la Rochelle, Pierre(-Eugene) 21
Dujardin, Edouard (Emile Louis) 13
Durkheim, Emile 55
Eluard, Paul 7, 41
Fargue, Leon-Paul 11
Feydeau, Georges (Leon Jules Marie) 22
France, Anatole 9
Gide, Andre (Paul Guillaume) 5, 12, 36
Giraudoux, (Hippolyte) Jean 2, 7
Gourmont, Remy (-Marie-Charles) de 17
Huysmans, Joris-Karl 7, 69
Jacob, (Cyprien-)Max 6
Jammes, Francis 75
Jarry, Alfred 2, 14
Larbaud, Valery (Nicolas) 9
Leblanc, Maurice (Marie Emile) 49
Leroux, Gaston 25
Loti, Pierre 11
Martin du Gard, Roger 24
Mirbeau, Octave 55
Mistral, Frederic 51
Moreas, Jean 18
Nizan, Paul 40
Peguy, Charles Pierre 10
Peret, Benjamin 20
Proust, (Valentin-Louis-George-Eugene-)
   Marcel 7, 13, 33
Rachilde 67
Radiguet, Raymond 29
Renard, Jules 17
Rolland, Romain 23
Rostand, Edmond (Eugene Alexis) 6, 37
Roussel, Raymond 20
Saint-Exupery, Antoine (Jean Baptiste Marie
   Roger) de 2, 56
Schwob, (Mayer Andre) Marcel 20
Sully Prudhomme 31
Teilhard de Chardin, (Marie Joseph) Pierre 9
Valery, (Ambroise) Paul (Toussaint Jules) 4,
   15
Verne, Jules (Gabriel) 6, 52
Vian, Boris 9
Weil, Simone (Adolphine) 23
Zola, Emile (Edouard Charles Antoine) 1, 6,
   21, 41

GERMAN
Andreas-Salome, Lou 56
Auerbach, Erich 43
Benjamin, Walter 39
Benn, Gottfried 3
Borchert, Wolfgang 5
Brecht, (Eugen) Bertolt (Friedrich) 1, 6, 13,
   35
Carossa, Hans 48
Cassirer, Ernst 61
Doblin, Alfred 13
Doeblin, Alfred 13
Einstein, Albert 65
Ewers, Hanns Heinz 12
Feuchtwanger, Lion 3
George, Stefan (Anton) 2, 14
Goebbels, (Paul) Joseph 68
Hauptmann, Gerhart (Johann Robert) 4
Heym, Georg (Theodor Franz Arthur) 9
Heyse, Paul (Johann Ludwig von) 8
Hitler, Adolf 53
Horney, Karen (Clementine Theodore
   Danielsen) 71
Huch, Ricarda (Octavia) 13
Kaiser, Georg 9
Klabund 44
Kolmar, Gertrud 40
Lasker-Schueler, Else 57
Liliencron, (Friedrich Adolf Axel) Detlev von
   18
Luxemburg, Rosa 63
Mann, (Luiz) Heinrich 9
Mann, (Paul) Thomas 2, 8, 14, 21, 35, 44, 60
Mannheim, Karl 65
Morgenstern, Christian 8
Nietzsche, Friedrich (Wilhelm) 10, 18, 55
Ophuls, Max 79
Plumpe, Friedrich Wilhelm 53
Raabe, Wilhelm 45
Rilke, Rainer Maria 1, 6, 19
Simmel, Georg 64
Spengler, Oswald (Arnold Gottfried) 25
Sternheim, (William Adolf) Carl 8
Sudermann, Hermann 15
Toller, Ernst 10
Vaihinger, Hans 71
Wassermann, (Karl) Jakob 6
Weber, Max 69
Wedekind, (Benjamin) Frank(lin) 7
Wiene, Robert 56

GHANIAN
Casely-Hayford, J(oseph) E(phraim) 24

GREEK
Cavafy, C(onstantine) P(eter) 2, 7
Kazantzakis, Nikos 2, 5, 33
Palamas, Kostes 5
Papadiamantis, Alexandros 29
Sikelianos, Angelos 39

HAITIAN
Roumain, Jacques (Jean Baptiste) 19

HUNGARIAN
Ady, Endre 11
Babits, Mihaly 14
Csath, Geza 13
Herzl, Theodor 36
Horvath, Oedoen von 45
Jozsef, Attila 22
Karinthy, Frigyes 47
Mikszath, Kalman 31
Molnar, Ferenc 20
Moricz, Zsigmond 33
Radnoti, Miklos 16

ICELANDIC
Sigurjonsson, Johann 27

INDIAN
Aurobindo, Sri 63
Chatterji, Saratchandra 13
Gandhi, Mohandas Karamchand 59

Nationality Index

Iqbal, Muhammad   28
Premchand   21
Tagore, Rabindranath   3, 53

INDONESIAN
Anwar, Chairil   22

IRANIAN
Hedayat, Sadeq   21

IRISH
A.E.   3, 10
Baker, Jean H.   3, 10
Cary, (Arthur) Joyce (Lunel)   1, 29
Dunsany, Lord   2, 59
Gogarty, Oliver St. John   15
Gregory, Isabella Augusta (Persse)   1
Harris, Frank   24
Joyce, James (Augustine Aloysius)   3, 8, 16,
   35, 52
Ledwidge, Francis   23
Martin, Violet Florence   51
Moore, George Augustus   7
O'Grady, Standish (James)   5
Riddell, J. H.   40
Shaw, Bernard   45
Shaw, George Bernard   3, 9, 21
Somerville, Edith   51
Stephens, James   4
Stoker, Bram   8
Synge, (Edmund) J(ohn) M(illington)   6, 37
Tynan, Katharine   3
Wilde, Oscar (Fingal O'Flahertie Wills)   1, 8,
   23, 41
Yeats, William Butler   1, 11, 18, 31

ITALIAN
Alvaro, Corrado   60
Betti, Ugo   5
Brancati, Vitaliano   12
Campana, Dino   20
Carducci, Giosue (Alessandro Giuseppe)   32
Croce, Benedetto   37
D'Annunzio, Gabriele   6, 40
Deledda, Grazia (Cosima)   23
Giacosa, Giuseppe   7
Jovine, Francesco   79
Lampedusa, Giuseppe (Tomasi) di   13
Malaparte, Curzio   52
Marinetti, Filippo Tommaso   10
Mosca, Gaetano   75
Papini, Giovanni   22
Pareto, Vilfredo   69
Pascoli, Giovanni   45
Pavese, Cesare   3
Pirandello, Luigi   4, 29
Saba, Umberto   33
Svevo, Italo   2, 35
Tozzi, Federigo   31
Verga, Giovanni (Carmelo)   3

JAMAICAN
De Lisser, H(erbert) G(eorge)   12
Garvey, Marcus (Moziah Jr.)   41
Mais, Roger   8
McKay, Claude   7, 41
Redcam, Tom   25

JAPANESE
Akutagawa, Ryunosuke   16
Dazai, Osamu   11
Futabatei, Shimei   44
Hagiwara Sakutaro   60

Hayashi Fumiko   27
Ishikawa, Takuboku   15
Masaoka Shiki   18
Miyamoto, Yuriko   37
Miyazawa Kenji   76
Mizoguchi, Kenji   72
Mori Ogai   14
Nagai Kafu   51
Natsume, Soseki   2, 10
Rohan, Koda   22
Santoka, Taneda   72
Shimazaki Toson   5
Yokomitsu Riichi   47
Yosano Akiko   59

LATVIAN
Rainis, Janis   29

LEBANESE
Gibran, Kahlil   1, 9

LESOTHAN
Mofolo, Thomas (Mokopu)   22

LITHUANIAN
Kreve (Mickevicius), Vincas   27

MEXICAN
Azuela, Mariano   3
Gamboa, Federico   36
Gonzalez Martinez, Enrique   72
Nervo, (Jose) Amado (Ruiz de)   11
Reyes, Alfonso   33
Romero, Jose Ruben   14

NEPALI
Devkota, Laxmiprasad   23

NEW ZEALANDER
Mander, (Mary) Jane   31
Mansfield, Katherine   2, 8, 39

NICARAGUAN
Dario, Ruben   4

NORWEGIAN
Bjornson, Bjornstjerne (Martinius)   7, 37
Bojer, Johan   64
Grieg, (Johan) Nordahl (Brun)   10
Hamsun, Knut   2, 14, 49
Ibsen, Henrik (Johan)   2, 8, 16, 37, 52
Kielland, Alexander Lange   5
Lie, Jonas (Lauritz Idemil)   5
Obstfelder, Sigbjoern   23
Skram, Amalie (Bertha)   25
Undset, Sigrid   3

PAKISTANI
Iqbal, Muhammad   28

PERUVIAN
Palma, Ricardo   29
Vallejo, Cesar (Abraham)   3, 56

POLISH
Asch, Sholem   3
Borowski, Tadeusz   9
Conrad, Joseph   1, 6, 13, 25, 43, 57
Peretz, Isaac Loeb   16
Prus, Boleslaw   48
Przybyszewski, Stanislaw   36
Reymont, Wladyslaw (Stanislaw)   5
Schulz, Bruno   5, 51

Sienkiewicz, Henryk (Adam Alexander Pius)   3
Singer, Israel Joshua   33
Witkiewicz, Stanislaw Ignacy   8

PORTUGUESE
Pessoa, Fernando (Antonio Nogueira)   27

PUERTO RICAN
Hostos (y Bonilla), Eugenio Maria de   24

ROMANIAN
Bacovia, George   24
Caragiale, Ion Luca   76
Rebreanu, Liviu   28

RUSSIAN
Aldanov, Mark (Alexandrovich)   23
Andreyev, Leonid (Nikolaevich)   3
Annensky, Innokenty (Fyodorovich)   14
Artsybashev, Mikhail (Petrovich)   31
Babel, Isaak (Emmanuilovich)   2, 13
Bagritsky, Eduard   60
Balmont, Konstantin (Dmitriyevich)   11
Bely, Andrey   7
Berdyaev, Nikolai (Aleksandrovich)   67
Blok, Alexander (Alexandrovich)   5
Bryusov, Valery Yakovlevich   10
Bulgakov, Mikhail (Afanas'evich)   2, 16
Bulgya, Alexander Alexandrovich   53
Bunin, Ivan Alexeyevich   6
Chekhov, Anton (Pavlovich)   3, 10, 31, 55
Der Nister   56
Eisenstein, Sergei (Mikhailovich)   57
Esenin, Sergei (Alexandrovich)   4
Fadeyev, Alexander   53
Gladkov, Fyodor (Vasilyevich)   27
Gorky, Maxim   8
Gumilev, Nikolai Stepanovich   60
Gurdjieff, G(eorgei) I(vanovich)   71
Guro, Elena   56
Hippius, Zinaida   9
Ilf, Ilya   21
Ivanov, Vyacheslav Ivanovich   33
Khlebnikov, Velimir   20
Khodasevich, Vladislav (Felitsianovich)   15
Korolenko, Vladimir Galaktionovich   22
Kropotkin, Peter (Aleksieevich)   36
Kuprin, Aleksandr Ivanovich   5
Kuzmin, Mikhail   40
Lenin, V. I.   67
Mandelstam, Osip (Emilievich)   2, 6
Mayakovski, Vladimir (Vladimirovich)   4, 18
Merezhkovsky, Dmitry Sergeyevich   29
Petrov, Evgeny   21
Pilnyak, Boris   23
Platonov, Andrei   14
Prishvin, Mikhail   75
Remizov, Aleksei (Mikhailovich)   27
Shestov, Lev   56
Sologub, Fyodor   9
Tolstoy, Alexey Nikolaevich   18
Tolstoy, Leo (Nikolaevich)   4, 11, 17, 28, 44,
   79
Trotsky, Leon   22
Tsvetaeva (Efron), Marina (Ivanovna)   7, 35
Zabolotskii, Nikolai Alekseevich   52
Zamyatin, Evgeny Ivanovich   8, 37
Zhdanov, Andrei A(lexandrovich)   18
Zoshchenko, Mikhail (Mikhailovich)   15

SCOTTISH
Barrie, J(ames) M(atthew)   2
Bridie, James   3

Brown, George Douglas **28**
Buchan, John **41**
Cunninghame Graham, R(obert) B(ontine) **19**
Davidson, John **24**
Frazer, J(ames) G(eorge) **32**
Gibbon, Lewis Grassic **4**
Lang, Andrew **16**
MacDonald, George **9**
Muir, Edwin **2**
Sharp, William **39**
Tey, Josephine **14**

SOUTH AFRICAN
Bosman, Herman Charles **49**
Campbell, (Ignatius) Roy (Dunnachie) **5**
Mqhayi, S(amuel) E(dward) K(rune Loliwe) **25**
Plaatje, Sol(omon) T(shekisho) **73**
Schreiner, Olive (Emilie Albertina) **9**
Smith, Pauline (Urmson) **25**
Vilakazi, Benedict Wallet **37**

SPANISH
Alas (y Urena), Leopoldo (Enrique Garcia) **29**
Barea, Arturo **14**
Baroja (y Nessi), Pio **8**
Benavente (y Martinez), Jacinto **3**
Blasco Ibanez, Vicente **12**
Echegaray (y Eizaguirre), Jose (Maria Waldo)
  4
Garcia Lorca, Federico **1, 7, 49**
Jimenez (Mantecon), Juan Ramon **4**
Machado (y Ruiz), Antonio **3**
Martinez Sierra, Gregorio **6**
Martinez Sierra, Maria (de la O'LeJarraga) **6**
Miro (Ferrer), Gabriel (Francisco Victor) **5**
Ortega y Gasset, Jose **9**
Pereda (y Sanchez de Porrua), Jose Maria de
  16
Perez Galdos, Benito **27**
Salinas (y Serrano), Pedro **17**
Unamuno (y Jugo), Miguel de **2, 9**
Valera y Alcala-Galiano, Juan **10**
Valle-Inclan, Ramon (Maria) del **5**

SWEDISH
Bengtsson, Frans (Gunnar) **48**
Dagerman, Stig (Halvard) **17**
Ekelund, Vilhelm **75**
Heidenstam, (Carl Gustaf) Verner von **5**
Key, Ellen **65**
Lagerloef, Selma (Ottiliana Lovisa) **4, 36**
Soderberg, Hjalmar **39**
Strindberg, (Johan) August **1, 8, 21, 47**

SWISS
Ramuz, Charles-Ferdinand **33**
Rod, Edouard **52**
Saussure, Ferdinand de **49**
Spitteler, Carl (Friedrich Georg) **12**
Walser, Robert **18**

SYRIAN
Gibran, Kahlil **1, 9**

TURKISH
Sait Faik **23**

UKRAINIAN
Aleichem, Sholom **1, 35**
Bialik, Chaim Nachman **25**

URUGUAYAN
Quiroga, Horacio (Sylvestre) **20**

Sanchez, Florencio **37**

WELSH
Davies, W(illiam) H(enry) **5**
Lewis, Alun **3**
Machen, Arthur **4**
Thomas, Dylan (Marlais) **1, 8, 45**

Nationality Index

ISBN 0-7876-2137-4